DUMBARTON OAKS TEXTS

III

THE CORRESPONDENCE
OF ATHANASIUS I
PATRIARCH OF CONSTANTINOPLE

LETTERS TO THE EMPEROR ANDRONICUS II
MEMBERS OF THE IMPERIAL FAMILY,
AND OFFICIALS

CORPUS FONTIUM HISTORIAE BYZANTINAE

CONSILIO SOCIETATIS INTERNATIONALIS
STUDIIS BYZANTINIS PROVEHENDIS DESTINATAE
EDITUM

VOLUMEN VII

ATHANASII I
PATRIARCHAE CONSTANTINOPOLITANI
EPISTULAE CXV AD IMPERATOREM
ANDRONICUM II
EIUSQUE PROPINQUOS NECNON
OFFICIALES MISSAE

EDIDIT, ANGLICE VERTIT,
ET COMMENTARIO INSTRUXIT
ALICE-MARY MAFFRY TALBOT

SERIES WASHINGTONENSIS
EDIDIT IHOR ŠEVČENKO

In aedibus Dumbarton Oaks
Washingtoniae, D.C.
MCMLXXV

THE CORRESPONDENCE
OF ATHANASIUS I
PATRIARCH
OF CONSTANTINOPLE

LETTERS TO THE EMPEROR ANDRONICUS II,
MEMBERS OF THE IMPERIAL FAMILY,
AND OFFICIALS

AN EDITION, TRANSLATION, AND COMMENTARY

by

ALICE-MARY MAFFRY TALBOT

Dumbarton Oaks
Center for Byzantine Studies
Trustees for Harvard University
Washington, District of Columbia
1975

In accordance with the rules adopted by the International Commission
for the Edition of Sources of Byzantine History,
the text and translation of this volume have been verified
by Ihor Ševčenko.

Distributed by
J. J. Augustin, Publisher
Locust Valley, New York 11560

LIBRARY OF CONGRESS CATALOG CARD NUMBER 74-28931; ISBN 0-88402-040-1
PRINTED IN GERMANY AT J. J. AUGUSTIN, GLÜCKSTADT

PREFACE

Manuscripts of the letters of Athanasius I, patriarch of Constantinople (1289–1293; 1303–1309), have been known for several centuries, and from time to time selected letters have been published. However, no systematic edition of his correspondence has ever appeared; no doubt, scholars have been discouraged by the large number of letters, by the difficulties of Athanasius' language, and by the disheartening proportion of pious exhortation to hard information.

Close study of Athanasius' correspondence, however, shows that it does warrant publication, especially for the picture it gives us of a man who figured prominently in Byzantine ecclesiastical and secular politics for twenty years. The events of Athanasius' two patriarchates are adequately described in the *Histories* of Pachymeres and Gregoras; the value of Athanasius' letters lies in the background they supply to the chroniclers' picture. For example, Pachymeres speaks of the strong ties between Athanasius and the Emperor Andronicus II, but in the letters we learn that their relations were not always amicable. Athanasius protests that the Emperor abandoned him during his struggle to retain the patriarchal throne, paid no attention to his memoranda, and refused to see him. We know from the *History* of Pachymeres that Athanasius led a crusade against bishops who abandoned their sees for the comfort and safety of the capital; in the letters we learn of the venality and indolence of these bishops, who spent their time carousing or engaging in profitable enterprise instead of attending church. Other sources tell us of the famine in Constantinople in the early fourteenth century and of Athanasius' efforts to alleviate the sufferings of the poor; only in his correspondence, however, can we read about his projects of creating commissions to supervise standards for bakeries and to control the sale of grain. The letters also provide glimpses of daily life in Byzantium: old ladies selling fish by the seashore; picnickers at St. Sophia leaving behind remains of their meal; noble women arrogantly preening themselves in the galleries of St. Sophia; a candidate for a bishopric catering to the episcopal electors by entertaining them with wine and melons.

The letters, moreover, contain interesting prosopographical information, introducing otherwise unknown personages such as John, abbot of Bera;

Dermokaïtes, Antiocheites, and Ploummes, members of the grain commission; Kokalas, lobbyist for the Jews; Philip Syropoulos, suspected of Arsenite sympathies; Paul the flutist, who loaned his house to the Patriarch of Alexandria as a place for ordinations; and Makrembolites, who was reduced to poverty by the oppression of the *megas dioiketes*. The letters also supply new information on more familiar figures; we learn that the metropolitan Luke of Bitzyne made a nice profit by lending church funds; that Nicephorus Moschopoulos of Crete came to the capital without asking the Patriarch's permission; that Cyril of Sardis had a vineyard, workshops, oxen, and a garden in Constantinople, in addition to his benefices; that the Patriarch Athanasius of Alexandria replaced an icon of Christ at the monastery of the Great Field with an image of the Emperor.

Out of the almost two hundred of Athanasius' letters, encyclicals, and sermons that survive in the principal manuscript, *Vaticanus Gr. 2219*, I have selected, for the purposes of this edition, the first 115 letters, most of which are addressed to the Emperor, to members of his family, or to imperial officials. The letters to the Emperor contain more material of historical interest than the works in the rest of the manuscript, many of which are moralizing sermons. Scattered among the homilies in the second part of the manuscript, however, are a number of important letters (addressed to bishops, to the clergy of St. Sophia, and to monks on Mt. Athos), which also warrant further study and the preparation of a critical edition.

The translation of Athanasius' correspondence has presented considerable difficulties, many of which I have been unable to solve to my satisfaction. The Patriarch's attempt to write in the elegant style demanded by the period often led him into long and complex sentences, which are hard to construe. A number of these sentences lack a main verb, or are characterized by faulty syntax and grammatical errors. After lengthy digressions, the Patriarch often failed to return to his original thought. I believe that many of these mistakes were caused by the necessity, because of his increasing blindness, to dictate his letters to a scribe. He was then unable to read over the finished version to correct either his own errors or those of the scribe. The Patriarch also delighted in the obscure allusions so treasured by fourteenth-century Byzantine authors. Some phrases are so ambiguous as to afford two possible interpretations; in these cases I have suggested an alternate translation in the commentary.

A word about the spelling of Greek names. When a name is familiar, I have used the English or Latinized form, e.g., Nicaea, Cyzicus, Nicephorus, Athanasius, Palaeologus. When the name is less well known, I have transliterated it directly from the Greek; thus, Melenikon, Akapniou, Bera, Moschopoulos, Choumnos.

The edition of the first one hundred letters was submitted to Columbia University in 1970 as a doctoral dissertation. The topic of an edition of the correspondence of Athanasius was suggested to me by my teacher, Professor

Ihor Ševčenko, formerly of Columbia University, and now of Dumbarton Oaks. I am extremely grateful to him for his constant advice and encouragement in the preparation of this publication, and for sharing with me his extraordinary knowledge of the Greek language and of fourteenth-century Byzantium.

I wish also to thank Father John Meyendorff, who relinquished his interest in preparing an edition of Athanasius' letters. Professors Cyril Mango, Herbert Hunger, Demetrius Georgacas, Dikeos Vayakakos, Haig Berberian, George Majeska, and the late Romilly Jenkins were kind enough to suggest solutions to specific problems.

The debt I owe the R. P. Vitalien Laurent will be evident from my extensive references to his articles on the Palaeologan period and to his monumental work on the acts of the Byzantine patriarchs from 1208–1309 (*Les regestes des actes du patriarcat de Constantinople*, I, *Les actes des patriarches*, fasc. IV, *Les regestes de 1208 à 1309* [Paris, 1971]) (hereafter, Laurent, *Regestes*), which appeared after the completion of my dissertation. This volume contains summaries of and commentary on all the letters and sermons in *Vaticanus Gr. 2219*, and proposes a chronological order for them. In revising my dissertation for publication I have benefited greatly from Laurent's conclusions.

I should also like to express my appreciation to Dumbarton Oaks for its support during the years 1966–1968, when I prepared the bulk of this edition in its superb library. I am also grateful to Dumbarton Oaks and to the Corpus Fontium Historiae Byzantinae for including in their joint series of texts and translations this edition of the letters of the Patriarch Athanasius. Special thanks are due members of the Editorial Department at Dumbarton Oaks—Julia Warner, Fanny Bonajuto, and Nancy Bowen—who patiently guided this paper through the press, and John Duffy who assisted me in proofing the Greek.

Finally, I wish to acknowledge with deep gratitude the encouragement and moral support of my husband, William Talbot, during the long years of preparing this edition.

Alice-Mary Maffry Talbot

Lake Erie College,
    Painesville, Ohio
Hiram College,
    Hiram, Ohio

TABLE OF CONTENTS

DUMBARTON OAKS TEXTS

III

THE CORRESPONDENCE
OF ATHANASIUS I
PATRIARCH OF CONSTANTINOPLE

LETTERS TO THE EMPEROR ANDRONICUS II,
MEMBERS OF THE IMPERIAL FAMILY,
AND OFFICIALS

GENERAL INTRODUCTION

I. THE LIFE OF ATHANASIUS

Sources for the Biography of Athanasius

1. Hagiographical Sources

Two *Vitae* of Athanasius were composed during the fourteenth century, when the cult of this Saint particularly flourished. The most important one has been attributed to Theoktistos the Studite,[1] and was edited by Athanasius Papadopoulos-Kerameus.[2] A less detailed biography, based on second-hand sources, was written by the Palamite monk Joseph Kalothetos.[3] Another hagiographical source is an unpublished *Oration on the Translation of Athanasius' Relics*, probably composed in the 1330's, which describes the burial of Athanasius, the translation of his remains, and numerous miracles associated with his relics.[4] In spite of the expected bias in favor of Athanasius, the evidence of the *Vitae* is quite reliable, and can frequently be confirmed by historical and epistolary sources.

[1] Cf. scholium in 15th-cent. manuscript of this *Vita*, cod. *Const. Chalc. mon. 64* (Istanbul Patriarchate Library, collection of monastery of Haghia Triada on Chalke, nunc 57, olim 64), fol. 39r. See also J. Meyendorff, *Introduction à l'étude de Grégoire Palamas* (Paris, 1959), 34 note 34; F. Halkin, *Bibliotheca Hagiographica Graeca*, I³ (Brussels, 1957), 71; and A. Ehrhard, *Überlieferung und Bestand der hagiographischen und homiletischen Literatur*, III (Berlin, 1952), 991.

[2] A. Papadopoulos-Kerameus, "Žitija dvuh' Vselenskih' patriarhov' XIV v., svv. Afanasija I i Isidora I," in *Zapiski istoriko-filol. fakul'teta Imperatorskago S.-Peterburgskago Universiteta*, 76 (1905), 1–51 (hereafter, *Theoctisti Vita Ath.*). An earlier abridged edition was prepared by H. Delehaye from a late and inferior manuscript, *Barberini VI, 22*; cf. H. Delehaye, "La vie d'Athanase, Patriarche de Constantinople," *Mélanges d'Archéologie et d'Histoire de l'Ecole Française de Rome*, 17 (1897), 39–75; reprinted in H. Delehaye, *Mélanges d'hagiographie grecque et latine*, Subsidia Hagiographica, Société des Bollandistes, 42 (Brussels, 1966), 125–49.

[3] *Calotheti Vita Athanasii*, ed. A. Pantokratorinos, in Θρᾳκικά, 13 (1940), 56–107 (hereafter, *Calotheti Vita Ath.*).

[4] This *Oration* is preserved in *Chalke 64*, fols. 157r–199r; cf. note 86 *infra*.

2. Historical Sources: Pachymeres and Gregoras

The two *Vitae* are our only sources for the biography of Athanasius prior to 1289, when he became patriarch of Constantinople. For information about his career after 1289 one can turn to the histories of George Pachymeres and Nicephorus Gregoras. Pachymeres, a contemporary of Athanasius, is a detailed but hostile witness, whose account unfortunately breaks off in 1307,[5] so that he provides no information on the mysterious events leading up to Athanasius' second resignation from the patriarchate in 1309. Nicephorus Gregoras, who wrote his *History* in the mid-fourteenth century, has left a less detailed but more impartial account of Athanasius' two patriarchates.

3. Epistolary Sources

The third source of biographical information is Athanasius' correspondence, consisting of letters to the Emperor Andronicus II, members of the imperial family, officials, bishops, clergy, and the monks of Mt. Athos. We are fortunate to have three such different perspectives on the life of Athanasius, especially since the three kinds of sources often confirm each other down to the smallest detail. The reliability of the *Vitae* as a source of factual information is particularly gratifying, and in the future may encourage even greater use by historians of hagiographical material.

THE LIFE

The future Patriarch Athanasius was born at Adrianople of pious parents named George and Euphrosyne, and was given the name of Alexius at his baptism.[6] The date of his birth is unknown, but it was probably *ca.* 1230–1235. When Alexius was still a child, his father died, and Euphrosyne was left with only one son to console her. Alexius displayed the usual saintly traits during his childhood, refusing to play with other children or to watch spectacles, and confining himself to meditation and reading holy books.[7]

---

[5] Cf. Pia Schmid, "Zur Chronologie von Pachymeres, Andronikos L. II–VII," *BZ*, 51 (1958), 82–86.

[6] *Theoctisti Vita Ath.*, 2–3; *Calotheti Vita Ath.*, 61; and Pachymeres, *Hist.*, II, 139.

[7] *Theoctisti Vita Ath.*, 3–4; *Calotheti Vita Ath.*, 62–63. The approximate date of Athanasius' birth can be calculated as follows. According to the *Vita* of Theoktistos, *ca.* 1275, when Bekkos' persecutions began, Athanasius had spent three years at Esphigmenou, made a trip to the Holy Land, paid extended visits to Latros and Auxentios, and had stayed eighteen years on Mt. Galesion, a total of at least 23 years. Since he would have arrived at Athos as a teenager before or around the year 1250, he must have been born *ca.* 1230–35. It follows that he would have been at least seventy-five when he died sometime after 1310; this tallies with his complaints in his letters about his old age (Letter 57, lines 14–15: ἐγὼ γὰρ καὶ γήρᾳ καὶ νόσῳ καὶ τὸ πλεῖον ἀπραγμοσύνῃ συζῶν; Letter 112, line 43: καὶ γήρᾳ καὶ ἀσθενείᾳ ταλαιπωροῦντες ...).

About the age of twelve, he left his widowed mother and set off for Thessalonica where he became a novice in his paternal uncle's monastery, and took the monastic name of Akakios. When his beard began to grow, he moved on to Mt. Athos, seeking greater opportunities for self-discipline and mortification of the body. After visiting various types of monastic communities on the Holy Mountain, he chose the cenobitic monastery of Esphigmenou, where he waited on tables in the refectory for two years. Akakios soon became distinguished by his asceticism, since he wore a hair shirt, never put on shoes or slept in a bed, and ate only the crumbs which fell from the table in the refectory.[8]

After a third year at Esphigmenou, when he served as cook, the monk Akakios made a quick tour of the Holy Land, including the desert monasteries of Jordan; on his return, he paid long visits to the monastic communities of Mt. Latros and Mt. Auxentios, where he met his distinguished older contemporaries Elias, Neilos the Italian, and Athanasius Lependrenos.[9] Akakios finally settled down at the monastery of St. Lazarus on Mt. Galesion. After eight years, he was honored with the rank of μεγαλόσχημος, changed his name again to Athanasius, and was ordained, against his will, as deacon and then presbyter. He also served the monastery as ecclesiarch for ten years.[10]

Around 1278, Athanasius moved on to Mt. Athos for the second time, but did not stay there long because of the persecutions of John Bekkos, Michael VIII's Unionist patriarch.[11] He returned to Galesion, where he associated with Galaktion and Isaac Garares, who were prominent opponents of Union. Growing restless again, Athanasius crossed back to Europe and went to the holy mountain of Ganos in Thrace. By now he had acquired a reputation as a holy man, and disciples flocked to him. At Ganos, the persecutions of Michael VIII finally caught up with Athanasius and he was whipped and beaten by a Unionist abbot sent to the mountain from Constantinople.[12] Kalothetos adds that Athanasius was also taken to the capital for a confrontation with the Emperor. Athanasius easily defeated Michael's arguments, but was nevertheless brutally punished.[13] This incident, however, closely resembles a hagiographical *topos*, such as is found in the lives of saints who were confessors in the iconoclastic period, and probably should not be accepted.[14]

---

[8] *Theoctisti Vita Ath.*, 4–6; *Calotheti Vita Ath.*, 62–63, 65, 69–70.

[9] *Theoctisti Vita Ath.*, 6–9; *Calotheti Vita Ath.*, 70–75.

[10] *Theoctisti Vita Ath.*, 9–10; *Calotheti Vita Ath.*, 75–77.

[11] *Theoctisti Vita Ath.*, 11–12; *Calotheti Vita Ath.*, 79–81.

[12] *Theoctisti Vita Ath.*, 12–13, 17–18; *Calotheti Vita Ath.*, 81–84.

[13] *Calotheti Vita Ath.*, 84–85.

[14] Confrontations between emperors and iconodule confessors are commonplace in hagiographical accounts of the 8th and 9th centuries; cf. the Patriarch Nicephorus' long dialogue with the Emperor Leo V in the *Vita Nicephori* of Ignatius the Deacon (PG, 100, cols. 92–108), and the dialogue of Euthymius of Sardis with Leo in the *Vita Euthymii* (ed. A. Papadakis, "The Unpublished Life of Euthymius of Sardis: Bodleianus Laudianus Graecus 69," *Traditio*, 26 [1970], 63–89).

Soon after Michael's death in 1282 and the succession of his son Andronicus II to the imperial throne, Athanasius was brought to Constantinople and introduced to the Emperor by the great droungarios Eonopolites.[15] Andronicus was greatly impressed by Athanasius' saintliness and installed him in the former monastery of the Great Logariastes on the hill of Xerolophos, so that he could see Athanasius frequently.[16] We know that Athanasius must have come to Constantinople by 1285, since the *Vita* by Kalothetos recounts that Athanasius attended the Council of Blachernae in 1285 which drew up a tome condemning the Unionist John Bekkos.[17]

At this time the empire was troubled not only by the struggle between supporters and opponents of the Union of Lyons, but also by continuing tension between Arsenites and Josephites.[18] In 1289 the Arsenites helped to bring about the resignation of the Patriarch Gregory, but failed in their attempt to secure the election of one of their number to the patriarchal throne. Their demands were so excessive[19] that Andronicus decided to choose the pious monk Athanasius as Gregory's successor. Both the *Vitae* and Pachymeres agree that Athanasius was at first reluctant to accept the position, but finally yielded to the pressure of the Emperor and synod.[20] During the days before Athanasius was ordained, Andronicus quickly learned what a controversial patriarch he had selected. Rumors of Athanasius' strict asceticism and harsh discipline ran rampant, and the Emperor was forced to hold two public meetings, at which witnesses testified for and against the patriarch-

---

[15] Pachymeres, *Hist.*, II, 107, 139.

[16] *Ibid.*, 108.

[17] Kalothetos' *Vita Athanasii* is the only source which mentions Athanasius' presence at this Council: ὁ τῆς ἀθανασίας ἐπώνυμος [i.e., Athanasius] ... τηνικαῦτα τῇ λαμπρᾷ καὶ μεγάλῃ συνόδῳ οὔπω μὲν τοῖς ἐπισκόποις συναριθμούμενος, τὰ πρῶτα δ' ὅμως παρά τε αὐτοῦ καὶ παρὰ τοῖς λογάσι φέρων τοῖς περὶ τὸν βασιλέα (*Calotheti Vita Ath.*, 87). This "healing council" (cf. *Calotheti Vita Ath.*, 87: δι' ἧς συνόδου οὐκ ὀλίγον τοῦ νοσοῦντος ἰάσατο) must be the Council of Blachernae, which has been convincingly assigned to the year 1285 by V. Laurent in "Les signataires du second synode des Blachernes," *EO*, 26 (1927), 129–49 (hereafter, Laurent, "Les signataires"). Although Pachymeres' account of the council gives no indications of chronology, he does place Athanasius' arrival in Constantinople (*Hist.*, II, 107–8) before his description of the signing of the tome against Bekkos (*Hist.*, II, 110–11).

[18] For an excellent study of the Arsenites, see V. Laurent, "Les grandes crises religieuses de Byzance. La fin du schisme arsénite," *BSHAcRoum*, 26, 2 (1945), 225–313 (hereafter, Laurent, "La fin du schisme arsénite"). See also I. Sykoutris, Περὶ τὸ σχίσμα τῶν Ἀρσενιτῶν, in Ἑλληνικά, 2 (1929), 262–332; 3 (1930), 15–44; and J. Troizky, *Arsenius, the Patriarch of Nicaea and Constantinople, and the Arsenites* (in Russian) (St. Petersburg, 1873).

[19] Cf. Laurent, "La fin du schisme arsénite," 247–49. The Arsenites insisted, among other conditions, upon the election of an Arsenite patriarch and the removal of Joseph's name from the diptychs. See the text of Arsenite demands to the Emperor, published by Laurent from *Par. Gr. 1302*, fol. B^r–B^v, at the end of his article "La fin du schisme arsénite," 286–87. Pachymeres summarizes the text in his *History* (II, 138–39).

[20] Pachymeres, *Hist.*, II, 139–40; *Theoctisti Vita Ath.*, 21, 23; *Calotheti Vita Ath.*, 88–89.

elect. The Emperor refused to listen to Athanasius' enemies, however, and the ordination took place in St. Sophia on October 14, 1289. Pachymeres, a hostile witness, describes several evil omens which took place at this ceremony, presaging the early expulsion of Athanasius from the patriarchal throne.[21]

All the sources, even the hagiographical ones, testify to the unpopularity of Athanasius' regime.[22] The Arsenites opposed Athanasius because he was a Josephite; the bishops opposed him because he sent them back to their sees,[23] and the monks opposed him because of the strict discipline he imposed and because he confiscated monastic funds.[24] Unfortunately for the Patriarch, his strongest supporter, the Emperor, made a tour of Anatolia from 1290 to 1293, and was thus absent from the capital for most of Athanasius' first patriarchate. Athanasius hoped that the Emperor's return would check the rising tide of opposition to his rule,[25] but by the time Andronicus arrived back in Constantinople, in June 1293, it was too late.[26] The hatred of Athanasius increased to such an extent that in October he was finally forced to resign.[27]

Pachymeres has left a detailed account of Athanasius' resignation, and has preserved the text of three pertinent documents. He describes the sequence of events as follows. Before Athanasius left the patriarchal offices, he composed two letters, one for the Emperor, and one which he hid in a hole at the top of a column on the left of the galleries of St. Sophia. In this second document Athanasius defended his conduct as patriarch, and asked to be anathematized if he had ever done or believed anything contrary to the canons and dogmas of the Church. On the other hand, if the charges against him were false, he

[21] Pachymeres, *Hist.*, II, 140–47.

[22] Cf. Pachymeres, *Hist.*, II, 148–49; Gregoras, *Hist.*, I, 180–82, 184; *Theoctisti Vita Ath.*, 27–28; *Calotheti Vita Ath.*, 90, 94–97.

[23] Gregoras, *Hist.*, I, 182; Laurent has suggested that several disaffected bishops joined the Arsenite faction in order to oppose Athanasius more effectively ("La fin du schisme arsénite," 242).

[24] Pachymeres, *Hist.*, II, 148–49; no doubt Athanasius confiscated monastic funds for a good purpose, for distribution to the poor. During his second patriarchate, he encouraged the Emperor to confiscate monastic and church land for distribution to soldiers; cf. Pachymeres, *Hist.*, II, 388–90.

[25] See Letter 115, lines 19–24.

[26] The date of Andronicus' return to Constantinople from Asia Minor has been long disputed. Pachymeres recounts that the Emperor left Nymphaeum and returned to the capital on June 28 (*Hist.*, II, 165). Pia Schmid, who has made an extremely useful study of Pachymeres' chronology, dates this event to 1294 ("Zur Chronologie von Pachymeres," 82). But according to Pachymeres (*Hist.*, II, 183) and Athanasius' Letter 115, the Emperor returned to Constantinople before Athanasius' resignation. We know that Athanasius resigned in October *1293*, since Pachymeres states that his first patriarchate lasted almost exactly four years, i.e., October 1289–October 1293 (*Hist.*, II, 177). J. Verpeaux also concludes that Andronicus returned to the capital in 1293; cf. "Notes chronologiques sur les livres II et III du *De Andronico Palaeologo* de Georges Pachymère," *REB*, 17 (1959) (hereafter, Verpeaux, "Notes chronologiques"), 169.

[27] Cf. Letters 111 and 115, lines 108–11.

subjected his false accusers to anathema together with "the man who was misled by them," no doubt a reference to Andronicus himself.[28]

In the first document, a letter addressed to the Emperor, Athanasius stated that he considered resignation to be uncanonical, but would yield to Andronicus' wishes.[29] He also asked the Emperor to send men to escort him from the patriarchal offices, since he feared for his personal safety.[30] Athanasius still hoped the Emperor would refuse to accept his resignation, but when guards arrived to escort him and to take over the patriarchal offices he realized that no hope remained. In the middle of the night, he made his way with the escort to the Golden Horn near the gate of Eugenius, and boarded a fishing boat to sail up the Golden Horn to the monastery of Kosmidion.[31] The next day he sent to Andronicus a formal resignation. The text of this letter of resignation as reproduced by Pachymeres[32] is different from the letter of resignation preserved in collections of Athanasius' correspondence (Letter 111),[33] and one must assume that the Patriarch composed two different versions. In any case, the Emperor accepted his resignation and sent him to his own monastery at Xerolophos, again under cover of night. The date was October 16, 1293, four years almost to the day since Athanasius had been ordained patriarch.[34]

Athanasius was succeeded by a gentle and simple monk, John of Sozopolis (1294–1303),[35] and was forced to look on helplessly from his monastery as his enemies gained power. The Patriarch Athanasius of Alexandria, who had been forced by his homonym to go into exile on Rhodes, returned to the capital and installed himself in the monastery of Christ Euergetes.[36] Cyril, metropolitan of Tyre, who had been elected patriarch of Antioch in 1287, but had not been recognized by Athanasius of Constantinople, finally received recognition in 1296.[37]

In September 1297 Athanasius again became a center of controversy, when some boy attendants of John XII discovered the hidden letter of excommunication while they were stealing baby pigeons from their nests in

---

[28] Pachymeres, *Hist.*, II, 169–73 (= Laurent, *Regestes*, no. 1553). The Patriarch John XII, upon reading the letter four years later, immediately suspected that Athanasius meant to include Andronicus among the targets of his anathema (Pachymeres, *Hist.*, II, 250).

[29] Pachymeres, *Hist.*, II, 173–74 (= Laurent, *Regestes*, no. 1554).

[30] *Ibid.*, 169 (= *ibid.*, no. 1555).

[31] *Ibid.*, 175.

[32] *Ibid.*, 175–76 (= Laurent, *Regestes*, no. 1556); cf. comments of Laurent, *Regestes*, 344.

[33] Laurent, *Regestes*, no. 1557.

[34] Pachymeres, *Hist.*, II, 177–78.

[35] *Ibid.*, 185.

[36] *Ibid.*, 203.

[37] V. Laurent, "Le patriarche d'Antioche Cyrille II (1287–c. 1308)," *AnalBoll*, 68 (1950) (= *Mélanges P. Peeters*, 2) (hereafter, Laurent, "Cyrille II"), 311, 316.

the galleries of St. Sophia.[38] They immediately showed the letter to the Patriarch John, who was extremely upset by it, "because he suspected that 'the misled man' against whom the curses were directed was none other than the Emperor himself."[39] Athanasius' scheme was a clever one: while still patriarch, he anathematized the Emperor; as a layman he had no power to release the Emperor from anathema; hence he would have to be reinstated as patriarch in order to clear the name of Andronicus.

After meeting with the bishops to discuss the dilemma,[40] the Emperor decided that his first step should be to approach Athanasius and ask him what his purpose was in writing the letter. Athanasius admitted readily to having written the anathematizing letter out of "meanness of spirit," but claimed that he had loosed the bonds of anathema immediately before his resignation, and that he regretted the discovery of the letter and the resulting disturbance.[41] Thus, the affair was officially settled without further difficulty, but Athanasius lost a great deal of prestige through the incident, which is of course not mentioned in either *Vita*. Gregoras, who is generally more favorable than Pachymeres to Athanasius, commented that the Patriarch's action was quite unworthy of his position, and that it "attached much blame on Athanasius, and at the same time checked the tongues of those who spoke on his behalf."[42]

It is noteworthy that Athanasius' formal statement repudiating the excommunications, whose text is preserved by Pachymeres,[43] is not included in any surviving collections of the Patriarch's correspondence. *Vat. Gr. 2219* includes instead a personal letter from Athanasius to Andronicus (Letter 2 = Laurent, *Regestes*, Appendix, no. 2), justifying his original letter of excommunication, written in 1293.[44] It is not clear whether Athanasius sent this letter to the Emperor before or after his "official" letter of repudiation, but in any case it seems evident that Athanasius was forced to concoct the tale that he had repudiated the excommunications before his resignation, when in fact he had done no such thing.

Meanwhile, the Arsenites were still plotting to gain control of the Church. In July 1302, John XII, discouraged by the hostility he faced, sent the Emperor a letter of resignation.[45] There ensued much discussion about the

[38] Pachymeres, *Hist.*, II, 249, 256. Gregoras writes that the discovery was made only a year after Athanasius' resignation (*Hist.*, I, 192), but Pachymeres' date is to be preferred, since he gives a specific month and year.

[39] Pachymeres, *Hist.*, II, 250.

[40] *Ibid.*, 251–52:

[41] *Ibid.*, 253–55.

[42] Gregoras, *Hist.*, I, 191–93.

[43] *Hist.*, II, 254–55.

[44] Cf. the remarks of Laurent in his *Regestes*, 568.

[45] Pachymeres states that John left the patriarchate on Friday, July 5, to retire to the monastery of the Pammakaristos, and that a few days later he sent his preliminary letter of resignation to the Emperor (*Hist.*, II, 341). July 5 fell on a Friday in 1303, not 1302, but we must assume that Pachymeres made a mistake in recording either the day of the week or the day of the month. John must have retired in July *1302*, since in June

validity of his resignation, since it was an act of anger and grief; while John lived in retirement at the monastery of Pammakaristos, his name was still commemorated in the diptychs, and his men ran the patriarchal offices.[46] It was to be almost a year, after countless intrigues and secret meetings, before a new patriarch was chosen. For the period July 1302 to June 1303, Pachymeres' *History* deals almost exclusively with ecclesiastical affairs, an emphasis which reflects the concern of the Emperor with solving the problem of the Arsenite schism and the succession to the patriarchate.[47]

John did not really wish to resign; he had drafted his letter of resignation in a moment of anger, and later indicated his willingness to return to the patriarchal throne. The Emperor, however, accepted the resignation, primarily because he saw an opportunity to restore peace to the Church by reconciling the Arsenite faction with a patriarch of their choice.[48] Thus, he held a secret meeting in the middle of the night with prominent Arsenites about the mechanics of transferring power to an Arsenite patriarch. In order to avoid alienating the Josephites, the Emperor insisted that the bishops who served under John XII be allowed to keep their positions. The Arsenite monks in turn demanded that the election of the new patriarch be entrusted to them. The agreement was drawn up in a formal document, and the Arsenites seemed assured of victory.[49]

In January 1303, however, the pious and superstitious nature of the Emperor led him to make a dramatic about-face and repudiate his agreement with the Arsenites. For, although Athanasius' anathema had been formally renounced in 1297, Andronicus continued to worry about it. Deep inside he felt that the best way to mollify the former Patriarch was to return him to his throne.[50] Athanasius, however, did not rely on the Emperor's conscience to secure his reinstatement. On January 15 he warned the Emperor privately that disaster threatened the city in three days' time, and indeed two mild earthquakes did take place on the 15th and 17th of the month.[51] Andronicus, amazed at the former Patriarch's powers of prophecy, was now convinced that Athanasius must be reinstated. After making a public speech in which

---

1303 he was succeeded by Athanasius. Pachymeres records that John sent his *final* resignation to the Emperor on Friday, June 21, 1303 (June 21 did fall on a Friday in 1303), and Athanasius was made patriarch on June 23, 1303 (*Hist.*, II, 382–84). The date of 1303 for Athanasius' accession is further confirmed by an entry in a catalogue of patriarchs (*Par. Gr. 1356*, fol. 282ᵛ); cf. V. Laurent, "La chronologie des patriarches de Constantinople de la première moitié du XIVᵉ siècle," *REB*, 7 (1950) (hereafter, Laurent, "La chronologie des patriarches"), 148.

[46] Pachymeres, *Hist.*, II, 347–49, 353.

[47] From the time of John's first resignation in early July 1302 (*Hist.*, II, 341ff.), Pachymeres included no discussion of external affairs until his description of Turkish raids in Anatolia during the summer of 1303 (*Hist.*, II, 388ff.)

[48] *Ibid.*, 349–53.

[49] *Ibid.*, 354–57.

[50] *Ibid.*, 301.

[51] *Ibid.*, 359–62.

he extolled the virtues of the prophet, who remained nameless, the Emperor led a great crowd of people to the monastery at Xerolophos. Only then did he dramatically reveal that the mysterious monk was none other than the former Patriarch Athanasius, who had been in retirement for almost ten years.[52]

Athanasius did not immediately agree to return to the patriarchal throne, pleading as an excuse his old age and declining health. Meanwhile the Emperor, in an extremely irregular proceeding, asked him to set up a court of mediation at the monastery, to make judgments especially in cases of oppression of the poor by the nobility.[53] The bishops, who had enthusiastically hailed Athanasius as patriarch at the monastery of Xerolophos, began to have second thoughts, as they remembered the harsh character of Athanasius' earlier patriarchate; so despite days of discussion, Andronicus did not succeed in persuading the bishops to accept his choice of patriarch.[54]

Further complications developed at the beginning of Lent, when John, claiming still to be patriarch, declared he would excommunicate anyone who tried to reinstate Athanasius.[55] The pious Emperor was now caught in a dilemma, since he feared Athanasius' anathema if he were not restored to the patriarchate, and John's excommunication if he were! It was not until June 21 that Andronicus was able to persuade John to repudiate his threat of excommunication. The Emperor could now proceed with a clear conscience to restore Athanasius to the patriarchal throne. Although a large number of bishops still refused to accept Athanasius, the Emperor disregarded them and went personally to Xerolophos to reinstate him as patriarch.[56] The date was June 23, 1303,[57] almost a full year since John had first resigned the patriarchate.

Athanasius desperately needed the Emperor's support during his second patriarchate, since from the very beginning half of the bishops refused to accept him and separated themselves from the Church.[58] He therefore demanded from the Emperor a promissory letter guaranteeing the freedom of the Church. In the draft of this letter, most probably prepared by Athanasius, Andronicus promised to submit to the Church in every matter that was legal and that conformed with the will of God, and to support the Patriarch in his ecclesiastical reforms, especially that of sending bishops back to their sees.[59] We have no way of knowing, however, whether or not Andronicus ever signed this letter.

[52] *Ibid.*, 363–68.
[53] *Ibid.*, 369–70.
[54] *Ibid.*, 370–75.
[55] *Ibid.*, 375–77.
[56] *Ibid.*, 383–84.
[57] *Ibid.*, 383. For the date of Athanasius' second accession to the patriarchate, see note 45 *supra*, and Laurent, "La chronologie des patriarches," 148–49.
[58] Pachymeres, *Hist.*, II, 384.
[59] γράμμα ὑποσχετικὸν τοῦ βασιλέως (= *Vaticanus Gr. 2219*, fols. 272v–274r), published by V. Laurent in his article, "Le serment de l'empereur Andronic II Paléologue au patriarche Athanase Ier, lors de sa seconde accession au trône œcuménique (Sept. [sic] 1303)," *REB*, 23 (1965) (hereafter, Laurent, "Le serment d'Andronic II"), 135–38.

The early years of the fourteenth century were a low point in the fortunes of the Byzantine Empire, as its shrinking territory was ravaged by the attacks of Turks and Catalans alike. Refugees flocked to Constantinople, food supplies in the capital dwindled, and a terrible famine began which lasted for several years.[60] At this time of crisis, Athanasius exerted every effort to alleviate the sufferings of the poor, and thus gained the support of the masses. He organized a commission to control grain supply and prices, and to supervise bakeries.[61] He set up soup kitchens on street corners, and arranged distributions of clothing to the poor.[62] After the fire of 1304 which destroyed the Kynegos quarter of Constantinople, he forced looters to return the property they had stolen, and set up a relief fund for those who had lost homes and possessions in the conflagration.[63]

Athanasius' actions in the ecclesiastical sphere were much less popular; indeed he failed to take any measures at all to reconcile the bishops, clergy, and monks who had become alienated during his previous regime. It was only thanks to the efforts of the Emperor that those bishops who had refused to agree to his election in 1303 were finally persuaded to accept him on Palm Sunday 1304.[64] The Patriarch of Alexandria, however, continued to refuse to recognize the election, and was finally forced to leave the capital by the Patriarch of Constantinople.[65] Athanasius accused other bishops of agitating for his deposition, and compelled several of them to leave the city.[66] He especially resented the grant of monasteries to displaced bishops, and on several occasions took them over for himself.[67]

During his second patriarchate Athanasius was also faced with a strike of the clergy of St. Sophia who rebelled because the patriarchal treasury did not have sufficient funds to pay them their customary salaries.[68] Moreover, there was substantial opposition to Athanasius in monastic communities, on the part of Arsenite sympathizers and of monks who objected to the Patriarch's insistence on ascetic discipline and to his approval of the confiscation of monastic property.[69]

[60] Pachymeres, *Hist.*, II, 412; *Theoctisti Vita Ath.*, 33–34.

[61] Grain supply and prices: Letters 72–74, 93, 100, 106; supervision of bakers: Letters 93 and 100.

[62] Cf. Letter 78; a sermon of Athanasius (*Vat. Gr. 2219*, fols. 166v–167v = Laurent, *Regestes*, no. 1632); *Theoctisti Vita Ath.*, 34–35; *Calotheti Vita Ath.*, 101.

[63] Cf. a sermon of Athanasius (*Vat. Gr. 2219*, fols. 168r–169r = Laurent, *Regestes*, no. 1631); Pachymeres (*Hist.*, II, 582–583) describes the fire and how Athanasius handed down decisions in cases arising from loss of property in the fire.

[64] Pachymeres, *Hist.*, II, 409.

[65] *Ibid.*, 409–10; 579.

[66] Cf. Letter 25, lines 17–20. We know that Athanasius drove from the capital the metropolitans of Crete and Sardis, as well as the Patriarch of Alexandria.

[67] Cf. Pachymeres, *Hist.*, II, 579–80, and commentary on Letter 69, lines 59–60 and 62–64.

[68] Pachymeres, *Hist.*, II, 642. Cf. also *Vat. Gr. 2219*, fols. 214v–222r = Laurent, *Regestes*, nos. 1767–73.

[69] Cf. Pachymeres, *Hist.*, II, 519, 618.

Despite the hostility by which he was surrounded, Athanasius was able, with imperial support,[70] to remain on the patriarchal throne for six years, until September 1309,[71] when he was forced to submit his resignation for the second time. The historical sources have recorded several trumped-up charges which were made against the Patriarch, including an attempt to frame him for lèse-majesté and/or Iconoclasm. The real reason behind Andronicus' consent to the final deposition of Athanasius, however, was the desire of the Emperor to bring an end to the Arsenite schism. Personal loyalty led Andronicus to support Athanasius for a long time against many charges, but in the end he decided that the only way to achieve peace within the Church was to remove the unbending Patriarch who refused to allow any compromise with the Arsenite faction.

The problem of Athanasius' second resignation is complicated by the fact that Pachymeres' History ends in 1307, so that for knowledge of the events of 1309 we have to rely on the less detailed History of Gregoras, the two Vitae, and Athanasius' own description of the course of events leading up to this abdication.[72]

The accounts of the Vitae, of Gregoras and of Athanasius himself, agree in broad outline on the story of the attempt to frame the Patriarch. Theoktistos' Vita recounts that Athanasius' enemies, led by a certain Iakobos (who is probably to be identified with Athanasius' rival for the patriarchal throne back in 1289),[73] placed under the Patriarch's footstool an icon bearing the images of the Virgin, Christ, the Cross, and the Emperors Andronicus and Michael, so that he would step on it unawares and could thus be charged with Iconoclasm and lèse-majesté. The Emperor and synod were not taken in by the trick and Iakobos was sentenced to imprisonment; still Athanasius decided to resign.[74] In his Second Letter of Resignation (= Letter 112), he gives this same story as the reason for his abdication. Fifty years later, Gregoras recorded an embroidered version of the incident, namely that the conspirators drew on the footstool a picture of Christ flanked by Andronicus on one side with a bit in his mouth and Athanasius on the other holding the reins![75]

According to the Vitae and the account of Athanasius' Letter of Resignation, then, the Patriarch decided to resign in despair after the incident of the footstool. He was also influenced in his decision by his advanced age and by

[70] Pachymeres frequently mentions the great favor in which Athanasius was held by the Emperor; cf. Hist., II, 519, 617.

[71] Cf. Laurent, "La chronologie des patriarches," 148.

[72] Nicephorus Choumnos cites complicity in a simoniacal ordination as the reason for Athanasius' resignation; see his Ἔλεγχος κατὰ τοῦ κακῶς τὰ πάντα πατριαρχεύσαντος Νίφωνος, ed. Boissonade, Anecdota Graeca, V, 259–60, and commentary on Letter 65.

[73] Cf. Pachymeres, Hist., II, 139, and Theoctisti Vita Ath., 37.

[74] Theoctisti Vita Ath., 37–38; Kalothetos' Vita tells the same story (102–3), but does not mention Iakobos by name.

[75] Gregoras, Hist., I, 258–59.

his increasing blindness.[76] Thus, in September 1309 Athanasius again retired to his monastery at Xerolophos.[77] The six-month delay before the election of his successor Niphon, an Arsenite sympathizer, in the spring of 1310[78] indicates that lengthy negotiations were necessary between the Emperor and the Arsenites, but within a year after Athanasius' abdication the schism between Arsenites and Josephites was healed.[79] On September 14, 1310, a dramatic ceremony of union took place in St. Sophia, and the forty-five-year schism was ended.[80]

Athanasius lived to see the Arsenites he so despised in reconciliation with the Church.[81] After September 1310, however, there is no further mention of Athanasius in the historical sources. Theoktistos' *Vita* states that he lived a long time after his abdication,[82] but it cannot have been much more than ten years, since he was certainly dead by 1323.[83]

Despite the hostility toward Athanasius on the part of bishops, clergy, monks, and officials, it is evident that he was greatly beloved by the people of Constantinople. Otherwise, it would be hard to explain how a man so reviled by his contemporaries soon came to be worshipped as a saint. Athanasius was buried by his disciples in a very damp plot of ground, presumably within the confines of the monastery at Xerolophos.[84] Three years later his disciples

[76] Letter 112, lines 40–44: διὰ ταῦτα καὶ τὸ ἐπιτεθὲν τῆς ἀρχιερωσύνης ἀξίωμα παραιτοῦμαι ... ὅτι καὶ γήρᾳ καὶ ἀσθενείᾳ ταλαιπωροῦντες, οὐδὲ αὐτὸ τὸ ὁρᾶν ἔχομεν. In the manuscript καὶ ... παραιτοῦμαι has been lightly crossed out, and the phrase is omitted in the Migne edition (PG, 142, col. 493B).

[77] Gregoras, *Hist.*, I, 258. Cf. also *Theoctisti Vita Ath.*, 41, and *Calotheti Vita Ath.*, 105–6.

[78] V. Grumel has established the date of Niphon's accession as May 9, 1310, on the evidence of a poem addressed to Niphon by Manuel Philes; see "La date de l'avènement du patriarche de Constantinople Niphon Ier," *REB*, 13 (1955), 138–39.

[79] The texts of the agreement were published by Laurent in an appendix to his article, "La fin du schisme arsénite," 288–313. One point of accord was that Athanasius was never again to serve as patriarch.

[80] Gregoras, *Hist.*, I, 261–62; see also a more detailed description in Niphon's Encyclical Letter (ed. Laurent, "La fin du schisme arsénite," 306–11), which also gives the date of the ceremony, September 14.

[81] Athanasius must still have been alive in 1310; otherwise the Arsenites would not have insisted that he was never again to be patriarch; cf. note 79 *supra*.

[82] *Theoctisti Vita Ath.*, 46. We need not, however, believe the testimony of the *Vita Ath.* (p. 48) that Athanasius lived to the age of 100, since Theoktistos lifted his description of Athanasius' death (including the figure 100 years) directly from Gregory of Nazianzus' *Funeral Oration for His Father* (PG, 35, cols. 1036C–37A).

[83] We can establish 1323 as the terminus ante quem of Athanasius' death from the following: A woman named Katenitzina was miraculously cured of an evil spirit by visiting the relics of Athanasius in the year that Brusa fell to the Turks, i.e., 1326; cf. Λόγος εἰς τὴν ἀνακομιδὴν τοῦ λειψάνου τοῦ ἐν ἁγίοις πατρὸς ἡμῶν Ἀθανασίου πατριάρχου Κωνσταντινουπόλεως, *cod. Const. Chalc. mon. 64*, fols. 195ᵛ–197ʳ. Since Athanasius had been dead three years when his perfectly preserved corpse was discovered and translated to the church of Christ the Savior, he must have died at least by 1323. See also note 85 *infra*.

[84] Λόγος εἰς τὴν ἀνακομιδήν, *cod. Const. Chalc. mon. 64*, fol. 163ᵛ.

decided to build a small vaulted chamber (ἀψίδα) over his tomb; but when they began to dig for the foundations, they discovered that his body had been perfectly preserved. Thus convinced of Athanasius' sanctity, his disciples removed the relics with reverence to the church of Christ the Savior (presumably the church at the monastery of Xerolophos), where he had expressed the wish to be buried.[85] The people soon came to consider Athanasius a saint and his relics became famous for their healing power. The fourteenth-century *Oration on the Translation of the Relics* gives an impressive list of thirty-two people who were cured or aided in some way by their faith in Athanasius.[86] The former Patriarch's memory was celebrated on the 28th of October.[87]

At the end of the fourteenth century, Athanasius' relics were still the object of great veneration. The Russian pilgrim Ignatius of Smolensk, for example, wrote of visiting Athanasius' monastery and of kissing his relics.[88] Nor does the history of Athanasius' relics end with the fall of Constantinople in 1453, for during the next year the relics were taken to Venice by a Venetian merchant in the belief that they were the remains of the fourth-century Patriarch of Alexandria.[89] The head was given to the church of San Girolamo, which was destroyed by fire in 1705; the rest of the relics were translated to the church of Santa Croce on the Giudecca.[90] In 1806, when an order of Napoleon suppressed the convent of Santa Croce, the nuns took the precious relics to San Zaccaria. In the twentieth century Athanasius' remains, still believed to be those of the fourth-century Church Father, were moved into the church proper and now rest on top of the second altar on the right. At present, these relics of an anti-Unionist Byzantine Patriarch, who despised all Latins, are the focal point of oecumenical services during the Week of Unity.[91]

---

[85] Λόγος εἰς τὴν ἀνακομιδήν, fols. 164ʳ–164ᵛ; cf. also ἡ ἀνακομιδὴ τοῦ λειψάνου, *cod. Const. Chalc. mon. 64*, fols. 146ᵛ–147ʳ. The church of Christ the Savior, in which Athanasius' relics were placed, must have been attached to the monastery at Xerolophos, since in the fifteenth century the Venetian merchant Zottarello stole the Saint's remains from a church in the region of Ascirolafo (= Xerolophos); cf. note 89 *infra*.

[86] Λόγος εἰς τὴν ἀνακομιδήν, fols. 157ʳ–199ʳ. Since the Λόγος gives the baptismal name and surname of most of the people who were miraculously healed, and often mentions their profession and the name of their native town or village, it is an important source for topography and prosopography of the first half of the 14th century. The terminus post quem for the composition of the Λόγος is 1326, since it mentions the fall of Brusa (fol. 196ᵛ), and it seems likely that the Λόγος was written in the late 1320's or 1330's. I am at present preparing an edition of the Greek text.

[87] Athanasius' memory is celebrated by the Greek Orthodox Church on the 28th of October (K. Doukakes, Μέγας Συναξαριστὴς πάντων τῶν ἁγίων τῶν καθ' ἅπαντα τὸν μῆνα 'Οκτώβριον ἑορταζομένων [Athens, 1895] [hereafter, Doukakes, *Synaxarion for the Month of October*], 455). Some manuscripts of his *Vita*, however, place his feast-day on October 24; cf. *Barberini VI, 22*, fol. 211, and *cod. Const. Chalc. mon. 64*, fol. 29ᵛ.

[88] S. P. Khitrovo, *Itinéraires russes en Orient* (Geneva, 1889), 138.

[89] D. Stiernon, "Le quartier du Xérolophos à Constantinople et les reliques vénitiennes du Saint Athanase," *REB*, 19 (1961), 165–88.

[90] *Ibid.*, 168–73, 182–83.

[91] *Ibid.*, 185–87.

The Patriarch Athanasius should be remembered as a crusader for much-needed ecclesiastical reform; unfortunately, his excessive zeal alienated every segment of the Church, to the extent that he was twice forced to abdicate and failed to achieve his goals. He was more successful as a true shepherd of his flock, concerned for both the material and spiritual welfare of Orthodox Christians. At a time of great crisis and suffering in Byzantium, the courts and soup kitchens of the Patriarch offered hope and sustenance to victims of social injustice and war.

II. ATHANASIUS' EDUCATIONAL BACKGROUND AND LITERARY STYLE

The historian Gregoras was judging Athanasius by his own standards when he wrote that the Patriarch had no knowledge of letters.[92] Gregoras really meant that Athanasius had no secular education, no knowledge of the Greek classics, of grammar, mathematics, or astronomy. The Saint's biographer Theoktistos readily admitted that Athanasius had not studied profane authors, but he did not consider this a disadvantage.[93]

As a child, Athanasius read and studied the Old and New Testaments; he must also have had access to some *Lives* of saints, since it is said that he decided to leave home and become a monk after reading the *Life of St. Alypios*.[94] Later, when he assumed monastic garb and visited the monasteries of Greece, Asia Minor, and the Holy Land, he had the opportunity to broaden his reading and to delve into the works of the Church Fathers. According to Theoktistos, Athanasius took advantage of his eighteen-year residence at the monastery of St. Lazaros on Mt. Galesion to read every book in the library three or four times.[95] A monastic library of the thirteenth century contained, on the average, perhaps fifty volumes; the works were almost all of a religious nature, such as Old and New Testaments, *synaxaria*, saints' *Lives*, patristic works, and liturgical books.[96]

The quotations in Athanasius' letters are just what one would expect from a man whose reading was limited to the holdings of a monastic library. His writings abound with phrases culled from the Old Testament, especially the Psalms and Prophets, and from the New Testament. One also finds in his letters occasional phrases taken from the works of the fourth-century Church Fathers, especially Gregory of Nazianzus. For the most part, however, these

---

[92] Gregoras, *Hist.*, I, 180.
[93] Cf. *Theoctisti Vita Ath.*, 26.
[94] *Ibid.*, 3–4.
[95] *Ibid.*, 10.
[96] Cf., for example, the inventories in Otto Volk's unpublished dissertation, *Die byzantinischen Klosterbibliotheken von Konstantinopel, Thessalonike und Kleinasien* (Munich, 1954) (hereafter, Volk, *Die byzantinischen Klosterbibliotheken*).

quotations are from well-known orations which were read in the churches on appointed days.[97] Thus, it is more likely that Athanasius became familiar with these works by hearing them read year after year during church services, than by reading them himself. Only rarely do Athanasius' letters go beyond John Chrysostom and the Cappadocian Fathers to include passages from Theodoret, John Climacus, Dionysius the Areopagite, and Epiphanius of Cyprus.[98] As patriarch, though, Athanasius was familiar with the canons of the Church and civil law,[99] and in three letters (49, 60, 61) he quoted from the chapter of the *Epanagoge* dealing with the duties of the emperor.

Compared with his erudite contemporaries, Nicephorus Choumnos, Theodore Metochites, and Maximus Planudes, Athanasius' background was woefully limited. Although he is reported to have studied eagerly the manuscripts at Galesion, we read in Letter 20 that he returned a book sent him by a friend, because neither he nor his disciples had any use for it. Perhaps it was too worldly for his tastes. Athanasius almost never used classical allusions, and, on the few occasions when he did refer to figures of antiquity (Proteus, Apollo, and Sardanapalus), it is probable that he was imitating Gregory of Nazianzus.[100]

One also suspects that, just as he had no doubt memorized the Psalms, he may have learned by heart portions of patristic works without studying in depth the theological complexities of their arguments, for one looks in vain in his writings for any discussion of theology or doctrine. Despite his hostility to Latins, for example, he never mentions the problem of the Procession of the Holy Spirit. Apparently, Athanasius did not have the intellectual capacity to deal with matters of theology, and his letters to the clergy and monks are concerned rather with matters of discipline. Nor is there any hint in his writings that he was a forerunner of hesychasm, or a master of the "psycho-technical" method of prayer, as he is described by Gregory Palamas.[101]

Although Athanasius had some knowledge of patristic literature, he had no formal literary training and his style lacks the smooth elegance of

[97] E.g., Letter 3, quotations from Greg. Naz., *Or.* XVI (read on Cheese-eating Sunday); Letter 12, Greg. Naz., *Or.* XXI (read on January 18, feast-day of St. Athanasius of Alexandria); Letter 44, Greg. Naz., *Or.* XIX (read December 22); Letter 47, Greg. Naz., *Or.* XI (read on January 10, feast-day of Gregory of Nyssa); Letter 66, Greg. Naz., *Or.* XIX (read on December 22), and *Or.* XL (read on January 7).

[98] Theodoret: Letter 69, lines 47–49; John Climacus: Letter 2, lines 57–58; Dionysius and Epiphanius: Patriarchal Letter, *Vat. Gr. 2219*, fols. 105ʳ–121ʳ (= Laurent, *Regestes*, no. 1738).

[99] Canons: e.g., Letters 62, line 4, and 91, lines 20–25; civil law: Letters 50, lines 45–46, and 21, *passim*.

[100] Cf. commentary on Letters 7, line 31; 64, lines 8–9; and 81, line 147.

[101] Cf. Gregory Palamas' *Défense des saints hésychastes*, ed. J. Meyendorff (Louvain, 1959), 99 (= *Triad*, I, 2, 12), and Meyendorff's comments on p. xli. A further indication that Athanasius was viewed as a spiritual predecessor to Palamas is the fact that both of his biographers, Theoktistos the Studite and Kalothetos, were Palamite monks.

the Church Fathers with whom he was familiar. The syntax of his letters is often disjointed and confused. For example, he frequently left sentences unfinished, especially in conditional sentences where he wrote a lengthy protasis, but omitted the apodosis.[102] Another common fault of his style is a lack of agreement in case between words and their modifiers if they are separated by any distance.[103] Athanasius' failure to produce neatly rounded periods, or even grammatical sentences, may be connected with the fact that his failing eyesight in his later years forced him to dictate his letters to a scribe.[104] He was certainly blind by 1309, when he gave the loss of his sight as a reason for his abdication,[105] and was probably already partially blind when he resigned for the first time in 1293, since his disciples read to him constantly during his retirement at the Xerolophos monastery.[106] Thus, we may presume that he was unable to read over his dictation, and consequently failed to realize that many of his lengthy sentences lacked a main verb, or that after digressions he frequently forgot to return to his original train of thought.

Athanasius was well aware that his educational background had not prepared him to write letters in the elegant style required by the Byzantine court, and apologized for his deficiencies.[107] Nevertheless, in his letters to the Emperor, he did attempt to write in a more elevated manner than that which he used in his sermons to the populace of Constantinople;[108] similarly, he quoted more liberally from patristic literature in letters to bishops than in letters to laymen.[109] Rhetorical questions abound in Athanasius' letters. A

---

[102] Cf. Letter 1, lines 15–17: καὶ εἰ καὶ μέμψιν ἐπάξει μοί τις, ... πρὸς τὸ τῆς βασιλείας ὕψος ... καταθρασυνθῆναι λαλεῖν — ἀλλὰ τί πάθω;

[103] Cf. Letter 1, lines 15–16: καὶ εἰ καὶ μέμψιν ἐπάξει μοί τις, ὡς τὰ ἐμαυτοῦ πενθεῖν καταλείψαντα; Letter 95, lines 22–24: καὶ τὸ πρόσφορον ἐκζητεῖν καὶ ἀπονέμειν αὐτῇ [the Church] ὡς δῶρον ἐποφειλόμενον, τὴν σὲ εἰς τοῦτο μαιευσαμένην.

[104] Cf. Theoctisti Vita Ath., 24: ἐν ταύταις ταῖς τῶν ἐπιστολῶν αὐτοῦ βίβλοις ἐμφέρονται κατηχήσεις τε καὶ διδασκαλίαι πολὺ μετὰ τοῦ ὠφελίμου τὸ χάριεν ἔχουσαι, ἃς οἰκείᾳ γλώσσῃ ὑπηγόρευσε.

[105] Cf. supra, p. xxv–xxvi note 76.

[106] Cf. Theoctisti Vita Ath., 31.

[107] Cf. Letter 73, line 39 (εἰ καὶ μὴ λέγειν ἀξίως πεπαίδευμαι), and Letter 86, lines 25–26 (εἰδήσεως ἄμοιροι πάμπαν καὶ παιδεύσεως ἀνακτορικῆς). Although this sort of apology is often a topos in Byzantine authors, in the case of Athanasius it is all too true.

[108] Athanasius' sermons to the people on the occasion of the famine and the Kynegos fire (Vat. Gr. 2219, fols. 166ᵛ–167ᵛ, 168ʳ–169ʳ = Laurent, Regestes, nos. 1631, 1632) are in a very simple and straightforward style, with no use of allusion or rhetorical devices. Cf. the remarks of Guilland about the writings of Gregoras, who also varied his style according to the erudition of his correspondent (Correspondance de Nicéphore Grégoras [Paris, 1927], xxi).

[109] For example, in letters to the metropolitan of Apameia (Vat. Gr. 2219, fols. 126ʳ–130ᵛ = Laurent, Regestes, nos. 1742–44, 1746), Athanasius quotes from Basil's Letter to Paregorius, Gregory of Nazianzus' Oratio XLIV, In Novam Dominicam, and Oratio XIX, and from the Vita Joanni Chrysostomi by Theodore of Trimithus. In a letter to the metropolitan of Sardis (Vat. Gr. 2219, fols. 158ᵛ–160ᵛ = Laurent, Regestes, no. 1750) he quotes from Gregory's Orations XIV and XLV, and canon 74 of the Quinisext Council.

favorite device is the use of τί δέ; or τί τοῦτο;, followed by the answer. In Letter 7 (lines 23–49), there are ten rhetorical questions in a row, and in Letter 69 (lines 199–212), eight follow one after another.

Another favored rhetorical device was his insertion of exclamatory parenthetical phrases, such as οὐαί μοι τῆς συμφορᾶς! (Letter 49, lines 13–14), ὦ τῆς ἀναισθησίας! (Letter 83, line 44), ὦ ζημίας! (Letter 88, line 20), and ὦ μοι τῆς δυστυχίας! (Letter 99, lines 13–14). He probably picked up these habits from Gregory of Nazianzus.[110]

The "manner indirect" was in great vogue among Byzantine writers, and whenever possible Athanasius made use of allusion; Athanasius of Alexandria is τὸν ἐξ Αἰγύπτου Πρωτέα (Letter 7, line 31), the Bulgarians are τοῖς τε περὶ τὸν Ἴστρον οἰκοῦσιν (Letter 81, line 166), a Lascarid is referred to as ἀπόγονον ... τῶν πώποτε βεβασιλευκότων τινός (Letter 81, line 50), Satan is ἐκείνου τοῦ θεῖναι τοῖς ἄστροις τὸν θρόνον βατταρίσαι τετολμηκότος (Letter 81, lines 59–60), Christians are τῶν ἀνάστασιν ἐλπιζόντων (Letter 69, lines 109–10), Moses is ὁ θεόπτης (Letter 62, line 65), Isaiah ὁ μεγαλοφωνότατος (Letter 19, line 3), and David ὁ θεοπάτωρ (Letter 43, line 30).

This frequent use of indirect allusion and confused syntax adds to the difficulties of understanding and interpreting Athanasius' writings; like many of his compatriots he wrote in such a way that it is often impossible to grasp the meaning of a passage unless one knows the historical background. His disciples, however, who were more interested in Christian zeal than in literary style and historical information, found the letters a source of inspiration and thus preserved them for posterity.

---

[110] For Gregory's use of rhetorical questions, cf. *Oratio* II, ογ´-οδ´ (PG, 35, col. 481A–C). For exclamations, cf. *Oratio* II, πα´ (*ibid.*, col. 488B): φεῦ τοῦ πάθους! and *Oratio* IV, πγ´ (*ibid.*, col. 609B): φεῦ τῆς πραγματείας! φεῦ τῆς ἀντιδόσεως!

CRITICAL INTRODUCTION

I. DESCRIPTION OF THE MANUSCRIPTS[1]

1. THE PRINCIPAL MANUSCRIPT

Vaticanus Gr. 2219 (Colonensis 58) (= V):

First half fourteenth century. Parchment (I, II, 274 Paper). 23.8 × 15.5 cm. Two flyleaves, 274 folios. Single column of 36 lines (fol. 5^r).

Collation: 5 × 8 (40), 6 (46), 8 (54), 6 (60), 4 × 8 (92), 7 (99), 21 × 8 (267), 6 (273), 1 (paper replacement — 274).

Hands: a) 1^r–89^v. Small, neat hand. Similar to *Vat. Gr. 2220* (1304/5 — A. Turyn, *Codices Graeci Vaticani saeculis XIII et XIV scripti* . . . [Vatican City, 1964], pl. 83) and *Urb. Gr. 126* (1315/16 — *ibid.*, pl. 91).

b) 93^r–99^r. Similar small hand, but more angular.

c) 100^r–273^v. Larger and bolder hand.

d) 274^r. Later hand.

e) Many of the letters' titles were added by yet another hand, V$^{r(ubricator)}$.

Decoration: Foliate headpiece in vermilion (1^r); ornate initials (93^r, 97^v, 148^r, 161^r, 163^v, 166^v, 169^r, 176^v, 178^r, 190^v, 210^r, 230^r, 246^r).

Inks: Brown for text; vermilion for titles, initial letters, and decorations.

Binding: Modern vellum.

Previous owner: Before entering the Biblioteca Vaticana, the manuscript was owned by Giovanni Cardinal Salviati (1490–1553). His name appears on fol. 273^v (Io. Car. de Salviati), and his seal on the flyleaves I and II.

---

[1] In the description of the manuscripts I have followed the system of H. Hunger's *Katalog der Griechischen Handschriften der Österreichischen Nationalbibliothek* (Vienna, 1961).

Contents:[2]

---

[2] For letters which are not included in this edition, I refer the reader to Laurent's *Regestes*, which includes the title and *incipit* of all the letters of Athanasius in *Vat. Gr. 2219*, and gives bibliography where pertinent.

210ʳ–211ʳ Letter on instruction of children — Laurent, *Regestes*, no. 1766.

211ʳ–214ʳ Letter about priests — Laurent, *Regestes*, no. 1761.

214ᵛ–219ʳ Letters to clergy of St. Sophia — Laurent, *Regestes*, nos. 1767–70.

219ʳ–219ᵛ Letter of Theophylact Libdikes, archon of the churches.

γράμμα ὑποσχετικὸν τοῦ ἄρχοντος τῶν ἐκκλησιῶν πρὸς τὸν πατριάρχην, ὅπως σχολάζῃ ὡς δεῖ, καὶ μάλιστα τῇ Κυριακῇ καὶ Σαββάτῳ καὶ πάσῃ δεσποτικῇ ἑορτῇ.

Inc. Ἐνδείᾳ καὶ ῥαθυμίᾳ πιεζομένων πολλῇ τῶν τοῦ κλήρου

Des. τοῦ βαθμοῦ οὗ ἠξίωμαι.

219ᵛ–220ʳ Letter to clergy of St. Sophia — Laurent, *Regestes*, no. 1771.

220ʳ–220ᵛ Letter of Andronicus to Athanasius.

γράμμα πρὸς τὸν βασιλέα, ἀναγκάσαντος τούτου διὰ τὴν ῥόγαν τῶν κληρικῶν (erroneous title; cf. Laurent, *Regestes*, p. 550).

Inc. Πάντως οὐκ ἀγνοεῖς τὸ ἀναρίθμητον

Des. ὁ τῆς ῥόγας καιρός.

220ᵛ–221ᵛ Letter to emperor about clergy — Laurent, *Regestes*, no. 1772.

221ᵛ–222ʳ Letter to clergy of St. Sophia — Laurent, *Regestes*, no. 1773.

222ʳ–222ᵛ Letter to new notaries — Laurent, *Regestes*, no. 1774.

222ᵛ–223ʳ Letter to priests — Laurent, *Regestes*, no. 1775.

223ʳ–228ʳ Two διδασκαλίαι — Laurent, *Regestes*, nos. 1776–77.

228ʳ–230ʳ Instructions for exarchs sent to the West — Laurent, *Regestes*, no. 1778.

230ʳ–232ʳ Encyclical to people of Anatolia — Laurent, *Regestes*, no. 1589.

232ʳ–235ʳ διδασκαλία — Laurent, *Regestes*, no. 1779.

235ʳ–244ᵛ Two διδασκαλίαι to Mt. Athos — Laurent, *Regestes*, nos. 1590, 1604.

244ᵛ–246ᵛ Two letters to *protos* of Mt. Athos — Laurent, *Regestes*, nos. 1605, 1602.

246ᵛ–255ʳ Letters to Lavra on Athos — Laurent, *Regestes*, nos. 1615, 1617–18.

255ʳ–258ʳ Letter on the death of the *protos* — Laurent, *Regestes*, no. 1656.

258ᵛ–260ʳ Letter to Xeropotamos — Laurent, *Regestes*, no. 1640.

260ʳ–261ᵛ Letter to Metaxopoulos, abbot of Lavra — Laurent, *Regestes*, no. 1659.

261ᵛ–268ʳ Letter to monks of Athos — Laurent, *Regestes*, no. 1657; extract, fols. 265ᵛ–267ʳ, ed. Laurent, in *REB*, 28 (1970), 109–10.

268ʳ–269ʳ Letter to abbot of Lavra and *protos* of Athos — Laurent, *Regestes*, no. 1658.

269ʳ–269ᵛ Reply to Athonite monk Myron — Laurent, *Regestes*, no. 1619.

269ᵛ–272ᵛ Reply to Mt. Athos — Laurent, *Regestes*, no. 1780.

272ᵛ–274ʳ Promissory letter of Andronicus II to Athanasius (ed. V. Laurent, in *REB*, 23 [1965], 135–38).

Comments:

Vaticanus Gr. 2219, containing 181 letters and homilies and one Νεαρά by Athanasius (plus three letters addressed to him), is the oldest and most complete manuscript of the works of the Patriarch. Although it may well be contemporary with Athanasius, there is no question of its being an autograph,[3] since the Patriarch is known to have dictated his correspondence to a scribe.[4]

It is quite possible that V was copied by three of Athanasius' disciples, soon after his death. These scribes would have assembled all the letters of the Patriarch they could find, and made a collection of them to serve as inspirational reading,[5] not as a historical record. It is probable that the original letters were on loose sheets; this would explain why the endings of two letters (32 and 76) are missing.

The letters, all of which can be dated to the interregnum (1293–1303) or Athanasius' second patriarchate (1303–9), are not arranged in chronological order,[6] but are grouped rather according to addressee. Thus, most of the first 115 letters (fols. 1r–89v) are addressed to the Emperor, members of his family, or officials, although two homilies and a Novel appear to have been inserted at random in this part of the manuscript. The letters to the Emperor seem to follow some chronological arrangement, since Letters 1 and 2 can be dated 1299/1300 and 1297, respectively, and are thus among the earliest letters, and many of the letters at the end of this group obviously belong at the end of Athanasius' second patriarchate, 1309–10 (e.g., Letters 89, 95, 109, and 112–15). There are many deviations within this rough chronological sequence, however; for example, the first Letter of Abdication (Letter 111), dated 1293, should be the first letter in the manuscript instead

---

[3] Some autograph manuscripts of Byzantine letters do survive; for example, two manuscripts of the correspondence of Manuel Kalekas are in the author's hand (*Vat. Gr. 1879* and *1093*); cf. R.-J. Loenertz, *Correspondance de Manuel Calecas* (= Studi e Testi, 152) (Vatican City, 1950), 14.

[4] Cf. *supra*, p. xxx and note 104.

[5] The title of the collection of Athanasius' letters indicates this inspirational purpose: τοῦ ὁσίου ... 'Αθανασίου ... ἐπιστολαὶ πρός τε τὸν αὐτοκράτορα καὶ πρὸς ἑτέρους πολὺν τὸν θεῖον ζῆλον ἐμφαίνουσαι. Theoktistos' *Vita Athanasii* also mentions the edifying nature of the letters: ἐν ταύταις ταῖς τῶν ἐπιστολῶν αὐτοῦ βίβλοις ἐμφέρονται κατηχήσεις τε καὶ διδασκαλίαι πολὺ μετὰ τοῦ ὠφελίμου τὸ χάριεν ἔχουσαι (p. 24). In another passage Theoktistos wrote that he found two of Athanasius' sermons particularly inspiring: τοσαύτην δὲ τὴν ὠφέλειαν ἐμποιοῦσαι τοῖς ἐντυγχάνουσιν, ὅσην ἴσημι κἀγὼ κἀκ τούτων πολλὴν δρεψάμενος τὴν ὠφέλειαν (p. 25).

[6] Several collections of Byzantine letters are arranged in chronological order. The R. P. R.-J. Loenertz has shown, for example, that the letters of Manuel Kalekas were copied in strict chronological sequence in the principal manuscript, *Vat. Gr. 1879* (*Correspondance de Manuel Calecas*, 16–17). The same editor has proved that in the manuscripts of Demetrios Kydones contemporaneous letters tend to be grouped together, although the letters are not arranged in strict chronological order (R.-J. Loenertz, *Démétrius Cydones, Correspondance* [= Studi e Testi, 186] [Vatican City, 1956], xii).

of near the end of the section; Letter 2 should be before Letter 1; Letters 43, 79, and 96, which can all be dated to 1307, are widely separated in the manuscript; Letter 93 should be placed before Letter 73.[7] After the group of letters to the Emperor come three other groups, letters to bishops (121^r–160^v), to the clergy of St. Sophia (204^r–222^r), and to Mt. Athos (235^r–272^v), separated by homilies and letters to miscellaneous addressees.

The titles of many of the letters have been added by another hand (V^r). This scribe did not know standard Greek very well and made numerous orthographical and grammatical mistakes in the superscriptions.[8] In some cases the title makes no sense because the scribe took it directly from a phrase in the letter without understanding it.[9] In a few instances the titles are incorrect; Letter 75, for example, which urges Irene to become reconciled with her husband, the Emperor, is entitled γράμμα πρὸς τὸν αὐτοκράτορα περὶ τοῦ παρ' ἐλπίδα συμπεσόντος τῆς Δεσποίνης ὁ θάνατος (sic). The correct title, as was suggested by a scholiast on folio 75^v of *Par. Gr. 137* (a sixteenth-century manuscript of Athanasius' letters), should be γράμμα πρὸς τὴν βασίλισσαν περὶ τοῦ δεῖν αὐτὴν ὁμονοεῖν τῷ συζύγῳ. In some titles, on the other hand, the scribe has provided information which is not included in the text of the letters; for instance, there is no mention of Niphon or of Cyzicus in Letters 89 or 95, yet the titles indicate to the reader that these letters allude to Athanasius' rivalry with the metropolitan of Cyzicus. Similarly, the title of Letter 1 tells us that it was written to the Emperor while he was in Thessalonica, although there is no mention of Thessalonica in the body of the text. This suggests that V^r was a contemporary of Athanasius, and familiar with his career.

2. The Secondary Manuscripts

a) *Parisinus Suppl. Gr. 516* (former no. 2933) (= S):

Sixteenth century. Paper. 29.9 × 16.3 cm. Three flyleaves, 329 folios. Single column of 23 lines (fol. 162^r).

---

[7] On the basis of internal evidence, Laurent has proposed dates for about seventy-five of the letters and sermons in the manuscript, and has presented these in chronological order in his *Regestes*. Although Laurent and I independently arrived at the same chronology for most of the letters, for the purposes of this edition I preferred to retain the order of the manuscript, since dating on internal evidence is a tricky business at best, and the evidence in many of the letters is slim or non-existent.

[8] E.g., Letter 1, πρὸς τὸν αὐτοκράτορα, ὄντος ἐν Θεσσαλονίκῃ; Letter 35, γράμμα πρὸς τὸν αὐτοκράτορα ἀναφαίρων τὰ συμβαίνοντα ἐν τῇ Ἀνατολῇ παρὰ τῶν αἱμοβόρων Μογαβάρων; Letter 29, γράμμα πρὸς τὸν αὐτοκράτορα τὸ ἀναρτῆσθαι μετὰ Θεὸν ὅσα δὴ δεξιὰ καὶ εὐώνυμα τῷ κατὰ πνεύματι πατρί. See the remarks of Laurent, *Regestes*, viii.

[9] E.g., the title of Letter 80 is γράμμα πρὸς τὸν αὐτοκράτορα περὶ τοῦ ἃ ἀναφαίρειν οὐχ ἕνεκεν φίλων ἢ συγγενῶν ἢ δώρων ἢ δόξης ἀλλ' ἀμφότερα ἀπαραίτητα αὐτόχρημα οὔσας σοι τὴν βασίλειον, a garbled version of lines 20–22: εἰδὼς ἀμφότερα ἀπαραίτητα τῇ ἐκ Θεοῦ βασιλείᾳ σου χρηματίσοντα· αἰτήσεις δὴ τὰς ἐμὰς αὐτόχρημα κόσμον βασίλειον οὔσας σοι. The eye of V^r apparently skipped a line in *Vat. Gr. 2219* from ἀπαραίτητα to αὐτόχρημα.

Collation: 41 × 8 (328), 1 (329).

Hand: Same as *Par. Gr. 137*.

Watermark: Blacksmith (Italy, 16th cent.);[10] cf. C. M. Briquet, *Les filigranes. Dictionnaire historique des marques du papier dès leur apparition vers 1282 jusqu'en 1600* (Paris, 1907), no. 7558.

Decoration: Headpieces at each new author.

Inks: Brown ink for text; vermilion initial letters and headpieces.

Binding: Green leather.

Previous owner: François de Noailles, bishop of Aix (1519–85); ex libris 1r (f. de noailles. e[vesque] d'acqs). When Noailles went to Constantinople in 1572 as the French ambassador, he loaned the manuscript to Arnaud du Ferrier (1508–85); cf. IIIv.[11]

Contents:

1r–110v Gelasius of Cyzicus, *History of the Council of Nicaea*.

111r–119v Theodore, presbyter of the monastery of Raithu, *On the Incarnation of Christ*.

120r–189r Athanasius, patriarch of Constantinople, Letters 1–69.

189v–192r Athanasius, Νεαρά (PG, 161, cols. 1064–67).

192r–243v Athanasius, Letters 70–115.

243v–255r Athanasius, Letters (= Laurent, *Regestes*, nos. 1627, 1748, 1750, 1766, 1619).

256r–280v Letters I–V and XVII of Cyril of Alexandria.

281r–288v St. Gregory of Nazianzus, *Exposition of the Stories Which He Mentioned in His Orations*.

289r–329v Nonnus, *Exposition of the Same*.

b) Neapol. Gr. II B 26 (olim Farnesianae Bibliothecae) (= N):

Paper. 24 × 34.5 cm. 149 numbered folios.

For a description of this manuscript, see G. Pierleoni, *Catalogus Codicum Graecorum Bibliothecae Nationalis Neapolitanae*, I (Rome, 1962), no. 64, pp. 188–90.

---

[10] Thus, S cannot be a 15th-cent. manuscript as listed in Omont's catalogue; cf. H. A. Omont, *Inventaire sommaire des manuscrits du supplément grec de la Bibliothèque Nationale* (Paris, 1883), 58.

[11] *Par. Suppl. Gr. 516*, flyleaf IIIv: "Ce petit livre a esté consigné à Monsieur de Montaignar, conseiller du Roy de sa court du parlament de Bordeaux ... pour estre mis entre les mains du Monsieur du Ferier du conseil privé du Roy et son ambassadeur à Venise. Lequel le jouira s'il luy plaist et le gardera jusques au retour de Monsieur de Noailles, évesque d'Acqs à qui ce livre appartient." The date of 1572 is thus a terminus ante quem for the copying of this manuscript. I wish here to express my gratitude to Dr. Gillian Jondorf of Howard University for her assistance in the transcription of this passage in old French.

N contains Athanasius' Letters 1–14 and part of 15 in two quires which are separated in the manuscript (fols. 10ᵃ–16ᵇ, 119ᵃ–126ᵇ). Since Letter 15 breaks off in N in the middle of the word ἀναφέρομεν, and P has the remaining text of the letter, it seems evident that N contains the missing first portion of P. Therefore it must be dated, like P, to the sixteenth century instead of to the fifteenth century as it is in Pierleoni's catalogue.[12] The dimensions of the two manuscripts are similiar but not identical.

c) Parisinus Gr. 137 (formerly Codex Telleriano-Remensis, 8 — Reg. 1890.2) (= P):

Sixteenth century. Paper. 22.2 × 32.8 cm. 265 folios. Single column of 28 lines (fol. 16ʳ).

Collation: 33 × 8 (264), 1 (265). The first two quires of this manuscript (Letters 1–14, and part of 15) were lost before binding, and are now incorporated in N.

Hand: Same as *Par. Suppl. Gr. 516.*

Watermarks: a) Blacksmith (Italy, 16th cent.); cf. Briquet, no. 7558 (e.g., fols. 2, 3, 6, 64, 67, 70–111).

b) Star (Italy, 16th cent.); cf. Briquet, no. 6097 (fols. 13–15).

c) Tulip (Italy, 16th cent.); cf. Briquet, no. 6683 (fol. 19, 66).

Decoration: 1ʳ — headpiece in black and vermilion.

Inks: Black for text; vermilion for initial letters of titles and texts.

Binding: Brown leather.

Previous owner: Before entering the French royal collection in 1700, the manuscript belonged to Charles Maurice LeTellier, archbishop of Rheims (1642–1710).[13]

Contents:

1ʳ–15ᵛ Catena in Job
16ʳ–28ᵛ Letters 15 (partial) — 34 of Athanasius
28ᵛ–69ʳ Letters 36–69 of Athanasius.
69ʳ–71ᵛ Νεαρά of Athanasius.
71ᵛ–99ᵛ Letters 70–93 of Athanasius.
99ᵛ–111ᵛ Letters 110–115 of Athanasius.
112ʳ⁻ᵛ Blank.
113ʳ–264ᵛ Homilies of St. John Chrysostom, Sisinnius, etc.[14]

---

[12] S. Cirillo notes in his 19th-cent. catalogue that the manuscript could be dated either to the fifteenth or sixteenth century; cf. his *Codices Graeci manuscripti Regiae Bibliothecae Borbonicae descripti atque illustrati,* I (Naples, 1826), 189.

[13] Cf. J. Gillet, *Charles-Maurice LeTellier, Archévêque-Duc de Rheims: Etude sur son administration et son influence* (Paris, 1881), 173.

[14] For a more detailed index of contents, see H. A. Omont, *Inventaire sommaire des manuscrits grecs de la Bibliothèque Nationale,* I (Paris, 1886), 16–17.

Comments:

The two Paris manuscripts contain fewer of Athanasius' works than V; S includes 120 Letters and the Νεαρά, P only 84 and the Νεαρά (plus 14 more letters in N). The copyist of these manuscripts omitted all the sermons and letters to the clergy and monks, and included only the Patriarch's letters to the Emperor, members of the imperial family, officials, and bishops. The two manuscripts are closely related, since both were copied by the same scribe on the same sixteenth-century Italian paper with a blacksmith watermark.

Not only is the handwriting of S and P similar, but it is evident also that the scribe made both copies from V. Many of the scribal errors in both manuscripts can be traced back to difficult readings or mistakes in the Vatican manuscript.[15] Furthermore, on several occasions where the scribe has inadvertently omitted several words in the Paris manuscripts, it is clear that his eye moved down two lines in V instead of one.[16]

The use of Italian paper in both S and P suggests that they were copied by a Greek scribe in Italy in the early or middle sixteenth century from Cardinal Salviati's fourteenth-century manuscript of Athanasius' letters. A very simple stemma results:

prototype (lost)

V

S   N+P

As will be discussed in greater detail below, the middle of the sixteenth century appears to be the most logical date for the copying of Athanasius' Letters, since interest in the question of episcopal residence was revived at this time and was a topic of controversy at the Council of Trent (1546–63).

3. OTHER MANUSCRIPTS

Four of Athanasius' Encyclical Letters (*Vat. Gr. 2219*, 100ʳ–121ʳ and 132ᵛ–158ᵛ) are included in folios 296ʳ–337ʳ of *Par. Gr. 1351A*, a fifteenth-century manuscript on paper.

[15] For example in Letter 62, line 73, V corrected τὸ δέ γε from τῇ δέ γε (fol. 43ᵛ). The correction so confused S that he wrote τʼ δέ γε (fol. 178ᵛ). In Letter 69, line 142, S miscopied τοὺς τῆς Νιτρίας as τοὺς τῆς νιτνίας, because V writes ν and ρ in a very similar fashion. Also in Letter 49, line 110, P copied V's mistake of repeating τῶν when he started a new page (fols. 34ᵛ–35ʳ), and wrote τῶν τῶν ἰχνῶν (fol. 43ʳ).

[16] Cf. Letter 112 where V (fol. 85ᵛ) has ὑπο⁴- | στρωννύντος καὶ τούτῳ Θεοῦ ὑπὸ πόδας αὐτοῦ τοὺς ἐχθροὺς ἴσα καὶ⁵ | λεανθέντι πηλῷ πλατειῶν. P skipped line 5 entirely, and wrote ὑπολεανθέντι (*sic!*) πηλῷ πλατειῶν (fol. 104ᵛ). Similarly, in Letter 75, V wrote κατὰ καιροὺς⁹ | ἰδικῶς καὶ κοινῶς ὑπομονῇ καὶ συνέσει καὶ προσευχῇ θυγατέρων τῆς¹⁰ | ἐκκλησίας (fol. 55ᵛ). P's eye skipped from καιροὺς of line 9 to ἐκκλησίας of line 11, and he wrote κατὰ καιροὺς ἐκκλησίας (fol. 76ᵛ).

Folios 145ʳ–280ᵛ of MS no. 288 (formerly no. 911) in the Patriarchal Library of Alexandria also contain a copy of Athanasius' longest encyclical letter (*Vat. Gr. 2219*, 100ʳ–121ʳ).[17] According to A. Papadopoulos-Kerameus, *ca.* 1903 a letter addressed to Nicephorus Moschopoulos, metropolitan of Crete (*Vat. Gr. 2219*, 130ᵛ–132ᵛ), was also included in a manuscript with the old number 911, between folios 159 and 160.[18] Papadopoulos-Kerameus, however, described the manuscript as a *Nomocanon*, which does not correspond to the description of no. 288/911 in Moschonas' catalogue. Either there has been some confusion in the numbering of the manuscripts, or the letter to Moschopoulos was inserted loosely in the manuscript and lost, since it is not included by Moschonas in his catalogue.

Athanasius' Novel, which was submitted to the Emperor in 1304, has been preserved in a variety of manuscripts: for example, *Par. Gr. 1351A* (296ʳ–298ʳ), *Par. Gr. 1356* (270ʳ–272ʳ), *Par. Gr. 1357A* (282ᵛ–283ᵛ), *Par. Gr. 1388* (397ʳ–399ᵛ), and *Vat. Gr. 847* (258ʳ–260ᵛ). *Vat. Gr. 856* contains the Novel on folios 234ʳ–236ʳ and the longest encyclical letter on folios 236ʳ–250ʳ.

There are also several manuscript copies of the First and Second Letters of Abdication (Letters 111–12). In addition to copies in S and P, the texts of the Letters of Abdication are preserved in Kalothetos' *Vita Athanasii*.[19] Theoktistos included only the First Letter of Abdication in his *Vita*.[20]

Other manuscripts of Athanasius' works may turn up in the future, as more collections of manuscripts are scientifically catalogued. Certainly not all of Athanasius' writings have been preserved in the manuscripts which survive today. We know of at least one sermon and one letter to the Emperor which are lost. For example, Theoktistos' *Vita Athanasii* mentions the *incipits* of two of Athanasius' sermons.[21] One of these sermons, beginning τὴν αἰχμα-λωσίαν τοῦ γένους, has survived in a unique copy in *Vat. Gr. 2219*, fols. 188ʳ–190ʳ; the other sermon, which begins δεῖπνον ἐν τοῖς εὐαγγελίοις, has not been preserved in any manuscript known to me. The lost letter to the Emperor (Laurent, *Regestes*, no. 1671) was entitled Ἀθανασίου Κωνσταντινουπόλεως τοῦ νέου ἐπιστολὴ πρὸς τὸν βασιλέα, and began ἡμεῖς, ἅγιε βασιλεῦ, εἰ καὶ πάντων ἀνθρώπων ἐσμὲν ἀνούστατοι καὶ ἁμαρτωλότεροι. It was preserved only in a fifteenth-century manuscript, no. 62 at the monastery of Megaspelaion in the northern Peloponnesus.[22] Unfortunately, the library of this monastery, including the unique copy of this letter by Athanasius, was completely destroyed by fire on July 17, 1934.[23]

---

[17] T. D. Moschonas, Κατάλογοι τῆς Πατριαρχικῆς Βιβλιοθήκης, Τόμος Α'. Χειρό-γραφα (Alexandria, 1945), pp. 258–59, no. 288.

[18] A. Papadopoulos-Kerameus, Νικήφορος Μοσχόπουλος, in *BZ*, 12 (1903), 217 note 2.

[19] *Calotheti Vita Ath.*, 96–97, 104–5.

[20] *Theoctisti Vita Ath.*, 28–30.   [21] *Ibid.*, 25–26.

[22] N. Bees, Κατάλογος τῶν ἑλληνικῶν χειρογράφων κωδίκων τῆς ἐν Πελοποννήσῳ μονῆς τοῦ Μεγάλου Σπηλαίου, Τόμος Α' (Athens, 1915), 61.

[23] M. Richard, *Répertoire des bibliothèques et des catalogues de manuscrits grecs* (Paris, 1948), 121. Only four manuscripts, all Gospel Books, were saved from the conflagration.

CRITICAL INTRODUCTION

II. PREVIOUS EDITIONS AND STUDIES
OF ATHANASIUS' CORRESPONDENCE

In the fourteenth century, Athanasius' letters and sermons were collected and read for spiritual inspiration. Theoktistos in his *Vita Athanasii* mentions "books" of Athanasius' letters;[24] he urges his readers to refer to these collections of letters,[25] and writes that he has derived great benefit from Athanasius' works, especially two sermons.[26] It is somewhat surprising therefore that only one fourteenth-century copy of Athanasius' Letters has been preserved.

Francisco Torres (ca. 1509–84)

In the sixteenth century, the question of the obligation of bishops to reside in their dioceses was hotly debated, and was one of the topics of controversy at the Council of Trent (1545–63). Since many of Athanasius' Letters contain exhortations to bishops to leave Constantinople and return to their sees, his works were of particular relevance during this reform–conscious period. As I have suggested above, the commissioning in the sixteenth century of two partial copies of Athanasius' correspondence (*Par. Gr. 137* and *Par. Suppl. Gr. 516*) is probably to be connected with the Council of Trent. It would seem significant that, in addition to letters to the Emperor, S also contains letters to the metropolitan of Sardis (fols. 243^v–245^v = Laurent, *Regestes*, no. 1750) and to the metropolitan of Crete (245^v–248^r = Laurent, *Regestes*, no. 1627), and a letter to a newly ordained bishop about to depart for his diocese (248^r–252^v = Laurent, *Regestes*, no. 1748).

Also at the time of the Council of Trent, a Spanish Jesuit named Francisco Torres (Turrianus) translated into Latin eight of Athanasius' letters on episcopal residence and included them as an appendix to his book *De Residentia Pastorum*, published at Florence in 1551.[27] Torres entered the service of Cardinal Salviati in Rome in 1540, and edited several patristic manuscripts in Salviati's library.[28] We may therefore presume that he used Salviati's copy of Athanasius' correspondence (now *Vat. Gr. 2219*) as the basis for his translations. Because of Torres' special concern with the problem of episcopal residence, he was appointed by Pope Pius IV as a papal theologian for the third session of the Council of Trent (1562–63) and took part in the debate on the obligation of bishops to remain in their sees.[29] It is tempting to suggest that on this occasion Torres commissioned the copying of two

---

[24] *Theoctisti Vita Ath.*, 24.

[25] *Ibid.*, 41.

[26] *Ibid.*, 25.

[27] F. Torres (Turrianus), *De Summi Pontificis supra Concilia auctoritate ... libri tres. Eiusdem de residentia pastorum jure divino scripto sancita ... liber, etc.* (Florence, 1551), 70–90.

[28] I. Onatibia, article on Torres in *New Catholic Encyclopedia*, XIV (1967), 206.

[29] *Ibid., loc. cit.*

additional manuscripts of Athanasius' letters (now *Par. Suppl. Gr. 516* and *Par. Gr. 137*) for use at the Council.

Jean Boivin de Villeneuve (1663–1726)

The French scholar Boivin de Villeneuve was the first to realize the *historical* importance of Athanasius' letters, and to publish excerpts from them in Greek. In the commentary on his 1702 edition of the *History* of Nicephorus Gregoras, Boivin listed a selection of titles of Athanasius' letters from P, which had been given to the Bibliothèque du Roi in 1700 by LeTellier. He also published transcriptions of Athanasius' First and Second Letters of Resignation (111–12), and an excerpt from the Letter about the Resignations (115).[30]

Anselmo Banduri (ca. 1670–1743)

A contemporary of Boivin, the Ragusan monk Banduri also concerned himself with the edition of certain of Athanasius' letters. Banduri was a student of Montfaucon, the father of Greek paleography, at St. Germain-des-Prés. He claimed that *ca.* 1705 he transcribed all of Athanasius' letters from P, and translated them into Latin,[31] but unfortunately no edition ever appeared. However, Banduri did include in the second volume of his *Imperium Orientale* (Paris, 1711) a complete list of the titles of eighty-four letters from P,[32] and published the transcriptions of ten, most of them accompanied by Latin translations (Letters 23, 36, 41, 65, 81, 89, 111–115).[33]

François-Jean-Gabriel La Porte du Theil (1742–1815)

La Porte du Theil, a curator at the Bibliothèque Nationale, began a serious study of Athanasius' correspondence, based again on P, but abandoned the task after transcribing twenty-one letters. Fortunately his notes are preserved at the Bibliothèque Nationale in *Par. Suppl. Gr. 971*, folios 107–157.[34]

---

[30] J. Boivin de Villeneuve, "Notae ad Nicephorum Gregoram," in *Nicephori Gregorae Byzantina Historia*, I (Paris, 1702), 755–58 and 762–63. Boivin did not give the number of the manuscript he used, but only described it as *Codex Regius, olim Tellerianus* (p. 755). However, from the folio numbers which he cited it is clear that he was referring to P.

[31] A. Banduri, *Imperium Orientale sive Antiquitates Constantinopolitanae*, 2 vols. (Paris, 1711) (hereafter, Banduri, *Imperium Orientale*), II, 962. La Porte du Theil challenged this claim of Banduri, and argued that Banduri merely copied Boivin's notes (*Par. Suppl. Gr. 971*, fol. 110). Banduri did publish seven more letters than Boivin, but it is impossible to determine whether he copied Boivin's unpublished transcriptions or made his own transcriptions from P.

[32] The second volume of *Imperium Orientale* consists of commentaries on the texts of manuscripts published in the first volume. The index of titles of Athanasius' letters is found on pp. 962–67. Banduri acknowledged his indebtedness to Boivin in compiling this list (p. 962).

[33] *Imperium Orientale*, II, 614–15, 968–86.

[34] La Porte du Theil, *Notices et extraits de manuscrits grecs*, III; cf. H. A. Omont, *Inventaire sommaire des manuscrits du supplément grec de la Bibliothèque Nationale* (Paris, 1883), 99.

They contain a few pages of general notes on the Life of Athanasius, drawn from Pachymeres, Gregoras, and Sphrantzes, and comments on the work of his predecessors Boivin and Banduri. La Porte du Theil also made a list of the titles of Athanasius' letters, and began to transcribe them. Like his predecessors, however, he made little effort to edit his transcriptions.

Other Editions

La Porte du Theil was the only scholar in the later eighteenth and nineteenth centuries who returned to the manuscripts of Athanasius' correspondence. All other compilers and editors confined themselves to reproducing the texts published by Torres and Banduri. J. A. Fabricius (1668–1736), for example, in his *Bibliotheca Graeca* merely copied Banduri's list of the titles of Athanasius' letters.[35] In 1885, J. P. Migne reprinted in his Patrologia Graeca Banduri's list of eighty-four titles from P, and the Greek texts and Latin translations of the ten letters which Banduri had transcribed and translated. Migne also included the eight Latin translations (with no Greek text) made by Torres for his *De Residentia Pastorum*.[36]

It is only in the twentieth century that Byzantine scholars have gone back to the manuscripts of Athanasius' letters. The publication of Theoktistos' *Vita Athanasii* in 1897 by Delehaye, and in 1905 by Papadopoulos-Kerameus, no doubt contributed to the revival of interest in the writings of this Byzantine Patriarch. Whereas Boivin, Banduri, and La Porte du Theil knew only P, in the past century more complete manuscripts have come to light. *Par. Suppl. Gr. 516* was included in Omont's catalogue of 1883, and in this century the R. P. Vitalien Laurent rediscovered the earliest and most complete manuscript of Athanasius' letters, *Vat. Gr. 2219*, which had lain in obscurity since the sixteenth century when it was used by Salviati and Torres. It was the intention of Laurent to prepare an edition of Athanasius' correspondence based on the Vatican manuscript,[37] but unfortunately his plans have not been realized, and he has published only two of the Patriarch's letters.[38] Laurent has, however, made extensive use of information from Athanasius' works in his numerous important articles on the early Palaeologan period, and has recently published very useful summaries of and commentary on Athanasius' letters in the fourth volume of *Les regestes des actes du patriarcat de Constantinople* (Paris, 1971).

[35] J. A. Fabricius, *Bibliotheca Graeca*, VIII (Hamburg, 1802), 51–55 [= Book V, chap. v]. The first edition of this series (1716–40) is inaccessible to me.
[36] PG, 142 (Paris, 1885), cols. 471–528.
[37] Cf. R. Guilland, "La correspondance inédite d'Athanase, Patriarche de Constantinople (1289–1293; 1304–1310)," *Mélanges Charles Diehl*, I (Paris, 1930) (hereafter, Guilland, "La correspondance inédite d'Athanase"), 123 note 1.
[38] In 1945 Laurent published Athanasius' letter to the monks of Xeropotamou (*Vat. Gr. 2219*, fols. 258v–260r) in *RHSEE*, 22 (1945), 285–86. In 1965 he published a promissory letter of Andronicus II which was most probably drafted by Athanasius; see "Le serment d'Andronic II," 124–39 (= *Vat. Gr. 2219*, fols. 272v–274r).

In the 1950's the texts of a few of Athanasius' letters were published by Gennadios, metropolitan of Helioupolis and Theira.[39] Although Gennadios used both S and V, he made no attempt to provide a critical edition, and his transcriptions contain numerous mistakes. Similarly, Demetrios Pallas' edition of six of Athanasius' letters,[40] based on S, contains so many errors as to be virtually worthless.

Studies

A few important articles on Athanasius' letters have appeared in the modern period. In 1930 Rodolphe Guilland published a study of *Par. Suppl. Gr. 516*, entitled "La correspondance inédite d'Athanase, Patriarche de Constantinople (1289–1293; 1304–1310)."[41] In this article he assessed the importance of Athanasius' correspondence, and sketched out the type of information provided by the writings of the Patriarch. A few years later appeared an article by the Rumanian scholar N. Bănescu, based on the more complete Vatican manuscript. Bănescu emphasized the great interest of Athanasius' correspondence because of its contributions to our knowledge of the social conditions of the Empire and of the struggle of the Byzantines with the Turks and Catalans.[42] In 1967 and 1968 Dr. Angeliki Laiou published two articles in *Byzantion* which discuss in detail three of Athanasius' letters (67, 78, and 84).[43] She has also included in these articles an edition and English translation of the three letters.

The most recent article on Athanasius, by J. Gill,[44] draws only on those excerpts from the Patriarch's correspondence which were published by Guilland and Bănescu.

[39] Gennadios of Helioupolis, 'Ορθοδοξία, 27 (1952), 113–20, 173–79, 195–98; 28 (1953), 145–50; 29 (1954), 5–10; 'Επ.'Ετ.Βυζ.Σπ., 22 (1952), 227–32; 'Ιστορία τοῦ Οἰκουμενικοῦ Πατριαρχείου, I (Athens, 1953), 364, 375–81, 392–93.

[40] D. I. Pallas, *Die Passion und Bestattung Christi in Byzanz, der Ritus — das Bild*, Miscellanea Byzantina Monacensia, 2 (Munich, 1965) (hereafter Pallas, *Die Passion Christi*), 299–307.

[41] *Mélanges Charles Diehl*, I (Paris, 1930), 121–40.

[42] N. Bănescu, "Le patriarche Athanase Ier et Andronic II Paléologue: Etat religieux, politique et social de l'empire," *BSHAcRoum*, 23 (1942), 28–56.

[43] A. Laiou, "The Provisioning of Constantinople during the Winter of 1306–1307," *Byzantion*, 37 (1967) (hereafter, Laiou, "The Provisioning of Constantinople"), 91–113, and "A Byzantine Prince Latinized: Theodore Palaeologus, Marquis of Montferrat," *Byzantion*, 38 (1968) (hereafter, Laiou, "Theodore Palaeologus"), 386–410. As this book was going to press, Dr. Laiou's book, *Constantinople and the Latins: The Foreign Policy of Andronicus II, 1282–1328* (Cambridge, Mass., 1972) (hereafter, Laiou, *Andronicus II*), which contains an edition of ten of Athanasius' letters in an appendix, was published by the Harvard University Press.

[44] "Emperor Andronicus II and Patriarch Athanasius I," *Byzantina*, 2 (1970), 13–19.

III. COMMENTS ON PRESENT EDITION AND CRITICAL APPARATUS

The following edition of Athanasius' letters is based on V, as the earliest, most complete, and most accurate manuscript. Since it is impossible to arrange the correspondence in strict chronological order, the edition follows the sequence of letters in V.[45]

In the first portion of the critical apparatus, the *Fontes*, I have listed the sources of Athanasius' quotations.

In the second portion of the apparatus I have listed the manuscripts in which the text of the letter appears, and have indicated any previous editions of the letter. The second part of the apparatus also contains variants found in S, N, and P, to indicate the nature of these apograph manuscripts, and to demonstrate that they were indeed copied from V. Readings of S, N, and P have been adopted in the text only when they correct an obvious error in V. When "codd." appears in the critical apparatus it indicates that the reading in the text is mine. Athanasius' Greek is full of grammatical errors, especially in the agreement of cases. I have not attempted to correct all these mistakes, but have left them in the text to retain the flavor of his language. In general I have rejected the reading of V only where I feel there has been a scribal error (perhaps going back to the original scribe who wrote down the Patriarch's dictation), for the most part iotacisms, e.g., εἰ for ἤ (Letter 2, line 6), οἶδεν for εἶδεν (Letter 3, line 33), or confusion of indicative and subjunctive, e.g., εἰσακούωμαι instead of εἰσακούομαι (Letter 17, line 77).

V usually limited his superscriptions to πρὸς τὸν αὐτοκράτορα. Another hand, Vr(ubricator), has supplemented these superscriptions with a brief indication of the contents of the letters. These additions have been relegated to the apparatus, since they are not part of the original text of the letters.

The orthography of V is excellent, so that in general the only tacit changes I have had to make are in the accentuation of enclitics, in which I follow Koster,[46] in the addition of the iota subscript, and in the division of words like καθ' ἑκάστην, τοῦ νῦν, etc., which are usually written καθεκάστην, τουνῦν in Late Byzantine manuscripts. The punctuation of the edition also differs from that of the manuscript.

[45] See my comments, *supra*, p. xxxvii note 7.

[46] A. J. Koster, *A Practical Guide for the Writing of Greek Accents* (Leiden, 1962), 24–26.

LIST OF ABBREVIATIONS

ActaSS: *Acta Sanctorum Bollandiana*
Actes de Xéropotamou: J. Bompaire, ed., *Actes de Xéropotamou*, Archives de l'Athos, III
(Paris, 1964)
Ahrweiler, "La région de Smyrne": H. Ahrweiler, "L'histoire et la géographie de la région
de Smyrne entre les deux occupations turques (1081–1317), particulièrement au
XIIIᵉ siècle," *TM*, 1 (Paris, 1965), 1–204
AnalBoll: *Analecta Bollandiana*
AnnUkrAcad: *The Annals of the Ukrainian Academy of Arts and Sciences in the U. S.*
AOC: Archives de l'Orient Chrétien
Arnakis, Οἱ πρῶτοι 'Οθωμάνοι: G. G. Arnakis, Οἱ πρῶτοι 'Οθωμάνοι. Συμβολὴ εἰς τὸ
πρόβλημα τῆς πτώσεως τοῦ ἑλληνισμοῦ τῆς μικρᾶς 'Ασίας *(1282–1337)*, in TF-
ByzNgPhil, 41 (Athens, 1947)

Banduri, *Imperium Orientale*: A. Banduri, *Imperium Orientale, sive Antiquitates Con-*
stantinopolitanae, 2 vols. (Paris, 1711)
Bănescu, "Le patriarche Athanase Iᵉʳ": N. Bănescu, "Le patriarche Athanase Iᵉʳ et
Andronic II Paléologue: Etat religieux, politique et social de l'empire," *BSHAc-*
Roum, 23 (1942), 28–56
BCH: *Bulletin de Correspondance Hellénique*
BNJbb: *Byzantinisch-neugriechische Jahrbücher*
Boissonade, *Anecdota Graeca*: J. F. Boissonade, *Anecdota Graeca*, 5 vols. (Paris, 1829–33;
reprint, Hildesheim, 1962)
———— *Anecdota Nova*: J. F. Boissonade, *Anecdota Nova* (Paris, 1844; Hildesheim, 1962)
Boivin, "Notae ad Nicephorum Gregoram": J. Boivin de Villeneuve, "Notae ad Nice-
phorum Gregoram," in *Nicephori Gregorae Byzantina Historia*, I (Paris, 1702)
Bratianu, *Etudes byzantines*: G. I. Bratianu, *Etudes byzantines d'histoire économique et*
sociale (Paris, 1938)
Bréhier, *Les institutions*: L. Bréhier, *Le monde byzantin*. II, *Les institutions de l'empire*
byzantin (Paris, 1949)
BSHAcRoum: *Bulletin de la Section Historique, Académie Roumaine*
BSOAS: *Bulletin of the School of Oriental and African Studies*
BZ: *Byzantinische Zeitschrift*

Calotheti Vita Ath.: Βίος καὶ πολιτεία τοῦ 'Αθανασίου Α' οἰκουμενικοῦ πατριάρχου (1289–
1293 καὶ 1304–1310) συγγραφεὶς ὑπὸ 'Ιωσὴφ Καλοθέτου μοναχοῦ, ed. Athanasios
Pantokratorinos, in Θρᾳκικά, 13 (1940), 56–107
Choumnos, Ἔλεγχος κατὰ τοῦ ... Νίφωνος: Nicephorus Choumnos, Ἔλεγχος κατὰ τοῦ
κακῶς τὰ πάντα πατριαρχεύσαντος Νίφωνος, ed. J. F. Boissonade, in *Anecdota*
Graeca, V, 255–83
CIC: *Corpus Iuris Civilis*, ed. R. Schoell (Berlin, 1904)
CMH: *Cambridge Medieval History*

Darrouzès, *Epistoliers byzantins*: J. Darrouzès, *Epistoliers byzantins du X*e *siècle*, AOC, 6 (Paris, 1960)
DDC: *Dictionnaire de Droit Canonique*
Δελτ.Χριστ.'Αρχ.'Ετ.: Δελτίον τῆς Χριστιανικῆς 'Αρχαιολογικῆς 'Εταιρείας
de Meester, *De monachico statu*: P. Placidus de Meester, *De monachico statu iuxta disciplinam byzantinam*, Codificazione canonica orientale, Fonti, 2nd ser. II, fasc. X (Vatican City, 1942)
Demetrakos, *Lexikon*: D. B. Demetrakos, Μέγα λεξικὸν τῆς 'Ελληνικῆς γλώσσης, 9 vols. (Athens, 1933–51)
Dölger, *Aus den Schatzkammern*: F. Dölger, *Aus den Schatzkammern des Heiligen Berges* (Munich, 1948)
——— *Regesten*, IV: F. Dölger, *Regesten der Kaiserurkunden des oströmischen Reiches. IV, Regesten von 1282–1341*, Corpus der griechischen Urkunden des Mittelalters und der neueren Zeit (Munich–Berlin, 1960)
——— -Karayannopoulos, *Byzantinische Urkundenlehre*: F. Dölger and J. Karayannopoulos, *Byzantinische Urkundenlehre. I, Die Kaiserurkunden* (Munich, 1968)
DOP: *Dumbarton Oaks Papers*
Doukakes, *Synaxarion for the Month of October*: K. Doukakes, Μέγας Συναξαριστὴς πάντων τῶν ἁγίων τῶν καθ' ἅπαντα τὸν μῆνα 'Οκτώβριον ἑορταζομένων (Athens, 1895)
DTC: *Dictionnaire de Théologie Catholique*

EO: *Echos d'Orient*
'Επ.'Ετ.Βυζ.Σπ.: 'Επετηρὶς 'Εταιρείας Βυζαντινῶν Σπουδῶν

GCS: Die griechischen christlichen Schriftsteller der ersten Jahrhunderte
Gennadios, 'Ιστορία τοῦ Οἰκουμενικοῦ Πατριαρχείου: Gennadios, metropolitan of Helioupolis, 'Ιστορία τοῦ Οἰκουμενικοῦ Πατριαρχείου, I (Athens, 1953)
Goar, *Euchologion*: J. Goar, *Euchologion, sive Rituale Graecorum* (Venice, 1730; reprint, Graz, 1960)
Guilland, "La correspondance inédite d'Athanase": R. Guilland, "La correspondance inédite d'Athanase, Patriarche de Constantinople (1289–1293; 1304–1310)," in *Mélanges Charles Diehl*, I (Paris, 1930), 121–40; reprinted in Guilland, *Etudes Byzantines* (Paris, 1959), 53–79

Harmenopoulos, *Hexabiblos*: C. Harmenopoulos, *Manuale legum sive Hexabiblos*, ed. G. E. Heimbach (Leipzig, 1851)
Herman, "Ricerche sulle istituzioni monastiche bizantine": E. Herman, "Ricerche sulle istituzioni monastiche bizantine. Typika ktetorika, caristicari e monasteri 'liberi'," *OCP*, 6 (1940), 293–375
Hunger, *Prooimion*: H. Hunger, *Prooimion, Elemente der byzantinischen Kaiseridee in den Arengen der Urkunden* (Vienna, 1964)

IRAIK: *Izvĕstija Russkago Arheologičeskago Instituta v' Konstantinopolĕ*

JA: *Journal Asiatique*
Janin, *Constantinople byzantine*: R. Janin, *Constantinople byzantine: Développement urbain et répertoire topographique²* (Paris, 1964)
——— *Géographie ecclésiastique*: R. Janin, *La géographie ecclésiastique de l'empire byzantin.* I. *Le siège de Constantinople et le patriarcat œcuménique.* 3, *Les églises et les monastères* (Paris, 1953)
Jannaris, *Historical Greek Grammar*: A. N. Jannaris, *An Historical Greek Grammar* (London, 1897)
JHS: *Journal of Hellenic Studies*
JÖBG: *Jahrbuch der Österreichischen Byzantinischen Gesellschaft*

Koukoules, Βυζαντινῶν Βίος καὶ Πολιτισμός: Ph. Koukoules, Βυζαντινῶν Βίος καὶ Πολιτισμός, 6 vols. (Athens, 1948–57)

Laiou, *Andronicus II*: A. Laiou, *Constantinople and the Latins: The Foreign Policy of Andronicus II, 1282–1328*, Harvard Historical Studies, 88 (Cambridge, Mass., 1972)
—— "The Provisioning of Constantinople": A. Laiou, "The Provisioning of Constantinople during the Winter of 1306–1307," *Byzantion*, 37 (1967), 91–113
—— "Theodore Palaeologus": A. Laiou, "A Byzantine Prince Latinized: Theodore Palaeologus, Marquis of Montferrat," *Byzantion*, 38 (1968), 386–410
Lampe, *Patristic Greek Lexicon*: G. W. H. Lampe, *A Patristic Greek Lexicon* (Oxford, 1961–68)
Laurent, "La chronologie des patriarches": V. Laurent, "La chronologie des patriarches de Constantinople de la première moitié du XIVe siècle," *REB*, 7 (1950), 145–55
—— "Cyrille II": V. Laurent, "Le patriarche d'Antioche Cyrille II (1287–c. 1308)," *AnalBoll*, 68 (1950) (= *Mélanges P. Peeters*, 2), 310–17
—— "La direction spirituelle à Byzance": V. Laurent, "La direction spirituelle à Byzance: la correspondance d'Irène-Eulogie Choumnaina Paléologine avec son second directeur," *REB*, 14 (1956), 48–86
—— "La fin du schisme arsénite": V. Laurent, "Les grandes crises religieuses de Byzance. La fin du schisme arsénite," *BSHAc Roum*, 26, 2 (1945), 225–313
—— "Un groupe de signatures épiscopales": V. Laurent, "Un groupe de signatures épiscopales," *EO*, 32 (1933), 318–23
—— *Regestes*: V. Laurent, *Les regestes des actes du patriarcat de Constantinople*. I, *Les actes des patriarches*, fasc. IV, *Les regestes de 1208 à 1309* (Paris, 1971)
—— "Le serment d'Andronic II": V. Laurent, "Le serment de l'empereur Andronic II Paléologue au patriarche Athanase Ier, lors de sa seconde accession au trône œcuménique (Sept. 1303)," *REB*, 23 (1965), 124–39
—— "Les signataires": V. Laurent, "Les signataires du second synode des Blachernes," *EO*, 26 (1927), 129–49
Lemerle, "Le tribunal du patriarcat": P. Lemerle, "Recherches sur les institutions judiciaires à l'époque des Paléologues. II, Le tribunal du patriarcat ou tribunal synodal," *AnalBoll*, 68 (1950) (= *Mélanges P. Peeters*, 2), 318–33
Le Quien, *OrChr*: Michel Le Quien, *OrChr*, 3 vols. (Paris, 1740)
Leutsch–Schneidewin: eds. E. L. Leutsch and F. G. Schneidewin, *Corpus Paroemiographorum Graecorum*, 2 vols. (Göttingen, 1839; reprint, Hildesheim, 1965)
Levi, "Cinque lettere inedite di Emanuele Moscopulo": L. Levi, "Cinque lettere inedite di Emanuele Moscopulo," *Studi italiani di filologia classica*, 10 (1902), 55–72
Loeb: The Loeb Classical Library
Λόγος εἰς τὴν ἀνακομιδήν: Theoktistos the Studite (?), Λόγος εἰς τὴν ἀνακομιδὴν τοῦ λειψάνου τοῦ ἐν ἁγίοις πατρὸς ἡμῶν Ἀθανασίου πατριάρχου Κωνσταντινουπόλεως, cod. Const. Chalc. mon. 64, fols. 157r–199r

Martini, *Manuelis Philae carmina inedita*: A. Martini, *Manuelis Philae carmina inedita* (Naples, 1900)
Matschke "Politik und Kirche": K.-P. Matschke, "Politik und Kirche im spätbyzantinischen Reich: Athanasios I., Patriarch von Konstantinopel 1289–1293; 1303–1309," *Wissenschaftliche Zeitschrift der Karl-Marx-Universität Leipzig, Gesellschafts- und Sprachwissenschaftliche Reihe*, 15 (1966), 479–86
MélUSJ: *Mélanges de l'Université Saint-Joseph, Beyrouth*
Michel, *Die Kaisermacht*: A. Michel, *Die Kaisermacht in der Ostkirche (843–1204)* (Darmstadt, 1959)
Miklosich–Müller: F. Miklosich and J. Müller, *Acta et diplomata Graeca medii aevi sacra et profana*, 6 vols. (Vienna, 1860–90)

Miller, *Manuelis Philae carmina*: E. Miller, *Manuelis Philae carmina*, 2 vols. (Paris, 1855–57)
Muntaner: R. Muntaner, *The Chronicle of Muntaner*, trans. Lady Goodenough, 2 vols. (London, 1920–21)
Muratori, RerItalSS: ed. L. A. Muratori, Rerum Italicarum scriptores

NachrGött: Nachrichten von der Akademie der Wissenschaften zu Göttingen, Philosophisch-historische Klasse

OCA: *Orientalia Christiana Analecta*
OCP: *Orientalia Christiana Periodica*
OrChr: *Oriens Christianus*
'Ορολόγιον: Τὸ μέγα 'Ορολόγιον περιέχον ἅπασαν τὴν ἀνήκουσαν αὐτῷ ἀκολουθίαν κατὰ τὴν τάξιν τῆς ἀνατολικῆς ἐκκλησίας, ed. M. I. Saliveros (Athens, n.d.)

Pallas, *Die Passion Christi*: Demetrios I. Pallas, *Die Passion und Bestattung Christi in Byzanz: Der Ritus—Das Bild* (= *Miscellanea Byzantina Monacensia*, 2) (Munich, 1965)
Panagiotakou, Τὸ Δίκαιον τῶν Μοναχῶν: P. I. Panagiotakou, Σύστημα τοῦ 'Εκκλησιαστικοῦ Δικαίου κατὰ τὴν ἐν 'Ελλάδι ἰσχυν αὐτοῦ. IV, Τὸ Δίκαιον τῶν Μοναχῶν (Athens, 1957)
Papadopoulos, *Genealogie der Palaiologen*: A. Th. Papadopoulos, *Versuch einer Genealogie der Palaiologen, 1259–1453* (Munich, 1938; reprint, Amsterdam, 1962)
Papadopoulos-Kerameus, Νικήφορος Μοσχόπουλος: A. Papadopoulos-Kerameus, Νικήφορος Μοσχόπουλος, in *BZ*, 12 (1903), 215–23
PG: Patrologiae cursus completus, Series Graeca, ed. J.-P. Migne
PL: Patrologiae cursus completus, Series Latina, ed. J.-P. Migne
Ps.-Kodinos, *Traité des Offices*: Pseudo-Kodinos, *Traité des Offices*, ed. J. Verpeaux (Paris, 1966)

REB: *Revue des Etudes Byzantines*
Rhalles–Potles: Σύνταγμα τῶν θείων καὶ ἱερῶν κανόνων, eds. G. A. Rhalles and M. Potles, 6 vols. (Athens, 1852–56)
RHSEE: *Revue Historique du Sud-Est Européen*
Rouillard–Collomp, *Actes de Lavra*: G. Rouillard and P. Collomp, *Actes de Lavra*, Archives de l'Athos, I (Paris, 1937)

Schmid, "Zur Chronologie von Pachymeres": Pia Schmid, "Zur Chronologie von Pachymeres, Andronikos L. II–VII," *BZ*, 51 (1958), 82–86
Ševčenko, "Anepigraphos": I. Ševčenko, "Le sens et la date du traité 'Anepigraphos' de Nicéphore Choumnos," *Bulletin de la Classe des Lettres et des Sciences Morales et Politiques, Académie Royale de Belgique*, 5th ser., 35 (1949), 473–88
———— *Etudes*: I. Ševčenko, *Etudes sur la polémique entre Théodore Métochite et Nicéphore Choumnos* (Brussels, 1962)
———— "Manuel Moschopulos": I. Ševčenko, "The Imprisonment of Manuel Moschopulos in the Year 1305 or 1306," *Speculum*, 27 (1952), 133–57

TFByzNgPhil: Texte und Forschungen zur byzantinisch-neugriechischen Philologie
Theoctisti Vita Ath.: *Vita Athanasii* by Theoktistos the Studite, ed. A. Papadopoulos-Kerameus, "Žitija dvuh' Vselenskih' patriarhov' XIV v., svv. Afanasija I i Isidora I," in *Zapiski istoriko-filologičeskago fakul'teta Imperatorskago S.-Peterburgskago Universiteta*, 76 (1905), 1–51
TM: *Travaux et Mémoires*

Tomadakes, Βυζαντινὴ Γραμματολογία: N. B. Tomadakes, Βυζαντινὴ Γραμματολογία *(1204–1453)*, I (Athens, 1957)
—— Σύλλαβος βυζαντινῶν μελετῶν καὶ κειμένων: N. B. Tomadakes, Σύλλαβος βυζαντινῶν μελετῶν καὶ κειμένων (Athens, 1961)
Treu, ed., *Planudis epistulae: Maximi monachi Planudis epistulae*, ed. M. Treu (Breslau, 1890; reprint, Amsterdam, 1960)
Triodion: Τριῴδιον Κατανυκτικόν, περιέχον ἅπασαν τὴν ἀνήκουσαν αὐτῷ ἀκολουθίαν τῆς ἁγίας καὶ μεγάλης Τεσσαρακοστῆς, 1st ed. (Rome, 1879)
Turrianus, *De residentia pastorum*: Francisco Torres (Turrianus), *De Summi Pontificis supra Concilia auctoritate ... libri tres. Eiusdem de residentia pastorum jure divino scripto sancita ... liber* (Florence, 1551), 70–90

Underwood, *The Kariye Djami*: Paul A. Underwood, *The Kariye Djami*, I–III (New York, 1966); IV (Princeton, N. J., 1975)

Verpeaux, *Nicéphore Choumnos*: J. Verpeaux, *Nicéphore Choumnos, homme d'état et humaniste byzantin (ca. 1250/1255–1327)* (Paris, 1959)
—— "Notes chronologiques": J. Verpeaux, "Notes chronologiques sur les livres II et III du *De Andronico Palaeologo* de Georges Pachymère," *REB*, 17 (1959), 168–73
VizVrem: *Vizantijskij Vremennik*
Volk, *Die byzantinischen Klosterbibliotheken*: O. Volk, *Die byzantinischen Klosterbibliotheken von Konstantinopel, Thessalonike und Kleinasien* (unpublished doctoral dissertation, Munich, 1954)
Vryonis, *Decline of Hellenism*: Sp. Vryonis, Jr., *The Decline of Medieval Hellenism in Asia Minor and the Process of Islamization from the Eleventh through the Fifteenth Century* (Berkeley, Calif., 1971)

Zachariä von Lingenthal, *Jus Graeco-Romanum*: K. E. Zachariä von Lingenthal, *Jus Graeco-Romanum*, 7 vols. (Leipzig, 1856–84)
Zepos, *Jus Graeco-Romanum*: J. and P. Zepos, *Jus Graeco-Romanum*, 8 vols. (Athens, 1931)
ZVI: *Zbornik Radova Vizantološkog Instituta, Srpska Akademija Nauka*

All citations of Byzantine historians refer to the Bonn edition, unless otherwise stated.

LIST OF SIGNS

TEXT

* * *	lacunae textus
⟨ ⟩	additiones ab editore factae
[ ]	uncis quadratis amplectuntur verba ab editore seclusa
† †	his crucibus corruptelae amplectuntur

APPARATUS

V	*Vaticanus Gr. 2219*
V^1, V^2	codicis V manus prima, secunda
V^x	manus codicis V de qua mihi nihil certi constat
V^r	codicis V rubricator
V^{mg}, V^{sv}	codex V in margine, supra versum
S	*Parisinus Suppl. Gr. 516*
N	*Neapol. Gr. II B 26*
P	*Parisinus Gr. 137*
( )	uncis rotundis amplectuntur solutiones compendiorum codicis

TEXT and TRANSLATION

ΤΟΥ ΟΣΙΟΥ ΠΑΤΡΟΣ ΗΜΩΝ ΑΘΑΝΑΣΙΟΥ ΠΑΤΡΙΑΡΧΟΥ
ΚΩΝΣΤΑΝΤΙΝΟΥΠΟΛΕΩΣ ΕΠΙΣΤΟΛΑΙ ΠΡΟΣ ΤΕ ΤΟΝ
ΑΥΤΟΚΡΑΤΟΡΑ ΚΑΙ ΠΡΟΣ ΕΤΕΡΟΥΣ, ΠΟΛΥΝ ΤΟΝ ΘΕΙΟΝ
ΖΗΛΟΝ ΕΜΦΑΙΝΟΥΣΑΙ

1. Πρὸς τὸν αὐτοκράτορα

Κύριε, εἰ ἧς ὧδε, οὐκ ἂν ἀπέθανέ μου ὁ ἀδελφός, φησί
που τὰ ἱερὰ λόγια· ἃ καὶ μικρὸν ὑπαλλάξας αὐτός, πρὸς τὸν ἅγιόν μου
αὐτοκράτορα, ὡς τοῦ Κυρίου χριστόν, «Κύριε βασιλεῦ, εἰ ἧς ὧδε, οὐκ
ἂν τῷ φύλῳ Χριστιανῶν τῶν ἀδελφῶν μου τοιαῦτα συνήντησε τὰ δεινά.
5 οὐκ ἂν ἡ κληρονομία Χριστοῦ, δι' ἣν καὶ θάνατον κατεδέξατο, δι' ἣν
οἱ τούτου αὐτόπται πολυτρόπους ἰδέας θανάτου ὑπέμειναν, καὶ ἅπας ὁ τῶν
ἁγίων χορὸς ὑπὲρ πλατυσμοῦ ταύτης, οὐ μόνον νηστείας καὶ ἀγρυπνίας,
ἀλλὰ καὶ τὰ ἑαυτῶν αἵματα κενῶσαι οὐ παρῃτήσαντο, καὶ ἧς σε ἄρχειν
10 προώρισε καὶ προέγνω καὶ βασιλεύειν, καὶ αὔξειν ταύτην καὶ συντηρεῖν,
καὶ νῦν, φεῦ, διὰ τὰς ἐμὰς ἁμαρτίας, παλαμναίοις Ἰσμαηλίταις κατήντησεν
εἰς κατάβρωμα, καὶ οἱ τῆς μακαρίας Τριάδος δοῦλοι καὶ λάτραι ἀθέοις
καὶ ταῦτα εἰς δουλείαν ἐγένοντο, καὶ τὸ αἷμα αὐτῶν ἡ βάρβαρος ὡς
ὕδωρ ἐξέχεε μάχαιρα.»
15 καὶ εἰ καὶ μέμψιν ἐπάξει μοί τις, ὡς τὰ ἐμαυτοῦ πενθεῖν καταλείψαντα, ἐπιλαθόμενόν τε τῆς οἰκείας ἐσχατιᾶς, πρὸς τὸ τῆς βασιλείας
ὕψος, καὶ ταῦτα μὴ ἐρωτώμενον, καταθρασυνθῆναι λαλεῖν—ἀλλὰ τί πάθω;
παρώρμησε γάρ με πρὸς τοῦτο τὸ τῶν πασχόντων φίλτρον Χριστιανῶν·
ἐγίνωσκον δέ ποτε καὶ τὴν σὴν ἁγίαν ψυχὴν εἰς τὴν τῶν Χριστιανῶν
20 ἐκκρεμαμένην προκοπὴν καὶ ἐπίδοσιν. πρὸς δὲ τούτοις, μήπως ἐμποδίζ-

---

1: 2 Joh. 11:32 ‖ 6 Ps. 78 (79):1 ‖ 13–14 Ps. 78 (79):3

1: V 1ʳ–1ᵛ. S 120ʳ–121ʳ. N 10ʳ–11ʳ.
1 post αὐτοκράτορα add. ὄντος (ὄντος SN) ἐν Θεσσαλονίκῃ VʳSN ‖ 5 Χριστιανὸν S ‖
16 ἐξεχέαι N ‖ 17 κατασαθσυνθῆναι (?) N

LETTERS OF OUR HOLY FATHER ATHANASIUS, PATRIARCH OF CONSTANTINOPLE, TO THE EMPEROR AND OTHERS, REVEALING HIS GREAT DIVINE ZEAL.

1. To the emperor

The Holy Scriptures say somewhere, «Lord, if thou hadst been here, my brother had not died». By changing this slightly, I ⟨could refer⟩ these words to my holy emperor, since he is the anointed of the Lord: «My lord emperor, if you had been here, such terrible misfortunes would not have befallen my Christian brethren. Nor would the patrimony of Christ—for which He died, for which His witnesses [i.e., the Apostles] endured many forms of death, for whose expansion the whole chorus of saints not only did not shrink from fasts and vigils, but did not even refuse to shed their own blood, and over which He predetermined and foreknew that you should reign and rule, and increase and preserve it—it would not now, alas, because of my sins, have ended up being devoured by the murderous Ishmaelites, nor would the servants and worshippers of the blessed Trinity have become slaves of godless men to boot, nor would the sword of the barbarian have 'shed their blood like water'».

And even if someone finds fault with me, because, ceasing to lament over my own affairs, and forgetting my own humble position, I am emboldened to address the emperor, when I have not even been asked ... But what can I do? My love for suffering Christians has driven me to this; and once upon a time I knew that your holy soul was intent upon the increase and prosperity of Christians. And in addition to this, lest certain flatterers

ωσι καί τινες τῶν κολακικωτέρων, ὑπέλαβον φθάνειν εἰς σὰς ἀκοὰς τὰ παρὰ τῶν ἐντὸς καὶ ἐκτὸς συμπίπτοντα τῷ ὁμοφύλῳ ἐπιζήμια. τὸ δὲ πλέον κινῆσάν με, μήπως ἐκ τῆς ὑποστολῆς τὸ μὴ εὐδοκεῖσθαι κατακρι-θῶμεν.

25   διὰ τοῦτο τοῦ κράτους σου καὶ ἀντιβολῶ, ἐπιφάνηθι τοῖς ποθοῦσί σε καὶ ταχύτερον. ἐξεγέρθητι εἰς ἐκδίκησιν· περίζωσαι τὴν ῥομφαί- αν σου ἐπὶ τὸν μηρόν σου μετὰ Θεὸν δυνατέ. ἀπόδος τοῖς γείτοσι τοῖς κακοῖς εἰς τὸν κόλπον αὐτῶν ἑπταπλάσια. κέρδησον τὸν τοῦ προφήτου μακαρισμόν, προσαράξας τῇ πέτρᾳ
30 τῶν ἀθέων τὰ νήπια πρὸς Θεοῦ κραταιούμενος. ἔσται δὲ τοῦτο πῶς; εἰ κελεύσεις ἀποστῆναι τῶν πονηριῶν ἡμῶν ἕκαστον, εἰ διδάξεις ἡμᾶς πράξει καὶ λόγῳ ἐν εὐσεβείᾳ καὶ δικαιοσύνῃ καὶ ἀληθείᾳ ἐξιλεοῦσ- θαι Θεόν. [fol. 1ᵛ] εἰ γὰρ οἱ βασιλεῖς τῆς γῆς τιμωροῦνται τοὺς μὴ αὐτοῖς πειθομένους συνδούλους καὶ ταῦτα, πῶς τοῦ μεγάλου Θεοῦ
35 ἐκφευξόμεθα τὴν ἐπὶ μαγείαις καὶ γοητείαις, πλεονεξίᾳ καὶ ἀδικίᾳ, μοι- χείᾳ τε καὶ πορνείᾳ, ἐπιορκίᾳ καὶ ψεύδει, τόκῳ καὶ δόλῳ, καὶ βλασφημίᾳ τῇ κατὰ τῆς ἀμωμήτου ἡμῶν πίστεως καὶ τοῦ ἁγίου βαπτίσματος, καὶ τοῖς ὁμοίοις αὐτῶν, φρικτὴν ἀγανάκτησιν, εἰ μὴ δι' ἀποχῆς τούτων καὶ μετανοίας ἀληθοῦς καὶ ἐπιστροφῆς; τίς τε ὁ διορθώσασθαι ταῦτα δυνά-
40 μενος μετὰ Κύριον, εἰ μὴ ὁ ἅγιος αὐτοκράτωρ μου, ἔχων εἰς τοῦτο παρὰ Θεοῦ σοφίαν καὶ πόθον καὶ δύναμιν; ἐξεγέρθητι οὖν μετὰ Θεοῦ δέομαι, καὶ διὰ Θεὸν ἐξεγέρθητι. ἐν τούτοις ἔντεινε καὶ κατευοδοῦ καὶ βασίλευε μετὰ ἀληθείας καὶ πραότητος καὶ δικαιοσύνης ὡς ἂν ὁδηγήσῃ σε θαυμαστῶς ἡ τοῦ Θεοῦ δεξιά. πρόσ-
45 θες τὸ μέγα τοῦτο καλλώπισμα τῇ βασιλείᾳ Ῥωμαίων ὑπὲρ Ἐζεκίαν καὶ Ἰωσίαν, τὸν περιούσιον λαὸν τοῦ Θεοῦ τῶν ἁλισγημάτων καθάρας ὡς κἀκεῖνοι εἰς δύναμιν, μὴ καὶ ἡμῶν Θεὸς ἐγκαλῇ, εἰ ὁ λαός μου ἤκουσέ μου, Ἰσραὴλ ταῖς ὁδοῖς μου εἰ ἐπο- ρεύθη, καὶ τὰ ἑξῆς. οἶδα πολλάκις πεζοπορούντά σε ἐν λιταῖς, οἶδα
50 ἐν ταῖς πρὸς Θεὸν παρακλήσεσι νήφοντα, καὶ τοῦτο δεῖγμα ποιοῦμαι τῆς πρὸς Θεόν σου ἐλπίδος καὶ πίστεως. διέγειρον πρὸς θεογνωσίαν ἡμᾶς, ταχὺ προκαταλαβέτωσαν οἱ οἰκτιρμοί σου βοᾶν πρὸς Θεόν. πάντως ἀντιδοξάσει σε καὶ αὐτός, οὐ μόνον ἐνταῦθα, ἀλλὰ κἂν ταῖς μετέπειτα γενεαῖς, καὶ στηρίξει τὴν βασιλείαν σου ἐν εἰρήνῃ καὶ δικαιο-
55 σύνῃ, καὶ παραπέμψει γενεαῖς γενεῶν, καὶ τῷ ἐπιγείῳ κράτει προσθή- σει καὶ τῆς βασιλείας τῆς ἐν οὐρανοῖς τὴν ἀπόλαυσιν.

26–27 Ps. 44 (45):4 ‖ 27–28 cf. Ps. 78 (79):12 ‖ 29–30 cf. Ps. 136 (137):9 ‖ 33 Ps. 2:2 ‖ 42–44 cf. Ps. 44 (45):5 ‖ 46 Ex. 19:5 ‖ 47–49 Ps. 80 (81):14 ‖ 52 Ps. 78 (79):8 ‖ 53 cf. I Reg. 2:30 ‖ 55 Is.58:12

---

21 φθάνει N ‖ σὰς] τὰς N ‖ 26 ἐξεγέρθητι N ‖ 30–31 ἔσται ... εἰ¹ om. N ‖ 31 εἰ¹]ἔτι S ‖ 35 ἐκφευξούμεθα S ‖ 36 πορνείᾳ] πονηρίᾳ N

1

stand in the way, I saw to it that you should hear about the misfortunes inflicted upon our fellow citizens by enemies without and within. An even more pressing motive was lest from my hesitation I be judged to be out of favor.

For this reason I beg your majesty, appear to those who yearn for you as quickly as possible; rouse yourself to vengeance. «Gird thy sword upon thy thigh», most mighty after God. «Repay your evil neighbors sevenfold into their bosom». Win the blessing of the prophet; strengthened by God, «dash against the rock the children of the godless». And how shall this come to pass? If you bid each of us abstain from wicked deeds, if you teach us by both word and deed to appease God with piety and justice and truth. For if «the kings of the earth» punish their fellow servants when they do not obey them in these respects, how shall we escape our great God's terrible wrath at magic and sorcery, greed and injustice, adultery and fornication, perjury and falsehood, usury and treachery, and blasphemy against our immaculate faith and holy baptism, and similar sins, except by avoiding these acts and by truly repenting and turning toward God? And who other than the Lord has the power to correct this situation, except my holy emperor, who has received wisdom and love and power from God for this very purpose? Therefore I beg of you, arise with God, and for the sake of God arise. In these affairs «bend thy bow and prosper and reign with truth and meekness and righteousness, and the right hand of God shall guide thee wonderfully». Add this great embellishment to the empire of the Romans, even more than Hezekiah and Josiah ⟨did⟩, and purify to the best of your ability, as they did, «the chosen people» of God from defilement, lest God reproach us, «If my people had hearkened to me, if Israel had walked in my ways», and so forth. I know that you often proceed on foot during prayerful processions, I know that you are sober in your supplications to God, and I consider this a proof of your hope and faith in God. Rouse us to knowledge of God, «let your compassionate feelings make haste» to cry out to God. And He will surely «glorify you in return», not only in this world, but in generations to come, and He will support your empire in peace and righteousness, and will transmit it «from generation to generation», and will add to your rule here on earth the enjoyment of the kingdom of heaven.

2

2. Πρὸς τὸν αὐτοκράτορα

Οἶδας, κύριε βασιλεῦ, ὡς πρὸ καιροῦ εὑρέθησαν γράμματα ἐν τῇ Μεγάλῃ Ἐκκλησίᾳ, ἐκ τῶν ὑπ᾽ ἐμοῦ γενομένων πρὸ τοῦ αὐτῆς ἐκβληθῆναί με. ἡ δὲ τούτων αἰτία ἐξ ἀθυμίας ἐγένετο τῶν παρανόμως ἀδικησάντων 5 με, καὶ τοῦ μὴ γινώσκειν πάπαν ὀρθοδοξοῦντα, εἰς τὸ ἀκοῦσαί με τὸ ἀδίκημα. καὶ πρόσσχες, ἄγιε βασιλεῦ, διατί κατεστράφη ἡ ἐκκλησία. ἡ γὰρ εἰς τοὺς πατριαρχεύσαντας, τὸν κύριν Ἀρσένιον, τὸν κύριν Ἰωσήφ, τὸν κύριν Γρηγόριον, γεγονυῖα ὕβρις καὶ ἀδικία, οὐκ εἰς ἐκείνους, ἀλλ᾽ εἰς τὸν εἰς τύπον αὐτοῦ ἐκείνους θέμενον ἐν τῇ ἐκκλησίᾳ ἀνέδραμεν. οὐ γὰρ 10 πάντοτε προσήκει τοῖς λεγομένοις ἀρχιερεῦσι πιστεύειν, ἀλλ᾽ [fol. 2ʳ] ὅταν τὰ λεγόμενα καὶ πραττόμενα παρ᾽ αὐτῶν ἀκολουθῇ τῷ θείῳ θελήματι. ἐπὶ ποίᾳ γὰρ νομίμῳ αἰτίᾳ τοὺς ῥηθέντας ἐξέβαλον πατριάρχας; οἱ δὲ διὰ τὸ ὄνομα μόνον συναγωνιζόμενοι τούτοις, καὶ μὴ τὴν ἀλήθειαν τοῦ Θεοῦ ἐκδικοῦντες, παρὰ Θεοῦ οὐκ ἀθωωθήσονται. ἔχουσι γὰρ καλουμέ- 15 νους ἀρχιερεῖς, καὶ τοὺς τὴν Ἰωάννου τοῦ φωστῆρος τῆς οἰκουμένης ἐπὶ κεφαλῆς δεξαμένους καθαίρεσιν, καὶ πρὸ τούτων Ἄνναν καὶ Καιάφαν, δι᾽ ἃ ἔρχεται καὶ ὀργὴ τοῦ Θεοῦ τοῖς βλέπουσι τὸ ἀδίκημα καὶ μὴ μαχομένοις ὀνόμασιν, ἀλλὰ ἀνόμῳ κρατουμένοις σιγῇ, τὴν δόξαν προκρίνασι τῶν ἀνθρώπων ὑπὲρ αὐτὴν τὴν ἀλήθειαν. 20 διὰ ταῦτα κἀγὼ τὸ ἀδίκημα τὸ ἐμὸν τῷ τοῦ πάπα Θεῷ ἐγγράφως τε καὶ ἀγράφως ἀνήγγειλα· οὐ γὰρ Ἀθανάσιον ἀβοήθητον, ἀλλ᾽ οἰκουμε- νικὸν πατριάρχην καὶ ἐκκλησίας καταστροφὴν ἔβλεπον, ἥτις καὶ φαίνεται σήμερον τοῖς μὴ τυφλώττειν θελήματι ὀρεγομένοις, μηδὲ τῆς ἀληθείας τὸ ψεῦδος θέλουσι προτιμᾶν. διατί δὲ καὶ ἀδικουμένου μου οὐκ ἀντέστη ἡ 25 βασιλεία σου, καὶ μᾶλλον ὅτι καὶ τοσαῦτά με ἀναγκάζων εἰς τὸ ἀναδέξασ- θαι τὴν φροντίδα ἐν τῷ τοῦ πειρασμοῦ καιρῷ; ὡς μηδέποτε γνωσθεὶς ὑπ᾽ αὐτῆς, ἐπελήσθην ἀπὸ ψυχῆς, ὅτε καὶ παρὰ τῶν ἀρχιερέων παρὰ πᾶσαν αἰτίαν ἠδίκημαι, αὐτῶν καὶ κλήρου καὶ μοναχῶν ἀποδράντων μου, ὡς καὶ διημερεύειν τοῖς ἀνακτόροις, καὶ τὰς παρά τινων κατ᾽ ἐμοῦ χεομένας 30 ὕβρεις καὶ λοιδορίας καὶ χλευασμοὺς καὶ συκοφαντίας κατατρυφώντων· πρὸς τούτοις καὶ παραιτήσασθαι καταναγκαζόμενος, οὐδὲ κἂν ἕνα εὑρίσκω τὸν συλλυπούμενον.

διὰ ταῦτα τοῦ ἁγίου θυσιαστηρίου ἐνώπιον στάς, χεῖρας καὶ ὄμματα πετάσας πρὸς τὸν Σωτῆρα, «Δέσποτα,» ἔφην, «οὐρανοῦ καὶ γῆς

2: 18–19 cf. Joh. 12:43

2: V 1ᵛ–3ʳ. S 121ʳ–123ʳ. N 11ʳ–13ʳ. Ed. Gennadios, Ὀρθοδοξία, 28 (1953), 148–150.
1 ante πρὸς add. τοῦ αὐτοῦ VʳSN ‖ post αὐτοκράτορα add. γράμμα περὶ τῶν ἀφοριστι- κῶν γραμμάτων ἅτινα εὑρέθησαν ἐν τῇ Ἁγίᾳ Σοφίᾳ, ζητοῦντες συγχώρησιν τοῦ πρώτου πατριαρχίου (πατριάρχου S) VʳSN ‖ 6 πρόσχες N ‖ ἤ²] εἰ VSN ‖ 11 ἀκολουθεῖ N ‖ 21 ἀνήγγειλα VSN¹: ἀνείγγειλα N

2. To the emperor

You are aware, lord emperor, that recently there were found in the Great Church some letters from among those which I had written before I was expelled from it. The reason for them was my despair on account of those who unjustly wronged me, and because I did not know any right-thinking priest (?) to listen to me with respect to the injustice ⟨I have suffered⟩. And pay attention, holy emperor, to why the Church has been destroyed. The insult and injustice inflicted upon the patriarchs Kyr Arsenius, Kyr Joseph and Kyr Gregory, did not revert to them, but to Him Who placed them in His form in the Church. For one should not always believe the so-called bishops, except when their words and deeds are in accordance with the divine will. For what lawful cause did they expel the above-mentioned patriarchs ? Those who collaborate with these ⟨bishops⟩ only because of their title, and do not defend the truth of God, will not be held guiltless by God. For they may refer to the fact that those who took upon their heads the deposition of John ⟨Chrysostom⟩, the illuminator of the world, and before them Annas and Caiaphas, were also called «arch-priests»; for which reason the wrath of God descends upon those people who observe wickedness and do not fight against people with titles, but are seized by unlawful silence, and prefer «the praise of men» to truth itself.

For this reason I declared the injustice against me to the God of the priest both in writing and aloud, for I realized that it was not Athanasius who was defenseless, but an oecumenical patriarch, and I saw the ruin of the Church, which is evident today to those who do not wilfully wish to put on blinders, or to give precedence to falsehood over truth. Why didn't your majesty protect me when I was wronged, especially since you forced me so much to assume responsibility ⟨for the Church⟩ at a time of trial ? But I was forgotten from your soul, as if I had never been known by you, and when I had been wronged by the bishops beyond any cause, and they and the clergy and the monks had fled from me, and spent all their days at the palace, and delighted in the insults and abuses and jests and libels directed at me by certain people; and in addition to this I was forced to abdicate, yet I did not find one person to share my sorrow.

Wherefore, standing in front of the holy sanctuary, and raising my eyes and hands to the Savior, I said: «Lord, Maker of heaven and earth and

35 καὶ πάντων δημιουργέ, εἰ κελεύσει σῇ καὶ βουλῇ ἐνεχειρίσθην τὴν
ἐκκλησίαν σου, ἄκουσον ἃ κατ' ἐμοῦ καὶ λέγουσι καὶ ψηφίζονται, καὶ
μᾶλλον τοὺς κρῖμα δίκαιον κρίνειν κεκελευσμένους παρὰ σοῦ τοῦ
Θεοῦ, καὶ τὸν λόγον τῆς ἀληθείας ὀρθοτομεῖν πανταχοῦ μνη-
μονευομένους, τοὺς ὧδε πάντας ἀρχιερεῖς ἐνεργοὺς καὶ ἀργούς, τὸν τοῦ
40 βασιλέως πνευματικόν, σὺν Γενναδίῳ καὶ Σελλιώτῃ καὶ τοῖς ὁμοίοις, εἰς
ἃ λέγουσι κατ' ἐμοῦ καὶ τοῖς ⟨ἃ⟩ λέγουσιν ἐνισχύουσιν. εἰ μὲν κατὰ γνώμην σὴν καὶ κανόνων τρακταϊσμὸν καὶ κρίσιν δικαίαν ἐξωθοῦσι τῆς ἐκκλησίας σου, αὐτὸς ὁ Θεὸς τῶν δυνάμεων, δὸς αὐτοῖς τὴν συγχώρησιν· εἰ δὲ
κωφαῖς καὶ ματαίαις διαβολαῖς—οὐδεὶς αὐτῶν οὐδεμίαν ὑπὲρ σοῦ (σὺ γὰρ
45 [fol. 2ᵛ] ἡ ἀλήθεια) ἐνεδείξατο ἔνστασιν, ἀλλ' ἐμπαθείας οἰκείας ἐκδικοῦντες καὶ ἀλλοτρίας, παρὰ πᾶσαν ἀλήθειαν—τοῦ οἰκείου αὐτῶν πατριάρχου ἀπέστησαν, τῷ ἑαυτῶν θρασυνόμενοι κρίματι, τὸν ἀπὸ τῆς ἁγίας καὶ
ζωαρχικῆς Τριάδος ἀφορισμὸν ἀφορίζω αὐτούς.»
　　　　ταῦτα ἐνώπιον τοῦ Θεοῦ ἐποίησα καὶ λόγῳ καὶ γράμματι, καὶ
50 ταῦτα ἕως τῆς σήμερον καὶ λέγω καὶ στέργω. μετὰ γοῦν τὸ ταῦτα γενέσθαι, τοὺς ἀναγκάζοντας τὴν παραίτησιν ποίαν αἰτίαν θέλουσι θεῖναί με
ἐρωτήσας, ἀκούσας τε τὸ «μὴ θέλειν σε τὸν λαόν», τοῦτο καὶ ἄκων ὡς παραίτησιν ἔδωκα. ἐθαύμασα δὲ τὴν ἐκ Θεοῦ βασιλείαν σου, πῶς ἑνὸς ἐκείνων
φανέντος γράμματος, τὴν ἣν αὐτοὶ ὤφειλον ζητεῖν λύσιν, εἴπερ ἔμελλε τού-
55 τοις περὶ Θεοῦ, αὐτὸς ἐζήτησας παρ' ἐμοῦ, καὶ ταῦτα γινώσκων,φιλοθε-
έστατε βασιλεῦ, ὡς οὐδέποτε οὐδεμία συγχώρησις τοῖς διακειμένοις πρὸς
τὸ ἀμετανόητον, κἂν διὰ χειλέων προβῇ· ἁμαρτία γὰρ πρὸς θάνατον
ἡ ἀμετανόητος. οὐ γὰρ Θεὸς μυκτηρίζεται, ἀλλ' ὃ σπείρει ἕ-
καστος, τοῦτο θερίσει. παρεσιώπουν δὲ ταῦτα ἵνα φανῇ ὅσον διὰ
60 τῆς ἐμῆς ἐκβολῆς τὴν ἐκκλησίαν αὐτοὶ βελτιώσωσι, διά τε τοὺς χειροτο-
νουμένους, ἵνα μὴ πλήττωνται τὴν συνείδησιν, καὶ ἵνα μὴ τὸν λαὸν τοῦ
Χριστοῦ οἱ σχιζόμενοι σχίσωσι. μετεχειρίσαντο γὰρ καὶ αὐτοὶ καί τινες
τῶν κοινωνικῶν τι τοιοῦτον λαβεῖν ἐξ ἐμοῦ, ἀλλ' οὐκ ἐδόθη τούτοις λαβὴ
μέχρι σήμερον, τοῦ Σωτῆρος μου χάριτι, παρ' ἐμοῦ κατὰ τῆς ἐκκλησίας
65 Χριστοῦ. ἐπεὶ δὲ νῦν τῶν ῥηθέντων τινὲς πρὸς τὸ τὴν καταστροφὴν ἐνεργεῖν τῶν ἀρεσκόντων Θεῷ, καὶ μηδὲ τῇ πολυημέρῳ μου κορεσθέντες σιγῇ,
ἀκμὴν διασύρουσι, πρὸς τοῖς ἄλλοις καὶ τὸ ὅλως τοῖς λαοῖς ὁμιλεῖν με, καὶ
ταῦτα τὴν τοσαύτην ὁρῶντες τῆς ἐκκλησίας καταστροφὴν καὶ ἀδικίαν καὶ
ἀνομίαν, ἐξ ἧς ἠγανάκτησε καὶ Θεός, καὶ τὴν κατὰ τοῦ Χριστωνύμου λαοῦ
70 πανωλεθρίαν ἐπήνεγκε, διέγειραν λέγειν με ὡς εἰ μὲν τὰς φιλονείκους ἐν-
στάσεις ἐάσαντες στῆσαι τὴν ἐκκλησίαν μετὰ Θεὸν ὡς δυνατὸν ἐπισπεύ-
σωσι, κἂν ὡς ηὑρίσκετο ὅτε ἡμᾶς αὐτῆς ἐξεδίωξαν, καὶ ἕκαστος τῇ ἰδίᾳ

---

35 cf. Ὁρολόγιον (ed. Saliveros), 101 ‖ 37 cf. Joh. 7:24 ‖ 38 II Tim. 2:15 ‖ 57–58 Schol.
66 in Johannes Climacus, scal. 26 (PG, LXXXVIII, 1052 D) ‖ 58–59 cf. Gal. 6:7

---

41 ἃ addidi ‖ 47 post ἀπέστησαν repetivit παρὰ πᾶσαν ἀλήθειαν et deinde delevit N ‖
60 τε] τι N ‖ 70 διήγειραν N ‖ 71 ἰάσαντες N ‖ 72 ηὕρισκεν S ‖ ὅτι N ‖ αὐτῆς
VSN¹: αὐτοῖς N ‖ ἐξεδίωξαν VSN¹: ἐξεδίωσαν N

all things, if indeed by your command and will I was entrusted with your Church, listen how they are speaking and voting against me; listen especially to those who have been ordered by you, O God, to 'judge righteous judgments,' and who are reminded on every occasion 'to divide rightly the word of truth,' that is, all the bishops here, both active and idle, the confessor of the emperor and Gennadius and Selliotes and their like, listen to what they say against me, and what they assert by what they say (?). If indeed it is according to your purpose and the usage of the canons and righteous judgment that they expel ⟨me⟩ from your Church, O God of hosts, grant them forgiveness. But if it is on account of their senseless and foolish slanders—not one of them has demonstrated any constancy on your behalf (for you are the Truth), but were only indulging their own and others' passions, in violation of all truth—that they revolted against their own patriarch, and are emboldened by their decision, then I excommunicate them from ⟨fellowship with⟩ the holy and lifegiving Trinity».

This I did in the sight of God in both speech and writing, and to this day I repeat and stand by these words of mine. Afterwards, when I asked those who were demanding my resignation what reason they wished me to give, and heard their reply that «the people don't want you», I gave this, albeit unwillingly, as the reason for my resignation. But I marvel at your majesty, why when one of those ⟨excommunicatory⟩ letters came to light, you yourself asked me for the absolution which they should have sought, if they had any concern with God, especially since you are well aware, O emperor most dear to God, that forgiveness can never be granted to the unrepentant, even if it is spoken with the lips, for «the unrepented sin is a sin unto death»; «God is not mocked: but whatsoever a man soweth, that shall he also reap». I kept quiet about these ⟨letters⟩ in order to see how much they would improve the Church by my expulsion, and also so that those who were ordained would not be pricked in their conscience, and so that the schismatics would not divide the people of Christ. For they and some of their cohorts were trying to get something of the sort out of me, but up to now, thanks to my Savior, they have not been given by me any opportunity for attacking the Church. But now when some of the above-mentioned people, in order to accomplish the ruin of those who are pleasing to God, are not satisfied with my long silence, but still ridicule me, in addition to other reasons, because I am always talking with the people, and ⟨they do⟩ this in spite of the fact that they see such great ruin and injustice and lawlessness of the Church, on account of which God has become angry and brought great destruction upon the Christian people, these people aroused me to say the following: if they abandon their contentious objections, and if with the help of God they hasten as quickly as possible to set the Church in order, as it was when they expelled me from the Church, and if each of them quickly returns to his see,

2, 3

ἐπισκοπῇ ταχὺ ἐπανασωθῇ, καὶ τῶν κακῶς γενομένων ἐπιστροφὴν ἀξίαν ἐνδείξονται, συγγνωσθήσονται· εἰ δ' ὡς εὑρίσκονται μείνωσιν (ἄνευ τοῦ
75 Ἡρακλείας, Μελενίκου, καὶ Ἀπαμείας καὶ Βρύσεως, καὶ ἑτέρων τριῶν), ἄλυτον αὐτοῖς τὸ ῥηθὲν ἐπιτίμιον κείσθω, καὶ ἐν τῷ νῦν αἰῶνι καὶ [fol. 3ʳ] ἐν τῷ μέλλοντι.

3. Πρὸς τὸν αὐτοκράτορα

Ὁ σταλεὶς ὑφ' ἡμῶν προσκυνῆσαι τὸ κράτος σου πρὸ μικροῦ ἐξεῖπεν ἡμῖν ὡς λελύπησαι μὴ εὐχόμενος ὑφ' ἡμῶν. εἰ γοῦν τοῦ ἁγίου μου μὴ ὑπερεύχομαι αὐτοκράτορος, καὶ μάλιστα νῦν, ὅτε πολλὰ τὰ λυποῦντα
5 συνέρρευσε, καὶ τῇ ποίμνῃ Χριστοῦ συνέπεσε πάνδεινα (ἃ καὶ ἀπίστοις συμβάντα ἀκάρδιος ἐλογίσθη καὶ ἄφρων ὁ τῇ φύσει μὴ συναλγῶν), καὶ εἰ μὴ ὀδύναι θανάτου πεπήγασι τῇ καρδίᾳ μου, καὶ ἡ ψυχή μου ἐκλείπει, οὔτε δοῦλός εἰμι τοῦ Χριστοῦ, οὔτε Χριστιανῶν μερίδι τετάξομαι. εἰ δὲ νυκτὸς καὶ ἡμέρας ἀπόστρεψον τὸν θυμόν σου, ἐν πικρίᾳ ψυχῆς βοῶ,
10 ἀφ' ἡμῶν, καὶ μὴ εἰς τοὺς αἰῶνας ὀργισθῇς ἡμῖν ὁ Θεός, τί πάθω ἀκούων τὸ οἴδαμεν ὅτι ἁμαρτωλὸν ὁ Θεὸς οὐκ ἀκούει, καὶ ἅμα νενουθέτημαι ὑπὸ τῆς Γραφῆς οὐ τῶν κατ' ἐμὲ μόνον ἁμαρτωλῶν, ἀλλὰ καὶ αὐτὰς τὰς τῶν δικαίων εὐχὰς ἐνεργουμένας ἰσχύειν;
διὰ τοῦτο τοῦ ἁγίου μου δέομαι αὐτοκράτορος, ἐπεὶ τὸ τῆς ἐπι-
15 τιμήσεως πατρικὸν καὶ ἀνουθέτητος πᾶσα ψυχὴ ἀδιόρθω-τος, δεξώμεθα ταύτην τὴν νουθεσίαν σωφρόνως, καὶ μὴ διὰ τῆς πρὸς ταύ-την ἀναισθησίας τὴν μείζω προσκαλεσώμεθα. ἐπιγνῶμέν τε τοῦ κακοῦ τὴν ὑπόθεσιν, καὶ πόθεν αἱ τοιαῦται πληγαί τε καὶ μάστιγες. τὸ γὰρ μηδὲ μετὰ τὴν πληγὴν σωφρονίζεσθαι
20 χαλεπώτερον· φάρμακον δὲ μέγα κακίας ὁμολογία καὶ φυγὴ τοῦ πταίσματος. καὶ μὴ λεχθῇ καὶ περὶ ἡμῶν, Κύριε, ἐμαστίγωσας αὐτούς, καὶ οὐκ ἐπόνεσαν. ἐπαίδευσας αὐτοὺς καὶ οὐκ ἠθέλη-σαν δέξασθαι παιδείαν, ἀλλὰ προφθάσωμεν ἐν ἐξομολογήσει

3: 9–10 Ps. 84 (85):5 ‖ 10 Ps. 84 (85):6 ‖ 11 Joh. 9:31 ‖ 13 cf. Jac. 5:16 ‖ 14–16 τὸ ... ἀδιόρθωτος Greg. Naz., *Or.* XVI, xv (PG, XXXV, 956A) ‖ 17–18 ἐπιγνῶμέν ... ὑπόθεσιν Greg. Naz., *ibid.*, xvii (PG, XXXV, 957A) ‖ 18–19 πόθεν ... μάστιγες Greg. Naz., *ibid.*, v (PG, XXXV, 940B) ‖ 19–20 τὸ ... χαλεπώτερον Greg. Naz., *ibid.*, xv (PG, XXXV, 956A) ‖ 20–21 φάρμακον ... πταίσματος Greg. Naz., *ibid.*, xvii (PG, XXXV, 957B) ‖ 21–23 Jer. 5:3 ‖ 23–24 Ps. 94 (95):2

3: V 3ʳ–3ᵛ. S 123ʳ–125ʳ. N 13ʳ–15ʳ.
1 ante πρὸς τὸν αὐτοκράτορα add. γράμμα VʳS ‖ post αὐτοκράτορα add. περὶ ἐπιστροφῆς καὶ μετανοίας τῆς πρὸς Θεὸν (τὸν Θεὸν S) καὶ περὶ τῶν υἱῶν αὐτοῦ καὶ ἀρχόντων μὴ τῇ δόξῃ τῇ βασιλείῳ σεμνύνεσθαι, ἀλλὰ τῇ δικαιοσύνῃ καὶ σωφροσύνῃ VʳS ‖ N scripsit γράμμα πρὸς τὸν αὐτοκράτορα post σωφροσύνῃ ‖ 3 ὑφ' ἡμῶν VN¹: ἀφ' ἡμῶν SN ‖ 16 σωφρόνως N ‖ 23 προφθάσομεν N

2, 3

and if they show sincere repentance for their wicked deeds, they will be forgiven ⟨by me⟩. But if they remain as they are, with the exception of the bishops of Herakleia, Melenikon, Apameia and Brysis, and three others, let the above-mentioned excommunication be laid upon them irrevocably, both now and forever more.

3. To the emperor

The man whom I recently sent to do obeisance to your majesty reported to me that you are distressed because you are not included in my prayers. If indeed I do not pray for my holy emperor, especially at a time like this, when many grievous events have occurred and terrible ills have befallen the flock of Christ (and even when such misfortunes befall pagans, any man who did not have natural compassion would be considered heartless and foolish), and if the pains of death do not pierce my heart, and if my soul is not faint, then I am neither a servant of Christ, nor to be included in the ranks of Christians. But if by night and day I cry in bitterness of soul, «Turn from us your anger», and «O God, be not wroth with us throughout the ages», what should I do when I hear the words «we know that God heareth not sinners» and at the same time I am admonished by the Holy Writ that not the prayers of sinners like me, but only «the effectual prayers of righteous men availeth much»?

For this reason I beg my holy emperor, since «chastisement is a paternal ⟨duty⟩ and every unadmonished soul is incorrigible», let us prudently heed this admonition, and let us not invite yet a greater ⟨chastisement⟩ through our disregard of this warning. «Let us discover the root of the evil and the cause of such plagues and scourges. For failure to be prudent after the blow strikes is even more dangerous; the great remedy against evil is confession and avoidance of sin». And let it not be said about us, «O Lord, thou hast scourged them, but they have not grieved; thou hast punished them, but they would not receive correction». Rather «let us come before God with

τὸ τοῦ Θεοῦ πρόσωπον. γενώμεθα Νινευῖται, μὴ Σοδομῖται.
25 θεραπεύσωμεν τὴν κακίαν, μὴ τῇ κακίᾳ συντελεσθῶμεν.
ἤκουσαν ἐκεῖνοι κηρύσσοντος Ἰωνᾶ, καὶ οὐ μόνον ἐπίστευσαν τῷ
Θεῷ ἄνθρωποι βάρβαροι, οὐδὲ νηστείᾳ καὶ κλαυθμῷ καὶ σάκκοις ἠρκέσ-
θησαν, ἀλλὰ τί; ἀπέστρεψεν ἕκαστος ἀπὸ τῆς ὁδοῦ αὐτῶν τῆς
πονηρᾶς, καὶ ἀπὸ τῆς ἀδικίας τῆς ἐν χερσὶν αὐτῶν. σκοπήσωμεν
30 ἐν αἰσθήσει, παρακαλῶ, ἑκάστης λέξεως δύναμιν, οὐχ ἵνα μόνον νοήσωμεν,
ἀλλ᾽ ἵνα καὶ πράξωμεν, λέγοντες, τίς οἶδεν εἰ μετανοήσει καὶ παρα-
κληθήσεται ὁ Θεός, καὶ ἀποστρέψει ἀπὸ ὀργῆς θυμοῦ αὐτοῦ;
καὶ εἶδεν ὁ Θεὸς τὰ ἔργα αὐτῶν, ὅτι ἀπέστρεψαν ἀπὸ τῶν
ὁδῶν αὐτῶν τῶν πονηρῶν, καὶ μετενόησεν ἐπὶ πάσῃ τῇ κακίᾳ
35 ᾗ ἐλάλησε ποιῆσαι αὐτοῖς, καὶ οὐκ ἐποίησεν. ἡμεῖς ἀκούσωμεν
τῆς φωνῆς Χριστοῦ τοῦ Θεοῦ ἡμῶν, ἵνα ὦμεν ἐκ τῶν προβάτων αὐτοῦ, καὶ
μὴ ἀκούσωμεν τί με λέγετε Κύριε, Κύριε, καὶ οὐ ποιεῖτε ἃ
λέγω ὑμῖν;
    ἀλλὰ τὴν μετάνοιαν, ἅγιε βασιλεῦ, τῶν Νινευϊτῶν [fol. 3ᵛ] καὶ
40 ἡμεῖς μιμησώμεθα. οὐδὲ γάρ, εἰ τοῦτο κελεύσεις, ὁ ἀπειθῶν εὑρεθήσεται·
εἰ δ᾽ (ὅπερ ἀπεύχομαι) εὑρεθῇ, βασιλικῆς πειραθήτω ἐνδίκου ἀγανακτήσεως. ἀρκεῖ τὰ ἑκάστῳ ἡμῶν ἁμαρτανόμενα ἐν κρυφῇ. διατί οὐκ εὐθύνονται
οἱ ἀνομοῦντες καὶ φανερῶς; ἢ οὐχὶ δι᾽ ἑνὸς ἁμαρτίαν ἔρχεται καὶ ἐπὶ
δήμους κακά; οὐχὶ Ἄχαρ παρανομήσαντος, ἡ τοῦ Ἰσραὴλ παράταξις
45 ἐμαστίζετο; οὐχὶ διὰ τὴν παρανομίαν τῶν υἱῶν ἀρχιερέως τοῦ Ἠλεί, αἱ
τοῦ Ἰσραὴλ φάλαγγες μαχαίρας ἐγένοντο παρανάλωμα, καὶ ὁ τούτων
πατὴρ ὡς μὴ ζηλώσας κατὰ Θεὸν μετ᾽ ὀργῆς ἐξώσθη καὶ τῆς ἱερωσύνης
καὶ τῆς ζωῆς; οὐχὶ διὰ ταῦτα καὶ ἡ τοῦ Θεοῦ κιβωτὸς βεβήλοις
ἐλήφθη χερσί;
50   διὰ τοῦτο παρακαλῶ τοῦ κρατίστου μου αὐτοκράτορος, διέγειρον
ἐν τοῖς θεαρέστοις ἡμᾶς καὶ μὴ θέλοντας. ἀνατειλάτω δικαιοσύνη ἐν ταῖς
ἡμέραις σου. σταθήτω κρίσις δικαία, σωφροσύνη πολιτευθήτω, βλυσάτω
ἔλεος καὶ ἀλήθεια, μή τι τῶν τῆς ταλανιζομένης πόλεως εὑρεθῇ ἐν τῇ πόλει τῇ σῇ, δόλος καὶ τόκος καὶ ἀνομία. καὶ πρῶτον τὸν οἶκον τὸν σόν,
55 καὶ οὕς σοι παῖδας Θεὸς ἐχαρίσατο, δίδαξον εὐσεβείᾳ πλέον καὶ δικαιοσύνῃ
ἢ τῇ βασιλείῳ σεμνύνεσθαι δόξῃ. ὁ μὲν γὰρ πλοῦτος καὶ ἡ τῆς βασιλείας
ὀφρὺς καὶ ἔθνεσι πρόσεστι καὶ θανάτῳ συγκαταλύεται· οἱ δὲ τὸν Κύριον
ἐκζητοῦντες παντὸς ἀγαθοῦ οὐκ ἐλαττωθήσονται. τοὺς ἄρχοντας δίδαξον μὴ εἶναι κλεπτῶν κοινωνούς, μηδὲ ἡττᾶσθαι ξενίοις καὶ δώ-

---

24–26 γενώμεθα ... Ἰωνᾶ Greg. Naz., Or. XVI, xiv (PG, XXXV, 953 B) ‖ 28–29 Jon.
3:8 ‖ 31–35 Jon. 3:9–10 ‖ 37–38 cf. Luc. 6:46 ‖ 44–45 cf. Jes. Nav. 7 ‖ 45–48 cf. I
Reg. 2–4 ‖ 48–49 cf. I Reg. 4:11 ‖ 54 cf. Ps. 54 (55):11–12 ‖ 59 Is. 1:23

---

33 εἶδεν scripsi, cf. Jon. 3:10 : οἶδεν VSN

3

thanksgiving»; «let us become Ninevites, not Sodomites. Let us cure wickedness and not be consumed by it. When Jonah preached, they listened», and not only did barbarous men have faith in God, nor were they satisfied with fasting and wailing and sackcloth, but what ⟨did they rather do⟩? «They turned every one from their evil way, and from the iniquity that was in their hands». I beg of you, let us consider carefully the meaning of each word, so as not only to understand but to act, saying, «Who knows if God will change His mind» and relent «and turn from His fierce anger? And God saw their works, that they turned from their wicked ways, and God repented of the evil which He had said He would do to them, and He did it not». Let us listen to the voice of Christ our God, so that we may be His sheep and not hear the words, «Why call ye me, Lord, Lord, and do not the things which I say unto you?».

So, O holy emperor, let us imitate the repentance of the Ninevites. For if you command this, no one will be found to disobey. And if one should be found (I pray this may not happen), let him experience the righteous imperial wrath. There are enough sins committed in secret by each of us. Why are those who openly break the law not chastised? Do not misfortunes befall nations because of the sins of one man? Is it not true that when Achar was disobedient, all the ranks of Israel were scourged? And did not the phalanxes of Israel perish by the sword on account of the transgression of the sons of the high priest Eli? As for their father, did not ⟨God⟩ wrathfully strip him of both the priesthood and life for not striving in accordance with God? And was not the ark of God seized by profane hands for these reasons?

Wherefore I supplicate you, my mighty emperor, rouse us to acts pleasing to God, even if we are unwilling; let righteousness shine forth in your days; let righteous judgment be established, let moderation be the rule, let mercy and truth pour forth, lest any of the characteristics of the unhappy city, such as «treachery and usury and lawlessness», be found in your city. First of all teach your household, and the children whom God has granted you, to take pride in piety and righteousness rather than in imperial glory. For wealth and pride in empire exist also among the pagans and come to an end with death; but those who seek the Lord are not deprived of any good. Teach the officials not to be «companions of thieves», nor to succumb to

60 ροις. τοὺς ἀρχιερεῖς ἐξαπόστειλον ἐν τιμῇ ταῖς λαχούσαις, ἵνα μὴ τούτων τὰ πρόβατα λυκόβρωτα γένωνται, ὡς ἀποίμαντα, καὶ φανερωθέντος
τοῦ ἀρχιποίμενος αἰσχυνθήσωνται. καὶ δὸς αὐτοῖς θάρσος, εἰ βλέπουσι
τῶν παραδυναστευόντων παρανομοῦντάς τινας, φιλαλήθως τῇ ἐκ Θεοῦ
βασιλείᾳ σου ἀναφέρειν, καὶ ἵνα θεοσεβεῖν διδάσκωσι τὸν λαόν, καὶ μὴ
65 μαγείαις καὶ γοητείαις καὶ ταῖς λοιπαῖς ἀνομίαις καὶ βλασφημίαις κα-
ταμιαίνωνται, δι' ἃ ἔρχεται ἡ ὀργὴ τοῦ Θεοῦ. εἰ οὕτω βιοῦν ἡμᾶς ἔργῳ
καὶ λόγῳ ῥυθμίσει ἡ ἐκ Θεοῦ βασιλεία σου, πάντες οἱ ταύτης εὐχόμενοι
οὐκ εἰς ἀέρα ἀλλ' εἰς αὐτὰ τὰ ὦτα λαλοῦντες Κυρίου εἰσακουσθήσον-
ται, καὶ τὸν θυμὸν αὐτοῦ ἐξ ἡμῶν ἀποστρέψει. ἐπιστρέψει τε τὰ κακὰ
70 τοῖς ἐχθροῖς εἰς τὸν κόλπον αὐτῶν ἑπταπλάσια καὶ ὑπὸ τοὺς
πόδας ὑποτάξει τοὺς σοὺς πάντα ἐχθρὸν καὶ πολέμιον, καὶ τὰ
ὅρια τῶν Χριστιανῶν πλατυνεῖ. εἰρήνης τε πλῆθος καὶ παντὸς ἀγαθοῦ
ἀνατελεῖ ἐν ἡμέραις σου, καὶ τὸ μνημόσυνόν σου εἰς αἰῶνας διαμενεῖ,
καὶ παραπέμψει τὴν βασιλείαν σου γενεαῖς γενεῶν, καὶ πρὸς τῇ ἐπι-
75 γείῳ βασιλείᾳ Χριστός, ὁ πιστῶς ὑπὸ σοῦ λατρευθείς, παρέξει καὶ τὴν
οὐράνιον.

4. ⟨Πρὸς τὸν αὐτοκράτορα⟩ [fol. 4ʳ]

Τὸ ἔρχεσθαι τὴν βασιλείαν σου πρὸς ἡμᾶς ὑπὲρ ἡμᾶς καὶ ὑπὲρ τὴν
ἡμετέραν προαίρεσιν γίνεται· ὅμως τοῦ λύεσθαι τὰς θεομισεῖς ἀδικίας τῇ
παρουσίᾳ αὐτῆς ἠνεχόμεθα. ἐπεὶ δέ, ὡς ὁρῶ, οὐ τοῦ παρόντος καιροῦ, ἀλλὰ
5 τοῦ μέλλοντος αἰῶνος χρῄζει ἡ λύσις αὐτῶν, διὰ τὸν Κύριον μὴ κοπιᾷ
πρὸς ἡμᾶς. ὅτι δὲ καὶ εὐχὴν παρὰ τῶν ἁμαρτωλῶν καὶ κατακρίτων ἡμῶν
ἡ ἐκ Θεοῦ βασιλεία σου ἀπαιτεῖ, πῶς οὐ θαυμάσω; εἰ γὰρ ἡμεῖς τὰ φίλα
καὶ ταῦτα Θεῷ παρ' αὐτῆς καὶ κοῦφα τοσοῦτον ὡς μηδὲ τῷ μικρῷ δακτύ-
λῳ, ἀλλὰ νεύματι μόνῳ δυνατὸν ἀφανίζεσθαι οὐκ εἰσακουώμεθα, πῶς
10 ὃν πάντα φρίσσει καὶ τρέμει, Θεὸν τῶν δυνάμεων, προσελθεῖν θαρρήσω
ἐγὼ ὁ ταλαίπωρος, παρὰ τῶν ὁμοιοπαθῶν ἀνθρώπων παρακουόμενος;
καὶ διὰ τὸν Κύριον, καθὼς ἀνενόχλητος ἤμην μέχρι καὶ νῦν, σῴζεσθαι
καὶ πάλιν ἐμοὶ ὑπὸ τῆς βασιλείας σου τὸ ἀτάραχον, οὐ μόνον τῆς παρου-
σίας, ἀλλὰ καὶ τοῦ μηνύματος.

68 I Cor. 14:9 ‖ 70 Ps. 78 (79):12 ‖ 70–71 cf. Ps. 8:7 ‖ 71–72 cf. Ex. 34:24 ‖ 73 Ps. 101
(102):13 ‖ 74 Is. 58:12

72 τε] τί S
4: V 4ʳ. S 125ʳ. N 15ʳ–15ᵛ.
1 γράμμα πρὸς τὸν αὐτοκράτορα ζητοῦντας (ζητοῦντος Ν¹) εὐχὰς (εὐχὴν Ν¹) παρὰ τοῦ
πατριάρχου add. VʳSN ‖ 8 αὐτῆς VSN¹: αὐτοῖς Ν

3, 4

bribes and gifts. Send the bishops with honor back to the sees assigned to them, lest their sheep be devoured by wolves, for lack of a shepherd, and lest they be ashamed when the Chief Shepherd reveals Himself. And give them the courage, if they see any authorities transgressing the law, to report the matter truthfully to your divine majesty, and that they may teach the people to revere God, and not be defiled by sorcery and witchcraft and other such transgressions and blasphemies, whence comes the wrath of God. If your divine majesty will guide us by both word and deed to live in this way, all who pray for your majesty will not «speak into the air», but to the very ears of the Lord, and will be heard, and He will avert His anger from us. He will return the evils of your enemies «sevenfold into their bosom», and «will subdue beneath your feet every» enemy and foe, and «He will widen the frontiers» of Christians. Abundance of peace and every good thing will shine forth in your days, and «your memory» will abide for centuries, and He will perpetuate your empire «through all generations», and Christ, Whom you so faithfully worship, will add the heavenly kingdom to your kingdom here on earth.

4. ⟨To the emperor⟩

It is above me and beyond my wish that your majesty should come to see me; but still I agreed so that these injustices hateful to God might come to an end through your presence. But since, as I see, the solution to these problems will not come at the present time, but in the world to come, for the sake of the Lord don't come to me. How shall I not marvel that your divine majesty seeks a prayer from me, sinner and condemned that I am? For if I am not heeded by your majesty in regard to matters pleasing to God, and so easy that you can make them disappear not just with your little finger, but with a mere nod, how can I, miserable creature that I am, have courage to approach the One at Whom everything shudders and trembles, the God of hosts, when I am even disregarded by men who suffer as I do? For the sake of the Lord, just as I led a tranquil existence up to now, let me not again be disturbed by your majesty, either through your presence, or through a message.

5. Πρὸς τὸν αὐτοκράτορα

Ἀλλὰ τίς κατ' ἀξίαν τῶν ῥαθύμων καὶ ἐμπαθῶν κατ' ἐμὲ εὐχαρισ-
τήσει καὶ ὑπερεύξεται τοῦ θεοστεφοῦς καὶ ἁγίου μου αὐτοκράτορος, καὶ
τῶν ἐπαίνων ὧν ἡμᾶς ἐκθειάζων διὰ Θεὸν ἀπίδῃ τὸ μέγεθος, σκώληκα
5 ὄντα ἐμὲ καὶ οὐκ ἄνθρωπον, οὐχ οἷον ὁ τοῦ Θεοῦ προφήτης ἐξεκε-
λάδησε θείῳ πνεύματι, ἀνάγων τὸ νόημα εἰς Χριστὸν τὸν Θεὸν ἡμῶν, ἀλλ'
οἷον τρέφει πηλὸς ἐν αὐτῷ εἰλισσόμενον, ὥσπερ κἀγὼ τῷ βορβόρῳ τῶν
ἡδονῶν; εἰ δέ γε πάλιν τὴν γλῶτταν κινήσει πρὸς τοὺς ἐχθραίνοντας καὶ
Χριστὸν καὶ τὴν ἐκκλησίαν αὐτοῦ, πόσης ἄρα αἰσχύνης καὶ ἀτιμίας
10 πληροῖ φιλαλήθως ἐκείνων τὰ πρόσωπα, εἰ καὶ νικώμενος τῇ φιλανθρωπίᾳ τὴν μάχαιραν οὐ κινεῖ ἣν θεόθεν φορεῖ, ἀλλ' εὐθυβόλως
μόνον τὴν γλῶτταν, τὴν ἐπιστροφὴν πρὸς τὰ κρείττω θεομιμήτως αὐτῶν καὶ τὴν μετάνοιαν ἐκδεχόμενος εἰ καὶ ὁ Αἰθίοψ οὐ θέλει λευ-
καίνεσθαι, ἀλλὰ δίκην ἀσπίδος κωφῆς ἐθελοκωφεῖ τὸ ἐὰν μὴ
15 ἐπιστραφῆτε, στιλβουμένην ὄψεσθε τὴν ρομφαίαν τοῦ ἐκ
Θεοῦ δυνατοῦ.

πλήν, ἅγιε βασιλεῦ, ὑπερεκπερισσοῦ ἐν τῷ βάλλειν δικαίως αὐτοὺς καὶ ἀναντιρρήτως ἡμᾶς ἐξεθάμβησας, καὶ χαρισθείη δόξα σοι πρὸς
Θεοῦ καὶ κράτος αἰώνιον. ἄρξου καὶ τοῦ δικαίου διὰ τὸν βασιλεύσαντά σε
20 δίκαιον Κύριον· ἐκεῖνος γὰρ μόνος ἑκάστῳ κατὰ τὰ ἔργα αὐτοῦ
ἀποδίδωσι τότε. τὴν δὲ βασιλείαν σου ἐν τῷ παρόντι καὶ δικάζειν καὶ
δικαιοῦν, τιμωρεῖσθαί τε καὶ εὐεργετεῖν, δικαίως ὁ δίκαιος ἐδικαίωσε.
μὴ οὖν, δι' αὐτὸν τόν σε δικαιώσαντα, ἀναβαλλώμεθα εἰς τὴν αὔριον,
ἀλλὰ κρίμα δίκαιον κρίνωμεν καὶ βασιλικόν· ἐξελώμεθα πένητα
καὶ [fol. 4ᵛ] πτωχὸν ἐκ χειρῶν στερεωτέρων αὐτῶν. διότι γὰρ
25 καὶ ἡμεῖς μὴ σπουδαίως εἰς τοῦτο τὴν ἐκ Θεοῦ βασιλείαν σου καὶ παρε-
καλέσαμεν καὶ κατηναγκάσαμεν, διὰ τοῦτο καὶ σκόλοψ ἀξίως ἐδόθη
ἡμῖν τῷ ποδί, καὶ ὅπερ πρὸ τῆς πληγῆς μὴ ἐσπεύσαμεν, μετὰ τὴν πληγὴν
ἐλθόντες εἰς νοῦν ἱκετεύωμεν, «διὰ τὸν Θεὸν διανάστηθι».

5: 4–5 cf. Ps. 21 (22):7 ‖ 9–10 cf. Ps. 82 (83):17 ‖ 11 cf. Rom. 13:4 ‖ 12 θεομιμήτως: cf. Ezech. 33:11 ‖ 13–14 cf. Apostolius I, 68 (Leutsch-Schneidewin, II,
258) ‖ 14 Ps. 57 (58):5 ‖ 14–15 cf. Ps. 7:13 ‖ 17 cf. Eph. 3:20, I Thess 3:10 ‖ 20–21 cf.
Rom. 2:6 ‖ 23 cf. Joh. 7:24 ‖ 23–24 cf. Ps. 34 (35):10 ‖ 26–27 cf. II Cor. 12:7

5: V 4ʳ–4ᵛ. S 125ʳ–125ᵛ. N 15ᵛ–16ʳ.
1 ante πρὸς add. γράμμα VʳSN ‖ post αὐτοκράτορα add. ἐπαινῶν καὶ ἐκθειάζων αὐτὸν
VʳSN ‖ 3 θεοστυφοῦς N ‖ 10–11 τῇ φιλανθρωπίᾳ VSN¹: τὴν φιλανθρωπίαν N ‖ 12–13
αὐτὸν N ‖ 15 στιλβομένην N

5. To the emperor

What person who is lazy like me and a slave to his passions can give thanks and pray in a worthy fashion on behalf of my holy God-crowned emperor, and can disregard the multitude of praises which he has heaped upon me for the sake of God, since «I am a worm and not a man», not such ⟨a worm⟩ as the prophet of God celebrated through the Holy Spirit, directing his reference to Christ our God, but such ⟨a worm⟩ as feeds upon and wriggles through the mud, so am I ⟨mired down⟩ in the muck of pleasures. And again if he [the emperor] moves his tongue against the enemies of Christ and His Church, truly «he will fill their faces» with shame and «dishonor», even if, overcome by his love for mankind, he does not brandish «the sword» which «he bears» as a gift from God, but moves only his tongue with exact aim, expecting them, in imitation of God, to turn to a better way of life and repent, although «the Ethiopian won't turn white», but like «a deaf asp» he turns a deaf ear to the precept, «If ye will not repent, ye will see furbished the sword» of him who is made strong by God.

However, holy emperor, you have amazed me «exceedingly» by smiting them righteously and without opposition, and may God grant you glory and eternal power. And make a beginning of righteousness for the sake of the righteous Lord Who made you emperor; for He alone «renders then to every man according to his deeds». The Righteous One has righteously ordained that at the present time your majesty should judge and ordain, and punish and reward. Therefore, for the sake of the One Who has justified you, let us not delay until tomorrow, but «let us make a righteous» and imperial «judgment». Let us rescue both «poor man and beggar from stronger hands than theirs». Because I did not zealously entreat and compel your majesty in this matter, for this reason «a thorn has pierced» my foot, as I deserve, and now after the disaster let me come to my senses and make the supplication which I did not strive to make before the disaster, ⟨namely⟩ «for the sake of God, arise!».

6. Πρὸς τὸν αὐτοκράτορα

Πάλιν ὡς καὶ πολλάκις παρακαλῶ, εἰσάκουσον τῆς φωνῆς μου δι'
αὐτὸν τὸν βασιλεύσαντά σε Χριστὸν τὸν ἐπὶ πάντων Θεόν. ἐξεγέρθητι εἰς
δικαίωσιν τῶν ἀδικουμένων, εἰς παίδευσιν τῶν ἁμαρτανόντων. κάθαρον
5 τὴν ἐκκλησίαν τῶν ῥυπασμάτων. μὴ λόγοις μόνον ἐλέγχῃς τὴν κακίαν
τῶν σχιζομένων· ἠγνόησαν γὰρ ὡς ὅτι τὸ χρηστὸν τοῦ Θεοῦ εἰς
μετάνοιαν ἄγει αὐτούς. κατὰ γοῦν τὴν τοιαύτην τούτων σκληρότητα
καὶ τὸ ἀμετανόητον τῆς καρδίας, γευσάσθωσαν δικαιοκρισίας βασιλικῆς
ἀγανάκτησιν. μνήσθητι τῶν τοῦ πέρυσι καιροῦ ἡμερῶν καὶ τῶν τοῦ νῦν.
10 καὶ μὴ θελήσωμεν τὰ ἀρξάμενα διὰ πέλαγος ἀγαθότητος ἀνοίγεσθαι θεῖα
σπλάγχνα, διὰ προσωποληψίαν ἢ ῥαθυμίαν, ἢ κολακείαν ἢ συγγένειαν
κλεῖσαι. διπλῶς γὰρ φθείρεται τὰ τῶν Χριστιανῶν, ἔξωθεν μὲν ὑπὸ τῶν
ἐχθρῶν, ἔνδοθεν δὲ ἀδικίας ὑπερβολῇ καὶ ἀκαθαρσίας. εἰ οὖν διαναστῇ ἡ
ἐκ Θεοῦ βασιλεία σου καὶ ποιεῖ σὺν Χριστῷ καὶ μετὰ τοῦ Χριστοῦ τὴν
15 διόρθωσιν, ὑπέρευγε τοῦ καλοῦ· εἰ δὲ διὰ τὰς ἐμὰς ἁμαρτίας ὀκνήσωμεν,
οὐαί μοι καὶ ἄλλο οὐδέν.

7. Πρὸς τὸν αὐτοκράτορα

Τῇ ἀγαθότητι τοῦ ἐκ μὴ ὄντος εἰς τὸ εἶναι παραγαγόντος
ἡμᾶς μεγάλου καὶ μόνου Θεοῦ, δίδοται ἑνὶ ἑκάστῳ κατὰ καιροὺς χάρις,
κατὰ τὸ μέτρον τῆς μεγάλης αὐτοῦ δωρεᾶς, καθὰ δοκῶ ἐχαρίσθη καὶ ἐν
5 ταύτῃ τῇ γενεᾷ τῇ ἐκ Θεοῦ βασιλείᾳ σου οὐ μόνον τὸ ὕψος τῆς βασιλείας
αὐτῆς, ἀλλὰ καὶ φρόνησις ἔξοχος εἰς τὴν ταύτης ἀρκοῦσαν κυβέρνησιν (ἐξ
ἧς πίστις ὀρθὴ εἰς Θεὸν καὶ ἀγάπη), πρὸς δὲ καὶ διάκρισις φαεινή, διαιρ-
οῦσα τὸ κρεῖττον ἀπὸ τοῦ χείρονος, καὶ στέργουσα μὲν τὸ κρεῖττον ἀπὸ ψυχῆς, μυσαττομένη δὲ πάλιν τὸ φαῦλον ὡς ἄξιον, καὶ ὅσα ἄλλα κατεπλου-
10 τίσθη ἄπειρα καὶ καλὰ ἡ ἐκ Θεοῦ βασιλεία σου, ἅπερ ἄλλος οὐδεὶς
καταπλουτεῖ σήμερον. εἰ δ' ἴσως ἐκ τούτων τι ἐδόθη τινί, δι' ἐνεργητικῆς
δυνάμεως στέρησιν ἄπρακτον μένον, ὀλίγην αὐχεῖ τὴν ὠφέλειαν. εἰ γὰρ
φανῇ λέων ὁ φοβερὸς ὀδόντων ἐκτὸς καὶ ὀνύχων, πῶς ἡ αὐτῷ ἐντεθεῖσα

6: 6–7 Rom. 2:4 ‖ 11–12 cf. I Joh. 3:17
7: 2 cf. λειτουργία Ἰωάννου Χρυσοστόμου (ed. Brightman), 340

6: V 4ᵛ. S 126ʳ. N 16ʳ–16ᵛ.
1 post αὐτοκράτορα add. γράμμα εἰς παιδείαν (παίδευσιν N) τῶν ἁμαρτανόντων καὶ δικαίωσιν τῶν ἀδικουμένων VʳSN ‖ 6 γὰρ om. S ‖ 16 οὐαί] οὐδέ S
7: V 4ᵛ–5ᵛ. S 126ʳ–128ʳ. N 16ᵛ, 119ʳ–120ᵛ.
1 ante πρὸς add. γράμμα VʳSN ‖ post αὐτοκράτορα add. περὶ τοῦ διεγεῖραι αὐτὸν τοῦ
ἀπελάσαι κακοποιοῦντας ἐκ τῆσδε τῆς πόλεως VʳSN ‖ 6 κυβέρνησις N

6. To the emperor

Again as so often I supplicate you, listen to my voice for the sake of Him Who made you emperor, Christ, God over all things. Rouse yourself to provide justice for the wronged, and punishment for sinners. Cleanse the Church from defilement, and do not refute the wickedness of schismatics with words alone; for they failed to realize that «the goodness of God leads them to repentance». In proportion therefore to their unyielding and unrepentant hearts, let them taste the wrath of imperial judgment. Remember the days of yesteryear and of today. Let us not wish as a result of personal prejudice or indolence or flattery or blood ties «to close the divine heart» which began to open because of the depths of His goodness. For Christianity is being destroyed in two ways, from without by enemies, and from within by excessive injustice and depravity. If therefore your divine majesty arises to make amends, together with Christ and with the aid of Christ, it will be a great blessing; but if we hesitate on account of my sins, woe is me and nothing else.

7. To the emperor

Through the goodness of the great and only God «Who led us from non-being to being», grace is granted to every person at different times, according to the measure of His great gift. Thus I think that in this generation not only the height of empire itself has been granted to your divine majesty, but also extraordinary wisdom to govern it sufficiently (from which comes your right faith in and love for God), and in addition your brilliant sense of discrimination, which distinguishes the better from the worse (so that in your soul you love the good, and loathe the base as it deserves), and all the other countless blessings with which your divine majesty has been endowed, blessings such as no one else today enjoys. But if it should happen that one of these ⟨assets⟩ was granted someone, but was not put to use because of a lack of effective power, he would boast of small benefit. For example, if a frightful lion should appear, but without teeth and claws, how will his inherent

ἰσχὺς γνωρισθῇ; οὕτω καὶ τοῖς ἀνενέργητον στερήσει δυνάμεως ἔχουσι
15 τί καλόν; οὐ μόνον ἐπαίνων μακράν, ἀλλὰ καὶ ψόγου ἐγγύς. τῇ δέ γε ἐκ
Θεοῦ βασιλείᾳ σου τέλεια καὶ ἀνελλιπῆ τὰ [fol. 5ʳ] ἐκ Θεοῦ χαρισθέντα
σοι, καὶ τῷ μόνον ὁρμῆσαι, ἀκωλύτως εἰς πέρας ἀγόμενα.

διὰ ταῦτα κλαίω καὶ σκυθρωπάζω πῶς, δι' ἐμὰς ἀνομίας, οὐκ
ἐνδείκνυται τὴν ὁρμὴν ἐν τοῖς ἄγαν καλοῖς καὶ φανερῶς θεαρέστοις ἡ ἐκ
20 Θεοῦ βασιλεία σου, καὶ ταῦτα ὡς οὔποτε ἄλλοτε τὴν ἀντίληψιν τὴν ἀπὸ
Θεοῦ χρῃζόντων ἡμῶν· ἣν ἄλλως οὐ κτήσασθαι δυνατόν, εἰ μὴ πάσῃ
δυνάμει οὐ λέγειν μόνον, ἀλλὰ μᾶλλον ἀποπληροῦν τὰ τούτῳ φίλα σπουδῇ.
ἢ γὰρ οὐ διότι ὁ τῆς μεγαλοπόλεως Ἱερουσαλὴμ ἄξιος βασιλεὺς Ἐζεκίας
ἐναργῶς τὴν ἔνδον ὀδύνην ἐν τοῖς κατὰ τοῦ μεγάλου Θεοῦ τοῦ Ῥαψάκου
25 ληρήμασιν ἐνδειξάμενος, διέρρηξε τὰ ἱμάτια, καὶ τῆς μεγάλης ταχὺ
ἀντιλήψεως ᾔσθετο, πρὸς δὲ καὶ προσθήκην ζωῆς ἐπεκτήσατο; διατί
οὖν ἡμεῖς τοὺς οὐδὲν ἐλάττω Ῥαψάκου τὸν μονογενῆ Υἱὸν καὶ Λόγον
Θεοῦ καὶ Θεὸν βλασφημοῦντας οὐκ ἀπηλάσαμεν; διατί τοὺς ὑπὸ τῶν
θείων πατέρων δικαίως ἀποκοπέντας καὶ παραδοθέντας τῷ ἀναθέματι
30 τοῖς ὀρθοδόξοις συναναστρέφεσθαι καὶ συνεῖναι κατεδεξάμεθα; διατί
καὶ τὸν ἐξ Αἰγύπτου Πρωτέα τὸν κατ' ἐκείνους μετατρεπόμενον τοὺς
καιροὺς καὶ πάντα γινόμενον διὰ τὴν τῆς ἐκκλησίας κατάλειψιν ἡμεῖς
συνεῖναι ἐπὶ τοσούτοις χρόνοις συνεχωρήσαμεν; καὶ εἰ μὲν δι' ἐλπιζομένην
ὠφέλειαν μείζω, καταδέξεταί τις καὶ ζημίαν μικράν, ἔχει λέγειν τάχα
35 καὶ τί ἐκ ταύτης δὲ τῆς μεγάλης ζημίας καὶ στυγηρᾶς; τί γὰρ ἐλεεινότε-
ρον τοῦ ταράσσειν μηχανωμένου τὴν ἐκκλησίαν Χριστοῦ, ὑπὲρ ἧς ἐκεῖνος
τὸ προσκυνητὸν ἐξέχεεν αἷμα, καὶ οἱ αὐτοῦ μαθηταὶ διὰ τὴν εἰρήνην
αὐτῆς; τί δὲ καὶ οἱ τὸν τάραχον ταύτης ἀπελάσαι δυνάμενοι καὶ μὴ
τοῦτο ποιοῦντες ἀπολογήσονται; διατί δὲ καὶ τοὺς τῇ ἐκ Θεοῦ βασιλείᾳ
40 σου συμβουλεύοντας ὧδε τοῦτον ἐᾶν παραδέχῃ, ἢ κουφότητι ἢ φιλίᾳ
ἀλόγῳ ἢ ἀχολήσει ταῦτα συμβουλευόντων, ἢ καὶ τὸ ἑαυτῶν φιλοτάραχον καλύπτειν σπευδόντων; διατί δὲ καὶ τοὺς ἀκολούθους αὐτῷ ἐν
τοιούτοις ἀρχιερεῖς συνάγειν τὰ τῶν ἐκκλησιῶν, καὶ ἐνταῦθα κακῶς
δαπανᾶν καὶ συμποσιάζεσθαι τούτῳ καὶ συνευφραίνεσθαι, καὶ ἀδεῶς
45 μυκτηρίζειν καὶ τὰ τῆς βασιλείας καὶ τὰ τῆς ἐκκλησίας, καὶ τοὺς τοῦ
λαοῦ μοχθηροτέρους ἢ κουφοτέρους καὶ χαιρεκάκους αὐτοῖς συναπ-
άγεσθαι εἴασας; καὶ ἵνα μὴ τἄλλα καθ' ἕκαστον λέγω, διατί μὴ ἐξω-
λόθρευσας ἐκ τῆς πόλεως ταύτης καὶ πάσης ὑπήκοον ὅσον τὸ
κατὰ σέ, τοὺς ἐργαζομένους τὴν ἀνομίαν ἀναφανδόν; ἀλλ' ἀνομία
50 καὶ ἀδικία καὶ ἀσωτία ἐν ταῖς πλατείαις αὐτῆς αὐλίζεται φανερῶς.

---

25 IV Reg. 19:1 ‖ 32 Hom., Od. 4, 417; Greg. Naz., Or. IV, lxxxii (PG, XXXV, 609A) ‖
47–49 cf. Ps. 100 (101):8 ‖ 49–50 cf. Ps. 54 (55):12

---

17 τῷ] τὸ VSN ‖ 20 βασιλείᾳ S ‖ 26 δὲ] δὴ S ‖ 28 βλασφημοῦντες N ‖ 32 κατάληψιν
N ‖ 40 ἐὰν VSN ‖ παραχέχῃ N ‖ 41 ἀσχολήσει SN fortasse recte

7

strength be recognized? Thus what good is there in those who do nothing because of the loss of their power? They are not only far from praise, but close to blame. The ⟨assets⟩ granted by God to your divine majesty are complete and unfailing, and if you only make a beginning, they carry through to the end without hindrance.

For this reason, I weep and sulk, ⟨in the reflection⟩ that on account of my transgressions your divine majesty does not manifest any zeal for actions which are good and clearly pleasing to God, and this at a time when we need the help of God as never before. And it is not possible to attain this ⟨assistance⟩ unless with all our might we not only speak, but rather accomplish with zeal deeds pleasing to Him. Was it not because Hezekiah, the worthy king of the great city of Jerusalem, clearly manifested his inner pain at the foolish babblings of Rhapsakes against the great God, and «rent his garments», that he quickly perceived His great help and also gained additional years of life? Why then have we not banished those who no less than Rhapsakes blaspheme the only begotten Son and Word of God, and God Himself? Why have we allowed those people who have been rightly rejected by the divine fathers and delivered to anathema, to associate and congregate with the orthodox? Why have we allowed that Proteus from Egypt, who changes according to the times and «assumes every shape», to associate with us for so many years after his abandonment of his church? And granted that for the hope of some greater gain one accepts slight harm, what can he show for this great and loathsome harm? For what is more pitiable than the man who contrives to disrupt the Church of Christ, for whose sake He shed His venerable blood, as did His disciples for the sake of its peace? What excuse will be given by those who are able to remove this source of trouble and do not do so? Why do you accept the counsels of those who advise your divine majesty to leave him here, when they either make these counsels through irresponsibility or unreasonable friendship or timidity, or strive to conceal their love of turmoil? Why did you allow the bishops who are his followers in such ⟨nefarious⟩ actions to collect church funds, and to spend them here for evil purposes, and to drink and make merry together with this man, and to jeer with impunity at both the empire and the church, and to be subverted together with the baser and more petty elements of the population and those who delight in the misfortunes of others?

So as not to go into further detail, why «didn't you root out» of this and every city as best you can those citizens who are openly breaking the law? But «lawlessness and injustice» and profligacy are plainly lodged «in its

22

7, 8

διὰ ταῦτα ἀκούομεν ὅτι ἐὰν ἐκτείνητε τὰς χεῖρας ὑμῶν πρός με,
οὐκ εἰσακούσομαι ὑμῶν, καὶ ὅτι ζη–[fol. 5ᵛ] τοῦσι τὸ πρόσωπον τοῦ
Θεοῦ αὐτῶν ὡς λαὸς δικαιοσύνην ποιῶν. τί δὲ καὶ ἀποκρινώμεθα,
λέγοντος τοῦ Θεοῦ, εἰ ὁ λαός μου ἤκουσέ μου, Ἰσραὴλ ταῖς ὁδοῖς
55 μου εἰ ἐπορεύθη, ἐν τῷ μηδενὶ ἂν τοὺς ἐχθροὺς αὐτῶν
ἐταπείνωσα καὶ ἐπὶ τοὺς θλίβοντας αὐτοὺς ἐπέβαλον ἂν τὴν
χεῖρά μου; μὴ οὖν διὰ τὸ πολὺ τῆς κακίας τοῖς καλοῖς ἐγχειρεῖν κατόκ-
νει, ἅγιε βασιλεῦ. ὁ γὰρ Θεὸς ἡμῶν, ὁ ὢν μετά σου, πῦρ καταναλίσ-
κον τὴν μοχθηρίαν ἐστίν. ὅπου γε καὶ εἰ μὴ πάντα ἦν δυνατὰ τῷ
60 πιστεύοντι, αὐτὸ τοῦτο τὸ καὶ ἐν τοῖς ὑπὲρ δύναμιν ἀγαθοῖς διὰ Θεοῦ
καὶ μετὰ Θεὸν ἐγχειρεῖν, πόσου μακαρισμοῦ παντὸς ὑπερκείμενον.
ἢ οὖν διὰ τὸν Θεόν, ἢ διὰ τὴν ἐνταῦθα ἀντάμειψιν ὑπὲρ τοῦ καλοῦ
καὶ ἐκεῖ, ἢ διὰ τὸ εἰς αἰῶνας μνημόσυνον, ἢ καὶ διὰ τὸ κοσμηθῆναί σε
πρὸς Θεοῦ μισοπόνηρον καὶ φιλάγαθον, διανάστηθι, δέομαι. μὴ λόγοις
65 μόνον τὴν κακίαν καταθροῇς, ἀλλ᾿ ἔργοις ἀνδρείως αὐτὴν ἐξολόθρευσον.
ἠγνόηται τοῖς κακοῖς ὅτι οὐδὲν ἄλλο ἐνταῦθα τὸ χρηστὸν τοῦ Θεοῦ
ἢ ἵνα εἰς μετάνοιαν βλέψωμεν· γνώτωσαν καὶ μετὰ Θεοῦ δικαίαν βασιλικὴν ἀγανάκτησιν. οὐδὲ γὰρ ἐν καιρῷ ἐξόδου χρεία ἐνδείξασθαι λόγους, ἀλλ᾿ ἔργα· οὐδὲ ὁ εὐτρεπιζόμενος σπεῖραι ἢ πλεῦσαι ἢ πολεμῆσαί
70 ποτε ἐπηνέθη, ἢ ὤνατό τι, ἀλλ᾿ ὁ σπείρας ἢ πλεύσας ἢ πολεμήσας ἢ
ἄλλο τι τῶν ἀγαθῶν ἐργασάμενος. εἰ δὲ καὶ οἱ τὴν ἀναβολὴν μεσιτεύον-
τες ἀγωνίζονται, ἀλλ᾿ οὐ λελάληκε Θεὸς ἐν αὐτοῖς· οὐδαμοῦ γὰρ ἐν
ἀγαθοῖς ἡ ἀναβολὴ ἀγαθή. εἰ γὰρ οὐ μικροῦ τὸ παρὰ μικρόν, τί εἴπωμεν
περὶ τοῦ μηδὲ μικρόν; εἰ οὖν ἔχειν τὸν Κύριον ἐγγύ σε ἡ βασιλεία σου
75 βούλεται, διανάστηθι. ἐδόθη σοι γὰρ παρ᾿ αὐτοῦ γνῶσις, σοφία, διάκρισις·
τὸ δὲ μεῖζον ἰσχὺς ἐν πᾶσι καλοῖς, καὶ ἔχεις τὸν Παντοδύναμον μετά
σου, ὃς στηρίξει, ἐνισχύσει, θεμελιώσει εἰς ἔμπρακτον διανάστασιν
παντὸς ἀγαθοῦ τὴν ἐκ Θεοῦ βασιλείαν σου.

8. ⟨Πρός τινα ἄρχοντα⟩

Ἵνα μὴ ὁ κομίζων τὸν λόγον ἄλλα ἀντ᾿ ἄλλων λαλήσῃ, τῷ γράμματι
ἐχρησάμεθα, τὰ ἡμᾶς λυποῦντα διὰ τούτου γνωρίσαι σοι, τῆς ἀντιλήψεώς

51–52 cf. Is. 1:15 ‖ 53 cf. Is. 58:2 ‖ 54–57 Ps. 80 (81):14–15 ‖ 58–59 Deut. 9:3, Hebr.
12:29 ‖ 59–60 cf. Marc. 9:23 ‖ 66–67 cf. Rom. 2:4

---

74 ἐγγύσαι S¹N
8: V 5ᵛ–6ʳ. S 128ʳ–128ᵛ. N 120ᵛ–121ʳ.
1 γράμμα πρός τινα (τὸν N) ἄρχοντα περὶ τῶν κελευσθέντων συλλέγειν εἰς κατάπλουν τοῦ
μεγάλου δουκὸς add. VʳSN ‖ ad τὸν scr. γρ(άφεται) πρός τινα Nˣᵐᵍ ‖ 3 γνωρίσω N

squares»; for this reason we hear that «If ye stretch forth your hands toward me, I will not hearken to you», and that they seek the face of their God «as a people that has done righteousness». What then shall we reply when God says, «If my people had hearkened to me, if Israel had walked in my ways, I should have put down their enemies very quickly, and should have laid my hand upon those that afflicted them»? Do not therefore, on account of the abundance of evil, hesitate to undertake good deeds, O holy emperor. «For our God», He Who is with you, «is fire which consumes» wickedness. Wherefore, even if «all things were not possible to him who believeth», this would be superior to every blessing, for the sake of God and with the help of God to attempt good deeds which are beyond your power.

Therefore, I beg of you, arise, either for the sake of God, or because of the rewards for good works both in this world and in the life hereafter, or for the sake of eternal memory, or to be honored by God as an enemy of evil and friend of virtue. Do not only shout down wickedness with words, but destroy it manfully with actions. The wicked have failed to realize that «the goodness of God» exists in this world for no other reason than that we turn «toward repentance». Let them also come to know righteous imperial wrath with the help of God. For at the time of departure [death?] one need not show his words, but his deeds. Nor has any man who was getting ready to sow or sail or fight ever received any praise or benefit, but rather the man who has sown or sailed or fought or done any other good deed. If there are some who strive to mediate a delay, God has not spoken in them. For a postponement of good deeds is never good. For if even a minor matter is not insignificant, what shall we say about a matter of major importance? If then your majesty wishes to have the Lord near you, arise. For knowledge, wisdom and discretion have been granted you by Him, but the greatest ⟨asset⟩ is strength in all good deeds; and you have with you the Almighty, Who will support, strengthen and steady your divine majesty in the active promotion of every good deed.

8. ⟨To a certain official⟩

To prevent the man who brings my message from saying one thing instead of another, I have made use of a letter with which to inform you of a matter grievous to me, since you are well aware that the threat which hangs

24

8, 9

σου ἐπισταμένης ὡς ἡ συμβᾶσα Χριστιανοῖς ἀπειλὴ δι' ἀθέτησιν ἐντολῶν
5 τοῦ μεγάλου Θεοῦ, ὡς καὶ τὸ στόμα Χριστοῦ μαρτυρεῖ, τοῦτο γάρ, φάμε-
νον, ἔστε γινώσκοντες, ὅτι πᾶς πόρνος ἢ ἀκάθαρτος ἢ πλεονέκτης, ὅς ἐστι λάτρις εἰδώλων, οὐκ ἔχει κληρονομίαν ἐν τῇ
βασιλείᾳ Χριστοῦ τοῦ μεγάλου Θεοῦ. εἰ οὖν κληρονομίας Χριστοῦ ἐκ
τῶν τοιούτων ἀλλοτριούμεθα, πάντως ἀλλότριοι καὶ βοηθείας ἐκείνου.
10 ἐν τούτοις τὴν καθ' ἡμᾶς οἰκουμένην ὡς οὔποτε κρατουμένην ὁρῶ. ἵνα
οὖν μὴ ἐκτρίψῃ Θεὸς πανωλεθρίᾳ τὸ πᾶν, ὅσον εἰς ἡμετέραν ἥκει καὶ
γνῶσιν καὶ δύναμιν, ἐπιμελώμεθα θεραπείας διὰ τὸν Κύριον. ἡ θεραπεία
δὲ τίς; τοὺς τῆς [fol. 6ʳ] κακίας ἐργάτας ἀπείργειν καὶ τούτων καὶ τῶν
ἄλλων θεομισῶν. εἰ γὰρ δι' ἑνὸς ἁμαρτίαν ἔρχεται ἐπὶ δήμους κακά, ὅταν
15 μικροῦ πάντες ποιῶμεν τοιαῦτα, πῶς οὐχὶ καὶ πάντες ἐκτριβησόμεθα;
καὶ ἵνα τἆλλα παρῶ, ὡς μηδὲ ὑμῖν ἀγνοούμενα, λέγω τὸ πραττόμενον σήμερον. ἄνδρας τινὰς κελευσθέντες συλλέξειν κωπηλατεῖν εἰς κατάπλουν τοῦ μεγάλου δουκός, οὐχ ὅσους ἡ χρεία ἀπῄτει συνέλεξαν, ἀλλ'
ὅσους ζωγρεῖσθαι δεδύνηνται. εἶτα τὸ ἱκανὸν λαμβάνοντες παρ' ἑκάσ-
20 του, ἐλευθερίας ἠξίουν. καὶ οὐ μόνον ἐνταῦθα, ἀλλὰ καὶ περὶ τὸ Ἱερὸν
ἄνω, ὡς ἐνωτίσθην, ἐνεργῆσαι τοῦτο ἐστάλησαν ἐν σπουδῇ. εἰ ὅσον
οὖν ἀρεστὰ τὰ τοιαῦτα Θεῷ, εἰ μὴ λάβῃ διόρθωσιν, κατὰ τοσοῦτον
ἀναμφιβόλως καὶ αὐτὸς ἀντιλήψεται τὰ ἡμέτερα.

9. Πρὸς τὸν αὐτοκράτορα

Ὅσον ἐσπούδασε μετὰ Κύριον ἡ ἐκ Θεοῦ βασιλεία σου τὴν ἐκκλησίαν καθάραι συγκοινωνίας τῶν Ἰταλῶν, οὐκ ἔστιν εἰπεῖν ὅσος ἀπόκειται
ταύτῃ μισθός. ἐπεὶ δὲ νῦν ἡ διὰ τὰς ἐμὰς ἁμαρτίας συμβᾶσα Χριστιανοῖς
5 συμφορὰ ἠνάγκασε νήσους δοθῆναι τῷ μεγάλῳ δουκί, δέομαι, ὅση σοι
δύναμις, ἵνα ἐκπέμπωνται παρ' αὐτοῦ κοινωνοὶ τῆς Χριστοῦ ἐκκλησίας.
εἰ γὰρ μὴ κοινωνοί, καὶ ὑμῖν πολὺ προξενήσουσι κρῖμα, καὶ τὸν ἐκεῖ
εὑρισκόμενον τῆς ἐκκλησίας λαὸν συγκοινωνὸν ποιήσουσι καὶ μὴ θέ-
λοντα. καὶ διὰ τὸν Κύριον γενέσθω τοῦτο μεγάλη φροντὶς τῇ ἐκ Θεοῦ
10 βασιλείᾳ σου, μήπως ἡμεῖς εὑρεθῶμεν ὑπεύθονοι τοσαύτης ζημίας.

8: 5–8 Eph. 5:5

---

6 ἔστε scripsi, cf. Eph. 5:5: ἴστε VSN || 13 τῆς τῆς V || 23 ἡμέτερα S: ὑμέτερα VN
9: V 6ʳ. S 128ᵛ–129ʳ. N 121ʳ. Ed. Bănescu, *BSHAcRoum*, 23 (1942), 45, note 1.
1 ante πρὸς add. γράμμα VʳSN || post αὐτοκράτορα add. δοθῆναι τῷ μεγάλῳ δουκὶ
κοινωνοὺς τῆς Χριστοῦ ἐκκλησίας VʳSN || 7 πολὺ VSN¹: πολλοὶ N || 8 ποιήσωσι VSN

8, 9

over Christians is to be attributed to our neglect of the ordinances of the great God, as the words of Christ bear witness, saying: «For this ye know, that no whoremonger, nor unclean person, nor covetous man, who is an idolater, hath any inheritance in the kingdom of Christ», the great God. If then we are deprived of the inheritance of Christ for such reasons, we will certainly be deprived of His help. Yet I see the land we inhabit in such straits as never before. Therefore, lest God wipe out everything with total destruction, let us attempt to remedy the situation, as much as our knowledge and power permit. And what is the remedy? To ward off the perpetrators of evil and of these and of other deeds which are hateful to God. For if on account of the sins of one man, evils come upon whole nations, when almost all of us are committing such ⟨wickedness⟩, how can we avoid being all destroyed?

And not to mention other incidents, which are well known to you, I will speak of that which occurred today. Certain people, who were ordered to conscript men to row on the voyage of the *megas doux* down ⟨the Sea of Marmara?⟩, conscripted not only as many as were needed, but as many as they could take captive. Then, after extracting from each one of them a sufficient sum, they allowed them to go free. And as I have heard, they were sent to do this with zeal not only here [in Constantinople], but also up ⟨the Bosporus⟩ in the vicinity of Hieron. In proportion, therefore, as such deeds are pleasing to God, if they do not receive correction, to such an extent without any doubt will He help us.

9. To the emperor

It is impossible to describe the reward that lies in store for your divine majesty for the efforts which you, after the Lord, have exerted to purge the Church from communion with the Italians. But now when the calamity which has befallen Christians on account of my sins has forced islands to be handed over to the *megas doux*, I entreat that as much as possible you send out with him communicants of the Church of Christ. For unless they are of our faith, they will both cause you great harm, and will convert to their faith the Orthodox Christians who are found there, even if they are not willing. For the sake of the Lord, let this be of great concern to your divine majesty, lest we be found responsible for such a great misfortune.

26

10, 11

10. Πρὸς τὸν αὐτοκράτορα

Οἶδεν ἡ ἐκ Θεοῦ βασιλεία σου ὅτι οὐδὲ πῶς οὐδὲ πότε αὐτὸς ἐν τῇ τοῦ Χριστοῦ ἐκκλησίᾳ εἰσήχθη ἐπίσταμαι, οὔτε τὸν παρ' αὐτοῦ λόγον ἀκήκοα κἂν φαῦλος κἂν μή. καὶ ἡ βασιλεία σου, διὰ τῆς χάριτος τοῦ Χριστοῦ
5 καὶ Θεοῦ μου, καὶ κριτὴς δίκαιος καὶ μάρτυς πιστὸς καὶ φιλόχριστος βασιλεύς· ὅσον οὖν κρίνεις καὶ μαρτυρήσεις καὶ παραστήσεις αὐτὸν τῇ τοῦ Χριστοῦ ἐκκλησίᾳ μετὰ τῶν εὑρισκομένων ἀρχιερέων, ἀναπαύομαι.

11. Πρὸς τὸν αὐτοκράτορα

Ὅσοις ἐχαριτώθη τοῖς ἀγαθοῖς παρὰ τοῦ ταύτην εὐεργετοῦντος μεγάλου Θεοῦ, διακρίσει τε καὶ λεπτότητι καὶ ζήλῳ δικαίῳ, ὃ ἡ τῶν γεννικῶν ἀνδρικωτάτη ἀνδρία οἶδε γεννᾶν, ἡ ἐκ Θεοῦ βασιλεία σου, οἶμαι
5 μὴ ἀγνοεῖν τοὺς καὶ ποσῶς βλέποντας· καὶ γένοιτο τὰ θεόσδοτα ταῦτα καλὰ ὡς φίλον ἐκείνῳ κινεῖν τὴν ἐκ Θεοῦ βασιλείαν σου. διὰ τοῦτο παρακαλῶ, ἡνίκα καλέσῃ καιρὸς στηλιτεύεσθαι τὴν κακίαν τινῶν φρυαττομένων κατὰ Θεοῦ καὶ βασιλείας καὶ ἐκκλησίας, μὴ παρεῖναι κἀμέ, φυλαττούσης τοῦτο τῆς βασιλείας σου ἄριστα, ἵνα μὴ ἔχωσι κακουργεῖν ὡς εἰσηγήσει [fol. 6�v]
10 ἡμετέρᾳ τὴν μοχθηρίαν αὐτῶν κινεῖ Θεὸς ἐκπομπεύεσθαι· ὅσον δὲ καὶ παθαίνομαι, μηδένα τὸν συλλυπούμενον βλέπων καὶ συναντιλαμβανόμενον ἀγαπητικῶς.

καὶ ὡς κεχρεωστημένον πιστοῖς ὑπηκόοις καὶ εὐνοοῦσι τῇ ἐκ Θεοῦ βασιλείᾳ σου, τῇ ψυχῇ μου δώῃ Θεὸς καὶ ὡς ἤθελον ἡμέραν καὶ νύκτα
15 συνεῖναι αὐτῇ· ἐμποδίζει με δὲ ἡ ταλαίπωρος σὰρξ καὶ τὸ ψῦχος καὶ ὁ πηλός, ἀκολουθοῦσι δὲ καὶ τὸ ὀλιγώτερον εἴκοσι, μὴ ἔχοντες ποῦ κοιμηθῆναι, ῥιγοῦντες καὶ ἐμπεπηλωμένοι. ἡ δὲ ἐμὲ δεχομένη κέλλα, εἰ ἦν δυνατὸν χωρεῖν ἐν αὐτῇ τὸν ὑπ' ἀνέμου κινούμενον μύλωνα, οἱ μοναχοὶ τῆς Χώρας πολὺν ἐκέρδαινον ἄλευρον. διὰ ταῦτα παρακαλῶ καὶ πάλιν
20 παρακαλῶ, καὶ τὴν ψυχρότητα τοῦ ἀέρος, καὶ τὸ ἐπικερδὲς τῆς ὁδοιπορίας ὁρᾶσθαι, καὶ τοὺς ἐκεῖθεν καρπούς, καὶ οὕτω ⟨μὴ⟩ κελεύειν τὴν ἐκ Θεοῦ βασιλείαν σου τὴν ὁδοιπορίαν ποιεῖσθαί με. εἰ γὰρ καταναγκάσω ὑπὲρ δύναμιν ἐμαυτὸν πρὸς τὸ ψῦχος καὶ τὴν ὑγρότητα, ἀπολέσω πάντως καὶ

10: V 6ʳ. S 129ʳ–129ᵛ. N 121ʳ–121ᵛ.
1 ante πρὸς add. γράμμα (ράμμα S) VʳSN ‖ 3 εἰσήχθην VSN ‖ παρ': num περὶ scribendum? ‖ 4 φαῦλοι VSN
11: V 6ʳ–6ᵛ. S 129ʳ–129ᵛ. N 121ᵛ–122ʳ.
1 ante πρὸς add. γράμμα VʳSN ‖ post αὐτοκράτορα add. εὐχαριστῶν αὐτὸν ὅτι ὅταν στηλιτεύεσθαι τοὺς κακουργοῦντας μὴ παρῆναι καὶ τὸν πατριάρχην, ἀλλὰ καὶ μᾶλλον ἤθελεν εἶναι σὺν αὐτῷ, ἐμποδίζετο δὲ διὰ τὸ ψῦχος καὶ τῇ πηλῷ VʳSN ‖ 2 τοῖς ἀγαθοῖς Vᵐᵍ ‖ 3–4 τῶν γενικῶν VSN ‖ 4 ἀνδρικωτάτων N ‖ 9 ἄριστον S ‖ 21 μὴ addidi

10. To the emperor

Your majesty is aware that I do not know how or when he was brought in to the Church of Christ, nor have I heard any word of him, whether he is base or not. Your majesty, by the grace of Christ my God, is a righteous judge and trustworthy witness and Christ-loving emperor. Therefore, however you judge and testify and commend him to the Church of Christ together with the bishops here, I will be satisfied.

11. To the emperor

I think that people of any perception are well aware of the blessings with which your divine majesty has been endowed by the great God Who favors you, with discretion and refinement and righteous zeal, which the most courageous valor of noble men is able to produce. And may your divine majesty use these God-given blessings in a manner pleasing to Him. For this reason, whenever the opportunity occurs to expose the wickedness of certain people who rebel against God and the Empire and Church, I ask that I not be present, since it is best that your majesty should take care of the matter, so that they may not be able to malign me by saying that it is at my instigation that God causes their wickedness to be exposed; and I do suffer this, since I see that no one shares my distress or assists me out of love.

Might God grant that I be with you day and night, as I wished, and as is an obligation for faithful subjects who are well disposed toward your divine majesty, but my wretched body and the cold and the mud hold me back, and I have at least twenty followers who have no place to sleep, and are freezing and covered with mud. If my cell were able to hold a windmill, the monks of Chora could grind a lot of flour. For these reasons I entreat, and again I entreat your majesty to consider the chill of the air and the advantage of the journey, and the profit to be gained therefrom, and thus bid me not to make the journey. For if I force myself beyond my endurance to face the cold and

ἣν ἔχω ὑγείαν καὶ δύναμιν, καὶ ὀδυνήσω μὲν ἐμαυτόν, λυπηθήσεται δὲ
25 καὶ ἡ ἐκ Θεοῦ βασιλεία σου, λίαν ἡμᾶς φιλοῦσα καὶ τὴν ὑγείαν ἡμῶν διὰ
Κύριον· ὃς καὶ ἐν πᾶσι τοῖς ἀγαθοῖς καταπλουτήσοι αὐτήν, στηρίξοι, σθε-
νώσοι, θεμελιώσοι, κινήσοι ὡς φίλον αὐτῷ, καὶ σὺν τῇ ἐπιγείῳ βασιλείᾳ
παρέξοι καὶ τὴν οὐράνιον.

12. Πρὸς τὸν αὐτοκράτορα

Ὀδύνη καρδιακή μοι καὶ λύπη ἐπικρατεῖ. διατί μὴ μετὰ τῶν
καταβαινόντων εἰς λάκκον καὶ αὐτὸς συνηρίθμημαι; ἀλλ' ἐναπελείφ-
θην τοιαῦτα ἰδεῖν, ἃ καὶ μνησθῆναι μόνον προεκπηδᾷ μου τὸ δάκρυον, τῶν
5 Χριστιανῶν τὴν πανωλεθρίαν, τὸ μὴ ἀντιλαμβάνεσθαι τοὺς ἀδικουμένους,
τὸ μὴ παιδεύεσθαι τοὺς πράττοντας τὰ αἰσχρά, τὸ μὴ καθαίρεσθαι
τοὺς θεοκαπήλους τοῦ ἱεροῦ. εἰ γὰρ σωματική τις ἀνωμαλία τινὶ
συναντήσει, οὐκ εἰς ἀναβολὰς ἀναπέμπει τὰ τῆς ἰάσεως. τὰ δὲ τὸ σῶμα τῆς
ἐκκλησίας Χριστοῦ καταβοσκόμενα ἀρρωστήματα μὴ σπουδάζειν ἰᾶσθαι
10 τοὺς τοῦ Χριστοῦ καὶ Θεοῦ ἡμῶν, πόσον αὐτὸς αὐτοὺς βαρυνθῇ, ἢ εἴπω
καὶ καταγνώσεται; ὁ γὰρ βασιλεύσας σε Κύριος οὐκ εἰς τὸ τοῦτο μὲν συντόνως πληροῦν τῶν εἰς δύναμιν ἀγαθῶν, τοῦτο δὲ παραπέμπειν ἀνα-.
βολαῖς, θεραπεύεται.

εἰς τοῦτο δὲ καὶ ἡμεῖς, τὸ διὰ μέσου διάστημα ἐκπηδῶντες, ὡς μηδὲ
15 πηλοῦ φροντίζειν, μηδὲ βροχῆς, ἐρχόμεθα συνεχῶς, μήπως παροραθῇ τι
τῶν δεόντων εἰς ἀκοὰς ἐμπίπτειν τῆς βασιλείας σου· ἃ συμπληρούμενα
μὲν θεραπεύει Θεόν, ὡς καὶ μὴ ἀναφερό [fol. 7ʳ] μενα, ἢ καὶ παραμελού-
μενα μετὰ τὸ σχεῖν τὴν ἀναφοράν, παροργίζει. διὰ ταῦτα σὲ γὰρ καὶ
Θεὸν οὐκ οἶμαι τινὰ τῶν ἀρξάντων Χριστιανοὺς τοσούτοις κατακοσμῆσαι
20 πλεονεκτήμασι, νοὸς λεπτότητι καὶ ὀξύτητι, καὶ φρονήματι σταθηρῷ, καὶ
ζήλῳ τῷ κατ' ἐπίγνωσιν, καὶ πρὸς τούτοις ἐπικλινῆ πρὸς οἶκτον
ψυχήν, ὡς οὐκ οἶδα τινά. ἀλλ' ἡ ἀνομία τῆς πτέρνης μου καὶ τῶν
κατ' ἐμὲ ἀνενέργητα καὶ μικροῦ ἀφανῆ τὰ τοιαῦτα θεόσδοτα καὶ μεγάλα
χαρίσματα κατεκράτησε· καὶ τί ἄλλο ἢ ἐγκατάλειψις φανερὰ τῷ λαῷ;

12: 2–3 Ps. 87 (88):5 ‖ 6–7 Greg. Naz., *Or.* XXI, xxxi (PG, XXXV, 1117C) ‖
21 Rom. 10:2; Greg. Naz., *Or.* XXI, xxi (PG, XXXV, 1105A) ‖ 22 Ps. 48 (49):6

---

26 καταπλουτήσοι VSN¹: καταπλουτήσει N
12: V 6ᵛ–7ʳ. S 130ʳ–131ʳ. N 122ʳ–123ᵛ.
1 ante πρὸς add. γράμμα VʳSN ‖ post αὐτοκράτορα add. διεγεῖρον αὐτὸν ὅπως βλέψει
(βλέψῃ SN) βασιλικὸν καὶ λεόντιον κατὰ τὸν (τῶν SN) ἀδικούντων VʳSN ‖ 7 εἰ] ἡ N ‖
10 τοὺς] τάς N ‖ 11 post ὁ N scr. δε et deinde delevit ‖ τὸ τοῦτο] τοῦτο τοῦτο N ‖ 16
συμπληρούμενα N

11, 12

the damp, I will completely lose what health and strength I do have, and will cause myself suffering, and will bring grief upon your divine majesty who loves me exceedingly and ⟨is anxious about⟩ my health for the sake of the Lord. And may He enrich you with all blessings and maintain you, give you strength, support you, and guide you as is pleasing unto Him, and may He grant you the heavenly kingdom in addition to the one here on earth.

12. To the emperor

Grief and sorrow overwhelm my heart. Why wasn't I numbered among «those that go down to the pit»? Instead I have been left behind to see such horrors that I begin to weep even at the thought of them, I mean the total destruction of Christians, the fact that victims of injustice receive no assistance, and that the perpetrators of dastardly deeds are not punished, and that «the temple is not cleansed of those who make merchandise of God». For if bodily indisposition affects a person, he does not postpone the treatment. Therefore when the followers of Christ our God do not hasten to cure the diseases which consume the body of the Church of Christ, will He not be distressed at them, or should I say condemn them? For the Lord Who made you emperor is not served by doing one possible good deed quickly and by postponing another one.

For this reason I come constantly, leaping over the intervening distance and taking no heed either of mud or rain, lest some matter be overlooked which should reach the ears of your majesty. For one worships God by attending to these matters, but if they are not reported, or are neglected even after the report is made, this angers God exceedingly. For this reason I do not think that God has adorned any Christian ruler with such advantages as He has adorned you, with a refined and penetrating mind, and with unwavering purpose, and with «zeal according to knowledge», and in addition with a soul inclined toward mercy, such as no one else I know. But «the iniquity of my heel» and of those like me has rendered such great virtues granted by God ineffective and almost invisible. And what are the people to believe except that

25 καὶ ἁρμόζον ἡμῖν, ὅ φησιν Ἡσαΐας, καλέσαι ἐν τῇ ἡμέρᾳ ἐκείνῃ
τὸν Θεὸν Σαβαὼθ κλαυθμὸν καὶ κοπετὸν καὶ ξύρησιν καὶ
ζῶσιν σάκκων, ὡς μὴ νομίζειν ἄλλως ἢ ἀλλαχόθεν κοπάσαι τὴν
καθ' ἡμῶν ἀγανάκτησιν.

　　διὰ τοῦτο παρακαλῶ, καὶ ἵνα βασιλέως μεγάλου καὶ εὐσεβεστάτου
30 καὶ φιλοχρίστου χρήσωμαι λόγοις, «παρακαλῶ, δέομαι καὶ ἀντιβολῶ»,
ἐπιστράφηθι. βλέψον βασιλικὸν καὶ λεόντιον κατὰ τῆς ἀδικίας, καὶ εἰς
τὴν αὐτῆς μετὰ Θεὸν ἐξολόθρευσιν διανάστηθι. ἡνίκα γὰρ σὺ ὁ Κυρίου
χριστὸς πρὸς τὴν ταύτης καταπολέμησιν καὶ ὧν ἐμνήσθημεν κακιῶν
ἐκτείνῃς τὰς χεῖρας, ἔχεις συμπολεμοῦντά σοι τὸν Παντάνακτα· οὗ τί
35 ἄν τις εἴποι μακαριώτερον τοῦ μετὰ Χριστοῦ καὶ διὰ Χριστὸν τὸν πόλε-
μον ἄρασθαι; τοῦτο καὶ πόλεμος ἱερὸς καὶ ἔνδειξις φανερὰ τῆς πρὸς
Θεὸν ἀγάπης καὶ πίστεως. εἰ δὲ καὶ πρὸς ἔλεον ὃν ἐζύμωσε τῇ ψυχῇ σου
ὁ τοῦ ἐλέους Θεὸς ἀποβλέψεις τοῦ πληροῦν τὰς αἰτήσεις τῶν προσφόρως
αἰτούντων, τοὺς δὲ προδιδόντας τὴν ἀλήθειαν καὶ τὸ δίκαιον πόθῳ
40 χρυσοῦ στηλιτεύσεις, πόση τούτου τοῦ ἔργου ἀποδοχὴ καὶ ἀντάμειψις
πρὸς Θεοῦ! διὰ ταῦτα, κύριε βασιλεῦ, διανάστηθι σὺν Θεῷ, διανάστηθι!
εἰ δ'(ὅπερ ἀπεύχομαι) παντελῶς ἡμᾶς ἀπώσατο ὁ Θεός, καὶ τοῦτό σοι
ἐν αἰσθήσει πάσῃ δεδήλωκε, πληροφόρησον καὶ ἡμῖν, ἵνα τοῦτο γινώσκοντες ἀποφηνάμενον τὸν Θεὸν παυσώμεθα αἰσχυνθέντες καὶ φοβη-
45 θέντες τῆς αὐτοῦ ἀγαθότητος δέεσθαι, ὑπέρ τε τῆς σωτηρίας ἡμῶν
καὶ τῆς συστάσεως καὶ διαμονῆς τοῦ Χριστωνύμου λαοῦ. καὶ οὐδὲ τὴν
βασιλείαν σου ἐνοχλήσομεν, ἀλλὰ τὰ πρόσωπα αἰσχύνῃ τῶν ἔργων
ἡμῶν καὶ ἐντροπῇ κατακαλυψάμενοι, κατακρύψομεν ἑαυτοὺς σιω-
πήσαντες.

13. ⟨Πρὸς τὸν βασιλέα κύριν Μιχαήλ⟩

　　Δεξάμενοι ἐκ μακροῦ τῆς βασιλείας σου πρόσταγμα ἠγαλλιάσθημεν
ὅσον οὐκ ἔστιν ἐκδιηγήσασθαι, περί τε τῶν ὑγειῶν αὐτῆς τῶν θεοπαρόχων
πεισθέντες, καὶ περὶ ἧς ὁ τῶν θαυμασίων ἡμῖν Θεὸς νίκης ἀπεχαρίσατο.
5 ἠνιάθημεν δὲ πῶς ὅλως ἰσχύουσι καθ' ἡμῶν οἱ μι-[fol. 7ᵛ] σοῦντες ἡμᾶς,
δι' ἄλλο οὐδὲν ἢ δι' ἀθέτησιν τῶν τοῦ Θεοῦ νόμων καὶ καταφρόνησιν, καὶ
πλέον οὐδέν. διὰ τοῦτο παρακαλῶ προηγουμένως τὴν βασιλείαν σας, μὴ

25–27 cf Is. 22:12

---

30 χρήσομαι N ‖ 45 δεῖσθαι N ‖ 48 ἐντροπῇ S
　　13: V 7ʳ–7ᵛ. S 131ʳ–131ᵛ. N 123ᵛ–124ʳ.
1 γράμμα πρὸς τὸν βασιλέα κύριν Μιχαὴλ ὅπως μὴ διὰ σώματος ἡδονὴν προδιδοῦντας (προδιδόντας S) τὴν βοήθειαν τοῦ Θεοῦ add. VʳSN ‖ 2 ἠγαλλιάθημεν VSN ‖ 7 σας VS¹:
σου　SN

12, 13

they have been abandoned? And it is fitting for us ⟨to do⟩ what Isaiah says, «that God Sabaoth called in that day for weeping and lamentation and baldness, and for girding with sackcloth», and not to think that we can appease God's wrath against us by any other means.

For this reason I beg of you, and to use the words of a great and most pious and Christ-loving emperor, «I beg, I entreat and supplicate you», change your ways. Fix an imperial and leonine gaze upon injustice, and with the help of God arise to destroy it. For whenever, O anointed of God, you stretch forth your hands to fight against injustice and the evils which we have mentioned, you have the Lord of all fighting on your side. And what would one call more blessed than to undertake a war with the help of Christ and for the sake of Christ? This is a holy war, and a clear indication of your love for and faith in God. And if with the mercy which the God of mercy leavened in your soul you will look to fulfil the requests of those who make appropriate petitions, and scorn those who betray the truth and justice through their greed for gold, how great will be your favor and reward from God as a result of this work! For these reasons, lord emperor, arise with God, arise! But if (and I pray this may not happen) God has completely spurned me, and has revealed this to you in all knowledge, let me know this, too, so that, in the knowledge that God has made this declaration, out of shame and fear I will cease to pray for His goodness, both on behalf of my salvation and for the protection and safekeeping of the Christian people. And I will not trouble your majesty, but covering my face in shame and embarrassment at my deeds, I will hide in silence.

13. ⟨To the emperor lord Michael⟩

When I received your majesty's command from afar, I rejoiced more than it is possible to tell, persuaded of the good health granted you by God, and of the victory which the God of miracles has granted us. I am grieved, however, at how our enemies always prevail over us, for no other reason than our neglect and scorn for the laws of God, and for this cause alone. Therefore first of all I entreat your majesty that it not be said of us, «Many times He

λεχθῇ καὶ περὶ ἡμῶν πλεονάκις ἐρρύσατο αὐτούς, αὐτοὶ δὲ
παρεπίκραναν αὐτὸν ἐν τῇ βουλῇ αὐτῶν. ὀφείλομεν γὰρ οὐ μόνον
10 δέεσθαι ἐκ ψυχῆς τοῦ μεγάλου Θεοῦ καὶ τῆς Θεομήτορος καὶ τῶν ἁγίων
αὐτοῦ, ἀλλὰ καὶ τὸ ὑπήκοον ἅπαν, καὶ πρότερον αὐτοὺς σωφροσύνης καὶ
δικαιοσύνης ὡς δυνατὸν ἀνθρώποις ἐπιμελεῖσθαι· οὕτω γὰρ ἕξομεν οὐ-
ρανόθεν βοήθειαν. πόσης γὰρ ἀδοξίας αἴτιος γίνεται ὁ διὰ σώματος ἡδονὴν
προδιδοὺς ἀγάπην Θεοῦ καὶ βοήθειαν καὶ ταῦτα διπλῆν! καὶ πόσης δόξης
15 ἐστὶ τὸ πεποιθέναι τινὰ ἐπὶ Κύριον, καὶ ἀνώτερον συντηρεῖν ἑαυτὸν φθορο-
ποιῶν ἡδονῶν! ἐχθροῖς γὰρ γίνονται φοβεροὶ οἱ τοῦτο κρατοῦντες καὶ
πᾶσιν ἐπέραστοι καὶ πεποθημένοι Θεῷ, οὐ μόνον ἐνταῦθα, ἀλλὰ καὶ ἐν
τῷ μέλλοντι. τοῦτο παρακαλῶ, τοῦτο εὔχομαι, τοῦτο ἐπιθυμῶ, πλουτισθῆναι τὴν βασιλείαν σας, ἐν τούτοις μεγαλυνθῆναι, ἐν τούτοις συντηρηθῆναι.
20 καὶ ὅσον ἐν τούτοις ἀκριβαζόμεθα καὶ φροντίζομεν τὰ καλά, καὶ πληροῦ-
μεν τὴν ἐργασίαν αὐτῶν, πάντας ἐχθροὺς συντρίψει ὁ ὕψιστος, καὶ τοῖς
ποσὶν ὑμῶν ταπεινώσει, καὶ κονιορτοῦ δίκην ἀπολικμήσει μακράν· ὃ
καὶ καταξιωθῶμεν ἰδεῖν πλουτισθῆναι ἐξ ὕψους τὴν ἐκ Θεοῦ βασιλείαν
ὑμῶν, πρεσβείαις τῆς Θεομήτορος.

14. Πρὸς τὸν αὐτοκράτορα

Τὰ τῷ γένει Χριστιανῶν συναντήσαντα ηὐχόμην πρὶν τοῦ ταῦτα
ἰδεῖν μετὰ τῶν καθευδόντων ἐν τάφοις λογίζεσθαι, ἢ κἂν κατὰ
δεύτερον σήμερον πλοῦν ἐν χηραμοῖς ὑπογαίοις καὶ ζόφῳ εἰσδύναι
5 ἐμαυτόν, καὶ τὸν κόσμον ἀποκλαιόμενον, καὶ μήτε ἀκούειν μήτε ὁρᾶσθαι,
ἢ τὰ τῆς ἐκκλησίας Χριστοῦ τοῦ Θεοῦ μου ἐπιστατεῖν· πλὴν τῷ δεδοξασ-
μένῳ δόξα Θεῷ, τῶν εἰς ἐμὲ πάντων ἕνεκεν τῆς ἀνομίας τῆς πτέρνης
μου κυκλωσάσης κἀνταῦθα δικαίως με. τί γὰρ καὶ γένωμαι, ἀγνοῶ,
μάρτυς Κύριος, οὔτε ψυχῆς ὠφέλειαν βλέπων ἐν ἐμαυτῷ, οὐδὲ ἄνεσιν σώμα-
10 τος. ἔξυπνος γὰρ γενόμενος ἐν νυκτὶ ἐπὶ μάρτυρι τῷ Θεῷ πολλάκις, ἔνθα
εἰμὶ οὐκ αἰσθάνομαι. διατί δὲ καὶ περιφέρεσθαι ἠνεσχόμην, ἵνα τάχα τύχω
καιροῦ εἰσακουσθῆναι δεόντως — εἰ καὶ οὐκ ἔτυχον — παρὰ τῆς ἐκ Θεοῦ
βασιλείας σου, ὑπὲρ τῆς συσχούσης δι' ἀνομίαν πανωλεθρίας τῇ Ῥωμαίων

13: 8–9 Ps. 105 (106):43
14: 3 cf. Ps. 87 (88):6 ‖ 3–4 Greg. Cypr. II, 21 et Diogen. II, 45 (Leutsch-
Schneidewin, I, 359; II, 24) ‖ 7–8 cf. Ps. 48(49):6

---

9 αὐτὸν VSN¹: αὐτῶν N ‖ 19 σας] σου N
  14: V 7ᵛ–8ᵛ. S 131ᵛ–133ᵛ. N 124ʳ–126ʳ.
1 ante πρὸς add. γράμμα VʳSN ‖ post αὐτοκράτορα add. περὶ τοῦ πολλάκις παρὰ βαλὼν
(παραβαλὼν SN) τοῖς ἀνακτόροις ὅπως ἀναφέρῃ (ante ἀναφέρῃ N scr. ἀφ et deinde delevit) τὰ εἰς θεραπείαν Θεοῦ, μὴ εἰσακουόμενος ἐστράφη (ἐτράφη N) κενός VʳSN ‖ 13 πα-
νολεθρίας N

13, 14

delivered them, but they embittered Him by their counsel». For not only should we pray from our hearts to the great God and the Mother of God and His saints, but so should all subjects, and they should first of all concern themselves with moderation and righteousness as much as is humanly possible; for in this way we will receive help from heaven. How disgraceful it is for a man to give up the twofold love and help of God for the sake of physical pleasures! And how glorious it is for a man to have faith in God and to rise above corrupting pleasures! For those who live in this way are fearful to their enemies, and beloved by all, and yearned for by God, not only in this world, but in the world to come. I beg of you, I entreat, I desire, that your majesty be endowed with this ⟨way of life⟩, and be magnified and maintained in these ⟨virtues⟩. And to the extent that we are strict in these matters and concern ourselves with virtuous actions, and bring them to fulfilment, God on high will crush all our enemies, and humble them at your feet, and scatter them to the winds like dust. And may we be deemed worthy to see your divine majesty enriched from on high with this blessing, through the intercessions of the Mother of God.

14. To the emperor

I hoped to be counted «among those who sleep in their tombs» before seeing these misfortunes which have befallen the Christian people, or second best to crawl into a dark hole underground these days, and as I weep for the world, neither to hear or be seen, rather than to manage the affairs of the Church of Christ my God. But glory be to the glorified God, since on account of all my ⟨sins⟩ «the iniquity of my heel» has justly «compassed me» in this world. And what will become of me, I do not know, the Lord is my witness, since I see in myself neither spiritual benefit, nor physical comfort. For often when I wake up in the night, with God as my witness, I do not know where I am. And why have I endured to go hither and yon in the hope that I might have a chance to be heard properly by your divine majesty—even though I have never gained ⟨such an opportunity⟩—concerning the total destruction which has befallen the Roman people on account of our lawlessness, and why

φυλῇ, καὶ πόθεν αὔξεται καθ' ἡμέραν καὶ πῶς, καὶ εἰς διέγερσιν παραθῆ-
15 ξαι ἐπιστροφῆς; ἐλπίσι νευρούμενος ἀγαθαῖς, ὡς εἴ γε νόμοις Χριστιανῶν
ἐτηροῦντο Χριστιανοὶ πολιτεύεσθαι, ἀδικίας κολαζομένης, μοιχείας τε καὶ
πορνείας καὶ πάσης παρανομίας, καὶ τὸ ἀρέσκειν βούλεσθαι [fol. 8ʳ]
ἡμᾶς ἑαυτοῖς καὶ τισίν, ἀλλὰ μὴ δικαιοσύνῃ καὶ ἀληθείᾳ, καὶ τὰ φίλα Θεῷ
εἰς δύναμιν ἐνεργεῖσθαι πρὸ παντὸς ἐθεσπίζετο, καὶ τῇ λαχούσῃ ἀρχιερέων
20 ἑκάστῳ καλῶς ἠναγκάζετο διατρίβειν, καὶ τὰ πρόβατα βόσκειν, ἀλλὰ μὴ ἑαυτῶν ἕκαστον, μηδ' ἐκ τῶν πτωχικῶν ἔχειν τὸ ἀβροδίαιτον (τί
γὰρ ὡς διάδοχοι ἀποστόλων ἐκείνων καὶ τετηρήκαμεν;), ἀφῄρει δειλίαν
πᾶσαν Θεὸς ἀφ' ἡμῶν, καὶ ἐν εὐθείᾳ βουλῇ τὰ ἔργα αὐτοῦ τὰ μεγάλα ἐν
ἡμῖν ἐπεδείκνυτο. οὐδὲ γὰρ τὰς τοῦ θείου πνεύματος παροπτέον ἡμῖν ἔδει
25 φωνάς, πρόσωπον, λέγων, Κυρίου ἐπὶ ποιοῦντας κακά, ὡς
καὶ παρεμβαλεῖ ἄγγελος Κυρίου κύκλῳ τῶν φοβουμένων
αὐτόν, ὅτι μηδὲ δυνατὸν ὑστέρημα εἶναι τοῖς φοβουμένοις
αὐτόν, οὐδὲ ἡ ἄμπελος τοῦ Θεοῦ ἐξεδόθη εἰς κοινὴν ὕβριν τοιαύτην, παντὶ
παραπορευομένῳ καὶ καταπάτημα.
30   ἀλλ', ὦ τῶν ἐμῶν συμφορῶν, πῶς καθ' ἑκάστην ὑπορρεῖ καὶ οἴχεται
τὰ ἡμέτερα! καὶ οὐδεὶς ὁ ἀποδυρόμενος, οὐδεὶς ὁ φροντίζων ἢ τῆς ζημίας
ἢ καὶ ὡς μέλλων λόγον δοῦναι Θεῷ, ὑπὲρ ὧν τοιαῦτα συναντᾷ καὶ συνήν-
τησεν. εἰ γὰρ μὴ ταῦτα ἐσπείραμεν, οὐκ ἂν ἐθερίζομεν.
εἰ δὲ φροντίζειν νομίζομεν, καὶ ἀλγεῖν διϊσχυριζόμεθα, τί τὸ εἰς θεραπείαν
35 Θεοῦ πραττόμενον ὑφ' ἡμῶν, ὡς ἂν ἀποστρέψῃ τὴν δικαίαν αὐτοῦ ἀφ'
ἡμῶν ἀγανάκτησιν; καὶ ὅταν δὲ παραβάλω τοῖς ἀνακτόροις, λόγοις μηδὲν
συντελοῦσι πρὸς τὰ δάκνοντα τὴν ψυχήν μου καὶ κατεσθίοντα τὸν καιρὸν
εἰς μάτην ἐξαναλώσας, βαρυθυμίας ἐπαναστρέφω μεστὸς καὶ συγχύσεως,
καθὰ καὶ τὴν σήμερον. καὶ γὰρ ἓξ ἐν τῇ Χώρᾳ ἡμέρας διατελέσας, ὡς ἄλ-
40 λοτε δέκα καὶ αὖθις ἑπτὰ ἢ ὀκτώ, μὴ κόπου, μὴ κακουχίας χειμῶνος δι'
ἐλπίδα φροντίσας, αἰσχύνης καὶ ἐντροπῆς καὶ δακρύων τὸ πρόσωπον πλη-
ρωθείς, ἐστράφην κενός.
εὔχεσθαι δέ με πολλάκις ἡ βασιλεία σου ἀξιοῖ· καὶ πῶς ἐνδέχεται,
ἅγιε βασιλεῦ, τινὰ εἰσακούεσθαι, τῶν θείων θεσμῶν ἀθετήσει τὸν δόντα
45 αὐτοὺς μικροῦ ὑπὸ πάντων ἐν γνώσει καθυβριζόμενον, δοῦναι φειδῶ τοῖς
ὑβρίζουσιν; ἢ πῶς οὐκ ἔσμεν ἐν φροντίδι τοῦ βασιλεύσαντός σε Θεοῦ, ἐν
ὁσιότητι καὶ δικαιοσύνῃ τὴν βασιλείαν ἰθύνειν σε θέλοντος, τοῦ εἰς δύναμιν τούτου τὸ θεῖον ἀποπληροῦν θέλημα, ἐπισταμένου σου διὰ ταῦτα εἰς
φιλοτίμημα βασιλείαν ἐκεῖ παρασχεθῆναί σοι τὴν ἀσάλευτον; ἀλλ'
50 εὐημερίαν ἢ ἄνεσιν ἀναμένωμεν τὰ φίλα αὐτῷ καὶ ἡμῖν κεχρεωστημένα

20–21 cf. Ezech. 34:2, 8 ‖ 25 Ps. 33 (34):17 ‖ 26–27 Ps. 33 (34):8 ‖ 27–28 cf. Ps. 33 (34):10 ‖
33 cf. Gal. 6:7 ‖ 49 Hebr. 12:28

---

18 ἑαυτοῖς] ὡς αὐτοῖς N ‖ 27–28 ὅτι μηδὲ ... φοβουμένοις αὐτὸν om. S ‖ 39 ἡμέρα
VSN

14

and how it increases every day, and ⟨in the hope of⟩ encouraging repentance ? Impelled by the good hopes that if Christians were to preserve the principle of living according to Christian laws, and if injustice, adultery and fornication and every sort of transgression were punished, as well as our wishing to please ourselves and certain people, but not ⟨to live⟩ in righteousness and truth, and if it were decreed that above all we should perform God-pleasing acts to the utmost of our ability, and if each of the bishops were rightly compelled to remain in the see assigned to him, and if all of them ⟨were compelled to⟩ «pasture their sheep, not themselves», rather than dining luxuriously off what rightly belongs to the poor—for what have we maintained as successors of the apostles of old ?—then God would remove all cowardice from us, and would show His great works in us in right counsel. Nor was it right for us to overlook the words of the Holy Spirit, which say «the face of the Lord is against them that do evil», and also «the angel of the Lord will encamp round about them that fear Him», «for there is no possibility of want to them that fear Him», nor was the vineyard of the Lord given over for such common abuse, to be trampled upon by all who passed by.

But, alas for my plight, how each day our fortunes ebb and decline! And no one deplores this, no one is concerned about the harm, or that he is going to have to render an accounting to God, for such misfortunes as have happened and are happening. For «if we did not sow these troubles, we would not reap their fruit». And if we think that we do care, and assert that we are distressed, what have we done in God's service that He should avert His righteous wrath from us ? And whenever I go to the palace, after spending my time in vain with words which accomplish nothing for the troubles which devour and consume my soul, I return filled with melancholy and confusion, as happened today. For after spending six days at Chora, as on another occasion ten days, and another time seven or eight, taking no heed of my trouble or of the hardships of winter because of my hopes, I returned empty-handed, my face filled with shame and embarrassment and tears.

Your majesty often asks me to pray ⟨for him⟩; but how, O holy emperor, is it possible for one to be heard ⟨in the demand⟩ that God spare those who insult Him, when by their disregard of the divine commandments almost everyone consciously insults the God Who granted these ⟨commandments⟩ ? Or how is it that we do not take thought for God Who made you emperor, and Who wishes you to guide the empire in holiness and righteousnesss, in order to fulfil His divine Will to the best of your ability, when you know that «the Kingdom ⟨of Heaven⟩ which cannot be moved» will be given you as a reward for these deeds ? Should we wait for a period of prosperity or ease to do works which are pleasing to Him and an obligation for us ? From what turn

ἐργάσασθαι; ἀλλ' ἐκ ποίας ἀποστροφῆς; ὅτι καὶ βλέπομεν ἐπὶ κεφαλῆς τὰ δεινὰ καὶ μὴ διορθούμενα· ὅμοιόν τι ποιοῦντες ἢ πάσχοντες ἀνθρώπῳ ἐμπεπτωκότι ἐν ὕδασι [fol. 8ᵛ] καὶ μὴ σπεύδοντι ἐν κινήσει χειρῶν εἰς δύναμιν διανήχεσθαι, εἴ πως ξύλου ἢ ῥίζης ἢ πέτρας ἢ τινὸς τοῦ σῴζοντος
55 ἐπιδράξηται, ἀλλ' ἀναμένει τὰ ὕδατα ξηρανθῆναι καὶ τότε τινὸς τῶν σῳζόντων κρατήσειν ἐπιμελήσασθαι.

διὰ ταῦτα τὸ τῇδε κἀκεῖσε ἐμπεριτρέχειν εἰς μάτην εἰδώς, οὐδὲ γὰρ μῆνα κἂν ἡμερῶν ἐν τόπῳ ἑνὶ ποιῆσαι ἐπίσταμαι, ἐξῆλθον ἐκ τῶν αὐτόθι μετὰ λύπης ὡς καὶ πολλάκις, οὐχ ὅτι ἀπέτυχον τῆς ἀποχερᾶς,
60 ἀλλ' ὅτι τὰ τῷ παμβασιλεῖ Χριστῷ φίλα πράττειν παρακαλῶν σε ἀποτυγχάνω. ἀπολέγομαι δὲ καὶ αὐτὴν τὴν ζωήν, καὶ μᾶλλον ὡς μὴ ἔχων τὸν συλλυπούμενον. ὅθεν τὰ περὶ τῆς ἐμῆς οὐθενίας, καὶ δι' ἃ κατεμπίπραμαι ὑπὲρ τῶν χρῃζόντων εὐεργεσίας καὶ ἄλλως ἀδικουμένων, τῷ φιλανθρώπῳ Θεῷ ἀναθέμενος, τοῦ μὴ δι' ὄχλου τῇ βασιλείᾳ σου, ἐπεὶ μηδὲ εἰσακούομαι,
65 βεβούλευμαι γίνεσθαι. ἐδόθη σοι γάρ, εἴπερ καὶ βούλει, καὶ γνώμη καὶ φρόνησις καὶ λεπτότης ἀπροσδεὴς τῶν καλῶν, καὶ τὸ εἰδέναι Θεόν, καὶ δι' ἃ συμπαθεῖ ἢ ὀργίζεται. εἰ δὲ καὶ ἡμᾶς ὑπὲρ τῆς σῆς βασιλείας καὶ δόξης καὶ σωτηρίας καὶ τοῦ λαοῦ βουλομένους συναγωνίζεσθαι προσεδέχου, μὴ δῶρα χρῄζοντας ἀπὸ σοῦ, μὴ φίλων ἢ συγγενῶν προκοπάς, μὴ
70 ἄλλην ἀντίχαριν, ἀλλ' ὑπὲρ τῆς σῆς καὶ τοῦ γένους ἀγάπης, ὡς οἶμαι, συνέφερεν. ἐπεὶ δὲ πολλάκις καὶ πολλὰ δοκιμάσαντες οὐκ εἰσακουόμεθα, ὡς μηδὲν βοηθεῖν ἐξισχύοντες τοῖς ἡμῶν ἀδελφοῖς καὶ συμπένησιν, ἐμαυτὸν κἀκείνους κέκρικα δέον κινεῖσθαι καὶ εἰς δύναμιν ἀποκλαίεσθαι· καὶ Κύριος ὁ Θεός, ὡς οἶδε, παρέξοι τὰ ἀγαθὰ τῇ ἐκ Θεοῦ βασιλείᾳ σου, καὶ
75 τῷ ὑπηκόῳ ἐν βουλῇ ἀγαθῇ.

15. Πρὸς τὸν αὐτοκράτορα

Εἰ καὶ ἀπαραμύθητα τὰ συμβάντα ἡμῖν, ὅτι θερίζομεν ἃ καὶ ἐσπείραμεν, ἀλλ' οὐκ ὀφείλει τὴν ἐκ Θεοῦ βασιλείαν σου εἰς πέλαγος

58 cf. Job 29:2
15: 2–3 cf. Gal. 6:7

53 ὕδασι VSN¹: ὕδατι N ‖ 55 τινὸς] τινὲς S ‖ 58 ἡμερῶν] ἢ μερῶν S ‖ 60 τὰ om. S ‖ 62 οὐθενείας N ‖ 64 τῇ βασιλείᾳ VSNˣ: τὴν βασιλείαν N ‖ 66 ante λεπτότης N repetivit φρόνησις et deinde delevit ‖ 68–69 προσδέχου VSN ‖ 74 καὶ om. N ‖ 75 ὑπηκό N
15: V 8ᵛ–9ʳ. S 133ᵛ–134ᵛ. N 126ʳ–126ᵛ (initium epistolae). P 16ʳ (finis epistolae).
1 post αὐτοκράτορα add. γράμμα περὶ τῶν ἀρχιερέων ὅτι οὐ μόνον ⟨οὐ⟩ συντρέχουσιν ἐν τῇ ἀγρυπνίᾳ, ἀλλὰ καὶ διασύρειν καὶ καταγελᾶν αὐτῶν, καὶ περὶ τοῦ ἔρχεσθαι μετ' αὐτοῦ ἐκ τῆς συγκλήτου ἕνα τινὰ ἀναφέρειν ὅσα παιδεύσεως χρῄζει VʳSN

14, 15

⟨of fortune⟩ will this come ? Because we see hanging over our heads terrible sins which are not corrected. Thus we would do or experience something similar to the man who has fallen into the water, and does not try to flail his arms and swim as vigorously as he can, in the hope that he may be able to grab hold of a piece of wood or a root or something which could save him, but waits for the water to dry up and then thinks of grabbing onto something which could save him.

Therefore, in the knowledge that my rushing around here and there is in vain, nor can I stay in one place for a month, I left there [the palace] sorrowfully as so often, not because I failed to gain my request (?), but because I achieved no result in asking you to perform deeds dear to Christ, the King of all. And I renounce this life, especially because there is no one who shares my sorrow. Wherefore I have resolved to refer to God Who loves mankind my worthless self and those who need charity and are otherwise wronged (for these matters are my ardent concern), and ⟨I have resolved⟩ not to trouble your majesty, since I am not heeded. For if you wish, knowledge and understanding and perfect refinement have been granted to you, and knowledge of God, and for what reasons He is compassionate or grows angry. If you had admitted me into your presence, I think it would have been profitable, since I wish to strive on behalf of your empire and glory and salvation, and on behalf of the people, and since I do not require any gifts from you, nor the advancement of friends and relatives, nor any favor, but ⟨come⟩ for the sake of my love for you and the nation. But since after numerous and various attempts I am not heeded, so that I am in no way able to help my brethren and fellow poor, I decided that it was necessary to move away and bewail my fate and theirs as best I can; and may the Lord God, as He knows how, provide your divine majesty and your subjects with blessings in good counsel.

15. To the emperor

Even if the events which befall us admit of no consolation, since «we are reaping what we have sown», still your divine majesty ought not to be sub-

ἀθυμίας καὶ βάθος ἀνελπιστίας καταβαπτίζεσθαι, τοῦ βασιλεύσαντός σε
5 Θεοῦ παιδεύειν καὶ πάλιν ἰᾶσθαι γνωριζομένου, εἰ καὶ τὰ λυπηρὰ ἐπεκτείν-
εται, ἐκ τοῦ βλέπειν τὴν ἐκ Θεοῦ βασιλείαν σου ὅτι ἐσπείραμεν πάντες,
καὶ οὐ πάντες λυπούμεθα. εἰ γὰρ ἐκλίναμεν εἰς ἐπιστροφὴν καὶ μετάνοιαν,
εἶχε μεταβαλεῖν ὁ πάντα ἰσχύων Θεὸς εἰς εὐφροσύνην τὰ λυπηρά. ἐπεὶ δὲ
τοσαύτη ἀναισθησία ἡμῶν κατεκράτησε, καὶ ἵνα ἐάσω τοὺς ἄλλους, αὐ-
10 τοὺς τοὺς ἀρχιερεῖς, ποσάκις ἠξίωσα ἵνα συνδράμωσιν ἐν τῇ ἀγρυπνίᾳ,
καὶ πλὴν ὀλίγων οὐ μόνον οὐκ ἔρχονται, ἀλλὰ καὶ διασύρειν ἡμῶν καὶ καταγελᾶν ἀναφαίνονται καὶ οἱ τάχα ἐλθόντες. ἐδεήθην αὐτῶν μετὰ τῆς ἀρχιερατικῆς στολῆς ἀγρυπνεῖν, ἀλλ᾽ οὐδόλως ἐφρόντισαν. ἐὰν οὖν [fol. 9ʳ]
οἱ τῆς ἐκκλησίας οὐ συντριβώμεθα, τί καὶ περὶ τῆς συγκλήτου τις ὑπο-
15 λάβοι;

διὰ ταῦτα, ἅγιε βασιλεῦ, τὴν μέριμνάν σου ἐπίρριψον ἐπὶ
Κύριον. οὐδὲ γὰρ παραβλέψει εἰς τέλος καὶ σὲ καὶ τὸν κλῆρον αὐτοῦ,
ἀλλ᾽ ἀντιλήψεται πάντως ἐν σπλάγχνοις ἐλέους αὐτοῦ πρὸς τὸ συμφέρον ἡμῖν. ἐγὼ γὰρ ἐνθυμούμενος πῶς διακείμεθα ἀναλγήτως, ἐπὶ
20 μάρτυρι τῷ Θεῷ, ἀγαπῶ καὶ εὔχομαι εἰ μὴ ἔζων· πλὴν τὰ ἐπελθόντα ἡμῖν
διὰ τὰς πάντων ἀπροσεξίας, ἀνατρέχει πάντα πρὸς τὴν ἐκ Θεοῦ βασιλείαν
σου. διὰ ταῦτα αὐτὸς ὁ Θεὸς ἀντιλήψεται καὶ παραμυθίαν παρέξει καὶ τὴν
μεταβολὴν τὴν εὐφρόσυνον, καὶ ἀναλόγως τῶν θλίψεων πολυπλασιάσει
σοι τὴν χαράν. μόνον μεγαλοψύχει καὶ ἀνδρίζου καὶ εὔχου, καὶ ὅση σοι
25 δύναμις διεκδίκει καὶ τὰ καλά. οὐδὲ γὰρ μόνον οἱ Φράγγοι βεβήλωσιν
θείων ναῶν * * * καὶ φθορὰν γυναικῶν, ἀλλὰ καὶ οἱ τάχα Χριστιανοί,
καὶ τῆς βασιλίδος ἐντός, λυττῶσι τοιούτοις, ἃ καὶ διὰ τὴν βίαν ἀναφέρειν
ἐμποδιζόμεθα. εἰ δέ γε καὶ ἀναφέρομεν, διὰ τῆς ἀναμονῆς καταλιμπάνεται
ἀνεκδίκητα, ἢ καὶ τινὲς φιλίᾳ ἢ δώροις μεσολαβοῦντες ἀμβλύνουσι τὴν
30 ἀλήθειαν.

εἰ οὖν ἕνα τινὰ τῶν ἀρχιερέων, ἢ τῆς συγκλήτου, ἢ ἱερέα ἢ μοναχὸν
εὐσυνείδητον οἶδεν ἡ βασιλεία σου, κέλευσον ἔρχεσθαι μετ᾽ ἐμοῦ ἐξετάζειν
διὰ Θεὸν καὶ ἀναφέρειν ὅσα παιδεύσεως χρῄζει, καὶ ὅσα προξενεῖ ζημίαν
τῇ ἐκ Θεοῦ βασιλείᾳ σου. καὶ διεγέρθητι ἐκδικεῖν τὸ δίκαιον, καὶ τὴν
35 σωφροσύνην καὶ τὸν ἔλεον, διὰ τοῦ ἐλέους σου· ἄλλως μὴ δυνατὸν εὐφραίν-
ειν τὸν βασιλεύσαντά σε Θεόν. ἐγὼ γὰρ εἰ μὴ ἄκρως ἐπιθυμῶ τὸ πρὸς
ἐπίδοσιν ψυχικὴν καὶ σωματικὴν καὶ δόξαν καὶ ἔπαινον σόν, καὶ δὴ καὶ
τοῦ ὑπηκόου, ἐπιλησθείη ἡ δεξιά μου καὶ τῷ λάρυγγί μου ἡ
γλῶσσά μου κολληθῇ. μὴ οὖν τὰ καλὰ δι᾽ ὄκνον ἢ διὰ πρόσωπα
40 ἀμελῶμεν, ὀρθῶς ἐλπίσαντες εἰς Θεόν.

16–17 Ps. 54 (55):23, I Pet. 5:7 ‖ 18 cf. Luc. 1:78 ‖ 38–39 cf. Ps. 136 (137):5–6

---

4 σε] ἐπὶ S ‖ 5 γνωριζομένου VS¹N: γνωριζομένους S ‖ 25 βεβηλῶσι N ‖ 26 post ναῶν
lacunam statui ‖ 28 post ἀναφέρο, Nˣᵐᵍ scr. λείπει ‖ post ἀναφέρο, incipit P ‖ 32 οἶδεν]
εἶδεν P ‖ 33 ὅσα¹] ὅτ P ‖ 35 ἐλέους] ἐλέου P

15

merged in a sea of despair and in the depths of despondency, since God Who
made you emperor knows how to punish and again how to remedy, even
if your majesty's grief is increased by seeing that we all have sowed ⟨evil⟩,
but are not all repentant. For if we turned toward repentance and conversion,
God, the all-powerful, would be able to transform our grief into joy. But since
such great insensitivity has taken hold of us, and not to mention the others,
how often have I asked the bishops to assemble for a vigil, and, with a few
exceptions, not only do they not come, but those who may come even appear
to mock and ridicule me. I asked them to keep the vigil in their bishops' robes,
but they paid no attention to me. If then we churchmen show no contrition,
what would one imagine ⟨the attitude of⟩ the senate to be ?

For these reasons, holy emperor, «cast your care upon the Lord»; for
He will not disregard you or His heritage until the end, but «in His tender
mercy» He will always help us, as is most expedient for us. And when I am
reminded of how we sit here unmoved by grief, with God as my witness,
I wish and pray that I weren't alive. The misfortunes which befall us on
account of the negligence of all men all revert to your divine majesty. For
these reasons God Himself will help and provide consolation, and a joyful
transformation, and in proportion to your sorrows He will multiply your joy.
Only act magnanimously and be of good courage and pray, and pursue the
good as much as you can. For it is not only the Franks who ⟨indulge in⟩
profanation of holy churches and the corruption of women, but also so-called
Christians, even within the Queen of Cities, commit outrages which I am
perforce prevented from mentioning. And even if I do report ⟨these outrages⟩,
they remain unpunished as the result of procrastination, or else certain
people intervene, out of friendship or influenced by gifts, and obscure the
truth.

If then your majesty knows a single bishop or senator, or a priest or
monk who is honest, bid him come with me to make an investigation for the
sake of God, and to report whatever is in need of correction and whatever is
causing harm to your divine majesty. And rouse yourself to pursue righteousness and moderation and mercy, through your mercy; for it is not otherwise
possible to gladden ⟨the heart of⟩ God Who made you emperor. And if I do
not desire exceedingly your spiritual and physical increase and glory and
praise, and that of your subjects, «let my right hand forget its skill and may
my tongue cleave to my throat». Therefore let us not neglect good works
through hesitancy or personal prejudices, but let us have our hopes rightly
in God.

16. Πρὸς τὸν αὐτοκράτορα

Οἶδεν ἡ ἐκ Θεοῦ βασιλεία σου πῶς σήμερον οἱ ἀρχιερεῖς εἰς οὐδὲν ἕτερον ηὑρίσκοντο καὶ εὑρίσκονται ὧδε, εἰ μὴ εἰς συμπόσια καὶ εἰς σχίσματα καὶ εἰς ταραχάς, ὡς καί τινες μοναχοί, καὶ ἵνα οἱ ἔχοντες ὑπο-
5 θέσεις, οἱ μὲν τοῦτον, οἱ δὲ ἐκεῖνον μεταχειρίζωνται εἰς βοήθειαν, ὡς καὶ προκαθημένους συνοδικῶς, οὐχ ἕνεκεν ἀληθείας πρὸς ἀλλήλους διαπληκτίζεσθαι. διὰ τοῦτο παρακαλῶ, ἐὰν ἠλέησεν ἡμᾶς ὁ Θεὸς καὶ τῶν ὧδε ἐξήγαγεν ἢ ἐξαγάγῃ τινὰς τῶν τοιούτων, μὴ πάλιν αὐτοὺς προσκαλώμεθα ἐπὶ βλάβῃ καὶ ταραχῇ. οἱ γὰρ λέγειν μαθόντες [fol. 9ᵛ] κακῶς, οὐ
10 μήποτε λαλήσουσιν ἀγαθά. τίς δὲ ἡ χρεία ἵνα ὁ χαρτοφύλαξ ἢ ὁ νῦν Ἀκαπνίου καταλάβωσιν ὧδε, ἢ ἄλλος ἐκ τῶν τοιούτων; μὴ λίπῃ ἐκεῖ ἐκείνοις τὰ πρὸς ζωήν; εἰ δὲ θέλομεν ταραχὰς ἀνάπτεσθαι ἐξ αὐτῶν ἡμεῖς, φέρωμεν ἐπάνω ἡμῶν ἃ καὶ μισήσαντες οὐ δυνησόμεθα ἀπορρίψαι. εἰ δὲ κελεύει ἡ βασιλεία σου ἵνα γνωρίσῃ πῶς διοικεῖ τὰ τοῦ Ἀκαπνίου, τὸν κύριν Ἠλίαν
15 ἐνόρκως ἐρώτησον, ὃν ἔχεις καὶ φιλαλήθη, κἀκεῖνος ἀναγγελεῖ διατί δὲ καὶ τὰ τοῦ Βήρας ἀββᾶ Ἰωάννου ὑπέρπυρα τριακόσια ἐν τῇ Θεσσαλονίκῃ οὐκ ἐζητήσαμεν.

17. Πρὸς τὸν αὐτοκράτορα

Τὰ παρά τισι μὲν εἰς παράβασιν θείων θεσμῶν πραττόμενα τολμηρῶς, ὑφ' ἡμῶν δὲ πῶς οὐκ οἶδα ἀνεκδίκητα καταλιμπανόμενα, μικρὰ καὶ μεγάλα, ἐν οἷσπερ σήμερον εὑρισκόμεθα τὰ ἡμέτερα κατηντήκασι. διὰ
5 τοῦτο, κἂν ἀπό γε τοῦ νῦν διαναστῆναι παρακαλῶ. καὶ γὰρ καὶ τῷ τῆς θείας δυνάμεως ῥήματι τὸ πᾶν κινεῖται καὶ φέρεται, ἀλλὰ βούλεται καὶ ἡμᾶς μὴ ἀργοὺς ὁρᾶσθαι, μηδὲ ἀπράγμονας, ὅτι μηδὲ κατὰ τὸ σωτήριον θέσπισμα ζῶντες ἐσμέν, μόνην τὴν τοῦ Θεοῦ δικαιοσύνην ζητοῦντες καὶ βασιλείαν, ἀλλὰ μὴ ἃ ὀρεγόμεθα.

17: 5–6 cf. Hebr. 1:3 ‖ 8–9 cf. Matt. 6:33

16: V 9ʳ–9ᵛ. S 134ᵛ–135ʳ. P 16ʳ–16ᵛ.
1 ante πρὸς add. γράμμα VʳSP ‖ post αὐτοκράτορα add. περὶ τῶν ἀρχιερέων τῶν εὑρισκομένων ὧδε ὅτι εἰς οὐδὲν ἄλλο εἰσίν, εἰ μὴ εἰς (εἰ S) σχίσματα καὶ συμπόσια (ὅτι ... συμπόσια om. P) VʳSP ‖ 5 ἐκείνων P ‖ 6 ροκαθημένους SP ‖ 8 ἐξαγάγῃ] ἐξάγῃ S ‖ 10 χορτοφύλαξ P ‖ 15 φιλαλήθει P ‖ 16 βύρας codd. ‖ 17 post ἐζητήσαμεν repetivit σαμεν P²
17: V 9ᵛ–10ᵛ. S 135ʳ–137ᵛ. P 16ᵛ–19ʳ. Ed. Laiou, Andronicus II, 336–338, no. 6.
1 post αὐτοκράτορα add. γράμμα ἀνιστορῶν αὐτὸν προόδους ποιεῖσθαι συχνότερον, καὶ μᾶλλον περὶ τὰ τείχη καὶ πύλας τῆς πόλεως, καὶ μὴ εἰσέρχεσθαι εἴσω τῆς πόλεως μεθ' ὅπλων τινά VʳSP

16, 17

16. To the emperor

Your divine majesty is aware how the bishops, as well as certain monks, have been and are staying here ⟨in the capital⟩ these days for no other reason than for drinking bouts and dissension and disturbances, and so that people who are bringing cases ⟨before the synod⟩ may make use of this or that ⟨bishop⟩ for assistance, so that even when the bishops deliberate at meetings of the synod, they squabble with each other for reasons alien to truth. For this reason, I beg of you, if God has had mercy on us and has removed or is removing some of these people from here, let us not invite them back to cause harm and confusion. For those who have learned to speak evil, will never speak good. What need is there for the *chartophylax* or the present ⟨abbot of the monastery⟩ of Akapniou to come here, or another of their ilk ? ⟨Are they afraid⟩ they won't have enough to live on there ? If we want them to stir up trouble, let us bring upon ourselves what we will not be able to get rid of even though we hate it. And if your majesty would like to learn how he administers Akapniou, question under oath Kyr Elias, whom you consider to be truthful, and he will tell you why we did not look in Thessalonica for the three hundred *hyperpyra* of Abbot John of Bera.

17. To the emperor

The fact that acts both great and small have been boldly committed by certain people in transgression of divine commandments, and have somehow been left unpunished by us, has resulted in our present fortunes. For this reason I bid you to bestir yourself, from this moment on. For although «everything is moved and upheld by the word of divine power», still He does not wish to see us lazy or idle, because we are not even living in accordance with the precept of salvation by «seeking only the righteousness and kingdom of God», and not our aspirations.

10　διὰ ταῦτα ἀνιστορῶ προόδους ποιεῖσθαι τὴν βασιλείαν σου συχνοτέρας, καὶ μᾶλλον περὶ τὰ τείχη καὶ πύλας τῆς πόλεως, καὶ ἐντὸς καὶ ἐκτὸς ὄκνου χωρίς, καὶ μηδὲ προφασιζομένους τὴν ὀλιγότητα, μηδὲ τὴν οἰκείαν ἀσφάλειαν, ὧν ὑμῖν Θεὸς ἐνεχείρισε, τούτῳ ἢ ἐκείνῳ καταπιστεύωμεν· ὀφθαλμοὶ γὰρ ὠτίων πιστότεροι. κέλευσον ὃ δίκαιον, τῆς πόλεως
15　εἴσω μηδένα μεθ' ὅπλων εἰσέρχεσθαι, καὶ μάλιστα τῶν Λατίνων. εἰς γὰρ ἀσφάλειαν μέγα καὶ τοῦτο, καὶ μηδὲ ὀκνῶμεν τὰ εἰς δύναμιν ἥκοντα ἡμετέραν ἀποπεραίνειν καλά, ὡς τὰ μείζω μὴ ἐξισχύοντες· μηδὲ παραπέμπωμεν εἰς τὴν αὔριον, τὸ μὴ δῴης εἰς σάλον τὸν πόδα σου, καὶ οὐ μὴ νυστάξῃ, ἀκουτισθέντες, ὁ φυλάσσων σε ἄγγελος. γενέσθω
20　φροντὶς εἰσαχθῆναι λαὸν εἰς ἀσφάλειαν, ὅτι μέγα τοῖς ἀντιπάλοις δέος καὶ τοῦτο. ὁ εὑρισκόμενος ἅπας λαὸς ὁμιλίας ἀπολαβέτω γλυκείας καὶ εὐχαρίστου (οἱ δὲ τῶν ἐν στρατείᾳ καὶ πλέον, εἰ δυνατόν) καὶ μικρᾶς ἀσχολήσεως ἢ σίτου ὀλίγου. εἰ δ' οὖν, κἂν μὴ διενοχλῶνται ἀτίμως παρὰ τῶν ἐνεργούντων καὶ τὰ οἰκεῖα ἁρπάζωνται. ἔχουσι γὰρ τὴν ὀφείλουσαν ὑποταγὴν καὶ
25　διάθεσιν, μοχθηρῶν ὀλίγων ἐκτός, κἂν καί τινες τῶν ἀποβλεπόντων μόνον πρὸς τὸ λαβεῖν ἐκταράττειν ἐπι-[fol. 10ʳ] χειροῦσι τὴν ἐκ Θεοῦ βασιλείαν σου κατ' αὐτῶν.

ὅτι δὲ ἀπὸ συμπαθείας, ὡς ἀπὸ τῆς βασιλείας σου ὁ Δοσίθεος ἤκουσεν, ἀναγκάζεσθαι ἀναφέρειν ἐμὲ ὑπὲρ ὧν μοι δοκεῖ ἐκπιέζειν ἀδίκως οἱ
30　τασσόμενοι ἐνεργεῖν, ὡς καὶ ὁ τῆς αὐλῆς πριμμικήριος, ἀλλά, μὴ ἀκριβῆ κατακαλύψω καὶ ἀληθῆ, εἴθε καὶ ἦν μοι ψυχὴ ἐλεήμων καὶ συμπαθής, καὶ μάλιστα κἂν τῷ νῦν δεομένῳ πολλῆς συμπαθείας καιρῷ· οὐ γὰρ ἠγνόησα, εἰ τοῦτο προσῆν μοι, ἀκμὴν μικρὰ αἰσθανόμενος. τοῦτο γὰρ τῇ ἐκ Θεοῦ βασιλείᾳ σου ἐχαρίσθη τὸ μέγα, ἡ συμπάθεια λέγω, ἀλλὰ καὶ κε-
35　χρεώσταται· ἐμοὶ δὲ (ἀληθεύω εἰς ταῦτα) καὶ ψυχρὰ ψυχὴ ἐνυπάρχει καὶ σκληρὰ καὶ ἀπόκροτος, κατὰ τὸν πρεπόντως ἐκεῖνον στηλιτευόμενον πλούσιον, εἰ μή με ἡ προφανὴς ὠμότης ἐκείνων, καὶ τὸ κατεσθίειν ὡς ἄρτον τοὺς πένητας ἀδεῶς — καὶ τῆς σῆς ᾐσθανόμην συμπαθοῦς ψυχῆς. ἐμοί τε τὸ κατεπεῖγον τοῦ χρέους εἰς δέος ὠθοῦν τοῦ οὐαί, ἀπό τε τοῦ
40　παρασιωπᾶν τὴν κακίαν, ἀπό τε τοῦ τὸ πικρὸν πικρὸν μὴ λέγειν, ἀλλὰ γλυκύ.

πλὴν ἀλλὰ δέομαι, πῶς τοὺς ἐπὶ πολλοῖς ἔτεσι τὰς πύλας φυλάσσοντας, καὶ παρὰ μηδενὸς τῶν ἐγχειρισθέντων τὴν κατ' αὐτῶν ἐξουσίαν καταγνωσθέντας, σήμερον ἢ διδόναι τὸ ἱκανόν, ἢ διώκεσθαι (καὶ εἰ παρ'
45　ἄλλου πλέον δοθῇ, κατακρίνονται), καὶ μάλιστα ἐν τοιούτῳ καιρῷ τοὺς μὴ

---

14 Apostol. XVIII, 71 (Leutsch-Schneidewin, II, 744) ‖ 18–19 Ps. 120 (121):3–4 ‖ 36–37 τὸν ... πλούσιον: cf. Luc. 16:19–31 ‖ 37–38 cf. Ps. 52 (53):5 ‖ 39–40 cf. Is. 5:20

---

13 ὑμῖν VSP¹: ἡμῖν P ‖ καταπιστεύωμεν S ‖ 16–17 ὑμετέραν codd. ‖ 24 γὰρ] δὲ P ‖ 29–30 οἱ τασσόμενοι] σιτασσόμενοι P ‖ 31 κατακαλύψει codd. ‖ 39 ἐμοί] ἐμός P ‖ 43 τῶν] ὧν P ‖ 44 ἢ²] εἰ P

17

Wherefore, I ask your majesty that without delay you make more frequent inspection tours, especially in the vicinity of the walls and gates of the city, both within and without, nor let us make excuses on account of the paucity ⟨of your retinue⟩ or personal safety, and entrust to this man or that those matters which God has entrusted to you; for «eyes are more trustworthy than ears». Order what is just, that no one, especially the Latins, should enter the city bearing arms. For this, too, is important for security, and let us not hesitate to accomplish the good deeds which are within our power, since we cannot accomplish those beyond ⟨our power⟩. Neither let us delay until the morrow, when we hear the words: «Let not thy foot be moved and the angel thy keeper will not slumber». Let it be your concern that the people be brought into safety, because this is a great source of fear to the enemy. Let all the people who are ⟨here⟩ enjoy pleasant and agreeable associations (?) (and let this be true to an even greater extent, if possible, for those who are performing military duty), and may they have a little work or a little grain. If this is not possible, at least may they not be disgracefully harassed by the tax-collectors and have their property seized. For they show the proper humble disposition (with the exception of a few rascals), even though certain people who think only of gain try to stir up your majesty against them.

⟨It is rumored⟩ that it is out of compassion—as Dositheus heard from your majesty—that I am compelled to make a report about those people who, it seems to me, are being unjustly oppressed by the men assigned to collect taxes, and by the *primicerius* of the court, but, lest I conceal the strict truth, would that I did have a merciful and compassionate soul, especially at a time like this which requires so much compassion; I would certainly know if I did have compassion, for I still retain some little perception. For this great gift, I mean compassion, has been granted to your divine majesty, but it is also an obligation for you; as for myself (and I speak the truth in this), I have a cold and harsh and unyielding soul, like the rich man ⟨of the parable⟩ who was justly exposed, except that their blatant cruelty, and the way «they devour» the poor with impunity «like so many loaves of bread»—and ⟨except that⟩ I have perceived your compassionate soul. And also the urgency of my obligation compels me to fear ⟨the prophet's cry of⟩ «Woe!», if I pass over evil in silence, and «do not call the bitter bitter but sweet».

I also ask this, how is it that men who have guarded the gates for many years, and have not been criticized by any of those who are entrusted with authority over them, today must either pay a sufficient sum, or be dismissed —and if a larger ⟨sum⟩ should be paid by another, they are condemned—and especially at a time like this, how is it that men who have given no evidence

μαρτυρίαν δόντας φυλακὴν τοιαύτην διὰ τὸ δοῦναι καταπιστεύεσθαι; εἰ
δὲ ὅτι τῆς ἐκ Θεοῦ βασιλείας σου κατενώπιον ἃ συνέρχονται τοῖς τοιούτοις λαλοῦσι, καὶ παρὰ τῶν αὐτοὺς συγκροτούντων ἐνευλογοῦνται, τί
θαυμαστόν, ἀεὶ τοῦ ψεύδους ἐκκεχυμένου, καὶ μάλιστα τοῖς περὶ τὸ λέγ-
50 ειν δεινοῖς ἐκ παιδεύσεως, εἰ μὴ ἐθέλουσιν ἀτενίζειν πρὸς τὸ ἀλάθητον
τοῦ κριτοῦ;

   δι' ἃ καὶ ταύτης ἀντιβολῶ πνεύματι μὴ πιστεύειν παντί, προ-
βαίνειν δὲ καὶ συχνότερον καὶ ἀκούειν καὶ βλέπειν, καὶ ὡς δέον διατιθέναι
κἂν τὰ ἐγγύς· οὐ γὰρ ἐκκόψαι ἡμᾶς τῶν δημοσίων τὴν εἰσφοράν—τὸ ἐκεῖ-
55 θεν δέος καὶ τὴν ἐπαινουμένην ἀσφάλειαν καὶ ὑποταγὴν συνεργοῦντες ἢ
ὀρεγόμενοι — ἀναφέρομεν (μὴ οὕτω μανείημεν!), οὐδὲ τοῦτον φιλοῦντες,
κἀκεῖνον ἀπεχθανόμενοι, οὐδὲ φιλίᾳ ἢ λήμματι χαριζόμενοι, ἀλλ', ὡς ὁ
πλάσας ἐπίσταται, συντηρεῖσθαι τὴν δόξαν τῆς βασιλείας ἣ ἐχαρίσθη τῷ
γένει Χριστιανῶν, μόνιμον καὶ διηνεκῆ καὶ ἐξηρημένην ἐκ τῶν εἰς δυσώ-
60 πησιν καὶ ἀρέσκειαν ὑφ' ἡμῶν πραττομένων Θεοῦ καὶ ἀναφέρομεν καὶ
ζηλοῦμεν καὶ ἐκκαιόμεθα καὶ εὐχόμεθα, καὶ ἵνα καὶ τῇ συγκλήτῳ τῇ ἱερᾷ
μὴ προσῇ ὅσα ὁ μεγαλοφωνότατος ὀνειδίζει ἀπὸ Θεοῦ τὴν Ἱερουσαλήμ·
οἱ ἄρχοντες [fol. 10ᵛ] σου ἀπειθοῦσι, φησίν, ἀγαπῶντες δῶρα,
διώκοντες ἀνταπόδομα, ὀρφανοῖς οὐ κρίνοντες, καὶ κρίσει
65 χηρῶν οὐ προσέχοντες.

   εἰ δὲ καὶ ἀνεξετάστως διακένῳ φιλοτιμίᾳ ἀναφέρειν τὰ ἁπλῶς
ἀκουόμενα νομιζόμεθα, καὶ τοσοῦτον ἢ ἑαυτοὺς ἠγνοήσαμεν ἢ τὸ ὕψος
τῆς βασιλείας ἢ τὴν ἀλήθειαν καὶ τὸ δίκαιον, ὃ ὀφείλεται καὶ τοῖς ὑπηρε-
τοῦσι τῇ βασιλείᾳ, καὶ δι' ἃ καὶ ἀντιλαμβάνονται πρὸς Θεοῦ τὰ ἡμέτερα,
70 καὶ μὴ διὰ φόβον Θεοῦ καὶ ἀγάπην καὶ τὸ ἔμμισθον χρέος τῆς βασιλείας,
καὶ τὴν τῷ ὑπηκόῳ πρεπούσαν διεξαγωγὴν καὶ τὸ ἐμοὶ ὀφειλόμενον ἀναφέρω, στελλέσθω διὰ Θεὸν εὐσυνείδητος ἄνθρωπος καὶ ταύτης πιστός, καὶ
μὴ τὴν ἀλήθειαν διαστρέφειν διὰ λῆμμα προσεθισθεὶς ἢ καὶ πρόσωπα,
σὺν ἐμοὶ ἐξετάσων ἅπερ ἀνέφερον ἢ ἀναφέρω. καὶ εἰ μὴ ὀλίγα ἐκ τῶν πολ-
75 λῶν καὶ ἐξεχόμενα ἀληθείας καὶ ζήλου καὶ ἐκδικήσεως, ἀλλ' ὀρέξεως ἢ
καὶ τάχα ἀκαίρου φιλανθρωπίας καὶ συμπαθείας φανῶσι, μηδὲ ἐν τοῖς
κατὰ ἀλήθειαν εἰσακούωμαι.

   μὴ οὖν ἐῶμεν τὰ πρέποντα καὶ ὀφείλοντα, ὅτι σωφρόνων τὸ κρίνειν
διὰ Θεὸν ἀνθρώπους μᾶλλον παραλυπεῖν, ἢ δι' ἀνθρώπους
80 Θεόν, καὶ μὴ δεδιέναι τὴν μοχθηρίαν τινῶν ἀποβλέποντας εἰς Θεόν, ἀγαθὸν εἰδότας μὴ ἐπ' ἄνθρωπον πεποιθέναι, ἀλλ' ἐπὶ Κύρ-
ιον, καὶ ἀγαθὸν ἐλπίζειν ἐπὶ Θεόν, μὴ ἐπ' ἄρχοντας. κατὰ

---

52 cf. I Joh. 4:1 ‖ 63–65 cf. Is. 1:23 ‖ 79–80 cf. Eph. 4:30 ‖ 80–82 cf. Ps. 117 (118):8–9

---

48 τί] καὶ P ‖ 49 ἐκκεχυμένου VSP: ἐγκεχυμένου S² ‖ 50 ἀλάθετον P ‖ 57 ἢ om. P ‖
58 ἢ] ἢ S ‖ 64–65 κρίσιν χειρῶν P ‖ 66 διακόνῳ P ‖ 70 φόβου P ‖ 77 εἰσακούομαι
codd. ‖ 78 σωφρόνων V¹P: σωφρόνως VS

17

⟨of competence⟩ are entrusted with such an important defence position because they have paid out a sum of money ? If it is because they ⟨dare to⟩ say in front of your divine majesty what is involved in such affairs (?), and because they are always being praised by their supporters, it is scarcely strange that they refuse to gaze at the ineluctable Judge, since lies are always being burbled forth, especially by men who are clever at speaking as the result of education.

For these reasons, I ask you «not to believe every spirit», but to go forth more often and listen and watch, and to arrange as necessary even matters which are near at hand. For I do not recommend that we abolish the payment of taxes (may I not be so rash), since I support and desire the respect and the praiseworthy security and obedience which results therefrom; nor ⟨do I make recommendations⟩ out of love for this man and hatred for that one, or as a favor influenced by friendship or bribes, but, as the Creator knows, I make my report and am zealous and ardently pray, so that the glory of the empire which has been granted to Christians may be preserved permanently and everlastingly and transcendently, as a result of the deeds which we do to please and entreat God. And ⟨I also pray⟩ that the words with which God, through the great-voiced ⟨Isaiah⟩, rebuked Jerusalem not be applied to the holy senate: «Thy princes are rebellious, loving bribes, seeking after rewards; not pleading for orphans, and not heeding the cause of widows».

If I am thought to report incidents simply from hearsay, and without investigation, through a vain desire for honor, and have been so ignorant of myself or your majesty or the truth and righteousness which servants of the empire have an obligation ⟨to uphold⟩, and on account of which we are helped by God, and if I do not make my report on account of fear of God, and my love for your majesty and my duty to you as a paid servant, and because it is the course of action which is fitting for a subject, and on account of my obligation, then for the sake of God send an honest man, who is loyal to your majesty, and who is not accustomed to twist the truth for the sake of a bribe or favoritism, to examine with me what I have reported or am now reporting. And if ⟨these incidents⟩ are not only a few out of many, and if ⟨my reports⟩ are not the result of truth and zeal and vengeance, but appear rather to be the result of personal desires or perhaps untimely philanthropy and compassion, then I should not be heeded in matters in which I do speak the truth.

Therefore let us not neglect what is meet and due, since wise men have decided that it is better «to cause grief to men for the sake of God, than to cause grief to God for the sake of men», and ⟨that we should⟩ look toward God and not fear the wickedness of certain people, in the knowledge that «it is better to trust not in man, but in the Lord», and «it is better to hope in the

46

17, 18

τῶν θείως γὰρ ζώντων ῥάβδον ἄλλως ἁμαρτωλῶν Ἰησοῦς ὁ ἡμέτερος
οὐκ ἐᾷ, ἀλλ᾽ ὅταν μὴ εἰς αὐτὸν καὶ ἃ κελεύει ὁρῶμεν, φοβερὸν ἄλλο τι τοῦ
85 θείου φόβου ὑπολαμβάνοντες. ἐξευμαρίζει γὰρ ὡς Θεὸς καὶ τὰ δυσχερῆ,
καὶ «σωτηρία σου» ταῖς ψυχαῖς ἡμῶν «ἐγώ εἰμι» λέγει, καὶ ἔργοις ἀποπληροῖ. διατί γὰρ κατεστραμμένην ὁρῶμεν τὴν ἐκκλησίαν καὶ ἀνεχόμεθα;
διατί ἀδικία, μοιχεία, πορνεία καὶ ὅσα τοιαῦτα πραττόμενα εἰς τὸ φανερὸν
οὐκ ἔχει ἐκδίκησιν; εἰ γὰρ καὶ ἀρχῆθέν εἰσι τὰ κακά, ἀλλὰ λαθραίως
90 πως καὶ κρυφιωδῶς, ὑπὸ τῶν νόμων καὶ παιδευόμενα καὶ ἀναστελλόμενα
καὶ καταισχυνόμενα· ἡνίκα δὲ ῥαθυμίᾳ ἢ ἐμπαθείᾳ ἢ λήμμασιν ἢ προσώποις ἢ καὶ καταφρονήσει ἡ ἀκρίβεια καὶ τὸ δίκαιον ἀπεμποληθῇ παρὰ
τοῖς προέχουσιν, ἀδύνατον μὴ ἐπάγεσθαι παιδείαν τὴν ἐξ ὀργῆς. καὶ ἴδοι
τις ἂν τοῦτο ἀρχῆθεν καὶ μέχρι παντός, εἰ θέλει λίαν ὁρᾶν, θαυμάζων δι-
95 καίως καὶ μεγαλύνων τῆς προνοίας τὸ ἄφυκτον· ὅπερ ἐπισταμένη ἡ ἐκ Θεοῦ
βασιλεία σου, εἰς τοῦτο διαναστήτω θερμότερον, Θεὸν ἔχων τὸν συναντι-
ληψόμενον καὶ τὴν Θεομήτορα.

18. Πρὸς τὸν αὐτοκράτορα

Οἷς μὴ ἐνεπιστεύσατο βασιλείαν ἀνθρώποις ὁ μέγας Θεὸς παρά τινων ἀδικούμενοι, τὴν ἐκδίκησιν ἐν τῷ μέλλοντι ἀναρτῶντες παραμυθοῦνται·
[fol. 11ʳ] οἷς δὲ κεχάρισται βασιλεύς, καὶ ταῦτα καὶ βασιλεὺς πολλῶν βασι-
5 λέων ὑπέρτερος χάριτι τοῦ Χριστοῦ, μισοπόνηρος λίαν καὶ φιλοδίκαιος, εἰ
μὴ βλέπωσι τὴν ἀλήθειαν καὶ τὸ δίκαιον ἐκδικούμενα ὑπ᾽ αὐτοῦ, ἀποθνήσ-
κουσιν ἀπὸ θλίψεως. διὰ ταῦτα παρακαλῶ, διὰ τὸν Θεόν, διὰ τὸ καλὸν τοῦ
δικαίου, τὸν ἀναχαιτισμὸν τῶν κακῶν. εἰς τὴν δύναμιν ἀποβλέπων τοῦ
Θεοῦ καὶ τὸ δίκαιον, τὴν ἀδικίαν καταπολέμησον πανταχοῦ, ἐν δὲ τῇ
10 ἐκκλησίᾳ καὶ κατ᾽ ἐξαίρετον, ὡς ταύτης εἶναι υἱὸς δοξασθεὶς καὶ ἀξιωθεὶς
πρὸς Θεοῦ, ὃ παρὰ πάσας τὰς βασιλείας τῆς γῆς συγκρινόμενον, ὡς ἥλιος
τῶν χωμάτων ὑπερανέστηκε.

καὶ εἰ μὴ εἰς πλέον ἡ παίδευσις γένηται, κἂν τριῶν νομισμάτων ἕκαστος τῶν κακοπραγούντων ἐντὸς ἢ καὶ πλησίον οἰκῶν τῆς ἐκκλησίας ζη-
15 μιωθήτω, ἢ ἑαυτοῦ χάριν, ἢ τῆς τῶν παίδων παρανομίας· καὶ ἵνα ἐάσω
τοὺς ὁρῶντας τὰ ἀπρεπῆ καὶ δακρύοντας, καὶ ταῦτα ἐν τῇ Ἁγίᾳ Σοφίᾳ,
καὶ τοῦ πολλῶν βασιλέων ἐν εὐλαβείᾳ καὶ φόβῳ Θεοῦ ὑπερτέρου δεχο-
μένου ἐν ἀκοαῖς τὰ τολμώμενα, ἐξ ὧν τινα ἐδηλώσαμεν. ἢ οὖν παιδευέσθω

83 cf. Ps. 124 (125):3

84 ἀλλ᾽ ὅτι P ‖ 88 πράττομεν P ‖ 94 θαυμάζω P ‖ 95 ἄφυτον P
18: V 10ᵛ–11ʳ. S 137ᵛ–138ʳ. P 19ʳ–19ᵛ
1 ante πρὸς add. γράμμα VʳSP ‖ post αὐτοκράτορα add. περὶ τοῦ ἵνα ἀναχαιτίζονται (ἀνα-
χετίζονται P) οἱ κακοπραγοῦντες, καὶ μὴ ἀναρτᾶν εἰς τὸ μέλλον, καὶ μᾶλλον ἐν κύκλῳ τῆς
Ἁγίας Σοφίας VʳSP ‖ 11 ἥλιος] ἢ et lacuna P

17, 18

Lord, not in princes». For our Jesus does not allow the «rod of sinners» ⟨to smite⟩ those who live piously, but ⟨it descends⟩ when we pay no attention to Him and His commandments, in the assumption that there is something more fearful than fear of God. For, as God, He smoothes over difficulties, and says to our souls, «I am your salvation», and carries out ⟨His promise⟩ with deeds. Why do we endure to see the Church destroyed ? Why are injustice, adultery, fornication, and other such deeds which are committed openly, not avenged ? Although evil has existed from the beginning of time, it has been kept in secret and darkness, since it is punished and restrained and dishonored by the laws; but when strict discipline and righteousness are sold out by the leading citizens on account of laziness or passion or bribes, or favoritism or scorn, it is inevitable that they will bring upon themselves the punishment of ⟨divine⟩ wrath. And one may see this from the beginning and for all eternity, if he really wishes to, rightly marvelling at and magnifying ineluctable Providence. Since your divine majesty knows this, rise more ardently to this task, with the help of God and the Mother of God.

18. To the emperor

When men to whom the great God has not given an emperor are wronged by certain people, they are consoled by the expectation that they will be avenged in the world to come; but when, through the grace of Christ, men have been granted an emperor (and indeed an emperor superior to many emperors, who is a great enemy of wickedness and lover of righteousness), they perish of sorrow if they do not see him defending truth and righteousness. Therefore, for the sake of God, for the good of righteousness, I ask that wicked people be restrained. Keeping in view the power and righteousness of God, fight injustice everywhere, especially in the Church, since you are glorified by God and deemed worthy to be Her Son and when this ⟨distinction ?⟩ is compared with all the empires of the earth, it towers above them as the sun above the dust of the earth.

And if the fine is not going to be increased, let each of the evildoers who lives either in or near the church be penalized at least 3 *nomismata*, either on his own account, or on account of the transgressions of his children; and I won't mention those who weep to see unseemly things, especially in St. Sophia, since you, who are superior to many kings in your piety and fear of God, hear of these daring deeds, some of which I have recounted. Therefore, either

ἡ ἀταξία, καὶ μὴ ἐν τῷ μέλλοντι ἀναρτῶμεν αὐτήν, ἢ εἰ ἀνεκδίκητα μένειν
20 κεκρίκατε δέον, γνωρισθήτω τοῦτο ἡμῖν, ἵνα μὴ ἐνοχλῶμεν τὴν ἐκ Θεοῦ
βασιλείαν σου. εἰ γὰρ ἀναφέροντες οὐκ εἰσακουόμεθα, ἵνα τί καὶ εἰς μάτην ὀχλώμεθα καὶ ἡμεῖς καὶ ὄχλησιν προξενῶμεν, ὡς τὰ μέλλοντα ἐκδι-
κεῖσθαι τῇ βασιλείᾳ σου ἀναφέροντες; ζητῶ δὲ καὶ τοῦτο ἵνα οὓς τάξει ἡ
βασιλεία σου ἐντὸς τῆς πόλεως ἐνεργεῖν τι, ἐνώπιον πολλῶν παραγγέλλῃς
25 ἑνὶ ἑκάστῳ αὐτῶν ὅτι «πρόσεχε πῶς μέλλεις ἐνεργεῖν, ὅτι ὁ πατριάρχης
μέλλει ἐρευνᾶν, μήπως ἀδίκως ἐνεργῇς, καὶ οὐχ ὡς ὁρίζεσαι ὑπ' ἐμοῦ».
λογίζομαι γὰρ ὅτι καὶ ὁ λόγος ἵνα συστέλλῃ αὐτὸν καὶ ἵνα ποιῇ αὐτὸν συντηρεῖσθαι.

19. ⟨Πρὸς τὸν αὐτοκράτορα⟩

Εἰ καὶ μὴ τῶν ἑπτὰ διακόνων ἐγώ, μηδὲ Κανδάκῃ συναναβάς, μηδὲ
συγκαθεσθεὶς ἐν τῷ ἅρματι, ἢ τὰ τοῦ μεγαλοφωνοτάτου μυσταγωγῆσαι
αὐτῷ, ἀλλά γε Φίλιππός εἰμι καὶ αὐτὸς ἐπίκλην Συρόπουλος, ὃς καὶ τοῦ
5 ῥήτορος νουνεχῶς τῆς ἐκκλησίας ἐνωτισθεὶς θεσπίζοντος τὰ σωτήρια
καὶ Ἰουδαίοις καὶ Ἕλλησι καὶ μάλα τῇ ἐκκλησίᾳ Χριστοῦ, ματαίας προφάσεις ἀποσεισάμενος, σωφρονῶ καὶ βοῶ· «τὸν ἅπαν δόγμα καὶ φρόνημα
μὴ φρονοῦν ὡς φρονεῖ καὶ δοξάζει ἡ ἁγία καὶ καθολικὴ καὶ ἀποστολικὴ
ἐκκλησία φρονοῦντα, καθυποβάλλω τῷ ἀναθέματι. καὶ πᾶσαν ἐρεσχελίαν
10 καὶ ἀπιστίαν τῶν Ξυλωτῶν, κατά τε τῆς ἐκκλησίας, κατά τε τῆς βασιλείας, φιλίαν τε [fol. 11ᵛ] καὶ συνοίκησιν φανερὰν καὶ κρυπτὴν Ἰγνατίου τοῦ
ῥακενδύτου, πᾶσί τε ἄλλοις ὁμοίοις, οἷς ἀμάρτυρος ἡ εὐσέβεια καὶ ἡ
ὀφειλομένη εὐλάβεια ὀρθοδόξοις καὶ μοναχοῖς, ἐκ ψυχῆς ἀποβάλλομαι.»

20. ⟨Πρός τινα ἀποστείλαντα βιβλίον⟩

Τὴν σταλεῖσαν βίβλον ἡμῖν ἀναπτύξαντες, τρυφὴν ἐγνώκαμεν οὖσαν
ψυχῆς οὐ ῥέουσαν, ἀλλὰ μένουσαν, καὶ μακαρίους ποιοῦσαν τοὺς ἀπλήστως
κατατρυφῶντας ἐν αὐτῇ. ὅθεν κἀμὲ καὶ τοὺς κατ' ἐμοῦ ἐρευνήσας, καὶ μὴ

19: 2–3 cf. Acta Ap. 8:27–28

---

19 ἀναρτῶμεν VSP¹: ἀναρτήσωμεν P ‖ 20 κεκρίκαμεν codd.
19: V 11ʳ–11ᵛ. S 138ʳ–138ᵛ. P 19ᵛ–20ʳ.
1 γράμμα πρὸς τὸν αὐτοκράτορα περὶ τοῦ ὀρθοῦ δόγματος add. VʳSP ‖ 4 εἰμι] εἰ μὴ P ‖
8 post ἁγία add. τοῦ Θεοῦ ἐκκλησία S ‖ 9 αἱρεσχελίαν codd.
20: V 11ᵛ. S 138ᵛ–139ʳ. P 20ʳ–20ᵛ.
1 γράμμα πρὸς τὸν ἀποστείλαντα βιβλίον χάριν κανισκίου καὶ στρέψαντα ταύτην ἐξοπίσω
add. VʳSP

19: Schol. ad 4, Φίλιππος ... Συρόπουλος: Hic scriptor hoc loco ait se vocari
Philippum cognomento Syropulum, scr. manus posterior in marg. P

18–20

let the transgression be punished, and let us not put it off to the future, or if you have decided that it is necessary for these actions to remain unpunished, let me know, so that I won't trouble your divine majesty any further. For if I am not heeded when I make my reports, why should I trouble myself to no purpose and cause annoyance by reporting to your majesty matters whose vengeance is always being postponed ? And this I ask too, that your majesty, in the presence of many ⟨witnesses⟩, instruct each one of the men whom you assign to collect taxes within the city: «Be careful how you go about collecting taxes, for the patriarch is going to make an investigation, lest you collect unjustly, and not as you are bidden by me». For I think that these words alone will restrain him and make him cautious.

19. ⟨To the emperor⟩

Even though I am not one of the seven deacons, nor did I mount or sit in the chariot together with Kandake, nor did I initiate him into mysteries of the great-voiced ⟨Isaiah⟩, still I am Philip, by surname Syropoulos. I listen with understanding to the orator of the Church who prophesies to Jews and to Greeks, and especially to the Church of Christ, and shaking off vain excuses, I soberly proclaim: «I subject to anathema anyone who believes any dogma or opinion which is not believed and approved by the Holy Catholic and Apostolic Church. Also I reject from my soul all the nonsensical and treacherous words of the Xylotes which are directed against the Church and the Empire, and I reject friendship and fellowship, whether manifest or secret, with the monk Ignatius, and with all other people of this kind, in whom there is no evidence of any piety or of the reverence owed by Orthodox Christians and monks».

20. ⟨To a man who sent a book⟩

When I opened the book which you sent me, I realized that it is not a transitory but an abiding delight to the soul, and it cheers those who find unending pleasure in it. Therefore, after questioning myself and my associ-

5 τοιαύτης ἐφιεμένους τρυφῆς εὑρηκώς, ἐταλάνισα μὲν ἐμαυτὸν καὶ τοὺς
σὺν ἐμοί, ἐξαπέστειλα δὲ καὶ τὴν δέλτον ὅθεν ἐπέμφθη μοι, λογισάμενος
ἀπρεπὲς τοιαύτην τρυφὴν κατασχεῖν, οὐκ ἀνενέργητον κεῖσθαι μόνον ἐν
τῇ θυρίδι, ἀλλὰ μικροῦ καὶ ὑπὸ τὸν μόδιον, καὶ πρὸς τῇ ἄλλῃ κακίᾳ
ἐκ στόματος ἀφαρπάσαι τῶν πεινώντων αὐτήν, καὶ διψώντων κατατρυφᾶν·
10 ὃ κακῶν ἐστι δούλων, καὶ τὸ τάλαντον τοῦ κυρίου κατακρυπτόντων
ἐπισφαλῶς. εὐχῶν οὖν δεομένῳ μοι, τιμιώτατε, εἰς ἕξιν ἐπιθυμίας φθάσαι
τοιαύτης ὡς δυνατὸν μὴ ἀποστερήσῃς μοι, ὡς ἂν ὁ διδοὺς τῷ εὐχομένῳ εὐχὴν ἀμφοτέροις παρέξοι σοῦ ταῖς τιμίαις εὐχαῖς.

21. Πρὸς τὸν αὐτοκράτορα

Τὸ συμβὰν τοῖς εὐγενεστάτοις, ἐπηρείᾳ ἐχθροῦ, τοῦ νομίμου χάριν
συνοικεσίου τούτων ἐπίμωμον, ἀμφοτέρων ζητούντων ἐν τούτῳ παρὰ τῆς
ἐκκλησίας διευλύτωσιν ἔννομον, καὶ μηδὲ τῶν ἀρχιερέων πρὸς συμφωνίαν
5 ὁρώντων, τάς τε συστάσεις ἐμοῦ τῶν μαρτύρων, ἐξ ὧν καὶ ἄμφω ἐδράζον-
ται, οὐκ ἀνισχύρους μόνον, ἀλλὰ καὶ διασεσεισμένας πάντῃ κατανοοῦντος.
ἐν πράγμασιν ἀμφισβητουμένοις δι' ἀπουσίαν γραμμάτων ἢ μαρτύρων
ἐχόντων τὸ βέβαιον, προχωρεῖν ἐπιστάμεθα ὃν κρίνουσιν ἱκανὸν οἱ τοῦ
δημοσίου ἐξόμνυσθαι, ἐν δέ γε τῇ ἐκκλησίᾳ τὸ φρίκης μεστὸν ἐπιτίμιον,
10 καὶ τοῖς ἔχουσι νοῦν ἀνυπόστατον, εἰ μὴ τῶν πάνυ ἀσυνειδήτων τις λογισ-
θῇ, λαμβάνειν τοῦτο εἰς κεφαλήν, εἰ δεήσει, διδόασιν· ὃ καὶ εἰς ἀκοὰς τῶν
ῥηθέντων εὐγενεστάτων πεσόν, ἐβασανίσθη καὶ ὑπεδέχθη, ὅπερ ἐμοὶ καὶ
θανάτου σωματικοῦ ἀσυγκρίτως βαρύτερον καταφαίνεται, μὴ τί γε χάριν
ζημίας ἢ κέρδους βιωτικοῦ, ὧν φύσις ἐστὶν ὑπορρεῖν ταχέως καὶ διαφθείρ-
15 εσθαι.
ὅθεν δίδωμι γνώμην βαράθρου τοιούτου λυτρώσασθαι ἀμφοτέρους
τὴν ἐκ Θεοῦ βασιλείαν σου, κελεύσασαν ἀποδοθῆναι πάντα τὰ μητρῷα
ἀνελλιπῆ, καὶ τὴν παῖδα τῇ οἰκείᾳ μητρί, καὶ τῷ ἀνδρὶ τὰ οἰκεῖα, καὶ ἀζημίως γενέσθαι τὴν τούτων διάζευξιν, καὶ μὴ τούτων τινὰ ἐαθῆναι ὑποπε-
20 σεῖν καταδίκῃ φρικτῇ, κρινούσης γὰρ ἀληθείας ἐκ τῶν μαρτύρων αὐτῶν
οὐκ ἔστι τις ἀξιόπιστος· εἰ δ' (ὅπερ ἀπεύχομαι) τις ἐκ τῶν ἀμφοτέρων, καὶ
μάλιστα ὁ ἐνάγων, ἕρμαιον κρίνει τοῦ ἀζημίου τὸ ἐπιτίμιον, καὶ τοῦτο ἢ
ἐλθέτω λαβεῖν [fol. 12ʳ] εἰ δοκεῖ, ἢ ἐγγράφως ἐκπέμψομεν.

20: 8 Marc. 4:21 ‖ 10 cf. Matt. 25:25 ‖ 12–13 I Reg. 2:9

8 ὑπὸ scripsi, cf. Marc. 4:21 : ἐπὶ codd. ‖ 12 δυνατοὶ P
21: V 11ᵛ–12ʳ. S 139ʳ–139ᵛ. P 20ᵛ–21ʳ. Ed. Gennadios, Ὀρθοδοξία, 27 (1952),
197–198.
1 ante πρὸς add. γράμμα VʳSP ‖ post αὐτοκράτορα add. διὰ τοῦ νομίμου τάχα συνοικεσίου,
ὄντως ἐπίμωμον, ζητούντων εὐλύτωσιν ἔννομον VʳSP

20, 21

ates, and not finding any of us desirous of such a pleasure, I deemed them and myself unhappy and returned the book to whence it came, thinking it unfair to keep such an object of delight, when it would not only lie unused in my window, but, so to speak, «under the bushel», and in addition to this injustice, to snatch it from the mouth of those who hunger for it, and thirst to delight in it (just like wicked servants «who hide the talent» of their master, to their own harm). Therefore, O best of men, to the best of your ability do not deprive me, who am in need of prayers, of attaining such a desire, so that «He Who grants his prayer to the suppliant» may provide us both with it, through your worthy prayers.

21. To the emperor

What has occurred to the noble couple, through the devices of the devil, with regard to their lawful marriage is reprehensible, since they both seek from the church a legal dissolution of their marriage, and the bishops do not arrive at any agreement, and I perceive that the testimony of witnesses, on which they both rest their cases, is not only invalid, but totally confused. In cases which are disputed because of the lack of documents or witnesses with certain proof, I understand that the case is won by the man whom civil magistrates judge competent to swear an oath, and in the ecclesiastical ⟨tribunal⟩, if necessary, they make a man swear under threat of that horrendous penalty which is intolerable to men of understanding (unless one is completely devoid of conscience). When these ⟨rules⟩ came to the attention of the abovementioned most noble couple, they were carefully examined and accepted, which seems to me incomparably more grievous than bodily death, especially if ⟨their decision⟩ is only for the sake of damages or material gain, whose nature it is quickly to fade away and disappear.

Wherefore I give my opinion that your divine majesty should save them both from such ruin, by ordering that all the mother's property be returned to her in its entirety, and that the child be given into the custody of her mother, and the husband's property should be returned to him, and their divorce should be effected without either party having to pay damages, and that neither of them should be allowed to fall subject to the terrible sentence, since, if truth were to judge, not one of their witnesses is trustworthy. But if, and I pray this may not happen, one of the two, especially the plaintiff, considers the censure of an innocent person a windfall (?), either let him come to get it, if he wishes, or I will send it in writing.

22. Πρὸς τὸν αὐτοκράτορα

Πολλάκις ἀναφέρω τῇ ἐκ Θεοῦ βασιλείᾳ σου πρᾶγμα ἀποβλέπον εἰς
σωτηρίαν ψυχῆς, ἀνέξοδον, μηδενὸς ἄλλου δεόμενον εἰ μὴ μόνης κελεύσεως.
καὶ διὰ τὰς ἐμάς, ὡς ἔοικεν, ἁμαρτίας παρατρέχει ὁ καιρὸς καὶ καταλιμ-
5 πάνεται ἀθεράπευτον. διὰ τοῦτο, παρακαλῶ, κἂν τὰ μὴ σκέψεως δεόμενα
ἢ ἐξόδου ἃς γίνωνται. εὑρίσκονται δὲ καὶ ἐντὸς τῆς πόλεως αἰχμάλωτος
λαὸς πολύς, καὶ ἔνι δέον νὰ συναντιλήψωνται οἱ δυνάμενοι, ἕκαστος καθὼς
προαιρεῖται. ζητῶ δὲ βουλὴν περὶ τῶν ἀρχόντων, ὡς ἄν, ἐὰν φανῇ καλόν,
πέμπω εἰς ἕνα ἕκαστον τῶν τοιούτων ἀρχόντων ἀναφορὰν χάριν τούτου,
10 ἢ ἐπειδὴ ἔγραψα κοινῶς γράμμα, ἵνα ἀναγνωσθῇ ἐν τῷ παλατίῳ συνηγ-
μένων πάντων, καὶ ὅσον καὶ οἷον προαιρεθῇ ἕκαστος. δύο γὰρ ζητῶ, ἢ ἵνα
προσλάβηται ἕκαστος κατὰ δύναμιν ὅσους προαιρεῖται μέχρι θέρους, ἢ
δώσῃ ὅσον προαιρεῖται.

23. ⟨Πρὸς τοὺς ἀρχιερεῖς⟩

Ἐπεὶ ἕκαστον τῶν ἱερωτάτων ἀρχιερέων πρὸς τὴν λαχοῦσαν πρό-
κειται ἀπελθεῖν, εἰσὶ δέ τινα κοινῆς δεόμενα ἱκεσίας πρὸς τὸν κρατοῦντα,
οἷον τὰ τῶν Λατίνων καὶ ὅπως ἀδεῶς διδάσκειν τούτους ἀκούομεν, καὶ
5 καταβλάπτειν τῶν ἀστηρίκτων πολλούς, οὐ δέον ἡμᾶς ἀθεράπευτον
τοῦτο καταλιπόντας ἀναχωρεῖν. καὶ δὴ καὶ περὶ τῶν Ἰουδαίων καὶ Ἀρμενίων, ὅπως ἐξέλθωσι, καὶ ὅσα τοιαῦτα ἔργα θεοφιλῆ ἱκεσίας κοινῆς δεόμενα, πρὸς δὲ καὶ διὰ τὴν κατεπείγουσαν ὥραν τοῦ θέρους. διὰ ταῦτα κελεύ-
σατε μετὰ τὸ γεύσασθαι ἡμᾶς τῇ Κυριακῇ συναχθῆναι καὶ ὁμοῦ ἀπελ-
10 θεῖν πρὸς τὸν αὐτοκράτορα. οὐ γὰρ οἶμαι τοῦτον παρόψεσθαι τὸ λυσιτελὲς
τῆς αἰτήσεως. μὴ οὖν διὰ τὸν Κύριον δι᾽ ὄκνον ἀπολειφθῇ τις. εἰ οὖν
κρίνετε δέον, συνέλθωμεν ἐν τῇ Χώρᾳ κἀκεῖθεν ὁμοῦ τοῖς βασιλεῦσιν
ἐντύχωμεν.

22: V 12ʳ. S 139ᵛ. P 21ᵛ. P hanc epistolam post epistolam XXIII scripsit. Ed.
Laiou, *Andronicus II*, 336, no. 5.
1 post αὐτοκράτορα add. γράμμα περὶ ἐλεημοσύνης ζητῶν βουλὴν περὶ τῶν αἰχμαλώτων
VʳSP ‖ 6 ἃς P ‖ 7 συναντιλήψονται VS ‖ 9 εἰς VˢᵛSP ‖ 13 δώσει codd.

23: V 12ʳ. S 139ᵛ–140ʳ. P 21ʳ–21ᵛ. P hanc epistolam ante epistolam XXII
scripsit. Ed. Banduri, *Imperium Orientale*, II, 615; Migne, PG, CXLII, 513–514.
1 γράμμα περὶ τοῦ συναχθῆναι τοὺς ἀρχιερεῖς ἐν τῇ Χώρᾳ, ὅπως κοινῶς ἀπελθεῖν πρὸς τὸν
αὐτοκράτορα χάριν ὠφελείας κοινῆς add. VʳSP ‖ 6 καταλιπόντος P ‖ 7 κοινῆς VS¹P :
τινῆς S ‖ 12 κρίνατε codd.

22. To the emperor

Often I petition your divine majesty about matters involving no expenditure of money, with a view to salvation of the soul and requiring nothing other than your command alone. But on account of my sins, as it appears, time passes and these problems are still ignored. Wherefore I beg of you, let some action be taken on those matters which require no consideration or expense. For example, there is within the city a great number of refugees, and those who have the means should help them, each in the way he prefers. Therefore I request a decree concerning the officials, that, if you agree, I will send to each one of these officials a report on this situation, or, since I have written an open letter, let it be read in the palace in the presence of all ⟨the officials⟩, and let each choose the amount and type ⟨of help⟩ he wishes ⟨to give⟩. For I seek two things, either that each assume the support of as many ⟨refugees⟩ as he can until summer, or that he give as much ⟨money⟩ as he wishes.

23. ⟨To the bishops⟩

Since each of the most holy bishops must soon go to his assigned see, and since there are certain matters which require a joint supplication to the ruler, such as the question of the Latins and the rumor that they are teaching with impunity, and are corrupting many of wavering ⟨faith⟩, we should not go away without attending to this. There is also the issue of the Jews and Armenians, that they should leave ⟨the capital⟩, and other such God-pleasing acts which require a joint supplication, and ⟨the factor of⟩ the oppressive summer weather. Wherefore, if you please after our meal on Sunday let us assemble and go together to the emperor. For I do not think that he will fail to see the advantage of the proposal. Therefore, for the sake of the Lord, let no one be absent through hesitancy. If then you judge it fitting, let us assemble at Chora, and from there go together to meet with the emperors.

24. Πρὸς τὸν αὐτοκράτορα

Οἷος ἡμᾶς ἐκ πολλοῦ ζῆλος οὐ μόνον κατέφαγεν, ἀλλὰ καθ' ἑκάστην, εἰπεῖν, κατεσθίει! κατανοούντων τὴν αὐθάδειαν τῶν πολλῶν, τῶν
πόρρω καὶ τῶν ἐγγύς, ὡς μὴ ἀποδιδόντων Θεῷ καὶ τῇ ἐκ Θεοῦ βασιλείᾳ
5 σου πρεπωδεστάτην τὴν ὀφειλὴν καὶ πόθον καὶ συνδρομὴν (τῇ ταλαιπώρῳ
ψυχῇ μου δώῃ Θεός). τεθαύμακα δὲ πῶς ὅλως περὶ τοιούτων οὐ στόμα
πρὸς στόμα ἀκήκοα παρ' αὐτῆς, ἀλλὰ διὰ μηνυτῶν. εἰ γὰρ καὶ πιστοὶ
καὶ εὐθεῖς καὶ φιλοῦντές εἰσιν οἱ πεμφθέντες, ἀλλ' ὅλως οὐ καταδέχομαι
περὶ τοιούτων αὐτοὺς ἐμπιστεύεσθαι, εἴ πως μὴ δόξῃ καὶ τούτοις διαφω-
10 νίαν εἶναί τινα μέσον ἐμοῦ καὶ τῆς ἐκ Θεοῦ βασιλείας σου. εἰδότος ἐμοῦ τὸ
ταύτης φιλόθεον καὶ ὀρθόδοξον (ἐν τούτοις γὰρ ὁ μὴ ἀνταγωνιζόμενος
ἐπιζήμιος), τούτων δὲ σῳζομένων, οὔ μοι δοκεῖ συνᾴδειν τινὰ καὶ συλλυ-
πεῖσθαι καὶ συναλγεῖν, εὐφραινομένῳ τε καὶ συνευφραίνεσθαι, καὶ ὑψου-
μένῳ συνανυψοῦσθαι, καὶ συγκαταφρονεῖσθαι καταφρονουμένῳ, ἐλο-
15 γίσθην ἄν, [fol. 12ᵛ] ὡς ἐμέ.

διὰ τοῦτο, παρακαλῶ, ἡνίκα τι τῶν τοιούτων εἰς τὰς αὐτῆς ἀκοὰς
ἀκουσθῇ, μὴ διὰ μηνυτοῦ (οὐ γάρ, ὡς ἔφην, ἀνέχομαι), ἀλλὰ στόμα πρὸς
στόμα δηλοῦσθαί μοι, ὅτι πολλοὶ κελαδεῖν διψῶσι τοιαῦτα καὶ πολυτρόπως. ἀλλ' ὁ τῆς ἀληθείας Θεὸς αὐτῇ τὰ ἡμέτερα παραστήσει σαφέστατα·
20 οὔ ποτε γὰρ τῆς βασιλείου δόξης τε καὶ τιμῆς προετίμησά τι, εἰ μὴ
ἐξέστην ἴσως τῶν οἰκείων φρενῶν.

καὶ ταῦτα μὲν οὕτως. πλὴν ἀναφέρω τῇ ἐκ Θεοῦ βασιλείᾳ σου, ὡς
⟨οὐ⟩ δυνατὸν ἐπὶ πλέον τὴν τῶν ἀρχιερέων ἐνταῦθα διατριβὴν ὑποφέρειν
με· οὔτε γὰρ ἔννομον, οὔτε εἰρήνην τῇ βασιλείᾳ, οὔτε τῇ ἐκκλησίᾳ
25 ποιοῦν, οὔτε πάλιν ἀνεύθυνον. καὶ πρὸ τοῦ ἀνακύψαι τὴν μάχην ὑπὲρ τοιούτων (οὐδὲ γὰρ τῆς μάχης ἐγώ), παρακαλῶ τὸ πρέπον γενέσθαι, ἵνα, τῆς
πρὸς ἀλλήλους μάχης ὄντες ἐκτός, τῷ Θεῷ τῆς ἀγάπης ἵλεων βλέπειν τῇ
τούτου ποίμνῃ ἐπιμελώμεθα.

24: 6—7 II Joh. 12 ‖ 17—18 II Joh. 12

24: V 12ʳ—12ᵛ. S 140ʳ—140ᵛ. P 21ᵛ—22ᵛ.
1 ante πρὸς add. γράμμα VʳSP ‖ post αὐτοκράτορα add. περί τινων ὑποθέσεων μὴ διὰ μηνυτῶν στέλλεσθαι, ἀλλὰ στόμα πρὸς στόμα VʳSP ‖ 5 πρεπωδεστάτη P ‖ 7 αὐτῆς V¹SP :
αὐτοῖς V ‖ 8 εὐθεῖς VS¹P : εὐθὺς S ‖ 12 οὔ μοι] οἴμοι P ‖ 14 συγκαταφρονεῖσθαι]
οὐ καταφρονεῖσθαι SP ‖ 23 οὐ addidi; cf. Ep. 28, 8—9: οὐδὲ ἐγὼ δύναμαι ὑποφέρειν τὴν
τούτων ἐνταῦθα διατριβήν ‖ 24 post βασιλείᾳ add. σου S, delevit S¹

24

24. To the emperor

How great is the zeal which not only has consumed me for a long time, but is daily consuming me, so to speak! For I perceive the rashness of the many, both near and far away, who do not render to God and to your divine majesty the fitting obligation and love and cooperation (may God grant to my wretched soul ⟨that I render these obligations⟩). And I marvel that I always hear from you about such matters, not «face to face», but through messengers. Even if the men you send are trustworthy and honest and friendly, still I do not like to trust them with such matters, lest there seem to them to be any disagreement between myself and your divine majesty. Since I know your love of God and right belief (for one who does not strive zealously in these affairs is blameworthy), as long as you maintain these virtues (?), it does not seem to me that there is anyone who sympathizes ⟨with you⟩ and shares your grief and sorrow, and shares your joy when you are joyful, and your exaltation when you are exalted, and your contumely when you are scorned, as I do (I would think).

For this reason I beg of you, whenever any such matter comes to your attention, not to tell me about it through a messenger (for as I have said I cannot endure it), but «face to face», because many people are anxious to proclaim such matters in various ways. But the God of truth will represent my situation to you most clearly; for I would never set anything before the imperial glory and honor, unless perhaps I went out of my mind.

So much for that. And I petition your divine majesty, because it is ⟨not⟩ possible for me to endure any longer the presence of the bishops here in the capital; for neither is it lawful, nor does it afford any peace to the empire or the church, nor again is it free from censure. And before strife breaks out over such matters (for I am not one to fight), I entreat that proper steps be taken, so that we may avoid internecine strife, and thus ensure that the God of Love look upon His flock with mercy.

25. Πρὸς τὸν αὐτοκράτορα

Πολλάκις ἀνέφερον τῇ ἐκ Θεοῦ βασιλείᾳ σου ὅτι ἐὰν μὴ ἕκαστος
τῶν ἀρχιερέων ἀποκαταστῇ τῇ λαχούσῃ αὐτῷ, τῇ ἐκκλησίᾳ τάραχος οὐκ
ἐκλείψει, οὐδὲ δημεγερσίαι, ὡς ἀπὸ βίας ἠβουλόμην βιάσαι ἵνα ἔχωσι τὴν
5 φροντίδα τῶν κρίσεων· οὐδεὶς γὰρ τῶν δυναστῶν μὴ πρότερον μεταχειρισ-
άμενος τούτους εἰς κρίσιν ἔρχεται. νῦν δὲ ὡς ἐγνώρισαν ὅτι τὰ ἱερὰ βουλόμεθα ἐξωνήσασθαι, καὶ ταῦτα βλεπόντων καὶ αἰχμαλώτους τὸ καθ᾽ ἡμέραν συρομένους, εἰς τὸ πωλεῖσθαι ἀντέστησαν, «διὰ τί μὴ ἡμῖν», λέγοντες,
«διδῶνται τοὺς κακοπαθοῦντας;» ἀλλ᾽ οὐδὲ ψήφους ποιῆσαι ἠθέλησαν σή-
10 μερον· «ἡμῖν μᾶλλον ἀνήκειν τὰς ἐκκλησίας· ὡς καὶ ὁ Κύριος ἔφη, μὴ
εἶναι καλὸν λαβεῖν τὸν ἄρτον τῶν τέκνων, καὶ βαλεῖν τοῖς
κυναρίοις·» οὕτως γὰρ τοῦτο αὐτοὶ ἑρμηνεύουσι. καὶ τί εἴπω; οὕτως
ἠθελήσαμεν τούτους ἡμεῖς; τί γὰρ γεγόνασιν ἃ συνῆξαν; ἀκούω γὰρ ὡς
ὁ Βιτζύνης εἰς ὀκτακόσια ἐξεδίδου κατ᾽ ἔτος τὰ τῆς ἐκκλησίας. τί δὲ ὁ Σάρ-
15 δεων; οὐχὶ ἀμπελῶνα ἔχει ἐνταῦθα καὶ ζευγηλατεῖον καὶ κῆπον καὶ ἐργαστήρια, πρὸς τούτοις καὶ ἀδελφᾶτα; τί δὲ ἡ ἐνέργεια τούτων ἐνταῦθα, ὅτι
κατέλιπον τὰς ἐκκλησίας αὐτῶν; οὐχὶ εἰς τὸ συνόδους ποιεῖν κατὰ τοῦ πα-
τριαρχεύοντος καὶ καλέσματα μετ᾽ ἀλλήλων καθὰ καὶ τὴν σήμερον; ἢ οὖν
κέλευσον ἕκαστον πορευθῆναι πρὸς τὴν λαχοῦσαν, ἢ οὐδέποτε παύσονται
20 στασιάζειν καὶ κατὰ τῆς ἐκκλησίας καὶ κατὰ τῆς βασιλείας. μὴ γὰρ ὁ
Φιλαδελφείας ἢ ὁ Νυμφαίου, οὐ δύνανται οἰκονομίαν ζητεῖν καὶ αὐτοί; εἰ
γὰρ διότι τὴν ἐκκλησίαν οὗτοι ἐτάραξαν καὶ ταράσσουσι, μισθοὶ αὐτοῖς
ἐποφείλονται, τοῦτο δύνανται ποιεῖν καὶ οἱ ἕτεροι, καὶ μάλιστα σήμερον.
εἰ δὲ θέλομεν τούτους τελεῖν, ἀπέμεινεν εἰς τὴν βασιλείαν σου· ἐγὼ γὰρ
25 οὐδέποτε τοῦτο ποιήσω.

26. ⟨Πρὸς τὸν μέγαν διοικητήν⟩ [fol. 13ʳ]

Γεγράφηκας τοῖς ἀρχιερεῦσι Θεοῦ, ὁ μέγας διοικητής, ὡς ὅτι τὰς
ἀπολογίας τὰς σὰς αὐτοὶ παραλογιζόμενοι, ἀποδοῦναι μόνον ἅπερ ἀφήρπα-
σας ἀναγκάζουσι. καὶ οὐ μέγα λέγειν τοιαῦτα τοὺς κατὰ σέ· τῆς γὰρ σῆς

25: 10–12 Matt. 15:26

25: V 12ᵛ. S 140ᵛ–141ᵛ. P 22ᵛ–23ʳ. Ed. Gennadios, Ἱστορία τοῦ Οἰκουμενικοῦ
Πατριαρχείου, I, 380–381; Tomadakes, Βυζαντινὴ Γραμματολογία, 124–125 et Σύλλαβος
Βυζαντινῶν Μελετῶν καὶ Κειμένων, 485–486.
1 ante πρὸς add. γράμμα VʳSP ‖ post αὐτοκράτορα add. περὶ τῶν ἀρχιερέων τῇ λαχούσῃ
ἀποκαταστῇ ἕκαστος VʳSP ‖ 18 καλλίσματα P ‖ 19 λαχοῦσαν] χαλοῦσαν P
26: V 12ᵛ–13ʳ. S 141ᵛ–142ʳ. P 23ʳ–23ᵛ.
1 γράμμα πρὸς τὸν μέγαν διοικητήν, ἵνα τὰ ἀδικήσαντα ἀποδῷ add. VʳSP ‖ 3 ἅπερ Vˢᵛ

25. To the emperor

I have often mentioned to your divine majesty that if every bishop does not return to his assigned see, the Church will not cease to be troubled by confusion and rebellion, because I wanted to force them [the bishops] to have some concern for legal proceedings; for none of the nobles comes to trial without first negotiating with these ⟨bishops⟩. And now when they learned that I want to sell sacred property, even though every day they see refugees dragging about, they opposed the sale, saying, «Why don't they give the wretches to us?». But today they weren't even willing to vote on it! «The churches belong to us, ⟨they say⟩; as the Lord said, 'it is not meet to take children's bread, and to cast it to dogs'». For this is the way they interpret this passage. And what can I say? Is this the way I wanted them to be? For what has happened to the funds they have collected? I hear that the bishop of Bitzyne used to lend out church funds for 800 ⟨gold pieces⟩ annually. And what about the metropolitan of Sardis? Doesn't he have a vineyard here and a yoke of oxen, and a garden and workshops, and benefices in addition to this? And why is the activity of these men centered here, when they have abandoned their sees? Is it not to hold synods against the patriarch, and to exchange invitations with each other as today?

Therefore, either bid each one go to the see assigned to him or they will never cease to stir up revolt against both the church and the empire. Won't the metropolitans of Philadelphia and Nymphaeum also be able to seek an accommodation ⟨here⟩? If then salaries are due these men because they have disturbed and continue to disturb the Church, then the others can do the same, especially at this time. If then we are to pay these men, it would be up to your majesty; for I will never do this.

26. ⟨To the great dioecete⟩

You have written to the bishops of God, O great dioecete, that the bishops who force you to return only the ⟨money⟩ you took are twisting your defense. But it is not important that people like you say such things, for

5 καταστάσεως ἄξια. παραλογισθεὶς γὰρ ταῖς ἀληθείαις αὐτὸς εὑρισκόμενος, καὶ πλεονέκτης καὶ ἄδικος, καὶ τῶν θείων ἐχθρὸς προσταγμάτων,
τί θαυμαστὸν εἰ καὶ λόγοις ἐνδιαστρόφοις σοφίζῃ; εἰ δὲ θέλεις (ὥσπερ
ἀνέχονταί σου τῶν λοιδοριῶν!) ἐπιτιμίῳ καταδικάσουσι, καὶ τῶν εἰς ἀκοὰς
ἀνθρώπων τὰ περὶ τοῦ Μακρεμβολίτου, κυαμοφάγον αὐτὸν καὶ ὄψου ἐθάδα
10 ταριχευτοῦ, βεβαιώσαντα, καὶ τοῦτό σοι δώσουσιν. ὅτι δὲ φῂς ὡς σωτηρίας χάριν ἀνθρώπων ἐλεεινῶς τὰ ἐκείνου εἴληφας ἐξ ἐκείνου, ἀπληστότατε
ἅμα καὶ ἀδικώτατε, ἔχει πρὸς τοῦτο καὶ ὁ Ἰούδας καυχήσασθαι, ὡς ἐπὶ
καλῷ πεποιηκέναι τὴν προδοσίαν· τοῦτο μὲν ὡς ὅτι ἀπέβη κοσμοσωτήριος, τοῦτο δὲ ὡς ὅτι καὶ χάριν τῶν ξένων τοῦ κεραμέως εἰσεποιήσατο
15 τὸν ἀγρόν. εἴ τι οὖν ἐμοὶ πείθῃ, ταυτὶ κατάλιπε τὰ ψυχρά, καὶ τῷ ἠδικη-
μένῳ σῷον ἀπόδος τὸ ὄφλημα, τοῦτο εἰδὼς ὅτι οὐ μὴ ἐξέλθῃς ἐκεῖθεν, εἴ
τι καὶ γένηται, ἕως καὶ τὸ ἔσχατον λεπτὸν ἀποδῷς.

27. Πρὸς τὸν αὐτοκράτορα

Τὰ μοναστήρια ἡ ἐκ Θεοῦ βασιλεία σου ἐτάχθη φροντίζειν αὐτῶν,
καὶ αἱ δουλεῖαι τῆς βασιλείας σου καὶ αἱ ἔξοδοι, τοῦ κόσμου εἰσὶ δουλεῖαι.
διὰ τοῦτο ὅσον κελεύσει, ἢ ἐκ τῶν χρυσοβούλλων ἢ τὰ ἐκτὸς ἐκείνων, καὶ
5 περὶ τὰ ὑπὲρ κυβερνήσεως κοσμικῆς, οὐκ οἶμαί τινα τῶν φρονούντων ὀρθῶς ἀντιλέξαι. τοῦτο δὲ ἀναφέρω, ἵνα γένηται κατὰ κρίσιν γεωργικήν, ὡς εἰ
μέλλουσι κατέχειν τὴν περίσσειαν οἱ κατέχοντες πρίν, δέον διδόναι μορ-
τήν· εἰ δὲ ἀφαιρεῖσθαι μέλλουσι ταῦτα, οὐ δέον μορτάζεσθαι, ὅτι καὶ τὴν
μορτὴν οἱ μέλλοντες ἐνεργεῖν οὐκ οἶδα εἰ μὴ λυμαίνονται, καὶ γίνεται ἡ
10 ζημία διπλῆ· πρὸς τὸ τὴν βασιλείαν γὰρ ἀδικεῖν, τάττονται καὶ αὐτοὶ ἐν
μοίρᾳ κλεπτῶν.

28. Πρὸς τὸν αὐτοκράτορα

Ἀναφέρω πολλάκις τὸ δοκοῦν ἀναγκαῖον τῇ ἐκ Θεοῦ βασιλείᾳ σου,
καὶ διὰ τὸν Θεὸν μηδὲν παρατρέχῃ. ἀνέφερον γὰρ καὶ πολλάκις, ὅπερ ἔνι

26: 14–15 cf. Matt. 27:7

---

9 κυαμοφάγοι P ‖ 10 δώσωσιν P; post δώσωσιν repetivit καὶ τῶν εἰς ἀκοὰς ... Μακρεμβολίτου P ‖ 13 ὅτι om. P ‖ 15 κατέλιπε S
    27: V 13ʳ. S 142ʳ. P 23ᵛ.
1 ante πρὸς add. γράμμα VʳSP ‖ post αὐτοκράτορα add. διὰ τὰ χρυσόβουλλα VʳSP
    28: V 13ʳ–13ᵛ. S 142ʳ–142ᵛ. P 23ᵛ–24ʳ.
1 ante πρὸς add. γράμμα VʳSP ‖ post αὐτοκράτορα add. ἵνα ἕκαστος τῶν ἀρχιερέων ἀπέλθῃ
πρὸς τῇ λαχούσῃ αὐτῷ VʳSP

they are typical of your condition (?). For since in truth you are the one who is found to reason falsely and to be greedy and unjust and an enemy of the divine commandments, what surprise is it if you also indulge in twisted reasonings ? But if you wish—as if they will endure your abusive language!— they will ⟨also⟩ impose a penalty on you, and you will suffer the same fate as is rumored to be the lot of Makrembolites (?), who is reduced to eating beans and salt pork. And when you say that it was for the sake of men's salvation that you mercifully took his [i.e., Makrembolites'] money from him, O most greedy and unjust of men, Judas could also boast that he had committed the betrayal for a good cause, on the one hand because he proved to be salutary for the world, on the other hand because it was for the benefit of «strangers» that he acquired «the potter's field». If then you heed me at all, put an end to this feeble joking, and return the money untouched to the man you wronged, in the full knowledge that in any case you will not leave that place [prison ?] until you repay the last cent.

27. To the emperor

To your divine majesty has been assigned responsibility for monasteries, and the duties performed—and expenses incurred—by your majesty with regard to monasteries are duties secular in nature. For this reason I do not think that anyone in his right mind will oppose whatever you command, either in chrysobulls or without chrysobulls, concerning secular administration. And I make this petition, that it come to pass, in accordance with agricultural law, that, if the former owners are going to keep the surplus land, then they should pay rent; however, if this ⟨land⟩ is going to be taken away, they should not pay rent on it, because it is very likely that those who are going to collect the rent will pocket it, and the damage will be twofold. For in addition to wronging your imperial majesty, they will be classed among thieves.

28. To the emperor

I often petition your divine majesty about matters which seem urgent, and for the sake of God let none of them pass by unnoticed. For I have often

28, 29

καὶ ἔννομον καὶ ἁρμόδιον τῷ καιρῷ, ἵνα ἕκαστος τῶν ἀρχιερέων ἀπέλθῃ
5 πρὸς τὴν λαχοῦσαν αὐτῷ καὶ συνάγῃ καὶ νουθετῇ τὸν λαόν, καὶ πρὸς ἀρέσκειαν Θεοῦ ἀγωνίζηται τούτους, καὶ πρὸς σύστασιν καὶ ἀσφάλειαν καὶ τοῦ
παρόντος καιροῦ. ὅθεν διπλοῦν τὸ καλόν· ἓν μὲν ὅτι πληροῦσι τὸ χρέος
αὐτῶν, ἕτερον δὲ ὅτι οὐδὲ ἐγὼ δύναμαι ὑποφέρειν τὴν τούτων ἐνταῦθα διατριβήν, ὅτι οὐδὲ εἰς τὴν ψυχὴν τούτων ἁρμόζει, οὔτε εἰς ἐμέ, οὔτε εἰς τὸν
10 λαόν, ἀλλ᾽ οὐδὲ τῷ νόμῳ τῷ ἐκκλησιαστικῷ. οὔτε γὰρ [fol. 13ᵛ] εἰς ἐπιστασίαν, οὔτε εἰς κρίσεις εὐθύτητα σῴζουσι· ποιοῦνται δὲ καὶ παρασυνάξεις
καὶ ἕτερα ἔξω τοῦ πρέποντος, καὶ καθ᾽ ἑκάστην ἐπὶ τὸ χεῖρον προκόπ-
τουσιν. ἦλθε γὰρ ὁ Κρήτης· κἂν ἦν δὲ καὶ συνήθεια, καὶ ἀπεστέλλομεν
ἐκκλησιαστικὸν καὶ εἰσῆγε τὸν ἐρχόμενον. νῦν δὲ ἀφῆκαν καὶ τοῦτο, καὶ
15 χωρὶς ὑπομνήσεως εἰσέρχονται. καὶ ἐν μὲν ταῖς λοιπαῖς πόλεσιν οὐ δυνατὸν
παρὰ γνώμην τοῦ ταύτης ποιμένος ἑτέρας πόλεως ἀρχιερέα ἐνεργῆσαι κἂν
τὸ τυχόν, ἐνταῦθα δὲ εἴ τι καὶ βούλεται ἕκαστος. διὰ τοῦτο παρακαλῶ,
μὴ ὑπάγῃ εἰς πλέον, ἀλλ᾽ ἐν ὅσῳ ἐσμὲν ἐν εἰρήνῃ, κέλευσον ἕκαστον ἀπελθεῖν, μήπως εἰς μάχην χωρήσωμεν καὶ ἐξέλθωσι καὶ μὴ θέλοντες.

29. Πρὸς τὸν αὐτοκράτορα

Φιλόζωος ὁ ἄνθρωπος ὤν, ὑγιαίνων ἐπιλανθάνεται, ὡς ἔχει φύσεως,
τὰ πραττόμενα ὑπ᾽ αὐτοῦ εἴτε αἰσχύνης, εἴτε καὶ δόξης, παραίτια· ἡνίκα
δὲ νόσῳ ἀπειλούσῃ θάνατον καθυποβληθῇ, τῶν τῇδε πάντων ἐπιλαθόμε-
5 νος, εὐγνώμων τῶν ἑαυτοῦ καθίσας κριτὴς ἐν τῷ ἐργαστηρίῳ τῆς συνειδήσεως, ὑποσχέσεις πρὸς τὸν ἀλάθητον καὶ ἀπροσωπόληπτον ποιεῖται κριτήν,
δι᾽ ἄλλο οὐδὲν ἢ ὑπὲρ σωτηρίας ἀγωνιῶν. τοῦτο, τῆς ἐκ Θεοῦ βασιλείας σου
δέομαι, τηρηθήτω καὶ ἐν ἡμῖν· καὶ τῶν πραγμάτων ψυχορραγούντων,
εὐγνωμόνως ἐπισκεψώμεθα πῶς ἵνα διοικηθῇ τὰ τῆς ἐκκλησίας καὶ τὰ
10 τῆς βασιλείας. καὶ εἰ μέλλει μὴ ἀπολέσθαι τὸ πᾶν σὺν ἡμῖν, ἀσφαλῆ λόγον
δῶμεν Θεῷ, κἂν ταῦτα τὰ τρία, ὅσον τὸ καθ᾽ ἡμᾶς, τηρηθήτω ἀσάλευτα,
δικαιοσύνη καὶ σωφροσύνη καὶ ἔλεος, καὶ τότε περὶ τῶν ἄλλων ὁ Θεὸς ἀντιλήψεται. μόνον ἡμεῖς μὴ μετατρεπώμεθα τοῦ καλοῦ, μὴ προσώποις, μὴ
σχέσει τῇ ἐξ αἱμάτων, μὴ δωρεαῖς ἢ ὑποσχέσεσι, μὴ δυναστείας δειλίᾳ.
15 οὐδεὶς γὰρ Θεοῦ δυνατώτερος. εἰ δὲ δυσχέρεια φαίνεται ἐκ τοῦ μὴ εἶναι

28: 12–13 II Tim. 3:13

---

18 εἰς] ὡς P

29: V 13ᵛ. S 142ᵛ–143ʳ. P 24ʳ–24ᵛ. Gennadios, Ἱστορία τοῦ Οἰκουμενικοῦ Πατριαρχείου I, 380–381; Tomadakes, Βυζαντινὴ Γραμματολογία, 125–126 et Σύλλαβος Βυζαντινῶν Μελετῶν καὶ Κειμένων, 486–487.
1 ante πρὸς add. γράμμα VʳSP ‖ post αὐτοκράτορα add. ἵνα τηρηθῶσιν ἀσάλευτον δικαιοσύνην καὶ σωφροσύνην καὶ ἔλεον VʳSP ‖ 12 δικαιοσύνην καὶ σωφροσύνην καὶ ἔλεον codd.

made the petition which is both lawful and suitable at this time, namely that each of the bishops should return to the see assigned to him, and gather together his people, and advise them, and train them to do what is pleasing to God, for the sake of their protection and security, especially at the present time. And the benefit therefrom is twofold: on the one hand, because they will fulfil their obligation; on the other hand, because I cannot endure their presence here, since it is neither fitting for their soul nor for me, nor for the people, nor is it even in accordance with ecclesiastical law. For they are not honest either in their administration or in their judicial decisions; but they instigate unlawful assemblies, and other unseemly acts, and every day «they get worse». For example, the metropolitan of Crete came, and it used to be my custom to send an ecclesiastic to escort the new arrival; but now they have even given this up and come without any notification or permission. In no other city is it possible for the bishop of another city to perform any function whatsoever contrary to the wishes of its bishop, but here everyone does whatever he wants. For this reason I beg you not to let this matter go any further, but while I keep my peace, order each one to return, lest we resort to violence and they have to leave against their will.

29. To the emperor

Since man clings to life, when he is healthy he forgets, as is natural, that his acts result either in shame or in glory; but when he falls victim to a possibly fatal disease, he forgets everything in this world, and sitting in the workshop of his conscience as a prudent judge of his own deeds, he makes promises to the Judge Whom nothing escapes and Who is no respecter of persons, and is anxious only for his own salvation. I beg of your divine majesty, let us maintain this principle. And since our affairs are in a dangerous state, let us consider prudently how the church and the empire should be governed. And if everything is not to perish with us, let us give our firm word to God, and if we maintain these three virtues as inviolate as we can, justice, moderation and mercy, then God will help us in other matters. Only let us not turn away from the good, either on account of personal favoritism, or blood ties, or bribes or promises, or fear of the powers that be; for no one is more powerful than God. And if difficulty should arise because supposedly there

τάχα τινὰ τὸν εἰς Θεοῦ ἀρέσκειαν ἐνεργήσοντα τὰ ῥηθέντα, ἐγὼ εὑρήσω μετὰ Θεὸν τὸν εἰς τοῦτο ὑπηρετήσοντα. καὶ οὕτω θεοδοξάστως ἡ ἐκ Θεοῦ βασιλεία σου φροντιεῖ μετὰ τῆς συγκλήτου τὰ τῇ βασιλείᾳ ἁρμόζοντα, μὴ τῶν προρρηθέντων ἀνθισταμένων. καὶ γὰρ εἰ ταῦτα πραχθῇ, ἔτι λαλοῦν-
20 τός σου πρὸς Θεὸν ἐμπράκτως, αὐτὸν ἀκούσεις βοῶντα, ἰδοὺ πάρ-
ειμι, καὶ τοῖς ἀγγέλοις αὐτοῦ ἐντελεῖται περὶ σοῦ, τοῦ
φυλάττειν σε ὡς ἂν μὴ προσκόψῃς πρὸς λίθον τὸν πόδα
σου. εἰ δὲ τὴν τῶν ῥηθέντων μὴ σπουδάσωμεν ἐργασίαν, προφάσεις προ-
φασιζόμενοι, δέον τοῦ συνορᾶν ὅτι καταφρονοῦντες καταφρονηθησόμεθα
25 παντελῶς.

30. Πρὸς τὸν αὐτοκράτορα

Εἰ μὲν ἐπέγνως, ἅγιε βασιλεῦ, τὴν ἐν τῇ ἀνατολῇ τῶν πόλεων ἐξολόθρευσιν, ὅπερ μὴ ἴδοιμεν, διατί μὴ καὶ τοὺς ἐκεῖ ἐνοικοῦντας ἐκέλευσας
[fol. 14ʳ] ἐξελθεῖν καὶ τὰ ὧδε καταλαβεῖν, ὡς τὴν πάντων ἀπὸ Θεοῦ
5 φροντίδα ἐγχειρισθείς, ἀλλὰ τοῖς ἀρχιερεῦσι μόνοις τοῦτο κεχάρισαι; εἰ δὲ
διὰ τῆς χάριτος τοῦ μεγάλου Θεοῦ τῇ ἐνούσῃ σοι ἐκ Θεοῦ φρονήσει καὶ
διακρίσει φιλανθρώπως οἶδας παιδεύειν ἡμᾶς τὸν Θεόν, οὐ πρὸς ὄλεθρον
ἀλλὰ πρὸς ἐπιστροφήν, τί μὴ ἐκέλευσας καὶ τοὺς ποιμένας ἐκείνων ἐν τοῖς
ἑαυτῶν ποιμνίοις εὑρίσκεσθαι, καὶ τοῦτο μὲν δι' εὐχῶν καὶ δεήσεων τῶν
10 πρὸς τὸν Θεόν, τοῦτο δὲ διὰ παραινέσεων ἢ καὶ ἐπιτιμήσεων, πρὸς ἀναμαρ-
τησίαν διατηρεῖν, καὶ οὕτως ἐξιλεοῦσθαι Θεὸν παρενέγκαι τὴν ἀπειλήν;
ἆρα εἰ πρόβατα ἐνεπίστευσας τῶν ποιμένων τινί, εἶτα ἐκεῖνα μὲν ἔγνως
μόνα καταλιπόντα, ἐκεῖνον δὲ οἰκείων ὀρέξεων καὶ ἀναπαύσεων φροντί-
ζοντα, πρὸς τῆς ἀληθείας αὐτῆς, παρέδραμες ἀτιμώρητον; εἶτα τῶν μὲν
15 ἀλόγων προβάτων ὁ μὴ φροντίζων ἀνεύθυνος οὐδαμῶς, τῶν δὲ τοῦ Χριστοῦ λογικῶν προβάτων ἐάσωμεν ἀνευθύνους τοὺς ποιμαίνειν ἐπιλιπόντας,
νῦν ἑαυτοὺς βόσκειν, ἀλλ' οὐ τὰ πρόβατα; καὶ ποίαν ἐκεῖ τὴν
ἀπολογίαν εὑρήσομεν; εὔχομαι μὴ ὀνειδισθῶμεν ὅτι πάντες τὰ ἑαυτῶν ζητοῦσιν, οὐ τὰ τοῦ Χριστοῦ Ἰησοῦ καὶ Θεοῦ. τί δὲ καὶ

29: 19–21 Is. 58:9 ‖ 21–23 cf. Ps. 90 (91):11–12
30: 17: cf. Ezech. 34:8 ‖ 18–19 Phil. 2:21

---

16 ῥηθέντα] τηρηθέντα P
30: V 13ᵛ–14ʳ. S 143ʳ–144ʳ. P 25ʳ–25ᵛ. Ed. Laiou, *Andronicus II*, 334–335, no. 2.
Hanc epistolam Latine vertit Turrianus in *De Residentia Pastorum*, 87–89; cf. Migne, PG,
CXLII, 525–526.
1 ante πρὸς add. γράμμα VʳSP ‖ post αὐτοκράτορα add. περὶ τῶν ἀρχιερέων ἵνα ἀπέλθῃ
ἕκαστος εἰς τὴν λαχοῦσαν αὐτῷ, ὅπως διδάσκῃ (διδάσκει Vʳ) τὸν λαὸν (τῶν λαῶν Vʳ) αὐτοῦ
VʳSP ‖ 3 καὶ τοὺς VS¹P : αὐτοὺς S ‖ 10–11 ἁμαρτησίαν S ‖ 12 ἆρα P ‖ 15–16 post
προβάτων om. ὁ μὴ φροντίζων ... λογικῶν προβάτων P

29, 30

is no one who will carry out the above-mentioned ⟨obligations⟩ in a manner pleasing to God, then with the help of God I will find the man who will thus serve. And thus your divine majesty, together with the senate, will consider what is fitting for the empire, to the greater glory of God, without any of the above-mentioned ⟨difficulties⟩ standing in the way. And if these deeds are accomplished, «while you are still actually speaking» to God, you will hear Him proclaiming, «Behold, I am here», and «He shall give His angels charge concerning you, to keep you, lest you dash your foot against a stone». But if we do not strive to accomplish the above-mentioned virtues, but make excuses, one must conclude that inasmuch as we show contempt, we ourselves will be utterly contemned.

30. To the emperor

If you were aware, O holy emperor, of the destruction of the cities in the East (from the sight of which may we be spared!), why didn't you order their inhabitants, too, to leave and come here, since you are entrusted by God with the care of all men, but granted this favor only to the bishops ? And if, in your divine wisdom and discretion granted you through the grace of the great God, you realized that God was punishing us because of His love for mankind, with the purpose of converting rather than destroying us, why didn't you order the shepherds of those people to remain with their flocks, to preserve their freedom from sin either by prayers and supplications to God, or by exhortations and reproaches, and thus appease God so that He would avert His threat? Surely if you entrusted sheep to a certain shepherd, and then you learned that he had abandoned the flock and was thinking only of his own pleasures and comforts, in the name of truth itself, would you allow him to go unpunished ? If then he who does not take care of his unreasoning sheep is in no way free from blame, will we permit those who fail to care for the reasoning sheep of Christ to «feed themselves but not their sheep», and ⟨will we then⟩ not blame them ? What excuse will we make in the world to come ? I pray that we may not be reproached because they «all seek their own, not the things which are Jesus Christ's» and God's. The bishop of Traianoupolis has taught us what

20 τὸ ἐκ τούτων ἐνταῦθα γινόμενον ὄφελος ἐδίδαξεν ὁ τῆς Τραιανοῦ; εἰ γὰρ
λιταῖς ὀκνοῦσι καὶ ἀγρυπνίαις, καταμωκῶνται δὲ καὶ ἡμῶν σπουδαζόντων
τοιούτοις, ἐκ τούτου τὸ πλέον νοεῖν ἀρκετὸν τοῖς νοῦν ἔχουσιν. οὐδὲ γὰρ
ἄλλο προτέρημα τούτοις ἢ τοῦ καταβιβάζειν πατριαρχεύοντας, καὶ δωροδοκεῖσθαι παρὰ τῶν κρινομένων, καὶ ὅσα ἐδίδαξε περὶ τούτων ἡμῖν ὁ
25 καιρός.

ἢ οὖν κελευσθήτωσαν ἀποκαταστῆναι τῇ οἰκείᾳ ἕκαστος ποίμνῃ, ἢ
μίαν ἡμᾶς παραχωρήσατε ποίμνην, ἀπελθεῖν εἰς αὐτήν. καὶ διδόαμεν ὅρ-
κον ὡς οὔποτε ἀποστῶμεν ἐκείνης ἐνταῦθα ἐλθεῖν. αὐτοὶ δὲ τὴν μεγαλό-
πολιν μερισάσθωσαν, καὶ γὰρ ὄντως ἐλεεινὸν ἐν ἄλλῃ μὲν πόλει τὸν ταύτης
30 ποιμένα ὡς δύναμις διοικεῖν, ἐνταῦθα δὲ μόνον ἀντικαθέζεσθαι τὸν βουλόμενον. ἀλλ᾽ εἴ τι ἐμοὶ πείθῃ, βασιλέων ὁ εὐλαβέστατος, θέλε μᾶλλον
τούτους λυπῆσαι καὶ μὴ Θεόν. καὶ γὰρ σήμερον εἴπερ ποτὲ δίκαιον
τῇ οἰκείᾳ ποίμνῃ συναποθνήσκειν αὐτούς. εἰ δὲ τούτοις τηρεῖν τὸ αἰδέσιμον
βούλει, ἀλλὰ μὴ τὸ ὀφειλόμενον, ἐγὼ τὸ ὑπὲρ αὐτῶν καταδεξάμενος
35 κρίμα, ἢ ἑκόντας ἢ ἄκοντας ἐξελάσω τῆς πόλεως, καὶ λόγον ὑφέξω Χριστῷ
τοῦ τοιούτου τολμήματος.

31. ⟨Περὶ τῶν ποιμένων⟩

Εἰ ἔχεται ἀληθείας ὁ λόγος, ὡς ὁ ποιμένος ἀποστερῶν ποίμνιον ἀμφοτέροις κίνδυνον προξενεῖ, χρεὼν μέχρις αἵματος
τῷ λογικῷ ποιμνίῳ Χριστοῦ ἐγκαρτερεῖν τὸν ποιμαίνοντα (εὐθύνης ἀσυμ-
5 παθοῦς ἀναμενούσης τὸν εἴργοντα), τῇ μεγάλῃ μόνῃ συνόδῳ ἑνὶ ἑκάστῳ
ἐνιαυτῷ εἰς ἀναγκαίων τινῶν θεωρίαν ἐπὶ μικρὸν διατρίβοντα, καὶ πάλιν
τῇ ποίμνῃ ἐπιταχύνοντα, εἰ πε-[fol. 14ᵛ] πίστευκεν ὑπὲρ ταύτης ὑφέξειν
λόγον τῷ ἀρχιποίμενι, καὶ μὴ ψευδώνυμος ᾖ, εἰ μή που ἀνάγκης ψυχωφε-
λοῦς ἕνεκεν μετάκλητος βασιλεῖ ἢ τῷ πατριαρχεύοντι γένηται. εἰ δ᾽ ἄλλως
10 δοκεῖ κἀκείνοις καὶ τῷ κρατοῦντι, οὐδαμῶς αὐτὸς ἐγώ, εἴ τι καὶ γένηται,

---

31–32 cf. Eph. 4:30
31: 2–3 locum non inveni ‖ 3 Hebr. 12:4

---

33 οἰκείᾳ VP : ἁγίᾳ S ‖ 34 τὸ ὀφειλόμενον S¹ : τί ὀφειλόμενον VSP
31: V 14ʳ–14ᵛ. S 144ʳ–144ᵛ. P 25ᵛ–26ʳ. Ed. Gennadios, Ἱστορία τοῦ Οἰκουμενικοῦ
Πατριαρχείου I, 364. Turrianus Latine vertit in De Residentia Pastorum, 89; cf. Migne, PG,
CXLII, 526–527.
1 γράμμα περὶ τοῦ μή τις ποιμένος ἀποστερεῖν ποίμνιον add. VʳSP ‖ 2 ἔρχεται P ‖ 10
οὐδαμὸς P ‖ εἴ τι καὶ] ἔτι καὶ SP

30: Schol. ad 21, καταμωκῶνται : κατακωμῶνται R. scr. manus posterior in
margine P ‖ ad 33, οἰκείᾳ (ἁγίᾳ S) : γρ(άφεται) οἰκείᾳ scr. manus posterior in margine S
31 : Schol. ad 10: εἴ τι καὶ (ἔτι καὶ P) : ὅτι κἂν R. scr. manus posterior in marg. P

30, 31

kind of «benefit» accrues from these men ⟨staying⟩ here. If they shrink from prayers and vigils, but make fun of me when I devote myself to such practices, for intelligent people this ⟨alone⟩ is sufficient for complete understanding. Their only accomplishment is to depose patriarchs, and to accept bribes from defendants, and such other things as the course of time has taught us about these men.

Therefore, either let them be ordered to return, each to his own flock, or else give me a flock to go to. And I give you my oath that I will never abandon it to come here. Let them divide the City among themselves, for it is really piteous that in any other city its shepherd administers to the best of his ability, but ⟨the bishop⟩ here is replaced by anyone who wishes. But if you heed me, O most pious of emperors, «wish to cause grief to these men rather than to God». For now if ever it is right for them to die together with their own flocks. But if you wish to maintain your reverence toward them, and not ⟨force upon them⟩ their duty, then I will take the decision about them upon myself, and will drive them out of the city, whether they are willing or not, and I will give an accounting to Christ for this daring act.

31. ⟨Concerning the bishops⟩

If the saying is true that he who deprives a flock of its shepherd causes danger to both, then the shepherd must remain with his reasoning flock of Christ «unto death» (and merciless punishment awaits anyone who prevents him); he should stay a short while at the great yearly synod alone for the investigation of certain important matters, and then should hasten back again to his flock, if he believes that he will render an accounting for this ⟨flock⟩ to ⟨our Lord⟩, the Chief Shepherd, and is not falsely called ⟨a shepherd⟩; unless, of course, he should be summoned by the emperor or patriarch for a spiritually beneficial reason. But if this does not meet with the approval of those ⟨bishops⟩ and the emperor, I will in no way go along with them,

66

ἔψομαι, ἢ εὐδοκήσω ποσῶς· οὐ γὰρ προφάσεων ἀνθρωπίνων καὶ ἀφορμῶν καὶ ὀρέξεων, ἀληθείας δὲ καὶ δικαιοσύνης καὶ θείων θεσμῶν ὑφέξειν εὐθύνας ἐσμὲν ὑπόχρεοι τῷ Χριστῷ.

32. Πρὸς τὸν αὐτοκράτορα

Θέλε μᾶλλον ἀνθρώπους καὶ μὴ Θεὸν λυπεῖν, λεγούσης μέμνησαι τῆς Γραφῆς. πλὴν τί τὸ δοκοῦν ὅλως βαρὺ τῇ ἐκ Θεοῦ βασιλείᾳ σου δικαιοσύνην καὶ σωφροσύνην καὶ ἔλεον τῷ ὑπηκόῳ νομοθετεῖν, οὐ μό-
5 νον οὐ ζημιούμενον, ἀλλὰ καὶ δι᾽ ἀγαθοεργίας τὸν ἔλεον ἕλκοντα τοῦ Θεοῦ; τί δὲ δικαιότερον, εἰ ἕκαστος κελευσθῇ τῶν ἀρχιερέων, ἑκὼν ἢ ἄκων, τῇ λαχούσῃ ἐπανελθεῖν; οὐ κανονικὸν καὶ κεχρεωστημένον; οὐχ ἁρμόδιον εἰς τὸ διεγεῖραι εἰς δέησιν τὸν λαόν, καὶ μάλιστα σήμερον; ποία γὰρ ἄλλη ἐλπὶς ὑπελείφθη Χριστιανοῖς; ἀλλ᾽ ὀρέγονται κατοικεῖν ἐν τῇ Πόλει· καὶ
10 μερισάσθωσαν ταύτην. ἀλλ᾽ ὀρέγονται διασύρειν καὶ ἡμᾶς, ἕνεκεν λιτῆς καὶ ἀγρυπνιῶν· εἰ τοῦτο δεινόν, εἰπάτωσαν καὶ ...

33. ⟨Πρὸς τὸν βασιλέα κύριν Μιχαήλ⟩

Εἰ καὶ μὴ δι᾽ ἄλλο τι κατάχρεοι ἦμεν ποθεινῶς διακεῖσθαι πρὸς σέ, καὶ τῆς σῆς βασιλείας διηνεκῶς ὑπερεύχεσθαι, ἀλλά γε διὰ τὸν δικαιώσαντά σε βασιλεύειν τοῦ Χριστωνύμου λαοῦ ἐπουράνιον βασιλέα, τὸ εἰς δύναμιν
5 ἧκον, εἰ καὶ μὴ κατ᾽ ἀξίαν,—ἡμᾶς παρεᾶν οὐ δοκῶ ἀτιμώρητον παρὰ τῷ τὰ κρυπτὰ εἰδότι Θεῷ, καὶ δικαίως καὶ ἀκριβῶς ταλαντεύσοντι. εἰ δέ γε πρὸς τούτοις καὶ τὰ ἐπίλοιπα ἀριθμεῖν δοκιμάσοι τις νουνεχῶς ἀγαθά, ἃ τῷ ἁγίῳ μου καὶ κρατίστῳ πρόσεστι βασιλεῖ καὶ φιλοτέκνῳ πατρί σου, καὶ τῷ φιλοπάτορι σοὶ καὶ γνησιωτάτῳ αὐτοῦ καὶ φιλτάτῳ καὶ ἰσοψύχῳ υἱῷ

32: 2 cf. Eph. 4:30

32: V 14ᵛ. S 144ᵛ. P 26ʳ. Hanc epistolam Latine vertit Turrianus in De Residentia Pastorum, 89–90; cf. Migne, PG, CXLII, 527–528.
1 ante πρὸς add. γράμμα VʳSP ‖ post αὐτοκράτορα add. ἑκὼν ἢ ἄκων τῇ λαχούσῃ ἀπελθεῖν τοὺς ἀρχιερεῖς VʳSP ‖ 3 τί] τῇ P ‖ 11 omnibus in codicibus caetera desunt
33: V 14ᵛ–15ʳ. S 144ᵛ–146ʳ. P 26ʳ–27ᵛ.
1 γράμμα πρὸς τὸν βασιλέα κύριν Μιχαὴλ ἵνα πρὸ τῶν μυρίων φροντίδων μελέτημα ἔχειν καὶ τί ὑπεσχέθημεν ἐν τῷ ἁγίῳ βαπτίσματι add. VʳS; ἐν τῷ ἁγίῳ βαπτίσματι γράμμα πρὸς τὸν βασιλέα κύριν Μιχαὴλ ἵνα πρὸς τῶν μυρίων φροντίδων μελέτημα ἔχειν καὶ τί ὑπεσχέθημεν P ‖ 3 σῆς] σὲ P ‖ 9 αὐτοῦ] αὐτῷ S ‖

whatever happens, nor will I in any way sanction their decision. For we have the obligation to Christ to be responsible not for human excuses and pretexts and desires, but for truth and righteousness and the divine commandments.

32. To the emperor

Remember the Scriptures which say, «Wish to cause grief to men rather than to God». Why does it seem wholly grievous to your divine majesty to legislate justice and moderation and mercy for your subjects, an act which not only causes no harm, but as the result of good works attracts the mercy of God ? And what could be more just than if each of the bishops were ordered to return to his assigned see, whether willing or not ? Is this not a canonical and obligatory act ? Is it not appropriate for them to rouse the people to supplication, especially at a time like this ? For what other hope is left to Christians ? But they wish to live in the City; so let them divide it among themselves. But they wish to make fun of me because of my prayers and vigils; if this is bad, let them also say ...

33. ⟨To the emperor lord Michael⟩

Even if I was obliged to be favorably disposed toward you, and to pray constantly and as fervently as I could for your majesty (if not in a worthy manner) for no other reason than for the sake of the King of Heaven Who deemed it right to make you emperor of the Christian people—I do not think that ⟨if I neglected to do so⟩, this would be unpunished by God Who knows all secrets and weighs out justly and accurately. And if in addition to this someone should attempt seriously to count up the other blessings which have been granted to my holy and most powerful emperor, your father, who is devoted to his son, and ⟨which have been granted⟩ also to you, his most legitimate and beloved son and mighty emperor, devoted to your father, like to him

10 καὶ κραταιῷ βασιλεῖ, ὑπὲρ τοὺς πάλαι Χριστιανῶν βασιλεῖς, τήν τε μεγάλην φιλοθεΐαν ὑμῶν καὶ εὐσέβειαν καὶ τὴν πρὸς τὰ θεῖα εὐλάβειαν, τὸ ὑπερανεστηκὸς τῆς φρονήσεως, καὶ τὸ εὐδιάκριτον, καὶ δὴ καὶ τὸ πρὸς τὸ ὑπήκοον συμπαθὲς ὑμῶν καὶ φιλάγαθον, τίνα ἄν τις πρεπόντως προσοίσει εὐχαριστίαν τῷ ἡμᾶς παρασχόντι βασιλεύεσθαι ὑφ' ὑμῶν παμβασιλεῖ Χρισ-
15 τῷ τῷ Θεῷ ἡμῶν, καὶ ὑμῖν εὐχὰς καὶ εὐγνωμοσύνην καὶ εὔνοιαν παρ' ὧν βασιλεύεσθαι οὕτως κατηξιώμεθα; καὶ δοξάζειν τὸν ὑπερδεδοξασμένον, καὶ ἀεὶ ἐξαιτεῖν παρ' αὐτοῦ τὴν διπλῆν πρὸς τὰ κρείττω τῶν λαμπρῶν βασιλέων ὑμῶν προκοπὴν καὶ ἐπίδοσιν.

διὰ ταῦτα, κύριε βασιλεῦ, ἀξιῶ πρὸ τῶν μυρίων φροντίδων ἃς
20 ἐπιφέρεται ἡ τοῦ κόσμου ἀρχή, μελέ-[fol. 15ʳ] τημα ἔχειν θεάρεστον ἧς κατηξίωσαι χάριτος τοῦ ἁγίου βαπτίσματος νηπιόθεν καὶ πρὸ τῆς βασιλείας αὐτῆς, καὶ πῶς ἀπετάξω μὲν τῷ ἐχθρῷ, συνετάξω δὲ τῷ Χριστῷ, ἃ καὶ ἀπαιτηθήσῃ ἀνελλιπῆ μετὰ τὴν τῆς πανηγύρεως ταύτης κατάληξιν. δι' ἃ καὶ εἰς δύναμιν ὡς συνετάχθη καὶ τηρηθέντα ἢ καὶ τηρη-
25 θησόμενα τὴν εὐδαιμονίαν τὴν ὧδε τηρήσει, καὶ τὴν ἐκεῖ βασιλείαν τὴν ὄντως ἀσάλευτον καὶ ἀγήρω καὶ ἀληθῆ καὶ ἀτελεύτητον μετὰ Θεοῦ συντηρήσει σοι.

τήρει οὖν τὴν καλήν σου συνείδησιν· μὴ παραδέχου τινὰ τῶν κολακικῶν, ἢ λογισμὸν ἀνθρώπων τινῶν, κἂν ἀξιώματι κοσμικῷ ἢ καὶ τῆς
30 ἐκκλησίας τύχῃ κατονομάζεσθαι, παρατιτρώσκειν αὐτὴν μέχρι καὶ τοῦ τυχόντος. τηρουμένης γὰρ καθηκόντως αὐτῆς, ἐν σκέπῃ τοῦ Θεοῦ τοῦ οὐρανοῦ ἀεὶ αὐλισθήσῃ καὶ σκεπασθήσῃ πτέρυξι ταῖς αὐτοῦ, ὑπέρτερός τε νυκτερινοῦ ἔσῃ φόβου, καὶ πετομένου βέλους ἡμερινοῦ, καὶ συνελόντα εἰπεῖν, πράγματος ἐναντίου παντός,
35 ὃ σκοτίας ἐστὶ διαπόρευμα, καὶ τοῦ ταύτης ἐφευρετοῦ· ἀλλ' οὐδέ τι ἐγγιεῖ τῶν κακούντων πρὸς σέ. κατανοήσεις γὰρ τότε τοῖς ὀφθαλμοῖς καὶ ὄψει τὴν πτῶσιν τῶν βουλομένων ἀνθίστασθαι, νοουμένων λέγω καὶ ὁρατῶν, καὶ μακάριος ὄντως ἔσῃ καὶ ζηλωτός, καὶ τὸ μνημόσυνόν σου εἰς γενεάς. καταφυγὴν αὐτὸς τὸν ὕψισ-
40 τον θέμενος, καὶ ὑπὸ τῶν ἁγίων ἀγγέλων αὐτοῦ ἐν ταῖς ὁδοῖς σου πάσαις δικαίως φανεὶς τειχιζόμενος, ἀσπίδα καὶ βασιλίσκον, δράκοντά τε καὶ λέοντα τὰ τῇ κακίᾳ ἀνήμερα, ὡς ἐγνωκὼς τὸ ὄνομα τοῦ μεγάλου Θεοῦ, καὶ κράζων αὐτόν, διαμείνῃς καταπατῶν, εἰσακουόμενος πρὸς Θεοῦ, ὃς καὶ μακρότητος ἐμπλή-
45 σει τὴν βασιλείαν σου ἡμερῶν, καὶ δείξει σοι ἀπεντεῦθεν αὐτοῦ τὸ σωτήριον· μεθ' οὗ καὶ συμβασιλεύσεις, πρεσβείαις τῆς Θεομήτορος.

33: 22–23 cf. Goar, Euchologion, 227 (Oratio ad faciendum catechumenum) ‖ 31–37 cf. Ps. 90 (91):1, 4–8 ‖ 39 cf. Ps. 101 (102):13 ‖ 39–46 cf. Ps. 90 (91):9, 11, 13–16

---

10 τοὺς] τοῖς P ‖ 12 τὸ²] τὰ P ‖ 22 ἀπετάξωμεν P ‖ 24 κατάληξιν] κατάληψιν codd. ‖ 28 τῶν] τὸν V

33

in spirit—more blessings than ever fell to the lot of any former Christian emperors, namely, your great love of God and reverence and piety for the divine, your superiority of mind and discretion, and in addition your benevolent and favorable attitude toward your subjects—then, what fitting thanksgiving could one offer up to Christ the King of all, our God, Who has granted to us to be ruled by you, and what suitable prayers and gratitude and favor could one offer to you by whom we have been deemed worthy to be ruled?—⟨We must⟩ both glorify the One Who is transcendently glorified and always seek from Him doubly great prosperity and increase for our resplendent emperors.

Wherefore, lord emperor, I ask that God-pleasing concern for the grace of Holy Baptism which you were deemed worthy to receive as a child, and for the way in which you «renounced the Enemy, but made promises to Christ» (whose fulfilment will be demanded of you unceasingly at the end of this time of rejoicing), take precedence over the myriad cares which rule of the world entails, and even over empire itself. Thus, if these promises which you made have been and will be kept to the best of your ability, they will maintain your prosperity here on earth, and will keep for you the kingdom of the next world which is truly immovable and ageless and true and eternal with God.

Therefore maintain your good conscience, and do not allow any flatterers or the views of certain men, even if they should happen to hold an official or ecclesiastic position, to violate your conscience even the slightest bit. For if ⟨your conscience⟩ is rightly maintained, «you shall always sojourn under the shelter of the God of heaven, and shall be sheltered by His wings, you shall be superior to any terror by night, or any arrow flying by day», in short, you will prevail over every evil thing which «walks in darkness» and over its inventor, «nor will anything harmful come near you». For then «you will observe with your eyes and see» the fall of those ⟨forces⟩ which wish to oppose you, I mean both intelligible and visible, and you will be truly blessed and enviable, and «your memory will endure for generations». «Making the Most High your refuge», and appearing righteously fortified «by His holy angels in all your ways», you will prevail, «trampling upon the asp and the basilisk, the dragon and the lion», savage in their wickedness, since «you» will «have known the name» of the great God, and since you proclaim Him, «you will be heard by Him». «He will satisfy» your majesty «with length of days», and henceforth «will show you His salvation», and you will rule together with Him, through the intercessions of the Mother of God.

34. ⟨Πρὸς τὴν Δέσποιναν τὴν Κεραμαρίαν⟩

Ἡνίκα τινὰ συμβῇ γνωρίσαι ἡμᾶς τὰ αὐτόθι καταλαμβάνειν, ὅσης
πληρούμεθα τῆς χαρᾶς, ἔχειν καιρὸν λογιζόμενοι διὰ γράμματος ὁμιλῆσαι
τῇ βασιλείᾳ σου, πιστώσεταί σε Χριστὸς ὁ βασιλεὺς καὶ Θεός σου,
5 νεφροὺς καὶ καρδίας ἐτάζειν εἰδώς. τὸ δ᾽ αἴτιον τῆς χαρᾶς ἡμῶν
ταῦτα τὰ κατὰ σὲ Θεοῦ οἰκονομίας μυστήρια, πῶς ἐκ μακρᾶς σε ἀνεκαλέ-
σατο γῆς, πῶς καὶ συμβασιλεύειν ἐκέλευσε τῷ κρατίστῳ καὶ ἁγίῳ μου
αὐτοκράτορι, πῶς τὰς τῆς εὐσεβείας ἀρχὰς ἀκραδάντους καὶ ἀνοθεύτους
τῇ εὐθυτάτῃ καὶ ἀγαθῇ σου ψυχῇ καὶ καρδίᾳ κεκράτηκε, πῶς πάλιν εὑρίσ-
10 κεσθαί σε ἐν τῷ καιρῷ τούτῳ εἰς ἀναγκαίων πραγμάτων κυβέρνησιν αὐτόθι ἐξέπεμψεν· ὅτι δὲ καὶ τῇ τῆς ἐκκλησίας εἰρηνικῇ ἑνώσει πολλὴν μετέρ-
χεσθαί σε μανθάνω τὴν μεταχείρισιν, πόσος σοι [fol. 15ᵛ] ὁ μισθὸς ἀποκείσεται παρὰ τοῦ τὰ διεστῶτα ἑνώσαντος ἐν εἰρήνῃ μεγάλου Θεοῦ, καὶ δια-
λύσαντος τὸν φραγμόν, οὐ δι᾽ ἀγγέλου, ἀλλὰ διὰ τῆς αὐτοῦ πρὸς ἡμᾶς
15 τοὺς ἀγνώμονας ἐπιδημίας ἁγίας μετὰ σαρκός!

ἐν τούτῳ τῷ ἔργῳ σκοπείτω ἡ βασιλεία σου τίνα εὐφραίνεις, σπουδά-
ζεις δὲ μετὰ τίνος, καὶ τίνι προσάγεις τοὺς * * *, τὴν εἰρήνην τῆς ἐκκλησίας τῇ συνετῇ σου μεταχειρίσει ποιοῦσα ἀσπάζεσθαι. πλὴν ἀλλὰ δέομαι,
τοὺς ἀναξίους κρίνοντας ἑαυτοὺς τοῦ τῆς εἰρήνης καλοῦ, μὴ κυβερνήσει
20 δῆθεν ἐλπίδος δωρεᾶς ἢ παρρησίας μετάδιδε· εἰς στηριγμὸν γὰρ οἱ ἄφρονες
τῆς αὐτῶν ψυχοφθόρου ἐνστάσεως δέχονται τὰ τοιαῦτα, οὐκ εἰς διόρθωσιν,
καὶ μᾶλλον οἱ ὑπ᾽ ἐκείνων πλανώμενοι· οὐ γὰρ ἀγνοίᾳ, ἵνα καὶ ἐλεῶνται,
ἀλλ᾽ ἐμπαθείᾳ ἀποδιΐστανται. εἰ δὲ διά τι τῆς ἐκκλησίας, τοῦ Θεοῦ δὲ μᾶλλον, ἀποκοπτόμενοι, πότε καὶ ἔσονται τοῖς κρατοῦσι πιστοί, κἂν σχη-
25 ματίζωνται τοῦτο ἐν δολιότητι; εἰ δὲ τὸν ἔλεον καλῶν πανταχοῦ ὁ ἀντιλέ-
γων ἐνίσταται, ἔχεις πολλὰς χήρας καὶ ὀρφανοὺς καὶ ἀδικουμένους παρά
τινων, ἐκεῖ δὴ τὸν ἔλεον· εὖ ποίησον τὸν κοινωνικόν, καὶ μὴ ἀντιλαβοῦ τὸν σχιζόμενον· μάχας καὶ ταραχὰς τοῦ κόσμου κατακρατεῖν
ἐπιθυμεῖ ὁ σχιζόμενος, ἅπαξ τὸν τῆς εἰρήνης Θεὸν ἀπωσάμενος ἐκ καρδίας
30 φιλονεικίᾳ κακῇ.

δένδρον ζωῆς ἡ ἐκκλησία Χριστοῦ· ὡς οὖν ἐκ δένδρου καλοῦ κλάδον
ἀποκοπέντα, μαραινόμενον κατ᾽ ὀλίγον, ἡ ξηρότης κατέλαβε καὶ ἔστι πυρὸς ἀνάλωμα, οὕτω κἀνταῦθα. ἡ δὲ βεβαίωσις αὕτη· πολλοὶ μετὰ τὴν ἔν-
σαρκον τοῦ Χριστοῦ καὶ Θεοῦ μου οἰκονομίαν τοῦ ζωηφόρου δένδρου, τῆς
35 ἐκκλησίας φημί, ἀπέκοψαν ἑαυτούς, ἢ δι᾽ αἵρεσιν ἢ διὰ σχίσμα. καὶ τὸ

34: 5 Ps. 7 (8):10 ‖ 13–14 cf. Eph. 2:14 ‖ 27–28 cf. Siracides 12:2,4

34: V 15ʳ–15ᵛ. S 146ʳ–147ʳ. P 27ᵛ–28ᵛ. Ed. Gennadios, Ἐπ.Ἑτ.Βυζ.Σπ. 22
(1952), 230–231.
1 γράμμα (ράμμα P) πρὸς τὴν δέσποιναν τὴν Κεραμαρίαν add. VʳSP ‖ 8 τὰς VS¹P ‖
τὰ S ‖ ἀνοθεύτους VSP¹ : ἀνοθεύτας P ‖ 12 ὁ om. S ‖ 17 post τοὺς lacunam statui ‖
24–25 σχηματίζονται P ‖ 25 δολιότητα P ‖ 32 ξυρότης SP

34

34. ⟨To the Despoina, Lady Maria⟩

Christ, your King and your God, Who knows how «to search the reins and hearts», will confirm the great joy with which I am filled, whenever some-one tells me that he is going to your residence, in the reflection that I have an opportunity to communicate with your majesty by letter. The cause of my joy is these mysteries of the way of God with regard to you, how He summoned you from a distant land, how He bade you rule together with my mighty and holy emperor, how He has maintained the principles of piety unshaken and unadulterated in your most honest and good heart and soul, and again how He has sent you there (?) at this time in order to arrange certain necessary affairs. But as I also learn that you are greatly involved in the attempts for peaceful union of the Church, how great will be your reward from the great God Who united differences in peace, and «removed the barrier», not by means of an angel, but by means of His holy sojourn in the flesh with us ungrateful people!

In this work let your majesty consider Whom you are making glad, and with Whom you are striving and to Whom you are bringing near the * * *, as you make them embrace the peace of the Church with your wise under-taking. But I beg of you, as for those who judge themselves unworthy of the good of peace, do not give them any gifts or access, misled by hope ⟨of their conversion⟩. For these foolish people, and especially those whom they have led astray, will consider such a step as support for their soul-destroying opposition, rather than considering it as a means of setting them on the right path. For they are in schism not as the result of ignorance (for which they might be forgiven), but as the result of passionate conviction. If then for some reason they cut themselves off from the Church, or rather from God, when will they be faithful to their rulers, even if they make a pretense of it in their crooked way ? If an opponent should object, crying out at every oppor-tunity about mercy, you have many widows and orphans and victims of injustice, ⟨show⟩ mercy to them; «be generous» to communicants ⟨of the Orthodox Church⟩, and «do not help» schismatics. The schismatic wants battles and confusion to rule the world, for he has utterly thrust away the God of peace from his heart through his evil contentiousness.

The Church of Christ is the tree of life. Therefore, just as a branch which has been cut off a healthy tree soon dries up and withers, and is consumed by fire, so it is in this case as well. The proof is this; many people, after the manifestation in the flesh of Christ, my God, cut themselves off from the life-giving tree, from the Church, I mean, either through heresy or schism. And

μὲν τῆς ζωῆς δένδρον, ἡ ἐκκλησία, ποτιζομένη ὑπὸ Χριστοῦ τοῦ Σωτῆρος μου καὶ φωτιζομένη, ἀνθεῖ· οἱ ταύτης δὲ ἀποστάντες ἀπώλοντο, ὡς ἑκόντες ἀπὸ Θεοῦ μακρύναντες ἑαυτούς. καὶ ταῦτα μὲν εἰς τοσοῦτον.

ὁ δὲ τῶν οἰκτιρμῶν Κύριος ἵλεων βλέψοι τῇ ἐκκλησίᾳ αὐτοῦ, ἣν ἡμῖν
40 ἐνεχείρισε, καὶ δυναμώσοι ἡμᾶς, καὶ συμβουλεύσοι καὶ συνετίσοι ὡς φίλον αὐτῷ τὸν Χριστώνυμον διεξάγειν λαόν. οὕτως γὰρ πάντως ἡ ἐκκλησία αὐτοῦ καὶ ὑμᾶς ἐν γήρᾳ βαθεῖ σὺν τοῖς θεοφρουρήτοις κλάδοις ὑμῶν συντηρήσοι ἐν πᾶσι καλοῖς, καὶ ὧδε συμβασιλεύοι ὑμῖν· ἐν τῷ μέλλοντι δὲ ἡμᾶς ἐκείνῳ συμβασιλεῦσαι καταξιώσοι, ἀμήν.

35. Πρὸς τὸν αὐτοκράτορα

Ἀεὶ ἀναλογιζόμενος καὶ φρόνησιν καὶ λεπτότητα καὶ ἄμετρον κόπον ὑπὲρ πολλούς, καὶ ψυχὴν συμπαθῆ, καὶ ὅσα ἀπὸ Θεοῦ ἡ ἐκ Θεοῦ πλουτεῖ βασιλεία σου, καὶ πάλιν ἀκινησίαν ὁρῶν καὶ ἀργίαν παντὸς [fol. 16ʳ]
5 ἀγαθοῦ, καὶ πᾶσαν κακίαν καθ' ἡμέραν ἐπὶ τὸ χεῖρον αὐξάνουσαν, εὔχομαι εἰ μετὰ τῶν ζώντων ἐλογιζόμην τὴν σήμερον· μικροῦ γὰρ δεύτερος χρόνος ἀφ' οὗ κεκρίκατε βλέπειν με. τί; ἐξ ὧν ἔκτοτε δι' ἐμοῦ Θεὸς ἐνεκάλεσε τῶν κακῶς πραττομένων ἡμῖν, ἃ καὶ ἐγγράφως ἀνέφερον, δι' ἃ καὶ ἀπέστρεψε τὸ πρόσωπον αὐτοῦ ἀφ' ἡμῶν καὶ κατάλειψιν ἀπειλεῖ τοῦ
10 παντὸς εἰ μὴ νήψομεν, ἐσπεύσαμεν διορθώσασθαι πορνείας ἡμῶν ἢ μοιχείας ἢ πλεονεξίας καὶ ἀδικίας; εἰ μὴ μᾶλλον καὶ προσεθήκαμεν. οὐχὶ ὅση ἀπὸ Ῥωμαίων σήμερον γῆ πενήτων ἐκπιεσμοῖς ἐκαλύφθη, καὶ πάσῃ ἀρρητουργίᾳ καὶ ἀδικίᾳ, δι' ἃ εἰς κόκκον σινάπεος, τὸ δὴ λεγόμενον, κατηντήκαμεν; διὰ τί δὲ καὶ τὰ συμβάντα ἐν τῇ Ἀνατολῇ καὶ συμβαίνοντα
15 μέχρι τοῦ νῦν καὶ τῇ Μακεδονίᾳ, φημί, πρὸς δὲ καὶ ἔνθα ὁ βασιλεὺς κύρις Μιχαήλ; καὶ πῶς διοικεῖται ὃν Χριστὸς ὁ Θεὸς ἐνεπιστεύσατό σοι λαὸν παρ' ἑκάστου; καὶ πῶς τοῦτον ἐν βρώσει ἄρτου, οἱ τὸν Κύριον μὴ ἐπικαλούμενοι κατεσθίουσιν; ἵνα ἐάσω τὴν ἐκ τῶν αἱμοβόρων ἢ Μογαβάρων πανωλεθρίαν. εἰ γὰρ καὶ κτηνῶν αὐτῶν δίκαιος οἰκτείρει
20 ψυχάς, οὐαί μοι, τοῖς κατ' εἰκόνα Θεοῦ τί συνέπεσε;

37–38 cf. Ps. 72 (73):27
35: 8–9 Ps. 9 (10):32 et 84 (85):5 ‖ 13 cf. Matt. 13:31 ‖ 17–18 cf. Ps. 13 (14):4

37 φωτιζομένη VS¹P, φωτιζομένοι S ‖ 40 συμβουλεύσοι] συμβουλεύοι VP, συμβασιλεύσοι S ‖ 42 ὑμᾶς] ἡμᾶς P ‖ 44 ἡμᾶς VS : ὑμᾶς PS¹
35: V 15ᵛ–16ᵛ. S 147ʳ–148ᵛ. P om. Huius epistolae partem edidit Gennadios, Ἐπ.ʿΕτ.Βυζ.Σπ., 22 (1952), 231–232; Tomadakes, Σύλλαβος Βυζαντινῶν Μελετῶν καὶ Κειμένων, 487–488.
1 ante πρὸς add. γράμμα VʳS ‖ post αὐτοκράτορα add. ἀναφαίρων (ἀναφέρων VˣS) τὰ συμβαίνοντα ἐν τῇ ἀνατολῇ παρὰ τῶν αἱμοβόρων μογαβάρων VʳS ‖ 8 ἡμῖν] ὑμῖν codd. ‖ 12 ἀπὸ] num ὑπὸ scribendum?

34, 35

the tree of life, the Church, given water and light by Christ my Savior, still blooms, but those who have apostatized from Her «have been destroyed», since of their own will «they have removed themselves far from God». But enough of this.

May the Lord of mercy look graciously upon His Church, which He has granted to me, and may He strengthen and counsel me and teach me how to lead the Christian people in a way pleasing to Him. May His Church thus always maintain you in ripe old age in the midst of all blessings together with your offspring, and deem all of us worthy to rule together with Him in the world to come, Amen.

35. To the emperor

Always when I consider your wisdom and subtlety and your countless labors on behalf of many people, and your sympathetic soul, and the other virtues with which God has endowed your divine majesty, and again when I see inertia and the absence of every good deed, and each day see every evil growing worse, I wish that these days I was reckoned ⟨by you to be⟩ among the living. For it is almost the second year since you have deigned to see me. What then? From the time when through me God rebuked our sins, which I detailed to you in writing, and on account of which «He has averted His face from us» and threatens to abandon all if we do not come to our senses, have we tried to reform our fornication and adultery, our greed and injustice? No! Rather we have added to them. Has not the whole Roman world been covered at this time with the oppression of the poor, and every base act and injustice, on account of which we have been reduced to the proverbial «mustard seed»? Why the events in Anatolia, and what is happening up to this moment in Macedonia, I mean, and also where the emperor Kyr Michael is? And how is the people whom Christ our God entrusted to you being governed by each? And how «do those who do not call upon the Lord eat» this ⟨people⟩ «like so many loaves of bread», not to mention the total destruction wrought by these bloodthirsty Almugavars? For if a just man has pity on the souls of the very beasts, O woe is me, what has befallen those who are made in the image of God?

διὰ τί δὲ ταῦτα μὴ οἶδεν ἡ βασιλεία σου εἰς ἀκρίβειαν, ἀλλὰ τοὺς
ταῦτα μηνύοντας ἀπωθεῖται, καὶ ἄγνωστα διαμένει τὰ ὄντως ἐλεεινὰ καὶ
δακρύων μεστά; ἢ εἰ καὶ εἰς ἀκοάς τι τούτων δοθῇ, ἡ ἀναβολὴ κατέλειψεν,
ὡς ἔοικε, τῶν ἐμῶν κακῶν, ἢ εἴπω κἀκείνων, τὰ σπλάγχνα κλειόν-
25 των Θεοῦ τὰ φιλάνθρωτα, καὶ αὐτὰ τῆς βασιλείας σου. καὶ εἴθε μὴ ἐζη-
τήθη ὕστερον ἐξ ἡμῶν πόθεν δὲ καὶ βοήθειαν καὶ εἰρήνην ἐλπίζομεν, ἢ ἐκ
ποίας ἐπιστροφῆς, ὅπου Θεὸν ὁμολογοῦντες εἰδέναι, τοῖς ἔργοις ἀρνούμε-
θα, ἐν δὲ τῷ καιρῷ τῶν κακῶν ἡμῶν, ὡς μηδὲν παραλείψαντες τῶν αὐτῶν
ἀρετῶν καὶ ἡμῖν δυνατῶν, «ἀνάστα», λέγομεν, ἢ «ἐλπίζομεν, καὶ σῶσον
30 ἡμᾶς». ὢ τῆς ἀναισθησίας! οὐδὲ γὰρ αὐτὸς ὁ Ἰὼβ εἶχε τοῦτο θαρρῆσαι,
ὁ καὶ περὶ τῶν υἱῶν ἀποστέλλων καὶ καθαρίζων, μήπως ἐκεῖνοι
κακὸν οὐ λέγω εἰ ἔπραξαν, ἀλλ᾽ εἰ ἐνενόησαν.

διὰ τί μὴ ἐνωτιζώμεθα μᾶλλον τὸ ἁρμόζον ἡμῖν ἐκ τῆς θείας
Γραφῆς, καὶ κἂν τῷ δέει διεγειρώμεθα, ἢ τὸ ἐντενεῖ τὸ τόξον αὐτοῦ,
35 ἕως οὗ ἀσθενήσουσιν οἱ αὐτοῦ παρακούοντες, ἢ τὸ ἐὰν μὴ ἐπιστραφῆτε, τὴν ῥομφαίαν αὐτοῦ στιλβώσει; εἰ οὖν δέχῃ με σύμβουλον, κἂν ἀπό γε τοῦ νῦν ζῶσαι ὥσπερ ἀνὴρ τὴν ζώνην καὶ τὴν
ῥομφαίαν σου, ῥῖψον τὸν ὄκνον καὶ τὴν μικροψυχίαν, καὶ τὸ εἰς ἀναβολὰς
τὰ πράγματα ἀναρτᾶν, καὶ τὸ αἰδεῖσθαί τινας ἢ χαρίζεσθαι. ὁ γὰρ λέγων
40 ὀλίγα, καὶ πράττων τῶν ὀφειλόντων πολλά, ἀξιέπαινος· ὁ λέγων δὲ μόνον,
ἀλλὰ μὴ πράττων, πάντως μικρὸν ἢ οὐδὲν τοῦ ἠχοῦντος [fol. 16v] χαλκοῦ διενήνοχεν. εἰπὲ καὶ αὐτὸς καὶ λόγοις καὶ πλέον τοῖς ἔργοις, ῥίψας
ἐν τῷ Θεῷ καὶ τῇ Θεομήτορι τὴν ἀδυναμίαν σου, ὅτι ἐν τῷ Θεῷ μου
ὑπερβήσομαι τεῖχος, καὶ δὴ καὶ τὸ προωρώμην τὸν Κύριον
45 ἐνώπιόν μου διὰ παντὸς πράττειν τὰ φίλα αὐτῷ, καὶ τὸ ἐκ δεξιῶν
μου ἐστίν, ἐν οἷς οὐ δεῖ με ὑπ᾽ αὐτοῦ ῥωννύμενον μὴ σαλεύεσθαι.
τότε γάρ σου ἀναμφιβόλως συναντιλήψεται, καὶ λαλήσει τὸ ἔντεινε καὶ
κατευοδοῦ καὶ βασίλευε πλὴν ἕνεκεν ἀληθείας καὶ πρᾳότητος καὶ δικαιοσύνης καὶ ἐλεημοσύνης καὶ κρίσεως, καὶ τῶν ὅσα φίλων
50 αὐτῷ. τότε γὰρ καὶ ἐν πάσῃ ἀγαθωσύνῃ ἐνισχύσει σε θαυμαστῶς ἐκ
δεξιῶν σου παρών, αὐτὸς Χριστὸς ὁ Θεὸς ἡμῶν, ὑπερασπίζων καὶ συν-
τηρῶν σου τὴν βασιλείαν ὑγιῆ καὶ πολυχρόνιον.

ἀναφέρω δεόμενος ἵνα μετὰ Θεὸν τηρῆται ἡ πόλις ἐν ἀσφαλείᾳ, πολεμίους λογιζομένων ἡμῶν τοὺς Μογαβάρους, καὶ ὡς δύναμις φροντίσαι
55 τούτων ἐλευθέρους δειχθῆναι Χριστιανούς, ἀγανακτοῦντος Θεοῦ, ὡς ἐν
τοῖς ἄλλοις ἡμῶν κακοῖς, καὶ ὑπὲρ αὐτῶν, καὶ μὴ ἀναβολὰς ἀναμένειν, ἀλλ᾽
ἐν τάχει, ὡς ἔφην, βουλευθῆναι τὰ δέοντα.

24–25 cf. I Joh. 3:17 ‖ 31–32 cf. Job 1:5 ‖ 34 καὶ κἂν cf. Nicholas Mysticus, *Ep.* XXXII
(PG, CXI, 205A) ‖ 34–35 Ps. 57(58):8 ‖ 35–36 Ps. 7:13 ‖ 37 cf. Job 38:3 ‖ 41–42 cf. I Cor.
13:1 ‖ 43–44 Ps. 17 (18):30 ‖ 44–46 cf. Ps. 15(16):8 ‖ 47–51 Ps. 44 (45):5

35

Why doesn't your majesty have accurate information on these events, but sends away those who report these happenings, so that these really pitiful calamities which provoke tears remain unknown? Or if any of these reports does come to your attention, as the result of procrastination it is neglected, since my evil deeds, or shall I say theirs, «close the bowels» of compassion of both God and your majesty. And I wish we were not asked later from what source we may hope for assistance and peace, or from what repentance, since we confess that we know God, but deny Him in our deeds, and in the time of our misfortunes, as if we had not neglected a single possible virtue, we say «arise» or «we have hope, save us». O what blindness! Not even Job himself was able to enjoy this confidence, for he used to «send his sons and purify them», not, I emphasize, lest they had committed some evil deed, but «lest they had evil thoughts in their minds».

Why don't we instead heed the fitting passages from the Holy Scriptures, and wake up at least from fear? Either «He shall bend His bow till they shall fail» who have not heeded Him, or «If ye will not repent, He will furbish His sword». If then you accept me as a counsellor, from this moment on «gird your loins like a man», and put on your sword, cast away hesitancy and pusillanimity, and stop putting things off, and fearing or favoring certain people. For he who says little and does many of the things which he ought is praiseworthy; but he who only speaks but does not do anything is little or no different from «sounding brass». Speak with words and even more with actions, casting off your weakness through the aid of God and the Mother of God, because «by my God I will pass over a wall», and also «I foresaw the Lord always before my face» to do what was pleasing to Him, and «He is on my right hand, that I should not be moved» when strengthened by Him. For then without any doubt He will help you, and will say «bend your bow, and prosper and reign, because of truth and meekness and righteousness» and mercy and judgment and whatsoever is pleasing unto Him. For then He will support you marvelously in all goodness, Christ Himself our God always present at your right hand, defending and preserving your majesty in good health and for many years.

I make this petition and ask that with the help of God we preserve the City in safety, by considering the Almugavars as our enemies, and that we undertake to the best of our ability to free Christians from them, for God is wroth with us on their account, as in our other misfortunes, and we should not delay, but, as I have said, the necessary measures should be quickly determined.

76

36. ⟨Πρὸς τὸν αὐτοκράτορα⟩

"Ότι μὴ τοὺς υἱοὺς παιδεύεις εἰς τὰ τῷ Θεῷ ἀρεστά· ὅτι τοῦ ὑπηκόου μὴ προνοῇ ὡς παίδων πατήρ· ὅτι ἐβεβηλώθη καὶ κατεβλήθη ἡ ἐκκλησία, ὡς μὴ μόνον οὓς ἀγνοοῦσιν, ἀλλὰ καὶ οὓς οἴδασιν ἀναξίους εἰσάγειν
5 τῷ βήματι· ὅτι οὐ μόνον ἀδίδακτος κατελείφθη ὁ κοινὸς λαός, ἀλλὰ καὶ
τῇ εἰσαγωγῇ ὡς οὐκ ὤφειλεν Ἰουδαίων καὶ Ἀρμενίων καταμιαίνεται· ὅτι
οἱ ἐνεργοῦντες οὐκ ἀνακρίνονται, ἀλλ' ἐν ἀκαθαρσίᾳ καὶ ἀδικίᾳ πορεύον-
ται· ὅτι ἐκρύβη ἡ ἀλήθεια καὶ δικαιοσύνη καὶ κρίσις καὶ ἔλεος· ὅτι ὁ τοῦ
Θεοῦ λαὸς εἰς Ἰσμαὴλ παρεδόθη διὰ μοιχείας, αἱμομιξίας, καὶ κτηνῶν καὶ
10 ἀρρένων μανίαν, καὶ τὴν ἀνυπόστατον βλασφημίαν καὶ γοητείαν καὶ ἀδικ-
ίαν· ὅτι οὐδέποτε ἄδεια ἀπωλείας ἐδόθη τοσαύτη μοναζούσαις καὶ μονα-
χοῖς· ὅτι δυνάμενος καὶ τὰ κοινὰ καὶ τὰ ἴδια διὰ Κυρίου καὶ μετὰ Κυρίου
ποιεῖσθαι καὶ κτᾶσθαι ταπείνωσιν τὴν ὑψοποιόν, προέκρινας τὸ ἀσύμβο-
λον· ὅτι ἐκπεμπομένου στρατοῦ, οὐκ ἔστιν ὁ νουθετῶν τούτους καὶ ἐκφο-
15 βῶν ὁδεύειν μετὰ Χριστοῦ, ἀλλὰ μοιχείαις καὶ ἁρπαγαῖς πρόσκεινται καὶ
κλοπαῖς, καὶ πόθεν ἕξουσι τὸ νικᾶν; ὅτι καταγινώσκοντες τὴν τῶν Ἰουδαίων ἀπειθείαν καὶ παρανομίαν, δι' ἣν ὠλοθρεύθησαν, ἀπειθοῦμεν ἡμεῖς
καὶ παρανομοῦμεν μειζόνως, ὅσον [fol. 17ʳ] συνδούλων ἐκεῖνοι καταφρονοῦντες, τοῦ δὲ Δεσπότου καὶ βασιλέως ἡμεῖς καὶ μεγάλου Θεοῦ. εἰ
20 οὖν τούτων μετὰ Θεὸν ὡς δυνατὸν σπουδάσεις τὴν ἄμειψιν, οὐ μόνον τῆς
ἀπειλῆς ὑπέρτερος ἔσῃ, μετὰ σοῦ δὲ καὶ τὸ ὑπήκοον, ἀλλὰ καὶ πρὸς ταύτῃ
τῇ βασιλείᾳ ἁρπάσεις καὶ τὴν οὐράνιον.

37. ⟨Πρὸς τὸν αὐτοκράτορα⟩

Ἡ τῆς ἀνομίας ἡμῶν καὶ ἀκαθαρσίας κραυγὴ πρὸς
Θεὸν ἀνέβη, οὐ τοῦ λαοῦ παντὸς μόνου, ἀλλὰ καὶ μᾶλλον μοναζόντων καὶ
ἱερέων. ἐντεῦθεν τοῦ Θεοῦ τῶν δυνάμεων ἀγανάκτησις καὶ ὀργὴ ἀνυπός-
5 τατος ἐπὶ κεφαλῆς ἡμῶν κρέμαται· καὶ οὐ μόνον ἐρχόμεθα εἰς συναίσθησιν ἐν οἷς εὑρισκόμεθα, ἀλλὰ καὶ ὡς τοῦ θείου θεραπευταὶ ἐκεῖθεν τὰ δο-

37: 2-3 cf. Jon. 1:2

36: V 16ᵛ–17ʳ. S 148ᵛ–149ʳ. P 28ᵛ–29ʳ. Ed Banduri, Imperium Orientale, II,
614–615; Migne, PG, CXLII, 511–514.
1 γράμμα πρὸς τὸν αὐτοκράτορα (post αὐτοκράτορα, ἂν scr. P, del. P¹) ἵνα παιδεύῃ
(παιδεύει Vʳ) τοὺς υἱοὺς αὐτοῦ (VʳSP¹, αὐτῷ P) εἰς τὰ τῷ Θεῷ ἀρεστὰ καὶ πᾶν τὸ ὑπήκοον add. VʳSP ‖ 9 εἰς scripsi: ἐξ codd. ‖ 11–12 μοναχοῖς scripsi, cf. Athanasius, Ep. 111,
19: μοναχαῖς codd. ‖ 13 ὑψοποιὸν VS¹P: ὑψοποιῶν S ‖ 22 ἁρπάσης codd.
37: V 17ʳ–17ᵛ. S 149ʳ–150ʳ. P 29ʳ–30ʳ. Ed. Laiou, Andronicus II, 335, no. 3.
1 γράμμα πρὸς τὸν αὐτοκράτορα περὶ ἐπιστροφῆς πρὸς Θεὸν καὶ ἵνα ἐπιγνῷ ἕκαστος τὰ οἰκεῖα καὶ τὰ κοινά, καὶ περὶ τοῦ τετρυγὼς (τετρυγὸς S, τετρυγῶς P) κτύπου ἐκείνου
add. VʳSP ‖ 2 κραυγὴ] αὐγὴ S

36. ⟨To the emperor⟩

The fact ⟨is⟩ that you do not instruct your sons in ways pleasing to God, and that you do not look after your subjects as a father should his children; that the Church has been profaned and attacked, so that not only through ignorance are unworthy men brought into the clergy, but also men who are known to be unworthy; that not only is the common people abandoned without any instruction, but they are defiled as they ought not to be by the introduction of Jews and Armenians; that fiscal agents are not investigated, but persist in their depravity and injustice; that truth and righteousness and judgment and mercy have disappeared; that the people of God have been delivered into the hands of Ishmael on account of their adultery, incest and perverted passion for sodomy and pederasty, and because of their intolerable blasphemy and sorcery and injustice; that never has such license for corruption been granted to nuns and monks; that although you were able to act in both public and private affairs and to acquire exalting humility through the Lord and with the help of the Lord, you preferred to do nothing (?); that when an army is dispatched, there is no one to admonish the men and to frighten them into marching with Christ, but they indulge in adultery and looting and thievery, and how will they then be victorious? that although we condemn the disobedience and transgression of the Jews, on account of which they were destroyed, we ourselves are even more guilty of disobedience and transgression, and just as they disregarded their fellow servants, so we disregard our Lord and King the great God. If then with the help of God you strive to the best of your ability for a change ⟨in these conditions⟩, not only will you rise above the threatened ⟨catastrophe⟩, and your subjects with you, but, in addition to this kingdom, you will also gain the kingdom of heaven.

37. ⟨To the emperor⟩

«The cry of our lawlessness and depravity», not only of all the people, but even more so of monks and priests, «has risen to God». Therefore the irresistible wrath and anger of the God of hosts hangs over our heads, and now not only do we realize the situation we are in, but as if we were servants of the

κοῦντα ἡμῖν αἰτοῦμεν αἰτήματα. καὶ λέγω ἐνώπιον τοῦ Θεοῦ τῶν δυνάμεων, εἰ μὴ αἱ θεοπειθεῖς καὶ πολλαὶ πρεσβεῖαι τῆς Θεομήτορος, δι᾽ ὀλίγων τινῶν λίαν εὐαριθμήτων δεομένων αὐτῆς, οὔτε αὕτη ἡ πόλις ἐσῴζετο
10 ἕως νῦν ἀπ᾽ αὐτῆς τῆς ιγ΄ ῆς τοῦ Δεκεβρίου, ἡνίκα ὁ τετρυγὼς ἐκεῖνος ἐγένετο κτύπος, οὔτε τὰ τῆς Ἀνατολῆς, ἀπ᾽ αὐτῆς τῆς Ἀνέας μέχρι τοῦ
Σκουταρίου. καὶ μὴ νομίσῃς ὡς δι᾽ ἐπιβολῆς στρατευμάτων ἰσχύσομέν τι·
λέγω γὰρ καὶ πάλιν ἐνώπιον τοῦ Θεοῦ, ὡς οὐδ᾽ ἂν αὐτὴ ἡ ἑσπέριος, εἰ ἦν
δυνατόν, ὅλη συνήχθη εἰς τὴν βοήθειαν. ἀλλὰ τί; ἐπιστροφὴ καὶ μετάνοια
15 εἰς δύναμιν πρὸς Θεόν, δι᾽ ἃ καὶ μακροθυμεῖ ἀναμένων.

εἰ οὖν βουλόμεθα καὶ ἑαυτοὺς καὶ τὸν κόσμον κερδῆσαι,
ἕκαστος ἐπιγνῶμεν καὶ τὰ οἰκεῖα καὶ τὰ κοινά, οἱ διοικοῦντες τὰ δημόσια
ἐξαιρέτως καὶ τὰ τοῦ κόσμου καὶ τὰ τῶν ἐκκλησιῶν· καὶ παυσώμεθα τῶν
κακῶν, τοὺς δὲ τοῦτο μὴ βουλομένους, παυέτω ἡ ἐξουσία. λέγω γὰρ πάλιν
20 ἐνώπιον τοῦ Θεοῦ τῶν δυνάμεων ὡς, εἰ γένηται ὁλόκληρος ἡ ἐπιστροφὴ
ὅσον τὸ κατὰ σέ, οὐ μόνον ἐλευθερίαν πάλιν ἡ ῥηθεῖσα γῆ τῆς Ἀνατολῆς
πλουτήσει καὶ ἀπολαύσει, ἀλλὰ συντρίψει καὶ τοὺς ἐπαναστάντας Ἰσμαηλί-
τας, καὶ τὰ ὅρια ἐκείνων δεσπόσει. εἰ δ᾽ (ὅπερ ἀπεύχομαι) μὴ τελεία γένηται ἡ ἐπιστροφή, ἀλλ᾽ ἐκ μέρους, ἐσεῖται καὶ ἡ εὐεργεσία ἐκ μέρους· εἰ δὲ
25 οὐδόλως, οὐδόλως, κἂν μυρίας ἐπιβολὰς στρατευμάτων ἢ καστελλίων
ἀνεγέρσεις ἐπινοήσωμεν. ἀλλὰ καὶ ὅπερ ἂν τῶν εἰς ἀσφάλειαν δοκούντων
μεταχειρισώμεθα, εἰς τὸ ἐναντίον ἐκβήσεται.

διὰ ταῦτα ἠθέλησα ὁ ἀνάξιος ἐγὼ τοῦ οὐρανοῦ καὶ τῆς γῆς ἀνοῖ-
ξαι τὴν θύραν, καὶ τοὺς ἐρχομένους [fol. 17ᵛ] παρακαλεῖν καὶ εἰς δύνα-
30 μιν νουθετεῖν πρὸς ἐπιστροφὴν καὶ μετάνοιαν. διὰ ταῦτα καὶ πεμφθῆναι
τινά, εἰ καὶ οὐκ εἰσηκούσθην, ὑπέμνησα πρὸς Ἀνατολήν, καὶ πάλιν παρακαλῶ καὶ τὰ ἴχνη κατασπάζομαι τῶν ποδῶν σου, βλέψωμεν πρὸς ἐπιστροφὴν καὶ μετάνοιαν βλέψωμεν· μηδὲ τὰς ὀρέξεις ζητῶμεν ἡμῶν, ὥσπερ ὁ κανικλείου, μὴ ζητῶν καταλλαγῆναι Θεῷ εἰς ὅσα τῇ ἐξουσίᾳ ἐχρήσατο
35 ἀσυμφόρως, ἀλλὰ μόνον γενέσθαι τοὺς γάμους, ὡς δυναμένους αὐτὸν τῶν
χειρῶν τοῦ Θεοῦ ἐξελεῖν. ζητήσωμεν τὰ ἀρέσκοντα τῷ Θεῷ, σπεύσωμεν
διορθῶσαι καὶ τὰ οἰκεῖα καὶ τὰ κοινά. πόθεν γὰρ ἐλπίζομεν ἀντίληψιν ἐκ
Θεοῦ, τῆς ἀνομίας ἀνερχομένης εἰς οὐρανούς; ταῦτα ἀναγγεῖλαί σοι ἐκε-
λεύσθην ἐνώπιον τοῦ Θεοῦ. εἰ μὲν οὖν εἰς ἀκουόντων ὦτα ἀνήγγειλα, τῷ
40 Θεῷ μου χάρις καὶ τῇ σῇ ἁγίᾳ ψυχῇ· εἰ δὲ βαρὺς φαίνομαι ἐνοχλῶν, δέομαι
πάλιν καὶ τοῖς σοῖς προσπίπτω ποσίν, ἵνα ἐάσῃς με καὶ μηνύειν καὶ βλέπ-
ειν· οὐδὲ γὰρ ἄξιος ἐγὼ ἐν ἀνομίαις συλληφθείς, καὶ ταλαίπωρος
ὢν καὶ ἀκάθαρτος, ὁρᾶσθαι παρά τινος, καὶ πολλῷ μᾶλλον παρ᾽ ὀρθοδόξου βασιλέως καὶ εὐσεβοῦς.

---

16 cf. Matt. 16:26 ‖ 28–29 cf. Ps. 77 (78):23 ‖ 34 cf. II Cor. 5:20 ‖ 42 cf. Ps. 50 (51):7

---

8 αἰθιοπειθεῖς SP, αἱ θεοπειθεῖς Pxmg ‖ 11 ἀνίας P ‖ 12 ἐπιβολῆς P ‖ 15 ἀναμόνων P
25 ἐπιβουλὰς S ‖ 26 τῶν VˢᵛSP ‖ 30 ταῦτα] τοῦτο S ‖ 33–34 ad ὁ κανικλείου P ˣᵐᵍ
scripsit litteram N. ‖ 36 τῷ] τὰ S

37

divine we make requests which seem good to us. And I say, in the presence of the God of hosts, if it were not for the numerous God-persuading intercessions of the Mother of God, because a few of us, many too few, prayed to Her, this city would not have been preserved until now from the 13th of December when that resounding blow occurred, nor even the eastern region from Anea itself as far as Scoutari. And do not think that we shall prevail by means of armed attacks, or I say again before God, even if the whole West, if it were possible, were to join to help us. What then is the solution? Turning toward God and repentance to the utmost of our ability, for which He is patiently waiting.

If then we wish to save both ourselves and the world, let each of us recognize our own ⟨duties⟩ and those toward the community, especially those who administer public affairs, both worldly and spiritual. And let us forsake wicked deeds, and as for those who are not willing to do this, let them be stripped of their authority, For again I say before the God of hosts that if everyone were to repent as much as you have, not only would the above-mentioned eastern region again attain and enjoy freedom, but it would crush the rebellious Ishmaelites and rule over their territory. But if (and I pray this may not happen) the repentance is not complete but only partial, then the benefit will be only partial; and if there is no repentance, there will be no benefit, even if we were to plan thousands of attacks by troops or the construction of castles. But whatever we should undertake as seemingly a measure of security, would turn out to the contrary.

Wherefore I, unworthy as I am, wished «to open the gate of heaven» and earth, and to entreat those who come ⟨to the gate⟩, and to urge them on, as best I can, to conversion and repentance. Therefore, even though I was not heeded, I suggested that someone be sent to the East, and again I beg you and clasp your feet, let us turn our eyes toward conversion and repentance. And let us not seek after our desires, as does the Keeper of the Inkstand, who does not seek to be reconciled with God, for all that he has used his authority harmfully, but only seeks after marriages as if they could save him from the hands of God. Let us seek what is pleasing unto God, let us hasten to make amends in both private and public affairs. For how shall we hope for help from God when our lawlessness rises to the heavens? I have been compelled to make these declarations to you before God. If then I have declared them into the ears of those who hear, thanks be to God and to your holy soul; but if I seem to be a grievous nuisance, then again I beg you and I fall at your feet, that you will relieve me from the role of observer and informer. For I, who am caught in transgressions and am wretched and depraved, am not worthy to be seen by anyone, much less by an orthodox and pious emperor.

38. Πρὸς τὸν αὐτοκράτορα

Παρακαλῶ, δέσποτά μου ἅγιε, ἵνα θεραπεύσῃς τὸν βασιλεύσαντά σε
Θεὸν τῶν δυνάμεων, καὶ κατὰ τὸ ἀρέσκον ἐκείνῳ ποιῇς ἰθύνεσθαι τὸ ὑπή-
κοον· καὶ εἰ ἀλήθειαν λέγει ὁ λέγων δίκαιος ὁ Κύριος καὶ δικαιοσύ-
5 νας ἠγάπησε, πολιτευέσθωσαν δικαιοσύναι ἃς ἀγαπᾷ. τῇ δὲ δικαιοσύνῃ
συνέζευκται καὶ ἔλεος καὶ ἀλήθεια, πλὴν οὐ λόγῳ, ἀλλ᾽ ἔργῳ. καὶ διὰ ταῦτα συμβασιλεύσεις Χριστῷ, εἰ ὅσον τὸ κατὰ σὲ ἃ ἐκεῖνος φιλεῖ ἐκπληροῖς,
καὶ ἔργοις παρρησιάσῃ φωνῆσαι πρὸς τὸ ὑπήκοον τὸ ἀξιομακάριστον τοῦτο, ἀπ᾽ ἐμοῦ ὄψεσθε καὶ οὕτως ποιήσετε. εἰ γὰρ γένηται τοῦτο,
10 καὶ συμβασιλεύεις οὐ μόνον ἀπεντεῦθεν Χριστῷ, ἀλλὰ καὶ αἰώνια. εἰ δὲ
συμβασιλεύεις, εὖ οἶδα καὶ συμπολεμήσει αὐτὸς ὁ Υἱὸς τοῦ Θεοῦ τοῦ
ζῶντος, καὶ πάντα ἐχθρὸν καὶ πολέμιον ὑπὸ τοὺς πόδας ὑποτάξει
τοὺς σούς, καὶ τῷ ὑποτάξαντι αὐτῷ τὰ πάντα Θεῷ καὶ Πατρὶ ὑπ-
έρτερόν σε παραστήσει τῶν βασιλέων τῆς γῆς. καὶ πάντες οἱ ζήσαντες εὐ-
15 σεβῶς κληρονόμοι φανήσονται τοῦ Θεοῦ, συγκληρονόμοι δὲ τοῦ
Δεσπότου Χριστοῦ. ὅσον αὐτὸς ὑπερέξεις παρά τε τοῦ ἀξιώματος
καὶ τῆς ὡς δυνατὸν ἐκπληρώσεως τῶν ἁγίων αὐτοῦ προσταγμάτων,
οὐδεὶς τῶν ἀνθρώπων τῶν σήμερον οἶδεν ὡς ἡ ἐκ Θεοῦ βασιλεία σου
ἀκριβέστερον· καὶ διὰ τὸν Κύριον μὴ προφανῶς ἀδικῶνται οἱ ἄνθρωποι.

39. Πρὸς τὸν αὐτοκράτορα

Παρακαλῶ τὴν βασιλείαν σου, ἐλέησον καὶ τὴν ψυχήν σου καὶ τὸν
λαόν σου. [fol. 18ʳ] ἃς γένηται δικαιοσύνη καὶ ἐλεημοσύνη, ἢ κἂν δικαιοσύνη, καὶ μὴ εἰς πλέον παροργίζηται ὑφ᾽ ἡμῶν ὁ ὑπεράγαθος καὶ φιλεύ-
5 σπλαγχνος Κύριος. μέγα γὰρ καὶ ἀσυγχώρητον τὸ δεινόν, τὸ μηδὲ μετὰ τὴν
τοσαύτην ἐλεεινὴν καὶ ἀφόρητον καὶ φρικώδη πληγὴν σπουδάζειν ἡμᾶς
σωφρονίζεσθαι, ἀλλ᾽ ἀναλγήτους διακειμένους, προσκαλεῖσθαι καὶ μείζω
διὰ τῆς πρὸς ταύτην ἀναισθησίας.

38: 4–5 Ps. 10 (11):7 ‖ 9 Jud. 7:17 ‖ 12–13 cf. I Cor. 15:27–28 ‖ 15–16 cf. Rom. 8:17

38: V 17ᵛ. S 150ʳ–150ᵛ. P 30ʳ–30ᵛ.
1 ante πρὸς add. γράμμα VʳSP ‖ post αὐτοκράτορα add. ἵνα πολιτεύεται δικαιοσύνη καὶ
ἔλεος καὶ ἀλήθεια VʳSP ‖ 8 παρρησιάσει VS, παρρησιάσα P ‖ 12 ὑποτάξῃ codd. ‖
16 τε] γε P ‖ 19 μὴ] δὴ P ‖ ἀδικοῦνται codd.
39: V 17ᵛ–18ʳ. S 150ᵛ. P 30ᵛ.
1 ante πρὸς add. γράμμα VʳSP ‖ post αὐτοκράτορα add. ἵνα μὴ ἀναβάλλῃ ποιεῖν τὰ καλά
VʳSP

38. To the emperor

I beg you, my holy master, to serve the God of hosts Who made you emperor, and to cause your subjects to be guided in a manner pleasing to Him; and if he who says «the Lord is righteous and loves righteousness» speaks the truth, let the righteousness which He loves be the rule; and righteousness is always coupled with mercy and truth, except not in word, but in deed. And thus you will rule together with Christ, if you fulfil what is dear to Him as best you can, and if your deeds will give you the assurance to declare to your subjects this blessed phrase: «Ye shall look at me and so shall ye do». For, if this occurs, not only will you rule together with Christ from this moment on, but forever. And if you rule together ⟨with Him⟩, I am sure that the Son of the living God will fight together with you, and «He will crush every foe» and enemy «beneath your feet», and He will commend you, as superior to all the kings of the earth, to God the Father «Who subjects all things to Himself»; and all those who have lived piously will appear as «the heirs of God, and joint heirs with our Lord Christ». No man today knows more accurately than your divine majesty how much you will prevail by your rank and by your fulfilment of His divine commands to the best of your ability; and for the sake of the Lord let men not be manifestly wronged.

39. To the emperor

I entreat your majesty, have mercy both on your soul and on your people. Let justice and mercy prevail, or at least justice, and let us not provoke the transcendently good and merciful Lord to even greater wrath. For it is a great and unforgivable sin for us not to strive to come to our senses after such a piteous, intolerable and terrible disaster, but to sit here unmindful of the danger and thus provoke an even greater ⟨disaster⟩ because of our insensitivity to this one.

40. Πρὸς τὸν αὐτοκράτορα

Τὴν βασιλείαν σου ὁ Θεὸς τοῦ Χριστιανικοῦ λαοῦ ἄρχειν ἐκύρωσε,
παρασχών σοι ἀναλογοῦσαν καὶ φρόνησιν καὶ ἰσχύν, ἵνα καὶ ψυχικῶς καὶ
σωματικῶς κατὰ τὸ ἀρέσκον αὐτῷ ἐν εὐνομίᾳ καὶ δικαιοσύνη ποιμάνης
5 αὐτούς. ὅρα δέ, ὡς εἰ πρὸς τὸν θεῖον σκοπὸν ἄρχεις αὐτῶν, πόσης ἐκεῖθεν
καταξιωθήσῃ δόξης παρὰ Θεοῦ καὶ λαμπρότητος. μὴ οὖν ἀναβάλλου ποιεῖν
τὰ καλά, μηδὲ ὄκνει. ἔχεις γὰρ καὶ αὐτὸς βασιλέα, κ α θ ὼ ς μ ε τ ρ ο ῦ μ ε ν
ἐ τ έ ρ ο ι ς, ἀ ν τ ι μ ε τ ρ ε ῖ σ θ α ι κ α ὶ ἡ μ ᾶ ς ὑπισχνούμενον. θεράπευε
οὖν αὐτῷ ἵνα θεραπεύσῃ σοι καὶ αὐτὸς καὶ ὧδε καὶ ἐν τῷ μέλλοντι.

41. ⟨Πρὸς τὸν αὐτοκράτορα⟩

Ῥαψάκου, τοῦ τῶν Ἀσσυρίων βασιλέως Σεναχηρεὶμ στρατηγοῦ,
λόγους ὀνειδισμοῦ κατὰ τοῦ ἐπὶ πάντων Θεοῦ ἐμέσαι τολμήσαντος, ὁ θεο-
φιλέστατος βασιλεὺς Ἐζεκίας οὐ τὰ ἱμάτια μόνον διέρρηξε, ζηλῶν ὑπὲρ
5 τοῦ μεγάλου Θεοῦ, ἀλλὰ καὶ τὴν βασιλικὴν ἀποδὺς ἐσθῆτα, ἠμφιάσατο
σάκκον· ὅθεν ἐπικαμφθεὶς ὁ Θεὸς τῶν δυνάμεων τὰς ἑκατὸν ὀγδοήκοντα
πέντε χιλιάδας ἀνεῖλε τῶν Ἀσσυρίων. ἡμᾶς δέ, ἅγιε βασιλεῦ, πῶς ἀντιλήψεται ὁ Θεὸς Σαβαώθ, ὅτι τὴν θεοκτόνον συναγωγὴν μὴ μόνον μέσον
καθέζεσθαι παραχωροῦμεν τῶν ὀρθοδόξων, μυκτηρίζοντας τὰ ἡμέτερα
10 (τὴν προσκύνησιν, λέγω, καὶ λατρείαν καὶ πίστιν τὴν πρὸς τὸν Κύριον καὶ
Θεὸν ἡμῶν Ἰησοῦν Χριστὸν καὶ τὰς εἰκονικὰς ἡμῶν εὐσεβεῖς προσκυνήσεις, καὶ ὅσα ἡ ἁγία καὶ ἄμωμος τῶν Χριστιανῶν πίστις πλουτεῖ μυστήρια), ἀλλ᾽ ὅτι καὶ διὰ δώρων πολλὴν αὐτοῖς τὴν ἰσχὺν παρέσχεν ὁ Κωκαλᾶς;
ὅτι εἰ καὶ τολμήσει τις τῶν Χριστιανῶν ἀπὸ ζήλου λαλῆσαι, τίς ὁ τῆς
15 φυλακῆς ἐκεῖνον λυτρώσων;
περὶ δὲ τῶν Ἀρμενίων ὅσα ποιοῦσι τοὺς πλησιάζοντας ὀρθοδόξους,
αἰσχύνομαι διηγήσασθαι, οἶδε Θεός· πλὴν ὅτι καὶ συναγωγὴν ἔχειν εἰς
προσευχὰς οὐ κωλύονται. εἰ δέ τις τῶν ὀρθοδόξων κἀκεῖ τολμήσει λα-

40: 7–8 cf. Matt. 7:2
41: 2–3 cf. IV Reg. 18:13–36 ‖ 3–7 cf. IV Reg. 19:1–35

40: V 18ʳ. S 150ᵛ–151ʳ. P 30ᵛ–31ʳ.
1 ante πρὸς add. γράμμα VʳSP ‖ post αὐτοκράτορα add. περὶ τοῦ αὐτοῦ VʳSP ‖ 3–4 καὶ
σωματικῶς om. P ‖ 6 καταξιωθείσῃ S
41: V 18ʳ–19ʳ. S 151ʳ–152ʳ. P 31ʳ–32ᵛ. Ed. Banduri, Imperium Orientale, II, 614;
Migne, PG, CXLII, 509–512.
1 γράμμα πρὸς τὸν αὐτοκράτορα περὶ τῶν θεοκτόνων Ἰουδαίων ἵνα ἐξέλθωσιν ἐκ τῆς πόλεως add. VʳSP ‖ 3 ἐμίσαι P ‖ τολμήσαντος] τολμήτος S ‖ 16 ποιοῦσιν VS ‖ 18 προσ-
ευχὴν P

40. To the emperor

God ordained that your majesty should rule over the Christian people, and granted you proportionate wisdom and strength, so that in both soul and body you might govern them with order and justice as is pleasing to Him. Consider, then, how great will be the glory and splendor of which you will be deemed worthy by God, if you rule them in accordance with the divine purpose. Therefore do not delay or hesitate to do what is right. For you yourself have a ruler Who has promised that «as we measure unto others, so shall it be measured again unto us». Serve Him therefore so that He will serve you, both here and in the world to come.

41. ⟨To the emperor⟩

When Rhapsakes the general of Senachereim, king of the Assyrians, dared to spew forth words of insult against the Lord of all, the most pious king Hezekiah not only rent his garments in his zeal for the great Lord, but removed his royal garb and donned sackcloth. Wherefore the Lord of hosts was moved to pity and slew 185,000 Assyrians. How then, holy emperor, will the Lord Sabaoth help us, when we not only permit, in the midst of Orthodox Christians, the assembly of a God-murdering congregation, people who sneer at our customs (that is, at our worship and adoration and faith in our Lord and God Jesus Christ, and our pious veneration of images, and all the mysteries in which the holy and immaculate faith of Christians abounds), but when also through bribes Kokalas has given them great power? And if any Christian out of zeal dares to protest, who will save him from jail?

As for the outrages which the Armenians perpetrate towards the neighboring Orthodox Christians, I am ashamed to tell that story, God be my witness. I'll say only so much, that they are not prevented from having a meetinghouse for their prayers, and if any orthodox person should dare to

λῆσαι, δι' ὀλίγων βασιλικῶν πολλὰ δυνήσονται οἱ Ἀρμένιοι. ὅτι δὲ καὶ διὰ
20 τὰς ἐμὰς ἁμαρτίας τῶν Χριστιανικῶν ἄρξαντες πόλεων Ἰσμα-[fol. 18ᵛ]
ηλῖται οὐδὲ σημαντῆρος ἦχον παραχωροῦσι Χριστιανοῖς, οὐδεὶς ἀγνοεῖ·
ἡμεῖς δέ, καὶ ταῦτα χάριτι Χριστοῦ τοῦ Θεοῦ τὴν ἐν Χριστῷ βασιλείαν
πλουτοῦντες, κατεφρονήσαμεν οὐ μόνον ποιεῖν ὅσα ἐποίησαν οἱ τῶν
Ἰσμαηλιτῶν πρέσβεις — καὶ ταῦτα οὐδαμηνοὶ καὶ παρὰ τοιούτων ἀπεσ-
25 ταλμένοι — ἀλλὰ καὶ φανερῶς ἐφ' ὑψηλοῦ ἀναβαίνοντες ὡς ἔθος ἔχουσιν ἐν
τῇ χώρᾳ αὐτῶν, τὰ μυσαρὰ αὐτῶν ἐκφωνοῦσι μυστήρια. ταῦτα καὶ τὰ
τοιαῦτα τολμώμενα συσκιάζουσιν οἱ ὁρῶντες, καὶ οὐ γυμνῶς ἀναφέρουσι
τῇ βασιλείᾳ σου, ἵνα τὸν ἔνθεόν σου ζῆλον ἐνδείξῃς.

δ ιὰ ταῦτα, ἅγιε βασιλεῦ, πῶς εἰσακούσεται ὁ Θεὸς τῶν εὐχῶν
30 ἡμῶν, εἰ καὶ ὅλως εὐχόμεθα; πῶς ἔτι λαλοῦντός σου ἐρεῖ, ἰδοὺ
πάρειμι; πῶς λαλήσει εἰρήνην ἐπὶ τὸν λαὸν αὐτοῦ; διὰ ταῦτα
ἵνα τοῖς σοῖς λόγοις χρήσωμαι, «παρακαλῶ, παρακαλῶ, παρακαλῶ» τὴν
βασιλείαν σου, διανάστηθι. ἐχέτωσαν οἱ ἀδικούμενοι κρίσιν, οἱ κακοπραγοῦντες τὴν ἀναχαίτισιν, οἱ τῆς δικαιοσύνης καὶ ἀληθείας τὴν ἀποδοχὴν
35 κ αὶ τὸν ἔπαινον. περίζωσαι τὴν ῥομφαίαν σου ἐπὶ τὸν μηρόν
σου μετὰ Θεὸν ἐν πᾶσι τοῖς ἀγαθοῖς, καὶ ἔντεινε καὶ κατευοδοῦ
καὶ βασίλευε ἕνεκεν ἀληθείας καὶ δικαιοσύνης καὶ ζήλου θεϊ-
κοῦ καὶ φρονήματος, ἵνα ἡ τοῦ Θεοῦ δεξιὰ θαυμαστῶς ὁδηγήσῃ
σε, ἵνα δοξάσῃ· τοὺς γὰρ δοξάζοντάς με δοξάζω, φησὶν ὁ Θεός,
40 καὶ οἶδα ὅτι δοξάσεις αὐτὸν ἐν καρδίᾳ. ἀλλ' ὅμως νόμος ἐστὶ Θεοῦ· τοὺς
κρυφίως αὐτὸν δοξάζοντας, κρυφίως ἀντιδοξάζει· τοὺς ἐνώπιον τῶν ἀνθρώπων, ἐνώπιον τῶν ἀνθρώπων, κατὰ τὸ ὅστις ὁμολογήσειεν ἐμοί,
ἐνώπιον τῶν ἀνθρώπων, ὁμολογήσω κἀγώ.

ἐν τούτοις εἰ σπεύσει μετὰ Θεὸν ἡ ἐκ Θεοῦ βασιλεία σου πρὸς ἐκ-
45 πλήρωσιν, οὐκ ὀκνήσομεν ἀναφέρειν καὶ περὶ τῶν λοιπῶν. κέρδησον οὖν διὰ
τὸν Θεὸν τὸ καλὸν καὶ ἅγιον ὄνομα. ζήλωσον ἀληθῶς, μὴ λόγῳ ἀλλ' ἔργῳ·
οὐ γὰρ λόγους ἐν καιρῷ ἐξόδου, ἀλλ' ἔργα χρεία ἐνδείξασθαι. γενοῦ Φ ι ν -
ε έ ς · ἐ ξ ί λ α σ α ι ὑ π ὲ ρ τ ῶ ν κ α κ ῶ ς γ ε ν ο μ έ ν ω ν ἵ ν α ἡ θ ρ α ῦ σ ι ς κ ο π ά σ ῃ,
ἵνα τὰ τῶν Χριστιανῶν ὅρια πλατύνῃ Θεός, ἵνα εὐθηνίαν τῶν χρειωδῶν
50 παρέξῃ πρὸς τὸ ὑπήκοον, ἵνα ὑπερμαχήσῃ σοι, ἵνα ὑπὸ τοὺς πόδας τοὺς
σοὺς καταλεάνῃ πάντα ἐχθρὸν καὶ πολέμιον δίκην κονιορτοῦ, ἵνα μακραίω-
νά σοι παρέξῃ ζωήν, ἵνα τὴν βασιλείαν παισὶ καὶ ἐγγόνοις σου διὰ τὰς σὰς
ἀρετὰς παραπέμψῃ γενεαῖς γενεῶν, [fol. 19ʳ] ἵνα σὺν τῇ ἐπιγείῳ βασιλείᾳ
παρέξῃ σοι καὶ τὴν οὐράνιον.

30–31 Is. 58:9 ‖ 31 Ps. 84 (85):9 ‖ 35–39 Ps. 44 (45):4–5 ‖ 39 I Reg. 2:30 ‖ 42–43 Matt.
10:32 ‖ 47–48 cf. Ps. 105 (106):30 ‖ 49 cf. Ex. 34:24

---

39 δοξάζω VS¹P : δοξάσω S ‖ 40 ἐστὲ P ‖ 48 κακῶς V¹S: καλῶς VP ‖ 50 παρέξει
VS ‖ ὑπερμαχήσῃ V¹S: ὑπερμαχήσοι VP ‖ 52 παρέξῃ V¹SP: παρέξοι V ‖ 54 παρέξει
VS

41

protest in that matter, too, the Armenians will exert a great deal of power with a few silver coins. Everyone knows that ⟨those⟩ Ishmaelites, who on account of my sins rule Christian cities, do not even allow Christians to strike the *semandron* there. But although we are endowed with this Christian empire through the grace of Christ our God, not only have we neglected to do what the envoys of the Ishmaelites did (good-for-nothings that they are, and sent by no better masters), but they openly climb up on high, as is the custom in their land, and shout forth their abominable mysteries. Witnesses of these and similar outrages conceal them and do not report the bald facts to your majesty, so that you might demonstrate your zeal inspired by God.

For this reason, holy emperor, how will God hear our prayers, if we pray at all ? How «while thou art yet speaking will He say 'Behold, I am here'» ? How «will He speak peace to His people» ? For this reason, to borrow your own words, «I entreat, I entreat, I entreat» your majesty, arise! Let victims of wrongdoing have a hearing, evil-doers be restrained, and men of righteousness and truth receive favor and praise. «Gird thy sword upon thy thigh» with the help of God in all good works, and «bend thy bow and prosper and reign, because of truth and righteousness» and divine zeal and courage, «so that the right hand of God shall guide thee wonderfully», and so that He will honor you; for God says, «I will only honor them that honor me», and I know that you will honor Him in your heart. However, God has a rule: He honors in secret those who honor Him in secret, and He honors in the presence of men those who honor Him in the presence of men. As He says, «Whosoever shall confess me before men, him will I confess».

Meanwhile, if you, your majesty, strive with the help of God to fulfil ⟨these duties⟩, I will not hesitate to petition about the other matters. Acquire then a good and holy name for the sake of God. Strive honestly, not in word, but in deed. For at the time of death, one should show deeds, not words. Be ⟨another⟩ Phinees. «Atone» for our evil deeds, so that «the slaughter will abate», and so that God may «broaden the territory» of Christians, so that He will supply an abundance of necessities to your subjects, so that He will protect you in battle, and grind down like dust under your feet every foe and enemy, so that He will grant you long life, and on account of your virtues will hand down the empire to your children and grandchildren, for generation after generation, and in addition to your terrestrial empire will grant you also the one in heaven.

42. [fol. 28�v] Πρὸς τὸν αὐτοκράτορα περὶ ἧς ὀφείλουσιν ἐπιμελείας
ἐνδείκνυσθαι οἱ βασιλεῖς πρὸς τὸ ὑπήκοον, ἐν ἀρχαῖς τῶν ἱερῶν καὶ ἁγίων
νηστειῶν — ἰνδικτιῶνος δ′

Πάντοτε μὲν δούλοις εὐγνώμοσιν ὀφειλὴ ἀνελλιπῶς καὶ ἀόκνως
5 πρὸς οἷα καὶ ὅσα κυρίοις δοκεῖ ἀγαθοῖς ὀρεκτὰ ἐν τούτοις νηφόντως ἐπαγωνίζεσθαι, κατ᾽ ἐξαίρετον δὲ ἡνίκα καὶ αἴσθονται τούτους ὀργιζομένους
δι᾽ ἀμέλειαν τούτων καὶ καταφρόνησιν. τότε γὰρ τότε προσῆκον οὐχ ὑπο-
πίπτειν καὶ δέεσθαι μόνον καὶ μεταμέλεσθαι δι᾽ ἐπιστροφῆς, ἀλλά τε καὶ
ὑφορᾶσθαι ἀσύγγνωστον καὶ πρεπώδη καὶ ἀφόρητον — καὶ δικαίαν ποιεῖ-
10 ται — τὴν ἐπεξέλευσιν· καὶ τοῦτο, εἴπερ ποτέ, σήμερον, μεταξὺ τοῦ μεγάλου καὶ μόνου Θεοῦ καὶ τοῦ κόσμου παντὸς βασιλέως γνωρίζωμεν, ὅσοι
μὴ πάντῃ καὶ ἀμβλυώττομεν.

διὰ τοῦτο ἀντιβολῶ, ἀνανήψωμεν, καὶ τοῖς ἄλλοις τὸν ὕπνον ἀποτι-
νάσσειν ἐκβιαζώμεθα, εἴ γε τὴν μῆνιν μὴ βουλοίμεθα ἐπιτείνειν ἐν τοῖς
15 ἡμῶν τὸν ἀνάλωτον πάθεσιν. ὅθεν δραξάμενοι ἀφορμῆς τὸ διάγγελμα τοῦτο τῆς μετανοίας τὸ σωτήριον καὶ κοινόν, ἡγησώμεθα ἴδιον ἕκαστος ἐν
πάσῃ ἀνακαινίσει καλοῦ, ὃ βασιλεῦσι καὶ μᾶλλον ὀφεῖλον ἑαυτῷ καὶ τῷ
ὑπηκόῳ καὶ εὔχεσθαι καὶ ζητεῖν. κέλευσον οὖν σὺν τοῖς ἄλλοις καλοῖς καὶ
τρανῶς διακηρυχθῆναι, μὴ βαλανείοις ἢ καπηλείοις τινὰ τῷ τῇδε καιρῷ,
20 ἀλλ᾽ ἐκκλησίαις ἐσχολακέναι ὀρθόδοξον πάντα ἐν ψυχικῇ συντριβῇ. ὅτι καὶ
τί συνηνέχθη ποτὲ τῷ μὴ ἐγκαίρως τῷ βαλανείῳ φοιτήσαντι, ὁ τῆς τεσσαρακοντάδος ἐλεεινὸς ἀνεδίδαξεν ἔκπτωτος.

ἅ με καὶ θράττει καὶ ἐκφοβεῖ τὰ πολλά, πῶς ἀπελήλαται ἡ ἀκρίβεια, καὶ ἐναντίοις ἀκριβασμοῖς οἱ ὀρθόδοξοι σὺν τοῖς ἄλλοις κἂν τούτῳ
25 προσκόπτομεν· τῶν γὰρ λογίων τῶν ἱερῶν εὐλαβῶς ὑποτιθεμένων (ἃ ὡς
καὶ πνεύματος θείου φωνὰς οὔκουν τὸν συνιόντα ποσῶς ἀμφιβάλλειν) καὶ
νύμφην ἐξέρχεσθαι τοῦ παστοῦ, καὶ τοῦ κοιτῶνος νυμφίον
τοιούτῳ καιρῷ, ἵνα νηστείᾳ καὶ προσευχῇ, καθά φησι Παῦλος ὁ
μέγας, ἐκ συμφώνου σχολάζωμεν, ὡς δή τι μέγα ἡμεῖς καὶ φρονοῦν-
30 τες καὶ δοκοῦντες θεοσεβεῖν, εἰσάγεσθαι μᾶλλον αὐτοὺς προτρεπόμεθα,
καὶ δοκοῦντες συνάγειν μετὰ Χριστοῦ, λέγειν οὐκ ἔχω εἰ μὴ καὶ
μᾶλλον σκορπίζομεν.

κἀντεῦθεν οἷα εὑρίσκεται τὰ τῆς ἐκκλησίας (ὢ συμφορᾶς!) ἀναλογιζόμενος, οὐκ αἰσχύνη καλύπτει μου μόνον τὸ πρόσωπον, ἀλλὰ καὶ οἱ
35 ὀφθαλμοὶ κατάγουσι δάκρυα. τί πρὸς τὰς εὐεργεσίας οἱ τά-[fol. 29ʳ] λανες
καὶ τὰ ὀφείλοντα φῶμεν μὴ ἐννοούμενοι; ἃ καὶ τὸν ἀκροώμενον μὴ εἰδώς,
ἁπάντων ζητούντων τὰ ἑαυτῶν, οὐ τὰ Χριστοῦ Ἰησοῦ, ὅπως

42: 21–22 Μηναῖον τοῦ Μαρτίου (Rome, 1898), 54 ‖ 27 cf. Joel 2:16 ‖ 28–29 cf. I
Cor. 7:5 ‖ 31–32 cf. Matt. 12:30 ‖ 37 cf. Phil. 2:21

42: V 28�v–29ʳ. S 152ʳ–153�v. P 32�v–33�v.
1 πρός] πρὸν S ‖ 14 ἐκβιαζόμεθα codd.

42

42. To the emperor concerning the attention which emperors should devote to their subjects; ⟨dispatched⟩ at the beginning of the sacred and holy fast days; 4th indiction

It is always the duty of grateful servants to strive constantly and without hesitation and soberly to fulfil the wishes of their good masters, especially when they perceive that these ⟨masters⟩ are angered because their desires have been disregarded and neglected. For at that time it is not only fitting to fall to one's knees and pray and repent by turning ⟨to God⟩, but also to suspect that their punishment—and God metes out justly—will be merciless and appropriate and unbearable. And let us, whosoever are not completely blind, realize today, if ever, that this is precisely what obtains between the great and only God and the emperor of the whole world.

For this reason I beg of you, let us come to our senses and let us force the others to shake off their sleep, if we do not want the One Who is untouched by passions to extend His wrath to our deeds. Therefore, let us take this opportunity, and let each of us believe that the message of repentance which has the power of salvation for everyone is his very own for every renewal of good; which message emperors especially ought to pray for and seek both for themselves and for their subjects. Command therefore together with other good works that it be clearly proclaimed that at this time no one should enter bathhouses or taverns, but every Orthodox Christian should spend his time in the churches in contrition of spirit. For the wretched man who was «excluded from the forty» has taught us the fate of a man who visited the bathhouse at an inopportune time.

What troubles and frightens me greatly is how strict discipline has been banished, and how we Orthodox Christians, in addition to our other sins, transgress the commandments to the contrary in this matter, too. For although the Holy Scriptures (which no one of understanding can in any way doubt, since they are the words of the Holy Spirit) piously enjoin «the bride to go forth from her closet, and the bridegroom from his chamber» at such a time, so «that», in the words of the great Paul, «with consent we may give ourselves to fasting and prayer», we, as if we believed we were doing something great and thought we were acting piously, urge them instead to be led in ⟨to the bridal chamber⟩, and when we think that «we are gathering with Christ», I should say rather that «we are scattering abroad».

Therefore when I think of the plight of the Church (what a misfortune!), not only does shame cover my face, but tears spring to my eyes. What can we wretched people say when we take no thought for good deeds and our obligations? Because I know no one who listens to these words, «since all seek their own, not the things which are Jesus Christ's», so that I may find some

88

42, 43

μικράν τινα τὴν ἀναψυχὴν ἐκδιηγούμενος εὕρω, ὃν δοκῶ μόνον ὑπολειφθῆ-
ναι ἀκροατὴν συνετόν, ἐξ ὧν ἀφελεῖν ἐπεισάγει Ἡσαίας τὸν
40 Κύριον Σαβαὼθ ἐκ Σιών, ἀνατίθημι οὐ μόνον τὸ συναλγῆσαι, εἰ καὶ
μέγα καὶ τοῦτό μοι, ἀλλά γε διαναστῆναι, περιζωσάμενον τὴν ῥομφαίαν ἐπὶ μηροῦ, τῇ ὡραιότητι καὶ τῷ κάλλει τῆς μισθαπο-
δοσίας νευρούμενος, τῇ παρὰ μόνου τοῦ κάλλει ὡραίου, εἰ οὕτω γε
καταπράττῃ, ἀποκειμένῃ σοι· ἐξ ὧν καὶ ἔντεινε καὶ κατευοδοῦ καὶ
45 βασίλευε μεγαλοπρεπῶς καὶ βασιλικῶς, ἕνεκεν ἀληθείας καὶ
πρᾳότητος καὶ δικαιοσύνης, ἐν τούτοις τῆς τοῦ Θεοῦ δεξιᾶς
θαυμαστῶς ὁδηγούσης σε, καὶ ἀνυψούσης μεγαλωσύνῃ διαβοήτῳ,
καὶ οὕτω προσλαμβανούσης ἐν πίονι γήρει καὶ τοὺς ἐκ σοῦ γενεαῖς
γενεῶν, ἐξῃρημένως δι' ἀμφοῖν συντηρούσης αὐτούς· γένοιτο, Κύριε,
50 γένοιτο.

43. Πρὸς τὸν αὐτοκράτορα περὶ αὐτοῦ καὶ αὖθις — ἰνδικτιῶνος ε'

Χρυσοῦ καὶ ἀργύρου καὶ λίθων τιμίων σωρὸν εἰ ὑποδείξας τις, ὑπές-
χετο νηπίῳ ἀφραίνοντι τοῦ χαρίσασθαι, τούτῳ δὲ ἐνεφάνισε καὶ στρουθὸν
ἐνδεσμούμενον λινῷ λεπτῷ, οὐδαμοῦ τὸ ἀμφίβολον ὡς ὁ παῖς τοῦ στρουθοῦ
5 —καὶ δάκρυα μᾶλλον ἢ ἐδέησε κατεβάλετο ἐγκρατὴς φανῆναι αὐτοῦ—διακα-
καῶς ἐκκρεμάμενος, τὰ δέ γε καὶ ὄντα καὶ τίμια τοῖς πολλοῖς εἰς οὐδὲν ἐ-
λογίσατο. τοῦτο εἰδείη τις ἀκριβῶς ψηλαφῶν τὰ ἡμέτερα, ἐν πᾶσι καλοῖς
οὕτω διακειμένων ἡμῶν, καὶ δὴ καὶ τῷ καιρῷ τῶν ἱερῶν νηστειῶν, καὶ
μάλα τῆς χάριτος σαλπίζειν οὐ παυομένης τοῦ πνεύματος, ἀποστολικῶς
10 καὶ προφητικῶς, ἐκεῖθεν τὸ συνετάφημεν τῷ Χριστῷ διὰ τοῦ
βαπτίσματος, ἐντεῦθεν τὸ ἐπιστράφητε πρός με ἐξ ὅλης
καρδίας ὑμῶν ἐν νηστείᾳ καὶ ἐν κλαυθμῷ καὶ ἐν κοπετῷ,
ὅτι ἐλεήμων καὶ οἰκτίρμων ἐστί, μακρόθυμος καὶ πολυέ-
λεος καὶ μετανοῶν ἐπὶ κακίαις ἀνθρώπων, καὶ τοσοῦτον διανιστᾶν
15 ὡς ἐξέρχεσθαι καὶ νυμφίον παραβιάζειν ἐκ τοῦ κοιτῶνος
αὐτοῦ, καὶ νύμφην ἀπὸ τοῦ ταύτης παστοῦ — ἀλλοτρόπως μὴ
εἶναι τὸν ἱλασμὸν ἐπιδίδοσθαι, οὗ εἰ μὴ ἐπιτύχοιμεν καὶ σήμερον μάλιστα,
οὐκ ἔστιν ἐν ἀμφιβόλοις ὡς ἀπολώλαμεν.

ἕνεκεν τούτων τῇ φροντίδι δαπανωμένους ἡμᾶς ὡς ἄρα τῇ μοιχα-
20 λίδι ἡμῶν γενεᾷ καὶ ἀπίστῳ μικροῦ τίς ὁ διακηρυκεύσων ἀξίως τὰ πρὸς
μετάνοιαν, [fol. 29ᵛ] ὡς ἂν ἐκ τοῦ ξένον τι καὶ στεντόρειον κεκραγέναι,

39–40 cf. Is. 3:1,3 ‖ 41–47 cf. Ps. 44 (45):3–5 ‖ 48 Ps. 91 (92):15
43: 10–11 cf. Rom. 6:4 ‖ 11–14 cf. Joel 2:12–13 ‖ 15–16 cf. Joel 2:16 ‖ 19–20 cf.
Marc. 8:38

43: V 29ʳ–29ᵛ. S 153ᵛ–154ᵛ. P 33ᵛ–34ᵛ.
5 ἢ] εἰ codd.

42, 43

small comfort through relating these matters, I propose to you (whom I
consider the only «intelligent hearer» left of those whom Isaiah declares that
«the Lord Sabaoth took away» from Sion), that you not only share my grief,
even if this is important to me, but that you also arise, «your sword girded
upon your thigh», impelled by «the comeliness and beauty» of the reward,
which is kept for you by Him alone Who is «fair in beauty», if you act in
this way. Wherefore, «bend your bow, and prosper, and reign» magnificently
and royally, «because of truth and meekness and righteousness, while the
right hand of God guides you wonderfully in these affairs», and exalts you
with celebrated greatness, and thus receives your descendants through all
generations «in a fine old age», preserving them transcendentally in both
⟨worlds?⟩, so be it, Lord, so be it.

43. To the emperor again about the same matter; 5th indiction

If someone were to show a foolish child a heap of gold and silver and
precious stones, and promised to give it to him, and then showed him a
sparrow caught in a fine net, there is no doubt that the child would cling
fervently to the sparrow, and would shed more tears than necessary in order
to gain possession of it, and would consider of no value those objects which
both are precious, and appear as such, to the many. We might also learn this
clearly by examining ourselves, for we behave in the same manner when faced
with all positive values, and especially at the time of the holy fast-days, when
the grace of the Spirit does not cease to proclaim in the words of the apostle,
«We are buried with Him by baptism», and in the words of the prophet, «Turn
to me with all your heart, and with fasting, and with weeping, and with
lamentation; for He is merciful and compassionate, long-suffering and plen-
teous in mercy, and repents of evils» of men; and ⟨when it does not cease⟩ to
rouse us to such an extent as to force «the bridegroom to go forth of his
chamber, and the bride out of the closet»—for it is not otherwise possible to
offer atonement, and if we do not receive it today, there is no doubt that we
are lost.

For this reason, I who am consumed with anxiety ⟨to find a man⟩ who
would worthily proclaim the road to repentance to «our adulterous» and all but
faithless «generation», so that he may be deemed equal to the task either by
shouting something strange and stentorian, or by sounding the trumpet in a

εὐπαράδεκτος νομισθῇ, ἢ ἐκ τοῦ φρικαλέον σαλπίσαι καθάπερ ἐν συντελείᾳ
ἣν καὶ πιστεύομεν δι' ἀγγέλου Θεοῦ, ὡς ἂν ἐκσφενδονηθῶμεν τῶν τάφων·
ξένης ἠχοῦς χρῃζόντων ἡμῶν, ὡς κάτω κυψάντων ἐξ ἐμπαθοῦς καὶ κτηνώ-
25 δους διαίτης, τοῦ βλέψαι κἂν πρὸς ὀλίγον εἰς οὐρανόν, τὴν λήμην περιαιρ-
ησαμένους τῶν ὀφθαλμῶν, στενάξαι καὶ τύψαι τὸ στῆθος, ἐξαιτουμένους
ἐν συντριβῇ, εἴ πως ὀψέ ποτε γνωριοῦμεν ἡμῶν τὸ μέγα ἀξίωμα καὶ
Χριστὸς ὑπὲρ τίνος ἀπέθανεν —
            ἐν τούτοις στρέφων τοὺς λογισμοὺς καὶ πόθεν εὕροιμι τὸν ἁρμόδιον,
30 κεκραγότος τοῦ θεοπάτορος πόρρωθεν ἐκλελοιπέναι τὸν ὅσιον,
ὁσιότητος διακόνημα φρονῶν τὸ ῥηθέν, οὐ διήμαρτον τῆς ζητήσεως,
μηδένα βεβαιωθεὶς ὑπουργῆσαι τῷ ἔργῳ πρεπόντως, ἐκτὸς τοῦ ἁγίου μου
αὐτοκράτορος, τῇ θελήσει τῇ ἀγαθῇ σὺν Θεῷ κεκτημένου καὶ τὸ δύνασθαι
σύνδρομον· καὶ δώη τούτῳ Θεὸς τὸ αὐτοῦ πρὸς ἀρέσκειαν καὶ φρονεῖν καὶ
35 προστάσσειν καὶ πράττειν, ἔχοντος ὄφλημα ταῦτα πληροῦν, οἷα τὸ ἀναπνεῖν ἄνθρωπον. οἷς καὶ ἀντιβολῶ μὴ ἐᾶσθαι τὰ πρόσφορα τῶν καλῶν, καὶ
μᾶλλον τῷ τῇδε καιρῷ κλεισθῆναι κελεύσει βασιλικῇ ἀπὸ πρωΐθεν Δευτέρας μέχρι πρωΐας Σαββάτου τὰ τῆς μεγαλοπόλεως πάντα βαλανεῖα καὶ
καπηλεῖα, καὶ σχολάσαι τοῖς θείοις ναοῖς ἄνδρας καὶ παῖδας σὺν γυναιξί,
40 καὶ βρῶσιν ἰχθύων παυθῆναι ἐν τῷ αἰγιαλῷ παρὰ τῶν γραϊδίων ἐνεργουμένην, ἀρκούντων ἀντὶ τούτων τοῖς ὀρθοδόξοις κολλύβων ἢ ὀσπρίων ἢ
ὀπωρῶν ἢ λαχάνων, ὡς ἂν τὸ διάγγελμα τῆς νηστείας δεξάμενοι εὐλαβῶς,
κριθῶμεν ἀποδεκτέοι Θεῷ, καὶ μεγάλας ἀντιμετρήσῃ ὁ ὑψιμέδων τὰς
ἀμοιβὰς τὰς χάριν θεοσεβείας τῇ ἐκ Θεοῦ βασιλείᾳ σου.

44. Πρὸς τὸν αὐτοκράτορα περὶ τῆς τῶν Χριστουγέννων ἑορτῆς

Τῶν πώποτε κατὰ γενεὰς ὑμνουμένων ἐλέους καὶ οἰκτιρμῶν καὶ
μεγαλοσύνης Θεοῦ τοῦ παμμέδοντος πρὸς τοὺς ὁμοίως ἡμῖν διὰ βίου δρα-
μόντας πρὸς ἀθέτησιν θείων θεσμῶν, θαυμάζειν μοι ἔπεισι τὰ πολλά,
5 ὅπως ἐκείνοις τοῖς φαύλοις ὁμοιωθέντες, ἢ καὶ ὑπεραρθέντες, μὴ κἂν τοῖς
κρείττοσι τῆς ἐκείνων ἐπιστροφῆς καὶ μεταβολῆς συμπράκται τυγχάνομεν,
κἀντεῦθεν τὰ σπλάγχνα τῆς ἀγαθότητος ἐν τῷ μὴ ἐπείγεσθαι πρὸς
μετάνοιαν ἀποκλείειν οὐ φρίττομεν, ἀλλὰ πάσῃ δυνάμει ὁ ἀθετῶν
ἀθετεῖ, ὁ ἀνομῶν ἀνομεῖ, πολὺ ἐν τοῖς φαύλοις τὸ ἰσχυρὸν ἐν-

30 cf. Ps. 11 (12):2
    44: 7–8 cf. I Joh. 3:17 ‖ 8–9 Is. 21:2

44: V 29ᵛ–30ᵛ. S 154ᵛ–155ᵛ. P 34ᵛ–35ᵛ.
1 post ἑορτῆς add. ζητῶν χορηγηθῆναι σεπτὸν πρόσταγμα προστάσσον ἐξ ὥρας ἑσπερινοῦ
Σαββάτου καὶ βασιλικῆς ἑορτῆς βαλανείῳ ἢ καπηλείῳ μὴ εἰσαχθῆναι πρὸς πότον (πόντον
S) τινά VʳSP

43, 44

terrifying manner, just as at the end of the world (when, we also believe, ⟨the trumpet will be sounded⟩ by an angel of God, so that we may be hurled forth from our graves); since we need a strange sound, bowed down as we are by our sensual and bestial behavior, to ⟨make us⟩ look ⟨up⟩, if only for a while, toward heaven, shedding the mist from our eyes, and to ⟨make us⟩ lament and beat our breasts, offering contrite supplications, if we ever should recognize our great honor, and realize for whose sake Christ had died. . . .

When I turn my thoughts to such topics and to where I might find ⟨such⟩ a suitable man, even if the ancestor of God [David] cried out long ago that «the godly man has failed», and I consider what I said to be a service of godliness, I have not failed in my search; for I have ascertained that no one has properly assisted in the task, with the exception of my holy emperor, who with the help of God has combined his good will with the ability ⟨to act⟩. And may God grant that he believe and command and act as is pleasing to Him, since he has the obligation to do these things, just as man must breathe. I ask that the offerings of good deeds not be neglected, and especially at this time that all the baths and taverns in the capital be closed by an imperial command from Monday morning to Saturday morning, and that men, women and children should spend their time in the holy churches, and should stop eating fish ⟨which is sold⟩ by the old women at the seashore. For instead of these foods, boiled wheat and pulse and fruits and vegetables are sufficient for Orthodox Christians, so that by piously accepting the proclamation of fasting, we may be judged acceptable to God, and so that the Ruler on High will recompense your divine majesty with great rewards, thanks to your reverence for God.

44. To the emperor, concerning the festival of Christmas

When for generations one has hymned the mercy and compassion and greatness which God, the Ruler of All, once showed toward those who like us went through life neglecting the divine ordinances, I marvel greatly how, although we resemble those people ⟨of old⟩ in base deeds, or even exceed them, we do not share their conversion and repentance through good deeds, and how we are not thus afraid «to shut up the bowels» of goodness by not hastening toward repentance. Instead «he that is treacherous deals treacherously ⟨and⟩ the transgressor transgresses» with all their might, and they show

10 δεικνύμενοι, ἐν δέ γε τοῖς κρείττοσιν ἐν καιρῷ οὐδὲν ἄμεινον διακείμενοι. κἀντεῦθεν ἡ ἀθυμία [fol. 30ʳ] μοι σθεναρὰ καὶ ἡ λύπη ἀπαρα-
μύθητος· ἣν καὶ προσαναθέσθαι θαρρῶν πρὸς μηδένα, ἀνενέγκαι διέγνων
συμφέρον τῇ ἐκ Θεοῦ βασιλείᾳ σου, μακρὰν ἰσχυούσῃ μετὰ Θεὸν
ἀπορραπίσαι τὰ ἀλγεινὰ καὶ ἐφάμαρτα.

15 καὶ ἐπεὶ τὰ τῆς ἑορτῆς ἐμποδών μοι προσγίνεται, ἀναφέρειν διέγνων
ὀλίγα, μὴ ἡμῖν, ἀλλὰ δῶρον ἑόρτιον προσενέγκαι Θεῷ, τῆς αὐτοῦ
ἐκκλησίας υἱῷ χρηματίζοντι, οὐ λίβανον, οὐδὲ σμύρναν, οὐδὲ
χρυσὸν (καιροῦ τοῦ τότε γὰρ ἦν ἐκεῖνα καὶ προσκυνήσεως), ἐξ ὧν δὲ προσήκει τοῖς καταξιωθεῖσιν ἀληθείᾳ καὶ πνεύματι προσκυνεῖν· ὧν
20 καὶ τὴν ἐκ Θεοῦ βασιλείαν σου τὸν πρῶτον εἶναι εὐχόμεθα, ὡς πρώτως
ἐκεῖθεν καὶ τηρηθέντα καὶ εὐεργετηθέντα.

πρὸς γοῦν τιμὴν τοῦ τετιμηκότος σε, σεπτὸν αἰτοῦμεν χορηγηθῆναι
καὶ ψυχῶν σωτήριον πρόσταγμα, ἐξ ὥρας προστάσσον ἑσπερινοῦ τοῦ Σαββάτου, ὃ ὅλως τολμήσων ἀνεῳγμένον ἐᾶν ἐργαστήριον, ἢ βαλανείῳ ἢ
25 καπηλείῳ μέχρι Κυριακῆς εἰσαχθῆναι πρὸς πότον τινά, ἢ ἄλλης βασιλικῆς
ἑορτῆς τὸ αἰδέσιμον τῆς ἡμέρας ὑβρίζοντα, ὑποκείσθω ζημίᾳ. ὁ δ᾽ ἄλλως
ἑσπερινῷ καὶ ὄρθρῳ καὶ λειτουργίᾳ αὐτῆς τῆς κυριωνύμου, ἢ ἄλλης μεγάλης δεσποτικῆς ἑορτῆς, μὴ θείοις ναοῖς προσεδρεύων εἰς προσκύνησιν καὶ
λατρείαν τοῦ ἐπὶ πάντων Θεοῦ, παιδευέσθω. ἢ οὐκ ὀρθόδοξος πᾶς, τὸ
30 πρωῒ παραστήσομαί σοι καὶ ἐπόψει με, λέγειν ὀφείλει καὶ πράττειν; τί γὰρ οἱ τάλανες ἄλλο πρὸς ἱκεσίαν καὶ προσάξομεν τῷ Θεῷ, οἱ μυρί-
οις καθ᾽ ὥραν τοῖς ἀτοπήμασιν ἐνεχόμενοι, καὶ μηδὲ κἂν τῇ κυριωνύμῳ, ἢ
καὶ τῇ ἄλλῃ βασιλικῇ ἑορτῇ, εἰς προσκύνησιν τοῦ τῶν ὅλων Θεοῦ συντρέχειν ἀγωνιζόμενοι; πῶς δὲ καὶ λέξομεν προσφυῶς, ἐγὼ δὲ ἐν τῷ πλή-
35 θει τοῦ ἐλέους σου εἰσελεύσομαι εἰς τὸν οἶκόν σου; ποῦ δὲ
καὶ πότε κατευθυνθῇ ὡς θυμίαμα ἡ ὑμῶν προσευχὴ ἐκείνου
ἐνώπιον; ὁ δέ γε μὴ παρρησιασθεὶς λέγειν, Κύριε, ἠγάπησα εὐπρέπειαν οἴκου σου καὶ τόπον σκηνώματος δόξης σου, πῶς
ὑπενέγκῃ τὸ μὴ συναπολέσῃς μετὰ ἀσεβῶν τὴν ψυχήν μου,
40 καὶ μετὰ ἀνδρῶν αἱμάτων τὴν ζωήν μου, εἰ δέ γε τοσαύτης
νωθρείας ἡμῖν ἐπικεχυμένης ἀναίσθητοι ὦμεν καὶ ἀνενέργητοι πρὸς τὰ
κάλλιστα; εἰ σπούδασμα ἐν τοιούτοις ἡ ἐκ Θεοῦ βασιλεία σου ἐπιδείξεται
ὀμματοῦν τὸν λαὸν ἐν τοῖς κρείττοσι, δύο τὰ μέγιστα κερδανεῖ, ἡμᾶς μὲν
πρὸς λατρείαν προτρεπομένη καὶ ζῆλον κατὰ Θεόν, καὶ τὸ ταύτης φιλόθεον
45 παριστῶσα ἐκ τῆς τοιαύτης ἐπιμελείας, ἐξ ἧς [fol. 30ᵛ] τὸν πάντων Θεὸν
πρὸς οἶκτον σαυτοῦ ἐν πᾶσι τοῖς σωτηρίοις κραταιῶς αὐτῆς ἀντιλαμβανόμενον καταπλουτίσεις αἰώνια.

16–18 cf. Greg. Naz., Or. XIX, ιβ′ (PG, XXXV, 1057C) et Μηναῖον τοῦ Δεκεμβρίου
(Rome, 1889), 581 ‖ 19 cf. Joh. 4:23 ‖ 29–30 cf. Ps. 5:4 ‖ 34–45 Ps. 5:8 ‖ 36–37 cf.
Ps. 140 (141):2 ‖ 37–40 Ps. 25 (26):8–9

---

31 προσάξωμεν codd. ‖ 34 λέξομεν S : λέξωμεν VP

44

great perseverance in evil deeds, but when there is an opportunity for good deeds, they show no improvement. For this reason my despondency is great and my grief inconsolable; and not daring to speak of it to anyone ⟨else⟩, I decided it would be expedient to make a petition to your divine majesty, who after God has the greatest power to drive far away misery and sin.

And since the feast day is upon us, I decided to submit a few matters to the one who is called the son of the Church, that you should offer a holiday gift not to me, but to God, «not frankincense or myrrh or gold» (for those ⟨gifts⟩ were ⟨appropriate⟩ for that other occasion and adoration), but ⟨gifts⟩ of the kind which are fitting for those who have been deemed worthy «to worship in truth and spirit». And I pray that your divine majesty may be the first of these, since you are the first of those who are supported and blessed by Him.

Therefore, for the honor of the One Who has honored you, I request that you issue a solemn proclamation, conducive to the salvation of our souls, commanding that, from the hour of vespers on Saturday until Sunday, anyone who dares to keep his workshop open, or goes into a bathhouse or tavern for a drink, or who on any other feast day of the Lord insults the solemn character of the day, will be subject to punishment. And also anyone who does not attend the holy churches for worship and veneration of the Lord of all, at vespers and matins and mass on Sunday and all other important feast days of the Lord, should be punished. Does not every Orthodox Christian have the obligation to say and practice ⟨the words⟩, «in the morning will I wait upon thee and thou shalt watch over me»? For what other expiation can we wretched people offer to God, if we hourly become entangled in myriad offences, and do not even strive on Sundays and other feast days of the Lord to assemble for veneration of the God of all? How can we fittingly say, «But I will enter into thine house in the multitude of thy mercy»? Where and when will «your prayer be set before Him like incense»? And as for the man who is not free to say, «O Lord, I have loved the beauty of thy house, and the place of the tabernacle of thy glory», how can he add the words, «Destroy not my soul together with the ungodly, nor my life with bloody men», if then, overcome by such indolence, we remain insensitive and do nothing for the good? If your divine majesty in such a situation would demonstrate a zeal that would make the people see superior values more clearly, you would gain two great advantages: first, you will encourage us to show veneration and zeal for God; secondly, you will show your love of God by such a concern, as the result of which you will eternally have the God of all as your mighty helper in all works of salvation out of His mercy for you.

45. Πρὸς τὸν αὐτοκράτορα προσκαλούμενος αὐτὸν ἐν τῇ πανσέπτῳ
κοιμήσει τῆς πανυπεράγνου Δεσποίνης καὶ Θεομήτορος

Ἡ τοῦ θεοφρουρήτου σου κράτους ἐκ φιλοθεΐας εὐλάβεια, δι' ἣν καὶ
ἀφίξεσθαι ἐν τοῖς ἀνακτόροις αἰτοῦμεν τῆς μεγαλωνύμου Σοφίας Θεοῦ,
5 μεγίστη τιμὴ τῇ ἐκκλησίᾳ Χριστοῦ, δι' ἣν καὶ ἀντιδοξάζειν ἐθέσπισεν
ἡ αὐτοαλήθεια τοὺς δοξάζοντας· τῷ τοι καὶ εὐφροσύνως ἀναπετάν-
νυσι πάσας τὰς πύλας, σὲ τὸν υἱέα αὐτῆς ὑποδεχομένη περιχαρῶς, καὶ
δήπου καὶ τοῖς κατηχουμενείοις αὐτοῖς εἰ κελεύσειας. εἰς δέ γε τῶν εὐγενῶν γυναικῶν εἰσδοχήν, πολύ μοι δοκεῖ ἀπαναίνεσθαι, ὡς ὅτι μὴ δι' εὐ-
10 λάβειαν καὶ αὐταῖς τὸ σκηνοῦν ἐν τοῖς κατηχουμενείοις, ὡς τάχα καιρὸν
προσευχῆς καὶ ἁγιασμοῦ καὶ διψώσαις καὶ ἁρπαζούσαις τὴν ἑορτὴν καὶ τὴν
ἄνοδον πρὸς τὰ θεῖα ἀνάκτορα, ἀλλ' ἕνεκεν μετεωρισμοῦ καὶ ἐνδείξεως,
ἵνα μὴ λέγω καὶ ὁράσεως ἐμπαθοῦς, οὐκ ἤθει ἐν καταβεβλημένῳ τῷ τὸν
ἔλεον ἕλκοντι, ἀλλ' ἐπηρμένῳ καὶ σοβαρῷ, χρυσοῦ ἐπιθέσει καὶ λίθων, καὶ
15 ἕνεκεν ἱματίων καλλωπισμοῦ, ἀγνοούσαις ὡς ὁ ἐξ ἀλλοτρίων καλλωπισμὸς
καὶ μὴ οἴκοθεν οὐκ ἐπαινετός, καὶ μᾶλλον τὸ ἐκ χρωμάτων καθωραΐζεσθαι,
πρὸς δὲ καὶ τῷ ἐκζητεῖν μὴ κοινῶς πεποιῆσθαι τὴν στάσιν τῷ ἐπιλοίπῳ
λαῷ τοῦ συνεύχεσθαι, ἀλλ' ὑψοῦ παρὰ τοὺς πολλοὺς καὶ αὐτοῦ τοῦ προσ-
κυνήματος ὕπερθεν. εἰ δ' ἴσως βεβούληνται καὶ συνεισελθεῖν καὶ συμ-
20 προσκυνῆσαι καὶ συστῆναι τῷ ἐπιλοίπῳ ὀρθοδόξῳ λαῷ, καὶ τῶν ταύταις
βεβιωμένων συγγνώμην αἰτήσασθαι, φρονήματι καταβεβλημένῳ — ὅτι
μηδ' ἐκ σοβαρότητος οἶδε προσνέμειν αὐτὸς ὁ τῆς ἐκκλησίας Θεὸς τὸν
ἔλεον καὶ ἁγιασμόν, ἀλλ' εὐλαβείᾳ καὶ συντριβῇ ἐκζεούσης καὶ κατανενυγ-
μένης ψυχῆς, τὰ πάντιμα καὶ μεγαλοπρεπῆ τοῖς οὕτω προσερχομένοις ἀεὶ
25 θεϊκῶς ἐπιδαψιλεύεσθαι — ὑπανοίγνυσι πάντως καὶ ταύταις, εἰ οὕτω πορ-
εύσονται, ἡ ἐκκλησία τὰς πύλας, ὡς ἔργῳ χρηματιζούσαις θυγατέρας
αὐτῆς. κἀκείνων εὐξαίμην ἂν ἔγωγε ἁπάσας γυναῖκας ὀρθοδοξούσας περὶ
ὧν ἡ Γραφή, πολλαὶ θυγατέρες ἐποίησαν δυνάμεις. καὶ μή μοι
τὸ ἔθος τὸ ἐκ μακροῦ προβεβλήσθω τισὶν εἰς δικαίωμα, εἰ τοῦτο διαφόρως
30 ἐπράττετο, ὅτιπερ εὐλαβείας καὶ ἀρετῆς καὶ φόβου τοῦ ἀκραιφνοῦς
εἰς Θεὸν οὐδὲν οὐδαμοῦ καὶ συμφέρον καὶ ἀρχαιότερον. [fol. 31ʳ]

45: 5–6 cf. I Reg. 2:30 ‖ 28 cf. Prov. 31:29

45: V 30ᵛ. S 155ᵛ–156ᵛ. P 35ᵛ–36ᵛ.
1 προσκαλούμενον S ‖ 2 πανάγνου S ‖ 8 αὐτοῖς] αὐτοὺς VS¹, αὐτὰς SP ‖ 17 κοινῶν
P ‖ 22 προσγέμειν S ‖ αὐτὸ P ‖ 28 θυγατέρες VSP¹: θυγατέραις P

45

45. To the emperor inviting him to the ⟨celebration of the festival of the⟩ most sacred Dormition of our most holy Mistress the Mother of God

The piety of your God-guarded majesty, which is motivated by your love of God (and on account of which I invite you to come to the shrine of the Great Wisdom of God), is a great honor for the Church of Christ, and on account of it ⟨God⟩ the Truth has decreed that «He glorifies those who give praise». Thus ⟨the Church⟩ gladly throws open all Her doors, joyfully receiving you Her son, even in the galleries themselves, if you should so bid. But it seems to me that we ought to refuse to receive the noble women there, because they do not take their place in the galleries from piety, as if they eagerly seized upon the holiday and the ascent to the holy shrine as an opportunity for prayer and consecration, but really for the sake of puffing themselves up and showing themselves off (not to mention for the sake of a sensual appearance), not in a downcast manner which would inspire mercy, but with a haughty and insolent attitude. Also they bedeck themselves with gold and precious jewels, and make a display of their clothes, failing to realize that embellishment from without rather from within is not praiseworthy, especially beautifying oneself with paints; and in addition they try to find ways to avoid standing with the other people that they might pray together, but stand high above the crowd, above their very prosternations. But if perhaps they would be willing to gather and worship together with the rest of the orthodox, and to ask pardon for their actions with a humble spirit (for the God of our Church does not dispense mercy and sanctification when faced with insolence, but always lavishes in a divine manner valuable and magnificent gifts upon those who approach Him with fervent souls, which are abject in piety and contrition), the Church will always open Her gates to these women, if they behave in this manner, as worthy indeed to be called Her daughters. And I wish all orthodox women resembled those of whom it is said, «many daughters have wrought valiantly». And let not ancient custom be cast in my face by certain people as justification, if different practices prevailed in the past, because there is nothing more fitting and hallowed by age than piety and virtue and pure fear of God.

46. Πρὸς τὸν αὐτοκράτορα διανιστῶν αὐτὸν πρὸς ἔλεον

Οἴμοι, κύριε βασιλεῦ, ὅτι διὰ τὸ ψυχικῶς νοσηλεύεσθαι συμπάσχω καὶ τῇ σαρκί· τὸ δέ μοι ἀφορητότατον, τὸ ἀνέλπιστον ἐκ τῶν ἔργων ὑποτοπάζειν τὴν ἴασιν χρηματίζειν μοι, καὶ τοῦτο ἐξ ἀταξίας διαίτης τῆς
5 ἐξ ἀμφοῖν, ὡς καθ' ἡμέραν προκόπτειν τοῖς χείροσιν. ὁ τοίνυν δυνάμενος ἐν ἀνθρώποις τὴν ἴασιν πρυτανεύσειν μοι, εἰ ὑπερτίθεται τοῦτο δι' ὄκνον, ἢ δι' ἐμὴν οὐθενότητα, οὐκ οἶμαι μὴ δίκας ὑφέξειν παρὰ τοῦ τὴν εἰς τοῦτο ἰσχὺν αὐτῷ χορηγήσαντος, ὅτι μὴ μεταδίδωσι ταύτης, ἐξ ἧς εἰλήφει αὐτὸς ἀκμητὶ πρὸς Θεοῦ δωρεᾶς. εἰ δέ γε κελεύεις, δηλοποιῶ σου
10 τῷ κράτει τὸν τὴν ἰσχὺν πλουτισθέντα κατὰ τῆς πιεζούσης ὀδύνης καὶ ἀθυμίας ἡμᾶς· καὶ εἰ βούλει, ὁ βασιλεύς μου, σὺ ἦσθα αὐτὸς καὶ τῶν καλῶν παροχεύς.

τὰ δὲ τῆς νόσου αὐξητικὰ ταῦτά εἰσι· τῶν συνδραμόντων ἐνταῦθα μέσον κεκαθικὼς λυπουμένων, καὶ μετ' ἀλλήλων φιλονεικούντων, ὁ μὲν
15 ὡράθη μοι σύνδακρυς, ὁ δὲ ὑπό του πληγείς, ὁ δὲ τὴν ἐσθῆτα καθημαγμένην, ἄλλος ἀφαίρεσιν ὑπαρχόντων ἀποκλαιόμενος, ἕτερος δυναστείαν παθῶν, καὶ μᾶλλον παρὰ τῶν ἐνεργούντων δημόσια (οἷς ὀφειλὴ βραβεύειν τὸ δίκαιον τοῖς ὁπωσδήποτε πάσχουσιν), ἵνα μὴ λέγω τοὺς παρὰ τῶν Ἰσμαηλιτῶν καὶ αὐτῶν Ἰταλῶν ἡμιθνεῖς ἀνασῳζομένους — εἶτα παρὰ τῶν
20 ὁμογενῶν γυμνουμένους ἀνηλεῶς, ὥνπερ τὴν συμφορὰν καὶ Ἰουδαῖος ἐθρήνησεν ἄν — διὰ κοινῆς ἀνομίας πληθὺν ἁλόντων αὐτῶν, καὶ Θεοῦ καταφρόνησιν, καὶ νόμων τῶν θείων μυκτηρισμὸν καὶ ἀθέτησιν.

τούτων οὐδεὶς τὴν μανίαν ἀναχαιτίσαι μετὰ Θεὸν εὐπορεῖ, ὥσπερ ἡ ἐκ Θεοῦ βασιλεία σου, πράττειν τὰ φίλα Θεῷ κατὰ δύναμιν πρώτως, καὶ
25 πάντας δι' ἀκριβοῦς πρὸς ταῦτα διανιστᾶν τῆς ἐρεύνης, καὶ δι' ἐπιστροφῆς καὶ δακρύων κοπάσαι Θεὸν τὴν ὀργὴν κοινῶς ἐκβοᾶν· τούτου γὰρ μὴ πραχθέντος, οὐκ ἔστιν ὁ ἐγγυώμενος τὴν μεταβολήν. ἐν τούτοις ἐπίβλεψον, ἅγιε βασιλεῦ, ἐν αἰσθήσει, καὶ μὴ παρόψῃ ἐπὶ πολὺ τὰ διὰ κακοπραγίας ἐπεισπεσόντα δεινά· φημισθήτω τὸ μέγα ἐπιμελείας τῆς σῆς καὶ νῦν καὶ
30 εἰς τὸ ἐξῆς. ἕνεκεν τούτων ἀντιβολῶ, ἀναχαιτίσωμεν τὴν ὀργήν, βελτίονα ποιησάμενοι τὰ ἐπιτηδεύματα. ἄξον εἰς πέρας ἑκάστῳ βιοῦν πρὸς τὸ δίκαιον καὶ τὸ ἔννομον. τὰς θείας ἐνωτισθῶμεν Γραφὰς ἐνηχούσας τὰ σωστικά, εἰ ταῦτα βουλοίμεθα διαπράττεσθαι· ἐπεὶ καὶ ἡμεῖς ἐπακοῦσαι
[fol. 31ᵛ] Θεὸν ἱκετεύοντες, οὐ τὸν ἦχον ἐνωτισθῆναι δεόμεθα, ἀλλ' ἀνυσ-
35 θῆναι τὸ ἔργον τῶν ἡμετέρων αἰτήσεων. τί δὲ καὶ τὸ εἰ θέλετε, λέγων, καὶ εἰσακούσετέ μου, τὰ ἀγαθὰ τῆς γῆς φάγεσθε, τὸ ἐνωτί-

---

46: 5 cf. II Tim. 3:13 ‖ 26 cf. Sirac. 48:10 ‖ 35–36 Is. 1:19

46: V 31ʳ–32ʳ. S 156ᵛ–158ᵛ. P 36ᵛ–38ᵛ.
28 παρόψει codd. ‖ 30 ἀναχαιτίσωμεν coni. Ševčenko; ἀναισχυντήσωμεν codd. ‖ 36 φάγεσθε P: φάγησθε VS

46. To the emperor, rousing him to mercy

Woe is me, lord emperor, since as a result of the affliction of my soul I suffer also in the flesh. But what is hardest for me to bear is my suspicion that it is hopeless to expect a cure through ⟨good⟩ deeds, and this is a result of the disorder of my way of life in both ⟨body and soul⟩, so that every day ⟨my illness⟩ «gets worse». Therefore if any man can provide me with a remedy, but puts if off through hesitation, or on account of my insignificance, I do not think that he will escape punishment at the hands of the One Who granted him power for this purpose, because he does not share this ⟨remedy⟩ which he received freely as a gift from God. If then you so bid, I will disclose to your majesty the identity of the man who is endowed with the strength ⟨to prevail⟩ against the sorrow and despondency which overwhelm me: You yourself, my emperor, if you will, are this man and ⟨this⟩ provider of blessings.

The ⟨conditions⟩ which aggravate my illness are as follows: as I sit here in the midst of a crowd of unhappy people who are quarreling with each other, I see one man in tears, another who has been struck by someone, another bemoaning his bloody clothing, another still, the loss of his property, yet another suffering from oppression, especially at the hands of those who collect the public taxes (who have an obligation to treat justly those who are in any way suffering), not to mention those who escape half-dead from the Ishmaelites and the very Italians—and then are mercilessly stripped by their own countrymen; their plight would bring tears even to a Jew—who were able to take them into captivity on account of the magnitude of general lawlessness, their disregard for God, and their scorn and neglect of the divine commandments.

After God, no one has the power to check the madness of these people as your divine majesty can, first by doing what is pleasing to God to the best of your ability, and by rousing everyone to this ⟨way of life⟩ with strict supervision, and by calling publicly with repentance and tears upon God «to abate His wrath». For if this is not done, no one can guarantee any improvement. Pay close attention to these matters, holy emperor, and do not disregard for long the terrible misfortunes which befall us because of our wicked deeds. Let the fame of your great concern be spread abroad now and in the future. For this reason I plead, let us restrain His wrath by improving our way of life. Bring it about that each person lives in accordance with righteousness and the law. Let us heed the Holy Scriptures which resound with precepts of salvation, if we wish to do these things, for, when we supplicate God to listen, we do not ask that the ⟨mere⟩ sound ⟨of our voices⟩ be heard, but that the substance of our petitions be fulfilled. As for the passage, «If ye be willing and hearken to me, ye shall eat the good of the land», does it mean to hearken

46

ζεσθαι λόγους, ἢ ἀνιχνεύειν τὰ ἐν τοῖς γράμμασι καὶ πάσῃ ἰσχύϊ πληροῦν;
εἰ γάρ που ἡ σὴ βασιλικωτάτη ψυχὴ ἐπινεύσοι πρὸς εὐεργέτησιν τῶν αὐτῆς
δεομένων ὑπανοιγῆναι χρηστότητος σπλάγχνα, ὑπόχρεως ὢν προσνέμειν
40 τὸ ὀφειλόμενον, καὶ τοῦ πιέζοντος ῥύεσθαι, ἀπήτησας καὶ τὴν ὀφειλήν, ὅτι
μηδὲ κατὰ χάριν σοι τὰ τοιαῦτα, ἀλλὰ κατὰ τὸ ἀπαραίτητον, καὶ ἀνθρώπῳ
παντί· καὶ κόσμος τοῖς βασιλεῦσι πρὸ παντὸς ἄλλου τὸ δίκαιον καὶ τὸ ἔλεος,
κἂν τούτῳ εὐφραίνων Θεῷ, πολυμερῶς εὐφρανθήσῃ, καὶ πολλῶν ὑπ'
ἐκείνου τῶν δωρεῶν πλουτισθείς, καὶ εὐχὰς καὶ ἐπαίνους παρὰ τοῦ ὑπη-
45 κόου κομίσῃ, ποθεινῶς καὶ ἡδέως πνεόντων σε.

μηδὲ παρέργως τῶν θείων εὐαγγελίων ἐπακροώμενος, ἃ παραδειγ-
ματίζει παρθένους μὴ φροντισάσας ἐλαίου ἀρκοῦντος αὐταῖς δι' ὅλης νυκτός, κἀκεῖθεν νυμφῶνος ἀποπεσεῖν, δακρύων ἀπαρακλήτων καὶ συμφορᾶς τοῖς παροδεύουσι καὶ ὁρῶσι ταλάνισμα· ὃ παρὰ τίνων πωλεῖται
50 ἢ καὶ κιχρᾶται, ὁ τὴν γλῶτταν καὶ τὴν ψυχὴν αὐτόχρημα ἔλεος, καὶ νῦν
συγκαλῶν τὴν βασιλείαν σου δι' ἡμῶν τῆς τοῦ Θεοῦ μεγάλης Σοφίας ἐν
ἀνακτόροις, καὶ πάντα ὀρθόδοξον, ψαλτῳδήματα ἐνωτισθῆναι τὰ ἐνταυθοῖ,
οὗτος ποιότητα τοῦ τοιούτου ἐλαίου καὶ φύσιν ἐδίδαξε, καὶ πωλεῖν
τοὺς προσαίτας τοὺς ὁδοῖς καὶ φραγμοῖς ἐρριμμένους καὶ πύλαις
55 ἐκκλησιῶν καθυπέδειξε παρακαθημένους· κἀκείνων μόνον τῷ
σώματι πτωχευόντων, πρὸς τούτῳ ἡμεῖς καὶ παντὸς ἀγαθοῦ, ὡς πωλεῖν ἢ
κιχρᾶν ἐστερῆσθαι ἐπὶ τοσοῦτον ἡμᾶς τοῦ καὶ εἰς βρῶσιν ἀρκοῦντος, ὡς
οἴμοι τοὺς κατ' ἐμὲ μηδὲ ρανίδος μιᾶς ἐξ ἔργων προμηθουμένους τυχεῖν.
καὶ εἴ μοι προσῆν καὶ ἐλαίου τοιούτου ποθὲν πορισμός, φειδωλῶς διαζῶντι
60 καὶ γνώμης ἀνελευθέρου τυχόντι, πρὸς τῷ μὴ πωλεῖν, οὐδὲ τοῦτο
κιχρᾶν προήχθην τινί, ἀποθήκας δὲ καθελεῖν, καὶ ἄλλας οἰκοδομεῖν ἐσπουδάκειν τῶν μὴ παραμενόντων εἰς παραφύλαξιν.

δι' ἃ καὶ τὴν ἐλεήμονα ἐννοήσας ψυχήν τε καὶ γνώμην τῆς ἐκ Θεοῦ
βασιλείας σου, εἰς τοῦτο ἀντιβολῶ· εἰ καὶ ἐλαίων πολλῶν εὐμοιρεῖ, οἵων ἐκ
65 Θάσου, ἐξ Ἄθω, ἐξ Ἕω, καὶ οὗ Κατελάνοι πιπράσκουσι, πρὸ τούτων καὶ
τῶν τοιούτων, ἐκείνου [fol. 32ʳ] μᾶλλον ἐπείχθητι τοῦ πρὸς ἐκείνην
τὴν νύκτα φωτίζοντος, καὶ τὴν ἐκεῖθεν ἐπιρροὴν μηδὲ νὺξ διακόψῃ,
μηδὲ ἡμέρα πρὸς τὸ ὁμόφυλον, μὴ ὅσαι βιωτικαὶ περιπέτειαι. ἀσέληνος γὰρ
τότε νύξ, καὶ χρεία πολλοῦ καὶ μάλιστα βασιλεῦσι φωτός, ὡς ἂν
70 φωτίζωνται καὶ οἱ συνιππεύοντες. αὐτοῦ τοῦ ἐλαίου πλησθήτω σου τὰ τα-
μεῖα, ὅτι τοῦτο πιαίνει, πρὸς δὲ καὶ φωτίζει καὶ δοξάζει τὸν ἔχοντα, καὶ

---

43 cf. Joh. Chrys., *In Phil.*, *cp. I*, *Hom. IV* (PG, LXII, 210) ‖ 47–48 cf. Matt. 25:1–13 ‖
48–49 cf. ps.-Joh. Chrys., *In parabolam decem virginum* (PG, LIX, 529) ‖ 54 cf. Luc. 14:23 ‖
55 cf. Joh. Chrys., *De Eleemosyna III* (PG, XLIX, 294) ‖ 61–62 cf. Luc. 12:18 ‖ 67 cf.
Greg. Naz., *Or. XIV*, λη' (PG, XXXV, 908 C) ‖ 69 cf. Joh. Chrys., *In Phil.*, *cp. I*, *Hom. IV*
(PG, LXII, 210)

---

44 πλουτισθείς coni. Ševčenko; πλουτισθῆς codd. ‖ 51 τῆς V¹SP: τοῖς V ‖ 55 μόνων
codd. ‖ 56 ἀγαθῷ codd. ‖ 61 προήχθη codd.

46

to the words, or to study the Scriptures diligently and fulfil them with all one's might ? If your most royal soul would deign to help those who call upon you to open your heart of goodness, since you are obliged to render ⟨to each⟩ what is due, and to rescue from the oppressor, you could claim your debt, because such deeds ⟨are not done⟩ by you for your own pleasure, but as an obligation, indispensable ⟨for you⟩ and for every man; and above all else righteousness and justice are an ornament for emperors. And in «making glad» thereby «the heart of God», you will be gladdened in many ways, and will be enriched by Him with many gifts, and you will receive many prayers and praises from your subjects, who regard you with fondness and affection.

Do not heed only cursorily the Holy Gospels which tell the parable of the virgins who did not think to bring enough oil to last them the whole night, and how they thereby failed to gain entrance to the marriage chamber, and are deemed worthy of «inconsolable tears» and ⟨victims of⟩ misfortune by those who pass by and see them. ⟨As for the question of⟩ «who sells» or lends this ⟨oil⟩: he who in very deed is mercy in both tongue and soul, even now summoning through me your majesty, and every Orthodox Christian, to the halls of the great Wisdom of God to hear the singing here, this man has taught the quality and nature of this kind of oil, and has shown that it is sold by the beggars who are cast into «the highways and hedges» and who «sit beside» the doors «of churches». For they are poor in body alone, but we, in addition to this, are poor in any good quality, so that we are utterly deprived of the chance of selling or lending even that oil that is used for food, because, alas, people like me do not even take thought to provide one drop for themselves through ⟨good⟩ deeds. If I ever did have a supply of such oil from somewhere, since I live selfishly and have a stingy disposition, in addition to not selling it, I was not even persuaded to lend it to anyone, but strove «to pull down my barns, and build greater» ones to protect that which is ephemeral.

Wherefore, mindful of the merciful soul and mind of your divine majesty, I make the following request: even if you have a supply of many kinds of oil, such as that from Thasos or Athos or the East, and the kind the Catalans are selling, instead of these ⟨oils⟩ and their like, be eager rather for that ⟨oil⟩ which will give light in that night, and «let not night» or day or any vicissitudes of life interrupt its flow to your fellow countrymen. For at that time the night ⟨will be⟩ moonless, and emperors especially «need much» light, so that those who ride with them may be illuminated. Let your storerooms be filled with this kind of oil, because it makes fat, and also illuminates and glori-

ἀνάλωτον συντηρεῖ δαιμόνων θηράτρων καὶ λύσσης ἀνθρώπων. τοῦτο καὶ
ἐσθιόμενον κατακόρως λαμπρύνει τὸν νοῦν, εὐφραίνει καρδίαν, καὶ
δὴ καὶ ὀφθαλμιῶσι φωτὸς φαεινοῦ χαρίζεται φῶς· σαρκὸς εὐρωστίαν, εὐεξ-
75 ίαν ψυχῆς, καὶ ὅσα ταῖς ἀληθείαις τίμιά τε καὶ μόνιμα τῇ φύσει φιλοτιμεῖ-
ται βροτῶν, τὸν ἀδόμενον ἀϊετῷ ἀνακαινισμόν.

τούτου γενέσθαι σε ὑπερπλήρη καὶ εὔχομαι καὶ ὀρέγομαι, καὶ φιλτάτοις καταλιπεῖν δόξαν τὴν ἔνθεν καὶ πλουτισμὸν ἀναφαίρετον· τοῦτο
ἀπαίρουσι καὶ τῶν τῇδε, πάντων τῶν ἄλλων ἐνταῦθα καταδυόντων δίκην
80 μολίβδου, συνάνεισι μεθ' ἡμῶν. ὑπὲρ τούτου καὶ αὖθις ἀντιβολῶ βασιλικώτερον κτήσασθαι τοῦτο καὶ ἀφθονώτερον, τοσοῦτον λιπαῖνον τὸν ἔχοντα
καὶ φωτίζον, ὡς καὶ μέσον νυκτῶν τῆς κραυγῆς ἧς αἰσθέσθαι κοινῶς προσδοκῶμεν, δίκην ἡλίου καταφωτίζειν τοὺς ἔχοντας. καὶ τούτου
σοι χρεία πολλοῦ, ὡς ἂν κἀκεῖθεν βασιλικῶς τοὺς αἰτοῦντας εὐεργε-
85 τῆς, βασιλέων τὸ ἰδιαίτατον· οὗ πάντες ἀξιωθείημεν, Θεὲ τοῦ παντός, εἰ τάχα ἠλπίκαμεν ἐπὶ σέ, τοῦ ἐλέους Θεέ, καὶ μάλιστα ὁ κρατῶν,
πρεσβείαις τῆς Θεομήτορος.

47. Πρὸς τὸν αὐτοκράτορα, ὅτι μὴ πρὸς εὐχὰς οἱ μετὰ τοῦ βασιλέως ἐν
τοῖς κατηχουμενείοις συνελθόντες, πρὸς δὲ τρυφὰς ἔβλεψαν

Ὁ τὴν γλῶτταν καὶ τὴν ψυχὴν χρυσοῦ παντὸς τιμαλφέστερος βασι-
λεῦς ὡς ἀεὶ συγκαλεῖται καὶ ἄρχοντας σήμερον καὶ πᾶσαν τὴν ἐκκλησίαν
5 πρὸς τὰ θεῖα ἀνάκτορα, ᾀσομένους εὐψύχως Χριστῷ τῷ παντάνακτι αἰωνίῳ, δοξάζοντι δόξῃ τοὺς τῇδε τῷ βίῳ αἰδεσθέντας αὐτὸν καὶ
δοξάσαντας· καὶ τοῦτο τοῖς συνδραμεῖν βουλομένοις συνορᾶν πρεπω-
δέστερον, τὸ τίς ἡ τοῖς ὀρθοδόξοις ὀφείλουσα ἑορτὴ καὶ ἁρμοδία τούτοις
πανήγυρις· οὐχ ὅπως τοῖς περιβόλοις τῶν θείων νεῶν οἷα χωρίοις
10 κραιπάλης ἀριστᾶν ἀναπέσωμεν, ἀλλ' ὅπως χεῖρας καὶ νοῦν ἀναρτᾶν
πρὸς Θεόν, οὐ μόνον παγίδων ἐχθροῦ τοὺς πιστοὺς ἀνωτέρους φυλάττεσθαι, ἀλλ' ἐξ ὅλης γηΐνης σκοτώσεως, καὶ βίου τοῦ τῇδε τυρβώδους περιπλανήσεως, ὡς ἂν μὴ καὶ στηλιτεύσῃ [fol. 32ᵛ] ὥς τινας καὶ τῶν πρὸ ἡμῶν
ἡ αὐτοαλήθεια, ὁ οἶκός μου, φάσκων, οἶκος ἐστὶ προσευχῆς,
15 ὑμεῖς δὲ αὐτὸν λῃστῶν πεποιήκατε σπήλαιον.

---

73 Ps. 103 (104):15 ‖ 76 cf. Ps. 102 (103):5 ‖ 82 cf. Matt. 25:6 ‖ 83–84 cf. Joh. Chrys.,
In Matt., Hom. *LXXVIII* (PG, LVIII, 712) et *In Phil.*, *cp. I*, Hom. *IV* (PG, LXII, 210) ‖
85 cf. Joh. Chrys., *In Phil.*, *cp. I*, Hom. *IV* (PG, LXII, 210)
47: 6–7 cf. I Reg. 2:30 ‖ 9–10 cf. Greg. Naz., *Oratio XI*, ε' (PG, XXXV, 837C) ‖
14–15 cf. Marc. 11:17

47: V 32ʳ–32ᵛ. S 158ᵛ–159ᵛ. P 38ᵛ–39ᵛ.
10 ἀριστεῖν codd.

46, 47

fies its possessor and preserves him invincible from the snares of demons and the rage of men. And when this ⟨oil⟩ is eaten, it makes the mind shine intensely, it «gladdens the heart», and gives light of bright light to those whose eyes are dim; it provides health for the body, a sense of well-being for the soul, and whatever honorable and enduring ⟨values⟩ are aspired to by human nature, the celebrated «rejuvenation of the eagle».

I pray and earnestly desire that you may be filled to overflowing with this ⟨oil⟩, and will bequeath to your loved ones the inalienable glory and wealth therefrom. And when we depart from this life, while everything else on this earth sinks like lead, it will rise together with us. For this reason I again ask you to acquire a royal and abundant supply of this ⟨oil⟩, since it so greatly fattens and illuminates its possessor, as to make its possessors shine like the sun «in the middle of the nocturnal cry» for which we are waiting together. And «you need much of this» ⟨oil⟩, so that with it you may benefit in a royal manner those who request it, as is «the special duty of emperors». And may we all be deemed worthy of it, O God of all, if we, and especially our ruler, have ever had hope in Thee, O God of mercy, through the intercessions of the Mother of God.

47. To the emperor, that those who accompany the emperor in the galleries do not come to pray, but to indulge themselves

He whose tongue and soul are more precious than all gold, today, as always, summons emperors and nobles and all the congregation of the church to the sacred halls, to sing heartily to Christ, the eternal Ruler of all, «Who glorifies with praise all those» who reverence and «glorify» Him in this life. And those who intend to assemble should consider what kind of festival is owed by Orthodox Christians, and what sort of celebration is appropriate for them. We should not recline and feast in the enclosures of sacred churches as if they were «places for drinking bouts», but should lift up our hands and thoughts to God, ⟨and pray that⟩ the faithful may be preserved not only from the snares of the devil, but from all earthly darkness, and from the confused wandering of life here on earth, so that ⟨Christ⟩ the Truth may not reproach us as He did some of our forebears, saying, «My house is a house of prayer, but ye have made it a den of thieves».

μὴ οὖν ἕνεκεν τοῦ τρυφῆσαι ἢ καὶ τὸ ὄμμα μετεωρίσαι συν-
δράμῃ τις, δέομαι, ἀλλ' ὅπως ψυχὴν εὐωχῆσαι τῇ ἀμβροσίᾳ τοῦ πνεύματος,
τὸ πρωῒ παραστήσομαί σοι καὶ ἐπόψει με, θαρρούντως φθεγ-
γόμενον. ἄνθρωποι γάρ, φησι, δύο ἀνέβησαν εἰς τὸ ἱερόν, οὐ
20 πάντως τρυφῆσαι ἀλλὰ προσεύξασθαι. ὃ καὶ τοῖς συνιοῦσι πανδαισίας
τρυφή, ἐξ ἧς καὶ τελώνης ἀπροσπαθῶς δεδικαίωται, ὡς ὀρθῶς ἀναβάς.
ταύτης τῆς εὐωχίας εἰ οὕτω τοῖς ἀνακτόροις συνίωμεν, καὶ εὖγε τῆς ἀναβάσεως, δεικνύντων κατὰ Χριστὸν τὸ ἐμπόρευμα, πρεπόντως τιμώντων
Χριστὸν καὶ τοὺς τοῦ Χριστοῦ. εἰ δέ τινες τῶν ἀφικομένων γαστρὸς
25 ἡδοναῖς ἀφίκοντο χαριούμενοι, ὃ καὶ τῇ προτεραίᾳ — τῶν συνειλεγ-
μένων ἐπαπελθόντων, ὀστέων τινῶν καὶ περιττωμάτων ἀπολειφθέντων
ἐκείνοις — ἡμεῖς τεθεάμεθα, τίνα τὴν ὄνησιν καὶ καρπώσονται οἱ
συντρέχοντες τούτῳ, καὶ κραιπάλης χωρία ποιούμενοι τὰ τῆς θείας
Σοφίας ἀνάκτορα; καὶ τίς ὁ αὐτοῖς ἐγγυώμενος εὑρήσειν ἄλλον καιρὸν
30 ἀναβάσεως καὶ θεώσεως τῆς ἐκ προσευχῆς; ἧς ἡμᾶς, εἰ βουλοίμεθα,
καὶ οἱ ἅγιοι μεσιτεύουσιν, ἀφίξεως ἄλλης τῷ ἱερῷ οὐκ ἐπαινετῆς,
ὅτι μηδὲ τὰ ἄχυρα πρὸς τὸν σῖτον, οὐδὲ θρύψις σαρκὸς πρὸς
ἱδρῶτας πνευματικούς.
μὴ τοίνυν, ἀντιβολῶ, πρὸς τοῖς ἄλλοις καὶ ἀνάγνως τελῶμεν
35 τὰ ἅγια, μηδὲ τὰ ὑψηλὰ ταπεινῶς, μηδὲ ἀτίμως τὰ πάντιμα.
πόσης γὰρ ἀμοιβῆς ἐποφθῆναι τινὰ εὐλαβῶς τοῦ Θεοῦ πρὸς προσκύνησιν,
ἄδηλον ὂν εἰ ζωῆς εὐμοιρήσει τυχεῖν τοῦ τοιούτου ἐσαύριον. ἀλλ' οὗτοι
γε ἀναμφίβολον ὡς τοὺς ἐν εὐλαβείᾳ θεμένους εἰσιτητὰ ἐν τοῖς θείοις
σηκοῖς, ἧχου κἀκεῖ τῶν ἑορταζόντων, μὴ συμπανηγυρίσαι αἰώνια· καὶ
40 φεῦ τῆς ἀναλγησίας εἰ πανηγύρεις ἐνταῦθα καταγελῶντες Ἑλλήνων
καὶ Ἰουδαίων, μὴ μόνοι τῶν ἄλλων ἡμεῖς, ὡς τῷ πνεύματι τῷ ἁγίῳ
δοκεῖ, καὶ πανηγυρίζομεν τοῦτο Χριστῷ τῷ Θεῷ καὶ δεσπότῃ, καὶ βασιλεῖς καὶ δεσπόται καὶ πᾶς ἐποφείλων πιστὸς καὶ ὀρθόδοξος· γένοιτο,
γένοιτο.

48. Πρὸς τὸν αὐτοκράτορα ὅτι μὴ προστάσσει ἀπελθεῖν ἕνα ἕκαστον τῶν
ποιμένων εἰς τὴν λαχοῦσαν αὐτῷ ποίμνην

Ἐπεὶ πρὸ καιροῦ ἠναγκάσθην ἐμαυτὸν ἐπαράσασθαι ἀπὸ παραλυπήσεως τῶν καλῶν ποιμένων, οἳ μηδεμίαν τῆς ποίμνης φροντίδα [fol. 33ʳ]

---

16 cf. Luc. 18:13 ‖ 18 cf. Ps. 5:4 ‖ 19–20 Luc. 18:10 ‖ 24–35 cf. Greg. Naz., Oratio XI,
ε'–ζ' (PG, XXXV, 837C-840A) ‖ 39 cf. Ps. 41(42):5 ‖ 40–41 cf. Greg. Naz., Oratio XI, ζ'
(PG, XXXV, 840A)

48: V 32ᵛ-33ʳ. S 159ᵛ-160ᵛ. P 39ᵛ-40ʳ.

47, 48

Therefore I ask that no one come ⟨to church⟩ for the sake of indulging himself, or «to lift up his eyes», but to feast his soul on the ambrosia of the Spirit, and to utter with confidence, «In the morning will I wait upon thee, and thou shalt look upon me». «For», ⟨Christ⟩ says, «Two men went up into the temple», not to feast, but «to pray»; and in this, for men of understanding, doth the luxury of a complete banquet reside, and thus was the publican impartially justified, because he went up rightly. If we assemble in this way at the imperial halls of such banqueting, then our approach is blessed, as we demonstrate that our wares are in accordance with Christ, and as we honor Christ and His servants in a fitting manner. But if certain people come «to delight in the pleasures of the stomach», as I saw yesterday—when the assembled multitudes departed, they left behind some bones and scraps—what benefit will they reap by assembling for this purpose, and turning the halls of Divine Wisdom into «places for drinking bouts»? And who will assure them that they will find another opportunity for «spiritual ascent» and to achieve through prayer «the deification, which the saints would procure» for us, if we would be willing? For a different approach to the temple is not praiseworthy, since «chaff is not praiseworthy compared with wheat», nor is «indulging the flesh» praiseworthy compared with spiritual labors.

Therefore I beg this of you: in addition to everything else, «let us not celebrate the holy ⟨mysteries⟩ in an impure fashion, nor exalted things in a degrading manner, nor honorable things dishonorably». For great is the reward for a man to be seen praying to God in a pious manner, since it is uncertain whether he will live long enough to earn such a reward again on the morrow. For it is not even certain that those enter the sacred precincts piously shall ⟨hear⟩ the «sound of celebrants» in the other world, and celebrate together with them forever. And alas for our insensibility, O emperors and despots, and every faithful Orthodox Christian who lies under this obligation, if we ridicule «the festivals of Greeks and Jews» here, but are the only ones not to hold this celebration for Christ, our God and Master, as seems good to the Holy Spirit; so be it, so be it.

48. To the emperor, that he does not order each of the bishops to go to the flock assigned to him

A while ago I was driven to curse myself because of my extreme vexation at those fine shepherds who give no thought to their flock, but, in the

5 ποιούμενοι, άλλ' ὅ φησιν ἡ Γραφή, ἑαυτούς, οὐ τὰ πρόβατα βόσκειν, στηλιτεύουσα τινάς—καὶ οὗτοι κερδῆσαι σπουδάζοντες, τὰς διατριβὰς ἀπεριμερίμνως ἐν τῇ βασιλίδι ποιούμενοι, καὶ ἀδείας βασιλικῆς ἔστιν
ὅπου καὶ φιλοτιμιῶν ἀξιούμενοι, ὀφείλοντες λόγον ἀσυμπαθῆ τιννύειν
αὐτῶν ἕκαστος· μὴ ἔχοντες ὅ,τι καὶ δράσαιμεν, ἡμᾶς καὶ τὴν ἐκκλησίαν
10 τυραννουμένην ἀποκλαιόμεθα, καὶ παρανομιῶν ὧν ἡ τούτων διατριβὴ ἐνταυθοῖ ἐξειργάσατο. πρὸς οἷς μηδὲ ἄνευ χαλκοῦ μαντεύεσθαι
Φοῖβον, ὡς καὶ συνεδριαζόντων πολλάκις ἀντιπίπτειν ἀλλήλοις ὑπὲρ
τῶν δικαζομένων, καὶ μέχρι καὶ ὕβρεων καταντᾶν, οὐχ ἵνα τὸ δίκαιον,
ἀλλ' ἵνα τὸν κῆνσον μὴ μάτην κομίσωνται. εἰ δέ γε καὶ περὶ ψήφων
15 συνέλθωσιν, οὔποτε ἀποστῇ παρ' αὐτοῖς ὁ οἴνου φροντίσας σὺν πέποσιν.
    εἰ οὖν διὰ ταῦτα ἐῶνται προσκαρτερεῖν εἰς αὔξησιν καὶ ἑδραίωσιν
τῶν ῥηθέντων, πῶς ἐπὶ τὸν λαὸν εἰρήνην λαλήσει ὁ Κύριος,
γεγενημένου τοῦ ἱερέως ὡς ὁ λαός; ἐν δέ γε τοιούτοις ταλαντευό-
μενοι, πόσῃ τῇ ἀθυμίᾳ βαλλόμεθα! εἰ γάρ που τῇ τῶν χηρευουσῶν ἀνομίᾳ
20 ἐκκλησιῶν ὡς ἐνεχόμενος δεδιὼς συγκαλέσω ἐναντίους τῷ ἔργῳ, ἀβασανίστους εἰσάξουσιν. εἰ τοῦτο μὴ πράξω, ποιμένων τὰ πλήθη ἐστερημένα
ἐπὶ πολὺ λυκόβρωτα γέγονεν. εἰ δ' ἄνευ τῶν ὑποπτευομένων τοῦ ἔργου ἁ-
ψόμεθα, ἀθετήσει κανονικῇ ἁλισκόμεθα. ἔνθεν καὶ τὴν ζωὴν ἀπολέγομαι,
τὰ αὐτὰ ἐξαιτούμενος· μὴ πλεῖον ἐάσθω, ἀντιβολῶ, τὰ τῶν ποιμένων τῆς
25 νομίμου μακρὰν καταστάσεως, ὡς τῆς βλάβης οὐ τῆς τυχούσης, ἀλλ' ὅλῃ
τῇ ἐκκλησίᾳ μεγάλην τὴν ἀμορφίαν ἐπεισαγούσης, καὶ ἐξ ἐκείνης τὸν ὄλεθρον καὶ τοῖς τούτοις ἐφησυχάζουσι, δυναμένοις καὶ ταῦτα προσδιορθοῦν
ἀσυγχώρητα.

49. Πρὸς τὸν αὐτοκράτορα

Ἐμοὶ ἀεὶ περὶ τὰ καλὰ καὶ μᾶλλον τὰ ἀναγκαῖα τυγχάνοντι λίαν
ἀμβλεῖ, μόλις ἐπῆλθεν ὑπόδειγμα ἀραρότως συντεινόν μοι εἰς νουθέτημα,
παρ' οὗ καὶ μικροῦ ἀπογνοὺς τὰ ἐμά, προήχθην τὸ ἐκφοβοῦν ἐκκαλύψαι
5 τουτί. οὔ μοι δοκεῖ ἀγνοεῖν τινὰ τῶν ὅσοι βάπτουσιν εἰς νοῦν, εἰ μή που
ταῖς πτέρναις φορεῖ τὸν ἐγκέφαλον, ὅσον ἀνέπνει καὶ ὅπως
ὑπερηγάπα καὶ οἵᾳ ἐδέδετο τῇ στοργῇ τοῖς υἱέσιν Ἠλεί· ἀλλ' ὅτι μὴ προε-
τίθει καὶ προετίμα τῶν τέκνων τοῦ Θεοῦ τὰ μαρτύ-[fol. 33ᵛ]ρια, ἐλεεινῶς
σὺν ἐκείνοις οὐ μόνον ἱερωσύνης, ἀλλὰ καὶ τῆς ζωῆς ἀπεστέρηται, δεῖγμα

48: 5–6 cf. Ezech. 34:2,8 ‖ 11–12 Leutsch-Schneidewin, II, 228 ‖ 14 cf. Matt. 22:19 ‖
17 Ps. 84 (85):9 ‖ 18 cf. Osee 4:9
49: 6 Demosthenes, Περὶ Ἀλοννήσου, 7.45; cf. Athanasius, Epp. 50, 19 et 58, 36–37 ‖
6–9 cf. I Reg. 2–4

24 τῆς] τοῦ P
49: V 33ʳ–35ʳ. S 160ᵛ–163ᵛ. P 40ʳ–43ᵛ.
1 ante πρὸς add. γράμμα VʳSP ‖ post αὐτοκράτορα add. ἵνα μὴ δι' ὑπέρθεσιν μένωσιν
ἀθεράπευτα ὅσα ἄττα μικρὰ ἀναφέρομεν, καὶ μὴ τῇ θυρίδι ῥιφέσθω μόνον τὰ γράμματα VʳSP

48, 49

reproving words of the Scriptures, «feed themselves, and not their sheep». Above all, they strive after gain, as they make their carefree residence in the capital, and from time to time ask the emperor for favors and honors, although each of them will have to pay the merciless penalty. Not knowing what else to do, I weep for myself and for the Church which is ruled by tyranny, and ⟨I weep⟩ for the outrages caused by their residence here. Furthermore, «Phoebus does not prophesy without a gift of copper»; thus, when they assemble ⟨for meetings of the synod⟩, they often argue with each other over the defendants, and even come to blows, not for the sake of justice, but so they won't have accepted bribes to no purpose. And if they meet for an election, a ⟨candidate⟩ who will bribe them with wine and melons is never far away.

If then for these reasons they are permitted to remain so as to increase and firmly establish the above-mentioned practices, how «will the Lord speak peace to His people», «when the priest has become like his flock»? Into what despair am I cast, caught as I am in this dilemma! For, on the one hand, if, out of my fear that I am responsible for the lack of order in dioceses which are bereft of bishops, I convoke ⟨bishops⟩ who oppose my plan, they will propose unqualified ⟨candidates⟩. If, on the other hand, I don't do this, the multitudes who have long been deprived of bishops will fall prey to wolves. But if I undertake my plan without those ⟨bishops⟩ who are under suspicion, then I will be guilty of disregard of the canons. Therefore I despair of life, making one and the same request: I beg of you, do not allow the bishops to reside far from the diocese allotted to them by law, since the harm is by no means slight, but is a great blemish upon the entire Church, and thus brings perdition to those who condone these unforgivable transgressions, although they have the power to correct them.

49. To the emperor

Although I have always been extremely sluggish with regard to good deeds, especially urgent ones, an incident recently occurred which urgently compelled me to reflect, after which I all but despaired of my situation, and was persuaded to reveal this terrible matter. I do not think there is anyone who has a drop of intelligence (unless «he wears his brain in his heels»), who does not know how Elei depended upon and loved his sons exceedingly and with what affection he was bound to them. But because he did not give precedence to and prefer the testimonies of God above his sons, together with them he was pitiably deprived not only of the priesthood, but also of life. And thus

10 αἰῶνι τιθεὶς τἄπαντι τοῦ μή τινα προτιμᾶν τολμηρῶς τῶν θεϊκῶν τὰ ἀνθρώπινα, ἢ σιωπῇ ἐπαράτῳ ἐφησυχάζειν ἐν οἷς θυμοῦται τὸ θεῖον καὶ παρο-
ξύνεται, ἐν μέρει κρινούσης τῆς Ἀληθείας συγκαταθέσεως εἶναι τὴν σιω-
πὴν ἐν κακοῖς ἢ καὶ χείροσιν. ὃ καὶ αὐτοὶ σχετλιῶμεν (οὐαί μοι τῆς συμφορᾶς!) ἰλύϊ τοιαύτῃ ἐμπεπαρμένοι δεινῶς διὰ μόνην ἀγάπησιν. τῆς γὰρ
15 κοινῆς ἀνομίας, ἀνυποίστου δίκην φλογός, τὴν ὅση ὑπὸ Ῥωμαίους δρατ-
τομένης διττῶς, καὶ μόνης μετὰ Θεὸν ἰσχυούσης, εἰ βούλει, τῆς ἐκ Θεοῦ
βασιλείας σου μὴ τὸ πᾶν ὑπ᾽ αὐτῆς, φεῦ, αἰσχρῶς ἀποτεφρωθῇ — ὡς πρότριτα τῶν σμικρυνόντων κακοβουλίᾳ τινῶν τῶν φέρειν τὰ σκῆπτρα λαχόντων τὰ Ῥωμαίων σχοινίσματα, ὡς ὅτι μὴ τὰ Χριστοῦ Ἰησοῦ,
20 ἀλλ᾽ ὀρέξεις οἰκείας προτιμησάντων, μηδέ γε τῷ τύφῳ ὑποκλινάντων
φιλήκοον οὓς εἰς ἐνώτισιν ὡς ἄρα ἐκείνοις καὶ προστεθεῖσθαι τὸ πᾶν,
τοῖς πρώτως ζητοῦσι δι᾽ ἔργων τὴν βασιλείαν καὶ τὴν δικαιοσύνην Θεοῦ, ὡς μὴ τά γε ἄλλως συμβασιλεύειν τούτοις ἀνέξεσθαι.
τοίνυν ὁμοίως ἐκείνῳ τῷ ἱερεῖ σήμερον καὶ ἡμεῖς, ἀφύκτῳ τῷ φίλτρῳ
25 τῷ περὶ ταύτην, υἱὲ ἀνθρώπου, σκοπὸν τέθεικά σε ἐπιλησθέντες,
σιωπῶμεν ὡς ἀβλεπτοῦντες ἐκ ταύτης τὰ τῆς ῥομφαίας, εἰ λάβοι
ψυχήν, τοῦ ἀναβοᾶν καὶ γυμνῇ, τὸ λεγόμενον, κεφαλῇ ἐκβιάζειν ὡς
δέον καὶ φίλον Θεῷ διοικεῖσθαι αὐτῇ τὰ κοινὰ καὶ τὰ ἴδια. ἀλλ᾽ εἴ που καὶ
τῶν πολλῶν ἄττα μικρὰ ἀναφέρομεν, τῷ τοῦ καιροῦ ἀνωμάλῳ, καὶ τῇ τῶν
30 ἀντικειμένων τοῖς δέουσιν ἐγρηγόρσει, καὶ δὴ καὶ ἀναβολῇ τῇ ἐσαύριον τῇ
κρατούσῃ τὰ νῦν (ἧς μέγα τὸ πῆμα περὶ τὰ καίρια), δι᾽ ὑπέρθεσιν ἔμεινεν
ἀθεράπευτα· καὶ ταῦτα σκοπὸς μὴ τὰ τυχόντα ἀνιστορεῖν με, ἀλλ᾽ ὅσα καὶ
σώματα καὶ ψυχὰς ὀλέσκειν τὴν ἀπραξίαν ἀρίδηλον. ἐν γοῦν καὶ τοῖς ἀναγ-
καίοις αὐτοῖς ἐπικρατοῦσαν παραδρομὴν αἰσθανόμενοι, ὡς δοκεῖν κενο-
35 λόγους ἡμᾶς καὶ εἰς ἀέρα λαλεῖν, ἀφορήτῳ λύπῃ κατακρατούμεθα,
καὶ μᾶλλον ὡς ἰσταμένων, φεῦ, ἐκ τοιούτων τῶν ἡμετέρων ἐπὶ ξυροῦ.
καὶ εἴ γε πατράσιν ὀφεῖλον υἱέσι τὰ τίμια ἀποθησαυρί-
ζειν, τί ἡμῖν τιμιώτερον καὶ χρεὼν τοῦ μὴ μόνον ἀνιστορεῖν, ἀλλ᾽ ἔστιν οὗ
καὶ βιάζεσθαι σε τὸν υἱέα τῆς ἐκκλησίας; πᾶσα ἀνάγκη θεοφιλῶς μὲν βιοῦν
40 ἐν τοῖς σοῖς, καὶ οἴκτῳ [fol. 34ʳ] ἴσα γνησίων υἱῶν φροντίζειν τῶν ὑπὸ
χεῖρα, ῥύεσθαι δὲ ἀνομίας διττῆς νομίμῳ ἐπεξελεύσει, εἰ συμβῇ ἐμπαγῆ-
ναι τινάς, οἰκτίζεσθαί τε ἀδικουμένους, καὶ πενομένους προῖκα καταπλουτεῖν, ἀλλὰ μὴ μάτην ἡμᾶς ἀναφέρειν τὰ λίαν ὀνήσοντα (εἰ ὅλως καὶ τὰ
ὑμῶν ἀκουστὰ αἰτήματα πρὸς Θεοῦ βουλοίμεθα γίνεσθαι, καθά που καὶ ἡ
45 θεία φωνή, ὡς μετροῦμεν ἀντιμετρούμενοι), ἃ Θεοῦ ἡμῖν ἐγκε-
λευομένου λαλεῖν καὶ μὴ σιωπᾶν, μηδὲ πάσχειν ὑποστολὴν ἡμέρας ὄψει

---

19 cf. Ps. 104 (105):11 ‖ 19–20 cf. Phil. 2:21 ‖ 21–23 cf. Matt. 6:33 ‖ 25 cf. Ezech. 33:7 ‖
26–27 cf. Ezech. 33:6 ‖ 27 Leutsch-Schneidewin, II, 85 ‖ 35 cf. I Cor. 14:9 ‖ 36 Leutsch-
Schneidewin, II, 392 ‖ 37–38 cf. II Cor. 12:14 ‖ 45 cf. Luc. 6:38 ‖ 46 cf. Ps. 55 (56):3–4

---

10 τἄπαντι] τὰ παντὶ codd. ‖ 13 κακοῖς] καλοῖς codd.

49

he set an example for all future generations never to dare to give precedence to the human over the divine, nor to pass over in accursed silence matters which enrage and provoke God, since Truth judges that silence in the face of evil or worse is a mark of approval. And this very thing we will bewail (alas for my misfortune!), since we are bogged down terribly in the mire of personal affection. For universal lawlessness, like an irresistible flame, has enveloped all the Roman territory twice over, and only you, your divine majesty, after God, are able, if you will, to keep everything from being shamefully reduced to ashes by it. Recently certain of those whose lot it is to bear the scepter have reduced Roman territory through the bad advice of some people, giving preference «not to the things of Jesus Christ», but to their own desires; nor in their arrogance did they lend an attentive ear to the advice that «everything is added to those who seek first of all through their works the kingdom and righteousness of God», since otherwise He will not endure to rule together with them.

Therefore today, just like that priest [Elei], because of my irresistible affection for your majesty, I forget ⟨the precept⟩ «son of man, I have set thee as a watchman», and keep silence, as if disregarding ⟨the warning⟩ «the sword, if it take a life...», and refrain from shouting and from forcing you with the proverbial bare head to administer both public and private affairs as is right and pleasing to God. But whenever I do report certain small matters out of many, because of the troubles at this time and the vigilance of my opponents against necessary measures, and because of the prevailing habit these days of postponing matters to the morrow (and in emergencies this causes great harm), they have remained unattended to through delay. And it is not my intention to report minor incidents, but matters in which failure to act will clearly destroy both bodies and souls. Even in these matters of utmost necessity, when I perceive the prevailing attitude of negligence, so that I seem to babble in vain and «to speak into the air», I am overwhelmed with unbearable sorrow, especially since as a result we are in an extremely precarious position.

And if indeed «fathers ought to lay up honorable things for their sons», then what could be more honorable and necessary for me than not only to make inquiries, but even on occasion to exert pressure on you as the Son of the Church ? You have the obligation to live your own life in love of God, and to look after your subjects compassionately as if they were your own children, and to save them with lawful punishment from twofold lawlessness, if any of them should happen to be ensnared ⟨in vice⟩, and to take pity on victims of injustice, and to enrich the poor at your own expense, but I should not report in vain matters of great importance—if we wish *your* petitions as well to be heard by God, since the Holy Scriptures say «as we measure it shall be measured unto us»—and these matters should not be subject to any delay because of «the early hour» or hesitation, since God charges us to speak and not keep

ἢ ὄκνῳ. ἀναβόησον γάρ φησιν ἐν ἰσχύϊ, καὶ μὴ φείσῃ· ὡς
σάλπιγγος ὕψωσον τὴν φωνήν σου· καὶ ἀνάγγειλον τῷ
λαῷ μου τὰ ἁμαρτήματα αὐτοῦ, καὶ τῷ οἴκῳ Ἰακὼβ τὰς
50 ἀνομίας αὐτῶν. ἐμὲ ἡμέραν ἐξ ἡμέρας ζητοῦσι, καὶ γνῶναί
μου τὰς ὁδοὺς ἐπιθυμοῦσιν· ὡς λαὸς δικαιοσύνην πεποιη-
κὼς καὶ κρίσιν Θεοῦ αὐτοῦ μὴ ἐγκαταλελοιπώς, αἰτοῦσί
με νῦν κρίσιν δικαίαν καὶ στόματι μόνον ἐγγίζειν ἐπιθυ-
μοῦσι Θεῷ, ὅλως μὴ φροντιζόντων ὑμῶν τῶν ἐν χερσὶ παρεισπράξεων.
55 καὶ ἵνα τἆλλα ἐάσω τῶν ὑμετέρων, πορνείας, φημί, καὶ μοιχείας καὶ ἀδικίας καὶ ἀλέκτους ἀρρητουργίας, τὸ ποιμένων ἐκτὸς ἀνεκτὸν ἡγεῖσθαι τὴν
ποίμνην Χριστοῦ ἐκ πολλοῦ ἀνθρώποις καὶ δαίμοσιν ἀφειδῶς εἰς κατάβρωμα κεῖσθαι (ὀφεῖλον ὑμῖν ἀναγκαῖον ἡγεῖσθαι οἷα τὸ ἀναπνεῖν), ἀλλὰ τὸ
διαρρήγνυσθαι καὶ διαρρηγνύειν τῆς ἐκκλησίας Χριστοῦ (ὢ τῆς ζημίας!)
60 τοῖς ὅσοι καὶ βουληθεῖεν συνδρομὴν καὶ ἄδειαν δίδοσθαι, ἀνθρώπων πρόσωπα λαμβανόντων ὑμῶν, μὴ αἰδουμένων ἐν προτιμήσει τοῦ κενωθέντος
ἁγίου καὶ πανολβίου αἵματος, ἐκείνου τοῦ θεορρύτου, ἑνώσεως ἕνεκεν τῶν
διϊσταμένων, καὶ δὴ καὶ τοῦ μὴ νομίμως διεξάγεσθαι τὰ ἀνθρώπινα, καὶ
παρὰ τίνος ἐδόθη καὶ τίσι τοῖς λόγοις.
65   οὐ δέον φρονεῖν διὰ ταῦτα ἐκκαυθῆναι καὶ τὴν ὀργήν; καὶ ὤ μοι
τῆς συμφορᾶς καὶ τῆς ὀφειλῆς! πότε καὶ γὰρ δοῦλοι ἀχρεῖοι τῇ
τηρήσει τῶν διατεταγμένων παρρησιασθῆναι θαρρήσομεν; καὶ εἴθε διὰ
νομίμων ἀποβολὴν πρὸς ἀξίαν κατεγινώσκομεν ἑαυτῶν, τὴν ὀργὴν ἐκδεχόμενοι! ἢ γὰρ ἂν ἐβλέψαμεν πρὸς διόρθωσιν, καὶ μὴ ἔργων χωρὶς ἀντί-
70 ληψιν ἀνεμένομεν, μόνον ἔλεον τοῦ κριτοῦ, ἀλλὰ μὴ καὶ τὴν κρίσιν προσά-
δοντες. ἢ οὐχ ὑπὲρ τὴν τῶν Σοδόμων ἄνεισι πρὸς Θεὸν ἡ ὑμετέρα κραυ-
γή, ἐξ ὧν μικροὶ καὶ μεγάλοι, ἄνδρες τε καὶ γυναῖκες, καὶ ἄρχοντες καὶ
ἀρχόμενοι τὰ χείριστα ἀσπαζόμεθα; τί δέ; οὐχ ὑπόχρεοι ἕκαστος τὸν πλησίον καὶ [fol. 34ᵛ] ἑαυτὸν ἀναγκάζειν βιοῦν ὡς τὰ λόγια (καὶ μᾶλλον οἱ
75 προύχοντες καὶ ἔργῳ καὶ λόγῳ) τὰ φάσκοντα, ἐπεφάνη ἡ χάρις τοῦ
Θεοῦ ἡ σωτήριος πᾶσιν ἀνθρώποις, παιδεύουσα ἡμᾶς, ἵνα
ἀρνησάμενοι τὴν ἀσέβειαν καὶ τὰς ἐπιθυμίας τὰς κοσμικάς,
(πρόσχωμεν τί ἀκούομεν!) σωφρόνως καὶ δικαίως καὶ εὐσεβῶς
ζήσωμεν ἐν τῷ νῦν αἰῶνι, ἀπεκδεχόμενοι τὴν μακαρίαν
80 ἐλπίδα καὶ ἐπιφάνειαν τῆς δόξης τοῦ μεγάλου Θεοῦ καὶ
σωτῆρος ἡμῶν Ἰησοῦ, ὃς ἑαυτὸν ὑπὲρ ἡμῶν δέδωκεν; οὕτω
γὰρ διαζώντων, ἠλπίζετο τὸ ὅταν ὁ Χριστὸς φανερωθῇ, ἡ ζωὴ
ἡμῶν, τότε καὶ ὑμεῖς σὺν αὐτῷ φανερωθήσεσθε ἐν δόξῃ.
ὑπέρευγε τῆς τοιᾶσδε θεώσεως, ἧς καὶ ἀντιβολῶ μὴ ἐκπέσωμεν, μηδέ γε

47–53 Is. 58:1–2 ‖ 53–54 cf. Is. 58:2 et 29:13 ‖ 66 Luc. 17:10 ‖ 71–72 cf. Gen. 18:20 ‖
75–81 Tit. 2:11–14 ‖ 82–83 Col. 3:4

---

73 τὸν] τῶν codd.

49

silence. For He says, «Cry aloud and spare not; lift up thy voice as with a trumpet, and declare to my people their sins and to the house of Jacob their iniquities. They seek me day by day, and desire to know my ways, as a people that had done righteousness, and had not forsaken the judgment of their God; they now ask of me righteous judgment, and desire to draw nigh to God only with their mouth», but all the while you take no heed at all of the illegal exactions of which you are guilty. And I will not mention your other sins, fornication, I mean, and adultery and injustice and unspeakable perversions, and your belief that it is tolerable for the flock of Christ to remain long without shepherds, and to lie pitiably as an easy prey for men and demons (when you should believe that ⟨having shepherds⟩ is as necessary as breathing), and ⟨your belief that it is tolerable⟩ to aid and abet anyone who wishes to separate from and to cause schism in the Church of Christ (O what misfortune!), while you show personal prejudice, and are not ashamed, in showing preferences, of the holy and most blessed blood which was shed for us, flowing from a god, for the sake of unifying the schismatics, and are not ashamed when mankind is not being governed lawfully, and ⟨when we do not consider with awe⟩ by Whom ⟨this mandate⟩ was given and with what words.

Doesn't one have to conclude that it is for these reasons that His wrath has been kindled? Alas for my misfortune and obligation! When will we «worthless servants» make bold to speak freely because we have abided by the commandments? Would that we might worthily condemn ourselves because of our rejection of lawful behavior, and await His wrath! For then we would seek to mend our ways and would not expect succor without action on our part, singing only of the mercy of the Judge, and not of His judgment. Has not your cry arisen to God even above that of the Sodomites, because we cling to iniquity, whether young or old, male or female, ruler or ruled? What then? Does not each person, especially those who are leaders in word and deed, have the obligation to force himself and his neighbor to live in accordance with the words which say: «the grace of God that bringeth salvation hath appeared to all men, teaching us that, denying ungodliness and worldly lusts» (let us pay attention to these words!), «we should live soberly, righteously, and godly in this present world; looking for that blessed hope, and the glorious appearing of the great God and our Savior Jesus, Who gave Himself for us»? For, if we lived in this way, it was hoped that «when Christ, Who is our life, shall appear, then shall ye also appear with Him in glory». Blessed be this deification! I pray that we may not fail to attain it, nor from now on let us prefer shame-

110

49

85 τὰ ἐπονείδιστα ἀπεντεῦθεν προκρίνωμεν. ὁ λαὸς οὗτος, φησί, τοῖς
χείλεσί με τιμᾷ, ἡ δὲ καρδία αὐτῶν πόρρω ἀπέχει ἀπ'
ἐμοῦ· μάτην δὲ σέβονταί με, καὶ τί με λέγετε Κύριε, Κύριε,
καὶ οὐ ποιεῖτε ἃ λέγω ὑμῖν; καὶ ὁ μὴ ἀγαπῶν με τὸν λόγον
μου οὐ τηρεῖ, ὡς αὖθις καὶ ὁ ἀγαπῶν με τὰς ἐντολάς μου
90 τηρήσει, καὶ ἐγὼ καὶ ὁ Πατὴρ ἐλευσόμεθα, καὶ ὅσα ἑξῆς, καὶ
εἰ ταῦτα οἴδατε, μακάριοί ἐστε ἐὰν ποιῆτε αὐτά. ἀλλ' ὤ μοι,
πρὸς τούτοις μὴ γένηται ὅτι καὶ ἔφαγεν Ἰακὼβ καὶ ἐνεπλήσθη,
καὶ ἀπελάκτισεν ὁ ἠγαπημένος. εἰ γάρ τι τῶν ἐπαράτων ποτὲ
συγκεκαλυμμένως ἐπράττετο, ἄρτι ἀναφανδὸν ἐνεργούμενα ἀνακόπτει
95 οὐδείς. τίς γὰρ τὰ τῆς ἐκκλησίας, τίς τὰ τῆς πολιτείας, εἰ ὡς φίλον Θεῷ διεξάγεσθαι πολυπραγμονεῖ καὶ συνίστησιν; ἢ οὐχ ἡ βασιλεία ἐπιστασία ἐστὶ καὶ ὁρίζεται ἔννομος; οὐ λόγον ὑφέξομεν ἕκαστος τῷ τοῦ
κόσμου παραγωγεῖ εἰς ὃ πεπιστεύμεθα, εἰ ὡς φίλον ἐκείνῳ καὶ διῳκήκα-
μεν, καθὰ ἐκφοβεῖ ὁ τὸ τάλαντον εἰληφώς, οὐχ ὅτι μὴ προσαπώλεσε
100 δεχθείς, ἀλλὰ διὸ καὶ μὴ προσεξείργαστο ἐκδοθείς; εἰ δέ που τινὰς ὀνειδίζει ὡς ὅταν ἀπέκτενεν αὐτούς, τότε ἐξεζήτουν αὐτόν, εἰ ἡμεῖς
μηδὲ τότε ἀλλ' ἔτι καὶ τῇ κακίᾳ ἐμπλατυνόμεθα, τί καὶ πεισόμεθα; καὶ
πόθεν μὴ δεδοίκαμεν τὸ οὐαὶ οἱ ἐπισπώμενοι ὡς σχοινίῳ μακρῷ
τὰς ἁμαρτίας αὐτῶν, καὶ τὰς αὐτῶν ἀνομίας οἷα ζυγῷ ἱμάντι
105 δαμάλεως, ὧν εἰ στραφέντες ὡς δέον στενάξομεν ἕνεκεν, σωθησόμεθα.
ταῦτα εἰ ἀληθεύων φημί, μὴ τῇ θυρίδι αἰτῶ τὸ γράμμα ῥιφήτω,
φοβοῦντος ἄκρως ὑμᾶς τοῦ ἐὰν μὴ ἐπιστραφῆτε, τὴν ῥομφαίαν
αὐτοῦ στιλβώσει θεσπίζοντος, καὶ μάλα διψῶντος Θεοῦ, ἕως ἐσμὲν ἐν
τοῖς ζῶσιν, εἰλικρινῆ πρὸς αὐτὸν ἐνδείξασθαι πάντας τὴν ἐξ ἔργων μετά-
110 νοιαν· ἐφ' ᾗ, ἀξιῶ, τῶν [fol. 35ʳ] ἰχνῶν ἐφαπτόμενος, μὴ μόνον διαναστῆναι, ἀλλὰ διαναστῆσαι καὶ ἡμᾶς καὶ πᾶν τὸ ὑπήκοον, εἰς ὑπόδειγμα κεχρη-
μένους ἀρίστως ἡμᾶς τοῖς Νινευΐτῶν, καὶ μάλα διαπρεψάσης ἐν πλείστοις
τῆς βασιλείας ὑπὲρ πολλούς, βασιλικώτερον ἅμα καὶ ἀνδρικώτερον ἐν τοῖς
κρείττοσι. καὶ τοῦτο ῥᾷστον αὐτῇ τῇ ἐκ Θεοῦ βασιλείᾳ σου, ἐπεὶ μηδὲ
115 ἄκριτα τὰ ἡμῶν, καὶ ἡμεῖς οὐκ ἀθάνατοι, συγκλείσαντος ὧδε Θεοῦ καὶ βίον
καὶ πρᾶξιν, δικαίαν δὲ μόνην ἐκεῖ τῶν πεπραγμένων ἐξέτασιν· ἐφ' οἷς ὁ
ἀφροντιστῶν ταλανίσει τῷ τότε πολλὰ ἑαυτὸν ἀκαίρως καὶ καταμέμψεται.
ἔνθεν παρακαλῶ, μὴ ὀνειδισθῶμεν ὡς βαρυκάρδιοι· ἕως δὲ
μᾶλλον καιρός, θεραπεύσωμεν τὴν κακίαν καὶ οὐ μὴ τῇ
120 κακίᾳ συντελεσθῶμεν, ἔχοντες στήλην ἁλὸς ἀπείρους τῶν πρὸ
ἡμῶν. φοβηθῶμεν ἢ αἰδεσθῶμεν ἢ ἀγαπήσωμεν τὸν καθ' ἡμέραν παρακα-

---

85–87 Is. 29:13 ‖ 87–88 cf. Luc. 6:46 ‖ 88–89 Joh. 14:24 ‖ 89–90 cf. Joh. 14:23 ‖ 91
Joh. 13:17 ‖ 92–93 Deut. 32:15 ‖ 96–97 *Epanagoge*, Tit. I, 1 ‖ 99 Matt. 25:24 ‖ 101 Ps. 77
(78):34 ‖ 103–105 cf. Is. 5:18 ‖ 107–108 Ps. 7:13 ‖ 111–114 Jon. 3 ‖ 118 Ps. 4:3 ‖ 119–120
cf. Greg. Naz., *Oratio* XVI, ιδ' (PG, XXXV, 953 B) ‖ 120 cf. Gen. 19:26

---

110 τῶν] τῶν τῶν VP ‖ 113 τῇ βασιλείᾳ codd.

ful actions. ⟨The Lord⟩ says, «This people honors me with their lips, but their heart is far from me; but in vain do they worship me», and «why call ye me, Lord, Lord, and do not the things which I say unto you ?», and «he that loveth me not keepeth not my sayings», and again «he that loveth me will keep my commandments», and «I and my Father will come, etc.», and «if ye know these things, happy are ye if ye do them». But woe is me, may there not be added to these the words, «Jacob ate and was filled, and the beloved one kicked». For if in the past any accursed deed was done in secret, now there is no restraint even on sins committed openly. Who makes it his business to ensure that the Church and State are being governed in a manner pleasing to God ? Is not «kingship a legal authority», and thus defined ? Will not each of us have to render an accounting to the Creator of the world for that which has been entrusted to us, whether we have administered it in a manner pleasing to Him ? Accordingly, the man who «had received the talent» arouses fears in us; he does so, not because after receiving the talent, he did not lose it, but because he made no interest on what he had been given. If God reproaches certain people because «when He slew them, then they sought Him», what shall we suffer if we do not ⟨seek Him⟩ even then, but still increase our iniquity ? And why don't we fear the words: «Woe to them that draw sins to them as with a long rope, and iniquities as with a thong of the heifer's yoke»; if we turn away and lament on account of these sins as we should, we will be saved.

If I speak the truth when I make these remarks, I beg of you, let not my letter be tossed into a pigeon-hole, since God threatens that «if ye will not repent, He will furbish His sword», and desires that, as long as we are among the living, we all show Him our sincere repentance by our deeds. Clasping your feet, I beg that you not only rouse yourself to repentance, but also rouse me and every subject, using the Ninevites as an excellent example, especially their king who distinguished himself above the masses in many ways, being more kingly and more manly in good deeds. And this is extremely easy for your divine majesty, since our affairs are subject to judgment, and we are not immortal, but God brings to an end our life and work in this world, and in the world to come there is only a righteous examination of our deeds. He who ignores this will deem himself extremely unfortunate at that time when it is too late, and will reproach himself.

Wherefore, I beg of you, let us not be rebuked for «slowness of heart»; while we still have time, «let us heal our iniquity, and not be consumed by it», and end up with a «pillar of salt», through our failure to learn from the experience of our predecessors(?). Let us fear or respect or love the One Who

λοῦντα ἐπιστράφητε πρός με, ὡς ἂν ἐνεργῶς ἐπιστρέψωμεν αὐτὸν
πρὸς ἡμᾶς. εἰ γάρ που καὶ προσκυνήσομεν τοῦτον ἐν φόβῳ, καὶ προσπέσο-
μεν καὶ προσκλαύσομεν, ταχὺ χαριεῖται τὰ εὐκταῖα ἡμῖν, καὶ θάρσος καὶ
125 νίκην καὶ σωτηρίαν παρέξει. εἰρήνην τὴν ὄντως λαλήσει ἐπὶ τὸν
τούτου λαόν, ἅμα καρδίᾳ εἰλικρινεῖ πρὸς αὐτὸν ἐπιστρέψοιμεν. καὶ τοσοῦτον τῆς σῆς φροντιεῖ καὶ ὑπερασπιεῖ βασιλείας, ὡς τοῖς αὐτοῦ μεταφρένοις τοιαύτην ἐπισκιάζειν διηνεκῶς καὶ ψυχαγωγεῖν, σὺν
ἅμα τῇ βασιλείᾳ τῇ τῇδε καὶ τὴν οὐράνιον χαριζόμενος· γένοιτο, γένοιτο,
130 γένοιτο, Κύριε.

50. Πρὸς τὸν αὐτοκράτορα περὶ τῶν ἐγγιζουσῶν ἡνωμένως οἰκιῶν μετὰ
τῶν θείων καὶ σεβασμίων ἐκκλησιῶν, ὅπως ἔνι τοῦτο λίαν ἐφάμαρτον

Εἰ τῶν φρονίμων παρ' Ἕλλησιν ἐξετέθη βιωφελῆ τοῖς λαοῖς καὶ
σωτήρια, δεχθέντα τοῖς μετὰ ταῦτα εἰς νόμων ἀκρίβειαν, πόση καὶ οἷα
5 ἡμῖν τοῖς πιστοῖς ὀφειλή, ἐγνωκόσιν ὡς θέμις Θεὸν καὶ τὰ τούτου προσ-
τάγματα, καὶ πράξει καὶ λόγῳ συνιστᾶν τὰ θεοφιλῆ! εἰ δὲ τοῖς πᾶσι καὶ
πάντῃ, πολλοῦ γε καὶ δεῖ ἀσυγκρίτως καὶ μάλα καταπλουτεῖν κἂν τούτοις
τὸ ὑπερανεστηκὸς τῇ ἐκ Θεοῦ βασιλείᾳ σου, ᾧ παρέθεντο τὸ πολύ,
περισσότερον ὄφλειν, ὡς διδάσκει τὸ θεῖον θεσπιώδημα. ὅθεν κεῖσθαι
10 ἀντιβολῶ ταύτῃ δεύτερα πάντα τοῦ θείου σκοποῦ, καὶ μόνον ἀνυπερθέτως
πληροῦν τὰ πρὸς τὸ θεῖον ἀναφερόμενα καὶ ἀγάπης ἐλπίδι καὶ ἀμοιβῆς,
προσθήκῃ καὶ τάχους διὰ τὴν ἄριστον συμβουλήν, φαμένου μὴ χρᾶσθαι
μηδόλως τοῦ συνετοῦ καὶ σοφίᾳ πεπλατυσμένου |τῷ ἄπιθι ὅλως καὶ τῷ
ἐπάνηκε, τῆς φύσεως τὸ [fol. 35ᵛ] τεχθὲν ὑστεριζούσης εἰδέναι· εἰ
15 δ' ἄρα καὶ τῶν βιωσομένων ἐπὶ μακρῷ, καὶ τότε ἔθεντο ἄμεινον· ὃ καὶ
προσῆκον, ὡς ἔφην, καὶ ἰδιαίτατον πρὸ παντὸς τῇ ἐκ Θεοῦ βασιλείᾳ σου,
λογιζομένη βασιλικῶς καὶ νηφόντως τὰ ἐκεῖθεν αὐτῇ φιλοτιμηθέντα, καὶ
ὁσημέραι φιλοτιμούμενα μυρία εὐεργετήματα· ὃ καὶ τοῖς πᾶσι χρεών,
τοῖς μὴ τῇ πτέρνῃ φοροῦσι, βαβαὶ συμφορᾶς, τὸν ἐγκέφαλον.
20 εἰ καὶ μὴ ἴσμεν τὰ πάντα, ἀλλὰ μέτρια τούτων ἢ ἐχέφρων ἐγγράφει καὶ
ἡ εὐγνώμων καὶ μὴ τῇ ἀπονοίᾳ βεβυθισμένη συνείδησις, εὐεπηβόλως
εἰδυῖα μὴ τοσαῦτα τὰ παραχθέντα, ὅσα τὰ ἀποκείμενα, εἰ βαίνειν πρὸς
τὸ εὐθὲς βουληθείημεν καὶ θεάρεστον· καὶ τούτων ἑνὸς καὶ μεγάλου

---

122 Joel 2:12 ‖ 125–126 cf. Ps. 84 (85):9 ‖ 127–128 cf. Ps. 90 (91):4
50: 8–9 Luc. 12:48 ‖ 13–14 cf. Prov. 3:28 ‖ 19 Demosthenes, Περὶ Ἀλοννήσου, 7.45;
cf. Athanasius, *Epp.* 49, 6 et 58, 36–37

---

122 ante ἐπιστρέψωμεν add. αὐτὸν V
50: V 35ʳ–35ᵛ. S 163ᵛ–164ᵛ. P 43ᵛ–44ᵛ.
13 τῷ²] τὸ codd. ‖ 22 βαίνειν V¹SP: βαίνει V

49, 50

daily begs us, «Turn to me», so that we may actively cause Him to turn toward us. For if we worship Him in fear, and fall at His feet and weep, He will quickly grant our prayers, and will give us courage and victory and salvation. «He shall speak true peace to His people», as soon as we turn toward Him with a sincere heart. And He will look after and defend your majesty so much as to «overshadow you with His shoulders» constantly and guide your soul, granting you the heavenly kingdom together with the kingdom here on earth. So be it, Lord, so be it, so be it.

50. To the emperor concerning the buildings which are adjoining the holy and revered churches, that this is a great sin

If even among the pagans prudent men expounded to the people profitable and saving ⟨precepts⟩ which were accepted by later generations as strict law, then how great an obligation do we faithful ⟨Christians⟩ have to act in a God-pleasing manner, both in word and deed, since we know God and His commandments in the right way! And if ⟨this is⟩ indeed ⟨an obligation⟩ for everyone everywhere, then it is especially necessary for your divine majesty to be incomparably endowed with these ⟨virtues⟩, since the Holy Scriptures teach us that «a man to whom men have committed much incurs a greater debt». Wherefore I ask of you that everything be secondary to the divine purpose, and that without delay you accomplish those ⟨actions⟩ which relate to the divine, with the hope of both ⟨His⟩ love and a reward. And make haste, ⟨heeding⟩ the excellent advice of that intelligent man of broad wisdom who said never to use the words «Go away» and «Come back», since nature is reluctant «to know what is brought forth» ⟨on the morrow⟩. But if one should be one of those who are going to live for a long time, even for that occasion they have established something better. And this, as I have said, is particularly fitting for your divine majesty, when you consider in a royal and sober fashion the countless favors which have been granted you by Heaven, and are still being granted every day; and this is also an obligation for everyone who does not (O woe!) «wear his brain in his heel». Even if we aren't aware of every ⟨blessing⟩, still the prudent and reasonable conscience which is not plunged into despair registers a moderate number of them, with the keen realization that those ⟨blessings⟩ which have ⟨already⟩ been delivered are not so great as those which lie in store ⟨for us⟩, if we would be willing to proceed in a way that is right and pleasing to the Lord. And one of these great and ex-

προσδοκησίμου ἁγιασμοῦ τοῦ εὐπρέπειαν οἴκου Κυρίου ἐρᾶν καὶ
25 αἰδεῖσθαι, ἧς ἀναμφίβολον καὶ συνάντημα ταῖς ψυχαῖς, μὴ συναπόλ-
λυσθαι μετὰ ἀσεβῶν, μηδὲ μετὰ αἱμάτων ἀνδρῶν αὐτῶν τὴν
ζωήν, ἀλλ' ἄριστον τούτοις προσεῖναι καὶ διπλοῦν φιλοτίμημα, ἐν ἐκκλησίαις εὐλογεῖν τὸν Θεόν, τὸ νῦν ἔχον ἐνθάδε, τῇ δὲ τῶν πρωτο-
τόκων ἐκεῖ.
30   κἀντεῦθεν ἀντιβολοῦμεν πρὸς τῇ ἐνθέῳ σπουδῇ καὶ κεραίαις ἐν
ἐρυθραῖς τῇ ἐκκλησίᾳ καὶ τοῦτο ἀφοσιώσασθαι εἰς ἀσφάλειαν, μὴ
ἐγγίζειν τινὰ ἀναιδῶς καὶ πλεονεκτικῶς τὴν οἰκίαν αὐτῇ· ὅπου καὶ τῇ
τυχούσῃ ἠπειλήθη τῷ ἅρπαγι προσεγγίζειν τὸ τοῦ προφήτου οὐαί,
τὸ δέ γε κατεπεμβαίνειν θείου ναοῦ καὶ κοινοποιεῖν, φρικτὰ καὶ πλεῖστα
35 τὰ ἐπιτίμια, εἰ καὶ καταπεφρόνηται πάντα τῷ ἀσεβεῖ πλεονέκτῃ
εἰς βάθος εἰσδύντι κακῶν, οἷς μηδὲ τὰ κατὰ τὸν Ὀζὰν ἐκεῖνον
ὑποφρίττειν φρικτά. εἰ τοίνυν τοὺς μεμηνότας τοσοῦτον καθ' ἑαυτῶν
οἰκτείρας τῆς συμφορᾶς ἀνακόψεις, καὶ τοῖς θείοις ναοῖς ἀπονεμεῖς
τὸ σεβάσμιον τῆς περικύκλῳ φιλοκαλίας, ὅσος σοι ὁ ἐκεῖθεν μισθός, ὅσος
40 ὁ ἔπαινος παρ' ὅσοις τὸ εὐλαβὲς συντετήρηται, ὅσον εἰς τοὺς αἰῶ-
νάς σοι τὸ μνημόσυνον, οὗ τὸν δίκαιον ἀπολαῦσαι ἡ θεία
Γραφὴ μεμαρτύρηκε, καὶ ὅση τῆς συνειδήσεως πάλιν ἡ εὐφροσύνη,
τιμῶντα ναοὺς τοῦ σὲ πολυτρόπως τετιμηκότος, εὐτόνως ἀποτιννύντα
τὴν ἀμοιβήν, ἣν ἅπαξ ὀφείλει ὁ παραχθεὶς πρὸς τοῦ κρείττονος· εἰ δέ
45 τις καὶ κατεπείγοι στενοχωρία, κἂν τὸ ᾀδόμενον νόμιμον γλώσσαις
πολλῶν ἀποδιϊστᾶν ἀπὸ τοῦ ναοῦ ἰχνῶν ποσὸν δύο καὶ δέκα.

51. Πρὸς τὸν αὐτοκράτορα συμπάθειαν ἐξαιτῶν τοῖς
ἀπολύσασιν ἐξ εἱρκτῆς τὸν Παξῆ [fol. 36ʳ]

Τὸ ὀλέθριον ἄνδρα ἐξαποστεῖλαι, τὸν ἢ χειρωσάμενον
μάχῃ ἢ πρὸς δεσπότην ἐλθόντα πρὸς παραφύλαξιν, ἢ πρὸς Μιχαίου προ-
5 βᾶσα σκῆψις ποτὲ πρὸς τοῦ Ἀχαάβου κριθεῖσα, ἐπιτίμιον εἶναι θανάτου πεφώρακε, καθὼς ἀριδήλως ἡ τῶν Βασιλειῶν ὑπηγόρευσε, καὶ
ἔργῳ εἰς ἑαυτὸν ἐπειράθη ὁ πράξας ἐκεῖνο ἀσυμπαθῶς τῆς δεινῆς
ἀνταμείψεως. ἔνθεν περὶ τῶν ὠλισθηκότων τοιαῦτα, τῇ συμπαθεῖ
διακρίσει τεθαρρηκότες, συνάμα τοῖς ὧδε εὑρισκομένοις ἀρχιερεῦσι

24–27 cf. Ps. 25 (26):8–9 ‖ 28–29 cf. Hebr. 12:23 ‖ 33 cf. Is. 5:8 ‖ 35–36 cf. Prov. 18:3 ‖
36–37 cf. II Reg. 6:1–7; I Paralip. 13:5–10 ‖ 40–41 cf. Ps. 111 (112):6
   51: 3 cf. III Reg. 21:34, 42

51: V 35ᵛ–36ʳ. S 164ᵛ–165ᵛ. P 44ᵛ–45ʳ.
2 ἀπολέσασιν SP ‖ Παξῆ] παταξῆ S ‖ 3 τὸ] τὸν P ‖ 4 ἐλθόντα conj.: λαβόντα codd.;
num προσλαβόντα δεσπότην scribendum? ‖ ἡ] ἢ codd.

50, 51

pected sacred privileges is «to love» and respect «the beauty of the house of the Lord», as a result of which comes unambiguous confirmation «for souls, that they will not be destroyed together with the ungodly, nor their life with bloody men», but they will receive the best reward, a twofold one, to praise God in churches, both now in this world, and in «the ⟨church⟩ of the first-born» in the world to come.

Therefore, I request that, in addition to your divinely inspired zeal, this, too, be written down formally in red letters as security for the church, that no one should shamelessly and greedily place a building next to ⟨a church⟩; for the prophet threatens «woe» to the rapacious man who builds near even an ordinary ⟨building⟩, and the punishments are numerous and dreadful for infringing on the property of a holy church and defiling it, even though all these ⟨punishments⟩ «mean nothing to the ungodly» and covetous man «who descends into a depth of evils», and therefore he does not even shudder at the horrible fate of Uzza. If then you take pity on those who are so insanely harming themselves, and if you restrain them from self-destruc-tion, and grant to holy churches the honor of surrounding beauty, the Holy Scriptures testify to the reward you will thereby receive, and how you will be praised by those who keep piety ⟨in their hearts⟩, and how «your memory will endure for ages as the reward of a just man», and again how joyful will be your conscience, as you pay honor to the churches of the One Who has honor-ed you in many ways, and vigorously repay the reward, as is the obligation of everyone who has been created by the Almighty. And if any difficulty should present itself, then there is the law well known by many that ⟨a building⟩ should be a distance of twelve paces from a church.

51. To the emperor, asking clemency for those who allowed Paxes
to escape from prison

The trap set long ago by Micah ⟨and⟩ the judgment once rendered by Ahab revealed that there is a penalty of death for «allowing the escape of a man appointed to destruction», who has either been captured in battle or has come to a ruler for protection, as the Book of Kings clearly indicated, and the man who committed that ⟨offense⟩ [Ahab] mercilessly experienced by deed the dread retribution himself. Therefore, since I have confidence in your compassion and discretion, together with the bishops who are here I decided

10 πρεσβείαν προσάξαι διέγνωμεν περὶ τούτων, ὅπερ ἐν ἄλλοις μὴ πε-
ποιήκαμεν, τῇ ἐκ Θεοῦ βασιλείᾳ σου ἵλεων ἐπιβλέψαι αὐτοῖς, καὶ μὴ
ἀξίαν ἐπάξαι τῆς ἐκείνου τοῦ στυγητοῦ ἀπροσέκτου ἀποβολῆς· μηδ'
ἕνεκεν τῆς τοῦ βδελυροῦ ἀπωλείας θεράποντας ἀγαθοὺς δικαίαν τὴν
τιμωρίαν ἀποτιννύναι καταδικάσῃ, ἀπροσεξίᾳ ληφθέντας, οὐ πονηρίᾳ, καὶ
15 δόλον τοσοῦτον ἀγνοίᾳ ἢ παροινίᾳ μὴ ὡς δέον φωράσαντας, συγγνώμης
ὀφειλομένης, ὡς Κύριον καὶ αὐτῆς ἐχούσης ἐν οὐρανοῖς, τὸν ἀφίεσθαι
ἀφιεῖσι θεσπίσαντα· ὃς καὶ τὸ συμπαθὲς καὶ φιλάγαθον ἀποβλέψας
τῆς σῆς βασιλικωτάτης, καί, μάλιστα ἐν τοσούτοις, ὑψηλῆς διακρίσεως,
ἀλύτοις ἀλυκτοπέδαις οὐ βραδυνεῖ συμποδίσαι τὸν ἀλιτήριον καὶ ἀλάσ-
20 τορα πάντῃ καὶ ἀσεβῆ, ὅπου ἄρα καὶ διατρίβει. εἰ δέ τι κατὰ τοῦ κράτους
καὶ σκαιωρῆσαι ἐπιχειρήσειν ὁ ἄθεος ἤλπισε, τὴν αὐτοῦ ἀδικίαν ῥαδίως
καταβιβάσει Θεὸς τῇ βαρβαρώδει ἐκείνου κεφαλῇ καὶ ψυχῇ, αὐταῖς
συνεξολοθρεύσας ἐκεῖνον φονώσαις βουλαῖς, καὶ εἱρκτῇ αἰωνίῳ προσ-
δήσας, τοσαύτης ἀναδοχῆς καὶ πολλῶν τῶν εὐεργεσιῶν, καί, τὸ μέγισ-
25 τον, τὸν θεοστυγῆ τοῦ θείου λουτροῦ ἐκμυκτηριστὴν ἀναφανέντα, καὶ
πρὸς κύλισμα βορβόρου ὥσπερ ὗν ἀγαπήσαντα λούεσθαι,
καὶ κύνα καθάπερ φιλήσαντα ἐμφορεῖσθαι τοῦ μυσαχθοῦς
αὐτοῦ ἐξεράματος. οὗ γε καὶ χάριν ὡς θεϊκῶν δωρεῶν τὸν βέβηλον
καταπαίξαντα τῷ αἰωνίῳ Χριστὸς ὁ Σώτηρ μου τοῦτον ἀξίως κατα-
30 βαπτίσει πυρί.

52. Περὶ τοῦ ὅπως δεῖ συνδραμεῖν ἐν τῷ τοῦ Σωτῆρος ἅπαντας
ἐνταφιασμῷ — πρὸς τὸν αὐτοκράτορα

Εἰ τῷ τοῦ Ἰσραὴλ ἐνταφιασμῷ οὐκ ἦν εἰκάζειν ἀπολειφθῆναί τινα
τῶν ἐν Αἰγύπτῳ παραδυναστευόντων, μὴ σύνδακρυν συνδεδραμηκέναι ἐπ'
5 ἀνθρώπῳ καὶ ταῦτα ἀλλοεθνεῖ, κελεύσει μὲν Φαραώ, θεραπείᾳ δὲ τῇ
πρὸς Ἰωσήφ, τίνα τὸν λόγον δῶμεν ἡμεῖς, εἰ μὴ ὀψὲ τὸ πρὸς Σάββα-
τον πάντες σπεύσωμεν ἐκδραμεῖν, μὴ βασιλεῖς καὶ ἄρχοντες μόνον,
φρικτὰ μυστήρια κατοψόμενοι τοῦ μακαρίου καὶ μόνου δυνάστου καὶ
βασιλέως, ἀλλὰ καὶ σὺν ἱερεῦσιν ἡγούμενοι ἐν τῇ μητρὶ τῶν ἐκκλησιῶν
10 τὴν παναγίαν σφαγὴν καὶ τὸν ζωηρὸν ἐντα-[fol. 36ᵛ] φιασμὸν προσκυνῆσαι καὶ ἀλαλάξαι τοῦ Σωτῆρος ἡμῶν Ἰησοῦ Χριστοῦ, ὃν δι' ἡμᾶς ὑπήνεγ-
κε θέλων, ὑφ' οὗ ἐζωώθημεν καὶ τὴν Ἐδὲμ ἀπελάβομεν; εἰ δ' ἔστι

16–17 cf. Matt. 6:14 ‖ 26–28 cf. II Pet. 2:22
52: 3–4 cf. Gen. 50:7 ‖ 6–7 cf. Matt. 28:1 ‖ 12 cf. *Triodion*, 712, 714

---

14 καταδικάσει codd. ‖ 16 αὐτῆς V¹SP: αὐτοῖς V ‖ 28 post αὐτοῦ repetivit αὐτοῦ S, del. S¹
52: V 36ʳ–36ᵛ. S 165ᵛ–166ʳ. P 45ʳ–45ᵛ. Ed. Pallas, *Die Passion Christi*, 299–300.
2 πρὸς τὸν αὐτοκράτορα VᵐᵍSP ‖ 12 ἔστι VSP¹: ἔτι P

51, 52

to undertake a mission to your divine majesty on behalf of those people who have committed a similar offense (I have never done so on other occasions), ⟨to ask you⟩ to look upon them with mercy, and not to punish them for carelessly allowing that despicable man to slip through their hands. May your majesty not condemn good servants to pay the just penalty on account of the escape of that abominable man, for they were guilty of carelessness, not wickedness, and it was through ignorance or drunkenness that they did not discover such a trick as they should have, and your majesty should pardon them, since even your majesty has a Lord in heaven Who has decreed that «He forgives those who forgive». And when He sees the compassion and goodness of your most royal and lofty discretion, especially at such a time, He will not be slow to bind with unbreakable fetters the utterly miserable and impious wretch, wherever he may be. And if the godless man hoped to undertake some mischief against the state, God will easily bring down his injustice upon his barbarous head and soul, destroying him together with his murderous plots, and confining in an eternal prison this God-loathed man who is revealed to have held in derision such a fine reception and numerous favors, and, worst of all, holy baptism, a man who loves «like a sow to wash by wallowing in the mire», and «like a dog loves to take his fill of his loathsome vomit». For this reason Christ my Savior will justly baptize this defiled man in eternal fire, since he has mocked the gifts of God.

52. To the emperor that everyone should assemble for the entombment of the Savior

If it is impossible to imagine that any of the rulers of Egypt was missing at the burial of Israel ⟨Jacob⟩, or did not assemble in tears for a man of another nation at that, at the command of the Pharaoh on one hand, and out of respect for Joseph on the other, what reason shall we give if we do not all hasten to assemble «at the end of the Sabbath» at the Mother of Churches, not only emperors and officials, but also abbots and priests, to witness the awesome mysteries of our blessed and only Ruler and King, to venerate and proclaim loudly the all-holy sacrifice and the life-giving entombment of our Savior Jesus Christ, which He was willing to endure for our sake, by which «we were quickened» and received Eden? If there is any reason that your

52, 53

κώλυμα τὸ ἀπεῖργον τὴν ἐκ Θεοῦ βασιλείαν σου, δυνατὸν ἀναπληρωθῆναι
τῇ τοῦ Δεσπότου ἐπιδημίᾳ· εἰ δ' ἔστι καί τις κωλύμη τῷ προεστῶτι, τινὲς
15 τῶν εὐλαβεστέρων ἐξ ἅπαντος ὑπ' αὐτοῦ σταλήτωσαν. ὅθεν καὶ δέον
τοῖς δομεστίκοις μάλιστα τοῖς μεγάλοις τῆς τοῦ Θεοῦ Μεγάλης Σοφίας
συναγεῖραι πάντας τοὺς ψαλτῳδούς, εἰς τὸ τὰ σωτήρια ἀλαλάξαι παννύχιον, χαρᾷ καὶ φόβῳ καὶ πόθῳ διεγηγερμέναις ψυχαῖς, ὡς ἂν τὸ μέγα
ἔλεος τοῦ Θεοῦ πλουσίως πᾶσι καταπεμφθῇ.

53. Πρὸς τὸν λαὸν ἅπαντα, παρακαλῶν συνδραμεῖν ἐν τῷ τοῦ Σωτῆρος
ἐνταφιασμῷ

Εἰ τὰ ἄνω Χριστὸς μὴ λιπὼν πρὸς ἡμᾶς τοὺς μακρὰν κατελήλυ-
θεν ἑκουσίῳ τῷ πάθει, τὸ τῆς ἡμῶν ὀφειλῆς ἐξαλεῖψαι χειρόγρα-
5 φον, — συνδραμεῖν μηδαμῶς βασιλεῖς καὶ πλουτοῦντες καὶ πένητες
κατοκνήσωμεν, δέομαι, ἐκπλαγῆναι, δοξάσαι, προσκυνῆσαι, δακρύσαι
καὶ ᾆσαι ὁσίως τοῦ φρικτοῦ ἐνταφιασμοῦ τὰ μυστήρια, ἵν' ἐντεῦθεν
συναισθανθῶμεν τοῖς παραδόξοις μεγαλεῖα Θεοῦ, καὶ ὅθεν καὶ ὅπως
παρὰ πάντας ἀνθρώπων υἱοὺς ὁ τῷ κάλλει ὡραῖος μονώ-
10 τατος ἀκαλλὴς καὶ ἀνείδεος ὦπται, ὡς ἔφησε πρόρρησις ἡ
προφητική. πόθεν γὰρ ἄλλως καὶ αὐτοῖς ἐνεργῶς βασιλεῦσι προσγε-
γένηται συνιέναι τὰ θεῖα θελήματα, καὶ παιδείας ὀρθῆς τοὺς κριτὰς
τῆς γῆς ἅπαντας δυνατῶς περιδράξασθαι, ὡς ἂν δυσώδους κἀντεῦθεν
ἰλύος τῶν γεηρῶν ἐνηχούντων τῷ τότε σαλπίγγων εὑρεθῶμεν καθύ-
15 περθεν, μήπως Κύριος ὀργισθεὶς ἀπολεῖσθαι δικαίας ὁδοῦ
παρεάσῃ ἡμᾶς;
ὧν ἡμῶν ἕνεκεν τὰ πολλὰ τῷ παμβασιλεῖ καὶ εἰπεῖν καὶ ἐκπέμψαι
ἐμέλησε καθ' ὁδοὺς καὶ φραγμοὺς ἀναγκάζειν εἰστρέχειν τὸ
γένος τῶν ἀνακτόρων εἰς πλήρωσιν· οὗ καὶ τῶν δούλων ὡς δοῦλοι
20 ἀχρεῖοι καὶ ἔσχατοι πάντῃ ἡμεῖς ὑμᾶς ἀξιοῦντες παρακαλοῦμεν,
ἀνιστοροῦντες ἅμα καὶ ἀναγκάζομεν. καὶ μή μοι, ἀντιβολῶ, δραμεῖν καὶ
γενέσθαι ἐντὸς παρακούσητε, μηδὲ πρόφασιν ἀτελῆ ἢ ζευγῶν ἢ ἀγροῦ
προϊσχώμεθα, μηδ' αὐτὴν τὴν νεόνυμφον. μηδ' αὖ εἰσελθεῖν ἀκαλ-
λώπιστοι πάλιν ἐνέγκωμεν, ὡς δεδέσθαι καὶ πόδας καὶ χεῖρας
25 τοῖς ἐκεῖ νυμφικῶς μὴ ἐστάλθαι καταθαρροῦντας τὴν εἴσοδον, καὶ
λίμναις ἐκριπτουμένους πυρὸς (ὃ μὴ καὶ πάθοι τις ἐξ ἡμῶν, Χριστὲ

53: 4–5 Col. 2:14 ‖ 9 Ps. 44(45):3 ‖ 10 cf. Is. 53:2,3; *Triodion*, 710. ‖ 12–15 cf.
Ps. 2:12 ‖ 18 cf. Luc. 14:23 ‖ 19–20 Luc. 17:10 ‖ 22–23 cf. Luc. 14:18–20 ‖ 24 Matt. 22:13 ‖
26 cf. Rev. 19:20; 20:14, 15

53: V 36ᵛ–37ʳ. S 166ʳ–167ʳ. P 45ᵛ–46ᵛ. Ed. Pallas, *Die Passion Christi*, 300–302.
11 ἐνεργὸς VSP ‖ 18 καθ'] καὶ codd. ‖ εἰστρέχειν] εἰσ- add. Vˢᵛ ‖ 23 προϊσχόμεθα codd.

52, 53

majesty cannot come, your place could be taken by the Despot. And if the leader of the service cannot attend, let him send some of those who are most pious in every way. In addition the great domestics should assemble all the psalm-chanters of the ⟨Church of the⟩ Great Wisdom of God to sound loudly the songs of salvation throughout the night, their souls roused by joy and fear and love, so that the great mercy of God may be sent down in abundance upon all.

53. To all the people, asking them to assemble for the ⟨ceremony of the⟩ entombment of the Savior

If Christ had not left the celestial world and descended to us, distant though we were, to suffer willingly in order «to blot out the register» of our debts—I entreat you, let us in no way hesitate to assemble, whether emperors or rich or poor, and to marvel, glorify, venerate, lament and sing in a holy manner the mysteries of the awesome entombment, so that we may thereby perceive the wondrous and incredible works of God, and whence and how He Who alone is «more beautiful than the sons of man» was seen «ugly and misshapen», as the prophet predicted. For in what other way will emperors actively comprehend the divine wishes, and will all the judges of the earth take vigorous hold of right punishment, so that thereby we may rise above the foul-smelling slime of earthly matter when the trumpets sound, lest «the Lord become angry» and allow us «to perish from the righteous way»?

It has been the concern of the King of All to say many of these things for our sakes, and to send ⟨disciples⟩ «into the highways and hedges» «to force» the people «to enter» and fill the ⟨divine⟩ precincts. And we, as the «unworthy» and utterly least of the servants of His servants, entreat you and beg you, and by telling you this we compel you. Do not, I pray, disregard my command to assemble with haste and enter the church, nor let us offer the vain excuse of «teams of oxen» or «a piece of land», or even «a new bride». Furthermore, let us not suffer to enter without the proper attire, since those who dare to enter without being clothed in wedding raiment «are bound hand and foot» by the people there and are cast into «lakes of fire» (which fate I pray

53, 54

βασιλεῦ καὶ Θεὲ τοῦ παντός), ὡς δὲ μᾶλλον στολῇ ἀπεντεῦθεν τῇ τοῦ νυμφῶνος ἀξίᾳ περιδήσαντες ἑαυτοὺς [fol. 37ʳ] εὐμενῶς εἰσδεχθείημεν·
μήτε περιτυχόντες, ὦ τῆς ζημίας, ἐντεθειμένας τὰς πύλας, καταγνωσ-
30 θῶμεν κρούειν ἀνόνητα, δυσφήμῳ ἐκεῖθεν ὀνειδισμῷ καὶ δεσποτικῷ
ἀξίως ἐπεγκαλούμενοι τῷ ἀκαίρῳ τοῦ κρούματος.
    ὧν ἕνεκεν κατασκέψασθαι συγκαλοῦμεν καὶ τὸν ἅγιον ἐνταφιασμὸν
κατιδεῖν τὴν ἐκ Θεοῦ βασιλείαν σου, εἰ μὴ τὸ ἀντίξουν ἀναγκαιότερον.
ἴσως τότε σου κἂν ὁ Δεσπότης τὸν τόπον ἀναπληρούτω ὁ εὐτυχὴς καὶ παν-
35 ευτυχέστατος. Ναζιραίων πληθὺν ἐν στολῇ ἱερᾷ παραστῆναι καὶ ᾆσαι ἐξόδια κατανύξει πρεπούσῃ καὶ φόβῳ καὶ πόθῳ καὶ δάκρυσι διατάττομεν,
ἵνα σβέσωμεν δάκρυσι δάκρυα. διὸ ταχὺ πρὸ νυκτὸς ἐπεισδράμωμεν, ὁ
ποιμὴν σὺν ποιμνίῳ θεόφρονι· οἱ γὰρ ὕστερον ὧδ᾽ ἐπιφθάνοντες ἐν-
δεκάτῃ μισθὸν οὐ κομίσονται, οὗ, Χριστὲ καὶ Θεέ, μὴ ἐκπέσωμεν.

54. Πρὸς τὸν αὐτοκράτορα περὶ τοῦ αὐτοῦ

    Τίνι καὶ δάκρυσιν ἠβουλόμην ἢ μέλανι μᾶλλον χαράξαι, εἰ ἦν
μοι ἐξόν, τὰ λυποῦντα καὶ ἀποκναίοντα σήμερον, εἰ μή γε τῇ συμπαθεῖ καὶ
πρὸς οἶκτον ἑτοίμῃ ἐκ Θεοῦ βασιλείᾳ σου; γινώσκων αὐτῆς τὸ φιλόπονον
καὶ φιλήκοον ἐν τοῖς ἀγαθοῖς καὶ πρὸς ἔλεον ἕτοιμον, πλουτούσης τὸ
5 κλαίειν μετὰ κλαιόντων καὶ χαίρειν μετὰ χαιρόντων, καὶ
λίαν αὐτοῦ ἐφιεμένης ψυχῆς δι᾽ εὐθύτητα, τοῦ τάχους πρὸ τοῦ κληθῆναι ἱππασαμένης συντόνως καταλαβεῖν τοῦ Θεοῦ τὰ ἀνάκτορα, ὡς ἂν σὺν
ἡμῖν ἁρμοζόντως συναλγήσῃ καὶ συνδακρύσῃ καί τι τῶν πρὸς ὄνησιν ἐφ-
10 εύρῃ, μὴ ἄλλοις τυχὸν ἐφικτὸν τῇ πολλῇ ἀτυχίᾳ τῆς φύσεως. καὶ ὅπως
ποσάκις βεβουλημένου Θεοῦ περιθάλψαι κοινῶς καὶ ἰδίως βροτούς, ὡς
ὄρνις αὐτῆς τὰ νοσσία, οὐ μόνον οὐ τεθελήκαμεν πεφευγότες ἐξ
ἔργων, ἀλλά, φεῦ, καὶ κατὰ καιρὸν αὐτὸν τὸν ζωῆς ἀρχηγὸν ἀνόμοις συν-
τεταχότες, τῇ τοῦ φθόνου κραιπάλῃ, βαβαί, τυφωθέντες, θανάτῳ παρα-
15 δεδώκαμεν. μηδ᾽ αὐτὸ τὸ ταφῆναι, ὡς ἑνὶ τῶν τραυματιῶν καὶ εἰς
λάκκον καταβαινόντων, τὸν καλύψαντα οὐρανοὺς ἀρετῇ
χαρισάμενοι, ἀλλ᾽ ἀνείδεον καὶ γυμνὸν καὶ νεκρὸν τῷ ξύλῳ τετανυκότες, καὶ χεῖρας καὶ πόδας ὀρωρυγμένον, καὶ λόγχῃ πλευρὰν νενυγ-
μένον, ἐάσαντες ἄταφον, τῶν οἴκοι φροντίζειν, ὡς μή τινος γεγονότος

38–39 cf. Matt. 20:9
    54: 2 cf. Nicholas Mysticus, *Epistola V* (PG, CXI, 45) ‖ 6 Rom. 12:15 ‖ 12 Matt.
23:37 ‖ 15–16 cf. Ps. 29(30):4 ‖ 16 cf. Hab. 3:3 et *Triodion*, 733 ‖ 17 cf. *Triodion*, 710 ‖
18–19 *Triodion*, 713, 714

---

29 μήτε VP: μή ποτε S ‖ 35 αζιραίων codd.
    54: V 37ʳ–37ᵛ. S 167ʳ–167ᵛ. P 46ᵛ–47ʳ. Ed. Pallas, *Die Passion Christi*, 302–304.
8 ἱππασαμένου codd. ‖ 17–18 τετανυκότες codd.

53, 54

that none of us may suffer, O Christ our King and God of all), but rather may we henceforth clothe ourselves in garb suitable for the bridechamber, and be graciously received; nor, alas, may we find the doors shut, and be condemned to knock in vain, and be justly rebuked with shameful reproaches by our Lord because we knocked too late.

For these reasons I ask your divine majesty to observe and witness the holy entombment, unless it is absolutely impossible. Perhaps in that case the fortunate and most fortunate Despot could take your place.

I enjoin the multitudes of Nazarenes to appear in sacred garments and to sing the hymns to the Departed with appropriate contrition and fear and love and tears, so that we may quench tears with tears. Therefore let us assemble quickly before nightfall, the shepherd together with his godly-minded flock. For those who arrive here later will not receive their reward «at the eleventh hour», and I pray, O Christ and God, that we may not be deprived of it.

54. To the emperor about the same matter

To whom would I wish to write, with tears instead of ink if I could, about the matters which distress and vex me these days, if not to your divine majesty, who is always compassionate and quick to pity? For I know your diligence and attention to good works, that you are eager to grant mercy, and are endowed with the attribute of «rejoicing with them that do rejoice, and weeping with them that weep», and desire Him (?) greatly on account of the rectitude of your soul, and would quickly mount a horse, even before the summons, and come immediately to the halls of God, so that you might share my grief and tears in an appropriate manner, and find something of benefit, which was not possible for others probably through the many misfortunes of nature. As so often when God has wished to envelop mortals in His warmth, both publicly and privately, as «a bird her nestlings», not only have we been unwilling and avoided ⟨good⟩ works, but alas on one occasion, deluded, O woe, by the intoxication of envy, we made a covenant with lawless men and delivered unto death the very Source of Life. Nor did we even grant burial, which is awarded to slain men and to those «that go down to the pit», to Him «Who covered the heavens with virtue». Instead we stretched Him on the Cross, «misshapen» and naked and «dead», and left Him unburied; His hands and feet pierced through, and «His side stabbed» with the lance, to tend to business at home, as if nothing new had happened, and we all busy ourselves

54, 55

20 καινοῦ, ματαίως (φεῦ τῆς ἀπάτης!) ἕκαστος σπουδαιολογούμεθα, μικρὰ
ἢ οὐδὲν ἐξετάζοντες περὶ τῶν πραχθέντων, μήπως ἐκ τούτων ἐπικερδῆ
ἀνακύψῃ ἡμῖν ἐπιβάλλοντα.
εἰ τοίνυν συγκατανεύσει καὶ συγκατάθηται συνδραμεῖν, [fol. 37ᵛ]
ὡς ἔφην, τοῖς ἀνακτόροις, τὸ μὲν πολὺ ἐξ ἡμῶν, ὡς οἷά τινι τῶν ἀκεσω-
25 δύνων, τῇ λαμπροτάτῃ ἐπιστασίᾳ αὐτῆς, τῆς λύπης ἀναλωθῇ, δοξασάσης
αὐτῆς ἐν τιμῇ τὸν αὐτὴν βασιλεύσαντα, καὶ παρ' οὗ βασιλεύουσι
βασιλεῖς καὶ γῆς δι'αὐτοῦ ἐπιδράττονται τύραννοι· κἀντεῦθεν καὶ ἄμφω βασιλικῶς τῷ παμβασιλεῖ τελεσάμενοι τὸν ἐνταφιασμὸν σὺν τῷ δήμῳ παντὶ ἁγιασθησόμεθα, «ἀνάστα, Κύριε», δεηθέν-
30 τες αὐτοῦ, «καὶ μάλιστα νῦν ἐξελέσθαι ἡμᾶς τῶν δεινῶν, ὁ πανεύ-
σπλαγχνος». ἐξὸν ἀναμφήριστον πάντως [μὴ] τυχεῖν δαψιλῶς τῶν αἰτήσεων, διψῶντος αὐτοῦ πολλαχῶς ἡμῖν ἐπιχέειν τὰ ἐλέη, εἰ ὡς δύναμις
πρὸς αὐτὸν ἐπιστρέφοιμεν.

55. Πρὸς τὸν αὐτοκράτορα

Εἰ καὶ πάντα τὰ ἔθνη καὶ πάντας τοὺς ἐν ἀξίᾳ προσκυνῆσαι καὶ
γνῶναι τὰ πάθη Χριστοῦ ἡ σοφία Θεοῦ συγκαλεῖται ἐτήσιον, κατ' ἐξαίρετον σήμερον σὲ τὸν ταύτης υἱόν — ὃν προγνώσει προώρισε Κύριος, ὃν
5 συνέσει καὶ οἴκτῳ ἡ ἐκκλησία βασιλικῶς ἐμαιεύσατο, ὃν καὶ ἄρχειν καὶ
βασιλεύειν θαυμασίως ἐτιθηνήσατο, καὶ σοφῶς ἐδικαίωσεν — οὐ φαι-
δρῦναι καὶ μόνον τῇ παρουσίᾳ τὰ θεῖα ἀνάκτορα, ἀλλ' ἐγκύψαι καὶ
μάλα πρὸς ἄγνωστον γνῶσιν, τὴν τῶν πάντων φρικτῶν μυστηρίων ἐκ-
πλαγησόμενον δύναμιν, κἀντεῦθεν σοφίας πλησθῆναι καὶ θείου φρονή-
10 ματος, τοῦ δουλεύειν Κυρίῳ ἐν φόβῳ τῇ ἐννόμῳ ζωῇ καὶ νηφούσῃ ψυχῇ,
πρὸς τὰ φίλα Θεῷ ἐν στοργῇ διεγείρειν καὶ ποδηγεῖν ἐν σπουδῇ καὶ τὸ
ἅπαν ὑπήκοον, πρὸς τὸ δράξασθαι θείας παιδείας, προφητικῆς,
ἀποστολικῆς, εὐαγγελικῆς, ὡς ὀρθοδόξοις ἐξόν, μήπως ἐπὶ πολὺ
ὀργισθῇ Κύριος, ὡς ἡ πεῖρα ἡμῖν παριστᾷ· ἀλλ' ὁμοῦ ψυχικῇ συντριβῇ
15 ἱκετεύσωμεν τὸ ἱλάσθητι Κύριε, ἄνες Κύριε, κόπασον Κύ-
ριε· μὴ ἐλέγξῃς ἡμᾶς τῷ θυμῷ σου, μηδὲ παιδεύσῃς ἡμᾶς
ἐν ὀργῇ. καὶ εἰ τούτοις κοινῶς εὑρεθῶμεν ἐνασμενίζοντες καὶ ὅλη

26–27 cf. Prov. 8:15–16 ‖ 29 cf. *Triodion*, 734
55: 12–14 cf. Ps. 2:12 ‖ 15–16 ἱλάσθητι ... κόπασον Κύριε: Greg. Naz., *Or.* XVI, ιβ'
(PG, XXXV, 952A) ‖ 16–17 cf. Ps. 6:2; 37(38):2

---

31 μὴ uncis inclusi
55: V 37ᵛ. S 167ᵛ–168ʳ. P 47ᵛ–48ʳ. Ed. Pallas, *Die Passion Christi*, 304–305.
1 ante πρὸς add. γράμμα VʳSP ‖ post αὐτοκράτορα add. προσκαλούμενον (προσκαλούμενος
Vʳ) αὐτὸν ἐν τῷ ἐνταφιασμῷ τοῦ Σωτῆρος VʳSP ‖ 5 καὶ¹ om. S ‖ 10 τῇ VS¹P: τε S ‖
11 καὶ ποδηγεῖν] ἐποδηγεῖν P

to no purpose (alas for the deceit!), making few or no enquiries about what has been done, whether some advantage might result to us therefrom.

If then you approve and agree that we should assemble, as I have said, at the ⟨sacred⟩ precincts, most of my grief will be assuaged, as if by a healing potion, on account of your illustrious auspices, as you glorify with honor Him Who made you emperor, and by Whom «kings reign and monarchs rule the earth». And thus we shall both be blessed together with all the people because we have royally celebrated the entombment of the King of all, praying to Him: «Arise, O Lord, especially now to rescue us from a dread fate, All-merciful One». For there is no doubt we will have our petitions abundantly granted, since He is eager to shed manifold mercies on us, if we turn toward Him with all our might.

55. To the emperor

If the wisdom of God bids all nations and all men of rank to venerate and recognize yearly the sufferings of Christ, then particularly today ⟨it bids⟩ you, Her son (whom the Lord with His foreknowledge preordained, whom the Church royally brought into the world with understanding and pity, and whom She wondrously reared and wisely justified to rule and reign), not only to adorn the holy shrine merely with your presence, but especially to seek out the ineffable knowledge, to be astonished by the power of all the awesome mysteries, and thus to be filled with wisdom and divine understanding, to serve the Lord in awe with a law-abiding life and sober spirit, to exhort with love and guide with zeal all your subjects toward what is pleasing to God, so that they may «accept the divine correction» of the prophets, the apostles and the Gospels, as is possible for right-thinking people, «lest the Lord wax angry» for a long time, as experience shows us. And let us supplicate all together with contrite souls, saying «Be merciful, Lord, cease, Lord, abate, Lord. Rebuke us not in thy wrath, neither chasten us in thine anger». And if we are found to please Him with these joint prayers, and turn toward

καρδία πρὸς αὐτὸν ἐπιστρέφοντες, ἕνεκεν τούτου τῇ ἐκ Θεοῦ βασιλείᾳ
σου ἔντεινε, λέξει, καὶ κατευοδοῦ καὶ βασίλευε ἀληθείας
20 ἕνεκεν καὶ πρᾳότητος καὶ δικαιοσύνης, θεϊκῇ δεξιᾷ θαυμαστῶς καθοδηγουμένη· τῷ δέ γε λαῷ εἰρήνην λαλήσει,
καὶ ἀγαθοῖς ἀνταμείψεται καὶ πρὸς ἅπαν καλὸν διηνεκῶς ἐπιδαψιλεύσεται.
γένοιτο, Κύριε, γένοιτο.

56. Πρὸς τὸν αὐτοκράτορα

Εἴ ποτε καὶ βασίλισσαν νότου σοφίας ἕνεκεν Σολομῶν-
τος ἐκ περάτων μὴ κατοκνῆσαι τὰ ἱερὰ συνδραμεῖν ὑφηγήσατο
λόγια, βοτανῶν καὶ ῥιζῶν ἐνεργείας καὶ φύσεις ἀκουσομένην, τὰ ὀλίγον
5 ὀνήσοντα, πόσης ἀναλγησίας τοῖς τοῦ θείου τυχοῦσι βαπτίσματος καὶ
νωθείας ἐπιβλα-[fol. 38ʳ] βοῦς μὴ συντρέχειν ἐν ἑορταῖς, εὐγενεῖς τε καὶ
δυσγενεῖς, ἀνακτόροις στοργῇ τοῦ Παμμέδοντος, οὐχ, ὡς ἔφην, ἀναμαθεῖν
βοτανῶν καὶ ῥιζῶν ἐνεργήματα, ἀλλ' ὡς (εὖγε τῆς δωρεᾶς!) εἰς Θεοῦ
παρακύπτειν ἐντεῦθεν μυστήρια. ἔνθεν τὸ ζέον καὶ πρόθυμον περὶ
10 πάντα τὰ κάλλιστα καὶ φιλόθεον καὶ φιλέορτον ἐπιστάμενοι τῆς ἐκ Θεοῦ
βασιλείας σου, ὡς ἵνα καὶ ἄρτι προτροπῇ τοῖς πολλοῖς πρὸς τὰ κρείττω
ἀναφανῇ, ἀξιοῦμεν καὶ συγκαλοῦμεν αὐτήν, συνάμα καὶ τῇ εὐσεβεστάτῃ Αὐγούστῃ εἰ δυνατόν, οὐ πρὸς δεῖπνα καὶ ὄψα καὶ γεηρὰς ἀναπαύ-
σεις καὶ τέρψεις, πρὸς δὲ θεῖα ἀνάκτορα καὶ περίκλυτον τέμενος τῆς με-
15 γάλης Θεοῦ Λόγου Σοφίας, πρὸς παράστασιν ὑπὲρ πᾶν ἀσυγκρίτως τὴν
ὄνησιν φέρουσαν, πρὸς ψυχῆς φωτισμὸν εἰ βουλοίμεθα καὶ τοῦ σώματος,
ἀντιμετροῦντος τοῦ φιλοδώρου ὑμῖν τὸ διὰ μέσου διάστημα καὶ αὐτά που
τὰ βήματα, τήν τε μετ' αὐτὴν εἴσοδον νῆψιν, τὴν δ' ἐξαγόρευσιν τῶν
κρυπτῶν, πρὸ δὲ τούτων ἐξαίτησιν θεϊκῆς ἀρωγῆς (ἧς ὁ μὴ χρῄζων
20 ἀκμὴν οὐ γεγένηται καὶ μᾶλλον οἱ ἐξικνεῖσθαι λαχόντες ὑψηλοτέρας τῆς
στάσεως), φαιδρύναι ὑμᾶς δι' ἀμφοῖν τὴν πανήγυριν, καὶ τὸν πόθον ἀφ-
οσιῶσαι τῇ πανυμνήτῳ εἰς δύναμιν ⟨(ὃ τοῖς μετ' εὐλαβείας καὶ φόβου
Θεοῦ εἰσιοῦσι προσγίνεται)⟩, οὐ πρὸς τὸ μετεωρίσαι τὴν ὄψιν καὶ πρὸς
διάχυσιν βλέψαι τῆς δομήσεως τῶν ἐπάλξεων [(ὃ τοῖς μετ' εὐλαβείας
25 καὶ φόβου Θεοῦ εἰσιοῦσι προσγίνεται)], οὐδ' ὁμιλίαις ἀκαίροις ἢ ποσῶς
καὶ χρειώδεσι τὸ τῆς νυκτὸς ἐκπεράσαι διάστημα, οὐδὲ κολακεῦσαι

19–21 cf. Ps. 44(45):5 ‖ 21 Ps. 84 (85):9
56: 2–3 cf. Matt. 12:42 ‖ 4 βοτανῶν ... φύσεις: cf. III Reg. 5:13 ‖ 8–9 cf. Greg.
Naz., *Or.* XXXI, η′ (PG, XXXVI, 141 B

56: V 37ᵛ–38ʳ. S 168ᵛ–169ʳ. P 48ʳ–48ᵛ.
1 post αὐτοκράτορα add. περὶ τοῦ αὐτοῦ et deinde erasit Vʳ ‖ post αὐτοκράτορα add.
προσκαλούμενον ἐν τῇ πανσέπτῳ κοιμήσει τῆς ὑπεραγίας θεοτόκου VʳSP ‖ 2 βασίλισσα P ‖
19 ἀρωγῆς VS¹P: ἀναγωγῆς S ‖ 20 γένηται P ‖ 22–25 ὃ ... προσγίνεται post ἐπάλξεων
seclusi et addidi post δύναμιν

55, 56

Him with all our heart, in consequence He will say to your divine majesty, «Bend thy bow and prosper and reign, because of truth and meekness and righteousness», and you will be «led wondrously by the right hand» of God, and «He will speak peace to the people», and He will reward them with good things, and will lavish every blessing forever. So be it, O Lord, so be it.

56. To the emperor

If the Holy Scriptures tell us that «the queen of the south» did not hesitate to come «from the uttermost parts ⟨of the earth⟩ for the sake of the wisdom of Solomon», to hear what was of little benefit, the properties and natures of herbs and roots, then what insensitivity and pernicious laziness it is for those who have received holy baptism (whether of noble or humble birth) not to assemble on feastdays, with love, at the palace of the Ruler of All, not as I said, to learn the properties of herbs and roots, but thereby «to observe the mysteries of God» (what a great gift!). And since I know that your divine majesty is zealous and eager for everything that is beautiful, and is a lover of God and feastdays, so that you may now appear in order to incite the multitudes to improvement, I ask and invite you, together with the most pious Augusta if possible, not to banquets and delicacies and to worldly pastimes and pleasures, but to the holy shrine and celebrated precinct of the Great Wisdom of God the Word, to a ceremony which will bring incomparably more benefit that anything else for enlightenment of the soul, if we should wish, and of the body, since the generous ⟨Lord⟩ rewards you for the distance traversed and, I suppose, for your very steps, for a solemn attitude after you enter ⟨the church⟩, for the confession of your secrets, and above all for a prayer for divine aid (and there has never yet been anyone who did not need it, especially those whose lot it has been to attain higher stations in life). ⟨So I invite you⟩ on two counts: to add luster to the celebration ⟨through your presence⟩, and to devote your love to the continually-hymned Virgin as much as you can (as is characteristic of those who enter with piety and fear of God), but not to raise your eyes and gaze at the extent of the construction of the ramparts, and not to pass the night in untimely conversations, or even in

56–58

γαστέρα τοῖς βρώμασι τοῖς καταργουμένοις, κατ' ἐκείνους ὧν Θεὸς
ἡ κοιλία, οἷς καὶ τὸ ἑορτάζειν οὐχ ὡς τῷ θείῳ δοκεῖ πνεύματι· ἀλλὰ
τὸ μέγα ἀναλογίσασθαι τῶν ἀπορρήτων Θεοῦ οἰκονομιῶν, καὶ πρὸς θείας
30 ἐννοίας πτερύξασθαι, καὶ ὅπως καὶ ἡ πηγὴ τῆς ζωῆς ἐν μνημείῳ
τίθεται, ἐξ οὗ τοῖς βροτοῖς τὴν πρὸς οὐρανοὺς εὐθυβόλως ἀν-
εστήλωσε κλίμακα, τὴν ἄνοδον θαυμασίως ἡμῖν ἐγκαινίσασα.

57. Πρὸς τὸν αὐτοκράτορα

Τὴν τῶν ὀρθοδόξων Χριστιανῶν βασιλείαν ὁ ἐπὶ πάντων Θεὸς τῇ
σῇ βασιλείᾳ καταπιστεύσας, οὐ κατὰ τὰς τῶν ἐθνῶν βασιλείας καὶ ταύτην, ἀλλὰ κατὰ συνείδησιν διεξάγεσθαι καὶ κέκρικε καὶ φιλεῖ, ὡς ἂν
5 ὀσφρανθείς σου τῇ ταύτης καλῇ διεξαγωγῇ, πρὸς ταύτῃ καὶ τὴν οὐράνιον
ὡς δή τι παρέξῃ σοι τροπαιούχημα. καὶ γένοιτο, γένοιτο ταύτῃ, ἀ-
γρύπνοις πρεσβείαις τῆς Θεομήτορος. καὶ τούτου γε ἕνεκεν ἐδεήθην καὶ
δέομαι ἐν ἡμέραις τῆς βασιλείας σου ἐλευθερίας καταπολαῦσαι τὴν ἐκκλησίαν Χριστοῦ, ἀλλὰ μὴ εἰς τὸ διηνεκές, οἷά τι τῶν οἰκτροτάτων
10 στρουθίων, ἀμφοτέροις ποσὶν [fol. 38ᵛ] ἐν ῥάμμασι πεδηθεῖσαν, καὶ νηπίοις δοθεῖσαν, ἀντὶ τοῦ ἀναπτῆναι εἰς ὕψος, οἴμοι, τοῖς χώμασι κατα-
σύρεσθαι. εἰ δὲ οὕτως ἀμεταθέτως μένειν ἐκρίθη, καὶ οὐδ' ἄν, εἴ τι καὶ
γένοιτο, ἀναγκάσει μεταβουλεύσασθαι, ὁ βουλόμενος, οὕτως ἐχούσης
αὐτῆς, ὀνόματι φροντιζέτω. ἐγὼ γὰρ καὶ γήρᾳ καὶ νόσῳ καὶ τὸ πλεῖον ἀ-
15 πραγμοσύνῃ συζῶν, εἴθε τῆς ἀσθενείας τῆς ἐμαυτοῦ φροντίζειν ἐνίσχυον.

58. Πρὸς τὸν αὐτοκράτορα

Εἰ καὶ διά τι ποιούμεθα ἢ καὶ διά τινας πλειστάκις ἀναφοράς,
καὶ πρὸ αὐτῆς τῆς πατριαρχείας καὶ μετ' αὐτήν, ἀλλ' οἶμαι μηδένα τὸν
ἡμέτερον νοῦν καταλήψεσθαι, ὡς οὐ διά τι ἀνθρώπινον ἀλλὰ μόνης χάριν

27–28 Phil. 3:19 ‖ 30–32 cf. Μηναῖον Αὐγούστου (Rome, 1901), 406

57: V 38ʳ–38ᵛ. S 169ʳ–169ᵛ. P 48ᵛ–49ʳ.
1 ante πρὸς add. γράμμα VʳSP ‖ post αὐτοκράτορα add. περὶ ἐλευθερίας τοῦ καταπολαῦσαι
τὴν ἐκκλησίαν (τῆς ἐκκλησίας S) Χριστοῦ VʳSP ‖ 6 παρέξει codd.
58: V 169ᵛ–39ʳ. S 169ᵛ–170ʳ. P 49ʳ–50ʳ.
1 ante πρὸς add. γράμμα VʳSP ‖ post αὐτοκράτορα add. περὶ οὗ (οὖ Vʳ) ἀναφέρομεν οὐ διὰ
τι ἀνθρώπινον, ἀλλὰ μόνης χάριν ἀγάπης καὶ δόξης καὶ ὀφειλῆς (καὶ δόξης ... ὀφειλῆς
om. SP) VʳSP

necessary ones, nor to pamper your stomach with useless (?) foods, like those «whose God is their belly», who don't even celebrate feastdays in accordance with the Holy Spirit. But the important thing is to reflect upon the secret arrangements of God, and to spread one's wings toward divine thoughts, and how the «Fountain of Life is placed in a tomb», from which She has set up for mortals «a ladder leading directly to heaven», wondrously inaugurating the ascent for us.

57. To the emperor

The God of all Who entrusted the empire of orthodox Christians to your majesty has decided and wishes that it be administered not like the pagan kingdoms, but in accordance with conscience, so that when He becomes aware of your good administration of it, He may also grant you the heavenly kingdom as a victor's crown of sorts. So be it, so be it, through the vigilant intercessions of the Mother of God. And for this reason I have entreated you and I entreat you now that during the period of your reign the Church of Christ enjoy freedom, and not forever, like a pitiful sparrow, have both feet tied with string, and be given to children, and instead of flying up into the sky, alas, be dragged along on the ground. But if it is your decision that it should remain thus unalterably, and nothing that happens will force ⟨you⟩ to change your mind, since ⟨the Church⟩ is in this condition, then let anyone who wishes take on ⟨this⟩ nominal position. For I spend my life for the most part ⟨overwhelmed by⟩ old age and disease and inaction, and would that I had the chance to care for my own infirmities.

58. To the emperor

Although I have frequently made petitions about a certain matter or certain people, both before and after my patriarchate, still I am afraid that no one will understand my purpose, that it is not for any personal reason, but

5 ἀγάπης καὶ δόξης καὶ ὀφειλῆς, ἣν ὀφείλει ὀρθόδοξος πᾶς πρὸς ὃν ἐδικαίωσε βασιλεύειν Θεὸς ὀρθοδόξως καὶ ὀρθοδόξων καὶ ὄντως ὀρθόδοξον
ἐννόμως καὶ δικαιότατα· οὐχ ὅπως φανῶμεν σπεύδοντες τὰ πολλὰ δύ-
ασθαι παρὰ βασιλεῖ (μὴ οὕτω μανείημεν, ὡς δόξης ἡττᾶσθαι τοιαύτης
ἐφέσει), οὐδ' ὅτι τῆς ἡμετέρας ἐσχατιᾶς, ἢ πάλιν τοῦ ὕψους τῆς ἐξου-
10 σίας τῆς βασιλείου καὶ τῆς εἰς ἄκρον περιφανείας ἐπιλελήσμεθα· οὐδ'
ὅτι φιλίᾳ ἢ συγγενείᾳ ἢ κέρδει ἢ ὀρέξει φερόμενοι τῇ τυχούσῃ, ἢ σχέσει
προσώπων τινῶν. καὶ τοῦτο μετὰ τὸν μόνον ἐν οὐρανῷ πιστὸν μάρτυς ὄντως πιστὸς καὶ ἀξιόπιστος μάλα, ὡς ἐν ἀνθρώποις οὐδείς, ἡ ἐκ
Θεοῦ βασιλεία σου, καὶ ἡ ταύτῃ προσοῦσα ἐπιφανὴς καὶ μεγάλη λεπτότης
15 καὶ φρόνησις καὶ διάκρισις· ἃ καθορῶντες ἡμεῖς ἐν αὐτῇ, καὶ βλέποντες
τῶν ἀνθρώπων, μεγάλων ὁμοῦ καὶ μικρῶν, τὸ πρὸς τὰ τοσαῦτα οὐ μὴν
ἀσύμβατον μόνον, ἀλλὰ καὶ ἐλλιπὲς καὶ ἀνόμοιον, ἀγάπης ζήλῳ πιμ-
πράμενοι ποσῶς ἀναφέρομεν (πρὸς ἃ καὶ εἰσακουόμενοι, μισθὸν λογιζόμεθα προξενεῖν πρὸς Θεοῦ, ὡς τὸ ὀφεῖλον αὐτῇ καὶ ἡμῖν πρεπόντως
20 προβαῖνον καὶ καλῶς περαινόμενον), ἔστι δ' ὅτε καὶ ἀπὸ δέους, μήπως
τινῶν κακοσχόλῳ σιγῇ καὶ τρόπῳ δολίῳ, ἢ καὶ παροξυσμῷ ἐκ κακούργου
ἀναφορᾶς (ἔπαθε γὰρ τοῦτό ποτε βασιλεύς, καὶ ταῦτα ψάλλων ἐν
πνεύματι), κελεῦσαι ἢ μὴ ἄλλο τι παρὰ τὸ δέον ἀναγκασθῇς· ἐπείπερ
καὶ ὁ μεγάλως ὑψώσας σε τῇ τοσαύτῃ περιωπῇ ἀναμφιβόλως ποιήσεται
25 τῶν αὑτοῦ καὶ σοῦ τὴν ἀνάκρισιν θελημάτων, ἐν ἀπαιτήσει ἀκριβασμοῦ,
καθὰ καὶ νόμος ἀνθρώποις κεφαλαίου καὶ εἰσφορᾶς.

ἕνεκεν τούτων ἡμεῖς ἀναφέρειν ἔστιν ὅπου καὶ ἀναιδῶς φίλτρῳ δόξης
τῆς σῆς τῆς διπλῆς εἰ φαινοίμεθα, καὶ βαρεῖς τῷ μὲν κράτει τῆς βασιλείας
ἀνιστοροῦντες, μὴ λήθῃ, μηδὲ συγ-[fol. 39ʳ] χύσει τὸ πρεπωδέστατον
30 παρεᾶν κρίνοντες πρόσφορον, μήπως ἐκ παροράματός τι προχωρήσῃ
τῶν μὴ φίλων Θεῷ καὶ βασιλεῖ καὶ ταῦτα τοιούτῳ, ὅτι μηδὲ μετρία ἐκ
τῶν τοιούτων ἡ βλάβη καὶ ἡ ὠφέλεια· καθὰ καὶ τὸ ὑπήκοον παρακαλοῦμεν, ὑποτιθέμενοι ὅσον ὀφείλει κἀκείνοις καὶ εἰρηναίαν περιποιεῖν καὶ
σώμασι καὶ ψυχαῖς καὶ ὅλῳ τῷ βίῳ αὐτῶν σωτηριώδη ἀσφάλειαν.
35 ἐν τούτοις ἡμῶν σπουδαζόντων, πῶς οὐ δυσχερανοῦμεν ὑπερορώ-
μενοι, πιστευομένων ὑπὲρ ἡμᾶς (ἃ συμφοράς!) τῶν ἐν ταῖς πτέρναις φορούντων συνείδησιν, οἷς τὰ ἐκεῖθεν δικαιωτήρια ὤτων
διάκενος κρότος πιστεύεται, ἓν μόνον κτωμένων διὰ σπουδῆς ἔνοικον,
καθόλου κτᾶσθαι τὸν μαμωνᾶν, οὐ μόνον ὡς ἔτυχεν, ἀλλὰ καὶ μεθ' ὅρκων,
40 ὅπερ οὐκ ἀνεκτὸν λογιζόμεθα. εἰ οὖν ἕνεκεν τῶν ῥηθέντων ὀδυνῶμαι παρακουόμενος, παυσάσθω τὸ αἴτιον. εἰ δέ γε ἴδιον πάθος ἐν ὑποκρίσει διεκ-

---

58: 12–13 cf. Ps. 88(89):38; Rev. 1:5 || 22–23 cf. I Cor. 14:15 || 36–37 cf. Demosthe-
nes, Περὶ Ἀλοννήσου, 7.45, et Athanasius, *Epp.* 49, 6, et 50, 19

---

21 παροξυσμῷ coni. Ševčenko; παροξυσμοῦ codd. || 23 ἀναγκασθῇς coni. Ševčenko;
ἀναγκασθεὶς codd. || 27 ὅπου] ὅπως P || 30 προχωρήσει S

58

only for the sake of the love and praise and duty which every Orthodox Christian owes to the truly orthodox man whom God has made to rule in an orthodox manner over the orthodox, with law and justice. Nor ⟨do I make petitions⟩ in order to appear to be striving for great influence over the emperor (may I not be so insane as to be overcome by the desire for such glory), nor have I forgotten my lowly position and the height of the imperial authority and its supreme glory, nor am I influenced by friendship or kinship or greed or ordinary desires, nor by my love for certain people. And of this your divine majesty, after the One «trustworthy Witness in heaven», is a truly trustworthy and credible witness as no other man, because of your manifest and great refinement and wisdom and discretion. And when I see these qualities in you and realize that the rest of mankind, old and young alike, not only is disparate in these respects, but is dissimilar and lacking ⟨in these characteristics⟩, I make a certain number of petitions because I am consumed by the fire of love—and when they are heeded, I consider that they procure a reward from God, since what is the duty of your majesty and my own self is suitably advanced and brought to a good conclusion—sometimes, however, ⟨I send petitions⟩ out of apprehension, lest, through the baneful silence and treacherous ways of certain people, or excited by a malicious report (for this once happened to a king, and one «singing in the spirit» at that), you be forced to order or forbid things which are not proper ⟨to order or forbid⟩. For He Who raised you to such a lofty position will, without a doubt, make a close examination of His wishes and of yours, demanding a strict reckoning, just as is men's custom about the payment of taxes (?).

For these reasons, if on occasion I appear to make petitions in a shameless manner because of my desire for your glory in both ⟨worlds⟩, and if I seem heavy-handed to your majesty in my investigations, or do not deem it expedient to allow the most appropriate course of action to be passed over through forgetfulness or confusion, ⟨it is⟩ lest through an oversight something happen to such a great emperor which is not pleasing to God, because the harm or profit from such actions is enormous; in the same way I entreat your subjects, showing them what an obligation they have to maintain the security of peace and salvation in both body and soul, throughout their lives.

When I am devoting my efforts to these affairs, why should I not take it ill when I am disregarded, and people «who carry their consciences in their heels», alas, are heeded more than I am myself? These people believe that the judgments of the world to come are a hollow rattling in their ears, and they acquire only one thing through their zeal, an exclusive search for gain, not in a haphazard manner, but with sworn oaths. This I find intolerable. If then it is on account of the above reasons that I suffer when I am not heeded, let the cause come to an end. But if someone suspects that I am hypocritically avenging

δικεῖν ὑπολάβῃ μέ τις, οὐ μέγα, εἰ ἄφρων καυχώμενος εὑρεθῶ. καυχήσομαι γὰρ ἐν Χριστῷ, ἐν αὐτῷ δυναμούμενος, περισσεύειν καὶ ταπεινοῦσθαι εἰδώς, καὶ λαλεῖν καὶ σιγᾶν, καὶ
45 χορτάζεσθαι καὶ πεινᾶν, καὶ κτᾶσθαι καὶ ἀποκτᾶσθαι, καὶ τοῦ γένους τὴν σωτηρίαν διψᾶν ἐν τῷ σταυρῷ τοῦ Κυρίου μου· ἅπερ καὶ κρίσει δικαίᾳ καὶ ἀρετῇ ἀναφέρω τῇ ἐκ Θεοῦ βασιλείᾳ σου. εἰ γὰρ ὑπόχρεοι οἱ πολλοὶ τῆς προκοπῆς τοῦ λαοῦ τῆς διπλῆς, ἀλλ' οὕτως οὐδεὶς ὡς ἡ ἐκ Θεοῦ βασιλεία σου.

59. Πρὸς τὸν αὐτοκράτορα

Τοῦ Κυρίου μου λέξαντος εἰ ἐν τῷ μαμωνᾷ τῷ ἀδίκῳ πιστοὶ οὐκ ἐγένεσθε, τίς ὁ παρέξων ὑμῖν τὸ ἀληθινόν; καὶ εἰ δοκεῖ τὰ τῆς ἀληθείας εἶναι τοῦ μαμωνᾶ, ἀλλ' οἶμαι τοῦ τῇδε
5 βίου τὸ πᾶν ὑπὲρ τὸν μαμωνᾶν τελεῖν καὶ τὸ ἄδικον. διὰ τοῦτο τῆς ἐκ Θεοῦ βασιλείας σου δέομαι, τῶν ἰχνῶν αὐτῆς ἐφαπτόμενος, ὡς ἔχεις ἐν τούτοις καιρόν, τὰ ἀληθῆ καὶ αἰώνια κέρδανον. αἰσχύνην ἐπένδυσον τοὺς ἐχθροὺς σὺν τοῖς κόλαξι· τῶν ψεύδεσθαι φρονηματευομένων ἐντροπῆς τὰ πρόσωπα πλήρωσον. οἱ διψῶντες τὴν ἀδικίαν καὶ
10 ἁρπαγήν, καὶ κέρδος οἰκεῖον λογιζόμενοι τὴν τοῦ γένους συμφορὰν καὶ ἐν βρώσει ἄρτου ἐπιθυμοῦντες καταφαγεῖν τὸν λαὸν τοῦ Θεοῦ, ἀρίστῃ ψήφῳ δικαιοσύνης χαίρειν εἰς μάτην ἐξελεγχθήτωσαν· οἱ ἐν μανίᾳ ἀκολασίας καὶ βορβόρῳ ἰλυσπώμενοι σωφροσύνης φαρμάκῳ θεραπευέσθωσαν καὶ μὴ θέλοντες. οἱ κλέπτειν τετολμηκότες ἢ φόνοις ἢ
15 γοητείαις ἢ ἐπιλοίπῳ προστετηκότες [fol. 39ᵛ] ἀρρητουργίᾳ δικαζέσθωσαν δικαιότατα.

τούτων γὰρ ἕνεκεν καὶ Θεὸς ἐνέδυσε τὴν ἰσχὺν τὴν ἐκ Θεοῦ βασιλείαν σου, εἰς τὸ τοὺς νόμους αὐτοῦ καὶ τὴν ἐκκλησίαν διεκδικεῖν ἀνδρικώτατα. ἕνεκεν τούτων καὶ τὴν μάχαιραν ἐνεχείρισεν, ὁ
20 στρέφειν καὶ τὴν εὐώνυμον κελεύσας τῷ παίοντι. ἀπείροις σε

---

42 cf. II Cor. 12:11 ‖ 42–43 καυχήσομαι . . . Χριστῷ: cf. Phil. 3:3 ‖ 43–45 ἐν αὐτῷ . . . πεινᾶν : cf. Phil. 4:12–13 ‖ 45 κτᾶσθαι . . . ἀποκτᾶσθαι: cf. Greg. Naz., Or. XL, λβ' (PG, XXXVI, 404C)
59: 2–3 cf. Luc. 16:11 ‖ 7–8 cf. Ps. 131(132):18 ‖ 9 cf. Ps. 82(83):17 ‖ 11–12 cf. Ps. 13(14):4 ‖ 17 cf. Sir. 17:3 ‖ 19–20 cf. Matt. 5:39

---

42 εὑρεθῶ S ‖ 43 δυναμούμενος VS¹P: δυνάμενος S ‖ 47 εἰ] οἱ P
59: V 39ʳ–40ʳ. S 170ᵛ–172ʳ. P 50ʳ–51ᵛ. Ed. Laiou, Andronicus II, 335–336, no. 4.
1 ante πρὸς add. γράμμα VʳSP ‖ post αὐτοκράτορα add. περὶ τῶν διψώντων ἐν βρώσει ἄρτου καταφαγεῖν τὸν λαὸν τοῦ Θεοῦ, καὶ συναλγεῖν αὐτὸν ἐν τοῖς ἐπερχομένοις ἀνιαροῖς ὑπὲρ φίλων καὶ συγγενῶν VʳSP ‖ 5 ante τῆς add. τὸ S ‖ 7 ἐπένδυσον] ἐπέρδυσε P
14 φόνοις] φόροις P

58, 59

my own suffering, it is not important, if I am found to be «a fool in glorying». For «I will glory in Christ», «taking my strength from Him, knowing how to abound and how to be abased», how to speak and how to be quiet, «to be satisfied and to hunger», «to possess and to lose possessions», and to long for the salvation of the nation through the Cross of my Lord. These ⟨qualities⟩ I recommend to your divine majesty together with righteous judgment and virtue. For although the multitudes are responsible for the twofold progress of the people, no one ⟨has such responsibility⟩ as your divine majesty.

59. To the emperor

Since my Lord said, «If ye have not been faithful in the unrighteous mammon, who will grant you the true riches ?», and if God's own things are things of the mammon, then surely everything of this life on earth belongs to the realm of the mammon and of injustice. For this reason, I beg your divine majesty and clasp your feet, while you still have time, gain the true and eternal ⟨riches⟩. «Clothe both enemies» and flatterers «with disgrace»; «fill with shame the faces» of those who presume to lie. As for those who thirst after injustice and greed, and consider the misfortune of the nation to be their gain, and who «desire to eat up the people of the Lord as they would bread», let them be condemned by the noble vote of justice to gloat in vain. Let those who crawl in the mud, as the result of their passion for licentiousness, be cured with the remedy of moderation, willing or not. Let those who have dared to steal or who are involved in murder or sorcery or other unspeakable deeds be judged most righteously.

It was because of these people that God «clothed» your majesty «with strength», so that you might defend courageously His laws and Church. Because of these people He, Who bade us «turn the left cheek» to the man who strikes us, entrusted you with the sword. He Who is transcendently good has

ἀγαθοῖς ὁ ὑπεράγαθος καθωράϊσε. τήρησον τούτου τὰ δικαιώματα· ἐν τούτοις ἡμᾶς καὶ μὴ θέλοντας ὤθισον. εὔφρανον τὸν ποιήσαντα· πλῆσον ἕνεκεν τούτων χαρᾶς καὶ τοὺς ὄντως φιλοῦντάς σε, καὶ μὴ διά τι τῶν γεηρῶν, ἵνα δὲ καὶ αὐτὸς ἐν Χριστῷ τι καυχήσωμαι, τῆς
25 φωνῆς μου εἰσάκουε· τὸ ἀξίωμά μου εἰσερχέσθω ἐνώ-
πιόν σου. οὐ γὰρ εὑρές τινα ὡς ἐμὲ τὸν φιλοῦντά σε, καὶ τὴν σὴν εὐφροσύνην οἰκείαν ποιούμενον τὴν σωτήριον, οὐδὲ τὸν ἐν τοῖς ἐπερχομένοις
ἀνιαροῖς ὡς ἐμὲ συναλγοῦντά σοι, ἢ τὸν δόξης καὶ σωτηρίας τῆς σῆς κη-
δόμενον ὡς ἐμέ, εἰ καὶ πολλοῖς σχηματίζεται τὸ φιλεῖν. ὡς ἀπόλοιτο ἡ
30 ὑπόκρισις, ἢ καὶ σαφῶς ἐξελέγχεται, εἰ τῆς ἐλπίδος ἀποσφαλῶσιν οἱ ταύτῃ προσκείμενοι.

ἕνεκεν τούτων ἀντιβολῶ, ζῶσαι ὥσπερ ἀνὴρ τὴν ὀσφύν
σου, δυναμούμενος ἐν Χριστῷ· εἰς Θεοῦ παράταξιν ἀριθμήθητι. ἀρίστευ-
σον κατὰ πάντων ὧν ἐχθραίνει Θεός. περίζωσαι τὴν ῥομφαίαν
35 σου, ὅσα μὴ φίλον ἐκείνῳ καὶ τοὺς τεκταίνοντας τὰ τοιαῦτα ἀκρατῶς
συγκόπτων καὶ ἀφειδῶς τῷ κράτει τοῦ σταυρωθέντος. τότε καὶ γὰρ
ἐνωτίσῃ ἀπ᾽ οὐρανοῦ, ἐν τούτῳ νίκα κατὰ παντός, μὴ ὑπὸ φίλων
καὶ συγγενῶν, μὴ ὑπὸ δυναστείας τῶν ὀφειλόντων ἀνακοπτόμενος·
πάντα γὰρ δυνατὰ τῷ πιστεύοντι. ἐπικοπτέτω σοι μέριμνα
40 μὲν ἡδονήν, τὴν λύπην δὲ πάλιν ἡ κρείττων ἐλπίς. λέγε τεθαρρηκώς,
ἰδοὺ Κύριος, Κύριος· τίς κακώσει με; εἰπέ, Κύριος ἐμοὶ
βοηθὸς καὶ οὐ φοβηθήσομαι τί ποιήσει μοι ἄνθρωπος.
ἔχε θαρρούντως ἀγαθὸν πεποιθέναι ἐπὶ Κύριον, ἢ πεποιθέναι ἐπ᾽ ἄνθρωπον. πίστευσον ἐν αἰσθήσει ὅτι Κύριος
45 ἐστὶν ὃς διασκεδάζει βουλὰς ἐθνῶν, πρὸς δὲ καὶ λαῶν,
καὶ ἀρχόντων βουλὰς ἀθετεῖ, μόνη δὲ μένει δεδοξασ-
μένη εἰς τὸν αἰῶνα ἡ τούτου ἁγία βουλή. παρρησιάσθητι
πρακτικῶς, καὶ μάλιστα νῦν ἐν ἡμέρᾳ τῶν θλίψεων, ἵνα ἴδωμεν ἐπὶ σοὶ
τὸ ἐπικάλεσαί με ἐν ἡμέρᾳ θλίψεώς σου, καὶ ἐξελοῦμαί
50 σε καὶ δοξάσεις με.

τί με παραλυπεῖς ἀγωνιζόμενον ἐν τοῖς ὑπὲρ σοῦ, καὶ γνησίως σοι
συλλυπούμενον, ὥσπερ ἐκ διαμέτρου μὴ ποθῶν εἰσακούειν μου; εἰ γάρ
τινος κέρδους ἢ δόξης ἐμῆς ἢ φίλων ἢ συγγενῶν ἕνεκεν ἢ ἀνέσεως καὶ οἰκείων ὀρέξεων, ἃ [fol. 40ʳ] καὶ πολλάκις ἀποχαρίζῃ τισί, δι᾽ αὐτὸν τὸν
55 Θεὸν μηδαμοῦ μηδόλως ποτὲ εἰσακούσῃ μου, μηδ᾽ ἔριφόν μοι παρ-
έξῃς εὐφρανθῆναι μετὰ τῶν φίλων μου. εἰ δ᾽ ἕνεκεν τοῦ Θεοῦ

---

24 cf. Phil. 3:3 ‖ 24–25 cf. Ps. 129(130):2 ‖ 25–26 cf. Ps. 118(119):170 ‖ 32–33 Job 38:3 ‖
34–35 Ps. 44(45):4 ‖ 37 Eusebius, *Vita Constantini*, ed. Heikel, GCS, VII, 21 ‖ 39 Marc.
9:23 ‖ 41 cf. Is. 50:9 ‖ 41–44 Ps. 117(118):6, 8 ‖ 44–47 cf. Ps. 32(33):10–11 ‖ 49–50 Ps.
49(50):15 ‖ 55–56 cf. Luc. 15:29

---

30 ἢ] ἢ codd. ‖ 38 ἀνακοπτόμενος VSP¹: ἀνακοπτώμενος P ‖ 55 εἰσακούσῃ VS¹P:
εἰσακούσει S ‖ 55–56 παρέξεις codd.

59

adorned you with countless blessings. Preserve His ordinances, and encourage us toward this end even against our will. Make glad the heart of the Creator, and for these reasons fill with joy the hearts of those who love you truly, and not because of any material reward; and so that «I», too, «may rejoice in Christ, hear my voice! Let my petition come before you». For you have not found anyone who loves you as I do, and who makes his own your joy in salvation, or anyone who commiserates with you as I do at the grievous events which afflict us, or who is concerned for your glory and salvation as I am, although many people make a show of loving you. May their hypocrisy be destroyed, which is laid patently bare, whenever those who hoped ⟨for some reward⟩ fail to see their hopes fulfilled.

For these reasons, I entreat you, «gird your loins like a man», finding your strength in Christ. Be numbered in the ranks of God. Prevail over all who have God as their enemy. Through the power of the One Who was crucified, «gird your sword», and relentlessly and mercilessly strike all things which are not pleasing to God, together with those who contrive them. For then you will hear from heaven, «'In this prevail' over all!», when you are restrained neither by friends or relatives or by pressures from fulfilling your obligations; «for all things are possible to him that believes». Let deliberation check your pleasures, and again let a stronger hope check your grief. Say confidently, «Behold, the Lord, the Lord! Who will hurt me?». Say, «the Lord is my helper, and I will not fear what man shall do to me». Be assured that «it is better to trust in the Lord than to trust in man».Believe deeply that it is the Lord Who «frustrates the counsels of the nations, and He also brings to nought the counsels of the peoples and of princes; but only His holy counsel endures and is glorified forever». Speak out with vigor, especially now in the day of afflictions, so that we may see ⟨directed⟩ toward you the words, «Call upon me in the day of affliction, and I will deliver you, and you shall glorify me».

Why do you cause me great grief when I labor on your behalf, and genuinely commiserate with you, but, as if you were diametrically opposed to me, you are not willing to listen to me? If ⟨I make petitions⟩ for the sake of my own profit or glory, or for the sake of friends or relatives or luxury or personal desires (which you often grant to certain people), by God Himself, do not ever by any means heed me, or grant «me a kid to make merry with my friends». But if ⟨I make petitions⟩ for the sake of God and the things of God,

καὶ τῶν τοῦ Θεοῦ, καὶ ὧν ὀφείλεις ἀπαραιτήτως αὐτῷ, δόξης τε καὶ μεγαλωσύνης καὶ σωτηρίας τῆς σῆς, δι' ἃ καὶ παρὰ Κυρίου, εἰ πείθῃ,
ἕψεταί σοι καὶ δόξα καὶ σωτηρία καὶ ἀντίληψις ταχεινὴ καὶ τιμή, τί μὴ
60 ἐπαγωνίζῃ ἐν ὅσῳ κύριος εἶ καὶ συναγωνιζομένους εὕρηκας καὶ ἡμᾶς ὑπὲρ
τῶν σῶν προθυμότατα; ἔστι γὰρ ἀναμφίβολον ὡς, ⟨εἰ⟩ ὑπὲρ ὧν ἐξαιτοῦ-
μεν προθύμως ἀποπληροῖς τὰ εἰς δύναμιν (ὅτι μηδὲ ζητοῦμεν τὰ ὑπὲρ
δύναμιν), Θεὸς μυριοπλασίως εὐφρανεῖ καὶ μεγαλυνεῖ, στηρίξει τε καὶ
σθενώσει τὴν ἐκ Θεοῦ βασιλείαν σου, ἀραρότως ὑπερασπίζων αὐτῆς καὶ
65 ὧδε καὶ ἐν τῷ μέλλοντι.

60. Πρὸς τὸν αὐτοκράτορα

Καὶ λίαν ὀλίγοι τῶν ἐν γῇ βεβασιλευκότων τετυχήκασιν εὐκλεῶς
καθαψαμένου ἐν ἀγαθοῖς τῶν αὐτῶν καρδιῶν τοῦ Θεοῦ, οἱ καὶ ὑπερφερεῖς
τῆς πρώτης εὐεργεσίας, τῆς βασιλείας φημί, καὶ ὅσα τῶν γεηρῶν. τῆς
5 τοσαύτης οὖν εὐτυχῶς δωρεᾶς ἀπολαύσασα καὶ ἡ ἐκ Θεοῦ βασιλεία σου μὴ
ἀνεχέσθω, ἀντιβολῶ, τοὺς καρποὺς τῷ τὰ τοιαῦτα χαρισαμένῳ μὴ
ἀξίους ἀποτιννύειν, μὴ δι' ὄκνον, μὴ διὰ τὸ τῶν ὑπηρετούντων κακόβου-
λον· ὅτι μηδὲ ἠγνόηται τοῖς νοοῦσι ποσῶς τὸ τῆς σῆς βασιλείας περὶ τὰ
καλὰ μεγαλόψυχον, ὁ ζῆλος ὁ κατ' ἐπίγνωσιν, τοῦ δικαίου ἡ
10 ἔφεσις, τοῦ ἐλέους πρὸς τοὺς ἀξίους τὸ πρόθυμον, ἡ παρ' ἐλπίδα συμπάθεια πρὸς τοὺς πταίοντας, καὶ συνελόντα εἰπεῖν, τὸ πρὸς ἅπαν καλὸν
τῆς καλῆς σου ψυχῆς σύντονον καὶ ὀξὺ καὶ διάπυρον.

διὰ τοῦτο παρακαλῶ, τὰ ὑψηλὰ καὶ θεόσδοτα ταῦτα ἐπικοπτέσ-
θωσαν μηδαμῶς, μὴ πραγμάτων περιπετείαις, μὴ δυσκολίᾳ καιροῦ, μὴ ἀ-
15 καίροις φιλοτιμίαις, μὴ σχέσεσι συγγενῶν, μὴ ἀρχόντων θρασύτητι,
μὴ φορολόγων ἀπανθρωπίᾳ, μὴ ὅσαις ὁ τῆς ζωῆς ἀντίδικος [εἰς]
ἡμῶν πάγαις ἁλίσκειν ἐπιχειρεῖ τοὺς λίαν μὴ βλέποντας, σκορπίων
ἐπάνω καὶ ὄφεων δυναμοῦντος ἡμᾶς τοῦ Σωτῆρος δεδυνημένους
πατεῖν. οὕτω βιούντων καὶ γὰρ οὐ μόνον ἐνταῦθα ἡμῖν συνέσεται
20 ὁδοποιῶν καὶ προπολεμῶν καὶ ὑπερασπίζων, ὁ μέχρι καὶ συντελείας, ὡς ἔφη, ἡμῖν συνεσόμενος, ἀλλ' ὅλως καὶ ἐκτυπώτερον ἀσ-
τράπτων τότε τῇ δόξῃ τῇ πατρικῇ, καί σε δικαίως καταγλαΐζων, ὡς

60: 6–7 cf. Luc. 3:8 ‖ 9 cf. Rom. 10:2 ‖ 15–16 cf. Greg. Naz., Or. XIV, ζ' (PG,
XXXV, 864C–865A) ‖ 17–19 cf. Luc. 10:19 ‖ 20–21 cf. Matt. 28:20 ‖ 21–22 cf. Luc. 17:24 ‖

---

58 πείθῃ VSP¹: πείθει P ‖ 61 εἰ addidi ‖ 61–62 ἐξαιτοῦμεν] ἐξαιτοῦμαι P ‖ 63 μυριοπλασίως VS¹P: μυριοπλάσιος S
60: V 40ʳ–41ʳ. S 172ᵛ–174ᵛ. P 51ᵛ–54ʳ.
1 ante πρὸς add. γράμμα VʳSP ‖ post αὐτοκράτορα add. περὶ δωρεᾶς ἧς αὐτὸς ἀπολαύσας
μὴ ἀνεχέσθω τῷ τὰ τοιαῦτα χαρισαμένῳ Θεῷ μὴ ἀξίους ἀποτιννύειν καρπούς VʳSP ‖ 16 εἰς
uncis seclusi ‖ 17 πάγας codd.

59, 60

for the sake of your glory and magnificence and salvation which you indubitably owe to Him, through which ⟨things⟩, if you heed me, you will receive from the Lord glory and salvation and swift succor and honor, why don't you exert every effort inasmuch as you are master, and since you have found me most eager to share your struggle ? For there is no doubt that ⟨if⟩ you readily accede to my requests which are within your power (since what I am asking for does not exceed it), God will ten thousandfold gladden and magnify, support and strengthen your divine majesty, steadfastly protecting you both here and in the world to come.

60. To the emperor

Extremely few earthly rulers have gloriously attained the God Who fastens on their hearts with blessings (?), and they excel in the supreme blessing (?), I mean the empire, and all that is terrestrial. Therefore, since your divine majesty is fortunate to enjoy such a gift, do not, I pray, endure not to repay with «worthy fruits» Him Who granted you such blessings, either as the result of hesitation, or through the bad advice of your ministers. For there is no one with any intelligence who is unaware of your majesty's generosity in good causes, of your «zeal according to knowledge», your desire for justice, your eagerness to extend mercy to those who deserve it, your compassion beyond expectation for those who go astray, in short, the intense and keen ardor of your good soul for every good work.

Wherefore, I pray, don't allow any of these lofty and divinely granted virtues to be curbed, not by reversals of circumstances, nor by the difficulty of the times, nor by inopportune ambitions, nor by ties of kinship, nor by «the audacity of nobles, or the inhumanity of tax-collectors», nor by such traps as those with which the adversary of our life tries to ensnare the blind, since the Savior has given us power «to tread on serpents and scorpions». For if we live in this manner, He will not only be with us in this world to lead our way and fight on our behalf and defend us, He Who, as He said, will be with us «until the end», but also in the world to come when He will «shine» ever more brightly with the glory of the Father, and will glorify you right-

τὴν πίστιν τετηρηκότα καὶ τὸν δρόμον τετελεκότα, καὶ
τὰ θεῖα ἠκριβωκότα εἰς ἄκρον ἐντάλματα, κρηδέμνῳ τῷ [fol.
40ᵛ] βασι-
25 λείῳ ἐγκαταστέψας δικαιοσύνης καὶ ὁσιότητος, ἐν δόξῃ ἀναφαιρέτῳ καὶ
ἀσυγκρίτῳ τιμῇ, ὑπέρ τε τῶν χαρισθέντων σοι πλεονεκτημάτων, καὶ τὸ
ἐννόμοις ἐπιστασίαις ἰθύναι τὴν βασιλείαν ὑπὲρ τὸ πᾶν ἀεὶ στέρξ-
αντι, καὶ τῷ νυμφῶνι ἐκείνῳ συνεισελθεῖν τῷ παμβασιλεῖ ἐν πανάγνῳ
τραπέζῃ καὶ ἀμβροσίᾳ συνεστιαθησόμενον, καὶ τυχόντα τοῦ μακαρισμοῦ·
30 μακάριος γάρ, φησιν, ὃς φάγεται ἄριστον ἐν τῇ βασιλείᾳ
τῶν οὐρανῶν.

τῷ γοῦν διψῶντι προσθεῖναί σοι δόξαν ἐν δόξῃ ἀνεκλαλήτῳ
μεγάλῳ Θεῷ πόθῳ συντρέχοντες καὶ αὐτοὶ οἱ ἀνάξιοι, οὐ δωρεᾶς ἐφιέμενοι, ὡς ὁ ἀπὸ Θεοῦ μαρτυρήσει μοι βασιλεύς, οὐκ ἀντιδόσεως, οὐκ
35 ἐπαίνων, οὐκ ἄλλου τῶν ἀνθρωπίνων τινός, οὔτ᾽ αὖθις ἐλάττωσιν πλούτου
τῇ βασιλείᾳ πραγματευόμενοι, ἢ καὶ φιλονεικοῦντες ἰδίαν συστήσασθαι
δόξαν ἡμῖν, ἐκ φίλων ἢ ἀλλοτρίων, ὡς ὁ ἐτάζων καρδίας καὶ νεφροὺς ἐπίσταται· ὅτι μηδὲ ἡμῖν ἐγνώσθη διαφορὰ οἰκείου καὶ ἀλλοτρίου,
ἢ πένητος ἢ πλουσίου, ὡς ἐν μὲν ἐν Χριστῷ οἱ πάντες δεδιδαγμένοι
40 ἐκ θεοπνεύστου Γραφῆς, κατόπιν δὲ μᾶλλον τοῦ θείου σκοποῦ βαδιού-
μενοι τοῦ καὶ σὲ βασιλεύσαντος, καὶ πρὸς ταύτῃ τῇ ἐπικήρῳ παρέξειν
διψῶντος καὶ τὴν οὐράνιον, οὗ καὶ ἡμεῖς δοῦλοι ἀχρεῖοι. ὅθεν τῷ
δέει τῷ πρὸς ἐκεῖνα καὶ τῷ φίλτρῳ δὴ τῷ πρὸς σὲ ἀσχέτως κινούμενοι,
ἀναφέρομεν ὅτε καὶ ὅσα καὶ ἀναφέρομεν.

45 μὴ γοῦν τοιαῦτα οὐτιδανὰ αἰτοῦντες παρακουώμεθα, κράτιστε βασιλεῦ καὶ φιλανθρωπότατε· εἰ γὰρ καὶ τἄλλα τῶν τριωβολιμαίων ἡμεῖς καὶ
ἄξιοι οὐδενός, ἀλλ᾽ ὅσον καὶ δόξης ἐπιποθοῦμεν καὶ σωτηρίας τῆς σῆς
ἐκκαιόμενοι, τῇ ἡμετέρᾳ ψυχῇ παρέξοι Θεός. καὶ μηδὲ οὕτω μανείημεν
πώποτε ὡς ἐξάξαι παρακαλεῖν διακρίνειν τὸν φυλακῆς ἄξιον, ἢ ἀζημίως
50 διάξαι τὸν ζημίᾳ ὑπεύθυνον. ἀλλ᾽ εἴ τι γε καὶ αἰτοῦμεν ἐν τοῖς τοιούτοις,
τὸ μόνον μὴ πάσχειν τινὰ ἐκ διαβολῆς, οὐδέ γε ἀπολαῦσαι τιμῆς τὸν μὴ
τίμιον, ἢ καὶ εὐεργετεῖσθαι τὸν παρωσάμενον τὴν εὐεργεσίαν δι᾽ ἔργων,
ὅπου γε καὶ τοιαῦτα αἰτησαμένοις ἀπεχαρίσω τισίν. ἢ οὖν δυσωπείτω τὸ
εὔκαιρον τῆς αἰτήσεως, τῷ κρατοῦντι καὶ μόνον τὴν ὄνησιν φέρον, ἤ, ⟨εἰ⟩
55 ἄξιοι μὴ ἐσμέν, ἀλλὰ τῇ ἐκκλησίᾳ πάρεχε τὴν τιμήν, ἣν φιλεῖς καὶ ἐφίλη-
σας, καὶ παρ᾽ ἧς ἀναμφίλεκτος καὶ βεβαία σοι ἡ ἐλπὶς κρατύνεσθαι πρὸς
Θεοῦ τὸ βασίλειον, καθ᾽ ὅσον λόγος αὐτὴν παρὰ τῆς βασιλείας κρατύνεσ-
θαι· [fol. 41ʳ] ὅτι καὶ θεία φωνή, τοὺς δοξάζοντάς με δοξάσω,
καὶ ἀτιμάσω τοὺς ἀτιμάζοντας.

---

23 II Tim. 4:7 ‖ 27 cf. *Epanagoge*, Tit. I, 1 ‖ 30–31 cf. Luc. 14:15 ‖ 32 cf. Sir. 45:20 ‖
37–38 Ps. 7:10 ‖ 39 cf. Rom. 12:5 ‖ 42 Luc. 17:10 ‖ 58 I Reg. 2:30

---

48 παρέξει codd. ‖ 54 εἰ addidi ‖ 57–58 post κρατύνεσθαι repetiverunt πρὸς Θεοῦ τὸ
βασίλειον, καθ᾽ ὅσον λόγος αὐτὴν παρὰ τῆς βασιλείας κρατύνεσθαι codd.

60

eously, as one who «has kept the faith, and finished the course», and scrupulously observed the divine commandments, and after He will have crowned you with the imperial headdress of righteousness and holiness in inalienable glory and incomparable honor, on account of the favors already granted you, and since you have always wished above all to guide «the empire with legal authority», and to come together with the King of all to that bridalchamber, to feast together on ambrosia at the all-holy table, and receive His blessing; for He says, «Blessed is he that shall eat a meal in the Kingdom of Heaven».

Thus, unworthy though I am, I concur with the great God Who desires to «grant you glory» upon unspeakable glory; not ⟨that I am⟩ desirous of a gift, as the divine emperor will testify on my behalf, or of a reward, or praises, or any other human ⟨ambition⟩, or strive to diminish the wealth of the empire, or ⟨am⟩ eager to acquire glory for myself with the help of friends or strangers(?), as «He Who searches the reins and hearts» knows. For I recognize no difference between friend and stranger, or rich and poor, since we are taught by the divinely inspired Scriptures that we are all «one in Christ», and should proceed in accordance with the divine purpose of the One Who made you emperor, and Who is anxious to grant you the heavenly kingdom in addition to this transitory one, and of Whom we are the «worthless servants». Therefore it is because of my fear of God, and because I am irresistibly swayed by my love for you that I make my reports, when and whatever I report.

O most mighty and generous emperor, do not ignore me when I make my trifling requests; for even if in other respects I am worthless and deserve nothing, still may God grant my request when I am inflamed with desire for your glory and salvation. And may I never be so insane as to beg you to decide to release a man who deserves imprisonment, or to dismiss without punishment a man who deserves it. But if I should request something in this category, then ⟨it is⟩ only that someone not suffer from slander, not that a dishonorable man should enjoy honors, or that someone who has rejected kindness through his deeds should be the recipient of kindness, even if you have granted such favors to others who have made petitions. Either, then, let the appropriateness of my request speak for itself, since it brings profit to the ruler and to him alone, or ⟨if⟩ I am not worthy, at least grant this favor to the Church which you love and have loved, and through which you have undisputed and certain hope that God will strengthen your empire to the same extent that ⟨the Church⟩ is strengthened by the empire. For the Divine Voice says, «I will only honor them that honor me» and dishonor them that dishonor me.

138

60, 61

60 καὶ ἵνα τἄλλα ἐάσω τὰ κατ' ἐμὲ μεστὰ ἀπαραμυθήτου παραλυπήσεως χρηματίζοντα, ὡς ὑπὲρ σοῦ καὶ δόξης τῆς σῆς προσκαίρου
καὶ αἰωνίας γονυπετοῦντα, καὶ παρορώμενον ἀθεράπευτον, ποσάκις ἡ ἐκ
Θεοῦ βασιλεία σου τῷ ἑταιρειάρχῃ ἐπέταξεν, εἴ τι πρὸς ἡμῶν περὶ
ὑποθέσεως διαμηνυθῇ, ἢ συνέρχεσθαι μεθ' ἡμῶν πρὸς ἀληθείας φανέρ-
65 ωσιν, ἢ τῶν διαμηνυθέντων ποιεῖσθαι δικαίαν καὶ ἀληθῆ τὴν διόρθωσιν,
οὐ χάριν ὀρέξεως ἡμετέρας, ἀλλ' ὅτι καὶ θέλημα τοῦτο Θεοῦ καὶ δόξα
βασιλικὴ καὶ τιμὴ καὶ σωτηρίας ἀσφάλεια, ἐπεὶ καὶ τὸ ἀγαπᾶν κρίσιν
βασιλέως τιμή; ὃ καὶ γενέσθω τῇ βασιλείᾳ σου δι' ἐρεύνης. εἰ κἂν
προσάπαξ πεποίηκε τοῦτο, ἀλλ' ἵνα οἰκείου κέρδους τινὸς ὀσφρανθῇ —
70 οὔ μοι δοκεῖ πρὸς στέαρ γαλῆ ταχύτερον ἐκπετάζεσθαι — εἰ καὶ
ἡνίκα προσέρχεται προσκυνήσων τὴν ἐκ Θεοῦ βασιλείαν σου, πλατεῖαν οὐκ
οἶδα πόθεν συρραψάμενος τὴν ἀλωπεκῆν, καὶ εἴσω περικρυπτόμενος ταύτης, ἀσφαλείᾳ ὅ, τι πολλῇ τῶν λόγων τῷ μειλιχίῳ, ὡς εὔνους καὶ ταπει-
νολογῶν, ὑποκλέπτειν τὴν εὔνοιαν σχηματίζεται, ὡς εἶναι καὶ τοῖς
75 ἀκριβαζομένοις τὰ κατ' αὐτὸν λίαν δυσθήρατος· ὅ με μειζόνως ἐκπλήττει
καὶ ἀποκναίει, εὐδοκιμοῦσαν τῇ ξένῃ καταστολῇ τὴν ὑπόκρισιν, οἴμοι, κα-
τανοοῦντός μου. καὶ τοῦτό μοι δι' εὐχῆς ὡς ἂν ὁ ἀποκαλύπτων
βαθέα, συνδέσμους τε ἀναγγέλλων καὶ λύων κρατού-
μενα, κρατήσῃ σου τῆς καρδίας, καὶ κρατύνῃ ἐκδηλότερον τὰ ἑκάστου
80 καταφωτίζων τὴν ἐκ Θεοῦ βασιλείαν σου, ἵνα μὴ πονηρία, εἰς βλάβην
καὶ ταῦτα πολλὴν ἀφορῶσα καὶ ζημίαν ἀπαραμύθητον, διπλόη κεκαλυμ-
μένη εἰς τέλος κατακαυχήσηται.

61. Πρὸς τὸν αὐτοκράτορα

Τὸ μόνον θελῆσαι Θεὸν πρᾶξιν εἶναι καὶ συντετελεσ-
μένην, ἀμφιβάλλειν οἶμαι μηδένα τῶν τοῦ Θεοῦ· κἀκείνου θεμελιοῦν
ἐν τῇ πέτρᾳ τὴν ἐκκλησίαν θεσπίζοντος, ὡς μήποτε κατισ-
5 χύσειν αὐτῆς μηδ' ᾅδου πύλας αὐτάς, εὐδόκιμον ὤφθη μετ' οὐ
πολὺ τοῦ ταύτην καὶ βασιλείῳ καταστέψαι περιωπῇ, ὡς ἂν ἐξυπηρετου-
μένη ἐν πᾶσι τοῖς θεαρέστοις καὶ ὑπ' αὐτῆς κρατύνῃ τε καὶ κρατύνηται,

---

67–68 cf. Ps. 98(99):4 ‖ 70 Zenobius II, 79 (Leutsch-Schneidewin, I, 53); Diog. III, 83
(Leutsch-Schneidewin, I, 230) ‖ 77–78 cf. Dan. 2:22 (Theodotion) ‖ 78–79 cf. Dan. 5:12
(Theodotion)
61: 2–3 Greg. Naz., Or. XVI, ιβ' (PG, XXXV, 952A) ‖ 4–5 cf. Matt. 16:18

61: V 41ʳ–42ᵛ. S 174ᵛ–176ᵛ. P 54ʳ–56ʳ.
1 ante πρὸς add. γράμμα VʳSP ‖ post αὐτοκράτορα add. περὶ τοῦ ἀναγκάζειν τοὺς ἀρχιερεῖς προσκαρτερεῖν τὴν ποίμνην αὐτῶν καὶ ποιμένην (ποιμένειν SP) καλῶς τὸν λαὸν τοῦ
Θεοῦ VʳSP

60, 61

Now—not to mention other incidents concerning me and which fill me with inconsolable grief, such as when I fall on my knees to pray on your behalf and for your glory, both temporal and eternal, but am overlooked and ignored—how often, when I have reported to you about the matter, has your divine majesty ordered the hetaeriarch either to accompany me in an investigation of the truth, or to arrange a just and true redress of things which I have reported, not to satisfy my personal desires, but because this is the will of God and brings glory and honor and the assurance of salvation to your majesty, since it is «the honor of a king to love judgment»? And may your majesty go into this matter himself. Even if the hetaeriarch should have done this once, it was in order to sniff out some personal gain; I don't think «a weasel» ever leaped «at suet» more quickly. ⟨This is so,⟩ even if, whenever he comes to do reverence to your divine majesty, he sews together a broad fox skin from somewhere, and concealing himself inside it, with the utmost security because of his gentle words, he schemes to win your favor, pretending to be a well-disposed and humble man, so that those who investigate the charges against him find him extremely hard to catch. This astonishes and annoys me greatly, since I see, alas, that hypocrisy thrives in its strange garb. And my fervent wish is that He Who «reveals the depths» and «answers difficulties and solves hard questions», may have a claim on your heart, and may give strength to your majesty, and cast greater light on every individual, so that wickedness, which leads to great harm and to irreparable damage, may not triumph in the end, concealed in a cloak.

61. To the emperor

I do not think that any man of God doubts that «God has only to will it for a deed to be instantly accomplished»; and when He decreed to found «the Church upon rock», so that «not even the gates of Hell would prevail against it», soon after He resolved to crown Her with the supreme imperial power, so that ⟨the Church⟩ might be served in all matters pleasing to God, and ⟨thus⟩ might support and be supported by ⟨the imperial power⟩, ful-

τῶν θείων ἀποπληροῦσα λειτούργημα νόων, ἰσχύϊ τοῦ ἀπο–[fol. 41ᵛ]
σῷζειν διηνεκῶς δυναμένου τὴν ἐκκλησίαν Χριστοῦ, ἐξευμαρίζουσα
10 ὅσον πρόσφορον, ὡς δή που τὰ πνεύματα τὰ λειτουργικὰ ἕνεκεν τῶν μελλόντων σωτηρίαν κληρονομεῖν, οὐ μόνον ὀλβίους
ἐντεῦθεν τοὺς βασιλεύοντας ταύτης, ἀλλά γε καὶ τοὺς ὑπ᾽ αὐτῆς βασι-
λευομένους μακαρίους ἀποδεικνύουσα, ὡς μᾶλλον τῶν θείων οὐδὲν προτιμῶντας ἀνθρώπινον, ἀλλ᾽ ὅλῃ ἰσχύϊ τὸ εὐσεβὲς καὶ θεάρεστον, καὶ
15 στρέφειν ἀγωνιῶντας ἀεὶ κατὰ νοῦν τὸ προωρώμην τὸν Κύριον
ἐνώπιόν μου διὰ παντός, καὶ τὰ τούτου ἑξῆς.

ἔνθεν τὰ περὶ ὧν πυθέσθαι ἡμᾶς ἐκελεύσθη ὁ καθηγούμενος
παρὰ τῆς ἐκ Θεοῦ βασιλείας σου, δεδοίκαμεν διακρῖναι ἄλλο μηδὲν παρὰ
τὰ θεσμοθετηθέντα τοῖς ὑπηρέταις τοῦ Λόγου καὶ μαθηταῖς, καὶ τοῖς
20 ἐκείνων ὁμόφροσι, καὶ ὡς ἔδοξε τῷ ἁγίῳ πνεύματι καὶ αὐτοῖς, καταπυκ-
νῶσαι τὴν ἐκκλησίαν ποιμέσιν (ἀλλ᾽ οὐ μισθίοις), μὴ ζητοῦσι τὰ
ἑαυτῶν, τὰ δὲ Χριστοῦ Ἰησοῦ, ἠφειδηκέναι μὲν ἑαυτῶν, τῇ δὲ
ποίμνῃ ἐπαγρυπνεῖν, ἐξάξειν τῆς ἐξουσίας τοῦ σκότους αὐτὴν
καὶ τῶν κοσμικῶν ἐπιθυμιῶν, καὶ ζῶντι λατρεύειν ὡς δέον Θεῷ
25 καὶ ἀληθινῷ, ὡς μήτε τρυφήν, μήτε τιμὴν ἐκζητεῖν, χήραν τὴν ἐν
σπατάλῃ τεθνάναι καὶ ζῶσαν, καὶ δὴ καὶ τοὺς τὴν γαστέρα
θεοποιοῦντας ἐχθροὺς ἀποφηναμένοις τοῦ σταυροῦ τοῦ δεσπο-
τικοῦ. εἰ δέ γε μὴ ἐδεδοίκειν ἐπιμνησθῆναι καθαπτομένης κἀμοῦ ἀποφάσεως, ἐξέρρηξα ἂν καὶ ἃ ἡ αὐτοαλήθεια ἀπεφήνατο, σὺν οἷς ἐννοῶν καὶ τὸ
30 εἰ φιλεῖς με, ποίμαινέ μου τὰ πρόβατα, Πέτρῳ καὶ ταῦτα
λεχθέν· περαιτέρω βαίνειν ἰλιγγιῶ, καὶ τίς ὁ ἰσχύσων εἰς ἀντέκτισιν
τὴν ποιμαντικὴν ἐπιδείξασθαι τοῦ φίλτρου τοῦ πρὸς Χριστόν;

ἐν τούτοις ὀφείλειν δοκῶ ἡμᾶς ἀναγκάζειν τὴν ἐκ Θεοῦ βασιλείαν
σου, καὶ ταῦτα διεκδικεῖν ἐξ ἡμῶν, μήπως οὐ βαίνομεν ἢ σπουδάζομεν ὡς
35 ἐτάχθημεν καὶ συνεταξάμεθα, πλάτος δοθείσης αὐτῇ καὶ γνώσεως καὶ
ἰσχύος τοῦ εἰσπράττειν ἐξ ὅλης τῆς ποίμνης νηφόντως ἅπαν ἔννομον καὶ
θεάρεστον, καὶ τοῦτο δόξαν ἡγεῖσθαι Θεοῦ καὶ οἰκείαν τρυφὴν καὶ ἐπίδοσιν, ὡς ἂν εἰς σωτήριον προτροπὴν ἀνιστᾶν, τῷ ἐξόχως ἀντιλαμβάνεσθαι,
τῶν τοιούτων τοὺς ἐραστάς, ἵν᾽ ἐγκαίρως καυχήσῃ καὶ τὸ ἐμοὶ δὲ
40 λίαν ἐτιμήθησαν οἱ φίλοι σου ὁ Θεός· τῶν δέ γε παραχαράττειν
ἐπιχειρούντων καὶ πρὸς οἰκείαν ῥαστώνην τὰ θεῖα μεταπλαττόντων,
ἀποστροφὴν τὴν ἔνδικον ἐπιδείκνυσθαι, καὶ οὕτω στηλιτευθέντες τὸ
καθῆκον ἀσπάσονται.

10–11 cf. Hebr. 1:14 ‖ 15–16 Ps. 15(16):8 ‖ 21–22 cf. Phil. 2:21 ‖ 23 Coloss. 1:13 ‖ 24
Tit. 2:12 ‖ 25–26 cf. I Tim. 5:6 ‖ 26–27 cf. Phil. 3:18–19 ‖ 30 cf. Joh. 21:16 ‖ 39–40
Ps. 138(139):17

---

8 θείων] ἐθνῶν S ‖ 9 ἐξευμαρίζουσαν codd. ‖ 20 αὐταῖς S ‖ 28 καθαπτομένης] καὶ
καθαπτομένης S ‖ 38 τῷ] τὸ codd.

61

filling the service of God through the power of Christ Who is constantly able to preserve the Church. For ⟨the Church⟩ eases the path of everything expedient, since «the ministering spirits» ⟨are⟩ «for them who shall be heirs of salvation». Consequently not only does She provide blessedness to the rulers of this ⟨empire⟩, but renders the subjects of the empire blessed as well, inasmuch as there be nothing human which they set before the divine, but with all their might they give precedence to piety and pleasing God, and strive always to keep in mind ⟨the words⟩, «I foresaw the Lord always before my face», and so forth.

Therefore as for the matter which your divine majesty bade the abbot communicate to me, I hesitate to make any decision other than that which was laid down by the servants and disciples of the Word, and by like-minded people, and in a way that seemed good to them and to the Holy Spirit; ⟨namely⟩ to stud the Church thickly with shepherds (but not with hirelings!), «who do not seek their own advantage, but that of Jesus Christ»; to reck not of themselves, but to keep vigil over their flock, to lead them away from «the power of darkness» and «worldly lusts», and to worship the true and living God in a fitting manner, so as not to seek luxury and honor, but to reveal that «the widow who lived in pleasure was dead», and that those «who make gods of their bellies» are «enemies of the Cross» of our Lord. If I were not afraid to mention the decree which incriminates me as well, I would burst out with the pronouncements of [God] the Truth Itself, under which I would also subsume the words spoken to Peter, «If thou lovest me, feed my sheep». But my head whirls and keeps me from going beyond this; anyhow who will be able to show that his priesthood is a form of paying one's debt in love for Christ ?

Now I think your divine majesty ought to oblige us in such matters, and to make these claims on us, ⟨to find out⟩ whether we proceed or strive as we have been bidden and have pledged. For you have been granted in full the knowledge and strength to exact soberly from the entire flock everything that is lawful and pleasing to God, and to consider that such demands are for the glory of God and your own thriving and progress; consequently, you can provide, through assiduous pursuit of such things, a salutary incitement for the lovers of such ⟨virtues⟩, so that you may boast at the proper time «but thy friends, O God, have been greatly honored by me». But when people try to debase and twist that which is divine for their own comfort, you should show your righteous aversion, and when they are thus reprimanded, they will embrace their duty.

τίνος γὰρ ἕνεκεν ἄλλου, παρακαλῶ, βασιλείᾳ τὴν ἐκκλησίαν Θεὸς
45 καθω-[fol. 42ʳ]ράϊσεν, ἢ δι'ἐπιστασίαν ὁριζομένην δικαίαν καὶ ἔννομον; εἰ δέ που καὶ ῥαθυμίᾳ ἐκ τοῦ μὴ ἀγαπᾶν ἢ φοβεῖσθαι Θεὸν ἠμελήθη
τοῖς πρὸ ἡμῶν, καὶ ὑπέμεινε σύγχυσιν τὰ ὀφείλοντα σωτηρίας τοῖς ὀρθοδόξοις, ἀλλ' ὀφείλομεν διδαχθῆναι ἐκ τοῦ αὐτῆς ἐπιστημονάρχου τὸ θέλεις
μὴ φοβεῖσθαι τὴν ἐξουσίαν; τὸ ἀγαθὸν ποίει, καὶ ἕξεις
50 ἔπαινον ἐξ αὐτῆς. τί γὰρ εἰς ἀναχαίτισιν τῆς κακίας καὶ προτροπὴν ἀρετῆς τούτου ἁρμοδιώτερον; εἰ δέ, φησι, τὸ κακὸν ποιεῖς,
φοβοῦ. εἰ οὕτω γὰρ διακείμεθα, λελέξεσθαι οἶμαι καὶ περὶ σοῦ πρὸς
Θεοῦ, ὡς εὗρον Δαυὶδ κατὰ τὴν καρδίαν μου, ὃς ποιήσει
πάντα τὰ θελήματά μου. καὶ τίς ὁ μισθὸς ἐπὶ τούτοις; ἡ γὰρ
55 χείρ μου συναντιλήψεται αὐτῷ, καὶ ὁ βραχίων μου
κατισχύσει αὐτόν, καὶ τὰ τούτοις ὁμόστιχα.

τῷ τοι καὶ τὸ ποιμένας τιμᾶν, εἰ ἐν οἷς ἐνετείλατο ἡ αὐτοαλήθεια
ἐν ζήλῳ ἐπειγομένους ἐκτρέχειν ὁρᾷς θεϊκῷ, καὶ εἰ χάρισι τοὺς τοιούτους
καὶ εὐεργεσίαις καταφαιδρύνειν ἐπείγῃ, τῶν ἐπάθλων ὑπέρευγε!, πρὸς
60 ζῆλον πολλοὺς παραθήξων ἀγαθουργίας τοιαύτῃ τιμῇ, εἰ δή που καὶ μάλα
ἀποπληροῖεν τὸ ὁ ποιμὴν ὁ καλὸς τὴν ψυχὴν αὐτοῦ τίθησιν
ὑπὲρ τῶν προβάτων· τοῖς δέ γε μὴ πεφρικόσιν, ἀλλ' ἔργοις ἀσπασα-
μένοις τὰ ἐναντία, καθὰ καὶ τὰ λόγια, ὁ μισθωτὸς δὲ καὶ οὐκ ὢν
ποιμήν, οὗ οὐκ εἰσὶ τὰ πρόβατα ἴδια, θεωρεῖ τὸν λύκον
65 ἐρχόμενον, καὶ ἀφίησι τὰ πρόβατα καὶ φεύγει, ἆρα τί τοῖς
τοιούτοις ὀφείλει; οὐχ ἡ ἀποστροφὴ ἡ προσήκουσα εἰς αἴσθησιν ἐπανῆξαι
κἂν δι' αὐτῆς τοῦ προσήκοντος; ἢ οὐ τὸ διαστέλλειν ἀναμέσον τοῦ
κατορθοῦντος καὶ παραβαίνοντος δικαιοσύνης Θεοῦ μετοχή, πρὸς ζῆλον
διανιστῶσα τῶν ὀφειλόντων, καὶ κακίας ἀποφυγήν; τὸν γὰρ τοῖς θείοις
70 ἐμπαροινοῦντα ἀξίως ὁ μὴ ἐπεξερχόμενος, οὐχ οἶδα τί καὶ ἀπολογήσεται.
ὁ γάρ τοι τῆς ποίμνης ἀπανιστάμενος εὐπαθήσων αὐτός, πότε κατόψεται
ῥομφαίαν τὴν ἐρχομένην; πότε τῇ σάλπιγγι σημανεῖ
μήπως λάβῃ ψυχήν; εἰ μή που καὶ μῦθος δοκεῖ τὰ τοιαῦτα, τὸ
βόσκουσιν οἱ ποιμένες ἑαυτούς, οὐ τὰ πρόβατα, ποῦ
75 δὲ καὶ δίκαιον, τὸν τὰ πρόβατα καταλείψαντα φιλαυτίας σκοπῷ, φροντίζειν
ἡμᾶς ἐγχειρεῖν τούτῳ ἕτερα; ἢ οὐχ, ὅπερ ἀπεύχομαι, εἰ ἡ σκοτομαίνα
καταλάβῃ κἀκεῖνα, οὐχ ἕτερα ἀπαιτήσει, φροντίζων μήπως ἀπολειφθῇ
μεθ' ὧν ἐλαλήθη τὸ στέαρ αὐτῶν συνέκλεισαν;
ὧν ἕνεκεν ὀφείλομεν καὶ πενθεῖν τοὺς πτέρναν αἴροντας τοι-
80 αύτην κατὰ Θεοῦ, καὶ ἔξω που βάλλοντας τοὺς λόγους [fol. 42ᵛ]

44–46 cf. *Epanagoge*, Tit. I, 1 ‖ 48–52 Rom. 13:3–4 ‖ 53–54 Acta 13:22 ‖ 54–56 Ps.
88(89):22 ‖ 61–65 Joh. 10:11–12 ‖ 72–73 cf. Ezek. 33:6 ‖ 74 Ezek. 34:8 ‖ 76 cf. Ps.
10(11):2 ‖ 78 Ps. 16(17):10 ‖ 79 cf. Joh. 13:18 ‖ 80 cf. Ps. 49(50):17

---

53 Θεόν codd. ‖ 58 ὁρᾷ codd. ‖ 78 συνέκλεισαν scripsi; cf. Ps. 16(17):10; συνέκλεισεν codd.

61

For what other reason, I ask, did God adorn the Church with «an empire», if not for the ⟨exercise of⟩ «protection» ⟨over it⟩, termed «just and legal»? And even if through lack of love or fear of God our predecessors took no heed of this on account of indolence, and the Orthodox allowed that which required salutary action to fall into a state of disorder, still we ought to be taught by the ⟨emperor, that⟩ *epistemonarch* ⟨of the Church⟩, the words, «Wilt thou then not be afraid of the power? Do that which is good, and thou shalt have praise of the same». For what is more effective than this to check evil and encourage virtue? «But», ⟨the Holy Writ⟩ continues, «if thou do that which is evil, be afraid». For if we are this way, then I think God will say about you, too, «I have found David a man after my own heart, who shall fulfil all my will». And what is the reward for this? «For my hand shall support him and mine arm shall strengthen him», and verses like this.

Therefore if you honor bishops, when you see them hastening to sally forth with divine zeal as bidden by God, and if you strive to glorify such ⟨bishops⟩ with favors and benefits, then bravo for such rewards, for by such honors you will incite many of them to zeal for good works; provided, that is, they carry out the injunction, «the good shepherd giveth his life for the sheep». But as for those who are not afraid, but through their deeds cling to a diametrically opposed way of life, in the words of the Scriptures, «but he that is an hireling, and not the shepherd, whose own the sheep are not, seeth the wolf coming, and leaveth the sheep and fleeth», what is their due? Is not aversion the most expedient way to bring them to realization of their duties? Or is not ⟨the touchstone⟩ to distinguish between the upright person and the transgressor to be found in participation in God's righteousness, which rouses us to zeal for our duty, and avoidance of iniquity? I do not know what defense will be made by the man who does not suitably punish those guilty of sacrilege. For if a man abandons his flock in order to live in comfort, when will he see «the sword coming»? When will he «sound the trumpet, lest ⟨the sword⟩ take a soul»? Unless such tales be legend, that «shepherds feed themselves, and not their sheep», how is it right for us to entrust yet other sheep to a man who has abandoned his flock for selfish purposes? Is it not true that if «the moonless night» should seize those ⟨sheep⟩ (and I pray this may not happen), he will demand others, taking care lest he be left behind with those of whom it has been said, «they have enclosed themselves with their own fat»?

For these reasons we ought to mourn for those «who raise up their heels» so violently against God, and who «cast out His words»; may we be

ἐκείνου, ὧν τῆς μερίδος ῥυσθείημεν. εἰ δέ γε καὶ συναινεῖν εὑρεθῶ τοῖς
τοιούτοις, ἐχθρὰ τὰ τοιάδε Θεῷ ἐπιστάμενος, τῷ καιρῷ τῆς ἀνάγκης τί
καὶ γενήσομαι; ὅθεν πενθῶ τὰ ἐν Ἀγκύρᾳ καὶ Πισιδίᾳ καὶ ὅσα ἐν πόλεσι
ταῖς ἡμῶν ταῦτα παθεῖν δυστυχῶς ἐξεγένετο, κατάβρωμα ἐαθέντα
85 καὶ θηρίοις καὶ πετεινοῖς. περὶ τίνων δὲ καὶ ἀγανακτήσεως καὶ
παραλυπήσεως ῥήματα ὡς ἐκ προσώπου ἐλέχθη Θεοῦ, ὦ, οἱ ποιμένες οἱ ἀπολλύντες τὰ πρόβατα τῆς νομῆς, καὶ ποιμένες πολλοὶ διέφθειραν τὸν ἀμπελῶνα μου; ὅνπερ ἱδρῶσι
πολλοῖς καὶ σφαγίοις συνειλεγμένον τοῖς πρότερον
90 Χριστοῦ καὶ μετὰ Χριστόν, ἡμεῖς ἀνέσεως χάριν οἰκείας διεπω-
λήσαμεν. τοῦτο πολλὴν ἐμποιεῖ μοι τὴν σύγχυσιν, καὶ πῶς οὐδεὶς τῶν
ἀρχόντων ἡμᾶς ἐκβιάζει τὸ ὀφειλόμενον, καὶ τοῦτο λύπη ἐμοὶ καὶ πόνος
ἀπαραμύθητος καὶ φροντίς. τί τότε τῷ ἀρχιποίμενι ἀπολογησόμεθα; εἰ
δέ γε κοῦφον τοῖς ἄλλοις, ἡμεῖς δὲ τῆς τοιαύτης συνέσεως ἐφικνεῖσθαι οὐ
95 δεδυνήμεθα, ὥστε ἡγεῖσθαι ἀνεύθυνα ταῦτα, ὡς τισὶν ἀρεστά· τοῦτο ἡμῖν
πληροφορείτωσαν (τοῦτο γὰρ καὶ αἰτοῦμεν Θεόν), ἐν οἷς καὶ εἰς ὅσον τοῦ
θείου σκοποῦ διημάρτομεν.

62. Πρὸς τὸν αὐτοκράτορα

Οἷα τοῖς νόμοις καὶ τοῖς κανόσι δοκεῖ τοῦ ἐλευθεριάζειν τὴν
ἐκκλησίαν καὶ εὐτακτεῖν, πρώτως αὐτὴν εὐτακτοῦσαν καὶ ὅροις ἰδίοις
ἱστῶσαν ἀρκεῖσθαι καὶ ἕκαστον, πρὸς οἷς μηδὲ ὑπὲρ τὸ ἑξάμηνον
5 ποίμνης ἰδίας ἐκτὸς ἀναστρέφεσθαι τῶν ποιμένων τινά, τὸν λόγον τῇ ποίμνῃ ἀνελλιπῶς ἐν ἑορταῖς ὑφηγεῖσθαι τῆς σωτηρίας, τῇ δὲ ἀναστασίμῳ
καὶ κατ᾽ ἐξαίρετον, καὶ ὅσα ἐπίλοιπα, ἃ μηδένα λεπτότερον καὶ ὀξύτερον
ἐνορᾶν μηδὲ δύνασθαι, μήτε μὴν ἐκπληροῦν, ἢ ἐποφείλειν τὴν τήρησιν
τούτων τῶν θεαρέστων [τοῦ] ἀπαιτεῖν ὡς πάντη χρεὼν τῇ ἐκ Θεοῦ βασι-
10 λείᾳ σου· ὧν ἕνεκεν καὶ κεχάρισαι ὑπὸ Θεοῦ εἰς ἀρχήν, ἵνα, εἰ ὑπὲρ νόμους
ζῆν μὴ καταδεχόμεθα, ὡς ἐξήνυστο καὶ τῇ σῇ κατὰ γενεάς, αὐτὸς τὴν
μέσην ἄγης ἡμᾶς καὶ βασιλικὴν τὴν ἐν νόμῳ ὡς πρὸς Θεὸν ἄγουσαν,
ὅτι καὶ τὸ μικρὸν βαδίζειν παρὰ τοὺς νόμους, πάντως παράνομον.

84–85 cf. Jer. 7:33 ‖ 86–87 Jer. 23:1 ‖ 87–88 Jer. 12:10 ‖ 88–90 Greg. Naz., Or. XXI,
κδ´ (PG, XXXV, 1108C–1109A)
  62: 4 can. 16, α´ καὶ β´ σύνοδος ‖ 11–12 cf. Greg. Naz., Or. XLII, ις´ (PG, XXXVI,
476C)

94 τῆς] τοῖς P
  62: V 42ᵛ–43ᵛ. S 176ᵛ–178ᵛ. P 56ʳ–58ʳ.
1 post αὐτοκράτορα add. περὶ τῶν ἀρχιερέων ἐνδιαιτᾶσθαι ἕκαστον τῇ λαχούσῃ, καὶ μὴ
ποιεῖν πλέον ἐξαμηνηνέον ἐκτὸς ὡς τοῖς νόμοις δοκεῖ καὶ κανόσι, καὶ μὴ κατοικεῖν τῆς
βασιλίδος ἐντός VʳSP ‖ 9 τοῦ uncis secludavi ‖ 10 κεχάρισται SP ‖ 11 μὴ om. S ‖
12 ἄγεις codd.

delivered from their ranks. And if I should be found to be in agreement with such people, although I know that such actions are hostile to God, what will become of me in the time of necessity? Wherefore I mourn for the events in Ankyra and Pisidia, and such misfortunes and sufferings as have occurred in our cities, the people abandoned as «food for the wild beasts and birds». And about whom were spoken words of exasperation and grief, as from the face of God, «Woe to the shepherds that destroy the sheep of their pasture», and «many shepherds have destroyed my vineyard»? This vineyard which «was collected with much toil and sacrifice by those before and after Christ» we have sold for the sake of our own comfort. This causes me great distress, especially the fact that none of our rulers compels us to fulfil our duty, and this is for me a source of grief, pain beyond consolation, and concern. What defense will we make to the Chief Shepherd in the world to come? And even if it seems unimportant to other people, I have not yet come to the point where I believe that such actions are blameless, because they are condoned by certain people. And may they inform me (for this I ask also of God) in what way and to what extent I have failed to attain the divine purpose.

62. To the emperor

With respect to what the laws and canons provide concerning the freedom and good government of the Church, first of all, everyone should be contented when She enjoys good order and rests upon Her own rules; in addition, no bishop should spend «more than six months» away from his own flock, but on feastdays, and especially on the Day of Resurrection, he should unfailingly teach his flock the Word of Salvation; and so on. And no one is more clever or eager than your divine majesty to observe or to execute, or indeed to fulfil or be obliged to demand the minutest and due maintenance of these God-pleasing ⟨acts⟩. For these reasons you have been granted authority by God, so that, since we are not allowed to live above the laws, as has been accomplished by you (?) for generations, you yourself may lead us in lawfulness «on the middle and royal ⟨road⟩» which leads to God, because even a slight transgression of the laws is completely unlawful.

τοῦτο τεθαρρηκὼς καὶ αὐτὸς σπούδασμα θεῖναι εἴπερ τι τὴν ἐκ
15 Θεοῦ βασιλείαν σου, κἂν τἄλλα ἠμελημένος ἐγὼ καὶ ἐκλελυμένος, ὡς
νωθὴς καὶ βραδύς, φροντίζειν τῆς ἐκκλησίας Χριστοῦ δυνάμει τεθάρρηκα.
ἐπεὶ δὲ πρὸς τοῖς ἄλλοις κακοῖς οἷς ἠκρωτηριάσθη [fol. 43ʳ] τὰ τῶν
πιστῶν, οἴμοι, πεφθάκει καὶ τὰ τῆς ἐκκλησίας, καὶ μᾶλλον αὐτονομίᾳ
ἢ νόμοις ὀρεγομένων ἀκολουθεῖν τῶν πολλῶν, καὶ τοῦτο ἔδοξεν ἀνεκτὸν
20 τὸ πάντῃ καὶ πάντως ἀσύμφορον, ἵνα μὴ τῶν ὀλιγοψύχων κριθῶμεν, ἀναχωρεῖν κεκρικότες ζητεῖν τὰ ἡμέτερα. γνωρίζω καὶ ἀναφέρω, εἰ κελεύοις,
κατὰ τὸ σοὶ δυνατὸν ἐλευθέραν ἐν πᾶσι τηρεῖσθαι τὴν ἐκκλησίαν, καὶ
ταύτης αὐτὸς προπολεμεῖν ἐν Χριστῷ, καὶ ἕκαστον τῇ λαχούσῃ ἐνδιαιτᾶσθαι, καὶ τοὺς τὰ σκάνδαλα καὶ τὰς ταραχὰς ἀγαπῶντας ἀνακυκᾶν, ἢ
25 ἔν τισι χηραμοῖς καταδύντας καθάπερ τῷ σκότει τῇ ἀφανείᾳ καλύπτεσ-
θαι, ἢ ἀπελαύνεσθαί που μακράν, ὅτι μηδὲ ποτὲ συνοικεῖν ἐχίδνῃ τινὰ
ἐχέφρων ἐφάνη ποσῶς συναινῶν.

εἰ δ᾽ οὕτως δοκεῖ καὶ τοιᾷδε ἐν καταστάσει τὴν ἐκκλησίαν, καὶ μὴ
ἄγειν ἀλλ᾽ ἄγεσθαι, μηδὲ κελεύειν ἀλλὰ κελεύεσθαι, μηδὲ δεσπόζειν τῶν
30 ταύτης ἀλλ᾽ ὑπὸ τῶν τυχόντων δεσπόζεσθαι, ἐν οἷς καὶ τῷ βουλομένῳ
ἀρχιερεῖ εἰς κλῆρον προνοίας προσνενεμῆσθαι καὶ κατοικίας, τῆς βασιλίδος ἐντὸς κατατρυφᾶν ἀδεῶς, καὶ βίου ἐντεῦθεν τὸν πορισμὸν ἀπαιτεῖν·
πρὸς δέ γε καὶ τὸν ποιμένα αὐτῆς ἀντικαθεζομένους ἔχειν αὐτούς, καὶ ἀν-
τιποιμαίνοντας καὶ ἀντινομοθετοῦντας ἐν πάσῃ ἀδείᾳ, ὅπου γε οὐδὲ τὸ
35 διδάσκειν ἐνορίᾳ παρεχωρήθη καὶ τῇ τυχούσῃ τοῖς νόμοις, εἰ μὴ ἄρα τῇ
ἑαυτοῦ· καὶ ἵνα τἄλλα ἐάσω, εἰ μόλις διαναστῶμεν ἢ ἀγρυπνῆσαι ἢ
λιτανεῦσαι, τοσούτου κινδύνου ἐπικειμένου ἡμῖν, καὶ μικροῦ καταδυο-
μένων τῶν ὀρθοδόξων, διὰ νομίμων ἀθέτησιν, τῷ πελάγει τῶν συμφορῶν
(τίνι γὰρ ἄλλῳ τὴν σήμερον δέον κεχρῆσθαι;), ἐκεῖνοι καθήμενοι οἴκοι,
40 οἷα μὴ γεγονότος καινοῦ μηδενός, τὰς ὀρέξεις αὐτῶν καὶ τὰ κέρδη λογί-
ζονται, καὶ πρὸς μὲν τὰς ἐπιστασίας καὶ τὰ τοιαῦτα ἰσχυροὶ καὶ εὐήκοοι,
πρὸς δέ γε συνάξεις καὶ προσευχὰς ἀπρονόητοι καὶ ἀπρόθυμοι, τῷ σώματι
ἀσθενεῖς καὶ καταπεπονημένους ἀνακηρύττοντες.

εἰ δέ τις ἐφάνη χειρὶ βασιλείῳ στρατάρχης ταινιωθῆναι τιμῇ, εἶτα
45 τοὺς ὑπ᾽ αὐτὸν στρατιώτας καὶ ὑπὲρ τὰ συνήθη καταναγκάζει τούτῳ
δασμοφορεῖν καὶ ὅλῃ συνάγειν χειρί, ἐκστρατείας δὲ κηρυχθείσης τὸ
νοσεῖν σχηματίζεσθαι, καὶ καθήμενον οἴκοι καὶ κατατρυφῶντα ἐκμυκ-
τηρίζειν καὶ τοὺς στρατευομένους, τοῦ μὴ εὐθύνας ὑφέξειν αὐτὸν ἐφάνη τι
ἀδικώτερον; ὃ καὶ ἡμῖν πρὸ τῆς ἐχθὲς κηρυχθὲν ἐξελθεῖν εἰς λιτήν, τοῖς
50 δεσπόταις προ-[fol. 43ᵛ] τιμητέον ἐκρίθη τῆς πρὸς Θεὸν προσευχῆς, διὰ
μόνον τὸν ὀβολόν, ἐπιστασίᾳ παρασπονδύλιος.

εἰ οὖν κελεύσει τοῦ κράτους σου εἷς ἕκαστος αὐτῶν πορευθῇ τοῦ
οἰκείου φροντίδα λαοῦ ἐκζητεῖν, ἀγαθόν· εἰ δ᾽ ἔχειν ὡς ἔχουσι καὶ αὐτοὶ
καὶ ὅσα τὴν ἐκκλησίαν ἐπίμωμα ἐκθλίβει ἀνέχῃ καὶ συγχωρεῖς, κἂν τούτῳ

---

16 νωθεὶς P ‖ 17 καλοῖς codd. ‖ 31 προσνενεμῆσθαι V¹SP: προνενεμῆσθαι V ‖ 39 ἐκεῖνοι]
καὶ κεῖνοι P ‖ 54 ἀνέχει P

62

⟨Precisely⟩ because I have boldly assumed that this above all is a cause of concern for your divine majesty, I have ventured, even if I am a negligent and dissolute man in other respects because of my laziness and indolence, to take charge of the Church, drawing my strength from Christ. And when to the other evils through which the fortunes of the faithful have declined was added, alas, the problem of the Church, especially since most people wish to live by their own rules, rather than in accordance with the laws, I decided to put up even with this totally intolerable thing, so that I may not be judged a man of little courage, by deciding to retire to look after my own affairs. I declare and recommend, if you are agreeable, that to the utmost of your ability you should maintain the freedom of the Church in all areas, and you yourself should be Her champion in Christ, and each ⟨bishop⟩ should reside in his assigned see, and those who love to stir up scandals and disturbances should either disappear down some hole to be concealed there by obscurity as dark as night, or should be banished far away somewhere, for no sensible person has ever been found who would agree to live with a viper.

But if you decide that the Church ⟨should remain⟩ in such a condition, and that She should not lead but be led, nor command but receive commands, nor be mistress of Her own affairs, but be ruled by anyone whatsoever—and incidentally *pronoiai* (?) and residences have been granted to any bishop who wishes as an allotment, and they make merry in the capital with impunity, and seek their livelihood here. If, moreover, ⟨it should be suffered that they⟩ sit instead of the patriarch and perform his pastoral duties and enact his legislation with all license, although it is against the law ⟨for a bishop⟩ even to teach in any diocese except his own; and, to omit other matters, if I only set out (?) to keep vigil or join processions of supplication, seeing that such danger threatens us, and we Orthodox Christians are all but submerged in a sea of calamities because of our disregard of the law (for what other recourse do we have these days ?), they sit at home, as if nothing new had happened, and think of their appetites and profits. When it is a question of administrative authority and the like, they are able-bodied and willing, but they show no concern or eagerness for services of worship or for prayers, declaring that they are weak and weary in body.

If someone were endowed by the emperor with a general's dignity, and then forced the soldiers under his command to pay him more tribute than usual and to collect it in whole armfuls, but when a campaign was announced, feigned illness, and sat at home in comfort while mocking those on campaign, what could be more unfair than for him not to have to give an accounting for his actions ? But when I recently announced that they should go forth for a procession, the prelates preferred their oppressive (?) administrative duties over prayer to God, all for the sake of the obol.

If your majesty were to order each one of them to go and take care of his own people, it would be a good thing. But if you permit and allow both their shameful ways and the circumstances which afflict the Church to continue,

55 ἡμεῖς τοῦ Σωτῆρός μου χάριτι μαθόντες καὶ ὑστερεῖσθαι καὶ περισσεύειν, καὶ χορτάζεσθαι καὶ πεινᾶν, οὔθ᾽ ἡμεῖς καταβαρυνθῶ-
μεν, οὔτ᾽ αὐτήν, ὡς νομίζω, καταβαρύνωμεν, δωρεὰς ἀπαιτοῦντες καὶ
λόγους χρυσοβουλλείους καὶ κτήματα καὶ ζητήματα ὥς τινες· ἀρκέσει
καὶ γὰρ ἡμῖν ἀντὶ πάντων ὁ κοινὸς καὶ ἐμὸς Ἰησοῦς, εἰ καὶ δοῦλος
60 ἀχρεῖος τούτου ἐγώ, καὶ μὴ δεσπότης τοιούτου κληθῆναι διὰ μεγάλην
ἀναξιότητα ἄξιος.
    τί δέ; μαθεῖν ἐξαιτῶ τὸ κωλῦον τοὺς νόμους διεκδικεῖσθαι τοὺς
τοῦ Θεοῦ, τῷ βουλομένῳ καταπεφρονημένους. ἔστι δὲ ὅπου καὶ ὑπὲρ τούτων τὰς ὑποσχέσεις τοῦ βίου μακροτέρας ποιούμεθα, καιρὸν ἀδείας ἐκ-
65 δέχεσθαι, ἵνα τότε κἀκείνων ὦμεν ἐκδικηταί. εἰ οὖν ταῦτα καὶ τῷ θεόπτῃ
ἐκέκριτο, τὸν ξυλευόμενον ἐν Σαββάτῳ οὐκ εἴα γενέσθαι ἐν
ἐρήμῳ λιθόλευστον, ἀλλ᾽ ἀνέχεσθαι τῶν παρανομούντων ἐνομοθέτει,
ἕως τῇ γῇ τῆς ἐπαγγελίας, ἐν ᾗ καὶ μητρόπολις τούτοις ἠλπίζετο
καὶ νεώς, ὑποσχέσει καὶ ταῦτα Θεοῦ ἀνεμένετο. εἰ δέ γε ταῦτα μὴ ἐξεδί-
70 κει, οὐκ ἄν, προτυπώσει τοῦ σταυρικοῦ μυστηρίου, ἡ νίκη
ἐκείνῳ τοῦ μυσαροῦ Ἀμαλὴκ καὶ πανώλου ἐδόθη ἡ περιβόητος. τί δὲ ὁ
Ἠλεὶ ταῖς τῶν παίδων παρανομίαις καιρὸν καρτερῶν διορθώσεως, ἐν
οἷσπερ μὴ ἔδει μακροθυμῶν, καὶ ἀπώνατο; τὸ δέ γε ὑπερυψῶσαν τὸν
Ἀβραάμ, οὐχ ἡ ταχίστη ὑπακοὴ ὧν κελεύει Θεός, εἰ δοκεῖ καὶ ξενίζουσα;
75 εἰ οὖν σπεύσωμεν ὑπακούειν Θεοῦ, τῶν τοὺς δοξάζοντάς με
δοξάσω ἀναμφιβόλως γνωσθείημεν (οὗ μοι δοκεῖ τι ἄλλο μακαριώτερον), καθάπου καί, ἐὰν θέλητε, φήσας, ὡς μόνου τοῦ θέλειν οὐκ
ἐξαρκοῦντος, καὶ εἰσακούσητέ μου ἐπήνεγκεν, οἵτινες τότε καὶ τὰ
τῆς γῆς ἀγαθὰ φάγοιεν· ᾧ δόξα καὶ κράτος, τιμὴ καὶ προσκύνησις,
80 καὶ μεγαλωσύνη εἰς τοὺς αἰῶνας, ἀμήν.

63. Πρὸς τὸν αὐτοκράτορα παρακαλῶν εὐεργεσίας τυχεῖν τὸν Οἰναιώτην

    Εἰ καὶ τὴν μαρτυρίαν λαμπρὰν τὴν ἐπ᾽ ἀγαθοῖς ἐπιστάμεθα, ἀλλ᾽
ἔστιν ὅπου πολὺ τὸ ἀσύγκριτον καὶ αὐτῇ τῆς λαμπρότητος, καὶ ἡ δόξα τοῦ
μαρτυροῦντος αὐτὴν ἀπειργάσατο· ἔνθεν καὶ εἰ ἀπαράμιλλον εἰς παράδειγ-
5 μα, καθ᾽ ὅσον τὰ θεῖα καὶ τὰ ἀνθρώπινα, ἀλλ᾽ οὖν γε εἰρήσεται εἰς δεῖγμα
ἡ μαρτυρία Κυρίου πρὸς τὸν προφήτην καὶ πρόδρομον. [fol. 44ʳ] τοίνυν καὶ

55–56 cf. Phil. 4:12 ‖ 59–60 Luc. 17:10 ‖ 66–67 cf. Num. 15:32 ‖ 68 cf. Hebr. 11:9 ‖ 70
cf. Exodus 17:8–16, et Greg. Naz., Or. XXXII, ιϛ′ (PG, XXXVI, 192C) ‖ 75–76 I Reg.
2:30 ‖ 77–79 cf. Is. 1:19
63: 3–6 cf. Joh. 5:31–37 (?)

56–57 καταβαρύνομεν codd. ‖ 59 κονὸς P ‖ 62 τοὺς] τοῦ P ‖ 73 τὸ V¹, τῇ V, τ᾽ S, τῆς
P ‖ 75 τῶν V¹, τὸ V, τῷ SP
63: V 43ᵛ–44ʳ. S 178ᵛ–179ʳ. P 58ʳ–58ᵛ.

62, 63

then, since by the grace of my Savior I have learned both «to suffer need and to abound, and to be full and to be hungry», I will not be despondent, nor, as I think, will I impose a burden upon you, by asking for gifts and chrysobulls and estates and various claims, as some people do. For Jesus, Who belongs to everyone and to me, will do for me above all, even if I am His «unworthy servant», and am not worthy to be called prelate of Christ because of my great unworthiness.

What then ⟨is my request⟩ ? I demand to know what prevents the laws of God from being defended when they are disregarded by anyone who wishes. And sometimes we make pledges ⟨to act⟩ on their behalf ⟨within a delay⟩ longer than a lifetime, waiting for an opportune moment, so that at that time we may defend them. If then this had been the decision of ⟨Moses⟩, who saw God, and he had not let «the man who collected wood on the Sabbath be stoned in the wilderness», but if he had ordained instead that one should tolerate the transgressors until «the promised land», in which they hoped to build a city and temple, then this, too, would have remained mere promise by God. If Moses had not punished this ⟨transgression⟩, that celebrated victory over the loathsome and abominable Amalek would not have been granted to him through the «prefiguration of the mystery of the Cross». What benefit did Elei gain from waiting for an opportunity to chastise the transgressions of his sons, showing patience when he shouldn't have ? Wasn't Abraham exalted because of his speedy obedience to God's commands, even if this obedience seemed strange ?

If then we strive to obey God, we shall be included without any doubt among those ⟨of whom God said⟩, «I will honor them that honor me», and I do not think there is anything more blessed; just as after He said, «If ye be willing», He added, since wishing alone is not sufficient, «and hearken unto me», whereupon they «would eat the good of the land». To Him be glory and power, honor and veneration and majesty forever, Amen.

63. To the emperor requesting that Oinaiotes be the recipient of largess

Although we all know that testimony concerning the good is a splendid thing, still on occasion the splendor of the testimony is incomparably ⟨great⟩, and is due to the glory of the Witness Himself. Therefore, even if it is inapplicable as a parallel, inasmuch as divine and human affairs cannot be compared, still I will mention as an example the testimony of our Lord compared with that of the Prophet and Forerunner (?). Thus also with regard to men, it

πρὸς ἀνθρώπους οὐκ ἴσον, ἀλλὰ καὶ μάλα ὑπερανέστηκεν, ἐπαινεῖσθαι τινὰ
παρὰ τοῦ τυχόντος, καὶ τούτων ἐπιτυγχάνειν καὶ παρ' αὐτῆς τῆς ἐκ Θεοῦ
βασιλείας σου, διά τε τὸ ὕψος καὶ τὸ φιλάληθες, διά τε τὴν πεῖραν καὶ
10 τὴν λεπτότητα, ἐξ ὧν καὶ ἦθος καταλαβεῖν ὡς ἄλλος οὐδεὶς ἀνδρῶν
δυνατὸν ἐξ ὀλίγων τὴν βασιλείαν σου· τούτου, συμβὰν οὐκ οἶδα πῶς, ἀπολαῦσαι καὶ εὐτυχῆσαι ἐξεγένετο καὶ τῷ Οἰναιώτῃ, ὃς καὶ τῆς βασιλείας
καὶ τῆς ἐκκλησίας ἐκ μέρους ὡς παρ' αὐτῆς μεμαρτύρηται. τοῦτον πεινῶν-
τα τὴν σήμερον ἐκ πολλῶν στοχασάμενοι, ὅμως σιγῶντα γνώμῃ ὡς
15 ἔοικεν εὐχαρίστῳ, καὶ ὅτι καὶ δι' αἰδοῦς καὶ πόθου διακείμενος φαίνεται
πρὸς αὐτήν, ὅσον εἰς ἡμετέραν κατάληψιν ἥκει γνωρίσαντες, συνάμα τούτῳ
λιταζόμεθα πρὸς τὴν βασιλείαν σου, ὡς μόνην μετὰ Θεὸν ἰσχύουσαν φυγα-
δεῦσαι τὸ τῆς πενίας δεινὸν καὶ ἀπαραμύθητον, εἰ καὶ αὐτὸς φιλονεικεῖν
ἡμῖν εἴωθεν, ἡνίκα τι κελευσθῇ πρὸς ἡμᾶς διαπορθμεῦσαι τῶν ἀναγκαίων,
20 πλήν γε τὸ φιλοδέσποτον δυσωπεῖ πρὸς ἄριστον βασιλέα καὶ πάντη ὀρθο-
δοξότατον· οἷσπερ οὐ μόνον οὐκ ἐγκαλοῦμεν, ἀλλὰ καὶ συμπρεσβεύομεν,
ὅτι μηδὲ οἱ λόγοι ἐν οἷς ἀνταίρει ἡμᾶς τοσοῦτον περὶ ψυχῆς τῆς μακαρίας
καὶ ἀθανάτου, καὶ κολασθησομένης ἢ εὐεργετηθησομένης ἀθάνατα χάριν
κακίας ἢ ἀρετῆς. μὴ οὖν ἐκπέσωμεν τῆς δεήσεως, πολλοὺς εἰδότες αἰ-
25 τησαμένους καὶ ταχυτέραν καὶ πλείονα τὴν εὐεργεσίαν, ἐπιτυχόντας καὶ
τῆς δεήσεως.

64. ⟨Πρὸς τὸν αὐτοκράτορα⟩

Ὁ λαμπρᾷ τῇ βοῇ ἀνακτόροις Θεοῦ πρὸ μικροῦ τερετίσας τερπνῶς
τὰ ὀρθόδοξα, καὶ τοῖς ὀρθοδόξων ὠσὶν εὐηχέστατα, βεβληκὼς ἐν ἀραῖς
τοὺς τὰ σκαιὰ φρονήσαντας, εὐλογίαις δὲ αὖ τοὺς υἱοὺς εὐλογίας, πρὸ
5 τῆς τοῦ κόσμου καταβολῆς τῷ Θεῷ καὶ Πατρὶ ἐγνωσμένους
εὐλογημένους, αἰωνίαις ἐν μνήμαις ἐγκαταστέψαντος, ὁ αὐτὸς
παραστὰς νῦν ἡμῖν ἀπαιτεῖ φιλοτίμημα, προβαλλόμενος τάχα καὶ μέγα
δικαίωμα, ὡς τὸ ἄτερ χαλκοῦ μηδὲ Φοῖβον ἐκεῖνον τὸν παρ'
Ἕλλησι μέγαν ἐθέλειν μαντεύεσθαι. ἀλλ' ἐπεὶ τὸ μὴ αἴρειν
10 χαλκὸν ἐν ζω-[fol. 44ᵛ] στῆρσιν ὀρθῶς κελευσθέντων ποτέ, καὶ
ὑμεῖς ἐν τῷ βίῳ τῷ τῇδε συνταξάμενοι φαίνεσθε, τῷ κοινῷ πλουτοδότῃ
σταθέντι πρὸς τοῦ Θεοῦ τὸν ῥηθέντα πεπόμφαμεν τοὺς νόσῳ πενίας πιεζομένους δεινῶς ἐμβριμήματι βασιλείῳ λυτροῦσθαι, ὡς μηδόλως ἀντοφ-

---

64: 4–5 cf. I Pet. 1:20 ‖ 6 cf. *Synodikon*, ed. Migne, PG, CXX, 728 C–Dff. ‖ 8–9
Leutsch-Schneidewin, II, 228 ‖ 9–10 cf. Marc. 6:8

---

11 τοῦτο codd. ‖ 18 φιλονεικεῖν coni. Ševčenko: φιλονείκως codd.
64: V 44ʳ–44ᵛ. S 179ʳ–179ᵛ. P 58ᵛ–59ʳ.
1 γράμμα πρὸς τὸν αὐτοκράτορα ὅπως τυχεῖν φιλοτίμημα τὸν τερετίσαντα ἐν τῇ ἁγίᾳ τοῦ
Θεοῦ ἐκκλησίᾳ τὸ συνοδικόν add. VʳSP ‖ 2 ὁ om. P ‖ 11 ὑμεῖς VSⁱP: ἡμεῖς S

63, 64

is not the same thing, but there is a great difference whether a man is praised by an ordinary person, or whether he receives these praises from your divine majesty, because of your lofty position and love of truth, and also because of your experience and subtle refinement, as a result of which your majesty, as no one else, can grasp a man's character from only a few indications.

It has happened somehow that this ⟨approval⟩ has been received and enjoyed by Oinaiotes, who has been attested to [i.e., granted a favor?] by your majesty, and on the part of the Church, too, as ⟨he has been⟩ by your majesty. Since I guess from many indications that he is hungry these days, but still seemingly remains silent with a thankful attitude, and since I have ascertained to the best of my knowledge that he appears to look upon you with respect and love, together with him I entreat your majesty, who with the help of God is alone able to banish the inexorable terror of poverty, even if he used to argue with me whenever he was ordered to bring me an important message, still his loyalty ⟨speaks for itself and⟩ entreats an excellent and in every way most orthodox emperor; and not only do I not blame him for this ⟨opposition⟩ but endorse his petition, since the words with which he opposes me concerning the blessed and immortal soul, which is going to be punished or blessed eternally by virtue of its evil or good nature, are not of such great import. Therefore, let me not be disappointed in my request, since I know that many people before me have requested both more immediate and greater benefits, and have been granted their petition.

64. ⟨To the emperor⟩

Not long ago in the palace of God a man with a sonorous voice gave a delightful rendition of the ⟨Synodikon⟩ of Orthodoxy, a most pleasant sound to the ears of the orthodox as he cursed men of crooked thoughts, and crowned with blessings «in eternal memory» the sons of blessing who are known to be blessed by God the Father «before the foundation of the world». This man now stands before me and asks for some compensation, putting forward the great justification that «not even Phoebus» of old, who was great among the Greeks, was willing «to prophesy without a gift of bronze coin». But since ⟨the twelve disciples⟩ were once rightly enjoined «not to take bronze coin in their purse», and you, too, ⟨said I to the petitioner⟩, appear to have renounced this life, I have sent the above-mentioned man to ⟨you⟩ the common benefactor who has been established by God to grant readily as a result of your great munificence, by merely wishing it, that those who are heavily burdened by the disease of poverty may be saved by solemn imperial order,

θαλμεῖν τὴν πενίαν αὐτοῖς χαρίζεσθαι, ῥᾶστα, ἐκ μόνου τοῦ βούλεσθαι,
15 ἐξ ἀρίστης φιλοτιμήσεως· δι' ὃν οὐ χαλκοῦ παροχὴν ἐξαιτούμεθα, ἀλλ'
εὐροίζου χρυσοῦ, τοῦ λαμπρότατα στίλβοντος, παρ' οὗ, ἐλέει Θεοῦ καὶ
κελεύσει, καὶ στήλη αὕτη καὶ εἰκὼν ὁρᾶται δεικνῦσα τὴν ἐκ Θεοῦ βασιλείαν σου.

65. Πρὸς τὸν αὐτοκράτορα κατὰ αἰσχροκερδῶν

Πάντων ἐφιεμένων τοῦ πλείονος σήμερον, καὶ μᾶλλον ὅτι μηδένα
διὰ παιδεύσεως σωφρονίζομεν τῶν ἐσθιόντων ἐν βρώσει ἄρτου
τὸν τοῦ Κυρίου λαὸν καὶ ἰδιοποιουμένων καὶ τὰ τῆς βασιλείας ἀμφο-
5 τέραις χερσί, κἂν ἡ παροῦσα ὑπόθεσις ὡς δέον ψηλαφηθήτω διὰ τὸν Κύριον, καὶ μὴ διὰ τῶν ἐκτυφλουμένων ξενίοις ἡ ἀλήθεια ἀθετείσθω καὶ τὸ
ἔννομον καὶ τὸ δίκαιον. μηδὲ τοσοῦτον καταφρονείσθω ἡ ἐκκλησία τῶν
προσόντων αὐτῇ προνομίων, εὐκόλως ὑπὸ παντὸς βουλομένου κερδαίνειν
πεπλασμένῃ ὑποβεβλῆσθαι διαβολῇ, ἀλλ' ἀξίως ἐπιτιμάσθω ἐπάρατος
10 πᾶς, εἴτε Θεοφάνης, εἴτε οἷός ἐστιν ὁ χρώμενος τῇ αἰσχροκερδείᾳ καὶ τῇ
διαβολῇ, καὶ κατὰ τῆς ἀληθείας χωρῶν, καὶ ταύτης καταψευδόμενος,
μεθ' ὧν καὶ οἱ ἐπὶ τοσοῦτον θαρρήσαντες νῦν τοῦ συγκαλύψαι ξενίοις καὶ
τοιαύτην μιαιφονίαν ἐλεεινήν, ὅτι μηδὲ ἡ θεία δίκη ἐπινυστάξει μέχρι
παντὸς τοῖς ταῦτα κατατολμῶσιν, οἵτινες καί εἰσιν. ἕνεκεν τούτων καὶ
15 αὖθις ἐξέτασιν δέομαι καὶ ἐκδίκησιν πρὸς τῆς ἐκ Θεοῦ βασιλείας σου ἀρ-
ρεπῆ γενηθῆναι καὶ ἄοκνον, μὴ παραδιεφθορότων καὶ τῇ κακίστῃ φιλαρ-
γυρίᾳ γόνυ κλινάντων, δι' ἣν καὶ Ἰούδας ἐμεγαλύνθη ἐπισφαλῶς, ὡς προσ-
άδεσθαι πανταχοῦ καὶ διηνεκῶς. εἰ δὲ μὴ διεκδικοῦμεν, ἀλλ' ἀνεχόμεθα
παρασιωπᾶν τὰ τοιαῦτα, Θεῷ τῷ δικαιοκρίτῃ ἀνεύθυνα οὐ διαμενεῖ.

66. Πρὸς τὸν αὐτοκράτορα

Εἰ καὶ μὴ ἐν χειροποιήτοις ναοῖς Θεὸν περικλείεσθαι
τὸν πληροῦντα τὸ πᾶν (τοῦτο γὰρ οἶμαι τὸ κατοικεῖν),

65: 3–4 cf. Ps. 13(14):4
66: 2–3 μὴ ... Θεὸν et τὸ κατοικεῖν: cf. Acta 17:24 ‖ 3 τὸν ... πᾶν: cf. Eph. 1:23 ‖

65: V 44ᵛ. S 179ᵛ–180ʳ. P 59ʳ–59ᵛ. Ed. Banduri, *Imperium Orientale*, II, 983–984;
Migne, PG, CXLII, 503–504.
1 ante πρὸς add. γράμμα VʳSP ‖ post αὐτοκράτορα add. καὶ τῶν προνομίων τῆς ἐκκλησίας
VʳSP

66: V 44ᵛ–46ʳ. S 180ʳ–182ᵛ. P 59ᵛ–62ʳ.
1 ante πρὸς add. γράμμα VʳSP ‖ post αὐτοκράτορα add. περὶ τῶν θείων ναῶν τιμᾶν καὶ
λαμπρύνειν καὶ ὡραΐζειν, καὶ μὴ ἐμμένειν τινὰ κατηχουμενείοις, καὶ μὴ οἴκους τινῶν ἐγκολλᾶσθαι τοῖς θείοις ναοῖς VʳSP

so that poverty does not stare them in the face. I do not ask a gift of bronze for this man, but of gold which rings true and shines brightly, on which, by the mercy and bidding of God, is seen an image and picture of your divine majesty.

65. To the emperor against those who make base gains

Today when everyone seeks more, and especially because we do not chasten with punishment any of those who «devour the people of the Lord like ⟨so many loaves of⟩ bread» and grab with both hands the property of the empire, for the sake of the Lord let the present matter be examined in a proper manner, and let not the truth and lawfulness and righteousness be disregarded by those who are blinded by bribes, nor let the Church be so slighted of her privileges as to be easily subject to the slanders fabricated by everyone who is desirous of gain. But let every accursed person be suitably punished, whether it is Theophanes, or anyone like him who indulges in base gain and slander, and proceeds against the truth, and makes a pretence of it, as well as those who have now made so bold as to conceal through bribes such a pitiable murder. For God in His judgment will not be forever nodding in the case of perpetrators of such deeds, whoever they may be. Wherefore I again ask that your divine majesty institute an investigation and provide a firm and prompt legal redress, resisting corruption and surrender to basest greed (through which Judas, to his own harm, gained great fame so that he is sung of everywhere continually). For if we do not take corrective legal measures, but allow such matters to be passed over in silence, an accounting for them will still have to be rendered to God the righteous Judge.

66. To the emperor

Even if the Scriptures teach that God «Who fills all» is not confined «in temples made with human hands» (for I think this is what «dwell» means), but

ἐκδιδάσκει [fol. 45ʳ] τὰ λόγια, ἀλλά γε τοὺς ἀνεγηγερμένους θείους ναοὺς
5 εἰς δόξαν Θεοῦ καὶ ὀνομασίαν, οὐ τοί γε μόνον τοὺς ἀνεγείραντας,
ἀλλὰ καὶ τοὺς ἐκ πόθου τιμᾶν καὶ λαμπρύνειν καὶ ὡραΐζειν κειμηλίοις
καὶ ἀναθήμασι καὶ ὅσοις χεὶρ ἀνθρωπεία ἰσχύει ποιεῖσθαι ὁσίως προθυμουμένους, ἀνέκφραστον φράσαι πηλίνοις ἐν στόμασι τὴν ἀντάμειψιν ὁποία αὐτοὺς ὑποδέξεται. τὸ δέ γε τούτων καὶ χάριεν, ὡς μηδὲ
10 ἀπείργειν καὶ πένητας εὐπορεῖν ὁμοίως ἐν τούτοις τοῖς ἔχουσι, καὶ κατόπιν
ὁδεύειν διὰ πενίαν πιέζουσαν, πλουτοῦντας ἐξ ἀληθῶν ὑποδειγμάτων τὸ
βέβαιον· ἐν ἄλλοις μὲν τὴν διαφορὰν τοῦ πλουτεῖν καὶ
τοῦ πένεσθαι, ἐν δέ γε τοῖς πρὸς τὸ θεῖον τὸν προθυμότερον
πλουσιώτερον. ἐπεὶ καὶ τοῖς προσαγηοχόσι χρυσὸν καὶ λίθους
15 τιμίους, πηγνύντος Μωσέως ποτὲ τὴν σκηνήν, οὐκ ἀπὸ συνεισ-
φορᾶς πρὸς τὸ θεῖον ἐξεγένετο καὶ τοῖς πένησι, τρίχας εἰσενεγκοῦσιν
αἰγείας ὡς ἠνωτίσμεθα, ὧν οὐδὲν εὐωνότερον, ἐκδιδάσκων καὶ τοὺς
ὁρῶντας τοῦ παναγάθου τὸ ὑπεράγαθον, εἰ μόνον ἐκ πόρων δικαίων καὶ
χειρῶν καθαρῶν ἡ τυχοῦσα προσαγωγή.
20   ὅπου γε καὶ τοῖς μόνον ἀξιωθεῖσιν ἀγαπᾶν καὶ νοεῖν εὐπρέπειαν οἴκου Κυρίου, οὐ μόνον κἀκείνοις ὑπερβαίνουσαι νοῦν
ἀμοιβαὶ ἀπόκεινται, ἀλλὰ καὶ ὥς τι ποιοῦσι τῶν ἀμιμήτων καὶ μέγα, ἱκε-
σίαι διηνεκεῖς ὑπὲρ τούτων ἀπὸ πάσης τῆς ἐκκλησίας πρὸς τὸ θεῖον
ἑκάστοτε ἀναφέρονται· εἰ καὶ μεμετρημένοι οἱ τούτων καὶ τῶν λίαν ὀλίγων
25 οἱ αἰσθανόμενοι, καθὰ καὶ τοῖς εἰσιοῦσι μετ' εὐλαβείας καὶ πίστεως καὶ
φόβου τοῦ πρὸς Θεὸν ἐξακούονται. τοῦτο τὸ μέγα καὶ σπάνιον τοῖς πολλοῖς
καὶ σοὶ τῷ θεοστεφεῖ καὶ ἁγίῳ μου βασιλεῖ χαρισθὲν πρὸς Θεοῦ, καὶ μάλα
τῇ καθ' ἡμᾶς μοιχαλίδι τὰ πρὸς Θεὸν καὶ ῥαθύμῳ καὶ πονηρᾷ
γενεᾷ, εἰ καὶ ὡς δέον οὐ διαφαίνεται τοῖς πολλοῖς (ὅτι μὴ μόνον τῷ
30 καρδίας ἐτάζοντι καὶ νεφρούς), τοῖς νυστάζουσιν ὄντως ἡμῖν περὶ
τὰ καλὰ ἢ ἀμβλυώττουσιν, ἀνορέκτως ἐχόντων ἡμῶν τὰ θεόσδοτα μεγαλ-
ύνειν τοὺς ἔχοντας καὶ ζηλοῦν καὶ μιμεῖσθαι (εἴθε δὲ καὶ τῷ φθόνῳ μὴ
διεβάλλοντο εἰς ἄκρον κακίζοντες), ὡς μόνη ἐξὸν καὶ διάτορον ἐκβοᾶν τῇ
ἐκ Θεοῦ βασιλείᾳ σου, καὶ τοῦτο ἡγεῖσθαι καὶ ἔχειν εἰς σεμνοπρέπειαν
35 ὑπὲρ αὐτὸ τὸ διάδημα, τὸ ἠγάπησα, Κύριε, εὐπρέπειαν οἴκου σου,
καὶ ἔχειν καὶ βλέπειν καὶ λέγειν καὶ καλλονὴν [fol. 45ᵛ] σκηνώματος
δόξης σου (ἐξ ὧν ὁ ζῆλος τοῦ οἴκου σου καταφάγεταί με
ταύτῃ προσγίνεται), καὶ ἐπιτηδεύμασι παριστᾶν, ὅπερ τοῦ λέγειν πολλῷ
τιμαλφέστερον καὶ μακαριώτερον.

---

8 cf. Joh. Damasc., *Hom.* 5 (PG, XCVI, 649 A) ‖ 12–14 Greg. Naz., *Or.* XL, κε′ (PG,
XXXVI, 393 D–396 A) ‖ 14–17 Greg. Naz., *Or.* XIX, η′ (PG, XXXV, 1052 B–C) ‖
20–21 cf. Ps. 25(26):8 ‖ 21 cf. Phil. 4:7 ‖ 28–29 cf. Matt. 12:39 ‖ 29–30 Ps. 7:10 ‖ 35–37
Ps. 25(26):8 ‖ 37 Ps. 68(69):10

---

7 ἀναθήμασι S ‖ 16 εἰσενεγκεῖν P ‖ 18 μένον P ‖ 33 ἄκραν P ‖ 35 ὑπὲρ ... εὐπρέπειαν
om. S ‖ Κύριε om. P ‖ post οἴκου σου καὶ repetivit τοῦτο ἡγεῖσθαι P, et deinde delevit

66

still, with regard to the divine churches which have been erected to the glory and name of God, it is not possible to express with our «mouths of clay» the reward which awaits not only the builders, but also those who were eager in a holy manner, because of their love ⟨for God⟩, to honor and make resplendent and adorn ⟨the churches⟩ with treasures and dedications and whatever the human hand is able to fashion. The nice thing about this is that the poor are not prevented from enjoying ⟨this reward⟩ as much as people of means, nor do they have to take second place because of their grinding poverty, since according to true examples they are wealthy in the assurance ⟨of salvation⟩. «For in other matters there is a distinction between riches and poverty», but in divine affairs «the most zealous man is the most wealthy». For both people who brought «gold and precious stones when Moses was setting up the tabernacle» and the poor people who, as we hear, offered «goats' hair», than which nothing is cheaper, made a contribution to the divine; and thus ⟨Moses⟩ taught the bystanders the transcendent goodness of the All-good One, if only the offering is from honest sources and clean hands.

Wherefore as for those who alone are deemed worthy «to love» and contemplate «the beauty of the house of the Lord», not only do rewards «which surpass understanding» lie in store for them, but, inasmuch as they have done something great and inimitable, constant supplications to the divine are offered on their behalf by the entire Church on every occasion; and even though those who are aware of it are limited in numbers and there are extremely few of them, in the same way ⟨these supplications⟩ are heard, just as are ⟨the prayers⟩ of those who enter ⟨church⟩ with piety and faith and fear of God. This is the great gift, which is rarely found in most people, but has been granted by God to you my holy and divinely crowned emperor, and indeed to our indolent and «wicked generation which is adulterous» in things divine; ⟨it is so⟩ even if this is not as clear as it should be to the many (but only to the One Who «searches the hearts and reins»), since we are drowsy or short-sighted about good works, and reluctant to magnify and emulate and imitate those who have gifts granted by God (would that they were not led astray by envy, and did not utter foul reproaches); it follows that your divine majesty alone is able to proclaim loudly and to maintain and believe that even more important for dignity than the diadem itself are the words, «Lord, I have loved the beauty of thy house», and to maintain and observe and speak of the beauty «of the tabernacle of thy glory» (as a consequence of which the phrase, «zeal for thy house has consumed me», also applies to you), and to represent this with actions which are far more valuable and blessed than words alone.

156

66

40 ἔνθεν καὶ τῆς τοῦ θείου πνεύματος δόξης καὶ χάριτος τῆς
τὸν Βεσελεὴλ ἐμπλησάσης ἐκεῖνον, ἐπιδραξάσης καὶ ἄκρως καὶ κατα-
κρατησάσης σου τῆς ψυχῆς, κἂν τοῖς θείοις ἀξίως παραθηξάσης, ὡς οὔποτε τῶν προβεβασιλευκότων καὶ πρὸ τῶν ἡμετέρων καιρῶν εὐλαβείᾳ
τινά, κειμηλίοις καὶ ἀναθήμασιν ἀκορέστως κατακοσμεῖν τὴν σκηνήν,
45 καὶ παντοίως ποικίλλειν οὐ παύῃ βασιλικώτερον (ἥνπερ ὁ Κύριος
ἔπηξεν ἀλλ᾿ οὐκ ἄνθρωπος)· πρὸς οἷς καὶ τῷ πόθῳ καὶ τῇ
λεπτότητι τὰ μήπω ἐπιγνωσθέντα ἐπεξεργάσασθαι ὑψηλῶς καὶ πολυτελῶς,
οἷα καὶ ὅσα ταῖς τῆς ἱεραρχίας στολαῖς, ἢ πατριαρχικαῖς, εἰπεῖν οἰκειότε-
ρον, πρὸς τὸ τῶν θείων ὑπούργημα λαμπρῶς ἐξεγένετο, καὶ κόσμον τῇ
50 ἐκκλησίᾳ Χριστοῦ ἀναφαίρετον ἀποθησαυρίζειν εὐσεβείας καὶ εὐλαβείας
καὶ εὐταξίας καὶ στολισμοῦ, εἰ Θεὸς ἐφορᾷ τὰ ἡμέτερα, ἕως καὶ ἥλιος τὴν
γῆν, φεραυγῆ καὶ ἐξαίρετα καὶ ἀνελλιπῆ, ἐξ ὧν καὶ τοῖς νῦν καὶ μετέπειτα
ἐποφείλεται τῷ ἁγίῳ μου αὐτοκράτορι εὐχῶν καὶ ἐπαίνων ἑσμός, τῶν
ὅσοι μὴ μεμήνασι, καὶ διηνεκὴς ἀποκείσεται. δόξαν δὲ παρέξει σοι Κύριος
55 καὶ μεγαλοπρέπειαν τὴν διπλῆν, καὶ πάσας τὰς αἰτήσεις σου
τὰς θεοφιλεῖς ἐκπληρῶν, ἐλέους τοῦ πρωϊνοῦ ἐμπλήσει.
ἐξαποστελεῖ τέ σοι ἐξ ἁγίου βοήθειαν καὶ πιανθῇ σου τὰ
καλλιερήματα, μιμνησκόμενος τούτων καὶ ἐν ἡμέρᾳ θλίψεως ἀντιλαμβανόμενος καὶ ῥυόμενός σε τὸν χριστὸν αὐτοῦ
60 ὁρωμένων καὶ νοητῶν τῆς μανίας. καὶ τοῖς αὐτοῦ μεταφρένοις
ἐπισκιάζων σοι (ὅ,τι ποτέ ἐστι θεῖα μετάφρενα), τοῖς τε εἰς
μάτην ἐχθραίνουσι τούτου ἡ χεὶρ εὑρεθείη, τῆς ἐκείνων
σκαιότητος ἀνώτερον συντηροῦσα, κἀκείνους ὡσεὶ πηλὸν πλατειῶν
ὑπὸ πόδας σοὺς ἐκλεαίνουσα, καὶ ἐν πίονι γήρει καταξιοῦσα
65 τῆς βασιλείας τῶν οὐρανῶν.
ἐν τούτοις οὖν ἐξαιτῶ μὴ καὶ τὰ τῶν θείων ἀπ᾿ ἄρτι νεῶν ἐᾶσθαι
ἀνεπιμέλητα (ὅτι μηδὲ μικρὸν τὸ μικρὸν παρὰ τοῖς μεγάλοις), μὴ ἐμμένειν
τινὰ κατηχουμενείοις, μὴ οἴκους τινῶν ἐγκολλᾶσθαι τοῖς θείοις ναοῖς, ὃ
τῶν ἀρχόντων οὐδεὶς τῷ οἴκῳ αὐτοῦ κατεδέξατο πώποτε, εἰς ὕβριν τῶν
70 θείων ναῶν κατατολμᾶσθαί τισιν. εἰ δέ που ἐκ τούτων ἀντιστραφῆναι
[fol. 46ʳ] δεήσει εἰς τιμὴν καὶ ἐλευθερίαν τῶν θείων ναῶν, ἡμεῖς ἀποτίσο-
μεν, ἡμᾶς λυτροῦντες κἀκείνους καταδίκης φρικώδους τῆς τοῖς κατα-
φρονηταῖς κειμένης ἐκεῖ. ὅσον γὰρ τὸ δεινὸν τοῖς τὰ θεῖα κοινοποιοῦσι,
καὶ ὅσος ἡμῖν ἐποφείλεται ζῆλος, ἐδίδαξεν ἡ αὐτοαλήθεια, ἀπορραπίσασα

40–41 cf. Ex. 31:3 ‖ 44–46 cf. Hebr. 8:2 ‖ 55–56 cf. Ps. 19(20):6 ‖ 56 cf. Osee 6:5(4) ‖
57–59 cf. Ps. 19(20):2–4 ‖ 59 Ps. 19(20):7 ‖ 60–61 cf. Ps. 90(91):4 ‖ 61–62 cf. Ps. 3:8 et
20(21):9 ‖ 63–64 cf. Ps. 17(18):43 ‖ 64 Ps. 91(92):15

---

48 οἷα καὶ ὅσα ... στολαῖς om. P ‖ 53 ἑσμὸς codd. ‖ 57 ἐξαποστελεῖ τέ] ἐξαποστελεῖταί
P ‖ πιανθῇ P ‖ 59 καὶ om. P ‖ 60 τοῖς] τῆς P ‖ 71 post δεήσει vacuum in codicibus ‖
73 κειμένοις codd.

66

Therefore, since the glory and grace «of the Holy Spirit, which filled» Beseleel of old, have also seized your spirit and hold it fast, and encourage you worthily in sacred affairs, like none of those who ever ruled with piety before our time, you do not cease to decorate insatiably in a royal manner and to adorn in a varied fashion with precious offerings «the tabernacle, which the Lord pitched, and not man». And in addition as a result of your love ⟨for the Church⟩ and your refined taste, you have munificently sponsored the production of stately and elaborate ⟨furnishings⟩, such as have never been seen before, like the vestments for bishops, or for the patriarch (to speak more personally), for the service of the divine, and you have stored up for the Church of Christ an inalienable adornment of piety and reverence and ceremony and decoration, which will keep their brilliance and distinction and abundance as long as the sun ⟨shines⟩ on the earth, if God watches over our affairs; and because of these ⟨gifts⟩ a stream of prayers and praises is owed to my holy emperor by present and subsequent generations, whosoever has not gone mad, and will be stored up for you unceasingly. And the Lord will grant you glory and twofold magnificence, and by «fulfilling all your petitions» which are pleasing unto God, He will fill you with «the mercy of the morning». And «He will send you help from the sanctuary, and your sacrifices will be increased, and remembering them in the day of affliction, He will help you» and deliver you, «His anointed one», from the madness of things both visible and intelligible. And as «He overshadows you with His shoulders» (whatever «divine shoulders» are), «let His hand be found by those who are your enemies without cause», preserving you above their wicked ways, and «grinding» them under your feet «like the mud of the streets», and «in a fine old age» deeming you worthy of the kingdom of heaven.

Therefore at this point I ask you from now on not to allow the holy churches to stand neglected (for even a small matter is not small in important affairs), nor allow anyone to remain in the upper galleries, nor permit the houses of certain people to be built adjoining the holy churches; ⟨nor permit⟩ what no official has ever allowed to happen to his house, to be ventured by certain people, as an outrage to the holy churches. If then it is necessary to turn away from these practices for the sake of the honor and freedom of the holy churches, we will pay the necessary price, redeeming ourselves and them, too, from the frightful judgment in the world to come which awaits those who have scorned ⟨the divine⟩. For we are taught the terrible ⟨punishment⟩ of those who encroach on sacred property, and how much zeal we must show, by Christ Himself, Who struck with «a scourge» the base traffickers in divine

75 φραγελλίῳ τοὺς ἀναιδεῖς καὶ θεοκαπήλους, τοῦ μὴ ποιεῖν ἐμπορίου
οἴκους τοὺς τοῦ Θεοῦ.

εἰ οὖν λάβοιμεν πρόσωπα, προτιμῶντες φιλίας ἀνθρώπων Θεοῦ, οὐκ
οἶδα τί καὶ πεισόμεθα· οὐδὲ γὰρ ἀτιμώρητα τὰ τοιαῦτα εἰάθη ποτέ. εἰ δέ
που μνησθῆναι πρὸς ταῦτα καὶ ἁγίων φωνῶν δοκεῖ καὶ προφητικῶν, ὧδέ
80 ποι ἀκούσωμεν· τάδε λέγει Κύριος, ἀνθ᾽ ὧν ὁ οἶκός μού
ἐστιν ἔρημος, ὑμεῖς δὲ διώκετε ἕκαστος εἰς τὸν οἶκον
αὐτοῦ· διὰ τοῦτο ἀνέξει ὁ οὐρανὸς ἀπὸ δρόσου, καὶ ἡ
γῆ ὑποσταλῇ δοῦναι τὰ ἐκφόρια αὐτῆς. καὶ ἐπάξω ρομφαίαν ἐπὶ τὴν γῆν, καὶ ἐπὶ τὰ ὄρη, καὶ ἐπὶ τὸν σῖτον,
85 καὶ ἐπὶ τὸν οἶνον, καὶ ἐπὶ τὸ ἔλαιον, καὶ ὅσα ἐκφορεῖ
ἡ γῆ, καὶ ἐπὶ τοὺς ἀνθρώπους, καὶ ἐπὶ τὰ κτήνη, καὶ
ἐπὶ πάντας τοὺς πόνους τῶν χειρῶν αὐτῶν· ὧν τῆς τοιαύτης
τόλμης οἱ ἀφεξόμενοι καὶ ἑτέρους ἀπείργοντες ἐν τοῖς θείοις μὴ διαζῆν
πλημμελῶς, οὐ μόνον αὐτοὺς ἀλλὰ καὶ τοὺς πειθομένους ἐξαιρήσονται τῶν
90 ἀνιαρῶν, καὶ ὡς ἔκδικοι καὶ νουθετηταὶ τῶν καλῶν πολλοὺς τρυγήσουσι
τοὺς μισθούς, καὶ ἀνέκφραστον δρέψονται τὴν ἀντάμειψιν, δοξάζειν
ὑποσχομένου Θεοῦ τοὺς δοξάζοντας. κἂν τούτοις ἀγάμενος τὸ πρόθυμον καὶ μεγαλοφυὲς τῆς σῆς βασιλείας Θεὸς πρὸς τὰ κρείττω καὶ
τελεώτερα, οἷα πιστότατον λάτριν, αὐχήμασι καταστέψει ἀναριθμήτοις,
95 καὶ ὧδε κατ᾽ ἄμφω πολυωρήσας, καὶ τοῦ νυμφῶνος οἰκήτορα καταστήσει,
τῆς βασιλείας δηλονότι τῶν οὐρανῶν· γένοιτο, γένοιτο, γένοιτο, Κύριε.

67. Πρὸς τὸν αὐτοκράτορα ὅπως μὴ παντὶ βουλομένῳ λέγειν πιστεύῃ

Συνέσει κεκοσμημένην τὴν ἐκ Θεοῦ βασιλείαν σου πλήρη καὶ ἀνά-
λογον τῇ ἀρχῇ, δέομαι μὴ ὑπέχειν τὰς ἀκοὰς βουλομένῳ παντὶ λαλεῖν ἐμπαθῶς. τί γάρ, ἅγιε βασιλεῦ, καὶ ὀνήσει, ἀλλ᾽ οὐ μᾶλλον ἐξαφανίσει ἡμᾶς,
5 τὸ ἄσπορον ἐαθῆναι τὴν γῆν, τῶν ἡμετέρων ἐκβιαζόντων ἁμαρτημάτων
τὴν ἀγαθότητα τοῦ Θεοῦ συμφοραῖς ἐν ποικίλαις ἢ καὶ μαχαίρᾳ παραδι-
δόσθαι ἡμᾶς; καὶ ἀντὶ τοῦ ἡμᾶς δεικνύειν ἐπιστροφὴν ἀξιόχρεων καὶ
μετάνοιαν ἀξιόλογον, καὶ τῶν ματαίων ἡμῶν ἐπιτηδευμάτων ἀποστῆναι

75–76 cf. Joh. 2:15–16 ‖ 80–87 Agg. 1:9–11 ‖ 91–92 cf. I Reg. 2:30

---

75 φραγελλίῳ scripsi, cf. Joh. 2:15: φραγγελίῳ codd. ‖ τούς] τάς P ‖ 78 εἰάθη] εἴσθη P ‖
80 ἀκούσωμεν codd. ‖ 94 τελειώτερα S ‖ 95 πολιωρίσας codd.
67: V 46ʳ–46ᵛ. S 182ᵛ–183ʳ. P 62ʳ–62ᵛ. Ed. A. Laiou, *Byzantion*, 37 (1967), 108–
109.
1 post πιστεύῃ add. μηδὲ κωλύειν τοὺς καλλιεργοῦντας (καλιεργοῦντας Vʳ) τὴν γῆν VʳSP ‖
5 ἄσπορον] ἄπονον S

things, so that «they would not make the houses of God houses of merchandise».

If then we are influenced by personal bias, and prefer the love of men to that of God, I do not know what our fate will be; for such offenses have never been allowed to go unpunished. And if it seems a good idea to recall the holy words of the prophets on this subject, let us listen to them now: «Thus saith the Lord, because my house is desolate, and ye run every one into his own house; therefore shall the sky withhold dew, and the earth shall keep back her produce. And I will bring a sword upon the land, and upon the mountains, and upon the corn, and upon the wine, and upon the oil, and all that the earth produces, and upon the men, and upon the cattle, and upon all the labors of their hands.» Those who refrain from such rashness, and prevent others from living in an outrageous fashion on sacred property, will deliver not only themselves but those that heed them from their plight, and as defenders and advisors of the good they will reap many rewards, and will enjoy indescribable compensation, since God has promised «to glorify those who glorify» Him. Thus God, in admiration of the magnanimity and zeal of your majesty for the best and most perfect, will crown you with countless glories as His most faithful worshipper, and thus exalting you in both ⟨worlds⟩, He will make you to dwell in the bridechamber, that is in the kingdom of heaven. So be it, so be it, so be it, Lord.

67. To the emperor that he should not believe everyone who wishes to speak

I beg your divine majesty, adorned with complete wisdom in proportion to your authority, not to listen to everyone who wishes to speak passionately. For leaving the land unplanted, holy emperor, will bring more destruction than profit, seeing that it is our sins which force the goodness of God to deliver us over to various misfortunes, or even to the sword. And instead of demonstrating substantial conversion and marked repentance, and instead of vigorously turning aside from our foolish pursuits and wicked ways, so that

εὐτόνως καὶ τῶν πονηριῶν, ἵνα κοπάσῃ ἡ θραῦσις, καὶ ἵνα ἀλ-
10 λήλους ὀψώμεθα [fol. 46ᵛ] εἰς ἀγάπης παροξυσμὸν καὶ
ἔργων καλῶν καὶ θεοφιλῶν, μάλιστα ἀσχολούμεθα εἰς πενήτων ἐκπιεσμούς, καὶ τὸ ἄδικον καὶ φιλοκερδὲς τῶν λυττώντων ἐν τοῖς τοιούτοις
ἐξάπτομεν, ἐν συμφοραῖς ἀλλοτρίαις ἀποκερδαίνειν ἐπειγομένων,
καὶ πορισμῷ ἐπαράτῳ (φεῦ τῆς ζημίας!) σεμνυνομένων, καὶ εἰς μάστιγα
15 ἀνθρώπων λογιζομένων, ἀληθείας κρινούσης, οὐκ εἰς ὠφέλειαν.

πίστευσον, ἅγιε βασιλεῦ, οὐ πρὸς ἡμᾶς ἐπιφέρει τοὺς πολεμίους ἀ-
φθονία τῶν χρειωδῶν, ἀλλ᾽ ἡμῶν ἀκαρπία καὶ τὸ ὀπίσω πορεύεσθαι
τῆς καρδίας τῆς πονηρᾶς ἡμῶν ἕκαστον. καὶ εἴθε τοὺς διψῶντας
τοιαῦτα μὴ παρεχώρησας, ἀλλ᾽ ἐκέλευσας ἐμβριθῶς τοῦ πάντα τὸν εὑρισ-
20 κόμενον κακοπράγον συντριβὴν ὑπέχειν καὶ ἀτιμίαν καὶ ὄλεθρον (ἦν γὰρ
ἂν οὕτω ὁ τῆς δικαιοσύνης Θεὸς καὶ τῆς ἀγαθότητος ἱλεούμενος τὰ ἡμέτερα), ἀλλὰ μὴ ἀναστέλλειν, καὶ οὕτω πικρῶς, τοὺς γεωργεῖν ἐργάζεσθαι
τὰ χρειώδη προθυμουμένους, ἐναντία τῶν δωρεῶν τοῦ Θεοῦ. ἢ οὐχὶ διὰ
τοῦτο πρὸς τὸ μᾶλλον εὐχαριστεῖν καὶ δοξάζειν καὶ πρὸς ἀγαθοεργίαν
25 πᾶσαν ἐπείγεσθαι, ὅτι καὶ πονηροὺς ἡμᾶς ὄντας καὶ πάσης κακίας συντό-
νους ἐργάτας εἴπερ ποτέ, ὑετὸν ἡμῖν ἐχαρίσατο τὴν σήμερον πρώϊμον; κέλευσον οὖν, ἢ πειθοῖ ἢ βίᾳ, ἡμᾶς ἀγαθοεργεῖν· εἰ δ᾽ οὖν, ἀλλὰ κἂν
τοὺς τὴν γῆν γεωργοῦντας μὴ κώλυε. λέγω γὰρ τοῦτο καὶ λέγειν οὐ παύσομαι, ὡς ὅτι οὐ τὰ χρειώδη, οὐχ ὁ ἡμέτερος πλοῦτος, οὐχ ἡ ἐκείνων ἰσχύς,
30 ἢ ἡ ἐμπειρία ἡ ἐν πολέμοις, οὐ μὰ τὸ ναί, ἀλλὰ ὁ πρὸς τὴν ἁμαρτίαν σπου-
δαῖος καὶ ἀνεπίστροφος ἔρως ἡμῶν πλεονάζει τὰ εἰς ἡμᾶς ἐπώδυνα καὶ
ὀλέθρια.

68. Πρὸς τὸν αὐτοκράτορα

Ὅτι ἡ ἐξ ἁμαρτημάτων κοινῶν ἀνάγκη καὶ βία τὰ ἡμέτερα κομιδῇ
ἀπεστένωσε, πρὸς ζημίας καὶ ἀλλοκότους ἐξόδους καὶ κώμας καὶ τὰς πόλεις ἡμῶν συνελάσασα, καὶ συνάντημα παρὰ προσδοκίαν, οἶμαι μηδένα τῶν
5 καὶ ποσῶς συνιέντων ἀμφαγνοεῖν· ὅτι δὲ πάλιν οὐκ ἀλλαχόθι, ἀλλ᾽ ἐκ τῶν
ἡμετέρων καὶ βίᾳ ἐρανίζεσθαι τὰ πρὸς ἔξοδον ὁπωσδήποτε ἀρνηθείη οὐδείς. πλὴν ἀλλὰ δέον εὐσπλάγχνως ἐπάγειν καὶ συμπαθῶς ὡς καυτῆρας

67: 9 cf. Ps. 105(106):30 ‖ 9–11 Hebr. 10:24 ‖ 13 cf. Greg. Naz., Or. XVI, ιθ′ (PG,
XXXV, 960 B) ‖ 17–18 cf. Jer. 3:17 ‖ 26–27 cf. Joel 2:23 et Jer. 5:24

---

9 εὐτόνως] forsitan corrige ἐντόνως ‖ 10 ὀψόμεθα codd. ‖ 28 λέγω] λέγων S ‖ 29 οὐχ¹
Vsv
68: V 46ᵛ–47ʳ. S 183ʳ–184ʳ. P 63ʳ–63ᵛ.
1 ante πρὸς add. γράμμα VʳSP ‖ post αὐτοκράτορα add. περὶ τῶν ἰταμῶν καὶ (om. S)
αἱμοχαρῶν καὶ πλουτούντων (S¹, πλουτοῦντας VʳSP) τὸ κακόβουλον VʳSP ‖ 3 ἀλλοκό-
τας S

67, 68

«the slaughter might abate» and we might see ourselves «stirring up one another to love, and to good and pious works», we rather indulge in oppression of the poor, and kindle the injustice and greed of those who rage in such ⟨oppressions⟩, who hasten to benefit «from the misfortunes of others», and pride themselves on their accursed gains, alas, and are in truth counted among the scourges of mankind, rather than among its benefactors.

Believe me, holy emperor, it is not abundance of provisions which brings the enemy upon us, but the barrenness ⟨of⟩ our ⟨souls⟩, and the fact that each of us «walks behind a wicked heart». And would that you did not yield to those who yearn for this sort ⟨of profit⟩, but would issue a stern command that every evildoer who is found out should suffer ruin and disgrace and destruction (for thus the God of justice and goodness would have pity on us), rather than to ⟨be able⟩ pitilessly, nullifying the gifts of God, to restrain those who are eager to till the soil in order to earn their living. Or is it not true that ⟨we should⟩ offer more thanksgiving and praise, and strive to accomplish all good deeds, in gratitude for this ⟨blessing⟩, that today He granted «us unseasonably early rain», even though now more than ever we are wicked and eager perpetrators of every evil? Therefore urge us to do good deeds, either by permission or force. And in any case do not prevent people from tilling the earth. For I say now and will not cease to say, that it is not our food supplies, nor our wealth, nor the strength of the enemy, nor their experience in warfare, no by George, but it is our passionate and unrepentant love of sin which multiplies the grievous and ruinous misfortunes which befall us.

68. To the emperor

I do not think there is anyone with any intelligence who does not know that, because of the sins of us all, necessity and violence have wholly straitened our affairs, bringing damage and unusual expenses and unexpected calamities upon our cities and towns; nor again would anyone deny that the funds for expenses must in any case be collected not elsewhere, but from our own resources, even by the use of constraint. But still one should apply the hot irons with mercy and compassion, since they are irons applied to us all,

κοινούς, καὶ μηδὲ πρός τινος τῶν ἀσυμπαθῶν ἰταμοῦ καὶ αἱμοχαροῦς καὶ
πλουτοῦντος πολὺ τὸ κακόβουλον ἐνεργεῖσθαι, οἵους καὶ τὸ παρεληλυθὸς
10 ἀπήλεγξε [fol. 47ʳ] τοῦ καιροῦ Σικελοὺς καὶ ζωμεῖς, ἐρυσίβης καὶ
κάμπης μηδὲν ἢ μικρὸν ἀποδέοντας, ὧν καὶ αἱ πράξεις πρὸς ταῖς λοιπαῖς
ἁμαρτίαις ἡμῶν τὰς ἀνυποίστους ταύτας ἡμῖν συμφορὰς προσεπήνεγκαν.
ἔνθεν τὸ κράτος ἀντιβολοῦμεν τῆς ἐκ Θεοῦ βασιλείας σου, μὴ τῇ ἐκείνων
ὠμότητι καὶ πρὸς τὸ ἑξῆς προχωρῇ τὰ δεινά, ἀλλὰ τῇ καταπλουτισθείσῃ
15 αὐτῇ πρὸς Θεοῦ εὐσπλαγχνίᾳ τοῦ γένους καὶ οἴκτῳ καὶ ἡμερότητι, ὃ καὶ
τοῖς βλέπουσιν οὐκ ἠγνόηται, διεξαγέσθω καὶ τὰ πολιτικά.

πρὸς οἷς εὐεργετηθῆναι ἀντιβολοῦμεν καὶ γονάτων ἁπτόμεθα ταύτης, τὸ ὅσοις προενομεύθη μέλαθρα ἢ σκηναὶ τῆς πόρτης ἐκτός, εἰ ἐτησίως
καὶ ἀταράχως τὸ ὄφλημα καταβάλλονται, μὴ παντελῶς αὐτῶν ἐξοστρα-
20 κισθῆναι, ὡς ἐντεῦθεν ποριζομένοις γυναιξὶ καὶ παισὶ καὶ αὐτοῖς τὴν
τροφήν. ἐπεὶ καὶ μετὰ Θεὸν ἀπ' αὐτῆς καὶ τῶν ταύτης χαρίτων τῶν εὐερ-
γετικῶν ἡ ζωὴ αὐτοῖς προσδοκήσιμος, καὶ ἐκ ταύτης μετὰ Θεὸν ἐλπίσαντες καὶ ἐλπίζοντες, ἀλλ' ὅσον φανῇ τῇ φιλαγάθῳ βασιλικῇ διακρίσει καὶ
μεστῇ οἰκτιρμῶν, καὶ τούτοις ἐτησίως εἰς φόρον καταβαλέσθαι προστάξῃ,
25 ἀλλὰ μὴ ἀποστῆναι τελέως, εὐγνωμόνως ἀποπληροῖεν. μὴ οὖν ἄλλως, καὶ
αὖθις δεόμεθα, τὰ τοῦ πράγματος ἀποβῇ, ἐν τούτῳ κειμένου πολλοῦ τοῦ
μισθοῦ πρὸς Θεοῦ, καὶ εὐχῶν καὶ εὐχαριστίας τῆς πρὸς ἡμῶν τῇ οἰκτίρμονι ἐκ Θεοῦ βασιλείᾳ σου.

69. ⟨Πρὸς τὸν αὐτοκράτορα⟩

Τὸν μετ' ὀργῆς ἐκδικοῦντα δικαίας Θεόν, ἐν οἷς
κακῶς πράσσουσιν οἱ κακεργατοῦντες, διάκονον εἶναι τὸ στόμα
Χριστοῦ καὶ Θεοῦ βεβαιοῖ· ὅτι δὲ οἱ καλῶς καὶ ὡς φίλον ἐκείνῳ
5 διακονήσαντες βαθμὸν ἑαυτοῖς περιποιοῦνται καλὸν καὶ
παρρησίαν πολλὴν τῇ πίστει τῇ ἐν Χριστῷ Ἰησοῦ,
φανερόν. τί δὲ πρὸς ἀπολογίαν εὑρήσει ὁ πρὸς αὐτὸ τοῦτο τὴν μάχαιραν
χειρισθεὶς πρὸς Θεοῦ, καὶ μὴ κατὰ τὸ θέλημα τοῦ χειρίσαντος ἀνασείων

68: 10–11 cf. Joel 2:25
69: 2–4 cf. Rom. 13:4 ‖ 4–6 I Tim. 3:13

---

12 προσεπήνεγκαν] προσεπήρειαν P ‖ 19 καταβάλονται codd. ‖ 20 αὐτοῖς SP ‖ 22 προσ-
δοκόσιμος P ‖ 24 προστάξει codd. ‖ 25 ἀποπληροῖ P ‖ 27 καὶ om. P
69: V 47ʳ–50ᵛ. S 184ʳ–189ᵛ. P 63ᵛ–69ʳ.
1 γράμμα πρὸς τὸν αὐτοκράτορα πρὸς τοὺς χειρισθέντας φορεῖν τὴν μάχαιραν πρὸς Θεοῦ,
καὶ μὴ κατὰ τὸ θέλημα τοῦ χειρίσαντος ἀνασείων αὐτήν, ὅσα εἰς χόλον Θεοῦ παρορᾷ καὶ
ζημίαν ψυχῶν, καὶ περὶ τοῦ Τύρου καὶ τοῦ Ἀλεξανδρείας ὅπως ἐξέλθωσιν ἐκ τῆς πόλεως add.
VʳSP

68, 69

and the collection of taxes should not be entrusted to heartless people, who are reckless and murderous and full of bad advice, men whom past experience showed to be worthless Sicilians and blood-thirsty fellows, who are little or no better than «corn-rust and locusts», whose actions, in addition to the rest of our sins, have brought these unbearable misfortunes upon us. Wherefore I entreat your divine majesty not to allow the calamities resulting from their cruelty to go any further, but let civil affairs be administered with the compassion for the nation and mercy and gentleness which your majesty has received from God, as is well known to those who have eyes.

In addition I beg to be granted the following favor, and clasp your knees, that those people to whom huts or tents have been granted outside the gates, should not be driven from them if they pay the annual rent without any fuss, since from them they procure food for their wives and children and themselves. But since except for God they can expect to survive only through your assistance and generous favors, and except for God their only hope now, as it did in the past, lies in you, they would pay gladly whatever amount will seem fair to your good and royal discretion, which is full of compassion, and whatever you order them to pay as an annual rent, but don't turn them out completely. And again I beg of you, may this affair not be resolved differently, for there is at stake in this a great reward from God, and my prayers for and gratitude to your merciful divine majesty.

69. ⟨To the emperor⟩

The words of Christ confirm that «he who avenges God with righteous anger, when workers of iniquity do evil deeds, is, by this token, the minister of God». And it is obvious that those «who have served Him well», and as is pleasing unto Him, «purchase to themselves a good degree and great boldness in the faith which is in Christ Jesus». But what excuse will be made by the man who has been entrusted by God with the sword for this very purpose, but does not brandish it for total revenge in accordance with the will of the

αὐτὴν εἰς τελείαν ἐκδίκησιν; τοῦτο καὶ ὁ τῷ προφήτῃ Μιχαίᾳ μὴ ὑπακού-
10 σας, αὐτὸν πατάξαι κεκελευσμένος καὶ δῆθεν φεισάμενος, μαρτυρεῖ. οὐ
γὰρ τοῦ φιλανθρώπου φιλανθρωπότερον δέον εἶναι τινὰ σχηματίζεσθαι,
πειθόμενον τῷ θεσπίζοντι οὐδεὶς ἀγαθός, εἰ μὴ εἷς, ὁ Θεός.
ἃ οὖν ὁ Θεὸς ἁγίως ἐκέλευσε καὶ σωτηριωδῶς, τὸ ἀξίως παιδεύεσθαι φημὶ τοὺς κακούς, διασκεδάζειν οὐ δεῖ. τίς γάρ, εἰπέ μοι,
15 Μωσέως πρᾳότερος; [fol. 47ᵛ] ἀλλ᾽ ὅμως τὸν ξυλευσάμενον ἐν
Σαββάτῳ βληθῆναι λίθοις παρέδωκε. τί δέ; Φινεὲς οὐ ζήλῳ θείῳ
συνεκκεντήσας τῷ ὁμοεθνεῖ τὴν Μαδιανίτιν, τὴν ἐκ θείας
ὀργῆς ἐκόπασε θραῦσιν καὶ αἰωνίως δοξάζεται; εἰ δέ τις τὰ εἰς αὐτὸν
ἀνατρέχοντα καταφρονητικῶς παρορᾷ, ἢ ἀκολούθως τῇ ἐντολῇ συγχωρεῖ,
20 τοῦτο ἐπαινετόν· ἃ δὲ ὁρᾷ εἰς Θεοῦ παραλύπησιν καὶ ζημίαν ψυχῶν, εἰ
μὴ ἐπεξέρχεται μετὰ ζήλου, ἐλεεινότατον. εἰ δὲ καὶ τὸ ταπεινοῖ
ἄνδρα πενία παρακρουσάμενός τις, πλησμίως παραχωρεῖ τοῖς
ταράκταις τὰ ζωαρκῆ ἐπιρρεῖν, ἵνα καὶ ἄλλους δι᾽ εὐεργεσιῶν ὁπλίσωσι
συμμαχεῖν αὐτοῖς, οὐδὲν διαφέρει τοῦ θάλπειν ἐν κόλπῳ ὄφιν τινά· εἰ γάρ
25 τι μικρὸν συστραφῇ, πάντως δῆξιν ἐμποιήσει. τί δὲ καὶ τὸ εὖ ποίησον
εὐσεβεῖ, τοῦ δὲ ἀσεβοῦς μὴ ἀντιλαβοῦ παρὰ τῇ Γραφῇ; καὶ
γοῦν τῷ τὰ ἡμέτερα ἕκαστον ἕως νῦν ἐκδικεῖν καὶ ὑπὲρ τὸ δέον, τῶν δὲ
θείων πάντῃ καταφρονεῖν, ἀπολώλαμεν, σκεπτόμενοι δῆθεν οἰκονομεῖν,
καὶ ἐῶντες οἰκοδομεῖν.
30 διὰ τοῦτο ἑτερότροπος νόμος Κυρίου ἐξῆλθεν ἐξ Ἱερουσαλήμ, καὶ λόγος Κυρίου ἀποπεφοίτηκεν ἐκ Σιών, καὶ ποιμένες πολλοὶ τὸν ἀμπελῶνα τῆς ἐκκλησίας διέφθειραν. τίς
γὰρ ἐφρόντισε καταστροφὴν τὴν αὐτῆς, ἀπὸ τῆς τοῦ πατριάρχου κυροῦ
Ἀρσενίου ἡμέρας, ἢ θρηνεῖν πρὸς Θεὸν ὑπὲρ ταύτης, εἰ μὴ ἄλλως ἠδύνατο
35 βοηθεῖν, ἢ δυνάμενος τὴν σύστασιν ταύτης ἀνελλιπῶς ἠγωνίσατο πρό τινὸς ἄλλου μετὰ Θεόν, ἵνα καυχήσηται καὶ αὐτὸς ἐν καιρῷ ἀνάγκης ἢ καὶ
θανάτου, μνήσθητι, Κύριε, ὡς ἐπορεύθην ἐνώπιόν σου
μετὰ ἀληθείας, ἐν καρδίᾳ ἀληθινῇ, καθὼς ἐθάρρησέ τις
καυχήσασθαι, ἵνα καταξιωθῇ καὶ τὸ ἤκουσα τῆς φωνῆς σου πρὸς
40 τοῦ Θεοῦ ἐνωτίσασθαι;
διὰ ταῦτα λυποῦμαι τὰ μέγιστα, διεσπασμένην ὁρῶν τὴν νύμφην
Χριστοῦ, καὶ πάνυ ὀλίγους τοὺς συναλγοῦντας αὐτῇ, λύπῃ τε καὶ πτωχείᾳ
πιεζομένους, τοὺς δὲ καταστρέφοντας ἐν ἀφθονίᾳ πολλῇ καὶ χαρᾷ. καὶ μὴν
ἐν βεβαίῳ μοι ἤκουσται ὡς ὦφθαι τῶν σχιζομένων τινὶ αὐτὸς ὁ Σωτὴρ

9–10 III Reg. 21:35–36 || 12 Matt. 19:17 || 13–14 locum non inveni || 15 cf. Num. 12:3 ||
15–16 cf. Num. 15:32 || 16–17 cf. Greg. Naz., Or. XIV, γ′ (PG, XXXV, 861A) || 18 cf.
Ps. 105(106):30 || 19 cf. Luc. 11:4, Matt. 6:12 || 21–22 Prov. 10:4 || 25–26 cf. Sirac. 12:2,
4, 5 || 30–31 cf. Mic. 4:2 || 31–32 Jer. 12:10 || 37–38 Is. 38:3 || 39 Is. 38:5

24 τοῦ] τὸ codd. || 26 εὐσεβεῖ scripsi, cf. Sirac. 12:2; εὐσεβῆ codd.

69

One Who entrusted it to him ? The man who did not heed the prophet Micah, when he was ordered to strike him, but spared him, also bears witness to this; for one should not make a pretence of loving man more than the Lover of Man, but should heed the One Who declares, «there is none good but one, that is, God». Therefore one should not mock the salutary and holy precept of God, namely that «the wicked should be punished as they deserve». For tell me, who was «meeker than Moses» ? Yet even he handed over to be stoned «that man who cut wood on the Sabbath». What then ? Did not Phinees in his divine zeal «stab his fellow countryman together with the Madianite woman», and thus «abate the slaughter» caused by divine wrath, for which he is eternally praised ? If someone disregards as of little account matters affecting himself, or, in accordance with the commandment, permits them to happen to him, this is praiseworthy. But it is most pitiable if he does not pursue with zeal matters which cause grief to God and harm to our souls. And if, moreover, one pays no heed to the proverb, «poverty brings a man low», and allows troublemakers to have an abundance of the necessities of life, so that through their own benefactions they might arm others to form an alliance with them, it is no different than for someone to cherish a serpent at his breast; for if it is squeezed even a little, it will bite him. And what about the words of the Scriptures, «Do good to the pious man, but do not help the impious one» ? Indeed because up to this point each of us has defended our own interests even more than is necessary, but has totally despised sacred matters, we are undone, presumably bent that we are on the principle of accommodation, but in fact neglecting that of edification.

For this reason a different sort of «law of the Lord went forth from Jerusalem, and the word of the Lord» departed «from Sion», and «many shepherds have destroyed the vineyard» of the Church. For who has been concerned to lament to God the decline of ⟨the Church⟩ ever since the time of the patriarch Kyr Arsenius, if he could help in no other way, or, if he did have the strength, struggled unceasingly for her protection more than anyone else except God, so that he too might boast at a time of necessity or death, «Remember, O Lord, how I have walked before thee in truth, with a pure heart» (as someone once made bold to boast), and so that he may also be deemed worthy to hear God say, «I have heard thy voice» ?

Therefore I am extremely distressed when I see the bride of Christ thus torn asunder, and that very few share her pain (and these are burdened with sorrow and poverty), while the destroyers ⟨of the Church⟩ enjoy abundance and good cheer. Indeed I truly heard that the Savior Himself, hanging on the Cross, appeared in a vision to one of the schismatics, and His holy

45 κρεμάμενος ἐν σταυρῷ, διεσπασμένης ἐν μέρεσι πέντε τῆς ἁγίας αὐτοῦ
σαρκός. ἀνοιμώξαντος οὖν γοερὸν τοῦ ὁρῶντος, καὶ τὸν τολμητὴν τοῦ φρικώδους ζητοῦντος, «ὑμεῖς», τὸν Σωτῆρα φάναι πρὸς τὸν ζητοῦντα, «'Αρείῳ
ὁμοιωθέντες εἰς δύναμιν, πλὴν ὅσον ἐκεῖνος μὲν τὸν χιτῶνά μου, ὑμεῖς δὲ
τὴν σάρκα ὡς ὁρᾷς διεθήκατε.» καὶ ὑπολάβοι τις ἄν, ὡς ἐγώ φημι, τὴν
50 πρώτην ῥῆξιν τὴν μετὰ τῶν [fol. 48ʳ] 'Ιταλῶν ἕνωσιν· δευτέραν τὴν τῶν
'Αρσενιανῶν· τρίτην δὲ καὶ τετάρτην Αἰγυπτίων καὶ Τυρίων, καὶ ὅσοι
ἐκεῖθεν σὺν τούτοις πρὸς ἡμᾶς ἐνεδη⟨μή⟩σαντο ἐπὶ καταστροφῇ τοῦ κα-
λοῦ· πέμπτην πρὸς τούτοις τὸν λαμπρὸν ὁρμαθὸν τῶν καλῶν ἱερέων, καὶ
τὸν διεγηγερμένον αὐτῶν ἐπὶ σφετέρῳ κακῷ καὶ ἐπὶ καταλύσει τῆς ἐκ-
55 κλησίας συνασπισμόν· καὶ γοῦν ἑνὸς ἐξ αὐτῶν «εἰς βεβαίωσιν» λόγος ᾀδόμενος τὴν αὐτῶν κατάστασιν βεβαιοῖ. ποίας γὰρ καταστροφῆς φείσονται οἱ
τάφον ἀνεῳγμένον τὸν λάρυγγα ἔχοντες; ἢ τί δυσωδέστερον
ὁ τάφος ἐρεύξεται τοῦ ὄνου ἐσαγισμένον παρεικάσαι μὴ φρίξαντος, ὡς
λόγος, τὰ πάντιμα; ἢ πρὸς τί ἀποβλέπει καὶ ἡ τοῦ Τύρου ἐν τῇ 'Οδηγη-
60 τρίᾳ ἀναστροφή; πάντως εἰς ὄλεθρον τῆς οἰκείας ψυχῆς, εἰς ὄλεθρον τῶν
ὁρώντων καὶ ἀκουόντων, εἰς λύμην τῶν τῆς μονῆς καὶ εἰς καταπολέμησιν
καὶ λαθραίαν καὶ φανεράν, ὡς βλέπομεν, τῆς ἀβοηθήτου ἐκκλησίας. τὰ δὲ
τοῦ λεγομένου 'Αλεξανδρείας κατά τε Θεοῦ καὶ τῆς οἰκείας ψυχῆς καὶ τῶν
ἀτύχων μονῶν ἐγχειρήματα, †καὶ τῆς ὡς† δίκην ἀγρίας θυέλλης ἀναπ-
65 τομένης ταῖς αὔραις τοῦ πονηροῦ, ὑπ' αὐτοῦ διεσκεμμέναις τέχ-
ναις καὶ μηχαναῖς κατὰ τῆς ἐκκλησίας, ἐπαγαλλομένου τῇ καταδύσει
αὐτῆς, οὐ δυνήσομαι εἰ θελήσω καὶ διηγήσασθαι κἄν τι τῶν μυριοστῶν
ἐξειπεῖν, πλὴν ὅτι κεκράτηκε καὶ λελάληκεν ὁ τῶν θαυμασίων
Θεός, ἣν καὶ κεκράτηκε καὶ παρέθηξε γλῶσσαν καὶ καρδίαν, θριαμβεῦ-
70 σαι καὶ στηλιτεῦσαι τούτου ὅσα καὶ δεῖ, ἵνα μὴ λανθάνειν εἰς τέλος πονηρία
δόξῃ κατακαυχήσασθαι.
ὅθεν καὶ μᾶλλον ἀσχάλλω, πῶς τοῖς λαχοῦσι τὸ κρίνειν καὶ τὸ
δίκαιον διανέμειν ἀπὸ Θεοῦ, ἐκεῖνο μόνον ἔαται ἀδίκαστον, τὸ μὴ προβὰν
εἰς φανέρωσιν. ἐν δὲ τοῖς νῦν ὑβρισταῖς οὐχ ἁπλῶς τὰ αὐτῶν ἀκουόμενα,
75 ἀλλὰ καὶ ψηλαφηθέντα καὶ τρανωθέντα πολλάκις, καὶ ἀκοαῖς πεσόντα
πολλῶν, καὶ τὴν ποιότητα τῆς καταστροφῆς, τοῖς μὴ βουλομένοις
τυφλώττειν τῇ τῶν καλῶν καταδύσει δίκην ἡλίου φαινούσης, ὁ κολάζων
δικαίως, πάντως οὐδείς· καὶ οὐ μόνον ⟨οὐ⟩ καταδικάζονται, ἀλλὰ καὶ τῆς
προτέρας εὐεργεσίας καὶ παρρησίας ἐπαπολαύουσι (παθαίνεται γὰρ ταῦτα

47–49 cf. epistola Alexandri episcopi Alexandrini, Theodoretus, *Eccl. Hist.*, I, 4 (ed.
Parmentier [Leipzig, 1911], 9–10); Nic. Call. Xanthopoulos, *Eccl. Hist.*, VIII, vii (PG,
CXLVI, 32D) ‖ 56–57 cf. Rom. 3:13 ‖ 65 cf. Greg. Naz., *Or.* XXI, ιδ' (PG, XXXV, 1096C) ‖
68–69 cf. Ps. 76(77):15

---

45 διεσπασμένοις codd. ‖ 49 ὑπολάβει codd. ‖ 52 ἐνεδημήσαντο coni. Ševčenko; ἐνεδήσαντο
codd. ‖ 64 καὶ ... ὡς non satis perspicio, cf. *Ep.* 81,85: δίκην θυέλλης ὡς ἐκ τυφῶνος
δεινοῦ ‖ 76 ποιότητα coni. Ševčenko, πιότητα codd. ‖ 78 οὐ² addidi

69

flesh was torn into five pieces. When the witness ⟨of the vision⟩ lamented mournfully, and asked who had dared to commit this dreadful deed, the Savior said to him: «It is you, who resemble Arius as much as is possible, except that he did this only to my tunic, whereas you all have done it to my flesh, as you see». One would assume, I think, that the first tear was union with the Italians, the second tear is by the Arsenites, the third and fourth are by the Egyptians and Tyrians, and their associates who have come to us from those places in order to destroy the good. The fifth in addition to these is that shining cluster of fine priests, and the conspiracy devised by them for their own misfortune and for the dissolution of the Church. For indeed a famous speech by one of them, called «In confirmation», does confirm their stand. For what destruction will be spared by those whose «throat is an open sepulchre»? What does the sepulchre vomit forth that is fouler than the man who did not shrink to compare the most holy objects with a saddled ass, as the story goes? Or what is the ⟨expected⟩ outcome of the residence of the metropolitan of Tyre at the monastery of the Hodegetria? Total destruction of his own soul, the destruction of those who see and hear him, the defilement of the inhabitants of the monastery, and, as we ⟨plainly⟩ see it, a secret and open war against the helpless Church. As for the attacks of the so-called patriarch of Alexandria against God and his own soul and the hapless monasteries, like a wild storm (?) stirred up by «the gales of the Devil», who rejoices in the downfall of the Church caused by the tricks and machinations he contrives against Her, I could not tell and recount the ten thousandth part, even if I should wish, were it not that «the God of marvels» has taken hold and spoken through a certain heart and tongue, ⟨namely mine⟩, of which he took hold and which he sharpened to triumph over and scorn this ⟨evil man⟩, however it is necessary, so that wickedness may not in the end appear to triumph undetected.

Wherefore I am especially distressed that men who have been appointed by God to judge and to distribute righteousness ⟨usually⟩ only allow to escape judgment ⟨a crime⟩ which has not been brought to light, but in the case of the present offenders, there is absolutely no one who justly punishes their crimes, not simply the ones which are reported, but frequently even crimes which have been investigated and clearly revealed, which are indeed common knowledge, or the enormity of ⟨their moral⟩ ruin which shines as brightly as the sun for those who do not wish to close their eyes to the decline of the good. And not only are they ⟨not⟩ condemned, but they enjoy their former benefits and access ⟨to the emperor⟩—Abbakoum also speaks passion-

80 καὶ Ἀββακούμ), τοῖς δὲ ἀσθενέσι καὶ λύμη προσγίνεται, καὶ καταθράττει
πολλοὺς ἢ ζητεῖν Κοιρανίδας ἢ ἐκείναις ἀνατιθέναι τὸ πᾶν.

ἐγὼ δὲ ἐν τῷ Θεῷ μου τὰ τοιαῦτα μὲν [fol. 48ᵛ] ὑπερ-
βήσομαι· ὃ δέ μοι πρέπον ζητεῖν, διηγήσομαι· τῶν λίαν ἀδικωτάτων
δοκῶ, τὸ ἑκάστην τῶν πόλεων τοῖς τῶν Ῥωμαίων σκήπτροις ὑποτελῆ,
85 μὴ ἐπ' ἀδείας ἔχειν ἄλλης ποιμένα ἐν τῇ μὴ ὑποκειμένη
χειροτονεῖν, ἢ τινὸς κατεξουσιάζειν, ἢ καὶ τὸ τοῦ ταύτης ποιμένος
σιωπᾶν ὄνομα, ἐν δὲ τῇ βασιλίδι κατὰ πολὺ πράττεσθαι. εἰ δέ γε ποτὲ καὶ
ψῆφος συνοδικὴ τι τοιοῦτον κατ' οἰκονομίαν ἐνέδωκεν, ἀγαπητικῇ καὶ
κοινῇ διασκέψει καὶ ἀφορώσῃ πρὸς σωτηρίαν, οὐ πρὸς ἀπώλειαν, οὐδὲ τὸ
90 πρὸς τὸ ἀντικαθέζεσθαι καὶ κατεξανίστασθαι τῆς πνευματικῆς εὐταξίας
καὶ ποιμένος κανονικοῦ· εὑρήσω καὶ γάρ, εἰ ζητήσω, τοὺς βουλομένους
ἐντὸς τῆς μεγαλοπόλεως, εἰδήσεως ἄνευ, οὐχ ἱερεῖς μόνον χειροτονήσαν-
τας ἔξω τοῦ δέοντος, ἀλλὰ καὶ ἐπίσκοπον, ὡς ἔθος Ἀλεξανδρεῦσιν ἐν
οἴκῳ Παύλου χοραύλου τινός, ἵνα ἐάσω τὰ τῶν ἐμπαθῶς καθημένων
95 μοναχῶν καὶ μοναζουσῶν, ἅτινα διὰ τούτων ἢ δι' ἐκείνων φέρεται
ἀδιόρθωτα.

τί δέ, εἰ ὅτε τῷ Τύρου δοκεῖ ἱερεῖς ἀποπαύειν καὶ διακόνους, ἢ τῷ
Ἀλεξανδρείας δέχεσθαι οὓς ἐθέλοι καταλόγῳ ὀρθοδοξούντων, καὶ ἀπο-
βάλλεσθαι ἄλλους, καὶ συνόδου καὶ πατριάρχου τῶν ὧδε καταφρυάτ-
100 τεσθαι, τοῦ μὴ κρίνεσθαι ὑπ' αὐτοῦ, αὐτὸν δὲ τὰ ἡμέτερα ταλαντεύειν ἐν
ἐξουσίᾳ, ὡς ἄλλον Θεόφιλον; πλὴν αἱ δοκοῦσαι τοιαῦται οἰκονομίαι, ὡς
ἔφην, κατέστρεψαν τὴν οἰκοδομήν, καὶ εἰ μὴ βλέψομεν πρὸς τὴν τούτων
διόρθωσιν, καὶ πλέον ἰσχύσουσι.

διὰ τί δὲ καὶ σχηματισαμένου τοῦ Τύρου, ἢ ἄλλου τινὸς τοιούτου,
105 ἐξελθεῖν τῶν ὧδε, τινὲς ἐμποδίζουσι, συμβουλευόντων τῶν τῆς εἰρήνης
τάχα δοκούντων καὶ ἡμετέρων, τῇ δὲ ἀληθείᾳ ὁμοίως ἐκείνοις περιθαλ-
πόντων τὸ φιλοτάραχον ἐν καρδίαις κατὰ τῆς ἐκκλησίας Χριστοῦ, ὅτι μὴ
οἰκουμενικὴν προξενήσωσι ζημίαν ἢ ταραχήν; ἀλλὰ μὴ γένοιτο τοῦτο,
Χριστὲ βασιλεῦ, ὡς ἀπρονόητα οὕτως ὑπολαμβάνειν τινὰ τῶν ἀνάστασιν
110 ἐλπιζόντων, τοῦ ἐν θελήσει κεῖσθαι τοῦ Τύρου καὶ τοῦ Ἀλεξανδρείας καὶ
τῶν ὁμοίων ἐκείνοις, ἐπιφέρειν ὅτε καὶ θέλουσι Χριστιανοῖς ὄλεθρον· καὶ
μὴν μυριοπλασίως τὴν κακίαν καὶ πονηρίαν καὶ συσκευὴν ὁ Σατάν, οὐκ
Ἀλεξανδρέων μόνον ἢ καὶ Τυρίων, ἀλλὰ καὶ πάντων τῶν ἀπ' αἰῶνος καὶ
μέχρι συντελείας κακῶν. εἰ δὲ τὸ πέλαγος τῆς κακίας ἀδυνατεῖ, κἂν
115 πρὸς χοίρου σταγὼν τί δυνήσεται; πλὴν οἱ ταῦτα τερατευόμενοι μάταιοι,
ὡς μὴ χαλινοῖς προνοίας προσκυ-[fol. 49ʳ] ροῦντες ὁδηγεῖσ-
θαι τὸ πᾶν· οὐδὲ γὰρ ἔστι κακία ἐν πόλει, ἣν οὐκ ἐποίησε
Κύριος, ἕκαστον δέον φρονεῖν τὴν ἐξ ἡμετέρων ἁμαρτημάτων, φημί,

---

82–83 cf. Ps. 17(18):30 ‖ 85–86 cf. Can. Apost. 35 ‖ 116–117 cf. Greg. Naz, Or.. XVI, ε′
(PG, XXXV, 940 B) ‖ 117–118 cf. Amos 3:6

---

115 χοίρους codd. ‖ 116 προσκυνοῦντες SP

69

ately about this—and corruption taints the ⟨morally⟩ weak and provokes many either to seek *Koiranides* or to entrust everything to these ⟨books⟩.

But «by my God I will pass over» such matters, and will tell what it is proper for me to seek. For I consider it extremely unjust that in every other city subject to Roman rule «the bishop» of another ⟨city⟩ «does not» have the right «to perform ordinations in a city not subject to him», or to exercise authority over someone, or to omit to mention ⟨in the diptychs⟩ the name of the bishop of that city, but here in the capital this is a frequent occurrence. And if ever a vote of the synod permitted such a thing by way of accommodation, it was for the purpose of charitable and general discussion with a view to salvation, not perdition, nor with a view to sitting in opposition and revolting against spiritual order and a canonically elected bishop. For if I look around, I can find people who in the capital, without notification, have not only ordained priests in an improper fashion, but even a bishop, as is the habit of the Alexandrians in the house of a certain flutist Paul, not to mention the actions of the monks and nuns who are passionately inclined, actions which remain uncorrected either by the former or by the latter (?).

What about the metropolitan of Tyre, who thinks he can relieve priests and deacons of their duties, or the patriarch of Alexandria, who decides to accept whomever he likes in the ranks of orthodox, and to reject others, and to behave insolently toward the synod and patriarch here in the capital, refusing to be judged by him [the patriarch of Constantinople], while at the same time he himself weighs my actions in authority, like a second Theophilus ? But as I have said, such apparent accommodations have destroyed the structure ⟨of the Church⟩, and if we do not attempt to remedy the situation, they will prevail even more.

Why, when the metropolitan of Tyre (or his like) makes a pretence of leaving here, do certain people prevent them, following the advice of those who appear to be men of peace and on our side, but, in truth, like the others, nourish in their hearts a love of stirring up trouble against the Church of Christ, except that they bring about *universal* harm and disorder ? May it not happen, O Christ our King, that any person who has hope in the Resurrection may assume that it is possible for the metropolitan of Tyre and the patriarch of Alexandria and their like to desire to bring destruction upon Christians whenever they want, without the nod of Providence! Satan himself ⟨brings about⟩ ten thousand times worse injustice and wickedness and intrigue, ⟨encompassing⟩ not only that of Alexandrians and Tyrians, but also of all evil people from the beginning to the end of the world, ⟨yet he, too, cannot bring these evil deeds about⟩ without the nod of Providence. And if ⟨Satan⟩, the sea of wickedness, is powerless, how will a drop coming from swine have any power ? But those who speak of these marvels are foolish men, since they do not affix validity to the fact that everything «is guided by the bridle of Providence». For «in a city there is no evil which the Lord has not wrought», I mean, everyone must bear in mind the destructive punishment which

παρὰ τοῦ τιθέντος ζυγῷ τὰ ἡμέτερα κακωτικὴν ἐπεξέλευσιν. καθ᾽ ὅσον
120 γὰρ ἔξω τῶν θείων θεσμῶν εὑρισκόμεθα, ἀναλόγως τῶν θείων κριμάτων
τὸ ἀψίνθιον ἐκροφήσομεν νῦν ἢ καὶ ὕστερον· οὐδὲ γὰρ λείψει τοῖς ἁμαρ-
τάνουσιν ἡ διὰ πονηρῶν ἀγγέλων ἀποστολή. ὅθεν καὶ δεῖ, οὐκ
ἐκεῖνον ἢ τοῦτον, ἀλλὰ τὸν ἐπόπτην τῶν ὅλων φοβεῖσθαι Θεόν· καὶ οὐδένα
ἄλλον φοβηθησόμεθα εἰ ὡς αὐτῷ ἀρεστὸν διατιθέναι τὰ ἐν χερσὶ σπεύδο-
125 μεν. οἱ γὰρ ἀποθεραπεύειν κακοὺς μηχανώμενοι, ἀζημίως ὀφείλουσι τοῦτο
δρᾶν, οὐκ ἐπὶ παροργισμῷ τοῦ Θεοῦ.
καὶ σκόπει, παρακαλῶ· κατέλαβε διὰ τὰς ἐμὰς ἁμαρτίας ἡ ἐνθήκη
τῶν δέκα πληγῶν. ἀπήλαυσε δόξης βασιλικῆς καὶ τῶν τῆς συγκλήτου·
ἐπλήσθη ὁ κόλπος αὐτοῦ δωρεῶν· δουλεύειν αὐτῷ καὶ μοναὶ ἀνδρῶν εἰς τὸ
130 σωθῆναι τάχα συναθροισθέντων ἐδόθησαν. εἰ μὲν διὰ τὴν τούτου ἀπώλειαν ἐγεγόνει τὸ εὐεργέτημα, σιωπῶ, πρὸς τὸν σκοπὸν ἐκβάντος τοῦ
πράγματος· εἰ δὲ δι᾽ ἃ ἐφορᾷ Θεὸς ἀγαθά, ἔδοξεν εὐεργετηθῆναι,
ἄκουε οὐρανέ, καὶ ἐνωτίζου ἡ γῆ· ἐπικατάρατος δὲ πᾶς ὁ
λέγων γλυκὺ τὸ πικρόν.
135 εἰπὲ δέ, καὶ ὁ τούτῳ προσκείμενος οὐ διὰ ταῦτα ἀλλότριος ἐγεγόνει
τῆς κλήσεως, ἧς εἰς κενὸν ὀνομάζεται; ἐν δεῖγμα ἐρῶ τῆς τούτου φιλοθεΐ-
ας· τὸν Κύριον ἡμῶν καὶ Θεὸν Ἰησοῦν Χριστὸν ἐν εἰκόνι ἱστάμενον
εἰς τὸ προσκυνεῖσθαι ἐν τῇ μονῇ τοῦ Μεγάλου Ἀγροῦ, ὁ δικαίῳ σταλεὶς
παρ᾽ αὐτοῦ οὐκ ἔφριξεν ὁ θεοστυγὴς διασπάσαι καὶ στήλην βασιλικὴν κο-
140 λακείᾳ ἀντιστηλῶσαι τυφλούμενος. εἰ δὲ καὶ παρὰ γνώμην τούτου εἴποις
γενέσθαι, τί πεποίηκε γνούς; πλὴν καὶ οἱ λέγοντες συναπορραγῆναι τούτῳ
τὰ πέρατα, ὁ κλῆρος Ἀλεξανδρείας εἰσὶν ἢ οἱ ἐπίσκοποι; τοὺς τῆς Νιτρίας
γὰρ μοναχοὺς ὁ τούτου ὁμότροπος ἀνεστάτωσεν. ἀλλὰ ὁ Ἀντιοχείας; ἀλλὰ
ὁ Ἱεροσολύμων καὶ οἱ ὑπ᾽ αὐτούς; ἀπορραγῆναι δὲ ἔχει μεγάλη στρατο-
145 πεδάρχισσα, μεγάλη δομεστίκισσα, καὶ Σιδηριώτισσα καὶ ὅσαι τοιαῦται;
τί δέ; καὶ σήμερον οὐκ ἀποδιΐστανται; τί δὲ καὶ οἱ παραβάλλοντες τούτῳ
καὶ τάχα ἡμέτεροι ἢ καὶ σύντροφοι λόγῳ; ἕνεκεν λόγου; οὐδαμῶς!
ἕνεκεν ἀρετῆς; καὶ τίς ὁ σήμερον ἀγαπῶν ἀρετήν; ἓν μόνον ἐστὶν ὑπολα-
βεῖν, [fol. 49ᵛ] διὰ τρόπου ὁμοίωσιν, ὅτι καὶ φίλον ἀεὶ τῷ ὁμοίῳ
150 τὸ ὅμοιον.
διὰ τοῦτο δέον τὸν συνιόντα καθέζεσθαι καταμόνας καὶ θρηνεῖν
πρὸς Θεόν, πῶς ἐσμικρύνθημεν, πῶς ἐσμὲν ταπεινοί, διὰ τὰς ἁμαρτίας
ἡμῶν, μικροῦ παρὰ πάντα τὰ ἔθνη, καὶ ταῖς τῶν πολλῶν παρασυρόμεθα
εὑρεσιλογίαις. τί γάρ; οὐχὶ τὴν ἐκκλησίαν ἡμεῖς ἐῶμεν καταστραφῆναι;
155 τί γὰρ ὁ Χαλκηδόνος; οὐκ ἐξήντλησε τὰ τοῦ Κοσμιδίου, ὡς καὶ μέχρι νῦν
οἱ πολλοὶ τοῦ Ξιφιλίνου τοῦτον ὀνομάζειν ἀρχιερέα; οὐχὶ κάθηται πλησίον

---

122 cf. Ps. 77(78):49 ‖ 133 Is. 1:2 ‖ 133–134 cf. Is. 5:20 ‖ 149–150 cf. Arist., *Ethica Nicomachea*, 1165ᵇ 17

---

123 ἐκείνων ἢ τούτων codd. ‖ 124 εἰ] ἢ codd. ‖ 142 νιτνίας S ‖ 155 τί] τίς codd.

comes as a result of our sins from the One Who weighs our deeds on the balance scale. For to the extent that we transgress divine ordinances, to such an extent will we swallow the bitter wormwood of divine judgment either now or later; for sinners will not escape the «message by evil angels». Therefore we must fear not this or that ⟨person⟩, but God Who oversees all things; and then we will fear no one else, if we hasten to arrange matters at hand in a manner pleasing to Him. For those who try to heal the wicked ought to do this without causing any harm and without provoking God to anger.

Just look, I beg of you; on account of my sins, the entire gamut of ten plagues has overwhelmed us. He [i.e., the patriarch of Alexandria] has enjoyed honor from the emperor and from the members of the senate; his lap has been filled with gifts, and monasteries of men who had supposedly gathered together for salvation were handed over to him as slaves. If this largesse was given to him on account of his wickedness, then I keep silence, since the measure has fulfilled its purpose; but if it was decided to reward him on account of good qualities, looked upon by God, then «Hear, O heaven, and hearken, O earth», for accursed is everyone who calls «the bitter sweet.»

Tell me then, wasn't the accomplice of this man [the patriarch of Alexandria] deprived for these reasons of the title which he was given to no purpose? I will tell you one example of this man's love of the divine: the God-hated agent whom he sent did not hesitate to destroy the image of our Lord and God Jesus Christ, represented on an icon in order to be venerated, in the monastery of the Great Field, nor did he hesitate to set up an image of the emperor in its place in blind flattery. If you should say that the incident took place without the knowledge of the aforementioned ⟨patriarch of Alexandria⟩, then what has he done, having once learned ⟨about this⟩? Those who say that the ends ⟨of the world⟩ will split off in schism together with this man, do they mean the clergy or the bishops of Alexandria? For a man of similar persuasions upset the monks of Nitria. Or do they mean the patriarch of Antioch, the patriarch of Jerusalem and their followers? Will the wife of the great stratopedarch and the wife of the great domestic, and Sideriotissa and their like split off in schism? What? Aren't they in schism already today? And why do people who are supposedly on our side or my nominal friends go over to this man [the patriarch of Alexandria]? Is it for the sake of wisdom? By no means! For the sake of virtue? And who loves virtue these days? One must assume that it is for only one reason, similarity of manner, since «like is always attracted to like».

For this reason the man of understanding must sit by himself and lament to God how our circumstances have been reduced, how we are humbled on account of our sins, almost more than any other nation, and how we are led astray by the sophistical arguments of the many. But why? Are we not allowing the Church to be destroyed? What about the metropolitan of Chalcedon? Did he not exhaust the ⟨resources⟩ of the Kosmidion monastery, so that even now people call him high priest of Xiphilinus? Doesn't he reside near

ἡμῶν, καὶ οἱ βουλόμενοι εἰς ὕβριν τῆς ἐκκλησίας πρὸς αὐτὸν συναθροίζονται; τί δὲ ὁ Σάρδεων; οὐχὶ τὸν ἱερουργοῦντα ἐκώλυσεν ἀναφέρειν συνήθως τὸ ὄνομα ὡσαύτως καὶ οἱ λοιποί; εἰ οὖν πλουτοῦντες αὐτοὶ καὶ τοὺς αὐτοῖς
160 προσκειμένους εὐεργετοῦντες, καὶ κατερευγόμενοι ἐκ τῶν τῆς ἐκκλησίας, πότε καὶ παύσονται; καὶ εἰ δέον εὐεργετεῖσθαι αὐτούς, μήποτε κακοὶ γένωνται, ἐπεὶ ἐγένοντο ταῦτα ἔχοντες, ἄλλας ὀφείλομεν εὐεργεσίας δοῦναι αὐτοῖς; ἀλλ᾽ οὗτοι οἱ λόγοι τῶν μὴ συναγόντων μετὰ Χριστοῦ.
πλὴν δέομαι, λόγῳ δοκιμάσας, ἐξωσθήτωσαν ὁ Χαλκηδόνος, ὁ
165 Περγάμου καὶ οἱ λοιποί, μὴ ἐχέτωσαν τὰ τῶν ἐκκλησιῶν, ἢ καὶ ὁ Ἀλεξανδρείας, ἵνα γνωρίσωμεν τίνες ἀποσπασθήσονται σήμερον ἐξ ἡμῶν ἀκολουθῆσαι αὐτοῖς· ὅτι δὲ καὶ οἱ σκαιωροῦντες τισὶ τὰ κακά, εἰ μὴ ἀπολυθῇ ἄνωθεν, εἰς μάτην κατεφλυάρησαν, ἀναμφίλεκτα· καὶ τούτου πολλὰ τὰ μαρτύρια — οὐ μόνον τὸ ἠριθμῆσθαι τὴν τρίχα, ἀλλ᾽ οὐδὲ
170 πίπτειν στρουθίον τῇ πάγῃ προνοίας χωρὶς τὸ σμικρότατον — καὶ δὴ καὶ τοῖς μὴ παραπαίουσιν ἑκοντί, ἡ τοῦ θεοστυγοῦς Θεοκτίστου καὶ τῶν ὁμοίων ἐκείνῳ σπουδαία πρὸς Ῥώμην ἄφιξις, καὶ ὅσα τοιαῦτα ὁ χρόνος παρέστησε.
διὰ τοῦτο μὴ διδῶνται τὰ τῶν ἐκκλησιῶν τοῖς μαχομένοις τῇ ἐκκλη-
175 σίᾳ, μὴ εὑρίσκωνται ταύτης ἐγγύς. ἢ οὐκ ἐξερχομένων ἡμῶν ἐν λιταῖς καταμωκῶνται ἡμῶν ἐνώπιον τοῦ λαοῦ, ὡς διὰ τοῦτο ἔρχονται τὰ δεινά; πῶς οὖν ἐπινεύσει Θεὸς ἐν τοιούτῳ λαῷ ἀγαθά; μέχρι δὲ τίνος ἀνεξόμεθα καὶ ἡμεῖς, εὐεργετουμένους βλέποντες τοὺς ὑβρίζοντας; εἰ μὲν γὰρ ἀδικοῦσι, μὴ εὐεργετῶνται· εἰ δὲ λαλοῦσι καλῶς, τί μὴ καὶ εἰσακούονται; εἰ δὲ
180 διὰ τοῦτο εὐεργετοῦνται, ἵνα μόνον ὑβρίζωσι, τί τοσοῦτον ἡμεῖς προσκεκρούκαμεν, ὡς κεῖσθαι τοῖς εὐεργετουμένοις εἰς ὕβριν καὶ καταπάτημα;
εἰ οὖν θελήσει ἡ ἐκ Θεοῦ βασιλεία σου ἔχειν τὴν ἐκκλησίαν Χριστοῦ ἐλευθέραν αὐτῆς τὴν ἐλευθερίαν [fol. 50ʳ] καὶ ἀκλινῆ ἐν αὐτοῖς τοῖς πνευματικοῖς ἐν οἷς περιέρχονται αἱ ψυχαί, αἱ ἐκκλησίαι καὶ αἱ μοναί,
185 ἀπεχομένην τῶν ἀνηκόντων τῷ δημοσίῳ, ἐκ μέτρου τοῦτο θεάρεστον. οὕτω γὰρ καὶ ὁ ταύτην κατέχων οὐκ ἀθυμήσει, ὡς παρά του ἐμποδιζόμενος πρὸς τὰ κάλλιστα, καὶ σπουδαίως μετὰ Θεὸν κινηθήσεται πρὸς τὰ φίλα Θεοῦ καὶ σωτήρια τοῦ λαοῦ, καὶ τὰ τῆς βασιλείας πάλιν, ὡς βασιλεῦσι δέον ὀρθοδοξοῦσι καὶ ἡγεμόσι πεμπομένοις ὑπὸ τοιούτων, θεαρέστως
190 διοικηθήσεται.
καὶ ταῦτα διῆλθον, οὐ κατεξουσιάζειν θέλων καὶ ὀφρῦν αἴρειν, ἢ κέρδους γλιχόμενος κοσμικοῦ — οὔ, μὰ τοὺς ὑπὲρ ἀρετῆς τῶν πατέρων ἀγῶνας καὶ τὴν αὐτῶν βάδισιν! — ἀλλὰ τὸ πρέπον τῇ ἐκκλησίᾳ καὶ ταῖς ψυχαῖς κράτιστον χρεωστῶν καὶ λέγειν καὶ βλέπειν, καὶ πραττόμενον ἀ-

---

163 cf. Matt. 12:30 ‖ 169–171 cf. Matt. 10:29–30

159–160 τοῖς ... προσκειμένοις codd. ‖ 166 ὑμῶν codd. ‖ 171 προσπαίουσιν codd., παραπαίουσιν coni. Ševčenko ‖ 187 κινηθῇ codd.

69

me, and those who wish to abuse the Church gather round him? What about the metropolitan of Sardis? Didn't he prevent the celebrant of the liturgy from mentioning ⟨my⟩ name as is customary and done by others? If then these people are growing wealthy, and benefitting their supporters, and spewing forth (?) church property, when will they cease? And if ⟨it is argued⟩ that they have to receive benefits so they won't turn to wicked ways, since they have become ⟨wicked⟩ even though they have these rewards, should we give them yet other rewards? But these ⟨would be⟩ the words of people «who do not gather with Christ».

But I beg of you, having proved ⟨my point⟩ through reasoning, have the metropolitans of Chalcedon and Pergamum and the others expelled, don't let them or the patriarch of Alexandria control the churches, so that we may learn which people will leave us these days to follow them. And there is no doubt that those who devise evil against certain people have chattered in vain, unless ⟨their actions⟩ are sanctioned by heaven. And there are many proofs of this—not only that «our very hairs are numbered», but that «not even the tiniest sparrow falls into a snare without divine foreknowledge»—for those who are not purposefully out of their minds (?), such as the hasty arrival in Rome of the God-hated Theoctistus and his like, and similar examples which our age has shown us.

For this reason, don't let churches be granted to enemies of the Church. Don't even let them get near Her. Isn't it true that, when I go forth in religious processions, they mock me in front of the people, ⟨saying⟩ that it is for this very reason that misfortunes befall us? How then will God grant blessings to such a people? And how long can I endure to see that those who insult ⟨the Church⟩ are granted favors? For if they do wrong, they shouldn't be rewarded; but if they speak well, why aren't they heeded? And if they are rewarded for this reason only, that they may inflict abuse, what offense have I given that I should lie down and be insulted and walked over by recipients of ⟨your⟩ favor?

If then your divine majesty wishes the Church of Christ to remain utterly free and untroubled in the spiritual sphere, in which men's souls, churches and monasteries dwell, and exempt from the ⟨taxes⟩ which are owed to the fisc, this would be immeasurably pleasing to God. For thus the man in charge ⟨of the Church⟩ will not despair because he is prevented by someone ⟨from advancing⟩ toward the best, and with the help of God he will proceed vigorously toward that which is dear to God and brings salvation to the people, and once more the empire will be administered in a manner which is pleasing unto God, and as is behooving to orthodox rulers and to officials despatched by such ⟨rulers⟩.

I have discussed these matters, not out of the desire to exercise authority and show my superiority, nor yearning for worldly profits—no! by the struggle of the Fathers for the sake of virtue, and by their way of life!—but because I have the obligation to observe and say what is fitting for the Church

195 γαπᾶν. εἰ δὲ μὴ οὕτω δοκεῖ, ἐμπαθέσι δὲ λόγοις τινῶν προκρινοῦμεν
ἀκολουθεῖν, τὸ συνεῖναι τὰ κράτιστα ἀρχῆθεν τῷ κόσμῳ, ἐμφράξει
τούτων τὰ στόματα πάλιν τὸ στόμα Χριστοῦ, τὰ τῆς ἁμαρτίας
ὀψώνια ἀπ' ἀρχῆς θάνατον εἶναι ἀποφηνάμενον.

τί γὰρ τὸ ἐξῶσαν τοῦ παραδείσου τὸ γένος ἡμῶν; τί τὸ τοὺς
200 καταράκτας ἀνοῖξαν, καὶ μικροῦ ἀποπνῖξαν τὸ πᾶν; τί τὸ σεισμοὺς καὶ
λιμοὺς καὶ καταβάσιον πῦρ ξενίζοντι τρόπῳ, καὶ σφαγὰς ἀνεκδιηγή-
τους ἀπεργασάμενον; οὐχὶ ἡ τῶν τῷ Θεῷ δοκούντων ἀθέτησις; τί δὲ τὸν
πρωτότοκον Ἰσραήλ, ᾧ θάλασσα παραδόξως ἐρράγη, καὶ νεφέλη ὡδήγησε
καὶ στῦλος πυρός, καὶ ἄρτον ἀγγέλων ἐτράφη, καὶ πέτρας μάλα ἡδὺ
205 μέλι ἐθήλασε, καὶ ὅσα ἑξῆς εὐηργέτηται, τί τὸ τὰ φρίκης ταῦτα μεστὰ
καὶ ἐκστάσεως ἀντιστρέψαν εἰς ἐναντίωσιν; οὐχ ἡ ἁμαρτία καὶ καταφρόνη-
σις τῶν καλῶν; τί δὲ τὸ τὴν θεομαρτύρητον ἐκείνην ἱερωσύνην καὶ τὴν
δόξαν καὶ τὴν ὕστερον βασιλείαν καὶ τὰς ἄνωθεν ὑποσχέσεις ἀφείλατο τοῦ
τοσούτου λαοῦ; οὐχὶ τὸ τὰ νόμιμα παριδεῖν, θαρρῆσαι δὲ πόλεων ὀχυρώ-
210 μασι καὶ πλήθει λαοῦ καὶ πλούτῳ βαθεῖ, ἐξ ὧν εἰς ὕβρεις προφητικὰς καὶ
θανάτους, καὶ τὸ τοῖς ψευδοεποῦσιν εὐκόλως ὑπέχειν τὸ οὖς, καὶ καταμω-
κᾶσθαι τοὺς τοῦ Θεοῦ ἄφρονας, ἐξεκυλίσθησαν;

εἰ ταῦτα φέρεσθαι οὕτω καὶ νῦν τῇ βασιλείᾳ καὶ τῇ συγκλήτῳ
δοκεῖ, καὶ τῷ τῆς ἐκκλησίας τάχα πληρώματι — τὰ ψόγου ἐπέκεινα ἀνεκ-
215 δίκητα καὶ ἀναμὶξ ἀδιόρθωτα, ὡς καταφθείρεσθαι [fol. 50ᵛ] ὑπ' ἀλλήλων
— κἂν γνωσθήτω μοι τὸ ἐν ποίοις καὶ μέχρι πόσου ἐκτείνειν μοι τὴν φροντίδα παρεκελεύσθην, καὶ ἀπέχεσθαι τῶν λοιπῶν, καὶ τὸ ἀρεστόν μοι
ἢ τὸ ἦκον εἰς δύναμιν, Θεοῦ διδόντος, καταπραχθήσεται. οὐ γὰρ ἐᾷ με
κατεμπιπρᾶν τὰ τοῦ Θεοῦ κρίματα, μήπως ἐξ ἀμελείας ἐμῆς τὸ πρέπον
220 ἀπεσιώπησα. εἰ δὲ ἄλλοις ἁρμόζειν ⟨καὶ⟩ ἀκούειν ἐτάχθησαν παρὰ τοῦ
ἐξουσιάζοντος, ἐκτὸς τῆς τούτων εὐθύνης εἰμί, πλὴν εἰ καὶ γῆ ἐγὼ
καὶ σποδός, ἀλλὰ τοῦτο ἀξιωθείην πρὸς τὸν ἐμὸν Δεσπότην καὶ Κύριον
Ἰησοῦν Χριστόν (ἔστι μοι δι' εὐχῆς), συμφρονεῖν καὶ συμφθέγγεσθαι τῷ
εἰπόντι, τί γάρ μοι ὑπάρχει ἐν τῷ οὐρανῷ, καὶ παρὰ σοῦ
225 τί ἠθέλησα ἐπὶ τῆς γῆς; αὐτῷ ἡ δόξα εἰς τοὺς αἰῶνας, ἀμήν.

196–197 cf. Ps. 106(107):42 ‖ 197–198 Rom. 6:23 ‖ 201 Sap. 10:6 ‖ 204 Ps. 77(78):25 ‖
221–222 Gen. 18:27 ‖ 224–225 Ps. 72(73):25

---

220 καὶ addidi

69

and best for souls, and to approve this when it is accomplished. But if another view should prevail, and we should prefer to go along with the passionate words of certain people that «the best existed in the world from the beginning» (?), the words of Christ will once more stop their mouths by declaring that from the beginning «the wages of sin are death».

What was it that cast our people out from Paradise? What opened the cataracts and all but drowned everything? What caused the earthquakes and famines and the «fire which descended» in a strange fashion, and indescribable slaughter? Was it not our disregard of God's will? And what about firstborn Israel, for whom the sea unexpectedly opened up, and who were led by a cloud and pillar of fire, and nourished by the bread of angels, and sucked the sweet honey of the rock, and were blessed in many other ways, what turned against them these horrible and astounding misfortunes? Was it not their sins and scorn of the good? What was it that took away from such a people that sanctity and glory which were witnessed by God and their later kingdom and the promises from heaven? Was it not because they scorned the laws, and trusted rather in the fortifications of their cities and in the numbers of their people, and in their great wealth, from which they slid down to insulting prophets and killing them, and readily listening to men who spoke falsely, and foolishly mocking the people of God?

If it now seems best to your majesty and the senate and even the faithful of the Church to manage affairs in this way—that affairs which are worthy of blame beyond measure should be unpunished and uncorrected, all mixed up together so as to infect each other with corruption—let me know within what limits and for how long I am bidden to continue my responsibility, and that I should withdraw from the rest, and that which is pleasing to me or within my power will be accomplished, God willing. For ⟨thoughts of⟩ the judgments of God do not cease to torment me with fire, for fear that through negligence I have omitted to mention what is fitting. But if they [the bishops?] have been instructed by the ruler [i.e., Andronicus] to conform to (?) ⟨and⟩ obey others, I am not responsible for them. And although «I am earth and ashes», may I still be deemed worthy of this, to join in the sentiments and words of the one who said to my Master and Lord Jesus Christ (and this is possible for me through prayer), «For what have I in heaven, but thee? And what have I desired on earth beside thee?». Glory be to Him forever, Amen.

70. ⟨Πρὸς βασιλεῖς τε καὶ ἄρχοντας, ἱερεῖς καὶ μονάζοντας⟩

Αἰσχύνη μεγάλη ἐμοὶ καὶ τοῖς κατ' ἐμέ, ὅτι βαρβάροις ἀνθρώποις
τοῖς Νινευΐταις μῆνις Θεοῦ, παρ' ἀγνῶτος καὶ ταῦτα, διαγγελθεῖσα, οὐ
τριημέρου νηστείας, οὐδὲ σποδοῦ καὶ σάκκου μόνον, ἀλλὰ καρδιακῇ
5 συντριβῇ καὶ πάσης κακίας ἀποβολῇ τὴν ἀγαθότητα [fol. 52ᵛ] τοῦ
⟨τῆς ἀγαθότητος⟩ πελάγους πρὸς συμπάθειαν εἵλκυσαν. ἡμεῖς δέ, τί παθόντες οὐκ οἶδα, οὐ ψιλῇ ἀκοῇ ἀλλ' ἔργοις ὁρῶντες τὰ φρικωδέστατα, καὶ
πολλὴν ἀγανάκτησιν πρὸς Θεοῦ εἰς ἡμᾶς ὑπεμφαίνοντα, τελοῦμεν ἀπηλ-
γηκότες, ὁμοῦ καὶ ἄρχοντες καὶ ἀρχόμενοι, καὶ σὺν ἀνδράσι γυναῖκες, ὡς
10 προσθήκη μᾶλλον κακίας τῷ σφετέρῳ κακῷ ἀνδρειούμενοι.
ἔνθεν, παρακαλῶ, γρηγορήσωμεν· ὑπ' ἀλλήλων διαναστῶμεν· ἀποστῶμεν τῶν φαύλων· στεναγμοὺς ἐκ βάθους πρὸς τὸν πανεύσπλαγχνον ἀ-
ποπέμψωμεν· ὑπόσχεσιν δῶμεν ὡς δύναμις πρὸς μετάνοιαν, καί, εἴ γε δοκεῖ, ἐξέλθωμεν καὶ γυμνῷ τῷ ποδὶ μετὰ τῶν θείων εἰκόνων ἐν κατα-
15 νύξει λιτάζοντες, καὶ μᾶλλον μονάζοντες. δόξαν μοι κράτιστον τοῦτο
ὑμῖν ἀναθεῖναι, εἴ πως κοινῇ συναινέσει ποιμένες καὶ ποίμνια, καὶ ὅσοις
ἐν ἀκοαῖς ὑπάρξει τοῦτο πεσεῖν, ἔργῳ καὶ λόγῳ, ἀντιβολῶ, φανερῶς τε
καὶ ἀφανῶς πρὸς ἀληθῆ μετάνοιαν ἐπειχθείημεν. εἰ δὲ κελεύει καὶ ὁ κραταιὸς καὶ ἅγιος αὐτοκράτωρ μου συμπονῆσαι ἡμῖν, οὐ μόνον⟨οὐκ⟩ἀπᾷδον,
20 ἀλλὰ καὶ εὔλογον· εἰ δ' οὖν, ὁ πανευτυχέστατος καὶ θεοφιλὴς Δεσπότης
ἀναπληρούτω τὸν τόπον ἐκείνου εἰς δόξαν Θεοῦ.

71. Πρὸς τὸν αὐτοκράτορα παρακινῶν ἐλθεῖν ἐν τῷ
ἐνταφιασμῷ τοῦ Σωτῆρος

Εἰ τὴν τοῦ Νότου βασίλισσαν ἐκ περάτων δραμεῖν
ἐπαινούμενος ἔρως ἀνέφλεξε, σοφίας ἀκουσομένην τῷ μετ' ὀλίγον
τεθνηξομένῳ δοθείσης, ποδαπὴ τοῖς πιστοῖς ὀφειλὴ ἀνακτόροις τῆς
5 θείας σοφίας ἐπιφθάνειν, οὐ συνεχέστερον μόνον, ἀλλὰ καὶ ἀπνευστί,
τὸ λεγόμενον, τοῖς σωτηρίας ἐξεχομένοις ἐν ὑψηλῷ συγκαλούσης
κηρύγματι, ὑποτιθέναι σὺν τοῖς λοιποῖς καὶ ὅσα θεοπρεπῶς ἐτελεσιουρ-

70: 2–6 cf. Jon. 3
71: 2–3 cf. Matt. 12:42, Luc. 11:31, III Reg. 10:1–10 ‖ 5–7 cf. Prov. 9:1–3

70: V 52ʳ–52ᵛ. S 192ʳ–192ᵛ. P 71ᵛ–72ʳ. Ed. Pallas, Die Passion Christi, 305–6.
1 γράμμα συγκαλῶν βασιλεῖς τε καὶ ἄρχοντας, ἱερεῖς καὶ μονάζοντας ἵνα γυμνῷ τῷ ποδὶ
ἐξέλθωσι μετὰ τῶν θείων εἰκόνων λιτάζοντες add. VʳSP ‖ 2 ἐμοὶ] ἐμὴ S ‖ 4–5 καρδιακὴ
συντριβὴ codd. ‖ 5 ἀποβολὴ codd. ‖ 6 τῆς ἀγαθότητος addidi; cf. Epp. 6, 10; 82, 64–65;
89, 9 ‖ ὑμεῖς S ‖ 8 τελοῦμεν] γελοῦμεν P ‖ 16 ποιμένες VS¹P: ποιμέναις S ‖ 19 καὶ] ὁ
P ‖ οὐκ addidi ‖ ἀπᾴδων VS ‖ 21 δόξαν S
71: V 52ᵛ–53ʳ. S 192ᵛ–193ᵛ. P 72ʳ–72ᵛ. Ed. Pallas, Die Passion Christi, 306–7.
4 ὀφείλει codd. ‖ 6 τοῖς] τῆς S

70. ⟨To emperors and nobles, priests and monks⟩

It is a great shame to me and people like me that, when the wrath of God was announced to barbarous men, the Ninevites, and by a stranger to boot, not only by fasting for three days or with ashes and sackcloth, but also by their contrition of heart and rejection of all evil did they attract the goodness of ⟨God⟩, that sea ⟨of goodness⟩, to compassion. But for some reason, although we not merely hear, but actually see the most horrifying occurrences, indicating to us the great wrath of God, we are insensitive, rulers and ruled alike, and men together with women, as if we were drawing reassurance from adding further evil to the evil of our own.

Wherefore I beg you, let us awaken; let us be roused by each other; let us stand aloof from base people. Let us send up lamentations to the All-merciful One from the depths ⟨of our hearts⟩. Let us promise to repent as much as we can, and, if you agree, let us go out with bare feet, especially the monks, to hold a procession in contrition with the holy icons. It has seemed very important to me to suggest this to you, so that somehow by common consent we all, shepherds and their flocks, and whosoever happens to hear this, may hasten to true repentance, in both word and deed, I pray, and both in public and in private. And if my mighty and holy emperor would be willing to share our self-mortification, it would not only be fitting, but praiseworthy; otherwise, let the most fortunate and God-loving Despot take His Majesty's place for the glory of God.

71. To the emperor, urging him to come to the ⟨ceremony of the⟩ entombment of the Savior

If praiseworthy passion inflamed «the queen of the south» to hasten «from the ends» ⟨of the earth⟩ «to hear the wisdom» which was granted to a man who was soon to die, then how great an obligation is there for the faithful not only to come immediately, but without even drawing a breath, as the saying goes, to the halls of Holy Wisdom Who «summons with a loud proclamation» those who cling to salvation, to enjoin Her sons to listen, among other things, to what has been accomplished in a manner befitting the divine

178

71, 72

γήθη εἰς μνήμην τῇ μόνῃ μεγαλωνύμῳ Σοφίᾳ Θεοῦ καὶ ἐνυποστάτῳ,
τὰ ὑπὲρ ἔννοιαν τοῖς υἱέσιν ἐξακουτίζεσθαι· καὶ πρό γε τῶν ἄλλων τῇ ἐκ
10 Θεοῦ βασιλείᾳ σου, φιλεόρτῳ καὶ φιλοθέῳ εἴπερ τινί, καὶ μόνῃ μικροῦ
συναισθήσει πνεούσῃ τῶν τοῦ Θεοῦ μεγαλείων τὰ ἀνυπέρβλητα, ὡς ἂν τὰς
ὑψώσεις αὐτοῦ πανηγυριζούσῃ τῇ ἐκκλησίᾳ συμφαιδρύναι τῇ παρουσίᾳ
καὶ συνδοξάσαι παρασκευάσῃ πρὸς μίμησιν τὸ ἀπαράμιλλον ταύτης
καὶ ἐπιτεταμένον τοῖς ἀγαθοῖς, τῷ ὑπηκόῳ προΐσχουσα τὸ μέγα τοῦ
15 μυστηρίου καὶ ἀπόρρητον καὶ ἀνέκφραστον, οὐ κατοπτεύσοντι μόνον τοῦ
ἐνταφιασμοῦ τὰ ἀνήκουστα καὶ ἐκστατικά, ἀλλά γε καὶ ὅσα τοῦ τότε
καιροῦ ἀπανθρώπῳ καὶ μιαιφόνῳ ὁρμῇ [fol. 53ʳ] κατεπράχθη ἀνθρώποις
συμπαθείᾳ ψυχῆς παραστῆσαι, καὶ τῇ ἀειπαρθένῳ Μητρὶ τοῦ Θεοῦ συνθρηνῆσαι, καὶ τίς ὁ τῷ μνήματι προσκυλίσων τὸν λίθον
20 ἰδεῖν, καὶ μηδ' οὕτως ἀναχωρεῖν ὡς τῶν θείων φιλοθεάμονα, ἀλλὰ
μᾶλλον συμπαραμεῖναι καὶ μύρα κομίσαι, εἴ πως ἐπόψει τὸν λίθον
ἠρμένον καὶ τὸν τῷ λίθῳ ἐπικαθήμενον, τὸν ὅτῳ δήποτε θόρυβον τῆς ἡμετέρας ψυχῆς καταστέλλοντα, ὡς ἂν ἀναστάντα προσκυνήσωμεν τὸν Χριστόν, τὸ δὲ χαίρετε ἀκουσόμενοι, οὐ μακραῖς ταῖς ἐλπίσιν εἰς
25 Γαλιλαίαν ἰδεῖν, ἀλλ' ἐντὸς ἡμῶν εἶναι ἀναμφιβόλως πιστεύσωμεν, εἰ
ὅσα ἡμῖν διὰ τῶν θείων εὐαγγελίων θεσπίζει τηρήσαιμεν, εἰ μάλιστα
καιομένην ἐν τούτοις τὴν καρδίαν κτησόμεθα, οὐ μόνον τῇ
κλάσει τοῦ ἄρτου ἐπιγινώσκοντες τοῦτον, ἀλλ' ἐνοικοῦντα
πελάγει φιλανθρωπίας ἡμῖν καὶ ἐμπεριπατοῦντα διηνεκῶς πλουτιζόμενοι.

72. Πρὸς τὸν αὐτοκράτορα περὶ τοῦ γεγονότος εἰς τὸν λαὸν λιμοῦ

Πρώην διερχομένων ἡμῶν τὰς ὁδούς, ἄλλος ἄλλο τι τῶν πενήτων
ἐζήτει ἡμᾶς, νῦν δὲ ὁμοφώνως ἀποδυρόμενοι ὑπὲρ σίτου, πάντες μικροῦ
ἵνα μὴ ἐξέρχηται τῆς μεγαλοπόλεως παρακαλοῦσιν ἐλεεινῶς, καὶ ὅρκοις
5 καταδεσμοῦσι πρὸ αἰτήματος ἄλλου παντὸς πρὸς τῆς ἐκ Θεοῦ βασιλείας
σου, τὴν ἀναφορὰν ὑπὲρ τοῦ σίτου ποιεῖσθαί με. τῇ συμφορᾷ δὲ τῇ τούτων
καὶ αὐτὸς συνθρηνῶν ἅμα καὶ συναλγῶν καὶ πειθόμενος, στοχαζόμενός
τε τὰ ἐκ σιτοδείας δεινὰ συναντήσοντα τοῖς ἐμοῖς ἀδελφοῖς καὶ συμπένησι,
καὶ τὸ ἀποβησόμενον πάλιν ἐκ τοῦ τοιοῦδε κακοῦ πάθος τοῖς ὑπολειφθεῖ-
10 σιν ἐκ τῆς διὰ τὰς ἐμὰς ἁμαρτίας συμβάσης Χριστιανοῖς ἀπειλῆς, τῆς ἐκ

19 cf. Matt. 27:60 ‖ 21 cf. Triodion, 723 ‖ 21–22 cf. Matt. 28:2 ‖ 24 cf. Matt. 28:9;
Triodion, 718 ‖ 24–25 cf. Matt. 28:10 ‖ 27 cf. Luc. 24:32 ‖ 27–28 Luc. 24:35

9 υἱέσιν VS¹ˢᵛ P: υἱέσι S ‖ 15 κατοπτεύσοντα codd. ‖ 22 ὁτιδήποτε SP ‖ 24 δὲ om. SP
72: V 53ʳ–53ᵛ. S 193ᵛ–194ᵛ. P 72ᵛ–74ʳ. Ed. Laiou, Andronicus II, 338, no. 7.
9 πάθος VS¹P: πάθους S

71, 72

to commemorate the unique, glorious and incarnate Wisdom of God, to things beyond understanding. And this is a duty above all for your divine majesty, a lover of festivals and of God if there ever was one, who almost instinctively is inspired by the incomparable mighty works of God; so that you may offer as an example to be imitated and praised your unrivalled and passionate zeal for good works by brightening with your presence the festivities through which the Church glorifies God. You will thus offer your subjects the great, secret, and ineffable mystery, as they not only will see the inconceivable and ecstatic ⟨ceremony of the⟩ entombment, but also will witness with compassionate soul what was done by the men of that time through an inhuman and murderous impulse, and share the sorrow of the ever-virgin Mother of God, and see who «will roll the stone to the sepulcher», and they should not simply depart, just as a spectator interested in watching divine spectacles, but should rather remain and «bring precious ointments», in the hope that they may see the stone rolled away, and the ⟨angel⟩ sitting on the stone, who represses the tumult of any man's soul, so that we may worship the risen Christ, and hear His words «All hail», not with remote hopes of seeing Him «in Galilee», but so that we may believe without question that He is within us, if we only observe the precepts of the Holy Gospels, especially if we acquire meanwhile «a burning heart», «knowing Him» not only «in the breaking of bread», but as One dwelling and walking among us because of His abundant love for mankind.

72. To the emperor concerning the famine which is afflicting the people

Formerly when I walked through the streets, one poor person would ask me for one thing, another for another, but now they complain as if with one voice about the grain, and almost everyone entreats me piteously that it not leave the capital, and bind me with oaths to put before any other request to your divine majesty a petition about the grain. I myself share their sorrow and suffering, and am persuaded of the plight of these people, and ⟨am able⟩ to estimate the distress which will befall my brethren and fellow poor, on account of the scarcity of food. And again as I estimate the suffering which such an evil will cause to the survivors of the threat to the Christians which has occurred on account of my sins, I entreat your divine majesty to heed

Θεοῦ βασιλείας σου δέομαι ἐνωτίσασθαι ἐν αἰσθήσει τὰς ἐμὰς ὑπὲρ σίτου
κἀκείνων φωνάς, καὶ μὴ παραχωρεῖν τοῖς ξενίοις ἢ νόσῳ πλεονεξίας ἢ καὶ
φιλίας ἁπλῶς, προτιμῶντας τὸν χρυσὸν τοῦ Χριστοῦ, ὃς διαθρύπτειν
πεινῶσι τὸν ἄρτον, ἀλλὰ μὴ προτιμήσει χρυσοῦ ἀποκτένειν τοὺς τοῦ
15 Χριστοῦ ἐνετείλατο. τί γὰρ αὐτοὺς ὠφελήσει, ἐὰν κερδή-
σωσιν ὅλον τὸν κόσμον (ὅπερ ἀδύνατον), ζημιωθῶσι δὲ τὴν
οἰκείαν ψυχήν; κερδῆσαι μὲν γὰρ ὅλον τὸν κόσμον τῶν ἀδυνάτων τινά·
ζημιωθῆναι δὲ ἕκαστον τὴν οἰκείαν ψυχήν, εἰ θέλει, τῶν δυνατῶν.
ὁπόσης αἰσχύνης καὶ ψόγου ὑπὲρ ἀδυνάτου κακοῦ προδοῦναί τινα τὸ δυνα-
20 τὸν ἀγαθόν, τῶν ὀλίγων τὸ ἀγνοεῖν. [fol. 53ᵛ] δέον γὰρ ἔχειν αὐτοὺς κατὰ
νοῦν τὸ πλοῦτος ἐὰν ῥέῃ, μὴ προστίθεσθαι καρδίαν, καὶ
πλοῦτος ἀδίκως συναγόμενος ἐξεμεθήσεται, καὶ οἱ βουλόμενοι πλουτεῖν εἰς πειρασμὸν καὶ παγίδα τοῦ διαβό-
λου ἐμπίπτουσι, καὶ τὸ ὁ τιμιουλκῶν σῖτον δημοκατάρατος·
25 εὐλογία δὲ εἰς κεφαλὴν τοῦ μεταδιδόντος.
    ταῦτα παρὰ τῆς ἐκ Θεοῦ βασιλείας σου δέομαι, ἢ διδαχθήτωσαν
ἢ ἐπιτιμηθήτωσαν, καὶ τὸ μὴ πεποιθέναι ἐπὶ ἀδηλότητι πλούτου, ἀλλ' ἐπὶ τῷ ζῶντι Θεῷ, τῷ πλουσίως ἡμῖν εἰς
ἀπόλαυσιν ἀγαθὴν πάντα παρέχοντι. ὅτι δεινὸν καὶ πέρα δεινῶν
30 ἐμὲ μέν, μετὰ τῶν συμπενήτων μου ἀδελφῶν καὶ πτωχῶν, προσπίπτειν
καὶ δέεσθαι βασιλέως μεγάλου εὐσεβεστάτου, ὀρθοδόξου καὶ φιλοχρίστου,
ἐλεήμονος ὑπερβολικῶς καὶ τῇ τῆς οἰκείας ψυχῆς συμπαθείᾳ καὶ ἀγαθότητι ἐπικαμπτομένου τῇ θλίψει τοῦ ὑπηκόου καὶ συμφορᾷ, τοῖς τοσούτοις
δὲ ἀγαθοῖς ὀλίγα κατακαυχᾶσθαι δῶρα καὶ ξένια, καὶ τὸν ποθητὸν ἡμῖν
35 σῖτον, ὡς μὴ ὤφειλεν, ἐκκενοῦντα τῆς πόλεως. καὶ ταῦτα μὴ ἀγνοούντων
τὴν μέλλουσαν ἐπιπίπτειν ἀνίατον νόσον καὶ συμφορὰν τοῖς πενομένοις
ἡμῖν οἱ τὰ πολλὰ ἔχοντες, καὶ τὴν ἁρπαγὴν τοῦ πτωχοῦ ἐν
τοῖς οἴκοις, καὶ τὰ ἑαυτῶν ἑκόντες ἀποκλείοντες ὦτα, τοῦ μὴ ἀκοῦ-
σαι τὸν ὑπὸ τοῦ Κυρίου στηλιτευόμενον διὰ τὸ τὰς ἀποθήκας γρη-
40 γορεύειν κακῶς καθελεῖν, εἰς μειζόνων ἀνέγερσιν. πρὸς ταύτην τὴν
νόσον οὐκ ἄρχων, οὐχ ἱερεύς, οὐ Λευίτης ἐπάξει τὴν ἰατρείαν, ἀλλὰ
μόνη ἡ ἐκ Θεοῦ βασιλεία σου μετά τινος Σαμαρείτου, ὃς καὶ τὸν ὑπὸ
τῶν λῃστῶν πληγέντα οὐ παρέδραμε βδελυξάμενος. αὐτὸς γὰρ καὶ τῇ ἐκ
Θεοῦ βασιλείᾳ σου δύο δέδωκε τὰ δηνάρια, τὴν εὐσέβειαν καὶ

72: 13–14 cf. Is. 58:7 ‖ 15–17 cf. Marc. 8:36 ‖ 21 Ps. 61(62):11 ‖ 22 Job 20:15 ‖
22–24 I Tim. 6:9 ‖ 24–25 Prov. 11:26 (Th.); cf. F. Field, ed., Origenis Hexaplorum Quae
Supersunt, II, 333 ‖ 27–29 cf. I Tim. 6:17 ‖ 37–38 cf. Is. 3:14 ‖ 39–40 cf. Luc. 12:18 ‖
41–42 cf. Luc. 10:31–33 ‖ 44 cf. Luc. 10:35

---

17 οἰκείαν VSP¹: οἰκίαν P ‖ 19 ὁπόσης] ὢ πόσης codd. ‖ 21 καρδίαν scripsi; cf. Ps.
61(62):11; καρδία codd. ‖ 25 εὐλογίαν S ‖ 31 δέεσθαι VP, δεῖσθαι S, δείσθαι S¹ ‖
35 ἐκκενοῦντα] ἐκκεντοῦντα VS, ἐκκεντοῦνται P ‖ 39–40 γρηγορεῖν codd. ‖ 40 ἀνέργεσιν
P ‖ 41 οὐχ ἱερεύς] ἀρχιερεύς S ‖ 43–44 τῆς … βασιλείας P

72

and register in your mind my and their pleas for grain; and do not yield to bribes, either through the disease of greed or simply of friendship, preferring gold to God Who ordered «the bread to be distributed among the hungry», but not that one should kill the people of God because of one's love of gold. «For what shall it profit them, if they shall gain the whole world» (which is impossible), «but will lose their soul?» For it is impossible for someone to gain the whole world, but it is possible for everyone to lose his own soul, if he wishes. Very few people are unaware of the shame and blame which results from betraying a possible good for an evil which cannot be obtained anyhow. For they should keep in mind the words, «If wealth should flow in, set not your heart upon it», and «wealth unjustly collected shall be vomited up», and «they that will be rich fall into the temptation and snare of the devil», and «he who raises the price of grain is cursed by the people; but blessing be on the head of him that gives it».

I make this request of your divine majesty: either let them be taught or rebuked, and do not have faith «in uncertain riches, but in the living God, who giveth us richly all things to enjoy». Because it is terrible and worse than terrible for me and my brethren, my fellow poor and beggars, to fall at your feet and entreat you, a great and most pious king who is right-thinking and a lover of Christ, who is exceedingly merciful and is swayed by the sympathy and goodness of his own soul, and by the sorrow and affliction of his subjects, while a few gifts and bribes triumph over such good qualities, and drive the grain we yearn for out of the city as should not happen. In addition let the rich realize the incurable disease and affliction which is about to befall us needy people, and that «the spoils of the poor are in ⟨their⟩ houses», as, of their own accord, they close their ears so as not to hear about the man mocked by the Lord, because in his misplaced eagerness he «tore down his barns» in order to build «greater ones». The cure for this disease will be found neither by ruler nor «priest» nor «Levite», but only by your divine majesty together with a certain Samaritan [i.e. God] who did not pass by with loathing the man wounded by thieves. For He gave your divine majesty

45 τὴν βασίλειαν. αὐτὸς καὶ τὸ ἐφ᾽ ὅσον ἐποιήσατε ἑνὶ τούτων τῶν
ἐλαχίστων, ἐμοί, βοᾷ, ἐποιήσατε. καὶ ἐν τῷ ἐπανέρχεσθαι τοῦτον
τὴν βασιλείαν παρέξει σοι ἣν ἐπορεύθη λαβεῖν, κἂν οἱ τυχόντες πολῖται
δοῦναι αὐτῷ οὐκ ἠθέλησαν, ἣν εἶχε μὲν ὡς Θεός, ἔχει δὲ ὡς θεάνθρωπος
καὶ βασιλεύων τοῦ οὐρανοῦ καὶ τῆς γῆς· καὶ τοῦ στεναγμοῦ τῶν πενήτων
50 καὶ τῆς ταλαιπωρίας ἐθέσπισεν ἕνεκεν ἀναστήσεσθαι· αὐτῷ ἡ δόξα εἰς
τοὺς αἰῶνας, ἀμήν.

73. Πρὸς τὸν αὐτοκράτορα περὶ τοῦ αὐτοῦ καὶ αὖθις

῞Ηνπερ ἀναφορὰν πεποιήμην ὑπὲρ σίτου, κράτιστε βασιλεῦ, διὰ
Θεὸν μὴ ἐπιλησθῶ, ὡς ἂν μὴ ἄλλῳ τινὶ τῶν ἀρχόντων τὴν διοί–[fol. 54ʳ]
κησιν τὴν περὶ τοῦ σίτου ἐκχωρηθῇ τοῦ οἰκονομεῖν, ἐκτὸς οὗ ἀνέφερον
5 εὐλαβοῦς, καὶ δοθῇ καὶ ἡμέτερος μοναχός, καὶ ἵνα μηδὲ αὐτὸς ἐπιτιμίου
χωρίς, τοῦ μὴ πρὸς πρόσωπα, μὴ πρὸς χάριν, μὴ πρὸς φιλίαν, μὴ πρὸς
δῶρα καὶ ξένια, τὰ καὶ σοφῶν ὀφθαλμοὺς ἐκτυφλοῦντα,
ἀλλ᾽ ἕνεκεν οἴκτου καὶ ἀληθείας Θεοῦ καὶ δικαιοσύνης, μήτε μὴν συγχω–
ρεῖν ἐξωνεῖσθαι τὸν σῖτον τοὺς τοῦτον διψῶντας τιμιουλκεῖν (οἱ
10 καὶ ἐπάρατοι ἐπιμίσγοντες ἄχυρα ἢ σῖτον διασαπέντα, ἢ ὅσα αὐτοῖς
ὁ Σατὰν ὑποτίθεται), τὰς τοῦ Χριστωνύμου λαοῦ συμφοράς, ὦ ζημίας!,
ἐξωνουμένους ἐλεεινῶς· εἰδυίας τῆς ἐκ Θεοῦ βασιλείας σου, ὡς εἰ καί που
περί τινων ὄντων ἐν βίᾳ πρὸς αὐτὴν πεποιήμην ἀναφοράν, ἀλλ᾽ οὔποτε κατ-
ηνάγκασα· ἐν δέ γε τοῖς νῦν, ὡς ὄντος κοινοῦ ναυαγίου, τὸ κοινῆς συμφο–
15 ρᾶς παραμύθιον οὐχ ἁπλῶς ἀναφέρω, ἀλλ᾽ ἀξιῶ καὶ καταναγκάζω, καὶ
εἰ μὴ εἰσακουσθῶ, τῇ συνέσει θαρρῶν καὶ ὀργίζομαι.

βλέψον οὖν εἰς Θεὸν τὸν τὴν χεῖρα ἀνοίγοντα ἐμπιπλᾶν·
βλέψον υἱέσιν ἀπόροις καὶ ἀδυνάτοις, καί, τὸ μειζόνως συνθρύπτον ἐμέ,
λιμώττουσιν ἄρτου· καὶ φιλοτέκνου πατρὸς ὀφειλὴν καὶ δυνατοῦ ἐνδειξά–
20 μενος, βλέψον ψυχῆς βασιλικωτάτης οἷον ὀφείλει βασιλικὸν ἐν τοιούτοις
ἐνδείκνυσθαι φρόνημα, καὶ βαθυτέρους τρόπους οἰκονομίας, μὴ ῥαδίους
πολλοῖς· καὶ εἰ μή που τῶν ἐν τῇ Νέᾳ θαυμαστωθέντων πρὸς μέτρον πεφθάκειμεν, τοῦ ηὐχόμην νεανιεύσασθαι (ὦ ψυχῆς μακαρίας!) ἀνάθεμα εἶναι ἀπὸ Χριστοῦ (ὀλίγων γὰρ τοῦτο τῶν πάνυ καὶ ὀλι–

45–46 Matt. 25:40
73: 7 cf. Deut. 9–10 ‖ 9–10 cf. Prov. 11:26 (Theodotion) ‖ 17 cf. Ps. 103(104):28 ‖
23–24 Rom. 9:3

73: V 53ᵛ–54ᵛ. S 194ᵛ–195ᵛ. P 74ʳ–74ᵛ. Ed. Laiou, *Andronicus II*, 339–340,
no. 10.
1 ante πρὸς add. γράμμα VʳSP ‖ post αὖθις add. καὶ μὴ πωλεῖν τινὰν σῖτον (σίτου P)
ἄνευ εἰδήσεως καὶ (VʳS¹P, ἐκ S) τοῦ πατριάρχου VʳSP ‖ 8 post δικαιοσύνης unum
verbum, fortasse οἰκονομεῖν, deest ‖ 12 ἐξωνουμένοις VS ‖ 18 συνθρύπτ P ‖ 19 π(ατ)ρ(ὸ)ς
πρὸς SP ‖ 20 οἷον] οἶνον P ‖ 22–23 πεφθάκειμεν VSP¹: πεφθάκαμεν P

«the two pence», piety and empire, and cries out, «Inasmuch as ye have done
it unto one of the least of these, ye have done it unto me». And on His
return He will give you the kingdom which He came to receive, even if the
people of that time weren't willing to give to Him that which He had as God,
and which He also has as man made God and ruler of heaven and earth; and
He has decreed that He will arise again on account of the groans and misery
of the poor; to Him be glory for ever and ever, Amen.

73. To the emperor concerning the same matter again

O mighty emperor, for the sake of God may I not be forgotten with
respect to the petition I made to you concerning grain, so that no other
official except the pious man I mentioned may be permitted to control the
administration of the grain supply (and so that one of my monks may also
be included), and even he should not be without injunction that he will not
⟨administer⟩ with personal bias, nor as a favor, nor out of friendship or as a
result of «gifts» and bribes, «which blind the eyes even of wise men», but for
the sake of mercy and the truth of God and righteousness, and so that he will
not allow grain to be bought up by men who are anxious to raise its price,
but ⟨in fact⟩ miserably buy up the misfortunes of the Christian people
(moreover, these accursed people mix in chaff or rotten grain, or whatever
else Satan suggests to them). Your divine majesty is aware that although
I have made petitions about certain individuals in straits, I have never bela-
bored the issue. But in the present circumstances, since the whole people has
been shipwrecked, I do not simply petition for the relief of a general disaster,
but I insist and am adamant, and if I am not heeded, I will get angry,
trusting in my own conscience.

Look therefore to God «Who opens His hand to give you your fill»; look at
your children in want and need, who are (and this is most grievous to me of all)
starving for bread. And indicate to them what are the duties of a mighty father
devoted to his children; be mindful of the royal attitude a most royal soul
has the obligation to demonstrate, and of the more profound ways of accommodation, which are not easy ⟨to follow⟩ for everyone. And even if we never
attain the stature of those who are magnified in the New Testament, so as to
say boldly (O blessed soul ⟨that did say this⟩!) «I could wish that myself
were accursed from Christ» (for this is attained only by a few and rarely),

25 γάκις), ἀλλά γε κἂν τῶν ἐν τῇ Παλαιᾷ μὴ κατόπιν βαδίσωμεν, δυσωπῶ,
ἢ οὐδὲ ἐκθειάσαι ἀδυνατοῦμεν Μωσέα, εἰ μὲν ἀφεῖς τὴν ἁμαρτίαν αὐτοῖς πρὸς Θεὸν δυσωποῦντα, ἄφες· εἰ δ'οὖν, ἀλλ'
ἐξάλειψόν γε κἀμὲ ἐξ ἧς γεγράφηκας βίβλου. καὶ ἄλλος,
μὴ κατισχύσητέ με παρακαλεῖν ἐπὶ τῇ συντριβῇ τῆς
30 θυγατρὸς τοῦ γένους μου, καὶ ἄλλος, ἄφετέ με πικρῶς
ἀποκλαύσασθαι. τί δὲ ὁ μέγας Δαυὶδ ἐπὶ τῇ θηλάτῳ ὀργῇ; οὐχὶ
ταύτην ἐκάλει πρὸς ἑαυτόν; εἰ ἐγὼ ὁ ποιμὴν ἐκακοποίησα,
φάσκων, τὸ ποίμνιον τί πεποίηκεν; ἐπ'ἐμὲ γενέσθω ἡ
χείρ σου, καὶ ἐπὶ τὸν οἶκον τοῦ πατρός μου; καὶ πλείους
35 εἶχον ἐξαριθμήσασθαι, εἰ μή που πρὸς οἶκον σοφίας καὶ οἴκτου ἐχάραττον
ἔμπλεων καὶ μόνον διψῶντα λαβεῖν ἀφορμήν, μακρὰν τῶν ῥηθέντων γινώσκων ἐμέ, καὶ συστελλόμενος ταῦτα ὑποτιθέναι [fol. 54ᵛ] ἢ καὶ πλείω
λαλεῖν, τοῦ μήπως ὀφλήσω καὶ γέλωτα. τούτου γε χάριν εἰσακουσθῆναι
ἀντιβολῶ, εἰ καὶ μὴ λέγειν ἀξίως πεπαίδευμαι.

74. Πρὸς τὸν αὐτοκράτορα περὶ τοῦ αὐτοῦ

Εἰ καὶ ἕνεκεν αὐχημάτων πατρῴων, κράτιστε βασιλεῦ, καὶ
ἀδελφῶν ἀδικίας καὶ σωφροσύνης ὑπερφυοῦς, ὥς τι ἀσύγκριτον ἐδόθη
καὶ μέγα τῷ Ἰωσὴφ ἡ σιτοδοσία πρὸς τοὺς ὁμογενεῖς, ἡμεῖς (ἐξόδου καὶ
5 κόπου χωρίς) μὴ ἀποστερηθῶμεν αὐτῆς, μηδὲ διά τι τῶν ἀνθρωπίνων
ἀποβαλώμεθα, δέομαι· ὑπὲρ ἧς ἅπας λόγος τοῖς συνιοῦσι καὶ ἅπαν μυστήριον, τὸ τίμιον ταύτης καὶ ἀναγκαῖον, γνωριζόμενον ἐν τῷ μέλλοντι. τί
γὰρ τοῦ πεινῶσί τινα διαθρύπτειν τὸν ἄρτον μακαριώτερον;
στέρξον οὖν τὴν ἀγαθωσύνην ἧς Θεός σοι τὸ κράτος παρέσχετο·
10 καὶ μόνον λόγῳ εἰπέ, καὶ καταισχυνθήσονται μὲν οἱ πλούτισμα καὶ τρυφὴν
καὶ ἀδιάδοχον δόξαν λογιζόμενοι τὸ τιμιουλκεῖν χρειώδη πάντα· ἡσθήσον-
ται δὲ καὶ ἀγαλλιάσονται οἱ πρός τε Θεὸν καὶ μετὰ Θεὸν διακρίνοντες δεξιῶς, καὶ λεῖα βλέποντες, καὶ ἐλπίζοντες καὶ δὴ καταλειφθέντες εἰς
χεῖρας τὰς σάς, ἰσχύος ἐξ ἀνθρωπίνης ἀπροστάτευτοι πάμπαν καὶ
15 ἄποροι, καὶ πάντες κατεπτηχότες καὶ μηδὲ γρύξαι δυνάμενοι πρὸς ἀμυθή-

---

26–28 cf. Exodus 32:32 || 29–31 Is. 22:4 || 32–34 cf. II Reg. 24:17
74: 8 cf. Is. 58:7 || 13 cf. Prov. 12:13ᵃ

---

26 ἢ] ἢ VS || ἐκθειάσαι VSP¹: ἐκθιάσαι P || 28 κἀμὲ scripsi; cf. Exodus 32:32; κἀμοῦ
codd. || 36 καὶ καὶ S || λαβὴν S
74: V 54ᵛ. S 195ᵛ–196ʳ. P 74ᵛ–75ᵛ. Ed. Laiou, *Andronicus II*, 338–339, no. 8.
1 ante πρὸς add. γράμμα VʳSP || post αὐτοῦ add. καὶ περὶ μὴ τιμιουλκεῖν χρειώδη πάν-
τα (om. P, χρειώδη πράγματα S) VʳSP || 8 μακαριώτερα P || 9 στέργον P || 12–13
post δεξιῶς repetivit καὶ ἀγαλλιάσονται S, et deinde delevit || 15 πάντας VP

still let us not lag behind the people of the Old Testament, I entreat, or else we should be unable to worship and admire Moses who begged God, «If thou wilt forgive their sin, forgive it; and if not, blot me out of thy book which thou hast written»; and as another man said, «labor not to comfort me for the breach of the daughter of my people», and again «leave me alone to weep bitterly». And what did the great David say at the time of divine wrath? Did he not call it on himself, saying, «If I the shepherd have done wrong, what has my flock done? Let thy hand, I pray thee, be upon me, and upon my father's house». And I could enumerate many more ⟨examples⟩, if I were not writing to ⟨your majesty⟩ in whom wisdom and mercy dwell, and who desires only to seize upon a point of departure; but since I know that I am far from ⟨the qualities⟩ which I quoted above, I restrain myself from making these suggestions or speaking further, lest I become a laughing stock. For this reason I beg you to heed me, even if I have not been taught to speak in a worthy manner.

74. To the emperor about the same matter

O mighty emperor, when Joseph was entrusted with the distribution of grain to his countrymen, this was something extraordinary, ⟨and done⟩ because he was the pride of his father, and because of his brothers' injustice, and his own unusual virtues. I beg of you, let us, ⟨who have this office⟩ without effort and expense, not be deprived of this office, nor let us lose it for any earthly reason. For men of understanding devote all their thoughts and secret purposes to this ⟨purpose of feeding their countrymen⟩, which is both honorable and necessary, and will be recognized in the world to come. For what is more blessed than for someone to «distribute bread to the hungry»?

Therefore accept gladly the goodness the exercise of which God has bestowed on your majesty. Only say the word, and you will put to shame those who consider it a source of profit and luxury and perpetual glory to raise the prices on all necessary provisions. But you will give pleasure and joy to those who make decisions in the right spirit, according to God and with the help of God, and to those whose «look is gentle», and who hope and indeed have been put in your hands, completely unprotected from human abuse and without resources, and afraid, all of them, and not even able to utter a

τους μακρηγορίας τῶν σοφῶν πρὸς τὸ ἀδικεῖν· δι᾽ οὓς καὶ τὸ βασιλεύεσθαι
ὑπ᾽ ἀνθρώπων ἀνθρώπους Θεὸς ἐδικαίωσε, μήπως καθὰ οἱ ἰχθύες
ὁ μείζων τῶν ἐλαχίστων αὐθαδῶς ποιῆται κατάποσιν.

ἕνεκεν τούτων, ἀντιβολῶ, ἀνθρώπους λυπῶμεν καὶ μὴ
20 Θεόν, πεποιθότας τῷ πλούτῳ (ἀλλὰ μὴ πένητας), Θεῷ δοκοῦντας
δουλεύειν καὶ μαμωνᾷ δυνατόν. ἢ οὐκ ἀναντιρρήτως ἅπας ἀλυκτοπέδαις τοῦ μαμωνᾶ πεδηθεὶς αὐτόχρημα καθορᾶται εὐαγγελίων
μυκτηριστής; ἐπίστηθι οὖν τοῖς τοιούτοις βασιλικώτερον, δέομαι·
ἔλεγξον, ἐπιτίμησον, ἀποστράφηθι· ἔνδυσαι τὴν προσήκουσαν λεοντῆν εἰς
25 δόξης αἰωνιζούσης καταστολήν· καὶ οὕτω διακειμένων ἡμῶν,
ὑπερασπίσαι ἐξεγερθήσεται ὁ παμμέδων, ὡς δυνατὸς καὶ
κεκραιπαληκὼς ἐξ οἴνου, πατάξων εἰς τὰ ὀπίσω σου
τοὺς ἐχθρούς, καὶ εἰς αἰώνιον ὄνειδος ταῖς μετέπειτα γενεαῖς
ὑποθήσων.

75. ⟨Πρὸς τὴν βασίλισσαν Εἰρήνην⟩

Ὡς χαίρειν μετὰ χαιρόντων ἀνεπιφθόνως πιστοῖς
ὀφειλή, οὕτω καὶ κλαίειν μετὰ κλαιόντων, εἰ καὶ μὴ περισσοτέ-
ρως, εἰπεῖν, ἡ θεία ἡμᾶς ἐκπαιδεύει Γραφή· εἰ δὲ ἐν ἀνθρώπῳ παντὶ κε-
5 χρεώστηται, [fol. 55ʳ] ἐν ὑπερέχουσι μάλιστα. διὰ τοῦτο καὶ τὸ πρὸς τοῖς
πολλοῖς λυπηροῖς τῇ ἐκ Θεοῦ βασιλείᾳ σου συμπεσὸν παρ᾽ ἐλπίδα καὶ μικροῦ ἀπιστούμενον τοῖς τοῦ γάμου εἰδόσι τὴν δύναμιν, τὸ εὑρίσκεσθαί τι
μεταξὺ τοῦ χαρισθέντος σοι πρὸς Θεοῦ νυμφίου καὶ βασιλέως, ὑμῶν ὀφειλόντων ἐκ περισσοῦ καὶ μᾶλλον, τῇ ἀλύτῳ ἑνώσει τῇ θαυμασίως ἀρχῆθεν
10 ἐν σπλάγχνοις ἐλέους δεδωρημένη τῷ γένει ὑπὸ Θεοῦ, ἐκτρέχειν
πρὸς ἕνωσιν ἀδιάρρηκτον καὶ στοργήν, καὶ ἐξ ἐκείνου τοῦ φίλτρου ὅσα καὶ
εἴ τι παρεμπίπτει ἀνιαρὰ συναντᾶν διαλύεσθαι, οἷα καὶ σκότος πρὸς τοῦ
φωτὸς τοῦ μεσημβρινοῦ.

ἀλλ᾽ (ὦ τῶν ἐμῶν συμφορῶν!) πῶς τὰ τῶν πειρασμῶν καὶ τοῦ φθό-
15 νου ἐν πᾶσι κατακρατεῖ τοῖς βιωτικοῖς, ὡς καὶ σχέσεως φυσικῆς τὸ θαυ-

---

17 cf. Hab. 1:13–14 ‖ 19–20 cf. Eph. 4:30 ‖ 21 cf. Matt. 6:24 ‖ 25 Is. 61:3 ‖ 26–28 cf.
Ps. 77 (78):65–66
75: 2–3 Rom. 12:15 ‖ 10 Luc. 1:78

75: V 54ᵛ–55ᵛ. S 196ʳ–197ᵛ. P 75ᵛ–76ᵛ.
1 πρὸς τὸν αὐτοκράτορα VSP (falsa inscriptio) ‖ ante πρὸς add. γράμμα VʳSP ‖ post
αὐτοκράτορα add. περὶ τοῦ παρ᾽ ἐλπίδα συμπεσόντος (συμπεσόντως VʳS) τῆς δεσποίνης ὁ
θάνατος VʳSP ‖ ad titulum scripsit ψεύδεται, γράμμα πρὸς τὴν βασίλισσαν περὶ τοῦ δεῖν
ὁμονοεῖν τῷ συζύγῳ Pˣᵐᵍ ‖ 5 τὸ] τῇ S ‖ 6–7 μικρὸν S ‖ 8 ὑμεῖν P ‖ 12 εἴ τι] ἥτει
codd. ‖ συνανιᾶν P ‖

74, 75

sound in rebuttal of the unspeakably long-winded explanations of those who are clever at villainy. It is for the sake of these people that God decreed that men should be ruled by men, lest «like fishes» the stronger swallow up the weaker with impunity.

For the sake of these people, I beg of you, «let us not grieve God» but rather men, not poor men, but those who put their trust in wealth, and believe that «it is possible to serve both God and mammon». Is it not true that everyone who is undeniably bound in the fetters of mammon is seen right away to be a scorner of the Gospels? Therefore, I beg of you, fix your imperial attention on these people; rebuke them, punish them, turn away from them. Put on the lion-skin which befits you as «a garment of» eternal «glory», and when we have adopted this attitude, the Ruler of all «will arise» to defend us «like a mighty man who has been heated with wine, to smite your enemies in their hinder parts, causing them to be eternally reproached» by subsequent generations.

75. ⟨To the empress Irene⟩

The Holy Scriptures teach us that it is the duty of the faithful ungrudgingly «to rejoice with them that do rejoice and weep with them that weep», if not excessively, so to speak (?); and if this is an obligation in the case of every human being, it is especially important in the case of people of prominence. Wherefore the unexpected misfortune which has befallen your divine majesty, in addition to your many other troubles, and almost not to be believed by those who know the power of marriage, namely the rift between you and the bridegroom and emperor granted you by God, while you both have a special obligation to embrace indivisible union and affection, on account of the indissoluble union which in the very beginning was marvelously granted to mankind by God in «the mercy of His heart»—and because of that love, whatever grievous troubles should happen to befall you should be dispersed like darkness by the noonday light.

But, alas for my woes, how temptation and jealousy prevail throughout life, so as to overcome the wonder of natural love! Wherefore, before your

μαστὸν περιγίνεσθαι! ὅθεν καὶ πρὸ τοῦ ἀποσωθῆναι τὴν βασιλείαν σου
τοῖς ἐνταῦθα, μηδ᾽ ἀκριβῶς διδαχθεὶς τὰ ἐν μέσῳ, ἃ τοῖς μεσολαβεῖν βουλομένοις τὰ πρὸς εἰρήνην γινώσκειν χρεών, ἀμφοτέρων τῷ πόθῳ καὶ τῇ
τιμῇ καὶ τῇ σωτηρίᾳ φλεγόμενος, τῶν λίαν ἐλογισάμην ἀνιαρῶν μὴ ὡς
20 δύναμις δεηθῆναι ἀπελαθῆναι τὴν μέσον ὑμῶν διάστασιν πολυήμερον. καὶ
πρῶτα μὲν συνεσκιασμένως ὡς δοκοῦν κατηνάγκαζον· ὡς δὲ ἐλέει Θεοῦ
ἐπανελθεῖν ἐγένετο καὶ τὴν βασιλείαν σου, καὶ φανερῶς ἐβιάσαμεν καὶ
πολλάκις, οὐ μόνον ὑπεραλγοῦντες τῶν θείων θεσμῶν δυναστευομένων,
ἀλλὰ καὶ ὑπὲρ τῶν ἀσυγκρίτων ὑμῶν καὶ γνώμῃ καὶ ἀξιώματι, ἐν οἷσπερ
25 ὁ καλλωπίσας Θεὸς ὑμᾶς ἐζωγράφισε τοῖς καλοῖς. τὰ σπλάγχνα σπαράσσομεν ὅπως μὴ κἀνταῦθα ἀσυγκρίτοις ὑπεροχαῖς ἐξ ἀγάπης κατὰ παντὸς
τοῦ λυποῦντος ὑπέρκεισθε, τῆς ὁμονοίας ὑμῶν ἐν τοῖς θεαρέστοις, καὶ
ὁμοζωίας καὶ εὐταξίας νόμου χρηματιζούσης τῷ κόσμῳ καὶ λύχνου πρὸς
σωτηρίας ὁδὸν ἐμβιβαζούσης καὶ τὸ ὑπήκοον· καὶ τοῦτο καὶ βασιλεῦσι καὶ
30 πᾶσιν ἀνθρώποις χρεών, λατρεύειν προαιρουμένοις καὶ θεραπεύειν καὶ δοξάζειν Θεόν. πλὴν εἰ καὶ μὴ διετηρήθη δι᾽ ἀμαρτίας ἐμὰς καὶ ὑμῖν, καὶ
μέγα τὸ λυπηρὸν καὶ ἀπαραμύθητον, ἀλλ᾽ ἡ σύνεσις ἡ πολλὴ ἡ προσοῦσα τῇ βασιλείᾳ ὑμῶν πρὸς Θεοῦ, καὶ ὁ πόθος καὶ ἡ ἀγάπη ἡ τηρεῖσθαι
ὀφείλουσα ἀδιάρρηκτος, κἂν ὁπωσδήποτε καὶ λυττήσῃ ὁ βασκαίνων
35 Βελίαρ τοῖς ἀγαθοῖς, παρ᾽ ὧν καὶ τὴν παραλύπησιν ὀξύνεσθαι πέφυκεν,
ἐκ [fol. 55ᵛ] τούτων καὶ μᾶλλον ὀφείλει ἐν πρᾳότητι παραμένειν καὶ
καταστέλλειν τὴν λύπην, καὶ Θεὸν ἐξαιτεῖν παρασχεῖν τὴν ὁμόνοιαν.
      ὅθεν ἀντιβολῶ καὶ τοὺς διαξαίνειν τὰ ἀηδίζοντα ἐγχειροῦντας
μηδαμῶς παραδέχεσθαι, ἐν ἐλπίσιν ἐντρεφομένη χρησταῖς, καὶ τὸ πᾶν ἀν-
40 αρτᾶν τῷ Θεῷ μετασκευάζοντι πάντα μόνῳ τῷ βούλεσθαι,
καὶ τοῖς φιλοῦσιν ὑμᾶς ἐξαιτεῖν πρὸς δεήσεις θερμότερον διανίστασθαι,
καὶ πρὸς δύναμιν ἀγαθοεργεῖν, καὶ δανείζειν Θεῷ καὶ μάλιστα
σήμερον, καὶ τῇ μνήμῃ ἐνδυναμοῦσθαι τῶν ᾀδομένων παρὰ τῇ θείᾳ Γραφῇ,
ποιῆσαι δύναμιν πρὸς συμφέρον κατὰ καιροὺς ἰδικῶς ἢ κοινῶς ὑπο-
45 μονῇ καὶ συνέσει καὶ προσευχῇ θυγατέρων τῆς ἐκκλησίας, ἢ καὶ ψυχὰς
κερδησάντων συνεύνων ἐν τρόπῳ χρηστότητος, καὶ τούτοις τὴν σὴν ἀνα-
κτᾶσθαι ἁγίαν ψυχὴν πρὸς τὸ εὔελπι· καὶ μὴ τοσούτοις τοῖς ἀγαθοῖς πρὸς
Θεοῦ κομισθεῖσα καταδέχου δι᾽ ὀλιγοψυχίαν ἀθυμίαις καὶ λύπαις ὑπὲρ τὸ
δέον βαπτίζεσθαι, πειραθέντων καὶ πιστευόντων ἡμῶν τὰ ἀδύνατα
50 παρ᾽ ἡμῖν, κοῦφα καὶ δυνατὰ παρὰ τῷ Θεῷ, εἰδυῖα εἴπερ τις

---

40 cf. Amos 5:8 et Greg. Naz., *Or.* XLII, ε΄ (PG, XXXVI, 464 B) ‖ 42 cf. Prov. 19:17 ‖
44 cf. Ps. 59(60):14 ‖ 49–50 cf. Luc. 18:27

---

16 πρὸς P ‖ 20 ἀπελασθῆναι S ‖ 22 ἐγίνετο P ‖ 23 δεσμῶν S ‖ 25–26 σπαράσσομεν
ὅπως] σπαρασσομένῳ πῶς codd.; forsitan lege σπαρασσόμενοι πῶς? ‖ 28 σωτηρίας V¹SP:
σωτηρίαν V ‖ 37 καταστέλειν V ‖ 39 παραδέχησθε codd. ‖ χρησταῖς V¹S: χρυσαῖς
VP ‖ 42 δύναμιν scripsi; cf. Ps. 59 (60):14; δύναμις codd. ‖ 44–45 ἰδικῶς ... θυγατέρων
τῆς om. P ‖ 48 κομισθεῖσαν codd.

75

majesty arrived here, when I was not even yet precisely informed of the circumstances (which must be known by those who wish to bring about a reconciliation), inflamed by my love for both of you, and by my concern for your honor and salvation, I considered it intolerable not to pray as much as I could that the lengthy separation between you come to an end. And first of all I applied persuasion by veiled hints, as seemed right to me, and when by the mercy of God it happened that you returned, I began to apply open and constant pressure, not only because I was aggrieved on account of the abuse of divine ordinances, but also for the sake of your blessings of mind and position, with which God, like a painter, adorned you. My heart is torn that here, too, given your incomparable qualities, you are not able to make your love surmount every distressing incident; and yet your harmony in God-pleasing actions and your life together and well-ordered existence is [i.e., should be] a law to the world at large, and to your subjects a lamp, leading them on the road to salvation; and this is necessary both for rulers and for all men who choose to venerate and worship and glorify God. But if on account of my sins you have not maintained this, and the grievance is great and not capable of consolation, still a great understanding has been granted to your majesty by God, and great the desire and love which ought to be preserved unbroken (even if the jealous Beliar should rage at your blessings, as a result of which irritation is usually exacerbated), and therefore you should abide in meekness and restrain your grief and ask God to grant you harmony.

Wherefore I ask you not to receive those people who attempt to exacerbate an ⟨already⟩ unpleasant situation, but, nourished by good hopes, entrust everything to God «Who transforms all things by His will alone», and ask those who love you to rouse themselves to more ardent supplications, and do good works to the best of your ability, and «lend unto God» especially now. Be strengthened by the memory of those who are celebrated in the Holy Scriptures, «strive valiantly» as is expedient according to the occasion, either in private or in public, with the ⟨help of the⟩ patience and understanding and prayers of daughters of the Church, or of couples who have gained their souls on account of their goodness, and through these virtues restore your holy soul to good hope. And since you have received so many blessings from God, do not allow yourself through faintheartedness to be submerged in excessive despair and grief. For through experience we believe that «what is impossible for us is» easy and «possible for God», and you know, if

τῶν βουλομένων βαδίζειν πρὸς τὸ σωθῆναι, καὶ τῷ πάντοτε χαίρειν προσεῖναι ἀδιαλείπτως προσεύχεσθαι καὶ εὐχαριστεῖν ἐν παντί. βιούσης γὰρ οὕτω εὐχαριστίᾳ καὶ φόβῳ Θεοῦ, αὐτὸς κρατήσει τῆς δεξιᾶς σου Χριστός, ὁδηγῶν πρὸς τὰ κρείττω καὶ τελεώτερα, καὶ ἀ-
55 φράστως δοξάσει δοξάζουσαν ὡς ὑπέσχετο τοὺς δοξάζοντας, καὶ πρὸς τῇ δόξῃ καὶ βασιλείᾳ τῇ ἐπιγείῳ, καὶ τὴν ἐν οὐρανοῖς σοι χαρίσεται.

76. Πρὸς τὸν αὐτοκράτορα

Εἰ ᾔδειμεν λυπουμένην τὴν ἐκ Θεοῦ βασιλείαν σου ἐν οἷς ὀρθοδόξοις οὐ δέον, οὔποτε συνηλγήσαμεν· ἀλλ᾽ ἐπεὶ κατὰ λόγον εὑρίσκῃ παρα-
λυπούμενος, οὐκ οἶμαι μὴ συναλγεῖν τὸν ἀκούοντα, εἰ μὴ πάντῃ τῶν ἀναισ-
5 θήτων ἐστίν. ἀλλὰ τί καὶ πρὸς τὰ τοιαῦτα διαπράξεταί τις, οὐκ οἶδα πόθεν καὶ πῶς ἐθισθέντων τῶν δυνατῶν πρὸς τὸ τούτοις ἀρέσκον ἐκφέρεσθαι, ἀλλὰ μὴ πρὸς ὅσα θυμήρη Θεῷ ἐπισπεύδειν, καὶ τοῖς αὐτοῖς ἀξιοῦσι τοιαῦτα ὡς συμβούλους σωτηριώδεις ὑπείκειν εὐχαριστίᾳ τῇ
πρὸς Θεόν; δι᾽ ὃν οἱ ποθοῦντες αὐτοὺς ὑποτίθενται, ἔστιν οὗ καὶ βιάζονται,
10 τὰ θεοφιλῆ· καὶ κέρδος οἰκεῖον ὀφείλειν λογιζομένους ἐν οἷς ὑπακούουσιν,
ἀλλὰ μὴ ὥσπερ εὐεργετοῦντες τοὺς ἐν [fol. 56ʳ] Χριστῷ φιλοῦντας αὐτοὶ
διακείμενοι· χάριν δὲ μᾶλλον τούτοις ὁμολογεῖν, ὡς εἰς κέρδος προτρεπο-
μένοις ἐκείνους σωτήριον, μηδεμίαν εὐεργεσίαν εἰς ἑαυτοὺς ἐξ ἐκείνων αἰ-
τούμενοι, ἀλλὰ τὴν τῶν ψυχῶν ἐκείνων καὶ εὐχόμενοι καὶ βιάζοντες προ-
15 κοπήν· οὓς καὶ ὡς εὐεργέτας ἐχρῆν ὑπακούειν καὶ ἀγαπᾶν, κἄν τι δοκῇ
τῶν ἐπιζημίων τοῦ πλούτου τοῦ φθειρομένου ἡ βελτίστη εἰσήγησις, ὅπου
καὶ ἰατρείαις σωματικαῖς καὶ ἡδοναῖς ἀλλοκότοις πολλὰ τοῖς φιλοσωμά-
τοις καταναλίσκεται χρήματα. εἰ δὲ ἐν τοῖς ἐπιζημίοις οὐ προτιθέασι
ζημίαν χρημάτων οἱ ἐμπαθεῖς, τί μὴ περιφρονήσῃ ὁ συνετός, συνιὼν ἀπο-
20 δόσθαι τῶν φθειρομένων πρὸς τὸ κερδῆσαι τὰ μὴ φθειρόμενα; ἀλλ᾽ ἐπεὶ
μὴ ζητοῦμεν κερδῆσαι τὰ μέλλοντα κόπῳ καὶ μόχθῳ, ἀλλὰ μόνον τοῖς
φθειρομένοις συνδαπανώμεθα, τοῦ πρώτως κεκελευκότος Θεοῦ
τὴν βασιλείαν ζητεῖν μὴ αἰδούμενοι, συνεξέλιπε διὰ τοῦτο καὶ ἡ
ἀπὸ Θεοῦ τοῖς γνησίως αὐτὸν φοβηθεῖσι καὶ ἀγαπήσασι δωρεὰ καὶ ἀντί-
25 ληψις.
    διὰ ταῦτα τὸ πᾶν ἐπληρώθη κακίας, καὶ ἀντὶ δικαιοσύνης καὶ σω-
φροσύνης καὶ ἀληθείας πολιτεύεται τἀναντία, καὶ ἡ ἀδικία ὡς δικαιοσύνη

51–53 cf. I Thess. 5:16–18 ‖ 55 cf. I Reg. 2:30
76: 8 cf. Sap. 16:6 ‖ 22–23 cf. Matt. 6:33

---

51 βαδίζειν] βαπτίζειν S ‖ τῷ] τὸ V ‖ 56 χαρίσηται codd.
76: V 55ᵛ–56ʳ. S 197ᵛ–198ᵛ. P 76ᵛ–77ᵛ.
1 ante πρὸς add. γράμμα VʳSP ‖ post αὐτοκράτορα add. περὶ τοῦ ὅσα θεοφιλῆ οἱ ποθοῦντες
ὑποτίθενται καὶ βιάζουσι, κέρδος οἰκεῖον ὀφείλειν εἶναι λογιζομένους VʳSP

75, 76

anyone does of those who wish to proceed toward salvation, that in addition to «rejoicing evermore», we should also «pray without ceasing», and «in every thing give thanks». For if you live thus in thanksgiving and fear of God, Christ Himself will hold your right hand and lead you on to greater perfection, and He will marvelously «glorify» you who glorify Him as He promised to «those who glorify Him», and in addition to your earthly glory and empire He will grant you that in the heavens.

76. To the emperor

If I knew that your divine majesty was grieving over something not proper for Orthodox Christians, I would never share your sorrow. But since you are distressed for good reason, I do not think that anyone who heard you would not share your sorrow, unless he had no feelings at all. But, to take another example, what can one do in the following situation, if in some way, I know not how, the mighty ones have become accustomed to rush after what is pleasing to them, rather than striving for what is pleasing to God, and in gratitude to God obeying those who, as «counsellors of salvation», ask them ⟨to do⟩ such ⟨God-pleasing deeds⟩ ? It is for the sake of God that those who love them suggest, and often force upon them, a way of life pleasing to God. And they ought to consider (?) it to be to their own profit if they pay heed, and not to have the attitude that they are doing a favor for those who love ⟨them⟩ in Christ. Instead they ought to be grateful to these people, for urging them on to the gain of salvation, and not asking any favor of them for themselves, but praying for and forcing the progress of their souls. And they ought to heed and obey them as their benefactors, even if the most laudable investment (?) of wealth should appear to them to bring about some loss, seeing that people who indulge their bodies spend a great deal of money on physical remedies and unusual pleasures. If then people who are slaves to their passions do not consider it a waste of money ⟨to spend it⟩ on harmful thing s, why shouldn't the intelligent man scorn ⟨money⟩, since he realizes that he is paying that which is corruptible in order to gain that which does not suffer corruption ? But since we do not seek to gain the world to come with toil and labor, but are only wasting away together with that which is corruptible, because we do not revere God Who bade us to «seek the kingdom first», for this reason even those who have genuinely feared and loved God have been deprived at the same time of His rewards and help.

For these reasons everything has been filled with evil, and instead of righteousness and moderation and truth, their opposites prevail, and injustice

192

σπουδάζεται. εἰ δέ τι καὶ ἀναφέρομεν περὶ ταύτης τῷ ἁγίῳ μου αὐτοκράτορι, ἢ διὰ τὸ πολὺ τῶν φροντίδων, ἢ καὶ δι' ἕτερόν τι ὅπερ ἀγνοῶ, μὴ εἰσ-
30 ακουόμενοι, σιωπῶμεν, αἰδούμενοι καὶ λυπούμενοι τοῦτον ἐπὶ πλεῖον
ὀχλεῖν, καὶ ἀθεράπευτα μένει τὰ θεραπείας καὶ θρήνων καὶ ὀδυρμῶν ἄξια.
ὅθεν ἐξαπορῶν τοῖς συμβαίνουσι καὶ καταβαπτιζόμενος λύπῃ, πῶς ἀνθρώπων οἱ πλεῖστοι χάριν εὐημερίας ψηλαφῶσι γινώσκειν τὰ ἐφετὰ βασιλεῦσιν, ἵνα τῇ τούτων ἀποπληρώσει δεικνύντες τὸ εὔνουν, τύχωσιν εὐεργεσιῶν
35 τῶν ἀνθρωπίνων, οἱ δέ, τὰ φίλα Θεῷ γινώσκοντες καὶ ὅσα ζητεῖ παρ'
ἡμῶν (ἃ πληροῦντες στεφάνους, παραβαίνοντες δὲ τιμωρίας τρυγῶμεν καὶ
ὧδε καὶ ἐν τῷ μέλλοντι), προκρίνομεν τὴν ζημίαν τοῦ κέρδους, καὶ τιμῆς
ἀτιμίαν, ἀδοξίαν τε δόξης, καὶ παρρησίας αἰσχύνην, ἀναφέρειν δεῖν ἔγνων
τῇ σῇ εὐγενεῖ καὶ βασιλικωτάτῃ ψυχῇ καὶ οἰκτίρμονι, ἵνα κἂν τὰ...

77. ⟨Πρὸς τὸν αὐτοκράτορα⟩ [fol. 56ᵛ]

Μέρος ἀρχῆθεν καὶ τοῦτο λατρείας θεοσεβοῦς καλῶς ὀρθοδόξοις
κριθὲν ἀνεγείρειν θείους ναοὺς καὶ μονύδρια καθιστᾶν κατὰ δύναμιν, λιμέ-
να ψυχῶν βουλομένων ἀποδιδράσκειν τρικυμιῶν τῶν βιωτικῶν εὐτρεπί-
5 ζοντας, εἶτα τῇ κατὰ τόπους καθολικῇ ἐκκλησίᾳ καὶ τῷ ταύτης λαχόντι
φροντίζειν καταπιστεύοντας, ὡς τοῖς θείοις κανόσι διαγορεύεται, φροντίζειν καὶ ἐπιδόσεως καὶ συστάσεως καὶ τῶν κατοικησάντων πνευματικῆς
ἀνακρίσεως καὶ πολιτείας θεοφιλοῦς· εἰ δέ που καὶ ὑφαρπάζειν τὰ ἐκεῖ
ἀφιερωθέντα Θεῷ ἐπισφαλῶς εἰς ὄλεθρόν τις τῆς οἰκείας ψυχῆς δοκιμά-
10 σει, ἀπείργειν ὡς δύναμις, ἢ τὸ βαρὺ τῆς ἱεροσυλίας ὑποτιθέντος, καὶ ὅτι
καθὼς οἱ ἀφιεροῦντες κτήσεις Θεῷ, ἢ ἄργυρον ἢ χρυσόν, ἀναφαίρετον
ἔχουσι τὸν μισθόν, καὶ οἱ ὁπωσδήποτε ἀποσπῶντες ἀναμφιβόλως τῷ τῆς
ἱεροσυλίας ἁλίσκονται κρίματι. εἰ δ' ἐν τούτοις μὴ εἴη καταπειθὴς πρὸς
τοὺς ἰθύνειν λαχόντας σκῆπτρα ἀπὸ Θεοῦ, ζητοῦσιν ἀντίληψιν, ὡς ἂν ἐκεῖ-
15 θεν τῷ κράτει καὶ τὸν ἱεροσυλοῦντα ἐξέλωνται ἀνομίας, καὶ τῇ ἐκκλησίᾳ
δοθῇ τὸ τίμιον ἀναποσπάστως κατέχειν τὰ ἀφιερωθέντα Θεῷ. ὅθεν, ὡς
οἶδε Θεός, καὶ ἡμεῖς τῶν τῆς ἐκκλησίας Χριστοῦ λαχόντες ἐνέχεσθαι, οὔτε
προσφέρεσθαί τι ἐξ ἁρπαγῆς ὀρεγόμεθα ταύτῃ, ἐγνωκότες μὴ ἥδεσθαι
προσφορᾷ Θεὸν τῇ ἐξ ἁρπαγῆς, οὔτε τῶν βουλομένων ἁρπά-

77: 18–19 cf. Sirac. 31 (34):19

39 epistolae finis deest omnibus in codicibus
77: V 56ᵛ–57ʳ. S 199ʳ–200ʳ. P 78ʳ–78ᵛ.
1 γράμμα πρὸς τὸν αὐτοκράτορα περὶ τοῦ καλῶς ὀρθοδόξοις κριθὲν ἀνεγείρειν θείους ναούς,
εἶτα τῷ κατὰ τόπους φροντίζειν λαχόντι καταπιστεύειν ὡς οἱ θεῖοι κανόνες διαγορεύουσιν
(διαγορεύουσι Vʳ) add. VʳSP ‖ 7 καὶ συστάσεως om. S

76, 77

is the goal, as if it were justice. But if I report anything about this to my holy emperor, either because of your many cares, or for some other reason of which I am unaware, I am not heeded and so keep silence, ashamed and distressed to trouble you any further, and matters worthy of concern and tears and lamentation are left neglected. Therefore, since I am at a loss about present events and plunged into despair at the way most men, for the sake of their own prosperity, try to find out what rulers want, so that by fulfilling these ⟨desires⟩ and thus making a show of their good will, they may receive worldly benefits, and ⟨since I also despair at how⟩ others of us, although we know what is pleasing to God and what He seeks from us—that if we fulfil ⟨His commandments⟩ we will receive crowns, and if we transgress ⟨them⟩ we will be punished, both here and in the world to come—still prefer the loss to the gain, and dishonor to honor, and lack of glory to glory, and disgrace to bold speech, I decided that it was necessary to make a petition to your kind and most royal and merciful soul, so that [the rest of the letter is missing].

77. ⟨To the emperor⟩

It has been rightly ordained from the beginning as a part of pious worship that Orthodox Christians should construct as many holy churches and establish as many monasteries as possible, thus providing a haven for those souls which yearn to escape the stormy seas of life, and then to entrust ⟨them⟩ to the local ⟨diocese of the⟩ catholic Church, and to the man appointed to Her charge, as is expressly stated by the holy canons. He should concern himself with the advancement and protection and the spiritual examination and God-loving behavior of their inhabitants. And if anyone should attempt to seize the objects there dedicated to God, at a great peril and to the destruction of his own soul, ⟨the bishop⟩ should prevent him as best he can, reminding him either of the grave sin of sacrilege, or of the fact that, just as people who dedicate to God their possessions, whether silver or gold, have their inalienable reward, so people who remove them in any way whatsoever are without any doubt found guilty of the crime of sacrilege. And if in these matters he [the sacrilegious person] should fail to obey those into whose hands God entrusted the rule ⟨of the Church⟩ [i.e., the bishops], they seek assistance, so that, first, in such a way they may deliver the sacrilegious person from his transgression of the law—this for the sake of the State—, and second, so that the Church may be granted the honor of keeping irrevocably those objects which are dedicated to God. Wherefore, as God well knows, I, who have been charged with responsibility for the property of the Church of Christ, desire neither to offer it anything which is stolen, since I know that «God takes no pleasure in an offering of stolen property», nor can

20 ζειν τὰ ταύτης ἀνέχεσθαι δεδυνήμεθα, θείῳ βαλλόμενοι φόβῳ τοῦ μὴ
εὐθύνην ἐκ σιωπῆς ἡμετέρας ἀσυμπαθῆ τοῖς ἁρπάζουσι προξενήσωμεν.
ὅθεν καὶ πρὸ μικροῦ συνέβη συνοδικῶς τινι προσελθόντι [fol. 57ʳ]
κατηγορῆσαι ἀναίδην ἡμῶν, πῶς ἐν τῷ περὶ τὴν Ἀπάμειαν πατριαρχικῷ
μονυδρίῳ ἀναισχύντως γυναίῳ τὸν προεστῶτα τοῦ μονυδρίου ἐκ πολλοῦ
25 συνοικεῖν, πληροφορεῖν δὲ καὶ πάντας ὡς ἐν εἰδήσει τοῦ πατριάρχου καὶ
τῶν ἐξάρχων οὕτω καθέζεσθαι. ὁ καὶ μαθόντες, τοῦ μὲν πτώματος τὸν
ἁλόντα, τὴν δὲ μονὴν μιασμοῦ, καὶ βλάβης τοὺς συνειδότας ῥυσθῆναι
φροντίσαντες, τῇ μονῇ τῆς τοῦ κόσμου Δεσποίνης καὶ Θεομήτορος τῆς
Εὐεργέτιδος ὄντως γειτονευούσῃ διέγνωμεν διὰ γράμματος παραδοῦναι
30 καὶ εἴ τι ἐκέκτητο, ἵνα καὶ μοναζόντων ὑπάρξῃ διατριβὴ εὐλαβῶν
ἀποδιδόναι ἐντεύξεις Θεῷ, προσευχάς, δεήσεις, εὐχαριστίας ὑπέρ τε τῆς βασιλείας ὑμῶν, καὶ τῶν ἐν ὑπεροχῇ
καὶ τοῦ κόσμου παντός. νῦν δὲ προσελθόντες ἡμῖν ἀποκλαίονται ὡς δυναστ-
ευόμενοι παρά τινων τῶν τῆς ἐκ Θεοῦ βασιλείας σου. ὁ καὶ διέγνωμεν
35 ἀναφέρειν αὐτῇ, ἵνα, εἰ λέγουσιν ἀληθῆ, κελεύσει τῆς ἐκ Θεοῦ βασιλείας
σου, ἔχωσι μὲν εἰρήνην οἱ μοναχοὶ πρὸς τῷ ἀζημίῳ, οἱ δ' ἐφιέμενοι ἀλλοτρίων κελευσθῶσιν ἀπέχεσθαι ἀδικεῖν καὶ μᾶλλον τῶν ἀφιερωμένων Θεῷ.
καὶ τούτου γε χάριν πρὸς τῇ βασιλείᾳ τῇ ἐπιγείῳ, ὁ τῆς δικαιοσύνης καὶ
τοῦ ἐλέους Θεὸς καὶ τῆς ἐπουρανίου καταξιώσειεν.

78. Πρὸς τὸν αὐτοκράτορα

Τῶν δοθέντων τῇ πρὸς Θεοῦ βασιλείᾳ ὑμῶν οἰκονόμοι καλοὶ
χρηματίζειν ὀφείλοντες, καὶ δανείζειν τὸν ἔλεον τούτῳ διὰ
μέσον πενήτων ἀναγκαίως σπουδάζειν, ὡς ἂν τῷ τοσούτοις ὑμᾶς κα-
5 ταστέψαντι καὶ δοξάσαντι, εὐχαρίστοις φωναῖς καὶ εὐγνώμοσι, καὶ τοῖς
ἔργοις πρὸ τούτων, τὸ εὔγνωμον ἐπιδεικνύησθε, ἵνα καί, ὁπηνίκα ὁμιλεῖν
αὐτῷ προσευχόμενοι ἔρχησθε, σπουδάζητε λέγειν ἐν παρρησίᾳ ἃ ψυχῶν
εὐλαβῶν καὶ Θεὸν ἐγνωκότων ὡς δεῖ, καὶ ὥς που φησὶν ἡ Γραφή, τὸ
ἐξ αὐτοῦ καὶ δι' αὐτοῦ καὶ εἰς αὐτὸν τὰ πάντα, ᾧ καὶ
10 ἡ δόξα ἀπέραντος, ὡς κἀντεῦθεν ἀρίστῳ φρονήματι καταβεβλημένῳ καὶ
ταπεινῷ τὰ σὰ ἐκ τῶν σῶν σοὶ προσφέρομεν κατὰ πάντα
καὶ διὰ πάντα βοᾶν, καὶ γεραίρειν καὶ εὐλογεῖν καὶ ὑμνεῖν, εὐχαρίστως

31–32 cf. I Tim. 2:1–2
78: 2 I Pet. 4:10 || 3–4 cf. Prov. 19:17 || 9 Rom. 11:36 || 11–12 cf. Paralip. I, 29:14,
et λειτουργία τοῦ Ἰωάννου Χρυσοστόμου (Brightman, 329)

---

21 εὐθύνην V¹SP: εὐθύνειν V || ἡμετέρας VSP¹: ἡμέρας P || 30 εἴ τι] ἔτι SP
78: V 57ʳ–58ʳ. S 200ʳ–201ʳ. P 79ʳ–80ʳ. Ed. Laiou, Byzantion, 37 (1967), 109–110.
1 ante πρὸς add. γράμμα VʳSP || post αὐτοκράτορα add. περὶ τοῦ πρόνοιαν προνοῆσαι τὸν πα-
τριάρχην ἀθῆραν ἐψεῖν περὶ τῶν πτωχῶν, καὶ ζητῆσαι ξύλα τὰ τὸ πῦρ τρέφοντα VʳSP ||
4 ἡμᾶς S || 6 ἐπιδείκνυσθε codd. || 6–7 ἵνα ... ἔρχησθε om. P || 7 σπουδάξει τὲ P

77, 78

I tolerate those who wish to seize the property of the Church. For I am gripped with divine fear lest as a result of my silence I bring merciless punishment on the thieves.

Thus a while ago a man happened to come before the synod and denounced us without restraint because at the patriarchal monastery near Apameia the *proestos* of the monastery had shamelessly cohabited with a woman for a long time, and he assured everyone that he [the *proestos*] indulged in such a cohabitation with the knowledge of the patriarch and the exarchs. When we learned this, thinking to deliver the guilty man from his sin, the monastery from its scandal, and the accomplices from their defilement, we decided to hand the monastery and all its possessions over by means of a letter to the neighboring monastery of the Mistress of the World and Mother of God, the Euergetis, so that there would be an opportunity for pious monks to offer up «entreaties to God, prayers, supplication and thanksgiving on behalf of your majesty and those in authority» all over the world. But now they [the monks] come to me and complain that they are being abused by certain of your divine majesty's officials. Wherefore I have decided to make this report to you, so that if the monks are speaking the truth, by the command of your divine majesty they may be left in peace and not suffer any losses; but those who desire the possessions of others should be ordered to refrain from wrongdoing, and especially ⟨to keep away⟩ from offerings dedicated to God. And thanks to this may the God of righteousness and mercy deem you worthy of the heavenly kingdom in addition to the one you have here on earth.

78. To the emperor

You have the obligation to be a «good steward» of what has been granted ⟨by God⟩ to your divine majesty, and to strive of necessity «to lend mercy to Him through the poor», in order to demonstrate with cries of thanksgiving and gratitude, and above all with deeds, your thankfulness to the One Who has crowned you and glorified you with so many blessings, and so that, whenever you come to speak with Him in prayer you may strive to pronounce confidently the words of pious souls which have known God in a right way, and ⟨to say⟩ as the Scriptures say somewhere, «everything is from Him and through Him and to Him» and to Him be eternal glory, so that then you may proclaim in a suitably humble and downcast attitude, «we offer to Thee Thine Own from Thine Own in all and through all», and honor and bless

δοξάζοντας ἔργῳ καὶ λόγῳ, ὅπως σὺν τοῖς ἐνταῦθα ὑμῖν κἂν οὐρανοῖς συν-
τηρηθῇ τὸ διάδημα. καὶ γένοιτο τοῦτο, Θεὲ τοῦ παντός, δι᾽ ἀγαθοερ-
15 γίας συντόνου ὡς δυνατὸν τοῖς ἐνταῦθα ἐπὶ [fol. 57ᵛ] καρπίαν ὑμῖν
πλουτισθῆναι καὶ τὰ οὐράνια, καὶ ταύτῃ τῇ πεποιθήσει ῥωννυμένους ἡμᾶς
ἀναφέρειν θαρρούντως ἃ τοὺς ἐκεῖ προξενοίη μισθούς, τοῖς καὶ (ὑπέρευγε
τῆς εὐκλείας!) συγκληρονόμοις Χριστοῦ χρηματίσασι.
    πρὸς δὲ ταῦτα τὸ νῦν κεκινήμεθα. ἀλλὰ πῶς ἐξομολογησόμεθα
20 τὰ ἡμέτερα; ἢ μᾶλλον ἀποκλαυσόμεθα, ἀνενέγκαι θελήσαντες πρὸς μικρὸν
τῶν πενήτων τὴν συμφοράν, καὶ τῆς ἡμῶν καταγνόντες ἀσπλαγχνίας καὶ
φειδωλίας καὶ φιλαυτίας, καὶ ὅτι μηδὲ τῇ τοῦ Ἰωσὴφ κατακλώμεθα
συντριβῇ, καὶ μήπως καὶ ζῶντας ἀσυμπαθῶς καὶ μακρὰν τοῦ καὶ πᾶσιν
ὀφείλοντος οἴκτου καταπίῃ ἀξίως ἡ γῆ; εἰς κόρον κατατρυφῶντος
25 ἐμοῦ καὶ ὑπὲρ τὴν χρείαν, τῶν δὲ πενήτων οὐ μόνον τοῖς ἄλλοις πιεζομένων, ἀλλ᾽ ἤδη καὶ τῷ λιμῷ καὶ τῷ κρύει τρυχομένων καὶ διαφθειρομέ-
νων, οὐ δεξιώσασθαι τούτους καὶ ἐπενδῦσαι ὡς δέον ἡ ἡμετέρα ψυχὴ ἐδικαίωσεν ἡ ἀσυμπαθής, ἀλλ᾽ οὐδ᾽ ἐκ τῶν τῆς ἐμῆς τραπέζης
ἀποπιπτόντων ψιχίων μεταδιδόναι ποσῶς βεβούλημαι ὁ ταλαίπωρος,
30 οὗτοί γε καθ᾽ ἡμέραν πρὸς τῶν θείων Γραφῶν κωμῳδούμενος, ἀλλ᾽ ἤδη
καὶ πρὸς τῶν θείων εὐαγγελίων ἱστορούντων μοι ἃ δι᾽ ὠμότητα ἀσπλαγχνίας τῷ ἐκεῖ στηλιτευομένῳ πλουσίῳ συνέβη.
    ἔνθεν καὶ ἔδοξέ μοι ὀψὲ τάχα ὑπὲρ πενήτων φροντίδα ποιῆσαί τινα·
καὶ ἡ φροντὶς ἁρμοδία τῇ προαιρέσει μου, ἥ, ὡς ἐγώ, καὶ αἱ ἐμαὶ παρο-
35 χαὶ πρὸς τοὺς πένητας καὶ ψυχραὶ καὶ μικροπρεπεῖς. ἀλλὰ μὴ τίς με
ταπεινολογεῖν ὑπολάβῃ· ἀληθεύω γὰρ ἐν Χριστῷ, βαβαί, ὁ τοσαῦτα παρὰ
Θεοῦ καὶ λαβὼν καὶ ἐλπίζων, ὁ κελευσθεὶς τὸν πλησίον ὡς ἑαυτὸν ἀγαπᾶν, καὶ κρέμασθαι ὅλον τὸν νόμον ἐν ταῖς δυσὶν
ἐντολαῖς διδαχθείς! τίς δέ μοι καὶ ἡ πρὸς τοὺς πένητας πρόνοια; ἀθῆραν
40 ἐψεῖν προενοησάμην τοῖς ἀπόροις καὶ ταλαιπώροις· καὶ ταύτης, ὡς ἔφην,
ἀρξάμενος, πρὸς βραχὺ (ὦ τῆς ἐμῆς συμφορᾶς!) ἐπιλελοίπει μοι καὶ τὰ
τρέφοντα ξύλα τὸ πῦρ. ὧν γε χάριν ἀντιβολῶ κελευσθῆναι τοῖς ὀρεινόμοις
πρὸς τῆς ἐκ Θεοῦ βασιλείας ὑμῶν ἄδειαν δοῦναι ἡμῖν τοῦ μετακομίσειν
οὐχ ὅσα καὶ βεβουλήμεθα, ἀλλ᾽ ὅσα δοκεῖ τοῖς δεσπόταις. καὶ ταῦτα
45 κελεύσετε, ἵνα κἀκεῖθεν ὑμῖν ὁ μισθὸς πρὸς Θεοῦ, ὡς ὅτι καὶ τοῖς τὸ ἀγαθὸν βουλομένοις καὶ ὁπωσδήποτε μὴ ἰσχύουσι, δαψιλῆ παρέχητε [fol. 58ʳ]
χεῖρα πρὸς τὴν τῶν βελτιόνων ἀποπεράτωσιν· καὶ οὕτω μὴ μόνον ἐξ ὑμετέρων ἀλλὰ καὶ ἐκ τῶν ἀλλοτρίων νομιζομένων καλῶν, ὑμῖν ὁ μισθαπο-
δότης κερδηθείη Θεός.

---

18 cf. Rom. 8:17 ‖ 19 cf. Ps. 74 (75):2 ‖ 22–23 cf. Amos 6: 6 ‖ 24 cf. Num. 16:30, 32 et
Ps. 105(106):17 ‖ 28–29 cf. Matt. 15:27 ‖ 32 cf. Luc. 16:19–26 ‖ 37–39 cf. Matt. 22:39–40

---

15 ἐπικαρπίαν codd. ‖ 17 τοῖς] οἷς codd. ‖ 18 χρηματίσασι VSP¹: χρηματίσασαι P ‖
19 κεκινήμεθα VS¹P: κεκτήμεθα S ‖ 35 σμικροπρεπεῖς P ‖ 41 ἐπιλελοίπει VS¹P:
ἐπιλελείπει S

and celebrate Him, glorifying Him thankfully in word and deed, so that you may wear the diadem both here and in Heaven. And may this come to pass, O God of all, that, through the vigorous accomplishment of good deeds as much as is possible to those dwelling in this world, you be granted the enjoyment of the heavenly kingdom, and that I be strengthened by this conviction so as to boldly proclaim what ⟨sort of conduct⟩ will bring rewards in the life hereafter, especially for those who are called «joint-heirs with Christ» (O what blessed glory!).

I have now been moved ⟨to do these things⟩. But how shall I confess my failings? Or shall I not rather weep for my condition, when I wanted to reduce the sufferings of the poor, but observed my heartlessness and stinginess and selfishness, and the fact that I am not overwhelmed «with the contrition of Joseph», and ⟨my fear⟩ lest the earth swallow me up as I deserve, since I live without compassion, far removed from the mercy which is the duty of all men? For although I am stuffed to satiety, and beyond my needs, while the poor are not only oppressed by other ⟨calamities⟩, but are also crushed and destroyed by famine and cold, my cruel soul did not consent to receive and clothe these people as it should have, nor, wretch that I am, was I even willing to share with them «the crumbs which fall from my table», no indeed, although I was ridiculed every day by the Holy Scriptures, and also by the Holy Gospels which tell me the fate of the rich man who was mocked in the hereafter because of his cruel lack of mercy.

Wherefore I decided, too late perhaps, to concern myself with the poor, and ⟨the extent of⟩ my attentions matched my character; that is, just as I am, so my offerings to the poor were both cold and insignificant. But let no one suspect that I belittle myself; for I swear by Christ that I am telling the truth, alas, I who have received and hope for so much from God, I who have been bidden «to love my neighbor as myself», and have been taught that «on the two commandments hangs all the law»! And what was my charity to the poor? I decided to have gruel boiled for the needy and miserable, and, as I said, after beginning this, I soon ran out of even enough wood to keep the fires going, alas for my ill fortune! Therefore, I entreat your divine majesty to order that the foresters be free to bring me ⟨wood⟩, not as much as I want, but as much as is decided upon by the rulers. And give this command so that you may be rewarded by God for this action, too, because to those who wish ⟨to accomplish⟩ good deeds, but have not the means, you extend a bountiful hand which helps to bring the deeds to completion. And thus may God, Who grants rewards, be attained by you, not only as a result of your own deeds, but of the deeds of others which are considered good.

79. Πρὸς τὸν αὐτοκράτορα

Εἰ μέγα τι ᾐτησάμεθα τὴν ἐκ Θεοῦ βασιλείαν σου, πῶς τῆς
αἰτήσεως ἐπετύχομεν, ὁπότε ἐννόμως καὶ ἐγκανόνως τῷ τοιούτῳ προσκείμενοι μέχρι καὶ νῦν οὐκ εἰσακουόμεθα; τί γὰρ μὴ ἕκαστος τῶν ἀρχιερέων,
5 ὡς τοῖς κανόσι δοκεῖ, τῇ τοῦτον λαχούσῃ προσκαρτερεῖ; τίς δὲ ὁ μὴ κέρδους χάριν αἰσχροῦ καὶ ξενίων ἢ ἀνέσεως καὶ σπατάλης τούτους ὑπειλη-
φὼς παρεδρεύειν τῇ βασιλίδι, θείων κατορχουμένους θεσμῶν, ἐκ παρεισπράξεων πληθυσμοῦ; τί δὲ μὴ — καὶ τῶν τοῦ κλήρου ὀλίγων τινῶν
ἀφηνιαζόντων τῆς ἐκκλησίας, καὶ ὥσπερ οὐ κατὰ χρέος, κατὰ δὲ χάριν εἰσ-
10 ερχομένων, ὅτε καὶ βούλονται καὶ ὡς βούλονται, καὶ ἄλλους ἐκδιδασκόν-
των τὸ αὔθαδες, τὸ μήτε ὑπηρεσίαν ἀποπληροῦν, μήτε στολῇ ἁρμοδίῳ τῇ
ἐκκλησίᾳ καθωραΐζεσθαι; ἀλλὰ πρὸς μέμψεις καὶ γογγυσμοὺς τὴν διάνοι-
αν ἔχοντες, ἕνεκεν ὀφφικίων καὶ ῥόγας ὑπὲρ ὧν οὐ κεκοπιάκασιν, ὡς ἀδικούμενοι τὰ μεγάλα καταστενάζουσι. πρὸς τίνος δὲ καὶ κριθῆναι ἑτέρου
15 δικαίως ἐπιδραμούμεθα, ὡς ἐφορῶντος Θεοῦ, εἰ μὴ παρὰ τοῦ τῆς
ἐκκλησίας υἱοῦ τῆς ἐκ Θεοῦ βασιλείας σου, ἣν καὶ ἀδικουμένην μὴ δικαιοῦν τὸ κρῖμα βαρύ; ἢ οὐχὶ ἐκ τοῦ μὴ ἐκφέρεσθαι τὰς κρίσεις εὐθεῖς,
ἡ βλάβη τῇ οἰκουμένῃ μεγάλη ἐξεγένετο κατὰ γενεὰς ὡς καὶ σήμερον;
ἔνθεν ἐν ὅσῳ καιρὸν ἔχομεν, χεῖρα παρέξωμεν καὶ τῇ ἐκκλησίᾳ καὶ
20 ἀδικουμένῳ παντὶ ἐν εὐθύτητι. καὶ γὰρ ἐξανθούσης δικαιοσύνης καὶ
ἀληθείας, ἀναμφιβόλως κακία πᾶσα ἐκμαρανθήσεται, καὶ οὕτω συνά-
γοντες ὦμεν μετὰ Χριστοῦ.

80. Πρὸς τὸν αὐτοκράτορα

Οἱ ὀρθοδόξων ἀνάκτων δεόμενοι πρὸς εὐεργεσίας αὐτοὺς διεγεῖραι
θεοτερπεῖς, ἢ ἐκείνων αὐτῶν ἕνεκεν πράττουσι τοῦτο, ἢ φίλων ἢ συγγενῶν
ἢ δώρων ἢ δόξης χάριν κενῆς. εἰ οὖν δι' ἓν τῶν ῥηθέντων αἰτοῦμεν καὶ
5 ἡμεῖς, ὁπότε αἰτοῦμεν τὴν ἐκ Θεοῦ βασιλείαν σου τὸ εὐεργετεῖν, μηδ' ὅπωσ-

79: 21–22 cf. Matt. 12:30
80: 7 cf. Rev. 2:23

79: V 58ʳ. S 201ʳ–201ᵛ. P 80ʳ–80ᵛ. Ed. Laiou, *Andronicus II*, 334, no. 1.
1 ante πρὸς add. γράμμα VʳSP ‖ post αὐτοκράτορα add. ὅπως ἕκαστος τῶν ἀρχιερέων τῇ
λαχούσῃ προσκαρτερῇ, καὶ περὶ τῶν (τῆς S) τοῦ κλήρου ἀφηνιαζόντων ἕνεκεν ὀφφικίων
καὶ ῥόγας VʳSP ‖ 13 οὐκ ἐκοπιάκασιν P ‖ 17 ἢ P ‖ 19 παρέξομεν codd.
80: V 58ʳ–59ʳ. S 201ᵛ–202ᵛ. P 80ᵛ–81ᵛ.
1 ante πρὸς add. γράμμα VʳSP ‖ post αὐτοκράτορα add. περὶ τοῦ ἃ ἀναφέρειν (ἀναφαίρειν
VʳSPˣ)οὐχ ἕνεκεν φίλων ἢ συγγενῶν ἢ δώρων ἢ δόξης, ἀλλ' ἀμφότερα ἀπαραίτητα αὐτόχρημα οὔσας σοι τὴν βασίλειαν VʳSP

79. To the emperor

If I were to ask an important favor of your divine majesty, what chance have I of being granted the request, since up to now I have not been heeded when I have made lawful and canonical petitions? Why doesn't each of the bishops remain in the see assigned to him, in accordance with the canons? Who has not understood that it is for the sake of base gain and bribes or comfort and wanton luxury that these men stay in the capital, as they trample upon the divine commandments through a multitude of illegal exactions? And what about the few members of the clergy who rebel against the Church, and come ⟨to services⟩ as if it were not a duty, but a favor, when and as they wish, and teach their boldness to others, not to fulfil one's duties, for example, nor to adorn oneself with garments suitable for church? Rather they have their mind on complaints and grumblings about the official positions and salaries for which they have performed no work, and groan loudly as if they had been wronged. To whom else will we run to be justly judged, with God watching over, if not to your divine majesty, the son of the Church? For it is a serious crime not to avenge ⟨the Church⟩ when She is wronged. Or is it not true that because right judgments were not carried out, great harm has befallen the world throughout the generations, even as now? Wherefore, while we still have the opportunity, let us offer our hand in righteousness both to the Church and to every wronged person. For when justice and truth flourish, there is no doubt that all evil will wither away. May we thus be people «who gather with Christ».

80. To the emperor

Those who entreat orthodox rulers in order to spur them to good works which are pleasing to God, do this either for their own sake, or for the sake of friends or relatives or gifts or vainglory. Thus if I should ever make a request for one of the above-mentioned reasons, when I ask for a favor from your

οὖν ὁρκίζω εἰσακουσθῆναί με. εἰ δέ γε πεπληροφόρηται πρὸς αὐτοῦ
[fol. 58ᵛ] τοῦ τὰς καρδίας ἐτάζοντος καὶ νεφροὺς δι’
οὐδὲν τῶν ῥηθέντων καταναγκάζειν με, λείπεται μόνον τὸ δι’ ἀγάπην
ἀσύγκριτον τοῦ ἀγαπωμένου. εἰ δέ τις καὶ χάριν μισθοῦ τῷ τὰ βέλτιστα
10 προξενοῦντι τινὶ ἐκδέξεται τὸν τὸν ἔλεον ἐπισπεύδοντα, ἀλλ’ οἶμαι πάλιν
τὸ κέρδος ὀλίγον ἢ καὶ οὐδέν. τί γὰρ ἄρα, καὶ ἀληθείας κρινούσης, φιλοτέκνου μητρὸς ὑποστάσει ὀνήσει ἐν φιλτάτῳ υἱῷ καὶ περιποθήτῳ καὶ
κάλλει ὡραίῳ ἐπεύχεσθαι, εἰ τούτοις προσῇ καὶ ἀνδρία καὶ εὐεξία καὶ
φρόνησις καὶ τρυφὴ καὶ ἱματίων καλλωπισμὸς χρυσοπάστων, καὶ ὡραϊσμα
15 πᾶν παντοδαποῦς πλουτισμοῦ; καὶ τί τὸ πρὸς ἀποδοχὴν ἐκείνην κινοῦν καὶ
ὠθοῦν τῷ φιλτάτῳ προσεῖναι τὰ τῇδε, εἰ μὴ μόνη ἀγάπη ἀνόθευτος, ἐξ
ἧς ὡς οἰκεῖα ἐκείνης τὰ τοῦ υἱοῦ, εἰ καὶ μὴ ταύτης καταλογίζεται, ἐπεὶ
μηδὲ ἴσμεν ἐγγύτερον ἄλλον τῇ φύσει τινὰ ἑαυτοῦ;
   δι’ ἃ καὶ ἀντιβολῶ, τὴν μισθαποδοσίαν τὴν ἐκ τοιούτων ἢ καὶ τὴν
20 ὀφειλὴν αὐτὴν προτιθείς, εἰδὼς ἀμφότερα ἀπαραίτητα τῇ ἐκ Θεοῦ βασιλείᾳ σου χρηματίσοντα· αἰτήσεις δὴ τὰς ἐμὰς αὐτόχρημα κόσμον βασίλειον
οὔσας σοι καὶ σωτήριον μὴ ἀποποιοῦ ὑπερθέσεσιν, ἢ ἐκ τούτων ὀλίγα τινὰ
καὶ μικρὰ παρεκλέγου, παραλιμπάνων τὰ πλείω καὶ μεγάλα καὶ ἀσυλλό-
γιστα, τινὰ δὲ ὀλίγα εἰς βραδυτῆτας ἀναρτηθείς, ἃ τῇ ἀργίᾳ πρὸς λήθης
25 κατολισθαίνει βυθούς, εἴ τι καὶ Σολομῶντι τῷ τὴν σύνεσιν ἄκρῳ πειστέον. πειστέον καὶ γάρ, ἐπεὶ καὶ τοῖς πρὸς ἀλήθειαν εὐλαβέσι καὶ συνετοῖς
λίαν ὠφέλιμος ἡ παραίνεσις· οὗ κἂν τοῖς ἄλλοις καὶ ἡ τοῦ μὴ ἀπόσχῃ
εὖ ποιεῖν ἐνδεῆ, φωτίζουσα καὶ συνετίζουσα, καὶ μάλα ὡς ὅτι μηδὲ
τῇ φύσει προσῇ ἡ τῶν ὄντως ἑρμαίων ἐργασία διηνεκής, ἀλλὰ μόνος και-
30 ρὸς ὁ παρὼν ἐνδεής· ὁ δὲ μέλλων (φεῦ τῆς ζημίας!), εἰ μὴ ὀρθῶς ἐπειχθῶ-
μεν τοῖς κρείττοσι, τῆς δικαίας ἀνταποδόσεως.
   ἀλλ’ οὐδὲ τοὺς ἐκ φίλτρου καὶ μόνου καταναγκάζοντας ταύτην, ὡς
δοκῶ, καθ’ ἡμᾶς εὑρήσεις ἀεί, ἢ παρὰ τὸ ἐκκακοῦν μὴ εἰσακουομένους
ἐπὶ πολύ, καὶ σιγὴν κἀντεῦθεν ἀσπάσασθαι, εἴ τε τυχὸν καὶ διὰ τὸ
35 προσόν μοι ὠκύμορον, ἀψαμένῳ ταῦτα καὶ γήρως, καὶ τῆς εὐκόλως ἐξα-
πατώσης νέους ἐλπίδος τῷ πλήθει τῶν ἡμερῶν μακρὰν ἀπορραπισθείσης
ἡμῶν. εἰ δέ γε εὑρήσειν ἢ κατέχειν πολλοὺς τοὺς φιλοῦντας ὑπὲρ ἡμᾶς βε-
βαίως [fol. 59ʳ] ὑπολαμβάνει ἡ ἐκ Θεοῦ βασιλεία σου ὡς παρορᾶσθαι ἐντεῦθεν ἡμᾶς, εὐξαίμην ἂν τοῦτό σοι προσεῖναι καὶ αὐτὸς ἔγωγε. ἀμφιβάλ-
40 λω δὲ ὅμως καὶ τὸ πρᾶγμα οὐ συνορῶ· τὸ δέ γε συνοῖσον καὶ ἀπλανὲς
ἐμβατεύσοι τῇ ταύτης καρδίᾳ Θεὸς ὁ παντέφορος.

---

13 Ps. 44(45):3 ‖ 24–25 cf. Sap. 16:11 ‖ 27–28 Prov. 3:27

---

11 καί¹ VˡˢᵛSP

80

divine majesty, I earnestly entreat you not to heed me. But if indeed it is confirmed by the One Who «searcheth the reins and hearts» that I make my demands for none of the above mentioned reasons, then the only ⟨reason⟩ left ⟨for my entreaty⟩ is my incomparable love for my beloved ⟨emperor⟩. And if someone expects that the One Who promotes mercy [God] will be the reward of the person who offers the best [Andronicus], even then the gain ⟨to the one who expects=Athanasius⟩ is little or nothing. For in truth how will it benefit the property of an adoring mother to pray for her dear and beloved and beautiful son, that in addition to these qualities he may possess courage and good health and intelligence and luxuries and cloaks shot with gold, and be adorned with every sort of wealth? And what kind of return is it that moves and stirs her ⟨to wish⟩ that her son should possess these things, if not her pure love alone, as a result of which she considers her son's possessions as her own, even if they are not reckoned as hers, since we do not know anyone who has closer natural ties ⟨to her⟩ than he does?

Wherefore I make ⟨the following⟩ request, keeping uppermost in mind the reward for such ⟨deeds⟩, or the very obligation ⟨to perform them⟩, since I know that both will be indispensable for your divine majesty: do not put off with delays my petitions which are indeed an imperial adornment for you and lead to salvation, or select only a few minor petitions and pass over without consideration the numerous important ones, and defer decision on a few matters, which through neglect sink down to the «depths of oblivion», if one is to believe Solomon, that summit of wisdom. And he must be believed, since advice is extremely profitable for men who are wise and revere the truth. For it is to him that we owe, among others, this illuminating and edifying proverb, «Refrain not from helping one that is needy», especially because by laws of nature it is impossible constantly to produce true strokes of fortune, but only the imperfect present is the time ⟨for action⟩; the future, alas, ⟨will be a time⟩ of just retribution, unless we strive for the better in the right way.

But, in my opinion, you will not always find people who make demands upon you from love alone, as I do, or, because they lose heart when they are ignored for a long time, therefore lapse into silence; perhaps it is because I have few years remaining to me, since I have reached old age, and have thrust far away from myself the hope of long life which readily deludes young people. But if you, your divine majesty, are firmly convinced that you will find or hold many people who love you more than I do, so that you can disregard me, I too would hope that you might enjoy this blessing. But I am doubtful and cannot envision such a possibility. And so may God, Who oversees all things, implant in your heart an expedient and unerring ⟨course of action⟩.

81. ⟨Πρὸς τὸν αὐτοκράτορα⟩

Χάρις κἂν τούτῳ σὺν τῇ λοιπῇ ἀγαθοπρεπεῖ θεουργίᾳ τῇ φύσει τῇ
μακαρίᾳ, ὅτι τὴν ἐκκλησίαν ἱερωσύνῃ καὶ βασιλείᾳ ἁρμοζόντως κατέστε-
ψεν, ὡς ἂν ὑπ' ἀμφοῖν ἐκ ζήλου κραταιουμένη κυπρίζοντας βότρυς περ-
5 κάζῃ, ἀξίους καὶ πλήρεις τῶν θείων ληνῶν, ἀφ' ἑαυτῆς ὀμφακίζον ἅπαν
ἀπορραπίζουσα, ὡς τοῦτο κἀντεῦθεν εἰσόμεθα· τῆς γὰρ Χριστοῦ ἐκκλησίας, σὺν ταῖς λοιπαῖς θεϊκαῖς δωρεαῖς, ἐπιδαψιλευομένης ἀνθρώποις ἐκ
δεξιᾶς ἱεραρχικῆς καὶ τὸ μέγα τουτὶ καὶ πανάγαστον τῆς ἱερωσύνης
ἀξίωμα—οἷστισιν ὀφειλὴ τὸ πρώτως ὀρθοδοξεῖν εἰς Θεόν, καὶ αἵματος
10 μέχρις διεκδικεῖν ὅσα φίλον αὐτῷ, καὶ δὴ καὶ τηρεῖσθαι πιστοὺς τοῖς
θεόφροσιν αὐτοκράτορσι, καὶ εὐλαβῶς καὶ πεφυλαγμένως δικαιοσύνῃ καὶ
σωφροσύνῃ καὶ ἀληθείᾳ βιοτεύειν ἐπείγεσθαι, ὡς ἔργῳ καὶ λόγῳ παντὶ
εἰς παίδευμα κεῖσθαι χρηστόν, καὶ ἅλας τυγχάνειν καὶ φῶς τῷ
ἐπιλοίπῳ λαῷ, καὶ μάλα πρὸ τῶν λοιπῶν τὸ εὔνουν ὑποτιθέναι τῇ βασι-
15 λείᾳ, ὡς ἔφην, τηρεῖν τοῖς λαοῖς, ὡς ἐπιβλέπειν λελαληκότος τοῦ τῆς
εἰρήνης Θεοῦ πραέσι καὶ πειθηνίοις ἂν καὶ πιστοῖς, δεήσεις αὖ καὶ ἐντεύξεις, εὐχαριστίας καὶ προσευχὰς πυκνὰς αὐτοὺς ποι-
ουμένους ὀφειλομένως, ὑπέρ τε τῆς βασιλείας καὶ τῶν
ἐν τέλει καὶ ἑαυτῶν, καὶ τοῦ κόσμου παντός, ὡς ἂν ἐν ἠρέμῳ ἐκεῖ-
20 θεν ζωῇ δίκην ἐσόπτρου πιστοὺς ὑπεμφαίνοιεν ὁποίας δέοι ἀναστροφῆς
τοῖς αὐχοῦσι λατρεύειν τῷ ἀληθεῖ καὶ ζῶντι καὶ μόνῳ Θεῷ, καὶ ἐπιεικείᾳ
σεμνοπρεπεῖ τὸ Χριστώνυμον σύνταγμα εἰς πᾶν ἀγαθὸν ἐξ ὧν ἐνεργοῦσιν
αὐτοὶ συνελαύνοιεν.

ἀλλά γε κἂν τούτοις ὡς ἐν ἀμπέλῳ φύεσθαι βάτον ἠκού-
25 σαμεν, καὶ ἕνα προδότην τῶν τοῦ μεγάλου Σωτῆρος Χριστοῦ
μαθητῶν βεβήλῳ γεγενημένον ἴσμεν παρατροπῇ, γνώμῃ τινὶ σκαιο-
τρόπῳ, καί τις Ἰωάννης τὰ νῦν, Δριμὺς τὸ ἐπίθετον, τοῦ βήματος ἕνα
προσμαρτυρῶν ἑαυτόν, κακίας ἐκβλύσαι ἐξήχθη, πολὺ τὸ δριμὺ [fol. 59ᵛ]
καὶ ἐπόζον τῇ πολιτείᾳ πιστῶν καὶ ὀλέθριον, καὶ ταῦτα κλήσει τῇ ἱερᾷ
30 ὑποκρυπτόμενος πανουργότερον, ὡς ἄν τις κῳδίῳ καὶ λύκον περικαλύψειεν.
οὐκ οἶδα ἐκ ποίων βαράθρων τε καὶ τριόδων ἀνασωθεὶς πρὸ καιροῦ ἐπ'
ἀπωλείᾳ τῇ ἑαυτοῦ, καὶ ὅσους υἱοὺς ἀπωλείας καὶ τούτῳ καταπει-

---

81: 9–10 Hebr. 12:4 ‖ 13 cf. Joh. Chrys., *De Sacerdotio* VI, iv (PG, XLVIII, 681) ‖
15 cf. Ps. 101(102):18? ‖ 16–20 cf. I Tim. 2:1–2 ‖ 24–26 cf. Greg. Naz., *Or.* XXI, ιδ' (PG,
XXXV, 1097A) ‖ 32 cf. Joh. 17:12 et II Thess. 2:3

81: V 59ʳ–61ᵛ. S 202ᵛ–207ʳ. P 81ᵛ–86ʳ. Ed. Banduri, *Imperium Orientale*, II,
970–975; Migne, PG, CXLII, 483–492.
1 γράμμα τοῦ πατριάρχου στηλητευτικὸν περὶ Ἰωάννου τινός, Δριμὺς τὸ ἐπίθετον, προσεταιρισάμενος συμμορίαν ἐπάρατον κατά τε τῆς ποίμνης Χριστοῦ, κατά τε τῆς ἐκκλησίας
καὶ τοῦ θεοστεφοῦς αὐτοκράτορος add. VʳSP ‖ 4 κρατουμένη SP ‖ 8 ἱεραρχικῆς]
ἀρχιερατικῆς P ‖ 29 ἐπόζον] ἐπήζον SP, ἐπίζον P¹

81

81. ⟨To the emperor⟩

Grace be to the Blessed Nature, because, together with the rest of His divine work which befits the good, He suitably crowned the Church with both the priesthood and kingship, so that supported by both with zeal She might ripen the blooming grapes, full-bodied and worthy of the holy wine troughs, rejecting from Herself every unripe grape, as we will know from what is to follow ⟨in this report⟩. For the Church of Christ, together with other divine gifts, has bestowed on mankind from Her hierarchical right hand this great and praiseworthy honor of priesthood; and it is the first duty of priests to hold correct doctrine concerning God, and to defend «unto blood» whatsoever is dear unto Him and to remain faithful to godly-minded emperors, and to strive to live piously and with due caution in justice and prudence and truth, so as to be a good example in every word and deed, and to be «salt and light» to the rest of the people, and especially, as I have said, to urge the people to be well disposed toward the emperor, since the God of peace has said that «He watches over» the meek and obedient and faithful; in addition ⟨priests⟩ ought to make «supplications and intercessions, thanksgiving and frequent prayers on behalf of the emperor and officials» and themselves and the whole world, so that by leading «a peaceful life» they may demonstrate like a mirror to the faithful what sort of life must be led by those who assert that they are devoted to the true and living and only God, and so that with dignified virtue they may urge on the Christian troops to every good deed by the example of their own actions.

But as «we have heard that thorns grow in a vineyard», and as we know that «one of the disciples» of the great Savior Christ through profane aberration and as the result of a twisted mind became «a traitor», so now a certain John, with the surname of Drimys [i.e., Bitter], who claims to be a member of the clergy, has been tempted to spew out evil, causing much bitterness and evil smell and harm to the community of the faithful, and even more wickedly has hidden behind his holy title, like a wolf clothed in sheepskin. After emerging some time ago from I don't know what pits and places of ill repute for his own destruction, together with as many «sons of perdition» obedient to

θεῖς ἐπέδειξεν ὁ καιρός, τὴν βασιλίδα καταλαμβάνει, οἷα τις ἐρυσίβη, καὶ
βασιλεῖ τῷ ἁγίῳ ἐμφανισθεὶς καὶ εἰσδεχθεὶς δεξιῶς, ὡς δῆθεν εἶναι
35 τῶν εὐλαβῶν, καὶ φιλοτιμηθεὶς ὑπὲρ τὴν ἀξίαν· δι' ὃ ἐπεφήμιζεν ἑαυτῷ
ἱερωσύνης οἶμαι ἀξίωμα, ἕλκειν σκεπτόμενος διὰ τούτου πολλὴν πρὸς αὐτὸν
τὴν ἀναδοχήν, εἰωθότος τιμᾶν τὰ θεῖα καὶ τοὺς τοῦ Θεοῦ μεγάλαις ἀνα-
δοχαῖς καὶ βασιλικαῖς τοῦ ἁγίου μου αὐτοκράτορος, ἀπό γε φιλοθεΐας καὶ
εὐσεβείας καὶ εὐλαβοῦς καὶ ἡμέρου ψυχῆς, ὡς οὔποτε τῶν ἀνέκαθεν βασι-
40 λέων ἄλλῳ τινὶ ἐν τοῖς θείοις. κἂν τούτῳ τὸ εὐλαβὲς μεμαρτύρηται, ὡς
τοῦτο τούτου τῷ κράτει πεφιλοφρόνηται ὑπερβολῇ καλοκἀγαθίας καὶ ἡμε-
ρότητος, ὡς ἵνα κἂν τούτῳ συνᾴδων εἴη τῷ μεγάλῳ Δαυῒδ τὸ λίαν
ἐμοί, ὁ Θεός, οἱ φίλοι σου ἐτιμήθησαν.
    ἀλλ', ὦ ψυχῆς ἀναισχύντου καὶ πάντη σκαιᾶς! ἀντὶ γὰρ ὀφειλούσης
45 εὐγνωμοσύνης τῇ εὐποιΐᾳ, ἐξ ἧς καὶ θῆρας ἴσμεν μεταβεβλῆσθαι, τὸν
θεῖον φόβον καὶ ὅρκους ἀπορραπίσας ἀφ' ἑαυτοῦ ὁ λίαν δριμὺς καὶ
δυσθάνατος, καὶ ὁμοίους αὐτῷ προσεταιρισάμενος κατά τε τῆς ποίμνης
Χριστοῦ, κατά τε τῆς ἐκκλησίας, καὶ τοῦ θεοστεφοῦς αὐτοκράτορος, ρα-
ψῴδημα δόλου καὶ τυραννίδος συνθέμενος (φεῦ τῆς ἐρεσχελίας!) ὁ ἄθλιος
50 ἀπόγονον εἶναι τῶν πώποτε βεβασιλευκότων τινός, ὃν οὐδὲ γεννηθῆναι,
οὐδὲ παρά τινος θεαθῆναι ἢ ἀκουσθῆναι ταῖς ἀληθείαις καὶ μέχρι σήμερον
ἄνθρωπος ἠνωτίσθη ποσῶς — τραγέλαφος οἶμαι τις ἀνυπόστατος, ἢ καθά
που τὰ λόγια, ὅτε ἡ θάλασσα ἐμαιοῦτο, σὺ ἐτήρησας τοκε-
τοὺς τραγελάφων ἀκηκοώς — ἔνθεν πρεσβύτερα μὴ ὀκνεῖν διακη-
55 ρυκεύειν ὑπὲρ αὐτοῦ καὶ μείζονα, γέλωτος κωμῳδίαν ἀξίαν ἢ μᾶλλον
δακρύων πολλῶν ἑαυτῷ καταχαριζόμενος, καὶ τοῖς προχείρως ἐκ μοχθηρίας τοιαῦτα πιστεύουσι καὶ κρατύνουσιν. ὅθεν καὶ μᾶλλον μυρμηκο-
λέων εὑρέθη κακός, κακῶς ὀλεσκόμενος ἀποτυχὼν τῆς βορᾶς,
ὅς, μετ' ἐκείνου τοῦ θεῖναι τοῖς ἄστροις τὸν θρόνον βατταρίσαι τετολμη-
60 κότος, τὰ τοιαῦτα [fol. 60ʳ] προσονειρῶξαι οὐκ ἔφριξε, μεθ' οὗ καὶ
συνηριθμῆσθαι καὶ συντετάχθαι διὰ τὴν μίμησιν, ὡς ἐξ ὧν εἰργάσατο
ἀποδείκνυται.
    κἀκεῖθεν ὁμόφροσι τούτῳ τισὶ τὰ τῆς πλάνης αὐτοῦ καὶ ἀποστα-
σίας καταπιστεύσαντα, καὶ ἀκοαῖς πονηραῖς λόγους διακομίσαντα πονη-
65 ρούς, τὰ αὐτοῦ βδελυρὰ σκαιωρήματα ἐν τῇ πόλει καὶ ταῦτα τοῦ κράτους
ἐνσπείρας ὁ δείλαιος, συμμορίαν ποιεῖται ἐπάρατον· οἳ καὶ μήπω διακορεῖς
τῇ τοσαύτῃ μανίᾳ γενόμενοι, ἔτι ὠδίνοντες τὰ κακά, τοῦ μόνοι ἐνταῦθα
λυττᾶν μεθ' ὧν ᾠκειώσαντο μικρὸν λογιζόμενοι, μειζόνως ἐν κακουργίᾳ
δραμεῖν συνέλαβον πόνον τοῦ ἀνομίαν ἀποτεκεῖν, ὡς ἂν μειζόνως
70 ἐκπολεμῶσαι αὐτοὺς καὶ Θεὸν ἐπισπεύδοντες, τοὺς κύκλῳ ἡμῶν ἀθέους

42–43 Ps. 138(139):17 ‖ 53–54 cf. Job 39:1 ‖ 57–58 cf. Job. 4:11 ‖ 69 cf. Ps. 7:15

---

33 τις] τι S ‖ 42 τὸ om. P ‖ 44 σκιᾶς SP ‖ 45 θύρας S ‖ 58 βορᾶς scripsi; cf. Job
4:11; βορρᾶς codd. ‖ 65 καὶ ταῦτα: num legendum κατὰ?

him as time has later shown, he arrived at the capital, like a wheat-rust, appeared before the holy emperor, and was received courteously as a supposedly pious man, and was honored more than he deserved, for he asserted that he was from the ranks of the clergy, thinking, I believe, thus to gain for himself great liberality from my holy emperor, who is accustomed to honor divine things and the people of God with great and royal liberality, because of his love of God, and his piety, and his reverent and peaceful soul, as none of the emperors before him in religious matters; and his piety was demonstrated in this affair, too, for on this occasion the emperor showed great hospitality with extraordinary nobility and kindness, so that he [the emperor] might sing together with the great David, «But thy friends, O God, have been greatly honored by me».

But what a shameless soul, wicked in every way! For instead of the gratitude which is owed in return for good deeds, as a result of which even wild beasts are known to change ⟨their temperament⟩, that fierce and deadly man cast aside fear of God and his oaths, and together with rogues like himself plotted against the flock of Christ, against the Church, and the God-crowned emperor; for the wretch composed a tale of treachery and tyranny (alas what foolish nonsense!) that he was a descendant of one of the former emperors, although in truth no one has ever heard of his birth, nor was he seen or heard by anyone up to this day. I think he is the nonexistent «goat-stag», or as the Scriptures say somewhere, «When the sea raged, you heard and observed the births of goat-stags». Wherefore he does not hesitate to declare even older and greater claims for himself, providing a comedy worthy of laughter or rather of many tears for himself and for those who rashly believe and maintain such things out of depravity. Wherefore he has been found out to be rather an evil «ant-lion who dies a miserable death for lack of food», who did not shudder to dream of such deeds together with the one who dared to stammer that he had placed his throne among the stars, and with whom he should be numbered and ranked on account of his imitation, as is shown by his actions.

And then having entrusted to certain like-minded men the secrets of his deviation and revolt, and conveying wicked words to wicked ears, the cowardly wretch spread his loathsome machinations even in the capital of the empire (?), and formed an accursed conspiracy. These men, in no way satisfied even with this extent of madness, brought forth yet more villainy, and considering it of little account to rage here alone with their associates, they also undertook the labor of a course of greater evil so as «to bring forth lawlessness». Thus, promoting a greater war between God and themselves,

καὶ ἀσεβεῖς εἰς ἄσπονδον μάχην τὴν κατὰ τοῦ Κυρίου καὶ τοῦ χριστοῦ αὐτοῦ καὶ ὅλου συντάγματος Χριστωνύμου συγκαλέσαι ἐπ' ἀπωλείᾳ κοινῇ εἰς ἀντίληψιν τὴν ἑαυτῶν ἐψηφίσαντο. καὶ τοῦτο ἐξήνυσαν ἄν, εἰ μὴ συνέχεε τούτων τὰς μηχανὰς ὁ θανάτου ἐκτρέπων σκιὰν εἰς ζωὴν
75 τοῖς ἐλπίδας βεβαίας ἀναθεμένοις αὐτῷ, ὃς καὶ τὸν πόνον αὐτὸν ταῖς αὐτῶν κεφαλαῖς ἐνδίκως ἐπέβαλε, καὶ λίθον κυλίειν ἐφ' ἑαυτῶν αὐτοῖς ἐξεγένετο. οἷς καὶ ἐπέλθοι μεθ' ὧν συμμάχων καὶ εἵλοντο, Χριστὲ βασιλεῦ καὶ Θεέ (τῆς ποίμνης εὐσπλάγχνως μνησθείς, ἧς ἐκτήσω τῷ πάθει σου), οἷα καὶ ὅσα τῷ Ὡρὴβ ἐκείνῳ καὶ τῷ Ζεβεὲ καὶ τῷ
80 Σαλμανάν, καὶ τοῖς ἄρχουσι τοῖς ἐκείνων φρυαξαμένοις ὑπερηφάνως, οἷα καὶ οὗτοι, τοῦ Θεοῦ τὰ ἁγιαστήρια.

ἐκ μηδενὸς τοῦ δικαίου ἢ ἀφορμῆς ἢ γένους ἢ τρόπου βασιλειῶντος δριμυτάτου Δριμέος καὶ ὄντως θεοστυγοῦς, ἐπιλησθέντος καὶ ἑαυτοῦ, καὶ ἃ μηδ' ὄναρ ἰδεῖν ἐφικτόν, διακένως ἐπὶ τὸ δράξασθαι κατασπεύσαντος,
85 καὶ δίκην θυέλλης ὡς ἐκ τυφῶνος δεινοῦ, διαταράξαι καὶ καταδύσαι πρὸς ἀπιστίας βυθὸν ὅσον ὑπόσαθρον εὗρε καὶ δύσνουν τῇ βασιλείᾳ ἐκ τοῦ λαοῦ, Θεῷ δέ, καὶ πρότερον καὶ μᾶλλον ἀπὸ τῶν Ξυλωτῶν — ἐξ ἀφορμῆς εὐλόγου οὐδεμιᾶς εἰς τοῦτο ἐλθών, ἢ ἐκ τοῦ φρονηματισθῆναι καὶ μόνου, καθά που ὁ τῇ Γραφῇ προσαδόμενος ἄφρων, μετὰ τῶν ἀκολούθων αὐτῷ φρεν-
90 απατηθεὶς ὁ ἐξάγιστος, ὡς ὅτι οὐκ ἔστι Θεός· ἐξ οὗπερ καὶ διεφθάρη βδελυχθεὶς καὶ διαπαιχθεὶς ὡς στρουθίον οἰκτρόν, ὁ φαντασθεὶς ἐμφανίσαι ἑαυτόν, [fol. 60ᵛ] ἕως ᾠετο, ὑπὲρ Θεοῦ φοβερώτατον, οἷα πίτυος ἁπτόμενος μῦς, συνάμα καὶ οἷσπερ ἑάλω κακῶς προσεταιρισάμενος, ἐκεῖθεν μυκτηρισθέντας καὶ ἀναφωνήσει προφητικῇ·
95 ἐβασίλευσαν γάρ, φησίν, ἑαυτοῖς καὶ οὐ δι' ἐμοῦ, ἦρξαν καὶ οὐκ ἐγνώρισάν με· μηδὲν τούτων λαβόντες εἰς νοῦν οἱ ἐμβρόντητοι καὶ ὁ τούτων ἀπαιδευτότατος προεστώς, ὁ χθὲς τοῦ βήματος ἕνα φημίζων ἑαυτόν, καὶ σήμερον ξιφηφόρος διψήσας φανῆναι, καὶ φαντασθεὶς ἁρματηλατεῖν σκηπτοῦχος (ὢ δίκη!) ὁ τολμητίας, ἀναδοθεὶς αὐ-
100 θωρὸν τοῖς ὁμοίοις αὐτῷ τὴν δυσσέβειαν, μόνῃ θαρρήσας ἀπάτῃ κωφῇ καὶ ματαίας διαβολῆς. ὡς ὅτι τῶν ἡμετέρων οὐδὲν ἀθεεί, καὶ ὅτι σκληρὸν τὸ πρὸς κέντρα λακτίζειν αὐτοὺς καί τι ἐκ τοῦ δι' ἐμοῦ βασιλεῖς βασιλεύουσι διδασκόμεθα· ἃ καὶ μὴ συνιέντες οἱ ἀλιτήριοι, οὐδ' ὅτι ἡμῶν καὶ αἱ τρίχες ἠριθμημέναι ἐκεῖθεν τῆς κεφαλῆς,
105 ἢ ὁ αὐτῶν πρωτουργός — περὶ τούτων γὰρ τάχα κατηύξατο καὶ ὁ θεῖος

---

74 cf. Ps. 106(107):14 ‖ 75–76 cf. Ps. 7:17 ‖ 76–77 cf. Prov. 26:27 ‖ 79–80 cf. Iud. 7:25; 8:1–21; Ps. 82(83):12 ‖ 81 cf. Ps. 82 (83):13 ‖ 89–90 cf. Ps. 13(14):1 et 52 (53):2 ‖ 91 cf. Job 40:24(29) ‖ 93 cf. Leutsch-Schneidewin, I, 206, 275; II, 189 ‖ 95–96 Osee 8:4 ‖ 102 cf. Leutsch-Schneidewin, II, 128, 379, 628 ‖ 102–103 Osee 8:4 ‖ 104 cf. Matt. 10:30

---

74 συνέχει SP ‖ 75 τοῖς] τῆς S ‖ 79 Ὡρὴβ scripsi, cf. Ps. 82(83):12; Ῥὴβ codd. ‖ 92 ὑπὲρ] ἅπερ codd. ‖ 93 οἷσπερ ἑάλω] οἷς περιάλω P ‖ 96 μηδὲ codd. ‖ 99 τολματίας SP ‖ 99–100 ὡθωρὸν P ‖ 102 τι om. P ‖ 105 ὁ om. P

81

they resolved to convoke all the godless and impious men in our midst to help them in an implacable battle against the Lord and His anointed [the emperor] and all the Christian troops, to bring about the destruction of us all. And they would have accomplished their object, if their machinations had not been confounded by the One Who turns the «shadow of death» into life for those who place firm hopes in Him. He justly turned «their mischief against their own heads», and it resulted that «they rolled the stone upon themselves». And may there befall them and their allies, O Christ King and God (mercifully remembering the flock which you acquired by your sufferings), such a fate as befell Oreb of old and Zebee and Salmanan, and their nobles who, like these men here, insulted «the sanctuaries of God».

The most fierce Drimys, truly hated by God, aiming at the imperial throne through no just reason of lineage or character, forgot himself, and strove in vain to grasp that which it is not even possible to see in a dream, and like a gust from a terrible typhoon he tried to stir up and to plunge into the depths of disloyalty any rotten elements of the population which he found ill-disposed toward the emperor and God, and above all and foremost from among the Xylotes. And he entered upon this scheme for no sensible reason, but from presumption alone, just like «the fool» who is celebrated in the Scriptures, that accursed man, demented like his followers, ⟨said⟩ that «there is no God», for which he was destroyed, loathed and «mocked at like a pitiful sparrow», he who had conceived of showing himself, as he thought, more fearful than God, was like «a mouse who touched pitch», together with the evil companions with whom he was caught; they are ridiculed by the declaration of the prophet, «They have made kings for themselves, but not by me; they have ruled, but they did not know me». The gaping fools thought of none of these things, nor did their utterly stupid leader, who yesterday proclaimed himself a member of the clergy and today has shown himself anxious to appear as bearer of the sword and imagines himself, that brazen man, driving a chariot and carrying a scepter (O justice!), who straightway imparts impiety to men like himself, taking confidence only in the deceit of senseless and vain slander. That none of our affairs occurs without the aid of God, and that it is hard for them «to kick against the pricks», we are taught to some extent by the phrase «by me kings reign»; but neither these wretched men, nor their leader, understand these words, nor that by Him «the very hairs of our head are numbered». For even the divine David invoked God

Δαυΐδ, ἀποπεσάτωσαν, λέγων, ἀπὸ τῶν διαβουλίων αὐτῶν·
κατὰ τὸ πλῆθός τε τῶν ἀσεβειῶν καὶ ἀπιστιῶν αὐτῶν
αὐτοὺς ἔξωσον. καὶ εἰ μὴ μετάνοιαν ἐπιδείξονται ταχεινήν, δηλαδὴ τῆς
τῶν πιστῶν ὁμηγύρεως, καὶ συλληφθήτωσαν ἐν τῇ ὑπερηφανίᾳ
110 αὐτῶν, καὶ ἐξ ἀρᾶς καὶ ψεύδους, μέχρι καὶ συντελείας, διαγ-
γελήσονται, γνόντες εἰ βούλοιντο, οἱ ἀπωλολεκότες καρδίαν,
πῶς ὁ Θεὸς δεσπόζει καὶ συντηρεῖ, καὶ φροντίζει καὶ περιέπει ὑπερασπίζων τὸν εὐσεβῆ καὶ θεόφρονα καὶ σταυροφόρον ἡμῶν καὶ πραῆ καὶ
φιλόχριστον ἄνακτα, ἐνηχῶν εἰς νοῦν αὐτῷ θεϊκῶς τὸ εἰ βούλοιο
115 ταῖς ὁδοῖς μου πορεύεσθαι, τοὺς ἐχθραίνοντάς σοι
θήσομαι ἐν τῷ μηδενί, καὶ χεῖρα ἐπιβαλῶ τιμωρὸν
μαχομένοις σοι. καὶ γὰρ οὐ μόνον ἐνύσταξαν οἱ ἐπιβεβηκότες
τοῖς ἵπποις, οἱ τῷ Δριμεῖ συνεκβακχευθέντες ἤτοι τῇ ἀλογίᾳ, οἱ καὶ
ἀλόγων αὐτῶν ἀλογώτεροι, ἀλλ᾽ ἤδη καὶ ὕπνωσαν ὕπνον αὐτῶν,
120 καὶ οὐχ εὗρον οὐδέν, ἀπὸ ἐπιτιμήσεως πάντως τῆς θείας ὀργῆς,
παραδειγματισθείσης τῆς ἀνομίας αὐτῶν ὡς μάτην χανόντων, καὶ
πρός γε τῇ ἁμαρτίᾳ καὶ ἀπωλείᾳ ᾗ αὐτοὺς ἐμβεβλήκασι καὶ διηνεκῆ ὀφλή-
σουσι γέλωτα.

οἷς οὐδὲ δυνατὸν παρ᾽ ἀνθρώπου ἀξίαν συμψηφισθῆναι τὴν τιμω-
125 ρίαν, ἢ [fol. 61ʳ] παρὰ μόνου Θεοῦ, πρὸς τὸ τοῦ ἔργου τούτων ὠμὸν καὶ
ἀσύγγνωστον, καὶ ἀθεώτατον καὶ ὀλέθριον, εἴ τις ἡμῶν νουνεχῶς τὸ τοῦ
ἀθέου τολμήσαντος διασκέψεται ἀποτέλεσμα. ὧν καὶ ἡμεῖς, ἐνδίκως
ὁμοῦ καὶ ἐνθέσμως, μετὰ τῆς περὶ ἡμᾶς τῶν ὧδε λαχόντων ἱερωτάτων
ἀρχιερέων θείας καὶ ἱερᾶς συνόδου, τοῦ Σάρδεων καὶ ὑπερτίμου, τοῦ
130 Χαλκηδόνος καὶ ὑπερτίμου, τοῦ Περγάμου καὶ ὑπερτίμου, τοῦ Βιτζύνης
καὶ ὑπερτίμου, τοῦ Ἀχυράους καὶ ὑπερτίμου, τοῦ ἀρχιεπισκόπου Χριστουπόλεως, καὶ τοῦ ἀρχιεπισκόπου Δέρκου, συμπαρόντων καὶ τῶν θεοφι-
λεστάτων ἐπισκόπων τοῦ Ῥαιδεστοῦ, πρὸς δὲ καὶ τοῦ Χαριουπόλεως,
τὸ τόλμημα μυσαχθέντες τὸ ἀθεώτατον καὶ ἀναίσχυντον, πάσης ἀπογυμ-
135 νοῦμεν ἱερωσύνης αὐτὸν τὸν θῆρα τὸν δυτικὸν καὶ δριμύν, σπορέα
φρικτῶν ζιζανίων ὑπάρξαντα τοιούτων — εἰ καί ποτε ταύτης ἠξίωτο, ἀλλὰ
μὴ μάτην καὶ ταύτης κατετυράννει, ἐν λόγῳ μόνῳ ψιλῷ, πρὸς ἐξαπάτην
τῶν ἁπλουστέρων, τιμὴν κἀντεῦθεν ὁ ἄτιμος ἑαυτῷ ποριζόμενος, ὡς ὁ τρό-
πος ἀπήλεγξεν, [ἑαυτῷ] ἀδεῶς τὰ ὑπὲρ ἑαυτὸν φημιζόμενος — σὺν τούτῳ
140 καὶ τὸν ἀκόλουθον, ὃν ἡ Μύρα Λυκίας προήνεγκεν, οἷα λύκον ἀσυμπαθῆ
τοῖς προβάτοις Χριστοῦ προσενεχθῆναι ὁρμήσαντα· πρὸς δὲ καὶ ἀλύτῳ καὶ
τούτῳ, μετὰ τοῦ πρωταιτίου Δριμέος σὺν πᾶσι τοῖς ἀκριβῶς εἰδόσι τὸ

106–108 cf. Ps. 5:11 ‖ 109–111 cf. Ps. 58(59):13 ‖ 111 Is. 46:12 ‖ 114–117 cf. Ps. 80(81):
14–15 ‖ 117–120 cf. Ps. 75 (76):6–7 ‖ 121 Leutsch-Schneidewin, II, 121

---

106 ἀποπεσέτωσαν V ‖ διαβολίων SP ‖ 108 ἐπιδείξωνται S ‖ 115 μοι S ‖ 119 αὐτὸν P ‖
122 ἁμαρτίᾳ] ἅματο S ‖ 130–131 τοῦ Περγάμου ... Βιτζύνης καὶ ὑπερτίμου om. S ‖
139 ἑαυτῷ uncis inclusi ‖ 142 δρομέος P

81

against them, saying, «Let them fail of their counsels; cast them out according to the abundance of their ungodliness» and their disbelief. And if they do not demonstrate swift repentance, ⟨so as to become⟩, that is, ⟨members⟩ of the company of faithful, «Let them be even taken in their pride. And for their cursing and falsehood shall they be denounced» until the end of the world, for «the corrupt of heart» know if they wish how God rules and preserves and cares for and treats well and defends our pious, godly-minded, cross-bearing, gentle and Christ-loving ruler, instilling in his mind with divine inspiration the words, «If you are willing to walk in my ways, I will reduce your enemies to nothing, and will lay an avenging hand upon those who fight against you». For not only did «the riders on horses slumber», those who revelled together with Drimys or Unreason in Bacchic frenzy, more irrational even than dumb beasts, but «they» even «slept their own sleep and found nothing», clearly «as punishment» of divine wrath, which made an example of the law-lessness of these people who «opened wide their jaws in vain», and in addition to the sin and destruction into which they have cast themselves, they will be the object of constant ridicule.

If one of us were thoughtfully to consider the consequences of the godless ventures of this man, ⟨he would realize that⟩ it is not possible for man, but only for God, to decide upon a worthy punishment for these men, because of the cruel, unforgivable, ungodly and deadly nature of their deeds. Thus in a just and lawful fashion, together with the divine and holy synod of those most holy bishops who happen to be here, the most honorable metro-politan of Sardis, the most honorable metropolitan of Chalcedon, the most honorable metropolitan of Pergamum, the most honorable metropolitan of Bitzyne, the most honorable metropolitan of Achyraus, the archbishop of Christoupolis and the archbishop of Derkos, together with the bishops of Rhaidestos and Charioupolis who are most dear to God, in disgust at their most ungodly and shameless crime, I strip of all priestly rank this fierce beast from the West, the seed of terrible darnel—that is, should he ever have possessed such rank, rather than appropriated it to himself in a tyrannical way, just by mere assertion, to deceive the simple-minded, deriving by such means, too, honor for himself, dishonorable though he is, as his manner has shown, spreading rumors about himself with impunity; in addition to him, ⟨I strip of priesthood⟩ his accomplice from Myra of Lycia, who burst forth against the sheep of Christ like a merciless wolf. And in addition we bind him in equally irrevocable excommunication together with Drimys, the prime

210

81

φόνιον βούλευμα, καὶ μὴ σπεύσασιν εἰς φανέρωσιν, ἐνδεσμοῦμεν ἀφορ-
ισμῷ· ἀλλὰ καὶ οἷς ἀπό γε τοῦ νῦν φωραθῇ λύσσης τοιαύτης καὶ ἀθείας καὶ
145 ἀπιστίας ἐγχείρημα, τούτῳ τῷ φρικαλέῳ τοῖς μὴ ἐξεστηκόσιν ἐμπε-
δοῦμεν ἀφορισμῷ, ὅτι μηδ' ἄλλο δριμύτερον ἢ πικρότερον τῷ Δριμεῖ
Ἰωάννῃ καὶ τραγελάφῳ καὶ τῷ αὐτοῦ ἀκολούθῳ Σαρδαναπάλῳ, καὶ
τοῖς ὁμόφροσι τούτων. ἐν λόγῳ ξενίου δι' ἃ κατεπράξαντο, ἔδοξε τῇ συνόδῳ παρασχεθῆναι τούτοις τῇ ἱερᾷ ἀξίως τῆς ἐργασίας αὐτῶν, ὡς πτέρ-
150 ναν ἐπᾶραι τετολμηκότων κατά τε τῆς ἐκκλησίας, κατά τε τῆς βασιλείας καὶ κατὰ τοῦ ὁμοφύλου παντός· μηδέ γε ἐπόπτην οἱ δείλαιοι σωτηρίας
αὐτῶν καὶ ζωῆς ἔχειν τὸν παντεπόπτην Θεὸν δοκιμάσαντες, ἀλλ' ὄντως
συκίνην ἐπικουρίαν [fol. 61ᵛ] ἐπὶ κεναῖς καὶ ματαίαις ἐλπίσιν αἰωρη-
θέντες καὶ κεπφωθέντες ἐλεεινῶς, καὶ τῷ ἀρχαίῳ συναποστάτῃ Σατᾶν
155 ἑαυτοὺς ἀναθέμενοι, κἀκείνου τῶν συμβουλῶν πληρωθέντες, ὡς καὶ εἰς
ἔργα φενακισθῆναι προβῆναι τὰς φλυαρίας αὐτῶν, οἱ ἐπάρατοι πᾶσαν γῆν
τὴν ὑπὸ Ῥωμαίων ἀρχὴν (ὢ τῆς ἀπάτης!) ὡς νοσσιὰν καταλελειμμένην
διακένως ἐλπίσαντες καταλήψασθαι, καθά που καὶ τούτων ὁ εἰσηγήτωρ
Σατᾶν ποτὲ φαντασθεὶς τὴν ὑπ' οὐρανόν, ἔλαθεν ἑαυτὸν καὶ σκότος ἀντὶ
160 φωτὸς κεχρημάτικε, καὶ στάσεως τῆς ἐπουρανίου ὁ βδελυρὸς ἀξίως τὰ
ὑποχθόνια ἀντηλλάξατο. ἅπερ καὶ τοῖς ῥηθεῖσι τὰ νῦν αὐτοῦ ὀπαδοῖς
σπουδαίως ἐξείργασται, ἐλπίδων ἀπορραγέντων θεϊκῶν, καὶ ταύτας
ἀθέοις κυσὶν ἀναρτησάντων τῶν δυσσεβῶν, ἀπεμπολήσει φρικῶδὲ ὅσον
τὸ κατ' αὐτοὺς τῆς μεγάλης κληρονομίας Χριστοῦ, καὶ ἀθετήσει ὀρθοδο-
165 ξίας, καὶ προδοσίᾳ τοῦ ὁμοφύλου αἰσχρᾷ, ἐν ἀθέοις πρεσβευομένους Ἀμα-
ληκίταις καὶ Ἰταλοῖς, τοῖς τε περὶ τὸν Ἴστρον οἰκοῦσιν, οὐκ οἶδα εἰ
τάχα πρὸς τῇ κλήσει ἀσπαζομένοις καί τι τῶν Χριστοῦ.
    ἐν τούτοις συνάμα καὶ τῇ συνόδῳ τῇ ἱερᾷ, μίαν τὴν αἴτησιν ἐξαιτοῦ-
μεν τῷ κρατίστῳ καὶ γαληνῷ, καὶ πρὸς εὐεργεσίας γεγεννημένῳ τὰς ἀν-
170 θρωπείας οὐ τιμωρίας, κρατίστῳ καὶ ἁγίῳ μου αὐτοκράτορι, τοὺς νόμους
εἰς συστολὴν τῆς κακίας ἀπ' ἄρτι παρρησιάσασθαι, αὐτούς τε τοὺς
κακεργάτας καὶ τοὺς ἄλλως ἑαλωκότας αἰσχροῖς ἢ καὶ μετέπειτα ἁλωσί-
μους, γνωρίζειν ἑαυτοὺς τὴν νόμιμον ἀγανάκτησιν, τὸν ἔκδικον
εἰς ὀργὴν τῷ πράσσοντι τὸ κακὸν καὶ εἰκῇ μὴ φοροῦντα
175 τὴν μάχαιραν τετάχθαι ἐν διακόνοις Θεοῦ, ἀποφηναμένου Παύλου τοῦ θείου καὶ θεοκήρυκος. ἔνθα γὰρ φόβος, ἐκεῖ συντήρησις ἐνταλμά-
των, τῶν θείων καὶ ἀνθρωπίνων φημί· ὡς ἂν τηρούντων τὴν εὐνομίαν
ἡμῶν εἰς δόξαν οὖσαν Χριστοῦ τοῦ δικαίου κριτοῦ, τὴν βασιλείαν ἀνεπιβού-
λευτον κρατυνεῖ παλάμῃ τῇ θεϊκῇ, λιταῖς ἁγίαις τῆς Θεομήτορος, καὶ
180 πάντα λαὸν τὸν Χριστώνυμον, ᾧ δόξα, κράτος, τιμὴ καὶ μεγαλωσύνη,
εἰς τοὺς αἰῶνας, ἀμήν.

149–150 cf. Joh. 13:18 ‖ 153 Leutsch-Schneidewin, II, 210 ‖ 173–175 cf. Rom. 13:4

149–150 πτέρναν] πτέραν P, ad πτέραν add. γρ(άφεται) πτέραν Pˣᵐᵍ ‖ 153 κεναῖς
VSP¹: καιναῖς P ‖ 163 φρικώδη P ‖ 167 ἀσπαζομένους codd. ‖ 170 μου] μοι codd. ‖
172 αἰσχραῖς codd. ‖ 174 φοροῦντι codd. ‖ 176 τήρησις S

81

instigator, and all those who knew of his murderous plot and did not hasten to reveal it. And also from now on, whoever is found guilty of such a crime of madness and godlessness and treason, we bind with this excommunication which is frightful to anyone in his right mind, because there is nothing more fierce or bitter than John Drimys, the goat-stag, and his side-kick Sardanapalus, and their accomplices. And by way of reward for their deeds, the holy synod has decided that these people should be punished as is deserved by people who have dared «to lift up their heel» against the Church, against the Empire, and against all their fellow-citizens. These wretched men did not even try to have God, the overseer of all, as overseer of their salvation and life, but rather pitifully relied on and became ensnared in empty and vain hopes of «useless help», and devoted themselves to Satan, their fellow rebel from of old. And filled with his counsels, so that they were tricked into believing that their foolish talk would materialize in deeds, the accursed men hoped in vain that they would seize all the land which is under Roman rule, like an abandoned nest (O what deceit!), just as when their leader Satan once imagined that ⟨he would gain⟩ all the world beneath the heavens, it escaped him, and he was called darkness instead of light, and the abominable fellow deservedly exchanged his place in heaven for the underworld. These same results have now been zealously accomplished by his above-mentioned followers, for deprived of divine hopes, these impious men have attached their hopes on godless dogs, through their frightful sale, as much as lay within their power, of the great inheritance of Christ, and through their disregard of orthodoxy, and through their shameless betrayal of their fellow citizens, and have sent envoys to the godless Amalekites and Italians, and to the inhabitants of the banks of the Danube, who, for all I know, possess hardly any Christian trait except for the mere name.

Meanwhile, together with the holy synod, I make one request of my mighty and serene and holy emperor, born to confer benefits, not punishments, on mankind, that from now on the laws for the repression of evil be vigorously enforced, and that evil-doers and those who are caught now or later in base deeds should be made aware of the wrath of the law, since the divine Paul, the herald of God, has declared that «he who is a revenger to execute wrath upon him that doeth evil, and beareth not the sword in vain», has been ranked among «the ministers of God». For where there is fear, there I say divine and human commands are obeyed, so that if we preserve our good order which is to the glory of Christ, the righteous Judge, He will keep the empire and all the Christian people safe from attack in His divine hand, through the holy prayers of the Mother of God, and to Him be glory, power, honor and magnificence forever, Amen.

82. ⟨Πρὸς τὸν αὐτοκράτορα⟩

Ὀδυνώδους ψυχῆς ἱκεσίους φωνὰς ὑπὲρ οἴκτου κοινοῦ, βασιλεῦ, μὴ
παρόψει μηδαμῶς, θεοδόξαστε, ὁ τὴν σύνεσιν ἄκρος καὶ πρὸς ἐπιείκειαν
καὶ εὐλάβειαν ἀπαράμιλλος, ὁ τὴν κρίσιν καὶ τὴν ἰσχὺν πρὸς ἐπιμέ-
5 λειαν ἔργων θεοπειθῶν σὺν Θεῷ στολισθείς, καὶ περιζωσάμενος ἀνδρικώτερον καὶ βασιλικώτερον ἐργασίᾳ θεοφιλεῖ, τὸν εἰς τέλος καταβληθέντα
κλῆρον Χριστοῦ μεγαλοψύχῳ ὁρμῇ μὴ βραδύνας ἀνασώσασθαι, παροράσει
ἀποδοθέντα θείων θεσμῶν, καὶ τὴν ἐκ παρανομιῶν κακὴν ἧτταν ἀποτιννύντα δεινῶς, πιεσμῷ πολυτρόπῳ καὶ μαχαίρᾳ καὶ συγκλεισμῷ καὶ λιμῷ
10 καὶ αἰχμαλωσίᾳ καὶ ὅσων ἑτέρων πεπείραται, ὡς πάντῃ ὀλιγωθῆναι καὶ
ἀσθενῆσαι καὶ εὑρεθῆναι τοῖς βουλομένοις κοινῶς εἰς ὕβριν καὶ καταπάτημα, ἐπελθούσης κατὰ μικρὸν τῆς καταστροφῆς ἐκ τῶν ἀρξάντων τῶν
σκήπτρων κατὰ καιρὸν καὶ τῶν ἀρξάντων τῆς ἐκκλησίας, πρό γε παντὸς
ἄλλου μὴ δι' ἐρεύνης ποιουμένων τὰς θείας φωνὰς ὀρθοδοξούντων πρὸς
15 ὦτα, μηδ' ἐκ πάσης προσαπαιτεῖσθαι τῆς ποίμνης ὑπ' ἀμφότερον τοῦ
ἁρμοδίου εἰς τοῦτο, κατὰ χρέος ἀποδιδόναι τὸ σιτομέτριον,
ἐκπαιδεύοντος ἔργῳ καὶ λόγῳ οὐκ εἰς τὸ λέγεσθαι μόνον τὰς θείας
φωνὰς ἡμῖν χαρισθῆναι, εἰς δὲ μᾶλλον τὸ πράττεσθαι, κἀκεῖθεν
πλουτιζομένους καὶ τὴν ἀντίληψιν πρὸς Θεοῦ ἀναφαίρετον· καὶ εἴ γε
20 συνετηρεῖτο, ὑπήρξαμεν ἂν ἀναμφιβόλως τῆς βασιλείας υἱοί, καὶ
ἐνταῦθα διακορεῖς τῶν τῆς γῆς ἀγαθῶν καὶ παντοίοις ἐχθροῖς φοβεροί·
ἀλλ', οὐαί, μὴ ἐπιστρεφόμενοι φρικωδῶν ἀπειλῶν καὶ φωνῶν, τῶν
ἀρθήσεσθαι, φεῦ, ἐκ τοῦ Ἰσραὴλ βασιλείαν, εἰς ἡμῶν νουθεσίαν
κἀκείνων αἰσχύνην, ἐξ ἀκαρπίας δοθησομένην τοῖς ἔθνεσι. καὶ
25 τούτων εἰ ἐδεδίαμεν τὴν ἀποβολήν, ἀπεδίδρασκεν ἀφ' ἡμῶν τὰ εὑρηκότα
κἀκείνους περιαλγῆ καὶ ὀλέθρια, καὶ τὴν πέρα δεινοῦ παντὸς συμφοράν
— εἶτα καὶ κατὰ Παῦλον τὸν μέγαν, εἰ οὐκ ἐφείσατο τῆς καλ-
λιελαίου ὀρθῶς συνιέντες καὶ [fol. 67ʳ] δεδιότες τί τὸ ἑξῆς. ἀλλ',
ὦ συμφορᾶς, ἀντὶ τοῦ συντηρῆσαι τὴν χάριν ζωῇ πνευματικωτέρᾳ, καὶ
30 ἔργοις δοξάσαι τὸν δόντα, πρὸς τοὐναντίον ἐτράπημεν, ἀπολαύειν ἀπατη-
θέντες τῶν δωρεῶν, καὶ χωρὶς τοῦ ποιεῖν μετανοίας καρπούς,
παρομοίως ἐθνῶν μὴ εἰδότων Θεόν, σωματικώτερον καὶ ἀγνω-
μονέστερον καὶ τῷ δόγματι μόνῳ τῶν ἔργων ἐκτὸς οὐ καλῶς ὑπελάβομεν
σῴζεσθαι. καὶ αὐτό, εἰ μή τι παρεμπέσοι, τῶν εἰωθότων ἀποξηραίνειν
35 ὡς ἄρριζον, ἡμῶν μὴ φροντιζόντων οὐδόλως τῶν ἕνεκεν ἀσφαλείας

82: 16 cf. Luc. 12:42 ‖ 20 Matt. 13:38 ‖ 23—24 cf. Matt. 21:43 ‖ 27—28 cf. Rom. 11:
21, 24 ‖ 31 Matt. 3:8 ‖ 32 cf. I Thess. 4:5 ‖ 34—35 cf. Matt. 13:6

82: V 66ᵛ—68ʳ. S 207ʳ—209ᵛ. P 86ʳ—89ʳ.
1 γράμμα πρὸς τὸν αὐτοκράτορα διεγείρων αὐτὸν εἰς σύστασιν τῆς ἐκκλησίας καὶ ἐννόμου
ζωῆς πᾶν τὸ ὑπήκοον add. VʳSP ‖ 4—5 ἐπιμέλειαν] ἐμμέλειαν codd. ‖ 8—9 ἀποτιννύντων
codd. ‖ 15 ἀμφοτέρου P ‖ 26 πειραλγῆ codd. ‖ 28 καὶ καὶ V

82. ⟨To the emperor⟩

Do not disregard the cry of a sorrowful soul in supplication for mercy on us all, O emperor glorified by God, who are superior in intelligence and unrivalled in fairness and piety, who have been adorned with judgment and strength for undertaking with God works of trust in God. Girding yourself in a courageous and imperial manner through God-pleasing works, you have not hesitated to rescue with a generous impulse the patrimony of Christ which has been completely overwhelmed, and sold out because of their neglect of divine ordinances, and who are atoning wretchedly for their transgressions with a miserable downfall, with all sorts of afflictions, murder, imprisonment, famine and captivity, and such other sufferings as they have experienced, so that they are utterly reduced and weakened and find themselves publicly insulted and abused by anyone who wishes. The disaster was gradually brought on by the rulers of the empire and the rulers of the church at the time, above all because they did not strive to bring God's words into the ears of the orthodox, nor did they require of the entire flock what is appropriate for such a purpose, on both counts (?), «to give their measure of grain» as they should, teaching in word and deed that the Holy Scriptures have been given us not only to be spoken aloud, but to be practiced, and only then will we be blessed with the aid of God which will stay with us for all time to come. And if we had kept ⟨the appropriate teaching⟩, we would undoubtedly have been the «children of the kingdom», and in this world we would have been filled with the bounties of the earth, and would have inspired fear in every kind of enemy. But, O woe, we heed not the dreadful threats and declarations ⟨which state⟩, as a warning for us and to Israel's shame, that «the kingdom shall be taken» from Israel, alas, because it did not bear fruit, and «will be given to the Gentiles». And if we had feared the loss which these people ⟨experienced⟩, then we would have escaped their painful and disastrous fate, and unspeakable misfortune—and also if we had rightly understood the words of the great Paul, «If He spared not the good olive tree», and if we feared what follows upon these words. But, to our misfortune, instead of maintaining His favor through a more spiritual life, and glorifying with ⟨good⟩ works the Giver thereof, we have turned in the opposite direction and deceived ourselves into consuming His gifts, and in the manner of «the Gentiles which know not God» we have wrongly assumed that salvation comes without «bringing forth the fruits of repentance», in a fleshly and senseless way, and through belief alone without works. And such doings are one of those things which «without a root will wither», unless something intervenes, since we take no heed at all of the words of the Gospel which were laid down

σωτηριώδους κειμένων φωνῶν εὐαγγελικῶν ⟨πρὸς⟩ τὸ μὴ προσκόπτειν
πρὸς ὄλισθον, οἷον τὸ ὅστις ὁμολογήσει, φησίν, ἀλλὰ μή, ἀθετήσει
τῶν ὀφειλόντων, πρὸς τῷ μὴ ἀναμένειν βασάνους, ὡς ἡ φύσις τοῦ πράγματος ἔχει, ⟨καὶ⟩ ἀποδοχὴν καὶ συντήρησιν ἐκ Θεοῦ προσδοκᾶν· πρὸς
40 τοσαύτας φρικτὰς ἀποφάσεις καὶ ἀπειλὰς (ὢ ζημίας!) πλαγιάζειν ἀφόβως
ὑμᾶς διὰ ταὐτεμπάθειαν· ὁ καὶ μίαν τῶν ἐντολῶν, θεσπιζούσης
τῆς θείας φωνῆς, λύσας καὶ διδάξας, κληθείη ἐλάχιστος,
βασιλείας διαπεσεῖν δηλονότι καὶ ἀπερρίφθαι πρὸς Γέενναν, καὶ ἐὰν
μὴ περισσεύσῃ ἡ δικαιοσύνη ὑμῶν, καὶ οὐ πᾶς ὁ λέγων
45 μοι Κύριε, Κύριε, καὶ πολλοὶ ἐροῦσί μοι ἐν ἐκείνῃ τῇ
ἡμέρᾳ, καὶ τὸν ἀκούοντα καὶ ποιοῦντα τοὺς λόγους,
φρόνιμον εἶναι, καὶ μὴ ὄψεσθαι τὴν ζωὴν τοὺς τῷ Υἱῷ
ἀπειθοῦντας, (ἃ καὶ τοῖς ἔχουσιν ὦτα πεφιλοτίμηται), καὶ ἔργων
χωρὶς τὴν πίστιν νεκράν, καὶ ὅσα τοιαῦτα· ὧν μὴ φρίττοντες
50 τὴν ἀλήθειαν ἐκ τοῦ σφόδρα ἡμᾶς προσηλῶσθαι τῇ γῇ, ἀρκούντως ἐκρίθη
τὸ καὶ μόνον ἐν δέλτοις ἡμῖν ἀποτεθησαυρίσθαι ὅσα μέλλει ἐλέγχειν ἡμᾶς,
ὡς τοῖς πρὶν ἡ Δεκάλογος, μηδ' ὅτι ἡμῖν ἐνετάλθη ἐρευνᾶν τὰς Γραφάς,
ἀλλ' ὁμοῦ ἱερεὺς καὶ λαὸς (ὢ δεινῆς συμφορᾶς!) τοῖς παροῦσι κεχή-
ναμεν, παρωσάμενοι ἄνω βλέπειν, ὡς δηλοῖ καὶ τὸ ἄνθρωπος μὴ ἐξ
55 ἔργων τὴν πίστιν, ἀλλ' ἐν μόνῃ ὁμολογίᾳ ἐπιζημίως βρενθύεσθαι,
μηδ' αὐτὴν τὴν ἀποβολὴν τῶν τοσούτων καλῶν δι' ἀθέτησιν νόμων παθεῖν,
ἀλλ' ἐλπίζοντες χορηγεῖσθαι ἡμῖν πρὸς Θεοῦ τὴν εὐημερίαν, οὗ οὐκ ἠδέσ-
θημεν, οὐδὲ ἠγαπήσαμεν, οὐδὲ ὑπηκούσαμεν, οὗ γε καὶ χάριν ὁρῶμεν ἐπὶ
τοσοῦτον ἀπωσάμενον καὶ ἀφεστηκότα μακράν· καὶ τίς οἶδεν
60 εἰ ἐπιστρέψει καὶ ὑπο-[fol. 67ᵛ] λείψεται εὐλογίαν ἡμῖν τοῖς
ὑπολειφθεῖσι τῆς ἀμέτρου ἀγνωμοσύνης καὶ ἀνομίας, καθά που τὰ λόγια;
πλὴν ἀλλὰ πάντας ἀντιβολῶ, κἂν ἀπό γε τοῦ νῦν ἀνανήψωμεν, καὶ
τῶν ὀφθαλμῶν τὴν λήμην διάρωμεν· ἑαυτοὺς ἀνακαλεσώμεθα τῆς
ἀκαίρου περιπλανήσεως, τῶν οἰκτιρμῶν ἐπιρρίψαντες τῷ πελάγει Θεοῦ
65 καὶ τῆς ἀγαθότητος. πρὸς μετάνοιαν ἔργῳ καὶ λόγῳ καὶ δάκρυα βλέψωμεν
ἕκαστος, ὅτι τούτου χάριν ἀκμὴν μὴ κατεπόθημεν αὔτανδροι, ἵνα καὶ τῇ
ζημίᾳ καὶ τῇ πληγῇ καὶ τῷ δέει συναισθανθέντες τὸν δυνάμενον σῴζειν δι'
ἔργων ζητήσωμεν. ἀνθρωπίνων βουλῶν καὶ μεταχειρίσεων μὴ ἐμμείνωμεν
ἀδηλότητι, μηδ' εἰς μάτην εἰρῆσθαι δοκῶμεν τὸ εἰ μὴ φυλάξοι Κύριος
70 πόλιν, εἰς μάτην ἐπαγρυπνεῖν τὸν φυλάσσοντα. ἀνόθευτον
πρὸς Θεὸν ἀσπασώμεθα τὴν ἐπιστροφήν, χαρισθείσης συνέσεως καὶ ἰσ-

---

37 Matt. 10:32 ‖ 41–44 Matt. 5:19–20 ‖ 44–46 Matt. 7:21–22 ‖ 46–47 cf. Matt. 7:24 ‖
47–48 cf. Joh. 3:36 ‖ 48–49 Jac. 2:26 ‖ 53 cf. Osee 4:9 ‖ 54–55 cf. Jac. 2:24, 26 ‖ 59 cf. Ps.
9:22 ‖ 59–60 Joel 2:14 ‖ 69–70 Ps. 126(127):1

---

36 πρὸς addidi ‖ 38 τῷ] τὸ codd. ‖ 39 ante ἀποδοχήν, καὶ addidi ‖ 39–41 πρὸς ... ταὐτεμπάθειαν non satis perspicio ‖ 41 ὁ codd. ‖ 51 ὑμῖν codd. ‖ ὑμᾶς codd. ‖ 52 ὑμῖν codd. ‖
54–55 ὡς δηλοῖ ... βρενθύεσθαι non satis perspicio ‖ 57 ὑμῖν codd. ‖ 63 λήμμην codd.

for the sake of our sure salvation, so that we would not fall into a snare—for example, the words, «Whoever shall confess»—and not for the purpose of our disregarding our obligations and not expecting torments, as would be natural, but rather expecting to be accepted and supported by God, and because of the same feelings you fearlessly turn (alas) toward such dread decisions and threats (?). For the Holy Scriptures declare that «he who breaks one of the commandments and teaches ⟨this⟩ would be called the least», that is, he will fall from the kingdom ⟨of heaven⟩ and be cast into hell, and «except your righteousness shall exceed», and «not everyone that says to me, Lord, Lord», and «many will say to me in that day», and «he that hears the sayings and does them is a wise man», and «those that believeth not the Son shall not see life» (and these sayings are zealously followed by those who have ears), and «faith without works is dead», and the like. We do not fear the truth ⟨of these words⟩ because we are too closely tied to the earth; rather we have decided that it was enough if things by which we are to be scrutinized were merely recorded for us in books, as the Decalogue had been for the Jews of old. Nor have we decided that we have been charged to examine the Scriptures, but «people and priest» alike (O terrible misfortune!) we are involved in the present, neglecting to look toward heaven, as is revealed by the passage, «man» boasts to his peril that «faith» is not «from works», but in confession alone; ⟨and we hope⟩ that we will not be deprived of such blessings because of our disregard of the laws, but that God will grant us prosperity, even though we have not venerated or loved or obeyed Him; and for this reason we see Him rejecting us so much and «standing far away». And «who knows if He will return and leave a blessing» to those of us who are left behind because of our excessive arrogance and lawlessness, as the Scriptures say somewhere ?

But I entreat everyone, at least from now on let us come to our senses and remove the mist from our eyes; let us call ourselves back from our untimely wandering, and cast ourselves into the sea of God's mercy and goodness. Let each of us turn our gaze tearfully toward repentance, in both word and deed, since it is for that reason that we have not been totally consumed, men and all, only so that coming to our senses as a result of the loss and harm and our fear, we might seek through our deeds the One Who is able to save us. Let us not cling to the uncertainty of human counsels and undertakings, nor let us seem to say to no purpose, «except the Lord keep the city, the watchman watches in vain». Let us sincerely turn toward God, since intelligence

χύος ἀνελλιποῦς τοῦ πτερῶσαι καὶ ἀνυψῶσαι τὸν λαὸν τοῦ Θεοῦ δι' ἐννόμου
ζωῆς τὴν ἧτταν ἀνακαλέσαι. κηρυχθήτω τῇ πολιτείᾳ πολιτεύεσθαι ἔλεον
καὶ ἀλήθειαν, δικαιοσύνην καὶ σωφροσύνην καὶ κρῖμα, καὶ τοῖς τολμήσασι
75 παραβαίνειν νόμιμος ἐπεξέλευσις καὶ βασιλική, ἵνα καὶ τῶν πρὸ σοῦ καὶ
τῶν μετὰ σὲ βασιλέων ἀσυγκρίτως ὑπεραρθῇς, καὶ τῷ πρώτῳ ἐν βασιλεῦσι
τῶν ὀρθοδόξων εἰς γνήσιον λογισθήσῃ υἱὸν (δι' ἔλλειψιν θείου ζήλου
ἀποδοκιμασθέντων τῶν ἐξ ἐκείνου), εἰ καὶ τὰ τῆς δυσχερείας ἐκείνου πρὸς
μετάθεσιν τοῦ σεβάσματος ἀσύγκριτα τοῖς ὧδε, καὶ οὐ τοσοῦτον δυσεπι-
80 κράτητον τὸ τὰ τῆς ἐκκλησίας Χριστοῦ, εἴ τι καὶ παρερρύη τῷ χρόνῳ,
ἀνασώσασθαι δυνήσῃ ὑπ' ἐκείνου δυναμωθείς.

κἀντεῦθέν σοι πρὸς ταῖς ἀπὸ Θεοῦ δωρεαῖς καὶ τοῦ αἰτήματος
χαρισθῇ τὸ ὀλίγον, ὃ ἐν ὀλίγῳ διεσήμανας ῥήματι, τὴν εἰς ἄκρον εὐδαιμονίαν ἐνταῦθα παντὸς ἀγαθοῦ, καὶ ζωῆς τῆς μελλούσης ἐκεῖ τὴν ἀπό-
85 λαυσιν, μηδαμῶς τὰ τῆς ἐκκλησίας ἐῶν παραφθείρεσθαι, καὶ μάλα τὰ τῶν
ἀρχιερέων πρὸς τοῖς λοιποῖς εἰς νουθέτησιν τοῦ λαοῦ. λαλήσει γὰρ τότε
εἰρήνην Θεὸς ἐφ' ὑμᾶς καὶ πρὸς πᾶν τὸ ὑπήκοον, εἰ ἔργοις καρδίας
πρὸς αὐτὸν ἐπιστρέψομεν, καὶ τὸ τόξον αὐτοῦ κατ' ἐχθρῶν
ἐντενεῖ καὶ εἰς τὸ [fol. 68ʳ] μὴ ὂν ἀσθενήσουσι. καὶ τοῖς
90 σοῖς ὑποτάξοι ποσὶ τὸ ἐχθρὸν καὶ πολέμιον, καὶ τῆς ποίμνης τὰ ἁρπαγέντα
ἐπανασώσοιτο, τῶν δίκην λεόντων προσπηδησάντων τῇ ποίμνῃ
τὰς μύλας συντρίψας. πλουτισμοῦ καὶ εἰρήνης καὶ μακρότητος ἡμερῶν ἐμπλήσοι καὶ καταστέψοι τὴν ἐκ Θεοῦ βασιλείαν σου, καὶ τῷ σῷ ὑπηκόῳ ὡς ἕνεκεν τούτων προθυμηθέντι παρέξοι τὰ ἀγαθὰ καὶ σωτήρια. κἀν-
95 τεῦθεν καὶ λάλημα γενεαῖς γενεῶν χρηματίσει τὰ σά, καὶ εἰς πόθον τοὺς
πάντας ἐξεγερεῖ τὸν πρὸς σὲ καὶ εὐχὰς καὶ ἐπαίνους· καὶ αἰώνιος μνήμη
ὑπάρξεις τῇ ἐκκλησίᾳ καὶ διπλῶς δοξασθήσῃ ἀναφαιρέτῳ τῇ δόξῃ, καὶ
νῦν καὶ ἐν τῷ μέλλοντι· γένοιτο, Κύριε, γένοιτο.

83. ⟨Πρὸς ποιμένας⟩

Ἄρχειν λαχόντες κρίμασι θείοις τῆς ἐκκλησίας Χριστοῦ, οὐχ ὡς
ἀρέσκον ἡμῖν οὕτω τὰ ταύτης διενεργεῖν δυνατὸν κατεξουσιάζειν, ἢ
πιπράσκειν ἢ καὶ καταχαρίζεσθαι, ἀλλ' ὡς τῷ Πνεύματι τῷ ἁγίῳ δοκεῖ,
5 καὶ τοῖς ὑπ' αὐτοῦ ἐμπνευσθεῖσι νενομοθέτηται σωτηρίως, καὶ ὀφείλομεν
καὶ εὐχόμεθα. τῶν γοῦν τῇ ταύτης φροντίδι προκειμένων ἐνεργειῶν, κρα-

---

86–88 cf. Ps. 84(85):9 ‖ 88–92 cf. Ps. 57(58):7–8

83: V 68ʳ–69ʳ. S 209ᵛ–211ʳ. P 89ʳ–90ᵛ.
1 γράμμα πρὸς ποιμένας μὴ προσκυροῦσθαι πρός τινας μονὰς τὰς ὑπὸ χεῖρα αὐτῶν, ἢ
πιπράσκειν ἢ καὶ καταχαρίζεσθαι, εἰ μὴ ὡς νενομοθέτηται ἐγκανόνως add. VʳSP

82, 83

and unfailing strength has been granted us to excite and exalt the people of God through a lawful life to make good their defeat. Let it be proclaimed that mercy and truth, righteousness and moderation and judgment should prevail in the state, and that lawful and imperial punishment ⟨will be meted out⟩ to those who dare to break the law, so that you may be incomparably exalted above the emperors before you and after you, and be considered as a true son of the first orthodox ruler (since his successors have been disowned because of their lack of divine zeal), even if the difficulty ⟨of his task⟩ of changing the religion is not comparable to the present situation; and strengthened by him, you will be able with less difficulty to restore ⟨the power of⟩ the Church of Christ, even if it has been reduced somewhat by the passage of time.

Thus in addition to your other gifts from God, you will be granted a small part of the request which you indicated in a few words(?), great abundance of every blessing in this world, and enjoyment of life hereafter in the world to come, if you do not allow the Church to be corrupted in any way, especially with regard to the duty of bishops to instruct the people, in addition to their other tasks. «For then God shall speak peace» to you and all your subjects, if through our works «we turn our hearts toward Him», and «He shall bend His bow» against our enemies, «and reduce them to nothingness». And may He subdue your enemy and foe beneath your feet, and return the ⟨sheep⟩ snatched from the flock, «breaking the cheek-teeth» of those who attack the flock «like lions». May He fill and crown your divine majesty with riches and peace and length of days, and provide blessings and salvation for your subjects who have exerted themselves for the sake of these things. Thus you will be spoken of by generation after generation, and He will rouse everyone to love for you and to prayers and praises, and you will be eternally remembered by the Church, and will be doubly glorified with irrevocable glory, both now and in the world to come; so be it, Lord, so be it.

83. ⟨To bishops⟩

Since we have been appointed by divine decision to rule over the Church of Christ, we should not use our authority to manage Her property in accordance with our personal wishes, either to sell it or give it away, but it is both our obligation and ardent desire ⟨to do so⟩ as seems proper to the Holy Spirit, and as has been ordained by those inspired by ⟨the Spirit⟩ for our salvation. Of the duties involved in caring for ⟨the Church⟩, most important

τίστη δοκεῖ μοι καὶ ἡ διοίκησις τῶν σεμνείων, εἰ καὶ πρότριτα ἐπελήσθη,
οἷα καὶ πᾶν ἀγαθὸν τῶν ὀρθῶς ὁροθετηθέντων τῇ ἡμῶν γενεᾷ, ὁποίῳ τῷ
λόγῳ τὰς μονὰς ἐγηγέρθαι, ἢ προσκυροῦσθαι ἑτέραν ἑτέρᾳ· ἃ οὐκ ἀνεύ-
10 θυνα ἔμοι γε, εἰ μὴ καὶ τοῖς αἰτοῦσι καὶ τοῖς παρέχουσιν ἀπαντᾷ ἐγκανόνως, ὅσον καὶ ὁ τὸ θέλημα τοῦ κυρίου εἰδώς, καὶ τοῦτο μὴ
καὶ νηφόντως διαπραττόμενος, τῶν πολλὰς δαιρομένων ἀναμφιβόλως γενήσεται· ὅτι μηδ᾽ ἀθεεὶ συνέστη τὰ τῶν μονῶν, ἀλλ᾽ ἕνεκεν
τῶν θείᾳ συνάρσει ἐκφυγόντων Σοδόμων καὶ ἐμπρησμοῦ τοῦ ἐκεῖθεν, οἷς
15 καὶ μὴ μεριμνᾶν ἐθνικῶς καὶ τοῖς παροῦσι προστετηκέναι, ζητεῖν δὲ
μόνην τὴν βασιλείαν, καὶ εἰ μὴ πᾶσα ἀνάγκη, μηδὲ τῶν
ἀναγκαίων ἐφάπτεσθαι, οἷς ἐσταυρῶσθαι τὸν κόσμον,
καὶ τῷ κόσμῳ αὐτούς. ὧν γε καὶ χάριν ἡ τὸ πᾶν [fol. 68ᵛ] θαυμασίως διϊθύνουσα πρόνοια, φιλοθέων ψυχῶν ἁπτομένη, κατοικίας ἐκείνης
20 εἰς δόξαν Θεοῦ ἀνιστᾶν παρορμᾷ, ὡς σπουδάζουσι ζῆν ὑπὲρ τὰ
ὁρώμενα.

ἀλλ᾽ (ὢ δεινῆς συμφορᾶς!) πῶς ἡ πλεονεξία τινάς, καθὰ καὶ τὸν
τοῦ Χαρμῆ, ἀνέπεισεν ἀδεῶς καὶ τῶν Θεῷ ἀφιερωμένων ἀπονοσφίζεσθαι,
καὶ πρὸς οἰκείας ὀρέξεις μεθέλκειν ὅσα μὴ θέμις· καὶ ἃ παρὰ τῆς
25 ἀνοιγομένης χειρὸς καὶ πᾶν εὐδοκίας ζῶον ἐμπιπλώσης
ἀρίστως εἰς κατοικίαν ἁγίων, τινὲς ἀδεῶς εἰς οἰκείαν περιουσίαν καὶ
χρῆσιν ὁπωσδήποτε προσλαμβάνοντες ἐκ μεταχειρίσεως τοῖς ἑαυτῶν
προστιθέασιν, ἀνιχνεύοντες ὅσα πρὸς ἐμπαθείας ἀπόλαυσιν συντείνει
αὐτοῖς, οὐχ ὅπως ἐγκατοικῆσαι φροντίζοντες ἐν ἀσκήσει πρὸς Θεοῦ εὐα-
30 ρέστησιν, ἀλλ᾽ ἵνα τῶν φθειρομένων σίτου καὶ οἴνου καὶ τῶν
λοιπῶν πλησμίως ἐπαπολαύσωνται, τὸ οὐαί, οἱ ἐμπεπλησμένοι
μηδὲ ἐνωτιζόμενοι, τὴν ἐν αὐταρκείᾳ προκρίνοντες βιοτὴν μετὰ τοῦ
καθελῶ μου τὰς ἀποθήκας ἀφρόνως κομπάζοντος, καὶ τοῦ λέγοντος τῇ ψυχῇ ἔχεις πολλὰ ἀγαθὰ κείμενα, καυχώμενοι τῇ αἰσ-
35 χύνῃ, φεῦ, ἐν ζημίᾳ διπλῇ, καὶ τὰ θείῳ παγέντα σκοπῷ προσηλοῦντες τῷ
μαμωνᾷ, καὶ δῆθεν ἐκ τούτου καὶ μισθοὺς ἐκδεχόμενοι τῶν ἔμπροσ-
θεν ἀνθρώπων κλειόντων τὴν βασιλείαν, πρὸς τῷ κωλύειν καὶ
ἑαυτοὺς καὶ τοὺς βουλομένους, ἀποκερδαίνοντες τὸ οὐαί. καὶ εἰ τὰ
δικαίως κτηθέντα ἀποκτᾶσθαι εὐκόλως, καὶ μὴ ὀρέγεσθαι τῶν τοῦ
40 πέλας, καὶ ἀπὸ πλεονεξίας ὁρᾶν καὶ φυλάττεσθαι, ἐν προσχήματι ἐργασίας καλῶν πλεονεξίᾳ δουλεύομεν, ζητοῦντες ἐν ὑποκρίσει
τὴν βασιλείαν, οἱ ὅλως προστετηκότες τῇ γῇ, καὶ προσχήματι ἀρετῆς

83: 11–13 cf. Luc 12:47 ‖ 15–16 cf. Matt. 6:33 ‖ 16–17 cf. Greg. Naz., *Or.* XX,
α' (PG, XXXV, 1065A) ‖ 17–18 cf. Gal. 6:14 ‖ 20–21 cf. Greg. Naz., *Or.* XX, α' (PG,
XXXV, 1065A) ‖ 24–25 cf. Ps. 144(145):16 ‖ 30 Greg. Naz., *Or.* XIV, κα' (PG, XXXV,
885A) ‖ 31 Luc. 6:25 ‖ 33–34 Luc. 12:18–19 ‖ 36–38 cf. Matt. 23:13 ‖ 40 cf. Luc. 12:15 ‖
41–42 cf. Matt. 6:33

---

7 ἐπελήθη P ‖ 12 τῶν] τὰς P ‖ 20 σπαδάζουσι P ‖ 22 δυνῆς P ‖ 35 θεῖα P ‖ 37 τῷ]
τὸ P

seems to me to be the administration of monasteries, even if recently, like every other good thing which was rightly laid down for our generation, it has been forgotten for what reason monasteries have been constructed, or one attached to another; and I am to blame if those who ask for ⟨monasteries⟩ and those who grant them do not act in accordance with the canons, just as «he who know his lord's will», and does not soberly carry it out, «will undoubtedly become one of those who is beaten with many stripes». For monasteries were not organized without the aid of God, but for the sake of those who with divine assistance have fled Sodom and its flames, who do not think pagan thoughts and cling to earthly possessions, but «seek» only «the kingdom» ⟨of God⟩, and «except in extreme need, do not even partake of necessities», «unto» whom «the world is crucified, and they unto the world». It is for the sake of these people that Providence, which marvelously guides everything, takes hold of God-loving souls and urges them to build dwelling-places for the glory of God, as they strive «to live above that which is visible».

But, alas, what a grievous misfortune! How greed has beguiled certain people, like the son of Charmi, to steal without scruple ⟨property⟩ dedicated to God, and to satisfy their own appetites with such things as are not lawful; and the ⟨gifts⟩ which come from the «opened hand, which satisfies the desire of every living being» in the best way, for the dwelling place of holy people, are taken, without scruple and for their own advantage and use, by certain people who should be merely administering them, and are added to their own property ⟨instead⟩. They search out whatever will contribute to their sensual enjoyment, and are not concerned with inhabiting ⟨the monasteries⟩ in an ascetic manner so that they may please God, but that they may enjoy to satiety «food and wine and other corruptible» ⟨pleasures⟩. Nor do they heed the warning, «Woe unto you that are full», but prefer a life of self-sufficiency together with the man who foolishly boasted, «I will pull down my barns», and who said to his soul, «you have many goods stored away». But they glory in their shame, alas, causing twofold harm, by attaching to mammon that which has been established for a divine purpose, and indeed in consequence they receive the rewards of those «who shut up the kingdom ⟨of heaven⟩ against men», in addition to preventing both themselves and those who wish ⟨from entering⟩, thus bringing upon themselves the cry of «woe!». And while ⟨it is⟩ easy to lose ⟨even⟩ what is justly acquired, and ⟨one should⟩ not covet the property of one's neighbor, and ⟨should⟩ «take heed and beware of covetousness», we pretend to be performing good works, but are ⟨actually⟩ slaves of greed, hypocritically «seeking the kingdom», although we are always clinging to the earth, and while we pretend to be virtuous, we are enveloped in sensuous

τῇ ἐμπαθείᾳ ἐμπλατυνόμεθα, φρεναπατοῦντες ἢ τάχα φρεναπατώμενοι,
καταλεῖψαι τοῖς μεθ' ἡμᾶς (ὢ τῆς ἀναισθησίας!) οὐ ζωὴν ἁγιοπρεπῆ
45 καὶ ψυχῶν ἐπιμέλειαν ἣν ἕκαστος ἀπαιτησόμεθα, ἀλλὰ βίον κατεγνωσ-
μένον, καὶ δαπάνην σητῶν.
    εἰ δέ που ἐγκύψας τινὶ θεῖος ἔρως φανῇ, ἢ ἀπο-[fol. 69ʳ] τάξασθαι
κόσμῳ ἢ ἀνεγεῖραι μονήν, ἢ βελτιῶσαι καταπεσοῦσαν, πολλὴ γενέσθω
τούτῳ φροντὶς μὴ τοῖς τυχοῦσι καταπιστεῦσαι — ἀλλὰ θεοφιλῶς τὸ ἔργον
50 μεταχειρίσασθαι, τὸν εἰπόντα εἰδὼς πολλοὶ ἐροῦσί μοι ἐν ἐκείνῃ
τῇ ἡμέρᾳ καὶ τὰ ἑξῆς — ἀλλὰ τοῖς ἀνοθεύτως προαιρουμένοις δουλεύειν Θεῷ. ὅτι τὸ ἐλεεῖν καὶ διδόναι ἀνθρώπῳ παντὶ ἀξιάγαστον· τὸ δὲ
λόγῳ στρατείας σιτηρέσιον τάξαι τισὶν ἐκ τῶν τοῦ δεσπότου, τοῖς μηδὲ
ὅπλων ὀνομασίαν ἐνωτισθεῖσιν, ἃ τὸ στρατιωτικὸν ἀμφιέννυται, οὐ μόνον
55 ἡ χλεύη πολλὴ μετὰ τιμωρίας, ἀλλὰ καὶ ἡ ἄνοια καταγέλαστος. ὁ δὲ
ἀδιαφόροις εἰς κατοικίαν ἀσκητῶν διδοὺς καταγώγιον, πολλῷ τῶν
ῥηθέντων τιμωρίαν ὑπομενεῖ. ἔνθεν οὐδὲ ἡμῖν ἀνεκτὸν ἐκδιδόναι μονάς,
τῷ πάντων Θεῷ ἀνατεθειμένας, λαϊκοῖς ἀπεριμερίμνως ἢ ἀδοκίμοις μονά-
ζουσιν, εἰ μὴ δεδώκασι πεῖραν οἱ μέλλοντες ἐνοικεῖν τὴν κλῆσιν μὴ κατα-
60 ψεύδεσθαι, εἰδότων τῶν συνιέντων κρείσσονα ἕνα ποιοῦντα
θέλημα τοῦ Κυρίου παρανομούντων μυρίων.

84. Πρὸς τὸν αὐτοκράτορα

    Εἰ καὶ μηδὲν μοχθήσασιν ὑπὲρ τοῦ καλοῦ τὴν βασιλείαν Θεὸς οἷς
ἐξελέξατο ἐνεπίστευσε, ποίαν ἄρα κἀκεῖ τὴν μακαριότητα ἀπολήψονται
οἱ πρὸς τῇ εὐσεβείᾳ καὶ τὴν ἐν νόμῳ ζωὴν ἐπιμελησάμενοι καὶ ἑαυτοὺς
5 πάσῃ δυνάμει καὶ τὸ ὑπήκοον διαζῆν, μόνην τὴν πίστιν ἐπιστάμενοι
νεκρὰν τῶν ἔργων χωρίς! διὰ ταῦτα, ἅγιε βασιλεῦ, τοῖς ὑφ' ὑμᾶς
θεοὶ χρηματίζοντες, ἑκάστῳ τὸ πρόσφορον ψυχῇ καὶ σώματι νέμειν, οὐ
τὸ πρὸς ἡδονήν, ἐποφείλετε. εὐθύνεται γὰρ ἕνεκεν τούτων ἐκεῖ καὶ τέκνων
πατήρ, καὶ δούλων δεσπότης, ἐπίσκοπός τε τῆς ἐκκλησίας, καὶ τοῦ ὑπη-
10 κόου ὁ βασιλεύς.

---

46 cf. Greg. Naz., *Or.* XIV, ιζ' et XVI, ιθ' (PG, XXXV, 877 B et 960 C) ‖ 50–51 Matt.
7:22 ‖ 60–61 cf. Sirac. 16:3
84: 5–6 cf. Jac. 2:26 ‖ 7 cf. Ps. 81(82):6

---

51 ἀνοθεύτοις P ‖ 56 post πολλῷ unum verbum, fortasse περισσοτέραν ve αὐστηροτέραν,
deest ‖ 58 ἀνατιθεμένας S
84: V 69ʳ–70ᵛ. S 211ʳ–213ᵛ. P 90ᵛ–92ᵛ. Ed. Laiou, *Byzantion*, 38 (1968), 404–6.
1 ante πρός add. γράμμα VʳSP ‖ post αὐτοκράτορα add. περὶ τοῦ περιποθήτου δεσπότου
υἱοῦ αὐτοῦ Ἰωάννου VʳSP ‖ 2 καλοῦ VSP¹: λαοῦ P ‖ 3 κἀκεῖ VSP¹: καλεῖ P ‖
6 ὑφ' ὑμᾶς V¹S, ὑφ' ἡμᾶς V, ἐφ' ὑμᾶς P

83, 84

pleasures, deceiving ⟨others⟩ or perhaps deceiving ourselves that we will bequeath to our descendants (oh, what lack of perception!) not the pious life and concern for our souls which will be asked of each of us, but a despicable life and a «feast for moths».

But if ever a divine passion should come and appear to someone, either to renounce the world, or to build a monastery or repair one that is falling down, let him be very careful not to entrust ⟨the matter⟩ to any chance person—but to undertake the task with love of God, in the knowledge that He said, «man will say to me in that day», and so forth—but to those who genuinely choose to serve God. For it is admirable to have mercy on and to give to every man; but to give an allowance, on the pretext of their military service, to certain of the Despot's men who have never heard the name of weapons which soldiers bear, is not only worthy of scorn and punishment, but is ridiculous stupidity. And the man who grants to unconcerned people an establishment where ascetics dwell will be punished much ⟨more⟩ than the above-mentioned. Wherefore I cannot bear to hand over unconcernedly to laymen or to inexperienced monks monasteries which have been dedicated to the God of all, unless those who are going to inhabit them show proof that they are not false to their name, for men of understanding realize that «one man who does the will of the Lord is better than ten thousand who go against His will».

84. To the emperor

If God has entrusted the empire to His elect even if they have not labored at all on behalf of the good, ⟨consider⟩ what happiness will be enjoyed in the world to come by those who have exerted every possible effort that they themselves and their subjects may live piously and in accordance with the law, since they realize that «faith alone, without works, is dead»! Therefore, holy emperor, you, who are given the name of god by your subjects, have the obligation to bestow on each of them what is expedient for his soul and body, not what is pleasurable. For the sake of these rewards in the world to come (?), a father guides his children, a master his servants, a bishop his church, and the emperor his subjects.

τούτων ἕνεκεν ἀναφέρειν καὶ μὴ ἐρωτηθεὶς ἐγχειρῶ. φήμη περι-
κτυπεῖ τοῖς ὠσὶ τῶν πολλῶν τοῦ περιποθήτου χάριν υἱοῦ τῆς ἐκ Θεοῦ βασιλείας σου δεσπότου κύρου Ἰωάννου, ὡς ἀναγκάζεσθαι τοῦτον παρὰ τῆς
περιποθήτου αὐτοῦ μητρὸς καὶ δεσποίνης, συναινέσει καὶ τῆς ἐκ Θεοῦ
15 βασιλείας σου, τῆς γονικόθεν αὐτῇ ἀνηκούσης διεκδραμεῖν, καὶ [fol. 69ᵛ]
ζητῆσαι κατάρξαι τῶν Φράγγων ἀρχῆς. καὶ τί τὸ κωλύον, θειότατε
βασιλεῦ, μὴ γνώριμα καὶ ἡμῖν ἐγίνετο τὰ τοιαῦτα; ἢ οὐχ ὑπερεκκαιόμεθα
ἕνεκεν τῆς ὑμῶν σωτηρίας καὶ προκοπῆς καὶ μεγαλωσύνης καὶ ἐπαίνου καὶ
πλουτισμοῦ; καὶ εἰ μὴ διὰ τὸ διακόνημα τοῦ σκοποῦ τὸ ἡμῖν ἐντεθὲν
20 τοῦ σημαίνειν τῇ σάλπιγγι, μήπως λάβοι ψυχὴν ὁ ἐχθρός
(ἄνθρωποι γὰρ καὶ ὑμεῖς καὶ ἀσφαλείας ἤχου σωτηριώδους ἐπιδεεῖς, καὶ
τῶν ἄλλων μακρῷ ζηλωτότεροι τοῖς ἐχθροῖς), ἀλλά γε καὶ ἐκ τοῦ φιλεῖν
ἀσυγκρίτως ὑμᾶς καὶ τὴν σωτηρίαν ὑμῶν, δοκοῦμεν τὸ δίκαιον φέρεσθαι
πρὸ τῶν ἄλλων εἰς τὸ ἐξακριβοῦσθαι πνευματικῶς τὰ τοιαῦτα εἰς δέον,
25 νομίζοντες — ἃ μὴ γινόμενα βλέποντες, πῶς οὐκ οἶδα, οὐ φορητὴν τὴν
ζημίαν ἡγούμεθα — καὶ πάντως οὐ τὸ τυχὸν εἰς ὠφέλειαν συμφροντιστὰς
καὶ συλλήπτορας, κἂν τοῖς πνευματικοῖς, εἴποι τις, κἂν τοῖς κατὰ
σῶμα πλουτεῖν τὸν ἐχέφρονα.

ἀλλ' εἴπωμεν περὶ ὧν καὶ ἠρξάμεθα· ὀφειλὴ τοῖς γονεῦσι
30 θησαυρίζειν τοῖς τέκνοις, ἀλλά γε τοῖς ὀρθοδόξοις καὶ συνετοῖς,
ἐν πρώτοις καὶ πρώτως τὰ αἰώνια καὶ ἀκήρατα, εἶτα καὶ τῶν ῥεόντων
ὅσα καὶ ὅθεν μὴ παροργίζει Θεόν, μηδὲ τῶν προλεχθέντων λυμαντικά.
οὐδὲ γὰρ οἶμαι ἀνέχεσθαι μὴ μετὰ τοῦ ἁγίου Δαυῒδ τὴν ἐκ Θεοῦ βασιλείαν
σου πεπαρρησιασμένη βοᾶν τῇ ψυχῇ πρὸς Θεὸν τὸ καὶ γὰρ τὰ
35 μαρτύριά σου μελέτη μου ἐστί· καὶ αἱ συμβουλίαι μου τὰ
δικαιώματά σου, ὅπως ἐπιτυγχάνῃ καὶ τὰ ἑξῆς τῆς δεήσεως. συμβουλίαι δὲ καὶ μαρτύρια πάντως τοῦ μεγάλου Θεοῦ τὸ τί ὠφελήσει
ἄνθρωπον ἐὰν ὅλον τὸν κόσμον κερδήσῃ, καὶ ζημιωθῇ
τὴν ψυχὴν αὐτοῦ; καὶ τὸ συμφέρει μονόφθαλμον εἰς τὴν
40 ζωὴν εἰσελθεῖν, ἢ δύο ὀφθαλμοὺς ἔχοντα, εἰς τὴν Γέενναν, καὶ τὸ ἠγάπησαν οἱ ἄνθρωποι μᾶλλον τὴν δόξαν τῶν
ἀνθρώπων ὑπὲρ τὴν τοῦ Θεοῦ.

τίς γὰρ ὁ ἐγγύας δοῦναι θαρρῶν περὶ τοῦ ῥηθέντος, εἰ κἂν τηρήσῃ
τὴν πίστιν ἀμώμητον ἐν τοιαύτη νεότητι, καὶ ἀλλοδαπεῖ γῇ βαρβάροις κατ-
45 οικουμένη, καὶ ἔθνει κατάκρως ὑπερηφάνῳ καὶ ἀπονενοημένῳ τὰ μέγιστα; εἰ δὲ καὶ πᾶσα ταῖς ἀληθείαις ἡ βασιλεία τῆς γῆς ἐξῆν δοθῆναί τινι,
καὶ πρὸς ταύτῃ ζωὴ χιλίοις ἐν ἔτεσι, θάνατος δὲ μετὰ ταῦτα, καὶ [fol. 70ʳ]

19–20 cf. Ezek. 33:2–6 ‖ 29–30 cf. II Cor. 12:14 ‖ 34–36 Ps. 118(119):24 ‖ 37–39 Marc.
8:36 ‖ 39–41 cf. Matt. 18:9 ‖ 41–42 cf. Joh. 12:43

---

17 ἐγίνετο VSP¹: ἐγένετο P ‖ ἢ P ‖ 21 ἡμεῖς codd. ‖ 23 ὑμᾶς VSP¹: ἡμᾶς P ‖ 27
εἴποι SP: εἴπῃ VS¹P¹ ‖ 32 λυμαντικά V, λημαντικὰ S¹P, λημαντικὰ S ‖ 36 δεήσεως]
διηγήσεως P ‖

84

For these reasons I have undertaken to submit this petition even though I have not been asked. The rumor is being spread among the multitudes that your divine majesty's dearly beloved son, the Despot Kyr John, is being compelled by his dearly beloved mother, the Despoina, with the consent of your divine majesty, to hasten to the land which is hers by inheritance, and to seek to rule over Franks. And what were the reasons, most divine emperor, that prevented my being notified of all this? Am I not ardently concerned for your salvation and prosperity and greatness and glory and wealth? And not only because of the duty of watchman which has been assigned to me, «to signal with the trumpet», lest the enemy «take a soul» (for you, too, are human, and need the security of the saving blast, since you are much more envied than others by our enemies), but also because of my incomparable love for you and your salvation, I think it right that first of all such a project be properly examined from the spiritual point of view—but I see that somehow this has not occurred and consider that it causes intolerable harm—and I certainly believe that it is of great benefit to a prudent man to have advisors and assistants both in spiritual affairs, as one might say, and in matters of the body.

But let me return to what I began to discuss. «It is an obligation for parents to store up for their children», especially those who are right-thinking and wise, first and foremost that which is eternal and undefiled, and secondly such transitory things as do not provoke God to anger by their quantity or origin, or turn out to the detriment of the former. For I doubt that your divine majesty would endure not to proclaim to God with a confident soul, together with the holy David, «for thy testimonies are my meditation, and thine ordinances are my counsellors», so that you may achieve the rest of the prayer. Now assuredly the ordinances and testimonies of the great God are, «What shall it profit a man, if he shall gain the whole world, and lose his own soul?», and «It is better to enter into life with one eye, rather than into hell-fire having two eyes», and «The men loved the praise of men more than the praise of God».

For who will dare to give assurance about the ⟨young man⟩ who is under discussion, that at such a tender age he will maintain his faith unblemished in a foreign land inhabited by barbarians and by an utterly insolent nation which has lost all sense? And if in truth it were possible to give someone the entire kingdom of the earth, and in addition life for a thousand years, to be

σὺν αὐτῷ τῷ θανάτῳ καὶ μακρυσμὸς ἐκ Θεοῦ, συνήνεσεν ἄν τις ἄρα κἄν
τῷ ἐχθρῷ τῶν καὶ ποσῶς πιστευόντων Θεῷ, καὶ ποῦ τὰ ἡμέτερα κεῖται
50 εἰδότων κατὰ ἀλήθειαν; εἰ δὲ μὴ πάσης τῆς γῆς, ἐλαχίστου δὲ μέρους καὶ
ἀμφιβόλου καὶ τούτου ῥιψοκινδύνου, τί καὶ πείσονται ἄρα οἱ ἄλλο τι
προκρίνειν τοῦ θείου φόβου καὶ τῆς ἐν οὐρανοῖς βασιλείας καὶ ἀσφαλείας
τῆς ὀρθοδόξου καταδεχόμενοι; ἢ οὐχὶ πρὸς τοῖς ἄλλοις οἷς σε Θεὸς καθωράϊσε, καὶ ἕνεκεν τούτου τοῦ μεγίστου κλέους τοῦ ὑπὲρ εὐσεβείας, φημί,
55 δι' ἀνδρίαν ψυχῆς ἐν τοῖς φθάσασι μεμαρτύρηκεν ἐνθέῳ τῇ δόξῃ σε καταστέψας, καὶ ἀναφαιρέτῳ διαγωνίσματι ἐραστὴν εὐσεβείας διάπυρον, θεραπείας γονέων ὑπεριδεῖν καὶ ὀρέξεως φίλων καὶ συγγενῶν, ἐν οὕτω
τεταραγμένῳ καιρῷ, ἐν τῇ τῆς βασιλείας ἀρχῇ;

τί δὲ καὶ ὀνήσει σου ὁ φίλτατος τὴν ψυχήν, ἢ τί καὶ τῇ βασιλείᾳ προσ-
60 οίσει τῇ σῇ, εἰ καὶ τῶν γενεῶν ἐκείνων κατάρξει πασῶν, ἀκράδαντον δὲ
μὴ συντηρεῖ τὴν εὐσέβειαν, μηδὲ εἰδότων ἡμῶν ἀκριβῶς οἷα τὰ μεταξὺ
συναντήσει, τὴν ἡμετέραν ἀσφάλειαν καταπροδιδόντων, οὐ τὴν τοῦ σώματος μόνον, ἀλλὰ καὶ τῆς ψυχῆς; πῶς δὲ καὶ μὴ ἠκροασάμεθα ἐπὶ
ῥέοντι πλούτῳ μὴ προστιθέναι καρδίαν, καὶ Παύλου μάλιστα
65 τοῦ μεγάλου ἀποσοβοῦντος τοὺς βουλομένους πλουτεῖν μήπως
εἰς πειρασμὸν καὶ παγίδα ἐμπίπτωσιν; εἰ γὰρ πλούσιοι
ἐπτώχευσαν καὶ ἐπείνασαν, τί τὸ τοῦ ἀσφαλοῦς ἀσφαλέστερον
τοῦ μὴ ἐλαττοῦσθαι παντὸς ἀγαθοῦ τοὺς ἐκζητοῦντας τὸν
Κύριον; ὃ καὶ ἡμεῖς ἐγκολπούμενοι τοῦ ἀβεβαίου ἐκφύγωμεν.

70 ἀλλ' εἴποι τις τάχα διὰ κυβέρνησιν μήπως παραλυπήσῃ τὴν μητέρα
καὶ δέσποιναν· ἀλλὰ καλὸν ἐν τοιούτοις ἀμφιταλάντοις γονεῖς λυπεῖν
καὶ μὴ Κύριον, ὅτι πλειστάκις γονεῖς πολλοὺς ἀπώλεσαν ὧν ἐφίλουν,
καὶ τῇ κολάσει παρέπεμψαν. ἀλλ' ὡς ἐκεῖθεν σωματικὴν ἀναμενοῦντες
βοήθειαν; ἀλλὰ πειθώμεθα παραινέσει μᾶλλον θεοφιλῶν, ματαίαν
75 ἀνθρώπων βοήθειαν ἀποδεικνυούσαις σαφῶς, ἵνα ἐν τῷ Θεῷ θαρρούντως
ποιώμεθα δύναμιν. οὕτω γὰρ καὶ αὐτὸς ἐκμυκτηριεῖ ἢ καὶ ἐξολοθρεύσει
τοὺς βουλομένους [fol. 70ᵛ] ἐκθλίβειν ἡμᾶς.

διὰ τοῦτο παρακαλῶ, τοῦ φιλτάτου φιλτάτως ἀντιλαμβάνεσθε, ἐν
οἷς δοκεῖ θεαρέστοις αἰτεῖν τὸν μεγαλόφρονα καὶ φιλότεκνον πατέρα καὶ
80 μεγαλόψυχον βασιλέα. ἀλλ' οὐδὲ νῦν εἰς ὄψιν ἐλθεῖν ἐκεῖνον τῆς πεφιλ-
μένης μητρὸς καὶ δεσποίνης, ἀμφοτέροις συνοῖσον ὁρῶ. εἰ γὰρ ταύτης μὴ
ὑπακούσει ὡς μητρὸς ἢ δέσποιναν αἰδεσθείς, μειζόνως παραλυπήσει. καὶ
εἰ ἐκ μικροψυχίας, ἢ καὶ ὑποβολαῖς τραχυτέρως ὁμιλήσει, ἢ καὶ ἀραῖς καθ-
υποβαλεῖ, καὶ ἀμφοτέροις ἀσύμφορον· εἰ δὲ οἷα συμβαίνει ἀναισχυντότε-
85 ρον ἀποκρίνασθαι, τοῦτο δεινότερον. ὅθεν καὶ κρίνω ἁρμόζον ἐπικαλέσασ-

---

63–64 Ps. 61(62):11 || 65–66 I Tim. 6:9 || 66–69 cf. Ps. 33(34):11 || 71–72 cf. Eph. 4:30

---

53 ἢ P || 57 ὑπερδεῖν S || 62 ὑμετέραν codd. || 64 καρδίαν scripsi, cf. Ps. 61(62):11; καρδία
codd. || 70 εἴπει S || 77 ὑμᾶς VSP¹: ἡμᾶς P || 80–81 πεφιλημένης P || 83 εἰ] ἢ codd.

84

followed by death, but death would be accompanied by separation from God, would this be granted, even to his enemy, by anyone who has any faith in God, and knows where our true interests lie? And if it is not the whole earth, but only the smallest part, and this uncertain and risky, what will be the fate of those who dare to set anything before fear of God and the kingdom of heaven and the security of the orthodox ⟨faith⟩? Is it not true that, in addition to the other blessings with which God has adorned you, because of your great renown, on account of your piety I mean, and because of the courage of your soul on that previous occasion, He has crowned you with divine glory, and testified that you are an ardent lover of piety because of your unending struggle ⟨for the faith⟩, so that you disregarded the duty owed to parents, and the wishes of friends and relatives, at such a troubled time, at the beginning of your rule?

How will your beloved son profit your soul, or what will he contribute to your empire, even if he does rule over all those nations, but does not preserve his piety unshaken? And if we will not know exactly what intervening events may occur, and thus will endanger the security, not only of our body, but also of our soul? Why did we not heed ⟨the advice⟩ «not to set our heart on transitory wealth», especially since the great Paul warned those «who wished to get rich, lest they fall into temptation and a snare»? For if ⟨it is true that⟩ «rich people became poor and went hungry», what is more certain than the certainty that «those who seek after the Lord will not lack any good thing»? Let us avoid uncertainty by keeping this in our hearts.

But perhaps someone might say, for the sake of discipline (?), ⟨that he should depart⟩, lest he cause great grief to his mother, the Despoina. But in such cases, all things being equal, it is better «to grieve parents than God», because on many occasions parents have caused the ruin of many of their loved ones, and sent them to hell. Or is it perhaps that we will expect from there [the West] some physical assistance? But let us trust rather in the counsels of those who love God, which show clearly the futility of human aid, so that we may confidently find our strength in God. For thus He will mock or destroy those who wish to oppress us.

Therefore I beg of you, help your dearly beloved with love in such of his requests made of a generous and devoted father and of a magnanimous emperor which seem God-pleasing. But for the time being I think it better for both that he not come into the presence of his beloved mother, the Despoina. For if he does not heed her as a mother, or respect her as the Despoina, he will cause her even greater grief. And if out of meanness of spirit she should speak harshly, with innuendoes, or should curse him, it would not profit either of them. And if it should occur that he replied rather shamelessly, so much the worse. Wherefore I judge it fitting for you to appeal with yearning

226

84, 85

θαι πόθω τὸν εἰρηνάρχην Σωτῆρα Χριστόν, ἵνα καὶ τοῦ   τῶν εἰ-
ρηνοποιῶν ἐπιτύχῃ μακαρισμοῦ ἡ ἐκ Θεοῦ βασιλεία σου, τὴν εἰρήνην
καὶ ἀμφοτέροις εὐχαῖς καὶ μεταχειρίσεσι πατρικαῖς καὶ βασιλικαῖς, ὡς
ὅλος αὐτὸς τοῦ Θεοῦ τῆς εἰρήνης, μεθ᾽ οὗ καὶ συναντιληψομένου εἰρήνης
90 καὶ ἀγάπης τῆς φυσικῆς ἐμπλησθείης διηνεκῶς πανοικεῖ. εἰ δὲ καὶ κόπον
καὶ βάρος εἰρήνης ἕνεκεν τῆς κοινῆς καὶ ἀγάπης καὶ ὁμονοίας ὑπομενεῖς,
ἕξεις ἀνταμειβόμενον τὸν τῆς ἀγάπης Θεόν, καὶ τὴν ὑπερέχουσαν
πάντα νοῦν εἰρήνην παρέξοντα τῇ ἐκ Θεοῦ βασιλείᾳ σου· γένοιτο,
γένοιτο, φιλανθρωπίᾳ καὶ χάριτι τοῦ τῆς ὁμοουσίου ἁγίας Τριάδος
95 ἑνὸς Χριστοῦ Ἰησοῦ τοῦ Σωτῆρος μου, πρεσβευούσης τῆς Θεομήτορος.

85. Πρὸς τὸν αὐτοκράτορα ὅπως ἡ Δέσποινα βαρέως ἔσχε κατὰ τοῦ υἱοῦ
αὐτῆς τοῦ πανευτυχεστάτου Δεσπότου

Τῆς μητρὸς καὶ Δεσποίνης, οὐκ οἶδ᾽ ὅθεν αἰτίας ἀπὸ τίνος, κατὰ τοῦ
πανευτυχεστάτου Δεσπότου μὴ ἀλύπως διακειμένης, λογιζομένου, λίαν
5 τοῦτο δοκεῖ πρὸς αὐτὸν βαρὺ καὶ ὀλέθριον· καὶ νωχελίας σφοδρᾶς, εἰ μὴ τὸ
τάχος ἐκδράμοι εἰς προσκύνησιν τὴν ἐκείνης ἐκμειλίξασθαι τὸ ἀλγοῦν,
κελεύσει τοῦτο καὶ συνεργίᾳ τῆς ἐκ Θεοῦ βασιλείας σου. εἰ οὖν μή ἐστιν
ὑπόνοια τὸ δοκοῦν, ἀλλὰ πρόφασις ἀληθής, δέον αὐτῇ ἐποφθῆναι τὸν ἀμφοτέροις κεχαρισμένον καὶ φίλτατον, καὶ ταχύτερον· τοῦτο μὲν ὡς τῷ
10 φίλτρῳ τῷ φυ-[fol. 71ʳ] σικῳ πιεζόμενον, καὶ ἄριστον ἐπὶ τέκνοις
εὐφραινομένην μητέρα ὁρᾶσθαι φρονίμως ὑπολαμβάνοντα· τοῦτο δὲ καὶ
Θεοῦ δεδιττόμενον κέλευσιν, τοῦ γονέας τιμᾶν προθεσπίσαντος. ὧν
τινων χάριν καὶ σταλῆναι, ὡς ἔφην, ταχύτερον ἐξαιτεῖται θερμῶς τῆς ἐκ
Θεοῦ βασιλείας σου. εἰ οὖν ἐστι καιρὸς (τοῦτο γὰρ οἶδας ὑπὲρ ἡμᾶς), καὶ
15 ἡμεῖς συνδεόμεθα, καὶ μᾶλλον ὡς ὅτι, καθὰ βεβαιοῖ, καὶ ἐνόρκοις δεσμοῖς
εἰς αὐτὸ ἑαυτὸν καθυπέβαλεν· εἰ δ᾽ οὐ δίδωσιν ὁ καιρὸς τελεσθῆναι τὸ κα-
ταθύμιον, τῶν ῥηθέντων ὁπωσδήποτε ἡ θεραπεία ἀνυσθήτω παρὰ τῆς ἐκ
Θεοῦ βασιλείας σου.

86–87 cf. Matt. 5:9 ‖ 92–93 cf. Phil. 4:7
85: 12 cf. Ex. 20:12

85: V 70ᵛ–71ʳ. S 213ᵛ–214ʳ. P 92ᵛ–93ʳ.
5 νωσχελίας S

84, 85

to Christ our Savior, the Prince of peace (so that your divine majesty may achieve the blessing of «the peacemakers») for peace between the two of them (?) through the prayers and efforts of a father and emperor, since you are wholly of the God of peace, and with His help may you be filled with peace and natural love eternally, together with all your family. For if you endure toil and grief for the sake of mutual peace and love and harmony, you will be rewarded by the God of love Who will grant to your divine majesty «the peace which passeth all understanding». So be it, so be it, through the love for mankind and the grace of one member of the consubstantial Holy Trinity, Christ Jesus, my Savior, through the intercession of the Mother of God.

85. To the emperor, that the Despoina was annoyed with her son, the most fortunate Despot

Since his mother the Despoina, for what reason I cannot tell, is ill disposed toward the most fortunate Despot, when he reflects upon this, it seems to him an extremely grievous and mortal blow; and ⟨it would be a sign⟩ of extreme apathy if he did not hasten to pay his respects to her and to appease her grief, and this with the approval and bidding of your divine majesty. If then his impression is not merely ⟨the result of⟩ suspicion, but a true reason, it is imperative that she see ⟨the son⟩ who is beloved and most dear to you both, as soon as possible; on the one hand because he is driven by (?) his natural affection, and reasonably assumes that it is best for mothers to be seen rejoicing in their children, on the other hand because he fears the command of God Who has bade us «to honor our parents». For these reasons, as I have said, he earnestly entreats your divine majesty to send him ⟨to her⟩ as soon as possible. If then this should be opportune (for you know this better than I), I join him in this request, especially because, as he affirms, he has subjected himself to binding oaths in this respect. If, however, no opportunity presents itself for his desire to be accomplished, in any case your divine majesty must find a solution to the above-mentioned problem.

86. Πρὸς τὸν αὐτοκράτορα

Πολλάκις προσμαρτυρεῖν ἠκηκόειν τὴν ἐκ Θεοῦ βασιλείαν σου τὰ
περὶ τοῦ φιλτάτου καὶ πανευτυχεστάτου δεσπότου καὶ πάντη ἀξιεπαίνου
καὶ μάλιστα δι' εὐλάβειαν, ὡς ὅτι οὐ μόνον τῇ βασιλείᾳ ἀλλὰ κἂν τῇ ἐκκλη-
5 σίᾳ πολλὴν ἐμφαίνει τὴν γνησιότητα καὶ σπουδήν. διά τοι τοῦτο πρὸς τῷ
ἐπαίνῳ τῷ τῶν ὁρώντων καταπεμφθείη ἀπὸ Θεοῦ καὶ πᾶν ἀγαθὸν καὶ σωτήριον. τοῦ δέ γε τοιούτου τινὰ ἀποκναίοντα τοῦτον αἰσθανθέντες ποσῶς
καὶ ἡμεῖς, σιωπᾶν ἐδόξαμεν οὐκ ἀνεύθυνον, ἀλλ' ἀναφέρειν πρὸς τὸν ὀφείλοντα καὶ δυνάμενον τὰ τοῦτον θράττοντα ἀπελάσαι, καὶ παρέξαι τὴν
10 εὐθυμίαν μετὰ Θεὸν κἂν τούτῳ τῷ μέρει τῇ ἐκείνου ψυχῇ. τὰ δέ γε ἄρτι
παραλυποῦντα ἐκεῖνον οὐ δίκαια μόνον εἰπεῖν, ἀλλὰ καὶ ἀναγκαῖα καὶ
ἀπαραίτητα. τί γάρ, εἰ καὶ μὴ ἀναλόγως πρὸς τὰς ἐξόδους αὐτῷ τῆς
ζωῆς καὶ τοῦ ἀξιώματος καὶ τῶν ὑπ' αὐτὸν ἐξ οἰκονομίας τινὸς προνοεῖται,
δυνηθῇ διαπράττεσθαι; ταῦτα τῷ θάρρει τῷ πρὸς ἡμᾶς, εἰ καὶ λίαν πεφυ-
15 λαγμένως καὶ εὐλαβῶς συντηρεῖ ἑαυτόν, ὡς μή τι γογγυστικὸν ἐμφῆναι,
ἢ ποσῶς ὑπονοηθῆναι, τὰ νῦν ἐκ θάρρους, ὡς ἔφην, καὶ τῆς βίας παρορμη-
θείς, τῇ φίλῃ συνέσει καὶ ἡμερότητι μετ' αἰδοῦς ἐξεκάλυψεν, ἀναφορὰν
ποιῆσαι καὶ ἡμῶν διὰ γράμματος, καὶ στεῖλαι τῇ πανευσεβεστάτῃ
Αὐγούστῃ καὶ κυρίᾳ αὐτοῦ καὶ μητρί, συμπρεσβεῦσαι δὲ καὶ ἡμᾶς ἀρκοῦ-
20 σαν πρὸς τὰ ῥηθέντα ὑπὲρ [fol. 71ᵛ] τοῦ ταύτης υἱοῦ ποιήσασθαι ἐπιμέλειαν, ὡς μᾶλλον ἐκείνῃ ἀνακειμένου, καὶ κεχρεωστημένης ἐκεῖθεν κατὰ
πολὺ τῆς αὐτοῦ κυβερνήσεως καὶ τῆς ἐπὶ τὸ κρεῖττον ἀναγωγῆς, τοῦτο
καὶ τοῦ μεγάλου Παύλου δηλοῦντος, ἐκ πόρων δικαίων τοῖς τέκνοις
παρὰ πατέρων ἐπιτηρεῖσθαι θησαύρισμα.
25 ἔνθεν μεταχειρίσασθαι μὴ εἰδότες ὡς δέον τὸ αἴτημα, εἰδήσεως ἄ-
μοιροι πάμπαν καὶ παιδεύσεως πέλοντες ἀνακτορικῆς, μήπως χωρὶς συμ-
βουλῆς (ἐπεὶ καὶ πολέμιον τὸ ἀσύμβουλον) ἀτελῶς ἀνενέγκωμεν τὰ ῥηθέντα, καὶ τῇ μὴ πρὸς τὸ δέον μεταχειρίσει τὰ καλὰ παρεμποδισθῇ, καὶ τῇ
πολλῇ βουλῇ ὑπάρχειν τὴν σωτηρίαν ἐπιμνησθέντες, μηδένα
30 τῶν ἐπὶ γῆς εἰδότες σύμβουλον θαυμαστὸν τῶν τοιούτων, καὶ ἵνα
καὶ νομισθῶμεν ἀκροαταὶ συνετοί, κἀντεῦθεν μικρὸν θηρεύσωμέν
τι δοξάριον, τῇ ἐκ Θεοῦ βασιλείᾳ σου ἀναφέρω, τὸ πότε καὶ πῶς πείθεσθαι
ταύτην τὰ περὶ τούτου, ἀρκούμενος τῇ προστάξει σου· καὶ πῶς ὀφείλει
γραφῆναί τε καὶ πεμφθῆναι, καὶ ὅσα δεῖ καὶ ὡς δεῖ ἐξείπῃ ἡμῖν, μηδὲν
35 ἐαθῆναι τῶν πρὸς ἀξίαν, μηδὲ ῥηθῆναί τι παρ' ἀξίαν ἐν οὕτω προσώποις
φιλτάτοις καὶ ὑπερέχουσιν, ἐντεῦθεν τὴν θεραπείαν ἀπαντῆσαι τῶν
αἰτημάτων ἀπροσδεῆ τὸ σύνολον ἠλπικότες μετὰ Θεόν, παρ' οὗ πανοικεὶ
φρουρηθείητε.

86: 23–24 cf. II Cor. 12:14 ‖ 28–29 Prov. 11:14 ‖ 30–31 Is. 3:3

86: V 71ʳ–71ᵛ. S 214ʳ–214ᵛ. P 93ʳ–94ʳ.
1 ante πρὸς add. γράμμα VʳSP ‖ post αὐτοκράτορα add. περὶ τοῦ δεσπότου καὶ υἱοῦ αὐτοῦ
Ἰωάννου ἀναλόγως πρὸς τὰς ἐξόδους καὶ τοῦ ἀξιώματος ἔχειν καὶ τὰς οἰκονομίας VʳSP ‖
31 θηρεύσομεν codd.

86

86. To the emperor

I have often heard your divine majesty bear witness to the character of the most beloved and most fortunate Despot, who is deserving of praise in all respects, but especially on account of his piety, since he reveals great sincerity and zeal, not only for the empire but also for the Church. For this reason, may God bestow on him all blessings and salvation, in addition to the praise of those who behold him. Since I have learned from him that certain problems are worrying him greatly, I have decided that it would be wrong for me to remain silent, but that I should refer the matter to the one who has both the obligation and capability to remove his vexing problems, and who can, after God, bring cheer to his soul in this affair. It is not only right that I speak of those matters which are now troubling him, but necessary and vital. For how can he manage, if some arrangement is not made for him to be granted an income commensurate with his living expenses, and the expenses entailed by his position, and the expenses of his household? Now, as a result of his confidence in me, even if he takes care to be cautious and discreet, so as not to appear to complain or to offer grounds for suspicion, now, as I have said, spurred on by confidence and the force of necessity, he has disclosed his problem ⟨to me⟩ with respect, as a result of his intelligence and his mild disposition, and ⟨wants⟩ me to prepare a petition, and send it to the most pious Augusta, his lady and mother, and he wants me to join him in his entreaty that she make suitable arrangements for her son for the above-mentioned needs, since he is dependent for the most part on her, and therefore she is greatly responsible for his support and good upbringing, as was pointed out by the great Paul when he said that money from just sources «should be stored up by fathers for their children».

Wherefore, not knowing how to handle the petition properly, since I have absolutely no knowledge of or training in palace etiquette, lest for lack of advice I make the abovementioned request to no avail (since lack of advice is dangerous), and lest a happy conclusion be forestalled by my clumsy handling of the situation, since I remember that «safety lies in much advice», and know that no one here on earth is such a «marvelous counsellor» in such matters ⟨as yourself⟩, and so that I may be considered an «intelligent listener» and seek some little repute therefrom, I ask your majesty ⟨to advise me⟩ when and how she [the empress] should be persuaded about this matter, and I will be satisfied with your recommendation. And ⟨tell me⟩ how ⟨the petition⟩ should be written and dispatched, and the proper content and style, and let nothing be left out that is appropriate to the dignity, nor let anything be said that is not appropriate to the dignity of people who are so closely related and distinguished, for I hope that in this way he [the Despot] may attain on the whole sufficient fulfilment of his requests, with the help of God, in Whose safekeeping may you be with all your family.

87. Πρὸς τὸν αὐτοκράτορα

Νομίζω καὶ τῶν ἀθέων πολλὴν ἀποσῴζειν πρὸς τά γε αὐτοῖς
λατρευόμενα καὶ τοὺς τούτων θεραπευτὰς τὴν τιμήν, ἀλλά γε τῶν ἡμετέρων, οἷς ἡ ἀλήθεια καὶ τὸ φῶς ἐβραβεύθη, ἐμέλησεν οὐδαμῶς περὶ τούτων,
5 ὡς κἂν τοῖς ἄλλοις καλοῖς, ποθησάντων ἡμῶν τὴν πώρωσιν τῆς
καρδίας, ἐκ τοῦ μύσαι τοὺς ὀφθαλμούς, ὡς ἂν μὴ ἐπιστραφέντες ἰάσεως
τύχωμεν. εἰ δέ που καὶ παραδείγματι ἁρμοδίῳ πρὸς τὸ μή τινα ἀμφιβάλλειν δέον τὴν συμφορὰν βεβαιῶσαι, οὐ μακρὰν ἐκζητήσομεν, ἀλλ' ἐξ ὧν ὁ
χρόνος οἶδεν ὁ καθ' ἡμᾶς, καὶ ἐνταῦθα· συνέβη οὐ πρὸ πολλοῦ ἕνα τῶν
10 περικλύτων ναῶν ἀτημέλητον ὁραθῆναι καὶ ἀσκεπῆ, ἐφ' ὃν σὺν πολλοῖς
ἐκτυπώμασι [fol. 72ʳ] θείοις προσῆν καὶ ἡ τοῦ Σωτῆρος θεανδρικὴ καὶ
προσκυνητὴ εἰκών· ἐν ᾧ τῶν λαχόντων διενεργεῖν ἀναγαγεῖν τινα προτρε-
ψάμενον τοῦ πατάξαι λαξευτηρίῳ — τῆς σῆς ἀνοχῆς, Ἀγαθέ — τὸ
θεανδρικὸν ἐκτύπωμα πρὸς καταστροφήν, τῶν κάτωθεν κατακεκραγότων
15 τοῦ ἀσεβοῦς καὶ βαλλόντων τῷ ἀναθέματι· οὗ καὶ τῆς δίκης ἐπὶ πολὺ μὴ
ἀνασχομένης, ὡς πρός τινος ὠθισθεὶς πρὸς τὰ κάτω, ἐλεεινῶς τὴν
ἀθλίαν ψυχὴν ἀπεστέρηται.

εἰ οὖν τοιούτοις ἀνθρώποις ἐγχειρίζονται τὰ δημώδη, τί πρὸς ἀνθρώπους ἐκεῖνοι καὶ δράσειαν, οἱ Θεοῦ μὴ φειδόμενοι; εἰ δέ που καὶ σήμερον
20 τὴν ὠμότητα τῶν πολλῶν μὴ συνέστελλεν ἡ προσοῦσα τῇ ἐκ Θεοῦ βασιλείᾳ
σου ἀσύγκριτος ἡμερότης καὶ πρὸς τὰ θεῖα εὐλάβεια, οὐδὲν τῶν ἀθέων ἢ
καὶ θηρίων ἀποδέειν ἐκρίθησαν, οἷς εἰ καὶ μὴ προσῇ ἀναχαίτησις, τὸ
κρῖμα κοινόν.

διὰ τοῦτο ἀντιβολῶ, ἐπεὶ δι' ἐμὰς ἀνομίας ὧν ἐπλούτει ἡ ἐκκλησία
25 ἐκ θυέλλης βαρβαρικῆς ἐγεγύμνωτο, καὶ ὃ κατελείφθη βραχοφάγου κα-
λούμενον, κελευσθῆναί τινα ὑπ' αὐτῆς ἀναδέξασθαι τοῦτο, ὡς ἂν μή, δι'
ἣν πρὸς ἡμᾶς οἱ διενεργοῦντες ἐπιθάλπουσιν ἀηδίαν ἐξ ὧν ἐξελέγχονται
παρ' ἡμῶν, τοῖς τῇ ἐκκλησίᾳ ὑποκειμένοις ἀφειδῶς δι' ἡμᾶς καταχρήσων-
ται. ἀρκεῖ γὰρ ἡμῖν ἡ εὐθύνη τῶν ἡμετέρων· ἵνα τί καὶ τοῖς ἄλλοις παραί-
30 τιοι συμφορᾶς χρηματίσωμεν; ἐπεὶ μὴ ὡς πάλαι τὸ σέβας τῇ ἐκκλησίᾳ
προσῆν, ὡς οἱ τοῦτο γινώσκοντες βλέπουσι, καὶ οἷα τοῖς πρὸ ἡμῶν ἐτηρεῖτο αἰδημοσύνη, καὶ ὅση τοῖς ὑπ' αὐτῶν στελλομένοις, καὶ ὧν καὶ ἡ
ἐκκλησία ἐπεξουσιάζει, ἀλλὰ νῦν ὁ βουλόμενος ἀδεῶς κατατρέχειν τῶν
ἐνεργούντων, ἢ διαρπάζειν, ἢ διαβάλλειν, οὐκ ἔχει τὸν ἀναστέλλοντα, ὀχ-
35 λούντων εἰς μάτην ἡμῶν, εἰ καὶ δόξομεν ἀναφέρειν, βασιλικὰς ἀκοάς.

87: V 71ᵛ–72ᵛ. S 214ᵛ–216ʳ. P 94ʳ–95ʳ.
1 ante πρὸς add. γράμμα VʳSP ‖ post αὐτοκράτορα add. περὶ τοῦ προτρεψαμένου λαχόντος
(λαχόντως VʳS) διενεργεῖν τὰ δημώδη καὶ ἀγαγεῖν τινα λαξευτηρίῳ πατάξαι πρὸς καταστροφὴν τοῦ Σωτῆρος ἐκτύπωμα καὶ περὶ τοῦ αὐθαδισθέντος ἁρπάσαι τὸν σῖτον (σίτον Vʳ)
VʳSP ‖ 10 περικλύτων] περικυκλούντων S, ἀπερικλύτων P ‖ 27 ἐξελέγχωνται S

87. To the emperor

I think that even pagans treat with great honor both the objects they worship, and the priests that attend to these objects, but as for us, to whom the Truth and Light have been awarded, we care not a bit about these things, as in the case of other blessings, since we have desired rather «blindness of heart», by closing our eyes, so that we would not be healed through repentance. And if it should be necessary to provide proof of our miserable state with a suitable example, so that no one will have any doubts, we will not have to look far, but to an incident witnessed in our time and ⟨right⟩ here. Not too long ago one of our famous churches, to which belonged the theandric and venerable icon of the Savior and many other holy images, could be seen in a state of neglect and without a roof. And a state official was ordered to climb up in this ⟨church⟩ for the purpose of smashing this image of God-Man with an adze, so as to destroy it (Oh, how great was Thy forbearance, my good Lord and God), while the people standing below cried out against the impious fellow and cursed him. And his punishment was not long delayed, since someone pushed him to the ground where he pitiably gave up the ghost.

If then public offices are entrusted to such people, how will they treat simple men, when they do not even spare God? And if even today your divine majesty's incomparable gentleness and reverence for sacred objects will not check somewhat the cruelty of many ⟨such people⟩, they will decide to be just like pagans or wild beasts; and unless they are constrained, we will all share in their guilt.

Therefore, since on account of my sins the Church has been stripped of Her possessions by a barbarian gale, and what has been left is but a mouthful, I ask that someone be ordered by your majesty to protect this ⟨portion that remains⟩, so that the state officials may not mercilessly devour the property of the Church on my account, since they nurse a grudge against me because of the charges I make against them. For responsibility for my ⟨own affairs⟩ is enough for me; why should I be the cause of other people's ruin? For now the Church does not have the same respect that it had before, as can be seen by those who know such things, nor do I enjoy the same respect as did my predecessors and their emissaries, and the same applies to church property; now there is no one to restrain any state official who wants to indulge in bullying with impunity or in confiscating ⟨church property⟩ or in false accusations, since I myself, if I decide to submit a petition, disturb the emperor in vain.

τί γὰρ καὶ κατὰ τοῦ τὸν σῖτον ἁρπάσαι αὐθαδισθέντος χιλίοις
μεδίμνοις πρὸς τοῖς ὀκτακοσίοις, δι' ὄχλου γενόμενοι τὰ πολλά, ἀνύσαι ἰσ-
χύσαμεν; εἰ δ' ἐν τοῖς τῆς ἐκκλησίας καὶ ἡμετέροις τοσοῦτον ἰσχύομεν, τί
[μὴ] δράσωμεν πρὸς δικαίωσιν τῶν ἐγγὺς ἢ μακρὰν ἀδικίᾳ πιεζομένων
40 τινῶν; εἰ μὲν οὖν ἕνεκεν εὐλαβείας [fol. 72ᵛ] καὶ ὀφειλῆς καὶ τιμῆς προσηη-
κούσης τῇ ἐκκλησίᾳ ἐτηρεῖτο τοῖς πρὸ ἡμῶν τὸ αἰδέσιμον, οὔ μοι πολὺ τὸ
λυποῦν, Θεοῦ τοῦ τῆς ἐκκλησίας τοὺς δοξάζοντας ταύτην ἀντι-
δοξάζοντος· εἰ δὲ προσώποις ἀπεχαρίζοντο χάριν αἰσθήσεως, ὡς ἂν
μὴ ἀμφιγνοῆται τὸ μέσον ἐμοῦ καὶ τῶν πρὸ ἐμοῦ, κἀκεῖθεν τὸ χρῆμα τῆς
45 ταπεινώσεως οὐδεὶς ὁ ἡμῶν ἀφαιρούμενος.

88. Πρὸς τὸν αὐτοκράτορα

Ὡς ἂν μὴ τῶν μεμψιμοίρων καὶ ὦν τὸ στόμα τάφος ἀνεῳγ-
μένος καὶ πικρίας μεστὸν καὶ ἀρᾶς διά τινα ὄκνον τὴν χειρίστην ὁρμὴν ἐρε-
θίσωμεν, τοῖς ἱεροῖς ἀποστόλοις ἀόκνως πεπληρώκαμεν τὸ λειτούργημα,
5 τοῦτο τῆς ἐκ Θεοῦ βασιλείας σου μὴ ἀνασχομένης, ἀνέορτον παρεᾶσαι τὴν
πάντη αἰδέσιμον φιλεόρτοις πανήγυριν καὶ ἑορτὴν ἀξιάγαστον, καὶ (εὖ γε
τῆς ὑψηλῆς περὶ τὰ χρηστὰ διακρίσεως καὶ ὁρμῆς!) ὄφλημα διδασκάλοις
ἀποδιδόναι καὶ γέρας, καὶ πᾶσι τοῖς τοῦ βαπτίσματος τοῦ ἁγίου τυχοῦσι
μὴ παραλείπειν ὡς δυνατὸν ἐκδιδασκούσης τὸ ἀξιόχρεων· πρὸς οἷς καὶ
10 προσαγωγὴν θαυμασίαν, τὸν πολύτιμον καὶ ποικίλον ποδήρη, καὶ μάλα
τῇ ἱερᾷ λειτουργίᾳ πανάγαστον, κρειττόνως τῶν προβεβασιλευκότων
προσενεγκάμενος, μικροῦ καὶ ἀμίμητον.

καὶ τί τὸ ἐντεῦθεν; ὑπόχρεων θεῖναι τὴν ἱερὰν ξυνωρίδα, θατέρου
πρεσβεύοντος ὑπὲρ σοῦ, ὡς ἄν σοι καὶ παρεχθείη θεόθεν ἰσχὺς κατ' ἐχ-
15 θρῶν νοουμένων καὶ ὁρατῶν, καὶ πρώτως σου τὴν ζωὴν ῥυθμισθῆναι καθ'
εἱρμὸν τῶν ἐκείνου ἐπιστολῶν, τοῦ δέ γε θατέρου, ὡς τὰς κλεῖς
ἐγκεχειρισμένου, τῆς Ἐδέμ σοι παρέξειν τὴν ὑπάνοιξιν, ἣν ὁ προπάτωρ καὶ οἱ φύντες ἐκεῖθεν μὴ φροντίσαντες ἐγκολπώσασθαι τῶν ἐπιστολῶν, ἐπεί γε κἀκείνοις ὁ ἄγραπτος νόμος αὐτὰ τὰ τῶν ἐπιστολῶν ὑπετίθει,

---

42–43 I Reg. 2:30
88: 2–3 cf. Rom. 3:13 ‖ 16–17 cf. Μηναῖον τοῦ Ἰουνίου, 389

---

37 ὀκτασίοις P ‖ ἀνίσαι S ‖ 39 μὴ uncis inclusi ‖ 43 post αἰσθήσεως, lacuna omnibus
in codicibus ‖ 44 ἀμφιγνοῆται VˣSP: ἀμφιγνοεῖται V
88: V 72ᵛ–73ʳ. S 216ʳ–217ʳ. P 95ʳ–96ʳ.
1 ante πρὸς add. γράμμα VʳSP ‖ post αὐτοκράτορα add. περὶ τῶν μὴ θελησάντων ἵνα
ἐκτελεσθῇ ἡ ἑορτὴ τῶν θείων ἀποστόλων, αὐτὸς δὲ μὴ ἀσχόμενος (leg. ἀνασχόμενος ?) ἐᾶσαι,
ἀπέστειλε καὶ προσαγωγὴν τῇ ἱερᾷ λειτουργίᾳ τὸν πολυτίμητον καὶ ποικίλον ποδήρη VʳSP ‖
14 ἰσχὺν codd. ‖ 15–16 καθ' εἱρμὸν VSP¹: καθ' ἡμῶν P

87, 88

For what was I able to accomplish with respect to the man who had the insolence to seize 1800 *medimnoi* of grain, despite the fact that I importuned you greatly? And if I have so little authority in the affairs of the church and my own affairs, what shall I be able to achieve to defend the rights of those both near and far who are weighed down by injustice? If then the reverence shown to my predecessors was due to piety, a sense of obligation, and honor owed to the *Church*, this grieves me little, since God of the Church «glorifies those who glorify» Her; but if they ⟨showed this reverence⟩ to ⟨them as⟩ *individuals*, to make it perceptible [i.e., so that it might become apparent] what a huge distance separates me from my predecessors, then in this case, too, nobody can take away from me the claim to humility.

88. To the emperor

So as not to provoke, through any hesitation, the contemptible attack of faultfinders and those whose «mouth is an open sepulchre» and filled with bitterness and curses, I celebrated unhesitatingly the service for the Holy Apostles, since your divine majesty could not allow to leave uncelebrated this marvelous *panegyris* and festival which is revered by everyone to whom feast days are dear, and (praised be your lofty discrimination and impulses with reference to good things!) ⟨ordered⟩ that due honor be paid to ⟨the Two⟩ Teachers; you ⟨also⟩ teach that all those who have received holy baptism should, to the best of their ability, insist on fulfilling what is worthy of fulfilment. And in addition, surpassing all the emperors before you, you brought a wondrous offering, the precious and beautifully decorated vestment, which is certainly marvelous for the holy liturgy, all but inimitable.

And what is the consequence of this? It made the holy pair indebted to you, Paul to intercede on your behalf, so that God may grant you strength against your enemies, both intelligible and visible, and that above all you may order your life in accordance with his epistles, and Peter, inasmuch as he is «entrusted with the keys», to open up for you ⟨the gates of⟩ Paradise, which were most rightly shut, alas, in the faces of our forefather and his descendants, because they did not take care to keep in their hearts ⟨the teachings of⟩ the epistles, since they, too, could derive from unwritten law

20 ἑαυτοῖς (ὢ ζημίας!) ἀπέκλεισαν ἐνδικώτατα. πρὸς τούτοις εἰ εὐδοκεῖ, ἔστιν οὗ καὶ ἡμᾶς ἀναγκάζει ἡ ἐκ Θεοῦ βασιλεία σου κατὰ κέλευσιν βαίνειν τῶν θείων ἐπιστολῶν, σκοποῦ τοῦ πληρῶσαι τὸν οἶκον, θελόντων καὶ μὴ θελόντων ἡμῶν, οὔ τοί γε μόνον τὰ τῆς Ἐδὲμ ἀλλά γε καὶ ἡ οὐράνιος βασιλεία, ὡς κἀνταῦθα ἡ ἐπὶ γῆς ἀμογητί σοι [fol. 73ʳ]
25 ἐπῆλθεν, εἴ πέρ τινι ἄλλῳ προμνηστευθήσεται.

οὗ γε καὶ χάριν ὡς δοῦλοι ἀχρεῖοι ἡμεῖς καὶ γονάτων ἁπτόμεθα καὶ ἀντιβολοῦμεν ἐνωτίζεσθαι τὸν κελεύοντα βαπτισθέντι παντί, μετανοεῖτε· ἤγγικε γὰρ ἡ βασιλεία τῶν οὐρανῶν, καί γε τοῦ θεοκήρυκος Παύλου καταλλάγητε τῷ Θεῷ ἀξιοῦντος, ἐχθραί-
30 νοντες οἷς ἐχθραίνει, καὶ δραττόμενοι τῶν θεοφιλῶν, ὡς ἕνεκεν τούτων τὸν ἁμαρτίαν μὴ γνόντα πεποίηκεν ἁμαρτίαν ὑπὲρ ἡμῶν, ἵνα σωθῶμεν ἡμεῖς, πολλὰ ἰσχυούσης ὁμολογίας τοῦ πταίσματος καὶ φυγῆς, ἐν οἷς γινώσκει Θεὸς ἡμετέροις, καὶ ἡ ἑκάστου συνείδησις· εἰ δ' ἴσως τὸ κράτος κελεύει τῆς ἐκ Θεοῦ βασιλείας σου ἀνιστορεῖν καὶ
35 ἡμᾶς τοὺς τῆς σωτηρίας ἐφιεμένους καὶ δόξης, ἐξ ὧν εἰς χόλον Θεοῦ οὐ καλῶς δραττόμενοί τινες ἀφορμῆς, μεγάλως πρὸς τὰ κοινά, παρὰ γνώμην τὴν σήν, ὀλισθαίνουσιν, ἑαυτοὺς ἀπολλύντες, καὶ αἷμα ἀθῷον ἐκχέοντες, ἀδεῶς ἀλλ' οὐ κρύφα τὰ χείριστα πράττοντες ὧν ἕνεκεν οἶδα καὶ Θεός σοι τὴν μάχαιραν ἐνεχείρισε, πιστεύσας σοι ταύτην εἰς ἐκδίκησιν τῶν
40 κακοποιῶν, καὶ ἔπαινον τῶν ἀγαθοποιῶν καὶ ἀντίληψιν.

89. ⟨Πρὸς τὸν αὐτοκράτορα⟩

Ἡνίκα τινὰ τῶν ἐν δίκαις συνεχομένων παρὰ μεγάλων συμβῇ πρὸς ἡμᾶς σταλῆναι προσώπων, ἀκουσθῆναι τὴν δίκην ἐκείνων συνοδικῶς ἀξιούντων, οὐ πρὸς ἀναβολὰς χωροῦμεν καὶ ὑπερθέσεις τῶν πεμψάντων
5 χάριν, ταχέως ἐπιμελούμενοι καὶ ὡς δέον φροντίζοντες. εἰ δ' ἐπ' ἀνθρώπων ἐν κρίσει διαφορὰ καὶ προτίμησις, ὁποία ἀναμφιβόλως καὶ ἀσυγκρίτως ἐν τοῖς ὑπὲρ Θεοῦ ἐποφείλεται, μεγάλοις τε καὶ μικροῖς, ὅς γε καὶ τοὺς ἐμπαροινοῦντας καὶ ἀφραίνοντας τὰ εἰς αὐτὸν δυνατὸς ὢν ἐπεξέρχεσθαι καὶ διεκδικεῖν, ἀγαθωσύνης πελάγει δοκιμάζων τὸν πόθον ἡμῶν πρὸς τὸ

21–22 cf. Luc. 14:23 ‖ 26 Luc. 17:10 ‖ 28 Matt. 3:2 ‖ 29–31 II Cor. 5:20–21 ‖ 32–33 cf. Greg. Naz., Or. XVI, ιζ' (PG, XXXV, 957 B) ‖ 39–40 cf. Rom. 13:4 et I Pet. 2:14

22 τὸν VS¹P: τῷ S ‖ 23 οὗ P ‖ 27 ἀντιβαλοῦμεν S
89: V 73ʳ–73ᵛ. S 217ʳ–217ᵛ. P 96ᵛ–97ʳ. Ed. Banduri, Imperium Orientale, II, 984–985; Migne, PG, CXLII, 503–6.
1 γράμμα πρὸς τὸν αὐτοκράτορα περὶ τοῦ κυροῦ Νίφωνος (νύμφωνος S, νύφωνος P) ὄντος (ὄντως Vʳ) Κυζίκου διὰ τὰς κατηγορίας τὰς ἀκουσθέντας περὶ αὐτοῦ add. VʳSP ‖ 8 ἐμπαροινεῖν καὶ ἀφραινεῖν codd.

the very teachings of the epistles. And in addition, if your divine majesty encourages and sometimes also «compels» me to proceed in accordance with the bidding of the holy epistles, with the purpose of «filling the house» ⟨of God⟩, whether I wish it or not, then not only paradise but also the heavenly kingdom will be procured by you, if by anyone, just as the ⟨kingdom⟩ here on earth came to you without any toil.

Therefore as an «unworthy servant» I clasp your knees and entreat you to heed the one who bade every person who is baptized, «Repent, for the kingdom of heaven is at hand», and to heed Paul, the herald of God, who prayed «Be ye reconciled to God», hating those who are His enemies, and holding close those who are dear to God, since it is for the sake of these people that «He hath made Him to sin for us Who knew no sin», that we might be saved, since «confession and avoidance of sin» are of great avail, and also the conscience of each, in those deeds which God knows to be ours (?); and if perhaps it should please your divine majesty, as one who desires your salvation and glory, I will tell you how certain people provoke the wrath of God by wickedly seizing an opportunity, and, against your will, have made serious mistakes in public administration, to their own destruction, and shed innocent blood, and openly and with impunity commit the most dastardly deeds; and I know that it is for these reasons that God delivered the sword into your hand, entrusting it to you «that you might punish evildoers, and praise» and assist «them that do well».

89. ⟨To the emperor⟩

Whenever it occurs that a person detained in a lawsuit is sent to me by important people, who ask that the case be tried before the synod, out of regard for those that sent him, I do not resort to delays and postponements, but rather swiftly take charge of the case and attend to it properly. But if there is ⟨such⟩ a difference and preference in judgment in the case of men, then it is incontrovertibly and absolutely an obligation in both great and small matters relating to God, Who, although He Himself is able to take vengeance on and punish those who are abusive and act offensively in matters referring to Him, still with a sea of goodness He puts our zeal for justice and

236

10 δίκαιον καὶ φιλάδελφον, εἰ ἐπιμελούμεθα ἁμαρτίας ἐλευθεροῦν ἀδελφούς,
ἀνθρώποις παρέπεμψε τὴν δικαίαν ἐκδίκησιν, μηδὲν προτιμᾶν ἐντειλάμενος
ἀληθείας.

διὰ τοῦτο τὰ φθάσαντα ἡμετέραις πεσεῖν ἀκοαῖς μὴ ὥς τι τῶν εὐ-
καταφρονήτων ἐάσωμεν ἀνενέργητα, μηδὲ καιροῦ ὑπερθέσει, ὅπως ἐπι-
15 λησθῶμεν, [fol. 73ᵛ] ἢ ἐξ ἄλλων φροντίδων παραδράμῃ ἡμᾶς ἀνεκδίκητα,
τῶν τοιούτων ὑφέξειν τὸν λόγον μὴ ἀγνοοῦντες. εἰ γάρ τις τὸν προσκόπ-
τοντα εἰς αὐτὸν ἢ ζημιοῦντα ἀνέξεται, τῶν ἐπαινουμένων ἐστίν· εἰ δὲ
χρήσεται τούτῳ ἐπὶ συνδούλοις, οὐδὲ μέμψεως ἔξω οὐδὲ ἀνεύθυνον. εἰ δὲ
καὶ πρὸς τοὺς κυρίους προσβλέπει τοῦ κρίνοντος, ἐπικίνδυνον, ὅτι μηδὲ
20 αὐτὸς ὁ πανάγαθος ἀδικεῖσθαί τινα ἐπαινεῖ, καὶ εἰ λίαν ἐστὶ φιλάνθρωπος, ἀλλὰ κίρνησι τὸν τρυγίαν αὐτοῖς τοῦ θυμοῦ ὀκνηρῶς τῶν δεσποτικῶν
ποιουμένοις ἐξέτασιν.

ἔνθεν ὡς ἂν καὶ φροντίδος καὶ ἁμαρτίας ἐκλυτρωθῶμεν (τῶν γὰρ
λίαν βαρέων τὰ ἀκουσθέντα), ἅπερ καὶ πρώην ἀνέφερον, ζητῶ καὶ τὰ
25 νῦν· τηρηθῆναι τῶν δύο τὸ ἕν, ἢ τηρηθῆναι παρὰ τῆς ἐκ Θεοῦ βασιλείας
σου, τῶν ἀμφοτέρων συνοψισθέντων, τοῦ κατηγόρου καὶ καθ᾽ οὗ ἡ
κατηγορία, ἢ ἐμπιστεύσασθαι τοῦτο ἡμῖν ὀλίγων τινῶν παρουσίᾳ, κατα-
κοῦσαι τῶν ἀμφοτέρων· ἀναχωρῆσαι γὰρ ἄλλως ἐν τῇ λαχούσῃ κἀκείνῳ
ἀσύμφορον καὶ ἡμῖν.

90. ⟨Πρὸς τὸν αὐτοκράτορα⟩

Πόμα θεοτερποῦς εὐφροσύνης λογικῶν καὶ νικητικῶν ἰδρώτων
σωτηρίας χάριν ψυχῶν κεκεράκει ἀνενεγκὼν ὁ τῆς εὐαγοῦς ὑφηγούμενος λαύρας τῆς ἐν τῇ πέτρᾳ ἡδραιωμένης, ἥτις ἐστὶν ὁ Χριστὸς καὶ
5 Θεός· καὶ τό γε θαυμασιώτερον, ὡς ἐν τοσαύτῃ φροντίδι καὶ συνοχῇ τοῦ
κόσμου καταλαμβανομένη καὶ ἑλκομένη ἡ ἐκ Θεοῦ βασιλεία σου, οὐδ᾽ ἐνταῦθα ἐκρίθη αὐτῇ ἀνεκτόν τινι τῶν πρωτείων ἑτέρῳ παραχωρεῖν, ὅπου
προσάξαι Θεῷ, εἰπεῖν, δυνατὸν ἀπολωλὸς πρόβατον. ἀλλὰ χάρις
κἂν τούτῳ τῷ Παντάνακτι καὶ Θεῷ βασιλεῖ τῶν δυνάμεων, προεγνωκότι
10 τὰ τῇδε καὶ προορίσαντι, καὶ θείᾳ θεοφανείᾳ καὶ τὴν σὴν ψυχὴν κατα-
στράψαντι, ὃν ἔκρινεν ἱκανὸν πρὸς τὴν τοῦ κόσμου κυβέρνησιν, ἕνεκεν

90: 2–3 cf. Ps. 101(102):10 ‖ 8 Luc. 15:6, Matt. 15:24

---

13 φθάσοντα P ‖ 27 παρουσίᾳ VS¹P: παρρησία S
    90: V 73ᵛ–74ʳ. S 217ᵛ–218ʳ. P 97ʳ–97ᵛ.
1 γράμμα εὐχαριστήριον πρὸς τὸν αὐτοκράτορα ὄντος ἐν ταύτῃ τῇ φροντίδι τοῦ κόσμου, μὴ
τῶν πρωτείων ἑτέρῳ παραχωρεῖν περὶ τοῦ ἀκουσθέντος αὐτῇ ἀπολωλότος προβάτου add.
VʳSP ‖ 2 πόμα coni. Ševčenko; πῶμα coni. Laurent; cf. Ps. 101 (102):10; ὄμμα codd. ‖
4 λαύρας codd. ‖ ἡδραιωμένης VʳSP: ἡδραιωμένοις V

89, 90

brotherhood to a test, to see if we try to free our brethren from sin, and has handed over to men the pursuit of law, bidding us prefer nothing to truth.

Wherefore we must not allow the matter which reached my ears to go neglected as if it were contemptible, nor must it pass by unpunished, either by postponement, so that we forget it, or because of any other worries, since we should be aware that we shall have to give an accounting for such ⟨omissions⟩. For if someone suffers a man to offend or harm him⟨self alone⟩, he is among the praiseworthy; but if he adopts the same attitude when these actions affect his fellow servants, he does not escape blame or responsibility. And if the matter is in regard to the masters (?) of the judge, it is dangerous because not even God, Who is completely good, praises a man for being wronged, even if He loves mankind greatly, but He mixes the wine of anger for those who reluctantly examine affairs that relate to God.

Therefore, so that we may be freed from anxiety and sin (for the reports are of extreme gravity), I now ask the same thing that I previously requested: that one of two courses be followed, either that the case be taken up by your divine majesty, and the plaintiff and defendant be submitted to a confrontation, or that the matter be entrusted to me, together with a few select people, to hear both sides. For it would be unbecoming both for him and for us, if he should return to his see in any other way.

90. ⟨To the emperor⟩

The abbot of the holy Lavra, which is founded on the rock which is Christ and God, by means of his petition has «mingled the draught» of God-pleasing joy with the sweat of spiritual and victorious labors for the sake of the salvation of souls. And what is even more marvelous is that your divine majesty, even though you are occupied and distracted by so much concern and sense of responsibility for worldly affairs, still you cannot bear to yield the prize to anyone here on earth, whenever it is possible for you to bring to God «a lost sheep», so to speak. But thanks be also to the Ruler of all, God the King of hosts, Who foreknew and foreordained affairs here on earth, and Who dazzled your soul with a holy vision of God. He deemed you capable of

τῶν μελλόντων κληρονομεῖν βασιλείαν, τοῦ ψηλαφητοῦ
σκότους τῶν σχιζομένων ἁρπάζειν Ἰσραηλίτας, καθά που καὶ
Μωσέα καὶ Παῦλον τὸν μέγαν ἐν φωτισμῷ τοὺς ἁλόντας τῇ σκοτομήνῃ
15 φωτίζειν ἐκπέμψαντι. καὶ εἴης μοι ἀπεράντοις αἰῶσι τῇ ἐκκλησίᾳ Χριστοῦ
χρη–[fol. 74ʳ] ματίζων καὶ πηγὴ καὶ ζωὴ καὶ πρόμαχος καὶ ἀσφάλεια,
εἴ πως σὺν πᾶσι τοῖς ἀγαθοῖς καὶ πρὸς τῇ τῶν ἀπολωλότων προβάτων
ἐπιστροφῇ διακέοιτο ἐπιπονώτερον καὶ φιλανθρωπότερον, δι' οὓς ἔκλι-
νεν οὐρανοὺς καὶ κατέβη Θεός, δι' οὓς ἐν πολλοῖς ἀδελφοῖς
20 ἐκλήθη πρωτότοκος, δι' οὓς ὁ παρὼν πανταχοῦ καὶ τὰ πάντα
πληρῶν οὐκ ἀπηξίωσε κατελθεῖν ἐν κατωτάτοις τῆς γῆς, ἐκ
κοιλίας Ἅιδου τὸ γένος ῥυσόμενος· δι' οὓς καὶ τοὺς συνεργοῦντας
τοιοῖσδε τοῦ συνάγειν μετὰ Χριστοῦ, καθὰ καὶ τὴν ἐκ Θεοῦ βασιλείαν σου, ἀσυγκρίτοις ὑπεροχαῖς καὶ διαδήματι δόξης καταστέψειεν ἀ-
25 θανάτῳ, καὶ τούτῳ συνεῖναι τῇ διαιωνιζούσῃ καταξιώσοι καὶ ἀπεράντῳ
μακαριότητι.

91. ⟨Γράμμα περὶ μοναχῶν⟩

Εἰ καὶ μέχρι τοῦ νῦν ἀγνωσίαν Θεοῦ, πῶς οὐκ οἶδα, παθόντες τινὲς
ἀνομεῖν ἑκοντὶ ᾑρετίσαντο, ὡς καὶ θείων κανόνων συνοδικῶν ὁδηγίας
καὶ καταστάσεως χάριν σωτηριώδους ἀποφάσεις φρικτὰς καταπάτημα
5 θεῖναι καὶ καταφρόνημα, τοῦ τοσούτου δεινοῦ μηδενὸς τῶν ἀρχιερέων τῶν
εἰς τοῦτο κειμένων, καταιγίδος τοσαύτης, ἐπιμέλειαν πεποιημένου, πυρι-
φλέκτων δὲ τῶν πλειόνων κατασταθέντων ἐξ ἐπαράτου σιγῆς (τῶν τῷ λαῷ
παρανομουμένων ὑφέξειν ἀναμφιβόλως τὸν λόγον ποιμένας, εἰ μὴ διάτορον ἐξελέγχοιεν καὶ νυκτὸς καὶ ἡμέρας διαμαρτύροιντο), ἀλλὰ τούτου
10 τοῦ δυσαχθοῦς εἰς συναίσθησιν, οἴμοι, τοῦ Θεοῦ ἐλεοῦντός με, αἰσ-
θανθεὶς καὶ αὐτὸς ἔγωγε, καὶ παράβασιν θείων θεσμῶν καταγνούς,
καὶ εἰδὼς καὶ λόγων καὶ ἔργων εὐθύνας ἐποφείλειν ἀσυμπαθῶς ὀρθόδοξον
ἅπαντα, πολλῷ δὲ μᾶλλον παραβάσεις εὐαγγελίων καὶ ἀποστολικῶν καὶ
κανονικῶν, ὑποσχέσεις ποιοῦμαι ἀπ' ἄρτι Θεοῦ κατ' ἐνώπιον καὶ ἀγγέλων
15 ἁγίων καὶ τῆς συνόδου, μὴ ἁλῶναι ὡς ψεύστης ἀπ' ἄρτι τῶν ἐμῶν ὁμο-
λογιῶν καὶ πρὸς αὐτὸν τὸν Θεὸν συνταγῶν, τῇ δυνάμει θαρρῶν τοῦ
Σωτῆρός μου. μέχρι παντὸς ἀνεπίληστον περιφέρω τὸ μέλλον τοὺς παρα-

---

12 cf. Hebr. 1:14 ‖ 12–13 Ex. 10:21 ‖ 13 cf. Matt. 15:24 ‖ 18–19 II Reg. 22:10; Ps.
17(18):10 ‖ 19–20 cf. Rom. 8:29 ‖ 20–21 cf. Eph. 4:10 ‖ 21 Ps. 138(139):15 ‖ 21–22 Jon.
2:3 ‖ 23 cf. Matt. 12:30

---

16 χρηματίζειν codd.
91: V 74ʳ–74ᵛ. S 218ᵛ–219ʳ. P 97ᵛ–98ʳ.
1 γράμμα περὶ μοναχῶν τῶν καταπάτημα τῶν θείων κανόνων ἑκοντὶ ᾑρετισάντων καὶ ἀπο-
φυγόντων τῆς οἰκείας μονῆς add. VʳSP

ruling the world, for the sake of «those who are going to inherit salvation»,
and to rescue the Israelites from the «palpable darkness» of the schismatics,
just as He sent Moses and the great Paul to illuminate with light those who
were caught in the darkness of a moonless night. And you would be, for
countless generations, the fountainhead and life and bulwark and protector
of the Church of Christ, if somehow, together with all your good works, you
would show greater concern and love for mankind through the restoration of
lost sheep, for whose sake God «bowed the heavens and came down», for whose
sake He was called «the firstborn among many brethren», for whose sake He
Who is present everywhere and «fills all things» did not refuse to descend
«into the depths of the earth», to save our people «from the belly of hell». For
their sake may He crown with incomparable honors and with the eternal
crown of glory your divine majesty and those who assist him in such works
by «gathering with Christ», and may He deem you worthy to dwell together
with Him in perpetual and everlasting blessedness.

91. ⟨Letter concerning monks⟩

Even if up to now certain people, I know not how, have suffered ignorance of God, and have chosen the lawless paths of their own accord, so as
to trample and despise the instructions of holy synodical canons and their
awesome decisions concerning a way of life leading to salvation, while none
of the bishops appointed for such purpose has paid attention to such an
evil, such a great storm, but most of them are liable to burn in hell-fire on
account of their accursed silence (and bishops surely will bear the responsibility for the transgressions of their flock, if they do not clearly rebuke them
and protest night and day), still as I indeed did perceive and realize the situation which was exceedingly grievous, God having mercy on me; since I realized the transgression of divine ordinances; and since I was aware that every
Orthodox Christian must without any sympathy render an accounting for
his words and deeds, and even more for transgressions ⟨of the command-
ments⟩ of the Gospels and the apostles and the canons; henceforth I promise
before God and the holy angels and the synod, with confidence in the power
of my Savior, that hereafter I will not be caught failing to live up to my
professions and covenants with God. I shall never forget the future fire which

βάτας τῶν λόγων τῶν ἐν πνεύματι λαληθέντων Θεοῦ διαδέχεσθαι πῦρ, τῆς
θεοπνεύστου γραφῆς, ἐξ ἧς καὶ τὸ μὴ μεταβαίνειν τινὰ τῆς οἰκείας μονῆς
20 ἐμπεδοῦν τὸν σωθῆναι βουλόμενον, οὑτωσὶν ἐπὶ λέξεως βεβαιούσης· εἴ
τις, φησί, μοναχὸς τῆς ἰδίας ἀποδράσας μονῆς, εἰς ἕτερον μεταπέσῃ μοναστήριον ἢ εἰς κοσμικὸν εἰσκωμάσῃ
καταγώγιον, αὐτός τε καὶ ὁ τοῦτον ὑποδεξάμενος ἀφω-
ρισμένος εἴη, ἕως ἂν ὁ ἀποφυγὼν ἐπανέλθῃ ἐξ ἧς κακῶς
25 ἐξέπεσε μονῆς.

92. Πρὸς τὸν αὐτοκράτορα

Τοῖς βασιλεύουσι πολυτρόπως τῶν ἐν τῇ γῇ παρὰ πάντων δωροφο-
ρεῖσθαι τὰ τῶν ἄλλων τούτοις τερπνά, τὰ πράγματα παρεστήσατο· πλὴν
ἀλλ' ἡμεῖς τὰ ἐκείνοις τερπνὰ ἐκζητοῦντες ἐν ἑαυτοῖς, οὐδ' ὀλίγων ἐτύ-
5 χομεν, ὡς ἂν καὶ προσοῖσαι τοῦ πόθου ἀφοσιώσει τῇ ἐκ Θεοῦ βασιλείᾳ
σου, ὅπου κἀκείνων οὐ χρείαν ἔσχες τῶν ἀγαθῶν, πλουτοδοτεῖν καταστὰς
πρὸς τοῦ τὰ δίκαια κρίνοντος· ὃ δέ μοι προσῇ καὶ ἁρμόζον καὶ ἀναγκαῖον
προσενέγκαι τῇ ἐκ Θεοῦ βασιλείᾳ σου καὶ χρηζούσῃ καὶ ὀφειλούσῃ ἐν
τούτῳ πλουτεῖν, καὶ ὡς ἔπος καὶ ἀμφοτέροις ἐποφειλόμενον, τὸ μὲν λέγειν
10 ἡμᾶς καὶ βιάζειν καὶ ἀξιοῦν ἁρμόζον ὑμῖν, τὸ ὑπακούειν δὲ καὶ πληροῦν
διηνεκὴς αὐτῇ καὶ πλοῦτος καὶ σπούδασμα, καὶ τῶν ἐν εὐσεβείᾳ διαλαμ-
ψάντων καὶ ἀρετῇ ὡς ἄλλο τοῦ βίου μηδὲν ἰδιαίτατον, οὐχ ὅπως τοπάζιον
ἢ χρυσίον, ἀλλ' ἀσυγκρίτως ἐκείνων καὶ ἀναγκαῖα καὶ τιμαλφέστερα.
καὶ «τί τοῦτο;», εἴποι τις ἄν. τὸ ἀνηρτῆσθαι μετὰ Θεὸν ὅσα τῇ ἐκ Θεοῦ
15 βασιλείᾳ σου κατὰ πνεῦμα πατρί, τὸ θαρρεῖν ἀπερικαλύπτως αὐτῷ ὅσα δὴ
τῶν ὑπὸ σὲ δεξιὰ καὶ εὐώνυμα, τὸ πλουτεῖν ἐν πληροφορίᾳ ὁμιλίας τὰς
πρὸς αὐτὸν ὑπὲρ ἅπαντας, ἐπεὶ καὶ κατὰ τὴν πίστιν ἐπιγίνεται καὶ
ἡ δωρεὰ τοῦ ἀγαθοῦ πνεύματος. τούτοις πλουτεῖν σε ἀντιβολῶ, τοιούτοις σεμνύνεσθαι, τοιούτοις ἐγκαλλωπίζεσθαι, ἀδιστάκτως
20 καὶ τῶν ἀρξάντων πρὸ σοῦ. τί γὰρ λάφυρα καὶ στρατόπεδα καὶ χρυσοῦ
καὶ ἀργύρου αἱ μὴ παραμένουσαι θημωνίαι, καὶ ὑποκύπτοντα ἔθνη καὶ
πόλεις, ἃ καὶ πρὸς ἔπαρσιν οἶδεν ἁρπάζειν τοὺς μὴ πλουτήσαντας τὰ ῥη-

91: 20–25 κανὼν δ' τῆς ἐν Κωνσταντινουπόλει α' καὶ β' συνόδου (Rhalles-Potles, II,
659)
92: 12–13 cf. Ps. 118(119):127 ‖ 17 Matt. 9:29 ‖ 18 cf. Acta 2:38

21 τις] τε P ‖ ἀποδρασάσης P
92: V 74ᵛ–75ʳ. S 219ʳ–220ʳ. P 98ʳ–99ʳ.
1 ante πρὸς add. γράμμα VʳSP ‖ post αὐτοκράτορα add. τὸ ἀναρτῆσθαι μετὰ Θεὸν ὅσα δὴ
δεξιὰ καὶ εὐώνυμα τῷ κατὰ πνεύματι πατρί VʳSP ‖ 5 ἀφοσιώσῃ codd. ‖ 10 ἡμᾶς] ὑμᾶς
codd. ‖ ὑμῖν] ἡμῖν codd.

91, 92

awaits transgressors of the words of God spoken through the Spirit, since the divinely inspired passage, which also asserts that anyone who wishes to be saved should not move from his own monastery, declares as follows, word for word: «If», it says, «a monk runs away from his own monastery and transfers to another monastery, or ends up in a worldly resting-place, both he and the one who receives him are to be excommunicated until the run-away monk returns to the monastery which he wickedly left».

92. To the emperor

Events have shown that those who rule over the people on earth should be presented by everyone in various ways with the belongings of others which are pleasing to them. But when I looked in myself for gifts pleasing to them, I found not even a few to offer to your divine majesty with a show of affection, since you had no need of those blessings, as you have been appointed by the righteous Judge to dispense riches. But I do have something which is both suitable and necessary to offer to your divine majesty, since you both need and ought to abound in it, and one might say that both of us have an obligation, on the one hand I should speak and compel and demand what is fitting for you, and on the other hand you ought constantly to show your abundant zeal to heed ⟨me⟩ and carry out ⟨my suggestions⟩. And this ⟨characteristic⟩, like nothing else in life, is the distinguishing feature of men who are conspicuous for their piety and virtue, not like «topaz or gold», but incomparably more important and valuable than them. «Just what is this characteristic?», one might ask. It is for your divine majesty to refer everything after God to your spiritual father [Athanasius], to entrust undisguisedly to him whatsoever you rule whether on the left or right, to converse more frequently with him than with all other men, since «the gift of the Holy Ghost» comes «according to one's faith». I entreat you to abound in this ⟨spiritual wealth⟩, to pride yourself on it, and to adorn yourself with it with less hesitation than those who ruled before you (?). For what good are spoils and military encampments and ephemeral heaps of gold and silver, and subject nations and cities, since He has the power to snatch them away from those who do not have the abovementioned ⟨spiritual riches⟩, and destroy

θέντα; τούτοις ἐμπλατυνθῆναι αὐτὴν διηνεκής μοι ἡ δέησις· ὁ τούτοις
ὀχυρωθεὶς πάντα τὰ ἐν χερσὶ διάξει πνευματικῶς, τὸ ἀξίωμα ὅσον τὸ πισ-
25 τευθὲν ταπεινότερον κατοπτεύσει καὶ πάντη ὀξύτερον, καὶ τὸ πιστευθὲν
ὅσον καὶ αὐτὸν τὸν πιστεύσαντα, καὶ εἰ πρὸς τὸ αὐτῷ ἀρεστὸν ἡ τοῦ κόσμου ὁλκὰς διϊθύνοιτο, πρᾶγ-[fol. 75ʳ] μα φρίκης μεστὸν ἐννοούμενον, ὅπως
οἱ μὲν διὰ ταύτης τῆς δωρεᾶς καὶ τῆς ἀληθινῆς βασιλείας εὑ-
ρεθήσονται κληρονόμοι, οἱ δὲ ἐτασθήσονται τὰ τῆς παρεισπράξεως,
30 ὡς τὸ τούτοις δοθὲν μὴ ἐπεργασάμενοι, τὸ μετὰ Θεὸν ὁραθῆναι τῷ ὁμοφύλῳ θεούς· ἃ πολλῆς ἀσφαλείας ἐνδέει πατρικῆς καὶ συνάρσεως καὶ
εὐθύτητος, ἃ καὶ μόνον προσῇ πνευματικῷ κατὰ ἀλήθειαν, οὐ τοῖς πρὸς
χάριν λαλοῦσι καὶ εὐκόλως ὑπονοθεύειν διά τι τῶν ἀνθρωπίνων τὴν ἀλήθειαν καὶ τὸ δίκαιον, ἀλλ' ᾧ ἐνυπάρχει τὸ προορᾶν δεξιόθεν τὸν
35 Κύριον ὡς ὑπὸ τοῦ μηδόλως κραδαίνεσθαι. ἔνθεν ὡς ἀσυγκρίτοις ὑπεροχαῖς προαχθεῖσαν πρὸς τοῦ Θεοῦ τὴν ἐξ αὐτοῦ βασιλείαν σου,
κἄν τούτῳ διατεθήτω, ἀντιβολῶ, τῶν πώποτε μνημονευομένων εἰς τοῦτο
τὸ ἀγαθὸν ἐνεργέστερον. εἰ γὰρ τὴν περιουσίαν τοῦ κόσμου τις
ἅπασαν περιβάλλεται, τὰ δὲ τίμιον τοῦτον ποιοῦντα καὶ μετ' αὐτοῦ
40 συναπαίροντα μὴ κερδήσει, καλὸν εἰ οὐκ ἐγεννήθη μηδὲ ἀπήλαυσεν.

93. Πρὸς τὸν αὐτοκράτορα

Ὥσπερ ἡλίου τὸ φέγγειν καὶ θάλπειν τὸ ἰδιαίτατον, οὕτω καὶ βασιλείῳ περιωπῇ δικαιοσύνη καὶ εὐνομίᾳ τῶν πόλεων· κἀντεῦθεν τῷ δήμῳ ἐκ
δικαιοπραγίας καὶ σωφροσύνης κοινῆς ὁ τοῦ Θεοῦ ἔλεος, ἐξ ὧν καὶ ἐπίκοι-
5 νος πλουτισμός, φιμουμένων δικαιοσύνη πλεονεκτῶν ἀεὶ τὰ κοινὰ θησαυρίζειν ἐπισφαλῶς ἰδιοποιουμένων, καὶ τῷ λαῷ τοῦ Θεοῦ προστριβόντων
πενίαν ἐξ ἁρπαγῆς καὶ ὠμότητος. ἔνθεν εἰ μέχρι καὶ νῦν οὐ προήχθη
καταναγκάσαι πρὸς πλήρωσιν αἰτημάτων τὴν ἐκ Θεοῦ βασιλείαν σου,
ποιεῖσθαι δὲ μόνην ἀναφορὰν τῇ αὐτῆς διακρίσει ἀνατιθέντα, ἀλλὰ νῦν
10 ὑπὲρ εὐνομίας καὶ εὐθύτητος, ὅπως προσῇ ἀναφαίρετος τῇ βασιλίδι τῶν
πόλεων, οὐ μόνον ἀντιβολῶ καὶ βιάζω, ἀλλὰ καὶ βιάζειν οὐ παύσομαι κατ'
ἐξαίρετον ἀναθεωρεῖσθαι τὰ τῶν γεννηματικῶν καὶ τῶν ἄρτων εἰς δικαίαν
ἐξώνησιν καὶ ἡ τούτων ἐπιστασία πρὸς τῶν εὐλαβεστέρων τινός· ὅθεν
οὐκ οἶμαι εὑρεῖν εὐλαβέστερον καὶ πιστότερον Δερμοκαΐτου τοῦ σεβαστοῦ.

28–29 Jac. 2:5 || 31 cf. Ps. 81(82):6 || 34–35 cf. Ps. 15 (16):8 || 38–40 cf. Matt. 16:26

---

39 τίμια codd.
93: V 75ʳ–75ᵛ. S 220ʳ–220ᵛ. P 99ʳ–99ᵛ. Ed. Laiou, Andronicus II, 339, no. 9.
1 ante πρὸς add. γράμμα VʳSP || post αὐτοκράτορα add. περὶ τοῦ ἀναθεωρεῖσθαι τὰ τῶν
γεννηματικῶν καὶ τῶν ἄρτων εἶναι εἰς δικαίαν ἐξώνησιν VʳSP || 14 καὶ πιστότερον]
ἀπιστότερον S

92, 93

them ? It is my constant prayer that you increase in your possession of this ⟨spiritual wealth⟩. For he who is fortified by this ⟨wealth⟩ will administer everything in his power in a spiritual manner, and will view more humbly and in every way more keenly the position entrusted to him, both the trust he has received and the One Who entrusted it to him, and ⟨see⟩ whether the ship of state is being guided in a manner pleasing to Him, reflecting on the awesome fact that some men, as a result of this gift, will become «heirs of the true kingdom», but others will be brought to trial for their malpractice, because they did not take advantage of the ⟨asset⟩ granted them, ⟨that is⟩ to be considered after God as gods by their countrymen. This requires much paternal assurance and assistance and direction, which qualities accrue only to a truly spiritual ⟨father⟩, not to those who speak only to curry favor, and to lightly debase truth and righteousness for worldly motives, but to the man who «sets the Lord before him on his right hand, so as not to be shaken at all by Him». Therefore I ask your divine majesty, who has been promoted by God with incomparable distinctions, at this time to devote more energies toward this worthy goal than anyone who has come down in memory. For if someone possesses all the riches of the world, but does not acquire that ⟨spiritual wealth⟩ which makes him honorable and which departs with him ⟨from this world⟩, it would be better if he had never been born, and had never enjoyed ⟨those advantages⟩.

93. To the emperor

Just as it is the particular function of the sun to shine and give warmth, so the particular function of the imperial power is the exercise of justice and of good order in the cities; and thus the mercy of God is bestowed upon the people when there is public righteousness and prudence, from which also result public enrichment, when justice restrains the profit-seekers who are always hoarding for themselves public ⟨property⟩ at great risk ⟨to their souls⟩, and who inflict poverty on the people of God by their rapaciousness and cruelty. Wherefore, although up to this time I have not gone so far as to force your divine majesty to fulfil my petitions, but have only made reports referred to your discretion, now, so that good order and righteousness may firmly abide in the Queen of Cities, not only do I supplicate and demand, but I will not cease to demand, that above all the honest purchase of grain and bread be carefully controlled, and that this supervision be carried out by a man noted for his honesty. Wherefore I do not think you will find anyone more honest and trustworthy than Dermokaïtes the *sebastos*.

15   διὰ τοῦτο ἵνα καὶ ἔθει βασιλικῷ χρήσωμαι, «παρακαλῶ, παρακαλῶ,
παρακαλῶ» ταχθῆναι αὐτῷ πρὸς τῆς ἐκ Θεοῦ βασιλείας σου εὐεργεσίας
[fol. 75ᵛ] προμήθειαν, πολλὰ συντελοῦντα πρὸς τὸ τῆς εὐνομίας ἀσυγκρίτως καλόν, μεγάλην τῆς πολιτείας ὑποστάσης ζημίαν ὑπὸ τοῦ λιμοῦ, ὡς
μικροῦ τὴν περιουσίαν Ῥωμαίων ἐν ταῖς χερσὶ τῶν Λατίνων χρυσίου καὶ
20   ἀργυρίου εἰσενεχθῆναι. τὸ δὲ μεῖζον ἡ τούτων ὀφρύς, ἐπεγγελώντων
ἡμῖν ἐξ ἀγερωχίας καὶ τοσοῦτον ὑπερφρονεῖν ὡς τὰς γυναῖκας τῶν
πολιτῶν ἀντάλλαγμα σίτου λαμβάνειν φρυαττομένους, ὅπερ μὴ ἴδοιεν.

ἕνεκεν τούτου ἀντιβολῶ, τῇ τοιαύτῃ σπουδῇ ἐπιμελείᾳ τῆς ἐκ Θεοῦ
βασιλείας σου μὴ ἐπὶ πλέον κατακαυχήσωνται, ἀλλ' αἰσχύνην ὡς
25 διπλοΐδα ὁ τὰς βουλὰς τῶν ἐθνῶν περιτρέπων ἐπενδύῃ
αἰωνίως αὐτοῖς.

94. Πρὸς τὸν αὐτοκράτορα

Ὅτι τῶν ἱερῶν ἀρετῶν οὐ πᾶσαι μόνῃ τῇ φύσει ἀλλὰ καὶ τῇ προαιρέσει ἀπεχαρίσθησαν, ἀραρότως αὐτὰ τὰ πράγματα παριστᾷ, ὡς ἂν τὸ τῇ
φύσει κατασπαρὲν ἀγαθὸν τῇ πανσόφῳ σοφίᾳ καὶ ἡμέτερον καταφαίνηται,
5 ὡς ὑφ' ἡμῶν ἐνεργούμενον, καὶ τοῦτο πρὸς τὸ διψῶντως διψᾶσθαι τὴν
σωτηρίαν ἡμῶν. ἔνθεν οἱ οἷς ἐδόθη τὰ θεῖα ἐνεργήσαντες σπέρματα εἰς
ζωῆς ἐξανάστασιν ἀναστήσονται, τῆς κρυπτομένης νυνὶ πρὸ
τοῦ νόμου καὶ μετὰ νόμον φημί, ἀδελφὰ καὶ συμπράξαντες ἅμα καὶ συμφρονήσαντες.

10   ὡς δ' οὖν ἐν πολλοῖς τῇ πρὸς Θεοῦ ἐξεγένετο βασιλείᾳ σου τῷ θεόπτῃ καὶ θειοτάτῳ Μωσεῖ κοινωνεῖν ἐν τοῖς κρείττοσι, δειξάτω κἂν
τούτῳ τὸν χαρακτῆρα σαφέστατα, ἵν' ὡς ἐκεῖνος τῆς δεκαπλήγου τῶν
Αἰγυπτίων ἀνώτερον τὸ ὑπήκοον ἀνεσώσατο, καὶ ἡ ἐκ Θεοῦ βασιλεία
σου τῆς ἀμειδοῦς δυναστείας τοῦ Σικελοῦ τὸ ὀρθόδοξον· οὐδαμῶς τῶν
15 πληγῶν ἀπαράβλητον ὑπολήψεσθαι [τούτου] τινὰ τὴν σκληρὰν καὶ ἀγέρωχον τούτου ψυχήν, οὐδὲ μόνῃ μιᾷ τῶν τότε πληγῶν, ἀλλὰ πάσαις, ⟨πάσας⟩

93: 24–25 cf. Ps. 32 (33):10 et 108(109):29
94: 7 cf. Joh. 5:29, Col. 3:3, et Greg. Naz., Or. XVI, θ' (PG, XXXV, 945 B)

---

25 ἐπενδυεῖ codd.
94: V 75ᵛ–76ʳ. S 220ᵛ–221ᵛ.
1 ante πρὸς add. γράμμα VʳS ‖ post αὐτοκράτορα add. διὰ τοῦ Σικελοῦ ἵνα μὴ ἐνεργῇ δουλείας
δημοτελεῖς διὰ τὸ ὠμὸν (ὁμὸν Vʳ) καὶ ἀπάνθρωπον VʳS ‖ 2 μόνη] μόναι codd. ‖ 6 τὸ
διψῶντως coni. Ševčenko, τοῦ διψῶντος codd. ‖ 7 οἱ οἷς coni. Ševčenko; εἰ οἷς codd. ‖
8–9 ἀδελφὰ . . . συμφρονήσαντες non satis perspicio; fortasse legendum ἀγαθὰ . . . συμφρονήσαντες? cf. Joh. 5:29 et Greg. Naz., Or. XVI, θ' (PG, XXXV, 945 B) ‖ 15 τούτου uncis
inclusi ‖ 16 πάσας addidi

93, 94

Therefore, to adopt an imperial usage, «I entreat, I entreat, I entreat» that your divine majesty entrust to him the responsibility for this worthy undertaking, for it will contribute much to the incomparable blessing of good order. For the state is suffering great harm from the famine, since the Romans' fortune, both gold and silver, has almost all ended up in the hands of the Latins. But the worst is their arrogance as they laugh at us haughtily, and despise us so much that they boast of receiving favors from the wives of citizens in payment for grain (may this not happen!). For this reason I ask that your divine majesty see to it that they not gloat any more in such undertakings (?), but that He Who upsets «the counsels of the nations may cover them» eternally «with confusion as with a mantle».

94. To the emperor

Facts themselves are a dependable proof that not all of the holy virtues are granted by nature alone, but are also the result of deliberate choice, so that the good implanted in our nature by all-wise wisdom may appear to be ours, too, inasmuch as we have had some effect on it, and this with a view to eagerly seeking our salvation. Therefore if those people to whom the divine seeds have been granted act upon them, they will arise «in a resurrection of life», which is now «hidden» before the law and after the law, I mean, since they both act and think in a manner akin ⟨to God⟩ (?).

Therefore since on many occasions it has happened that your divine majesty has resembled in matters of Higher Order the most holy Moses, who saw God, may you demonstrate this characteristic most clearly in this affair, too, so that, as he of old delivered his people from the ten plagues of the Egyptians, so may your divine majesty deliver the Orthodox people from the grim tyranny of the Sicilian. Everyone will agree that his harsh and arrogant soul is comparable to the plagues, and not only to one of those plagues,

έξικνουμένην μικρού κακουργία καὶ ἀθεότητι· εἰς ἐφόδιον ἄλλο μὴ κεκτη-
μένοις μηδὲν τῆς προκειμένης φρικτῆς ἐκείνου ἐξόδου πρὸς τὸν μέλλοντα
κατεπείξειν τῷ διαχωρισμῷ τῆς ψυχῆς ἀσυμπαθῆ καὶ ἀπότομον, ἢ τὸ δράξ-
20 ασθαι τῆς οἰκείας ὑπήνης χερσὶ καὶ πρὸς αὐτὸν ἐξειπεῖν, ὡς «ἢν ὁρᾷς πο-
λιάν, ἄγγελε τοῦ Θεοῦ, πατριαρχῶν ἐξελεύκανα καὶ ἐλίπανα καὶ ἐπλάτυνα
ἀφορισμοῖς καὶ ἀραῖς», τοῦ ἀγγέλου κομίζοντος τούτῳ τὴν [fol. 76ʳ] οὕ-
τωσὶν ἐπὶ λέξεως ἔχουσαν· «ὦ γηραλέε καὶ ἄφρων, ταύτῃ τῇ
νυκτὶ (τῷ περιέχοντι τοῦτον σκότῳ φημί), τὴν ψυχήν σου ἀπαι-
25 τοῦσιν ἀπὸ σοῦ· ἃ δὲ ἐλογίσω παρανοσφίσασθαι καὶ τρυφῆσαι καὶ
ἀπολαῦσαι, καὶ σπαταλῆσαι ἡδυπαθῶν, τίνι ἔσται;» ὅτι μηδ' ἄλλο
μηδὲν ἔχει προσμαρτυρήσειν αὐτὸς ἑαυτῷ καὶ ποσῶς ἀγαθόν, εἰ μὴ
θηριωδίαν δεινὴν καὶ μανίαν, ὡς μικροῦ καὶ τὴν φύσιν αὐτὴν ἀπεχθάνεσ-
θαι, ὅτι τοιοῦτον κακὸν εἰς φῶς αὐτῇ προηγάγετο.
30 ἕνεκεν τούτων ἀντιβολῶ, εἰ καὶ πρός τινων δυσωπίας τυγχάνειν
σπουδάζεται, καὶ εἰ σεπτοῖς ἐνεργεῖν ἐνεγράφη καὶ κατηλέχθη προστάγμασι, ψευσάσθω ὁ λυμεὼν ἑαυτῷ, ὑπ' αὐτῆς τῆς μισοπονήρου καὶ συμπαθοῦς σῆς ἁγίας ψυχῆς διειργόμενος, τοῦ τῶν ὅλων παραγωγέως καὶ
νομοθέτου δυσωπουμένης τὸ θεσπιώδημα· καὶ τοῦτο τῆς ἀπονοίας τοῦ
35 Σικελοῦ προτιμᾶν, προτιθέντος καὶ τῆς θυσίας τὸν ἔλεον. καὶ
λύκος ἀπελεγχθήτω μάτην χανών, τὸ τοῦ λόγου, ὡς ἂν τῶν ἐλπίδων
ἀποσφαλεὶς γνωρίσῃ Θεὸν ἐφορᾶν τὰ ἀνθρώπινα, καὶ μὴ ἐῶντα
εἰς τέλος τὴν πονηρίαν κατακαυχήσασθαι.

95. Πρὸς τὸν αὐτοκράτορα

Καθ' ὅσον τιμιωτέρα τοῦ σώματος ἡ ψυχὴ καὶ τῶν προσύλων τὰ
ἐπουράνια, κατὰ τοσοῦτον τὸ εὐνομεῖν τῶν πολιτικῶν τὰ τῆς ἐκκλησίας
ὀρθοδόξῳ παντὶ καὶ μάλιστα βασιλεῦσι σπουδάζειν, καθὰ καὶ τὸ ἀνα-
5 πνεῖν, ἀεὶ ἐποφείλεται. καὶ τοῦτο (ὦ συμφορᾶς!) οἱ πολλοὶ παρὰ μικρὸν
ἀφῃρήμεθα, ζητούντων πάντων τὰ ἑαυτῶν, ἀλλὰ μὴ τὰ
τοῦ Χριστοῦ Ἰησοῦ. δι' ἃ οὐδεὶς ἀντερεῖ ὡς ὅτι τοῖς ὀρθοδόξοις τῆς

23–26 cf. Luc. 12:20 || 35 cf. Osee 6:6 || 36 Diogen. VI, 20 (Leutsch-Schneidewin, I, 273);
Greg. Cypr. IV, 15 (Leutsch-Schneidewin, II, 21); Apostol. X, 85 (Leutsch-Schneidewin, II,
510) || 37 cf. Zach. 9:1
95: 6–7 Phil. 2:21

23 ἄφρον codd. || 27 ἔχειν codd.
95: V 76ʳ–76ᵛ. S 221ᵛ–222ᵛ.
1 ante πρὸς add. γράμμα VʳS || post αὐτοκράτορα add. διὰ τὰ λαληθέντα παρὰ τοῦ μοναχοῦ
διὰ τὸν Κυζίκου μὴ παραδράμωσιν ἀνεξέταστα VʳS

94, 95

but to all of them, since it encompasses almost ⟨all of them⟩ with its villainy and impiety.

For I (he ?) possess no other defense against the frightful death that awaits him, against the merciless and cruel ⟨angel⟩ which is going to hasten him to the separation of his soul, than to grasp my (his ?) beard in my (his ?) hands, and to say to ⟨the angel⟩, «This gray hair which you see, O angel of God, I made white, anointed and broadened with patriarchal excommunications and curses», when the angel brings him ⟨a verdict⟩ whose tenor is word for word as follows: «Thou aged 'fool, in this night'» (I mean in the darkness surrounding him), «'thy soul shall be required of thee.' And then 'whose shall be' the things which you thought to appropriate for yourself and to feast upon and enjoy and squander luxuriously ?». For he cannot testify to any good in himself, but only to his terrible brutality and ferocity, so that nature is all but disgusted with herself, because it was through her that such wickedness was brought to light.

For these reasons I ask, even if he tries to gain the respect of certain people, and has been inscribed and registered in imperial *prostagmata* as a state functionary, let that agent of destruction be deceived ⟨in his hopes⟩, and be excluded by your holy and compassionate soul which hates evil, and reveres the pronouncement of the Creator of all things and Lawgiver; and one should prefer this to the madness of the Sicilian, since ⟨the prophet⟩ puts «mercy» before «sacrifice». And let him be exposed as the proverbial «wolf which opens its jaws in vain», so that disappointed of his hopes he may realize that «God watches over the affairs of mankind», and does not allow wickedness to triumph in the end.

95. To the emperor

Inasmuch as the soul is more precious than the body and heavenly things are more precious than material things, to such an extent every orthodox person, especially emperors, should always strive, just as we breathe, to make sure that the good governance of the Church is of greater concern than that of the State. But, woe is me, most of us have been deprived of this ⟨attitude⟩, since «all seek their own, not the things which are Jesus Christ's». Therefore no one will deny that Orthodox Christians are suffering greatly,

μάστιγος τὸ πολύ, ἐκ τοῦ μὴ τὰ τῆς ἐκκλησίας, ὡς θέμις καὶ ὡς ἄνωθεν
ἤρξατο, διϊθυνθῆναι καὶ τοῖς μετέπειτα, ὡς καὶ τοῖς ὦτα ἀκούειν
10 πεπλουτηκόσι τὰ ποιμέσιν ἀπειληθέντα διὰ τοιάδε οὐκ ἀμφηγνόηται, πρὸς
τῆς θείας Γραφῆς καὶ ἀεὶ κωμῳδούμενα, εἰ καί τισιν ὡσεὶ λῆρος καὶ μάλιστα καὶ λαχόντων ποιμαίνειν καταπάτημα φρικτὸν ἐφωράθησαν, μὴ συνιέντων ἢ δεδιότων ἡμῶν πρὸς τοῖς ἄλλοις πνευματολέκτοις καὶ τὸ ποιμένες ἠφρονεύσαντο καὶ τὸν Κύριον οὐκ ἐξεζήτησαν·
15 διὰ τοῦτο οὐκ ἐνόησε πᾶσα ἡ νομὴ αὐτῶν ἀλλὰ διεσ-
κορπίσθησαν.

πλὴν εἰ καὶ τοῖς ἐπὶ τῆς Μωσέως καθέδρας κεκαθικόσιν ἡμῖν τοσαύτη ἐπηκολούθησε κάρωσις, ὡς κἀντεῦθεν καὶ τὴν [fol.
76ᵛ] τῶν θείων χρησμῶν καταφρόνησιν, ἀλλ' ἀνεπαίσθητα οὐκ εἰάθη παρὰ
20 Θεοῦ τὰ ἡμέτερα, ἀλλ' ἕνεκεν τούτου ἡ ἐκκλησία Χριστοῦ πεπλουτήκει τὸν
ἐν φρονήσει καὶ εὐλαβείᾳ καὶ διακρίσει ὑπέρλαμπρον σὲ ἐπιστημονάρχην,
ὡς δέον εἰδότα τὰ θεῖα τιμᾶν καὶ ἐπεκδικεῖν καὶ αἰδεῖσθαι καὶ τὸ πρόσφορον ἐκζητεῖν καὶ ἀπονέμειν αὐτῇ ὡς δῶρον ἐποφειλόμενον, τὴν σὲ εἰς
τοῦτο μαιευσαμένην, καὶ εἰς τόδε προενεγκοῦσαν καὶ συντηροῦσαν, καὶ
25 δεῖξαι πιστευομένην, εἰ μὴ ὅσον τὸ καθ' ἡμᾶς παραλείψομεν, τῆς βασιλείας τῶν οὐρανῶν κληρονόμον τῆς ὄντως ἀδιαδόχου καὶ ἀσαλεύτου καὶ
πανολβίας, καὶ ἰσχύος καὶ δόξης ἐμπλήσασαν.

ἔνθεν ἀντιβολῶ, μὴ ὡς ἔτυχε καὶ τὰ πρὸς τοῦ μοναχοῦ λαληθέντα,
πολλὴν ἀπειλοῦντα τὴν βλάβην, παραδράμοιμεν ἀνεξέταστα, μηδὲ βρα-
30 δύνῃ. εἰ γὰρ αὐτὸν καταλήψεται θάνατος ἢ τυχὸν καὶ μεταναστεύσει,
πολὺν δισταγμὸν συνειδήσεσιν ἐμβαλεῖ τῶν ἀκριβαζομένων, ἀλλὰ δὴ καὶ
τῶν Ξυλωτῶν καὶ τῶν ἄλλως ὀρεγομένων ζητεῖν ἀφορμάς, εἰ μὴ τὴν
ἐξέτασιν ἀκριβασαμένων ἐλευθερίως καὶ φιλαλήθως ἡμῶν ἡ ἀδικία
ἐμφράξει τὸ στόμα αὐτῆς. ὅτι τῶν σωτηρίας ἐφιεμένων, οὐ μόνον
35 τὸ κοινωνεῖν, ἀλλ' οὐδὲ τὸ φιλιάζειν, τοῖς κατὰ τῶν ἁγίων εἰκόνων
λυττῶσιν, ἀνέξεταί τις. καὶ εἰ μὴ δίκαιον κρίνομεν κρῖμα ἐλευθερίως καὶ
φιλαλήθως, ὡς ἢ τὸν κατηγορηθέντα ἀθῷον φανῆναι, ἢ τὸν κατήγορον
ἀληθεύειν, καὶ μὴ τοσοῦτον ταῖς ἡμετέραις ἐναπομεῖναι ψυχαῖς ἀνεξέταστ-
ον, ἀλλὰ τυχεῖν φιλαλήθως τὸ πρᾶγμα συνεξετάσεως καὶ ἐλευθερίου, ***,
40 λύπης, ὡς οἶδε Θεός, τὴν ψυχήν σου συμπληρωσάσης κἂν τούτῳ, ὅπως δι'
ἁμαρτίας ἐμὰς ἀλλεπαλλήλου τοῦ σάλου τῇ ἐκκλησίᾳ συμπίπτοντος, καὶ
οὕτω ζεόντων αὐτῇ τῶν κυμάτων, καὶ συνεχῶς προσαρασσομένων ταῖς
αὔραις καὶ μηχαναῖς τοῦ ἐχθροῦ, καὶ μέχρι τῆς σήμερον.

13–16 Jer. 10:21 || 17–18 cf. Matt. 23:2 || 33–34 cf. Ps. 106(107):42 || 42–43 cf. Greg. Naz.,
Or. XXXI, ιδ' (PG, XXXV, 1096C)

---

9 διϊθύνθη VS || 13 πν(ευματ)ολέκτοις V: π(ατ)ρολέκτοις S || 18 κάρωσις] κάκωσις
S || 19 ἀνεπαίσθητα] ἀνεπήσθητα V, ἀνεπίσθητα S || 20 τούτῳ S || 20–21 τῶν ...
ὑπερλάμπρων VS || 29–30 βραδύνει VS || 38 καὶ] ἵνα S || 39 post ἐλευθερίου lacunam
statui

95

because the Church has not been administered by subsequent generations rightfully and as it was ruled in the beginning. Surely those who have ears to hear are aware of the threats against shepherds for such deeds, and the constant ridicule of the Holy Scriptures, even if ⟨these threats⟩ have turned out to be horribly trampled by certain people to whom the words seem nonsense, and especially by some of those to whom bishoprics have been assigned. For in addition to other words of the Spirit, we neither understand nor fear the passage, «the shepherds have become foolish and have not sought the Lord; therefore the whole pasture has failed, and the sheep have been scattered».

But if we who «sit in Moses' seat» have been overcome by such paralysis that scorn for the divine pronouncements is the result, still God does not allow our affairs to go unperceived, but for this very reason the Church of Christ has been endowed with you as *epistemonarch*, resplendent in wisdom and piety and discretion, since you know how to honor divine things properly and to defend and respect ⟨the Church⟩ and to seek what is fitting and to present it as a gift due Her, Who was midwife to you and brought you forth for this purpose and preserves you; and we all are confident that She will show you to be heir of the eternal and immovable and blessed kingdom of heaven (if we don't omit our part); and She has filled you with strength and glory.

Wherefore I ask that we not in a careless fashion leave uninvestigated the accusations of the monk which portend great harm, and let not this affair drag on. For if death should overtake him, or if he should by chance move away, it will cause much hesitation to the consciences of those who are making the investigation, and also for the Xylotes and those who are otherwise anxious to seek pretexts, unless «injustice shall stop her mouth», because we have conducted a free and truthful investigation. For no one who desires salvation will endure either to be in communion with, or to be friends with, those who rage against the holy icons. And if we do not judge a righteous judgment freely and truthfully, so as either to reveal the innocence of the defendant or to substantiate the plaintiff, and so that such a matter may not remain in our souls uninvestigated, but may receive true and free examination, — even if meanwhile grief fills your soul, as God knows, while storm after storm falls upon the Church on account of my sins, and the waves thus seethe, and constantly dash against Her as a result of «the gales» and machinations «of the enemy», even up to this day.

96. Πρὸς τὸν αὐτοκράτορα

Ἡμῶν καθημένων συνοδικῶς, παρέστησαν ἄνδρες καὶ νεανίσκοι
ὀλολύζοντες καὶ ἀποκλαιόμενοι τὸν τοῦ μακαρίτου ἐκείνου καὶ πανευτυχεστάτου Δεσπότου θάνατον, ὡς καὶ πολλοὺς τῶν ὁρώντων κινῆσαι εἰς
5 δάκρυα, τὸ μὲν ἐκείνου τὸν χωρισμόν, [fol. 77ʳ] τὸ δὲ καὶ τὴν ἔκτοτε
τούτους πιέζουσαν ἔνδειαν, καὶ ζητοῦντες ἀναδοχήν. ἐπεὶ γοῦν πάντων οἱ
ὀφθαλμοὶ μετὰ Κύριον πρὸς τὴν ἐκ Θεοῦ ἐλπίζουσι βασιλείαν σου, καὶ
ἡμεῖς συμπαρακαλοῦμεν, συνικετεύομεν, συνδακρύομεν καὶ γονάτων
ἁπτόμεθα, μὴ ἐαθῆναι τὸ πένθος ἐπὶ πολὺ τοῖς τὸν αὐτῶν ἀποβεβληκόσι
10 δεσπότην, καὶ ταλαιπώροις ἐκ τούτου διπλῶς, καὶ μᾶλλον τῇ πλέον δυστυ-
χεστάτῃ ἤπερ εὐτυχεστάτῃ περιποθήτῳ νύμφῃ τῆς ἐκ Θεοῦ βασιλείας
σου, διά τε τὸν ἄωρον θάνατον τοῦ ὡραίου ἐκείνου ἰδεῖν, καὶ τὴν
παρὰ καιρὸν καὶ ἐλπίδα καὶ ὥραν ἀναφθεῖσαν αὐτῇ κάμινον τῆς χηρείας,
ὦ Θεοῦ πάντα βλέποντες ὀφθαλμοί, ὁρῶσαν δὲ νῦν καὶ τοὺς φιλοῦντας
15 ἐκεῖνον καὶ τῶν ἐκείνου νευμάτων ἐκ πόθου ἐξηρτημένους ἀνάγκη λιμοῦ
καὶ πενίας ἀποσπωμένους αὐτῆς. καὶ ἔδοξε τοῖς εὑρισκομένοις ἀρχιερεῦσιν
ἐνταῦθα ἀπὸ πολλῆς συμπαθείας συνδραμεῖν μεθ' ἡμῶν περὶ τούτου,
καὶ πρὸς τὴν ἐκ Θεοῦ βασιλείαν σου πολλὴν τούτου χάριν προσενεγκεῖν
τὴν παράκλησιν. ἀλλ' ἵνα μὴ βάρους προσθήκη ταῖς πολλαῖς καὶ ἀναριθ-
20 μήτοις ὀχλήσεσιν, ἃς ὁ σήμερον ἐπιφέρει καὶ παρ' ἐλπίδα καιρός, καὶ ἡ
ἄφιξις ἡ ἡμῶν εὑρεθῇ, ἀνεχαιτίσθημεν τῆς ὁρμῆς, ἐλπίζοντες καὶ πιστεύ-
οντες ὡς καὶ πλεῖον ἡμῶν τὰ σπλάγχνα τῆς ἐκ Θεοῦ βασιλείας σου κάμπ-
τειν τὸν χωρισμὸν τὸν ἐκείνου, καὶ τὴν κάμινον τῆς χηρείας, ὡς ἔφην, τῆς
περιποθήτου συμβίου τοῦ εἴπερ ποτὲ νῦν πανευτυχεστάτου Δεσπότου, ὡς
25 πρὸ ὥρας ἀπαλλαγέντος τῆς σφαλερᾶς ἁλμυρίδος τῆς τῇδε ζωῆς — ἵν' ἔχῃ
ἐν παρρησίᾳ πρὸς τὸν Δεσπότην εἰπεῖν καὶ Σωτῆρα διὰ τρόπων εὐθύτητα,
«ἐστέρησας, Δέσποτα, τῶν ἐπιγείων ἡμᾶς, μὴ στερήσῃς καὶ τῶν ἐπου-
ρανίων»—βλεπούσης καὶ καμπτομένης καὶ εἰς δάκρυα κινουμένης διηνεκῶς,
καὶ ὑπὲρ τῆς τῶν ὑπηρετησάντων ἐκείνῳ δεξιῶς καὶ ἀδόλως πιεζούσης
30 ἐνδείας. ὅθεν πρὸς τῇ συμπαθεστάτῃ καὶ εὐεργετικωτάτῃ ψυχῇ τῆς ἐκ
Θεοῦ βασιλείας σου καὶ τὴν ἡμετέραν πρὸς οἶκτον ἀναφορὰν ἀναφέρομεν, μὴ ἐπὶ πλέον τὰ λυπηρὰ βραδυνῇ, ἐχούσης μετὰ Θεὸν δυνατὸν
μεταμεῖψαι εἰς εὐθυμίαν τῆς ἐκ Θεοῦ [fol. 77ᵛ] βασιλείας σου.

96: 12 cf. Gen. 39:6

96: V 76ᵛ–77ᵛ. S 222ᵛ–223ᵛ.
1 ante πρὸς add. γράμμα VʳS ‖ post αὐτοκράτορα add. περὶ τῆς βασιλίσσης γυναικὸς
δεσπότου τοῦ Ἰωάννου καὶ τῶν ἀνθρώπων αὐτοῦ VʳS ‖ 20 παρ' ἐλπίδας V ‖ καιρός]
καινός S ‖ 24 εἴπερ] ἤπερ VS ‖ 25 ἵν' ἔχῃ] ἣν ἔχει VS ‖ 32 ἐχούσης] S praebet
lacunam duarum litterarum ante -ούσης

96

96. To the emperor

While the synod was in session, some men and youths appeared, weeping and lamenting the death of the blessed and most fortunate Despot, so as to move to tears many of us who saw them, as they bewailed both his death and the need which has weighed heavily upon them ever since ⟨his death⟩, and sought some redress. Since next after the Lord the eyes of all men turn toward your divine majesty in hope, I join them in their supplication, entreaty and lamentation, and clasp your knees, ⟨asking⟩ that you not allow to continue for long the distress of these men who have been deprived of their master (and are doubly miserable for this reason), and especially of your divine majesty's dearly beloved daughter-in-law, ⟨whose title should be⟩ «most unfortunate» rather than «most fortunate», because of the untimely death of that young man who was «handsome to look upon», and the unseasonable, unexpected, and untimely furnace of widowhood which has been lit for her, O eyes of God which see everything; and now she sees those who loved him, and hung upon his orders because of their love, torn away from her by the pressure of hunger and poverty. The bishops here, in their great compassion, decided to meet with me regarding this matter, and to present an ardent petition to your divine majesty on this subject. But for fear that our arrival might seem one more burden in addition to the numerous and countless cares which these times have inflicted upon you unexpectedly, we checked our impulse, in the hope and belief that the feelings of your divine majesty will be stirred, to a greater extent than we could do so, by the Despot's death, and by the furnace of widowhood, as I said, of the dearly beloved wife of the now, if ever, all-fortunate Despot, who was delivered before his time from the perilous bogs of this life (so that on account of the righteousness of his ways, he may say confidently to the Lord and Savior, «Thou hast deprived me, Master, of earthly ⟨rewards⟩, so do not deprive me of those in heaven»); she is swayed and constantly moved to tears when she observes the poverty which presses hard upon those who served him adroitly and faithfully. Wherefore I present this piteous petition to the exceedingly compassionate and munificent soul of your divine majesty, so that their grievous plight may not continue any longer, since your divine majesty, after God, is able to change ⟨grief⟩ into joy.

97. ⟨Πρὸς τὸν αὐτοκράτορα⟩

Ἀναφέρω καθὰ καὶ τὸ πρὶν περὶ τῆς Δεσποίνης τῆς πρὸς Θεοῦ συζύγου σοι δοθείσης, ἵνα τοῦ γάμου τὸ τίμιον καὶ τὴν σωφροσύνην τὴν ὀφείλουσαν ἀπαιτεῖσθαι παντὶ ὀρθοδόξῳ κερδήσωμεν, καὶ μὴ μεγάλην
5 ἐντεῦθεν καὶ ὀφείλοντι καὶ διψῶντι καὶ εὐχομένῳ τὴν σωτηρίαν τὴν σὴν προσεῖναί μοι παραλύπησιν, ἐκ τοῦ ψιθυρίζειν τινὰς τὰ ἐπίψογα ἕνεκεν βασιλέως γνώμην ὁμοῦ καὶ ψυχὴν κεκτημένου βασιλικά, καὶ μᾶλλον διὰ θυμὸν ἐξ ἁμαρτιῶν τὸν ἡμᾶς ἐκπιέζοντα. καὶ τοῦτο καὶ ὁ τῶν ἱερῶν νηστειῶν καιρὸς ἀπαιτεῖ, τῷ ῥυσαμένῳ ἡμᾶς τῷ αἵματι τῷ τιμίῳ
10 βασιλεῖ καὶ Θεῷ καρποφορίαν ἑκάστῳ ἐν τῇ ἁγίᾳ ἀναστασίμῳ προσάξαι εἰς δύναμιν. εἰ οὖν σὺν ἄλλοις καλοῖς καὶ ἡμεῖς τὴν σωφροσύνην καὶ τὴν ἐκ ταύτης εἰρήνην προσφέρομεν, ἀποδοχῆς ἀξιώσει, καὶ τοῖς ἐκεῖνον ἠγαπηκόσι συντάξει. χαροποίησον οὖν τὸν ποιήσαντα, καὶ τοὺς φιλοῦντάς σε ἐκ ψυχῆς, πληρώσας ἡμῶν τὴν χαράν.

98. Πρὸς τὸν αὐτοκράτορα

Χάριτας ἐποφείλοντες πολλαχόθεν κἂν τούτῳ Θεῷ τῷ δόντι σε βασιλέα τοῖς ὀρθοδόξοις, τοῦτο μὲν ὡς παντοίοις κατεστεμμένῳ τοῖς ἀγαθοῖς, τοῦτο δὲ ὡς καὶ τῇ ἐκκλησίᾳ Χριστοῦ ἀσυγκρίτως ἠγαπημένῳ,
5 καὶ χάριν ἀγάπης τῆς πρὸς αὐτὴν καὶ ἡμᾶς τὰ πολλά. ἐξ ὧν καὶ ἡμῖν ἐπὶ πλεῖστον ἡ ὀφειλὴ τὸ παντοίως τὴν σωτηρίαν ὑμῶν καὶ ἐπίδοσιν ἐν παντοίοις καλοῖς, καὶ κραταίωσιν καὶ τὸ ἄμεμπτον τῷ αἰῶνι τῷ μέλλοντι καὶ τῷ νῦν ἐπεύχεσθαι καὶ διψᾶν. οὗ γε καὶ χάριν ἀνιστοροῦμεν καὶ νῦν τὰ δοκοῦντα πρὸς τὸ συμφέρον, παντοίως κατακοσμεῖσθαι ἐπαίνοις καὶ ἀρετῇ
10 πρὸς δόξαν τοῦ βασιλεύσαντος ⟨σε⟩ ἐφιέμενοι. εἰ γὰρ πᾶσιν ἐσμὲν ὀφειλέται ἀγάπην ἀποπληροῦν καὶ τιμήν, ἐν οἷς μὴ Θεὸς ἀτιμάζεται, πόσῳ γε μᾶλλον βασιλεῦσιν ὀρθοδοξοῦσι καὶ Θεὸν ἀναπνέουσιν (ὃ χαρισθείη ὀρθοδοξοῦσι μέχρι καὶ συντελείας, Θεὲ τοῦ παντός);
ἕνεκεν τούτου ἀναγκαῖον νομίζω ἐλθεῖν με αὐτόθι, εἰ τοῦτο κελεύ-
15 σει ἡ ἐκ Θεοῦ βασιλεία σου, ἢ ἐν τῇ Χώρᾳ, ἢ ἐν τῷ τῶν ἁγίων πάντων ναῷ, πλήν, εἰ κελεύεις, ταχύτερον. ἡ δὲ αἰτία, μήπως καὶ θορυβῆται ὁ λο-

---

97: 9 cf. I Pet. 1:19

97: V 77ᵛ. S 223ᵛ–224ʳ.
1 γράμμα πρὸς τὸν αὐτοκράτορα περὶ τῆς δεσποίνης ὅτι οὐ συνέρχεται πρὸς αὐτὴν διὰ τὸ τοῦ γάμου καλόν add.   VʳS ‖ 6 μοι] με   VS ‖ 8 ante ἡμᾶς add. εἰς   S ‖ 12–13 ἀγαπηκόσι S
98: V 77ᵛ–78ʳ. S 224ʳ–224ᵛ.
1 ante πρὸς add. γράμμα   VʳS ‖ post αὐτοκράτορα add. περὶ ὁμονοίας καὶ εἰρήνης τῆς πρὸς Θεοῦ συζύγου καὶ ἕνωσιν δοθείσης αὐτῷ   VʳS ‖ 4 ἠγαπημένῳ] ἠγαπηκότι VS ‖ 6 ὑμῶν   V¹S : ἡμῶν   V ‖ 10 σε addidi ‖ 15 πάντω   V

97. To the emperor

As before I bring up the matter of the Despoina, the wife given to you by God, that we may attain the honor of the marriage and the continence which ought to be asked of every orthodox person, so that great grief may not afflict your humble servant, who has the obligation to yearn and pray for your salvation, from the whispered reproaches of certain people against an emperor who possesses imperial wisdom and soul alike, and especially because of the ⟨divine⟩ wrath which afflicts us on account of our sins. Moreover, the season of holy fasting requires each of us to bring as many offerings as we can on Easter Day to the King and God Who saved us with «His precious blood». If then together with other bounties we offer continence and the peace which results from this, He will deem us worthy of reward and will ordain it for those who have loved Him. Rejoice therefore Him Who made you and those who love you in their soul by filling us with joy.

98. To the emperor

We owe thanks for many reasons for this as well to God, for granting us you as an emperor to Orthodox Christians, since you are crowned with all sorts of blessings, and are incomparably loved by the Church of Christ, because of your great love for Her, and for us as well. For this reason we have a great obligation to pray for and desire your salvation and increase in every kind of blessing, and your strength and purity both now and in the world to come. Wherefore at this time I will tell you what I think is expedient, since I want you to be adorned in every way with praises and virtue, to the glory of Him Who made ⟨you⟩ emperor. For if we have the obligation to pay the debt of love and honor in all things in which God is not dishonored, how much greater an obligation this is for emperors who believe true doctrines and draw their inspiration from God (and may this be granted to men of orthodox belief until the end of the world, O God of all)!

For this reason, if your divine majesty is agreeable, I think I should come there [to the palace], or to Chora, or to the church of All Saints, and as quickly as possible, if you agree. The reason, lest your thoughts be troubled (?),

γισμός, ἵνα τὰ [fol. 78ʳ] πρὸς ὁμόνοιαν καὶ εἰρήνην φροντίσῃς τῆς πρὸς
Θεοῦ σοι δοθείσης συζύγου, καὶ ὅσα συνεύνοις ἁρμόζει πρὸς ἀγάπην καὶ
ἕνωσιν, καθὰ περὶ γάμου καὶ Παύλῳ δοκεῖ τῷ μεγάλῳ, ἀναγκαιότερον
20 πάντων τεθεσπικότι τὴν εἰρήνην καὶ τὸν ἁγιασμόν, γινωσκού-
σης μετὰ Θεὸν τῇ ἐνούσῃ συνέσει καὶ διακρίσει τῆς ἐκ Θεοῦ βασιλείας
σου καὶ τὸ δίκαιον ταύτης, καὶ τὸ τῆς γνώμης καὶ τὸ τοῦ γένους κατὰ πάντα ὑπέροφρυ, καὶ τοῦ καιροῦ τὸ ἀνώμαλον ὑπὲρ πάντας, καὶ εἰδυίας
καὶ δυναμένης πρὸς εἰρήνην καὶ σωτηρίαν μεταμεῖψαι πανσόφως τὰ στα-
25 σιάζοντα.

99. Πρὸς τὸν αὐτοκράτορα

Τῶν ἑκάστοτε γινομένων συνοδικῶς ὑποθέσεων λίαν ὀλίγα τις
εὕροι μὴ χρῄζοντα τοῦ πίπτειν εἰς ἀκοὰς τῆς ἐκ Θεοῦ βασιλείας σου, διά
τε ταλαιπωρίαν πολλὴν καὶ ἀνάγκην τῶν ἐμπιπτόντων ἐν συμφοραῖς,
5 διά τε τὸ δυσπειθὲς τῶν πολλῶν καὶ ἀγέρωχον, ἔστιν οὗ καὶ τὸ δυσδιάκρι-
τον τοῦ δικαίου, ἄλλο τι κρινόντων πολλῶν τοῦ δεξιοῦ δεξιώτερον. οὗ
χάριν ὁ κρίνειν μέλλων ἡμᾶς προεθέσπισε κρίμα δίκαιον κρίνειν
τοὺς κρίνοντας, ὡς ἐν ᾧ κρίματι κρίνομεν κριθησόμενοι·
ἐντεῦθεν καὶ μέγαν τὸν λόγον τοὺς κρίνειν λαχόντας ὀφείλειν ἀποτιννύναι,
10 καὶ μᾶλλον οἷς ἐχαρίσθη καὶ πλεῖστα εὐεργετήματα, ἐξ ὧν καὶ τῆς
ἐξουσίας καὶ τῆς θεογνωσίας καὶ τῆς συνέσεως τὰ ἐξαίρετα. ἐξ ὧν ἀναφέρειν ἀναγκαζόμεθα οἱ οἰκτείροντες τοὺς ἐμπίπτοντας, καὶ μᾶλλον ὅσα
ὑπὲρ ἡμᾶς ὡς κοῦφα τῇ βασιλείῳ περιωπῇ καὶ ὀφείλοντα. ἀλλ᾽, ὤ
μοι τῆς δυστυχίας!, ὅπως ἐκ τῶν μυρίων ὀλίγα προαγόμενοι ἀνα-
15 φέρειν, καὶ ἀποκρίσεως ἀποπίπτομεν, ἐξ ὧν οὐδὲ στέλλειν τινὰ εὐ-
μοιρῶ, τῇ στάσει καὶ σιωπῇ κατοκνούντων τῶν στελλομένων. εἰ δέ γε μὴ
ἦν τὰ ἀναφερόμενα ὄφλημα ἀλλὰ χάριτες, τὸ λυποῦν οὐκ ἀπαραμύθητον·
εἰ δὲ μὴ αἵρεσις ἢ φιλανθρωπία καὶ σπλάγχνα τοῖς χρῄζουσιν ἀνοιγόμενα,
ἀλλὰ μᾶλλον ἀνάγκη καὶ ἀπαραίτητον ὄφλημα, οὐκ οἶδα τί γένωμαι,
20 αὐτοῦ τοῦ μεγάλου Δεσπότου θεσπίζοντος καὶ τῶν μικρῶν μὴ
καταφρονεῖν, εἰ δι᾽ ἄλλο μηδέν, ἀλλ᾽ ὡς βλέποντας τοὺς ἀγ-
γέλους ἐκείνων ἐν οὐρανοῖς τὸ τοῦ Θεοῦ καὶ Πατρὸς
(ὅ, τι ποτέ ἐστι) πρόσωπον. ἔνθεν πολιορκοῦμαι καὶ λέγειν καὶ
σιωπᾶν. [fol. 78ᵛ]

98: 20 Hebr. 12:14
99: 7 cf. Joh. 7:24 ‖ 8 cf. Matt. 7:1 ‖ 20–23 cf. Matt. 18:10

---

24 μεταμεῖψαι VS¹: μεταλῆψαι S
99: V 78ʳ. S 224ᵛ–225ʳ.
1 ante πρὸς add. γράμμα VʳS ‖ post αὐτοκράτορα add. ὅτι περὶ τῶν ὑποθέσεων ὧν
ἀναφέρει πρὸς αὐτὸν οὐδὲ ἀποκρίσεως ἀξιοῦται VʳS ‖ 8 ᾧ] τῷ S

98, 99

is that you may take thought to bring about concord and peace with the wife granted you by God, and whatever else is fitting for husbands and wives with respect to love and union, in accordance with the precepts about marriage of the great Paul, who decreed that «peace and holiness» are most necessary of all. For your divine majesty, after God, thanks to your inherent wisdom and discretion, realizes your spouse's rights, and her arrogance and that of her nation in all things, and the unusual difficulties of these times, and in your great wisdom you know how and are able to change discord into peace and salvation.

99. To the emperor

One would find very few of the matters discussed in the synod on each occasion which did not need to come to the attention of your divine majesty, both on account of the great suffering and need of those who have fallen upon evil times, and on account of the refractory and insolent attitude of the many. In addition there are difficult judicial decisions, since many people judge that something else is more right than the right. For this reason our future Judge decreed that those who judge «should judge righteously», since «with what judgment we judge, we shall be judged»; wherefore those whose lot it is to judge have to pay a great reckoning, especially those to whom many blessings have been granted, of which the most noteworthy are authority, knowledge of God, and wisdom. Since I take pity on those who have fallen ⟨into misfortune⟩, I am compelled to make petitions especially about those problems which are beyond my power, but are easy, and indeed obligatory, for an emperor. But, alas for my misfortune, although I have been induced to petition about only a few cases out of thousands, I still do not receive a reply, and for this reason I cannot even send anyone, since my messengers are unwilling to go, for they have to stand around for a long time and are met with silence. If my reports were not an obligation but rather a favor, my grief would not be so inconsolable. But if philanthropy and mercy toward the needy are not a mere matter of choice, but rather a necessity and indispensable obligation, I do not know what will become of me, since the great Lord Himself has decreed that we should «not despise the little ones», if for no other reason than that «their angels in heaven do behold the face» (whatever it is) «of God the Father». Wherefore I am blocked both from speaking and from keeping silence.

100. Πρὸς τὸν αὐτοκράτορα

Τὸ μέγα τοῦτο καλὸν καὶ σωτήριον τὸ κελευσθὲν πρὸς τῆς ἐκ Θεοῦ
βασιλείας σου ἀναθεωρεῖσθαι τοὺς ἀρτοπώλους, τίνες καὶ πόσοι καὶ πῶς
ὠνοῦνται καὶ πῶς οὗτοι πιπράσκουσι, καὶ τὰ κατάγοντα πλοῖα τὰ τῶν
5 γεννηματικῶν, ἵνα μὴ ἐξωνῶνται ταῦτα σιτῶναι καὶ σιτοκάπηλοι, ἀλλ᾽ ὁ χρήζων, ἐκεῖνος πορίζηται, καὶ τὸ τὰ μέτρα τηρεῖσθαι τοῦ μὴ
μέτρα δισσὰ καὶ στάθμια πολιτεύεσθαι (κειμένης ἐκείνοις προφητικῆς ἀρᾶς), ἀνταμείψαιτο ὁ Παμμέδων πρὸς τοῖς τοσούτοις καλοῖς
ἐν ἀπειρομεγέθεσι δωρεαῖς τὴν ἐκ Θεοῦ βασιλείαν σου. ὃ καὶ ἀντιβολῶ
10 συντηρεῖσθαι διηνεκῶς, εἰς δόξαν Θεοῦ τοῦ δοξαζομένου ἐν εὐνομίαις, εἰς
αἰώνιον ἔπαινον καὶ μισθὸν ἀναφαίρετον τῆς ἐκ Θεοῦ βασιλείας σου, εἰς
κυβέρνησιν ἐπιμελῆ καὶ προνοητικὴν τοῦ ὑπηκόου παντός, εἰς φανέρωσιν
μεγαλοψυχίας, ἣν οἱ καιροὶ οὐκ ἐῶσι φανῆναι.

καὶ ἐπεὶ τὰ καλὰ κόπῳ μὲν κτῶνται, πόνῳ δὲ κατορθοῦνται,
15 ἐκλεγῆναι δέομαι τοὺς εἰς τοῦτο ἁρμοζόντως ὑπηρετῆσαι καὶ καθαρείως
μετὰ σεβαστοῦ τοῦ Δερμοκαΐτου. ἐξελέγησαν οὖν παρ᾽ ἡμῶν εἰς τοῦτο δύο
ἐκ τῶν δημάρχων, Ἀντιοχείτης λεγόμενοι καὶ Πλουμμῆς, καὶ τούτους,
καὶ ὅσους εἰς τὸ ἔργον εὑρήσομεν ἐν ὑπολήψει ἁρμοδίους, κελευσθῆναι αἰτοῦμεν παρὰ τῆς ἐκ Θεοῦ βασιλείας σου διὰ τὸ ἀσφαλέστερον πρὸς τὸ ἔρ-
20 γον, ἵνα καὶ φόβῳ καὶ συνειδήσει ἐργάζωνται τὸ καλόν· καὶ τοῦτο ἡμῖν δι᾽
εὐχῆς χαρισθῆναι τῇ ἐκ Θεοῦ βασιλείᾳ σου, τοὺς ὑπ᾽ αὐτῆς κελευομένους
ὑπηρετεῖν, πρὸς ἅπαν βιωφελές, ὡς τῷ Θεῷ ἀρεστὰ καὶ αὐτῇ, ἐξυπη-
ρετῆται τὰ ὑπ᾽ αὐτῶν ἐκπληρούμενα· γένοιτο, Κύριε, γένοιτο.

101. ⟨Πρὸς τὸν αὐτοκράτορα⟩

Οὐκ ἴσα προσκρούειν τὰ τῆς εὐθύνης τινὰ τῶν πρὸς βασιλέως εὐ-
εργετουμένων μεγάλως πρὸς τοὺς τὰ μέτρια, οὐδ᾽ ἴσον ὀλίσθημα τῶν συνέσει κεκοσμημένων, πρὸς τῶν τυχόντων ἑνός· οὐδὲ τοῦ καταστάντος πρὸς
5 τὸ νομίμοις ἐπεκδικεῖν καὶ κρατύνειν δεσποτικῶς, μᾶλλον κατὰ τῶν

100: 5–6 cf. Greg. Naz., Or. XVI, ιθ' (PG, XXXV, 960 B) et ibid., Or. XLIII, λδ'
(PG, XXXVI, 544 A) ‖ 7 cf. Prov. 20:10, 23

100: V 78ᵛ. S 225ʳ–226ʳ.
1 ante πρὸς add. γράμμα VʳS ‖ post αὐτοκράτορα add. περὶ τοῦ σεβαστοῦ Δερμοκαΐτου καὶ
τῶν δημάρχων ὧν ἐξελέγησαν ἀναθεωρεῖσθαι περὶ τοῦ μὴ μέτρα (μέτρῳ S) δισσὰ καὶ
στάθμια πολιτεύεσθαι, ἔχουν ἀναδοχὴν παρ᾽ αὐτοῦ VʳS ‖ 14 ἐπεὶ] ἐπὶ S ‖ 22–23 ἐξυ-
πηρετεῖται VS ‖ 23 τὰ] καὶ VS
101: V 78ᵛ–79ʳ. S 226ʳ–226ᵛ.
1 γράμμα πρὸς τὸν αὐτοκράτορα περὶ τοῦ περισσότερον ἀπαιτεῖσθαι ᾧ τὸ πολὺ παρέθεντο
add. VʳS ‖ 5 lege νομίμως?

100. To the emperor

Since this great good which leads to salvation has been commanded by your divine majesty, namely that supervision be made of bakers, who they are and how many, and how they buy and sell, and also that the ships which transport the grain be closely supervised, so that public buyers of grain and grain dealers do not buy up the cargoes, but rather that the needy individual should be able to procure it himself, and that also the measures be controlled so that no one use «double weights and measures» (for the curse of the prophet is laid upon them), may the Ruler of all reward your divine majesty for such good deeds with countless gifts. And I ask that these measures be maintained perpetually, to the glory of God Who is extolled through good order, for the eternal praise and inalienable reward of your divine majesty, for the careful and provident governing of all your subjects, to reveal your magnanimity which the times do not ⟨normally⟩ allow you to reveal.

And since good deeds are achieved with toil and are accomplished with labor, I ask that men be chosen to serve together with Dermokaïtes the *sebastos* to achieve this purpose suitably and irreproachably. And therefore I have selected for this task two of the demarchs, named Antiocheites and Ploummes, and, so that we may be sure that their work will be better performed, I request that these men, and whomsoever we find to be by reputation suitable for the task, be ordered by your divine majesty to act honestly through fear and conscientiousness. And I also pray that it may be granted to your divine majesty that the men ordered by you to serve may accomplish their duties to a completely useful purpose and as is pleasing to God and yourself. So be it, Lord, so be it.

101. ⟨To the emperor⟩

It is not the same thing when one who is greatly benefited by an emperor commits an irregularity in rendering his accounts, and when one of those who have been benefited only moderately does the same; nor is the guilt of those who are adorned with wisdom equal to that of an ordinary person; nor ⟨is it meet⟩ for a man who has been appointed to avenge the laws and to govern in the manner of a Ruler to go instead against the laws,

νόμων χωρεῖν, τοῦ εἰπόντος ἡμῶν αἰδουμένων περισσότερον ἀπαιτεῖσθαι, ᾧ καὶ παρέθεντο τὸ πολύ.

ἔνθεν παρακαλῶ, ὡς καιρός, εὐγνώμονες ὦμεν περὶ τὸν πλάστην
καὶ εὐεργέτην καὶ συνοχέα, καὶ ἀπείρων ἡμᾶς [fol. 79ʳ] ἐμπιπλῶντα
10 τῶν ἀγαθῶν, πρὸς δέ γε τοῖς πᾶσι καὶ βασιλεύσαντα βασιλείᾳ οὐ τῇ
τυχούσῃ, ἀλλ᾽ αὐτῇ τῇ ἀρίστῃ βασιλειῶν τῶν ἐν γῇ, ὑπὲρ ἧς καὶ τὸ
αἷμα ἐξέχεεν, ἵνα πεπαρρησιασμένως ἐμφανισθῶμεν καὶ παραστῶμεν
καὶ προσκυνήσωμεν τότε τούτῳ· καθ᾽ ὅσον ἐπαισχυνθῶμεν ἐνταῦθα
αὐτὸν καὶ τοὺς λόγους αὐτοῦ, καὶ τὸ ὑπήκοον ἐπαισχύνεσθαι
15 τούτους, ὡς δυνατόν, παρασκευασώμεθα, μὴ ἀγνοοῦντες ὡς ὅτι πολλάκις
πρὸς τοῖς ἐκείνῳ ὀφείλουσιν ὀβολόν, ὀβολὸν καὶ οὐ μαργαρίτην προσίεται.

102. ⟨Πρός τινας τῶν ἀρχόντων⟩

Ἔδοξε τοῖς φοβουμένοις Θεὸν κληρονόμους γενέσθαι τῆς θείας
φωνῆς κελευούσης ἐπείνασα καὶ ἐδώκατέ μοι φαγεῖν, λυτρώσασθαι δὲ τὰς ψυχὰς τῆς ἐλεεινῆς καὶ φρικτῆς ἀποφάσεως, τῆς πο-
5 ρεύεσθε ἀπ᾽ ἐμοῦ οἱ κατηραμένοι, ἐπείνασα γὰρ καὶ
οὐκ ἐδώκατέ μοι φαγεῖν θεσπιζούσης. διὰ τοῦτο ἀντιβολῶ
πλουσίους καὶ πένητας, λαϊκοὺς καὶ μονάζοντας, κερδῆσαι τὴν πρὸς
Θεοῦ εὐλογίαν, καὶ τῆς ἀπευκταίας ἀποφάσεως λυτρωθῆναι, καὶ κατὰ
δύναμιν ἀναδέξασθαι, πρὸς ἣν ἐχαρίσθη ἀπὸ Θεοῦ εὐπορίαν, εἰς κυ-
10 βέρνησιν ὁμοπίστων ὀνόματα τόσα, καὶ ταῦτα ἐγγράψαι τῷ γράμματι τῷ
παρόντι, ἵνα γνόντες τοὺς ὑπολειπομένους, τῷ κρατίστῳ καὶ ἁγίῳ μου
ἀναφέρωμεν αὐτοκράτορι κἀκείνων ποιήσασθαι πρόνοιαν.

103. Πρὸς τὸν αὐτοκράτορα

Ὅτι μὴ ἠγνοήθη τοῖς καὶ ποσῶς συνιοῦσι τοῦ σφάλματος τὸ πολύ,
ὡς ὅτι καὶ μείζων τοῦ ἀφεθῆναι ἡ τοῦ Γλυκέος αἰτία καὶ τοῦ ἑταίρου

101: 6–7 cf. Luc. 12:48 ‖ 9–10 cf. Ps. 102 (103):5 et Ps. 106 (107):9 ‖ 11–12 cf. Matt.
26:28 ‖ 13–14 cf. Marc. 8:38
102: 3 Matt. 25:35 ‖ 4–6 Matt. 25:41–42

---

12 ἐμφανιστῶμεν S
102: V 79ʳ. S 226ᵛ.
1 γράμμα πρός τινας τῶν ἀρχόντων πτωχοὺς κατὰ δύναμιν ἀναδέξασθαι εἰς κυβέρνησιν add.
VʳS ‖ 8 Θεοῦ scripsi: Θεὸν codd. ‖ 12 ἀναφέρομεν S
103: V 79ʳ–80ʳ. S 226ᵛ–228ʳ.
1 ante πρός add. γράμμα VʳS ‖ post αὐτοκράτορα add. ὅπως εὕρωσι συμπάθειαν οἱ συν-
δραμῶντες (συνδραμόντες S) τῶν ἐπιβούλων τῆς βασιλείας VʳS ‖ 3 μείζων V¹S: μεῖζον V

101–103

if we respect the One Who said that «more is required of him unto whom much is given».

Wherefore I ask, while there is time, let us be grateful to our Creator and Benefactor and Supporter, «Who fills» us with countless «good things»; and Who, in addition to all these ⟨blessings⟩, has made you to rule not any ordinary kingdom, but this the best of all kingdoms on earth, on behalf of which «He shed His blood», so that we may appear before Him and present ourselves and adore Him with confidence at that time ⟨of the Last Judgment⟩. ⟨We shall accomplish it⟩ inasmuch as «we are ashamed of Him and His words» here on earth, and prepare our subjects to be «ashamed» of them as well, since we are fully aware that many times from those who owe Him an obol, He accepts an obol and not a pearl.

102. ⟨To certain officials⟩

It seemed good to those who fear God to become heirs of the divine voice which commands: «I was an hungred, and ye gave me meat», and to save their souls from the pitiable and terrible sentence which decrees: «Depart from me, ye cursed ... for I was an hungred and ye gave me no meat». Wherefore I ask that rich and poor, laymen and monks, gain the blessing of God, and be saved from the abominable sentence, and assume ⟨responsibility for⟩ the support of a number of fellow believers, in proportion to the prosperity which has been granted you by God, and inscribe these names on the present letter, so that I may know which ones are left out, and may petition my mighty and holy emperor to make provision for them.

103. To the emperor

No one who has any understanding of the magnitude of the crime will deny that the guilt of Glykys and his partner is too great to be forgiven—

αὐτοῦ (ἐπάρατον ἄνδρα καὶ πάντη ὀλέθριον, οὗ οἱ μὲν πόδες εἰς τὸ
5 αἷμα ἐκχέαι ὀξεῖς, καὶ εἰρήνην διαταράξαι μανίᾳ καὶ ἐπινοίᾳ δαιμονιώδει πορίμώτατος, ὡς λυττῆσαι κατὰ τῆς εὐσεβείας αὐτῆς), καὶ λη-
θάργῃ ἢ κάρῳ ἑαλωκέναι τοσοῦτον, ὡς καὶ πάροδον εἰς φυγὴν παρα-
σχέσθαι τῷ ἀναιδεστάτῳ, τίς ἀντερεῖ; εἰ καὶ πᾶσι φιλοῦσι Χριστόν,
καὶ εἰδόσιν ἐκείνου τὸ σκολιὸν δι᾽ εὐχῆς ματαιῶσαι, κἀκείνου καὶ τῶν
10 ὁμοίως ἐκείνῳ ἐπᾶραι πτέρναν βεβουλημένων κατὰ τοῦ κράτους
τῶν ὀρθοδόξων γενέσθαι παγίδα αὐτοῦ ταῖς ὁδοῖς, καὶ ὀλίσθημα
σκότους τοῖς τούτου διαβουλίοις, ὡς ἀλήθειαν καὶ εἰρήνην τὸν μυσαρὸν
καὶ πίστεις ἐνόρκους ἠθετηκότα, καθέξει τε τοῦτον στενοχωρία
καὶ θλῖψις καὶ ταλαιπωρία καὶ σύντριμμα, τῆς αὐτὸν ὑπο-
15 δεξομένης Γεέννης [fol. 79ᵛ] ἐκεῖ προοίμιον ἐναργέστατον, ὡς τοῖς
θείοις ἐμπεπαιχότα τὸν ἐναγῆ· πρὸς δ᾽ αὖ τῇ λοιπῇ μοχθηρίᾳ καὶ ἄνακτα
σταυροφόρον καὶ τῶν πώποτε βασιλέων διαφορώτατον ἐν συνέσει θωπεί-
αις βεβουλημένον παραλογίσασθαι (καὶ μὴ γνόντα τὸν κακοδαίμονα ὡς
τὴν σήμερον ἐν τῇ γῇ τὸν κρατοῦντα τῇ τοῦ ὑψίστου εἴπερ ποτὲ
20 στοιχεῖσθαι καὶ κατοικεῖν βοηθείᾳ, κἀντεῦθεν θαρρούντως
αὐλίζεσθαι σκέπῃ τοῦ οὐρανίου Θεοῦ, ἐξ οὗ καὶ πεπαρρησιασμένως λέγειν πρὸς τὸν Θεὸν ἀντιλήπτωρ μου εἶ καὶ κα-
ταφυγή μου, ἐκεῖνον πεπλουτηκότα ἀπὸ κοιλίας μητρός, παγίδος
ἐκ θηρευτῶν καὶ ἔργου καὶ λόγου ταραχώδους ῥυόμενον),
25 τοσούτων ἠλογηκότα τὸν ἀλάστορα εὐεργετημάτων, καὶ οὐδὲ ἴσα κυνὸς
φανέντα περὶ τὸ φιλοδέσποτον τὸν τῇ γνώμῃ κυνώδη, καὶ τῇ ψυχῇ τερα-
τώδη καὶ τῇ ἰδέᾳ, καὶ ἐπίψογον πάντη καὶ βδελυρόν, καὶ πρὸς τοσοῦτον
ἐλάσαντα αὐθαδείας ὡς καὶ τῷ θείῳ λουτρῷ ἐμπαῖξαι ἀναιδευσάμενον,
ὥς τι ὗς ἐν ῥινὶ ἐνώτιον χρύσεον, ἢ κύων στραφεὶς
30 ἐνεῶς πρὸς τὸ οἰκεῖον ἐξέραμα, ψεῦδος προκρίνας τῆς ἀληθείας, καὶ τοῦ παρὰ Θεοῦ βασιλέως ἀναριθμήτων χαρίτων ἐλεεινὴν
ἀποπλάνησιν, προκρίνας ἐγκυβισταν τῷ βορβόρῳ ὁ ἀποστάτης
τῆς ἀθεΐας ὡς μονιὸς ἄγριος.

ὅθεν οὐ δέον ἕνεκεν ἀσεβοῦς καὶ θεοστυγοῦς εὔνουν ἀπώσασθαι
35 δοῦλον κλαπέντα ἐκ ῥαθυμίας, καὶ τὸν δόλον καὶ τὴν κακοτεχνίαν τοῦ
παλαμναίου ἐκείνου ποσῶς μὴ φωράσαντα, καὶ μεθοδείᾳ δαιμονιώδει
ἐκείνου διαγρυπνῆσαι στερηθέντα, πλεῖστα τὰ δυσωποῦντα πρὸς ἱλασμὸν
καὶ συγκινοῦντα ἡμᾶς — τὸ προσὸν εὐσυμπάθητον κλεπτομένοις ἀγνοίᾳ ἢ

103: 4–5 cf. Ps. 13 (14):3 et Rom. 3:15 ‖ 10 cf. Joh. 13:18 ‖ 11–12 cf. Ps. 34 (35):6 ‖
13–14 cf. Is. 8:22 et 30:6 ‖ 14 Ps. 13 (14):3 et Rom. 3:15 ‖ 19–21 cf. Ps. 90 (91):1 ‖
22–23 Ps. 90 (91):2 ‖ 23–24 cf. Ps. 90 (91):3 ‖ 29 cf. Prov. 11:22 ‖ 29–30 cf. Prov. 26:11
et II Pet. 2:22 ‖ 32 cf. II Pet. 2:22 ‖ 33 Ps. 79 (80):14

10 βεβουλημένον codd. ‖ 13 τούτων S ‖ 25 τοσοῦτον S ‖ 29 ὅστις ἰὸς codd. ‖ 30 ἐννέως
codd. ‖ 33 ἀθεΐας] ἀληθείας S ‖ 38 καὶ συγκινοῦντα ἡμᾶς scripsi: συγκινούντων ἡμῶν
codd. ‖ προσὸν] πρὸς τὸν S

103

O what an accursed and utterly abominable fellow, whose «feet are sharp enough to shed blood»; for he is most resourceful at disturbing the peace with demonic frenzy and invention, so as to fight against piety itself—still we have been caught up in such lethargy and torpor as to provide this most despicable creature with a means of escape. If everyone who loves Christ, and knows the devious schemes of that man, ardently wishes to confound them and sets a snare in the path of that fellow and his like, who wanted «to lift up their heel» against this nation of Orthodox Christians, and if his treacherous road is made «dark and slippery», then «anguish and trouble» and «destruction and misery» will be the lot of this abominable man who has rejected truth and peace and sworn pledges; and this will be a most clear prelude to the hell which awaits him in the world to come, since he is an accursed man who has mocked at divine things.

And in addition to his other wicked deeds, he tried to mislead with flattery a cross-bearing ruler, who is distinguished for his wisdom above all kings that have ever ruled—since that evil man did not realize that our present ruler more than any ruler before him is established on earth and «dwells there with the help of the Highest», and thus confidently «sojourns under the shelter of the God of Heaven», wherefore he can say boldly, «Thou art my helper and my refuge» to God Who has richly endowed him ever since he left his mother's womb, and he is «delivered from the snare of hunters and from every troublesome matter» and deed—and the wretch disregarded the many favors ⟨he had received⟩, and although he is of a dog-like disposition, he did not even show the gratitude of a dog for his master, but he is monstrous both in soul and in shape, in every way an object of censure and abomination. Furthermore he went to such extremes of audacity as to mock shamelessly at holy baptism, and like a «gold ring in the nose of a pig» or «a dog» dumbly «turning to his own vomit again», he preferred falsehood to truth, and pitiful deceit to the countless favors ⟨he received⟩ from the divine emperor; apostate that he is, he preferred «to roll in the mud» of godlessness like «a solitary wild boar».

Wherefore one should not, on account of an impious man, despised by God, thrust away a well-disposed servant who was led astray by carelessness, and did not fully realize the treachery and malice of that miscreant, and was deprived of his ⟨normal⟩ vigilance by that man's diabolic wiles. Many factors cry out for mercy and move us to sympathy: the compassion of your holy

γνώσει τῇ σῇ ἁγίᾳ ψυχῇ, τὸ πανοῦργον ἐκείνου καὶ φονικόν, καὶ τὸ τῶν
40 ἐπταικότων ἁπλοῦν καὶ ἀκέραιον, τὴν κοινὴν τῶν ἀρχιερέων ὑπὲρ αὐτῶν
ἱκεσίαν, τὸ δὲ καὶ δυσωπητικώτερον τούτων, τὸ ἐν μέρει νομίζεσθαι τὸν
Γλυκὺν παρακαταθήκης πρὸς ἐκείνου τοῦ ἀοιδίμου, φημί, καὶ γνησίου
υἱοῦ τοῦ ἐν μακαρίᾳ τῇ λήξει βασιλέως Ῥωμαίων γεγενημένου κυροῦ Θεοδώρου τοῦ Λάσκαρι, τοῦτον παρατεθῆναι τῇ ἐκ Θεοῦ βασιλείᾳ σου, ὃν
45 καὶ φιλοτιμίαις ἀφοσιοῦσθαι καὶ μετὰ [fol. 80ʳ] θάνατον δέον αὐτῇ (καθὰ
πρὸς τοῖς ἄλλοις ὑπῆρξε καὶ τοῦτο καλοῖς τῷ πραοτάτῳ Δαυΐδ, χάριν
τῶν συμπεσόντων ἐκείνῳ κρίμασι θείοις ἀνιαρῶν, οἷς τὰ δυστυχῆ παρ'
ἐλπίδα ἐν τῇ τῇδε ζωῇ, καὶ αἱ ἀνώμαλοι περιπέτειαι ψυχὰς φιλαγάθους
καὶ μετὰ τέλος πρὸς ἔλεον κάμπτουσιν), ὡς τούτου γε χάριν αὐτῇ καταλεί-
50 ψαντα τὸν Γλυκὺν τοῦ ἀπολαῦσαι βασιλικῶν δωρεῶν· κἀκείνῳ τὴν χάριν
διδούς, θεραπεύσεις Θεόν, τῆς ἐκείνου μνησθεὶς τληπαθοῦς βιοτῆς,
ὡς τοῦ καὶ πᾶσι κεχαρισμένου ἀνθρώποις καὶ ζώοις ἐστερημένου φωτός,
οἷα τὰ τοῦ Θεοῦ κρίματα, πάντων πρὸς οἶκτον κινούντων τὴν ἐκ Θεοῦ
βασιλείαν σου, καὶ τούτων γε χάριν μὴ παρόψῃ τὴν δέησιν.

104. Πρὸς τὸν αὐτοκράτορα

Τῆς ἀναγεννησάσης τῷ θείῳ βαπτίσματι καὶ εἰς τόδε προενεγκού-
σης μεγαλειότητος ἐκκλησίας Χριστοῦ, αὐτοῦ, φημί, τοῦ μεγάλου Θεοῦ
καὶ Σωτῆρος μου Ἰησοῦ Χριστοῦ, τὴν ἐκ Θεοῦ βασιλείαν σου προορίσαν-
5 τός τε καὶ ἐκλεξαμένου καὶ δικαιώσαντος βασιλεύειν τοῦ Χριστωνύμου
λαοῦ, ὀφειλὴν δικαίαν ὀφείλουσαν τούτῳ τὴν ἐκ Θεοῦ βασιλείαν σου τὸ
μηδέν τι προτιμᾶν τῶν βιωτικῶν τῆς συστάσεως καὶ τιμῆς τῶν ἐκκλησιῶν, καὶ ὑπὲρ τούτων ἀγρύπνως ἐπαγωνίζεσθαι, δέομαι τοῦ μεγάλου
Θεοῦ τὴν αὔξησιν τῶν τοιούτων καὶ παντὸς ἀγαθοῦ παρ' ἐκείνου προσ-
10 γίνεσθαι τῇ καρδίᾳ τῆς ἐκ Θεοῦ βασιλείας σου, ἐπισταμένης ἐν ἀκριβείᾳ
αὐτῆς, ὡς ἡ ἀθέτησις τῶν ὀφειλόντων τῇ ἐκκλησίᾳ ἀκριβασμῶν, εἴπερ
τι ἄλλο, τὴν καθ' ἡμῶν κεκίνηκε καὶ κινεῖ ἀγανάκτησιν.

τῆς γὰρ ἐκκλησίας συνισταμένης ἐν τῷ καλῷ, εἰ ὅλως συμβαίη
τινὰ ἔξω βαδίσαι τῶν ὀφειλόντων Χριστιανοῖς, εἰ μή που πάντη νοσήσει
15 ἀνίατα, ἰατρευθήσεται πάλιν καὶ εἰσδεχθήσεται παρ' αὐτῆς· εἰ δ'(ὅπερ
ἀπεύχομαι) τὸ ἀνίατον ἀγαπήσει, πάλιν ἡ ἐκκλησία ἔπαθε μὲν ζημίαν, συνίσταται δέ, καὶ ἔχει ἐν ἑαυτῇ θεραπευόμενον τὸν Θεόν. εἰ δέ γε κοινῶς
ἐκκλίνει τῶν θεαρέστων ἡ ἐκκλησία, ἀφέστηκεν ἀπ' αὐτῆς ὁ Θεός,

---

42 φημί] φωνὴ S ‖ γνησίου S ‖ 54 παρόψει codd.
104: V 80ʳ–80ᵛ. S 228ʳ–229ʳ.
1 ante πρὸς add. γράμμα VʳS ‖ post αὐτοκράτορα add. περὶ τοῦ μὴ προτιμᾶν τῶν βιωτικῶν τῆς συστάσεως καὶ τιμῆς τῶν ἐκκλησιῶν VʳS

103, 104

soul for those who have been deceived either in ignorance or knowingly, the wickedness and bloodthirstiness of that man, and the simplicity and integrity of those who have been deceived, the joint supplication of the bishops on their behalf, and the most forceful argument of all, that Glykys was considered to be a ward of that famous and noble son of the late emperor of the Romans, Kyr Theodore Laskaris, I mean, and that he was commended to your divine majesty, and it was proper for you to devote honors to him, even after his [John's] death (just as in addition to his other good works the most gentle David possessed this ⟨virtue⟩, too, thanks to the grievous misfortunes which befell him through divine judgments; for as a result of these ⟨judgments⟩ unexpected calamities in this life and capricious reversals of circumstance move good souls to mercy on a man even after his death), for this reason he entrusted Glykys to you to enjoy imperial favors; and in granting ⟨the late prince⟩ this favor, you will serve God, being mindful of his wretched existence, deprived of the light which is granted to all men and beasts (such are the judgments of God!). Since all these ⟨arguments⟩ move your divine majesty to pity, for these reasons do not overlook my petition.

104. To the emperor

Since you have been reborn in holy baptism and brought to this peak of greatness by the Church of Christ, I mean, by Jesus Christ, the great God Himself and my Savior, Who foreordained and chose and decided that your divine majesty should rule the Christian people, your divine majesty has a just obligation to Him to set nothing in this world before the protection and honor of the churches, and to strive vigilantly on their behalf. ⟨And⟩ I ask the great God to grant increase of such ⟨virtues⟩ and every good thing to the heart of your divine majesty, since you are well aware that more than anything else disregard of the commandments owed to the Church has provoked and continues to provoke His wrath against us.

For when the Church is flourishing, if it were to occur that someone should deviate from his Christian duty, unless his disease is completely incurable, he will be healed and received again by the Church. Even if (and I pray it may not happen) he should prefer the incurable ⟨disease⟩ [the schism?], the Church suffers harm, to be sure, but continues to flourish and has God in Her midst as Supreme Healer. But if the Church in general turns away from God-pleasing actions, God stands aloof from Her, and justly

ὀνειδίζων δικαίως ἡμᾶς, ἱερεῖς οὐκ εἶπαν «ποῦ ἐστιν ὁ Θεός;»

20 καὶ οἱ τοῦ νόμου μου ἀντεχόμενοι οὐκ ἠπίσταντό [fol. 80ᵛ]
με· ὃ καὶ συνέβη μικροῦ σήμερον.

ἐπεὶ δὲ σωτήριον ζῆλον ὑπὲρ αὐτῆς ὁ ὑπεράγαθος Κύριος ἀνῆψεν
ἐν τῇ καρδίᾳ τῆς ἐκ Θεοῦ βασιλείας σου, γένοιτο ταύτης ἀξιωθῆναι παρὰ
Θεοῦ καὶ τὰ τῆς ἐκκλησίας ἰδεῖν καὶ τὰ τῆς βασιλείας ἀναδραμεῖν πρὸς
25 τὸ βέλτιον. οὐ γὰρ διὰ τὴν βασιλείαν ἡ ἱερωσύνη ἀπεχαρίσθη τῷ Χριστωνύμῳ λαῷ, ἀλλὰ διὰ τὴν ἱερωσύνην ἡ βασιλεία, ἵνα πρὸς τὸ ἀρέσκον
Θεῷ τῇ ἔξω χειρὶ κρατύνουσα ταύτην καὶ περιέπουσα καὶ συνιστῶσα,
ἀντικρατύνηται πάλιν αὐτὴ καὶ συνίσταται αὐξομένη ὑπὸ Θεοῦ. διὰ ταῦτα
καὶ ὅσον ἂν ἐμπνευσθῇ πρὸς Θεοῦ τῇ καρδίᾳ τῆς βασιλείας σου ἀρέσκον
30 Θεῷ, καὶ τῇ αὐτοῦ ἐκκλησίᾳ ἐπάγον σύστασιν καὶ πρὸς τὰ κρείττω βελτί-
ωσιν καὶ πράττειν καὶ λέγειν τὴν ἐκ Θεοῦ βασιλείαν σου, οὐκ ἀποδέχομαι
μόνον, ἀλλὰ καὶ εὔχομαι πρὸς Θεοῦ πλουτισθῆναι καὶ τοῦτο καὶ ἄλλο
πᾶν ἀγαθὸν τῇ ἐκ Θεοῦ βασιλείᾳ σου.

105. ⟨Πρός τινας τῶν ἀρχιερέων⟩

Τὸ οἰκονομεῖν τοὺς λόγους ἐν κρίσει τῆς τελειότητος ἴδιον· ἡμεῖς
δὲ οὐ μόνον μὴ πεφθακότες τὸ τέλειον, ἀλλὰ καὶ τῶν ἀτελῶν ἀτελέστερον
διακείμενοι, ἵνα μὴ τῶν οἰκονομούντων καταγινώσκωμεν, ἢ οἰκονομεῖν
5 γνωματευόντων, πάλιν ἡμῶν θεῖναι τὸ στόμα φυλακὴν βεβουλήμεθα, ἕως ἂν τοῖς οἰκονομοῦσι δοκεῖ — οἰκονομεῖν γὰρ αὐτοὺς τὰ ἡμῖν
μὴ ἀρέσκοντα, εἴτε ἐξ ἀτελείας ἡμῶν, εἴτε καὶ ἄλλως πῶς, ἀσθενοῦμεν
ἀκολουθεῖν — ἄλλως τε ἵνα μὴ καί τινας τῶν ἐνταῦθα οἰκούντων παρα-
λυπήσωμεν· οὐδὲ γὰρ ἀνέχονται οἱ Ἰουδαῖοι ἡμῶν ἀπελθεῖν ἐν τῇ τοῦ
10 Θεοῦ ἐκκλησίᾳ καὶ τὰ τῶν ἁγίων παθῶν τοῦ Κυρίου μου ὡς ἔθος ἀναφωνεῖν. ἢ οὐχὶ καὶ αὐτοὶ πρωτότοκος εἶναι αὐχοῦσιν υἱός, καὶ οἱ
πατέρες αὐτῶν ὑπὸ τὴν νεφέλην ἦσαν, καὶ διὰ τῆς θα-
λάσσης διῆλθον, καὶ εἰς τὸν Μωϋσῆν ἐβαπτίσθησαν; εἰ
οὖν μηδὲ λειτουργεῖν ἡμᾶς ἀνέχονται ἄλλοι, εἰ μὴ καὶ τῷ Ῥώμης δόξῃ
15 καὶ ὡς ἐκείνῳ δοκεῖ, δέον ἡμᾶς λογιζόμεθα καθέζεσθαι οἴκοι τοῦ φροντί-

---

104: 19–21 Jer. 2:8
105: 5 cf. Ps. 38 (39):2 ‖ 11 Luc. 2:7 ‖ 11–13 cf. I Cor. 10:1–2

---

28 αὐτῇ S ‖ συνιστᾶται VS
    105: V 80ᵛ–81ʳ. S 229ʳ–229ᵛ.
1 γράμμα πρός τινας τῶν ἀρχιερέων ὅπως γνωριοῦσι τῷ βασιλεῖ ὅτι ὁ πατριάρχης βεβαρυ-
μένως (βεβαρυμένος S) ἐστὶ διὰ τὸν Κυζίκου add. VʳS ‖ 5 γνωματευόντων coni. Ševčenko:
γνωματεύοντες codd. ‖ 11 ἢ S ‖ 15 δόξει codd.

104, 105

reproaches us: «The priests said not, 'Where is the Lord?', and they that held by my law knew me not»; and this almost happened today.

But since the Lord, in His great goodness, has kindled in the heart of your divine majesty salutary zeal on behalf of the Church, may it come to pass that you be deemed worthy by God to see improvement in the fortunes of the Church and of the empire. For priesthood was not granted to Christian people for the sake of empire, but empire for the sake of priesthood, so that if the empire in a manner pleasing to God supported the Church with the secular arm and honored and protected Her, the empire in turn would be supported and protected and increased by God. Therefore, whatsoever God inspires in your majesty's heart that is pleasing to God, and whatever your divine majesty may do or say that brings protection and improvement to His Church, I not only accept, but pray that your divine majesty may be richly endowed by God with these ⟨virtues⟩ and all other good works.

105. ⟨To certain of the bishops⟩

To control one's words in a judgment is a characteristic of perfection. But since I not only have not attained perfection, but am even more imperfect than the imperfect, so as not to condemn those who follow the principle of accommodation, or, rather, pretend to follow it, I prefer once more «to keep my mouth with a bridle», as long as seems good to the accommodators—for either on account of my imperfection, or for some other reason I am unable to go along with them when they arrange compromises displeasing to me—⟨and I keep silence⟩ also so as not to distress certain people living here. For the Jews, too, are against my entering the church of God and proclaiming the holy sufferings of my Lord as is customary. But isn't it true that even they boast that He is a «firstborn son», and that «their fathers were under the cloud, and passed through the sea, and were baptized with Moses»? If then other people won't let me celebrate the liturgy unless the ⟨bishop⟩ of Rome agrees and in the manner approved by him, I think that I should sit at home and

266

ζειν τὰ ἑαυτῶν. εἰ γὰρ ἀπέλθωμεν ἐν τῇ ἐκκλησίᾳ, τοῖς πυθομένοις τί τὸ τῆς ἀλειτουργησίας οὐκ ἔχομέν τι ἀποκρίνασθαι. εἰ οὖν δοκεῖ ἀμφοτέροις ἵνα γνωρίσητε καὶ τῷ βασιλεῖ, γενέσθω· εἰ δὲ μή, γινώσκετε τοῦτο μόνοι ὑμεῖς. οὐ γὰρ ἴσμεν τῆς ἐκκλησίας Χριστοῦ, ὡς ὁρῶ, πολλοὺς
20 ὀρεγο–[fol. 81ʳ] μένους τὸ ἀκατάλυτον.

106. Πρὸς τὸν αὐτοκράτορα περὶ τῶν σιτοκαπήλων καὶ αἰσχροκερδῶν

Ἀδικίαν ἐμίσησα καὶ ἐβδελυξάμην μετὰ τοῦ θεσπεσίου Δαυῒδ ἀπὸ ψυχῆς κατακαυχᾶσθαι τὴν ἐκ Θεοῦ βασιλείαν σου ἀμφιβάλλει οὐδεὶς ὁ γινώσκων αὐτήν· καὶ τοῦτο οὐκ ἐξ ὑμῶν, Θεοῦ τὸ
5 δῶρον, εἰ προστεθῇ καὶ τὸ λεῖπον. ὁ γὰρ τοιαύτην σοι συμπαθῆ καὶ ὑπερφυῆ, εἰ θελήσεις, ἐν τοῖς καλοῖς χαρισάμενος, καὶ ταινίᾳ καὶ δόξῃ καταστέψας βασιλικῇ, καὶ φορεῖν εἰς δέον τὴν μάχαιραν ὕψωσε. μὴ οὖν διὰ τὰς ἐμὰς ἁμαρτίας ἡ μάχαιρα μείνῃ σήμερον ἀνενέργητος διχοτομεῖν τὸ δίκαιον καὶ τὸ ἄδικον· καὶ ἵνα τἄλλα ἐάσω, τὸν σῖτον καὶ οἶνον
10 ὃν Θεὸς ἐχορήγησεν εἰς κυβέρνησιν τοῦ λαοῦ καὶ τῶν βασιλικῶν δουλειῶν, οἱ ἐκ τοῦ μαμωνᾶ πλουτοῦντες ἀποκλεῖσαι ταῦτα εἰς ὄλεθρον τῶν πενήτων οὐκ ὤκνησαν, τοῖς τούτων ἐκπιεσμοῖς ἐπαράτου τυχεῖν πλουτισμοῦ ἐφιέμενοι, ὅτι καὶ ὁ τιμιουλκῶν σῖτον δημοκατάρατος. διὰ τί γὰρ πρὸς τῷ μηδὲν ὠφελεῖν καὶ λυμεῶνες τοῦ Χριστωνύμου πληρώματος
15 γινόμενοι οὐκ ἀναχαιτίζονται; εἰ μὲν οὖν εἰς τοῦτο λύσιν τινὰ ποιήσει ἡ ἐκ Θεοῦ βασιλεία σου, χάρις Θεῷ. εἰ δ'οὖν, μὰ τὸν ἐλθόντα καλέσαι ἁμαρτωλοὺς εἰς μετάνοιαν, συναθροῖσαι βούλομαι τὸν λαόν, ἀφορισμὸν ἐπ' ἄμβωνος καὶ ἀνάθεμα ἐκφωνῆσαι σιτοκαπήλῳ παντί, καὶ οὕτως οἴκαδε ἀπελθεῖν, μηδὲν ἄλλο εἰπὼν εἴ τι καὶ γένηται. συμφέ-
20 ρει γάρ μοι σφαγὴν ὑπομεῖναι ἢ τοσαύτας ὁρᾶν ἀδικίας τῇ πολιτείᾳ Χριστιανῶν αἳ οὐδὲ ἐν τοῖς ἔθνεσι, ⟨καὶ⟩ σιωπᾶν.

106: 2 Ps. 118 (119):163 ‖ 4–5 Eph. 2:8 ‖ 7 cf. Rom. 13:4 ‖ 13 Prov. 11:26 (Theodotion) ‖ 16–17 cf. Matt. 9:13

106: V 81ʳ. S 229ᵛ–230ʳ.
1 ante πρὸς add. γράμμα VʳS ‖ post αἰσχροκερδῶν add. ἀναγνωσθὲν καὶ ἐν τῇ Ἁγίᾳ Σοφίᾳ ἐν μέσῳ τοῦ δήμου VʳS ‖ 21 καὶ addidi

look after my own affairs. For if I enter the church, I will have no reply to those who inquire why I am not celebrating the liturgy. If then you both decide to make this known to the emperor, so be it. Otherwise, keep this to yourselves. For as I see it, I do not know many people who desire the perpetuity of the Church of Christ.

106. To the emperor, concerning grain-dealers and profiteers

No one who knows your divine majesty doubts that you exult in your soul along with the divinely inspired David, saying, «I hate and abhor unrighteousness». «And that ⟨is⟩ not of yourselves; it is the gift of God», if I may complete the quotation. For the One Who has granted you among your blessings such a compassionate and extraordinary ⟨soul⟩, whenever you have the will ⟨to employ it that way⟩, has also crowned you with the diadem and imperial glory, and has exalted you «to bear the sword» for needful purposes. Let not that sword, on account of my sins, today remain powerless to sever the just and unjust. To omit other matters, those who are enriched by Mammon have not hesitated to hoard the grain and wine which God has furnished for the support of the people and ⟨payment for⟩ imperial services, and this to the ruin of the poor. For it is by the oppression of these ⟨poor people⟩ that they wish to acquire their accursed wealth, accursed because «he who raises the price of grain is cursed by the people». Why is there no check on these people who are not only of no use, but are the ruin of the Christian flock? If your majesty finds some solution to this problem, thanks be to God; otherwise, by the One «Who came to call sinners to repentance», I intend to gather together the people, and from the pulpit to declare excommunication and anathema on every grain-dealer, and then go home, saying nothing further, no matter what happens. For it is better for me to be killed than to keep silent, when I see in a Christian state injustices which are not to be found even among pagan nations.

268

107. Πρὸς τὸν αὐτοκράτορα

Ἐὰν διὰ τὸν ἄνθρωπόν του λόγον δοῦναι χρεωστεῖ τῷ Θεῷ τοῦ
οἴκου ὁ κύριος, πολλῷ μᾶλλον δι' υἱοὺς καὶ θυγατέρας. διὰ τοῦτο παρακαλῶ, καὶ μάλιστα ἐν τοιούτῳ καιρῷ, ἵνα ἐξακριβάζηται καὶ περὶ τῶν
5 ἰδίων υἱῶν ἡ ἐκ Θεοῦ βασιλεία σου. φήμη γὰρ κρατεῖ περὶ τοῦ Δεσπότου
Κυροῦ Κωνσταντίνου, ὁπλισμένον ἐν ἅρμασι κατὰ νύκτα, συνεργοῦντος
αὐτῷ τοῦ υἱοῦ τοῦ ἐπάρχου ἐκείνου, κακῶς ἀναστρέφεσθαι. ὅσον δὲ καὶ τὸ
ἄτιμον καὶ τὸ κρῖμα, λέγειν οὐκ ἔχω, καὶ μᾶλλον ὡς ἔφην ἐν τοιούτῳ
καιρῷ, ἡνίκα ἄνθρωπος συνετὸς καὶ τῆς ἰδίας ἐγκρατεύσηται γυναικός, εἰ
10 ὅλως ὁρᾷ τὰ συμβάντα Χριστιανοῖς. διὰ τοῦτο παρακαλῶ, ὀργισθῶμεν
ἡμεῖς τοὺς τοιούτους, ἵνα τῆς θείας ὀργῆς αὐτοὺς [fol. 81ᵛ] ἐκλυτρώσω-
μεν. τοὺς γὰρ μὴ παιδευομένους ὑπὸ τῆς ἐξουσίας, βαρυτέρα γενήσεται
ἡ ἐκ τοῦ μείζονος ἐπεξέλευσις· πλὴν κἂν οἱ ῥηθέντες ὅσοι κἂν ἄλλοι τινὲς
παιδευέσθωσαν.

108. Πρὸς τὸν αὐτοκράτορα

Εἰ καὶ σαθρᾷ ἀκοῇ αἰσθέσθαι ἦχον βροντῆς καθαρῶς οὐ
προσγίνεται, ἀλλά γε τοῖς ὑγιαίνουσιν, οὐ μόνον χρήσιμον τὸ βροντᾶν, ὡς
οἱ ταῦτα ἐξητακότες, ἀλλὰ καὶ ἀναγκαῖον, φασί· κατεπτηχέναι γὰρ
5 ἐκ τοῦ ἤχου τὰ ὕδατα λέγουσιν. ὀψὲ γοῦν καταβροντώσης τοὺς ἐμ-
βροντήτους τῆς ἐκ Θεοῦ βασιλείας σου, ἐσήμανεν ὁ τερπνὸς ἦχος ἐκείνης
καὶ περί τινος πένητος ὑβρικότος τινὰ τῶν ὀνομαστῶν· περὶ οὗ καὶ ἅπερ
δοκεῖ τοῖς λόγοις τοῖς ἱεροῖς, ὀλίγα χαράξας τῇ ἐκ Θεοῦ βασιλείᾳ σου
πέπομφα, φάσκοντα οὕτως· εἰ μή τις ἀποσταίη τῆς ἁμαρτίας,
10 μετανοεῖν οὐ πιστεύεται, οὔτε δέχεται εἰς μετάνοιαν.
μετάνοια γάρ ἐστι τὸ μεταμέλεσθαι τὸν ἁμαρτήσαντα ἐφ' οἷς ἥμαρτε καὶ
δάκνεσθαι ἐπ' αὐτοῖς. ὁ δὲ ἐπιμένων τῇ ἁμαρτίᾳ οὔτε μεταμέλεσθαι πιστεύεται, οὔτε δάκνεσθαι, ἀλλὰ καὶ ἥδεσθαι ταύτῃ.

108: 2 cf. Greg. Naz., *Or.* XLI, ς' (PG, XXXVI, 437 B) || 4–5 cf. Ps. 76 (77):17–19
et 103 (104):6–7 || 9–10 locum non inveni

107: V 81ʳ–81ᵛ. S 230ʳ.
1 post αὐτοκράτορα add. γράμμα περὶ τοῦ υἱοῦ αὐτοῦ καὶ δεσπότου κυροῦ Κωνσταντίνου
VʳS

108: V 81ᵛ. S 230ʳ–230ᵛ.
1 ante πρὸς add. γράμμα VʳS || post αὐτοκράτορα add. περὶ δημηγορίας αὐτοῦ ὄντως καὶ
τοῦ πατριάρχου ἐκεῖ ἐν τῷ παλατίῳ VʳS || 2 σαθρὰ V

107. To the emperor

If the master of a house is obliged to give an accounting to God for his man-servant, then so much more ⟨is he obliged to render such an accounting⟩ for his sons and daughters. For this reason I beg of you, and especially at this time, that your majesty make diligent inquiry about his own sons. For there is a current rumor that the Despot Kyr Constantine is wickedly swaggering about at night, fully armed, together with the son of the prefect. I have no words to express the disgrace and sin ⟨of such behavior⟩, especially, as I have said, at such a time when a wise man should even abstain from intercourse with his own wife, if he considers the afflictions of Christians. For this reason I beg of you, let us bring our wrath to bear upon these ⟨young⟩ men, so as to save them from divine wrath. For those who are not punished by ⟨earthly⟩ authority, the vengeance of the Divine ⟨authority⟩ will be even more severe; so let the abovementioned, as well as certain others, and as many as they may be, be punished.

108. To the emperor

To be sure, it is not possible for ⟨people with⟩ «poor hearing» to perceive clearly «the sound of thunder»; however, for those with unimpaired faculties, thundering is not only useful, but indeed necessary, as those who have examined these matters say. For they say that even the waters have cowered at the sound. Recently indeed when your divine majesty was thundering against gaping fools, your pleasant voice mentioned a certain poor man who had insulted a notable. As for the opinion of divine Scriptures on this matter, I have written a few lines and sent them to your divine majesty, namely that «if one does not turn away from sin, he is not considered to have repented, nor is he accepted as truly repentant». For true repentance consists of the sinner feeling regret for his sins and being vexed by them; but he who persists in sin is not considered to be repentant, or grieved, but to take pleasure in it.

109. Πρὸς τὸν αὐτοκράτορα

Τοῦ Θεοῦ τῆς εἰρήνης τὸ εἰς δύναμιν σπουδάζειν τὴν ἐκ Θεοῦ
βασιλείαν σου προκόπτειν τὴν ἐκκλησίαν σαφές· καὶ εἴθε τοῦτο καὶ τοῖς
πρὶν ἐσπουδάζετο, ἢ κἂν ἡμῖν πρὸ μικροῦ. πλὴν τὰ ζητήματα τῶν πολλῶν
5 ὀρέξεις ἰδίας νοῶ, καὶ ἀνταμείψεις φιλίας σωματικῆς, κἂν εἶχον κροτῆσαί
τινας, πλὴν ἀναφέρω.

εἰ γὰρ διὰ τὸ μὴ ἐκπεσεῖν ἐμπαθείας οἰκείας τινὲς κατὰ τῆς ἑαυτῶν
ψυχῆς ἐχώρισαν εἰς τὸ σχίζεσθαι, εἰ ἀξιοῦμεν αὐτοὺς μόνον τῶν ἑνουμέ-
νων εὑρίσκεσθαι καὶ μὴ κωλύεσθαι παρ᾽ ἡμῶν τῶν οἰκείων ἐμπαθειῶν
10 ἀπολαύειν, τρόπον τινὰ συνεργεῖν αὐτοῖς εἰς τὸ βλάπτον γινόμεθα· καὶ
τοῦτο σόφισμα λογίζομαι τοῦ ἐχθροῦ, τὸ ὅπερ τῇ διαστάσει οὐκ ἴσχυσε.
τότε γὰρ πρὸς ἐκείνους τὸ κρῖμα ἀπέβλεπε μόνον· νῦν δὲ κυβερνοῦντες ἡμεῖς
αὐτούς, τὰ αὐτοῖς καταθύμια γίνεται. εἰ μὲν γὰρ τὰ προδήλως ἐμπαθῆ
ἀθετήσαντας προσηκάμεθα, εἰκὸς ὡς ἐξ ἀναξίου ἐξάγειν ἄξιον
15 ἑτερπόμεθα· εἰ δὲ χαριζόμεθα τούτοις τὰ μήτε πρὸς σωτηρίαν ὁρῶντα,
μήτε οἰκοδομοῦντά τινα, λυποῦμεν [fol. 82ʳ] τὸν λέγοντα τίς ἐστιν
ὁ εὐφραίνων με, ὁ λυπούμενος ἐξ ἐμοῦ; τοιαύταις γὰρ
λύπαις καὶ λυποῦσιν οἱ τοῦ Θεοῦ καὶ λυποῦνται· τὰ δ᾽ ἄλλως ἔχοντα
λυπηρὰ τοῦ κόσμου εἰσὶ καὶ οὐ τοῦ Θεοῦ.

110. Πρὸς τὸν αὐτοκράτορα

Κράτιστε, θεόστεπτε, θεοδόξαστε, θεοκυβέρνητε, δέσποτά μου,
ἅγιε βασιλεῦ· ἀντίληψις εἴη τῇ βασιλείᾳ σου πρὸς Θεοῦ κραταιά, καὶ
τροπαιούχημα μέγα κατὰ παντὸς πολεμίου νοουμένου καὶ ὁρατοῦ. εἰ
5 πάπαν καὶ τῶν τυχόντων τοῦ καιροῦ καθήψαντο τὴν σήμερον τὰ δεινά,
τοῖς τὰ σκῆπτρα λαχοῦσιν ἰθύνειν τῶν ὀρθοδόξων οὐκ οἶμαι μὴ δραστικώτερον καὶ ἀφορητότερον ὅσα καὶ οἷα τῶν κοινῇ παρανομιῶν καὶ νομίμων
καταπατήσεως χάριν καθ᾽ ἡμῶν ἀπελύθη παρὰ τοῦ δίκαια κρίνοντος.
καὶ οὐκ ἔστι τῷ καὶ ποσῶς συνιόντι μὴ ἀκριβῶς αἰσθανθῆναι ὡς μάλιστα
10 βασιλέων τὰ τοιάδε καθάπτεται· ὅπου καὶ τὸ ἡμέτερον τῶν οὐδαμινῶν

109: 14 cf. Jer. 15:19 ‖ 16–17 II Cor. 2:2

109: V 81ᵛ–82ʳ. S 230ᵛ–231ʳ.
1 ante πρὸς add. γράμμα   VʳS ‖ post αὐτοκράτορα add. περὶ τοῦ μὴ εὑρίσκειν τινὰς φιλίας
σωματικῆς καὶ χάριν τούτου χωρίζεσθαι εἰς τὸ σχίζεσθαι   VʳS ‖ 5 κἂν] καὶ codd.
110: V 82ʳ–84ʳ. S 231ʳ–234ᵛ. P 99ᵛ–103ʳ.
1 post αὐτοκράτορα add. et deinde delevit περὶ δημηγορίας αὐτοῦ ὄντως τοῦ πατριάρχου
ἐκεῖ ἐν τῷ παλατίῳ Vʳ; postea scr. γράμμα διεγείρων βασιλεῖς καὶ ἄρχοντας καὶ πᾶν τὸ
ὑπήκοον πρὸς ἐπιστροφὴν πρὸς Θεὸν καὶ μετάνοιαν VʳSP ‖ 9 τῷ] -ὸ P ‖ 10 βασιλεύων codd.

109. To the emperor

It is clear that your divine majesty is laboring to the utmost to promote the increase of the Church of the God of peace. Would that this had been a concern of your predecessors, or indeed that we had been recently concerned. But I consider the problems raised by many people to be expressions of private passions and the requitals of mundane friendship; and I could strike some of them, but I will only make a report.

If as a result of not escaping their private passions certain people, to the harm of their souls, have separated off into schism, and if I then demanded only that they return to the fold, but did not prevent them from indulging their desires, in a way I would be coöperating with them to their harm; and I think this is a trick of the devil, which has failed to succeed because of my keeping them at a distance (?). For in the latter case, the crime could be attributed to them alone, but in the former case I would be in authority over them, and their desires would be fulfilled. If I should admit to communion those who have clearly rejected their passions, it would stand to reason that I did it because I rejoiced at having «changed an unworthy person into a worthy one». But if I give them things which lead neither to salvation, nor to edification, I would grieve the one who said, «Who is he that makes me glad ⟨but⟩ the same which is made sorry by me ?». For it is with such sorrows that men of God cause sorrow and are made sorry. Other kinds of sorrows belong to the world and not to God.

110. To the emperor

My mighty lord, holy emperor, crowned by God, glorified by God, guided by God. May God grant your majesty mighty succour and great victory against every foe, both intelligible and visible. If these days the misfortunes of our times have fallen upon a Pope of inconsequential people, ⟨then⟩ I believe that ⟨the wrath⟩ which has been released against us by the righteous Judge, on account of our general transgressions and trampling of hallowed customs, ⟨must fall⟩ even more harshly and unbearably upon those whose lot it is to rule over Orthodox Christians. And any man of understanding must perceive that such ⟨disasters⟩ assail emperors especially. Wherefore, to ex-

272

110

ἵν᾽ ἐξείπω, εὐκταῖόν μοι ἦν καὶ ἐπίχαρτον, εἰ τοῖς καταβεβηκόσιν
εἰς λάκκον προσελογίσθην, πρὶν ἐν τῷ γένει ἡμῶν τοιαῦτα ἰδεῖν τὰ
πρὸς συμφορὰν ἀπαράβλητα, ἐκδοθὲν τὸ ὀρθόδοξον τοῖς ἀθέοις δι᾽ ἐντολῶν καταπάτησιν, ὡς οὐ μόνον τινῶν ἑκοντὶ τὸ σέβας ἀρνησαμένων
15 μοχθηρίας ὑπερβολῇ, ἀλλὰ καὶ ἀκόντων συνελαθέντων εἰς τοῦτο τῇ ἀν-
υποστάτῳ ἀνάγκῃ ὑπὲρ ἄμμον τῷ ἀριθμῷ, τοῦ πλάσαντος, φεῦ, ἐκσφεν-
δονηθέντων, ἀπὸ τοῦ πάντα τὰ ἔθνη ἐπισυνάξαι ἐπὶ σταυροῦ παλάμας ἐκ-
τείναντος.

κ̄αὶ οἱ ἕλκειν ἐξ ἡμετέρας ἀναστροφῆς ἀγαθῆς καὶ ἀθέους ὀφείλον-
20 τες, ἐκ τοῦ μὴ ἀναστραφῆναι ἀξίως τῆς κλήσεως, ἀσεβῶν δουλείᾳ κατε-
δικάσθημεν, τὴν ἐλευθερίαν προδόντες ὀρέξεσι σαρκικαῖς τὴν διπλῆν, καθὰ καὶ τῶν πάλαι τινές, τῶν διὰ τοῦ τιμίου Σταυροῦ χαρισθέντων
πιστοῖς πλατυσμοῦ καὶ τροπαίων καὶ ὅσης εὐημερίας ἀνεπαισθήτως
καὶ ἀχαρίστως διατεθέντες, ἀθετήσει τῶν θείων εὐαγγελίων καὶ νόμων,
25 ἀποβεβλήκεσαν καὶ πλατυσμοῦ καὶ τροπαίων καὶ εὐτυχίας, πρὸς τῷ τῶν
ἀρχῆθεν τῷ γένει παρασχεθέντων ἀντιλήψεων καὶ χαρίτων ἀνεπαισθήτως διατεθῆναι καὶ ἀχαρίστως, καὶ θείων εὐαγγελίων καὶ νόμων ἀπε-
πλανήθησαν, ὃ διὰ τοῦ τιμίου Σταυροῦ ἐβραβεύθη αὐτοῖς τροπαιούχημα
ὡς μικροῦ τὴν ὑπ᾽ οὐρανὸν τῷ εὐσεβήσαντι πρώτως ἐν βασιλεῦσι κα-
30 [fol. 82ᵛ] θυποτάξαντος. εἴ γε συνετηρήθη τοῖς διαδόχοις ἐκείνου ἡ
εὐσέβεια καὶ εὐλάβεια καὶ ἡ λοιπὴ τῶν νομίμων ἐκπλήρωσις, οὐκ ἄρα τῆς
μοναρχίας τὸ λεῖπον προσετέθη αὐτοῖς, ἀλλ᾽ ὄλλοιτο ἡ κακία καὶ ἡ
ταύτης καταβολή· μὴ γὰρ θελησάντων ἐκείνων τὴν βασιλείαν καὶ
τὴν δικαιοσύνην πρώτως ζητεῖν τοῦ Θεοῦ, κἀντεῦθεν
35 αὐτοῖς τὸ πᾶν προστεθήσεσθαι, ἀλλ᾽ ἐπάρσει καὶ φρυαγμῷ
ἐπιλησθέντες ὅτι εἰσὶν ἄνθρωποι, φυσηθέντες ἢ πρὸς ἀποστασίαν τοῦ
αὐτοὺς βασιλεύσαντος, ἢ εἰ μὴ τοῦτο, ἀλλά γε πρὸς ὕβριν τῶν θείων
θεσμῶν καὶ καταπάτησιν καὶ ἀθέτησιν, ὡς στόματι μὲν εἰδέναι
ὁμολογεῖν Θεόν, τοῖς δ᾽ ἔργοις ἀρνεῖσθαι, ἄπορα ἐκείνοις
40 διὰ τὴν ἀπόνοιαν καὶ τὰ πόριμα γέγονεν.

ἐκ τούτου στενοχωρεῖσθαι συνεχωρήθη κατὰ μικρὸν τῇ πασῶν
ἀσυγκρίτως τῇ γῇ βασιλειῶν βασιλείᾳ καὶ τῇ τὸ κράτος αὐτῇ συντηρεῖσθαι δεδυνημένη ἀσάλευτος. εἰ καθ᾽ ὅσον τοῦ δόντος Χριστοῦ ἀνοθεύτως
τηρεῖ σὺν τῇ πίστει τῇ ὀρθοδόξῳ καὶ τὰς ἁγίας αὐτοῦ ἐντολάς, συνδιαιω-
45 νίζειν καὶ τὴν εὐημερίαν αὐτὴν καὶ τὴν βασιλείαν μέχρι καὶ συντελείας αἰῶνος, ὡς ἐπηγγείλατο· καθ᾽ ὅσον δὲ ἡ ἀποβολὴ τῆς πίστεως
ἢ τῶν ἔργων, κατὰ τοσοῦτον καὶ τὰ τῆς ἀντιλήψεως ἄπορα. καὶ εἴθε κἂν

110: 11–12 cf. Ps. 27(28):1 || 33–35 cf. Matt. 6:33 || 38–39 cf. Tit. 1:16 || 45–46 cf.
Matt. 28:20

---

17 πάντα] πάπαν P || 24 νόμων] νέμων P || 25–27 ἀποβεβλήκεσαν ... καὶ νόμων om.
P || 25 τῷ] τὸ codd. || 28 ὁ P || 30 γε] τε P || 35 προστεθείσεσθαι S

110

press my humble opinion, I would wish and rejoice to be numbered among those «who descend into the ditch», rather than to see such incomparable calamities befall our nation, Orthodox Christians delivered unto the godless because of their transgression of the commandments, since not only have certain people, in an excess of wickedness, repudiated piety of their own accord, but also countless numbers (even more than the grains of sand) of unwilling people have been driven to this by irresistible necessity, alas, cast by a sling away from the Creator, the One Who stretched out His hand on the Cross to gather together all the nations.

And we, who ought to attract the godless by our good behavior, have been condemned to serve impious men because we did not live worthily of the ⟨Christian⟩ name, but betray our twofold freedom with passions of the flesh, just like certain people of old, who had an imperceptive and ungrateful attitude toward the increase and victories and prosperity granted to the faithful through the venerable Cross, and because of their disregard of the holy Gospels and commandments they were deprived of this increase and victory and good fortune; and in addition to failing to perceive and appreciate the assistance and favors which have been granted to our people from of old, they went astray from the holy Gospels and laws. This victory was awarded to them through the venerable Cross Which made most of the earth subject to the first Christian emperor. And if his piety and reverence and fulfilment of traditional customs had been continued by his successors, not only would rule over the rest of the world have been granted to them, but wickedness and its foundations would have utterly perished. For they were not willing «to seek first the kingdom and righteousness of God», and thus have «everything added unto them», but in their insolence and arrogance they forgot that they were human beings, and either puffed themselves up to rebel against the One Who made them emperor, or else to abuse and trample upon and disregard the divine ordinances, so that with their tongue «they profess that they know God, but with their works they deny Him», and because of their senseless rebellion that which was fertile became barren.

For this reason the empire which surpassed all empires on earth, and which had been able to maintain its power unshaken, was allowed to shrink slowly in territory. This is so, since, inasmuch as ⟨the Empire⟩ sincerely keeps the holy commandments of Christ the Giver together with the Orthodox faith, prosperity will last as long as the empire, «until the end of the world», as has been announced. If, on the other hand, the empire rejects both faith and works, it will be deprived in direct proportion of His succour. I wish that

οὕτω παιδευόμενοι ἐπεστρέφομεν, τὸ κρῖμα τοῦ μόνου Θεοῦ φοβηθέντες
ἢ αἰδεσθέντες, ἐτρέχομεν πρὸς μετάνοιαν, ἀναμφιβόλως ἐγγυωμένης τῆς
50 μετανοίας καὶ ὧδε εὐημερίαν καὶ σωτηρίαν καὶ πᾶν ἀγαθόν. ἃ τοῖς
κρατοῦσι χρεὼν τῷ Χριστωνύμῳ πληρώματι συνεισάγειν πρὸ ἄλλου παντός, ἀπαιτεῖν πρεπωδέστατον ἔργα καὶ πίστιν τὴν εἰς Θεὸν τὰ ἀνόθευτα,
καὶ ταῦτα δραστικώτερον ἐκδικεῖν, εἰ ταῦτα παραβαθεῖεν, ὡς διακόνους Θεοῦ φοροῦντας τὴν μάχαιραν, ἐκδίκους τῷ τὸ
55 κακὸν πράσσοντι εἰς ὀργήν, μετρούντων οἷα καὶ ὅσα διὰ παράβασιν ἐντολῶν καὶ νόμων Θεοῦ ἀνθρώποις συνήντησε.

διὰ τί γάρ, τὴν πίστιν χωρὶς τῶν ἔργων νεκρὰν ἐπιστάμενοι, μὴ τῶν θεαρέστων ἔργων ἐπιμελώμεθα, ἀλλ' ὥσπερ εἰ μὴ ἀνέμενε
κρίσις καὶ ἀνταπόδοσις Γεέννης καὶ βασιλείας, ὦ ζημίας!, πολιτευόμεθα;
60 καὶ ταῦτα εἰδότων τῶν καὶ ποσῶς [fol. 83ʳ] συνιέντων τοὺς αἰδεσθέντας
ἀρχῆθεν Θεὸν καὶ τιμήσαντας κἀνταῦθα δοξαζομένους, καὶ αἰωνίαν
τὴν τούτων μνήμην καὶ ἀνέκφραστον τὴν ἀποκειμένην μακαριότητα, τοὺς
δέ γε ἐν ἀφοβίᾳ Θεοῦ καὶ σκότῳ βαθεῖ ἐκδεδωκότας αὑτούς, καὶ πρὸς φῶς
μετανοίας ἀνανῆψαι μὴ βουληθέντας, εἰ καὶ βίου ἀπάτῃ ἐξυψωθέντας ἐδό-
65 κει, ἀλλὰ μετ' ἤχου αὐτῶν καὶ ἡ μνήμη ἀπώλετο. μὴ βουλομένων ἡμῶν ἐνωτίζεσθαι ἃ διὰ προφητῶν Θεὸς ἐνετείλατο, ἃ διὰ τῶν
ἁγίων εὐαγγελίων καὶ ἀποστόλων καὶ διδασκάλων (τίνα γὰρ εἰς συναίσθησιν μὴ ἀγάγῃ τὰ ἱερὰ λόγια, ἔχουσι Μωσέα καὶ τοὺς προφήτας,
ἀκουέτωσαν αὐτῶν καὶ ζησάτωσαν;), πάντως οἱ παρακούοντες πόθεν
70 ζησόμεθα; ὡς γὰρ ὀφθαλμοὶ Κυρίου ἐπὶ δικαίους, καὶ τὰ ἑξῆς·
οὕτω καὶ πρόσωπον Κυρίου ἐπὶ ποιοῦντας κακά, τοῦ
ἐξολοθρεῦσαι ἐκ γῆς αὐτῶν τὰ μνημόσυνα, καὶ εἰς μνημόσυνον αἰώνιον ἔσται δίκαιος· οὐ φοβηθήσεται γὰρ
ἀπὸ ἀκοῆς πονηρᾶς, καὶ μακάριος ἀνὴρ ὁ φοβούμενος
75 τὸν Κύριον· ἐν γὰρ ταῖς αὐτοῦ ἐντολαῖς θελήσει σφόδρα.

ἔνθεν παρασυρόμενοι οἱ πιστοί, ὡς ἵνα μὴ σὺν τῷ κόσμῳ
κατακριθῶμεν παιδευόμενοι, οὐδ' ὅπως ἐπιστρεφόμεθα· ἐξ ὧν καὶ
μυκτηρισμὸς καὶ χλεύη τοῖς κύκλῳ ἡμῶν γεγενήμεθα. καὶ οὐδὲ ἀπό γε
τοῦ νῦν, ὦ τῆς ἀναισθησίας!, διακενῆς ἀνομεῖν πεφροντίκαμεν, καὶ μακρὰν
80 γεγονότες δι' ἁμαρτίας ἐνεργουμένας ἀπὸ Θεοῦ, ἐν καιρῷ ἀναγκῶν, ὡς
τῶν θείων ἀνελλιπῶς προσταγμάτων ἐκπληρωταί, «εἰς ἀντίληψιν», λέγομεν, «ἀνάστηθι, Κύριε», ὃν οὐ φιλοῦμεν (ὁ γὰρ μὴ ἀγαπῶν με,
φησίν, οὐ τηρεῖ τοὺς λόγους μου), οὗ μὴ στέργομεν, οὗ μὴ

53–55 cf. Rom. 13:4 ‖ 57 cf. Jac. 2:26 ‖ 61 cf. I Reg. 2:30 ‖ 65 Ps. 9:7 ‖ 68–69 Luc. 16:29 ‖
70 Ps. 33 (34):16 ‖ 71–72 Ps. 33(34):17 ‖ 72–74 Ps. 111(112):6–7 ‖ 74–75 Ps. 111(112):1 ‖
76–77 I Cor. 11:32 ‖ 82–83 Joh. 14:24

48 ἐπιστρέφομεν SP ‖ 49 ἐτρέχομεν] καὶ τρέχομεν SP ‖ ἐγγυωμένοις S ‖ 53 εἰ] καὶ
codd. ‖ 54 φοροῦντες P ‖ 70 ζησώμεθα P ‖ 78 νυκτηρισμὸς P

110

we would change our ways as a result of this punishment, either fearing or respecting the judgment of the One God, and would hasten toward repentance, since without any doubt repentance would guarantee prosperity and salvation and every blessing in this world.

Rulers should bring these ⟨truths⟩ to the Christian people before anything else, and should demand most fittingly sincere works and faith in God, and should exact punishment most vigorously, if these principles should be transgressed, as «ministers of God who bear the sword, revengers to execute wrath upon him that doeth evil», taking into account the number and kind ⟨of punishments⟩ that have befallen mankind because of its transgression of the commandments and laws of God.

When we know «that faith without works is dead», why don't we take care to act as is pleasing unto God, but, O woe, behave as if no ⟨Day of⟩ Judgment and the reward of Hell or the kingdom ⟨of heaven⟩ awaited us ? Especially when people of any intelligence realize that those who have revered and honored God from of old «are glorified» in this world, and that they will be remembered eternally, and that ineffable blessedness awaits them, but as for those who have delivered themselves into the depths of darkness in their lack of fear of God, and who are not willing to come to their senses ⟨and move⟩ toward the light of repentance, even if in the deceit of life they thought they were exalted, still «their memory has been destroyed with a noise». Since we are not willing to listen to what God has commanded through His prophets, and through the holy Gospels and apostles and teachers (for who is not led to understanding by the holy passage, «they have Moses and the prophets; let them hear them» and live ?), and are completely disobedient, how shall we live ? For, as ⟨the saying goes⟩, «The eyes of the Lord are over the righteous», and so forth, so also ⟨that other one⟩, «The face of the Lord is against them that do evil, to destroy their memorials from the earth», and «The righteous shall be in everlasting remembrance, he shall not be afraid of any evil report», and «Blessed is the man that fears the Lord : he will delight greatly in His commandments».

Therefore we faithful are being swept away, since we do not repent in any way, although we are punished so «that we should not be condemned with the world»; and thus we are mocked and scorned by those around us. And even now we have not realized that we are senselessly transgressing the law (O what blindness!), and, although we are estranged from God because of the sins we have committed, at the time of need, as if we had unfailingly kept His holy commandments, we say, «Arise to help ⟨us⟩, O Lord», even though we do not love Him (for He says «he that loveth me not keepeth not my sayings»), nor do we respect or fear Him, or heed His threats and command-

276

110

τρέμομεν, οὗ οὐκ ἐνωτιζόμεθα ἀπειλῶν ἢ ἐπαγγελιῶν. ἐν τούτοις
85 εὑρισκομένων ἡμῶν, εἰ ἐν ζῶσιν ἐσμὲν ἠγνοήκαμεν, καὶ μᾶλλον ὡς καὶ
μηδὲν ἐνεργούμενον πρὸς ἐπιστροφὴν ἀποβλέποντες, ἀλλὰ πάντας καὶ
πάντα ἐπὶ τὸ χεῖρον προκόπτοντα. κἀντεῦθεν ὡς οἶμαι ἀρίστως
ὁρῶσα δονεῖσθαι τὸ πᾶν, ὡς δύναμις ποιουμένη τὴν ἄλλην ἀνήκουσαν
μεταχείρισιν, καὶ πρὸς τῆς ἐκκλησίας ἐντεύξεις αἰτεῖς καὶ παρακελεύῃ
90 καὶ προσευχάς· καὶ εὖ γε τῆς πεποιθήσεως, ἀλλ᾽ ὅρα, θεόστεπτε, καὶ τὸ
προσιστάμενον τοῖς γὰρ τὸν ὕψιστον τιθεμένοις καταφυγήν,
ἀφθάστῳ σπουδῇ προεκκλίνειν ἀπὸ κακοῦ καὶ ποιεῖν ἀγαθόν,
μὴ τάχα [fol. 83ᵛ] καὶ ἀκουσαίμεθα τί με λέγετε Κύριε, Κύριε,
καὶ οὐ ποιεῖτε ἃ λέγω ὑμῖν;
95   εἰ γάρ που μὴ εἰσενέγκωμεν τὸ ἡμέτερον, ἀλλὰ μόνον ἐκλιπαροῦ-
μεν, εἰ τάχα καὶ λιπαροῦμεν, τοιοῦτον δοκῶ τὸ ἐγχείρημα, ὡς εἴ τινι τῶν
ἀρίστων ποτὲ ἰητρῶν, ἀκμαία πλευρῖτις ἀνδρὶ εὐεκτοῦντι καὶ ἰσχυρῷ καὶ
νεάζοντι συμπεσοῦσα, ἐπέτρεψέ τις ἐξουσιάζων μὴ ἅψασθαι ὕδατος, ἀλλ᾽
οἴνου ἀκράτου κατακόρως κορέννυσθαι, μήτε φλέβα τοῦ τεμεῖν, μήτε
100 τῶν ῥύσιν ῥαγδαίαν ἀνακοπτόντων αἱματηράν, ἢ ὅσα τῇ τέχνῃ πρὸς
ἀναχαίτισιν τοῦ νοσήματος ἐξευρέθη ποσῶς καταπράξασθαι, καὶ οὕτω
διακειμένου τοῦ κάμνοντος, ἀπαιτεῖν πρὸς τοῦ ἰητροῦ ἀσφαλῆ καὶ ταχεῖαν
τὴν ἴασιν. εἰ οὗτος οὐ τῶν τυχόντων, ἀλλὰ καὶ τῶν ἐξησκημένων εἰς ἄκρον
τὰ Εὐκλείδου καὶ Γαληνοῦ, οὐ πρὸς χλεύην καὶ κόπον κενὸν ἀπέβλεπε τοῦ
105 τεχνίτου καὶ κωμῳδίαν καὶ γέλωτα καὶ τῆς νόσου ἐπίτασιν;
        εἰ γάρ τις καὶ νῦν εἰρήνην καὶ εὐστάθειαν τῷ κόσμῳ αἰτεῖ, καὶ πάν-
των καταβολὴν πολεμίων, πῶς καὶ εἰσακουσθήσεται, παροργίζων τοῖς
ἐναντίοις ἀπὸ μικροῦ ἕως μεγάλου τῷ διδόντι τῷ εὐχομένῳ
εὐχήν, ἀναιδῶς ἐνεργούμενα πρόπτον τὰ Θεῷ ἐπαχθῆ καὶ μηδενὸς ἀνα-
110 κόπτοντος, πορνείας καὶ ἁρπαγάς, μοιχείας, ἀρρητουργίας καὶ γοητείας,
ἀδικίας καὶ ψεύδη, ἀκαθαρσίας καὶ πενήτων ἐκπιεσμούς, καὶ ὅσα θεομη-
νίαν ἢ καὶ πανωλεθρίαν ἐπεσπάσατο κατὰ γενεάς; ἐν τούτοις τίς ἐπετίμη-
σεν ἢ ἀνεχαίτισεν ἐξ αὐτοῦ ἢ τοῦ γείτονος; ἃ ἕως καὶ ἐνεργοῦνται, οὐδ᾽ εἰ
κατὰ τὸν ἱερὸν ἐκεῖνον Ἱερεμίαν ηὑρίσκετό τις, εἰ μὴ βλέψομεν πρὸς
115 μετάνοιαν, εἰσηκούσθη· ὅπου κἀκεῖνος, τῇ συμφορᾷ καμπτομένου τοῦ
γένους, καὶ πλεῖστα λιταζομένου, ὀδυνώδους ἐπέτυχεν ἀποκρίσεως,
καὶ σὺ μὴ προσεύχου περὶ τοῦ λαοῦ τούτου, ὅτι οὐκ
εἰσακούσομαί σου· ἢ οὐχ ὁρᾷς τί αὐτοὶ ποιοῦσιν ἐν ταῖς
πόλεσιν Ἰούδα, καὶ ἐν ταῖς διόδοις Ἱερουσαλήμ; ὅτι
120 μηδὲ ἰσχύειν δικαίου εὐχὴν μὴ ἐνεργουμένην ἠκούσαμεν.

---

87 cf. II Tim.3:13 ‖ 91 cf. Ps. 90(91):9 ‖ 92 cf. Ps. 33(34):15 ‖ 93–94 cf. Luc. 6:46 ‖
108–109 I Reg. 2:9 ‖ 117–119 Jer. 7:16–17 ‖ 120 cf. Jac. 5:16

---

88 δονεῖσθαι] δωρεῖσθαι P ‖ 96 εἰ τάχα καὶ λιπαροῦμεν om. P ‖ 112 ἢ om.   S ‖ 115
κἀκεῖνος V¹S:κἀκείνου VP

110

ments. When we find ourselves like this, we don't know if we are even among the living, especially since we see nothing done with a view to repentance, but everyone and everything «waxing worse and worse». And therefore I think that it is for the best, when you, ⟨O emperor⟩, see everything in a state of turmoil, that, after taking other appropriate measures to the best of your ability, you request and encourage prayers and intercessions on the part of the Church. And praised be your confidence, but consider, O divinely crowned one, the obligation of those «who make the most High their refuge» to «turn away from wickedness and do good» with unrivalled zeal, lest we hear ⟨the words⟩, «Why call ye me, Lord, Lord, and do not the things which I say unto you ?».

For if we do not contribute our share ⟨of good deeds⟩, but only make earnest prayers, if indeed we do pray, I think that such an endeavor is ⟨as fruitless⟩ as if ⟨the following happened to⟩ one of the best doctors ever: a young man, who was strong and in good condition, was stricken with severe pleurisy; and some man in authority bade the patient not to touch water, but to quench his thirst liberally with undiluted wine, and did not allow ⟨the doctor⟩ to cut his veins, or ⟨do anything⟩ to check the uncontrolled flow of blood, or to use any remedy which has been devised by the ⟨medical⟩ profession to control the disease; then, when the ill man was in this condition, that man asked our doctor to bring about a sure and speedy recovery. If this ⟨doctor⟩ were not a hack, but a man well versed in the works of Euclid and Galen, wouldn't he regard that «specialist» as an object of ridicule and derision and laughter, whose efforts were in vain, and even aggravated the disease ?

And if at the present time we entreat for peace and tranquillity in the world, and the suppression of all enemies, how will we be heeded, when ⟨all of us⟩, young and old, provoke to anger with contrary acts «the One Who answers the prayers of suppliants», and when no one checks shameless actions which are clearly repugnant to God, fornication and rape, adultery, acts of lewdness and sorcery, injustice and falsehood, depravity and oppression of the poor, and whatsoever has brought divine wrath or total destruction throughout the ages ? Who has rebuked or restrained either himself or his neighbor in such actions ? And as long as they are continued, even if someone like holy Jeremiah of old should be found, he would not be heeded, unless we repent. Even he, when, overwhelmed by the misfortune of his people, he was praying constantly, received the grievous reply: «Pray not for this people, for I will not hearken unto thee. Seest thou not what they do in the cities of Juda, and in the streets of Jerusalem ?». For we have heard that «the ineffectual prayer of a righteous man availeth not».

εἰ οὖν δράμωμεν πρὸς ἐπιστροφήν, παυσάμενοι τῶν αἰσχρῶν, εἰ γὰρ θέλετε καὶ εἰσακούσετέ μου, φησί, τὰ ἀγαθὰ τῆς γῆς φάγεσθε, σπεύσωμεν, ἀξιῶ, τὸ ἐπόμενον ἐκφευξόμενοι. ἐπι- στράφητε πρός με, οὐ λόγῳ καὶ μόνῳ ἀλλ' ἔργῳ, καὶ ἐπιστραφή- 125 σομαι πρὸς ὑμᾶς. πόσης εὐκλείας, τὸ καὶ τὰ τῇδε ἡμᾶς κερδῆσαι καὶ τὰ αἰώνια, καὶ πόσης, ὤ, συμφορᾶς ἀμφοτέρων διαπεσεῖν! [fol. 84ʳ] μὴ ἀπατώμεθα, σπείροντες φαῦλα, ποτὲ θερίσαι χρηστά. εἰ μὴ βλέψομεν πρὸς διόρθωσιν, τίς ὁ ἡμῶν προστησόμενος; Νῶε, φησί, καὶ Δανιὴλ καὶ 'Ιὼβ θυγατέρας αὐτῶν καὶ υἱοὺς παράνομα δρῶντας 130 οὐ μὴ ἐξέλωνται τῆς κολάσεως. διὰ τοῦτο ζητήσωμεν τὸν Θεόν· ἐγγύς, φησί, Κύριος πᾶσι τοῖς ἐπικαλουμένοις αὐτὸν ἐν ἀληθείᾳ. διαναστήσωμεν οὖν ἔργῳ καὶ λόγῳ ἀλλήλους πρὸς τὴν ἐν νόμῳ ζωήν, ὡς γὰρ ἐπιστρέψομεν πρὸς αὐτὸν τὰς καρδίας, οὕτω λαλήσει εἰρήνην ἐπὶ τὸν τούτου λαόν, καὶ σωτηρίαν 135 καὶ σύνεσιν καὶ ἰσχὺν τοῖς βασιλεῦσιν ἡμῶν.

τοὺς ἄρξαντας ἐξ αἰῶνος σκοπήσωμεν, ὅπως οἱ θεαρέστως βιώσαν- τες, εὐκλεέστατοι· οἱ δ' ἔξω σκοποῦ τοῦ αὐτοὺς βασιλεύσαντος ἀπάτῃ κλα- πέντες τοῦ βίου διέπρεψαν, κατεπόθησαν ἀδοξίᾳ καὶ αἰωνίῳ πυρὶ κατὰ τὸν ἀποτηγανιζόμενον πλούσιον. πόση γὰρ δόξα τοῖς βασιλεῦσι τοῖς τὴν 140 ἐμπιστευθεῖσαν αὐτοῖς ἐξουσίαν ὡς φίλον τῷ παρασχόντι καθυπουργήσα- σι, τῶν ἀπ' αἰῶνος ἀνθρώπων καὶ ἀγγέλων ἐνώπιον εὖ δοῦλε ἀγαθὲ καὶ πιστὲ ἀκουσομένοις αὐτοῖς πρὸς Θεοῦ!

αἰδεσθῶμεν καὶ φοβηθῶμεν Θεόν, ἀγαπήσωμεν, ἀγαπώμενοι, διψῶντος καὶ ἀγαπῶντος ἡμῶν τὴν ἐπιστροφήν. ἀκουσθήτω τῇ μεθ' ἡμᾶς 145 γενεᾷ καὶ περὶ ἡμῶν τὸ καὶ εἶδε, φησίν, ὁ Θεὸς ἐπὶ Νινευϊτῶν, ἐπειδὴ ἐκ τῶν πονηριῶν αὐτῶν ἀπέστρεψεν ἕκαστος καὶ ἀπὸ τῆς ἀδικίας τῆς ἐν χερσὶν αὐτῶν, καὶ μετεμε- λήθη ἐπὶ τῇ κακίᾳ ᾗ ἐλάλησε τοῦ ποιῆσαι αὐτοῖς. ἐγ- γίσωμεν τούτῳ δι' ἔργων καὶ ἐγγιεῖ ἡμῖν: οὗ καὶ ἀξιωθείημεν, 150 βασιλεῖς καὶ λαός, πρεσβείαις τῆς πανυμνήτου Δεσποίνης ἡμῶν καὶ Κυρίας καὶ Θεοτόκου, καὶ πάντων τῶν ἀπ' αἰῶνος ἁγίων εὐχαῖς, βασι- λέων ὁ συνετώτατος καὶ ἐπιεικέστερος.

121–123 Is. 1:19 ‖ 123–125 Zach. 1:3 ‖ 128–130 cf. Ez. 14:20 ‖ 131–132 Ps. 144(145):18 ‖ 133–134 cf. Ps. 84(85):9 ‖ 139 cf. Luc. 16:19ff. ‖ 141–142 cf. Matt. 25:21, 23 ‖ 145–148 cf. Jon. 3:8, 10 ‖ 148–149 cf. Jac. 4:8

---

130 ζητήσομεν P ‖ 137 οἷ] οἱ codd. ‖ 139 δόξῃ P ‖ 151 καὶ¹ om. S

110

If then we hasten toward repentance, and cease our shameful acts, ⟨after hearing⟩ the words, «If ye be willing and hearken unto me, ye shall eat the good of the land», I beg of you, let us strive to avoid ⟨the threat⟩ which follows. «Turn to me» not in word alone, but in deed, «and I will turn to you». What glory for us to gain both life here on earth and eternal life, and what misfortune to be deprived of both! Let us not deceive ourselves that by sowing evil, we will some day reap good. If we do not try to mend our ways, who will be our guardian? «Not even Noah and Daniel and Job», says the Lord, «can save from hell their sons and daughters who have acted unlawfully». Therefore let us seek God; «the Lord is near», it is said, «to all that call upon Him in truth». Therefore let us rouse each other with words and deeds to a law-abiding existence, for as «we turn our hearts toward Him, thus will He speak peace to His people», and salvation and wisdom and strength to our emperors.

Let us reflect on the rulers from the beginning of the world, how those who lived in a manner pleasing to God achieved the greatest glory; but those who, contrary to the purpose of the One Who made them to rule, distinguished themselves by being seduced by life's deceit, were swallowed up in disgrace and eternal fire, like the rich man who roasts ⟨in hell⟩. How glorious it is for emperors, who have used the authority entrusted to them in a manner pleasing to the One Who granted it, to hear from God, «Well done, thou good and faithful servant», in the presence of men and angels from the time the world began!

Let us revere and fear God, let us love Him, my beloved, since He anxiously awaits and desires our repentance. And let the generation which succeeds us hear about us what was said of the Ninevites, that «God saw ⟨their works⟩, when they turned each one from their evil ways, and from the iniquity that was in their hands, and He repented of the evil which He had said He would do to them». «Let us draw nigh unto Him» through our works, «and He will draw nigh unto us». And may we, emperors and people alike, be deemed worthy of Him, through the intercessions of our eternally celebrated Mistress and Lady, the Mother of God, and through the prayers of all the saints from the beginning of the world, O most wise and equitable of emperors.

111. Παραίτησις τῆς πρώτης πατριαρχείας αὐτοῦ

Τῆς Χριστοῦ ἐκκλησίας οἷς αὐτὸς οἶδε κρίμασι τὴν φροντίδα
δεξάμενοι, οὐκ ἐξησφαλίσθημεν τοῦ μήτε τοὺς σχιζομένους τῆς ἐκκλησίας Χριστοῦ καὶ ὑβριστὰς αὐτοῦ τιμωρεῖν, μήτε τοὺς ἀκαθαρσίαις,
5 μοιχείαις τε καὶ πορνείαις ἑαλωκότας ἀναχαιτίζειν. ἠγνοήσαμεν δὲ ὅτι καὶ
τὰ πονηρὰ ἀντὶ ἀγαθῶν ἀντιστρόφως οἱ φαῦλοι ἀνταποδιδόναι προαιρούμενοι τοῖς ἄρχουσιν, ὡς ἐννόμως ζῆν ἀναγκάζοντας, [fol. 84ᵛ] καιροῦ
δραξάμενοι, ἀπηνεῖς εἰσπράττονται δίκας αὐτούς, ἐν οἷς ποτὲ διῳκήκασι·
καὶ ταῦτα μηδὲ τοῖς ἐνεργοῦσι σήμερον τὰ δημόσια τοιαύτας ἐν οἷς
10 ἐνήργησαν ὑπεχόντων εὐθύνας, ὅσα ἢ κακοτρόπῳ γνώμῃ ἢ ἀγνοίᾳ κατὰ
τοῦ δικαίου πεπαρῳνήκασιν. ἀλλ᾽, ὦ τῶν ἐμῶν κακῶν!, ὡς μηδὲ κἂν ἴσα
τούτοις ἐξισωθῆναι καὶ τὰ ἡμέτερα. καὶ εἰ καὶ πόθεν ταῦτα ἐπῆλθεν ἡμῖν,
ἄδηλα τοῖς πολλοῖς, ἀλλ᾽ οὐχὶ καὶ τῷ Θεῷ. ὁ γὰρ εἰπεῖν παρρησιασά-
μενος πρὸς Θεόν, ὁ ζῆλος τοῦ οἴκου σου κατέφαγέ με,
15 εἶπε καὶ τὸ οἱ ὀνειδισμοὶ τῶν ὀνειδιζόντων σε ἐπέπεσον
ἐπ᾽ ἐμέ. οὐδὲ γὰρ ἡμετέρων μόνον ταῦτα σφαλμάτων ἀντέκτισις, καὶ
χάρις Θεῷ. καὶ ἡμεῖς μὲν ἀδικούμενοι οὕτως, οὐκ ἀδικούμεθα, ὅτι τὸν
μὴ ἑαυτὸν ἀδικοῦντα, οὐδεὶς δύναται παραβλάψαι· ἡ

111: 14–16 Ps. 68(69):10 ‖ 17–18 Joh. Chrys., *Liber quod qui seipsum non laedit, nemo
laedere possit*, PG, LII, 459–460

111: V 84ʳ–85ʳ. S 234ᵛ–236ʳ. P 103ʳ–104ᵛ. Ed. Boivin, *Notae ad Nicephorum
Gregoram*, 757–758; Banduri, *Imperium Orientale*, II, 968; Migne, PG, CXLII, 479–484.
Pantokrator 251, ed. Athanasios Pantokratorinos, Θρακικά, 13 (1940), 96–97 (=K);
Iberon 50 (=A) et Barberini VI (22) (=B), ed. Papadopoulos-Kerameus, *Theoctisti
Vita Ath.*, 28–30. Cf. Pachymeres, *Hist.*, II, 169–175 (=Pach.).
2 post τῆς add. γὰρ Pach. ‖ 3 δεξάμενος K ‖ ἐξησφαλισάμεθα KAB ‖ τοῦ] τὸ K ‖
4 αὐτοῦ] αὐτῆς Pach.; om. K ‖ 5 ἠγνοήκαμεν A ‖ 5–8 καὶ τὰ πονηρά ... διῳκήκασι] καὶ
οἱ πατριαρχεύοντες τοιαύτας εὐθύνας ὑπέχουσι παρὰ τῶν ἐπὶ σφάλμασιν αὐτῶν εὐθυνθέντων
καὶ τῶν τούτοις ὁμοίων εἰς ἃ διῳκήκασι Pach. ‖ 6–7 προαιρούμενοι om. VSPAB ‖ 7 ante
καιροῦ add. καὶ K ‖ 8 ἐν] ἀφ᾽ K ‖ 9 τῶν ἐνεργούντων K ‖ ἐν om. KAB ‖ οἷς] αἷς K ‖
10 ὑπεσχόντων K ‖ post ἢ² add. καὶ Pach. ‖ 12 καὶ³ om. K ‖ ταῦτ᾽ K ‖ 13 ἃ δῆλα K ‖
τῷ om. Pach. ‖ εἰπὼν Pach. ‖ 14 post Θεὸν add. ὅτι Pach. ‖ 15 τὸ om. Pach. ‖ 16 οὐδὲ]
οὐ Pach. ‖ μόνον ταῦτα σφαλμάτων] σφαλμάτων ταῦτα μόνον K ‖ μόνον om. Pach. ‖ 17 καὶ
om. Pach. ‖ οὐκ om. Pach.

111: 2 Pachymeris *Historia* (II, 169–170) huius epistolae alium initium praebet: δύο
τινὰ ἐφάνη πρὸς καταβολὴν τῆς ἐκκλησίας, εἰς ὠφέλειαν δῆθεν αὐτῆς ἐπινοηθέντα, ἐξ ἐπιβου-
λῆς τῶν ἐπιχαιρόντων τοιούτοις, ἐν μὲν τὸ τὸν Βέκκον ἐλθεῖν εἰς τὸ διαλεχθῆναι καὶ τάχα κα-
ταγνωσθῆναι καὶ ἡττηθῆναι, ὃ ἀμήχανον ἦν τοῦ λαοῦ μεμηνότος καὶ τὸ γλυκὺ πικρὸν ἐχόντων
τε καὶ λεγόντων, δεύτερον, ἡνίκα τῷ Ὑακίνθῳ ἐξερωρήθη ἁπανταχοῦ τῆς Ῥωμαίων προσκαλεῖσθαι κατὰ τῆς ἐκκλησίας οὓς εὕρισκεν οὐ συνειδήσει, οὐ νόμοις θεοῦ τεθραμμένους,
ἀλλ᾽ ἀγυρτώδεις καὶ τριωβολιμαίους τινάς, καὶ ἱκανοὺς καταστρέψαι τὴν ἐκκλησίαν Χριστοῦ,
καὶ ὅσα παρέλαβεν, ἀλόγῳ θράσει καὶ διαβολῇ καὶ ὕβρει, ἐν οἷς εἶχον ἐκεῖνοι τὸ ἰσχυρόν. καὶ
ἔτι, ὡς ἔοικεν, ἔμελλε τοῖς δυσὶν ἐκείνοις κακοῖς καὶ τρίτον ἀναφυῆναι, ὃ καὶ διὰ πλῆθος
ἡμετέρων ἁμαρτιῶν τῇ ἡμετέρᾳ συνέβη ἡμέρᾳ καὶ καθ᾽ ἡμῶν ἐστρατεύσατο· τῆς γὰρ Χριστοῦ
ἐκκλησίας οἷς αὐτὸς οἶδε κρίμασι τὴν φροντίδα δεξάμενοι, κτλ.

111

111. Resignation from his first patriarchate

When I took charge of the Church of Christ (by a decision whereof He Himself knows the reasons), I did not make sure either to punish those who were in schism with the Church of Christ and abused Him, or to restrain those who were caught in wanton acts of adultery and fornication. For I did not realize that base people choose to repay their rulers in an opposite manner, i.e. with evil for good; because ⟨these spiritual rulers⟩ forced them to live within the bounds of the law, those cruel people, whenever they can seize the opportunity, bring ⟨the rulers⟩ to trial about their former administration. ⟨They do this⟩ even though these days government officials don't have to give such an accounting for their operations, for the abuses of justice which they have perpetrated either through evil intentions or ignorance. But, alas for my misfortune, my case is not the same as theirs, nor can it even be compared. And even if the masses don't understand how these events befell me, God understands. For he who ventured to say to God, «the zeal of thine house has eaten me up», also said, «the reproaches of them that reproached thee are fallen upon me». For these events are not retribution for my sins alone, thanks be to God. And although I may be a victim of injustice, I am not in fact wronged, because «no one can harm a person who does not wrong him-

ἐκκλησία δὲ πάλιν ὑβρίσθη καὶ ἐζημίωται. τίς δὲ ἡ ζημία; τῶν μοναχῶν
20 καὶ μοναζουσῶν καὶ τοῦ λοιποῦ Χριστωνύμου λαοῦ, τῶν μὲν λόγῳ,
τῶν δὲ καὶ βίᾳ βλεψάντων πρὸς τὸ σεμνότερον, ὡς καταιγὶς ἀγρία ἀθρόον
ἐπεισπεσοῦσα, ἡ καθ' ἡμῶν ὕβρις πρὸς τὰ πρότερα ἔτρεψεν. ἡ δὲ ὕβρις καὶ
τὸ αὐτῆς λυπηρόν, τὸ μὴ κατὰ τῆς αὐτῶν ὑπολήψεως μόνον, καὶ τὸ λίθους κρατῆσαι βαλεῖν ἡμᾶς καὶ ἀναθεματίσαι, καὶ ὅσα σωματικῆς
25 ἐστιν ὕβρεως ἐπειπεῖν, ἀλλ', οἴμοι!, καὶ κατ' αὐτοῦ τοῦ σεβάσματος.
δι' ὃ καὶ φημί, εἰ ἐφρόνησα πώποτε ἢ φρονῶ ἢ φρονήσω τῆς ἁγίας
Χριστοῦ τοῦ Θεοῦ ἐκκλησίας ἀλλότριον φρόνημα, ἀνάθεμά μοι ἀπὸ Χριστοῦ τοῦ Θεοῦ καὶ παντανάθεμα καὶ κατανάθεμα. εἰ δὲ ὡς οἱ τοῦ Κυρίου
μου Ἰησοῦ ἐδογμάτισαν καὶ παραδεδώκασιν ἅγιοι μαθηταὶ καὶ ἀπόστολοι,
30 καὶ οἱ τούτων διάδοχοι θεοφόροι πατέρες, καὶ ὡς ἡ ἁγία ἐκκλησία Χριστοῦ
τοῦ Θεοῦ ἡμῶν ἐδέξατο, πιστεύω καὶ προσκυνῶ καὶ δέχομαι καὶ ἀσπάζο-
μαι καὶ κηρύττω, εἴ τι δὲ ταύτης ἐχθρὸν καὶ ἀλλότριον, παραπέμπω τῷ

---

19 δὲ² om. K ‖ 20 τοῦ om. Pach. ‖ 22 πρότερα Pach.; ἀσεμνότερα VˣBK; σεμνότερα
VSPA ‖ ἔτρεψεν] ἔστρεφεν Pach. ‖ post ἔτρεψεν add. αὐτοὺς K ‖ post δὲ add. γε K ‖
23 αὐτῶν] ἡμῶν Pach. ‖ 24 σωματικῶς K ‖ 25 ἐστιν om. Pach. ‖ 26 πώποτε] ποτε
KAB ‖ 32 ταύτης] ταύταις K ‖ καὶ] ἢ A

---

32 Pachymeris *Historia* (II, 171–173) huius epistolae aliam finem praebet: διὸ καὶ φημί,
εἰ σύνοιδα ἐμαυτῷ πορνείᾳ ἢ μοιχείᾳ ἢ ἀρρενομανίᾳ ἑαλωκέναι, καὶ εἰ ἐφρόνησα πώποτε ἢ
φρονῶ ἢ φρονήσω ἀλλότριον φρόνημα τῆς ἐκκλησίας Χριστοῦ τοῦ θεοῦ μου, ἀνάθεμά μοι
ἀπὸ Χριστοῦ, καὶ ἡ μερίς μου σὺν τῷ προδότῃ καὶ τοῖς τὸν κύριόν μου σταυρώσασιν. εἰ δὲ
ὀρθῶς καὶ πιστῶς με λατρεύοντα καὶ φρονοῦντα, καὶ ἀποβαλλόμενον ἐκ ψυχῆς ὃ μὴ δοξάζει
ἡ ἐκκλησία μηδὲ παρέλαβε, συκοφαντῆσαι οὐκ ἔφριξαν γλῶσσαι λέγειν μαθοῦσαι κακά, ὅσοι
καὶ οἵτινες εἶεν, ἔχω αὐτοὺς καθὰ ὁ κανών, καὶ ἀπὸ τῆς ζωαρχικῆς τριάδος ἀφωρισμένους.
ὅτι δὲ βιασθέντες ἀλλ' οὐ βιάσαντες ἐτέθημεν εἰς τὴν ἐκκλησίαν, ἐλπίδι εἰρήνης καὶ ὠφελείας κοινῆς, οὐ προέβη δὲ κατὰ τὰς ἐλπίδας ὅσον διωκήσαμεν, οὕτω συμφέρον ἡμῖν κατε-
φαίνετο, μάρτυς θεός, καὶ ὃ μὴ ὡς κακὸν ἀλλ' ὡς πρέπον ἐπράττομεν. πλὴν εἰ ἐν ᾧ μέτρῳ
μετροῦμεν ἀντιμετρηθησόμεθα, τὴν τούτων διάκρισιν ἀνατίθημι τῷ ἁγίῳ βασιλεῖ καὶ τοῖς
ἀρχιερεῦσι ἐνώπιον τοῦ θεοῦ, καὶ εἴτε ἀποδοχῆς εἴτε εὐθύνης κριθῶμεν, στέργομεν, καὶ ὡς
ἐκ θεοῦ τὴν τῶν τούτων κέλευσιν ἐκδεχόμεθα. ἕτερον, εἰ καὶ ὁποῖόν ἐστιν ἑκάστου τὸ ἔργον
τῇ ἡμέρᾳ ἐκείνῃ δηλοῦται, χάριν τῆς δυσφημίας ἣν ἐξήμεσε καθ' ἡμῶν ὁ διάβολος λέγομεν.
εἰ σύνοιδα ἐμαυτῷ πορνείᾳ ἢ μοιχείᾳ ἢ ἀρρενομανίᾳ ἑαλωκέναι, καὶ εἰ ἐφρόνησα πώποτε ἢ
φρονήσω ἀλλότριον φρόνημα καὶ ἀπᾷδον τῆς ἐκκλησίας Χριστοῦ τοῦ θεοῦ καὶ κυρίου μου,
καὶ εἰ μὴ ὡς οἱ ἅγιοι μαθηταὶ καὶ ἀπόστολοι τούτου παραδεδώκασι καὶ οἱ διάδοχοι τούτων
θεοφόροι πατέρες, ἰδικῶς καὶ συνοδικῶς, καὶ εἰ μὴ ἅπαν ἑτερόδοξον φρόνημα, ὃ μὴ παρέλαβε καὶ κρατεῖ ἡ ἐκκλησία Χριστοῦ, παραπέμπω τῷ ἀναθέματι, ἀνάθεμά μοι ἀπὸ Χριστοῦ,
καὶ ἡ μερίς μου σὺν τῷ προδότῃ καὶ τοῖς τὸν κύριόν μου σταυρώσασιν. εἰ δὲ ὀρθῶς καὶ
πιστῶς με λατρεύοντα καὶ φρονοῦντα καὶ ἀσπαζόμενον καὶ κηρύττοντα διαβολαῖς μέ τινες
τοιαύταις διέβαλον, ὅσοι καὶ οἵτινες εἶεν, ἐκκήρυκτοι τῆς ἐκκλησίας Χριστοῦ, καὶ ἀλύτῳ
ἀφορισμῷ τῷ ἀπὸ τῆς ζωαρχικῆς καὶ μακαρίας καὶ ἁγίας τριάδος ἡ μετριότης ἡμῶν
ὑποβάλλει αὐτούς, καὶ ἀρᾷ ἀναθέματος καὶ τὸν τοιούτοις παρασυρέντα εἰς τὸ βλάψαι καὶ
ἀδικῆσαί με. ὡς δὲ τοῖς ἀδίκοις καὶ βλασφήμοις αὕτη ἀρὰ παρὰ θεοῦ, οὕτω καὶ τοῖς
φειδομένοις τὴν γλῶσσαν καὶ ἀλήθειαν ἀγαπῶσι καὶ λέγουσιν ἡ τοῦ θεοῦ εὐλογία καὶ σκέπη
περικυκλώσοι καὶ ὧδε καὶ ἐν τῷ μέλλοντι.

111

self». But it is the Church that is insulted and harmed. And what is the harm ?
The abuse flung against me like a furious storm has caused a whole group of
monks, nuns and other Christians, who had been persuaded either by reason
or by force to live in a more seemly fashion, to return to their former ways.
But the most painful part of the abuse for me is that they not only attack my
own convictions, and carry stones around to throw at me, and curse me, and
inflict every physical injury one could mention, but, alas, they also ⟨outrage⟩
religion itself.

Wherefore I declare: if I have ever held, or hold now, or at any time in
the future, a belief hostile to the holy Church of Christ our God, may I suffer
anathema from Christ our God, a most inclusive anathema and the worst
anathema! But if I believe and worship and accept and embrace and proclaim
⟨the same beliefs⟩ as were laid down and handed on by the holy disciples and
apostles of my Lord Jesus, and their successors, the divinely inspired Fathers,
and as were received by the Holy Church of Christ our God, and if I send
to anathema any ⟨belief⟩ which is hostile and alien to this ⟨Church⟩, let

ἀναθέματι, οἱ κατ' ἐμοῦ ἀκονήσαντες γλώσσας, καὶ τοιαύτας
ἀθέους φωνὰς ἐρευξάμενοι διαβολῆς καὶ συκοφαντίας, ἐκκήρυκτοι οἱ τοι-
35 οῦτοι ἐκκλησίας Χριστοῦ, καὶ ἀλύτῳ ἀφορισμῷ ἐκ τῆς ζωαρχικῆς Τριάδος καὶ ἡμεῖς αὐτοὺς ὑποβάλλομεν καὶ ἀρᾷ ἀναθέματος.
    ἐπεὶ δὲ νόμος τῇ ἐκκλησίᾳ Χριστοῦ ἑκόντας ἄρχειν ἑκόν-
των, ἡμεῖς δὲ δυναστικῶς [fol. 85ʳ] ἐδόξαμεν ἄρχειν, καὶ διὰ τοῦτο ἀπώ-
σαντο, ἀπωσάμενοι τοῦ ποιμαίνεσθαι ὑφ' ἡμῶν, καὶ ἡμεῖς ποιμαίνειν αὐ-
40 τοὺς παραιτούμεθα, κατὰ τὸν εἰπόντα κλήρῳ ἀνυποτάκτῳ καὶ
λαῷ ἀπειθεῖ ἀποτάσσομαι, δεόμενος ἐκ ψυχῆς ἡμῖν τε καὶ αὐτοῖς
ἵλεων ἔσεσθαι τὸν Θεόν. τὰ δὲ ἡμέτερα ἄγοιτο ὅπου καὶ βούλοιτο ὁ ἐν
Τριάδι ὑμνούμενος Κύριος, πρεσβείαις τῆς Θεομήτορος, τῶν νοερῶν Θεοῦ
λειτουργῶν καὶ πάντων τῶν ἀπ' αἰῶνος ἁγίων ἡμῶν. καὶ οἱ ἀρχιερεῖς
45 εἰ μὲν κανονικῶς εἶπαν καὶ ἔπραξαν, καὶ δικαίως μου ἀπεκόπησαν, ἵλεως
οὕτως Θεὸς εἴη καὶ αὐτοῖς· εἰ δὲ μή, τοῖς ῥηθεῖσιν ἐπιτιμίοις ὑπεύθυνοι
ἔστωσαν, καὶ αὐτοὶ καὶ οὓς ψευδῶς ὑποσύρουσι καὶ ὑφ' ὧν παρεσύρησαν.
    εἶχε δὲ καὶ «'Αθανάσιος ἐλέῳ Θεοῦ ἀρχιεπίσκοπος Κωνσταντινου-
πόλεως Νέας 'Ρώμης, καὶ οἰκουμενικὸς πατριάρχης, ἰνδικτιῶνος ζ'».
50 εἶχε καὶ μολυβδίνην βοῦλλαν πατριαρχικὴν καὶ κάτωθεν ταῦτα· «τούτοις στοιχῶ
ἐνώπιον Θεοῦ καὶ ἀνθρώπων, τούτοις ἐμμένα. εἴ τι δὲ ἄλλο εἴπω ἢ
πράξω ἐκτὸς τῶν ὧδε γεγραμμένων, ἄστοργον ἔχω καὶ βίας καὶ τυραννίδος ἔργον, μὴ συνειδὼς ἐμαυτῷ χάριτι Χριστοῦ ἀργίας τι ἔγκλημα —
ἰνδικτιῶνος ζ' ης.»

---

33 cf. Ps. 63(64):4 ‖ 37–38 cf. I Pet. 5:2 et Greg. Naz., Or. II, ιε' (PG, XXXV, 425A) ‖
40–41 locum non inveni ‖ 48–49 cf. Pachymeres, Hist., II, 174: εἶχε γὰρ "'Αθανάσιος ἐλέῳ
Θεοῦ ἀρχιεπίσκοπος Κωνσταντινουπόλεως νέας 'Ρώμης καὶ οἰκουμενικὸς πατριάρχης." ‖
51 ff. cf. Pachymeres, Hist., II, 174–175: ἣν δ' ἔτι φερόμενον καὶ ἄλλο τι ἐν κρυπτῷ γράμματι, ὅπερ οὐκ οἶδα εἰ προσετέθη ὕστερον παρὰ τῶν ἐκείνῳ προσκειμένων, ὡς "κἂν εἴ τι
ποιήσω παρὰ ταῦτα, ἄστοργον ἔχω καὶ ἔξω τῆς ἡμετέρας γνώμης, κἂν αὐτὴν ἐγχαράξω μου
τὴν παραίτησιν."

---

34 ἐξερευξάμενοι B ‖ 35 καὶ ἀλύτῳ] ἀλύτῳ δὲ KAB ‖ 37 ἐπεὶ δὲ] ἐπειδὴ K ‖ post
ἐκκλησίᾳ om. Χριστοῦ K ‖ 40 κατὰ τὸν εἰπόντα] λέγοντες AB ‖ 40–41 κατὰ ... ἀποτάσσομαι om. K ‖ 41 ἀποτασσόμεθα AB ‖ δεόμενοι KAB ‖ ἡμῖν KAB : ὑμῖν VSP ‖
τε om. KAB ‖ 42 δ' ἡμέτερα K ‖ ὅποι K ‖ 43 ante Θεοῦ add. τοῦ K ‖ 44 ἀπ' αἰῶνος
om. KAB ‖ ἡμῶν om. KAB ‖ 45 εἴπε KAB ‖ μου om. KAB ‖ 47 παρασύρουσι KAB ‖
48 εἶχε δὲ καὶ om. KAB ‖ 49 ἰνδικτιῶνος ζ' om. KAB ‖ μολιβδίνην SP ‖ εἶχε καὶ
μολυβδίνην βοῦλλαν πατριαρχικὴν καὶ κάτωθεν ταῦτα om. KAB ‖ 52 καὶ² om. K ‖
53 μὴ συνειδὼς] οὐ γὰρ σύνοιδα K ‖ 54 ἰνδικτιῶνος ζ' ης om. KAB

111

those who «sharpen their tongues» against me, and spew forth such impious cries of slander and false accusation, be expelled from the Church of Christ, and I impose upon them indissoluble excommunication from the life-giving Trinity, and the curse of anathema.

But since it is a law of the Church of Christ for «men to rule willingly over willing subjects», and I am considered to have been ruling arbitrarily, and for this reason they have rejected me, and refused to have me for their shepherd, then I resign from being their shepherd, following the example of the man who said: «I bid farewell to an unrestrained clergy and disobedient congregation», praying from my soul that God will be gracious to me and to them. As for my own affairs, may the Lord Who is celebrated in the Trinity conduct them as He will, through the intercessions of the Mother of God, of the intelligible ministers of God and of all our saints since the beginning of the world. As for the bishops, if their words and actions have been in accordance with the canons, and if they have justly rejected me, may God be gracious unto them. Otherwise, may they be subject to the above-mentioned punishments, they themselves and those whom they have falsely misled, and those by whom they were misled.

⟨The document⟩ also read: Athanasius, by God's mercy archbishop of Constantinople, the New Rome, and Oecumenical Patriarch—7th indiction. It also had a patriarchal seal in lead, and underneath the following words: I stand by these words, in the sight of God and of men; by these words I abide. If I should say or do anything except what is written here, I consider it a heartless act of violence and usurpation, nor am I aware that there is any grounds for accusation in my abdication, thanks be to Christ—7th indiction.

286

112. Παραίτησις τῆς δευτέρας πατριαρχείας

Τῆς Χριστοῦ ἐκκλησίας οἷς αὐτὸς οἶδε κρίμασι καὶ δευτερόπρωτα
τὴν φροντίδα διαδεξάμενοι, τοῖς εἰς τοῦτο προτρεψαμένοις ἀρχιερεῦσιν
ὑμῖν (ὑμεῖς γὰρ ἐκεῖνοι), ὡς καὶ περὶ ἡμῶν προνοησαμένοις τὰ κρείττω
5 ὁ τῆς ἐκκλησίας Θεὸς ἀνταμείψαιτο, καὶ μάλιστα τῷ θεοστεφεῖ βασιλεῖ
καὶ ἁγίῳ μου αὐτοκράτορι, ἀρχῆθεν περὶ τὴν ἐκκλησίαν ἐνδειξαμένῳ
τὸν κατ᾽ἐπίγνωσιν ζῆλον καὶ σπουδὴν καὶ ἀναδοχὴν καὶ καθ᾽
ἑκάστην ἐνδεικνυμένῳ ἀρίστη φρενί· δι᾽ ἣν καὶ ἡμῶν οὐ διέλιπε κήδεσθαι,
ἐπαίνοις καὶ εὐφημίαις καταγεραίρειν, καὶ στολαῖς ἱεραρχικαῖς καὶ ἱεραῖς
10 εἰκόσι ταῖς μετὰ κόσμου καὶ εὐεργεσίαις ἀσυγκρίτως τὴν ἐκκλησίαν
καταπλουτῶν, ὡς οὔποτε τῶν πατριαρχούντων τινὸς τοιούτων ἐπαπο-
λαῦσαι πρὸς τῶν ἀνέκαθεν εὐσεβῶν καὶ ὀρθοδόξων αὐτοκρατόρων, εἰ
μήπου καὶ τὴν παρίσωσιν πρὸς τῷ τούτου πατρὶ κατὰ πνεῦμα, τῷ μεγάλῳ
φημὶ καὶ ἰσαποστόλῳ, εἰκάσειεν ἄν τις, ἐν ταῖς κατὰ τὸν ἐν ἁγίοις ἐκεῖνον
15 τιμαῖς [fol. 85ᵛ] ἱερώτατον Σίλβεστρον, εἰ κἀκείνου τὸ μέσον πρὸς
τὰ ἡμέτερα ὅσον ἀκτῖνος ἡλιακῆς τοὺς πρὸς αὐτὴν ἀτενίζοντας. δι᾽ ἃ καὶ
πλουσιοπαρόχως ἀνταμειφθείη πρὸς τοῦ Παντάνακτος καθὰ τῷ μεγάλῳ
ἐκείνῳ ἐν βασιλεῦσι τὰ γέρα, καὶ πρώτῳ ἐν ὀρθοδόξοις, ὑποστρωννύντος
καὶ τούτῳ Θεοῦ ὑπὸ πόδας αὐτοῦ τοὺς ἐχθροὺς ἴσα καὶ λεανθέντι
20 πηλῷ πλατειῶν, ἐν δέ γε τῇ βασιλείᾳ Χριστοῦ ἐκείνῳ συνευωχεῖσθαι
καὶ ἐν Θεῷ γάννυσθαι.

ἀλλ᾽ ὅπερ καὶ λέγειν ἐξώρμημαι, πρὸς τὸ τῆς ἱεραρχίας ἀνατε-
θέντες ἡμεῖς ὑψηλόν, οὔτε διηγωνίσμεθα πρὸς τὸ μέγα πρεπόντως, οὔτε
ἐδόξαμεν τοῖς πολλοῖς, ἀλλὰ καὶ δύσχρηστοι πλέον παρ᾽ ὅσον καὶ εὑρισκό-
25 μεθα. καὶ δὴ πρὸς τοῖς ἄλλοις οἷς καὶ προσωνειδίκασι τὸ ἐν ὑποκρίσει
βιοῦντας ἡμᾶς, οὐδὲ κατὰ τῆς ἁγίας καὶ ἀμωμήτου ἡμῶν πίστεως συκοφαντῆσαι ἐφείσαντο. οἷς, Θεὲ τοῦ παντός, ὁ ἐλθὼν εἰς τὸ πλάνης καὶ
ἀσεβείας βροτοὺς ἐκλυτρώσασθαι, ἐν τῇ δικαιοσύνῃ σου ἀντιμέτρησον·
καὶ ἡ ῥομφαία αὐτῶν εἰσέλθοι εἰς τὰς καρδίας αὐτῶν, εἰ
30 ἐγὼ ἐπὶ σὲ ἐπερρίφην ἀπὸ γαστρός· καὶ μᾶλλον τοῖς περὶ
τὸν Ἰάκωβον, τοῖς ἐπαράτοις καὶ πάντη θεοστυγέσιν, οἳ καὶ καθάπερ ἀπεχ-

112: 7 cf. Rom. 10:2 ‖ 19–20 cf. Ps. 17(18):43 ‖ 29 Ps. 36(37):15 ‖ 30 cf. Ps.
21(22):10–11

112: V 85ʳ–86ʳ. S 236ʳ–237ᵛ. P 104ᵛ–106ʳ. Ed. Boivin, *Notae ad Nicephorum
Gregoram*, 762–63; Banduri, *Imperium Orientale*, II, 976–978; Migne, PG, CXLII, 491–496.
Haec epistola etiam invenitur in ms. Pantokrator 251, ed. Athanasios Pantokratorinos,
Θρακικά, 13 (1940), 104–105 (=K).
3 ἀρχιερεῦσιν om. K ‖ 7 καὶ³ om. K ‖ 8 ἀρίστῳ K ‖ 9 καταγεραίρων K ‖ 13 τὸν ...
πατέρα K ‖ 13–14 τὸν μέγαν...ἰσαπόστολον K ‖ 16 δι᾽ ἅ] διὰ S ‖ 18–19 -στρωννύντος...
ἴσα καὶ om. P et scripsit ὑπολεανθέντι ‖ 19 ante πόδας add. τοὺς K ‖ 21 Θεῷ] αὐτῷ K ‖
22 ἐξώρμημα S ‖ 22–23 ἀνατιθέντες S ‖ 23 πρὸς τὸ μέγα om. K ‖ 25 καὶ² om. K ‖
26 ἁγίας καὶ om. K ‖ ἡμωμήτου P ‖ 27 ante πλάνης add. ἐκ K

112

112. Resignation from the second patriarchate

Since I received charge of the Church of Christ a second time (by a decision whereof He Himself knows the reasons), may you bishops who supported me (for you are the ones), and who provided the best for me, be rewarded by the God of our Church, and ⟨may He reward⟩ especially the God-crowned Emperor, my holy ruler, who from the first displayed «zeal according to knowledge» concerning the Church, and ardor and patronage, and showed each day that he was endowed with exceptional wisdom, on account of which he never ceased to concern himself about me, to honor me with praises and acclaim, and enriched the Church with priestly garments and ornamented sacred icons and with incomparable benefits, such as no patriarch ever enjoyed from the pious and orthodox emperors of old, unless one were to liken him to his spiritual father, the equal of the apostles I mean [Constantine], in his honors to the most holy Silvester, who is now among the saints, even if the difference between him and myself is that between a ray of the sun and those who behold it. Wherefore may he [Andrònicus] be richly rewarded by the Almighty, just as he [Constantine] who is ranked great among emperors and first among orthodox was honored by God; may He lay his [Andronicus'] enemies at his feet like «the earth which is trampled in public places», and may he [Andronicus] feast together with Him in the Kingdom of Christ and rejoice in God.

But as I started to say, when I was put upon the pinnacle of the hierarchy, I did not labor at the great task as I should have, nor did I give this appearance to the many, but appeared ⟨to them⟩ to be even more intractable than I am. And in addition to the reproaches that they made against me for living in hypocrisy, they did not even hesitate to attack my holy and blameless faith. O God of all, Who came to save men from error and impiety, requite these men in Thy justice! «Let their sword enter into their own hearts», if I «was cast on thee from the womb». And especially ⟨take vengeance on⟩ Jacob and his cohorts, accursed and despised by God. They, in their hatred

θανόμενοι τῷ ἐπὶ πάντων Θεῷ δικαιώσαντι καὶ ἡμᾶς καλεῖσθαι ἀπὸ
Χριστοῦ, καὶ μὴ ἔχοντες ὅπως ἐκεῖνον ἀμύνονται, κατὰ τῆς ἱερᾶς ἐκείνου
θεανδρικῆς καὶ προσκυνητῆς εἰκόνος, τῆς ἐρημώσεως τὰ βδελύγ-
35 ματα, ὦ τῶν ἐμῶν κακῶν, λυττῆσαι οὐκ ἔφριξαν, πρὸς δὲ καὶ τῆς παν-
αχράντου Δεσποίνης ἡμῶν Θεοτόκου καὶ τοῦ τύπου τοῦ θείου καὶ
ζωηφόρου σταυροῦ, δι' οὓς καὶ ἀνάθεμα πᾶσιν αἱρετικοῖς ἐκβοῶ ἀπὸ
Θεοῦ Παντοκράτορος, καὶ Χριστιανοκατηγόρῳ παντὶ τῷ μὴ ἀξιοχρέως
μετανοήσαντι.

40   διὰ ταῦτα καὶ τὸ ἐπιτεθὲν τῆς ἀρχιερωσύνης ἀξίωμα παραιτοῦμαι
καὶ τῆς ὑμῶν ἱερότητος δέομαι μὴ πρὸς ἐμποδισμὸν ἐνστῆναι τινά, δι' αὐτὸν τὸν Χριστόν, ὅτι μηδὲ δυνατὸν ἄλλο τι φρονῆσαι ἀπ' ἄρτι ἡμᾶς, εἴ
τι καὶ γένοιτο, ὅτι καὶ γήρᾳ καὶ ἀσθενείᾳ ταλαιπωροῦντες, οὐδὲ αὐτὸ τὸ
ὁρᾶν ἔχομεν. ἀλλὰ πρόσιτε, ἀξιῶ, τῷ ἁγίῳ μου αὐτοκράτορι ἐκδυσωπῆσαι
45 κἀκεῖνον ὑπὲρ ἐμοῦ, πλέον ἁπάντων τῆς ἐκκλησίας τὴν μέριμναν τρέφ-
οντι, συγκροτεῖν ἐξαιτοῦντες καὶ συντρέχειν ὑμῖν ἐν παντὶ καὶ μᾶλλον
εἰς ἐρεύνης πνευματικῆς ἀναζήτησιν, ὡς ἂν τὸν ἁρμόδιον ταῖς ὑμετέραις
εὐχαῖς καταπέμψοι τῇ ποίμνῃ Χριστὸς εἰς ἐπίσκεψιν ἱερέων καὶ μοναζόντων καὶ λαοῦ Χριστωνύμου τοῦ σύμπαντος. πρὸς δὲ [fol. 86ʳ] τούτοις,
50 ἐπεὶ τὸν ἐν μέσῳ εἰκὸς εὑρισκόμενον καὶ λυπεῖν καὶ λυπεῖσθαι παρὰ
τινῶν, τοὺς λυπήσαντας ὁπωσδήποτε καὶ τοὺς ὑφ' ἡμῶν λυπηθέντας
συγχωρήσεως ἀξιώσοι καὶ ἀμφοτέρους ὁ ἐπὶ τὸ σῶσαι τὸ πλάσμα φιλανθρώπως παραγενόμενος, καὶ κρατύνειε τὰ τῶν ὀρθοδόξων, καὶ σκαιωρίας
περιφυλάξοι παντοίας καὶ ποιμένας καὶ ποίμνια, ἕως τὴν γῆν ὁ ἥλιος
55 ἐφορᾷ, πρεσβείαις ἀλήκτοις τῆς τὸν ἥλιον τῆς δικαιοσύνης σωματωσάσης
Θεόν.

       τοῖς ἱερωτάτοις ἀρχιερεῦσι Θεοῦ καὶ τοῖς ἐνδοξοτάτοις τοῖς τῆς
συγκλήτου βουλῆς, καὶ τοῖς ἐντιμοτάτοις τοῦ κλήρου ἱερεῦσι καὶ μονάζουσι, τοῖς τε στρατευομένοις καὶ τοῖς τῆς πολιτείας, πλουσίοις τε καὶ
60 πενομένοις καὶ ἀνδράσι καὶ γυναιξί, πᾶσι διηνεκῶς χορηγεῖσθαι τὸ τοῦ
Θεοῦ ἐπεύχομαι ἔλεος. εἶτα καὶ πᾶσιν ἀντιβολῶ μὴ ὡς ἔτυχε προσ-
ταλαιπωρεῖν κοπιῶντας τῇ ἐν ᾗ παροικοῦμεν ἐσχατιᾷ, τῆς σοφίας Θεοῦ
ἐπάνω ὅρους κειμένης καὶ τηλαυγούσης τοὺς ἕνεκεν φωτισμοῦ πρὸς
αὐτὴν ἐπιτρέχοντας· πλὴν καὶ ὑμῖν ἀντιμετρηθείη πρὸς τοῦ τῆς ἀγάπης

34–35 Daniel 9:27 ‖ 63 cf. Matt. 5:14

34 ante θεανδρικῆς add. καὶ K ‖ 40 καὶ τὸ ἐπιτεθὲν ... παραιτοῦμαι KV, delevit Vˣ,
om. SP ‖ 41 ὑμῶν K: ἡμῶν VSP ‖ δέομαι VS¹P: δαίομαι S ‖ 42 ἡμᾶς ἀπ' ἄρτι K ‖
42–43 καὶ εἴ τι K ‖ 43 καὶ³ om. K ‖ 44 πρόσετι K ‖ 46 συγκρατεῖν K ‖ 47 ἡμετέραις
K ‖ 48 καταπέμψῃ K ‖ Χριστοῦ K ‖ 52 ἀξιώσοι K: ἀξιώσει VSP ‖ καὶ om. K ‖ 53
κρατυνεῖ codd. ‖ σκευωρίας K ‖ 54 παντοίας] πάντας K ‖ ὁ om. K ‖ 56 Θεόν] Θεοτόκου
K ‖ 57 τοῖς ἱερωτάτοις ἀρχιερεῦσι Θεοῦ ... πάντων ἁγίων σου om. K; hoc loco novam
epistolam inc. VSP ‖ 60 πᾶσι] καὶ πᾶσι Χριστιανοῖς ὀρθοδόξοις K ‖ 61 post ἔλεος caetera
om. K ‖ 63 τοὺς V¹: τῆς VSP ‖ 64 ὑμῖν] P scripsit ἡμᾶς et deinde delevit

112

of the God of all, Who deemed it right for me to be called a Christian, and not being able to work their vengeance upon Him, did not shrink from attacking His holy theandric and venerable image, «abomination of desolation» ⟨that they were⟩, (alas for my misfortunes!). And in addition ⟨they als oattacked the image of⟩ our immaculate Lady the Mother of God, and the representation of the divine and life-giving Cross; through them I pronounce anathema from God the Almighty against all heretics and against every accuser of a Christian who does not worthily repent.

For these reasons, I resign the office of archbishop with which I have been endowed, and ask, for the sake of Christ Himself, that none of you prelates stand in the way, because from now on I cannot change my mind, whatever happens, since I am wearied by old age and illness, nor am I even in possession of my sight. But I ask of you, approach my holy emperor, and entreat him on my behalf, since he cares for the Church more than anybody, and ask him to help you and coöperate with you in every way, and especially in a search of spiritual investigation, so that Christ may send to His flock a man who fits your specifications to watch over priests and monks and all Christian people. In addition, since it is probable that a man in the center of affairs [Athanasius] both grieves and is grieved by some people, may He Who came to save Creation through His love for mankind deem worthy of forgiveness both those who in any way grieved me and those who were grieved on my account. And may He uphold Orthodox Christians, and preserve from all mischief both shepherds and their flocks, as long as the sun shines on the earth, through the unceasing intercessions of the One Who gave birth to God, the Sun of Righteousness.

I pray that the mercy of God may be granted unceasingly to the most holy bishops of God, and to the most illustrious members of the senate, to the most honorable priests of the clergy and to the monks, to soldiers and civilians, to rich and poor, men and women. Then I ask of you all that you not labor without design in these last days in which we are living, since the wisdom of God «sits upon the mountain» and shines upon those who run toward it for the sake of enlightenment; but rather ⟨I wish⟩ that you be rewarded by

65 Θεοῦ ὅσον καὶ δι' ἀγάπην κεκοπιάκατε, καὶ ἡ ἀντάμειψις ἀμφοτέροις
δαψιλευθείη, ἐπεὶ καὶ ἡμεῖς τῷ περὶ ὑμᾶς ἀλύτῳ συνδούμενοι πόθῳ, οὐχ
ὡς ἔτυχε διεστήσαμεν αὐτοὺς ἀφ' ὑμῶν, ἀλλ' ὥς που ὁ μεγαλοφωνότατος
ὑποτίθεται, ἃ ὁ Θεὸς ὁ ἅγιος βεβούλευται, τίς διασκε-
δάσει; ἐκείνου γὰρ κρίναντος ἀναξίους ἡμᾶς καὶ θέας καὶ ὁμιλίας αὐτῆς
70 τῶν φιλτάτων, πειθαρχεῖν καὶ ὑμᾶς ὀφειλόμενον, ὑπερεύχεσθαι μόνον ὑμᾶς
ἐξαιτοῦντες, μὴ κἀκεῖθεν ἀποζευχθείην τῶν πρὸς Θεοῦ φιλουμένων,
καὶ φιλτάτων ὑμῶν, μεθ' ὧν, υἱὲ Θεοῦ ζωοδότα, ταῖς στρατιαῖς καὶ ἡμᾶς
συγχορεῦσαι ταῖς οὐρανίαις εὐδόκησον, πρεσβείαις τῆς σὲ τεκούσης μητρός, καὶ ἀποστόλων καὶ τῶν μαρτύρων, καὶ πάντων ἁγίων σου.

113. ⟨Τῷ ἐπὶ τῶν δεήσεων⟩

Ὁ συνήθως στελλόμενος πρὸς ἡμῶν εἰς προσκύνησιν, ἄνθρωπε τοῦ
Θεοῦ, τοῦ κρατίστου καὶ ἁγίου μου αὐτοκράτορος, ὡς ἔθος ἐλθὼν πρὸ καιροῦ καὶ προσκυνήσας καὶ ἐξελθών, ἀνέμαθε πρός τινων ζητῆσαι σὲ τὸν
5 ἅγιόν μου αὐτοκράτορα φωνηθῆναι τοῦ ὑποστρέψαι τὸν ἀδελφόν, ἕνεκεν
τοῦ ἐρωτηθῆναι πῶς τὰ περὶ τῶν ψήφων ἐφάνη ἡμῖν, καὶ εἰ ἀπεδέχθη
καὶ τί ἐλαλήσαμεν περὶ τούτου· καὶ τὸ μὲν ψήφους προβῆναι ἢ μὴ προβῆναι ἡμεῖς ἕως νῦν ἐπὶ μάρτυρι τῷ Θεῷ οὔτε ἠκούσαμεν, οὔτε εἰπεῖν
πεφροντίκαμέν τι. τοίνυν εἰ καὶ τὸν τῆς ἀντιλήψεώς σου μὴ ἴσμεν σκο-
10 πόν, τίνος χάριν ὀρέγῃ μαθεῖν πῶς ἡμῖν τὰ περὶ τῶν ψήφων δοκεῖ ἐν
καρδίᾳ, καὶ τί καὶ λαλήσομεν, ἀλλά γε ὡς περὶ σοῦ λογιζόμενοι πάντῃ καλὰ
θεῖα ὁμοῦ καὶ ἀνθρώπινα, [fol. 86ᵛ] καὶ τοῦτο τῶν τι συνοισόντων εὑρεῖν,
ἐρᾶν τοῦ εἰς γνῶσιν ἐλθεῖν κεκρίκαμεν, καὶ μᾶλλον παρορμηθέντες πρὸς
τῶν λογίων τοῦ Πατρός, ἑτοίμους εἶναι διδόναι ἡμᾶς θεσπιζόν-
15 των λόγον αἰτοῦντι παντὶ περὶ τῆς ἐλπίδος τῆς ἐν ἡμῖν,
περὶ ἧς ἅπας λόγος καὶ ἅπαν μυστήριον. ἐν καὶ τοῦτο καὶ τῶν τιμιωτέρων,
τὰ τῶν ψήφων φημί, λογιζόμενοι, τῆς πρὸς αὐτοὺς πνευματικῆς δωρεᾶς
καὶ εὐεργεσίας καὶ ἐλπίδος καὶ χάριτος, ὡς ὀρεγόμεθα καὶ φρονοῦμεν καὶ
εὐχόμεθα περὶ τούτου καὶ λέγομεν ἀριδήλως γνωρίσαι σοι, τὸ ἐφετὸν καὶ
20 ἡμῖν λογισθὲν ὡς ἐνὸν ἰδιωτικῶς ἐχαράξαμεν. καὶ εἰ προτραπῶμεν, καὶ

68–69 Is. 14:27
113: 14–15 cf. I Pet. 3:15

71 ἀποζευχθεῖεν VSP ‖ 74 ante ἁγίων add. τῶν S
113: V 86ʳ–86ᵛ. S 237ᵛ–238ᵛ. P 106ʳ–106ᵛ. Ed. Banduri, Imperium Orientale, II, 985, et Migne, PG, CXLII, 505–506.
1 γράμμα σταλὲν τῶν ἐπὶ τῶν δεήσεων περὶ τοὺς ψήφους οὓς πεποιήκασι διὰ τὸν Κυζίκου
ὅπως ποιοῦσιν αὐτὸν πατριάρχην add. VʳSP ‖ 10 πῶς] τοὺς P ‖ 17 num lege αὐτοῦ, i.e.
Dei?

112, 113

the God of love to the extent that you have labored for the sake of love, and may the reward be lavished on both ⟨you and me⟩. For I, too, bound as I am to you by indissoluble love, have not separated myself from you without design, but in a manner proclaimed by the great herald [Isaiah]: «Who will bring to nought what the holy Lord has planned ?». For since He judged me unworthy either to see or to speak with those who are dearest to me, you must obey. And I ask only that you pray for me, so that in the next world I may not be separated from you who are beloved by God and most dear to me. O lifegiving Son of God, grant that we may rejoice together with You and with the heavenly host, through the intercessions of the Mother Who begot Thee, and of the apostles and martyrs and all Thy saints.

113. ⟨To the superintendent of petitions⟩

O man of God, the man whom I usually send to do reverence to my mighty and holy emperor, some time ago, after he came as usual and did reverence and left, then learned from certain people that you had asked the holy emperor to recall the monk, so that he might be questioned about my opinion on the election, whether I accepted it and what I said about it. But, with God as my witness,⟨I swear that⟩ up to this moment I have not heard whether the election has taken place or not, nor have I taken thought to say anything. Therefore even if I do not know the purpose of your helpful involvement, why you are anxious to learn my innermost feelings about the election, and what I will say, still, since I think that everything about you is good, whether divine or human, I have decided that you are passionately desirous to learn this, and will find it something of profit, especially since I am incited by the words of the Father which decree that «we should be ready to give an answer to every man that asketh about the hope that is in us», with which every word and every mystery is concerned. And since I consider the matter of the election to be one of the most important spiritual gifts and favors and hope and grace ⟨granted⟩ to them [the bishops], I have written down on a separate sheet my wishes and opinion to the best of my ability, so as to inform you clearly of my desires, thoughts, prayers and statements on this matter.

πέμψομεν· ἃ τῇ ἐνούσῃ σοι ἀξιοῦμεν παιδεύσει τε καὶ συνέσει διεξελθόντα,
εἰ μὲν συναντῶσαν τῷ μεγαλείῳ τῶν ψήφων τὴν ἡμετέραν εὑρήσεις συναίν-
εσιν καὶ διάθεσιν καὶ διάκρισιν, δηλώσεις ἀπεριφάνως· εἰ δὲ πόρρω τοῦ
πρέποντος (οὐ γὰρ πάντων ἡ γνῶσις), ἐν ἀγάπῃ καὶ τοῦτο ἡμῖν γνω-
25 ριεῖς. κἀντεῦθεν ἡμῖν καὶ συντηρηθείης πρὸς τοῦ Θεοῦ τῆς ἀγάπης ὑγιής
τε καὶ πολυχρόνιος.

114. ⟨Τῷ ἐπὶ τῶν δεήσεων⟩

Ἔδει τοῖς τὴν ἐκλογὴν ποιουμένοις πιστοῖς τοῦ ὃν εἰς τύπον
ἔχειν Χριστοῦ, οὗ κατηξίωνται μόνου καὶ πρώτου ἀρχιερέως καὶ θύματος,
μὴ ὅλως ὀρέξει καὶ διακρίσει ἀνθρωπίνῃ ἐπιχειρεῖν, νέμεσιν ὡς εἰδότας
5 τὴν ἄνω, ἐβασίλευσαν γὰρ ἑαυτοῖς, καὶ οὐ δι’ἐμοῦ, ἦρξαν
καὶ οὐκ ἐγνώρισάν μοι, ἀλλὰ καρδίᾳ μιᾷ καὶ ὁμοφροσύνῃ καὶ ἱκεσίᾳ
εἰλικρινεῖ καὶ ἀόκνῳ τὸν θεοκρίτως ἐκεῖθεν κριθέντα ἀναμφιβόλως τοὺς
τοῦ Θεοῦ ὑποδέχεσθαι, καὶ τότε πολλὴν καὶ ἀσύγκριτον εἶναι νομίζειν
ἡμῖν τὴν ἀποδοχὴν πρὸς Θεοῦ καὶ ἀντίληψιν, ἐπ’ αὐτῷ τὰς ἐλπίδας
10 καὶ μόνῳ τὰς τῆς διπλῆς σωτηρίας καὶ πιστεύοντας καὶ ⟨μὴ⟩ σα-
λεύοντας. καὶ ὄντως πίστεως πέρα καὶ συνέσεως τὰ τοιάδε καὶ ταπεινώσεως, καθὰ καὶ τοῖς ὑπηρέταις τοῦ λόγου, ὡς ἴσμεν,
διέπρακτο, ὡς πλουτοῦντας τῷ τότε ἀναντιρρήτως ἡμᾶς τὴν ἐκλογὴν θεο-
πάροχον, ἀνθρωπίνων ἐξηρημένην καὶ ξένην ἐπινοιῶν καὶ ὀρέξεων, συνε-
15 τῶς ἀποδιδρασκόντων καὶ τῶν τὰ θεῖα λαχόντων οἰκοδομεῖν, τῷ μὴ
ἁλῶναι ἐν συνειδήσει καὶ Θεοῦ ψευδομάρτυρας, ἀποκρίνοντες ἢ
ἐγκρίνοντες, οὓς μὴ ᾔδεισαν καὶ Θεὸν ἐγκρίνειν ἢ ἀποκρίνειν πρὸς τὸ
ἀξίωμα (τίς γὰρ ἔγνω νοῦν Κυρίου ποτέ, ἢ αὐτοῦ ἐγένετο
σύμβουλος;), πίστιν ἐν ἔργῳ δεικνύντες [fol. 87ʳ] τὸ ἐν
20 πάσῃ τῇ γῇ τὰ κρίματα τοῦ Θεοῦ, καὶ τὸ οὐχ ὡς ὄψεται
ἄνθρωπος, οὕτως ὄψεται καὶ Θεός.

οὕτω δὲ καὶ παραιτουμένου, ὡς ἔφην, τούτου τοῦ ἔργου τοῦ μεγάλου καὶ θαυμασίου καὶ θεαρέστου εἰς δόξαν Θεοῦ, ἀλλ’ οὐκ ἐπι-
νοίαις ἐπισφαλέσι κραδαινομένου ποσῶς πρός τινων, πάντως ἐν τούτῳ

114: 5–6 Osee 8:4 || 9–11 cf. Ps. 25(26):1 || 12 cf. Luc. 1:2 || 16 cf. I Cor. 15:15 ||
18–19 Is. 40:13 || 19 cf. Jac. 2:18 || 19–20 I Paralip. 16:14 || 20–21 cf. I Reg. 16:7

26 hanc notam addidit patriarcha: ὁ δεξάμενος καὶ ἀναγνούς, ἱππότην ἐκπέμψας μετὰ
σπουδῆς, λαμβάνει καὶ ὅσον ἡμῖν ἐφάνη πρὸς τὰς ψήφους ἁρμόδιον, ἔχον οὕτως.
114: V 86ᵛ–87ᵛ. S 238ᵛ–239ᵛ. P 106ᵛ–108ʳ. Ed. Banduri, Imperium Orientale, II,
985–986, et Migne, PG, CXLII, 505–510.
5 post τὴν "desunt reliqua" scripsit manus posterior in margine P, quamquam nunc nihil
deest || 10 μὴ addidi; cf. Ps. 25(26):1

113, 114

And if I am encouraged, I will send ⟨these thoughts⟩; I wish that you peruse them with your inherent culture and intelligence, and if you find that my approval and attitude and decision is in accordance with the importance of the vote, you should reveal it discreetly. But if it is definitely unsuitable (for not everyone has knowledge), let me know this too in ⟨a spirit of⟩ love. And may you thereby be preserved by the God of love in good health and long life.

Marginal remark by Athanasius: When he received this and read it, he sent in haste a messenger on horseback and received my opinion on the proper course for the election, as follows.

114. ⟨To the superintendent of petitions⟩

When the faithful are electing the man [i.e., the patriarch] whom they hold as a model of Christ, Whom alone they deem to be the first high priest and sacrificial victim, they should not be influenced by any human passion or consideration, since they are aware of the vengeance of heaven, because «they have made kings for themselves but not by me; they have ruled, but they did not make it known to me». But men of God, with one heart and in concord and with earnest and unwavering supplication, should accept without any hesitation the man chosen by God in heaven, and believe that then we will receive great and incomparable favor and assistance from God, if we entrust «our hopes» of twofold salvation «in Him» alone and «do not waver». And these affairs ⟨of the election⟩ are truly beyond faith and understanding and humility, just as we know was done by «the ministers of the word», for then we are incontrovertibly endowed with the election furnished by God, exalted above and removed from human purposes and desires, when those who have been assigned to provide divine edification [i.e., the bishops] wisely avoid being found out in conscience «false witnesses of God» by rejecting or approving ⟨a candidate⟩ without knowing whether God approves or rejects the decision («for who ever knew the mind of the Lord, or was His counsellor?»), but they should «show by their deeds their faith» that «the judgments of God are in all the earth» and «God sees not as man looks».

When one resigns from this great and marvelous and God-pleasing task in the manner I have described, for the glory of God, and not at all swayed by certain people with fallacious reasonings, truly in such a case (and

25 (εἴθε δὲ καὶ ἐν πᾶσι τοῖς ἐκ Θεοῦ χαρισθεῖσι πιστοῖς), ὡς ἀληθείας
ἀνατειλάσης ἐκ γῆς, οὐδεὶς ἀντερεῖ ὡς καὶ δικαιοσύνη ἀνακύ-
ψει ἐξ οὐρανοῦ· καὶ οὕτω Χριστοῦ χρηστότητα χορηγοῦντος,
καὶ πιστοῖς πηγάσει πᾶν ἀγαθὸν εὐλογίας ἀνελλιποῦς, θεοπειθῶν ἐξ εὐχῶν καὶ ἱκεσιῶν τῶν θεοπαρόχων πλουτιζομένοις διηνεκῶς. εἰ δέ
30 που ὀψὲ κατὰ τοῦ ποιμένος λαληθῆναι συμβῇ τῶν ὅσα τῶν ἀπευκταίων
καὶ ἀπαισίων (τὸ γὰρ ἀνάλωτον πάθεσι μόνου Θεοῦ), οὐχ ὑπ' ὀδόντα
τῷ βουλομένῳ λαλεῖσθαι ἐξὸν τοὺς κρατοῦντας ἐᾶν τὰ τοιάδε, ὡς
ἀπιστίας καὶ ἀπωλείας ζιζάνια, ἀτιμίας καὶ καταγνώσεως ἀπεράντου,
καὶ μελῶν ψωριούντων τῆς ἐκκλησίας τῷ σώματι ἐνιέντων τὴν ἀθεράπευ-
35 τον σῆψιν τοῖς ἀεὶ κνηθομένοις τὴν ἀκοὴν ἐν τοιαύτῃ ἀτίμῳ καὶ
ἐφαμάρτῳ διαφθορᾷ, ἀλλ' ὡς τῆς δίκης οὐκ ἄλλου, ἀλλὰ τοῦ μέλλοντος
οὔσης κρῖναι πᾶσαν τὴν γῆν ἐν δικαιοσύνῃ, φανερὰν καὶ
δικαίαν καὶ δυναστείας μακράν, συγκαλουμένου παντὸς τοῦ τῆς ἐκκλησίας
πληρώματος παρὰ τοῦ κρατοῦντος, ὡς ὁρῶντος Χριστοῦ καὶ ἀκροωμένου,
40 ἐξάκουστον καὶ λαμπρὰν τὴν κρίσιν καθίζειν· καὶ εἰ μεταξὺ τὰ τῆς καταδίκης θεσμοῖς καὶ κανόσι καὶ Θεοῦ κατ' ἐνώπιον γυμνασθέντα ἐπι-
κρατέστερα δόξῃ, ἐξωθεῖσθαι καὶ ἀφειδῶς καὶ ἀπαραιτήτως (μηδὲ τῆς
ἐκκλησίας ἀσμενιζούσης τὰς ὁπωσδήποτε παραιτήσεις), ὄνησιν τοῖς
μετέπειτα ἀσφαλείας σωτηριώδους ποιοῦν, τῷ δ' ἐκβληθέντι (εἰ μή που
45 καὶ μέμηνε), μνώμενον τρόπου μετάνοιαν.

εἰ δὲ ἐλέει Θεοῦ τοὐναντίον ἐκβῇ, καὶ ὁ πάλαι ἐξαιτησάμενος τὸν
δίκαιον καὶ ἀληθινὸν καὶ ἄμεμπτον καὶ θεοσεβῆ Σατὰν
κἀνταῦθα ἐν ταῖς καρδίαις ὅλως εἰσδὺς τῶν συκοφαντῶν, τὴν δυσώδη
ὀδμὴν κατὰ τοῦ ποιμένος ἠρεύξατο, τὰς ὑβριστικὰς καὶ δυσφήμους καὶ
50 φληναφώδεις φωνάς, μὴ μαλακῶς τὰ τοιαῦτα ἀλλὰ δικαιότερον ἐπεξερ-
γαζόμενοι, ὡς ἐπὶ ὕβρει Θεοῦ, καὶ φειδοῦς ἀπάσης ἀποστερήσωμεν, καὶ
καθ' ὅσον ἀγάπης καὶ ζήλου τοῦ πρὸς Θεὸν ἀπαραίτητος ὀφειλὴ τῷ πιστῷ,
ὡς ὅτι μὴ τὸν τυχόντα ἀρχιερέα, ἀλλ' αὐτὸν τὸν τῆς ἐκκλησίας Θεὸν τὸν
ἀνύβριστον ἐμωμήσατο καὶ ἐξύβρισεν, ἐκεῖθεν ἀναμφιβόλου καὶ τῆς
55 [fol. 87ᵛ] φωνῆς, τὸ ὁ ἀθετῶν ὑμᾶς, ἐμὲ ἀθετεῖ, καὶ τὸ
ἔμπαλιν.

ἐκ τούτων καὶ τῶν τοιούτων, τῶν ἐν ἀληθείᾳ, φημί, καὶ δικαιοσύνῃ
καὶ πίστει καὶ φόβῳ Θεοῦ πρὸς ἡμῶν γινομένων, ἀναλόγως συντηρηθῶμεν
καὶ φρουρηθῶμεν καὶ ἀναχθῶμεν, ὡς καὶ ὄντας ἐν πᾶσιν ἡμᾶς Χριστοῦ,
60 καὶ ἀκούοντας τοῖς ἔργοις τὴν πίστιν δεικνύναι, καὶ τὴν
σπουδήν, ἐφαμάρτου διπλόης ἀπηλλαγμένους, καὶ μάλιστα ἐν τοῖς τοῦ
Θεοῦ, καὶ ἀνθρωπίνων ὀρέξεων, κἀντεῦθεν ἐνδίκῳ καὶ θεαρέστῳ θυμῷ
τὰ ἡμῶν καὶ τὰ τῶν πέλας δικάζοντας.

25–27 cf. Ps. 84(85): 12–13 ‖ 35 cf. II Tim. 4:3 ‖ 37 cf. Ps. 8(9):9 ‖ 46–47 Job. 1:1, 8 ‖
55 Luc. 10:16 ‖ 60 cf. Jac. 2:18

---

29 πλουτιζομένης P ‖ 31 ὑπ' ὀδόντα coni. Ševčenko; ὑποδόντα codd. ‖ 32 ἐξὸν] ἐξ ὧν codd. ‖
35 καὶ om. S ‖ 41–42 ἐπικρατεστέρα codd. ‖ 45 μνωμένοις codd. ‖ 51 ἀποστερήσομεν codd.

114

I wish that this were true of everything granted by God to the faithful)
no one would deny that as «truth springs out of the earth, so shall righteousness look down from heaven», and thus Christ grants «that which is good», and
will pour forth to the faithful every good of unceasing blessing, and they will
be enriched constantly with gifts from God because of their God-persuading
prayers and supplications. If, however, at some late date deplorable and nega-
tive charges should be made against the shepherd (for God alone is untouched
by passions), the emperor should not allow such things to be said surreptitiously by anyone who wishes (for these things are darnels leading to loss of
faith and perdition, dishonor and boundless condemnation; and ⟨by them⟩
the festering members introduce the incurable gangrene into the body of the
Church, among people whose «ears» are «perpetually irritated» by such dis-
respectful and sinful corruption); but rather, considering that the judgment
belongs to no one else, but to the One Who is going «to judge all the earth in
righteousness», the whole congregation of the Church should be summoned
by the emperor, openly and justly and far removed from constraint, as if
Christ were looking on and listening, and he should convene an open and large-
scale trial. And if meanwhile the judgment should incline towards condemnation, when examined in the light of the commandments and canons, and in
the presence of God, then ⟨the accused shepherd⟩ should be repudiated freely
and irrevocably by an overwhelming opinion (for the Church does not look
favorably upon any abdications whatsoever); this would benefit with assurance of salvation both future generations and the man who has been deposed
(unless he has gone mad), and would solicit a change of behavior on his part.

But if, by the mercy of God, the opposite should occur, and Satan, who
of old demanded the surrender of the «just and true and blameless and pious»
man, should fully enter into the hearts of flatterers here, and spew forth
stinking accusations against the shepherd, namely insulting and libellous
and nonsensical cries, we should not investigate such matters gently, but
rather with justice, as God Himself is insulted, and we should deprive ⟨the
false accuser⟩ of all ⟨consideration of⟩ mercy, inasmuch as love and zeal
for God are an indispensable obligation for the faithful, because he has not
reproached and insulted any ordinary bishop, but the unassailable God of the
Church Himself, since the words are incontrovertible that «He that despiseth
you despiseth me», and the reverse ⟨is also true⟩.

As a result of these and similar ⟨deeds⟩ performed by us in truth, I mean,
and justice and faith and fear of God, may we accordingly be preserved and
protected and uplifted, since we belong to Christ in all things, and hear that
«we should show by our works our faith» and our zeal, far from any sinful
duplicity and earthly desires, especially in divine affairs, and judge ourselves
and our neighbors in a just and God-pleasing spirit.

115. Sine titulo

Τῆς Χριστοῦ ἐκκλησίας τὸ πρῶτον ἐπὶ μόνῃ τετραετίᾳ γενόμενοι,
ἄνθρωπε τοῦ Θεοῦ, ἐγκρατεῖς, ὡς ἠρώτησας, τοῦ ἁγίου μου αὐτοκράτορος
μὴ ἐνδημοῦντος τῷ τότε τῇ βασιλίδι τῶν πόλεων, ἀλλὰ περὶ τὴν Ἕω τὰς
5 διατριβὰς ποιουμένῳ, ἐκστρατείας κατεπειγούσης ἕνεκεν τῆς ἀπολυθεί-
σης παιδείας ἀπὸ Θεοῦ ὀρθοδόξοις δι' ἀθέτησιν προσταγμάτων εὐαγγελικῶν καὶ ἁγίων νόμων, τῆς ἀνυποστάτου, φημί, βαρβαρικῆς ἐκδρομῆς
καὶ κινήσεως· ἔνθεν μὴ ἔχων τὸν ἀντιλαμβανόμενον εἰς τὸ τὴν κληρου-
χίαν ἰθύνειν Χριστοῦ πρὸς τὰς εὐαγγελικὰς καὶ νομίμους φωνὰς καὶ
10 νομάς, ὅμως ὡς δυνατόν μοι, δωρεᾷ καὶ χάριτι τοῦ Σωτῆρος μου, πρὸς τὸ
δοκοῦν μοι θεάρεστον καταναγκάζειν οὐ κατενάρκουν λαϊκούς, ἱερεῖς
καὶ ἀρχιερεῖς καὶ μονάζοντας, καὶ ταῦτα πληθυνομένων ἑκάστοτε τῶν
ἀντικειμένων μοι, καὶ ἐνεδρευόντων ἀφανῶς τε καὶ προφανῶς, τιθέν-
των μοι σκάνδαλα ἐχόμενα τρίβου σκαιωρίᾳ σατανικῇ, καὶ
15 λόγους ὅ,τι πολλοὺς παρανόμους κατ' ἐμοῦ τεκταινόντων· μιᾷ καὶ
μόνῃ τῇ ἐπὶ τὸν Θεὸν ἐτρεφόμην ἐλπίδι καὶ ἀντιλήψει, ὡς ἂν τοῖς ἀνθισ-
ταμένοις κακῶς μεταμέλεια ἐπιλάμψῃ καὶ φόβος Θεοῦ καὶ ἀλήθεια,
παυσαμένους ψευδολογιῶν καὶ διαβολῶν, ὧν ὁ τοῦ ψεύδους πατὴρ ταῖς
αὐτῶν ἐνσπείρει ψυχαῖς, καὶ μᾶλλον εἰ καὶ ὁ κραταιὸς αὐτοκράτωρ μου
20 πρὸς τὴν βασιλεύουσαν ἀναζεύξει ταχύτερον, κἀντεῦθεν ἐξετασμὸς
φιλαλήθης καὶ φιλοδίκαιος καὶ φιλόθεος, καὶ ταῦτα πρὸς βασιλείου περιω-
πῆς ἐκφερόμενος, οὐκ ἀσεβεῖς ὀλέσει καὶ μόνον, καὶ πάντα τὰ
χείλη τὰ δόλια φιμωθήσονται, ἀλλὰ καὶ τὰ θρυλλούμενα μάτην
δαιμονιώδει ὑποβολῇ ὡς ἀπὸ πυρὸς ζωύφια πτερωτὰ φλογισθήσονται.
25 καὶ τὴν ἐκδίκησιν οὐ μόνον τῶν παρεληλυθότων ἐκεῖθεν, ἀλλὰ καὶ τὴν
ἀντίληψιν πρὸς τὰ πρόσω ἐντελῆ καὶ διηνεκῆ καὶ ἀκράδαντον, πρὸς
ἅπαν ἐθάρρουν καὶ ἐγχειρεῖν καὶ καταπλουτεῖν με θεάρεστον, καὶ τὴν μογ-
ήσασαν πρὸ πολλοῦ εὐαγγελικὴν καὶ κανονικὴν τῶν νομίμων ἁγίων θεσμῶν λαϊκοῖς καὶ [fol. 88r] μονάζουσι καὶ παντὶ τῷ τῆς ἐκκλησίας πληρώ-
30 ματι· ἐξ ὧν εἰς αἰχμαλωσίαν, ὡς ἔφην, καὶ ὕβριν ψυχικὴν καὶ σωματικὴν
ζημίαν ὁ περιούσιος ἐξεδόθη λαός. ὧν ἀλλοτρόπως ῥυσθῆναι
καὶ τῆς πρὶν εὐτυχίας, ὡς ὅτε ηὔγαζεν ὁ λύχνος τοῦ Θεοῦ ἐπὶ
κεφαλῆς τῆς τῶν πιστῶν κληρουχίας, ἐξυψωθῆναι καὶ εὐημερίσαι καὶ

115: 13–14 cf. Ps. 139(140):6 ||| 20–22 cf. Prov. 1:32 || 22–23 Ps. 11(12):4 || 31 cf.
Tit. 2:14 || 32 I Reg. 3:3

115: V 87v–89v. S 240r–243v. P 108r–111v. Ed. Banduri, Imperium Orientale, II, 978–980; Migne, PG, CXLII, 493–502; ed. partim Boivin, Notae ad Nicephorum
Gregoram, 764.
1 γράμμα περὶ τοῦ πῶς καὶ διατί τὰ τῶν παραιτήσεων, τῆς πρώτης, φημί, καὶ δευτέρας,
ἐγένοντο add. VrSP || 8 ἔχον P || 14 τρίβου scripsi; cf. Ps. 139(140):6; τρίβους codd. ||
30 αἰχαλωσίαν P || 32–33 ὡς ὅτε ... κληρουχίας om. S || 33 κεφαλῆς VSP1: κεφαλὴν P ||

115

115. ⟨Letter about my resignations⟩

In answer to your question, O man of God, when I took charge of the Church of Christ the first time, for a period of only four years, my holy emperor was not residing at that time in the Queen of Cities, but was in the east, since there was urgent need of a campaign on account of the punishment wreaked by God upon Orthodox Christians because of our disregard for the commandments of the Gospels and the holy laws; I am referring, of course, to the irresistible attacks and campaigns of the barbarians. Therefore, since I had no one to help me guide the patrimony of Christ in accordance with the commands and precepts of the Gospels and of the laws, still to the best of my ability, by the gift and grace of my Savior, I did not hesitate to compel laymen, priests and bishops, and monks ⟨to live⟩ in a manner which I thought pleasing to God. I did it even though my opponents constantly multiplied, and laid snares for me openly and in secret, and with Satanic mischief «set stumbling-blocks in my path», and concocted many stories against me, thereby transgressing the law; I was supported only by my hope in God and His succour, that my wicked opponents might be enlightened with repentance, fear of God and the truth, and might put an end to the lies and slanders which the father of falsehood instilled in their souls. And especially ⟨I hoped⟩ that if my mighty emperor should return quickly to the capital, and if there resulted «an investigation» inspired by the love of truth, righteousness and God, indeed an investigation carried out ⟨under the auspices of the⟩ imperial splendor, then it would not only «destroy the impious», and «all treacherous lips» would be silenced, but also that vain babbling prompted by the devil would be burned up like tiny winged insects in fire. And ⟨I was convinced⟩ that, when I was correcting the errors of the past and was bringing complete and continual and unshakeable assistance in the future, I was acting fruitfully, in a manner fully pleasing to God, especially ⟨when I was enforcing⟩ the evangelical and canonical ⟨way of life⟩ of the lawful holy commandments which had been abused for a long time by laymen and monks and the entire congregation of the Church; as a result of which, as I said, «the chosen people» was delivered into slavery, abuse of the soul, and bodily injury. And it is not possible for them to be saved from these ⟨misfortunes⟩ and to be raised again to their former happiness (when «the lamp of God» shone above the heads of the inheritance of the faithful) and to prosper and be supported through any

κρατυνθῆναι δι' ἐπινοίας καὶ ἐπιχειρήσεως ἀνθρωπίνης παντοίας ἀδύνα-
35 τον, εἰ μὴ διὰ μετανοίας εἰλικρινοῦς καὶ ἀνοθεύτου ἐπιστροφῆς πρὸς
Θεόν, καὶ συντηρήσεως τῶν θείων εὐαγγελίων καὶ νόμων, ὡς ὀνει-
διζόμεθα πρὸς τῆς θείας Γραφῆς· αὐτοί, φησίν, οὐκ ἐνέμειναν
ἐν τῇ διαθήκῃ μου, κἀγὼ ἠμέλησα αὐτῶν, λέγει Κύριος,
καὶ ὁ λαὸς οὐκ ἐπεστράφη ἕως ἐπλήγη, καὶ εἰ ὁ λαός μου
40 ἤκουσέ μου, ταῖς ὁδοῖς μου εἰ ἐπορεύθη, ἐν τῷ μηδενὶ
ἂν τοὺς ἐχθροὺς αὐτῶν ἐταπείνωσα, καὶ ἐπιστράφητε
πρός με, καὶ ἐπιστραφήσομαι πρὸς ὑμᾶς, καὶ μὴ ῥητίνη
οὐκ ἔστιν ἐν Γαλαάδ, ἢ ἰατρὸς οὐκ ἔστιν ἐκεῖ; διὰ τί
οὐκ ἀνέβη ἴασις θυγατρὸς λαοῦ μου, καὶ ὅσα τοιαῦτα θεσπίζει
45 τὸ πνεῦμα τὸ ἅγιον εἰς ἐξυπνισμὸν καὶ ποιμένων καὶ ποιμνίων, καὶ ἀπει-
λὴν καταφρονητῶν.

τίνος γὰρ ἕνεκεν ἄλλου τὴν φροντίδα τῆς ἐκκλησίας Χριστοῦ καὶ
αὐτὸς ἀναδέδεγμαι, εἰ μὴ τὰ τοιαῦτα καὶ φρονεῖν καὶ διδάσκειν, καὶ ὑπὲρ
τούτων προκινδυνεύειν, καὶ ὡς ἐγένετο; ἀλλὰ τὰ Χριστοῦ Ἰησοῦ καὶ τὰ
50 τῆς ἐκκλησίας αὐτοῦ πρὸς τῇ ὀρθοδοξίᾳ ὅσον τὸ κατ' ἐμὲ καὶ ῥυτίδος
καὶ σπίλου παντὸς ὑπερτέραν ὁρᾶσθαι τῷ νυμφίῳ αὐτῆς καὶ δεσπότῃ,
ὃ καὶ ποιμένι παντί, ἀλλ' οὐ μισθωτῷ ἀναπολόγητον ὄφλημα.
ἀλλά, βαβαί, συμπτωμάτων τῶν παρ' ἐλπίδα, τινῶν, ὡς ἔοικεν, ὀρθοδόξῳ
κλήσει σεμνυνομένων, χείλη δὲ δόλια ἐν καρδίᾳ ἀναβλυζόντων,
55 κακὰ καὶ πόρρω Θεοῦ.

καὶ γὰρ ὅτε τὴν ἐπὶ τὰ κρείττω μεταβολὴν ἐπιλάμψαι, διὰ τῆς τῶν
θείων θεσμῶν ἐκζητήσεως καὶ ἀνανεώσεως, εὔελπις ἤμην τῇ ἐπελεύσει
τοῦ αὐτοκράτορος, καὶ ἐκ τῶν συκοφαντωδῶν ἀρρητουργιῶν ἀναπνεῦσαι,
τότε μᾶλλον τὰ θεοστυγῆ τῶν διαβολῶν κεκραταίωνται καθ' ἡμῶν, ἀπορ-
60 ραγέντων μου οὐ μόνον τῶν ἀδελφῶν καὶ συλλειτουργῶν διὰ τὸ ζηλότυπον ὅτι κατηναγκάζοντο ὑφ' ἡμῶν παραμένειν ἕκαστος τῇ λαχούσῃ, ἀλλὰ
καὶ τῶν πλησίον καὶ φίλων, ὅτι μὴ πρὸς τὰς ὀρέξεις διεκείμην ἑκάστου,
πρὸς δὲ τὴν ἀλήθειαν καὶ τὸ δίκαιον τοῦ Θεοῦ, ὡς αὐτὸς μαρτυρήσει μοι.

ὅθεν καὶ σύνοδον καθίσαντες τῆς ἐκκλησίας ἐντὸς καθ' ἡμῶν,
65 καὶ ζητήσεις σκεψάμενοι, ὡς εἰ πρὸς ταύτας μὴ κατανεύοντα εὕρωσι,
μηδὲ αὐτοὶ πατριαρχεύειν με ἔχειν ὁμολογήσωσιν, ἡμῶν δὲ τὰ [fol. 88ᵛ]
τούτων ζητήματα μὴ ἀγνοησάντων ματαίαν πρόφασιν εἶναι, κἀντεῦθεν
ἀπωσαμένου αὐτοὺς τοῦ μὴ ἀνελθεῖν πρὸς ἡμᾶς, τοῦ σκέμματος ἀστοχ-
ήσαντες, πρὸς τὸ ἔργον χωρὶς ἀφορμῆς τοῦ ἐξῶσαι ἐχώρησαν παρὰ
70 πᾶσαν ἀλήθειαν τῆς ἐκκλησίας ἡμᾶς, ἀποσυνάγωγον θέμενοι τὸν πλησιά-

---

37–38 Jer. 38(31):32 ‖ 39 Is. 9:12 ‖ 39–41 Ps. 80(81):14–15 ‖ 41–42 Zach. 1:3 et Mal. 3:7 ‖
42–44 Jer. 8:22 ‖ 50–51 Eph. 5:27 ‖ 52 cf. Joh. 10:12 ‖ 54 Ps. 11(12):3

---

34 κρατυνθῆναι VS¹P: κραταιωθῆναι S ‖ 40 μου²] μοι P ‖ 46 καταφρονητῶν VSP¹:
καταφρονητὴν P ‖ 62 πλησίον VS¹P : πλησίων S ‖ 66 μηδὲ] μὴ δὴ S ‖ με] μὴ S ‖ μὲ
ἔχειν om. P

115

sort of human plan or undertaking, but only by means of sincere repentance and genuine turning toward God, and by keeping the holy Gospels and commandments, since we are reproached by the Holy Writ: «They abode not in my covenant, and I disregarded them, saith the Lord», and «the people turned not until they were smitten», and «If my people had hearkened to me, if it had walked in my ways, I should have put down their enemies very quickly», and «Turn to me and I will turn to you», and «Is there no balm in Galaad, or is there no physician there? Why then is not the health of the daughter of my people recovered?», and such other words as the Holy Spirit pronounces to rouse both shepherds and their flocks, and to threaten those who scorn ⟨His commands⟩.

For what other reason did I take upon myself responsibility for the Church of Christ, if not to hold and teach these ⟨doctrines⟩, and to brave danger for their sake, as it has turned out? But also ⟨in order that⟩, in addition to ⟨the mere preservation of⟩ orthodoxy, the affairs of Jesus Christ and His Church be seen by Her Bridegroom and Master without any «spot or wrinkle», as much as was within my power, since this is the indispensable obligation of «every shepherd, but not of a hireling». But alas for the unexpected misfortunes brought on by certain people who, as it seems, pride themselves on their orthodox name, but in their hearts gush forth with «treacherous lips» things evil and far from God.

For when at the return of the emperor I was hopeful that there would be a change for the better through examination and renewal of the divine ordinances, and that I would have a respite from the unspeakable charges of informers, then indeed the loathsome slanders against me gained strength, and not only my brethren and fellow ministers abandoned me because of my zeal at compelling each of them to remain in his appointed see, but also my neighbors and friends, because I was not interested in their desires, but in the truth and justice of God, as He Himself will testify on my behalf.

For this reason they convened a synod in the Church against me, and thought up certain demands, so that if I did not assent to them, they would not agree to keep me as patriarch. But since I realized that these demands were a false pretext, I therefore prevented them from approaching me. And since they failed in their scheme, they proceeded to expel me from the Church without any pretext, doing violence to every truth, and agreed that anyone of them who approached or talked with me would be expelled from the con-

σαι καὶ συλλαλῆσαι ἡμῖν ἐξ αὐτῶν συμφωνήσαντες. ὅτι μηδὲ βασιλεὺς τὸ
τυχόν, μηδέ τις τῶν συλλειτουργῶν ἀπᾷδον τὸ βούλευμα τοιοῦτον κρίνας
ἀντέστη, ἐταλανίσαμεν τὰ ἀνθρώπινα, πῶς μὴ πρὸ ὀφθαλμῶν οἱ ἄνθρωποι
τιθέμεθα καὶ Θεὸν ἐν οἷς κατὰ τῆς ἀληθείας φερόμεθα· τῶν μισούντων
75 τοῖς ἀνακτόροις ἀθροιζομένων ἐν εὐφροσύνῃ, εἰς τὸ τοὺς ἐκ διαβολῶν καθ᾽
ἡμῶν μώμους συστῆσαι καὶ κραταιῶσαι, ἵνα τὴν ἄδικον ἐκβολὴν ὡς
συνήθη καὶ νομίμην ἀποδείξωσι, καθὰ περὶ ὧν ἡ αὐτοαλήθεια, ἵνα
πᾶς ὁ ἀποκτείνας ὑμᾶς δόξῃ λατρείαν προσφέρειν τῷ
Θεῷ.
80   μηδενὸς πλησιάσαι τολμήσαντος ἔκτοτε, μόνον δὲ τῶν φυ-
λασσομένων τὰ μάταια καὶ ψευδῆ Ξυλωτῶν τῆς ἐκκλησίας ἐντὸς
συντρεχόντων ἑκάστοτε, καὶ λοιδορίαις καὶ ὕβρεσι καὶ ἀναθεματισμοῖς
καθ᾽ ἡμῶν χρωμένων μεγάλῃ φωνῇ, ὀψὲ δὲ καὶ μόλις ἑνὸς συγκλητικῶν
πρὸς ἡμᾶς ἀνελθόντος, καὶ τὰ τῆς κραυγῆς τῶν ἀρχιερέων καὶ τὰ φημι-
85 ζόμενα κατὰ τῆς ἡμῶν ὑπολήψεως ἀνυπόστατα καὶ μάταια καὶ
ψευδῆ (ὡς οἶδεν ὁ μέλλων κρῖναι πᾶσαν τὴν γῆν ἐν δικαιοσύνῃ)
ἐμβριθῶς διεξερχομένου καταπλῆξαι τάχα ἡμᾶς καὶ φοβῆσαι, ὡς εἴπερ ἐργάτην ἀναμφιβόλως ἠπίστατο τῶν φημιζομένων ἀνομημάτων
τῇ ὑπολήψει ἡμῶν, καὶ ὡς οἰκτείρων τάχα τῆς συμφορᾶς, μὴ καθαί-
90 ρεσιν πάθωμεν, ἀπῄτει παραίτησιν, τὸ τάχα κουφότερον, ὡς εἴ τις κτεῖναι
τινὰ σφαδάζων θυμῷ, συμπαθείας προσχήματι δῆθεν μόνον τούτου τὴν
κεφαλὴν ἐκτεμεῖν ἀποφήνηται.
        «ἀλλ᾽ ἡμεῖς, κῦρ ὁ μέγας,» εἰπόντες τῷ ἄρχοντι, «ἀδικούμενοι, ὡς
μηδὲν τῶν συκοφαντουμένων εἰδότες, κρίσιν ζητοῦμεν παρὰ κριτῶν Θεὸν
95 ἐχόντων πρὸ ὀφθαλμῶν, καὶ πῶς παραίτησιν δῶμεν; εἰ δὲ δῶμεν δυνασ-
τευόμενοι, ἐν τῷ κοινῷ κριτηρίῳ οὐκ ἐλεγχθήσεται ἡ ἀλήθεια, ἡνίκα
παρρησιάσεται Θεὸς ἐκδικήσεως, ἑνὸς τῶν φημιζομένων ἀτόπων παρὰ
πολλῶν, ὡς μανθάνομεν ἀπὸ σοῦ, καθ᾽ ἡμῶν, οὐχ ἕνα καὶ μόνον, ἀλλ᾽
ὅλων ἀρχιερέων δυνάμενον ὁρμαθὸν τῆς ἐκκλησίας ἐξῶσαι, εἴ γε τῆς
100 ἀληθείας τὸ ψεῦδος οἱ ἀκροαταὶ προτιμήσουσιν;»
        «ἀλλὰ μὴ τῇ σῇ καθαιρέσει,» φησί, [fol. 89ʳ] «καὶ οἱ ὑπὸ σοῦ
χειροτονηθέντες τοῖς λαϊκοῖς κριθῶσιν ἀπόβλητοι;»
        «σκῆψις ταῦτα,» ἀντείπομεν· «οἱ γὰρ ἡμῶν μὴ φειδόμενοι ἀδικεῖν,
ἑτέρων πῶς φείσονται;»
105   ὡς δὲ ὁ ἄρχων μηδὲν λαβὼν καὶ δὶς καὶ πολλάκις ἀπῆλθε, μηδενὸς
τῶν συλλειτουργῶν, μηδὲ τῶν τοῦ κλήρου, μὴ ἡγουμένου πρὸς ἡμᾶς παρα-
βάλλειν τολμῶντος ἐπὶ τοσαύταις ἡμέραις ἐκτὸς τῶν ἀρχιερέων ἑνός, τοῦ
τότε Γαγγρῶν· ᾧ κοινωσάμενοι περὶ τὴν παραίτησιν δι᾽ ἣν καὶ ἠναγκαζό-

---

77–79 Joh. 16:2 ‖ 80–81 cf. Jon. 2:9 ‖ 85–86 Jon. 2:9 ‖ 86 cf. Ps. 8(9):9

---

71 ὅτι] ἔτι   SP ‖ 72 ὑπᾷδων codd. ‖ κρῖναι   S ‖ 75 τοῖς] τὰ   SP ‖ 93 post κῦρ lacuna in
S ‖ 98 ἕνα] ἵνα   SP

115

gregation. Since neither the emperor, for one, nor any of my fellow ministers decided to oppose such a counsel as unworthy, I wept over human ⟨folly, pondering⟩ how we mortals do not keep God before our eyes when we act against the truth. And meanwhile my enemies gathered merrily in the palace to devise and increase the slanderous jests against me, in order to show that my illegal deposition was in fact in accordance with custom and lawful, just like those people about whom ⟨Christ⟩, the Truth Itself, said «that whosoever killeth you will think that he doeth God service».

From that time on no one dared to approach me, but the Xylotes, «guardians of vanity and falsehood», alone assembled within the Church on each occasion and loudly shouted abuses and insults and anathemas against me. But at length one of the senators came to me, and vehemently repeated the shouts of the bishops and the insinuations against my reputation, which were intolerable and «foolish and untrue»—as He knows Who is going «to judge the whole world in righteousness»—perhaps to bully and frighten me. And as if he knew without question ⟨that I was⟩ the worker of the unlawful deeds which were noised about against my reputation, and as if he pitied my misfortune, ⟨and feared that⟩ I might be deposed, he asked for my resignation, supposedly to make matters easier; as if someone desired with passionate impulse to kill a man, and then with a show of compassion decided to cut off only his head!

But I said to the official, «Great lord, I am the victim of injustice, since I know nothing of the charges against me, and I seek a trial by judges who have God before their eyes. How, then, am I to hand in my resignation? For even if I am forced to give it, will not the truth be revealed at the tribunal which we all must face, when the God of vengeance speaks freely, since just one of the unseemly charges made against me by many people, as I learn from you, would be sufficient to drive from the church not one alone, but all the archbishops, if indeed the listeners should prefer falsehood to truth».

He replied, «But if you are deposed won't the people repudiate those ⟨priests⟩ ordained by you?».

«This is a pretext», I answered. «For those who did not hesitate to wrong me will certainly not hesitate to wrong others».

But when the official accomplished nothing, even though he came back several times, none of my fellow ministers, none of the clergy, not even an abbot, dared to visit me all this time, except for one of the bishops, who was at that time the metropolitan of Gangra. And I consulted with him about the

μεθα, καὶ ἱερομονάχων προσκαρτερούντων δι' ἐκκλησίας, καὶ τὴν ἐξαφ-
110 θεῖσαν ὁρῶντες ἐξαίφνης τοσαύτην πυρκαϊὰν καθ' ἡμῶν παρὰ πάντων καὶ
ἐκπληττόμενοι, ἐνδοῦναι ἡμᾶς τῆς ἐνστάσεως συνεβούλευσαν, «εἰ μὲν ηὑρίσκοντο», λέγοντες, «καὶ τινὲς μετὰ σοῦ ἀντεχόμενοι τῶν ἀρχιερέων ὑπὲρ
ἀληθείας Θεοῦ καὶ κανονικῶς ἐδέχου μηνύματα, καὶ αὐτὸς ἐνίστασθαι
ὤφειλες καὶ κρίσιν ζητεῖν τοῖς ἀπαιτοῦσι παραίτησιν. ἐπεὶ δὲ παρὰ συγ-
115 κλητικοῦ, ὅρα, τίς τῶν ἐκδιωχθέντων ἀδίκως τῆς ἐκκλησίας πρὸ σοῦ, καὶ
ταῦτα λόγῳ καὶ βίῳ μεγάλων, καὶ ὑπὲρ σὲ ἀσυγκρίτων, κανονικῶς ἐξε-
βλήθη, ἀλλ' οὐχὶ ἐξουσιαστικῶς; διὰ τοῦτο Θεῷ πιστεύσας τὰ κατὰ σὲ καὶ
αὐτὸς τῷ ἐρχομένῳ τὰ ἡμέτερα δικαιῶσαι, παραιτησάμενος ἔξιθι, μὴ
καὶ πρὸς βαρυτέρας τινὲς τῶν μηχανορράφων συκοφαντίας χωρήσαντες,
120 πολλῶν ψυχὰς καὶ τὰς ἑαυτῶν καταβλάψωσιν.»

αὕτη ἐπὶ Θεῷ μάρτυρι τῆς παραιτήσεως τῆς πρώτης καὶ τῆς
δευτέρας ἡ συσκευὴ καὶ ὑπόθεσις, εἰ καὶ τὰ τῶν κατηγοριῶν ποικίλα καὶ
ἄνισα, ἐπεὶ δὲ οὐ δημοσίᾳ καὶ μόνον, ἀλλὰ καὶ οἴκοι, τοῦ ἱερᾶσθαι καὶ εὐλογεῖν καὶ διδάσκειν τοῖς τυχοῦσιν ἀπείργειν ἡμᾶς οἱ ἀρχιερεῖς ἐγκε-
125 λεύονται (ἅπερ οὐδὲ τῷ δυσσεβεῖ Γεωργίῳ, ἢ τοῖς φυλασσομένοις
τὰ μάταια καὶ ψευδῆ Ξυλωταῖς ποσῶς ἐπετίμησαν), μὴ ἑαυτοὺς
ἀκανόνιστα πράττειν καὶ ἄθεσμα τὴν κρίσιν φρίττοντες τοῦ Θεοῦ, ἢ
κἂν ἀνθρώπους αἰδούμενοι, ἀλλ' ἡμῖν ἐπιτρίβειν θαρροῦσι τὸ ἀκανόνιστον·
αὐτοὶ καὶ τοῖς πρὸς τῶν θείων θεσμῶν ἐπαράτοις καὶ ἀλλοτρίοις τῆς ἐκ-
130 κλησίας Χριστοῦ τὰς κεφαλὰς ὑποκλίναντες καὶ κανόνα δεξάμενοι, καὶ
τὸν ἐν μακαρίᾳ τῇ μνήμῃ πατριάρχην τῆς ἐκκλησίας Χριστοῦ καὶ ὁμολογη-
τὴν κύριν Ἰωσὴφ παρανάλωμα, ὅσον τὸ κατ' αὐτούς, τῆς μανίας τῶν
σχιζομένων γενέσθαι κατα-[fol. 89ᵛ] δεξάμενοι, καὶ ταῦτα καὶ μετὰ
θάνατον (ὅπερ οὐκ εἶδεν ὁ ἥλιος).

135 ἀναμείναντες ἐπὶ χρόνοις τοσούτοις ζητῆσαί τινα τῶν πρὸ ὀφθαλμῶν ἐχόντων Θεὸν πῶς καὶ πόθεν τοσαῦτα καθ' ἡμῶν ἐφρυάξαντο, καὶ
μηδένα τὸν συλλυπούμενον μηδὲ τὸν παρακαλοῦντα εὑρόντες, ἵνα καὶ κρίσιν δικαίαν ζητήσωμεν, ἐκχεῶ καὶ αὐτὸς τοῦ δι' ἐμὲ σταυρωθέντος
ἐνώπιον τὴν δέησίν μου, καὶ τὴν θλίψιν μου αὐτῷ ἀπαγ-
140 γελῶ, καὶ μᾶλλον ὡς τῆς κακίας ἐπιδιδούσης καὶ εἴργειν ἀναισχυντούσης
καὶ τῶν ἀναπνοῶν ἡμᾶς τὸ λεγόμενον, ὡς μὴ λειτουργεῖν, μὴ εὐλογεῖν, μὴ
διδάσκειν τινὰ τὰ πρὸς σωτηρίαν παραχωρούσης. ἄγοιτο οὖν, δέσποτα
καὶ Θεὲ τοῦ παντός, ὁ ἐν Τριάδι γινωσκόμενος καὶ ὑμνούμενος, ὅποι φίλον
σοι τὰ ἡμέτερα, πρεσβείαις τῆς ἀρρήτως καὶ ἀρρυπάρως σωματωσάσης
145 τὸν ἕνα τῆς παναγίας Τριάδος, καὶ πάντων τῶν ἀπ' αἰῶνος λελατρευκό-
των Θεῷ, καὶ τοιαῦτα παθόντων, ἀμήν.

125-126 cf. Jon. 2:9 ‖ 138-140 cf. Ps. 141 (142):3

---

115 ἐκδιωχθέντως P ‖ 123 ἱερᾶσθαι scripsi; cf. 1. 141; ἐρᾶσθαι codd. ‖ 127 φρίττοντος S ‖
129 τοῖς] τοὺς P ‖ 136 ἐφρυάξατο VP

115

resignation which I was being compelled to submit; the monks, too, who remained in the Church, when they saw such a sudden conflagration stirred up against me by everyone, were amazed, and advised me to give up my resistance. For they said, «If some people were to be found who would join you in your resistance to the bishops, for the sake of God's truth, and if you received summons in accordance with the canons, then you should resist, and ask for a trial by those who demand your resignation. But, since it is a senator ⟨who demanded your resignation⟩, consider, of those men who were unjustly expelled from the Church before you, who were distinguished for their words and for their lives, and incomparably superior to you, which one was thrown out in accordance with the canons, instead of by secular authority? Therefore, entrust your affairs to God Who will come to judge us, abdicate and retire, lest some of those crafty schemers devise even more grievous accusations, and destroy many souls, in addition to their own».

As God is my witness, this is the plot and story of my first and ⟨also⟩ of my second resignation, even if the charges were different and of unequal weight ⟨on the two occasions⟩, since ⟨this time⟩ the bishops are ordered to prevent me from celebrating mass or giving a blessing or teaching anyone, not only in public but also in private, a punishment which was not meted out even to the impious George, or to the Xylotes who are «guardians of vanity and falsehood». And they do not fear the judgment of God because they commit uncanonical and unlawful acts, nor do they have any respect for men, but ⟨instead⟩ dare to accuse *me* of uncanonical behavior. They bow their heads and accept their laws from men who are cursed by divine ordinances and alienated from the Church of Christ, and they have accepted, as far as they are concerned, that the patriarch of the Church of Christ and confessor Kyr Joseph, of blessed memory, be a victim of the madness of the schismatics, even after his death, something which the sun has never seen before.

After I waited for so many years to ask one of those who has God before his eyes how and why they were so insolent to me, and found no one to share my grief or to console me, so that I may seek righteous judgment, «I pour forth my supplication» before the One Who was crucified for my sake, and «I declare unto Him my affliction», especially since their wickedness increases and is shameless enough even to prevent me from breathing, as the saying goes, since they do not allow me to celebrate mass or to give my blessing or to teach anyone the path which leads to salvation. Therefore, O Lord and God of all, Who are known and praised in the Trinity, let me be guided in accordance with Thy will, through the intercessions of the One Who ineffably and immaculately gave birth to one member of the all-holy Trinity, and through the intercessions of all those who have worshipped God from the beginning of time, and have suffered such ⟨abuses⟩, Amen.

COMMENTARY

COMMENTARY

1.

Athanasius asks the Emperor to return to Constantinople from Thessalonica as soon as possible because of the threat to the empire from the Turks.

Laurent, *Regestes*, Appendix, no. 3

Date: April 1299–October 1300, when Andronicus was in Thessalonica for the marriage of his daughter Simonis to Stephen Milutin, kral of Serbia; cf. Pachymeres, *Hist.*, II, 283, 290; Laurent, *Regestes*, 569.

11 Ἰσμαηλίταις: The Turkish emirates which succeeded the Seljuk Empire of Rum were firmly established in western Anatolia by the end of the thirteenth century. According to Ottoman tradition, by 1299 Osman was sole ruler of an area including Dorylaeum (Eskişehir), Sögüt (Thebasion), the lake of Nicaea (Iznik Gölü) on the north, and Angelokoma (Inegöl) on the west; cf. Arnakis, Οἱ πρῶτοι Ὀθωμάνοι, 71.

45 Ἐζεκίαν: Cf. 4 Kings 18–19.

46 Ἰωσίαν: Cf. 4 Kings 21–23.

49 πεζοπορούντά σε ἐν λιταῖς: Andronicus frequently took part in the Patriarch's services of intercession; cf. Pachymeres, *Hist.*, II, 420–21.

2.

Athanasius justifies the letter of excommunication which he wrote in 1293, and states that he will not forgive the bishops unless they return to their sees.

Laurent, *Regestes*, Appendix, no. 2

2

Date: September 1297; this letter refers to the discovery four years after
Athanasius' first abdication of a letter of excommunication which
the Patriarch had hidden in a gallery of St. Sophia in October 1293;
cf. Pachymeres, *Hist.*, II, 249–57, my Introduction, pp. xx–xxi, and
Laurent, *Regestes*, 567. Gennadios of Helioupolis erroneously assigned
Letter 2 to October 1293 in his article, 'Η πρώτη ἀπὸ τοῦ θρόνου
ἀποχώρησις τοῦ πατριάρχου 'Αθανασίου Α', in 'Ορθοδοξία, 28 (1953),
145.

4 ἐξ ἀθυμίας: Cf. Pachymeres, *Hist.*, II, 254: ἐξ αὐτῆς τῆς κατασχού-
σης με ὀδύνης καὶ πικρίας παρακινηθείς.

5 πάπαν ὀρθοδοξοῦντα: Laurent translates this as «pope», but admits
that his interpretation presents certain difficulties, since Athanasius
was such a staunch anti-Catholic; cf. *Regestes*, 568.

7 'Αρσένιον: Arsenius, patriarch of Constantinople 1255–1259 and
1260–1265. Note that despite Athanasius' hostility to the Arsenite
faction, he sympathized with Arsenius as a patriarch who, like himself, was forced to abdicate.

'Ιωσήφ: Joseph, patriarch of Constantinople 1266–1275 and 1282–
1283.

8 Γρηγόριον: Gregory of Cyprus, patriarch of Constantinople 1283–
1289.

15 'Ιωάννου: John Chrysostom, patriarch of Constantinople 398–403 and
403–404, who was condemned at the Synod of the Oak Tree held
at Chalcedon in 403. The Emperor Andronicus used to compare
Athanasius with Chrysostom; cf. Gregoras, *Hist.*, I, 216.

16–17 "Ανναν καὶ Καιάφαν: Cf. Matt. 26:3, 57; Luke 3:2.

18 ὀνόμασιν ... ἀνόμῳ: Note the pun.

20 τῷ τοῦ πάπα Θεῷ: Laurent suggests that this is a reference to the
pope, or an ironic allusion to Athanasius, patriarch or «pope» of
Alexandria; cf. *Regestes*, 568.

39–40 τὸν τοῦ βασιλέως πνευματικόν: The only person who can be identified
as a confessor of the Emperor *ca.* 1293 is John-Cosmas of Sozopolis,
who became patriarch of Constantinople in 1294. He was made
spiritual confessor to the Emperor sometime before 1293; cf. Pachymeres, *Hist.*, II, 183.

40 Γενναδίῳ: Gennadios, archbishop of Justiniana Prima under Andronicus II. He was elected to the patriarchal throne in 1289, but did not accept the position (Pachymeres, *Hist.*, II, 139). Pachymeres mentions Gennadios as a prime mover in persuading Andronicus of the necessity of removing Athanasius from the patriarchate in 1293 (*Hist.*, II, 167). In 1293 Gennadios was again considered as a patriarchal candidate (Pachymeres, *Hist.*, II, 184), and thus had ample motivation for forcing Athanasius' resignation.

Σελλιώτῃ: Selliotes must be identified with the Sylaiotes who is reported by Pachymeres to have agitated together with Gennadios for the deposition of Athanasius in 1293; cf. note on Gennadios, *supra*. Lequien asserted he was called Sylaiotes because he was bishop of Syllaeum in Pamphylia (*Oriens Christianus*, I, 1020), but he was in fact a simple monk; perhaps he acquired the name because his family came from Syllaeum.

Sylaiotes is mentioned in Letter XXVII of Maximus Planudes (Treu, ed., *Planudis epistulae*, 44), and was also a forerunner of the hesychast movement; cf. Gregory Palamas, *Triads for the defense of the Hesychasts* (*Spicilegium Sacrum Lovaniense*, 29–30 [Louvain, 1959]), ed. J. Meyendorff, I, 2, 12, and II, 2, 3. See also Laurent, *Regestes*, 568.

75 Ἡρακλείας: Andreas, metropolitan of Thracian Heraclea (present day Marmara Ereğlisi, on the north shore of the Sea of Marmara) from *ca.* 1289 to at least 1303. Andreas is known from a synodal act preserved in the Athonite monastery of Xeropotamou, dated to a July in Athanasius' first patriarchate (*Actes de Xéropotamou*, no. 11, p. 97) and from an unpublished patriarchal act of June 2, 1294, found in *Laurent. Plut. V, 2*, fol. 386ᵛ.

In January 1303, the monk Menas approached this metropolitan of Heraclea for advice after hearing Athanasius' prophecy that divine wrath imminently threatened Constantinople. Andreas advised Menas to communicate the news directly to the Emperor (Pachymeres, *Hist.*, II, 360). Andreas would thus appear to be a member of the anti-Arsenite faction, which wished to restore Athanasius to the patriarchal throne, and it is not surprising that in 1297 Athanasius excluded him from his threats of general excommunication.

Μελενίκου: A diocese in northeastern Macedonia (present day Melnik in Bulgaria). The metropolitan mentioned by Athanasius may possibly be identified with Maximus, who is attested in a patriarchal act of June 2, 1294 (*Laurent. Plut. V, 2*, fol. 386ᵛ), or with John who was metropolitan of Melenikon in September 1315 (Miklosich–Müller, I, 14).

2,3

'Απαμείας: Under Andronicus II, Apameia, on the southern shore of the Sea of Marmara (near present day Mudanya), was the seat of a metropolitan. The name of the metropolitan mentioned in this letter is unknown, but he is probably the same man to whom Athanasius addressed several letters, urging him to return to his see and to make amends for certain injustices he had committed (cf. *Vat. Gr. 2219*, fols. 126ʳ–130ᵛ = Laurent, *Regestes*, nos. 1742–44, 1746).

Βρύσεως: A diocese located in eastern Thrace at present day Pinar Hisar. The bishop mentioned in this letter should perhaps be identified with Gerasimus, who was archbishop of Brysis in July 1315 (Miklosich–Müller, I, 6).

3.

To the Emperor, urging him to imitate the repentance of the Ninevites, teach piety to his children, and send the bishops back to their sees.

Laurent, *Regestes*, no. 1673

Date: mid-February 1303? See commentary on line 3.

3 λελύπησαι μὴ εὐχόμενος ὑφ'ἡμῶν: Athanasius may be referring here to the incident of January 1303, when Andronicus led a crowd of people to the monastery of Xerolophos where Athanasius was living in retirement, but the former Patriarch refused to pronounce a blessing (Pachymeres, *Hist.*, II, 369). Because of Athanasius' extensive use in this letter of quotations from Gregory of Nazianzus' *Oration* XVI, which was read on «Cheese-Eating Sunday», it is likely that he wrote the letter around the time of this Sunday, which fell on February 17 in 1303.

Laurent places the letter between the end of 1303 and 1305; cf. *Regestes*, 466.

24 γενώμεθα Νινευῖται, μὴ Σοδομῖται: Cf. Jon. 3 and Gen. 19.

44 Ἄχαρ παρανομήσαντος: Cf. Josh. 7.

45–48 διὰ τὴν παρανομίαν ... καὶ τῆς ζωῆς: Cf. 1 Kings 2–4.

48 ἡ τοῦ Θεοῦ κιβωτός: Cf. 1 Kings 4:3–11.

3–6

54–55 τὸν οἶκον τὸν σὸν καὶ ... παῖδας: Gregoras commented that Athanasius was not afraid to criticize the Emperor's own family (*Hist.*, I, 182); cf. Letters 36, 107.

4.

Athanasius, apparently in retirement, asks the Emperor not to disturb him again, by either a personal visit or a message.

Laurent, *Regestes*, Appendix, no. 4

Date: Laurent assigns this letter to November–December 1300, linking it with Letter 1, addressed to the Emperor in Thessalonica. I would prefer to link this letter with no. 3, which directly precedes it in the Vatican manuscript, and feel the letter refers rather to Andronicus' visit to Xerolophos in early 1303. See commentary *infra*.

6–7 εὐχὴν παρὰ τῶν ἁμαρτωλῶν ... ἡ ... βασιλεία σου ἀπαιτεῖ: Cf. commentary on Letter 3, line 3.

12 ἀνενόχλητος ἤμην: Probably an allusion to Athanasius' retirement to his monastery after his first patriarchate.

5.

Athanasius urges the Emperor to save the poor from oppression through righteous judgments.

Laurent, *Regestes*, no. 1674

4 ἀπίδῃ: For the replacement of the future indicative by the subjunctive in later Greek, cf. Jannaris, *Historical Greek Grammar*, App. IV, 8–10.

22 δικαίως ὁ δίκαιος ἐδικαίωσε: Note here Athanasius' use of the stylistic device of *figura etymologica* (σχῆμα ἐτυμολογικόν); cf. R. Volkmann, *Die Rhetorik der Griechen und Römer* (Leipzig, 1874), 407–8.

6.

Athanasius urges the Emperor to punish sinners and to cleanse the Church of defilement by schismatics.

Laurent, *Regestes*, no. 1675

7.

Athanasius praises Andronicus for the blessings he has received from
God, then scolds him because he does not make use of his power. The Emperor
should hasten to drive troublemakers out of the capital, especially the Patriarch
of Alexandria.

Laurent, *Regestes*, no. 1597

Date: between late 1303 and 1305, when Athanasius of Alexandria was
   expelled from the capital; cf. Pachymeres, *Hist.*, II, 579.

21–22 εἰ μὴ ... σπουδῇ: Anacoluthon.

23 Ἐζεκίας: Cf. 4 Kings 18–19, and Letter 41, lines 2–7.

26 προσθήκην ζωῆς: Cf. 4 Kings 20:6.

28–30 τοὺς ... συναναστρέφεσθαι καὶ συνεῖναι: Probably a reference to
   Armenians; cf. Letter 36, lines 5–6: ὁ κοινὸς λαὸς ... τῇ εἰσαγωγῇ
   ὡς οὐκ ὤφειλεν Ἰουδαίων καὶ Ἀρμενίων καταμιαίνεται.

31 τὸν ἐξ Αἰγύπτου Πρωτέα: A rare example of the use of classical
   allusion in Athanasius' correspondence, perhaps derived from Gregory of Nazianzus, *Oration* IV (PG, 35, cols. 586A, 609A). Proteus
   was an Egyptian «old man of the sea» who was able to assume a
   variety of shapes; cf. *Odyssey*, IV, 385 ff. Athanasius is alluding to
   Athanasius II, patriarch of Alexandria (1276–*ca.* 1316), who was
   one of the Constantinopolitan Patriarch's strongest opponents; cf.
   Chrysostomos of Athens, Ὁ Ἀλεξανδρείας Ἀθανάσιος Βʹ, in
   Ἐπ.Ἑτ.Βυζ.Σπ., 6 (1929), 3–13. A former monk on Sinai
   (Pachymeres, *Hist.*, II, 579), he was elected patriarch of Alexandria
   in 1276; since his see was in the hands of the Mamelukes, he went
   to Constantinople in 1278 and was presented by the Emperor
   Michael VIII with the monasteries of St. Michael at Anaplous and
   of the Great Field (Μεγάλου Ἀγροῦ) in Hellespont, as a residence and
   a source of income respectively. When his homonym Athanasius
   became patriarch of Constantinople in 1289, confiscated the monastery of the Great Field, and insisted that his name be commemorated
   at the monastery of St. Michael, the Patriarch of Alexandria went
   into exile on Rhodes (Pachymeres, *Hist.*, II, 203).
   He returned to the capital after Athanasius' first resignation
   from the patriarchate of Constantinople in 1293, and was allowed to
   live in the monastery of Christ Euergetes. In 1294 the Patriarch was

chosen by Andronicus to act as an emissary to the King of Armenia, in order to pursue negotiations about the marriage of Michael IX. The voyage to Cilicia, however, came to a sudden end when the ship bearing the imperial ambassador was captured by pirates near Phocaea, and the Patriarch was forced to escape by an overland route (Pachymeres, *Hist.*, II, 203–4; Treu, ed., *Planudis epistulae*, 110–11, 146).

The Patriarch of Alexandria naturally opposed Athanasius' return to the patriarchal throne and refused to accept his reinstatement in 1303 (Pachymeres, *Hist.*, II, 409; Gregoras, *Hist.*, I, 216–17). In 1305 the Patriarch of Alexandria was again forced to leave the capital (Pachymeres, *Hist.*, II, 579), and had several hair-raising adventures at the hands of Franks on the Greek mainland (Pachymeres, *Hist.*, II, 593–95). We may assume that he finally reached the μετόχιον of Sinai on Crete where he wished to retire. We know that he died sometime during the patriarchate of John XIII Glykys (1315–1319), because his successor Gregory II sent a letter to Glykys at the time of his election to the throne of Alexandria (Miklosich–Müller, I, 20–25).

Athanasius' hostile picture of the Patriarch of Alexandria as the originator of one of the five schisms which was tearing apart the Christian Church (Letter 69) is contradicted by the testimony of contemporaries who describe the Patriarch as a cultured and saintly man; cf. Gregoras, *Hist.*, I, 216, and Treu, ed., *Planudis epistulae*, 146. For the Alexandrian Patriarch's activity as a bibliophile, see T. C. Skeat, *The Codex Sinaiticus and the Codex Alexandrinus* (London, 1963), 31–33, and T. D. Moschonas, Κατάλογοι τῆς Πατριαρχικῆς Βιβλιοθήκης, Τόμος Α΄, Χειρόγραφα (Alexandria, 1945), nos. 12 and 34.

8.

Letter to an official concerning the conscription of oarsmen for the *megas doux* (Roger de Flor).

Laurent, *Regestes*, no. 1593

Date: between September 1303 and Christmas 1304; cf. commentary *infra*. Laurent first dates the letter between the end of 1303 and March 21, 1304, but gives no reason for this latter date (*Regestes*, 375). On the next page (376), however, he gives Christmas 1304, or even April 1305 as the *terminus ante quem*.

8, 9

17–18 εἰς κατάπλουν τοῦ μεγάλου δουκός: Andronicus II granted the title *megas doux*, or admiral of the fleet, in turn to three members of the Catalan Company which he had hired after the peace of Caltabellotta in 1302 to fight the Turks in Asia Minor. The title of *megas doux* was held by Roger de Flor from September 1303 to December 1304, and by Berenguer d'Entença from December 1304 until 1307. When Berenguer d'Entença died, he was succeeded as *megas doux* by Fernand Ximenes de Arenos; cf. R. Guilland, «Etudes de titulature et de prosopographie byzantines: Drongaire de la flotte, grand drongaire de la flotte, duc de la flotte, mégaduc», *BZ*, 44 (1951), 231–32; Pachymeres, *Hist.*, II, 395 and 498; Gregoras, *Hist.*, I, 232.

Since this letter is placed early in the collection of Athanasius' correspondence, we may assume that Athanasius is referring to Roger de Flor, the first and most famous Catalan *megas doux*, especially since the following letter, no. 9, clearly alludes to Roger. Therefore, Letter 8 should be dated between Roger's arrival in Constantinople in September 1303 and his promotion to the rank of Caesar in December 1304.

κατάπλους, «a downward voyage», means a voyage south; cf. ἄνω in line 21 of this letter, which means «up the Bosporus» or north. This letter could refer to any of the several occasions on which Roger de Flor sailed south from Constantinople: 1) in the fall of 1303, he sailed to Artaqui (present day Erdek, slightly west of Cyzicus) (Muntaner, II, 489; Pachymeres, *Hist.*, II, 399); 2) in March 1304 he went to Constantinople and returned to Artaqui *ca.* March 15 (Muntaner, II, 494; Pachymeres, *Hist.*, II, 419); 3) in October 1304 he visited Constantinople and then went to Gallipoli in November (Muntaner, II, 508). According to Muntaner, Roger visited the Byzantine capital again after Christmas (Muntaner, II, 508–9).

20 Ἱερόν: A port on the east coast of the Bosporus, north of present-day Anadolukavaği; cf. Janin, *Constantinople byzantine*, 485.

9.

Athanasius asks the Emperor to arrange that Orthodox Christians accompany Roger de Flor to the Greek islands which have come under his authority.

Laurent, *Regestes*, no. 1594

9

Date: probably the winter of 1303 or summer of 1304, when the Catalans were setting up headquarters on Chios and other Aegean islands; cf. Laurent, *Regestes*, 376.

2–3 τὴν ἐκκλησίαν καθάραι συγκοινωνίας τῶν Ἰταλῶν: An allusion to Andronicus II's repudiation in 1282 of his father's Unionist policy.

4–5 ἡ ... συμφορὰ ἠνάγκασε νήσους δοθῆναι τῷ μεγάλῳ δουκί: According to Guilland, from the time of Alexius I Comnenus the *megas doux* was chief admiral of the Byzantine fleet (*BZ*, 44 [1951], 222). Muntaner states that the title *megas doux* which was conferred on Roger also gave him authority over the Aegean islands: «Grand Duke is a title which means the same as prince and lord over all the soldiers of the Empire, with authority over the admiral; and *all the islands of Romania* [italics mine] are subject to him and also all the places on the seacoasts» (Muntaner, II, 483). On May 10, 1305, Berenguer d'Entença, Roger's successor as *megas doux*, in a letter to the Republic of Venice, called himself «by grace of God, megas doux of Romania, seigneur of Natolia and of the islands of the empire»; cf. *I Libri Commemoriali della Repubblica di Venezia*, ed. R. Predelli, I (Venice, 1876), 181; quoted by G. Schlumberger in *Expédition des Almugavars ou routiers catalans en Orient* (Paris, 1902), 129.

However, Muntaner also reports that after Christmas 1304 «it was so settled between the Caesar [Roger de Flor] and the Emperor, that the Emperor would give him all the kingdom of Anatolia and *all the islands of Romania* [italics mine]» (Muntaner, II, 508). Pachymeres' version of the story differs somewhat and states that in January 1305 Andronicus agreed to make Roger Caesar and to hand over all of Anatolia except the major cities (*Hist.*, II, 506).

I have not been able to find any confirmation in a Byzantine source that the title *megas doux* conferred authority over the islands, but it is not surprising, since the equivalent position in the Ottoman Empire, *kapudan pasha*, included responsibility for the Aegean islands and coasts of the Morea; cf. article on Kaptan Paşa in *Islam Ansiklopedisi* (Istanbul, 1955), VI, 206–7.

6 κοινωνοὶ τῆς Χριστοῦ ἐκκλησίας: Athanasius, an ardent opponent of Union, feared lest the Catalans attempt to convert the islanders to the Catholic faith. According to Muntaner, the Catalan fleet spent the winter of 1303 at Chios and visited neighboring islands (II, 493). Pachymeres also records visits of the Catalans to Chios, Lemnos, and Lesbos during the summer of 1304 (*Hist.*, II, 436).

10.

Athanasius writes to the Emperor about a third person who has been nominated for an ecclesiastical position, perhaps his successor as patriarch (cf. Laurent, *Regestes*, 566). Although Athanasius insinuates that this person is not of good character, he states that he trusts the Emperor's judgment and will accept his decision in the matter.

Laurent, *Regestes*, Appendix, no. 1

Date: Laurent ingeniously interprets the letter as Athanasius' reply to the Emperor, who had asked his opinion on the choice of John Cosmas as patriarch, and therefore dates the letter to the autumn of 1293. The letter could, however, refer to any number of ecclesiastical nominations made during Athanasius' patriarchate.

11.

Athanasius asks the Emperor to forgive him if he is not present when certain people are charged with rebellion against the Empire and Church.

Laurent, *Regestes*, no. 1634

Date: winter, 1305–1306; cf. Laurent, *Regestes*, 428, and commentary on lines 7–8 *infra*.

7–8 τινῶν φρυαττομένων κατὰ Θεοῦ καὶ βασιλείας καὶ ἐκκλησίας: No doubt a reference to the Arsenite-supported conspiracy of Drimys; cf. the phrase used in Letter 81, lines 47–48: κατά τε τῆς ποίμνης Χριστοῦ, κατά τε τῆς ἐκκλησίας, καὶ τοῦ θεοστεφοῦς αὐτοκράτορος.

16 ἀκολουθοῦσι δὲ καὶ τὸ ὀλιγώτερον εἴκοσι: Athanasius' disciples, described by Pachymeres as νήλιποί τινες καὶ ὠχρίαι καὶ κατεσκληκότες καὶ γυμνοὶ καὶ ἀπέριττοι (*Hist.*, II, 143–44).

17 ἡ δὲ ἐμὲ δεχομένη κέλλα: Athanasius is in temporary residence at the monastery of Chora, located near Edirne Kapi in the northern sector of Constantinople. For the definitive study of this monastery, see Underwood, *The Kariye Djami*.

17–19 εἰ ἦν δυνατὸν ... ἄλευρον: The pathetic state of the church and monastery at Chora in the early fourteenth century is recorded by Theodore Metochites, the eventual restorer of Chora; see his *Poem 1*,

11-13

vv. 1004–5, ed. M. Treu, *Dichtungen des Gross-Logotheten Theodoros Metochites* (Potsdam, 1895), 28. Cf. also Gregoras, *Hist.*, I, 459. Restoration of the church began sometime after 1312, probably *ca.* 1316 (cf. I. Ševčenko, «Theodore Metochites, the Chora, and the Intellectual Trends of his Time», *The Kariye Djami*, IV, *Studies in the Art of the Kariye Djami and Its Intellectual Background* [ed. P. A. Underwood], 90–91), and was completed by 1321; cf. Underwood, *The Kariye Djami*, I, 15. Note the pun χωρεῖν ... τῆς Χώρας.

24 ἣν ἔχω ὑγείαν καὶ δύναμιν: Athanasius' allusion to failing health is a further indication that this letter should be attributed to his second patriarchate.

12.

Athanasius begs the Emperor not to neglect his reports on injustice in the empire.

Laurent, *Regestes*, no. 1676

Date: winter, since Athanasius alludes to rain and mud. It may perhaps be more precisely dated to the month of January, since Athanasius quotes twice from Gregory of Nazianzus' *Oration in Praise of St. Athanasius of Alexandria*, which was read in churches on January 18, his feast day.

2–3 ὀδύνη καρδιακή ... συνηρίθμημαι: Athanasius wishes he were dead, a frequently expressed sentiment; cf. Letters 14 and 15.

6–7 τὸ μὴ καθαίρεσθαι τοὺς θεοκαπήλους τοῦ ἱεροῦ: Perhaps a reference to simoniacal priests; cf. the Promissory Letter of Andronicus, *Vat. Gr. 2219*, fol. 273ʳ: εἰ βουλήσεται ⟨the patriarch⟩ ... θεοκαπήλους ἐλαύνειν τοῦ ἱεροῦ (ed. Laurent, «Le serment d'Andronic II», 137, lines 46–47).

29–30 ἵνα βασιλέως ... παρακαλῶ, δέομαι καὶ ἀντιβολῶ: Apparently Andronicus frequently used this phrase; cf. Letter 41, line 32: ἵνα τοῖς σοῖς λόγοις χρήσωμαι, παρακαλῶ, παρακαλῶ, παρακαλῶ, and Letter 93, lines 15–16: ἵνα καὶ ἔθει βασιλικῷ χρήσωμαι, παρακαλῶ, παρακαλῶ, παρακαλῶ.

13.

Athanasius urges the Emperor Michael to renounce physical pleasures and lead a virtuous life.

Laurent, *Regestes*, no. 1610

Date: 1304 (?)

ad apparatum 1: Μιχαὴλ: Michael IX Palaeologus, son of Andronicus II
by his first wife, Anne of Hungary. He was crowned emperor on
May 21, 1295 and ruled as co-emperor until his untimely death in
1320.

2 πρόσταγμα: An imperial document to which the emperor affixed
short marks of validation, as contrasted with the chrysobull, the
only document which the emperor signed with his own hand; cf.
Dölger-Karayannopoulos, *Byzantinische Urkundenlehre*, 109–12. In
this instance, however, Athanasius is probably not using the word
πρόσταγμα in its technical sense.

3 τῶν ὑγειῶν: Athanasius had good reason to be concerned about
the health of the young co-Emperor who had suffered a nearly fatal
illness at Pegae in the fall of 1303 (Pachymeres, *Hist.*, II, 391–92).

4 νίκης: Michael's military campaigns were notoriously unsuccessful;
therefore, this rare victory may be attributed with some certainty
to Michael's Bulgarian campaign of 1304. On August 23, for example,
Michael made a successful attack on the Bulgarians near Adrianople
(Pachymeres, *Hist.*, II, 447). Laurent sees a possible allusion to
some victories over the Turks in Asia Minor in 1304; cf. *Regestes*,
398.

5 οἱ μισοῦντες ἡμᾶς: In the early fourteenth century, Byzantium was
surrounded by enemies on all sides, the Bulgarians in Thrace, the
Turks in Asia Minor, the Genoese and Venetians in the capital
itself, and the Catalan mercenaries who attacked the Byzantines as
frequently as they did the Turks.

6–7 δι' ἄλλο οὐδὲν ... καὶ πλέον οὐδέν: Athanasius did not attribute the
success of the Turks and other hostile powers to the superiority of
the enemy forces, but believed that the Byzantines were being
punished by God because of their immorality and lack of faith;
cf. Letters 36, 41, and 67.

13 σώματος ἡδονὴν: The historical sources give no clue as to the sort
of physical pleasure in which Michael was indulging.

14.

Athanasius complains to the Emperor that, although he frequently visits the palace to present petitions, Andronicus fails to act on his recommendations.

Laurent, *Regestes*, no. 1677

Date: winter, 1303–1309

2–3 ηὐχόμην ... λογίζεσθαι: Athanasius again uses this turn of phrase to express his bitter despair; cf. Letters 12 and 15.

28 ἡ ἄμπελος τοῦ Θεοῦ: The Church.

36 τοῖς ἀνακτόροις: The palace of Blachernae, in the northern corner of Constantinople, near the Golden Horn, was the usual residence of the Palaeologan emperors; cf. Janin, *Constantinople byzantine*, 123–30.

39 ἐν τῇ Χώρᾳ: Athanasius used to wait at the Chora monastery (which was only about 1000 meters from the Blachernae Palace) for a summons from the Emperor, because it was closer to the palace than the patriarchate or his monastery at Xerolophos. Thus if the Emperor did agree to grant him an audience, Athanasius could quickly make his way to the palace before the Emperor changed his mind.

42 ἐστράφην κενός: Athanasius was frequently frustrated in his attempts to communicate with Andronicus in person. In Letter 35, for example, he complains that the Emperor has not been willing to see him for almost two years! It appears that the Patriarch had no better luck with his efforts to communicate in writing, since in Letter 49, line 106, he pleaded with the Emperor not to toss his memorandum in a pigeonhole.

59 αὐτόθι: Probably the imperial palace at Blachernae, since, in correspondence, αὐτόθι refers to the residence of the addressee of the letter; cf. Darrouzès, *Epistoliers byzantins*, 400.

ἀποχερᾶς: The word ἀποχερά is not found in any dictionary, and may be a scribal error for ἀπόπειρα, since in this passage it apparently has the meaning of «attempt». Possibly ἀποχερά may be derived from the verb ἀποχεριάζω, meaning «to enclose something completely in one's grasp» (Demetrakos, *Lexikon*, I, 888–89).

61 ἀπολέγομαι δὲ καὶ αὐτὴν τὴν ζωήν: Cf. lines 2–3 *supra*.

73 κέκρικα δέον κινεῖσθαι: I.e., to leave Chora, where he has been waiting in vain for an audience with the Emperor.

15.

Athanasius complains to the Emperor about the unrepentant attitude of bishops and senators, and asks that an investigation be made of certain outrageous injustices committed by both Franks and Greeks.

Laurent, *Regestes*, no. 1611

Date: 1303–1309; Laurent (*Regestes*, 399) dates this letter *ca.* 1304–1305, in the belief that the Φράγγοι of line 25 are Catalans; in Letter 84, however, the term Φράγγοι clearly alludes to Italians; cf. line 16.

10 ἐν τῇ ἀγρυπνίᾳ: The ἀγρυπνία is a service which takes place during the night preceding a solemn feast day; cf. L. Clugnet, *Dictionnaire grec-français des noms liturgiques en usage dans l'Eglise grecque* (Paris, 1895), 3. Athanasius kept these vigils frequently, in an effort to appease the wrath of God; cf. Pachymeres, *Hist.*, II, 421 and 518.

11–12 διασύρειν ἡμῶν καὶ καταγελᾶν ἀναφαίνονται: Pachymeres tells us that Athanasius was ridiculed for believing his processions and vigils would save the empire, especially after fire broke out in the Kynegos quarter during the very evening of a day when Athanasius had led a religious procession (*Hist.*, II, 581–82).

12–13 μετὰ τῆς ἀρχιερατικῆς στολῆς: Athanasius also had difficulty in making the clergy wear himations to services; cf. Pachymeres, *Hist.*, II, 642; *Vat. Gr. 2219*, fols. 214ᵛ–221ᵛ (= Laurent, *Regestes*, nos. 1767–72).

14 τῆς συγκλήτου: By the fourteenth century the term σύγκλητος meant the government, the ministers assembled as a body; cf. Ševčenko, *Etudes*, 136 note 1, and R.-J. Loenertz, «Le chancelier impérial à Byzance au XIVᵉ et au XIIIᵉ siècle», *OCP*, 26 (1960), 294. See also A. Christophilopoulou, Ἡ σύγκλητος εἰς τὸ βυζαντινὸν κράτος, in Ἀκαδημία Ἀθηνῶν, Ἐπετηρὶς τοῦ ἀρχείου τῆς ἱστορίας τοῦ ἑλληνικοῦ δικαίου, 2 (1949).

15, 16

25 οἱ Φράγγοι: The Genoese and Venetians had taken over Byzantium's commercial supremacy in the twelfth century. Athanasius despised the Italians because they were Catholics and because their merchants grew rich by selling grain at exorbitant prices to the poor in Constantinople.

26 φθορὰν γυναικῶν: Athanasius may be here alluding to the sort of behavior recorded in Letter 93, lines 20–22, where he reports that Italian merchants boasted of receiving favors from Byzantine women as payment for grain.

16.

Athanasius attacks bishops and monks who stay in Constantinople, instead of returning to their dioceses or monasteries.

Laurent, *Regestes*, no. 1678

Date: 1303–1309

5–7 οἱ μὲν τοῦτον ... διαπληκτίζεσθαι: Athanasius is here alluding to the bishops' practice of accepting bribes from people whose cases were being tried before the synod; cf. Letters 25, lines 5–6, and 48, lines 12–14.

7–9 ἐὰν ἠλέησεν ... βλάβῃ καὶ ταραχῇ: Athanasius may be referring to the case of the Patriarch of Alexandria, who was forced to go into exile on Rhodes during Athanasius' first patriarchate, but returned to the capital after Athanasius' resignation in 1293; cf. Pachymeres, *Hist.*, II, 203.

10 ὁ χαρτοφύλαξ: The keeper of archives in Thessalonica. Laurent has suggested a possible identification with John Stavrakios, a correspondent of George of Cyprus; cf. *Regestes*, 470, and E. Kurtz, *Des Klerikers Gregorios Bericht über Leben, Wunderthaten und Translation der hl. Theodora von Thessalonich* (St. Petersburg, 1902), 94–104.

10–11 ὁ νῦν ᾿Ακαπνίου: The abbot of the monastery of Akapniou located in Thessalonica, probably to be identified with the Ignatius who wrote, *ca.* 1307, a Διήγησις ἐπωφελὴς περὶ τῆς θεανδρικῆς εἰκόνος τοῦ κυρίου ᾿Ιησοῦ Χριστοῦ τῆς φανερωθείσης ἐν τῇ κατὰ τῶν Θεσσαλονικέων μονῇ τῶν Λατόμων, συγγραφεῖσα παρὰ ᾿Ιγνατίου μοναχοῦ

τοῦ καθηγουμένου τῆς ἐν Θεσσαλονίκῃ μονῆς τοῦ 'Ακαπνίου; cf. Volk, *Die byzantinischen Klosterbibliotheken*, 115.

The monastery was involved in a dispute in 1294, when the synod restored to the metropolitan of Thessalonica jurisdiction over the church of the Archangels which had been usurped by the abbot of Akapniou; cf. Laurent, *Regestes*, no. 1565. Akapniou is also mentioned in *Regestes*, nos. 1530, 1531.

For literature on this monastery, see *EO*, 30 (1931), 91–95, and H.-G. Beck, *Kirche und theologische Literatur im byzantinischen Reich* (Munich, 1959), 223.

14 'Ηλίαν: An otherwise unknown personage.

16 Βήρας: The monastery of the Kosmosoteira at Pherrae in Thrace, near the present-day Turkish-Greek border. The monastery was founded in 1152 by Isaac Comnenus, the third son of Alexius I Comnenus. The *typikon* of the monastery was published by L. Petit, «Typikon du monastère de la Kosmosotira près d'Aenos (1152)», *IRAIK*, 13 (1908), 17–77. See also an unpublished M. A. thesis by N. Patterson at Columbia University in New York, «Byzantine Frescoes at Pherrai» (1964).

τοῦ . . . ἀββᾶ 'Ιωάννου: ἀββᾶς is another term for ἡγούμενος or ἀρχιμανδρίτης, the superior of a monastery; cf. Panagiotakou, Τὸ Δίκαιον τῶν Μοναχῶν, 344–45 and note 2, and de Meester, *De monachico statu*, 202. Athanasius' letter is the only source to mention this early-fourteenth-century abbot of the monastery at Bera. The mysterious incident involving three hundred gold nomismata is not recorded in the historical sources.

17.

Athanasius urges the Emperor to take action against external enemies. Andronicus should make personal inspection tours of the city, especially in the vicinity of the walls and gates, and no armed person should be allowed to enter the city.

Laurent, *Regestes*, no. 1612

Date: 1304–1305, when the security of the capital was menaced by the Catalan mercenaries of Roger de Flor; see commentary on line 15 *infra*, and Laurent, *Regestes*, 400.

17

12 μηδὲ προφασιζομένους τὴν ὀλιγότητα: I have translated this sentence as if προφασιζομένους were nominative. I have not emended the form of the participle because it seems likely that Athanasius here, as so often, confused his cases and dictated προφασιζομένους.

15 μάλιστα τῶν Λατίνων: Athanasius is probably referring to Catalans; cf. his warning in Letter 35, lines 53–57.

23-24 παρὰ τῶν ἐνεργούντων: The term ὁ ἐνεργῶν (or διενεργῶν), meaning fiscal agent, tax collector, first appeared in Byzantium in the twelfth century; cf. Miklosich–Müller, IV, 62–63 (the act is dated to 1133 by Ahrweiler, «La région de Smyrne», 128; see also 125–26, and her article «Recherches sur l'administration de l'empire byzantin au IXe–XIe siècles», BCH, 84 [1960], 88, 90, and 92).

28 Δοσίθεος: Unknown.

30 ὁ τῆς αὐλῆς πριμμικήριος: The primikerios of the court was a master of ceremonies at the palace, and played an especially important role at imperial receptions; he was thirty-third in rank in Pseudo-Kodinos' list of dignities (Traité des Offices, 138 and 179). On this title, see also R. Guilland, «Etudes de titulature byzantine: les titres auliques réservés aux eunuques», REB, 14 (1956), 122–57. The only primikerios of the court of this period who is known by name is Nestongos Doukas, who was subsequently promoted to the position of megas hetairiarches around June of 1304 (Pachymeres, Hist., II, 429). It is unlikely, however, that Nestongos Doukas is the object of Athanasius' attack, since the Patriarch granted him refuge when he fell into disgrace with the Emperor a short time later. Athanasius is probably referring, therefore, to Nestongos' successor, and the letter can thus be dated after the middle of 1304; cf. Laurent, Regestes, 400–1.

Guilland has suggested the possibility that the primikerios mentioned in this letter should be identified with Kassianos, who was megas primikerios ca. 1305–1307 (Guilland, ibid., 151–52; Pachymeres, Hist., II, 528, 549, 618), but the primikerios attacked by Athanasius is specifically described as primikerios of the court, not megas primikerios.

42-43 τοὺς ... τὰς πύλας φυλάσσοντας: The πορτάριοι, who guarded the city gates; cf. Constantine Porphyrogenitus, De cerimoniis, II, 52 (Bonn, I, 719), and R. Guilland, «Etudes sur l'histoire administrative de l'empire byzantin: Le comte des murs», Byzantion, 34 (1964) (hereafter, «Le comte des murs»), 21.

43 τῶν ἐγχειρισθέντων τὴν κατ' αὐτῶν ἐξουσίαν: The πορτάριοι were under the command of the δομέστικος τῶν τειχέων, who was charged with maintaining the fortifications of the city and commanding the soldiers entrusted with their defense, οἱ τειχειῶται; cf. *De cerimoniis*, *loc. cit.*; Ps.-Kodinos, *Traité des Offices*, 186; and Guilland, «Le comte des murs», 17–25.

44 ἢ διδόναι τὸ ἱκανόν, ἢ διώκεσθαι: Athanasius protests against the Byzantine custom whereby aspirants to official positions paid a fixed sum for the offices in exchange for the prestige of the position and a small annual pension. This system, however, provided an essential source of capital for the public treasury; cf. P. Lemerle, «'Roga' et rente d'état aux Xe–XIe siècles», *REB*, 25 (1967), 77–100; R. Guilland, «Vénalité et favoritisme à Byzance», *REB*, 10 (1952), 35–46; and G. Kolias, *Ämter- und Würdenkauf im früh- und mittelbyzantinischen Reich*, TFByzNgPhil, 35 (Athens, 1939). Athanasius, as a champion of the «little man», realized that this system made officials exact money in turn from their subordinates, in order to recoup their losses.

18.

Athanasius asks the Emperor to restrain the wicked conduct of evildoers, especially in St. Sophia.

Laurent, *Regestes*, no. 1679

10 ὡς ταύτης εἶναι υἱὸς δοξασθείς: Athanasius frequently referred to the Emperor as the son of the Church; cf. Letters 45, line 7; 49, line 39; 55, line 4; and 79, lines 15-16.

13–14 ἕκαστος τῶν κακοπραγούντων ... οἰκῶν τῆς ἐκκλησίας: Athanasius is apparently protesting here against people who were eating and sleeping in churches or in adjoining buildings, since this practice was forbidden by canon and civil law; cf. canons 74, 76, and 97 of the Synod in Trullo, and *Basilics*, Book V, Title 1, 11. Also see Athanasius, Letters 50 and 66, for similar complaints.

23–24 οὓς τάξει ... ἐνεργεῖν τι: In Athanasius' letters the verb ἐνεργεῖν often has the technical meaning «to collect revenue». Here he is warning the ἐνεργοῦντες or tax-collectors to perform their duties honestly; cf. commentary on Letter 17, lines 23-24.

19.

A letter of the deacon Philip Syropoulos, who has evidently been accused of Arsenite sympathies, declaring that henceforth he will remain faithful to the Orthodox Church, and renounce all association with the Arsenites. It would seem that the letter is included in the manuscripts of Athanasius' correspondence because the Patriarch drafted the text of the recantation, presented it to the deacon for his signature, and then forwarded it to the Emperor. For a parallel case, see the promissory letter of Andronicus II (*Vat. Gr. 2219*, fols. 272ᵛ–274ʳ, ed. Laurent, «Le serment d'Andronic II», 135–38), which was in all probability written by Athanasius. For similar recantations, cf. Miklosich–Müller, I, 346–47, 501–2, 503–5, 506–7.

Laurent, *Regestes*, no. 1680

2 τῶν ἑπτὰ διακόνων: A reference to the original seven deacons chosen by the Early Christian community at Jerusalem; cf. Acts 6:5.

Κανδάκη συναναβάς: In Acts 8:27 ff. it is recounted that one of the seven deacons, Philip, on his way to Gaza met an unnamed eunuch of the Ethiopian Queen Kandake (ἀνὴρ Αἰθίοψ εὐνοῦχος δυνάστης Κανδάκης τῆς βασιλίσσης Αἰθιόπων), and climbed into his chariot to explain to him a passage from Isaiah. Athanasius, who writes that Philip climbed into the carriage beside Kandake, evidently misunderstood the verse in *Acts* and thought that Κανδάκης was a masculine nominative form and the name of the eunuch.

3 τὰ τοῦ μεγαλοφωνοτάτου: The eunuch was reading Isaiah 53:7–8.

4 ἀλλά γε Φίλιππός εἰμι καὶ αὐτὸς ἐπίκλην Συρόπουλος: The deacon Philip Syropoulos is known only from this letter. However, the name of the Syropoulos family appears quite often in Byzantine sources of the thirteenth-fifteenth centuries. V. Laurent has published the seal of a John Syropoulos and lists five individuals in the thirteenth-fourteenth centuries who bore this name (*Les sceaux byzantins du Médailler Vatican* [Vatican City, 1962], no. 193, pp. 206–7). Stephen Syropoulos, a relative of Andronicus II, was an ambassador to the Venetians in 1324 (Miklosich–Müller, III, 100, 103, and 105), and Silvester Syropoulos, who attended the Council of Florence in 1439, was patriarch of Constantinople from 1463 to 1464. For other members of the Syropoulos family, cf. A. N. Diamantopoulos, Σίλβεστρος Συρόπουλος καὶ τὰ ἀπομνημονεύματα αὐτοῦ τῆς ἐν Φλωρεντίᾳ Συνόδου, in Νέα Σιών, 18 (1923), 267–68, and Ahrweiler, «La région de Smyrne», 119, 148.

19

Earlier scholars failed to realize that Athanasius wrote this letter to the Emperor in the name of a third person. In the eighteenth century, for example, La Porte du Theil thought that Athanasius' real name was Philip Syropoulos (*Par. Suppl. Gr. 971*, fol. 109). Guilland, who knew from the *Vita Athanasii* of Theoktistos that Athanasius' baptismal name was Alexius, and that he later assumed the monastic names of Akakios and then Athanasius (*Theoctisti Vita Ath.*, 4, 10), admitted he was baffled by Letter 19 («La correspondance inédite d'Athanase», 121 note 7). Cf. also Laurent, *Regestes*, 471–72.

I. Ševčenko was apparently the first person to realize that Athanasius and the deacon Philip Syropoulos were two different people; cf. «Manuel Moschopulos», 156 note 100.

4–6 τοῦ ῥήτορος τῆς ἐκκλησίας ... 'Ιουδαίοις καὶ "Ελλησι: St. Paul; cf. *Vat. Gr. 2219*, fol. 259ᵛ, where Athanasius also refers to Paul as ὁ ῥήτωρ τῆς ἐκκλησίας, and the Μηναῖον τοῦ 'Ιουνίου (M. I. Saliveros [Athens, 1926], 153), where Paul is called ὁ ῥήτωρ τῆς ἐκκλησίας τοῦ Χριστοῦ. For both Jews and Greeks, 'Ιουδαίους τε καὶ "Ελληνας, having heard the preaching of St. Paul, cf. Acts 19:10.

10 τῶν Ξυλωτῶν: «Xylote» was Athanasius' derisive name for the Arsenites, who referred to themselves as Zealots (cf. Γράμμα τῶν Ζηλωτῶν τὸ πρὸς βασιλέα, ed. Laurent from *Par. Gr. 1302*, fols. Bʳ–Bᵛ, in his article «La fin du schisme arsénite», 286–87). Athanasius apparently combined ξύλον with Ζηλωταί to make the pun Ξυλωταί, and to suggest the unyielding opposition of the Arsenites.

It has also been suggested by N. Panayotakis of the University of Jannina (in a conversation with the editor) that Ξυλωτής should be emended to Ξηλωτής, and connected with the verb ξηλώνω (the demotic form of ἐξηλῶ), meaning «to rend, tear, split». This would tie in well with the schismatic character of the Arsenites.

κατά τε τῆς ἐκκλησίας: The Arsenites wanted a member of their own faction to be elected patriarch, and were distressed at the choice in 1289 and 1303 of Athanasius, who proved to be an implacable opponent.

10–11 κατά τε τῆς βασιλείας: The Arsenite schism was also a reflection of the dynastic struggle between the Lascarids and Palaeologi. Since the Patriarch Joseph had crowned Andronicus II as emperor in 1272, it was clear that an Arsenite victory would endanger Andronicus' position on the throne; cf. Laurent, «La fin du schisme arsénite», 240–44.

19, 20

11-12 Ἰγνατίου τοῦ ῥακενδύτου: Syropoulos renounces friendship and fellowship with this Ignatius; therefore, one must assume that Ignatius is still alive and that he is an Arsenite. The epithet ῥακενδύτης, which further identifies Ignatius as a monk (cf. M. Treu, «Der Philosoph Joseph», *BZ*, 8 [1899], 43), was used by Gregoras to describe the Arsenites (*Hist.*, I, 261).

It is not possible, however, to identify this Arsenite Ignatius with any Ignatius who is known in the late thirteenth or early fourteenth century. Ignatius the Rhodian was an intimate of Arsenius, but he died soon after Arsenius' deposition in 1265 (Pachymeres, *Hist.*, I, 295). Another Ignatius, who signed the tome of the Second Council of Blachernae in 1285, must be excluded from consideration because he was not a monk, but metropolitan of Thessalonica (Laurent, «Les signataires», 145). As for Ignatius the Paphlagonian, who is mentioned in Letter 124 of Gregory of Cyprus (Ἐκκλησιαστικὸς Φάρος, 3 [1909], 290), there is no evidence as to whether he was an Arsenite or not; Sykoutris identifies him as an Arsenite (Ἑλληνικά, 2, p. 323), Laurent disagrees (Ἑλληνικά, 3, p. 466). For discussion of the identity of the various Ignatii, see the polemics between I. Sykoutris and V. Laurent in Ἑλληνικά, especially Laurent's «La question des Arsénites», Ἑλληνικά, 3 (1930), 463–70, and Sykoutris' rebuttal, Ἰγνάτιος ὁ Ῥόδιος καὶ Ἰγνάτιος ὁ Θεσσαλονίκης, in Ἑλληνικά, 5 (1932), 108–12.

20.

Athanasius returns a book which has been sent to him, since it is of no interest to him or his disciples.

Laurent, *Regestes*, no. 1681

ad apparatum 1: κανισκίου: synonym for δῶρον; cf. A. Vogt, ed., *Constantin VII Porphyrogénète, Le livre des cérémonies*, I (Paris, 1935), 154.

4 κατ᾽ ἐμοῦ: Unusual use of κατά with the genitive to mean «my associates»; cf. σὺν ἐμοί in line 6.

6 τὴν δέλτον: Originally a writing tablet, *deltos* came to mean a book in the mediaeval period; cf. R. Devreesse, *Introduction à l'étude des manuscrits grecs* (Paris, 1954), 2.

7–8 κεῖσθαι ... ἐν τῇ θυρίδι: For evidence that some of the Early Christian monks kept their few books on a windowshelf, see the *Verba Seniorum*, VI, xii (PL, 73, cols. 890D, 929D–930A, 933A).

21.

A noble couple has asked the synod to grant them a divorce, but the bishops are unable to come to any agreement on account of the confused testimony of the witnesses for both sides. It was the usual practice in such cases for the patriarchal tribunal to force the involved parties to make a declaration, under penalty of excommunication if they gave false evidence; cf. Lemerle, «Le tribunal du patriarcat», 325. Athanasius wishes to avoid subjecting the couple to the dire threat of excommunication, and therefore asks the Emperor to dissolve the marriage outside of court without either party being compelled to pay damages.

Laurent, *Regestes*, no. 1682

ad apparatum 1: εὐλύτωσιν: The word εὐλύτωσις is not listed in any dictionary except Lampe, *Patristic Greek Lexicon*, where it is defined as «payment or settlement of a debt» (571); here, however, it obviously has the same meaning as διευλύτωσιν in line 4, «dissolution of marriage», «divorce».

3–4 ἀμφοτέρων ζητούντων ... παρὰ τῆς ἐκκλησίας διευλύτωσιν ἔννομον: The patriarchal tribunal, composed of the patriarch and the synod of bishops, had jurisdiction over all marital cases, although it usually only handled cases of exceptional importance; cf. Lemerle, «Le tribunal du patriarcat», 321. The tribunal had no initiative in trying cases; the plaintiff or defendant had to request a hearing by the tribunal; cf. Lemerle, *ibid.*, 324; Miklosich–Müller, I, 32, and II, 238.

5 τῶν μαρτύρων: According to the *Epanagoge*, Title XX, chap. 27, a decree of divorce could not be granted without the testimony of seven adult Roman citizens (Zachariä von Lingenthal, *Jus Graeco-Romanum*, IV, 259).

9 ἐν δέ γε τῇ ἐκκλησίᾳ: I.e., in the patriarchal tribunal; cf. Miklosich–Müller, II, 300 and 448.

τὸ φρίκης μεστὸν ἐπιτίμιον: I.e., excommunication; cf. Miklosich–Müller, I, 67 and 389–90.

17–18 ἀποδοθῆναι πάντα τὰ μητρῷα ἀνελλιπῆ: Athanasius requests that the wife be allowed to keep her dowry. The husband could keep his wife's dowry after the divorce only if she were guilty of certain offences, such as treachery against the empire, adultery, going to

the theater and horseraces without her husband's permission, not coming home at night, or plotting against her husband's life; cf. *Epanagoge*, Title XX, chaps. 7–13 (Zachariä von Lingenthal, *Jus Graeco-Romanum*, IV, 256–57), and Harmenopoulos, *Hexabiblos*, IV, 15, pp. 580–82.

18 τὴν παῖδα τῇ οἰκείᾳ μητρί: According to the *Epanagoge*, Title XX, chap. 5, the mother was given custody of the children, if the father was judged to be the guilty party in the divorce (Zachariä von Lingenthal, *Jus Graeco-Romanum*, IV, 255).

τῷ ἀνδρὶ τὰ οἰκεῖα: At the time of marriage, the husband presented his wife with a gift of money or property. In case of divorce, the husband was allowed to keep this marriage settlement, unless he had plotted against the life of his wife, devised treachery against the empire, committed adultery in his own house, etc.; cf. *Epanagoge*, Title XX, chaps. 15–20 (Zachariä von Lingenthal, *Jus Graeco-Romanum*, IV, 257–58), and Harmenopoulos, *Hexabiblos*, IV, 15, pp. 582–86.

20 καταδίκη φρικτῇ: The penalty of excommunication.

22.

Athanasius asks that every wealthy noble either support a certain number of refugees until summertime, or contribute to a relief fund (cf. *Vat. Gr. 2219*, fol. 185ʳ = Laurent, *Regestes*, no. 1757).

Laurent, *Regestes*, no. 1684

Date: winter, *ca.* 1304–1305; cf. Letter 25.

6–7 ἐντὸς τῆς πόλεως αἰχμάλωτος λαὸς πολύς: Although αἰχμάλωτος usually means «captive», it can have the meaning of «refugee» (cf. P. Lemerle, *L'Emirat d'Aydin, Byzance et l'Occident* [Paris, 1957], 20 note 4), as here and in Letter 25; cf. Laurent, *Regestes*, 402. Hordes of refugees began to pour into Constantinople at the beginning of the fourteenth century as the Turks overran the western coast of Anatolia.

23.

Athanasius asks the bishops to join him when he presents a supplication to the Emperor about the problem of the Latins, Jews, and Armenians in Constantinople.

Laurent, *Regestes*, no. 1621

Date: probably summer 1305; see *infra*.

4 τὰ τῶν Λατίνων: Athanasius is worried about the teachings of the
Catholic Latins; this is probably a reference to the Minorite monastery
which was situated in a market place within the walls of Constantinople. Pachymeres relates that Athanasius became incensed at the
presence of the Franciscan monks and forced Andronicus to confiscate their property and expel the monks from Constantinople
(*Hist.*, II, 537–38). Dölger correctly dates the incident to the beginning of May 1305 (*Regesten*, IV, 45). Since this letter is apparently
connected with the expulsion of the Latin monks, and Athanasius
comments that it is summer (line 8), we can probably date the
letter to the summer of 1305.

    Laurent interprets the passage as a more general allusion to
the dangers of Latin propaganda spread by supporters of Union;
cf. *Regestes*, 415.

6–7 περὶ τῶν ᾿Ιουδαίων ... ὅπως ἐξέλθωσι: By the twelfth century,
the Jewish quarter at Constantinople, formerly located within the
walls at Chalkoprateia, had been moved across the Golden Horn
to the Pikridion quarter in Pera (present-day Hasköy); cf. D.
Jacoby, «Les quartiers juifs de Constantinople à l'époque byzantine»,
Byzantion, 37 (1967), 169, 175. *Ca.* 1165, the traveller Benjamin
of Tudela reported: «No Jews live among them inside the city
[Constantinople], for they have been transferred to the other side
of the strait. ... The place in which the Jews live is called 'Pera'»
(J. Starr, *The Jews in the Byzantine Empire [641–1204]* [Athens,
1939], 43, 231). At the time of the Fourth Crusade, the Jewish
quarter was still in Pera (cf. Geoffrey de Villehardouin, *La conquête
de Constantinople*, ed. and trans. E. Faral, I [Paris, 1938], § 159),
but after the recovery of Constantinople, there are references to
Jews living within the city proper, in the Vlanga quarter on the Sea
of Marmara (late thirteenth century: Treu, ed., *Planudis epistulae*,
Ep. XXXI, p. 52; *ca.* 1350: Stephen of Novgorod, trans. S. P. de
Khitrovo, *Itinéraires russes en Orient* [Geneva, 1889], 121).

    Michael VIII apparently ended the exclusion of Jews from
Constantinople proper as a result of his efforts to repopulate the
Byzantine capital; cf. J. Starr, *Romania: The Jewries of the Levant
after the Fourth Crusade* (Paris, 1949), 27.

    Andronicus continued his father's policy of toleration and
included in a chrysobull of 1319 a clause which states that the
Jews of Joannina were to enjoy the same privileges as other in-

23, 24

habitants of the city; cf. Miklosich–Müller, V, 83; N. Bees, «Über-sicht über die Geschichte des Judentums von Janina (Epirus)», *BNJbb*, 2 (Berlin, 1921), 159–77; P. Charanis, «The Jews in the Byzantine Empire under the First Paleologi», *Speculum*, 22 (1947), 75–77. Cf. also Janin, *Constantinople byzantine*, 259–60, and most recently Jacoby, *op. cit.*, 167–227, on the Jewish quarter in Con-stantinople. See Letters 36, 41, and 46 for further anti-Jewish sentiment on the part of Athanasius.

'Αρμενίων: Athanasius also wanted to exclude the Armenians from Constantinople proper. We must assume the existence of an Armenian quarter at Constantinople, although it is not attested in the sources, since it was Byzantine practice to seclude all non-Orthodox peoples in ghettoes; cf. Rhalles-Potles, V, 415, and Charanis, *op. cit.*, 76–77.

12 συνέλθωμεν ἐν τῇ Χώρᾳ: Just as Athanasius went to Chora to await a summons to an imperial audience, in the same way he suggested that the members of the permanent synod assemble at Chora before proceeding to the Blachernae Palace; cf. Letters 11 and 14.

24.

Athanasius urges the Emperor to confide in him directly, since he is sympathetic with the Emperor's problems.

Laurent, *Regestes*, no. 1623

Date: *ca.* 1305, the year of the plot of the Arsenite Drimys against the Em-peror; cf. commentary *infra*, lines 3–4, and Laurent, *Regestes*, 418.

3–4 τὴν αὐθάδειαν ... τῶν πόρρω καὶ τῶν ἐγγύς: Probably a reference to the Arsenites who were strong both in the capital and in Asia Minor; the inhabitants of Anatolia resented the usurpation of the throne by Michael VIII Palaeologus, and his transfer of the capital to Constantinople, and thus naturally supported the pro-Lascarid Arsenites. Cf. Laurent, «La fin du schisme arsénite», 235–36.

7 διὰ μηνυτῶν: Andronicus' use of messengers is an indication of the tension between Emperor and Patriarch.

23–24 ⟨οὐ⟩ δυνατὸν ... ὑποφέρειν με: Athanasius refuses to tolerate any longer the presence of bishops in Constantinople, because of their

24, 25

disruptive influence on the Church. Cf. Letter 28, lines 8–9: οὐδὲ ἐγὼ δύναμαι ὑποφέρειν τὴν τούτων ἐνταῦθα διατριβήν.

24 οὔτε γὰρ ἔννομον: A novel of Justinian, repeated in the *Basilics*, forbade bishops to be absent from their sees without permission of the emperor or patriarch; cf. Justinian's *Novel* 123, chap. 9 (*CIC*, III, 601–2), and *Basilics*, Book III, Title I, 15 (*Basilicorum Libri LX*, eds. Scheltema and van der Wal, Series A, I [Groningen, 1955], 88).

25.

An attack on bishops who have abandoned their sees and make their residence in the capital.

Laurent, *Regestes*, no. 1613

Date: *ca*. 1304–1305, since the metropolitan of Sardis has not yet left the capital.

4–6 ἵνα ἔχωσι ... εἰς κρίσιν ἔρχεται: Athanasius wants the bishops to be impartial judges when cases are tried before the synod. Cf. Letters 16, lines 4–7, and 48, lines 12–14, for similar complaints about the way in which the bishops are bribed or otherwise influenced by defendants and plaintiffs before their cases come to trial.

6–7 τὰ ἱερὰ ... ἐξωνήσασθαι: Athanasius would no doubt justify the sale of church property for the relief of refugees by citing Byzantine civil and canon law which permitted sale of sacred vessels, etc. for ransoming captives; cf. *Nomocanon* II, 2 (Rhalles–Potles, I, 108–9), and Justinian, *Novels* 65, 1, and 120, 10.

14 ὁ Βιτζύνης: Luke, metropolitan of Bitzyne, was a supporter of John XII Kosmas in the spring of 1303 (Pachymeres, *Hist.*, II, 377), and would therefore have incurred the wrath of Athanasius. Luke became metropolitan sometime after 1285, since Theodore was metropolitan of Bitzyne at the time of the Second Synod of Blachernae and signed the tome against John Bekkos; cf. Laurent, «Les signataires», 147 note 35. G. Bratianu's study of Bitzyne («Vicina: I. Contributions à l'histoire de la domination byzantine et du commerce génois en Dobrugea», *BSHAcRoum*, 10 [1923], 113–89) gives no information on Luke. An unnamed metropolitan of Bitzyne was a member of the synod which condemned Drimys in 1305 (Letter 81, line 130).

14–15 ὁ Σάρδεων: This metropolitan of Sardis, who was one of Athanasius' major opponents and is frequently mentioned in his Letters, is most probably to be identified with Cyril, metropolitan of Sardis and exarch of Lydia, who sometime between 1301 and 1305 authenticated a copy of a chrysobull of Andronicus II (dated 1298), preserved at the Lavra on Mt. Athos; cf. V. Laurent, «Un groupe de signatures épiscopales», 318–23. Laurent was able to narrow down the date of these signatures to between 1301 and 1315. I believe the *terminus ante quem* can be pushed back to 1305 for the following reason: Babylas of Ankara signed the copy of the chrysobull as πρόεδρος Φιλίππων καὶ Χριστουπόλεως. Yet, in 1305 an archbishop of Christoupolis attended the synod against Drimys (Letter 81, lines 131–32), and thus Babylas could no longer have been *proedros* of Christoupolis at this date.

Cyril did not become metropolitan of Sardis until after 1285, since at the Council of Blachernae Gerasimus of Corcyra was called πρόεδρος Σάρδεων; cf. Laurent, «Les signataires», 144 note 4. By July 1315, Cyril had been succeeded by Gregory as metropolitan of Sardis (Miklosich–Müller, I, 5).

Cyril was apparently unable to live in Sardis, because of the presence of the Turks of Saruhan (cf. Pachymeres, *Hist.*, II, 403–4), but was well established in Constantinople. He was still in the capital in October 1304 (PG, 161, col. 1065A), and was also a member of the synod at the trial of Drimys (Letter 81, line 129), but was forced to leave the capital shortly afterward. The Emperor granted him the see of Methymna κατ' ἐπίδοσιν (cf. *Vat. Gr. 2219*, fol. 132^r= Laurent, *Regestes*, no. 1627), and one may assume that the metropolitan went to live on Lesbos.

16 ἀδελφᾶτα: Pensions established in monasteries by wealthy benefactors usually for the support of monks, but occasionally granted to bishops who had lost their sees. There were two kinds of ἀδελφᾶτα: ἐξωμονίτατον, if the holder lived outside the monastery; ἐσωμονίτατον, if he lived together with the monks in the monastery; cf. E. Herman, «Die Regelung der Armut in den byzantinischen Klöstern», *OCP*, 7 (1941), especially 444–48.

20–21 ὁ Φιλαδελφείας ἢ ὁ Νυμφαίου: Athanasius suggests that the metropolitans of Philadelphia and Nymphaeum, who are remaining in their dioceses, may be tempted by the example of other bishops to come to Constantinople. Theoleptos, metropolitan of Philadelphia from 1283 to *ca.* 1324 (see Ševčenko, «Anepigraphos», 478–79 note 2, for the dates of this prelate and extensive bibliography),

was a man after Athanasius' own heart. He was a violent anti-Arsenite, a defender of the poor, and stayed in his diocese as much as possible. In early 1303, Theoleptos was in the capital (Pachymeres, *Hist.*, II, 358), but he must have returned to Philadelphia soon after, since he led the defense of his city against the Turkish siege of 1304. Choumnos tells in his *Funeral Oration* on Theoleptos how the brave bishop, a ποιμὴν τὴν ἑαυτοῦ ψυχὴν τιθεὶς ὑπὲρ τῶν προβάτων (John 10:11), saved the city single-handed from famine and capture ('Επιτάφιος εἰς τὸν μακάριον καὶ ἁγιώτατον μητροπολίτην Φιλαδελφείας Θεόληπτον, in Boissonade, *Anecdota Graeca*, V, 231–34). Gregoras somewhat more realistically informs his readers that Theoleptos was assisted in the relief of the siege by the timely arrival of the Catalan Company (*Hist.*, I, 221). Theoleptos seems to have stayed with his flock in the following years, since he was not in the capital in 1305, when the synod condemned Drimys (Letter 81).

Theoleptos adhered to the principle of ἀκρίβεια instead of οἰκονομία in 1310, when he refused to accept the reconciliation of the Arsenites with the Church. He remained in schism during the patriarchates of Niphon (1310–1314) and John XIII Glykys (1315–1319), and became reconciled with the Church only *ca.* 1321; cf. V. Laurent, «Les crises religieuses à Byzance: le schisme anti-arsénite du métropolite de Philadelphie (died *ca.* 1324)», *REB*, 18 (1960), 45–54. Theoleptos was spiritual advisor to Irene Choumnaina Palaeologina, daughter of Nicephorus Choumnos, the young widow of the Despot John Palaeologus; cf. *idem*, «Une princesse byzantine au cloître», *EO*, 29 (1930), 28–60.

ὁ Νυμφαίου: Athanasius must be referring either to Joseph, who was metropolitan of Nymphaeum in 1294 (*Laurent. Plut.*, V, 2, fol. 386ᵛ), or to Theodoulos, who held this position in 1315 (Miklosich–Müller, I, 14), unless yet a third prelate held the see of Nymphaeum between Joseph and Theodoulos. Like Theoleptos, this metropolitan of Nymphaeum was not a member of the synod in 1304 or 1305; cf. Letter 81, and Athanasius' Νεαρά, PG, 161, col. 1065. See Ahrweiler, «La région de Smyrne», 81–82, for a brief history of the see of Nymphaeum.

22–23: μισθοὶ αὐτοῖς ἐποφείλονται: Athanasius argues that if bishops stay in the capital, they should not be paid, since the law provided that if bishops did not return to their sees they would be deprived of financial support for their churches; cf. *Basilics*, Book III, Title 1, 16.

26.

The *megas dioiketes* has written to the members of the synod protesting his sentence, which is to repay the money he has taken. Athanasius warns the official that he has escaped with a light punishment, and that if he continues his protests and use of abusive language, the bishops will impose a penalty on him.

Laurent, *Regestes*, no. 1685

2 τοῖς ἀρχιερεῦσι Θεοῦ: The members of the synod who convicted the *megas dioiketes*.

ὁ μέγας διοικητής: According to Ps.-Kodinos, in the mid-fourteenth century the *megas dioiketes* was a minor palatine official of the sixteenth *pentas* who no longer performed any function (*Traité des Offices*, 185 and 323). Laurent suggests, however, that in the early fourteenth century the *megas dioiketes* still had the duties of tax official, and on this occasion had extorted some funds in the course of his work. The official attacked by Athanasius is probably to be identified with the tormentor mentioned by Manuel Moschopoulos in a letter of 1305; cf. Ševčenko, «Manuel Moschopulos», 138 and 147. It is impossible to assign a name with any certainty to this official, although he may perhaps be identified with the *megas dioiketes* Cabasilas who received letters from John Choumnos (Boissonade, *Anecdota Nova*, 211–13) and Michael Gabras (*Marc. Gr. 466*, fol. 78). Between 1316 and 1320, Ps.-John Chilas also addressed a letter to a *megas dioiketes* (*Par. Gr. 2022*, fols. 153ᵛ–155ʳ; ed. J. Gouillard, «Après le schisme arsénite: La correspondance inédite du Pseudo-Jean Chilas», *BSHAcRoum*, 25 [1944], 178, 203–7). See Ševčenko, «Manuel Moschopulos», 154–55 note 76, for other early-fourteenth-century allusions to a *megas dioiketes*.

Athanasius never hesitated to criticize government officials; cf. his attacks on the *primikerios* of the court in Letter 17, and on Nicephorus Choumnos, ὁ ἐπὶ τοῦ κανικλείου, in Letter 37.

4 οὐ μέγα ... τοὺς κατὰ σέ: Laurent proposes an alternative translation, «and people like you say it is not a large ⟨sum⟩» (*Regestes*, 474–75).

9 τοῦ Μακρεμβολίτου: The Makrembolites who was a victim of the *megas dioiketes* is known only from this letter. He was perhaps related to the theologian Alexius Makrembolites, who wrote several ascetic works in the 1340's; cf. I. Ševčenko, «Alexios Makrembolites

26, 27

and his 'Dialogue between the Rich and the Poor'», *ZVI*, 6 (1960),
187–228. A Michael Makrembolites is also known from the year 1300;
cf. Ἑλληνικά, 2 (1929), 382–83.

9–10 ὄψου ... ταριχευτοῦ: Salt pork; cf. *Ioannis Zonarae Lexicon*, ed.
I. A. H. Tittman (Leipzig, 1808), II, 1713: ταριχευτὸν ὄψον· ὁ καλού-
μενος λάρδος ἢ τὸ ἀπόκτιν. See also R. Cantarella, «Basilio Minimo.
II, Scolii inediti con introduzione e note», *BZ*, 26 (1926), 29. λάρδος
is the fat between the skin and meat of a pig; cf. Koukoules,
Βυζαντινῶν Βίος καὶ Πολιτισμός, V, 63 and note 4. ἀπόκτιν, ἀπόκτην,
and ἀπόκτιον, which must be synonyms for λάρδος, are not to be
found in the dictionaries.

27.

Since the Emperor is entitled to regulate the secular administration
of monasteries, no one will oppose any imperial measure dealing with secular
affairs in monasteries. Therefore Athanasius asks Andronicus to issue a decree
protecting monasteries from fiscal agents (οἱ ἐνεργοῦντες). If monasteries keep
surplus land (περίσσεια) which has been assigned them, then the tenants on
the περίσσεια should pay μορτή to the monks, who in turn pay taxes to the
imperial treasury. If the περίσσεια is taken away from the monastery, the
monks should not be accountable for the μορτή, since the fiscal agents will
probably appropriate the money for themselves, instead of forwarding it to
the imperial treasury.

Laurent, *Regestes*, no. 1686

2 τὰ μοναστήρια ... ἐτάχθη φροντίζειν αὐτῶν: This sentence does not
imply that all monasteries were under direct imperial control, but is
rather a *topos*, reminding the Emperor of his responsibilities in the
empire; cf. Hunger, *Prooimion*, sections on πρόνοια and φροντίς,
84–100.

6 κατὰ κρίσιν γεωργικήν: The same expression is found in an act
of 1266 (ποιήσητε καὶ εἰς αὐτὸ κατὰ τὴν γεωργικὴν κρίσιν), and is
translated by Dölger as «auf Grund bauernrechtlichen Entscheids»
(Dölger, *Aus den Schatzkammern*, 94, no. 34, lines 18–19).

7 τὴν περίσσειαν: περιττὴ γῆ, surplus land, in excess of the land recorded in the tax registers; cf. Dölger, *Aus den Schatzkammern*,
no. 43/44, line 142; Rouillard-Collomp, *Actes de Lavra*, no. 43, line 60.

27, 28

οἱ κατέχοντες πρίν: The monks; cf. Miklosich–Müller, IV, 219, 234, and 235.

7–8 μορτήν: Rent paid by free peasants for lease of land which was not fully cultivated; cf. W. Ashburner, «The Farmer's Law», *JHS*, 30 (1910), 99, §§ 9–10, and 32 (1912), 82–83, and Dölger, *Aus den Schatzkammern*, no. 109, line 13, and commentary on no. 102, line 25. See also Miklosich–Müller, IV, 145, 218, 220, 231, 235, 254; VI, 212.

9 οἱ μέλλοντες ἐνεργεῖν: Fiscal agents; cf. commentary on Letter 17, and Miklosich–Müller, IV, 218 and 219.

28.

Athanasius again asks the Emperor to force the bishops to return to their sees.

Laurent, *Regestes*, no. 1620

Date: between the end of 1303, when Athanasius began his second patriarchate, and 1305, when Nicephorus Moschopoulos was forced to go to Mistra.

4 ἔννομον: Cf. *Basilics*, Book III, Title I, 15.

5 νουθετῇ τὸν λαόν: Cf. canon 19 of the Synod in Trullo (Rhalles–Potles, II, 346).

8–9 οὐδὲ ἐγὼ δύναμαι ... διατριβήν: Cf. Letter 24, lines 23–24.

10 τῷ νόμῳ τῷ ἐκκλησιαστικῷ: The canons of the Church as well as civil law forbade the prolonged absence of a bishop from his see; cf. the fourteenth canon of the Apostles (Rhalles–Potles, II, 18) and the sixteenth canon of the First and Second Synod in the Church of the Holy Apostles (861) (Rhalles–Potles, II, 696–97).

10–11 οὔτε γὰρ εἰς ἐπιστασίαν ... εὐθύτητα σῴζουσι: Athanasius is here attacking bishops' dishonest management of monastic property.

11 οὔτε εἰς κρίσεις: An allusion to bishops who accepted bribes from the plaintiff or defendant in a case which was going to be tried before the synod; cf. Letter 16, lines 4–7, and Letter 25, lines 5–6.

28

13 ὁ Κρήτης: Nicephorus Moschopoulos, metropolitan of Crete *ca.* 1283
to sometime after 1322 (for these dates, see Laurent, «Les signataires», 145, and M. I. Manousakas, in Ἑλληνικά, 15 [1957], 238–43).
Since Crete had been occupied by the Venetians since the Fourth
Crusade, Nicephorus could not maintain his residence on the island;
cf. N. B. Tomadakes, Ὀρθόδοξοι ἀρχιερεῖς ἐν Κρήτῃ ἐπὶ Ἑνετοκρα-
τίας, in Ὀρθοδοξία, 27 (1952), 63–75, esp. 68–69. He therefore
spent much of his time in Constantinople (cf. Laurent, «Les signataires», 145, no. 12, and Pachymeres, *Hist.*, II, 349), although he
had been granted the see of Lacedaemonia κατ᾿ ἐπίδοσιν sometime
between 1285 and 1289; cf. Manousakas, *op. cit.*, 240.

In 1303 Nicephorus was a supporter of John Kosmas and an
opponent of the reinstatement of Athanasius, since he would force
bishops to leave the capital (Pachymeres, *Hist.*, II, 349). Once
Athanasius was successful in regaining the patriarchate, Nicephorus
tried to appease his wrath by spreading the rumor that he wished
to leave Constantinople. Athanasius took advantage of this rumor
to get rid of Nicephorus and sent him a letter of dismissal (*Vat.
Gr. 2219*, fols. 130ᵛ–132ᵛ [= Laurent, *Regestes*, no. 1627], ed. Papadopoulos-Kerameus, Νικήφορος Μοσχόπουλος, 217–19, and PG, 142,
col. 513ff.). Nicephorus had previously held the see of Methymna
on Lesbos as an additional source of revenue; the Emperor now
transferred the see of Methymna to the metropolitan of Sardis, and
in compensation gave Nicephorus an annual income of two hundred
gold pieces from a suffragan bishopric of Monemvasia.

Nicephorus did not leave the capital for Mistra until 1305,
since in October 1304 he was still a member of the synod; cf. Νεαρά
of Athanasius, PG, 161, col. 1065. He was a great benefactor of the
diocese of Lacedaemonia; several inscriptions record his restoration
of the cathedral church of St. Demetrius at Mistra, together with
his brother Aaron, as well as his construction of windmills and his
planting of olive groves and vineyards in the neighboring countryside. For edition of inscriptions, see G. Millet, «Inscriptions byzantines de Mistra», *BCH*, 23 (1899), 122–23; for commentary on the
inscriptions, see D. A. Zakythinos, *Le Despotat de Morée*, II (Paris,
1953), 183–87, and M. I. Manousakas, Ἡ χρονολογία τῆς κτιτορικῆς
ἐπιγραφῆς τοῦ ἁγίου Δημητρίου τοῦ Μυστρᾶ, in Δελτ.Χριστ.᾿Αρχ.
Ἑτ., Δ', α' (1959), 72–80.

By 1317 Nicephorus had returned to Constantinople, for in
April of that year he was present at a meeting of the synod in the
capital; he was replaced as *proedros* of Lacedaemonia by the metropolitan of Patras (Miklosich–Müller, I, 52–53).

Nicephorus, uncle of the philologist Manuel Moschopoulos (as
was shown by Treu, ed., *Planudis epistulae*, 208–12), was an active

28–30

bibliophile and generous benefactor of monastic libraries; cf. Ševčenko, «Manuel Moschopulos», 134 and note 15; Levi, «Cinque lettere inedite di Emanuele Moscopulo», 61, lines 32, 36; 62, line 30; 63, line 14; K. Amantos, "Αγνωστον ἀφιέρωμα τοῦ Νικηφόρου Κρήτης εἰς μονὴν τῆς Φωκαίας, in Μικρασιατικὰ Χρονικά, 2 (1939), 49–54; Papadopoulos–Kerameus, Νικήφορος Μοσχόπουλος, 220 and note 4; *idem*, Ἱεροσολυμιτικὴ Βιβλιοθήκη, II (St. Petersburg, 1894), 74–77 and 84–85; P. Papageorgiou, «Zwei iambische Gedichte saec. XIV und XIII», *BZ*, 8 (1899), 672–74; and, most important, M. I. Manousakas, Νικηφόρου Μοσχοπούλου ἐπιγράμματα σὲ χειρόγραφα τῆς βιβλιοθήκης του, in Ἑλληνικά, 15 (1957), 232–46.

The metropolitan of Crete was greatly admired by his contemporaries; cf., for example, Pachymeres, *Hist.*, II, 241, and Treu, ed., *Planudis epistulae*, 34. Athanasius, who had no interest in collecting books (cf. Letter 20) or in secular learning, was an obvious exception in his failure to appreciate Nicephorus.

15 χωρὶς ὑπομνήσεως: A bishop was supposed to notify the patriarch of his arrival in the capital, and to receive permission to stay from both the patriarch and the emperor; cf. *Basilics*, Book III, Title I, 15, and *Nomocanon*, Title VIII, chap. 2 (PG, 104, col. 1085A–B). Athanasius complains that this procedure is now disregarded.

29.

Athanasius urges upon the Emperor the pursuit of three virtues, justice, moderation, and mercy.

Laurent, *Regestes*, no. 1687

30.

Athanasius urges the Emperor to force bishops to return to their sees in Anatolia.

Laurent, *Regestes*, no. 1598

Date: The letter can be dated between the end of 1303 and 1305, the year in which Athanasius forced most of the bishops to return to their dioceses; cf. Pachymeres, *Hist.*, II, 518, 616, and Laurent, *Regestes*, 381, 418.

30, 31

2–3 τὴν ἐν τῇ ἀνατολῇ ... ἐξολόθρευσιν: During Athanasius' patriarchate, the troops of the various Turkish emirates overran western Anatolia and reached the Aegean; cf. Gregoras, *Hist.*, I, 214, and Arnakis, Οἱ πρῶτοι 'Οθωμάνοι, esp. 71–132.

20 ὁ τῆς Τραιανοῦ: The bishop of Traianoupolis, a city in Thrace near the right bank of the Maritza River. We know that a Makarios was metropolitan of Traianoupolis in 1294 (*Laurent. Plut. V, 2*, fol. 386ᵛ); it is more likely, however, that Athanasius is referring to his arch-enemy, Niphon of Cyzicus, who probably succeeded Makarios as *proedros* of Proconnesus and Traianoupolis. In his accusation of Niphon in 1314, Nicephorus Choumnos charged that after Niphon became patriarch in 1310 he refused to relinquish the sees of Cyzicus, Proconnesus, and Traianoupolis (Ἔλεγχος κατὰ τοῦ ... Νίφωνος, 278–79).

20–22 εἰ γὰρ λιταῖς ... ἡμῶν σπουδαζόντων τοιούτοις: Cf. Letters 15, lines 11–12, and 32, 10–11.

23–24 δωροδοκεῖσθαι παρὰ τῶν κρινομένων: The bishops acted as judges in the synod; many were apparently not averse to taking bribes; cf. Letters 16, lines 4–7; 25, lines 5–6; and 28, line 11.

31.

Athanasius writes that bishops may come to the capital to attend the annual meeting of the synod, but then should return immediately to their sees.

Laurent, *Regestes*, no. 1599

Date: between the end of 1303 and 1305; cf. Letter 30.

5 τῇ μεγάλῃ μόνῃ συνόδῳ: The early canons of the Church specified that the synod should meet twice each year; cf. the fifth canon of Nicaea I (Rhalles–Potles, II, 124–25), and the thirty-seventh Apostolic canon (Rhalles–Potles, II, 50). Later canons and civil legislation provided for only one meeting a year; cf. the eighth canon of the Quinisext Council (Rhalles–Potles, II, 324–25); *Novel* 137, chap. iv, of Justinian; and *Basilics*, Book III, Title 1, 17.

Parallel with the system of annual synods, there developed the system of a permanent synod, the σύνοδος ἐνδημοῦσα, which is attested as early as the fourth century; see J. Hajjar, *Le synode*

31–33

*permanent (*σύνοδος ἐνδημοῦσα*) dans l'église byzantine des origines au XIᵉ siècle* (= *OCA*, 164) (Rome, 1962), 21–43. At the time of Athanasius, the bishops used the custom of a permanent synod as an excuse for remaining in the capital the year round; thus Athanasius wished to abolish the permanent synod and revive the system of annual synods. Pachymeres writes that Athanasius expelled all the bishops 'from the capital and held synods of abbots (*Hist.*, II, 518, 643), but bishops apparently continued to come to Constantinople to attend an annual synod; cf. commentary on Letter 96, lines 16–17.

7–8 ὑπὲρ ταύτης ὑφέξειν λόγον τῷ ἀρχιποίμενι: Cf. Apostolic canon 39 (Rhalles–Potles, II, 54).

   9 μετάκλητος βασιλεῖ ἢ τῷ πατριαρχεύοντι: Cf. *Basilics*, Book III, Title 1, 15.

32.

Athanasius again urges the Emperor to force the bishops to leave the capital.

Laurent, *Regestes*, no. 1600

Date: between the end of 1303 and 1305; cf. Letter 30.

   5 ἕλκοντα: Note this late form of the neuter participle; cf. Jannaris, *Historical Greek Grammar*, § 823, pp. 206–7.

   7 κανονικὸν: Cf. Apostolic canon 14 (Rhalles–Potles, II, 18) and the fifteenth canon of the First Council of Nicaea (Rhalles–Potles, II, 145).

10–11 ὀρέγονται διασύρειν καὶ ἡμᾶς, ἕνεκεν λιτῆς καὶ ἀγρυπνιῶν: Cf. commentary on Letters 15, lines 11–12, and 30, lines 20–22.

  11 The letter stops abruptly in the middle of folio 14ᵛ, and Letter 33 begins immediately underneath; one must therefore assume that the text copied by the scribe had already lost its ending.

33.

Athanasius urges the Emperor Michael IX to remember the promises made at his baptism.

Laurent, *Regestes*, no. 1688

23 τῆς πανηγύρεως ταύτης: I.e., Christian life; cf. Clement of Alexandria, *Stromateis*, 7.7 (PG, 9, col. 469B): ἄπας δὲ ὁ βίος αὐτοῦ πανήγυρις ἁγία, and Methodius, *Symposium*, i.1 (PG, 18, col. 140A): πανήγυριν τὸν βίον ἡμῶν σοφῶν παῖδες εἰρήκασιν εἶναι.

34.

Athanasius praises the Empress Maria for her zeal in striving for unity
in the Church, and warns her against schismatics.

Laurent, *Regestes*, no. 1689

Date: probably 1303–1309, in any case after January 16, 1296, the date of
      Maria's marriage to Michael IX; on this date, cf. C. Marinescu,
      «Tentatives de mariage de deux fils d'Andronic II Paléologue avec
      des princesses latines», *RHSEE*, 1 (1924), 143; see also Schmid,
      «Zur Chronologie von Pachymeres», 84, and Ševčenko, «Theodore
      Metochites», *Kariye Djami*, IV (see *supra*, p. 317).

ad apparatum 1: Κεραμαρίαν: Rita, sister of Het'um II, king of Armenia (1289–
      1305), assumed the name Maria upon her conversion to the Greek
      Orthodox faith before her marriage to Michael IX (Pachymeres,
      Hist., II, 206).

   2–4 ἡνίκα τινὰ συμβῇ ... διὰ γράμματος ὁμιλῆσαι τῇ βασιλείᾳ σου: Atha-
       nasius is delighted to hear that someone is going to visit Maria
       and can carry a letter to her. Laurent has interpreted this sentence
       as referring to the arrival of Maria in Constantinople, but αὐτόθι
       usually means «over there», the residence of the addressee of the
       letter (cf. commentary on Letter 14, line 59). Athanasius' expression
       for arriving in Constantinople is ἐνταῦθα ἐλθεῖν (*Letter* 30, line
       28), or τὰ ὧδε καταλαβεῖν (Letter 30, line 4).

   6–7 ἐκ μακρᾶς ... γῆς: Cilician Armenia.

   11 τῇ τῆς ἐκκλησίας εἰρηνικῇ ἑνώσει: The Church of Cilician Armenia
       was officially united with Rome from 1198–1375, but retained its
       own ritual and dogma; cf. S. Der Nersessian, «The Kingdom of
       Cilician Armenia», in *A History of the Crusades*, eds. R. L. Wolff and
       H. W. Hazard (Madison, Wisconsin, 1969), II, 647–48. Both Rita-

34, 35

Maria and her sister Theophano were converted from the Armenian rite to Greek Orthodoxy in 1296. It is possible that Athanasius is alluding here to an attempt of the new Empress to persuade her fellow Armenians to join her in her conversion. It is more likely, however, that he is referring to some otherwise unknown efforts on the part of Rita-Maria to reconcile the Arsenites with the official Greek Church.

31 δένδρον ζωῆς ἡ ἐκκλησία Χριστοῦ: The Tree of Life, which was planted in the middle of Paradise (Gen. 2:9), is a symbol of immortality, and is thus an appropriate metaphor for the Christian Church, which also offers hope of immortality.

Athanasius also uses the Tree as a metaphor for the Church in an encyclical letter: ὁ τὴν ἐκκλησίαν σχίζων καὶ κατατέμνων Χριστοῦ, νενεκρωμένον τὸ μέλος ὡς τῆς οἰκείας ὁλομελείας ἀποτεμνόμενος καὶ κλάδος κατάξηρος τῆς τοῦ λοιποῦ δένδρου συμφυοῦς συνεχείας ὁλοτελῶς ἀποσπώμενος, καὶ τῶν αἱρετικῶν κατ' οὐδὲν διενηνοχώς (*Vat. Gr. 2219*, fol. 105ʳ).

35.

Athanasius complains that the Emperor fails to act on his reports, and warns him to view the Catalans as enemies.

Laurent, *Regestes*, no. 1630

Date: *ca.* 1304, since Andronicus still has faith in the Catalan mercenaries, whom he hired to fight the Turks in Anatolia; cf. commentary on lines 53–54. Possibly, however, first part of 1305 (before May); cf. arguments of Laurent, *Regestes*, 424.

ad apparatum 1: Μογαβάρων: One of the Greek names for Catalans, a corruption of the Castilian Almogavar, derived in turn from the Arabic *al-mughawir*, meaning «one who occupies himself much in raids or sudden attacks on enemies or upon the dwellings of enemies with armed horsemen»; cf. E. W. Lane, *Arabic-English Lexicon* (London, 1877), I, vi, 2308. The Greek form ἀμογάβαρος also exists (e.g., Pachymeres, *Hist.*, II, 393). Note the pun αἱμοβόρων (ἀ)μογαβάρων.

ad apparatum 1: τὰ συμβαίνοντα ... παρὰ τῶν αἱμοβόρων Μογαβάρων: The scribe who added this title misunderstood the letter; Athanasius mentions disasters in Anatolia and Macedonia, «not to mention

the destruction of the Catalans». In other words, he does not say specifically that the Catalans are causing the disasters in Anatolia.

6–7 μικροῦ γὰρ δεύτερος χρόνος ... : Evidence of the tension between Emperor and Patriarch; cf. Letter 14, where Athanasius complains that he has waited as long as ten days at Chora without being summoned to the palace for an audience with the Emperor.

14 τὰ συμβάντα ἐν τῇ ᾿Ανατολῇ: A reference to Turkish successes in Anatolia. Pergamum, for example, fell ca. 1303 (cf. Pachymeres, Hist., II, 318; H. Gelzer, Pergamon unter Byzantinern und Osmanen [Berlin, 1903], 91; and P. Wittek, Das Fürstentum Mentesche [Istanbul, 1934], 21), and Ephesus in 1304 (cf. P. Lemerle, L'Emirat d'Aydin, Byzance et l'Occident [Paris, 1957], 20 and note 4).

15 Μακεδονίᾳ: The term Macedonia was used by Byzantine writers to describe several different geographical areas, including Bulgaria and Albania, but most often it referred to present-day western Thrace; cf. K. Amantos, Παρατηρήσεις τινες εἰς τὴν Μεσαιωνικὴν Γεωγραφίαν, in ᾿Επ.῾Ετ.Βυζ.Σπ., 1 (1924), 44–45. Athanasius is probably referring to the area of the *theme* of Macedonia, which included Adrianople and Philippoupolis; cf. G. Ostrogorsky, *History of the Byzantine State* (Oxford, 1956), 172, and P. Lemerle, *Philippes et la Macédoine Orientale* (Paris, 1945), 123.

15–16 ἔνθα ὁ βασιλεὺς κύρις Μιχαήλ: In August 1304, Michael set forth from Constantinople to fight the Bulgarians in the vicinity of Adrianople; cf. Pachymeres, Hist., II, 447. Athanasius may be referring to this expedition.

18–19 τὴν ... Μογαβάρων πανωλεθρίαν: Since Andronicus had difficulties in paying the Catalan Company its promised wages, the mercenaries began to pillage and loot soon after their arrival. During the winter of 1303–1304, which they spent at Cyzicus, the Catalans terrorized the local inhabitants; cf. Pachymeres, Hist., II, 399.

21–22 διὰ τί δὲ ταῦτα μὴ οἶδεν ... ἀπωθεῖται: Pachymeres also recounts that the Emperor refused to listen to tales of the Catalans' deeds at Cyzicus (Hist., II, 420).

53–54 πολεμίους λογιζομένων ἡμῶν τοὺς Μογαβάρους: Athanasius urges the Emperor to consider the Catalans as enemies, rather than allies. Michael IX, like Athanasius, was very hostile to the Catalans, but Andronicus continued to have faith in them through 1304 (Pachymeres, Hist., II, 483).

36.

Athanasius lists the sins of omission of Andronicus and his subjects.
If the Byzantines strive to correct their faults, they will be saved from the
Turkish peril and the wrath of God.

Laurent, *Regestes*, no. 1639

Date: Laurent (*Regestes*, 434) suggests a date of *ca.* 1305–1306, because he
sees a possible allusion to the battle of Apros in lines 14–16; however, these might well be general remarks on the condition of the
Byzantine army.

2 ὅτι μὴ τοὺς υἱοὺς παιδεύεις: Cf. commentary on Letter 3, lines 54–55.

6 τῇ εἰσαγωγῇ ... 'Ιουδαίων καὶ 'Αρμενίων: Cf. commentary on
Letters 23 and 41.

7 οἱ ἐνεργοῦντες: Fiscal agents; cf. commentary on Letter 17, lines
23–24.

18–19 συνδούλων ... καταφρονοῦντες: This is no doubt an allusion to the
Jews' disregard of the prophets of the Old Testament, who warned
that God's wrath would punish Israel for its iniquity. The Christians
are even more guilty, inasmuch as they have disregarded not their
fellow subjects but God Himself.

37.

Athanasius writes the Emperor that the only way to save the empire
from the Turks is through prayer and repentance.

Laurent, *Regestes*, Appendix, no. 7

Date: between December 13, 1302, the date of the «resounding blow», and
Easter 1303, when Irene Choumnaina was married to the Despot
John Palaeologus; cf. commentary *infra*, and Laurent, *Regestes*,
572–73.

9–11 οὔτε αὕτη ἡ πόλις ἐσῴζετο ... ὁ τετρυγὼς ἐκεῖνος ἐγένετο κτύπος:
The meaning of the τετρυγὼς κτύπος in this phrase has long puzzled
scholars; cf. Bănescu, «Le patriarche Athanase Iᵉʳ», 43–44, and
Laurent, *Regestes*, 573–74. One first thinks that the terrifying event
might have been an earthquake, but no natural disaster is recorded

at this time. It would therefore seem that the phrase refers to an
enemy invasion; cf. Pachymeres' description of the ravages of the
Catalans, where he uses the word τετρυγός (*Hist.*, II, 500).

Athanasius may be alluding here to a Turkish attack on
Scutari, described as follows by the Catalan chronicler Muntaner:
«And what is more, the Turks had in truth made such conquests,
that an army of them came opposite Constantinople; there was not
more than an arm of the sea, less than two miles broad, between
them and the city, and they drew their swords and threatened the
Emperor, and the Emperor could see it all. Imagine with what
grief he beheld it. If they had had wherewith to cross this arm of
the sea, they would have taken Constantinople» (Muntaner, II, 488).
We may assume with some certainty that Muntaner is referring to
Scutari, since the Bosporus is slightly over two miles wide between
Scutari and Constantinople. Furthermore, in lines 11–12 of this letter
Athanasius states that the danger extended as far as Scutari. Unfortunately, Muntaner gives no date for the incident, except that
it occurred before September 1303, the date of the Catalan arrival
in Constantinople.

Pachymeres does not mention any such Turkish attack on
Scutari around this time; however, for the period June 1302–June
1303 Pachymeres described only internal affairs in Constantinople,
particularly the complicated ecclesiastical negotiations which took
place between the abdication of John XII in 1302 and the restoration of Athanasius to the patriarchal throne a year later.

11–12 τὰ τῆς 'Ανατολῆς ... μέχρι τοῦ Σκουταρίου: Gregoras writes that
the Turks reached the coasts of the Aegean in 1302 (*Hist.*, I, 214).

'Ανέας: Anea, a town on the western coast of Anatolia, lying opposite
Samos. Although the area around Anea was captured by Sasan
ca. 1302, the town itself remained in Byzantine hands; cf. Gregoras,
Hist., I, 214, and Lemerle, *L'Emirat d'Aydin*, 16–17, note 5.

13–14 αὐτὴ ἡ ἑσπέριος ... ὅλη συνήχθη: Athanasius warns the Emperor
not to trust in the Catalans to save the empire, for not even all
the armies of western Europe could defeat the Turks; only prayers
and repentance can avert the wrath of God.

22–23 τοὺς ἐπαναστάντας 'Ισμαηλίτας: Athanasius' use here of the verb
ἐπανίστημι reflects the Byzantine attitude that the Turks were
insurgents rather than a rival empire.

37–39

25–26 καστελλίων ἀνεγέρσεις: Cf. Gregoras, *Hist.*, I, 275, where Gregoras speaks of τὰ ἐν 'Ασίᾳ καὶ Εὐρώπῃ πολίχνια . . . ὅσα τε ἐκαινούργησε καὶ ὅσα ἐκ βάθρων ἀνήγειρε ⟨Andronicus II⟩.

33–34 ὁ κανικλείου: Nicephorus Choumnos, who was made ὁ ἐπὶ τοῦ κανικλείου, prefect of the scriptorium, *ca.* 1295. The ἐπὶ τοῦ κανικλείου was responsible for verifying the accuracy of documents copied by scribes, and inserted certain words in red ink to establish the authenticity of documents emanating from the imperial chancery; cf. Dölger–Karayannopoulos, *Byzantinische Urkundenlehre*, 29, 118.

Choumnos was one of Andronicus' most trusted ministers, and from *ca.* 1293 held the position of μεσάζων or imperial chancellor (on this title, see Ševčenko, *Etudes*, 6 note 4, and R. J. Loenertz, «Le chancelier imperial à Byzance», *OCP*, 26 [1960], 275–300). In the early fourteenth century, however, Choumnos' influence with the Emperor was gradually supplanted by that of Theodore Metochites, who succeeded Choumnos as μεσάζων *ca.* 1305/6; cf. Ševčenko, *Etudes*, 145–51, and *idem*, «Manuel Moschopulos», 155 note 83. For a complete study of Choumnos, see Verpeaux, *Nicéphore Choumnos*.

34–35 ζητῶν . . . μόνον γενέσθαι τοὺς γάμους: Nicephorus Choumnos had lofty ambitions for his children. He had originally hoped that his daughter Irene would marry Alexius of Trebizond, but the engagement plans fell through (Pachymeres, *Hist.*, II, 287–88). In consolation, Andronicus offered Irene the hand of his son, the Despot John. The marriage took place soon after Easter 1303 (Pachymeres, *Hist.*, II, 289, 378–79); for a discussion of this chronology, see commentary on Letter 96, lines 3–4. Sometime before 1310, Choumnos also succeeded in marrying his son John to a member of one of the Byzantine imperial families; cf. Verpeaux, *Nicéphore Choumnos*, 44 and note 5.

38.

To the Emperor, that righteousness, mercy, and truth should prevail in the empire.

Laurent, *Regestes*, no. 1690

39.

Athanasius reminds the Emperor of the need for repentance, especially after the terrible disaster which has befallen the empire.

Laurent, *Regestes*, Appendix, no. 9

Date: early 1303, if indeed the «piteous and terrible disaster» of lines 5–6
is the same as the τετρυγὼς κτύπος of Letter 37; cf. Laurent, *Regestes*,
576.

40.

Athanasius urges the Emperor not to hesitate to follow the right course.

Laurent, *Regestes*, no. 1691

41.

Athanasius protests the Emperor's toleration of religious worship by
Jews, Armenians, and Turks within the walls of Constantinople.

Laurent, *Regestes*, no. 1622

Date: after 1304, the date of the introduction of a new coin, the *basilikon*;
cf. commentary on line 19.

   2–7 'Ραψάκου ... τῶν 'Ασσυρίων: Cf. 4 Kings 18–19. In Letter 7
   Athanasius also urged Andronicus to follow the example of Hezekiah,
   king of Jerusalem.

   8–9 τὴν θεοκτόνον συναγωγὴν ... τῶν ὀρθοδόξων: The synagogue of the
   Jews who are called «deicides» because of their role in the Crucifixion
   of Christ; cf. τῶν θεοκτόνων 'Ιουδαίων in the title. See *supra*, commentary on Letter 23, lines 6–7, for a discussion of the transfer of some
   of the Jewish population from Pera to Constantinople proper under
   the Palaeologi. Planudes, writing in the late thirteenth century,
   mentioned the existence of a synagogue in the Vlanga quarter where
   the Jewish tanners were also concentrated (Treu, ed., *Planudis epistulae*, Ep. XXXI, p. 52). See Ch. Du Fresne Du Cange, *Constantinopolis
   christiana*, II (Paris, 1680), 163–64; Banduri, *Imperium orientale*,
   II, 613; and D. Jacoby, «Les quartiers juifs de Constantinople à
   l'époque byzantine», *Byzantion*, 37 (1967), 169, 190–91, for discussion
   of Jewish synagogues in Constantinople.

   11–12 τὰς εἰκονικὰς ἡμῶν εὐσεβεῖς προσκυνήσεις: Cf. the prohibition of the
   Ten Commandments, Exod. 20:4.

41

13 διὰ δώρων ... ὁ Κωκαλᾶς: Perhaps to be identified with the Kokalas who was *megas logariastes ca.* 1327. His daughter was married
to the *protovestiarios* Andronicus Palaeologus, who was the nephew
of the Emperor Andronicus II; cf. Cantacuzenus, *Hist.*, I, 232, and
Papadopoulos, *Genealogie der Palaiologen*, no. 50. In his *Chroniques
gréco-romanes* (Berlin, 1873), 529. C. Hopf states that Kokalas' first
name was George, without, however, quoting any source for this
information. According to Ps.-Kodinos, in the fourteenth century the
megas logariastes no longer fulfilled any function (*Traité des Offices*,
182).

16 'Αρμενίων: It is curious that there is almost no information in
contemporary Byzantine sources about the Armenian community
at Constantinople. We must assume that the Byzantine capital
contained a quarter of Armenian merchants such as is documented
at Kaffa; cf. W. Heyd, *Histoire du commerce du Levant au moyen-
âge*, II (Leipzig, 1936), 172. The Armenians in Constantinople were
viewed with suspicion by the Greek Orthodox Patriarch because
they did not accept the Council of Chalcedon; furthermore, the
Church of Cilician Armenia was officially united with the Roman
Church from 1198 to 1375, although it maintained the Armenian
rite; cf. Letter 34.

For an example of the hostility between the Armenian and Greek
inhabitants of Constantinople, cf. Pachymeres, *Hist.*, II, 520–21.

17 συναγωγὴν: The location of this Armenian church is not mentioned
in the sources. Michael Syrus records a precedent for the destruction of an Armenian church by imperial command, in the reign of
Alexius I Comnenus; cf. *Chronique de Michel le Syrien*, ed. and
trans. J.-B. Chabot, III (Paris, 1904), 185.

19 δι' ὀλίγων βασιλικῶν: The *basilikon* was a silver coin, worth 1/45
of a gold *hyperperon*, introduced by Andronicus II in 1304 in order
to pay his Catalan mercenaries; cf. V. Laurent, «Le *basilicon*, nouveau
nom de monnaie sous Andronic II Paléologue», *BZ*, 45 (1952), 50–58.

20–21 'Ισμαηλῖται οὐδὲ σημαντῆρος ἦχον παραχωροῦσι Χριστιανοῖς: A
σημαντήρ or σήμαντρον was a wooden board which was struck to
announce the beginning of a church service. It was used in place
of a bell, especially at monasteries; cf. Demetrakos, *Lexikon*, 6502.

Athanasius' letter is one of the earliest sources to mention a
Turkish prohibition of the use of the *semandron* to summon the
faithful to services. A decree of Sinan Pasha, the conqueror of
Ioannina, in 1431 gives specific permission for the use of the *seman-*

41

dron, and thus implies that the Turks usually forbade the practice in the lands they conquered (Miklosich–Müller, III, 283).

23–26 οἱ τῶν Ἰσμαηλιτῶν πρέσβεις ... μυστήρια: Athanasius' letter is the only Byzantine source which specifically mentions the existence of a mosque in Constantinople in the Palaeologan period, although there are several references to mosques in the capital from the eighth century until the Fourth Crusade; cf. Ch. A. Nomikou, Τὸ πρῶτο τζαμὶ τῆς Κωνσταντινουπόλεως, in Ἐπ.Ἑτ.Βυζ.Σπ., 1 (1924), 199–209; *De administrando imperio*, ed. Moravcsik–Jenkins (Budapest, 1949), 21, line 114; Nicholas Mysticus, *Epistola* 102 (PG, 111, col. 316B); and Nicetas Choniates, *Hist.*, II, 731, 733.

The mosque to which Athanasius alludes was built during the reign of Michael VIII, according to the fourteenth-century Arab historian Makrizi, who wrote *sub anno* 660/1262: «Lascaris [Michael VIII] députa vers le sultan [Baybars], afin de lui demander un patriarche pour les chrétiens Melkites. On nomma à cette dignité Reschid–Kahhal, qui fut envoyé vers l'empereur grec, accompagné de l'émir Fares-eddin-Akousch-Masoudi et de plusieurs évêques. Lascaris les combla d'honneurs et de présents; il montra à l'émir Akousch une mosquée qu'il avait fait construire dans la ville de Constantinople» (*Histoire des Sultans Mamlouks de l'Egypte*, trans. M. Quatremère, I [Paris, 1837], 177). Athanasius' letter thus confirms the testimony of the Arab historian.

The mosque was probably located in the walled Muslim quarter in Constantinople which is mentioned by the fourteenth-century Arab historian al-Jazari. Al-Jazari's account quotes the report of a merchant, ʻAbd Allah b. Mohammad of Sinjar, who lived in Constantinople from 1281–1293; for a translation of al-Jazari's text, see M. Izeddin, «Un texte arabe sur Constantinople byzantine», *JA*, 246 (1958), 453–57. The mosque would have been used by members of the Muslim community in Constantinople which included merchants such as ʻAbd Allah, and Muslim ambassadors to the Byzantine capital.

For further bibliography on the question of a mosque in Constantinople, see R. Jenkins, *Commentary on the De administrando imperio* (London, 1962), 78, and Janin, *Constantinople byzantine*, 257–59.

32 παρακαλῶ, παρακαλῶ, παρακαλῶ: Cf. Letter 93, lines 15–16 (ἵνα καὶ ἔθει βασιλικῷ χρήσωμαι, παρακαλῶ, παρακαλῶ, παρακαλῶ), and commentary on Letter 12, lines 29–30.

47–48 Φινεές: Cf. Num. 25:6–8 and Ps. 105 (106): 28–31.

42.

Athanasius asks the Emperor to order that during Lent no Orthodox Christian should frequent bathhouses or taverns.

Laurent, *Regestes*, no. 1646

Date: beginning of Lent (February) 1306; see commentary on lines 2–3.

2–3 ἐν ἀρχαῖς τῶν ἱερῶν καὶ ἁγίων νηστειῶν: — ἰνδικτιῶνος δ': During Athanasius' patriarchates, the fourth indiction coincided with the years 1290/91 and 1305/6. It seems likely that this letter should be dated to his second patriarchate, i.e., to the beginning of Lent 1306, since he makes the same recommendations which are found in his Νεαρά proposed in 1304. Cf. commentary on Letter 43. Laurent also opts for 1306, noting that in 1290/91 Andronicus was absent from the capital; cf. *Regestes*, 440.

19–20 μὴ βαλανείοις ἢ καπηλείοις τινὰ τῷ τῇδε καιρῷ ... ἐσχολακέναι: Cf. the Νεαρά proposed by Athanasius in October 1304, which prescribed that during Lent Orthodox Christians should μὴ καπηλείων μόνον καὶ βαλανείων ἀπέχεσθαι, ἀλλὰ πάσης σωματικῆς ἀνέσεως (PG, 161, col. 1067B).

21–22 ὁ τῆς τεσσαρακοντάδος ἐλεεινὸς ... ἔκπτωτος: An allusion to the forty Christians of Sebaste who suffered martyrdom under Licinius (308–323). The forty martyrs were condemned to stand naked in a lake overnight, while a hot bath was set up on the shore to tempt them. One of the Christians weakened and left the icy waters, but died upon reaching the warmth of the bathhouse; cf. O. von Gebhardt, *Acta martyrum selecta* (Berlin, 1902), 171–81.

30 εἰσάγεσθαι μᾶλλον αὐτοὺς προτρεπόμεθα: Athanasius is here criticizing Byzantines who married during Lent, since this practice was forbidden by the fifty-second canon of the Council of Laodicea (Rhalles–Potles, III, 219). This prohibition was reinforced by a synodal decision of the mid-thirteenth century; cf. Rhalles–Potles, V, 116.

43.

Athanasius again enjoins the Emperor to order a rigorous observance of Lent.

43, 44

Laurent, *Regestes*, no. 1663

Date: Lent 1307; see commentary on line 1.

 1 ἰνδικτιῶνος ε′ : During Athanasius' patriarchates, the fifth indiction coincided with the years 1291/92 and 1306/7. Because of the connection of this letter with the Νεαρά proposed by Athanasius in October 1304, it should be dated to his second patriarchate, i.e., to Lent 1307. Cf. commentary on Letter 42, and Laurent, *Regestes*, 459.

37–39 τῷ τῇδε καιρῷ κλεισθῆναι ... πάντα βαλανεῖα καὶ καπηλεῖα: Although Andronicus had confirmed in May 1306 Athanasius' Νεαρά, which ordered Orthodox Christians to keep away from bathhouses and taverns during Lent, the regulation was apparently not being observed; perhaps Athanasius hoped that by prescribing specific hours of closing (Monday morning to Saturday morning) the regulation would be more likely to be enforced.

 40 βρῶσιν ἰχθύων παυθῆναι: The eating of fish was forbidden during Lent; cf. Balsamon's commentary on the fiftieth canon of the Synod of Laodicea (Rhalles–Potles, III, 217) for prohibition of eating fish on fast days. In the fifteenth century, the Spanish traveller Pero Tafur commented that the Greeks ate no fish, but only shellfish, during Lent and other periods of fasting; cf. A. Vasiliev, «Pero Tafur and his Visit to Constantinople, Trebizond, and Italy», *Byzantion*, 7 (1932), 105.

ἐν τῷ αἰγιαλῷ: Cf. *Book of the Prefect*, chap. XVII, 3: οἱ ἰχθυοπράται τὴν ἐξώνησιν ποιείτωσαν ἐν τοῖς αἰγιαλοῖς καὶ ἐν σκάλαις ἀπὸ τῶν καταιρόντων πλοίων ... (Zepos, *Jus Graeco-Romanum*, II, 387).

 43 ὑψιμέδων: A high classical word used by Aristophanes and Pindar, but also found in a tenth-century *Hymn to the Virgin* by John Geometres (PG, 106, col. 868A: Ὕμνος ε′, 21). Cf. τοῦ παμμέδοντος in Letter 44, line 3.

44.

Athanasius urges the Emperor to issue an edict closing taverns, bathhouses, and workshops on the Sabbath.

Laurent, *Regestes*, no. 1665

44, 45

Date: a few days before Christmas (see title), probably in the year 1307, since this letter directly follows a letter dated to Lent of 1307; cf. Laurent, *Regestes*, 461. I would suggest that perhaps the letter might be dated even more precisely to December 22, since in lines 16–18 Athanasius quotes a passage which is found in the *Menaion* for December 22, and in Gregory of Nazianzus' *Oration* XIX, which is read on the same date.

3 Θεοῦ τοῦ παμμέδοντος: According to Lampe, *Patristic Greek Lexicon* (p. 1000), παμμέδων means «carefully, with careful thought», and παμμεδέων means «all-ruling». Athanasius, however, at least three times (see also Letters 56, line 7, and 100, line 8) uses παμμέδων in the sense of «all-ruling, almighty», following the pattern of ὑψιμέδων (Letter 43, line 43).

22–24 σεπτὸν αἰτοῦμεν ... ἐργαστήριον: Athanasius wants the Emperor to issue a *prostagma* ordering that workshops be closed from Saturday evening through all day Sunday; cf. *Novel* 54 of Leo VI, which ordered everyone to refrain from work on Sundays (Zepos, *Jus Graeco-Romanum*, I, 123–24).

24–25 βαλανείῳ ἢ καπηλείῳ: Athanasius wants to prohibit anyone from entering a bathhouse or tavern for the purpose of drinking, from Saturday evening through Sunday. Cf. Athanasius' *Novel* of 1304–1306 which ordered that bathhouses be closed from the ninth hour on Saturday (3 P.M.) until the ninth hour on Sunday; the same rules applied to taverns, except that they were also to be closed every night at sunset (PG, 161, col. 1066C–D). Athanasius' regulations for taverns were much stricter than those in the tenth-century *Book of the Prefect*, which provided that taverns must not open before the second hour of the day (7 A.M.), and must close by the second hour of the night (7 P.M.) on Sundays and major feast days (chap. xix, § 3, in Zepos, *Jus Graeco-Romanum*, II, 389).

Koukoules states that it was customary for Byzantines to eat and drink in the bathhouse after the bath, but presents no evidence later than the fourth century; cf. Βυζαντινῶν Βίος καὶ Πολιτισμός, IV, 456, and Τὰ λουτρὰ κατὰ τοὺς Βυζαντινοὺς χρόνους, in 'Επ. 'Ετ.Βυζ.Σπ., 11 (1935), 226–27.

45.

Athanasius invites the Emperor to the service at St. Sophia commemorating the Dormition of the Virgin.

45, 46

Laurent, *Regestes*, no. 1655

Date: *ca.* August 15, probably between 1305 and 1309, since the letter is similar to Letter 56, which can be dated to 1305 or later.

4 ἐν τοῖς ἀνακτόροις ... τῆς μεγαλωνύμου Σοφίας Θεοῦ: Originally the service commemorating the Dormition of the Virgin was celebrated at the church of the Virgin in Blachernae (Constantine Porphyrogenitus, *De cerimoniis*, ed. A. Vogt, I [Paris, 1935], 177); Andronicus II, however, issued a decree changing the location of the service to St. Sophia; cf. V. Grumel, «Le mois de Marie des Byzantins», *EO*, 31 (1932), 257–69.

8 κατηχουμενείοις: The *catechumeneia* are galleries in the triforium of a church; cf. Leo VI's *Novel* 73 (Zachariä von Lingenthal, *Jus Graeco-Romanum*, III, 171), which mentions τοῖς τῶν ἐκκλησιῶν ὑπερῴοις, ἃ πολὺς ἄνθρωπος κατηχούμενα καλεῖν ἔγνω. In St. Sophia these upper galleries were set aside for female worshippers from the time of the original construction of the church; cf. Procopius, *De aedificiis*, I.i., 56–58 (Loeb, VII, 24–26), and Paulus Silentiarius, "Εκφρασις τοῦ ναοῦ τῆς 'Αγίας Σοφίας, line 389 (ed. P. Friedländer, *Johannes von Gaza und Paulus Silentiarius* [Leipzig, 1912], 238). The emperor frequently ascended to the galleries on special occasions, e.g., Leo VI at the translation of the relics of Lazarus; cf. Arethas, *Oration* III, 105–6, eds. Jenkins, Laourdas, Mango, «Nine Orations of Arethas», *BZ*, 47 (1954), 24. At the time of his coronation the emperor ascended to the κατηχουμενεῖα to receive the acclamations of the people; cf. Cantacuzenus, *Hist.*, I, 202, and Ps.-Kodinos, *Traité des Offices*, 269, 1–2 (ἀνέρχεται εἰς τὰ λεγόμενα κατηχούμενα).

Here Athanasius is emphasizing the welcome the Emperor will be granted if he attends the service at St. Sophia; all the doors will be thrown open and the Emperor can ascend to the upper galleries if he wishes.

8–9 τῶν εὐγενῶν γυναικῶν: Athanasius will not offer such a cordial welcome to the noblewomen who come to church to show off their finery and to put on airs. This letter seems to indicate that in the fourteenth century the galleries were reserved for the noblewomen, while commoners stood below; cf. lines 17–19.

46.

To the Emperor, urging him to have mercy.

46

Laurent, *Regestes*, no. 1693

Date: between 1303 and April 1305, since, after the assassination of Roger de
Flor, Catalan merchants were forced to leave Constantinople; cf.
commentary on line 65.

13–14 τῶν συνδραμόντων ἐνταῦθα ... φιλονεικούντων: Athanasius preferred to make his residence at his own monastery at Xerolophos
rather than at the patriarchate. At the monastery (ἐνταῦθα) Athanasius held court sessions, dealing for the most part with cases of
oppression of the poor by officials and wealthy nobles; cf. Pachymeres, *Hist.*, II, 583. Andronicus had asked Athanasius to hold
court at the monastery as early as January 1303, six months before
he was restored to the patriarchate; cf. Pachymeres, *Hist.*, II, 369.

19 ᾽Ιταλῶν: Either the Catalans or the Genoese and Venetians. The
Byzantines suffered from the ravages of the Catalans in Anatolia
(and later in Greece), and from occasional attacks by Venetians and
Genoese in the capital itself; cf. Pachymeres, *Hist.*, II, 239, 322 ff.

20–21 καὶ ᾽Ιουδαῖος ἐθρήνησεν ἄν: For Athanasius' attitude toward the
Jews, cf. Letters 23, 36, and 41.

42 κόσμος τοῖς βασιλεῦσι ... τὸ ἔλεος: The rest of the letter is a play
on the words ἔλεος (mercy) and ἔλαιος (oil); cf. St. John Chrysostom,
De eleemosyna, III (PG, 49, col. 294) and *Homily IV on the Epistle
to the Philippians*, chap. 1 (PG, 62, col. 210).

50 ὁ τὴν γλῶτταν καὶ τὴν ψυχὴν ... ἔλεος: Probably a reference to St.
John Chrysostom, as the supposed author of the liturgy used in
Constantinople in the fourteenth century; Athanasius elsewhere
refers to John as ὁ τὴν γλῶτταν καὶ τὴν ψυχὴν χρυσοῦ παντὸς τιμαλφέστερος (Letter 47, line 3), and as τοῦ τὴν ψυχὴν καὶ τὴν γλῶτταν
χρυσοῦ (*Vat. Gr. 2219*, fol. 127ᵛ).

65 Κατελάνοι: This is not a reference to the Catalan Company of
mercenaries, but to Catalan merchants who established themselves
in Constantinople in the second half of the thirteenth century. The
Catalan merchants were discriminated against, since they had to
pay a tax of 3 percent on goods which they traded, whereas the Venetians and Genoese were exempt from all taxes, and the other Italian
states paid only a 2 percent tax. The Catalans maintained a consul
in the Byzantine capital; for example, a certain Dalmau Suner is
referred to as Catalan consul in the privilege issued in 1296 by An-

dronicus II, which established the 3 percent tax (Miklosich–Müller, III, 97–98; the date of 1290 in Miklosich–Müller is incorrect).

After the assassination of Roger de Flor in 1305, anti-Catalan feeling ran so high in the Byzantine empire that the Catalan merchants were forced to flee Constantinople for Gallipoli (Heyd, *Histoire du commerce du Levant*, I, 477; Muntaner, II, 538). By 1316, however, good relations with the Catalan merchants were reestablished and the tax on goods handled by Catalans was lowered to 2 percent; cf. Miklosich–Müller, III, 98–100; C. Marinescu, «Notes sur les Catalans dans l'Empire byzantin pendant le règne du Jacques II (1291–1327)», *Mélanges d'histoire du moyen âge, offerts à M. Ferdinand Lot* (Paris, 1925), 505–6.

47.

Athanasius asks the Emperor and his retinue to come to St. Sophia for services with the intention of praying, not feasting.

Laurent, *Regestes*, no. 1633

Date: Laurent assigns the letter to 1305–1306, but gives no reason for this date (*Regestes*, 426–27). He also places the letter at the end of January, since he interprets the first sentence as an allusion to the feast day of St. John Chrysostom, celebrated on January 27. It seems equally plausible, however, that this could be an allusion to the liturgy of St. John Chrysostom; cf. Letter 46, line 50. I prefer to date the letter *ca.* January 10, because of the extensive quotations from Gregory of Nazianzus' *Oration* XI, which was customarily read on Gregory of Nyssa's feast day; cf. Albert Ehrhard, *Überlieferung und Bestand der hagiographischen und homiletischen Literatur der griechischen Kirche*, I (Leipzig, 1937), 211.

3 ὁ τὴν γλῶτταν καὶ τὴν ψυχὴν ... τιμαλφέστερος: St. John Chrysostom; cf. commentary on Letter 46, line 50. See also Μηναῖον τοῦ Νοεμβρίου (Athens: Saliveros, 1926), 135, where John is described as κόσμον γλώσσῃ φαιδρύναντα, χρυσίου λαμπροτέρᾳ.

5 πρὸς τὰ θεῖα ἀνάκτορα: Athanasius' usual phrase for the church of St. Sophia, not the imperial palace as Laurent interprets it (*Regestes*, 427); cf. Letters 46, line 5, and 54, line 8 (τοῦ Θεοῦ τὰ ἀνάκτορα). which Laurent also translates as St. Sophia (*Regestes*, 487).

9–10 τοῖς περιβόλοις ... οἶα χωρίοις κραιπάλης: It was the custom of early Christians to celebrate the anniversary of a saint by holding

47, 48

an ἀγάπη or community meal in the church or chapel dedicated to that saint. This practice was attacked by Gregory of Nazianzus in his eleventh Oration, and in Epigrams 166–69 and 175. Several councils of the Church also forbade eating and drinking in churches; cf. the twenty-seventh canon of Laodicea, the sixtieth canon of Carthage, and the seventy-fourth canon of the Synod in Trullo (Rhalles-Potles, III, 194, 475; II, 476).

12 τυρβώδους: The word τυρβώδης is not found in the dictionaries, but must be an adjective meaning «tumultuous», derived from τύρβη («tumult, confusion, disorder»).

40–41 πανηγύρεις ἐνταῦθα ... Ἑλλήνων καὶ Ἰουδαίων: Athanasius is here attacking popular festivals which had survived from the time of the ancient Greeks and the Jews of the Old Testament. From the sixty-second canon of the Synod in Trullo we know that Byzantines continued to celebrate the Kalends and the Broumalia in the seventh century; canon sixty-five of the same council forbade Byzantines to leap over fires at the festival of the new moon (Rhalles–Potles, II, 448, 456–57). Balsamon, in his commentary on this canon, also describes the Byzantine custom of κληδόνες, or divination by extracting objects from a narrow-mouthed jug of water (Rhalles–Potles, II, 458–59). Although he claims this custom had died out in his time, it was still in evidence in the time of Athanasius (cf. *Vat. Gr. 2219*, fol. 139v), and is practiced in Crete to this day; cf. L. Oeconomos, *La vie religieuse dans l'empire byzantin au temps des Comnènes et des Anges* (Paris, 1918), 223–29.

48.

Athanasius once more urges the Emperor to make the bishops return to their sees.

Laurent, *Regestes*, no. 1694

7 ἀδείας βασιλικῆς: Andronicus encouraged the residence in Constantinople of certain bishops, such as the Patriarchs of Alexandria and Antioch, by granting them monasteries as headquarters; cf. Pachymeres, *Hist.*, II, 123, 203.

14 τὸν κῆνσον: An allusion to the «tribute penny» of the New Testament; cf. Matt. 22:19. Athanasius is referring here to the bitter arguments of the bishops over the decisions of the patriarchal tribunal, because

48, 49

some have been bribed by the defendant, and some by the plaintiff, and each bishop wants his man to win the case; cf. Letters 16, lines 4–7; 25, lines 4–6; 28, line 11; 30, lines 23–24.

15 ὁ οἴνου φροντίσας σὺν πέποσιν: This obscure allusion is clarified by a parallel passage in a letter to the metropolitan of Apameia (*Vat. Gr. 2219*, fol. 129ᵛ = Laurent, *Regestes*, no. 1744), where Athanasius derides the willingness of bishops to accept bribes in synodal elections: ⟨the story is told⟩ ὡς ὅτι ψῆφον ποτὲ γενέσθαι δεῆσαν, ἐκεῖθεν τοὺς ἐξελθόντας [i.e., ἐπισκόπους] οἴνῳ τινὸς καὶ πέποσι δεξιωσαμένου, ὅτι μὴ καὶ προέγνωσαν τοῦτον, μηδ' ἔθεντο συναρίθμιον τῷ ψηφίσματι, ἄλλος τὸν ἄλλον ἐπιμεμφόμενοι μετεμέλοντο, τῆς δέ γε φιλοξενίας δεδώκασι δεξιὰς μὴ στερήσειν μετέπειτα.

19–21 εἰ γάρ ... ἀβασανίστους εἰσάξουσιν: At this time when the bishop of a see died, frequently he was not replaced, but the bishop of a Turkish occupied see was granted the diocese κατ' ἐπίδοσιν. These absentee bishops remained in Constantinople, and never visited their own dioceses or the ones they had been assigned κατ' ἐπίδοσιν. Athanasius wanted the synod to elect new bishops for these «bereft dioceses», but was afraid that the members of the synod would elect unqualified candidates, since no one was willing to leave the safety of the capital.

22–23 εἰ δ' ἄνευ τῶν ὑποπτευομένων ... ἀθετήσει κανονικῇ ἁλισκόμεθα: On the other hand, if Athanasius selected bishops in the absence of those members of the synod whom he suspected of venality, he would be disobeying the canons of the Church which provided that bishops should be elected by all the members of the synod; cf. canon four of Nicaea I (Rhalles–Potles, II, 122) and the sixth canon of the Council of Sardica (Rhalles–Potles, III, 243). See also Balsamon's commentary on the latter canon: μετακαλοῦνται πάντες οἱ ἐνδημοῦντες κατὰ ταύτην τὴν τῶν πόλεων βασιλεύουσαν ἀρχιερεῖς, ὅταν ψῆφος ὀφείλῃ γενέσθαι ἐκκλησίας οἰασδήτινος, καὶ ἐμποδίζῃ [sic] ταύτην ἡ ἀποδημία τοῦ ἑνός (Rhalles–Potles, III, 246). The usual procedure was for the synod to select three candidates, one of whom was subsequently approved by the patriarch; cf. Gennadios, Ἱστορία τοῦ Οἰκουμενικοῦ Πατριαρχείου, 370.

49.

Athanasius complains that the Emperor ignores his memoranda.

Laurent, *Regestes*, no. 1695

49

5 ὅσοι βάπτουσιν εἰς νοῦν: For parallels to this curious phrase, meaning «to have a tincture of sense», «to have any understanding», cf. Nicetas Choniates, *Hist.*, 284, line 22–285, line 1, and *Novel* 24 of Alexius Comnenus (Zepos, *Jus Graeco-Romanum*, I, 306).

5–6 εἰ μή που ταῖς πτέρναις φορεῖ τὸν ἐγκέφαλον: Athanasius uses this quotation from Demosthenes' oration Περὶ Ἁλοννήσου (VII, 45) at least three times in his correspondence; cf. Letters 50, line 19, and 58, lines 36–37. We must assume that he knew this quotation because it had become proverbial in the Byzantine period, for one may well doubt that Athanasius ever read Demosthenes.

This phrase of Demosthenes was occasionally cited by Greek writers; cf. Hermogenes of Tarsus, Περὶ ἰδεῶν (*Hermogenis opera*, Teubner [1913], 255–56); Libanius, *Argumenta orationum Demosthenicarum* (*Libanii opera*, ed. R. Foerster, VIII [Leipzig, 1915], 619); *Eustathii Commentarii ad Homeri Iliadem*, ed. G. Stallbaum (Leipzig, 1829), § 1015, 43 (vol. III, 265).

7 Ἠλεί: The priest Elei allowed the iniquity of his sons to go unchecked; not only were his two sons slain in battle, but the priest himself died as a punishment from God; cf. 1 Kings 2–4. This passage can be interpreted in two different ways. On the one hand, Athanasius may identify himself with the priest Elei and consider Andronicus as his son, since the Emperor is the son of the Church; cf. line 39. Thus, Athanasius is torn between his love for the Emperor and the necessity of chastising him. On the other hand, Athanasius may identify Andronicus with Elei, and the Emperor's sons with the sons of Elei. On other occasions Athanasius chides the Emperor for his failure to chastise his sons; cf. Letters 36, line 2, and 107, lines 4–5.

7–8 Ἠλεί ... ἐλεεινῶς: Note the pun.

18–19 τῶν σμικρυνόντων ... τὰ Ῥωμαίων σχοινίσματα: This allusion is deliberately obscure, since Athanasius dared not make a specific accusation against any member of the imperial family. The Patriarch might be referring to Andronicus himself, who had introduced the Catalan Company into Byzantine territory, or to the Empress Irene, who sought to carve out appanages on the Greek mainland for herself and her sons. Gregoras severely attacked Irene's Western concept of the division of the territory of the empire; cf. *Hist.*, I, 233. See also H. Constantinidi-Bibikou, «Yolande de Montferrat, impératrice de Byzance», *Hellénisme contemporain*, 4 (1950), 425–42.

49, 50

40–41 ἴσα γνησίων υἱῶν φροντίζειν τῶν ὑπὸ χεῖρα: Cf. Letter 36, lines 2–3.

46–47 μηδὲ πάσχειν ὑποστολὴν ἡμέρας ὕψει ἢ ὄκνῳ: Cf. *Vat. Gr. 2219*, fol. 146ᵛ: μὴ δι' ὄκνῳ [ὄγκῳ ms.] μὴ ἐξ ὕψους ἡμέρας εἰργόμενοι.

96–97 ἡ βασιλεία ἐπιστασία ἐστὶ καὶ ὁρίζεται ἔννομος: Cf. *Epanagoge*, Title I, chap. 1 (ed. Zachariä von Lingenthal, *Jus Graeco-Romanum*, IV, 181): βασιλεύς ἐστι ἔννομος ἐπιστασία. See also Letter 61, lines 44–46: τίνος γὰρ ἕνεκεν ἄλλου ... βασιλείᾳ τὴν ἐκκλησίαν Θεὸς καθωράϊσεν, ἢ δι' ἐπιστασίαν ὁριζομένην δικαίαν καὶ ἔννομον;

106 μὴ τῇ θυρίδι αἰτῶ τὸ γράμμα ῥιφήτω: An indication of the tension which occasionally developed between the Emperor and Patriarch.

112 τοῖς Νινευΐτῶν: Cf. Letters 3 and 70, and Jonah 3.

50.

Athanasius urges the Emperor to issue a chrysobull forbidding the construction of buildings right against the walls of churches.

Laurent, *Regestes*, no. 1696

7 πολλοῦ γε καὶ δεῖ: Although in classical authors πολλοῦ δεῖ is an idiomatic expression meaning «there wants much», «far from it» (Liddell–Scott, 9th ed., 372), in this passage πολλοῦ should apparently be taken as an adverbial genitive absolute meaning «very», so that the phrase means «it is very necessary», «there is great necessity».

13 τοῦ συνετοῦ καὶ σοφίᾳ πεπλατυσμένου: Solomon, the author of the Book of Proverbs.

19 τοῖς μὴ τῇ πτέρνῃ φοροῦσι ... τὸν ἐγκέφαλον: Cf. commentary on Letter 49, lines 5–6.

30–31 κεραίαις ἐν ἐρυθραῖς: The emperor signed documents with special red ink to protect himself against forgeries; cf. Dölger–Karayanno-poulos, *Byzantinische Urkundenlehre*, 28–31.

34 κοινοποιεῖν: Athanasius here uses the word κοινοποιῶ in the sense of «to defile», rather than «to make common property»; cf. the ninety-seventh canon of the Synod in Trullo: τοὺς ἢ γαμετῇ συνοι-

50, 51

κοῦντας, ἢ ἄλλως ἀδιακρίτως τοὺς ἱεροὺς τόπους κοινοποιοῦντας (Rhalles–Potles, II, 536).

36 τὸν 'Οζὰν: Oza was struck dead by the Lord for touching the ark; cf. 2 Kings 6:1–7 and 1 Chron. 13:7–10.

45 τις ... στενοχωρία: Although it is possible to translate this passage «if lack of space should be a pressing problem», the translation «if some difficulty should present itself» makes better sense historically, since it is well known that by the fourteenth century there was no lack of open space for construction in Constantinople. From the time of the Latin Empire the population of the capital had steadily diminished (A. M. Schneider, *Die Bevölkerung Konstantinopels im XV. Jahrhundert*, NachrGött, 9 [1949], 233–44), and by the middle of the fourteenth century, when Ibn Battuta visited Constantinople, there were thirteen separate settlements within the walls, divided from each other by vacant lots or cultivated land; cf. Ibn Battuta, *Voyages*, eds. C. Defremery and B. R. Sanguinetti, II (Paris, 1854), 431–32. Athanasius anticipated that there would be objections to the proposed chrysobull on the part of people who wished to build next to churches for the sake of convenience or commercial advantage, not because there was no room elsewhere. This testimony is confirmed by the fourteenth-century Arab geographer Abulfeda; cf. *Géographie d'Aboulfeda*, trans. J. T. Reinaud, II, 1 (Paris, 1848), 315–16.

51.

Athanasius asks for the Emperor's clemency toward the men who inadvertently allowed Paxes to escape from prison.

Laurent, *Regestes*, no. 1644

Date: *ca.* 1306 (?); cf. commentary *infra* on line 2.

2 τὸν Παξῆ: Although the stress is on the wrong syllable, Παξῆς is apparently a variation of the Greek form πέκις or πάκις of the Turkish word *bey* (‮ڊك‬), pronounced *bak* in the mediaeval period; cf. G. Moravcsik, *Byzantino-Turcica*, II (Berlin, 1958), 250. The scribe took the foreign word παξῆς as a proper name, but it is more likely to be a title; cf. the confusion of the *De cerimoniis* (Bonn, 681), where the titles καναρτικεινος and βουλιας ταρκανος were taken as proper names, whereas they are in fact titles given to Bulgarian princes; cf. C. Mango and I. Ševčenko, «A New Manuscript of the

51

De Cerimoniis», *DOP*, 14 (1960), 248. Moravcsik gives no example of πέκης (or any form thereof) used as a proper name, although it is often used in conjunction with a proper name, e.g., Σολυμάμπαξις. In any case, Paxes must be a Turk who has escaped from prison.

Boivin, in his «Notae ad Nicephorum Gregoram» (p. 755), proposed that the traitor Paxes should be identified with the Tartar Koutsimpaxis who is known from the *History* of Pachymeres. Koutsimpaxis did incur the suspicion of treachery while on an embassy to the Alans (*Hist.*, II, 346, 574–75), but Pachymeres does not mention any imprisonment. Laurent has suggested that he was imprisoned upon his return from the embassy in 1305 and escaped in 1306; cf. *Regestes*, 438–39.

3–8 τὸ ὀλέθριον ... τῆς δεινῆς ἀνταμείψεως: the text of this passage is somewhat suspect since it requires at least two emendations to make sense grammatically. Moreover, Athanasius' interpretation of the story does not coincide exactly with the details set forth in the Old Testament. The Book of Kings relates that Ahab, king of Israel, defeated his archenemy Benhadad, king of Syria. Although Ahab had the opportunity to imprison Benhadad, he let him go (3 Kings 21:26–34). A prophet then declared to Ahab that anyone who allowed a prisoner to escape should be punished with death (3 Kings 21:38–43). Indeed Ahab was killed the next time he engaged in battle with the Syrians (3 Kings 22:29–36). In the Bible the prophet of chapter 20 is not named, but Athanasius assumes that he is the same as Micah, who figures prominently in chapter 22.

9 τοῖς ὧδε εὑρισκομένοις ἀρχιερεῦσι: The σύνοδος ἐνδημοῦσα.

16 αὐτῆς: I.e., τῆς βασιλείας σου.

20–21 τι κατὰ τοῦ κράτους καὶ σκαιωρῆσαι: Cf. commentary on line 2 *supra*.

21 ἄθεος: This epithet would fit Koutsimpaxes, who was a recent convert to Christianity from Zoroastrianism (Pachymeres, *Hist.*, II, 345).

22 τῇ βαρβαρώδει ἐκείνου κεφαλῇ καὶ ψυχῇ: This phrase further supports the identification of Paxes as a Turk.

24 τοσαύτης ἀναδοχῆς καὶ πολλῶν τῶν εὐεργεσιῶν: This description could also apply to Koutsimpaxes, who was pardoned by the Emperor after falling into the hands of the Byzantines, and later became one of Andronicus' retainers; cf. Pachymeres, *Hist.*, II, 345.

COMMENTARY   363

52.

Athanasius urges the Emperor and all Orthodox Christians to attend the ceremony of the Entombment of Christ.

Laurent, *Regestes*, no. 1697

Date: Easter Week, 1305 (?); cf. commentary on line 14.

1–2 ἐν τῷ τοῦ Σωτῆρος ... ἐνταφιασμῷ: Athanasius summons the Emperor and the people of Constantinople to attend the Orthros service of Holy Saturday, commemorating the death and entombment of Christ; cf. Letters 53–55 and 71. This service was held during the night of Good Friday-Holy Saturday. Athanasius' language in this and related letters is strongly reminiscent of the *Enkomia* which were sung around the *epitaphios* (for the text of these songs of praise, see *Triodion*, 710–27). It has therefore been suggested that the patriarchate of Athanasius should be a *terminus ante quem* for the insertion of these *Enkomia* in the Orthros service; cf. Pallas, *Die Passion Christi*, 64–66, 299–300. The fact that Athanasius devoted five letters to invitations to this service is perhaps an indication that it had taken on a new importance because of the addition of the *Enkomia*.

3 τῷ τοῦ 'Ισραὴλ ἐνταφιασμῷ: All the nobility of Egypt attended the funeral of Israel (Jacob), the father of Joseph; cf. Gen. 50:7.

9 τῇ μητρὶ τῶν ἐκκλησιῶν: St. Sophia.

10–11 τὴν παναγίαν σφαγὴν καὶ τὸν ζωηρὸν ἐνταφιασμὸν προσκυνῆσαι: Pallas has suggested that Athanasius is here referring to two icons, one of the ἄκρα ταπείνωσις of Christ (the «Christ of Pity», after the Crucifixion), the other of the burial of Christ; cf. *Die Passion Christi*, 38–39. He also proposes that the iconographical theme of Christ in the tomb was developed in connection with the addition of the *Enkomia* to the Orthros service (290–96).

14 τοῦ Δεσπότου: Although Constantine, Andronicus' son by Anne of Hungary, was also despot during Athanasius' second patriarchate, it is evident that Athanasius is here referring to the Despot John Palaeologus, Andronicus' son by Irene of Montferrat, since in the closely related Letter 53, lines 34–35, the Despot is called πανευτυχέσ-τατος, an epithet reserved by Athanasius for John; cf. Letters 85, lines 2 and 4; 86, line 3; 96, lines 3–4. John moved to Thessalonica

in 1303 after his marriage to Irene Choumnaina and died there in 1307 (Pachymeres, *Hist.*, II, 379; Gregoras, *Hist.*, I, 241), but he returned to the capital at the end of 1304 to serve as prefect of the city (Pachymeres, *Hist.*, II, 480 and 497). Thus, Letters 52 and 53 should probably be dated to successive years, 1305 and 1306.

τῷ προεστῶτι: This title was not assigned on a permanent basis, but at each service one of the members of the clergy was chosen as *proestos* and was charged with reading certain parts of the service; for example, he recited the Creed during the liturgy; cf. Θρησκευτικὴ καὶ ᾽Ηθικὴ ᾽Εγκυκλοπαίδεια, X, *s.v.* cols. 600–1.

16 τοῖς δομεστίκοις ... τοῖς μεγάλοις: These *megaloi domestikoi* were leaders of the first and second choirs; cf. Goar, *Euchologion*, 225.

17–18 παννύχιον: The vigil lasted through the night of Good Friday-Holy Saturday.

53.

Athanasius again urges the Emperor and the people of Constantinople to attend Good Friday services; cf. Letters 52, 54–55, and 71.

Laurent, *Regestes*, no. 1698

Date: Easter Week, 1306 (?); cf. commentary on *Letter* 52, line 14.

1 πρὸς τὸν λαὸν ἅπαντα: Although the title of this letter, in the hand of the original scribe, indicates that it was addressed to the people of Constantinople, the letter was also addressed to the Emperor; cf. lines 32–33. Pallas tried to obviate this difficulty by suggesting that the end of the letter (lines 32–39) really belongs at the end of Letter 52; cf. *Die Passion Christi*, 299–300. In that case, however, Athanasius would have twice in the same letter suggested that the Despot take the Emperor's place if necessary. It is more plausible that the title of Letter 53 is incorrect, and that the texts of Letters 52 and 53 should stand as they do in the manuscript.

34–35 ὁ Δεσπότης ... ὁ εὐτυχὴς καὶ πανευτυχέστατος: Cf. commentary on Letter 52, line 14.

35 Ναζιραίων: Monks; cf. *Suidae Lexicon*, ed. A. Adler, II (Leipzig, 1933), 434.

53-56

35-36 ἐξόδια: Hymns to the departed Christ sung during the Orthros service on Holy Saturday; cf. *Triodion*, 723, 729.

37 πρὸ νυκτός: Athanasius urges the people to come to the church before nightfall on Good Friday; those who are late will not be rewarded in Heaven.

54.

Another letter urging the Emperor to come to church the evening of Good Friday; cf. Letters 52, 53, 55, and 71.

Laurent, *Regestes*, no. 1699

Date: Easter Week, 1307 (?). Laurent has suggested (*Regestes*, 486) that Letters 52-55 represent invitations from four successive years. Since Letters 52 and 53, which mention the Despot John, can with some certainty be assigned to 1305 and 1306, then Letters 54 and 55 can probably be dated to 1307 and 1308 respectively.

19-20 ἐάσαντες ἄταφον ... ὡς μή τινος γεγονότος καινοῦ: Athanasius complains that the people do not come to the *epitaphios* ceremony on Good Friday. The ambiguous phrase ὡς μή τινος γεγονότος καινοῦ could be interpreted literally as meaning that the people fail to realize the importance of Christ's death, and go about their business as if nothing new had happened (cf. *Triodion*, 732: ὦ τῶν θαυμάτων τῶν καινῶν!), or could also be interpreted as referring to the introduction of the *Enkomia* in the Orthros service; cf. Pallas, *Die Passion Christi*, 65.

55.

Yet another letter urging the Emperor to attend church services on Good Friday; cf. Letters 52-54 and 71.

Laurent, *Regestes*, no. 1700

Date: Easter Week, 1308 (?); cf. commentary on date of Letter 54 *supra*.

56.

Athanasius invites the Emperor to attend the service at St. Sophia on August 15 in commemoration of the Dormition of the Virgin.

56

Laurent, *Regestes*, no. 1641

Date: shortly before August 15, 1305–1309 (?); cf. commentary on lines 12–13 *infra*.

2 βασίλισσαν νότου: The Queen of Sheba; cf. Letter 71, line 2.

σοφίας ἕνεκεν: A play on words, since the Emperor is invited to τὰ ἀνάκτορα τῆς Σοφίας; cf. Letter 71, lines 3–5.

12–13 τῇ εὐσεβεστάτῃ Αὐγούστῃ: The title Augusta could be held by several female members of the imperial family at the same time, for example, the mother and wife of the emperor, his sisters, and the wives of co-emperors; cf. A. Vogt, *Constantin VII Porphyrogénète, Le livre des cérémonies*. II, *Commentaire* (Paris, 1940), p. xv.

Laurent (*Regestes*, 436) identifies the Augusta of this letter as the Empress Irene, and suggests that some time between 1305 and 1309 she may have returned to Constantinople from Thessalonica, where she lived from 1303 to 1317 in estrangement from her husband. There is, however, no supporting evidence for this assumption in the *Histories* of Gregoras or Pachymeres. We know that Irene stayed in Thessalonica at least until 1305 (Pachymeres, *Hist.*, II, 557). Around 1305 or 1306 she attempted to leave Thessalonica for the capital, but was forced by the Catalan danger to turn back (Pachymeres, *Hist.*, II, 586–87). She was also in Thessalonica in 1307, when the Despot John died (Gregoras, *Hist.*, I, 241). It is possible, however, that at some point Irene made a quick trip to Constantinople in a final effort to become reconciled to her husband; see commentary on Letters 75, 97, and 98.

Rita-Maria, wife of Michael IX, is also referred to as Augusta by Pachymeres (*Hist.*, II, 405, 447, 525–26), but it does seem more likely that Athanasius is referring to Andronicus' wife than to his daughter-in-law.

14–15 τέμενος τῆς μεγάλης Θεοῦ Λόγου Σοφίας: For the celebration of the feast of the Dormition of the Virgin at St. Sophia, see commentary on Letter 45, line 4.

23–24 πρὸς διάχυσιν βλέψαι τῆς δομήσεως τῶν ἐπάλξεων: Two sources mention Andronicus' construction and restoration of the walls of Constantinople; cf. B. Meyer-Plath and A. M. Schneider, *Die Landmauer von Konstantinopel*, II (Berlin, 1943), 6 and 155. (1) Gregoras (*Hist.*, I, 275) speaks of τὰ τῆς Κωνσταντινουπόλεως τείχη ὅσα ἐκαινούργησε καὶ ὅσα ἐκ βάθρων ἀνήγειρε. (2) Nicephorus Callistus

56–58

Xanthopoulos praises Andronicus for his fortification of the capital in his address, προσφώνημα ἐν εἴδει ἐγκωμίου (PG, 145, col. 584D). Neither source, however, gives any date for this reconstruction. Thus, Athanasius' letter is important for its indication that work on the walls was in progress *ca.* 1305–1309.

57.

Athanasius threatens to resign from the patriarchate unless the Church is granted freedom.

Laurent, *Regestes*, no. 1701

8–9 ἐλευθερίας καταπολαῦσαι τὴν ἐκκλησίαν Χριστοῦ: When he begs for the «liberation» of the Church, Athanasius probably means that he wants complete control of the Church for himself, without interference from Arsenites, hostile bishops, and perhaps even the Emperor himself.

10–11 νηπίοις: An allusion to bishops who are destroying the Church, perhaps youthful appointees to metropolitan sees.

13–14 ὁ βουλόμενος, οὕτως ἐχούσης αὐτῆς, ὀνόματι φροντιζέτω: Athanasius again threatens to resign; cf. Letter 30. For ὀνόματι meaning «nominally», cf. *Theological Dictionary of the New Testament*, ed. G. Friedrich (Grand Rapids, Mich., 1967), *s.v.* ὄνομα, c, and Demetrakos, *Lexikon*, 5159–60, 3.

14–15 ἐγὼ γὰρ καὶ γήρᾳ καὶ νόσῳ ... συζῶν: Athanasius complained of ill health and old age even at the beginning of his second patriarchate; cf. Pachymeres, *Hist.*, II, 369.

58.

Once again Athanasius protests that it is not for his own personal advantage that he sends petitions to Andronicus, but rather for the good of the Emperor. Therefore he cannot understand why Andronicus pays less attention to his reports than to the advice of other men.

Laurent, *Regestes*, no. 1702

11 σχέσει: For σχέσις with the meaning of «love», cf. I. Ševčenko, «On the Preface to a Praktikon by Alyates», *JÖBG*, 17 (1968), 71 and note a, and Boissonade, *Anecdota Graeca*, II, 155 note 1.

22–23 ἔπαθε ... βασιλεύς, καὶ ταῦτα ψάλλων ἐν πνεύματι: An allusion to David, who was both king and psalmist. It is not clear to which incident in David's life Athanasius is referring; perhaps it is to David's command that Uriah, the husband of Bathsheba, be placed in the front lines of battle so that he would be killed; cf. 2 Kings 11:15.

26 κεφαλαίου: For κεφάλαιον as a tax, cf. Miklosich–Müller, IV, 86 and 249; VI, 253–54.

εἰσφορᾶς: For the meaning «payment of taxes», cf. Demetrakos, *Lexikon, s.v.* 5.

36–37 τῶν ... συνείδησιν: Cf. commentary on Letter 49, lines 5–6.

38–39 ἓν μόνον κτωμένων ... ἀλλὰ καὶ μεθ᾽ ὅρκων: Perhaps an allusion to witnesses in a lawsuit who were persuaded by bribes to perjure themselves.

46 τοῦ γένους τὴν σωτηρίαν: The concept of γένος, «the Greek nation», began to develop in Byzantium after the Fourth Crusade. The word is found in this sense already in the Lascarid Empire of Nicaea; cf., for example, a letter of John III Ducas Vatatzes written between 1237 and 1241 to Pope Gregory IX (cited in A. E. Bakalopoulos, Ἱστορία τοῦ Νέου Ἑλληνισμοῦ, I [Thessalonica, 1961], 67–68).

48 διπλῆς: I.e., material and spiritual progress.

59.

A letter in which Athanasius urges the Emperor to punish the wicked and help the oppressed so that he in turn will be helped by God. Again the Patriarch complains that he is ignored by Andronicus, even though he makes petitions to the Emperor out of the purest of motives.

Laurent, *Regestes*, no. 1703

4 τὰ τῆς ἀληθείας: God's own things, i.e., debts owed to the «rich man» of the parable.

59, 60

10 κέρδος οἰκεῖον λογιζόμενοι τὴν τοῦ γένους συμφοράν: An allusion to merchants who took advantage of the short supply of wheat in Constantinople in the early fourteenth century to charge exorbitant prices for grain. For Athanasius' use of γένος, cf. commentary on Letter 58, line 46.

60.

Since Andronicus has received so many blessings, he should try to repay God by stamping out wickedness in the empire. Athanasius again complains that Andronicus never heeds his petitions, or sends the hetaeriarch to investigate the abuses reported by the Patriarch.

Laurent, *Regestes*, no. 1654

Date: Laurent assigns the letter to the summer of 1306–1307, without explaining his reasons for this dating. I can find no internal evidence in the letter to indicate that it was written during the summer. If the hetaeriarch mentioned is indeed Nestongos Ducas (see commentary *infra*), then a date of 1307 is possible, since we know that the hetaeriarch was in Constantinople at that time (Pachymeres, *Hist.*, II, 627).

11 συνελόντα εἰπεῖν: The usual expression is συνελόντι εἰπεῖν.

37 ἐκ φίλων ἢ ἀλλοτρίων: An alternative translation for this phrase could be «through friends rather than strangers».

63 τῷ ἑταιρειάρχῃ: In the fourteenth century one of the functions of the hetaeriarch was to handle the reception of refugees; cf. Ps.-Kodinos, *Traité des Offices*, 178, 186; Pachymeres, *Hist.*, I, 321; and E. Stein, «Untersuchungen zur spät-byzantinischen Verfassungs- und Wirtschaftsgeschichte», *Mitteilungen zur osmanischen Geschichte*, 2 (1924), 41 note 3. Athanasius may have wanted the hetaeriarch to assist him in the investigation of refugee problems, such as housing, the famine, and abuses by tax collectors.

The only early-fourteenth-century hetaeriarch whose name we know is Nestongos Ducas, who was appointed great hetaeriarch in 1304; cf. Pachymeres, *Hist.*, II, 428–29; D. I. Polemis, *The Doukai* (London, 1970), 152 note 133; Laurent, *Regestes*, 449. One difficulty presents itself, however, in this identification: that Athanasius supported Nestongos in 1304 when he was suspected of conspiracy

60, 61

against the Emperor (Pachymeres, *Hist.*, II, 431), whereas in this letter he bitterly attacks the unnamed hetaeriarch.

61.

Athanasius reminds the Emperor that God established the empire to serve the Church. Therefore Andronicus should use his authority to encourage bishops to remain in their sees.

Laurent, *Regestes*, no. 1704

6 ταύτην καὶ βασιλείῳ καταστέψαι περιωπῇ, etc.: Athanasius believed that the role of the emperor was to serve and support the Church which had been established before the Empire; cf. Letter 104, lines 25–28.

17 ὁ καθηγούμενος: It is impossible to identify any further this abbot, who served as a liaison between the Emperor and Patriarch.

45–46 δι᾽ ἐπιστασίαν ὁριζομένην δικαίαν καὶ ἔννομον: Cf. *Epanagoge*, Title I, chap. 1: βασιλεύς ἐστιν ἔννομος ἐπιστασία, κοινὸν ἀγαθὸν πᾶσι τοῖς ὑπηκόοις (Zachariä von Lingenthal, *Jus Graeco-Romanum*, IV, 181). Cf. also Letter 49, lines 96–97: ἢ οὐχ ἡ βασιλεία ἐπιστασία ἐστι καὶ ὁρίζεται ἔννομος;

48 ὀφείλομεν διδαχθῆναι ἐκ τοῦ αὐτῆς ἐπιστημονάρχου: A reference to the Emperor who was called *epistemonarch* of the Church, as protector and guardian of the faith and ecclesiastical tradition; cf. Ch. Du Fresne Du Cange, *Glossarium ad scriptores mediae et infimae Graecitatis* (Breslau, 1891), I, col. 427, and Demetrakos, *Lexikon*, 2857.

For parallel passages, see Athanasius, Letter 95, line 21; Pachymeres, *Hist.*, I, 260–61; Balsamon, commentary on the twelfth canon of the Second Council of Antioch (PG, 137, col. 1312A). For further literature, see Laurent, *Regestes*, 491.

75–76 τὸν τὰ πρόβατα καταλείψαντα ... φροντίζειν ἡμᾶς ἐγχειρεῖν τούτῳ ἕτερα: The metropolitan of Sardis, for example, was given the bishopric of Methymna on Lesbos κατ᾽ ἐπίδοσιν, since he was unable to return to Sardis; cf. Athanasius' letter to Nicephorus Moschopoulos, ed. Papadopoulos-Kerameus, Νικήφορος Μοσχόπουλος, 219.

83 τὰ ἐν Ἀγκύρᾳ καὶ Πισιδίᾳ: After the Seljuk conquest of central Anatolia at the end of the eleventh century, the areas of Ankyra and

61

Pisidia were permanently lost to the Byzantine empire, and we may assume that the bishops of these dioceses spent much of their time in Constantinople; cf. a patriarchal act of April 1345: ἡ ἁγιωτάτη μητρόπολις τῆς Πισιδίας ἐπὶ πολλοῖς ἐστιν ἤδη τοῖς χρόνοις ἀρχιερατικῆς ἀμοιροῦσα ποιμανσίας καὶ ἐπισκέψεως, ἅτε δὴ καὶ τοῦ λαχόντος αὐτὴν ἱερωτάτου ἀρχιερέως ἐκείνου κωλυθέντος ὑπὸ τῆς ἐπισυμβάσης ἐθνικῆς ἐπικρατείας προσμεῖναι ταύτῃ δὴ τῇ κατ᾽ αὐτὸν ἐκκλησίᾳ (Miklosich–Müller, I, 242).

Athanasius bemoans the fate of the Christians in Ankyra and Antioch of Pisidia, suffering from Turkish oppression without any bishop to protect them and act as mediator with the Turks; cf., for example, the role of the metropolitan of Pisidia under Michael VIII, Makarios, who was on friendly terms with the Seljuk sultan Izzeddin (Pachymeres, *Hist.*, I, 259, 267; P. Wittek, «'Yasijioglu' Ali on the Christian Turks of the Dobrudja», *BSOAS*, 14 [1952], 259–60).

The Christian population of central Anatolia was in a particularly difficult position at this time, since the Seljuk Sultans of Rum had been reduced to vassals of the Mongol Ilkhanids after the battle of Kösedag in 1242, and there was constant fighting as various Turkish emirs began to carve out their own beyliks in areas no longer under Seljuk control. With the death in 1308 of Giyaseddin, son of Alaeddin Keykûbad II, the Seljuk Empire of Rum came to an end; cf. P. Wittek, «Deux chapitres de l'histoire des Turcs de Roum. I, Les traits essentiels de la période seldjoucide en Asie Mineure», *Byzantion*, 11 (1936), 285–302; Tamara Talbot Rice, *The Seljuks in Asia Minor* (London, 1961), 74–80; Sp. Vryonis, *The Decline of Medieval Hellenism in Asia Minor and the Process of Islamization from the Eleventh Through the Fifteenth Century* (Berkeley, Calif., 1971); and Cl. Cahen, *Pre-Ottoman Turkey. A General Survey of the Material and Spiritual Culture and History, c. 1071–1330* (New York, 1968), 303–14.

In 1285, Sabbas, metropolitan of Antioch of Pisidia, was present at the Second Synod of Blachernae, and signed the tome against Bekkos; cf. Laurent, «Les signataires», 145 no. 13. Sabbas was still metropolitan of Pisidia in October 1295 (Dölger, *Aus den Schatzkammern*, Act no. 100, p. 259), and sometime between 1301 and 1305 authenticated a copy of a chrysobull of Andronicus II (dated 1298), preserved at the Lavra on Mt. Athos; cf. Laurent, «Un groupe de signatures épiscopales», 318–23, and my commentary on Letter 25, lines 14–15. At this time he was also *proedros* of Ainos. We may assert then that the metropolitan of Pisidia who was a member of the synod in 1304 (PG, 161, col. 1065B) was still Sabbas. By December 1315 Sabbas had been replaced by Gregory as metropolitan of Pisidia (Miklosich–Müller, I, 40–41).

61, 62

We also know that Babylas, the metropolitan of Ankyra, resided in Constantinople during the early fourteenth century, since he supported John XII Cosmas in 1303 (Pachymeres, *Hist.*, II, 377) and was present at the synod in October 1304 (PG, 161, col. 1065B). Babylas of Ankara also signed the copy of Andronicus' chrysobull sometime between 1301 and 1305 as ὁ μητροπολίτης Ἀγκύρας ὑπέρτιμος καὶ ἔξαρχος πάσης Γαλατίας, πρόεδρος Φιλίππων καὶ Χριστουπόλεως Βαβύλας; cf. Laurent, «Un groupe de signatures épiscopales», 319.

62.

Athanasius again brings up the question of episcopal residence, and urges the Emperor to force bishops to return to their sees.

Laurent, *Regestes*, no. 1705

4 μηδὲ ὑπὲρ τὸ ἑξάμηνον: The sixteenth canon of the anti-Ignatian synod of 859/861 (called «the First and Second Synod») limited to six months the time a bishop was allowed to be absent from his see (Rhalles–Potles, II, 696).

5–6 τὸν λόγον τῇ ποίμνῃ ... τῆς σωτηρίας: Cf. the nineteenth canon of the Synod in Trullo (Rhalles–Potles, II, 346), which asserted that bishops should teach their people the Scriptures daily, and especially on Sundays.

20–21 ἀναχωρεῖν κεκρικότες ζητεῖν τὰ ἡμέτερα: Athanasius again hints that he may resign if the Emperor does not give him full authority over the Church; cf. Letter 57.

30 ἐν οἷς: «Incidentally», German «wobei»; cf. D. Tabachovitz, *Sprachliche und textkritische Studien zur Chronik des Theophanes Confessor* (Uppsala, 1926), 20.

31 προνοίας προσνενεμῆσθαι: A well-known passage in Pachymeres implies the assignment of πρόνοιαι to churches and monasteries in the early fourteenth century; cf. *Hist.*, II, 390. On this point, see also I. Ševčenko, «An Important Contribution to the Social History of Late Byzantium», *AnnUkrAcad*, II,4 (1952), 458.

32 καὶ βίου ἐντεῦθεν τὸν πορισμὸν ἀπαιτεῖν: Cf. Letter 25, lines 14–16: τί δὲ ὁ Σάρδεων; οὐχὶ ἀμπελῶνα ἔχει ἐνταῦθα καὶ ζευγηλατεῖον καὶ

κῆπον καὶ ἐργαστήρια, πρὸς τούτοις καὶ ἀδελφᾶτα; The canons of the Church forbade priests to have such worldly concerns; cf. the tenth canon of the Second Council of Nicaea (Rhalles–Potles, II, 587–88).

34–35 οὐδὲ τὸ διδάσκειν ... τοῖς νόμοις: Cf. the twentieth canon of the Synod in Trullo (Rhalles–Potles, II, 349), which forbids a bishop to preach publicly in a city which is not under his jurisdiction.

49–50 τοῖς δεσπόταις: Athanasius here uses the word δεσπότης to refer to bishops; cf. Demetrakos, *Lexikon*, 1818, and Lampe, *Patristic Greek Lexicon*, 339.

51 ἐπιστασία παρασπονδύλιος: The word παρασπονδύλιος is not found in the dictionaries, although Παρασπόνδυλος was a common Byzantine surname in the fourteenth century; cf. Cantacuzenus, *Hist.*, II, 525; Miklosich–Müller, III, 114. In the fifteenth century Ζωτικὸς Παρασπόνδυλος wrote a poem about the battle of Varna; cf. N. G. Svoronos, Τὸ περὶ τῆς μάχης τῆς Βάρνης ποίημα, in *Athena*, 48 (1938), 163–83. Svoronos (p. 172) interprets Παρασπόνδυλος, a compound formed of the preposition παρά (to the side) and the noun σπόνδυλος (vertebra, backbone), as a nickname meaning «with twisted neck». Here παρασπονδύλιος might mean «neck-twisting», «oppressive», or be a pun on the family name.

58 λόγους χρυσοβουλλείους: Michael VIII gave two monasteries to the patriarch of Alexandria ἀσφαλέσιν ἐμπεδώσεσι χρυσοβούλλοις; cf. Pachymeres, *Hist.*, II, 203.

65 τῷ θεόπτῃ: Moses.

71 τοῦ μυσαροῦ Ἀμαλὴκ καὶ πανώλου: Cf. Exod. 17:8–16, where Joshua won a victory over Amalek, because Moses had ordered the swift execution of a man who broke the Sabbath by collecting wood. During the battle, the Israelites were victorious over the Amalekites as long as Moses held up the rod. When his arms grew tired, they were supported by his brother Aaron and by Hur, so that his standing figure with outstretched arms may have resembled a cross; hence Athanasius' reference to a «prefiguration of the mystery of the Cross».

Athanasius' use of this Old Testament passage as a simile was apt, since Byzantium was the new Israel (cf. *Vat. Gr. 2219*, fol. 272ᵛ: ὁ ... νέος κληθεὶς Ἰσραήλ) and Byzantine writers occasionally used the term Ἀμαληκῖται to refer to the Turks; cf. Athanasius, Letter 81, lines 165–66, and Philes, *Poem* 44, line 68 (Martini, *Manuelis Philae carmina inedita*, 55).

If Andronicus, the new Moses (cf. Athanasius, Letter 94, lines 10–11), does not punish transgressors, he will never be victorious over the Turks. Philes used very similar language in a poem to the Emperor written sometime between 1305 and 1307, when the Turks were ravaging Thrace; cf. *Poem* XIV, lines 373–76 and 394–98, in Miller, *Manuelis Philae carmina*, II, 49–50.

71–72 ὁ ’Ηλεί: In his letters Athanasius frequently reminds the Emperor of the Old Testament priest who was deprived of his priesthood and his life because he did not chastise the transgressions of his sons (1 Kings 2–4); cf. Letters 3, lines 45–48, and 49, lines 6–9.

73–74 τὸ δέ . . . ξενίζουσα: A reference to Abraham's willingness to sacrifice Isaac (Gen. 22:1–14). Cf. Philes, *Poem* XIV, lines 416–18 (Miller, *Manuelis Philae carmina*, II, 51).

63.

Athanasius asks the Emperor to intercede on behalf of a certain Oinaiotes, who is starving.

Laurent, *Regestes*, no. 1706

1 τὸν Οἰναιώτην: Oinaiotes was a fairly common Byzantine surname. Under Michael VIII, an Oinaiotes served as ὁ τοῦ βασιλικοῦ κλήρου λαμπαδάριος (Pachymeres, *Hist.*, I, 290). It is possible that he is to be identified with the Oinaiotes of this Letter and/or with the George Oinaiotes who collaborated with the deacon and *sakellios* of St. Sophia, George Galesiotes, in translating into simpler language Nicephorus Blemmydes' speech on kingship (Βασιλικὸς ’Ανδρίας) to his pupil Theodore II Lascaris; cf. PG, 142, cols. 609–10. Two early-fourteenth-century correspondents of Michael Gabras, Michael and Macarius, also bore the surname Oinaiotes (unpublished letters in *Marc. gr. 446*, nos. 49, 293, 301); cf. Laurent, *Regestes*, 493.

64.

Athanasius asks the Emperor to grant a reward in gold coin to the man who sang so well the Synodikon of Orthodoxy.

Laurent, *Regestes*, no. 1707

64

Date: beginning of Lent, since the Synodikon of Orthodoxy has just been
sung.

ad apparatum 1: τὸ συνοδικόν: A liturgical text read on the Feast of Orthodoxy,
celebrated on the First Sunday of Lent. It was composed by the
Patriarch Methodius ca. 843, and has since undergone several modi-
fications. For the version in current use by the Orthodox Church,
see the *Triodion*, 240–46. The most recent edition of the Synodikon
is that of Jean Gouillard, «Le Synodikon de l'orthodoxie: édition
et commentaire», *TM*, 2 (1967), 1–313.

3–4 βεβληκὼς ἐν ἀραῖς τοὺς τὰ σκαιὰ φρονήσαντας: The Synodikon
declared anathema on iconoclasts and heretics, mentioning certain
patriarchs, ecclesiastics, clerics, and emperors by name.

4–6 τοὺς υἱοὺς εὐλογίας ... αἰωνίαις ἐν μνήμαις ἐγκαταστέψαντος: The
Synodikon blessed the memory of heroes of Orthodoxy, e.g., the
Patriarchs Germanus, Tarasius, Nicephorus, and Methodius.

8–9 ἄτερ χαλκοῦ μηδὲ Φοῖβον ... μαντεύεσθαι: Classical allusions are
rarely found in Athanasius' letters. He must have derived this proverb
from Gregory of Nazianzus' *Fourth Oration* (PG, 35, col. 661A),
from which he also probably derived the allusion to Proteus in
Letter 7; cf. commentary on Letter 7, line 31. See also remarks on
Letter 81, line 147. In general, all Athanasius' allusions to classical
texts can be traced to patristic intermediaries.

16 εὐροίζου χρυσοῦ: Athanasius may be referring to a gold nomisma
issued by Andronicus II between 1282 and 1295, which depicted
on the obverse the Emperor kneeling before Christ; cf. H. Goodacre,
A Handbook of the Coinage of the Byzantine Empire (London, 1957),
328, no. 9, and W. Wroth, *Catalogue of the Imperial Byzantine Coins
in the British Museum*, II (London, 1908), 614–16. After the association of Michael IX as co-emperor in 1295, the obverse depicted
Christ flanked by Andronicus and Michael; cf. remarks of Laurent,
Regestes, 494.

17–18 στήλη ... δεικνῦσα τὴν ἐκ Θεοῦ βασιλείαν σου: For the use of the
word στήλη, cf. Nicetas Choniates, *Hist.*, 522, where he writes that
Theodore Mangaphas ἀργύρεον κέκοφε νόμισμα τὴν οἰκείαν ἐγχαράξας
ἐν αὐτῷ στήλην. It has been suggested that στήλη refers to the
tall and slender figure of the standing Emperor (Dölger–Karayanno-
poulos, *Byzantinische Urkundenlehre*, 42), but all surviving gold coins
of Andronicus depict the Emperor kneeling; cf. Wroth, *op. cit.*, 614–25.

65.

Athanasius attacks certain people who are guilty of «base gain» and slander, and urges the Emperor to punish these offenders.

Laurent, *Regestes*, no. 1708

10 εἴτε Θεοφάνης: This Theophanes, who is singled out by Athanasius as possibly guilty of the charge of αἰσχροκέρδεια, is probably to be identified with the simoniac Theophanes mentioned in Nicephorus Choumnos' Ἔλεγχος κατὰ τοῦ κακῶς τὰ πάντα πατριαρχεύσαντος Νίφωνος, ed. Boissonade, in *Anecdota Graeca*, V, 259–60; cf. Boivin, «Notae ad Nicephorum Gregoram», 755 and 763. Choumnos recounts that Athanasius was deposed from the patriarchate because his retainer Theophanes had accepted gifts in return for an ordination, with the knowledge of the Patriarch. Because of Athanasius' reputation for strict integrity, it seems unlikely that he was involved in simony, and indeed in this letter he appears to be trying to disassociate himself from Theophanes by denouncing him for «base gain».

ὁ χρώμενος τῇ αἰσχροκερδείᾳ: In this letter αἰσχροκέρδεια apparently has connotations of simony; cf. 1 Peter 5:2 and the second canon of the Council of Chalcedon (Rhalles–Potles, II, 217).

13 τοιαύτην μιαιφονίαν ἐλεεινήν: Because Athanasius says that the αἰσχροκερδεῖς are «covering up such a pitiable murder», Laiou has connected this letter with the hoarding of wheat by ecclesiastical landowners («The Provisioning of Constantinople», 94 note 3), and it is possible that «the pitiable murder» might refer to the fact that poor people were starving to death as a result of the grain shortage. However, the μιαιφονία might simply refer to killing the Holy Ghost through simony, or something of the sort.

66.

Athanasius urges the Emperor to devote his attention to beautifying churches and preserving them from encroachment by other buildings.

Laurent, *Regestes*, no. 1709

Date: This letter should probably be dated to Christmas time, since Athanasius quotes from *Oration* XIX of Gregory of Nazianzus, which was read

66

on December 22, and from *Oration* XL, which was read on January 7. Moreover, the Christmas season would be an appropriate time for the Emperor to present gifts to the Church.

9–10 ὡς μηδὲ ἀπείργειν καὶ πένητας, etc.: Athanasius' argument here resembles that of Gregory of Nazianzus in *Oration* XIX, that even the poorest offerings are acceptable (PG, 35, col. 1052B–C).

41 τὸν Βεσελεὴλ: Beseleel was chosen by the Lord to make the furnishings for the tabernacle of the ark of the covenant; cf. Exod. 31:2ff.

44–45 κειμηλίοις ... βασιλικώτερον: Andronicus was an extremely pious emperor who bestowed lavish gifts upon churches; cf. Pachymeres, *Hist.*, II, 617, and Athanasius, Letter 112, lines 9–12.

48 ταῖς τῆς ἱεραρχίας στολαῖς ἢ πατριαρχικαῖς: The Patriarch emphasizes the uniqueness (τὰ μήπω ἐπιγνωσθέντα) of the episcopal vestments created under Andronicus' patronage. In another letter he also described a beautifully decorated priest's robe, which the Emperor presented to the Church, as «all but inimitable» (μικροῦ καὶ ἀμίμητον: Letter 88, line 12). Athanasius may be referring here to gold-figured embroidery, which came into vogue in the Palaeologan period, especially on fabrics designed for ecclesiastical use; cf. Volbach's essay on Byzantine textiles in *Byzantine Art, an European Art* (Athens, 1964), 466. In her book, *The Byzantine Tradition in Church Embroidery* (London, 1967), Pauline Johnstone suggests that embroidered fabrics were developed in the thirteenth and fourteenth centuries as an economical substitute for woven textiles (p. 10). Her attribution of most Palaeologan embroideries to imperial workshops in Constantinople (p. 58) would appear to be borne out by Athanasius' comments on the Emperor's encouragement of the manufacture of the new type of vestments.

Except for two unique late-twelfth-century eucharistic veils in the Halberstadt cathedral (Johnstone, *op. cit.*, pls. 85 and 86), the earliest embroideries date from Andronicus' reign. They include an *epitaphios* made *ca.* 1295 for the church of St. Clement in Ochrid (cf. G. Millet, *Broderies religieuses de style byzantin* [Paris, 1947], 89–90, and pls. CLXXVIII and CXCII,1), and the two eucharistic veils in Castell'Arquato (near Piacenza), which were made shortly before 1314 (*ibid.*, 72–73, and pls. CLIV–CLVI).

61 ὅ,τι ποτέ ἐστι θεῖα μετάφρενα: Athanasius might well wonder about the meaning of θεῖα μετάφρενα, since commentators on the Psalms

66

gave different interpretations of this phrase from Psalm 90. Cyril of Alexandria offered the straightforward explanation that μετάφρενα are shoulders: μετάφρενά που καθάπερ ἐγῷμαι τὰ ὑπαυχένια μέρη, καὶ τὰ ὡς ὤμοις ὑποδηλῶν, καὶ οὐχὶ δὴ πάντως τὰ νῶτα (*De adoratione*, XI, PG, 68, col. 736B). Commentaries by Athanasius of Alexandria and Ps.-John Chrysostom, on the other hand, give metaphorical interpretations of the phrase; cf. PG, 27, col. 1044, and PG, 55, col. 759.

66–67 μὴ καὶ τὰ τῶν θείων ἀπ' ἄρτι νεῶν ἐᾶσθαι ἀνεπιμέλητα: By the early fourteenth century many churches in the capital were in dilapidated condition and in need of repairs. Gregoras recounts that, although most emperors concentrate on building new churches because of their thirst for glory, Andronicus decided instead to spend his limited funds on the restoration of existing churches (*Hist.*, I, 274). Thus, in 1317 Andronicus had buttresses erected on the north and east sides of St. Sophia, to support walls dangerously weakened by earthquakes; cf. Gregoras, *Hist.*, I, 273. The Emperor also undertook repairs of the church of St. Paul near the Eugenius Gate (cf. Janin, *Géographie ecclésiastique*, 407) and of the church of the Holy Apostles (Gregoras, *Hist.*, I, 275).

For the most part, however, the imperial treasury was too poor to undertake major works of restoration, and private benefactors were responsible for the improvements made in several churches at this time. *Ca.* 1293, for example, Michael Glabas Tarchaneiotes and his wife had the church of the Theotokos Pammakaristos (Fethiye Cami) restored; cf. Janin, *Géographie ecclésiastique*, 218. Sometime between 1308 and 1321 Theodore Metochites, Andronicus' loyal minister, undertook the restoration and decoration of the church of Chora (Kahriye Cami). See Athanasius' Letter 11, lines 17–19, and my commentary for contemporary allusions to the ruinous condition of the Chora church and monastery before their restoration.

67–68 μὴ ἐμμένειν τινὰ κατηχουμενείοις: Both canon and civil law prohibited eating or sleeping within a church; cf. canons 74 and 76 of the Synod in Trullo, and *Basilics*, Book V, Title 1, 11. Canon 97 of the Synod in Trullo forbade anyone to cohabit with his wife in, or otherwise defile, the κατηχούμενα of a church (Rhalles–Potles, II, 536). Byzantines differed in their interpretation of the word κατηχούμενα in this canon. The Emperor Leo VI defined κατηχούμενα as the upper galleries of a church (Novel 73, ed. Zachariä von Lingenthal, *Jus Graeco-Romanum*, III, 171); Zonaras, on the other hand, felt the κατηχούμενα must be buildings attached to the church (Rhalles–

66, 67

Potles, II, 536). In Letter 45, Athanasius definitely uses the word κατηχουμενεῖα to mean the upper galleries of the church, so we should probably assume that he uses the word in the same way in this passage. In Letter 45, Athanasius states that he would like to prevent noblewomen from entering the galleries, because they delight in showing off their finery and in making their prayers above the rest of the crowd. In Letter 66, however, where he uses the verb ἐμμένειν, Athanasius is more likely to be attacking people who were actually sleeping in the galleries or otherwise defiling churches; cf. also lines 87–90.

68 μὴ οἴκους τινῶν ἐγκολλᾶσθαι τοῖς θείοις ναοῖς: Cf. Letter 50, where Athanasius asks the Emperor to issue a decree forbidding any building to be constructed close to a church, renewing Zeno's order that buildings should be constructed at least twelve feet apart; cf. *CIC, Codex Justinianus*, VIII, 10, 12, 2. The Patriarch was concerned lest the churches be defiled by improper acts in an adjoining building; cf. Zonaras' commentary on canon 97 of the Synod in Trullo (Rhalles–Potles, II, 536–37).

67.

Athanasius urges the Emperor not to forbid the peasants to cultivate their fields.

Laurent, *Regestes*, no. 1650

Date: autumn 1306; see commentary *infra*.

5 ἄσπορον ἐαθῆναι τὴν γῆν: In the fall of 1306 Andronicus, on the advice of his counselors, forbade Thracian peasants to sow grain, in order to prevent marauding Turks and Catalans from reaping the crops (Pachymeres, *Hist.*, II, 628). Pachymeres discusses the imperial measure immediately after his account of a Byzantine raid on the Catalans at Rodosto which took place in the autumn of 1306; cf. Laiou, «The Provisioning of Constantinople», 100–1.

16–17 ἀφθονία τῶν χρειωδῶν: Athanasius argues that it is not the wealth of Byzantium which attracts the enemy; rather the sins of the Byzantines have provoked God to anger, and hence He allows the Turks and Catalans to be victorious. Athanasius repeats this argument in the final sentence of the letter.

20 κακοπράγον: This word, with the accent on the penultimate as in the manuscripts of Athanasius' letter, is not in the dictionaries. From the context its meaning is clearly «evil-doer, villain». Demetrakos (*Lexikon*, 3548) lists only κακόπραγος, accented on the antepenultimate, and meaning «unfortunate, ill-starred».

22–23 μὴ ἀναστέλλειν ... τῶν δωρεῶν τοῦ Θεοῦ: Andronicus' policy did in fact cause great hardship to the Byzantines, since the capital soon began to suffer from famine when the usual Thracian grain supply was no longer available (Pachymeres, *Hist.*, II, 628). Still, Andronicus' «scorched-earth policy» was successful as a factor in the decision of the Catalans to move on to Macedonia, because provisions were so expensive and scarce in Thrace; cf. *Diplomatari de l'Orient Català, 1301–1409*, ed. A. Rubió i Lluch (Barcelona, 1947), 40, no. xxxiii, and Laiou, «The Provisioning of Constantinople», 104.

26–27 ὑετὸν ... πρώϊμον: This phrase, which means «morning rain» in its Biblical context, was translated by Bănescu as «la pluie d'aurore» («Le patriarche Athanase Iᵉʳ», 53). Laiou has suggested, however, that in this passage πρώϊμος must mean «unseasonably early», and that Athanasius was grateful for the rain since it would soften ground hardened by the summer heat and allow the Byzantines to begin to plow and sow earlier. She therefore dates this letter to October or November 1306; cf. «The Provisioning of Constantinople», 101. Laurent prefers a date in early autumn; cf. *Regestes*, 444.

68.

Athanasius agrees that the Byzantine Empire is in reduced circumstances, and has unusual expenses. He also agrees that Byzantine subjects must pay higher taxes to cover the deficit. He argues, however, that the collection of money should be entrusted to compassionate men, not to the bloodthirsty Catalans; cf. Letter 94.

Laurent, *Regestes*, no. 1624

Date: early 1305; cf. commentary *infra* on lines 8–9.

3 ἀλλοκότους ἐξόδους: The pay granted the Catalans drained the imperial treasury; cf. Gregoras, *Hist.*, I, 220.

8 ἰταμοῦ: Laurent suggests that ἰταμός is a pun on Ἰταλός; cf. *Regestes*, 418.

αἱμοχαροῦς: Cf. αἱμοβόρων Μογαβάρων of Letter 35, lines 18–19. Also cf. Philes, *Poem* 44, line 50 (Martini, *Manuelis Philae carmina inedita*, 54), where the Catalans are described as αἱμοχαρεῖς ἀνθρακεῖς.

8–9 μηδὲ πρός τινος τῶν ἀσυμπαθῶν ... ἐνεργεῖσθαι: The Catalans began to extort money from the Byzantines almost as soon as they arrived at Cyzicus in the fall of 1303 (cf. Pachymeres, *Hist.*, II, 399, and Gregoras, *Hist.*, I, 220–21). However, the use of the verb ἐνεργεῖσθαι in this letter implies that the Catalans had received authorization from the Emperor to collect taxes, rather than that they were indulging in indiscriminate plundering; cf. Letter 94, lines 31–32, where Athanasius specifically states that Roger de Flor was enrolled as a government agent σεπτοῖς ... προστάγμασι.

Therefore this letter can probably be dated to early 1305, since, according to Muntaner, when Roger de Flor was elevated to the position of Caesar he received authority to «impose tributes» (Muntaner, II, 507). Pachymeres also states that in early 1305, when the Emperor was trying to procure 100,000 *modii* of grain for the Catalans, both imperial agents and the Catalans themselves collected this tax in kind; cf. *Hist.*, II. 522–23.

10 Σικελούς: Another name for the Catalan mercenaries who had previously been in the service of Frederick II of Sicily. Neither Pachymeres nor Gregoras uses the term Σικελός for Catalan, but it is found in two letters of Manuel Moschopoulos and in the poetry of Manuel Philes; cf. Moschopoulos, *Letter to Acropolites* (ed. Ševčenko, «Manuel Moschopulos», 138), and the *Letter to Nicephorus Moschopoulos* (ed. Levi, «Cinque lettere inedite di Emanuele Moscopulo», 60); Philes, *Poem* 44, lines 7 and 80 (Martini, *Manuelis Philae carmina inedita*, 52 and 55). For other examples from Philes' poetry, cf. Ševčenko, «Manuel Moschopulos», 145–46.

ζωμεῖς: The plural of the noun or adjective ζωμεύς, which is not found in the dictionaries; one can postulate the form of this word, however, from the related words ζώμευμα, ζωμευτός, and ζωμεύω (Demetrakos, *Lexikon*, 3215). The word probably means «blood-thirsty» (cf. αἱμοχαρής and αἱμοβόρος, other adjectives used to describe the Catalans), since ζωμός can mean «blood» as well as «broth»; ζωμὸς μέλας or αἱματιά was an ancient Spartan dish made primarily from pork blood (Demetrakos, *Lexikon*, 116 and 3215), and ζωμός is used as a synonym for «bloodshed» in the *Characters* of Theophrastus, VIII, 7 (Loeb, 60): ταῦτα γὰρ λέγειν περὶ τῆς μάχης καὶ πολὺν τὸν ζωμὸν γεγονέναι.

15 τοῦ γένους: Cf. commentary on Letter 58, line 46.

18 προενομεύθη: The dictionaries give only the meaning of «ravage, plunder» for the verb προνομεύω. In this passage, however, Athanasius uses προνομεύω in the sense of «to grant a privilege» (from προνόμιον).

18–21 ὅσοις προενομεύθη μέλαθρα ἢ σκηναὶ τῆς πόρτης ἐκτὸς ... ποριζομένοις ... τὴν τροφήν: This passage apparently describes shopkeepers who set up stalls outside the city gates; cf. Guilland, «La correspondance inédite d'Athanase», 138.

69.

Athanasius demands that the patriarchs of Antioch and Alexandria leave Constantinople.

Laurent, *Regestes*, no. 1614

Date: between June 1303 and 1305. The Patriarch of Alexandria was forced to leave the capital by 1305; therefore this letter must be dated to 1305 or earlier. The confiscations by Athanasius of the monasteries assigned to the Patriarch of Alexandria took place *ca.* 1305 (cf. Schmid, «Zur Chronologie von Pachymeres», 85–86), not *ca.* 1308 as is assumed by Laurent («Cyrille II», 317) and Janin (*Géographie ecclésiastique*, 523). The *terminus post quem* of this letter must be June 1303, because the schism of the bishops and of the clerics of St. Sophia is described by Pachymeres in his account of Athanasius' second patriarchate. Laurent's date of 1304–1305 for this letter is based on somewhat different reasoning; cf. *Regestes*, 405–6.

ad apparatum 1: τοῦ Τύρου: Cyril, metropolitan of Tyre, was made patriarch of Antioch in 1287; cf. Pachymeres, *Hist.*, II, 56, and passage from Περὶ Μεταθέσεων (cited by Laurent in «Cyrille II», 311).

In 1288 Cyril went to Constantinople, but his election was not recognized either by the Patriarch Gregory III (1283–1289) or by his successor Athanasius (1289–1293), because of accusations that Cyril had taken communion with Catholic Franks and Cilician Armenians; cf. Pachymeres, *Hist.*, II, 123, and passage from Περὶ Μεταθέσεων (cited by Laurent in «Cyrille II», 311). Cyril therefore established his headquarters in the capital at the monastery of the Hodegetria, and waited there patiently until 1296, when his transfer to the see of Antioch was finally recognized by the Patriarch John XII (1294–1303); cf. Pachymeres, *Hist.*, II, 123, and Περὶ Μεταθέσεων (cited by Laurent, «Cyrille II», 311).

It is conceivable that Cyril was one of the bishops who forced Athanasius' resignation in 1293, since he would hope for recognition by Athanasius' successor. In any case, Athanasius, in retirement at the monastery of Xerolophos, must have looked upon the recognition of Cyril in 1296 with helpless fury. When Athanasius regained the patriarchal throne in 1303, he ignored the recognition of Cyril's election to the patriarchate of Antioch and almost always referred to him contemptuously as ὁ Τύρου.

Cyril must have died soon after 1306–1307. Pachymeres states that in 1305 Athanasius confiscated the monasteries granted to the Patriarch of Alexandria, and that he later took over control of the monastery of the Hodegetria, after Cyril's death (*Hist.*, II, 580). Cyril was still alive *ca.* 1306–1307, when the Patriarch of Alexandria had already been exiled and the Patriarch of Jerusalem was deposed (Pachymeres, *Hist.*, II, 615–16), but he must have died shortly afterward, since Pachymeres mentions his death in his *History*.

τοῦ Ἀλεξανδρείας: Athanasius II, patriarch of Alexandria (1276–1316). See commentary on Letter 7, line 31, for a biography of this opponent of Athanasius of Constantinople. In March 1304 several schismatic bishops were persuaded by the Emperor to reconcile themselves to the reinstatement of Athanasius; the Patriarch of Alexandria alone remained steadfastly in opposition to the restored Patriarch of Constantinople (Pachymeres, *Hist.*, II, 409).

9–10 ὁ τῷ προφήτῃ Μιχαίᾳ μὴ ὑπακούσας, αὐτὸν πατάξαι κεκελευσμένος: Cf. 3 Kings 20:35–36. In the Septuagint, the prophet is not specifically identified as Micah; cf. commentary on Letter 51, lines 3–8.

22–23 πλησμίως παραχωρεῖ τοῖς ταράκταις τὰ ζωαρκῆ ἐπιρρεῖν: Athanasius attacks the Emperor's policy of assigning monasteries in the capital to bishops who cannot or do not remain in their dioceses. The bishops are in Constantinople only to cause trouble, by agitating against the Patriarch.

28–29 σκεπτόμενοι δῆθεν οἰκονομεῖν, καὶ ἐῶντες οἰκοδομεῖν: One of Athanasius' rare attempts at a play on words; cf. lines 101–2: πλὴν αἱ δοκοῦσαι τοιαῦται οἰκονομίαι, ὡς ἔφην, κατέστρεψαν τὴν οἰκοδομήν.

33–34 καταστροφὴν ... ἀπὸ τῆς τοῦ πατριάρχου κυροῦ Ἀρσενίου ἡμέρας: A reference to the Arsenite schism, which split the Orthodox Church from 1265 to 1310.

41–42 διεσπασμένην ὁρῶν τὴν νύμφην Χριστοῦ: For the Church as the bride of Christ, cf. Origen, Τῶν εἰς τὸ κατὰ Ἰωάννην εὐαγγέλιον ἐξηγητικῶν,

fr. 45 (*Origenes*, 4, ed. E. Preuschen, GCS, 10 [Leipzig, 1903], 520);
Methodius, Συμπόσιον τῶν δέκα παρθένων, vii (PG, 18, col. 133B);
Gregory of Nyssa, Εἰς τὰ ᾄσματα τῶν ᾀσμάτων, *Homily* I (PG, 44,
col. 777C). For other examples of this metaphor, see Lampe, *Patristic
Greek Lexicon*, 928.

In the ninth-century Letter of the Three Patriarchs to Theophilus, the Church torn by strife between iconoclasts and iconodules
is represented as a woman with torn tunic; cf. L. Duchesne, «L'icono-
graphie byzantine dans un document du IXᵉ siècle», *Roma e l'Orien-
te*, 5 (1912–1913), 362–63.

47–49 ὑμεῖς ... ᾿Αρείῳ ὁμοιωθέντες, etc.: Arius was accused of tearing the
tunic of Christ (which had not been torn by the soldiers at the
Crucifixion; cf. John 19:23–24) in a letter written by Alexander,
patriarch of Alexandria (*ca.* 312–328), quoted in Theodoret's *History*,
I, 4 (ed. L. Parmentier, GCS, 44 [Berlin, 1954], 9–10), and in
Nicephorus Callistus Xanthopoulos, *Ecclesiastical History*, VIII, vii
(PG, 146, col. 32D).

49–50 τὴν πρώτην ῥῆξιν, τὴν μετὰ τῶν ᾿Ιταλῶν ἕνωσιν: The Union of the
Greek Orthodox and the Roman Catholic Churches at Lyons in
1274.

50–51 δευτέραν τὴν τῶν ᾿Αρσενιανῶν: For bibliography on the Arsenite
schism (1265–1310), see *Introduction*, note 18.

John Chilas also accused the Arsenites of tearing the tunic
and flesh of Christ; cf. his «Sur le schisme arsénite», ed. J. Darrouzès,
Documents inédits d'ecclésiologie byzantine, AOC, 10 (Paris, 1966),
357, line 19 ff.

51 τρίτην δὲ ... Αἰγυπτίων: For the schism of Athanasius of Alexandria, cf. commentary, ad apparatum 1 *supra*, and on lines 86–87
infra.

τετάρτην ... Τυρίων: Cyril, formerly metropolitan of Tyre, now
patriarch of Antioch, and his followers. Athanasius accused Cyril
of being in schism because he did not recognize Cyril's election to the
patriarchate of Antioch. There was also tension between the two
men over the monastery of the Hodegetria; cf. Pachymeres, *Hist.*,
II, 615.

53 πέμπτην ... τὸν λαμπρὸν ὁρμαθὸν τῶν καλῶν ἱερέων: An allusion
to the clerics of St. Sophia who refused to attend services or wear
proper vestments because they were not paid. Pachymeres describes
them as «seceding from the Church»: *Hist.*, II, 643; cf. also 384.

69

55–56 ἑνὸς ἐξ αὐτῶν ... λόγος ᾀδόμενος: The sources give no clue to the interpretation of this allusion.

58–59 τοῦ ὄνον ἐσαγισμένον παρεικάσαι μὴ φρίξαντος ... τὰ πάντιμα: The ὄνος ἐσαγισμένος is a symbol of stupidity; cf. Theodore of Cyzicus, *Epistula* 8, lines 12–14 (ed. Darrouzès, *Epistoliers byzantins*, 325).

59–60 ἡ τοῦ Τύρου ἐν τῇ Ὁδηγητρίᾳ ἀναστροφή: The monastery of the Θεοτόκου Ὁδηγητρίας (or τῶν Ὁδηγῶν) was located to the east of St. Sophia, near the seawalls, and was in existence by the early ninth century; cf. Janin, *Géographie ecclésiastique*, 208–16. The monastery was assigned to Cyril of Antioch as a headquarters upon his arrival in Constantinople in 1288 (Pachymeres, *Hist.*, II, 123; Περὶ Μεταθέσεων, ed. Laurent, «Cyrille II», 311). In all probability Cyril maintained his residence in this monastery until *ca.* 1306–1307.

Laurent has translated ἀναστροφή as «return» (cf. *Regestes*, 406), and misinterprets this passage in Athanasius as meaning, «To what will the return of the metropolitan of Tyre lead?». He therefore assumes that Athanasius evicted Cyril from the monastery during his first patriarchate (1289–1293), but that Cyril was able to return after Athanasius' abdication in 1293 («Cyrille II», 316).

Actually, however, ἀναστροφή can simply mean «dwelling», «abode», or «residence» (cf. Liddell–Scott, *s.v.* II, and Demetrakos, *Lexikon*, *s.v.* 3), and the sentence should be translated, «What is the result of the residence of the metropolitan of Tyre at the monastery of the Hodegetria?». This interpretation is supported by the testimony of both Pachymeres (*Hist.*, II, 123) and the anonymous treatise Περὶ Μεταθέσεων (ed. Laurent, «Cyrille II», 311) that Cyril had lived in the monastery of the Hodegetria for eight years (i.e., 1288–1296), when he was finally recognized as patriarch of Antioch. There is no evidence that Athanasius seized control of the monastery until after Cyril's death; cf. Pachymeres, *Hist.*, II, 580.

62–64 τὰ δὲ τοῦ λεγομένου Ἀλεξανδρείας κατά ... τῶν ἀτύχων μονῶν ἐγχειρήματα: Athanasius was extremely resentful of the fact that the Emperor had assigned the Patriarch of Alexandria monasteries which he could use as headquarters and sources of income. When Athanasius of Alexandria first came to Constantinople in 1278, Michael VIII assigned him the monastery of St. Michael at Anaplous and the monastery of the Great Field (Μεγάλου Ἀγροῦ) in Hellespont, near Cyzicus (Pachymeres, *Hist.*, II, 203). Since the monastery of St. Michael was located on the European shore of the Bosporus, between Bebek and Arnavutköy (Janin, *Géographie ecclésiastique*,

352), it is likely that the Patriarch of Alexandria used this monastery as his residence, and derived an income from the revenues of the monastery of the Great Field; cf. J. Pargoire, «St. Théophane le Chronographe et ses rapports avec St. Théodore Studite», *VizVrem*, 9 (1902), 44–48, 92–95, and B. Menthon, *Une terre de légendes. L'Olympe de Bithynie, ses saints, ses couvents, ses sites* (Paris, 1935), 198–99, 205–8.

During Athanasius' first patriarchate, after forcing the Patriarch of Alexandria to go into exile on Rhodes, he confiscated the monastery of the Great Field, and insisted that his name, instead of that of the Patriarch of Alexandria, be commemorated in the diptychs at the monastery of St. Michael. After Athanasius' abdication in 1293, the Patriarch of Alexandria returned to Constantinople from Rhodes and was assigned the monastery of Christ Euergetes as a headquarters by Andronicus II; cf. Pachymeres, *Hist.*, II, 203; Janin, *Géographie ecclésiastique*, 522–24; and J. Pargoire, «Le couvent de l'Evergétès», *EO*, 9 (1906), 231. In 1305, Athanasius again forced his homonym to leave the capital, and confiscated the monasteries of St. Michael at Anaplous and of Christ Euergetes; cf. Pachymeres, *Hist.*, II, 579–80.

78–79 τῆς προτέρας εὐεργεσίας καὶ παρρησίας ἐπαπολαύουσι: Athanasius complains to the Emperor about the favors and liberties enjoyed by dissident bishops. He is probably here referring specifically to Athanasius of Alexandria, who was granted another monastery by the Emperor, after the Patriarch of Constantinople had confiscated the monastery of the Great Field.

Gregoras writes that the Patriarch of Alexandria was held in great respect by the Emperor (*Hist.*, I, 216). After Athanasius of Alexandria's return from exile on Rhodes *ca.* 1294, he was entrusted by Andronicus with the important mission of negotiating for a suitable bride for the crown prince Michael (Pachymeres, *Hist.*, II, 203–4).

80 Ἀββακούμ: Habbakuk complained in his prophetic book (1:4) that no one was being punished for wrongdoing.

81 Κοιρανίδας: The Κοιρανίδες or Κυρανίδες is a Greek work in four books in which are collected recipes of medicine and magic. The treatise was probably compiled in the third or fourth century, but the earliest surviving text is a Latin translation dated 1169 of a lost Greek text; cf. L. Delatte, *Textes latins et vieux français relatifs aux Cyranides*, Bibliothèque de la Faculté de Philosophie et Lettres de l'Université de Liège, 93 (Paris, 1942), 3–5. Volume II (Paris, 1898)

69

of F. de Mély, *Les lapidaires de l'antiquité et du moyen âge*, contains an edition of the text of the *Koiranides* by C. E. Ruelle, and volume III (Paris, 1902) contains de Mély's translation of the text. The prologue of the treatise states that the book is the result of a compilation by Hermes Trismegistos (the Egyptian god of literature) from the book of *Kyranides* by Kyranos, king of Persia, and from a book by Harpokration of Alexandria.

The *Koiranides* were viewed with great suspicion by the Orthodox Church; cf. a patriarchal act of 1371 which condemned a certain Syropoulos for magical practices, and stated that the *protonotarios* of St. Sophia, Demetrios Chloros, had compiled a book of magic, based on the *Koiranides* and other magical treatises (Miklosich–Müller, I, 544).

85–86 μὴ ἐπ' ἀδείας ἔχειν ἄλλης ποιμένα ἐν τῇ μὴ ὑποκειμένῃ χειροτονεῖν: Cf. the thirty-fifth canon of the Apostles (Rhalles–Potles, II, 47), and canons thirteen and twenty-two of the Council of Antioch (Rhalles–Potles, III, 150–51 and 164–65).

86–87 ἢ καὶ τὸ τοῦ ταύτης ποιμένος σιωπᾶν ὄνομα: When Athanasius was restored to the patriarchate in 1303, about half the bishops refused to recognize him, and we may assume that they omitted his name from the diptychs; cf. Pachymeres, *Hist.*, II, 384. The metropolitan of Sardis was one of the bishops who refused to commemorate Athanasius; cf. lines 158–59 *infra*: τί δὲ ὁ Σάρδεων; οὐχὶ τὸν ἱερουργοῦντα ἐκώλυσεν ἀναφέρειν συνήθως τὸ ὄνομα ὡσαύτως καὶ οἱ λοιποί; In March 1304, most of the bishops ended the schism, but the Patriarch of Alexandria held out. Pachymeres recounts that he refused to commemorate the Emperor at this time (*Hist.*, II, 409), and we can be sure that he continued to refuse recognition of Athanasius.

93–94 ὡς ἔθος Ἀλεξανδρεῦσιν ἐν οἴκῳ Παύλου, χοραύλου τινός: The flutist Paul, in whose house the Patriarch of Alexandria performed ordinations, is known only from this letter. For the term χοραύλης, cf. Theodore of Nicaea, *Ep.* 39, 31 (ed. Darrouzès, *Epistoliers byzantins*, 306).

101 ὡς ἄλλον Θεόφιλον: Athanasius compares Athanasius of Alexandria with Theophilus, an earlier patriarch of Alexandria (385–412), who also agitated for the deposition of his rival patriarch in Constantinople. Theophilus was an ardent opponent of John Chrysostom, patriarch of Constantinople 398–403 and 403–404, and eventually procured his deposition at the Synod of the Oak in 403.

101–2 πλὴν αἱ δοκοῦσαι τοιαῦται οἰκονομίαι ... κατέστρεψαν τὴν οἰκοδομήν: Cf. *supra*, lines 28–29.

114 τὸ πέλαγος τῆς κακίας: Satan; God, on the other hand, is τὸ πέλαγος τῆς φιλανθρωπίας (cf. Letter 71, line 29), or τὸ πέλαγος τῆς ἀγαθότητος (cf. Letters 6, line 10; 82, lines 64–65; 89, line 9).

127–28 ἡ ἐνθήκη τῶν δέκα πληγῶν: An allusion to the «Egyptian», Athanasius of Alexandria; cf. Letter 7, line 31: τὸν ἐξ Αἰγύπτου Πρωτέα.

129–30 μοναὶ ἀνδρῶν ... ἐδόθησαν: The monasteries of the Great Field, St. Michael at Anaplous, and Christ Euergetes; cf. commentary on lines 62–64 *supra*.

135–36 ὁ τούτῳ προσκείμενος ... ἀλλότριος ἐγεγόνει τῆς κλήσεως, ἧς εἰς κενὸν ὀνομάζεται: Perhaps a reference to the metropolitan of Tyre, whose new title of patriarch of Antioch was not recognized by Athanasius.

138 ἐν τῇ μονῇ τοῦ Μεγάλου 'Αγροῦ: See commentary on lines 62–64 *supra*, for a discussion of this monastery.

138–39 ὁ δικαίῳ σταλεὶς παρ' αὐτοῦ: δικαίῳ, used adverbially and meaning «as an agent», «in lieu of», is the dative singular of δίκαιος (Du Cange, *Glossarium ad scriptores mediae et infimae Graecitatis*, I, col. 308), or of δικαῖος (Demetrakos, *Lexikon*, 2014, and de Meester, *De monachico statu*, 294, 305); cf. Miklosich–Müller, IV, 229 (ἀπέστειλα δικαίῳ μου τὸν γαμβρόν μου), 231 (ἐξαπέστειλε δικαίῳ αὐτοῦ ... τὸν κῦρ Λέοντα), and 256 (ὁ ἐνεργῶν τὸ θέμα τῶν Θρακησίων δικαίῳ τοῦ δημοσίου). See also J. Darrouzès, *Recherches sur les ὀφφίκια de l'Eglise byzantine*, AOC, 11 (Paris, 1970), 131 and note 1, 338 note 4, 340 note 1.

137–40 τὸν Κύριον ἡμῶν ... καὶ στήλην βασιλικὴν ... ἀντιστηλῶσαι: According to Athanasius, the agent of the Patriarch of Alexandria destroyed an image of Christ at the monastery of the Great Field, and replaced it with an image of the Emperor. It would seem that the Patriarch of Alexandria set up this imperial image at the Great Field in gratitude for this monastery which Michael VIII had granted him with a chrysobull; cf. Pachymeres, *Hist.*, II, 203. Literary evidence indicates that imperial images, such as those in the galleries of St. Sophia, were set up in churches and monasteries in gratitude for gifts and chrysobulls confirming privileges; cf. epigrams nos. 57 and 80 of John Mauropous of Euchaita (*Iohannis*

69

Euchaitorum Metropolitae quae in codice Vaticano Graeco 676 supersunt, eds. P. de Lagarde and J. Bollig [Göttingen, 1882], 34 and 39). I am indebted to Professor Cyril Mango for these references.

142–43 τοὺς τῆς Νιτρίας γὰρ μοναχοὺς ὁ τούτου ὁμότροπος ἀνεστάτωσεν: Cf. line 101 *supra*: ὡς ἄλλον Θεόφιλον. Theophilus of Alexandria infuriated the monks of the Nitrian desert by his denunciation of the writings of Origen at the Synod of Alexandria in 400. Eighty of the monks went to Constantinople to protest to the Patriarch John Chrysostom. Theophilus, however, managed to secure the deposition of his rival at the Synod of the Oak in 403; cf. the *Church History* of Sozomenus, VIII, 11–17, eds. J. Bidez and G. Ch. Hansen, GCS, 50 (Berlin, 1960), 364–73.

143 ὁ 'Αντιοχείας: This is the only place where Athanasius calls Cyril by his proper title.

144 ὁ 'Ιεροσολύμων: Athanasius III, who was patriarch of Jerusalem by 1303; cf. V. Grumel, «Notes de chronologie patriarchale», *Mélanges Mouterde*, 2 (= *MélUSJ*, 38) (Beirut, 1962), 264–67. Like the Patriarch of Antioch, he went to Constantinople to have his election confirmed, but as the result of charges brought against him *ca.* 1307 by Broulas, the bishop of Kaisareia in Phoenicia, he was replaced by his accuser; cf. Pachymeres, *Hist.*, II, 615–16, and Nicephorus Callistus Xanthopoulos, *Ecclesiastical History*, PG, 146, col. 1197.

144–45 μεγάλη στρατοπεδάρχισσα: Probably to be identified with Theodora Palaeologina, the wife of John Comnenus Ducas Synadenos, the *megas stratopedarches*; cf. Papadopoulos, *Genealogie der Palaiologen*, no. 11, p. 9, and D. I. Polemis, *The Doukai. A Contribution to Byzantine Prosopography* (London, 1970), 179–80. She was co-founder with her husband of the convent of the Θεοτόκος τῆς Βεβαίας 'Ελπίδος; cf. H. Delehaye, *Deux typica byzantins de l'époque des Paléologues* (Brussels, 1921), 144.

145 μεγάλη δομεστίκισσα: Probably Eugenia Palaeologina, who married the great domestic Syrgiannes before 1290, and lived until at least 1329; cf. Cantacuzenus, *Hist.*, I, 109. See also Papadopoulos, *Genealogie der Palaiologen*, no. 34a, p. 21; St. Binon, «A propos d'un *prostagma* inédit d'Andronic III Paléologue», *BZ*, 38 (1938), 143–46.

Σιδηριώτισσα: Probably the wife of Manuel Phakrases Sideriotes, who is mentioned in a poem of Philes (CV, lines 23–24, Miller,

Manuelis Philae carmina, I, 291), or of his relative John Phakrases Sideriotes, who was logothete τῶν ἀγελῶν under Andronicus II, and is known as a correspondent of Planudes; on these two personages, see D. M. Nicol, *The Byzantine Family of Kantakouzenos (Cantacuzenus)*, ca. *1100–1460* (Washington, D.C., 1968), 234–35.

155 ὁ Χαλκηδόνος: During the two patriarchates of Athanasius, several bishops followed each other in fairly rapid succession in the see of Chalcedon. In 1298, Theognostos signed an unpublished act as metropolitan of Chalcedon; cf. Laurent, «La fin du schisme arsénite», 312 note 1. By March 1303, Theognostos had been replaced by Symeon, who signed a letter of commendation at that date as ὁ μητροπολίτης Χαλκηδόνος καὶ ὑπέρτιμος (ed. Sp. Lampros, Κυπριακὰ καὶ ἄλλα ἔγγραφα ἐκ τοῦ Παλατίνου Κώδικος 367 τῆς Βιβλιοθήκης τοῦ Βατικάνου, in Νέος Ἑλλ., 15 [1921], 162, no. 55). According to Gennadios of Helioupolis, a year later Symeon was succeeded by Theodoulos, who signed a patriarchal act in 1304 as ὑπέρτιμος καὶ πρόεδρος Μαρωνείας; unfortunately Gennadios gives no source for this statement (Σκιαγραφία τῆς ἱστορίας τῆς μητροπόλεως Χαλκηδόνος καὶ ὁ ἐπισκοπικὸς αὐτῆς κατάλογος, in Ὀρθοδοξία, 19 [1944], 72). A metropolitan of Chalcedon signed the Νεαρά of Athanasius in 1304 (PG, 161, col. 1065B) and was present at the synod which condemned Drimys in 1305 (Letter 81), but his name is not mentioned. In 1310, the metropolitan of Chalcedon must have been pro-Arsenite, since he was one of seven prelates to whom Andronicus II addressed a chrysobull, guaranteeing that he would not alter or suppress any portion of the agreement he had made with the Arsenites (ed. Laurent, «La fin du schisme arsénite», 312–13). In any case, a Theodoulos was definitely metropolitan of Chalcedon by September 1315; cf. Miklosich–Müller, I, 14.

ἐξήντλησε τὰ τοῦ Κοσμιδίου: The monastery of the Kosmidion, dedicated to SS. Kosmas and Damianos, was located near the Blachernae Palace, at present-day Eyüp; cf. Janin, *Géographie ecclésiastique*, 296–99. The management of this monastery was apparently granted to the metropolitan of Chalcedon, who managed to exhaust its revenues. Laurent has suggested, however, that this allusion might indicate that the metropolitan of Chalcedon took the relics of St. Euphemia from the Kosmidion monastery to restore them to the church of St. Euphemia (near the Hippodrome), where he resided; cf. *Regestes*, 405, 407.

156 τοῦ Ξιφιλίνου: This allusion is obscure. Athanasius is perhaps referring to certain offices in the patriarchate called τὰ κελλία τοῦ

69

Ξιφιλίνου, which are mentioned in Nicholas Mesarites' description of the *Disputation* of August 30, 1206, between Greeks and Latins (ed. A. Heisenberg, *Neue Quellen zur Geschichte des lateinischen Kaisertums und der Kirchenunion. II, Die Unionsverhandlungen vom 30. August 1206* [Munich, 1923], 17). See also Janin, *Constantinople byzantine*, 178, 440, and *idem*, «Le palais patriarcal de Constantinople», *REB*, 20 (1962), 133 and 143. Laurent is also baffled by this reference; cf. *Regestes*, 407.

156–57 κάθηται πλησίον ἡμῶν: The church of St. Euphemia, which served as residence for the metropolitan of Chalcedon, was very close to the patriarchate; cf. A. M. Schneider, «Das Martyrion der hl. Euphemia beim Hippodrom zu Konstantinopel», *BZ*, 42 (1943–1949), 178–85, and R. Naumann and H. Belting, *Die Euphemia-Kirche am Hippodrom zu Istanbul und ihre Fresken* (Berlin, 1966), 17, 29–33.

158 τί δὲ ὁ Σάρδεων, etc.: See commentary on Letter 25, lines 14–15, for information on the metropolitan of Sardis, Cyril. He was one of the bishops who refused to include Athanasius' name in the diptychs; cf. commentary on lines 86–87 *supra*.

164–65 ὁ Περγάμου: Arsenius; he was metropolitan of Pergamum by May 1295, when he refused to sign an imperial rescript; cf. Pachymeres, *Hist.*, II, 200. He did sign an act of October 5, 1295, which is preserved at the monastery of Iberon on Mt. Athos (ed. Dölger, *Aus den Schatzkammern*, no. 100, line 3). In 1302 he was sent with Nicephorus of Crete and Athanasius of Alexandria to ask John XII whether he really wished to resign (Pachymeres, *Hist.*, II, 349). It is probable that Arsenius, like his fellow envoys, opposed the reinstatement of Athanasius as patriarch.

Arsenius ignored Athanasius' demand that he leave the capital until at least 1305, for we know that he was present at the synod which drew up the Νεαρά in 1304 (PG, 161, col. 1065B) and also attended the synod of 1305 which condemned Drimys (Letter 81). In any case it was difficult for Arsenius to return to Pergamum, which was in the hands of the emir of Karasi from 1302 or 1303; cf. Pachymeres, *Hist.*, II, 318; Gregoras, *Hist.*, I, 214; H. Gelzer, *Pergamon unter Byzantinern und Osmanen* (Berlin, 1903), 91. Arsenius was, however, also *proedros* of Ainos, so he may have sought refuge there (Miklosich–Müller, I, 5). Arsenius was metropolitan of Pergamum until at least September 1315; cf. Miklosich–Müller, I, 14. For further remarks on the career of Arsenius, see V. Laurent, «Le métropolite de Pergame Arsène, mélode et polémiste antilatin», *REB*, 15 (1957), esp. 126–29.

69, 70

171–72 ἡ τοῦ θεοστυγοῦς Θεοκτίστου ... σπουδαία πρὸς 'Ρώμην ἄφιξις: It
seems most likely that Athanasius is here referring to Theoctistus,
metropolitan of Adrianople (ca. 1278/1282–1283), an ardent supporter
of the Unionist Patriarch John Bekkos; cf. V. Laurent, «La liste
épiscopale du synodikon d'Andrinople», EO, 38 (1939), 23–24.
Theoctistus was deposed from his see ca. March 1283, and went into
exile in Byzantine territory. By 1289 he had fled to Rome, since in
that year he was a pensioner of the Holy See and signed several
letters of indulgence; cf. idem, «Un théologien unioniste de la fin du
XIIIᵉ siècle: Le métropolite d'Andrinople Théoctiste», REB, 11
(1953), esp. 188–92.

175–76 ἢ οὐκ ἐξερχομένων ἡμῶν ἐν λιταῖς ... ἔρχονται τὰ δεινά: On the
occasion of the Kynegos fire in 1305, for example, some people
mocked Athanasius because he had held a religious procession in the
morning, yet the disastrous fire broke out the same evening (Pachymeres, Hist., II, 582).

182–85 τὴν ἐκκλησίαν Χριστοῦ ἐλευθέραν ... ἀπεχομένην τῶν ἀνηκόντων τῷ
δημοσίῳ: For parallel phrases in thirteenth-century acts exempting
monasteries from taxes, cf. Miklosich–Müller, IV, 216 and 365.

216–17 κἂν γνωσθήτω μοι ... ἀπέχεσθαι τῶν λοιπῶν: Athanasius again
threatens to resign unless full control of the Church is restored to
him; cf. Letter 57.

220–21 εἰ δὲ ἄλλοις ... τοῦ ἐξουσιάζοντος: This sentence apparently means
that if the Emperor (ὁ ἐξουσιάζων) supports the bishops in their
rebellion against the Patriarch of Constantinople, then Athanasius
will no longer maintain responsibility for these bishops.

70.

Athanasius urges the Emperor to join him in a procession of contrition.

Laurent, Regestes, no. 1710

Date: ca. 1305–1306; cf. commentary on Letter 52, line 14.

3 παρ' ἀγνῶτος: The prophet Jonah; cf. Jonah 3:4–5.

70–72

14–15 ἐξέλθωμεν καὶ γυμνῷ τῷ ποδὶ ... λιτάζοντες: Athanasius held frequent processions in an effort to avert the wrath of God; cf. Pachymeres, *Hist.*, II, 581 and 631.

18–19 ὁ κραταιὸς καὶ ἅγιος αὐτοκράτωρ μου: The Emperor did not need much encouragement to join the Patriarch's processions, in fact, he himself requested them; cf. Pachymeres, *Hist.*, II, 420–21.

20 ὁ πανευτυχέστατος καὶ θεοφιλὴς Δεσπότης: The Despot John Palaeologus; cf. commentary on Letter 52, line 14.

71.

Athanasius invites the Emperor to Good Friday services.

Laurent, *Regestes*, no. 1711

Date: Easter week, just before Good Friday; cf. Letters 52–55.

2 τὴν τοῦ Νότου βασίλισσαν: The Queen of Sheba; cf. 3 Kings 10:1–10.

3 σοφίας ἀκουσομένην: A play on words, since the Emperor is invited to the ἀνάκτορα τῆς θείας σοφίας (lines 4–5); cf. Letter 56, lines 2–8. Cf. also ἐξακουτίζεσθαι in line 9.

3–4 τῷ μετ' ὀλίγον τεθνηξομένῳ: Solomon; cf. 3 Kings 11:43.

9 ἐξακουτίζεσθαι: Not in the dictionaries. The Septuagint has ἀκουτίζω.

18–21 παραστῆσαι ... συνθρηνῆσαι ... ἰδεῖν ... ἀναχωρεῖν ... συμπαραμεῖναι ... κομίσαι ... ἐπόψει: I have taken all these verbs as referring to τὸ ὑπήκοον of line 14, since κατοπτεύσοντι definitely refers to τὸ ὑπήκοον, and the construction οὐ ... μόνον ... ἀλλά γε καὶ suggests that τὸ ὑπήκοον is the subject of the following verbs as well. It is grammatically possible for the verbs to be taken as referring to the Emperor, but the phrase μύρα κομίσαι, an allusion to the women who came to anoint Jesus (cf. Luke 23:56), would seem to apply more appropriately to the congregation than to the Emperor.

72.

Athanasius begs the Emperor not to permit export of grain in the midst of famine.

Date: *ca.* 1306–1307

1 τοῦ γεγονότος εἰς τὸν λαὸν λιμοῦ: Although in the early fourteenth
century Constantinople was overcrowded with refugees from Anatolia, at first the famine was caused not so much by lack of food
supplies, as by inequity in the system of distribution; middlemen
who handled grain raised the prices so high that the poor could
not afford to purchase it. Cf., for example, the account of Muntaner
(II, 491–92), who visited the capital in the fall of 1303 and found Greeks
starving in the midst of plenty. Pachymeres cites the debasement of
coinage as another factor in the scarcity of provisions (*Hist.*, II, 494).

Later, however, the grain supplies in the capital were severely
reduced as the raids of Catalans and Turks destroyed many crops.
Muntaner (II, 530) records that from 1305 on the Catalans lived
off the food and wine they collected in raids of the countryside.
Therefore, in the fall of 1306 Andronicus decided to institute a
«scorched-earth policy» and forbade peasants to plant crops in the
vicinity of Constantinople; cf. Pachymeres, *Hist.*, II, 628 and Athanasius, Letter 67. The result was, however, an even greater scarcity
of grain in the capital (Pachymeres, *loc. cit.*).

3–4 ὑπὲρ σίτου ... ἵνα μὴ ἐξέρχηται τῆς μεγαλοπόλεως: Venetian and
Genoese merchants did a thriving trade by bringing wheat and
barley to Constantinople from the northern coast of the Black Sea
and then exporting it to Italy. Athanasius urges Andronicus to
enforce the policy established by his father, Michael VIII, who
forbade the Venetians to export grain to Italy if the price at Constantinople for 100 *modii* was over 50 hyperpers (the price would
be so high only when there was a shortage of grain in the capital);
cf. Laiou, «The Provisioning of Constantinople», 92–94, and Bratianu,
Etudes byzantines, 157–61.

12–13 μὴ παραχωρεῖν τοῖς ξενίοις ἢ νόσῳ πλεονεξίας ἢ καὶ φιλίας ἁπλῶς:
Andronicus was apparently being bribed by the Italians to allow
them to continue to export grain to Italy, despite the shortage in
the capital. In 1302 Andronicus had made a treaty with the Venetians, renewing the prohibition on export of grain if the price of
one *modius* rose to more than one hyperper; cf. Bratianu, *Etudes
byzantines*, 162.

13 προτιμῶντας τὸν χρυσὸν τοῦ Χριστοῦ: Puns are found only rarely in
Athanasius' writings. This particular play on words, however, is a

72, 73

common sentiment; cf. Gregory of Nazianzus, *Oration* XXI, 21 (PG, 35, col. 1105 A–B): ἐξωνεῖται δὲ τῶν ἐν τέλει τοὺς φιλοχρύσους μᾶλλον ἢ φιλοχρίστους, and John Geometres, *Poem* 21 (PG, 106, col. 873A): τὸν χρυσὸν φιλέων, φιλέειν ἔραμαι καὶ Χριστόν.

35 σῖτον ... ἐκκενοῦντα τῆς πόλεως: Another reference to exports of grain from the capital by Italian merchants.

41 οὐκ ἄρχων, οὐχ ἱερεύς, οὐ Λευΐτης: The allusion here seems to be twofold: 1) to the priest and Levite who passed by the man injured by thieves; 2) to the threefold Christian ministry of ἐπίσκοπος (ἀρ-χιερεύς), ἱερεύς, and διάκονος, since ἄρχων can mean bishop, and Λευΐτης can mean deacon; cf. Lampe, *Patristic Greek Lexicon*, 241 and 798. See also Clement of Rome, *Epistola ad Corinthios I*, chap. 40 (PG, 1, col. 289A), and *Constitutiones apostolicae*, II, 25, and VIII, 46 (PG, 1, cols. 668A–B and 1152B).

73.

Letter to the Emperor about the grain commission.

Laurent, *Regestes*, no. 1642

Date: probably during the famine of 1306–1307; slightly later than Letter 93.

3–4 τὴν διοίκησιν: One would expect ἡ διοίκησις here.

4–5 ἐκτὸς οὗ ἀνέφερον εὐλαβοῦς: A reference to Dermokaites the *sebastos*, whom Athanasius proposed in Letter 93 to head the grain control commission. For a discussion of the identity of Dermokaites, see commentary on Letter 93, line 14.

5 ἡμέτερος μοναχός: Athanasius wants one of his followers also to be a member of the commission.

8–9 μήτε μὴν συγχωρεῖν ἐξωνεῖσθαι τὸν σῖτον τοὺς τοῦτον διψῶντας τιμι-ουλκεῖν: Athanasius' wrath is directed not only at Italian exporters, but at local middlemen who raise the price of grain; cf. Pachymeres (*Hist.*, II, 460–61), who specifically mentions Athanasius' letters to the Emperor about profiteers.

10 ἐπιμίσγοντες ἄχυρα ἢ σῖτον διασαπέντα: The controls on merchants in the Palaeologan period had evidently deteriorated from the tenth century, when the *Book of the Prefect* strictly regulated the price

and weight of bread sold by bakers; cf. *Book of the Prefect*, XVIII, Zepos, *Jus Graeco-Romanum*, II, 388, and now Τὸ Ἐπαρχικὸν Βιβλίον, ed. J. Nicole (reprint, London, 1970), 53–55.

18 υἱέσιν ἀπόροις καὶ ἀδυνάτοις: Cf. Letter 36, lines 2–3, for the sentiment that an emperor's subjects are his children.

23–24 ἀνάθεμα ἀπὸ τοῦ Χριστοῦ: Athanasius' quotation makes sense only if we remember the rest of the verse: ὑπὲρ τῶν ἀδελφῶν μου, τῶν συγγενῶν μου κατὰ σάρκα, «for the sake of my brethren, my kinsmen in the flesh».

25 κἂν τῶν ἐν τῇ Παλαιᾷ μὴ κατόπιν βαδίσωμεν, etc.: The quotations which follow give examples of Old Testament figures who asked God to direct His wrath at themselves, rather than at their subjects.

35 οἶκον σοφίας καὶ οἴκτου: The Emperor.

39 εἰ καὶ μὴ λέγειν ἀξίως πεπαίδευμαι: Athanasius is aware of his deficiencies in the art of speaking and writing.

74.

Another letter complaining about Byzantine profiteers who are raising the prices on grain.

Laurent, *Regestes*, no. 1653

Date: *ca.* 1306–1307

2 αὐχημάτων πατρῴων: Jacob loved Joseph more than all his sons, because he was the son of his old age; cf. Gen. 37:3.

3 ἀδελφῶν ἀδικίας: Joseph's brothers sold him to Ishmaelite merchants who carried him off to Egypt; cf. Gen. 37:25–28.

σωφροσύνης ὑπερφυοῦς: Probably an allusion to the incident with Potiphar's wife (Gen. 39:1–19).

4 ἡ σιτοδοσία: Joseph, who was in charge of the storage and distribution of grain in Egypt during the famine, gave grain to his brothers when they came from Canaan to buy some food: cf. Gen. 41–45.

74, 75

4–5 ἐξόδου ... χωρίς: I.e., ἔχοντες; «we [Andronicus II] inherited the office of caring for our countrymen without the sacrifices to which Joseph had to submit». ἐξόδου could also be translated as «exile» or «journey» and refer to the exodus of the Israelites from Egypt.

11 τὸ τιμιουλκεῖν χρειώδη πάντα: Cf. Letter 73, 8–9: μήτε μὴν συγχωρεῖν ἐξωνεῖσθαι τὸν σῖτον τοὺς τοῦτον διψῶντας τιμιουλκεῖν.

16–17 τὸ βασιλεύεσθαι ὑπ᾽ ἀνθρώπων ἀνθρώπους Θεὸς ἐδικαίωσε, etc.: Athanasius argues that God established kings on earth to protect the weak from the stronger.

75.

Athanasius urges the Empress Irene to become reconciled with her husband Andronicus.

Laurent, *Regestes*, no. 1629

Date: 1305–1309 (?); see commentary *infra* on lines 16–17.

ad apparatum 1: γράμμα ... θάνατος: This superscription is obviously incorrect, since Irene did not die until 1317, and the letter refers to dissension in marriage, not death. Although the feminine participles used by Athanasius (line 39, ἐντρεφομένη; line 50, εἰδυῖα; line 53, βιούσης) could indicate that the letter was addressed to Andronicus (ἡ ἐκ Θεοῦ βασιλεία), as the title states and as was assumed by Guilland («La correspondance inédite d'Athanase», 128), the context shows that they must rather be understood as referring to Irene. A scholiast on *Paris. Gr. 137* (fol. 75ᵛ) has provided a more correct title for the letter: γράμμα πρὸς τὴν βασίλισσαν περὶ τοῦ δεῖν ὁμονοεῖν τῷ συζύγῳ.

8 τοῦ χαρισθέντος σοι πρὸς Θεοῦ νυμφίου καὶ βασιλέως: Andronicus.

14–15 τὰ τῶν πειρασμῶν καὶ τοῦ φθόνου: One of the primary reasons for dissension between the Emperor and Empress was their disagreement over the future of Irene's children, for whom she had great ambitions. Athanasius' mention of jealousy is an allusion to Irene's envy of the prerogatives of Andronicus' sons by his first wife, Anne of Hungary.

15 σχέσεως: For σχέσις with the meaning of love, cf. commentary on Letter 58, line 11.

16–17 πρὸ τοῦ ἀποσωθῆναι τὴν βασιλείαν σου τοῖς ἐνταῦθα: This letter seems to provide further evidence that Irene did return to Constantinople at some point between 1305 and 1309, after her separation from her husband, and move to Thessalonica in 1303; see commentary on Letter 56, 12–13, and Laurent, *Regestes*, 422–23.

17 μηδ' ἀκριβῶς διδαχθεὶς τὰ ἐν μέσῳ: The Emperor tried to keep quiet the discord between himself and Irene; cf., for example, Pachymeres, *Hist.*, II, 290: καὶ διὰ τοῦτο καὶ βασιλεῖ πολλή τις ἦν ἡ ἐχεμυθία περὶ τῶν τοιούτων.

21 πρῶτα μὲν συνεσκιασμένως ... κατηνάγκαζον: Athanasius apparently wrote another letter to Irene even before her return to the capital.

21–22 ὡς ... ἐπανελθεῖν ἐγένετο καὶ τὴν βασιλείαν σου, καὶ φανερῶς ἐβιάσαμεν: Athanasius began to apply greater pressure on the Empress after her return to Constantinople.

76.

Athanasius complains to the Emperor about certain powerful people who do not heed patriarchal admonitions, because they fail to realize that the Patriarch is their benefactor and trying to save their souls. He adds that, even though the Byzantines are guilty of manifold sins, Andronicus refuses to pay any attention to his memoranda or to correct the abuses reported by the Patriarch. The letter breaks off abruptly after this preamble to a petition.

Laurent, *Regestes*, no. 1712

7–8 τοῖς αὐτοῖς ... ὑπείκειν: I have translated this phrase as if it read τοῖς αὐτοὺς ἀξιοῦσι τοιαῦτα ⟨ποιεῖν⟩ ὡς συμβούλοις σωτηριώδεσι.

9 οἱ ποθοῦντες: Athanasius.

10 ὀφείλειν λογιζομένους: Athanasius has here apparently transposed the form of these two verbs, which should probably read ὀφείλοντας λογίζεσθαι.

24 τοῖς ... αὐτὸν φοβηθεῖσι καὶ ἀγαπήσασι: Andronicus II.

39 κἂν τὰ: The scribe broke off writing at the end of this preamble to a petition, leaving two blank lines on fol. 56ʳ and 1/4 blank page

76, 77

on fol. 56ᵛ. This would seem to indicate that the rest of the letter was missing in the original, and that the scribe hoped to find the missing page(s) and fill in the text later. In any case, since this collection of Athanasius' letters had a literary and inspirational principle, the preamble was considered of greater importance than the essence of the petition.

77.

Because of the misconduct of the abbot of a patriarchal monastery near Apameia, the synod has granted the property of that monastery to a neighboring monastery dedicated to the Virgin. Now imperial agents are seeking to confiscate some of this property newly acquired by the monastery of the Theotokos. Athanasius asks the Emperor to put an end to this harassment.

Laurent, *Regestes*, no. 1714

6 ὡς τοῖς θείοις κανόσι διαγορεύεται: Apostolic canon 38 entrusts authority over ecclesiastical property to bishops (Rhalles–Potles, II, 52). Cf. also Apostolic canon 41 (Rhalles–Potles, II, 57).

10 καὶ ὅτι: One expects ἢ ὅτι; cf. ἢ τὸ βαρύ in the same line.

23–24 ἐν τῷ περὶ τὴν Ἀπάμειαν πατριαρχικῷ μονυδρίῳ: The name of this Bithynian monastery is unknown. For discussion of the different kinds of patriarchal monasteries, see Herman, «Ricerche sulle istituzioni monastiche bizantine», 353–55.

24–25 ἀναισχύντως γυναίῳ τὸν προεστῶτα τοῦ μονυδρίου ἐκ πολλοῦ συνοικεῖν: This story of the *proestos* of the monastery is incidental to the letter; Athanasius mentions the case only to trace the history of the property which was transferred from the patriarchal monastery at Apameia to the neighboring monastery of the Mother of God.

24 τὸν προεστῶτα: The abbot; cf. Θρησκευτικὴ καὶ Ἠθικὴ Ἐγκυκλοπαίδεια, X, 600–1.

28–29 τῇ μονῇ ... τῆς Εὐεργέτιδος ὄντως γειτονευούσῃ: Perhaps to be identified with the monastery of the Theotokos near Peladarion (present-day Filadar), northeast of Apameia; cf. V. I. Kandes, Ἡ Προῦσα (Athens, 1883), 143. There was also a monastery of the Theotokos at Elegmoi (present-day Kurşunlu), east of Apameia,

but the full name of this monastery was μονὴ τῆς ὑπεραγίας Θεοτόκου τῶν Ἡλίου βωμῶν ἤτοι τῶν Ἐλεγμῶν; cf. the typikon of the
monastery, ed. A. Dmitrievskij, *Opisanie liturgičeskih rukopisej*, I
(Kiev, 1895), 715–69, and now, C. Mango, «The Monastery of St.
Abercius at Kurşunlu (Elegmi) in Bithynia», *DOP*, 22 (1968), 169 ff.

78.

Athanasius asks the Emperor to help him obtain a supply of wood for
his «soup kitchens».

Laurent, *Regestes*, no. 1638

Date: winter of 1306–1307. Although the capital suffered from food shortages
from 1302 on, as the result of the influx of refugees from Anatolia,
the worst famine was in the winter of 1306–1307, when no Thracian
grain was produced; cf. commentary on Letter 67. Laiou dates
this letter to October or November 1306 («The Provisioning of
Constantinople», 106–7), but it probably was not written any
earlier than December, since Athanasius speaks of the «bitter cold»
(line 26). Laurent places the letter at the end of 1305 or beginning of 1306, but does not give any reasons for this date.

20 ἀνενέγκαι ... πρὸς μικρόν: I have taken this phrase as meaning «to
reduce». It is possible, however, that ἀναφέρω should be taken in
its usual meaning of «to report», and the phrase translated, «I wanted
to report briefly the sufferings of the poor...».

39–40 ἀθῆραν ἑψεῖν προενοησάμην: ἀθήρα is a gruel, consisting of flour
boiled with oil; cf. Koukoules, Βυζαντινῶν Βίος καὶ Πολιτισμός, V,
39 and note 3. Athanasius' provisions for feeding the poor are
described in some detail in his διδασκαλία of *ca.* 1306–1307 (*Vat.
Gr. 2219*, fol. 166ᵛ = Laurent, *Regestes*, no. 1632), and in *Theoctisti
Vita Ath.*, 35.

42 τοῖς ὀρεινόμοις: These ὀρεινόμοι are probably to be identified with
the imperial foresters who are mentioned by Nicetas Choniates
(*Hist.*, 716). At the time of the Fourth Crusade these foresters
refused to allow the cutting of timber needed for ship construction,
on the grounds that logging operations would disturb the wild
game.

79.

Athanasius complains to the Emperor about the bishops who remain in Constantinople, and the clergy who are protesting about promotions and pay.

Laurent, *Regestes*, no. 1643

Date: *ca.* 1306–1307. The hostility of the clergy of St. Sophia toward the Patriarch came to a head in 1307 because they were receiving no pay or promotions whatsoever (Pachymeres, *Hist.*, II, 642); however, the letter should perhaps be dated to the previous year, because there are still bishops in the capital; cf. Laurent, *Regestes*, 438.

5 ὡς τοῖς κανόσι δοκεῖ: Cf. the fourteenth canon of the Apostles and the twenty-first canon of the Council of Antioch (Rhalles–Potles, II, 18, and III, 164).

5–8 μὴ κέρδους χάριν αἰσχροῦ ... ἐκ παρεισπράξεων πληθυσμοῦ: In other letters Athanasius is more specific about the ways in which bishops filled their pockets: through accepting bribes in return for favorable judicial decisions (cf. Letters 30, lines 23–24, and 48, lines 11–14), and by appropriating funds which they should have spent on the upkeep or improvement of monasteries or other properties under their administration (cf. Letters 62, lines 49–51, and 83, line 24 ff.). In Letter 65 there may also be allusions to simony and to grain hoarding and profiteering on the part of ecclesiastics.

8–9 τῶν τοῦ κλήρου ... ἀφηνιαζόντων τῆς ἐκκλησίας: Athanasius is here referring to the clergy of St. Sophia; cf. *Vat. Gr. 2219*, fol. 214ᵛ, where he addresses the rebellious clerics as τῆς περιωνύμου μητρὸς τῶν ἐκκλησιῶν, τοῦ Θεοῦ Λόγου Σοφίας φημί, θεοσεβέστατοι κληρικοί. Athanasius sent numerous letters to the Emperor and to the clerics themselves, complaining about their behavior; cf. *Vat. Gr. 2219*, fols. 204ʳ–211ʳ and 214ᵛ–221ᵛ (= Laurent, *Regestes*, nos. 1660, 1763–72). Pachymeres quotes a letter written by the clerics to Athanasius in which they speak of the συχναὶ γραφαί of the Patriarch (*Hist.*, II, 645).

9–10 οὐ κατὰ χρέος, κατὰ δὲ χάριν εἰσερχομένων: Cf. Pachymeres, *Hist.*, II, 643: διὰ ταῦτα γοῦν ἀμελῶς εἶχον καὶ σπανίως ἀπήντων εἰς τὴν ἐκκλησίαν καὶ ὡς εἰπεῖν ἀπεσχίζοντο.

11–12 μήτε στολῇ ἁρμοδίῳ τῇ ἐκκλησίᾳ καθωραΐζεσθαι: The *himation* was a long black overgarment worn by all members of the clergy; cf.

Symeon of Thessalonica, *De sacris ordinationibus*, chaps. 184 and 185 (PG, 155, cols. 393D–96B), and the recent work of Tano Papas, *Studien zur Geschichte der Messgewänder im byzantinischen Ritus*, Miscellanea Byzantina Monacensia, 3 (Munich, 1965), 31, 33. Athanasius insisted that the church officials wear the *himation* to church services; see Pachymeres, *Hist.*, II, 642.

13 ἕνεκεν ὀφφικίων καὶ ῥόγας: Athanasius had difficulty raising funds to pay church officials, and moreover was reluctant to pay the clerics because of their slack attendance at church services. Pachymeres, himself an official of St. Sophia, sympathized with his fellow clerics, and gave a very biased account of this struggle between the Patriarch and his subordinates (*Hist.*, II, 642). After the church officials complained to the Emperor, he decided that they should receive half pay, six or eight nomismata according to their rank (Pachymeres, *Hist.*, II, 642).

15–16 τοῦ τῆς ἐκκλησίας υἱοῦ τῆς ἐκ Θεοῦ βασιλείας σου: Athanasius frequently refers to the Emperor as the son of the Church; cf. Letters 45, line 7, and 49, line 39.

80.

Athanasius repeats his frequent claim that he presents petitions to the Emperor not for any personal profit, but on account of his love for the Emperor, whom he regards as a son. He therefore begs the Emperor to heed his requests, and hasten to fulfil them.

Laurent, *Regestes*, no. 1715

Date: During Athanasius' second patriarchate (1303–1309), on account of references to his old age (lines 34–35).

11–12 φιλοτέκνου μητρὸς ... ἐν φιλτάτῳ υἱῷ: The Church, represented by Athanasius, is the mother; the Emperor is the son. For other passages in which Athanasius refers to the Emperor as the son of the Church, see Letters 45, line 7; 49, line 39, and 79, lines 15–16.

12 ὑποστάσει: Means οὐσία, «property»; for this definition of ὑπόστασις, cf. *Scriptores originum Constantinopolitanarum*, ed. Th. Preger (Leipzig, 1901), 224, line 15.

81.

Athanasius and the synod excommunicate and expel from the priesthood John Drimys and other members of his conspiracy against Andronicus II.

Laurent, *Regestes*, no. 1636

Date: winter 1305–1306; cf. commentary *infra*.

ad apparatum 1: περὶ 'Ιωάννου τινός, Δριμὺς τὸ ἐπίθετον: John Drimys, who claimed to be a descendant of the Lascarids, led a conspiracy in 1305 to overthrow the Palaeologan dynasty (Pachymeres, *Hist.*, II, 592–93). The plot was discovered in time, and Drimys and his accomplices were tried before the synod, which defrocked and excommunicated them (Letter 81, lines 134–35, 139–44). This letter is a report of the Patriarch on the decision of the synod. Although the Emperor is not mentioned in the title of the letter, it is clear from the final paragraph (line 168ff.) that the report is addressed to Andronicus.

　　The Drimys family is known to have existed as early as the twelfth century, when Michael Acominatus, metropolitan of Athens, addressed a eulogy to one Demetrius Drimys, προσφώνημα εἰς τὸν πραίτορα Κῦρ Δημήτριον τὸν Δριμὺν ταῖς 'Αθήναις ἐπιστάντα (ed. S. P. Lampros, Μιχαὴλ τοῦ Χωνιάτου τὰ σωζόμενα, I [Athens, 1879], 157–79).

2–3 τῇ φύσει τῇ μακαρίᾳ: I.e., God; cf. Lampe, *Patristic Greek Lexicon*, 821, *s.v.* μακάριος, A.1.

3 ἱερωσύνη καὶ βασιλείᾳ: Here Athanasius has apparently taken Justinian's doctrine of ἱερωσύνη and βασιλεία, as formulated in the preamble to Novel 6 (*CIC*, III, 35–36), and applied it to the Church alone.

5 τῶν θείων ληνῶν: A metaphor for churches; cf. Athanasius of Alexandria, *Expositio in Psalmum 8:1* (PG, 27, col. 80D): αὗται [i.e., αἱ ληνοί] δὲ ἂν εἶεν αἱ ἐκκλησίαι, αἱ τοὺς τῶν κατορθούντων ἐν θεοσεβείᾳ δεχόμεναι καρπούς. For other examples, see Lampe, *Patristic Greek Lexicon*, 799–800.

13–14 καὶ ἅλας τυγχάνειν καὶ φῶς τῷ ἐπιλοίπῳ λαῷ: Cf. John Chrysostom, *De sacerdotio*, VI, iv (PG, 48, col. 681): φωτὸς γὰρ δίκην τὴν οἰκουμένην καταυγάζοντος, λάμπειν δεῖ τοῦ ἱερέως τὴν ψυχήν ... οἱ ἱερεῖς τῆς γῆς εἰσιν ἅλες.

27–28 τοῦ βήματος ἕνα προσμαρτυρῶν ἑαυτόν: Drimys claimed to be a
priest; cf. Pachymeres (*Hist.*, II, 593), who described Drimys as
ἱερωσύνης περικτᾶσθαι δόξας ἀξίωμα.

33–34 τὴν βασιλίδα καταλαμβάνει ... καὶ βασιλεῖ τῷ ἁγίῳ ἐμφανισθείς:
Cf. Pachymeres, *Hist.*, II, 592–93: ἔνθεν μέν τις τῶν ἐπιρρήτων ἐκ
δύσεως ... καὶ πρὸ χρόνων προσχωρήσας ἐκεῖθεν τῷ βασιλεῖ, ὁ
τοιοῦτος Δριμὺς τοὐπίκλην ... ὑπήρχετο τοὺς πολλούς. It is unclear what Pachymeres had in mind when he wrote that Drimys
came «from the west» (cf. line 135 of this letter where Drimys is
described as αὐτὸν τὸν θῆρα τὸν δυτικὸν καὶ δριμύν); did he mean the
western (i.e., European) parts of the Byzantine Empire, or more
specifically Epiros? See Ševčenko, «Manuel Moschopulos», notes 91
and 95, on this question. A few lines later Pachymeres mentioned
τῷ ἐκ δύσεως Μυζάκῃ (*Hist.*, II, 593), but unfortunately even less
is known about Myzakes than about Drimys! Cf. also Pachymeres,
Hist., I, 294, where he described the Arsenite monk Hyakinthos as
μοναχὸς ... ἐκ δύσεως. I. Sykoutris, in his article Περὶ τὸ σχίσμα
τῶν Ἀρσενιατῶν (in Ἑλληνικά, II, 2 [1929], 304), interprets this as
meaning that Hyakinthos came from Epiros.

35–36 δι' ὃ ἐπεφήμιζεν ἑαυτῷ ἱερωσύνης οἶμαι ἀξίωμα: Athanasius accuses
Drimys of claiming to be a priest in order to gain greater favor with
the pious Emperor. Later in the letter, when the Patriarch and synod
expel Drimys from the priesthood, they qualify their action with
the phrase, «if indeed he ever was a priest» (cf. lines 136–39).

49–50 ὁ ἄθλιος ἀπόγονον εἶναι τῶν πώποτε βεβασιλευκότων τινός: Drimys
claimed to be descended from the Lascarid family; cf. Pachymeres,
Hist., II, 593.

52 τραγέλαφος ... τις ἀνυπόστατος: This imaginary animal, the confla-
tion of a goat and stag, was used along with σκινδαψός (a word
without meaning, a «what d'ye call it») in treatises on philosophy
as terms to which no reality corresponds; cf. Elias, *Prolegomena
philosophiae* (*Commentaria in Aristotelem graeca*, XVIII, 1 [Berlin,
1900]), 3, 7–8, and David, *Prolegomena philosophiae* (*Commentaria
in Aristotelem graeca*, XVIII, 2 [Berlin, 1904]), 1, 16–17, quoted in
I. Ševčenko, «The Definition of Philosophy in the *Life of St. Constantine*», in *For Roman Jakobson* (The Hague, 1956), 450 note 5.
     Athanasius was no doubt familiar with this word from Gregory
of Nazianzus' *Oration* XXV, *In laudem Heronis philosophi*, 7 (PG, 35,
col. 1205B): ταύτης καρπὸς τῆς φιλοσοφίας, οὐ λόγῳ πλαττόμεναι

πόλεις (σκινδαψοί τινες, ὡς αὐτοί φασι, καὶ τραγέλαφοι, ἃ γλῶσσα μόνη συντίθησιν).

59–60 ἐκείνου τοῦ θεῖναι τοῖς ἄστροις τὸν θρόνον βατταρίσαι τετολμηκότος: Satan; cf. Rev. 12:7–9.

65 ἐν τῇ πόλει καὶ ταῦτα τοῦ κράτους: There is something curious about this phrase, which I have tentatively translated «even in the capital of the empire». Perhaps καὶ ταῦτα should be emended to κατὰ so that the phrase would read τὰ αὐτοῦ βδελυρὰ σκαιωρήματα ἐν τῇ πόλει κατὰ τοῦ κράτους ἐνσπείρας ὁ δείλαιος . . . .

79–80 τῷ Ὠρὴβ ἐκείνῳ καὶ τῷ Ζεβεὲ καὶ τῷ Σαλμανάν: These three Madianites were slain by Gedeon; cf. Judg. 7:25, 8:1–21, and Ps. 82 (83):12–13.

87 ἀπὸ τῶν Ξυλωτῶν: Drimys sought Arsenite support for his conspiracy. The Arsenite faction was traditionally anti-Palaeologan and pro-Lascarid, since the Patriarch Arsenius was the defender of the young Emperor John IV Lascaris, from whom Michael VIII Palaeologus usurped the throne; cf. Laurent, «La fin du schisme arsénite», 227–44. Because of their role in the conspiracy, the Arsenites were evicted, in the dead of winter, from their headquarters at the monastery of Mosele and from elsewhere in the city (Pachymeres, *Hist.*, II, 593).

129 τοῦ Σάρδεων: Cyril; cf. commentary on Letter 25, lines 14–15.

129–30 τοῦ Χαλκηδόνος: Symeon or Theodoulos (?); cf. commentary on Letter 69, line 155. It seems unlikely that this metropolitan who agreed in 1305/1306 to a condemnation of Arsenite conspirators can be identified with the pro-Arsenite metropolitan of Chalcedon who was assured by the Emperor in 1310 that he would not change any portion of his agreement with the Arsenites; cf. Laurent, «La fin du schisme arsénite», 312 note 1.

τοῦ Περγάμου: Arsenios; cf. commentary on Letter 69, lines 164–65.

τοῦ Βιτζύνης: Perhaps Luke; cf. commentary on Letter 25, line 14.

131 τοῦ Ἀχυράους: This anonymous metropolitan of Achyraous, a city of Bithynia, is mentioned only in this letter, and in some manuscript copies of the Νεαρά; cf. PG, 166, col. 1065B. See also the notice

of S. Petrides, in *Dictionnaire d'histoire et de géographie ecclésiastique*, I, 333.

131–32 τοῦ ἀρχιεπισκόπου Χριστουπόλεως: This archbishop of Christoupolis (present-day Kavalla in northern Greece) is probably the predecessor of Hierotheos, who is known from a patriarchal act of July 1315 (Miklosich–Müller, I, 5). In 1310 a metropolitan of Christoupolis (Hierotheos?) was among seven pro-Arsenite prelates who insisted that Andronicus guarantee his concessions to the Arsenites; cf. Laurent, «La fin du schisme arsénite», 312 note 6. Sometime between 1301 and 1305, Babylas of Ankara signed a copy of a chrysobull of 1298 as *proedros* of Christoupolis; cf. Laurent, «Un groupe de signatures épiscopales», 319, and my commentary on Letters 25, lines 14–15, and 61, line 83. By the time of this synod in late 1305 or early 1306, however, the see of Christoupolis was no longer granted to Babylas κατ' ἐπίδοσιν, but had regained an archbishop of its own.

132 τοῦ ἀρχιεπισκόπου Δέρκου: Perhaps to be identified with Makarios, who was a member of the synod during Athanasius' first patriarchate, and is also attested in 1294 in the cod. *Laurent. Plut. V, 2*, fol. 386ᵛ; cf. *Actes de Xéropotamou*, no. 11.

133 τοῦ ʽΡαιδεστοῦ: The name of this bishop of Rhaidestos is unknown; he is included anonymously in M. LeQuien, *Oriens Christianus*, I (Paris, 1740), 1129–30.

τοῦ Χαριουπόλεως: This bishop of Charioupolis is also unknown; he is listed without any name in LeQuien, *Oriens Christianus*, I, 1133–34.

135 αὐτὸν τὸν θῆρα τὸν δυτικὸν καὶ δριμύν: Cf. commentary on lines 33–34 *supra*.

140 τὸν ἀκόλουθον ὃν ἡ Μύρα Λυκίας προήνεγκεν: Drimys' accomplice from Myra must have been a priest, since he was defrocked by the synod. Perhaps he is to be identified with Luke, a metropolitan of Myra in the late thirteenth century, who may be tentatively linked with the Arsenites on the evidence of an act addressed by the Patriarch John XIII Glykys (1315–1319) to the metropolis of Myra: ὁ ἀπὸ τῶν αὐτόθι [Myra] παρὼν πρεσβύτερος Μιχαὴλ ὁ Ἄρχων ἀνέφερε πρὸς τὴν ἡμῶν μετριότητα, ὅτι σκανδαλίζονταί τινες ἐπ' αὐτῷ τε καὶ ἑτέροις πρεσβυτέροις, διὸ ἐχειροτονήθησαν παρὰ τοῦ θεοφιλεστάτου ἐπισκόπου Κυάνων, ὃν ἐχειροτόνησεν ὁ Λουκᾶς ἐκεῖνος ἀρχιερεύς

γενόμενος ἐν τῇ καθ᾽ ὑμᾶς τοιαύτῃ ἐκκλησίᾳ κατὰ τὸν καιρὸν τῆς ἐκκλησιαστικῆς ἐκείνης συγχύσεως καὶ ταραχῆς (Miklosich–Müller, I, 37). It seems likely that the ἐκκλησιαστικὴ ἐκείνη σύγχυσις καὶ ταραχή refers to the Arsenite schism, although it could possibly be the schism in the Church over the Union of Lyons. Luke is known only from this passage, although he may be the πρόεδρος Μυρέων mentioned in *Poem* CV, line 24, of Manuel Philes (ed. Miller, *Manuelis Philae carmina*, I, 291).

Note Athanasius' play on words in this sentence, τὸν ἀκόλουθον ὃν ἡ Μύρα Λυκίας προήνεγκεν, οἷα λῦκον ἀσυμπαθῆ. Is there also perhaps a pun on Λουκᾶς — λῦκος?

147 τῷ αὐτοῦ ἀκολούθῳ Σαρδαναπάλῳ: This must be the same accomplice from Myra. According to Greek tradition, Sardanapalus (the Greek form of Ashurbanipal) was the last king of Assyria, who wasted away his life in luxury and pleasure. The name Sardanapalus was used to describe an effeminate, debauched person; cf. Gregory of Nazianzus, *Poem on Virtue*, lines 612–16 (PG, 37, cols. 724–25). Blemmydes, in his essay *On Kingship*, also used Sardanapalus as an example of a king destroyed by indulgence in sensuous pleasures (PG, 142, col. 617A).

165–66 ἐν ἀθέοις πρεσβευομένους ᾿Αμαληκίταις καὶ ᾿Ιταλοῖς: Athanasius apparently uses indiscriminately the terms Λατῖνοι, ᾿Ιταλοί, and Φράγγοι to describe Roman Catholic Westerners; cf. Letters 9, line 3; 17, line 15; 84, line 16, and 93, line 19. Here the term ᾿Ιταλός must mean Catalan, since we know that Drimys did seek help from the Catalans in his attempt to overthrow the Palaeologan dynasty; cf. Pachymeres, *Hist.*, II, 593. Ševčenko concurs in this identification (cf. his article on «Manuel Moschopulos», 149), as does Laurent (*Regestes*, 431).

Drimys may also have tried to bring into his conspiracy some of the Turcopoles (᾿Αμαληκίταις) who had joined the Catalans in 1305. See commentary on Letter 62, line 71, for the Byzantine usage of ᾿Αμαληκῖται as a name for the Turks. Perhaps, however, one should not take too seriously this charge against Drimys of collaboration with Byzantium's archenemies; cf. Ševčenko, «Manuel Moschopulos», 149.

166 τοῖς τε περὶ τὸν ῎Ιστρον οἰκοῦσιν: These inhabitants of the Danube region are probably Bulgarians. During this period they were enjoying relative prosperity and freedom from Tatar and Byzantine pressure under the vigorous rule of Theodore Svetoslav (1298–1322);

81, 82

cf. *CMH*, IV, i, 535–37. This vague allusion could, however, also refer to Serbs, Hungarians, or Rumanians; cf. Laurent, *Regestes*, 430–31.

82.

Athanasius repeats his frequent theme that, since the misfortunes of the Byzantines are caused by their sins, the only hope for the empire lies in repentance and good works.

Laurent, *Regestes*, no. 1717

26 τὴν πέρα δεινοῦ παντὸς συμφοράν: As if dependent from ἀπεδιδράσκομεν ἄν.

41 ταὐτεμπάθειαν: Not in the dictionaries. A similar word, ταὐτοπάθεια, is defined by Liddell-Scott as «reflex signification» (αὐτοπαθὴς σημασία in Demetrakos, *Lexikon*, 7119).

76–77 τῷ πρώτῳ ἐν βασιλεῦσι … λογισθήσῃ υἱὸν: Byzantine emperors were usually hailed as «new Constantine», rather than «son of Constantine»; cf. O. Treittinger, *Die oströmische Kaiser- und Reichsidee nach ihrer Gestaltung im höfischen Zeremoniell vom oströmischen Staats- und Reichsgedanken* (Jena, 1938; reprinted Darmstadt, 1956), 130–31 and note 4. For example, Gregory of Cyprus addressed an encomium εἰς τὸν αὐτοκράτορα κυρὸν Μιχαὴλ τὸν Παλαιολόγον καὶ νέον Κωνσταντῖνον (Boissonade, *Anecdota Graeca*, I, 313), and John Chilas, metropolitan of Ephesus, addressed Andronicus II as ἰσαπόστολε νέε Κωνσταντῖνε in the preamble to an unpublished work contained in *Mosquensis* 368 (240), fol. 76, quoted by J. Darrouzès, in his *Documents inédits d'ecclésiologie byzantine*, AOC, 10 (Paris, 1966), 348 note on line 1.

There is a parallel, however, to Andronicus being addressed as «son of Constantine» in another work of John Chilas; cf. «Sur le schisme arsénite», ed. Darrouzès, *op. cit.*, 373, lines 12–15: Μόνος ὁ πάντων τῶν ὀρθοδόξων βασιλέων καὶ τούτου [Andronicus II] πατήρ, Κωνσταντῖνος ἐκεῖνος, ὁ ἰσαπόστολος βασιλεὺς καὶ μέγας οὐ τοσοῦτον τὸν πλατυσμὸν τῆς ἀρχῆς ὅσον τὸ μέγεθος τῆς βασιλείας κληθείς, τὸ τοιοῦτον ἔργον κατώρθωσεν. Cf. also Athanasius, Letter 112, lines 13–14, where he refers to Constantine as Andronicus' «spiritual father».

79–80 δυσεπικράτητον: An extremely rare word meaning «grasped with difficulty». According to H. Estienne's *Thesaurus Graecae linguae*,

II (Paris, 1833), col. 1747, it is found only in «Marcus Eremita, p. 894, A». I have not been able to determine to which edition of Marcus' works this citation refers.

90–91 τῆς ποίμνης τὰ ἁρπαγέντα ἐπανασώσοιτο: Athanasius still hopes that Arsenites and other dissidents may be induced to return to the fold.

83.

One of the responsibilities of bishops is to see that monasteries are administered in accordance with the canons. Athanasius complains that the greed of certain people (the bishops to whom the letter is addressed?) has led them to exploit the monasteries which they are administering. If someone builds a monastery, or restores one in ruins, he should take care to entrust it to true servants of God (i.e., to people who will not exploit the monastery). It is sheer folly to give σιτηρέσιον (the revenue from monastic lands granted as *pronoia*) to soldiers, and it is even worse to entrust monasteries to laymen or worthless monks.

Laurent, *Regestes*, no. 1718

Date: 1303? See commentary *infra* on lines 52–55.

10–11 ἐγκανόνως: When Athanasius states that bishops are responsible for seeing that grants of monasteries are made in accordance with the canons, he apparently has in mind the forty-ninth canon of the Council in Trullo (a repetition of the twenty-fourth canon of the Council of Chalcedon) which declared that monasteries were not to be granted to laymen; cf. Rhalles–Potles, II, 423. On the whole question of monastic properties, see P. Charanis, «The Monastic Properties and the State in the Byzantine Empire», *DOP*, 4 (1948), 53–118.

22–23 τὸν τοῦ Χαρμῆ: Not an allusion to a contemporary of Athanasius, as Laurent suggests (*Regestes*, 503), but a reference to Achar, the son of Charmi, who stole some of the spoils from Jericho which Joshua had dedicated to God; for this transgression he was stoned to death by the Israelites; cf. Josh. 6–7.

26–28 τινὲς ἀδεῶς ... τοῖς ἑαυτῶν προστιθέασιν: These charges are similar to those made in earlier centuries against χαριστικάριοι, laymen to whom monasteries were granted, but by the fourteenth century

the institution of χαριστίκιον no longer existed in Byzantium; cf. E. Herman, «Charisticaires», in *DDC*, III (1942), col. 617.

52–55 τὸ δὲ λόγῳ στρατείας ... ἡ ἄνοια καταγέλαστος: Athanasius protests against granting σιτηρέσιον, revenue from monastic lands granted as *pronoia*, to soldiers. Cf. Nicolas Cabasilas, Λόγος περὶ τῶν παρανόμως τοῖς ἄρχουσιν ἐπὶ τοῖς ἱεροῖς τολμωμένων, where government alienation of monastic property for military purposes is discussed (ed. I. Ševčenko, «Nicolas Cabasilas' 'Anti-Zealot' Discourse: A Reinterpretation», *DOP*, 11 [1957], 97, 100–1).

This letter may be related to the incident of 1303, when Andronicus considered confiscating monastic lands and distributing them to soldiers as *pronoia*. Pachymeres records that Athanasius condoned this alienation of monastic property under the pressure of military necessity, and sent the Emperor an olive branch to indicate his assent (*Hist.*, II, 390). A free translation of this difficult passage can be found in Charanis, «Monastic Properties», 111; see also the interpretation of Ševčenko in «Cabasilas», 157 note 125, and Elizabeth Fisher, «A Note on Pachymeres' 'De Andronico Palaeologo'», *Byzantion*, 40 (1970), 230–35.

It may be that Athanasius first wrote this letter attacking the imperial policy of confiscation of monastic property, and then later sent the olive branch, when he realized he could not change Andronicus' mind. If this letter is indeed a veiled attack on the Emperor, that would explain the extremely general and vague language in which it is couched.

53 τοῦ δεσπότου: Laurent interprets τοῦ δεσπότου as referring to the Emperor, and reads the phrase as τὸ δὲ τάξαι λόγῳ στρατείας σιτηρέσιον ἐκ τῶν τοῦ δεσπότου τισίν ..., and translates «to give pay, out of the Emperor's property, to soldiers ...» (*Regestes*, 502). I prefer to see in τοῦ δεσπότου an allusion to the Despot John Palaeologus (nowhere else does Athanasius call the Emperor δεσπότης), and leave the original word order, attaching τισίν τὸ ἐκ τῶν τοῦ δεσπότου, and translating «to certain of the Despot's men».

56–57 πολλῷ ... τιμωρίαν ὑπομενεῖ: A word like μείζονα or αὐστηροτέραν is apparently missing here.

84.

Athanasius asks the Emperor not to allow his son John to leave Byzantium and accept the succession to the marquisate of Montferrat.

84

Laurent, *Regestes*, Appendix, no. 8

Date: late spring or early summer of 1305; cf. Laiou, «Theodore Palaeologus», 403, and commentary *infra*.

Laurent places the letter before Easter 1303, arguing that the letter concerns a marriage project and therefore must have been written before John's marriage to the daughter of Nicephorus Choumnos in 1303; cf. *BZ*, 63 (1970), 170, and *Regestes*, 575. The letter, however, nowhere alludes to any marriage plans, and specifically states (line 15) that the Empress wants to send John to Montferrat. I therefore concur with Laiou's conclusion that the letter must be dated to 1305, when the Marquis of Montferrat died. It is true that John's marriage presented an obstacle to his inheriting the title (cf. Laiou, *op. cit.*, 394), but it is quite probable that Irene favored her eldest son for the succession until she was made aware of the problems involved; see commentary *infra* on lines 13–16.

6–7 τοῖς ὑφ' ὑμᾶς θεοὶ χρηματίζοντες: Not «you must behave as a God toward those who are under you», as Laiou translates (*op. cit.*, 407), but «you who are given the name of god by your subjects»: cf. Letter 92, lines 30–31: τὸ μετὰ Θεὸν ὁραθῆναι τῷ ὁμοφύλῳ θεούς. This concept of the king as god is derived from the celebrated verse 6 of Psalm 81 (82): ἐγὼ εἶπα: θεοί ἐστε. The θεοί in this psalm, in Psalm 49 (50):1, and in Exodus 22:28 were frequently interpreted as «kings, princes»; cf. Eusebius, *In psalmos commentaria*, LXXXI (PG, 23, col. 988B) and XLIX, 2 (PG, 23, col. 433D), and Chrysostom, *Expositio in psalmos*, XLIX (PG, 55, col. 241). The same interpretation was followed in the twelfth century by Euthymius Zigabenus (PG, 128, col. 853C): ἐγὼ δὲ προσεξεῦρον, ὅτι θεοὺς μὲν εἶπε τοὺς ἄρχοντας καὶ δικαστὰς ἐν τῇ βίβλῳ τῆς Ἐξόδου (22:28). For a full discussion of king as god, see E. H. Kantorowicz, «Deus per naturam, deus per gratiam: A Note on Medieval Political Theology», in *Selected Studies by Ernst H. Kantorowicz* (Locust Valley, N.Y., 1965), 121–37, esp. 126, 128–29. Cf. also Theodore of Nicaea, *Ep.* 35, lines 7–8, and Letter of the Patriarch Antony, 56–57 (ed. Darrouzès, *Epistoliers byzantins*, 302 and 345), and ed. Westerink, «Le Basilikos de Maxime Planude», *Byzantinoslavica*, 29 (1968), 36, lines 860–62.

13 δεσπότου κυροῦ Ἰωάννου: John Palaeologus, son of Andronicus II by his second wife Irene of Montferrat. He was born in 1286 and made despot on May 22, 1295, the day after the coronation of his half-brother Michael; cf. Pachymeres, *Hist.*, II, 197, and Papadopoulos, *Genealogie der Palaiologen*, 38, no. 61. I accept the chronology

84

established by Pia Schmid, «Zur Chronologie von Pachymeres», 83
and note 6.

13–14 τῆς περιποθήτου αὐτοῦ μητρὸς καὶ δεσποίνης: Yolanda of Montferrat
married Andronicus in 1285 and took the name of Irene; cf. Pachymeres, *Hist.*, II, 87–88, and Papadopoulos, *Genealogie der Palaiologen*,
35. Two studies have been devoted to this Byzantine empress:
Ch. Diehl, *Figures byzantines*, 2e série. *Princesses latines à la cour
des Paléologues* (Paris, 1938), 226–45, and H. Constantinidi-Bibikou,
«Yolande de Montferrat, impératrice de Byzance», in *Hellénisme
contemporain*, 4 (1950), 425–42.

Irene, who had great ambitions for her three sons, John,
Theodore, and Demetrius, and for her daughter Simonis, resented
the fact that Michael, Andronicus' son by his first wife, was heir
to the Byzantine throne. She begged Andronicus either to disinherit
Michael so that her sons could inherit the empire, or else to divide
the empire equally between the sons of both his wives (Gregoras,
Hist., I, 233–34). When Andronicus refused to yield to Irene's
wishes, she began to plan illustrious marriages for her children
which would assure each of them a small kingdom. In 1299, the
five-year-old Simonis was married to Uroš II Milutin of Serbia
(Gregoras, *Hist.*, I, 204; Pachymeres, *Hist.*, II, 275). Irene wanted
her eldest son John to marry the recently widowed Isabella, Princess
of Achaia (Pachymeres, *Hist.*, II, 290), but Andronicus' will prevailed
and John was married in 1303 to Irene, daughter of Nicephorus
Choumnos (Pachymeres, *Hist.*, II, 378–79). In 1306 Theodore was
married to Argentina Spinola, daughter of one of the two captains
of Genoa (Pachymeres, *Hist.*, II, 598).

At the time of this letter Irene was separated from her husband
and living in Thessalonica.

13–16 ὡς ἀναγκάζεσθαι τοῦτον ... ζητῆσαι κατάρξαι τῶν Φράγγων ἀρχῆς:
In January 1305 Irene and her sons fell heir to Montferrat when her
brother, the Marquis John I, died without issue. In March, envoys
came to Thessalonica from Montferrat to discuss the inheritance
of the marquisate. Since Irene did not choose to go to Montferrat
herself, she had to select one of her sons as successor to her brother;
cf. Benvenuto di San Giorgio, *Historia Montis Ferrati*, in L. Muratori, *RerItalSS*, XXIII (Milan, 1733), 408–13, 450–53.

From Athanasius' letter we learn that Irene's first choice was
her eldest son John. When news of the Empress' decision reached
the capital, Andronicus at first consented (συναινέσει καὶ τῆς ἐκ Θεοῦ
βασιλείας σου, lines 14–15), but was then dissuaded by the arguments
of the Patriarch. This is one of the rare occasions when we know

that the Emperor was actually influenced by a memorandum from the Patriarch.

Theodore Palaeologus writes in his autobiography that his brother John could not go to Montferrat, *quod jam matrimonio aderat copulatus, et aliis negotiis occupatus* (Benvenuto di San Giorgio, *op. cit.*, 453 B–C). The *negotia* which kept John in Byzantium may have been the duties connected with the position of eparch of Constantinople, which he assumed around this time; cf. Pachymeres, *Hist.*, II, 480 and 497. It is also possible that Andronicus hesitated to send his third eldest son to Montferrat because of his concern for the succession to the Byzantine throne; cf. Laiou, «Theodore Palaeologus», 392–93. He therefore urged that Demetrius, his youngest son, be designated as heir to the marquisate. Eventually Andronicus and Irene compromised on a third choice, their middle son, Theodore (Pachymeres, *Hist.*, II, 598).

43–44 τηρήσῃ τὴν πίστιν ἀμώμητον: Athanasius is worried that John might convert to Catholicism if he went to Italy. The Patriarch's anxiety was justified, since John's younger brother Theodore did abandon the Orthodox faith when he went to Montferrat (Gregoras, *Hist.*, I, 240).

44 ἐν τοιαύτῃ νεότητι: Since John was born in 1286, he would have been less than twenty years old at this time.

44–45 ἀλλοδαπεῖ γῇ βαρβάροις κατοικουμένῃ: Typical of Athanasius' violent anti-Latin prejudice.

53–58 ἢ οὐχὶ ... ἐν τῇ τῆς βασιλείας ἀρχῇ: Athanasius is here alluding to Andronicus' repudiation, at his accession in 1282, of the Union of Lyons which his father Michael had agreed to in 1274.

70 διὰ κυβέρνησιν: The translation of the word κυβέρνησις as used by Athanasius presents difficulties almost everywhere it occurs in his correspondence. In Letter 34, line 10 (εἰς ἀναγκαίων πραγμάτων κυβέρνησιν), κυβέρνησις evidently means «management, arrangement». In lines 19–20 of the same letter (κυβερνήσει δῆθεν ἐλπίδος), I have interpreted κυβέρνησις as «guidance». In this letter, κυβέρνησις apparently has the meaning of «discipline», whereas in Letter 86, line 22, the term seems to mean «financial support».

73–74 ἀλλ' ὡς ἐκεῖθεν σωματικὴν ἀναμενοῦντες βοήθειαν: Athanasius rejects any western help against the Turks; cf. Letter 37, lines 13–14.

80 οὐδὲ νῦν εἰς ὄψιν ἐλθεῖν, etc.: Athanasius suggests that John should
stay away from his mother for the time being, to avoid further
arguments.

85–93 ὅθεν ... τῇ ἐκ Θεοῦ βασιλείᾳ σου: Athanasius uses the word εἰρήνη
seven times in these two sentences, playing on the name of the Empress
Irene.

85.

Athanasius asks Andronicus to help effect a reconciliation between the
Empress Irene and their son John.

Laurent, *Regestes*, Appendix, no. 5

Date: Laurent dates the letter *ca.* 1301–1303, but I find his arguments
unconvincing (cf. *Regestes*, 571), and prefer a date of 1305. The
language of the letter suggests that John was in the capital, and
wished to leave to visit his mother in Thessalonica as soon as an
opportunity presented itself. John moved to Thessalonica in 1303
with Irene, but returned to Constantinople *ca.* 1305 to serve as
prefect of the city; cf. Pachymeres, *Hist.*, II, 480 and 497, and
commentary on Letter 84, lines 13–16.

In this letter Athanasius takes back the advice of Letter 84,
in which he recommended that John not see his mother. Now he
suggests that Irene be allowed to see her son as soon as possible.
Perhaps the Patriarch's earlier advice had only succeeded in creating
further tensions within the imperial family.

86.

Athanasius, requested by the Despot John to intercede with his mother,
the Empress Irene, in his petition for an increase in income, asks Andronicus
for clearance before committing himself. If the petition to Irene was ever
written, it has not been preserved.

Laurent, *Regestes*, Appendix, no. 6

Date: The Despot John is apparently living in the capital at the time of
this letter; it can therefore be dated to *ca.* 1305–1306, when he
returned to Constantinople to serve as prefect of the city; cf. Letters 84
and 85. Laurent dates this letter, like the two previous, to 1301–
1303.

4–5 κἂν τῇ ἐκκλησίᾳ πολλὴν ἐμφαίνει τὴν γνησιότητα καὶ σπουδήν: Cf.
Letters 52, 53, and 70 in which Athanasius suggests to Andronicus
that the Despot John take the Emperor's place at ceremonies if he
is unable to attend himself.

25–26 εἰδήσεως ἄμοιροι πάμπαν καὶ παιδεύσεως πέλοντες ἀνακτορικῆς: Cf.
Letter 73, line 39, where Athanasius remarks on his ignorance of
proper court rhetoric.

87.

Athanasius, infuriated at the confiscation of sacred property by fiscal
agents, asks the Emperor to appoint someone else to assume responsibility
for the small portion of church property which has survived the ravages of
invasion and internal corruption.

Laurent, *Regestes*, no. 1719

9–10 ἕνα τῶν περικλύτων ναῶν ... ἀσκεπῆ: This is perhaps a reference to
the church τῶν ἁγίων πάντων, whose roof fell in during the earthquake of June 1296; cf. Pachymeres, *Hist.*, II, 234, Gregoras, *Hist.*,
I, 202, and Janin, *Géographie ecclésiastique*, 403–4. Or Athanasius
might have in mind the church of Chora whose dome, by the early
fourteenth century, «either had collapsed or was in such shattered
condition that it had to be demolished and replaced by another»
(Underwood, *The Kariye Djami*, I, 17).

12 τῶν λαχόντων διενεργεῖν: Fiscal agents; cf. commentary on Letter 17,
lines 23–24.

13–14 πατάξαι λαξευτηρίῳ ... πρὸς καταστροφήν: This description of a
fiscal agent's attack on an icon is reminiscent of the destruction of
the Chalke image of Christ in 726; cf. *Vitas. Stephani junioris*
(PG, 100, col. 1085C). One must assume, however, that in the incident
described by Athanasius, the official was not motivated by iconoclastic
beliefs, but was trying to obtain revenues from the Church by
removing precious metals from the frame (?) of the icon. When
Niphon was deposed from the patriarchate in 1314, one of the charges
laid against him was that he had stripped the gold and silver from
an icon of the Virgin Mary; cf. Choumnos, Ἔλεγχος κατὰ τοῦ ...
Νίφωνος, 270.

24–25 ὧν ἐπλούτει ἡ ἐκκλησία ... ἐγεγύμνωτο: Athanasius is here referring
to the Church's loss of property and buildings in Anatolia as a

result of Turkish conquests; cf., for example, the letter of Matthew of Ephesus which describes the reduced circumstances of the see of Ephesus in 1339 (ed. Treu, *Matthaios Metropolit von Ephesos* [Potsdam, 1901], 54–55). For a more general discussion, see Vryonis, *Decline of Hellenism*, 311–23.

25 βραχοφάγου: βραχοφάγος is not in the dictionaries, but is probably the same word as βραχυφάγος, «one who eats sparingly»; cf. βραχυ-φαγέω and βραχυφαγία in Demetrakos, *Lexikon*, 1499. The translation «mouthful» was suggested by Laurent (*Regestes*, 503).

27–28 πρὸς ἡμᾶς οἱ διενεργοῦντες ... ἐξ ὧν ἐξελέγχονται παρ' ἡμῶν: Athanasius attacked the cruelty of Byzantine government agents in several of his letters: cf. Letters 17, lines 23–24 and 29–30; 18, lines 23–26; 36, lines 7–8; and 46, lines 16–18.

36 τοῦ τὸν σῖτον ἁρπάσαι αὐθαδισθέντος: An allusion to Byzantine profiteers who cornered the grain market and hoarded wheat until prices rose, so they could sell it at greater profit.

36–37 χιλίοις μεδίμνοις πρὸς τοῖς ὀκτακοσίοις: In classical antiquity, the *medimnos* was a dry measure of 51.84 liters. Six *modioi* equalled one *medimnos*. In the mediaeval period these two terms became confused; for example, Cedrenus, in a passage of his *History* (II, 373, 16), uses the word *medimnos* where he definitely means *modios*; cf. G. Ostrogorsky, «Löhne und Preise in Byzanz», *BZ*, 32 (1932), 320 note 3, and 322. Similarly, in the twelfth century, in a poem of Theodore Prodromus addressed to the sebastocrator Andronicus Comnenus, the poet mentions that he received twelve *medimnoi* of wheat four times a year. A variant reading for μεδίμνους, however, is μόδια; cf. D.-Ch. Hesseling and H. Pernot, *Poèmes prodromiques* (Amsterdam, 1910), II, 40–41, lines 24–28.

Zakythinos, in a study of this problem, has commented that μέδιμνος, as a more old-fashioned, archaizing word, usually replaces μόδιος, instead of the other way round; cf. his Περὶ τῆς τιμῆς τοῦ σίτου ἐν Βυζαντίῳ, in ᾿Επ.῾Ετ.Βυζ.Σπ., 12 (1936), 391. Thus we may conclude that Athanasius probably used μέδιμνος here as an archaizing synonym for μόδιος. However, Zakythinos' researches on the capacity of a *modios* have produced such contradictory evidence that it is only possible to state that the Byzantine *modios* was considerably larger than the Roman *modios* of 8.75 liters; cf. Dölger, *Aus den Schatzkammern*, note on Act 13, line 13.

88, 89

88.

Athanasius praises the Emperor's devotion to SS. Peter and Paul, for which he will be rewarded.

Laurent, *Regestes*, no. 1720

Date: shortly after the feast day of the Holy Apostles Peter and Paul, celebrated on June 29.

10 προσαγωγὴν θαυμασίαν ... ποικίλον ποδήρη: For Andronicus' generous presentation of vestments and other offerings to the Church, cf. Letter 66, lines 42–51; Letter 112, lines 9–11; and Pachymeres, *Hist.*, II, 617.

12 μικροῦ καὶ ἀμίμητον: See commentary on Letter 66, line 48, for the suggestion that Athanasius may be referring to embroidered vestments.

13 θατέρου: St. Paul.

16 τοῦ δέ γε θατέρου: St. Peter.

17–18 ὁ προπάτωρ: Adam.

19 ἐπεί γε κἀκείνοις ὁ ἄγραπτος νόμος ... ὑπετίθει: Here Athanasius suddenly realizes that Adam could not have known Paul's Epistles, and gets out of the difficulty by saying that the unwritten law already contained the doctrine of the Epistles.

89.

Athanasius reminds the Emperor that the synod tries cases justly and quickly, and begs that the present accusations against Niphon not go unexamined. He asks that the case be judged either by the Emperor, or by the Patriarch and some of the bishops, for, unless Niphon's name is cleared, it is not fitting for him to return to his see.

Laurent, *Regestes*, no. 1721

Date: *ca.* 1309, on the eve of Athanasius' second deposition from the patriarchate (?).

ad apparatum 1: τοῦ κυροῦ Νίφωνος ὄντος Κυζίκου: Niphon, metropolitan of Cyzicus, was Athanasius' successor on the patriarchal throne from May 9, 1310 to April 11, 1314; cf. V. Grumel, «La date de l'avènement du patriarche de Constantinople Niphon Iᵉʳ», *REB*, 13 (1955), 138–39. Formerly the abbot of the Lavra on Mt. Athos, Niphon became metropolitan of Cyzicus sometime between the imprisonment in 1288 of his predecessor Daniel (Pachymeres, *Hist.*, II, 129) and 1303, when he led the defense of Cyzicus against the Turks (Pachymeres, *Hist.*, II, 390).

Since we do not find the name of the metropolitan of Cyzicus among the members of the permanent synod in 1304 and 1305, we may assume that Niphon stayed in his diocese during those years to protect his flock from Turks and Catalans alike. At the time of this letter, however, he was in Constantinople.

Despite his diligence in performing his pastoral duties, Niphon apparently incurred Athanasius' wrath because of imputations of theft and simony, and because he was a moderate on the Arsenite question. It was exactly this conciliatory attitude which led Andronicus to select Niphon as Athanasius' successor, in order to end the Arsenite schism; cf. Laurent, «La fin du schisme arsénite», 251–56.

In 1314 Niphon was deposed from the patriarchate on the charge of committing various sacrileges (cf. Choumnos, Ἔλεγχος κατὰ τοῦ ... Νίφωνος), and he never forgave Andronicus for failing to defend him at this time. He finally got his revenge in May of 1328, when he advised Andronicus III to force his grandfather to retire (Gregoras, *Hist.*, I, 427–28).

If this letter can be placed *ca.* 1309, then Athanasius would have written it when he realized that his influence with the Emperor was waning and that he was threatened once again with deposition from the patriarchal throne. It is possible that the charges brought against Niphon at this time by a monk (cf. Letter 95) were at the instigation of Athanasius, who wished to eliminate his rival from consideration for the office of patriarch.

τὰς κατηγορίας τὰς ἀκουσθέντας: Niphon was evidently charged with «profanation of holy images»; cf. commentary on Letter 95, lines 35–36: τοῖς κατὰ τῶν ἁγίων εἰκόνων λυττῶσιν.

23–24 τῶν γὰρ λίαν βαρέων τὰ ἀκουσθέντα: Cf. Letter 95, lines 28–29: τὰ πρὸς τοῦ μοναχοῦ λαληθέντα, πολλὴν ἀπειλοῦντα τὴν βλάβην.

25–26 παρὰ τῆς ἐκ Θεοῦ βασιλείας σου: Athanasius is probably alluding not to the Emperor alone, but to the imperial tribunal, τὸ βασιλικὸν δικαστήριον or τὸ σέκρετον τῆς βασιλείας μου, which was reformed

89, 90

in 1296 by Andronicus II; cf. P. Lemerle, «Recherches sur les institutions judiciaires à l'époque des Paléologues. I, Le tribunal impérial», *Mélanges Henri Grégoire*, I (Brussels, 1949), 371. It would be more usual for the case of Niphon, as an ecclesiastic, to be tried by the patriarchal tribunal; and indeed, in 1314 Niphon was brought before the synod on charges of simony and sacrilege.

26 τοῦ κατηγόρου: Probably the monk mentioned in Letter 95, lines 28–29.

26–27 καθ' οὗ ἡ κατηγορία: Niphon; cf. Letter 95, lines 37–38: ἢ τὸν κατηγορηθέντα ἀθῷον φανῆναι, ἢ τὸν κατήγορον ἀληθεύειν.

90.

Athanasius praises the Emperor for his zeal for restoring lost sheep to the fold. In this case Andronicus has apparently influenced the ὑφηγούμενος of a monastery, perhaps an Arsenite, to renounce his opposition to the official Church.

Laurent, *Regestes*, no. 1722

3–4 ὁ ... ὑφηγούμενος: This unusual term is not included in the basic works on monastic organization, e.g., Panagiotakou, Τὸ Δίκαιον τῶν Μοναχῶν, and de Meester, *De monachico statu*. I have been able to find the term used in only one other Byzantine text, a thirteenth-century act of the Athonite monastery of Kutlumus; cf. *Actes de Kutlumus*, ed. P. Lemerle (Paris, 1946), no. 2, lines 16 and 19. In this act ὑφηγούμενος is apparently a synonym of καθηγούμενος, since both terms are used to refer to Theophanes, abbot of the monastery of Alopou.

τῆς εὐαγοῦς ... λαύρας ἐν τῇ πέτρᾳ ἡδραιωμένης: Identification of the *lavra* mentioned in this passage presents several difficulties. It could be *the* Lavra on Mt. Athos, founded by an earlier St. Athanasius in 963. The πέτρα would thus be an allusion both to the «rock», upon which the Universal Church is founded (here Christ, rather than Peter), and, more specifically, to the rocky promontory of Athos on which the Lavra was built. In a letter addressed to the monks of the Lavra, Athanasius refers to the monastery as τῇ εὐαγεῖ λαύρᾳ τοῦ θεσπεσίου πατρὸς 'Αθανασίου (*Vat. Gr. 2219*, fol. 252r).

It is more likely, however, that Athanasius is playing on the word πέτρα and referring to a monastery with πέτρα, or a deriva-

tion thereof, in its name. We know, for example, a monastery of Petra which existed on Athos by 1335; cf. Callistus, *Homily on Orthodoxy, Patm. 366*, 414ᵛ–415ʳ, quoted by J. Meyendorff, *Introduction à l'étude de Grégoire Palamas* (Paris, 1959), 61 and note 88. The most plausible candidate is the Constantinopolitan monastery τοῦ Προδρόμου ἐν τῇ Πέτρᾳ, which is frequently documented in the thirteenth and fourteenth centuries (Janin, *Géographie ecclésiastique*, 435–43). The term *lavra* usually was applied to a type of monastic foundation in an isolated area in which monks lived like hermits in separate cells, but were supervised by an abbot at a central monastery; cf. Du Cange, *Glossarium ad scriptores mediae et infimae Graecitatis*, I, col. 792, and de Meester, *De monachico statu*, 7, 72, 100. Apparently, on occasion, however, the term λαύρα was used interchangeably with μονή; cf. Pachymeres, *Hist.*, II, 203, where the monastery of St. Michael at Anaplous near Constantinople is called ἡ τῆς Λαύρας τοῦ ἀρχιστρατήγου μονή.

Cf. also *ActaSS Novembris*, 4 (1925), col. 662F, where the ninth-century monastery of St. Caesarius in Rome is referred to as Καισαρίου λαύρας (I am indebted to Professor Ihor Ševčenko for this reference). See the remarks of Laurent (*Regestes*, 506), who also opts for the monastery of Petra in the capital.

12–13 τοῦ ψηλαφητοῦ σκότους τῶν σχιζομένων ἁρπάζειν Ἰσραηλίτας: Andronicus has been appointed by God to rescue the Byzantines, the new Israelites, from the darkness of schismatics (Arsenites?).

13–14 καθά που καὶ Μωσέα: For another passage in which Athanasius compares Andronicus with Moses, cf. Letter 94, lines 10–11. Cf. also Philetos Synadenos, *Ep.* 9, 14–15 (ed. Darrouzès, *Epistoliers byzantins*, 256), and Hunger, *Prooimion*, 201–2.

91.

Athanasius reiterates the canonical ruling that monks should not leave their monasteries. (This letter should perhaps be connected with another of Athanasius' letters about a runaway Athonite monk, *Vat. Gr. 2219*, fols. 269ᵛ–272ᵛ = Laurent, *Regestes*, no. 1780.)

Laurent, *Regestes*, no. 1723

7–8 τῶν τῷ λαῷ παρανομουμένων ... ποιμένας: Cf. canon 39 of the Apostles (Rhalles–Potles, II, 54).

91–93

19 μὴ μεταβαίνειν τινὰ τῆς οἰκείας μονῆς: Cf. Gregoras, *Hist.*, I, 183, who recounts that Athanasius forbade monks to leave their monasteries except in cases of urgent necessity, and then only with the permission of their superior. See de Meester, *De monachico statu*, 393–98, on the question of monks leaving their monastery.

92.

Athanasius reminds the Emperor that he is his spiritual father, and therefore Andronicus should follow his advice at all times.

Laurent, *Regestes*, no. 1724

Date: perhaps toward the end of Athanasius' second patriarchate, when he was attempting to regain his weakening hold on the Emperor.

21 θημωνίαι: Note that the scribe has incorrectly placed the accent, which should be on the final syllable; cf. Liddell–Scott, *s.v.*

30–31 τὸ μετὰ Θεὸν ὁραθῆναι τῷ ὁμοφύλῳ θεούς: Cf. commentary on Letter 84, lines 6–7.

93.

Athanasius asks that Dermokaites be made head of the grain commission.

Laurent, *Regestes*, no. 1652

Date: *ca.* 1306–1307, the period of worst famine in Athanasius' second patriarchate; this letter is slightly earlier than Letters 73 and 100. Cf. remarks of Laurent, *Regestes*, 447.

2–3 ὥσπερ ἡλίου τὸ φέγγειν … τῶν πόλεων: For a similar comparison, see the chrysobull of John V Palaeologus, anno 1344, *Philotheu*, no. 8, ed. Regel, in *VizVrem*, 20 (1913), Supplement 1, p. 22, lines 1–4.

12 τῶν γεννηματικῶν: Here and in Letter 100, lines 4–5, Athanasius uses τὰ γεννηματικά as a synonym for the more usual τὰ γεννήματα, meaning «grain». I have not found this usage in the dictionaries or any other author. Compare, however, the use of the word γεννηματική in a chrysobull of John VII Palaeologus dated 1407: καὶ ταῦτα μὲν ἐφ᾽ ὅρῳ τῆς ἐμῆς ζωῆς λαμβανέτωσαν ἀκωλύτως, καὶ μεριζέσθω-

σαν ὥσπερ εἴπομεν τὴν δεκατίαν ἀπάσης γεννηματικῆς τῶν ζευγαρίων
μου κατασπορᾶς (*Actes de Xéropotamou*, 207, lines 24–25). The editor
Bompaire (p. 205) translates γεννηματικὴ ... κατασπορά as «le revenu
en nature tiré de l'ensemencement (céreals, légumes secs)».

12–13 ἀναθεωρεῖσθαι τὰ τῶν γεννηματικῶν καὶ τῶν ἄρτων εἰς δικαίαν ἐξώνησιν: Athanasius wants to have state control established over the
sale of grain and bread; such regulations existed in the tenth century
when the *Book of the Prefect* closely supervised the weight and price
of bread (chap. xviii, ed. Zepos, *Jus Graeco-Romanum*, II [1931], 388).

14 Δερμοκαΐτου τοῦ σεβαστοῦ: It is not possible to identify Dermokaites, as this was a fairly common name in the Middle and Late
Byzantine period. The name is found as early as the tenth century;
cf. Darrouzès, *Epistoliers byzantins*, 147–49, esp. note 55, and references in Laurent, *Regestes*, 447. A Michael Dermokaites, *pansebastos
sebastos*, is mentioned in a thirteenth-century (?) document in the
monastery of St. Paul on Mt. Latros, near Miletus. A tomb at Kariye
Cami (dated after 1330) contains the portrait of a woman whose
garment bears the monograms of the families of Dermokaites,
Asanes, and Palaeologus. Cf. Underwood, *The Kariye Djami*, I,
291–92, for these and other members of the Dermokaites family.
See also Papadopoulos, *Genealogie der Palaiologen*, notes 140, 141,
165. The only Dermokaites known from the reign of Andronicus II
is a correspondent of Gabras; cf. A. M. Zanetti and A. Bongiovanni,
Graeca d. Marci bibliotheca codicum manu scriptorum (Venice, 1740),
no. 440.

15–16 ἵνα καὶ ἔθει βασιλικῷ χρήσωμαι, «παρακαλῶ, παρακαλῶ, παρακαλῶ»:
cf. Letter 12, lines 29–30, and 41, line 32.

18–20 ὡς μικροῦ τὴν περιουσίαν 'Ρωμαίων ... εἰσενεχθῆναι: Athanasius
greatly resented the commercial supremacy of the Italians, who by
the Palaeologan period controlled the grain routes to Byzantium;
cf. G. Bratianu, «La question de l'approvisionnement de Constantinople à l'époque byzantine et ottomane», *Byzantion*, 5 (1929–30),
101. For comments on Athanasius' xenophobic attitude, see another
article by Bratianu, «Nouvelles contributions à l'étude de l'approvisionnement de Constantinople sous les Paléologues et les empereurs
ottomans», *Byzantion*, 6 (1931), 643–46.

21–22 τοσοῦτον ὑπερφρονεῖν ὡς ... σίτου λαμβάνειν: Cf. Letter 15, line 26,
where Athanasius complains that the Latins are guilty of φθορὰν
γυναικῶν.

94.

A petition to the Emperor requesting that he put an end to the reign of terror of a certain «Sicilian», almost certainly to be identified with the Catalan leader Roger de Flor; cf. Bănescu, «Le patriarche Athanase Iᵉʳ», 18–19; Laurent, *Regestes*, 395–96; and my commentary on line 14.

Laurent, *Regestes*, no. 1608

Date: early 1305; cf. commentary on Letter 68. Laurent prefers to place the letter in late 1304.

This letter presents several difficulties. An unusual number of emendations is required to make any grammatical sense of the text, and even with the aid of these corrections Athanasius' scheme of thought is somewhat difficult to follow.

2–3 ὅτι τῶν ἱερῶν ἀρετῶν ... τῇ προαιρέσει ἀπεχαρίσθησαν: For similar statements, cf. John Chrysostom, *Sermo IX in Gen.*, 5 (PG, 54, col. 628): οὐ φύσεως ἀλλὰ προαιρέσεως ἡ κακία καὶ ἡ ἀρετή, and Origen, *Comm. in Matt. 10:11* (PG, 13, col. 860C): οὐ γὰρ φύσις ἐν ἡμῖν αἰτία τῆς πονηρίας, ἀλλὰ προαίρεσις ἑκούσιος οὖσα κακοποιητική.

7–8 πρὸ τοῦ νόμου καὶ μετὰ νόμον: I do not understand the allusion here.

10–11 ἐν πολλοῖς ... τῷ θεόπτῃ καὶ θειοτάτῳ Μωσεῖ κοινωνεῖν: For the comparison of the Byzantine Emperor with Moses, cf. commentary on Letter 62, line 71.

14 τῆς ἀμειδοῦς δυναστείας τοῦ Σικελοῦ: ὁ Σικελός does not refer to an official named Sikelos, as Guilland assumed («La correspondance inédite d'Athanase», 138 note 1), but rather to a Catalan; cf. commentary on Letter 68, line 10, where Σικελούς also refers to the Catalan mercenaries hired by Andronicus II. The assumption that ὁ Σικελός is to be identified with the Catalan leader Roger de Flor is supported by a poem of Manuel Philes, which specifically refers to Roger as «Sicilian»; cf. his poem εἰς τὴν τοῦ Σικελιώτου Καίσαρος ἐκείνου σφαγὴν αὐθώρον (Miller, *Manuelis Philae carmina*, II, 288; title given by Martini, *Manuelis Philae carmina inedita*, 53). See commentary on Letter 68, lines 8–9, for discussion of Roger's cruel exactions from the Byzantine people.

18 τῆς προκειμένης φρικτῆς ἐκείνου ἐξόδου: An unconscious prophecy of Roger's murder at Gallipoli in May 1305 ?

23 ὦ γηραλέε ... : This phrase was evidently addressed by the angel to Roger, since the following sentence about greedy squandering must refer to Catalan extortion. Roger was a young man when he died, but Athanasius would have foreseen his death in old age.

31–32 εἰ σεπτοῖς ἐνεργεῖν ἐνεγράφη ... προστάγμασι: Cf. commentary on Letter 68, lines 8–9, where the verb ἐνεργεῖσθαι is also used.

95.

Athanasius urges the Emperor not to delay any longer an investigation of the charges of a certain monk against Niphon, metropolitan of Cyzicus; cf. Letter 89.

Laurent, *Regestes*, no. 1725

Date: *ca.* 1309 (?); cf. commentary on Letter 89.

3 τὸ εὐνομεῖν τῶν πολιτικῶν: After εὐνομεῖν a word like περισσότερον has apparently been omitted.

13 πνευματολέκτοις: πνευματόλεκτος is not found in the dictionaries, but, following the parallel of θεόλεκτος, it can either mean «uttered by the Spirit» or «chosen by the Spirit»; cf. Lampe, *Patristic Greek Lexicon*, 626.

17–18 τοῖς ἐπὶ τῆς Μωσέως καθέδρας κεκαθικόσιν ἡμῖν: A reference to the sluggish bishops who have neglected their duties. But if ecclesiastics fail to look after the Church, God has provided an emperor to supervise church affairs.

19 καταφρόνησιν: After καταφρόνησιν one would expect συνεπακολου-θῆσαι or the like.

21 ἐπιστημονάρχην: Cf. commentary on Letter 61, line 48.

28 τοῦ μοναχοῦ: This monk may well have been one of Athanasius' disciples who made accusations against Niphon in an effort to prevent him from succeeding to the patriarchate.

29–30 μηδὲ βραδύνῃ: The Emperor was apparently delaying Niphon's trial because he had decided on Niphon as a good compromise candidate for the patriarchate, and therefore opposed any investigation which might prove Niphon unsuited for the post.

95, 96

32 τῶν Ξυλωτῶν καὶ τῶν ἄλλως ὀρεγομένων ζητεῖν ἀφορμάς: Athanasius was worried that a postponement of Niphon's trial might
provide the Arsenites with grounds for accusation against himself.
The Arsenites evidently wanted a trial, so that Niphon could be
vindicated; if judgment were delayed, they might accuse Athanasius
of treating Niphon unfairly.

35–36 τοῖς κατὰ τῶν ἁγίων εἰκόνων λυττῶσιν: These charges of «defiling the
holy icons» do not mean that Niphon attacked the sacred images
themselves, but that he removed the gold and silver decorations
from icons. One of the charges made against Niphon in 1314 was
that he had stripped an image of the Virgin of thirty talents of
gold and silver (Choumnos, Ἔλεγχος κατὰ τοῦ ... Νίφωνος, 270).
Choumnos uses the same phrase as Athanasius to describe Niphon's
sacrilege: κατ᾽ εἰκόνος Χριστοῦ καὶ τῆς μητρὸς αὐτοῦ καὶ τῶν σεπτῶν
ὁμοίως εἰκόνων λυσσῶντα (ibid., 270).

37 τὸν κατηγορηθέντα: Niphon.

τὸν κατήγορον: The monk.

96.

Athanasius intervenes on behalf of the retinue of the recently deceased
Despot John Palaeologus, asking that its livelihood be supported by the
Emperor.

Laurent, Regestes, no. 1664

Date: 1307; see commentary on lines 3–4.

2 ἡμῶν καθημένων συνοδικῶς: A formulaic expression in patriarchal
acts; cf. Miklosich–Müller, I, 14 and 28.

ἄνδρες καὶ νεανίσκοι: Faithful retainers of the Despot John.

3–4 τὸν τοῦ ... Δεσπότου θάνατον: The Despot John died in Thessalonica in 1307, only four years after his marriage in 1303 to Irene,
the daughter of Nicephorus Choumnos; cf. Gregoras, Hist., I, 241.
Papadopoulos is a year off when he gives the dates of 1304 for John's
marriage and 1308 for his death (Genealogie der Palaiologen, 38,
no. 61); this is inconsistent with his correct date of March 1303 for
the death of the Augusta Theodora (op. cit., 4 and note 15), since

John was married very shortly after his grandmother's death (Pachymeres, *Hist.*, II, 379).

Ihor Ševčenko (in «Anepigraphos», 485–86), and, following him, Jean Verpeaux (in *Nicéphore Choumnos*, 44 and 48), give the correct dates of 1303 and 1307 for John's marriage and death, respectively. If, however, less than four full years passed from the time of John's marriage until his death, he must have died early in 1307, not late in that year as Verpeaux assumed; cf. *Nicéphore Choumnos*, 48.

10–11 δυστυχεστάτη ... νύμφη: Irene Choumnaina, who was tragically widowed at the age of 16; for her age in 1307, cf. Nicephorus Choumnos, Πρὸς τὴν ἑαυτοῦ θυγατέρα βασίλισσαν, ἐπὶ τῷ πάθει τῆς χηρείας, αὐτῆς ἑξκαιδέκατον ἀγούσης χρόνον, ed. Boissonade, in *Anecdota Graeca*, I, 293. Very soon after John's death, Irene entered the convent of Χριστὸς Φιλάνθρωπος; cf. Theodore Hyrtakenos, μονῳδία on the death of Nicephorus Choumnos, ed. Boissonade, *op. cit.*, I, 287. Irene adopted the monastic name of Eulogia (Ph. Meyer, «Bruchstücke zweier κτητορικὰ τυπικά», *BZ*, 4 [1895], 48), and contributed large sums of money towards the restoration of this double monastery; cf. Janin, *Géographie ecclésiastique*, 541–42, and V. Laurent, «Une princesse byzantine au cloître», *EO*, 29 (1930), 29–60.

δυστυχεστάτη ἤπερ εὐτυχεστάτη: Note Athanasius' pun on Irene's title as *basilissa*.

12 ἄωρον θάνατον: John was only about twenty years old when he died. His untimely death inspired Manuel Philes to write a monody (Miller, *Manuelis Philae carmina*, I, 388–414).

14–16 ὁρῶσαν δὲ νῦν καὶ τοὺς φιλοῦντας ἐκεῖνον ... ἀνάγκη λιμοῦ καὶ πενίας ἀποσπωμένους αὐτῆς: Laurent pointed out the paradox that Athanasius asked the Emperor to relieve the poverty of John's widow and retainers, when Irene was in fact a wealthy woman. He was forced to explain the apparent inconsistency by assuming that the Catalans destroyed the Choumnos property in the vicinity of Thessalonica («La direction spirituelle à Byzance», 83 note 6, and *Regestes*, 460). A careful perusal of Athanasius' letter, however, indicates that the Patriarch nowhere mentions Irene's poverty, but only refers to the distress of her husband's retainers.

Irene had received a large dowry upon her marriage to John (Pachymeres, *Hist.*, II, 287), and after his death she was still rich enough to give half her money to the poor and for the ransom of prisoners, and to use the other half to restore the monastery of Χριστὸς Φιλάνθρωπος; cf. Gregoras, *Hist.*, III, 238. Thus one may

96–98

conclude that Irene did not provide for these men because she felt it was the responsibility of the Emperor to support his son's retainers (especially since she was about to enter a convent), rather than because she did not have sufficient funds.

16–17 τοῖς εὑρισκομένοις ἀρχιερεῦσιν ἐνταῦθα: One must assume that the bishops were in Constantinople for the annual synod, since Athanasius had forced the bishops to leave the capital for their dioceses, and usually met with a synod composed of abbots (Pachymeres, *Hist.*, II, 643).

97.

Athanasius urges the Emperor to become reconciled to his wife Irene.

Laurent, *Regestes*, no. 1647

Date: Lent, before 1303, or 1306? Laurent prefers the latter date, on the assumption that Irene returned to the capital from Thessalonica in 1305; cf. *Regestes*, 442, and my commentary on Letter 56, lines 12–13.

ad apparatum 1: οὐ συνέρχεται πρὸς αὐτήν: Gregoras records that Andronicus loved his wife passionately during the first years of their marriage, but Irene's constant nagging about the destiny of her sons turned him against her so that he refused to share her bed (*Hist.*, I, 235).

3 τὴν σωφροσύνην: Athanasius may be discreetly urging Andronicus to give up his mistress. We know that the Emperor fathered at least two illegitimate children, Maria and Irene (Papadopoulos, *Genealogie der Palaiologen*, nos. 66 and 67).

8–9 ὁ τῶν ἱερῶν νηστειῶν καιρός: Athanasius suggests that Andronicus make a special effort during the Lenten season to effect a reconciliation with his wife.

98.

Athanasius suggests an immediate conference with Andronicus to discuss his marital problems.

Laurent, *Regestes*, no. 1648

Date: before 1303 or *ca.* 1306 ? Cf. commentary on Letter 97.

15 ἐν τῇ Χώρᾳ: Athanasius often used the Chora monastery for conferences; cf. Letter 23, in which he asks his bishops to meet him there.

15–16 ἐν τῷ τῶν ἁγίων πάντων ναῷ: A church built by Leo VI to the east of the church of the Holy Apostles; cf. Janin, *Géographie ecclésiastique*, 403–4. The church was severely damaged in the earthquake of June 1296; cf. Pachymeres, *Hist.*, II, 234. Athanasius' Letter indicates that the church must have been at least partially repaired by the early fourteenth century. By 1391 the church was totally abandoned, since John V Palaeologus quarried the ruins of the church to strengthen fortifications in the vicinity of the Golden Gate; cf. Ducas, *Hist.*, 47.

99.

Athanasius complains once more that the Emperor ignores his petitions.

Laurent, *Regestes*, no. 1726

6 τοῦ δεξιοῦ δεξιώτερον: I cannot find any source for this phrase which would appear to be proverbial.

18–19 εἰ δὲ μὴ αἵρεσις ἡ φιλανθρωπία ... ὄφλημα: An alternative interpretation of this passage would be to emend ἡ to ἤ, and translate, «But if it is not *parti-pris* or philanthropy and mercy toward the needy ⟨that moves me⟩, but rather necessity and the indispensable obligation...».

22–23 τὸ τοῦ Θεοῦ καὶ Πατρὸς (ὅ,τι ποτέ ἐστι) πρόσωπον: Chrysostom interprets this phrase from Matthew as meaning that the angels have access to God, can stand in His presence, and are held in honor; cf. *In Matt. Homil. LIX* (PG, 58, col. 579): ὅταν δὲ εἴπῃ, Τὸ πρόσωπον τοῦ Πατρός μου, οὐδὲν ἕτερον ἢ τὴν πλείονα παῤῥησίαν λέγει, καὶ τὴν πολλὴν τιμήν.

100.

Athanasius thanks the Emperor for setting up controls on bakers and the grain market, and suggests that two demarchs, Antiocheites and Ploummes, be selected to assist Dermokaites on the grain commission.

100

Laurent, *Regestes*, no. 1727

Date: *ca.* 1306–1307; later than Letter 93.

3–4 ἀναθεωρεῖσθαι τοὺς ἀρτοπώλους ... πιπράσκουσι: Athanasius thanks the Emperor for establishing regulations for bakers, such as had existed in the tenth century; cf. *Book of the Prefect*, chap. xviii, ed. Zepos, *Jus Graeco-Romanum*, II, 388. The Emperor has acted upon Athanasius' suggestion in Letter 93, lines 12–13, ἀναθεωρεῖσθαι τὰ τῶν γεννηματικῶν καὶ τῶν ἄρτων εἰς δικαίαν ἐξώνησιν. Thus this letter gives evidence of one of the few occasions on which we can be sure that Athanasius' pleas to the Emperor were actually heeded. See the remarks of Peter Charanis on the breakdown of the guild system in late Byzantium in his article, «On the Social Structure and Economic Organization of the Byzantine Empire in the Thirteenth Century and Later», *Byzantinoslavica*, 12 (1951), 151–52.

5–6 ἵνα μὴ ἐξωνῶνται ταῦτα σιτῶναι καὶ σιτοκάπηλοι, ἀλλ' ὁ χρῄζων ἐκεῖνος πορίζηται: The new regulations provide for the abolition of middlemen, who raised the prices on grain and exploited the poor.

6 τὸ τὰ μέτρα τηρεῖσθαι: It was traditional in the Byzantine Empire for bishops to assume responsibility for the control of weights and measures in each city; cf. *Novel* 128, chap. 15, of Justinian (*CIC*, III, 641): κελεύομεν ... τὰ αὐτὰ μέτρα καὶ σταθμὰ ἐν τῇ ἁγιωτάτῃ ἑκάστης πόλεως ἐκκλησίᾳ φυλάττεσθαι.

17 τῶν δημάρχων: The demarchs appear only rarely in fourteenth-century texts. Pseudo-Kodinos mentions the banners of the demarchs in his description of the celebration of Christmas at the palace (*Traité des Offices*, 196 line 33), and Gregoras tells how Apokaukos used the demarchs to stir up the people against Kantakouzenos in 1341 (*Hist.*, II, 608). R. Guilland envisions the demarchs in late Byzantium as police officers entrusted with maintaining law and order in the various quarters of the city; cf. *Etudes byzantines* (Paris, 1959), 105.

Note that Athanasius speaks of δύο ἐκ τῶν δημάρχων, although in the ninth century there were only two demarchs at a time; cf. J. B. Bury, *The Imperial Administrative System in the Ninth Century* (London, 1911), 105, 138. Perhaps in the fourteenth century all the δημοκράται, i.e., the demarchs and their subordinates, were called δήμαρχοι.

Ἀντιοχείτης ... καὶ Πλουμμῆς: These two men are otherwise unknown.

20–23 καὶ τοῦτο ἡμῖν ... ἐκπληρούμενα: Even with two emendations, the sense is unclear. Another possible translation is: «And I also pray that the men ordered by you to serve may be granted all necessary provisions by your divine majesty, so that they may accomplish their duties in a manner pleasing to God and yourself».

101.

Letter to the Emperor, reminding him that more is expected of those to whom much has been given.

Laurent, *Regestes*, no. 1728

6 τοῦ εἰπόντος ἡμῶν αἰδουμένων: I have interpreted τοῦ εἰπόντος as the object of αἰδουμένων, even though Athanasius elsewhere uses αἰδεῖσθαι with the accusative; cf. Letter 115, line 128.

102.

Athanasius asks more fortunate citizens to take on the support of their poor brethren.

Laurent, *Regestes*, no. 1729

Date: perhaps during the winter of 1306–1307, when Constantinople was in the grip of an especially severe famine.

10–12 καὶ ταῦτα ἐγγράψαι ... πρόνοιαν: Athanasius evidently circularized this document, and had people write their names beside the names of those whom they agreed to support. The Patriarch planned to ask the Emperor to provide for any poor people whose names were not checked off on the list. For a similar patriarchal relief project, cf. Letter 22.

103.

Athanasius asks the Emperor to be merciful to Glykys (Mr. Sweet), who was deceived by a wicked associate (Drimys [Mr. Bitter]?) into joining a conspiracy against the empire.

103

3 ἡ τοῦ Γλυκέος αἰτία: Glykys, not to be confused with John Glykys, patriarch of Constantinople from 1315–1319, has ingeniously been identified as Drimys by Laurent, who interprets this letter as a plea for mercy on behalf of the unnamed accomplice who was deceived into joining the conspiracy; cf. *Regestes*, 428–32. He has, however, disregarded the difficulty that, upon careful reading, the villain of the letter appears not to be Glykys, but his associate (cf. Ševčenko, «Manuel Moschopulos», 149), and at the end the petition asks clemency specifically on behalf of Glykys.

I would therefore prefer to identify the unnamed conspirator (= X) of this letter with Drimys, since he bears a number of similarities to the traitor described in Letter 81 (cf. Ševčenko, *op. cit.*, 156–57 note 104):

1. both men received many benefits from the Emperor, but ungratefully turned against him; cf. 81, lines 33–43, and 103, lines 25–26, 31.

2. both are connected with the Lascarid party; Drimys claimed to be a descendant of the Lascarids (81, lines 49–50), and X's associate, Glykys, is a ward of John IV Lascaris (103, lines 41–44).

3. both disregarded sworn oaths (81, lines 45–47, and 103, line 13).

4. X has «mocked at divine things» (103, lines 15–16), Drimys pretended to be a priest (81, lines 27–30, 35–36).

5. Athanasius uses the same phrase to describe their treachery: (81, lines 149–51) πτέρναν ἐπᾶραι τετολμηκότων κατά τε τῆς ἐκκλησίας, κατά τε τῆς βασιλείας καὶ κατὰ τοῦ ὁμοφύλου παντός (103, lines 9–11): κἀκείνου καὶ τῶν ὁμοίως ἐκείνῳ ἐπᾶραι πτέρναν βεβουλημένων κατὰ τοῦ κράτους τῶν ὀρθοδόξων.

42–44 τοῦ ἀοιδίμου ... υἱοῦ τοῦ ... κυροῦ Θεοδώρου τοῦ Λάσκαρι: John IV Lascaris (1258–1261), son of Theodore II Lascaris (1254–1258). Athanasius' respectful allusion to John IV, who was deposed by Michael VIII Palaeologus in 1261, may have been a rare effort to appease the pro-Lascarid Arsenites; cf. Ševčenko, «Manuel Moschopulos», 156 note 102. John IV was still alive in 1284 (cf. Pachymeres, *Hist.*, II, 103–4; Gregoras, *Hist.*, I, 173), but was presumably dead by 1305, when the impostor Drimys claimed to be a descendant of the Lascarids; cf. Pachymeres, *Hist.*, II, 593, and Ševčenko, «Manuel Moschopulos», 156 note 93.

52 τοῦ ... ἐστερημένου φωτός: The unfortunate John IV Lascaris was blinded in 1261, at the age of 10, after Michael VIII's coronation in Constantinople.

104.

Athanasius reminds the Emperor of his obligation to protect the Church, especially from the danger of schism, and to lend secular support to the policies of the Church and its Patriarch.

Laurent, *Regestes*, no. 1730

Date: 1309 (?); see commentary *infra* on line 21.

2–12 τῆς ἀναγεννησάσης ... ἀγανάκτησιν: My translation has somewhat glossed over the irregular syntax of this very long sentence.

13–17 τῆς γὰρ ἐκκλησίας ... θεραπευόμενον τὸν Θεὸν: If the Church remains staunchly orthodox, then it will be possible to bring back to the fold all but the most stubborn schismatics (Arsenites?). Even if a few persist in their schism, the Church will suffer some harm, but will continue to flourish.

17–18 εἰ δέ γε κοινῶς ἐκκλίνει ... ἀπ᾽ αὐτῆς ὁ Θεός: If, on the other hand, the Church abandons a course pleasing to God (i.e., if She comes under the control of Arsenite sympathizers), God will abandon Her.

21 ὃ καὶ συνέβη μικροῦ σήμερον: Athanasius has evidently learned of the Emperor's plan to placate the Arsenites by replacing his unyielding Patriarch with a compromise candidate. His deposition appears to be imminent, and therefore this letter should probably be dated to 1309, since Athanasius was forced to resign in September of that year.

25–28 οὐ γὰρ διὰ τὴν βασιλείαν ... αὐξομένη ὑπὸ Θεοῦ: Athanasius' remarks should be interpreted as a warning to the Emperor that God will withdraw His support from the empire, if the Emperor allows the Church to be handed over to Arsenite sympathizers.

105.

Letter to two bishops, asking them to inform the Emperor that he is distressed about the metropolitan of Cyzicus.

Laurent, *Regestes*, no. 1731.

Date: As Laurent has commented, «le contenu de cette lettre est assez sibyllin». I would place it toward the end of the second patriarchate (*ca.*

105, 106

1309), since I interpret the letter as a threat of resignation by Athanasius, and a statement of his distress about the choice of Niphon as his successor. Laurent, on the other hand, sees in the letter an allusion to charges of simony made against Niphon earlier in Athanasius' patriarchate; cf. *Regestes*, 512–13.

4 τῶν οἰκονομούντων: The allusion is apparently to accommodators who wished to end the fifty-year Arsenite schism in the Orthodox Church by selecting a patriarch acceptable to the Arsenites. Niphon, the metropolitan of Cyzicus, appeared to be an ideal compromise candidate; he was not himself an Arsenite, but sympathized with their cause (cf. Laurent, «La fin du schisme arsénite», 251). Athanasius, who was in any case an adherent of the principle of ἀκρίβεια, maintaining an inflexible policy regardless of circumstances, was especially opposed to compromise with his arch-enemies the Arsenites.

9–11 οὐδὲ ἀνέχονται οἱ 'Ιουδαῖοι ... ὡς ἔθος ἀναφωνεῖν: Here Athanasius is apparently drawing a parallel between his enemies and the Jews; both groups oppose his celebration of the liturgy.

10 τὰ τῶν ἁγίων παθῶν τοῦ Κυρίου μου: If this is an allusion to the ceremonies of Holy Week, rather than an allusion to the liturgy in general, this letter may be dated to Eastertime.

13–16 εἰ οὖν μηδὲ λειτουργεῖν ... φροντίζειν τὰ ἑαυτῶν: Athanasius complains that he cannot please anyone. Certain people are proposing accommodation with the Arsenites, the Jews don't want him to celebrate at all, and the Uniates want him to join the Church of Rome and use the Roman ritual. Therefore he will stay in his monastery at Xerolophos (οἴκοι), and not even go to church, so that he will not be embarrassed by people asking him why he isn't celebrating mass. This sentence should probably be interpreted as a threat of resignation.

106.

If the Emperor does not punish the grain dealers, who are hoarding grain at a time of famine, Athanasius will excommunicate them.

Laurent, *Regestes*, no. 1606

Date: *ca.* September 1304, since Pachymeres describes this letter in his *History* (II, 461) immediately before his account of the events of September 29, 1304.

From the similarities in wording between Athanasius' letter and Pachymeres' summary, one may conclude that Pachymeres heard this letter read aloud in St. Sophia. Pachymeres informs us that Athanasius' threats accomplished nothing, and that his enemies were able to add a further piece to the incriminating dossier which they were collecting against the Patriarch.

107.

Athanasius urges the Emperor to curb the scandalous behavior of his son Constantine.

Laurent, *Regestes*, no. 1732

Date: after 1293, when Constantine was made despot; see *infra*, commentary on lines 5–6. In this letter Constantine is depicted as a young man, perhaps twenty years old, sowing his oats. Since he was born between 1277 and 1282 (see commentary *infra*), the letter should probably be dated to the period of Athanasius' first retirement, 1293–1303, or to early in his second patriarchate.

2 ἄνθρωπόν του: Note that here Athanasius lapses into a demotic form.

4–5 περὶ τῶν ἰδίων υἱῶν: Cf. Letter 36, line 2, where Athanasius rebukes Andronicus because he does not instruct his sons in ways pleasing to God. Gregoras comments that Athanasius did not hesitate to attack the Emperor's own relatives (*Hist.*, I, 182).

5–6 τοῦ Δεσπότου κυροῦ Κωνσταντίνου: Constantine, Andronicus' second son by his first wife Anne of Hungary, must have been born between 1277, the date of Michael IX's birth, and 1282, the date of Anne's death (Pachymeres, *Hist.*, I, 499). It is possible to determine with greater precision the date when Constantine was made Despot. Pachymeres comments (*Hist.*, II, 181) that at the time of Constantine's engagement to the daughter of George Muzalon, *ca.* 1293, he was not yet Despot, but he had received the title by the time of his marriage in 1294 (cf. Verpeaux, «Notes chronologiques», 169–70). Thus, his elevation must have taken place in late 1293 or in 1294; cf. Guilland, «Etudes sur l'histoire administrative de l'empire byzantin; le despote», *REB*, 17 (1959), 60, who dates the promotion to 1292.

Papadopoulos, confused perhaps by the fact that Constantine was made despot of Thessalonica and Athos in 1321 (Gregoras,

107–109

Hist., I, 354; Cantacuzenus, *Hist.*, I, 129), mistakenly concludes that Constantine was not made despot until 1320 (*Genealogie der Palaiologen*, 37).

7 τοῦ υἱοῦ τοῦ ἐπάρχου: This «son of the eparch» may be the son either of Hypertimos or Chalkeopoulos, two eparchs who served under Andronicus II (Pachymeres, *Hist.*, II, 517). On the office of eparch, who had lost his functions by the fourteenth century, see Bréhier, *Les institutions*, 187–92; Bury, *The Imperial Administrative System*, 69; and Ps.-Kodinos, *Traité des Offices*, 178 and 321.

108.

Athanasius intervenes in the case of a poor man who insulted a notable.

Laurent, *Regestes*, no. 1733

109.

Athanasius reminds the Emperor that it is not sufficient for schismatics merely to return to the fold, but they must also repent and change their former way of life.

Laurent, *Regestes*, no. 1734

Date: Laurent (*Regestes*, 514–15) connects this letter with the reconciliation of some Arsenites with the official Church, and suggests a date of autumn 1304 (after Andronicus' speech of September 29 to former schismatics—Pachymeres, *Hist.*, II, 461–75), or 1306, after the suppression of the Drimys conspiracy.

7–8 διὰ τὸ μὴ ἐκπεσεῖν ... ἐχώρισαν εἰς τὸ σχίζεσθαι: Athanasius' language here is similar to his attacks on bishops who stayed in the capital for their personal comfort and pleasure; cf. Letter 30, lines 12–14, and Letter 62, lines 31–32 and 39–41. When he accuses the bishops of schism, it is not clear whether he is referring to prelates like the Patriarchs of Alexandria and Antioch who refused to recognize him, or to bishops who disliked the rigid discipline imposed by the Patriarch and therefore joined the Arsenite faction which was already a focal point of resistance to Athanasius; cf. Laurent, «La fin du schisme arsénite», 242.

8–10 εἰ ἀξιοῦμεν αὐτούς ... εἰς τὸ βλάπτον γινόμεθα: Athanasius explains to the Emperor why he is taking a hard line with schismatics.

110.

Athanasius reiterates his constant refrain that the Byzantines are being defeated by the Turks as punishment for their sins. The only salvation for the empire lies in sincere repentance.

Laurent, *Regestes*, no. 1735

Date: late 1303 or 1304, if indeed the allusion in lines 4–5 is to the «tragedy of Anagni» of September 1303; cf. Laurent, *Regestes*, 515.

4–5 εἰ πάπαν ... τὰ δεινά: Laurent interprets this as a reference to the humiliation of Pope Boniface VIII at Anagni.

12 ἐν τῷ γένει ἡμῶν: For the meaning of the term γένος, cf. commentary on Letter 58, line 46.

14–15 οὐ μόνον τινῶν ἑκοντὶ ... ἀκόντων συνελαθέντων: An allusion to spontaneous and forced apostasy to Islam. For remarks on the Islamization of the inhabitants of Anatolia, see Vryonis, *Decline of Hellenism*, esp. 339–43 and 351–402.

29 τῷ εὐσεβήσαντι πρώτως ἐν βασιλεῦσι: Constantine the Great.

87–92 κἀντεῦθεν ὡς οἶμαι ... ποιεῖν ἀγαθόν: Athanasius praises the Emperor's confidence in the efficacy of prayer, but advises him to act as well to stamp out evil in the empire.

96 τοιοῦτον δοκῶ τὸ ἐγχείρημα, etc.: In this simile, the good doctor represents either God or the Patriarch (cf. God the Healer in Letter 104, line 17), the patient is the declining Byzantine empire, and the «specialist» in authority represents the Emperor Andronicus.

Mr. John Duffy has kindly informed me that the description of the treatment of pleurisy is not derived from a specific ancient medical authority, but must be based on Athanasius' general knowledge.

97 ἰητρῶν: Athanasius uses the Ionic form here because he is vaguely aware that some Greek medical authorities wrote in the Ionic dialect. Cf. Symeon Magister's use of the term ἰητρῶν παῖδας in Letter 68, line 5 (ed. Darrouzès, *Epistoliers byzantins*, 140).

110, 111

104 Εὐκλείδου: The Alexandrian mathematician who flourished *ca.* 300 B.C. Athanasius, whose secular education was woefully limited, thought Euclid was a medical writer!

Γαληνοῦ: The second-century A.D. physician and author of medical treatises. He was a native of Pergamum who later became court physician to Marcus Aurelius. Galen, along with Hippocrates, stands for «doctor par excellence» in rhetorical writings.

111.

Athanasius abdicates from the patriarchal throne, threatening with excommunication those people who forced his resignation.

Laurent, *Regestes*, no. 1557

Date: The letter is dated to the seventh indiction, i.e., September 1293 to August 1294. The date can, however, be further narrowed down to on or before October 16, 1293, the date of Athanasius' first resignation from the patriarchate.

1 παραίτησις τῆς πρώτης πατριαρχείας αὐτοῦ: According to this superscription, this should be the letter of resignation which Athanasius sent to the Emperor from the monastery of Kosmidion on October 16, 1293, after fleeing from the patriarchal offices under cover of night; cf. Pachymeres, *Hist.*, II, 175. However, the text of this letter of resignation, which is included in collections of Athanasius' correspondence and in both *Vitae*, is totally different from the short letter which Pachymeres cites as Athanasius' letter of resignation (*Hist.*, II, 175–76 = Laurent, *Regestes*, no. 1556), and instead closely resembles the middle section of the letter which Athanasius hid in St. Sophia (Pachymeres, *Hist.*, II, 170–71 = Laurent, *Regestes*, no. 1553). Apparently Athanasius drafted two versions of his letter of resignation in 1293, only one of which came to the attention of Pachymeres. Both versions were signed by the Patriarch, and it is impossible to ascertain which letter was actually sent to Andronicus, or whether perhaps both were submitted. Laurent suggests (*Regestes*, 344) that the short letter was deemed unsatisfactory, and that Athanasius was asked to write a second version, the one reproduced in this edition.

2 οἷς αὐτὸς οἶδε κρίμασι: A formulaic expression; cf. Letter 112, line 2, and Miklosich–Müller, II, 188.

23-24 καὶ τὸ λίθους κρατῆσαι βαλεῖν ἡμᾶς καὶ ἀναθεματίσαι: Athanasius was not exaggerating the hostility toward him; cf. Pachymeres, *Hist.*, II, 168: ἄλλοι δὲ καὶ λίθους ἔβαλον φανέντος ἐκείνου [i.e., τοῦ πατριάρχου].

46-47 τοῖς ῥηθεῖσιν ἐπιτιμίοις . . . οὓς ψευδῶς ὑποσύρουσι: Unlike the letter hidden in St. Sophia, which, in addition to those people who had slandered the Patriarch, also anathematized τὸν τοιούτοις παρασυρέντα, presumably the Emperor (Pachymeres, *Hist.*, II, 173), this letter avoids a specific accusation of the Emperor by threatening excommunication of *all those* who had been led astray by Athanasius' enemies.

112.

Athanasius submits his resignation from the patriarchate for the second time.

Laurent, *Regestes*, no. 1666

Date: September 1309, when Athanasius abdicated from his second patriarchate; cf. Laurent, «La chronologie des patriarches», 148.

3-4 ἀρχιερεῦσιν ὑμῖν: This letter of resignation was addressed to the synod.

9-10 στολαῖς ἱεραρχικαῖς καὶ ἱεραῖς εἰκόσι: Cf. Letter 66. Andronicus' generous gifts to the Church are also mentioned by Pachymeres, *Hist.*, II, 617.

13-14 τῷ μεγάλῳ . . . καὶ ἰσαποστόλῳ: The Emperor Constantine the Great. For Constantine as the spiritual father of Andronicus, cf. Letter 82, lines 76-77.

15 Σίλβεστρον: Bishop of Rome (314–335).

31 τὸν Ἰάκωβον: Cf. *Theoctisti Vita Ath.*, 37: Ἰάκωβος δ'ἦν ὁ τὸν κυκεῶνα τῆς κακίας ταύτης κεράσας τῷ πατριάρχῃ . . . ὃς καὶ πάλαι τῆς καθέδρας ἦν ἐρῶν τῆς βασιλευούσης, εἰ καὶ τοῦ σκοποῦ διήμαρτε πάμπαν ὁ δυστυχής, εἱρκτὴν ἀφεγγῆ ἀντὶ θρόνου κληρωσάμενος.
This Iakobos is probably to be identified with the Iakobos who was *protos* of Mt. Athos and lost the patriarchal election of 1289 to Athanasius; cf. Pachymeres, *Hist.*, II, 139. Ivan Dujčev also identifies

112, 113

the Iakobos who intrigued against Athanasius in 1309 with the Iakobos who was an unsuccessful candidate for the patriarchate in 1289; cf. «Die letzten Jahre des Erzbischofs Iakobos von Achrida», *BZ*, 42 (1943–49), 377–83, esp. 380 ff.

33–37 κατὰ τῆς ἱερᾶς ἐκείνου θεανδρικῆς ... ζωηφόρου σταυροῦ: The conspirators placed under the Patriarch's footstool an icon depicting the Virgin, Christ, the Cross, and the Emperors Andronicus II and Michael IX; cf. Gregoras, *Hist.*, I, 258–59, and Introduction, *supra*, p. xxx.

43–44 οὐδὲ αὐτὸ τὸ ὁρᾶν ἔχομεν: Athanasius' blindness forced him to dictate his correspondence. For the effect on his literary style, cf. my remarks in the Introduction, *supra*, p. xxx.

47 εἰς ἐρεύνης πνευματικῆς ἀναζήτησιν: Athanasius asks the synod and Emperor to confer on the selection of a successor to the patriarchate.

52 συγχωρήσεως: In contrast to his first abdication, Athanasius now asks the Lord to forgive his enemies.

113.

Athanasius informs the superintendent of petitions that, if he so desires, he will send him in a separate letter his views on the election of a new patriarch.

Laurent, *Regestes*, Appendix, no. 12

Date: at the time of Niphon's election as patriarch on May 9, 1310; Laurent, who gives a somewhat different interpretation to this letter and letter no. 114, prefers a date shortly after the 9th of May; cf. *Regestes*, 579.

1 τῷ ἐπὶ τῶν δεήσεων: There were two different superintendents of petitions, one for the patriarch and one for the emperor. The ἐπὶ τῶν δεήσεων of the patriarchate registered all petitions addressed to the Church and reported them to the patriarch; cf. H.-G. Beck, *Kirche und theologische Literatur im byzantinischen Reich*, 115, 118, and J. Darrouzès, *Recherches sur les ὀφφίκια de l'Eglise byzantine*, AOC, 11 (Paris, 1970), 378–79. The imperial ἐπὶ τῶν δεήσεων was responsible for collecting petitions to the emperor; cf. Ps.-Kodinos, *Traité des Offices*, 183, and R. Guilland, «Le maître des requêtes: ὁ ἐπὶ τῶν δεήσεων», *Byzantion*, 35 (1965), 97–100.

It is clearly the imperial ἐπὶ τῶν δεήσεων who is addressed in this letter, since he has a messenger on horseback at his disposal. Moreover, Athanasius would have known the patriarchal ἐπὶ τῶν δεήσεων too well to praise him for his «inherent culture and intelligence».

5 τὸν ἀδελφὸν: One of Athanasius' monks whom he used as a messenger.

114.

Athanasius has second thoughts on his abdication, and protests his deposition from the patriarchate, saying that the people should accept without hesitation the patriarch chosen by God. He requests that the Emperor convene a public tribunal where he may appeal his case.

Laurent, *Regestes*, Appendix, no. 12 (Laurent treats 113 and 114 as one letter)

Date: *ca.* May 9, 1310.

2–3 ἔδει τοῖς ... ἔχειν Χριστοῦ: I have translated this phrase as if it read ... ἔχουσι Χριστοῦ.

38–39 συγκαλουμένου παντὸς τοῦ τῆς ἐκκλησίας πληρώματος παρὰ τοῦ κρατοῦντος, etc.: Laurent, who interprets the letter as a protest against the election of Niphon as patriarch, sees this passage as a demand that the Emperor convene a public tribunal where charges against Niphon may be examined (*Regestes*, 579–80). I understand the letter rather as a final attempt by Athanasius to regain the throne, by having the question of his deposition reexamined. If indeed the accusations against him are justified, then he will abide by his abdication. If, however, the charges against him are libellous, then his false accusers should be brought to justice.

46–47 τὸν δίκαιον ... θεοσεβῆ: This passage, in which Athanasius likens his plight to that of Job, is further evidence that he wants a trial for himself, not Niphon. Surely he would not deign Niphon worthy of comparison with Job.

115.

Athanasius explains the circumstances of his two abdications from the patriarchal throne.

115

Laurent, *Regestes*, Appendix, no. 11

Date: shortly after September 1309.

2 ἐπὶ μόνῃ τετραετίᾳ: Athanasius' first patriarchate lasted from October 14, 1289, to October 16, 1293.

3 ἄνθρωπε τοῦ Θεοῦ: The addressee of this letter may be the superintendent of petitions, who was also addressed as ἄνθρωπε τοῦ Θεοῦ in Letter 113, lines 2–3.

3–5 τοῦ ἁγίου μου αὐτοκράτορος . . . περὶ τὴν Ἕω τὰς διατριβὰς ποιουμένῳ: Andronicus II was absent from the capital during most of Athanasius' first patriarchate, since he was campaigning against the Turks in Anatolia. Andronicus left for Nymphaeum in early 1290 (?) (Pachymeres, *Hist.*, II, 153) and returned to Constantinople on June 28, 1293; cf. Pachymeres, *Hist.*, II, 165; Verpeaux, «Notes chronologiques», 169; and Ševčenko, *Etudes*, 139 and note 3.

18 ὁ τοῦ ψεύδους πατήρ: Satan.

59–61 ἀπορραγέντων μου οὐ μόνον τῶν ἀδελφῶν . . . τῇ λαχούσῃ: Athanasius' battle with the bishops over the question of episcopal residence began in his first patriarchate; cf. Gregoras, *Hist.*, I, 182.

64 σύνοδον καθίσαντες τῆς ἐκκλησίας ἐντὸς καθ᾽ ἡμῶν: Cf. Pachymeres, *Hist.*, II, 166.

80–81 τῶν . . . Ξυλωτῶν: The Arsenites were anxious to secure Athanasius' deposition, so that a member of their faction might succeed to the patriarchal throne.

107–8 τοῦ τότε Γαγγρῶν: This bishop must be Phocas, who was metropolitan of Gangra from at least 1285 until 1294. He is known from his signature on three acts, the Tome of the Second Council of Blachernae in 1285 (Laurent, «Les signataires», 145 note 9), a synodal decision from Athanasius' first patriarchate (*Actes de Xéropotamou*, 97, no. 11), and an unpublished act of June 2, 1294 (*Laurent. Plut. V, 2*, fol. 386ᵛ; cf. *Actes de Xéropotamou*, 96).

111–12 εἰ μὲν ηὑρίσκοντο . . . τῶν ἀρχιερέων: A possible alternate translation would be: «If certain of the bishops were to be found who would join you in your resistance...».

121–22 αὕτη ... τῆς παραιτήσεως τῆς πρώτης καὶ τῆς δευτέρας ἡ συσκευὴ καὶ ὑπόθεσις: Apparently Athanasius only discusses the circumstances of his first abdication in this letter, and then says that his second resignation was a similar story, only worse.

123–25 οὐ δημοσίᾳ καὶ μόνον ... οἱ ἀρχιερεῖς ἐγκελεύονται: When Athanasius was forced to resign from the patriarchate in September 1309, he was also deprived of his priesthood and was not allowed to perform any priestly functions, either publicly or privately in his monastery at Xerolophos (οἴκοι); cf. lines 141–42, and Letter 105.

125 τῷ δυσσεβεῖ Γεωργίῳ: A reference to Gregory of Cyprus, patriarch of Constantinople 1283–1289, whose baptismal name was George. Athanasius called George «impious» because of his pro-Unionist sympathies during the reign of Michael VIII, even though he repudiated the policy of Union after Andronicus' accession to the throne in 1282. Even after George–Gregory was forced to resign from the patriarchate in 1289, he was allowed to retain his priesthood; cf. Pachymeres, *Hist.*, II, 121–22.

132 κύριν Ἰωσὴφ: Patriarch of Constantinople (1266–1275; 1282–1283). The Arsenites demanded the removal of Joseph's name from the diptychs because of his persecution of Arsenite supporters during his patriarchate.

INDICES

I: Proper Names

'Αββακούμ (bibl.) **69**:80.

'Αβραάμ (bibl.) **62**:74.

Ἁγία Σοφία **2**:ad app. 1; **18**:16; **45**:4; **46**:51–25; **52**:⟨9⟩, 16; **56**:14–15; ⟨**71**:4–5⟩; **106**:ad app. 1.

Ἁγίων Πάντων, church in Constantinople **98**:15.

Ἄγκυρα **61**:83.

⟨'Αδάμ⟩ (bibl.) ⟨**88**:17–18⟩.

⟨'Αθανάσιος, patriarch of Alexandria⟩ ⟨**7**:31⟩; **69**:ad app. 1, 63, 97–98, 110, 165–66.

'Αθανάσιος, patriarch of Constantinople **111**:48.

Ἄθως **46**:65.

Αἰγύπτιοι **69**:51; **94**:13. Cf. 'Αλεξανδρεῖς.

Αἴγυπτος **7**:31; **52**:4.

Αἰθίοψ **5**:13.

'Ακαπνίου, monastery in Thessalonica **16**:10–11, 14.

'Αλεξάνδρεια **69**:ad app. 1, 63, 97–98, 110, 142, 165–66.

'Αλεξανδρεῖς **69**:93, 113. Cf. Αἰγύπτιοι.

'Αμαλήκ (bibl.) **62**:71.

'Αμαληκῖται (Turks) **81**:165–66. Cf. 'Ισμαηλῖται.

'Ανατολή **30**:2; **35**:ad app. 1, 14; **37**:11, 21, 31.

⟨'Ανδρέας⟩, metropolitan of Heracleia ⟨**2**:75⟩.

'Ανέα **37**:11.

Ἄννας (bibl.) **2**:16.

'Αντιόχεια, Antioch-on-the-Orontes **69**:143.

'Αντιοχείτης, demarch of Constantinople **100**:17.

'Απάμεια **2**:75; **77**:23.

Ἄρειος **69**:47.

'Αρμένιοι **23**:6–7; **36**:6; **41**:16.

'Αρσενιανοί ⟨**19**:10⟩; **69**:51; ⟨**81**:87⟩ ⟨**95**:32⟩. Cf. Ξυλωταί.

'Αρσένιος, patriarch of Constantinople **2**:7; **69**:34.

⟨'Αρσένιος⟩, metropolitan of Pergamum ⟨**69**:165⟩; ⟨**81**:130⟩.

'Ασσύριοι (bibl.) **41**:2, 7.

'Αχαάβ (bibl.) **51**:5.

Ἄχαρ (bibl.) **3**:44.

'Αχυράους, city in Bithynia **81**:131.

Βελίαρ (bibl.) **75**:35.

Βεσελεήλ (bibl.) **66**:41.

Βήρα, monastery in Thrace **16**:16.

Βιτζύνη **25**:14; **81**:130.

Βρύσις, city in eastern Thrace **2**:75.

Καιάφας (bibl.) 2:16–17.
Κανδάκη (bibl.) 19:3.
Κατελάνοι, Catalans   46:65. Cf.
   Μογαβάροι, Σικελοί.
Κοιρανίδες, Greek magical treatise
   69:81.
Κοσμίδιον, monastery in Constanti-
   nople 69:155.
Κρήτη 28:13.
Κύζικος, city in theme of Opsikion
   95:ad app. 1;   105:ad app. 1;
   113:ad app. 1.
⟨Κύριλλος⟩, metropolitan of Sardis
   ⟨25:14–15⟩; ⟨69:158⟩; ⟨81:129⟩.
⟨Κύριλλος⟩, metropolitan of Tyre
   and patriarch of Antioch ⟨69:ad
   app. 1, 59, 97, 104, 110, 143⟩.
Κωκαλᾶς 41:13.
⟨Κωνσταντῖνος⟩, Constantine I, em-
   peror 82:76–77; 110:29.
Κωνσταντῖνος, the Despot Constan-
   tine Palaeologus 107:ad app. 1, 6.
Κωνσταντινούπολις 111:48–49.

Λατίνοι 17:15; 23:4; 93:19.
Λευΐτης (bibl.) 72:41.

⟨Μακάριος⟩, archbishop of Derkos
   81:132.
Μακεδονία, theme 35:15.
Μακρεμβολίτης 26:9.
Μαρία, Rita-Maria, wife of Michael
   IX Palaeologus 34:ad app. 1.
Μέγας ᾿Αγρός, monastery in Hel-
   lespont 69:138.
Μελένικον, city in Macedonia 2:75.
Μιχαήλ, Michael IX Palaeologus,
   co-emperor   13:ad app. 1; 33:ad
   app. 1; 35:15–16.
Μιχαίας (bibl.) 51:4; 69:9.
Μογαβάροι, Catalans 35:ad app. 1,
   19, 54; ⟨46:65⟩; ⟨68:10⟩. Cf.
   Κατελάνοι, Σικελοί.
Μύρα, city in Lycia 81:140.

Μωσῆς (bibl.)   ⟨62:65⟩;   66:15;
   69:15; 73:26; 90:14; 94:11; 95:17;
   110:68.
Μωϋσῆς (bibl.) 105:13

Ναζιραῖοι, monks 53:35.
Νέα ῾Ρώμη, Constantinople 111:49.
⟨Νικήφορος Μοσχόπουλος⟩, metro-
   politan of Crete ⟨28:13⟩.
⟨Νικήφορος Χοῦμνος⟩, Keeper of
   the Inkstand ⟨37:33–34⟩.
Νινευΐται (bibl.)   3:24, 39; 49:112;
   70:3; 110:145.
Νιτρία 69:142.
Νίφων, metropolitan of Cyzicus 89:
   ad app. 1; ⟨95:ad app. 1⟩; ⟨105:
   ad app. 1⟩; ⟨113:ad app. 1⟩.
Νυμφαῖον 25:21.
Νῶε (bibl.) 110:128.

Ξιφιλῖνος 69:156.
Ξυλωταί, Arsenites 19:10; ⟨69:51⟩;
   81:87;   95:32;   115:81,   126. Cf.
   ᾿Αρσενιανοί.

῾Οδηγήτρια, monastery in Constanti-
   nople 69:59–60.
᾿Οζά (bibl.) 50:36.
Οἰναιώτης 63:1, 12.

Παξῆς, a Turk 51:2.
Παῦλος, apostle   ⟨19:4–5⟩;   42:28;
   81:175–76; 82:27; 84:64; 86:23;
   88:⟨13⟩, 29; 90:14; 98:19.
Παῦλος, a flute player 69:94.
Πέργαμον 69:165; 81:130.
Πέτρος, apostle 61:30; ⟨88:16⟩.
Πισίδια 61:83.
Πρωτεύς (Athanasius of Alexandria)
   7:31.

῾Ραιδεστός 81:133.
῾Ραψάκης (bibl.) 7:24, 27; 41:2.

II: Terms

ἀνάξιος, unworthy (Athanasius) 37:28; 60:33; 112:69.

ἀναστάσιμος (ἡμέρα), Day of Resurrection, Easter Day 62:6; 97:10.

ἀνατολή, the East 30:2; 35:ad app. 1, 14; 37:11, 21, 31.

ἀναφέρω, make a report, recommend, petition 3:64; 12:17; 14:ad app. 1; 15:ad app. 1, 27, 28, 33; 17:29, 56, 60, 66, 71–72, 74; 18:21, 23; 22:2; 24:22; 25:2; 27:6; 28:2, 3; 35:ad app. 1, 8, 53; 41:27, 45; 44:12, 15; 49:ad app. 1, 29, 43; 58:ad app. 1, 18, 27, 47; 60:44; 62:21; 73:4, 15; 76:28, 38; 77:35; 80:ad app. 1; 84:11; 86:8, 27, 32; 87:35; 89:24; 90:3; 96:31–32; 97:2; 99:ad app. 1, 11–12, 14–15, 17; 102:12; to reduce (?) 78:20; to relate, proclaim 50:11; 78:17; to offer 66:24; to mention 69:158.

ἀναφορά, report 12:18; 22:9; 58:2, 22; 72:6; 73:2, 13; 86:17; 93:9; 96:31; 109:6.

ἄνθρωπος, agent 17:72; man-servant 107:2; ἄ. τοῦ Θεοῦ 113:2–3; 115:3.

ἀντίδικος: ὁ τῆς ζωῆς ἀ., the adversary of life 60:16.

ἀπόστολος: οἱ ἀπόστολοι 14:22; 110:67; 111:29; 112:74; οἱ ἱεροὶ ἀπ., Peter and Paul 88:ad app. 1, 4.

ἀρχιεπίσκοπος, archbishop 81:131, 132; 111:48.

ἀρχιερεύς, bishop 2:10, 15, 27, 39; 3:60; 7:43; 10:7; 14:19; 15:ad app. 1, 10, 31; 16:ad app. 1, 2; 21:4; 23:ad app. 1, 2; 24:23; 25:ad app. 1, 3; 26:2; 28:ad app. 1, 4, 16; 30:ad app. 1, 5; 32:ad app. 1, 6; 51:9; 61:ad app. 1; 62:ad app. 1, 31; 69:156; 79:ad app. 1, 4; 81:129; 82:86; 91:5; 96:16; 103:40; 105:ad app. 1; 111:44; 112:3, 57; 114:3, 53; 115:12, 84, 99, 107, 112, 124; high-priest (Eli) 3:45.

ἀρχιερωσύνη, office of archbishop 112:40.

ἀρχιποίμην, Chief Shepherd (Christ) 3:62; 31:8; 61:93.

ἄρχων, official, noble 3:ad app. 1, 8; 8:ad app. 1; 22:8, 9; 47:4; 49:72; 52:7; 61:92; 66:69; 70:ad app. 1, 9; 73:3; 81:80; 102:ad app. 1; 110:ad app. 1; 115:93, 105; ruler 72:41; 111:7.

ἄσκησις, asceticism 83:29.

ἀσκητής, ascetic 83:56.

αὐγοῦστα, empress 56:13; 86:19.

αὐτοαλήθεια, the Very Truth (God) 45:6; 47:14; 61:29, 57; 66:74; 115:77.

αὐτοκράτωρ, emperor 1:1, 4, 40; 2:1; 3:1, 4, 14, 50; 4:1; 5:1, 3; 6:1; 7:1; 9:1; 10:1; 11:1; 12:1; 14:1; 15:1; 16:1; 17:1; 18:1; 19:1; 21:1; 22:1; 23:10; 24:1; 25:1; 27:1; 28:1; 29:1; 30:1; 32:1; 34:8; 35:1; 36:1; 37:1; 38:1; 39:1; 40:1; 41:1; 42:1; 43:1, 33; 44:1; 45:1; 46:1; 47:1; 48:1; 49:1; 50:1; 51:1; 52:2; 54:1; 55:1; 56:1; 57:1; 59:1; 60:1; 61:1; 62:1; 63:1; 64:1; 65:1; 66:1, 53; 67:1; 68:1; 69:1; 70:19; 71:1; 72:1; 73:1; 74:1; 76:1, 28–29; 77:1; 78:1; 79:1; 80:1; 81:1, 11, 38, 48, 170; 82:1; 84:1; 85:1; 86:1; 87:1; 88:1; 89:1; 90:1; 92:1; 93:1; 94:1; 95:1; 96:1; 97:1; 98:1; 99:1; 100:1; 101:1; 102:12; 103:1; 104:1; 106:1; 107:1; 108:1; 109:1; 110:1; 112:6, 12, 44; 113:3, 5; 115:3, 19, 58.

αὐτόπτης: αὐ. Χριστοῦ, witnesses of Christ, the apostles 1:7.
ἀφορίζω, excommunicate 2:48.
ἀφορισμός, excommunication 2:48; 81:143–44, 146; 94:22; 106:18; 111:35.

βάπτισμα, baptism 1:37; 33:ad app. 1, 21; 56:5; 88:8; 104:2.
βάρβαρος, barbarian 1:13 (of Turks); 84:44 (of Franks).
βασιλεία: ἡ ἐκ Θεοῦ β. σου, your divine majesty 2:53; 3:63–64; 4:7; 5:25; 6:13–14; 7:5, 10, 15–16, 19–20; 7:39–40, 78; 9:2, 9–10; 10:2; 11:4, 6, 13–14, 21–22, 25; 15:12–13, 74; 15:3, 6, 21–22, 34; 16:2; 17:26–27, 33–34, 47, 95–96; 18:20–21; 21:17; 22:2; 24:4–5, 10, 22; 25:2; 27:2; 28:2; 29:7, 17–18; 32:3–4; 35:3–4; 38:18; 41:44; 43:44; 44:13, 20, 42; 46:23–24, 63–64; 49:16–17, 114; 50:8, 16; 51:11; 52:13; 53:33; 54:3–4; 55:18–19; 56:10–11; 58:13–14, 47, 49; 59:5–6, 17–18, 64; 60:5, 62–63, 71, 80; 61:18, 33–34; 62:9–10, 14–15; 63:8–9; 64:17–18; 65:15; 66:33–34; 67:2; 68:13, 27–28; 69:182; 71:9–10; 72:5–6, 10–11, 26, 42, 43–44; 73:12; 75:6; 76:2; 77:34, 35–36; 79:2, 16; 80:5, 20–21, 38; 82:93; 84:12–13, 14–15, 33–34, 87, 93; 85:7, 13–14, 17–18; 86:2, 32; 87:20–21; 88:5, 21, 34; 89:25–26; 90:6, 23–24; 92:5–6, 9, 14–15, 36; 93:8, 16, 23–24; 94:10, 13–14; 96:7, 11–12, 18, 22, 30–31, 33; 98:15, 21–22; 99:3; 100:2–3, 9, 11, 19, 21; 103:44, 53–54; 104:4, 6, 10, 23, 31, 33; 106:3, 16; 107:5; 108:6, 8; 109:2–3; ἡ ἐκ Θεοῦ β. ὑμῶν 13:23–24; 78:43; ἡ πρὸς Θεοῦ β.

ὑμῶν 78:2; ἡ β. ὑμῶν 75:33; ἡ βασιλεία σου, your majesty 2:24–25; 4:2, 13; 5:21; 7:74; 10:4; 11:9; 12:16, 46–47; 13:2, 7, 19; 14:43, 64; 15:32; 16:13–14; 17:10, 28; 18:23, 23–24; 25:24; 27:5, 10; 33:45; 34:4, 16; 35:21, 25, 52; 39:2; 40:2; 41:28, 32–33; 46:51; 60:68; 63:11, 17; 75:16, 22; 104:29; 110:3; ἡ σὴ β. 33:3; 49:127; 57:2–3; 60:8; 66:93; empire 1:16, 45, 54; 3:56, 74, 75; 7:45; 11:8, 27; 14:47, 67; 17:58, 69, 71; 18:2, 11; 19:10–11; 24:25; 25:20; 29:10, 18; 33:21–22; 36:22; 41:22, 52, 53; 49:129; 57:2, 3; 60:4, 27, 36, 57; 61:44; 63:12; 65:4; 69:188, 208; 72:45, 47; 75:56; 77:38; 81:86, 150–51, 178; 84:2, 46, 59; 86:4; 101:10, 11; 103:ad app. 1; 104:24, 25, 26; 110:42, 45; kingship 49:96; 81:3; reign 57:8; 84:58; kingdom (of heaven) 1:56; 14:49; 33:25; 49:20; 60:30; 66:65, 96; 82:43; 83:42; 84:52; 88:24, 28; 92:28; 95:25–26; 110:33, 59; 112:20.
βασιλεύουσα, ἡ, Queen (of Cities), capital 115:20.
βασιλεύς, emperor (Andronicus II) 1:4; 2:2, 6, 56; 3:39; 5:17; 7:58; 10:5–6; 12:29, 41; 14:44; 15:16; 18:4–5; 30:2; 31:9; 33:8; 37:44; 41:7, 29; 42:11, 17; 46:2, 11, 28; 47:1; 58:8, 31; 60:34, 45–46, 68; 63:20; 66:27; 67:4, 16; 72:3; 73:2; 74:2; 75:8; 81:34; 82:2; 84:6, 10, 17, 80; 97:7; 98:3; 101:2; 103:31; 105:ad app. 1, 18; 110:3; 112:5; 115:71; (Michael IX) 13:ad app. 1; 33:ad app. 1, 10, 19; 35:15; (Theodore Lascaris) 103:43; (Hezekiah) 7:23;

41:4; (David) 58:22; (Senachereim) 41:2; (Christ) 33:4; 34:4; 36:19; 40:7; 52:9; 53:27; 69:109; 81:78; 90:9; 97:10; plural (gener.) 18:17, 30:31; 33:10; 38:14; 42:2; 46:42, 69, 85; 47:3–4, 42–43; 53:11; 69:188; 75:29; 76:33–34; 81:39–40; 82:76; 95:4; 98:12; 103:17; 110:ad app. 1, 10, 29, 139, 151–52; 112:18; (Andronicus and Michael) 23:12; 33:18; 52:7; 53:5; 69:70; 70:ad app. 1; 110:ad app. 1, 135, 150.

βασιλικόν, silver coin 41:19.

βασιλίς, Queen (of Cities), Constantinople 15:27; 48:7; 62:ad app. 1, 31–32; 69:87:79:7; 81:33; 93:10; 115:4.

βασίλισσα, empress 75:ad app. 1; 96:ad app. 1.

βῆμα, clergy 36:5; 81:27, 97.

βουλή, decree 22:ad app. 1, 8; council 112:58.

βοῦλλα, seal 111:50.

δέησις: ὁ ἐπὶ τῶν δεήσεων, superintendent of petitions 113:ad app. 1.

δένδρον ζωῆς, Tree of Life (Christian Church) 34:31, 36.

δέσποινα, title of empress 34:ad app. 1; 75:ad app. 1; 84:14, 71, 81, 82; 85:1, 3; 97:ad app. 1, 2; Mistress (epithet of Virgin) 45:2; 77:28; 110:150; 112:36.

δεσπότης, title (of emperor) 38:2; 110:2; (of Despot John Palaeologus) 52:14; 53:34; 70:20; 83:53; 84:ad app. 1, 13; 85:2, 4; 86:ad app. 1, 3; 96:ad app. 1, 4, 24; (of Despot Constantine Palaeologus) 107:ad app. 1, 6; plural (gener.) 47:43; (of Christ) 2:34; 36:19; 38:16; 47:42;

69:222; 96:26, 27; 99:20; 115:51, 142; bishop 62:50, 60; ruler 51:4; 78:44; master 84:9; 96:10.

δήμαρχος, demarch 100:ad app. 1, 17.

δημόσιον: οἱ τοῦ δημοσίου, civil magistrates 21:9–10; τὸ δημόσιον, the fisc 69:185; τὰ δημόσια, taxes 17:54; 46:17; public affairs 37:17; 111:9.

δημώδη, τά, public offices 87:18.

διάδημα, diadem 66:35; 77:14; 90:24.

διάζευξις, divorce 21:19.

διάκονος, deacon 19:2; 69:97.

διενεργεῖν, to be a state official, collect taxes 87:ad app. 1, 12, 27; manage, administer 83:3.

διευλύτωσις, dissolution (of marriage) 21:4.

δικαιοκρίτης, righteous judge (God) 65:18.

δικαίῳ, as an agent 69:138.

διοικητής: ὁ μέγας δ., great dioecete 26:ad app. 1, 2.

δομεστίκισσα: ἡ μεγάλη δ., wife of great domestic 69:145.

δομέστικος: οἱ μεγάλοι δ., great domestics (leaders of the choirs in St. Sophia) 52:16.

δοῦξ: ὁ μέγας δ., grand duke (Roger de Flor) 8:ad app. 1, 18; 9:ad app. 1, 5.

δυναστεία, pressure 59:38; tyranny 94:14.

δυνάστης, noble 25:5; ruler (Christ) 52:8.

δυτικός, western 81:135.

ἔγκλημα, accusation 111:53.

εἴδησις, notification 69:92; knowledge 77:25; 86:25.

ἐσχατιά, lowly position (of Athanasius) 58:9.

ἑταιρειάρχης, hetaeriarch 60:63.

εὐλύτωσις, dissolution (of marriage) 21:ad app. 1.

ἡγούμενος, abbot 52:9; 115:106.

θεοκήρυξ, herald of God (St. Paul) 81:176; 88:29.

θεοκρίτως, chosen by God 114:7.

θεοκτόνος, deicide, God-murdering (of Jews) 41:ad app. 1, 8.

θεοπάροχος, furnished by God 114:13–14, 29.

θεοπάτωρ, ancestor of God (David) 43:30.

θεοπειθής, God-persuading 37:8; 82:5.

θεόπτης, witness of God (Moses) 62:65; 94:10–11.

θεός, god (epithet of emperor) 84:7; 92:31.

θεοστεφής, god-crowned (of emperor) 5:3; 66:27; 81:ad app. 1, 48; 112:5.

θεοφρούρητος, God-guarded (of emperor and family) 34:42; 45:3.

θεόφρων, godly-minded 81:11.

θυσιαστήριον, sanctuary 2:33.

ἱερά, τά, sacred property 25:6.

ἱεράομαι, celebrate mass 115:123.

ἱεραρχία, hierarchy 66:48; 112:22.

ἱερεύς, priest 15:31; 37:4; 49:24; 52:9; 69:53, 92, 97; 70:ad app. 1; 72:41; 82:53; 112:48, 58; 115:11.

ἱερομόναχος, monk 115:109.

ἱερόν, τό, temple 47:31.

ἱεροσυλία, sacrilege 77:10, 13.

ἱερωσύνη, priesthood 3:47; 49:9; 81:3, 8, 36, 135; 104:25, 26; sanctity 69:207.

ἱκανός, capable 90:11; τὸ ἱ., a sufficient sum (of money) 8:19; 17:44.

ἰνδικτιών, indiction 42:3; 43:1; 111:49, 54.

ἰσαπόστολος, equal of the apostles (of Constantine) 112:14.

καθαίρεσις, deposition 2:16; 115:89–90, 101.

καθηγούμενος, abbot 61:17.

κανίκλειον: ὁ ἐπὶ τοῦ κ., the Keeper of the Inkstand 37:33–34.

κανίσκιον, present 20:ad app. 1.

κανονικός, canonical 69:91.

κανών, canon 2:42; 62:ad app. 1, 2; 77:ad app. 1, 6; 79:5; 91:ad app. 1, 3; 114:41; 115:130.

καστέλλιον, castle 37:25.

κατάκριτος, condemned (Athanasius) 4:6.

καταστολή, garb, garment 60:76; 74:25.

κατηγορία, charge, accusation 89:ad app. 1, 27; 115:122.

κατήγορος, plaintiff 89:26; 95:37.

κατηχουμενεῖα, τά, galleries 45:8, 10; 47:2; 66:ad app. 1, 68.

κέλλα, monastic cell 11:17.

κεραία, letter (?) 50:30.

κεφάλαιον, a tax 58:26.

κληρονομία: κ. Χριστοῦ, patrimony of Christ, Christians 1:6; 81:164.

κλῆρος, clergy 2:28; 69:142; 79:ad app. 1, 8; 111:40; 112:58; 115:106; heritage, patrimony 15:17; 82:7; allotment 62:31.

κληρουχία, patrimony, inheritance 115:8–9, 33.

κοίμησις, Dormition (of the Virgin) 45:2; 56:ad app. 1.

κοινοποιῶ, to defile, encroach on 50:34; 66:73.

κοινωνικός, communicant 34:27.

κοινωνός, communicant 9:ad app. 1, 6, 7.

κοσμοσωτήριος, savior of the world 26:13–14.

κράτιστος, powerful, mighty (of emperor) 3:50; 33:8; 34:7; 60:45; 73:2; 74:2; 81:169, 170; 102:11; 110:2; 113:3.

κράτος, power 5:19; 59:36; 62:79; 81:180; 110:42; state, empire 77:15; 81:65; 103:10; emperor 58:28; 68:13; 88:34; as form of address (emperor) 1:25; 3:2; 45:3; 46:9–10; 62:52; 74:9.

κρίσις, judgment, legal proceeding, trial 2:42; 3:52; 25:5, 6; 28:11; 36:8; 41:33; 49:70; 58:47; 60:67; 79:17; 82:4; 89:6; 105:2; 110:59; 114:40; 115:94, 114, 127, 137–38; κατὰ κρίσιν γεωργικήν, in accordance with agricultural law 27:6.

κριτήριον, tribunal 115:96.

κυβέρνησις, arrangement 34:10; guidance 34:19; discipline (?) 84:70; support 86:22; 102:ad app. 1, 9–10; 106:10; governing, government 7:6; 27:5; 90:11; 100:12.

κύριος, master 89:19; 107:3.

κύρις (gen. κυροῦ; acc. κύριν): ὁ κ. followed by first name: (emperors) Μιχαήλ 13:ad app. 1; 33:ad app. 1; 35:15; Θεόδωρος ὁ Λάσκαρις 103:43; (despots) Ἰωάννης 84:13; Κωνσταντῖνος 107:ad app. 1, 6; (patriarchs) Ἀρσένιος 2:7; 69:33; Γρηγόριος 2:8; Ἰωσήφ 2:7; 115:132; (bishops) Νίφων 89:ad app. 1; (others) Ἠλίας 16:14; 115:93.

λαγχάνω, happen to be here 81:128; ἡ λαχοῦσα (ἐπισκοπή), assigned

(diocese) 3:60; 14:19; 23:2; 25:ad app. 1, 3, 19; 28:ad app. 1, 5; 32:ad app. 1, 7; 30:ad app. 1; 48:2; 62:ad app. 1, 23; 79:ad app. 1, 5; 89:28; 115:61; ὁ λαχών, appointed 77:5, 14, 17; 83:2; 87:ad app. 1, 12; 95:12; 99:9; 110:6; 114:15.

λαϊκός, layman 83:58; 102:7; 115:11, 29, 102.

λαύρα, lavra 90:4.

λειτουργέω, celebrate mass 115:141.

λειτούργημα, service 61:8; 88:4.

λειτουργός, minister 111:44.

λεπτόν, small coin, "cent" 26:17.

λιτή, prayerful procession 1:49; 30:21; 32:10; 62:49; 69:175; prayer 81:179.

λουτρός: θεῖος λ., holy baptism 103:28.

λύσις, absolution 2:54.

μαρτυρία, testimony 63:2, 6.

μεγαλόπολις, (Jerusalem) 7:23; (Constantinople) 30:28–29; 43:38; 69:92; 71:4.

μεγαλοφωνότατος, great-voiced (Isaiah) 17:62; 19:3; 112:67.

μεγαλοψυχία, magnanimity 100:13.

μεγαλόψυχος, generous, magnanimous (of emperor) 82:7; 84:80.

μέγας, great (emperor) 12:29.

μέδιμνος, measure of grain 87:36.

μήνυμα, summons 115:113.

μητρόπολις, city 62:68.

μισοπόνηρος, enemy of evil (emperor) 7:64; 18:5; 94:32.

μονάζων, monk 37:3; 70:1, 15; 77:30; 83:58–59; 102:7; 112:48–49, 58–59; 115:12, 29.

μονάζουσα, nun 36:11; 69:95; 111:20.

μοναρχία, rule 110:32.

μοναστήριον, monastery 27:2; 91:22.

μοναχός, monk 2:28; 11:18; 15:31;
16:4; 19:13; 36:11–12; 69:95,
143; 73:5; 77:36; 91:ad app. 1,
21; 95:ad app. 1, 28; 111:19.

μονή, monastery 69:61, 64, 129,
138, 184; 77:27, 28, 98; 83:ad
app. 1, 9, 13, 48, 57; 91:ad app. 1,
19, 21, 25.

μονύδριον, monastery 77:3, 24.

μορτάζομαι, pay rent 27:8.

μορτή, rent 27:7–8, 9.

ναός, church 15:26; 43:39; 44:28;
47:9; 49:34, 38, 43, 46; 66:ad
app. 1, 2, 4, 66, 68, 70, 71; 77:ad
app. 1, 3; 87:10; 98:16.

νηστεία, fastday, fasting 42:3;
43:8, 42; 70:5; 97:8–9.

νόμισμα, gold coin 18:13.

νόμος, law 28:10; 46:22; 50:4;
59:18; 62:ad app. 1, 2, 10, 12, 13,
19, 35, 62; 69:30; 75:28; 81:170;
82:56; 84:4; 88:19; 94:8; 101:7;
110:24, 26, 56, 133; 111:37; 115:7,
36; rule (of God) 41:40; custom
58:26.

ὀβολός, obol 62:51; 101:16.

οἰκονομέω, follow the principle of
accommodation 69:28; 105:4, 6;
control 73:4; 105:2.

οἰκονομία, accommodation 25:21;
34:6; 69:88, 101; 73:21; manifestation (of Christ) 34:34; arrangement 56:29; 86:ad app. 1,
13.

οἰκονόμος, steward 78:2.

οἰκουμένη, world 2:15; 79:18.

ὀρεινόμος, forester 78:42.

ὀφφίκιον, official position 79:ad
app. 1, 13.

παλάτιον, palace 22:10; 108:ad
app. 1.

παμμέδων, Ruler of All (God) 44:3;
56:7; 74:26; 100:8.

πανάχραντος, immaculate (Virgin)
112:35–36.

πανευσεβέστατος, most pious (of
empress Irene) 86:18.

πανευτυχέστατος, most fortunate (of
Despot John) 53:34–35; 70:20;
85:2, 4; 86:3; 96:3–4, 24.

πανήγυρις, celebration, festival
47:9, 40; 56:21; 88:6; time of
rejoicing (i.e., Christian life)
33:23.

παντέφορος, who oversees all things
(God) 80:41.

πανυπέραγνος, most holy (Virgin)
45:2.

πάπας, priest (?) 2:5, 20; Pope
110:5.

παραδυναστεύοντες, authorities 3:63

παραίτησις, resignation 2:51, 52–53;
111:1; 112:1; 114:43; 115:ad
app. 1, 90, 95, 108, 114, 121.

παραιτοῦμαι, abdicate, resign 2:31;
111:40; 112:40; 114:22; 115:118.

παρακαταθήκη, ward 103:42.

πατριαρχεία, patriarchate 58:3;
111:1; 112:1.

πατριαρχεῖον, patriarchate 2:ad
app. 1.

πατριαρχεύω, to be patriarch 2:7;
25:17–18; 30:23; 31:9; 115:66.

πατριαρχέω, be patriarch 112:11.

πατριάρχης (of Constantinople) Athanasius 2:22, 46–47; 4:ad app. 1;
11:ad app. 1; 18:25; 69:99; 77:25;
78:ad app. 1; 81:ad app. 1; 105:ad
app. 1; 108:ad app. 1; 111:49;
Arsenius 69:34; Joseph 115:131;
Niphon 113:ad app. 1; plural
(gener.) 2:12; 94:21 (?).

πατριαρχικός, patriarchal 77:23;
111:50.

περίσσεια, surplus land 27:7.

συλλειτουργός, fellow minister
115:60, 72, 106.
συναγωγή, congregation (of Jews)
41:8; (of Armenians) 41:17.
σύναξις, service of worship 62:42.
συνοδικόν, liturgical text 64:ad
app. 1.
συνοδικός, of the synod 69:88; 91:3.
συνοδικῶς, in synod 16:6; 77:22;
89:3; 96:2; 99:2.
σύνοδος, synod of bishops 25:17;
31:5; 69:99; 81:129, 148–49, 168;
91:15; 115:64.
συνοικέσιον, marriage 21:ad app. 1,
3.
σύστασις, testimony 21:5; protection 28:6; 69:35; 77:7;
82:ad app. 1; 104:ad app. 1, 7, 30.
σχίζομαι, be in schism 69:44;
90:13; 109:ad app. 1, 8; 111:3;
115:133.
σχίσμα, schism 16:ad app. 1, 3–4;
34:35.

ταινία, diadem 106:6.
ταλαίπωρος, wretched (Athanasius)
4:11; 37:42; 78:29.
τριωβολιμαῖος, worthless (Athanasius) 60:46.
τύπος, representation 112:36; model
114:2.

υἱός: ὁ. τῆς ἐκκλησίας, son of the
Church (emperor) 18:10; 44:16–
17; 45:7; 49:39; 79:15–16; ὁ.
εὐλογίας, son of blessing 64:4.
ὑπεράγαθος, transcendently good
(Christ) 39:4.
ὑπέρπυρον, gold coin 16:16.
ὑπέρτιμος, most honorable (of archbishop) 81:129, 130, 131.
ὑπόθεσις, case (for trial) 16:4–5;
99:ad app. 1, 2; 115:122; matter
24:ad app. 1; 60:64; 65:5.

ὑπόμνησις, notification 28:15.
ὑπόστασις, property 80:12.
ὑφηγούμενος, abbot 90:3–4.
ὑψιμέδων, Ruler on High (God)
43:43.
ὕψος, lofty position (of emperor)
1:16–17; 7:5; 17:67–68; 58:9–10;
63:9.

φιλάγαθος, friend of virtue (emperor) 7:64.
φιλανθρωπία, love of mankind 99:18.
φιλάνθρωπος, lover of mankind (God)
14:63; 35:25; 69:11; 89:20–21;
112:52–53; (emperor) 60:46;
90:18.
φιλεύσπλαγχνος, merciful (Christ)
39:4–5.
φιλοδίκαιος, lover of justice (emperor)
18:5; 115:21.
φιλοθεΐα, love of God 33:11; 45:3;
69:136–37; 81:38.
φιλόθεος, lover of God (emperor)
2:55–56; 44:44; 56:10; 71:10;
115:21; (Christians) 83:19.
φιλοπάτωρ, loving one's father (of
Michael IX) 33:9.
φιλότεκνος, loving one's children
(of Andronicus II) 33:8; 73:19;
84:79.
φιλόχριστος, lover of Christ (emperor)
10:5; 12:30; 72:3; 81:114.
φόρος, payment 68:24.
φυλακή, jail, imprisonment 41:15;
60:49.
φυλάσσω: ὁ φυλάσσων τὰς πύλας,
guardian of the gates 17:42–43.
φωστήρ: ὁ φ. τῆς οἰκουμένης (John
Chrysostom) 2:15.

χαρτοφύλαξ, chartophylax (of Akapniou) 16:10.
χειροτονέω, ordain 69:86, 92–93;
115:102.

χηρεύω, be bereft of a bishop (of diocese) 48:19.
χοραύλης, flutist 69:94.
χριστός: χ. τοῦ Κυρίου, anointed of the Lord (of emperor) 1:4; 12:32–33; 81:71.
Χριστούγεννα, τά, Christmas 44:1.
χρυσοβούλλειος, pertaining to a chrysobull 62:58.

χρυσόβουλλον, chrysobull 27:ad app. 1, 4.

ψαλτῳδός, psalm-chanter 52:17.
ψῆφος, vote 25:9; 48:14; 59:12; 69:88; 113:ad app. 1, 6, 7, 10, 17, 22, ad app. 26.

III: Vocabulary

ἀβασάνιστος, unqualified 48:20–21.
ἀβλεπτέω, disregard 49:26.
ἀβροδίαιτον, luxurious diet 14:21.
ἀγαθοπρεπής, befitting the good 81:2.
ἀγερωχία, haughtiness 93:21.
ἀγήρως, ageless 33:26.
ἀδιάδοχος, eternal 95:26.
ἀδιάφορος, unconcerned 83:56.
ἀδόκιμος, inexperienced 83:58.
ἀζήμιος, without suffering any losses 77:36.
ἀζημίως, without payment of damages 21:18–19; without punishment 60:49.
ἀθεεί, without the aid of God 81:101; 83:13.
ἄθεος, godless, impious, pagan 1:12; 51:21; 81:70, 126, 127, 134, 163, 165; 87:2, 21; 110:13, 19; 111:34.
ἀθεότης, impiety 94:17.
ἀθήρα, gruel 78:ad app. 1, 39.
αἰγιαλός, seashore 43:40.
αἱμοβόρος, bloodthirsty (of Catalans) 35:ad app. 1, 18.
αἱμομιξία, incest 36:9.
αἱμοχαρής, murderous (of Catalans) 68:ad app. 1, 8.
αἵρεσις, heresy 34:35; matter of choice 99:18.
αἱρετικός, heretic 112:37.
αἰσχροκέρδεια, base gain 65:10.

αἰσχροκερδής, one who makes base gains, profiteer 65:1; 106:1.
αἰτία, guilt 103:3.
αἰχμάλωτος, refugee 22:ad app. 1, 6; 25:7.
ἀκανόνιστος, uncanonical 115:127, 128.
ἀκατάλυτος, perpetual 105:20.
ἀκέραιος, pure, innocent 103:40.
ἀκεσώδυνος, healing 54:24–25.
ἀκινησία, inertia 35:4.
ἀκμητί, freely 46:9.
ἀκραιφνής, pure 45:30.
ἄκρατος, undiluted 110:99.
ἀκρατῶς, relentlessly 59:35.
ἀκριβασμός, commandment 42:24; 104:11; strict reckoning 58:25.
ἀκρωτηριάζω, cut off, mutilate 62:17
ἄληκτος, unceasing 112:55.
ἀλλεπάλληλος, one upon another 95:41.
ἀλλοδαπής, foreign 84:44.
ἁλμυρίς, bog 96:25.
ἀλυκτοπέδαι, fetters 51:19; 74:21–22.
ἀλωπεκῆ, fox skin 60:72.
ἀμβλύς, sluggish 49:3.
ἀμεταθέτως, unalterably 57:12.
ἀμογητί, without any toil 88:24.
ἀμορφία, blemish 48:26.
ἀμπελών, vineyard 25:15; 61:88; 69:32.

ἀμφιτάλαντος, equal 84:71.

ἀναβλύζω, gush forth 115:54.

ἀναβολή, procrastination 35:23, 38, 56; 49:30; 89:4.

ἀναγωγή, upbringing 86:22.

ἀναδοχή, reception, liberality, redress, patronage 51:24; 81:37, 37–38; 96:6; 100:ad app. 1; 112:7.

ἀναζεύγνυμι, return 115:20.

ἀνάθημα, dedication 66:7, 44.

ἀνάκρισις, examination 58:25.

ἀνάλωτος, untouched 114:31.

ἀναμαρτησία, freedom from sin 30:10–11.

ἀναμφήριστος, without doubt 54:31.

ἀναντιρρήτως, incontrovertibly 114:13.

ἀναπνεύω, have a respite 115:58.

ἀναπνέω, to depend on, draw inspiration from 49:7; 98:12; to breathe 49:58; 95:4–5.

ἀναπολόγητος, indispensable 115:52.

ἀναποσπάστως, irrevocably 77:16.

ἀναστροφή, residence 69:60; mode of life, behavior 81:20; 110:19

ἀναφανδόν, openly 49:94.

ἀναχαίτισις, restraint 61:50.

ἀναψυχή, comfort 42:38.

ἀνέγερσις, construction 37:26.

ἀνεκλάλητος, unspeakable 60:32.

ἀνενέργητος, powerless 106:8.

ἀνεξέταστος, unexamined, uninvestigated 95:ad app. 1, 29, 38–39.

ἀνέορτος, uncelebrated 88:5.

ἀνεπαίσθητος, unperceived 95:19.

ἀνεπαισθήτως, with an imperceptive attitude 110:23, 26–27.

ἀνεπιφθόνως, ungrudgingly 75:2.

ἀντέκτισις, payment of debt, retribution 61:31; 111:16.

ἀντίδοσις, reward 60:34.

ἀντίληψις, help, assistance 7:20, 26; 37:37; 49:69–70; 59:59; 76:24–25;

77:14; 81:73; 82:19; 88:40; 110:3, 26, 47, 81; 113:9; 114:9; 115:16, 26; perception 8:3.

ἀντιστρόφως, in an opposite manner 111:6.

ἀνύβριστος, unassailable 114:54.

ἀνυπερθέτως, without delay 50:10.

ἀνύποιστος, unbearable 68:12.

ἀνυπόστατος, nonexistent 81:52; irresistible 110:16; 115:7; intolerable 115:85.

ἀνυπότακτος, unrestrained 111:40.

ἀπαραμύθητος, inconsolable 44:11–12; 63:18; 75:32; 99:17.

ἀπειρομεγέθης, countless 100:9.

ἀπερικαλύπτως, undisguisedly 92:15.

ἀπεριμερίμνως, in a carefree manner, unconcernedly 48:7; 83:58.

ἀπεριφάνως, discreetly 113:23.

ἀπνευστί, without drawing a breath 71:5.

ἀπόβλητος, rejected, repudiated 115:102.

ἀποδοχή, favor, reward 41:34; 80:15; 82:39; 97:12; 114:9.

ἀπολογία, defense 26:3; 30:18.

ἀποσοβέω, warn 84:65.

ἀποστροφή, aversion 61:42, 66.

ἀποσυνάγωγος, expelled from the congregation 115:70.

ἀποτεφρόω, reduce to ashes 49:17.

ἀποχερά, request (?) 14:59.

ἀπραγμοσύνη, inaction 57:14–15.

ἀπροσπαθῶς, impartially 47:21.

ἀπροστάτευτος, unprotected 74:14.

ἀραρότως, urgently 49:3; steadfastly 59:64; 94:3.

ἀργία, absence 35:4; abdication 111:53.

ἀργύριον, silver 93:20.

ἄργυρος, silver 43:2; 77:11; 92:21.

ἀριδήλως, clearly 51:6.

ἅρμα, weapon 107:6.

ἁρματηλατέω, drive a chariot 81:99.

ἀρρεπής, firm 65:15–16.

ἀρρυπάρως, immaculately 115:144.

ἀρτοπώλοι, bakers 100:3.

ἄρτος, bread 93:ad app. 1, 12.

ἀσκεπής, without a roof 87:10.

ἄσπορος, unplanted 67:5.

ἄστοργος, heartless 111:52.

ἀσύγκριτος, incomparable 63:3; 74:3; 75:24, 26; 80:9; 82:79; 87:21; 90:24; 92:35–36; 114:8; 115:116.

ἀσυγκρίτως, incomparably 82:76; 84:23; 89:6; 92:13; 93:17–18; 98:4; 110:42; 112:10.

ἀσύμβατος, disparate 58:17.

ἀσύμβολον, failure to act 36:13–14.

ἀσύμφορος, intolerable 62:20; unprofitable (?) 84:84; unbecoming 89:29.

ἀσυμφόρως, harmfully 37:35.

ἀσχέτως, irresistibly 60:43.

ἀσχόλησις, work 17:22.

ἀτενίζω, gaze, behold 112:16.

ἀτημέλητος, neglected 87:10.

αὐθωρόν, straightway 81:99–100.

αὔτανδρος, men and all 82:66.

αὐτόθι, there, the residence of the addressee 14:59; 34:2, 10–11; 98:14.

αὐτόχρημα, in very deed 46:50; 80:ad app. 1, 21; immediately 74:22.

ἄφθαστος, unrivalled 110:92.

ἀχόλησις, timidity 7:41.

ἄχυρα, chaff 47:32; 73:10.

ἀψίνθιον, bitter wormwood 69:121.

βαλανεῖον, bathhouse 42:19, 21; 43:38; 44:ad app. 1, 24.

βάπτω εἰς νοῦν, to have a drop of intelligence 49:5.

βάραθρον, pit 81:31.

βασκαίνω, be jealous 75:34.

βεβαίωσις, confirmation 69:55.

βιωφελής, profitable 50:3.

βότρυς, grapes 81:4.

βραχοφάγος, one who eats sparingly 87:25.

γάμος, marriage 37:35; 75:7; 97:ad app. 1, 3; 98:19.

γεννηματικά, grain 93:ad app. 1, 12; 100:5.

γένος, nation, people 14:2, 70; 17:59; 53:19; 58:46; 59:10; 68:15; 69:199; 75:10; 81:82; 90:22; 98:22; 110:12, 26, 116.

γεωργέω, till the earth 67:22, 28.

γῆρως, old age 57:14; 112:43.

γύναιον, woman 77:24.

γυνή, woman 15:26; 43:39; 45:9, 27; 49:72; 68:20; 70:9; 112:60; wife 93:21; 96:ad app. 1; 107:9.

δασμοφορέω, pay tribute 62:46.

δεκάπληγος, ten plagues (of Egypt) 94:12.

δέλτος, book 20:6; 82:51.

δευτερόπρωτα, a second time 112:2.

δημεγερσία, rebellion 25:4.

δημηγορία, address 108:ad app. 1.

διαβολή, slander 60:51; 65:9, 11; 81:101; 111:34; 115:18, 59, 75.

διάδοχος, successor 110:30; 111:30.

διάμετρος: ἐκ δ., diametrically 59:52.

διαξαίνω, exacerbate 75:38.

διάστασις, separation 75:20; distance 109:11.

διάτορος, piercing, clear 91:8–9.

διάχυσις, extent 56:24.

διεστῶτα, τά, differences 34:13.

δικαιωτήριον, judgment 58:37.

διπλόη, cloak 60:81; duplicity 114:61.

διχοτομέω, sever 106:8–9.

δόμησις, construction 56:24.

δονέομαι, be in confusion, commotion 110:88.

δριμύς, bitter, fierce 81:28, 46, 83, 135, 146.

δυσδιάκριτος, difficult to judge 99:5–6.

δυσεπικράτητος, grasped with difficulty 82:79–80.

δυσθήρατος, hard to catch 60:75.

δύσχρηστος, intractable 112:24.

δυσωπία, respect 94:30.

ἐγγύη, assurance 84:43.

ἐγρήγορσις, vigilance 49:30.

εἰσαγωγή, introduction 36:6.

εἰσδοχή, reception 45:9.

εἰσήγησις, investment (?) 76:16.

εἰσιτητός, accessible 47:38.

ἐκβολή, expulsion 2:60; 115:76.

ἐκδίδωμι, lend out 25:14.

ἐκδυσωπέω, entreat 112:44.

ἐκλιπαρέω, make earnest prayers 110:95–96.

ἐμβριθῶς, vehemently 115:87.

ἐμβρίμημα, solemn order 64:13.

ἐμβρόντητος, gaping fool 81:96–97; 108:5–6.

ἐμπαροινέω, be abusive 61:70; 89:8.

ἐμπεριπατέω, walk among 71:29.

ἐμπόρευμα, wares 47:23.

ἐνδημέω, reside 115:4.

ἐνδιάστροφος, twisted 26:7.

ἐνθήκη, gamut 69:127.

ἔνστασις, resistance, opposition 115:111.

ἔνταλμα, commandment 60:24; 81:176–77.

ἐνταῦθα, in this world 7:62, 66; 13:17; 14:8; 46:79; 60:19; 77:13, 15; 82:21, 84; 88:24; 90:6–7; 101:13; 110:61; here (in CP.) 8:20; 24:23; 25:15, 16; 28:8, 17; 30:20, 28, 30; 46:13; 75:17, 26;

81:67; 87:9; 96:17; 105:8; 114:48; in this case 34:33.

ἐνταυθοῖ, here 46:52; 48:10–11.

ἐνυπόστατος, incarnate 71:8.

ἐξαγόρευσις, confession 56:18.

ἐξευμαρίζω, ease, smooth 61:9.

ἔξοδος, departure, death 7:68; 41:47; 94:18; expense 22:6; 27:3; 68:3, 6; 74:4; 86:ad app. 1, 12.

ἐξολόθρευσις, destruction 30:2–3.

ἐξυπνισμός, awakening 115:45.

ἔπαλξις, rampart 56:24.

ἔπαρσις, destruction 92:22; insolence 110:35.

ἐπέλευσις, return 115:57.

ἐπιβολή, attack 37:12, 25.

ἐπίδοσις, increase, advancement 33:18; 77:7; 98:6.

ἐπιζήμιος, harmful 76:16, 18.

ἐπίθετον, surname 81:ad app. 1, 27.

ἐπίκηρος, transitory, ephemeral 60:41.

ἐπισφαλής, fallacious 114:24.

ἐπισφαλῶς, at great peril 77:9.

ἐπιτήδευμα, action, pursuit 66:38; 67:8; ἐπιτηδεύματα, τά, way of life 46:31.

ἐπίχαρτος, wherein one feels joy 110:11.

ἐπόζω, become stinking 81:29.

ἐργαστήριον, workshop 25:15–16; 29:5; 44:24.

ἕρμαιον, windfall (?) 21:22; stroke of fortune 80:29.

ἐρυσίβη, wheat-rust 81:33.

ἐσμός, stream 66:53.

ἔσοπτρον, mirror 81:20.

εὐαρίθμητος, few 37:9.

εὐδιάκριτον, τό, discretion 33:12.

εὐεπηβόλως, keenly 50:21.

εὐθηνία, abundance 41:49.

εὐκαταφρόνητος, contemptible 89:13–14.

εὐμοιρέω, have a supply of, possess 46:64; 47:37; 99:15–16.

εὐνομέω, to be well governed 95:3.

εὐπαράδεκτος, equal to the task 43:22.

εὑρεσιλογία, sophistical argument 69:154.

εὔροιζος, ringing true 64:16.

εὐτόνως, vigorously 50:43.

εὐωχία, banquet 47:22.

ἐφόδιον, defense 94:17.

ἕως, east 115:4.

ζευγηλατεῖον, 25:15.

ζηλότυπον, zeal 115:60–61.

ζημία, punishment 44:26; 60:50, 81; damage, harm 68:3; 69:ad app. 1, 20, 108; 83:35; 84:26; 93:18; 104:16; 111:19; 115:31; loss 76:19, 37; 82:67; ὦ ζημίας!, alas 73:11; 88:20; 110:59; φεῦ τῆς ζημίας!, alas 67:14; 80:30.

ζήτησις, demand 115:65.

ζιζάνιον, darnel 114:33.

ζωμεύς, bloodthirsty 68:10.

ζωΰφιον, tiny animal, insect 115:24.

ἡμιθνής, half-dead 46:19.

θεοκάπηλος, trafficker in divine things 66:75.

θεουργία, divine work 81:2.

θεοφόρος, divinely-inspired 111:30.

θεσπέσιος, divinely-inspired 106:2.

θέωσις, deification 49:84.

θημωνία, heap 92:21.

θῦμα, sacrificial victim 114:3.

θυρίς, window shelf 20:8; pigeon-hole 49:ad app. 1, 106.

θωπεία, flattery 103:17–18.

ἰητρός, doctor 110:97, 102.

ἰλύς, mire, slime 49:14; 53:14.

ἱππότης, rider 113:ad app. 26.

ἰσόψυχος, like in spirit 33:9.

ἰταμός, reckless 68:ad app. 1, 8.

ἴχνος, pace 50:46; foot 49:110; 59:6.

κακοπράγος, evildoer 67:20.

κακόσχολος, baneful 58:21.

κάλεσμα, invitation 25:18.

κάμινος, furnace 96:13, 23.

καπηλεῖον, tavern 42:19; 43:39; 44:ad app. 1, 25.

κάρος, torpor 103:7.

καρποφορία, offering 97:10.

κάρωσις, paralysis 95:18.

καταβολή, foundation 110:33; throwing down, suppression (?) 110:107.

καταγώγιον, resting-place 83:56; 91:23.

κατακόρως, liberally 110:99.

κατάλειψις, abandonment 35:9.

κατάληξις, end 33:24.

κατάληψις, apprehension, perception 63:16.

κατανάθεμα, worst anathema 111:28.

καταναρκάω, be sluggish, hesitate 115:11.

κατάνυξις, contrition 53:36; 70:14–15.

κατάπλους, downward voyage 8:ad app. 1, 17–18.

κατάποσις, swallowing 74:18.

καταπυκνόω, to stud thickly 61:20–21.

καταργέομαι, be useless (?), prohibited (?) 56:27.

καυτήρ, hot iron 68:7.

κειμήλιον, treasure 66:6, 44.

κῆπος, garden 25:15.

κόσμος, ornament 46:42; 66:49; 80:21; 112:10; world 33:20; 34:28; 37:16, 18; 42:11; 49:98; 64:5; 69:196; 72:16, 17; 75:28;

77:28, 33; 81:19; 83:17, 18, 48; 90:ad app. 1, 6, 11; 92:26–27, 38; 109:19; 110:76, 106.
κρήδεμνον, headdress 60:24.
κυαμοφάγος, eater of beans 26:9.
κυνώδης, dog-like 103:26.
κυπρίζω, bloom 81:4.
κῴδιον, sheepskin 81:30.
κώλυμα, obstacle 52:13.
κωλύμη, obstacle 52:14.
κωπηλατέω, to row 8:17.

λαξευτήριον, adze 87:ad app. 1, 3.
λεοντῆ, lion skin 74:24.
λήμη, mist 82:63.
ληνός, wine trough 81:5.
λῆρος, nonsense 95:11.
λιμός, famine, hunger 72:1; 78:26; 82:9; 93:18; 96:15.
λοιδορία, abusive language 26:8; 115:82.
λυμαντικός, destructive, detrimental 84:32.
λυμεών, agent of destruction 94:32; 106:14.

μακρηγορία, long speech 74:16.
μακρυσμός, separation 84:48.
μαμωνᾶς, mammon, material gain 58:39; 59:2, 4, 5; 74:21, 22; 83:36; 106:11.
μαργαρίτης, pearl 101:16.
μεγαλώνυμος, great 45:4.
μέλαθρον, hut 68:18.
μεμψιμοίρος, faultfinder 88:2.
μεσολαβέω, intervene 75:17.
μεταναστεύω, move away 95:30.
μετάφρενον, shoulder 66:60, 61.
μετεωρισμός, puffing oneself up 45:12.
μετοχή, participation 61:68.
μηχανορράφος, crafty schemer 115:119.
μιαιφονία, murder 65:13.

μικροψυχία, pusillanimity, meanness of spirit 35:38; 84:83.
μόλιβδος, lead 46:80.
μολύβδινος, leaden 111:50.

νέμεσις, vengeance 114:5.
νεῦμα, command, will 96:15.
νεώς, temple 62:69.
νόσημα, disease 110:101.
νόσος, illness 46:13; 57:14; 64:12; 72:12, 36, 41; 110:105.
νύμφη, daughter-in-law 96:11; ν. Χριστοῦ, bride of Christ, the Church 69:41.
νύμφιος, bridegroom 75:8; 115:51.
νυμφών, marriage chamber (Kingdom of Heaven) 46:48; 53:27–28; 60:28; 66:95.
νωχελία, apathy 85:5.

ξένιον, bribe 3:59; 65:6, 12; 72:12, 34; 73:7; 79:6; reward 81:148.
ξυνωρίς, pair (of apostles) 88:13.

ὀδμή, smell 114:49.
ὀδούς, tooth; ὑπ' ὀδόντα, surreptitiously 114:31.
οἰκία, building 50:1, 32.
οἰκοδομέω, edify 69:29; 109:16; 114:15.
οἰκοδομή, structure 69:102.
οἶνος, wine 48:15; 106:9; 110:99.
ὀλιγοψυχία, faintheartedness 75:48.
ὀλιγόψυχος, of little courage 62:20.
ὁλκάς, ship 92:27.
ὀμματόω, make see, furnish with eyes 44:43.
ὁμογενής, countryman 46:20.
ὀμφακίζω, be unripe 81:5.
ὄνομα, title 2:13, 18; name 41:46; 69:87, 159; 102:10; nominal position 57:14.
ὀνομαστός, famous, of note 108:7.

ὄνος: ὄ. ἐσαγισμένος, saddled ass 69:58.

ὁρμαθός, cluster 69:53; 115:99.

ὄφλημα, debt, obligation 26:15; 43:35; 68:19; 88:7; 99:17, 19; 115:52.

ὀφρύς, arrogance 93:20.

ὄψον ταριχευτόν, salt pork 26:9–10.

παίδευσις, education, culture 113:21; correction 15:ad app. 1, 33; π. ἀνακτορική, palace etiquette 86:26.

παλαμναῖος, miscreant 103:36.

πανάγαστος, praiseworthy, marvelous 81:8; 88:11.

πανδαισία, complete banquet 47:20.

παντανάθεμα, most inclusive anathema 111:28.

πανωλεθρία, total destruction 35:19.

παραγωγεύς, creator 49:98; 94:33.

παραδρομή, negligence 49:34.

παρανάλωμα, victim 115:132.

παρανοσφίζομαι, appropriate 94:25.

παρασπονδύλιος, oppressive (?) 62:51.

παρασύναξις, unlawful assembly 28:11.

παρατιτρώσκειν, violate 33:30.

παρατροπή, aberration 81:26.

παραφύλαξις, protection 51:4.

παραχαράττω, debase 61:40.

παρείσπραξις, illegal exaction 49:54; 79:7–8; 92:29.

παρίσωσις, close resemblance, equality 112:13.

παροινέω, abuse 111:11.

παροξυσμός, excitement 58:21.

παρόραμα, oversight 58:30.

παροχεύς, provider 46:12.

παροχή, gift, offering 64:15; 78:34–35.

παρρησία, access 34:20; 69:79; bold speech, confidence 76:38; 77:7; 96:26.

πέλαγος: π. τῆς ἀγαθότητος, God 6:10; 70:6; 82:64–65; π. ἀγαθωσύνης, God, 89:9; π. τῆς κακίας, Satan 69:114; π. τῶν συμφορῶν, 62:38; π. φιλανθρωπίας 71:29.

πέπων, melon 48:15.

περιαλγής, painful 82:26.

περίβολος, enclosure 47:9.

περίκλυτος, famous 87:10.

περιπλάνησις, wandering 47:12–13.

περίττωμα, scrap, leftover 47:26.

περιωπή, lofty position, supreme power 58:24; 61:6; 93:3; 99:13; 115:21–22.

περκάζω, ripen 81:4–5.

πῆμα, harm 49:31.

πλευρῖτις, pleurisy 110:97.

πλοῖον, ship 100:4.

πλοῦς: κατὰ δεύτερον π., second best 14:3–4.

πλουσιοπαρόχως, richly 112:17.

πλουτοδότης, benefactor 64:11.

πνευματόλεκτος, spoken by the Spirit 95:13.

πνέω + Acc., to regard 46:45.

ποδηγέω, guide 55:11.

πολιά, gray hair 94:20–21.

πολλοῦ γε καὶ δεῖ, it is very necessary (?) 50:7.

πολυπραγμονέω, to make it one's business, concern oneself 49:96.

πόμα, draught 90:2.

προαίρεσις, character 78:34.

πρόγνωσις, foreknowledge 55:4.

προῖκα, at one's own expense 49:42.

προκοπή, prosperity, progress 33:18; 58:48; 76:14–15; 84:18.

πρόμαχος, bulwark 90:16.

προσαγωγή, offering 88:ad app. 1, 10.

πρόσκαιρος, temporal 60:61.

προσκρούω, give offense, commit an irregularity 101:2.

προσονειρώσσω, dream 81:60.

πρόσυλος, material 95:2.
πρότριτα, recently 49:17–18; 83:7.
προῦπτον, clearly, manifestly 110:109.
πρωταίτιος, prime instigator 81:142.
πυρίφλεκτος, blazing with fire 91:6–7.

ῥαγδαῖος, uncontrolled 110:100.
ῥαψῴδημα, tale 81:49–50.
ῥῆξις, tear, schism 69:50.
ῥιψοκίνδυνος, risky 84:51.

σάλος, storm 95:41.
σεμνοπρέπεια, dignity 66:34.
σηκός, precinct 47:39.
σῆψις, gangrene 114:35.
σκαιοτρόπος, twisted 81:26–27.
σκαιωρία, mischief 112:53; 115:14.
σκέμμα, scheme 115:68.
σκηπτοῦχος, carrying a scepter 81:99.
σκῆψις, trap 51:5; pretext 115:103.
σκοτομήνη, moonless night 90:14.
σπέρμα, seed 94:6.
σπλάγχνα, bowels, heart 35:24; 44:7; 46:39; 75:25; 96:22; 99:18.
σπουδαιολογέομαι, to busy oneself 54:20.
στενοχωρία, difficulty (?) 50:45.
στεντόρειος, stentorian 43:21.
συγκατάθεσις, approval 49:12.
συγχώρησις, forgiveness 2:ad app. 1; 112:52.
σύζυγος, wife 75:ad app. 1; 97:3; 98:ad app. 1, 18.
συκοφάντης, flatterer 114:48.
συκοφαντία, false accusation 111:34; 115:119.
συλλήπτωρ, assistant 84:27.
σύμβιος, wife 96:24.
σύμβουλος, counsellor 35:36–37.
συμμορία, conspiracy 81:66.

συμπόσιον, drinking bout 16:ad app. 1, 3.
συμφροντιστής, advisor 84:26.
συναίσθησις, understanding 110:67–68.
συναποστάτης, fellow rebel 81:154.
σύναρσις, assistance 83:14; 92:31.
συνασπισμός, conspiracy 69:55.
σύνδακρυς, in tears 46:15; 52:4.
συνείδησις, conscience 33:28; 50:21, 42; 57:4; 58:37; 88:33; 95:31; 100:20; 114:16.
συνεισφορά, contribution 66:15–16.
συνεκβακχεύω, to revel in Bacchic frenzy 81:118.
συνελόντα εἰπεῖν, in short 33:34; 60:11.
συνεξέτασις, examination 95:39.
σύνευνος, consort 75:46; 98:18.
συνευωχέομαι, feast together 112:20.
συνιππεύω, to accompany on horse-back 46:70.
συνοχεύς, supporter 101:9.
συντέλεια, end (of the world) 43:22; 98:13; 110:45–46.
συσκευή, plot 115:122.
συστολή, repression 81:171.
σφάλμα, crime, sin 103:2; 111:16.
σφαδάζω, be excited 115:91.
σχέσις, love 58:11; 60:15; 75:15; relationship 29:14.
σχετλιάζω, bewail 49:13.
σωστικός, pertaining to salvation 46:33.
σωφροσύνη, continence 97:3, 11.

ταριχευτὸν ὄψον, salt pork 26:9–10.
ταὐτεμπάθεια, same feelings (?) 82:41.
τελώνης, publican 47:21.
τέμενος, precinct 56:14.
τερετίζω, sing 64:ad app. 1, 2.
τετραετία, period of four years 115:2.

466   INDICES